November 3–6, 2011
Atlanta, GA, USA

Association for
Computing Machinery

Advancing Computing as a Science & Profession

C&C'11

Proceedings of the 8th ACM Conference on

Creativity and Cognition

Sponsored by:

SIGCHI

In Cooperation with:

SIGART, SIGCAS, SIGGRAPH, SIGMM and SIGSOFT

Association for
Computing Machinery

Advancing Computing as a Science & Profession

The Association for Computing Machinery
2 Penn Plaza, Suite 701
New York, New York 10121-0701

ISBN: 978-1-4503-0820-5 (Digital)

ISBN: 978-1-4503-1399-5 (Print)

Additional copies may be ordered prepaid from:

ACM Order Department
PO Box 30777
New York, NY 10087-0777, USA

Phone: 1-800-342-6626 (USA and Canada)
+1-212-626-0500 (Global)
Fax: +1-212-944-1318
E-mail: acmhelp@acm.org
Hours of Operation: 8:30 am – 4:30 pm ET

Printed in the USA

C&C 2011 General Chair's Welcome

Welcome to the 8th ACM Conference on Creativity and Cognition (C&C 2011)! We are excited to have you join us. Each conference has a story, and I want to briefly share some parts of the story of C&C 2011 with you.

The story of C&C 2011 really begins with C&C 2009 at Berkeley with Nick Bryan-Kinns as the Chair. At C&C 2009, Georgia Institute of Technology had a strong and lively presence with about a dozen participants and about a score of papers, posters, and artworks. At a C&C 2009 party sponsored by the Georgia Tech GVU Center (http://www.gvu.gatech.edu/), my Georgia Tech colleagues and I became pleasantly aware that so many of us shared a common interest in creativity!

Upon returning from Berkeley in late fall of 2009, Brian Magerko and I, along with other Georgia Tech colleagues, won a small GVU seed grant for an initiative that we called Creativity + Cognition + Computation. We used this grant to start a seminar series as well as a faculty consortium that now has some fifty participants (http://dilab.gatech.edu/C3/index.html). We also used it to develop a proposal for organizing C&C 2011 at Georgia Tech, naturally selecting Creativity and Technology as the conference theme. In order to insure that C&C 2011 was intellectually diverse, we invited several colleagues from around the world to join the organizing team, including Jim Davies from Canada, Andres Gomez de Silva Garza from Mexico, Chien-Sing Lee then in Malaysia and now in Taiwan, Yukari Nagai from Japan, and Jane Prophet from the United Kingdom. Fortunately, in late spring of 2010, the C&C conference series steering committee led by Ernest Edmonds and Nick Bryan-Kinns accepted our proposal.

About a year back, in early fall of 2010, Local Chair Brian Magerko and I decided on the Academy of Medicine building on the outskirts of the Georgia Tech campus as the conference venue. The elegant building with a prime location had been only recently acquired by Georgia Tech and was undergoing thorough renovation. This also led us to select Hotel Renaissance as the conference hotel because it was right across the street from the Academy of Medicine building. About the same time, Finance Chair Alexandra Mazalek and I decided to make the registration fees for C&C 2011 in various categories to be the same as – and where possible – lower than those for C&C 2009.

Life, of course, rarely proceeds linearly! In early spring of 2011, we learned that renovation of the Academy of Medicine building was running behind schedule, and the building, which was scheduled to open in mid fall of 2011, will not open until after C&C 2011, perhaps in late fall of 2011, perhaps even later. This created a scramble to find another conference venue, but by spring 2011, all other Georgia Tech buildings suitable for C&C 2011 already had been booked for other fall events.

Fortunately, we were able to find the High Museum of Art (http://www.high.org/) as an alternative location. The Museum provides a beautiful venue for C&C 2011; it also rightly emphasizes the importance of the arts in the ACM Creativity and Cognition conference series. On the other hand, the change in venue from a Georgia Tech building with nominal cost to C&C 2011 to an off-campus, private building, put us behind our financial planning by a very substantial amount. The change in the conference venue shaped many of our subsequent decisions about C&C 2011.

That we nevertheless have put together a stimulating conference for you is due to the enterprise, commitment, and perseverance, and tenacity of my colleagues on the C&C 2011 organizational committee, program committee, advisory committee, and steering committee. I want to specifically acknowledge Ernest Edmonds and Linda Candy for sponsoring the Best Creative Communication Award, Ben Shneiderman for his general support and help in raising monies, Ellen Do for her general support and help in getting an US National Science Foundation grant in support of the Graduate Student Symposium, Fox Harrell for his leadership on the art program, and Jim Davies for doing the extra work of a program chair during the reviewing process without getting any credit for it!

Most of all, I want to thank student volunteers Evan Barba, Kurt Luther, Brian O'Neill and Jill Russek. They, together with Brian Magerko, Alexandra Mazalek, and administrative associate Gail Wynens, have put in enormous amounts of time, energy, and effort into organizing C&C 2011. Please join me in thanking them.

Now let the proceedings start and the fun begin!

Ashok K. Goel
Chair, C&C 2011

C&C 2011 Program Chairs' Welcome

The goal of the 8th ACM Conference on Creativity and Cognition (C&C 2011) is to foster disruptive new ideas in understanding human creativity in its many manifestations, in designing new interactive computing techniques to augment and amplify human creativity, and in using computational media technologies to explore new creative processes and artifacts in human endeavors ranging from the arts to science, from design to education, from research to practice to everyday life. The theme of the conference, as the conference website (http://dilab.gatech.edu/ccc/) states, is Creativity and Technology, as befits Georgia Institute of Technology, the host institution. We are pleased to share the conference program that follows in these proceedings with you, for we believe that it both promotes the conference theme and accomplishes the conference goal.

For C&C 2011, we received 144 full paper and 35 poster paper submissions. We also received 33 artworks for review. In addition, we received 21 paper abstracts for the Graduate Student Symposium. We also received several proposals for tutorial and workshops, and subsequently many papers for the accepted workshops. In all, we received about 260 creative articles in various categories. C&C 2011 is a good-sized conference!

Although we had organized a fair-sized program committee, the number of submissions nevertheless was larger than we had anticipated. Fortunately, a good number of external reviewers stepped up to help with the review process, though the conference program committee and the art program jury still did the bulk of the work. After much deliberation by the program chairs (and Jim Davies who allowed us to recruit him as a "volunteer" program chair, and Ellen Do, the Graduate Student Symposium Chair), we finally selected 32 full papers, 75 poster papers, 18 artworks, and 12 paper abstracts for the Graduate Student Symposium. To give some perspective on these numbers, we note that we accepted only 32 full papers out of the 144 submitted (or about 23%). C&C 2011 is a very competitive conference!

In addition to the above articles, these proceedings contain abstracts of four keynote addresses by Guy Claxton (creativity and learning), Sara Diamond (creativity and arts), Atau Tanaka (creativity and music), and Ben Shneiderman (social creativity). We are very excited to have the four keynote speakers join us at the conference.

These proceedings also contain abstracts of three workshops: Being there, Doing It: The Challenge of Embodied Cognition for Design (Chairs: Jelle van Dijk & Joep Frens); Semi-Automated Creativity: Software as a Creative Collaborator (Chair: Jimmy Secretan), and Beyond the Binding: Exploring the Future of the Book (Chairs: Natalie Freed, Jie Qi, Cristina Sylla, and Pedro Branco). These workshops add to the breadth of the conference.

The conference program also includes three panel sessions on Creativity and Technology that bring creative artists together with creativity researchers, as well as an evening of art exhibits and performances. This focus on art builds on the tradition of past C&C conferences, and adds intellectual diversity, energy and fun to the conference!

The quality of a conference is a direct function of the community that supports it: the quality of C&C 2011 reflects the quality, dynamism and vibrancy of the growing creativity and cognition research community. We thank all the authors who submitted their papers and artworks to the conference, the members of the program committee and the external reviewers who helped review the submissions, the workshop chairs who organized the workshops, and the keynote speakers. We are especially grateful to Jim Davies, Ellen Do, Chien-Sing Lee, the Workshops Chair and Andres Gomez de Silva Garza, the Tutorials Chair.

We hope you have as much fun reading these proceedings as we had putting them together!

Ashok K. Goel, Fox Harrell, Brian Magerko, Yukari Nagai & Jane Prophet

September 10, 2011

Table of Contents

Session 6: Affect

Session 7: Creativity & Technology – 2: Physical Presence

Session 7B: Collaboration

Session 8: Creativity and Art

Session 9: Perception

Session 10: Design - 2

Demo Session

Art Exhibits

Art Performances

Workshops

Graduate Student Symposium

C&C 2011 Conference Organization

General Chair: Ashok K. Goel, *Georgia Institute of Technology, USA*

Program Co-Chairs: Ashok K. Goel, *Georgia Institute of Technology, USA*
Fox Harrell, *Massachusetts Institute of Technology, USA*
Brian Magerko, *Georgia Institute of Technology, USA*
Yukari Nagai, *Japan Advanced Institute of Science and Technology, Japan*
Jane Prophet, *Goldsmiths College, University of London, UK*

Art Program Chair: Fox Harrell, *Massachusetts Institute of Technology, USA*

Tutorials Chair: Andres Gomez de Silva Garza, *Instituto Tecnológico Autónomo de México, Mexico*

Workshops Chair: Chien-Sing Lee, *National Central University, Taiwan*

Graduate Student Symposium Chair: Ellen Do, *Georgia Institute of Technology, USA*

Finance Chair: Alexandra Mazalek, *Georgia Institute of Technology, USA*

Publicity Chair: Jim Davies, *Carleton University, Canada*

Local Chairs: Brian Magerko, *Georgia Institute of Technology, USA*
Kurt Luther, *Georgia Institute of Technology, USA*

Webmasters: Brian ONeill, *Georgia Institute of Technology, USA*
Kurt Luther, *Georgia Institute of Technology, USA*
Jill Russek, *Georgia Institute of Technology, USA*

Email and Registration: Evan Barba, *Georgia Institute of Technology, USA*
Gail Wynens, *Georgia Institute of Technology, USA*

Program Committee: Anna Abraham, *University of Gießen, Germany*
Dor Abrahamson, *University of California, Berkeley, USA*
Michael Anderson, *Franklin & Marshall College, USA*
Banny Banerjee, *Stanford University, USA*
Steve Benford, *University of Nottingham, UK*
Olav Bertelsen, *University of Aarhus, Denmark*
Dorrit Billman, *NASA, USA*
Alan Blackwell, *Cambridge University, UK*
Nathalie Bonnardel, *Aix-Marseille University, France*
Will Bridewell, *Stanford University, USA*
Andreas Broeckmann, *Transmediale, Germany*
Amy Bruckman, *Georgia Institute of Technology, USA*
Winslow Burleson, *Arizona State University, USA*

Program Committee (cont'd): Gary Olson, *University of California, Irvine, USA*
Jack Ox, *University of New Mexico, USA*
Paul Pangaro, *Cybernetic Lifestyles, LLC, USA*
Rafael Pérez y Pérez, *Universidad Autónoma Metropolitana, Mexico*
Dana Plautz, *Mrs P Enterprises, USA*
Peter Ride, *University of Westminster, UK*
Mark Riedl, *Georgia Institute of Technology, USA*
Mark Runco, *University of Georgia, USA*
Demetrios Sampson, *University of Piraeus, Greece*
Mark Sandler, *Queen Mary University, London, UK*
Rob Saunders, *University of Sydney, Australia*
Jason Schmitt, *Oakland University, USA*
Jimmy Secretan, *Ad Summos, Inc., USA*
David Shamma, *Yahoo! Research, USA*
Edward A. Shanken, *University of Amsterdam, The Netherlands*
Carol Strohecker, *University of North Carolina, USA*
Masahiro Takatsuka, *University of Sydney, Australia*
Toshiharu Taura, *Kobe University, Japan*
Dan Ventura, *Brigham Young University, USA*
Ron Wakkary, *Simon Fraser University, Canada*
Leon Watts, *University of Bath, UK*
Rob Woodbury, *Simon Fraser University, Canada*
Geraint Wiggins, *Goldsmiths College, University of London, UK*
Jichen Zhu, *University of Central Florida, USA*

Art Program Jury: Ricardo Dominguez, *University of California, San Diego, USA*
Jeremy Douglass, *University of California, San Diego, USA*
Leah Gilliam, *Institute of Play, New York, USA*
Troy Innocent, *Monash University, Australia*
Erik Loyer, *USA*
Nick Montfort, *Massachusetts Institute of Technology, USA*
Mendi + Keith Obadike, *William Paterson University, USA*
Dave Surman, *Australian Centre for the Moving Image, Australia*
Paul Vanouse, *University at Buffalo, USA*

External Reviewers:

Inês Albuquerque
Alissa Antle
Michael Atwood
Erin Beatty
Karl Bergström
Peter Beyls
Mark Billinghurst
Marius Brade
Robert Burton
Licia Calvi
Benedita Camacho
Kristin Carlson
Erin Carroll
Oron Catts
Rongjuan Chen
Sheng-Chih Chen
Yee Chieh Chew
Sandra Coelho
Marcus Colman
Greg Corness
Amod Damle
Eleanor Dare
Nicholas Davis
Denise Doyle
Maher Elkhaldi
Mark Fuge
Florian Geyer
Elisa Giaccardi
Ian Gwilt
Hakim Hachour
Kim Halskov
Norkhairolizah Hamzah
Ronah Harris
W. Michelle Harris
Dew Harrison
Richard Hass
Michael Helms
Damian Hills
Simon Holland
Raquell Holmes
Chih-Pin Hsiao
Hung Pin Hsu
Yi Ji
Sara Jones
David Joyner
Nick Kelly
A. Baki Kocaballi
Kyu Han Koh
Maithilee Kunda
Carlos León
Lassi A Liikkanen
Rhema Linder
Gareth Loudon
Terence Love
Lynne MacLachlan
Lee Martie
Andrew Martin
Fred Martin
Anijo Mathew
Anthony McCaffrey
Keith McGreggor
Catarina Mota
Maurice Mulvenna
Janet Murray
Tim Murray-Browne
Eric Nichols
David Norton
Bryan Pardo
Anna Rabinowicz
Iulian Radu
Claudia Rebola
Corina Sas
Thecla Schiphorst
M.C. Schraefel
Orit Shaer
Moushumi Sharmin
James Sheridan
Jennifer Sheridan
Paul Sowden
Gerry Stahl
Jack Stenner
Cristina Sylla
Emmanuek Taiwo
Anthony Threatt
Meredith Tromble
Jelle van Dijk
Swaroop Vattam
Peter Wardrip
Andrew Webb
Bryan Wiltgen
Andy Wu
Lixiu Yu
Stanislaw Zabramski
Shahriman Zainal Abidin
John Zimmerman

Best Paper Award Committee: Janet Murray, Chair, *Georgia Institute of Technology, USA*
Mary Lou Maher, *University of Maryland at College Park, USA*
Jeannette Yen, *Georgia Institute of Technology, USA*

Honorary Advisory Committee: Sabir Khan, *Georgia Institute of Technology, USA*
Janet Kolodner, *US National Science Foundation*
Abir Mullick, *Georgia Institute of Technology, USA*
Janet Murray, *Georgia Institute of Technology, USA*
Nancy Nersessian, *Georgia Institute of Technology, USA*
David Rosen, *Georgia Institute of Technology, USA*
Jeannette Yen, *Georgia Institute of Technology, USA*

Conference Series Steering Committee: Nick Bryan-Kinns, *Queen Mary College, University of London, UK*
Linda Candy, *University of Technology, Australia*
Ernest Edmonds, *University of Technology, Australia*
Gerhard Fischer, *University of Colorado at Boulder, USA*
Tom Hewett, *Drexel University, USA*
Janis Jefferies, *Goldsmiths College, University of London, UK*
Ben Shneiderman, *University of Maryland at College Park, USA*

C&C 2011 Sponsor & Supporters

Sponsor: SIGCHI

In cooperation with: ACM SIGART, ACM Computers Society, ACM SIGGRAPH, SIGSOFT (Special Interest Group on Software Engineering), ACM SIGMM (Special Interest Group Multimedia)

Supporters: NSF, Georgia Tech, dilab (design & intelligence lab), creativity and cognition studios, intel, HIGH Museum of Art Atlanta

Creative-Mindedness: When Technology Helps and When it Hinders

Guy Claxton
Professor of the Learning Sciences
Co-Director, Centre for Real-World Learning
University of Winchester, UK

Creative-mindedness is the broad disposition to come up with a good idea when you need one, and work it through. It relies on a number of factors: the absence of beliefs that might cause one to neglect or misrepresent useful aspects of one's own mind; the possession of a rich and partly unsystematic neural compost of experience, snippets and understanding; an intuitive grasp of when and how to think clearly and precisely, and when and how to think vaguely and dreamily; an awkward but irresistible sense of wonderment and scepticism; patience and persistence in the face of confusion and frustration; and the ability to amass and deploy material, spatial, technological and social resources in a way that is fluidly appropriate to the evolving nature of the creative project. This last factor is perhaps the most important of all: the presence of mind to orchestrate both one's own mental resources and habits, and the affordances of the outside world, in a way that optimises their ability to mesh with themselves and with each other. Creativity means being smart about yourself, smart about the world, and smart about how to fit the two together.

In this presentation, I will explore and illustrate some of these factors, and show how their importance is underpinned by current research in cognitive and social neuroscience. I will argue that recent research in both embodied and extended 'mind' requires us to hold a more sophisticated and contingent view of creativity than is common in the many well-worn models that populate the worlds of both commercial and popular culture. We need to expand the idea of the creative individual as 'Cognition+ Tools' to include wider aspects of both the human body and the material world. The concepts of balance, fluidity and contingent optimisation turn out to be crucial to an understanding of real-world creativity.

Author Keywords
Learning dispositions, creative thinking

ACM Classification Keywords
F.m. Theory of Computation: Miscellaneous

General Terms
Experimentation

C&C'11, November 3–6, 2011, Atlanta, Georgia, USA.
ACM 978-1-4503-0820-5/11/11.

Studying Medium Effects on Children's Creative Processes

Sharon Lynn Chu Yew Yee, Francis Quek, Xiao Lin
Center for Human-Computer Interaction, Virginia Tech
2202 Kraft Drive, KWII Building (0106)
Blacksburg, VA 24061-0106
{sharilyn, quek, linxiao}@vt.edu

ABSTRACT

The Fourth Grade Slump, whereby children's creativity drops precipitously at around fourth grade, is a developmental phenomenon that begs for research to be done on ways to nurture children's creativity. We posit that due to its form and formal features, the use of the animated medium for creative activities can positively sustain the child's creativity throughout the Slump. We present a study that investigated how the animated medium (animation) mediates and influences the creative process of children in the third and fourth grade, using the digital print medium (storybook) as comparison. Analysis of the process was done at the structural and production level using mainly the method of discourse analysis.

Children were observed to go through different stages and sequences when creating stories using animation as opposed to the storybook medium. The strategies that the children adopted to create differed along six themes: the prevalence of *micro-activities*, an integrated and *activity-driven process* of story generation, a *focus on qualitative details* producing richer stories, a *broader imagination* in terms of the story world, the occurrence of *serendipitous creativity*, and a higher degree of *convergence and divergence* despite a low seeding level of ideas in story generation. While animation was seen to have certain limitations in the act of creating, it had a largely positive impact on the children's motivation and enthusiasm to engage in the creative activity. Our results have implications for the understanding of the creative process among elementary school children, a necessary first step for the proper design of systems to nurture and sustain children's creativity throughout the Fourth Grade Slump.

Author Keywords

Creativity, medium effects, fourth grade slump, children

ACM Classification Keywords

H.5.m. Information interfaces and presentation (HCI): Misc

General Terms

Human factors, Design

C&C'11, November 3–6, 2011, Atlanta, Georgia, USA.

INTRODUCTION

Creativity is of critical importance to us as individuals, as a society, and ultimately as cultures that span multiple generations. Recognized as "the driving force behind our greatest ideas, our most comprehensive solutions, and our most profitable enterprises" at the 2010 Creativity World Forum [1], this fundamental aspect of human beings stands as the key factor for the formation of a creative class that is becoming a distinguishing mark of global, post-industrial cities [2]. But it is not only those generally recognized as specially creative for whom this quality is important. Creativity plays a role in everyday life (what [3] call small 'c' creativity) – the plumber making-do with an alternate tool, the baker developing a cake-mix, and the technician devising a work-around to solve a technical problem. Indeed it is thought that creativity is needed for all acts of learning [4, 5]. Yet, since the 1990s, creativity levels have been steadily declining especially for children [6]. Many have started to make calls for action to bring back creativity into the current school system [6, 7].

The 'creativity crisis' however may be conflated by another phenomenon called the Fourth Grade Slump. From the beginning of speech, children show increasing creative activity, until about the fourth grade when many of them start to shy away from creative activities and behaviors. The Slump seems to be in effect until the mid-teens (at about the eight grade) [8] when some children are able to "discover themselves". Given the importance of creativity, we can ill-afford this loss of 'practice of creativity' at this critical turning point of child development.

Concurrently with the 'creativity crisis', we also see an increasing consumption of media among children. The Kaiser Family Foundation [9] reports that children of 8 to 10 years old spend an average of 8 hrs consuming media in a typical day, with the most serious increase occurring in total television consumption as opposed to print consumption that has remained constant over the past five years.

In this paper, we present a study to investigate how animated media mediates creative activity in the production of stories, for children in the Fourth Grade Slump. We are interested in the role of the medium in creativity for third and fourth graders. The literature on the subject is rather divided. While some suggest that visual animated media can motivate creative animation, others argue on the other hand that they absolve the consumer from imagination, and turn them into passive consumers. Given the increased exposure of children to media, we believe that creating with digital animated media may provide a positive means to nurture and sustain creativity throughout the slump among this new generation of digital natives.

The contribution of this study is three-fold: firstly, on a specific level, it shows how for children the animated medium positively modulates the creative process. Secondly, on a general level, it provides additional evidence that the type of medium used in creative activities has an effect on how creativity manifests itself. And thirdly, it suggests a way by which the 'practice of creativity' may be sustained during the Fourth Grade Slump. In the rest of this paper, we present relevant background about the Slump, literature investigating the effects of media consumption on creativity, and highlight the importance of the type of medium to creativity. We then present the research questions of this study, followed by our study design and findings.

RELEVANT BACKGROUND

The Fourth Grade Slump

A predominant hypothesis of why the Fourth Grade Slump occurs is developmental in nature. As defined by Torrance [8], the Fourth Grade Slump is a precipitous "decrement in all creative thinking abilities near the end of third grade or beginning of the fourth grade", that has been observed through intercultural longitudinal studies in many countries from the United States to Norway, India and Western Samoa. Apart from the more recent decline in creativity levels, this phenomenon has been discovered more than thirty years ago and remains a worrying gap for teachers [10].

Torrance [8] provides a three-part rationale for the Slump based on the profound changes that take place in the child's development during that period: social accommodation, peer approval, and the need for validation as the child comes into greater contact with society and her environment. This developmental social awareness leads a child to be more judgmental of her own work [11] and to engage in more critical self-evaluation of competence [12]. Such self-appraisals with respect to social norms and standards often lead to self-regulation of behavior [13]. Positive self-appraisals may then lead to greater involvement in creative behavior, and negative self-appraisals may result in self-doubt and possibly a decrease in or withdrawal from creative activity. This is illustrated by Henk & Melnick's [14] study on the activity of reading, whereby children who see themselves as poor readers "probably have not experienced much in the way of reading success".

One approach to addressing the Slump then is to identify an activity in which the child is willing to take part and where her self-evaluation is positive to encourage exercise of further creativity during that critical period. We hypothesize that animated media authoring (where the complexities of the technical media creation process such as generation of colors or character path definition are satisfactorily hidden) may satisfy the criteria of such an activity.

Media Effects on Creativity

The study of media effects is not new, especially in discipline like Communication or Media studies. Research has been carried out on the impact of different types of media on the child's cognitive processes as early as in the 1950s. The literature is replete with studies of media effects on higher mental functions such as learning, comprehension, recall or memory, and attention. However, the study of media effects on creativity received relatively less attention. Among studies that have been conducted, there has not been a consensus. On one hand, Greenfield et al. [15] found medium effects in favor of radio over the television (TV), and Watkins & Coulombe [16] found differences between print, radio and TV in terms of inferential elements. Valkenburg & Beentjes [17] also more recently found that a TV stimulus produced more novel stories for children aged 8 years and older than a radio stimulus. On the other hand, both Runco & Pezdek [18] and Rubeinstein [19] did not obtain any effects comparing radio and TV, and print and TV respectively. Despite the contradictory results, McLuhan's proposition that "the medium is the message" maintains that the medium can have an important impact on the content, processes and the environment.

Why Medium Matters

Based on neuroscience, Greenfield [20] highlights a dichotomy between "people of the book" and "people of the screen". Other theorists have suggested that there are complementary roles for our verbal/symbolic and visual systems. Baddeley [21] proposed that we have both a visio-spatial sketchpad and phonological loop in working memory. Paivio [22] advanced a "dual coding theory" by which "memory and cognition [are] served by two separate symbolic systems, one specialized for dealing with verbal information and the other for nonverbal information" [23]. Mayer [24] thus argues that using both visual and verbal channels improves our creative problem solving abilities. In fact, multimedia learning systems are built based on this very argument. It is worth noting that similarly, the media richness theory proposes that a communication medium is 'richer' when it transmits immediate feedback and a multiplicity of cues [25].

Nevertheless, among the various modes of representations Sheppard [26] claims the primacy of the visual. In the same way that media naturalness theory [27] adopts an evolutionary perspective to posit face-to-face communication as the most 'natural' medium, spatiality and visual images according to Sheppard have been "incorporated into our perceptual machinery by eons of evolution in a 3-dimensional world". Imagery therefore empowers us to obtain ideas and thoughts that are not "fully preserved by language" [23].

MEDIA AS TOOLS FOR CREATIVITY

We have shown the significance of studying creativity in relation to media, but it is necessary to point out three essential differences between previous media effects studies and the research described in this paper.

First, prior studies such as those mentioned earlier consider media as modes of communication. Thus their experiments manipulated the medium in which stories were presented while keeping neutral the medium in which the subjects were assessed. In our study, we adopt the perspective of media as tools provided by culture and enabling mediated activity. In that sense our understanding of media here is closer to Vygotsky's [4] concept of 'tools for thinking'. For Vygotsky, tools have properties that can change behaviors and thoughts. It would not be surprising therefore that as tools of cultural production, media possess the ability to influence the nature of our higher psychological processes, including our creativity, in their use.

Secondly, our study looks at how the intrinsic form of the medium mediates creativity. A medium can be said to consist of three components: a physical platform or hardware, a set of formal features, and content [28]. Even though the influence of content on creativity cannot be denied, "medium content is a fickle thing" [29] and easily enough be controlled by the user. We are instead interested in the medium's formal features, or the way that the representation of content using the differing symbolic makeup of verbal language, icons or visual signs, as well as the rules and conventions governing the interaction of the symbols, exercise influence on children's creative activity.

A review of the literature shows few prior studies that exactly investigate the effects of media as tools on creativity. One strand of research of greater relevance consists of studies performed during the popularization of personal computers. Cochran-Smith [30] summarizes work inquiring about the impact of using a word processor on the writing process as opposed to the use of pen and paper. Some of the qualitative findings of those studies reported the rise of "speculative thought", the tendency towards "impermanent writing", and the positive effect of "discouraging premature closure of divergent ideas" during the writing process.

The third point on which our study deviates from the previous studies mentioned is our focus on process rather than outcome. Studies of media effects mostly evaluate creativity in terms of the creative products, that is the stories generated by the children. Creativity has been conventionally studied using four different approaches: by looking at the product created, the process of creating, the person or the creator, or the environment of creation [19]. The emphasis of our study is on the creative process that takes place as the outcome is being produced. Although the 'objective' creativity of the work products is important as the basis for evaluation by others, studying creativity developmentally enables us to tease out the effects of the medium on children's behavior as a process.

Moreover, we look at creativity as 'situationally induced' [15], that is creativity motivated by current conditions and environmental factors, instead of creativity as an individual trait as measured by standardized tests. However to prove whether practicing situated creativity over an extended period of time will or can result in better creative individual abilities is out of the scope of this study. In a similar line of thought, we investigate creativity in the average child in an everyday context, as opposed to others who have looked at 'specialists in creativity', such as gifted children or artists who either have developed, stable creative processes or defined creative output.

Based on the preceding, we asked the following research questions with regards to the animated medium:

1. How does storytelling with animation qualitatively change children's creative processes?
2. How do children perceive storytelling with animation?
3. Do children produce more creative stories with animation?

STUDY DESIGN

Pre-Interview

Third and fourth graders were recruited from the after-school program of a local elementary school as participants. The main medium of study was the animated medium or animation, but we concurrently studied the digital print medium as well for control and comparison purposes. The print medium provides a contrasting mode of mainly textual information representation with regards to the mostly visual nature of animation. Results from a pre-interview lasting around half an hour conducted with a group of fourteen children at the school also provided us good confidence in the choice of the control medium. The print (textual) medium and the animated medium were seen to be a significantly different pair ($p<0.005$) in a survey of their perceived familiarity with various media including storybooks, cartoons, movies, comics and the internet. Familiarity has been described as consisting of five main factors: prior experience, repeated exposure, level of processing, study duration and forgetting rate [31]. We based our questions about familiarity with the different media on these five factors, and produce a scale with a reliable alpha coefficient of 0.77.

Main Study

Ten children from third or fourth grade, 5 girls and 5 boys, took part in the main study. Eight of them participated in the pre-interviews and two of them joined in only for the main study. The bulk of the study consisted of asking the children to create stories using the two media. They made use of the *Frames* software to create the animated stories. *Frames* [32] is a digital storytelling software that can be downloaded for free as a fully-featured evaluation version on the web. The children created the textual story with the Microsoft *PowerPoint* software, presented as a set of storybook slide templates to them (Figure 1).

Frames makes use of a frame-by-frame approach to allow one to create animations (Figure 1). Stories can be organized as a series of still frames (like a storyboard with sound). Authors can specify the duration that each frame stays active when the animation is played, and so, can create the illusion of motion by varying the placement of objects in consecutive frames. Objects can be obtained either from a library or can be created using drawing tools. They can be manipulated through rotation, flipping or resizing. *Frames* has been tested with children in several schools [32] and is easy to use even for younger children. By controlling the frame transitions, children can then create the effect of 'stop-motion-animation' or a slide-show story.

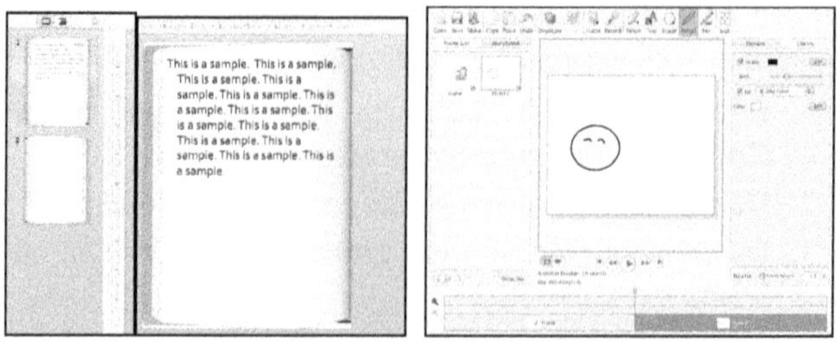

Figure 1. Screenshots of Powerpoint with storybook template (L) and Frames animation software (R)

The study was carried out in two sessions over two different days to prevent fatigue of the children from creating two stories in one session. To enable us to study the creative process, they worked in random groups of two or three as social interaction motivates externalization of thoughts into speech. In the first session, two pairs created animated stories and two pairs produced *Powerpoint* 'storybooks'. In the second session, two of the participants were not able to take part in the study, resulting in two groups of three children, one using the animation software and the other the *Powerpoint* software. Each group worked on a separate computer, and had a voice recorder placed nearby to capture the conversation during the story creation process.

The children's task was to continue and provide an ending to a given stimulus story beginning. Tasks that have been used in previous storytelling creativity studies can be classified as drawings, questions about a story, the use of standardized creativity tests such as the Torrance [8] tests, and story completions [17], which we used. We wrote two stimulus story beginnings that we ensured satisfied three criteria: that they were appropriate for the developmental age of the children, both in terms of language and content, that they were not close to experiences that only some of the children might has gone through before, and that they were more action-oriented than emotionally-driven. The stories had similar themes and were both around half a page in length with standard formatting, while still being different. The first story beginning related the story of living soap bars who have been placed in the cupboard by a family. One day the protagonist, a blue soap bar, decided to leave the cupboard to see the outside world. His cousin, a green soap bar, wanted to go with him. The second stimulus story introduced a set of Red, Blue, Yellow and Green living colored pencils belonging to a girl named Amy. They live in a box on Amy's desk. One day, they decided to visit the outer world. The step-by-step procedures of the study were as follows:

The children were grouped and each given a sticker with an ID code to paste on their shirt. They were separated into two groups according to the stimulus stories that they had to follow. Two researchers read out the stimulus stories to each group.

The children were then divided into their working pairs or groups of three. Those creating animations were sent to a different room than those creating the storybooks. Two researchers, one in each room, explained how to use the software (*Powerpoint* for the storybook group and *Frames* for the animation group) to the children. The children were given a print-out of the stimulus story that they had to follow, and asked to continue and end the story. One researcher remained in each room as an observer and took down notes of behaviors.

No formal time limit was imposed for the authoring sessions, but the amount of time that the children had to create the stories was determined by the arrival of their parents. Under these circumstances, the children had about 1.5hrs for the task. Individual post-interviews were conducted on the next day with each child separately. The children were asked about any problems that they might have had with the software, and to retell their own story.

Study Model

Figure 2 illustrates our study model. Demographics and familiarity with media were variables that we collected for the purpose of the pre-study. The possible confounds were controlled as described above: content familiarity through the use of the same stimulus stories for all the children, and usability of software through the use of a tested, off-the-shelf software. In the post-interviews, all the children also indicated that they had no problems using the software and did not find it hard to create the animations. We next describe the lower part of the model: methods used and the data analysis done.

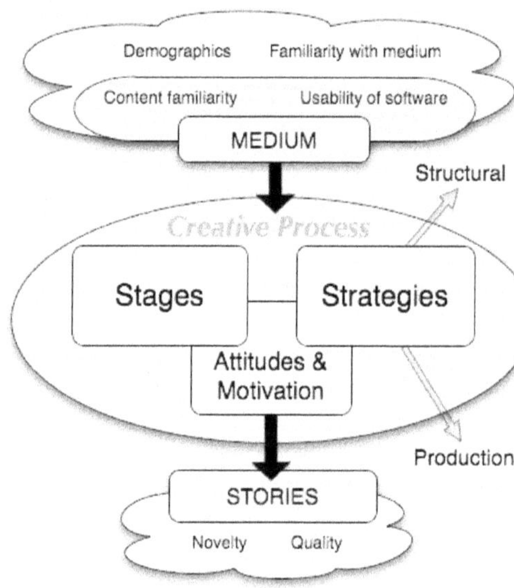

Figure 2. Study model

Data Analysis Methods and Metrics

As we mentioned above, evaluating outcomes was not a main focus of this study. We wanted to analyze the 'way in which' the authoring took place in-situ. A theoretically-driven discourse analysis was used to analyze the data collected to identify qualitative trends in the children's creative process. The coding process was conducted thus:

All the audio clips recorded during the story creation sessions were transcribed with associated speaker turn numbers, emphasis points and short event descriptions (e.g. playing the animation). A reference chain analysis as described in [33] was performed by four coders. Each was first allotted a transcript to analyze according to the following coding scheme of speech at three levels: *object*, where the reference is to a task-related entity; *meta*, which includes references to the talk being carried out (this includes speech referencing the process of story construction and not the stories being constructed themselves); and *para*, which references things and persons in the environment and includes discourse about the individual's perspective and opinions. The four coders then conferred and resolved any serious discrepancies in the different understandings of the coding scheme. We found that an *object* code in our case could refer either to talk about the Story or the Tool. The transcripts were then redistributed among the coders, and coded again with new understanding of the coding scheme.

After the reference chain analysis, an open coding was done on the transcripts to reveal categories and themes. Examples included 'distribution of roles', 'asking for help', 'setting up next scene', or 'searching the library'. All the instances of each code and theme were then grouped and analyzed for patterns using Coughlan & Johnson's [34] two perspectives of creative interaction as a guide.

The first perspective, structural interaction entails the practices and the structuring of the creative process. In this respect we looked at the different stages that the children went through to complete the task. The speech acts coded as *Para* and *Meta* helped in identifying patterns. The second, productive interaction is concerned with "low-level interactions", such as the generation, externalization and evaluation of ideas while working towards the final outcome. We thus looked at the different strategies that the children employed to generate ideas for their stories by employing Guilford's [35] concept of convergent and divergent thinking but given our interest in the process, we analyzed the concepts in a more qualitative manner.

Divergent thinking has been defined as "producing a variety of responses in which the product is not completely determined by the information given to the respondent" [36]. Several divergent thinking tests have been developed (e.g. Torrance Tests of Creative Thinking, Guilford's Alternative Uses Task). In our coding process, divergence was taken to be a proposition of a story idea that departs from previously presented material, either in the stimulus story or by other group members. It was however not taken to be equivalent to disagreements. If only a disagreement was manifested without a suggestion for a change, it was not counted as an instance of divergent thinking.

Convergent thinking refers to the process of following "a particular set of logical steps to arrive at one solution, which in some cases is the 'correct' solution [36], and has often been measured using the Mednick's Remote Associates Test. For our study, an instance of convergence entailed a proposition of a story idea that draws from, builds, follows or draws from what was presented before by the stimulus story or by another child. Apart from divergent and convergent thinking, we also coded a third element that we labeled as 'seeding'. The emergence of a story idea was categorized as seeding when it consisted of a proposition that did not draw from what has been presented before in any form. It should be noted that all story ideas were considered in the analysis, including ideas that were suggested but did not eventually make it into the final story. Furthermore, no assessment was done as to the originality of the story ideas during the coding process. A convergent idea could be as original or more original than a divergent idea, but if it drew from material presented in the past, it was still coded as convergence. The coding was done mainly in terms of how an idea shaped, directed or influenced the path of the creation of the final story product.

A further analysis was carried out for the children's retelling of their stories in the post-interviews. There were three storybooks and three animations produced. Although the stories were short, each story was first reduced to a 'narrative digest' [37] before being used for analysis so that they all had comparative value. Procedures to create a 'narrative digest' included reviewing the story and writing down the main events that happened in the story as a list of sequential story propositions. The retelling of the story by the child was then compared to the story's 'narrative digest' and checked for coverage of the propositions.

Finally, we used Amabile's [38] consensual assessment technique for the evaluation of the actual stories. Three teachers with experience dealing with children of the 8 to 10 year old age group were asked to be the judges. Teachers were chosen because as pointed out by Boden [39], it is not possible for one to "decide whether or not an act is genuinely creative" without being familiar with the conceptual space of the creator. The teachers were asked to judge the stories with the following instructions: they were asked to first go through all the six stories without any judging. They then had to preview each story again one by one and fill in an evaluation form for each. The ratings scale was exactly as Amabile's and included the dimensions of creativity, novelty, coherence, continuation and completion. Following Valkenburg and Beentjes [17], we grouped the first two dimensions into a story Novelty component, and the last three into a story Quality component. The next section of this paper describes our findings from the various analyses conducted.

FINDINGS

Structural Interaction: Stages of Creation

The creative process in the storybook and the animation sessions differed substantially. The development of the storybook happened in series consisting of four main steps: generating Ideas, Typing it into the *Powerpoint* storybook, working on Aesthetics, and correcting Language (Figure 2). Idea generation saw greater argumentation before a story idea was actually materialized in the form of text and typed in, as compared to the animation sessions where story ideas were mostly acted out immediately. Previewing story (in terms of reading aloud) and assessment of the story mostly

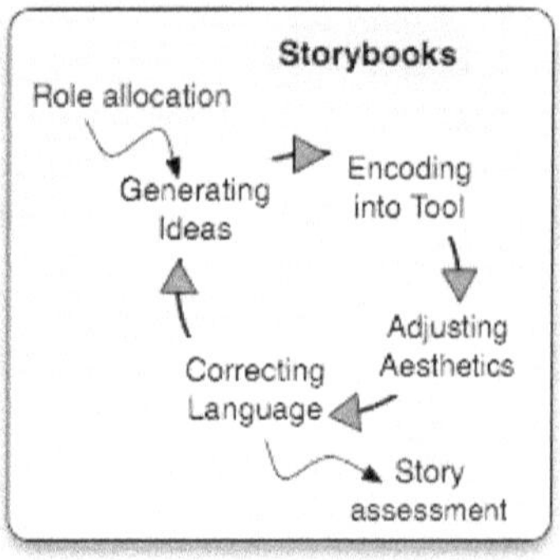

Figure 2. Stages of creative process for Storybooks

occurred towards the end of the creation process. Work distribution in the storybook session was done by turns. It was typically settled that one child would be the 'typist' and the other the 'idea generator'. Throughout the session then, the 'idea generator', despite having the logically more important role in the creative process, would often claim their turn to be the 'typist' after some intervals. The following extracts illustrate the typical role distribution procedure that took place across the storybook sessions:

"How about this Lisa? I type and you tell me what to type"

"So you (^) make up the text."

"No...Lisa...help meee. You got to tell me what to write."

"Ok can I just type from there from now on?"

In the animation sessions, the creative process took place mainly as alternating sequences of Idea generation, Previewing the story (playing the animation), Assessment and Fixing (using tool functions, e.g. undo, timing, placement) (Figure 3). During the process of generating ideas, the children were more inclined to openly state what they were thinking of doing. They seemed to clearly have pre-formed ideas of what was going to happen next in their story, and offered their 'plans' both when asked and even without prompting. For example, one of the child saying "on this one (referring to a frame) he needs to say 'Bye'" shows that she already had a picture of the story development in mind while creating the previous frame.

Children also started to preview their story much earlier in the process and much more frequently in the animation sessions, leading to what we call 'micro-assessments'. Rather than a concrete assessment phase at the end of the session, assessment was done more as a step-by-step process of short evaluations for each subtask, e.g. image placement, object appearance, sounds.

The micro-assessments created more opportunities to generate consensus throughout the creation process. As compared to the storybook sessions, negotiation of roles in the animation sessions was similarly more integrated in the process. We identified four main strategies that the children adopted to distribute work: by frame (each child does one frame), by task (e.g. choosing the color, placing the images) or by skill (e.g. drawing, making sounds). For instance, even though it

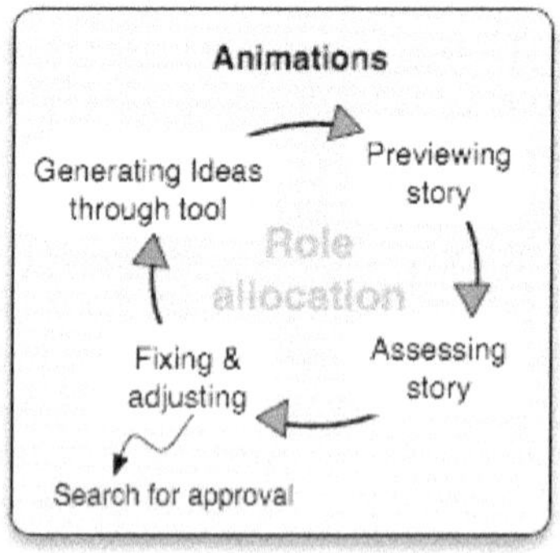

Figure 3. Stages of creative process for Animations

was not his 'turn' to work on the particular frame, a child interjected:

"Let me (^) do it, you're terrible (car honking sound)"

This flexibility in role negotiation and work distribution enabled all of the group members to stay active and interested throughout the sessions. It was also observed that children contested roles much more often than during the storybook sessions.

An additional 'stage' was seen in the animation sessions in terms of the search for approval. Children were eager to 'show off' what they have created, and were clearly confident that they did a good job. They repeatedly asked the researcher, who stayed as an observer and to help with any software-related problems, or other teams to watch their story, as *"it's really good"*. Two of the children also asked their parents to see their stories as they were leaving.

Production of Interaction: Strategies of Creation

Five main themes were uncovered in the analysis of the children's creative process using the animated medium through the coding of recurrent instances and patterns.

1. Micro-activities

The animation medium resulted in the story being told using micro-activities of creating different elements, e.g. sounds, objects. Even though they spent longer amounts of time on certain micro-activities (e.g. one group recorded a character script line four times to get it right in terms of loudness, clarity, speed, etc), it was clear that the children still had a macro-view of the story as a whole. In contrast, in the storybook sessions the story was generated through the use of prompting questions. Questions such as *"What happens next?", "What do they do?", "What are we going to write about?"* served as breakpoint that constantly appeared throughout the session and that pushed for a series of ideas built around a central topic each time. It seemed that the story was developed by the children in an amorphous manner as they go along, fashioned 'by-the-seat-of-their-pants' at each breakpoint.

2. Activity-driven integrated story generation

Story creation occurred in terms of specification of actions within the interface and without. They responded to the multiple cues and modes of stimuli enabled by the animation tool to make sense of the story, for instance through *placement of elements*, the *choice of objects* to include, *characters' speech and sound effects.*

Object placement: By placing and moving objects in the set-up of each story frame, the children molded the development of the story. For example, to tell the story that the main character is going out while the rest of the family is staying behind, the child verbalized her actions in the following way: *"That guy needs to be way up. Those guys need to be right there."* Action-based story creation was hence often accompanied by extensive gesturing and pointing at the screen. Space and time became a kind of 'medium' where the children's imagination was materialized.

Choice of objects: Searching for material to use in the story was done in two ways: the children either used existing images in the software library or drew their own objects. This search for objects, whether through library browsing or by deciding what to draw, became a focal point that led the children to make decisions on what to include in their story. It can be argued that the provision of ready-made 'sources of ideas' in the library is limiting to the child's imagination. For example, one of the groups saw the categories of items 'Animals' while browsing the library and decided to include a dog in their story. Hence, the categories may be said to 'limit' the possibilities the children considered. Contrariwise, library materials also served as epistemic prompts to scaffold individual and group creative activity. This is similar to the use of physical objects as inspirational devices to catalyst creative design [40, 41]. In the same group of children, we observed a feedback loop whereby the library informed and modulated the creativity of the children. In that one group's story, the dog was made to save the falling green crayon.

Characters' speech: The auditory mode of representation was found to be a key part of story construction. This, in itself, is unsurprising since it is difficult to carry the symbolic element of any narrative arc in animation alone. What was remarkable is that throughout the story creation process, the children did not explicitly (in speech) or directly (using straightforward words) discuss the overall arc of the story. In many instances across the animation sessions the children communicated story development through the process of creating sounds, from determining what to record, practicing the speech or sound effect to be recorded, recording the sound, to deciding where to place the sound:

"Ok wait, I wanna do a sound to that. He might be saying like "woah this suitcase is so heavy"

A: Wait let me practice. (dog sounds) Like that? (dog sounds) which one?
B: Big dog voice

In this way, the animation storytellers seem to be thinking through the tool. This is different from the storybook children who wrote 'on the fly' (without an overall narrative sketch), but did so in spurts where they formulated what to do next, and then proceeded to encode it by typing into the 'storybook'. The children even acted out sounds made by characters in the storybook sessions, but this remained as part of the idea generation process we identified earlier. The children had no way to include the sounds directly into the storybook, and the fundamental authoring loop of *Idea generation – Encoding with tool – Aesthetics – Correction* remained intact. The extract below of a child explaining to her partner that the story's main characters heard a singing voice in the storybook session is a clear example:

"So they're hearing this: Do you want to plaaayy" (singing)

3. Qualitative focus

Development of the story manifested itself with a focus on precise, qualitative details through the shaping of aesthetics (e.g. color, speed, size, thickness). This motivated the children to think of how the different objects in their story world look like qualitatively, for instance, discussing whether the book in the story should be rectangular or square, determining book size and color, or the type of dog.

Yet, manipulating aesthetic details at times did cause the process to be longer. One group spent a significant amount of time determining what was to be shown on the book cover, even though the book was not a major element in their story. They went from depictions of Jack and Jill, to the Three Little Pigs, with suggestions about the Three Musketeers and simple scribbles. Nevertheless, comparatively, spending time adjusting aesthetics in the creation of the storybook story was time lost on manipulating the tool (e.g. font size and spaces), whereas adjusting aesthetics in the creation of the animation was meaningful to the story itself, acting as means to induce the children to define or take decisions on certain story details.

Moreover, the focus on qualitative details made for much shorter stories with the animated medium, but richer in texture. If the stories were to be converted in text based on the details that the children paid attention to in their creative process using animation, they would be much more vivid stories than the storybook stories they wrote. Skilled adult writers have the necessary fluency (in the common sense of the term) to portray a story with expressive imagery using the written language. At fourth grade, children do not possess the sophistication in the written text yet, but the animated medium provides them with a 'language' that enables them to create similarly rich stories.

4. Broader imagination

The visual nature of the animation medium seemed to have the capability of serving as a stimulus for retention and to broaden the imagination of the child with respect to the story world. In the interviews conducted after the sessions, there was a large difference in the fidelity with which the children who did the storybooks could retell their story as compared to those who did the animations. The first group could retell their story with an accuracy of 41.8% (based on the number of propositions covered in the retelling over the total number of propositions in the 'narrative digest' of the story), whereas the second group did so with an accuracy of 63.3%. In fact, two of the children could not remember any of the propositions at all when asked to recount their storybook stories,

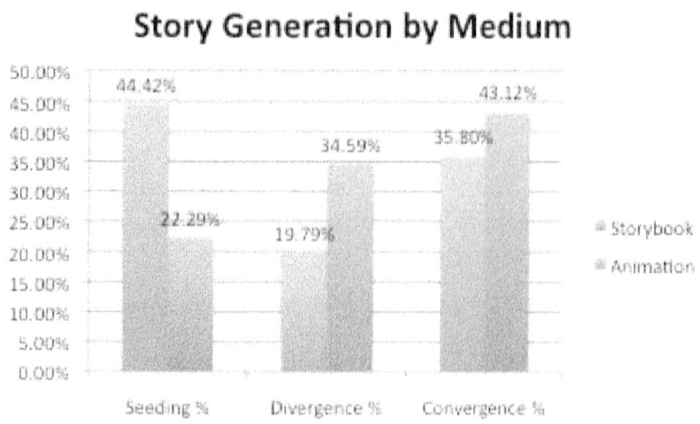

Graph 1. Seeding, divergence and convergence by medium

while two others recounted their animation stories with a full coverage of all the propositions.

5. Serendipitous creativity

The activity-based nature of the creation process with the animation medium led to idea generation by accident at various times, a strategy that was not present in the storybook authoring. This finding was also observed by Earles [42] when she studied the ad hoc creative process of a professional artist using digital software to produce her works of art. In the creative process of the artist, the computer "often introduces unexpected or accidental effects and elements, generally helping to create the compositional problem". While one group using the animation software was trying to draw a cupboard, they accidentally created a brown shape that they then imagined to be a shelf. The following conversation shows this serendipitous creativity:

A: Oh...how did that (^) happen?

B: Ooh that's good actually

A. That's good yea...it's like a shelf

B: Shadow. The shelf on it.

A: Yea we've got a shadow with the shelf. We can move the suitcase up there so he can be reaching down there

6. Story generation

Using the coding process based on the concepts of divergence and convergence as explained above, we found that more seeding (by 22.13%) occurred in the storybook sessions than in the animation ones, indicating that somewhat more ideas were put forward during the creation of the storybooks. However using the animated medium, the degree of both divergence (by 14.8%) and convergence (by 7.32%) of ideas was greater (Graph 1). These results may be explained by the five themes that we have described above. For example, low seeding may have been caused by the constraints imposed by the software, such as the search for objects in the library. The activity-driven property of the creative process may have on the other hand encouraged greater divergence and convergence by providing more discussion and decision points.

Attitudes and Perceptions

Hennessey [43] describes motivation as one of the key factors in creative behavior that needs attention. In fact, it is of even greater importance if we are to sustain creativity over an extended period of time throughout the Fourth Grade Slump. Amabile's [44] "principle of internal motivation for creativity" states that internal motivation like satisfaction and interest leads to the creative process, but external stimuli such as expectations and the offering of rewards hinder it. We thus need to look at children's reactions to the use of animation for creative activity.

A number of observations provide support for us to posit that story authoring using animation was more motivating for the children. The storybook sessions, which lasted on average 28 minutes (153 speaker turns), were much shorter than the animation sessions, which took an average of 48 minutes (417 speaker turns). The children became bored and restless quickly when making the storybooks, as we observed and as illustrated by the extract below from one of the group's conversation:

"That's all we have to do. We just have to write a middle and an end."

"Hurry let's write the story so we can get outside"

Children in the animation sessions conversely showed excitement and enthusiasm, gesturing, acting out, and were eager to present their story to others. Two children in fact explicitly remarked to their group during the sessions:

A: This is fun
B: I know

A: Kyra isn't this fun?
B: Yea...

The groups doing the animated stories wanted to keep going even when they were being picked up at the end of their after-school period. Several students requested that the researchers return another day to let them finish their stories.

Creative Products

The average rating given by the three teachers on Novelty (consisting of the dimensions of creativity and novelty) was slightly higher for the animated stories ($\mu = 3.72$) than for the storybooks ($\mu = 3.56$). For the Quality component (continuity, coherence, completion), the teachers rated the storybooks ($\mu = 4.44$) higher than the animation stories ($\mu = 3.96$). However, it would be unfair to draw out any conclusions from the lower Quality ratings for the animations given that both groups had the same amount of time to create the stories and the animated medium by nature requires a longer commitment of time to create. We reiterate here our point that our focus in this paper was about the process of creativity rather than the outcome. We believe that it is difficult to draw conclusions, although interesting, from mere assessments of finished products.

CONCLUSION

The study of creativity is not new, but with the rapid advancement of technologies, it is important that we pay close attention to how new media affect creativity. In light of the 'creativity crisis' that Robinson [7] warns us about and the developmental phenomenon of the Fourth Grade Slump, research is needed on ways to nurture children's creativity.

We posit that the use of the animated medium for creative activities is a good candidate to sustain the child's creativity throughout the critical times of the Fourth Grade Slump. Due to its form and formal features, the animated medium transforms the activity into one that the child is motivated to be involved in, that creates engagement and enthusiasm during the process, and that results in positive self-confidence in the created product. Media effects have long been studied but little research has been done on the creative processes that take place with media as tools of creative production, especially with children.

We presented a study on the effects of medium on the creative storytelling process by third and fourth grade children. We chose our target age group to address the Fourth Grade Slump where creative activity in the child declines precipitously. Given the exposure of children to video and other multimedia it is critical to investigate whether authoring in such new media would alter both the creative process as well as the motivation for creative activity. We compared children authoring animated stories using *Frames,* an animation authoring tool against children creating stories in text using *Powerpoint* with a 'storybook' template. To understand the process of creation, we recorded the children's discussions as they created their stories in both media.

Our results showed that the children adopted significantly different strategies in story construction. Both of the groups seemingly engaged in 'on-the-fly' story generation with no apparent overall story-arc design, generating each subsequent piece of story sequentially. However the storybook students took a more rigid loop of *idea generation – encoding (typing), –working on aesthetics (fonts and formats) – correcting grammar and spelling*. The animated story children took an *activity-driven* approach using the *medium as a thinking tool*, constructing each piece while working with the authoring program. Their authoring loop, *idea generation – previewing* (playing animation snippets), *assessment – fixing* (using tool functions), were smaller and the children seemed more fluid and interactive in the process. There was greater attention to detail and quality in the animations, and they had better recall of their stories in the post-interviews. We ascribe this recall and ability to picture their stories to having a *broader imagination* when creating in the medium. The animation tool also provided more opportunity for *serendipitous creativity* as the children trying to create something realized that their creations could be repurposed. There was no such observation among the storybook children. The animation groups also showed greater evidence of both divergent and convergent thinking, although more seeding of ideas was done in the storybook groups. We also saw evidence that motivation and enthusiasm were far higher in the animation groups. Yet, the creative process is complex. We recognize that other factors such as group dynamics and gender may have had an effect on the processes and strategies during the authoring sessions. It is however out of the scope of this paper to present an analysis of the role of social influences in the mediated creative process.

The power of the tool and its constituent symbolic system to change human higher mental functions has been highlighted by influential researchers such as Vygotsky and Leont'ev. Tools can therefore be of help to nurture children's creativity during the Slump. As we design and develop tools for that purpose, it is necessary that we first gain a full understanding of the influence that the medium of creation exerts on the creative process. In that sense, future work entails the analysis of medium effects on creativity in coupling with other important factors such as social relationships and group communication.

ACKNOWLEDGMENTS

This research has been partially supported by grants #IIS 0954048 "EAGER: Creative IT: Hyper Drama Storytelling: Engaging and Nurturing Creativity in K-12 Students", and CRI-0551610 "Interacting with the Embodied Mind". We also thank Sarah Quek who helped greatly in data coding.

REFERENCES

1. Creativity World Forum. *State of Creativity. 7th annual creativity world forum*. 2010 [cited 4/30/11]; From: http://stateofcreativity.com/events/cwf/about/.
2. Florida, R., *The Rise of the Creative Class: And How it's transforming work, leisure, community and everyday life,* 2002, New York: Perseus Book Group.
3. Gruber, H.E. and D.B. Wallace, *The case study method and evolving systems approach for understanding uniquely creative people at work*, in *Handbook of creativity*, R.J. Sternberg, Editor, 1999, Cambridge University Press.: New York. p. 93–115.
4. Vygotsky, L.S., ed. *Thought and Language, (Edited and translated by E. Hanfmann and G. Vakar)* ed. A. Kozulin, 1987, MIT Press: Cambridge.
5. Guilford, J.P., *Creativity.* American Psychologist, 1950. **5**: p. 444-454.
6. Bronson, P. and A. Merryman. *The Creativity Crisis*. 2010 [cited 2011 April 30]; From: <http://www.newsweek.com/2010/07/10/the-creativity-crisis.html>.
7. Robinson, K. *Do Schools Kill Creativity?* 2006; From: http://www.ted.com/index.php/talks/view/id/66.
8. Torrance, E.P., *Understanding te Fourth Grade Slump in Creative Thinking*, 1967. p. 444.
9. Roberts, D.F., U.G. Foehr, and V. Rideout, *Generation M: Media in the lives of 8-18 year-olds*, 2005, Kaiser Family Foundation Study.
10. Springen, K. *Fourth-Grade Slump*. 2007 [cited 4/30/11]; From: http://www.newsweek.com/2007/ 02/18/fourth-grade-slump.html.
11. Kirkpatrick, E.A., *Individual Tests of School Children.* Psychological Review, 1900. **5**(7): p. 274.
12. Ruble, D.N., *The acquisition of self-knowledge: A self-socialization perspective*, in *Contemp. topics in developmental psyc.*, N. Eisenberg, 1987, Wiley: NY.
13. Collins, W.A., *Development During Middle Childhood. The Years from Six to Twelve,* 1984, Washington, DC: National Academy Press.
14. Henk, W.A. and S.A. Melnick, *The Reader Self-Perception Scale (RSPS): A new tool for measuring how children feel*

about themselves as readers. The Reading Teacher, 1995. **48**(6 Res. Libr. Core): p. 470.
15. Greenfield, P., D. Farrar, and J. Beagles-Roos, *Is the medium the message? An experimental comparison of the effects of radio and television on imagination.* Jour. of Applied Develop. Psyc., 1986. **7**(3): p. 201-218.
16. Watkins, B. and J. Coulombe, *Children model the medium: Media forms in written narratives*, 1981, University of Michigan: Ann Arbor.
17. Valkenburg, P.M. and J.W.J. Beentjes, *Children's Creative Imagination in Response to Radio and Television Stories.* Journal of Communication, 1997. **47**(2): p. 21-38.
18. Runco, M.A. and K. Pezdek, *The Effect of Television and Radio on Children's Creativity.* Human Communication Research, 1984. **11**(1): p. 109–120.
19. Rubenstein, D.J., *Stimulating Children's Crativity and Curiosity: Does Content and Medium Matter?* Journal of Creative Behavior, 2000. **34**(1): p. 1-17.
20. Greenfield, S., *Creating Creative Brains*, in *Keynote address presented at CCI's Creating Value: Between Commerce and Commons Conference*2008: Brisbane.
21. Baddeley, A.D. and G. Hitch, *Working Memory*, in *The Psychology of Learning and Motivation: Advances in Research and Theory*, G.H. Bower, Editor. 1974, Academic Press: New York. p. 47--89.
22. Paivio, A., *Mental representations: a dual coding approach.* 1986, Oxford University Press.
23. Malaga, R.A., *The Effect of Stimulus Modes and Associative Distance in Individual Creativity Support Systems*, in *Proc. of the 32nd Hawaii International Conference on System Sciences.* 1999.
24. Mayer, R., *Multimedia Learning,* 2001, Cambridge, UK: Cambridge University Press.
25. Daft, R.L. and R.H. Lengel, *Organizational information requirements, media richness and structural design.* Management Science, 1986. **32**(5): p. 554-571.
26. Shepard, R.N., *Externalization of mental images and the act of creation*, in *Visual learning, thinking, and communication*, B.S. Randhava and W.E. Coffman, 1978, Academic Press: New York. p. 133-189.
27. Kock, N., *The psychobiological model: Towards a new theory of computer-mediated communication based on Darwinian evolution.* Organization Science, 2004, **15**(3): p. 327-348.
28. Subrahmanyam, K. and P. Greenfield, *Media Symbol Systems and Cognitive Processes*, in *The Handbook of Children, Media, and Development,* 2009, Blackwell Publishing Ltd. p. 166-187.
29. Brown, L.K., *Fiction for Children: Does the Medium Matter?* Jour. of Aesthetic Edu., 1988. **22**(1): p. 35-44.
30. Cochran-Smith, M., *Word Processing and Writing in Elementary Classrooms: A Critical Review of Related Literature.* Rev. of Edu. Res., 1991. **61**(1): p. 107-155.
31. Zhang, J. and A.A. Ghorbani, *Familiarity and Trust: Measuring Familiarity with a Web Site*, in *Proceedings of the 2nd Annual Conference on Privacy, Trust and Security,* 2004. p. 23-28.
32. Tech4Learning. *Frames: Everyone has a story to tell*, 2011 [cited 4/30/11]; From: http://www.tech4learning.com/frames.
33. McNeill, D., et al., *MIND-MERGING*, in *Expressing Oneself / Expressing One's Self: Communication, Language, Cognition, and Identity: A Festschrift in honor of Robert M. Krauss (11/8/07)*, E. Moresella, 2008, Taylor & Francis Pubs.
34. Coughlan, T. and P. Johnson, *Understanding Productive, Structural and Longitudinal Interactions in the Design of Tools for Creative Activities*, in *Creativity and Cognition,* 2009. p. 155-164.
35. Guilford, J., *The Nature of Human Intelligence.* 1967, New York: McGraw-Hill.
36. Runco, M.A. and S.R. Pritzker, *Encyclopedia of Creativity Vol. 1,* 1999: Elsevier.
37. Register, L.M. and T.B. Henley, *The Phenomenology of Intimacy* Journal of Social and Personal Relationships, 1992. **9**(4): p. 467-481
38. Amabile, T.M., *Social Psychology of Creativity: A Consensual Assessment Technique.* Jour. of Personality and Social Psychology, 1982. **43**(5): p. 997-1013.
39. Boden, M.A., *The Creative Mind: Myths and Mechanisms,* 2004: Routledge.
40. Heimdal, E. and T. Rosenqvist. *Textiles as tangible working materials in participatory design processes: potentials and challenges.* in *Proc. of the 11th Biennial Participatory Design Conference.* 2010.
41. Jacucci, G. and I. Wagner, *Performative roles of materiality for collective creativity*, in *Proceedings of the 6th ACM SIGCHI conference on Creativity & cognition.* 2007, ACM: Washington, DC. p. 73-82.
42. Eales, J.R.T., *Creativity in Action: Some implications for the design of Creativity Support Systems*, in *Proc. of 6th ACM SIGCHI New Zealand Chapter's CHI: Making CHI Natural,* 2005. p. 9-14.
43. Hennessey, B.A., *Creativity and Motivation in the Classroom: A Social Psychological and Multi-Cultural Perspective.*, in *Creativity: A Handbook for Teachers*, A. Tan, 2007, World Scientific: Singapore. p. 27–45.
44. Amabile, T., *Children's Artistic Creativity: Detrimental Effects of Competition in a Field Setting.* Personality and Social Psychology Bulletin, 1982. **8**: p. 573–578.

Combining Concept Maps to Catalyze Creativity

Lixiu Yu
Stevens Institute of Technology
Hoboken, New Jersey
lisayu1103@gmail.com

Jeffrey V. Nickerson
Stevens Institute of Technology
Hoboken, New Jersey
jnickerson@stevens.edu

ABSTRACT

Combining concept maps aids creative problem solving. In two studies, participants were presented with a story describing a problem and its solution. They were then asked to read an analogous problem and provide a solution. In order to facilitate transfer from the first story to the second, concept maps of the stories were elicited and participants instructed to combine them. The results show that participants were more likely to solve the problem when they produced and combined concept maps, as compared to a condition in which concept maps were used without combination, and compared to a condition in which no maps were used, but instead summaries were created and combined.

Author Keywords

Creativity, combination, concept map, analogy

ACM Classification Keywords

H5.3. Group and Organization Interfaces

ACM General Terms

Design

INTRODUCTION

How can designers be encouraged to come up with more creative ideas? There are three techniques that show particular promise: combination [26, 30, 35], analogical thinking [11], and visual representation [28, 32]. Can these three overlapping techniques work together? That is, can combining visualizations work to encourage creativity in the design process? In order to answer this question, we will first discuss the relationship between visual combination and creativity, and then discuss analogy.

Visual combination and creativity

What do we mean by combination? Combination has been defined as the merging of two or more concepts into one new idea [34], the mental synthesis of object parts [6] and the putting together the elements of a problem in a way that is not obvious [27]. In addition, it has been defined as the rearrangement of the elements within an existing problem [21]. Synthesizing these definitions, we describe combination as a process bringing together two or more separate things to produce a new object. In design, this combination process usually involves the visual: according to one study, 87% of the inventions examined used visual mental representations [29]. Furthermore, experiments have shown that the mental synthesis of a given set of visual objects produces creative designs [6].

The present study investigates the role of visual combination in creativity. Specifically, the catalyzing role of visual combination in analogical thinking is tested. We focus on analogical thinking because visual analogy is arguably an important cognitive strategy in the design process and there is evidence that creative analogies produce innovative designs [2, 31]. We now discuss how visual combination might help with analogical thinking.

Visual combination and analogy

Creative insights can be gained by noticing and applying an analogy from an understood domain of knowledge to a problem in a new domain [6, 8, 15, 31]. This process is called spontaneous transfer if it occurs without an explicit hint being given to the solver that the solution of the source problem can be applied to the target problem. A number of studies have investigated manipulations that trigger spontaneous transfers [3, 11, 22, 24]. Most of them were designed to encourage the formation of generalized schema: that is, multiple examples are used to encourage abstraction [1, 3, 7, 11]. We argue that analogical thinking can also be encouraged through a process of visual combination.

How does an analogy work? Analogical reasoning is a process of mapping relations between two disparate domains guided by multiple constraints [11, 15]. Specifically, knowledge may be represented in networks made up of nodes (things), attributes (the qualities of nodes), and relations (predicates that link two nodes together) [8]. The mapping between two conceptual systems, formed by finding similarity in the relations between these systems, is an analogy [9]. Specifically, by mapping the source conceptual system consisting of a problem and a solution, it becomes possible to fill in the solution slots of the targeted conceptual system.

Visual representation is an integral part of analogy [4, 25] and more generally is fundamental to design [23, 28, 32]. While there are many possible representations, we will focus on a particularly abstract one: conceptual maps. Such maps are set of nodes connected by lines. The nodes and lines are usually labeled, the nodes as noun phrases, and the lines as relations. Concept maps have been shown to be useful in the classroom, because they can promote the

C&C'11, November 3–6, 2011, Atlanta, Georgia, USA.

development of thinking skills by helping students organize knowledge. A concept map is simple to teach: the only syntactical elements are nodes, connectors and labels. Even with such a simple syntax, the maps can been used to portray abstract and complex systems [14, 16, 20, 33]. Thagard used such diagrams in his study of scientific creativity, showing how concepts in one field are applied in another in a process that leads to scientific discovery [30].

Predictions

Concept maps can be used to encourage the abstraction of a source problem and a target problem. The optimal abstract level of representation involves finding and preserving commonalities while deleting the differences between the analogs [11, 19]. In other words, such a process seeks to find a structural alignment between two mental representations [9]. Concept maps portray the overall structure of a concept system and require the constructer to develop an organized view of the concepts. Consequently, concept maps can be used as a technique to encourage abstract representation in the step we call the structure generation process.

This step is followed by a structure combination process, in which the solution system of the source is applied to the target problem. The target conceptual system is augmented. The theory of conceptual development claims that the development of new concepts results from the combination of existing concepts: such a conceptual change might involve deleting old concepts and adding new concepts [30]. In the combination process, people will draw upon the knowledge to be combined as well as their broader world knowledge to construct a causal reasoning chain [18]. And the combination of concepts often produces emergent attributes not found in the original concepts [18]. We predict that asking participants to combine concept maps may assist with the class of well-known insight problems, and it may help participants to discover analogs. That is, combining concept maps improves the ability of a person to notice the analogical structure within source and target problems and apply that structure to solve the target problem. The above discussion leads to the following hypothesis:

> Combining concept maps will increase the recognition of analogies.

This hypothesis was explored through two studies. In the first study, participants were given a variant of the Duncker radiation problem as the target problem [5]. All were asked to draw concept maps of the source and the target problem; those in the experimental condition were asked to draw a combined concept map prior to solving the target problem. The second study sought to solidify the findings of the first study, incorporating three conditions that sought to understand the importance of both combination and concept maps. In all, the experiments were designed to determine the extent to which concept maps and combination processes can improve insight in problem solving.

OVERALL METHOD

Much of creativity happens in response to open-ended problems, but the evaluation of creative work is fraught with difficulty, as experts often disagree [6]. There are problems, called insight problems, for which strong solutions exist, and for which the solutions generated are thought to be demonstrative of creative thought processes. In these studies, we first perform two experiments using such an insight problem.

We modified versions of the military problem and Duncker's radiation problem, frequently used in analogy reasoning research [5, 10, 11]. The military problem serves as the source analogy and the radiation problem serves as the target analogous problem that requires a solution. The military problem presented in the experiments was as follows:

A small country was ruled from a strong fortress by a dictator. The fortress was situated in the middle of the country, surrounded by farms and villages. Many roads led to the fortress through the countryside. A rebel general vowed to capture the fortress. The general knew that an attack by his entire army would capture the fortress. He gathered his army at the head of one of the roads, ready to launch a full-scale direct attack. However, the general then learned that the dictator had planted mines on each of the roads. The mines were set so that small bodies of men could pass over them safely, since the dictator needed to move his troops and workers to and from the fortress. However, any large force would detonate the mines. Not only would this blow up the road, but it would also destroy many neighboring villages. It therefore seemed impossible to capture the fortress.

However, the general devised a simple plan. He divided his army into small groups and dispatched each group to the head of a different road. When all was ready he gave the signal and each group marched down a different road. Each group continued down its road to the fortress so that the entire army arrived together at the fortress at the same time. In this way, the general captured the fortress and overthrew the dictator.

The radiation problem was presented as follows:

Suppose you are a doctor faced with a patient who has a malignant tumor in his stomach. Through an analysis of imaging data, you have determined that it is impossible to operate on the patient. However, unless the tumor is destroyed the patient will die. You know there is a kind of ray that can be used to destroy the tumor. If the rays reach the tumor all at once at a sufficiently high intensity, the tumor will be destroyed. Unfortunately, you also know that at this high intensity the healthy tissue that the rays pass through on the way to the tumor will also be destroyed. This destruction would be catastrophic. You would therefore like to use a lower intensity ray, because at lower intensities the rays are harmless to healthy tissue. Unfortunately, these lower intensity rays will not affect the tumor either.

These are close to the text of the original problems [11], modified to provide a similar level of detail in each of the prompts. The desired transfer from the military to the radiation problem is the following: split the high intensity ray into multiple low-intensity rays which are arranged to converge at the tumor from multiple angles simultaneously, similar to the way the general captures the fortress by converging his troops down multiple roads. This is called the *convergence* solution; it is difficult to discover [5, 11].

COMBINING MAPS EXPERIMENT

Method

Participants

A total of 28 master students participated in the present experiment. Participants registered for a masters-level course on systems design. Seventy-eight percent were male and 37% were part-time students.

The tasks of the experiment were given as part of in-class tests. A description of concept maps was provided in a lecture before the one in which the problem was given. All students were randomly assigned to one of the two conditions. There were 13 participants in the *map* condition and 15 in the *map then combine maps* condition. One participant's data in the *map then combine maps* condition was not included in the analyses due to his failure to follow instructions. All participants were given 30 minutes to work on the task.

Design and Procedure

In both of the two conditions, participants were presented with the military problem and the solution, then asked to draw a concept map:

Please draw a concept map for the military problem.

After that they were presented with the radiation problem and asked to draw a concept map for it, using near-identical instructions: "military problem" was replaced with "tumor problem"

The difference between the two conditions occurred in the last step. In the map condition, participants were asked to solve the radiation problem after they completed the two maps:

What type of procedure might be used to destroy the tumor with the rays, and at the same time avoid destroying the healthy tissue?

In the *map then combine maps* condition, participants were asked to draw a new concept map to combine the two concept maps for the military problem and the radiation problem before they were asked to solve the radiation problem. The prompt read as follows:

Please draw a new concept map to combine the two concept maps you just drew for the military problem and the tumor problem.

Results

Each participant's data consists of two parts: concept maps and the solution to the radiation problem. Each solution for the radiation problem was classified into two categories: convergence solutions and non-convergence solutions. Table 1 shows one example of each solution category.

Solution Type	Example
Convergence	Expose tumor to low-intensity rays coming from different directions. The focused power will be enough to destroy the tumor without affecting healthy tissue.
Non-convergence	The doctor might use the lower intensity rays to go through the healthy tissue and locate the tumor, and once there, increase the intensity, which the tumor is destroyed.

Table 1. Participant solution examples for the radiation problem.

Figure 1 shows the examples of concept maps drawn by participants for the two problems. Figure 2 shows an example of the combined concept maps drawn by participants.

We examined whether participants in the *map then combine maps* condition generated more convergence solutions to the radiation problem. The convergence solution frequencies are 9 out of 14 (64%) in the *map then combine maps* condition, and 2 out of 13 (15%) in the map condition, as shown in Figure 3. The small sample size does not lend itself to statistical inference. However, the general trend shows that many more participants generated convergence problems in the *map then combine maps* condition.

Discussion

This experiment was designed to examine the effect of the combination of the concept maps on problem solving. Consistent with our prediction, the results suggest that participants were more likely to generate convergence solutions when they drew and combined concept maps. Although the sample size was not big enough to perform significance tests on, the results still indicate that the process of generating concept maps and combining concept maps might help people with analogical mapping and thus trigger insight.

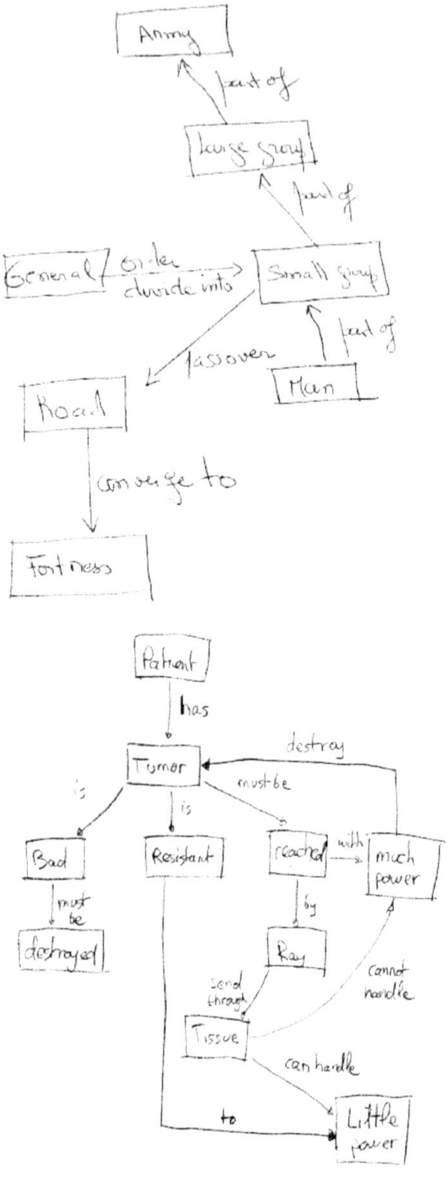

Figure 1. Concept maps drawn by the study participants: the top map represents the military problem and the bottom map represents the radiation problem.

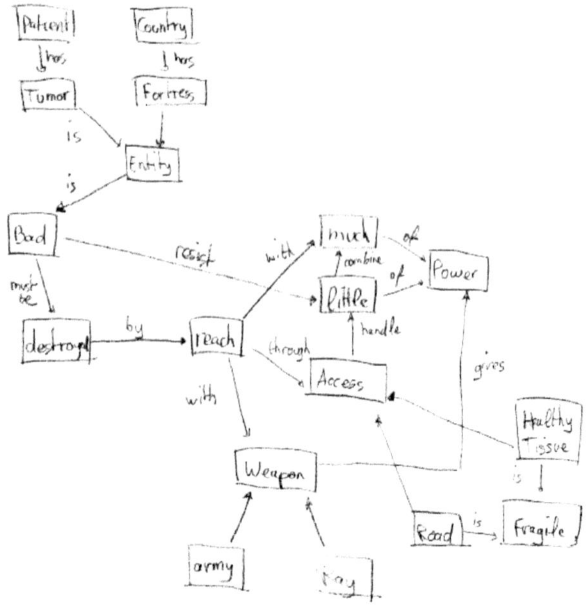

Figure 2. A combined concept map.

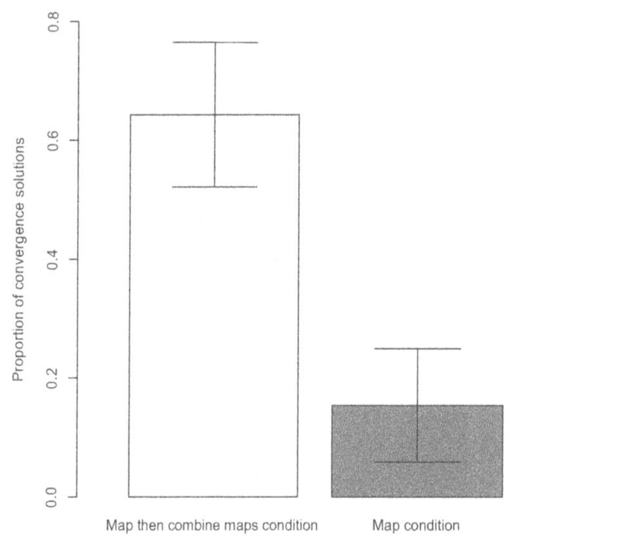

Figure 3. The convergence solutions frequencies in the *map then combine maps* condition and the *map* condition. Error bars show 95% percent confidence intervals.

However, one might argue that in the *map then combine maps* condition, the added combination step might serve as an implicit cue to prime participants to apply the solution of the military problem to the radiation problem. Therefore, the combination of concept maps is not necessarily the cause of the successful transfer. Another potential confounding variable is the amount of effort put into the two conditions. Participants in the *map then combine maps* condition might put more effort into the task because they were asked to draw an extra combined concept map, although all participants were given the same amount of time in the experiment and participants in the two conditions completed the tasks at about the same time.

Moreover, the experiment does not allow us to determine whether combining other representations would help, or whether it is the combination of a specific representation, concept maps, that led to improved performance. In particular, we want to know whether the combination of verbal descriptions would help with the analogy transfer. Consequently, we designed a follow-on experiment.

In this new experiment, we added a *combining scenarios* step to the *map* condition to equate the time on task and effort required between the two conditions and address the potential implicit cuing effect of the instruction to combine.

We also added a third condition in which participants were asked to first summarize the two problems instead of constructing concept maps. After performing the summarization task, they were asked to combine the two scenarios. This condition emulates the use of summarization in one of Gick and Holyoak's past studies [11], which was intended to provoke schema induction.

Overall, our experiment design allows us to test three different explanations for the increase in performance we saw in the first experiment. Specifically, it allows us to test if concept maps themselves promote transfer, with combination playing no contributing role. If true, the two conditions using maps should both outperform the summarization condition. The experiment also allows us to test if combination works regardless of the medium of representation, textual or diagrammatic, in which case all conditions should perform similarly. And the experiment allows us to test if, consistent with our hypothesis, the representation matters, so that combining concept maps, and not text, leads to increased performance, in which case the first condition will lead to higher performance than the other two. We will describe the experiment design in detail in the following section.

THE MAPS AND SCENARIOS EXPERIMENT

Method

Participants

A total of 120 online participants took part in this experiment. All participants were randomly assigned to one of three conditions. There were 40 participants in each condition. Participants were elicited from an online crowdsourcing market, Amazon Mechanical Turk [17]. Ages ranged from 19-59: the mean age was 30. Sixty-two percent were male, 70% were native English speakers, and 68% had a college degree. There were no significant differences in the demographics of the participants across the three conditions.

Design and Procedure

In the *map then combine maps* condition, participants were asked to draw concepts maps for the military problem and the radiation problem. After that they were asked to combine the two concept maps and then provide a solution for the radiation problem. The instructions used were as same as those used in the in-class experiment.

In the *map then combine scenarios* condition, participants were asked to draw concept maps for the military problem and the radiation problem. The instructions used were as same as that used in the in-class experiment. After that they were asked to combine the verbal statements of the two problems and then provide a solution for the radiation problem. (The instruction was: *Please combine the two scenarios*).

In the *summarize then combine scenarios* condition, participants were asked to summarize the two given problems (The instruction was: *Please summarize the scenario*) and then combine the verbal statements of the two problems and provide a solution for the radiation problem (The instruction was: *Please combine the two scenarios*).

Online participants don't necessarily understand the nature of concept maps, so we provided an illustration of a concept map in a different domain. The illustration was produced by the authors for a restaurant scenario, as shown in Figure 4 below.

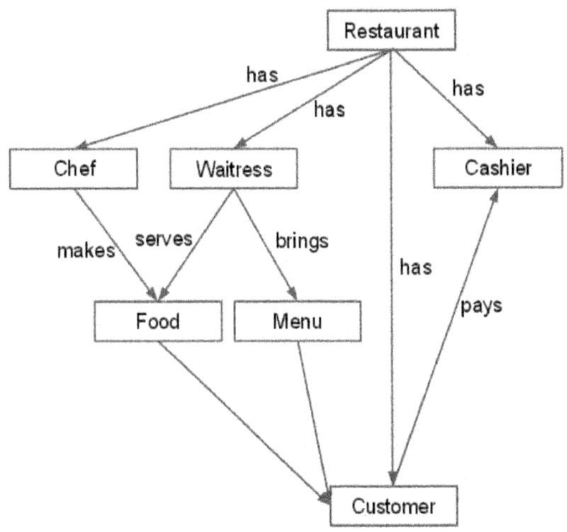

Figure 4. The illustrated concept map used in the experiment.

The drawing step in this experiment was performed by participants using the Google drawing application in Google Docs [13]. The drawing tool provides options to perform freehand sketching, vector line drawing, text entry, and shape drawing. Participants were directed to a Google document page already opened as a drawing interface.

Results

We collected three sets of data: the verbal summaries of the problems, the concept maps of the problems and the solutions to the radiation problem. Some participants were excluded from the analysis because they failed to follow the instructions. This set includes participants who didn't draw maps, summarize the problems or answer the questions. The proportion of the excluded participants was 33% for the *map then combine maps* condition and 23% for the *map then combine scenarios* condition. There were no participants excluded for the *summarize then combine scenarios* condition. Participants may have failed to complete the experiments due to either browser incompatibilities with the Google interface, or other issues related to mastering the interface.

The example below shows the summary of the military problem from one participant:

In order to take possession of the head-of-state's fortress in a small but diverse country, a rebel general divides his large body of soldiers into many discrete forces small enough not to trigger defensive traps--designed to respond only to large forces--along the roads to the citadel.

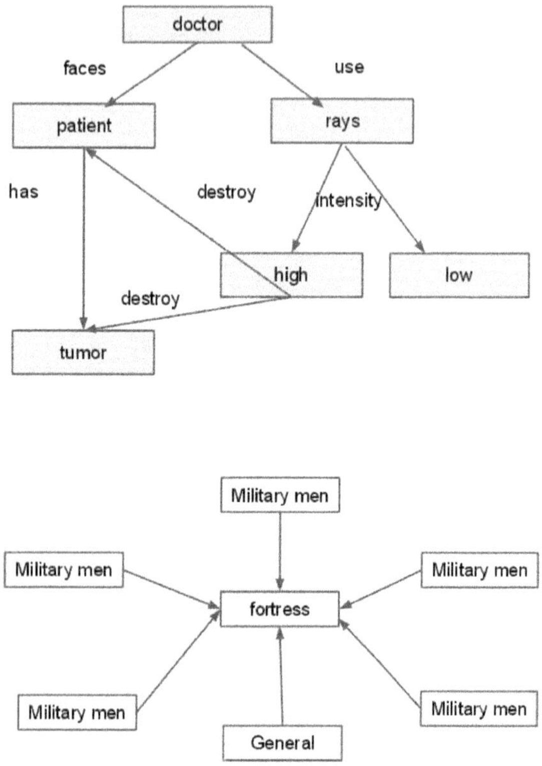

Figure 5. Concept maps from participants: the top one represents the radiation problem and the bottom one represents the military problem.

The example below shows a participant's unfruitful combination of the verbal statements for the two problems:

The General of an army decided to attack a fortress that is ruled by a dictator. There were many roads but all where fixed with mines. It can be related with the feelings of a Doctor who was in confusion whether to operate a patient for tumor. If the patient is treated with high intensity ray it will damage the cell, but low intensity beam will not cure the tumor. Like this the General was confused whether to attack the fortress or not.

The concept maps produced in the online experiment are more diverse than those produced in the in-class experiment, as illustrated by Figure 5 and Figure 6.

As with the first experiment, each solution for the radiation problem was classified into two categories: convergence solutions and non-convergence solutions. The convergence solution frequencies in the *map then combine map* condition, the *map then combine scenarios* condition and the *summarize then combine scenarios* condition are 30 out of 40, 19 out of 40 and 20 out of 40, as shown in Figure 7.

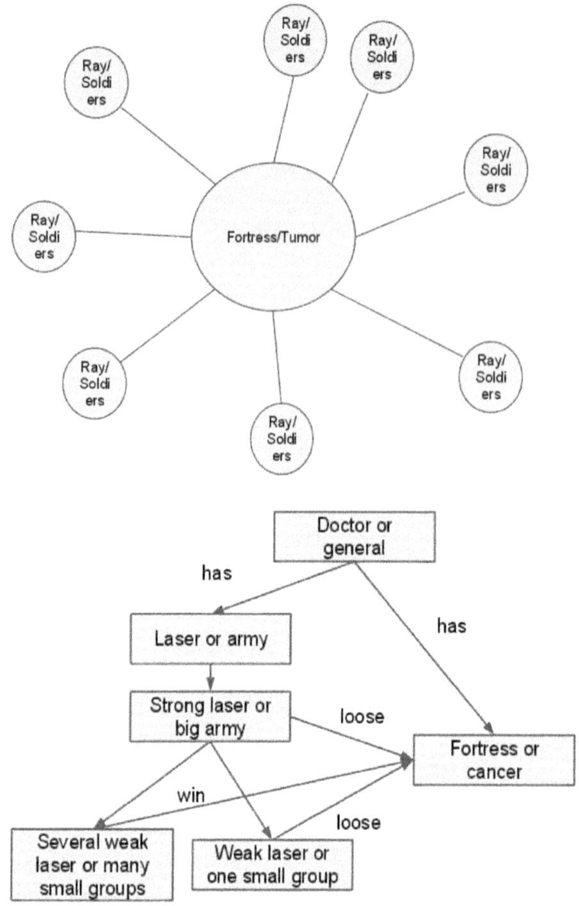

Figure 6. Two examples of combined concept maps.

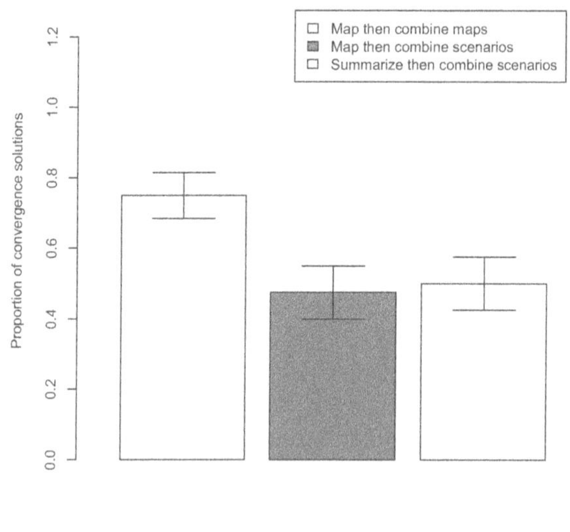

Figure 7. The convergence solution frequencies under the three different conditions. Error bars show 95% percent confidence intervals.

Proportion tests show that the convergence solution frequency in the *map then combine maps* condition is significantly higher than the frequency in the *map then combine scenarios* condition ($x^2(1, N=80)=5.27, P<0.01$) and also higher than the frequency in the *summarize then combine scenarios* condition ($x^2(1, N=80)=4.32, P<0.01$). There is no statistical difference in the frequency between the *map then combine scenarios* condition and the *summarize then combine scenarios* condition ($x^2(1, N=80)=0, P=1$). Thus, our hypothesis that combining concept maps will increase the recognition of analogies is supported.

DISCUSSION AND FINAL THOUGHTS

The experiments presented here explore the use of concept maps in creative problem solving. The results show that constructing and combining concept maps helps with transfer. Given this result, we would like to understand how combining the concept maps helps. While we provided no explicit instruction on how to combine the two concept maps, in looking at the concept maps, we found two common types of combination. The first type can be described as top-down combination. Participants picked the key concepts of each problem and put these pairs of concepts in the same concept box in the map, as illustrated by each diagram in Figure 6. Consistent with the schema induction assumption, this type of combination is an abstract structure mapping. By finding the commonalities and deleting the minor differences, the analogy can be noticed and the problem solved. The second type of combination is a bottom-up approach, as shown in Figure 2. The two concept systems maintain a certain level of independence in the combined map, while the corresponding concepts from the two disparate systems are matched up at the same level in the combined map and are connected through higher level concepts. This type of bottom-up one-to-one mapping allows the discovery of the attributes existing in the source problem but missing in the target. Future studies might test whether one approach is more effective than the other in particular situations.

In the experiment, we required participants to construct their own concept maps for the problems, based on the common assumption that the construction process assists in understanding, organizing and representing ideas [14]. Construction might help designers notice the mapping structures between the two different concept systems. However, if individuals have difficulties creating concept maps in the first place, these difficulties might constrain their later performance. Thus future research might consider presenting participants with well-constructed concept maps at the start, and then asking the participants to combine them. If this proves useful, but not as useful as constructing maps, then a process of fading (c.f. [12]) might be introduced, in which, through a series of training exercises, participants begin with provided diagrams and learn how to construct their own.

Can concept maps be helpful in open-ended design situations? Designers need to integrate systems; they also need to locate analogous cases so that they can reuse previous solutions. Combining concept maps is a technique that may serve both these needs. That is, the technique encourages abstraction and at the same time provides a way to bring together two or more separate ideas to produce a new concept or artifact.

In order to test this conjecture we might provide designers with problems that involve several concept domains and ask them to sketch the concept maps as a precursor to design. There are many design situations that call for knowledge about different domains: for example, architects may consider zoning, energy efficiency, traffic flow, and work collaboration issues, and each of these issues has associated with it a set of concepts. In contrast to the radiation problem, most design problems don't present clear analogies, and, even if they exist, they may not be important in generating new designs. Nevertheless, concept diagrams might prove useful even in situations in which analogies are not present. In particular, designers arguably integrate domains by finding common elements across domain structures. Then, concept maps might serve two purposes: structures identified in the mapping process might suggest integration points as well as analogies. To test this, a number of design situations can be presented to participants in different conditions, some asked to use concept diagrams, others asked to use other well-known design techniques.

In sum, our results suggest that combining concept maps may be a useful technique in problem solving. In particular, both students and online participants were better able to solve insight problems by combining concept maps. It was not the maps themselves, nor combination itself, but the *combining of concept maps* which led to better performance. Previous work has focused on the effectiveness of concept maps in education: our experiments suggest they may also be useful in other activities. Drawing a concept map elicits structure, and structure is important in not only educational, but also problem-solving and design activities.

REFERENCES

1. Bassok, M. and Holyoak, K. J. Interdomain transfer between isomorphic topics in algebra and physics. *Journal of Experimental Psychology: Learning, Memory, and Cognition.* 15, 1 (1989), 153.
2. Casakin, H. Visual analogy as a cognitive strategy in the design process: Expert versus novice performance. *Journal of Design Research.* 4, 2 (2004).
3. Catrambone, R. and Holyoak, K. J. Overcoming contextual limitations on problem-solving transfer. *Journal of Experimental Psychology: Learning, Memory, and Cognition.* 15, 6 (1989), 1147.
4. Davies, J. and Goel, A. K. Visual analogy in problem solving. *International Joint Conference on Artificial Intelligence.* 17(1), 1 (2001), 377-384.

5. Duncker, K. On problem-solving. *Psychological monographs*, 1945.
6. Finke, R. A., Ward, T. B., and Smith, S. M. *Creative cognition: theory, research, and applications.* MIT Press, 1992.
7. Fong, G. T., Krantz, D. H., and Nisbett, R. E. The effects of statistical training on thinking about everyday problems. *Cognitive Psychology.* 18, 3 (1986), 253-292.
8. Gentner, D., Brem, S., Ferguson, R., Wolff, P., Markman, A. B., and Forbus, K. Analogy and creativity in the works of Johannes Kepler. Creative thought: An investigation of conceptual structures and processes. 1997. 403-459.
9. Gentner, D., Holyoak, K. J., and Kokinov, B. N. *The analogical mind: perspectives from cognitive science.* MIT Press, 2001.
10. Gick, M. L. The effect of a diagram retrieval cue on spontaneous analogical transfer. *Canadian Journal of Psychology/Revue canadienne de psychologie.* 39, 3 (1985), 460.
11. Gick, M. L. and Holyoak, K. J. Schema induction and analogical transfer. *Cognitive psychology.* 15, 1(1983), 1-38.
12. Goldstone, R. L. and Son, J. Y. The transfer of scientific principles using concrete and idealized simulations. *The Journal of the Learning Sciences.* 14, 1(2005), 69-110.
13. Google Docs Drawing Application http://docs0.google.com/demo/edit?id=scACRQalm3t83kVISWPhWfrqx#drawing.
14. Halford, G. S. *Children's Understanding:: The Development of Mental Models*, 1993.
15. Holyoak, K. J. and Thagard, P. *Mental leaps : analogy in creative thought.* MIT Press, 1995.
16. Kinchin, I. M., Hay, D. B., and Adams, A. How a qualitative approach to concept map analysis can be used to aid learning by illustrating patterns of conceptual development. *Educational Research.* 42, 1 (2001), 43-57.
17. Kittur, A., Chi, E. H., and Suh, B. Crowdsourcing user studies with Mechanical Turk. In *Proc. SIGCHI conference on Human factors in computing systems. 2008.* 453-456.
18. Kunda, Z., Miller, D. T., and Claire, T. Combining social concepts: The role of causal reasoning. *Cognitive Science.* 14 (1990), 551-577.
19. Mackie, J. L. *The cement of the universe; a study of causation.* Clarendon Press, 1974.
20. McAleese, R. A theoretical view on concept mapping. *ALT-J.* 2, 1 (1994), 38-48.
21. Mumford, M. D., Mobley, M. I., Reiter-Palmon, R., Uhlman, C. E., and Doares, L. M. Process analytic models of creative capacities. *Creativity Research Journal.* 4, 2 (1991), 91-122.
22. Needham, D. R. and Begg, I. M. Problem-oriented training promotes spontaneous analogical transfer: Memory-oriented training promotes memory for training. *Memory & Cognition.* 19, 6 (1991), 543-557.
23. Novak, J. D. and Cañas, A. J. The theory underlying concept maps and how to construct and use them. Florida Institute for Human and Machine Cognition Pensacola 2008. [http://cmap. ihmc. us/Publications/ResearchPapers/TheoryCmaps/TheoryUnderlyingConceptMaps. htm].
24. Novick, L. R. Representational transfer in problem solving. *Psychological Science.* 1, 2 (1990), 128.
25. Pedone, R., Hummel, J. E., and Holyoak, K. J. The use of diagrams in analogical problem solving. *Memory & Cognition.* 29, 2 (2001), 214.
26. Simonton, D. K. *Creativity in science: chance, logic, genius, and Zeitgeist.* Cambridge University Press, 2004 .
27. Sternberg, R. J. and Davidson, J. E. *The nature of insight.* The MIT Press, 1995 .
28. Suwa, M. and Tversky, B. Constructive perception: A metacognitive skill for coordinating perception and conception. In *Proc. Cognitive Science Society*, 2003.
29. Thagard, P. Creative combination of representations: Scientific discovery and technological invention. In *Psychology of science*, R. Proctor and E. J. Capaldi, Eds Oxford University Press, forthcoming
30. Thagard, P. *Conceptual revolutions.* Princeton University Press, 1992 .
31. Vattam, S. S., Helms, M. E., and Goel, A. K. Nature of creative analogies in biologically inspired innovative design. In *Proc. Creativity and cognition.* ACM Press (2009).
32. Visser, W. *The cognitive artifacts of designing.* L. Erlbaum Associates, 2006 .
33. Wandersee, J. H. Concept mapping and the cartography of cognition. *Journal of Research in Science Teaching.* 27, 10 (1990), 923-936.
34. Welling, H. Four mental operations in creative cognition: The importance of abstraction. *Creativity Research Journal.* 19, 2 (2007), 163-177.
35. Yu, L. and Nickerson, J. V. Cooks or Cobblers? Crowd Creativity through Combination. In *Proc. CHI 2011*, ACM Press.

Kinesthetic Pathways: A Tabletop Visualization to Support Discovery in Systems Biology

Andy Wu, Jung-Bin Yim, Eric Caspary, Ali Mazalek, Sanjay Chandrasekharan, Nancy J. Nersessian
GVU Center, Georgia Institute of Technology
TSRB, 85 5th St. NW
Atlanta, GA 30318, USA
{ andywu, jyim, ecaspary3, mazalek }@gatech.edu, { sanjayan, nancyn }@cc.gatech.edu

ABSTRACT
We report on an ethnographic study of the work practice and discovery process in a systems biology lab, and outline a tabletop visualization that was developed based on this study, in collaboration with the researchers. The feedback from the researchers on the current prototype is presented, and ongoing revisions are outlined. We conclude with some of the challenges involved in developing such tangible visualizations for discovery.

Author Keywords
Pathways, systems biology, simulation, modeling, tabletop, HCI, tangible user interface, kinesthetic interaction

ACM Classification Keywords
H.5.2 [Information Interfaces and Presentation]: User Interfaces---*input devices and strategies, interaction styles, user-centered design*; I.6.7 [Simulation and Modeling]: Simulation Support Systems---environments.

General Terms
Design, Experimentation

INTRODUCTION

In August 2010, *Nature* published a paper where roughly 200,000 players of a videogame were included as authors. The paper reported how the re-representation of the protein-folding problem as a multi-player videogame, Foldit, allowed collaborative solving of the problem by ordinary people. It also proposed that such harnessing of people's visual and spatial reasoning abilities could be a new method to solve computationally-challenging scientific problems.

Much of the attention on Foldit has focused on the "citizen science" aspect [2], but equally important is its contribution to an understanding of how perception and action systems interact in creativity and cognition, particularly in relation to scientific discovery. A central component of the success of Foldit is its direct manipulation interface, which allows players to grasp and pull and move and twist different protein strands. This type of interface, where the user actively controls and explores objects on screen to develop an understanding, is common in educational applications in science (e.g. PhET [16]). But most scientific visualizations do not seek to support this type of kinesthetic interaction-based discovery [4]. Rather, they seek to represent data in new ways, and the insight is expected to come from the different visual perspectives on the data.

One of the reasons for the success of Foldit is the use of the kinesthetic interaction, which allows the motor system to work in tandem with the visual and imagination systems while solving spatial problems (for a detailed model of this interaction, see [1]. In this paper, we report a prototype system where we seek to extend such kinesthetic interaction for discovery to systems biology, particularly to the modeling and simulation of metabolic systems. This is a more complex and abstract problem than protein-folding, as the entities involved do not have spatial features. In the following section, we provide an outline of the practice and problems in a systems biology lab, based on a two-year ethnographic study. The next section outlines the prototype we have developed based on this study, and the feedback we have received from the lab members on the prototype. We conclude with some of the challenges involved in developing systems to support discovery in this domain and future work. The images in this paper are retrieved from different stages of the prototype. Since we have been trying different types of visualizations techniques, some of them are different from the current working system.

PRACTICE IN A SYSTEMS BIOLOGY LAB

In our current project we are studying problem-solving practices in two integrative systems biology labs. We focus here on one lab that does only computational modeling ("Lab G"). The modelers in Lab G are mainly from engineering fields, but work on building computational models of biochemical pathways, to simulate and understand phenomena as varied as Parkinson's disease, plant systems for bio-fuels, and atherosclerosis. The problems Lab G modelers work on are provided by outside experimental collaborators, who see modeling primarily as a method for identifying key experiments of scientific or

C&C'11, November 3–6, 2011, Atlanta, Georgia, USA.

commercial importance. The collaborators provide experimental data for modeling, and also data needed for developing pathway diagrams, or validating the model.

The modeling process can be classified into three phases – building, fitting/testing and perturbation – even though these phases overlap. In general, the model is built up in a 'ripple' fashion, with small models in the beginning, each going through these three phases. More elements are then added to these models, and these complex models then go through the three phases.

The Modeling Process

Lab G researchers mostly build ordinary differential equation (ODE) models of metabolic systems, which capture how the concentration levels of different metabolites in a given biological pathway change over time. The first step in this building process is the development of a pathway diagram, which shows the main reactions involved. The pathway diagram also captures positive and negative regulation effects, which specify how the presence of different metabolites has a positive or negative influence on different reactions (see Figure 1). The experimental collaborators usually provide a rough diagram of the pathway. But the modelers, who mostly come from engineering backgrounds, have to estimate the details of the pathway by themselves, particularly values of parameters related to metabolites, such as speed of change (kinetic order) and concentration level (rate constant), which are usually not measured by experimenters. This information is available in rough form (with varying degrees of reliability) from online databases, but most often these values need to be estimated, usually through iterative testing of the model, using a range of numbers as parameter values.

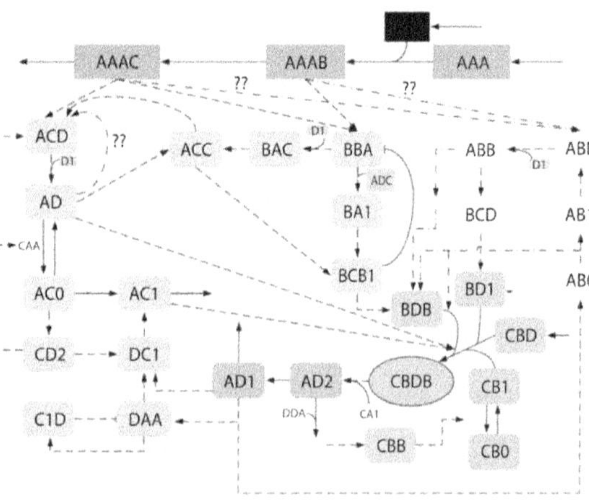

Figure 1. A sample pathway diagram. Metabolite names are replaced with alphabet characters. The dark lines indicate connections where material moves across nodes, the dotted lines indicate regulatory connections. The question marks show connections that are postulated by the modeler.

Modelers also add some components to the pathway, usually metabolites that are known to interact with the network provided by the experimenters. These components are found by reading and searching biology journal articles and databases related to the problem being modeled, and also based on results from preliminary models. Even though experimentalists provide much of the pathway, these additions based on literature searches are required, because the provided pathway does not identify all the components, and the regulatory influences they have on the reaction.

The pathway developed by the modeler thus brings together pieces of information that are spread over a wide set of papers, databases, and unreported data from the experimentalists. This pathway is usually trimmed, based on some simplifying assumptions, mostly to lower the mathematical and computational complexity involved in numerically solving the differential equations. After the trimming, differential equations are generated to capture the trimmed pathway. A variable is used to represent the metabolite, while the speed of its change (kinetic order) and its concentration level (rate constant) are represented by parameters, which can take many values. The next step involves estimating values for these parameters, and these values are then used to initialize simulations of the models. The simulation results are then compared to actual experimental results, to judge the 'fit' of the model.

Usually, modelers split available experimental data into two, one set is used to develop the model (training data), and the other set is used to test the completed model (test data). When the model data do not fit the test data, the parameters are "tuned" to get model results that fit. Once the model fits the test data, it is run through a series of diagnostic tests, such as stability (e.g. does not crash for a range of values), sensitivity (e.g. input is proportional to output) and consistency (e.g. reactant material is not lost or added). If the diagnostic tests fail, the parameters are tuned again, and in some cases, the pathway changed, until the model meets both the fit and diagnostic tests. Figure 2 provides a broad outline of the modeling process.

Lab G models do not have real-time dynamic visualizations. Parameter values are changed manually or using scripts. Results for different parameter values are compared using a deck of graphs, where each graph plots the concentration value of an element in the pathway across time. The modeler uses these graphs while discussing the model with collaborators and other team members. A significant chunk of the parameter estimation problem is tackled using optimization algorithms (such as simulated annealing and genetic algorithms), which automatically do the 'tuning' of parameters, by comparing the output values (for different parameter inputs) against a desired value. Importantly, the linear workflow suggested by the above description is very deceptive – the modeling process is highly iterative. For instance, to develop the pathway diagram, preliminary models are built using the network provided by the experimenters, and these are run using tentative parameter values, and the generated model data

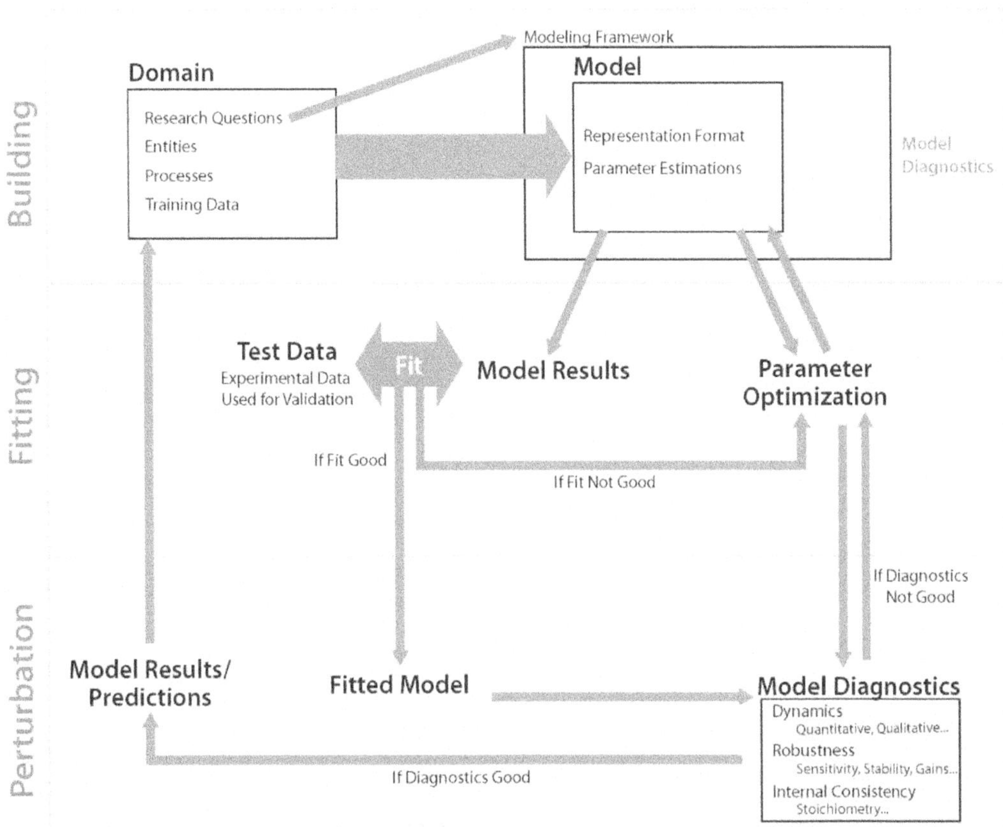

Figure 2. An outline of the modeling process in Lab G. Note that the 'building' phase involves both 'fitting' (of the training data) and perturbation (model diagnostics).

are fit to the training data. The parameter values are then revised based on this fit. If the model data do not fit after a large number of these parameter revisions – particularly if the data trends are the exact opposite of experimental data – the modeler will add some components to the network, based on elements that are known (in the literature) to be related to the pathway. There is also an instance where the modeling led to the discovery that an element (named X) in another pathway was influencing a biofuel pathway. Later experimental work by collaborators identified a candidate element for X. Thus, *some of the model's components – elements and values – are set by building and running the model itself.* These pathway revisions, and their justifications, are discussed with the collaborators, and if a revision is considered "reasonable" by the experimenter, it becomes a stable component of the pathway. This pathway identification process is usually "bottom-up," and creates a "composite" network, made up of parameter values and metabolites extracted from experiments in different species, different cell lines etc. This composite is usually unique, and does not exist anywhere else in the literature.

One of central problems the lab members face is the unavailability of rich, and dependable, data. In modeling, data are used for many purposes. One central use of data is to establish that the model captures a possible biological mechanism, and this is done by showing that the model's output matches the output from experiments (fitting data). A second use of data is to tune parameter values during the training phase of building the model. The fit with the experimental data from each training simulation can indicate how the model parameters need to be changed, to generate model data that fit the training data. This use is highly dependent on the type of data available. Most of the time, the available data are 'qualitative' in nature – usually how an experimental manipulation led to a change in a metabolite level from a baseline. Mostly, this is reported as a single data point, indicating the level going up or down, and then holding steady. However, when this type of "steady-state" data fits the results of the model, this fit does not indicate that the model has captured the biological mechanism. A range of parameter values can generate model results that fit such sparse data – the fit is not unique. Further, since the pathway is an approximation, the modeler is uncertain as to whether the lack of a unique and accurate solution is due to poor estimation of parameters, or because some elements are missing from her pathway.

Example Cases

As an example instance of modeling in this lab, consider G12, an electrical engineer by training, who is modeling atherosclerosis. When she started modeling, she had no background on atherosclerosis. Her experimental collaborators provided her a rough outline of the pathway, and she learned more about the pathway by reading papers. The initial papers were from the collaborating lab, but then she spread out using the reference lists of those papers. The data available were mostly steady-state data. Once she had read a number of papers, she started building rudimentary computer models and testing these using available data. She then added some components to the model based on connections in the literature. It is worth noting here that while her problem mostly concerned endothelial cells, some of her parameters were taken from experiments with neurons, a very different cell class, and a domain of research (neuroscience) that is not usually connected to research in endothelial cells. Some of her additions were considered "reasonable" by her experimental collaborators.

Estimating parameter values for her model was a tough problem, since the data were sparse. To get parameter values that generated model data that fit the training data, she ran a large number of simulations and compared the results with the training data. Finally, she arrived at a set of values that generated data that roughly matched the training data. Once this was done, she tested her model against the test data, and got a rough fit there as well. Based on this fit, she generated a number of predictions from the model, by changing the parameter values. Her experimental collaborators would test some of these predictions.

A second example is G11, a physicist with a Ph.D. in bioinformatics, who is modeling Parkinson's Disease (PD), particularly the dopamine pathway. He works closely with a neuroscience lab in a neighboring university, and he has access to all their data (excel files), which he uses to build his models. He has also suggested experiments based on his models, and the collaborators are currently testing some of these predictions. He, however, thinks the experiments take a long time, and as he is waiting for the results, he is trying purely mathematical approaches (such as Monte Carlo simulations) to develop a good model of PD. Apart from this 'phase lag' between modeling and experimentation, he also finds the experimental methods limiting. For instance, he can manipulate more than three variables in his model, and give very specific values to his variables (such as concentration of a metabolite in one stage of a reaction). Whereas in experiments, manipulating more than three variables is impossible, and there is no good way to ensure that concentration of the material in the cell is the same as what was specified in the model.

G10 has an electrical engineering background, and he is developing a model of the biosynthesis of lignin (a critical component of plant cell walls). The objective of the model is to provide insight on how the composition of lignin could be manipulated in such a way that the lignin breaks down easily to produce biofuel. A related objective is supporting the development of transgenic species where the lignin composition is optimal for biofuel production. This work is different from other work in the lab in two respects. One, G10 works with non-academic collaborators, particularly a company and a non-governmental organization. Secondly, G10's work deals with plant cells, while all others work with animal cells. In recent work, his modeling work showed that a product of another pathway (identified as X) has significant regulatory influence in the production of lignin. His collaborator has identified a candidate molecule that could play this regulatory role. Also, his modeling work suggests that some of the reactions are reversible, even though they have traditionally been considered as just forward reactions. These discoveries suggest that modeling has a self-illuminating effect, where the model can provide insight into the very pathways on which the model is based.

PATHWAYS

Based on this detailed understanding of the scientific practice in Lab G, we are working to develop a tangible tabletop visualization system to support discovery in systems biology, with a focus on developing an interface that would allow the researchers to explore parameters in a kinesthetic fashion, and thus estimate the parameters that would best fit model data with experimental data. The system also seeks to support modeling by experimentalists, who may not have a detailed understanding of the mathematical techniques, and also efficient collaboration between modelers and biologists.

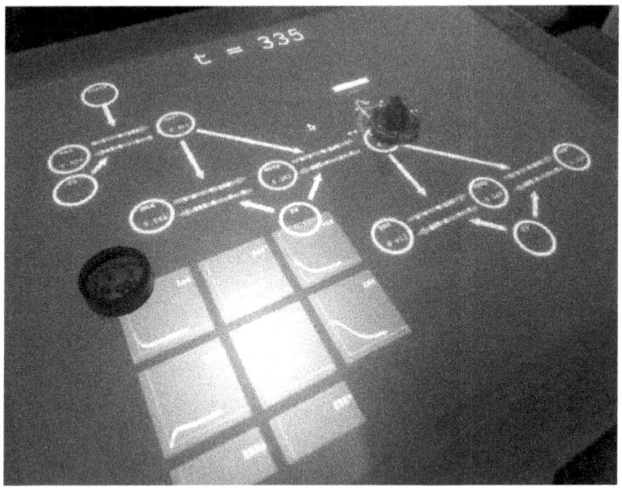

Figure 3. Pathways runs on an interactive tabletop display.

Pathways is a tangible visualization for systems biology. It works with an interactive tabletop display (see Figure 1). The interface shows a dynamic display of the pathway as the simulation is running. Manipulating objects on the table changes the concentration and kinetic order values in the simulation. Additionally, the interface provides a display of the graphs associated with the pathway, and also the possibility of creating the pathway and its associated equations by just drawing pictures on the table, or using objects to create nodes and arrows. The interface allows even a novice researcher to create a network and simulation from scratch, and see both the global changes (entire network) and the local changes (graphs) when she manipulates parameter values kinesthetically. In the following sections, we outline some related work, and describe the current prototype, then present the feedback from users, and how we are planning to revise the prototype based on this feedback.

RELATED WORK

Interactive Tabletop displays provide a large screen area and allow multiple people to work collaboratively. They are more friendly interfaces than traditional Graphical User Interfaces (GUIs), since people are familiar with working at tables. Also, people working at a table have virtually the same access to any spot on the table. In our research lab, we have built several interactive tabletop displays [11] capable of tracking multiple finger touches and tagged objects, as well as recognizing several gestures. The display surfaces of these tabletops measure nearly 55 inches diagonally. The tables use reacTIVision [7] as their core engine to read the inputs, and Multitouch for Java (MT4J) [12] as the application level Application Programming Interface (API) to integrate with other programs. Additionally, these interactive tabletops have Bluetooth and WiFi capabilities. It is also feasible to integrate smartphones with the tables. The display of the smartphone can be a separate window in which to show dynamic information.

On the visualization side, the Sensetable [15] is a sensing technology that tracks the positions and orientations of multiple objects on a tabletop display surface electromagnetically. It introduced several tangible visualization techniques. For example, using a "scoring process" to determine the importance of the content, Using a puck as an interactive medium, indicating the center of attention by darkening the less important information, using fisheye effects to provide more detailed information and semantic zooming. This interface provides more direct interaction between the human hand and the actual digital media than does a mouse manipulating GUI widgets. Sensetable also affords better collaboration between users than GUI interfaces. The capability of manipulating multiple objects allows different people to change different interface elements concurrently.

In recent years, many groups have developed tangible tabletop interfaces for a range of applications. An application close to our project is the use of tabletop visualization to control network models. IP Network Bench [10] is based on Sensetable and provides an interface for users to determine the balance between cost and performance in IP network design. Users can have real-time results by controlling the network model collaboratively with multiple controllers. Pico [14] is a Tangible User Interface (TUI) based tabletop surface that can track and move small objects on top of it. The position of these physical props represents and controls application variables for optimizing the configuration of cellular telephone network radio towers. The computer optimizes the network, while the user moves the physical props under the constraints of other physical objects.

LifeLines [17] visualizes the personal histories of various types of biographical data, such as medical and court records. These data are collected and converted into appropriate visualization to explore the personal histories. The linear time scale helps to provide an intuitive approach to visualize histories in different time scales, in months, weeks, days and even minutes. It always begins with a screen showing the overview of the record, and the user can use options, recalling tools or filters, to analyze complex records. Visualizing with different colors and thickness of lines, rescaling, and filtering allow users to focus on parts of the record and find out more details.

ThemeRiver [5] is another visualization representing thematic variation over time within a large collection of documents. The river flows from left to right within the context of a timeline, and the variation of data is depicted with different colors and width. This visual metaphor facilitates discovery by presenting data in an intuitive, easily ingested format and builds a relationship with user's perceptual and cognitive abilities. This tool is useful when the user needs to figure out trends, relationships, unexpected data, and structure in the data.

There are also other systems designed for visualizing biological pathways. VisANT [6] is a web-based software framework for visualizing the network models of biological interactions and relations. Users can import data from either their own data source, or from standard exchange format and they can be represented with millions of edges and nodes. The system not only provides analytical tools for extracting topological properties, but also supports customizing and modifying the network with user-defined sets. Another visualizing and modeling tool, iFBA (Integrated Flux-Balance Analysis) [3] has the advantage of flux balance models over traditional sets of ODEs that allows for analysis of the entire metabolic and regulatory networks. It also has the advantage of the ODE models to capture intracellular concentrations and short time-scale dynamics. iFBA approach has the potential to incorporate the advantages of both perspectives.

Cytoscape [18] is a software tool for integrating bio-molecular components and their interactions with expression profiles, phenotypes and other molecular states. It supports various automated network layout algorithms, and visualizes various sizes and colors of nodes and edges. The system is extensible by adding new plug-ins, which allows rapid development of additional visualization and computational analyses.

Karp [8] describes Pathways Tools, a software environment for creating a model-organism database that can integrate the evolving understanding of the genes, proteins, metabolic network and regulatory network of an organism. This paper supports our point that most visualization tools just re-represent data, they don't seek to support the process of fitting data. More broadly, our objective is to help people fit data, and estimate parameters. Visualizing the network is a step in that direction.

DESIGN

We interviewed our potential users to understand how they sketched a graphical pathway, and to see what other pathways look like. It was found that there is no standard method for drawing a pathway. One common characteristic of most pathways is the use of directed graphs. The nodes of these types of graphs are usually enzymes or molecules, and the edges are the reactions.

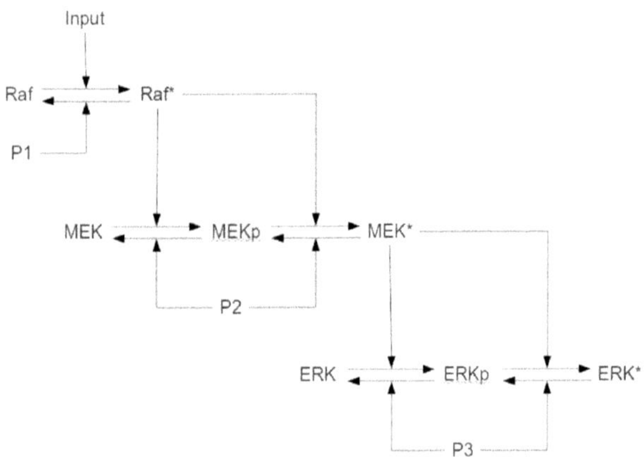

Figure 4. A draft of the MAP Kinase cascade. *Raf, Raf*, MEK, MEKp, MEK*, ERK, ERKp,* and *ERK are molecules. *Input, P1, P2,* and *P3* are enzymes.**

The default data running on our current implementation of Pathways is the MAP Kinase cascade in the MAPK/ERK pathway. There are 8 molecules and 4 enzymes in this pathway. A draft of the pathway from one systems biologist is shown in Figure 4.

Simulation

The underlying math of a pathway is a series of Ordinary Differential Equations (ODEs) that represent the producers and consumers in the chain reactions. Currently, systems biologists have to write programs to solve these ODEs. We expect them to interact with the graphical representation of the data once Pathways is completed. There are several mathematical libraries available for solving the ODE set. We tried two different approaches to create a sample pathway.

Graphical Pathways with Supporting Math

The idea is to allow the systems biologist to create a pathway on an interactive tabletop display. This can either be done using a graph description language or using the tools provided by our tabletop application. DOT [19], a language designed to describe graphs was used in the first prototype. DOT is good for describing complex graphs. To describe a graph, one has to use this syntax:

```
A -> B
```

This statement describes the start-node A, a directional edge from A to B and the end-node B. DOT is written in plain text and can be easily parsed by computer programs. However, one cannot describe a graph using this DOT without actually having a draft beforehand.

In the current system, a user drafts molecules by using the visual tools provided by the tabletop. After that, she creates reactions between molecules by dragging her finger from one molecule to another. The ODEs are generated when she creates the pathways. This approach is intuitive, but the user needs to have a rough pathway image in her mind in advance to create the graph. Another drawback of this approach is the freedom of creation can create unreasonable chemical chain reactions and unsolvable pathways. This problem is partially offset by the knowledge of our users, who are very familiar with their domain.

Math Equations with Graphics

Another approach is to allow the user to enter the ODEs. After that, the system generates the pathways based on the equations. Eventually, they have to approach the tabletop to interact with the visualizations on the tabletop surface. In this approach the user can concentrate on the numerical data and mathematical equations rather than on the visual representation of data. However, few people can think with ODEs only, especially when the pathway grows larger. Even if some claim they do, they most likely have graphical representations of data in their minds.

Visualization

There are benefits and drawbacks of using different types of visualization techniques. One design decision we needed to make was using abstract versus more organic looking pathways. An abstract visualization [8, 9] is very similar to a subway map. It gives users a clear overview of the pathways. However, we wanted to make the pathways look and feel more organic. For example, molecules should move and morph slowly like amoebas. A very structured abstract pathway similar to a subway map looks more robotic than organic.

Reactions

To show the reaction speed, we had several options. Changing the stroke weight of a reaction arrow based on its flux, namely the reaction speed, is a simple solution. Another similar visualization is to change the arrow color based on its data. However, these two methods do not always generate steady and clear visualizations. When the change is subtle, users can hardly tell the difference.

Another technique that is more perceivable to users is to use animations (see Figure 5). The animation moves small arrows one by one from one node to another. This would give users clearer feedback about the process. Other visualization options include using numerical presentations of flux, using pie charts to show normalized speeds, or using a progress bar to show the values.

However, except for the "numerical presentation", all alternatives have the problem of reflecting the actual data. In other words, users can hardly distinguish the subtle changes of values. Consequently, our final decision was to use animations to show the speed, since it provides the most obvious feedback.

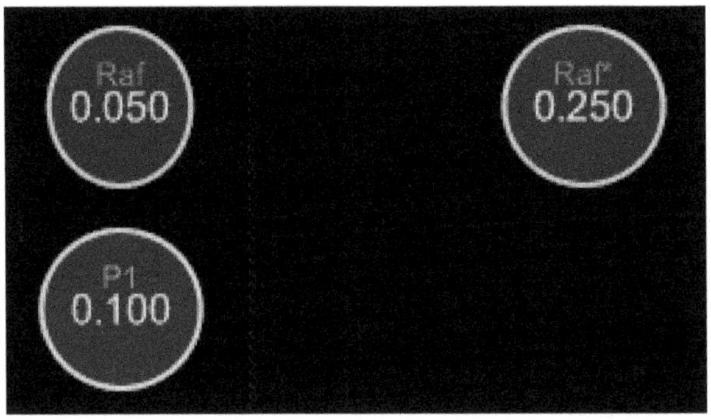

Figure 5. An image of three molecules "breathing". From their shapes, we can tell *Raf* was exhaling while *Raf and *P1* were most likely inhaling when they were captured.**

Molecules

We changed the size, the filled color and the stroke color of the molecules based on the concentration value in the beginning, but encountered similar problems – users can hardly tell the difference between different molecules. Therefore, we used similar animation techniques as above to visualize the molecules. The molecules move slowly and randomly in a confined area. They also "breathe" slowly by changing the width of the shape (see Figure 5). The stroke color of a molecule shows its type. Green is for molecules and yellow is for enzymes, which are also a different kind of molecule. The higher the concentration value, the deeper the "breath" a molecule makes. A molecule also has its name and concentration value on it. We added some red dots in one prototype to evaluate the visualization. The dots are generated randomly inside a molecule. The number of the dots reflects the concentration of a molecule.

Charts

According to Lab G researchers, the chart is the most important channel for them to understand a series of reactions under certain initial conditions. One of our goals was to allow them to work more effectively without frequently switching between charts, ODEs and the sketched pathways. Therefore, a chart is a supplementary tool in our application. Ideally, the researchers would read all information from the graphical representation of Pathways. Currently, a tangible object is used to control the charts' position.

The charts in Pathways show the concentration changes across time. In each single chart, the corresponding molecule's name and its concentration value at that time are shown. A vertical baseline moves when time passes. A user can compare the concentration values of different molecules at the same time (see Figure 6).

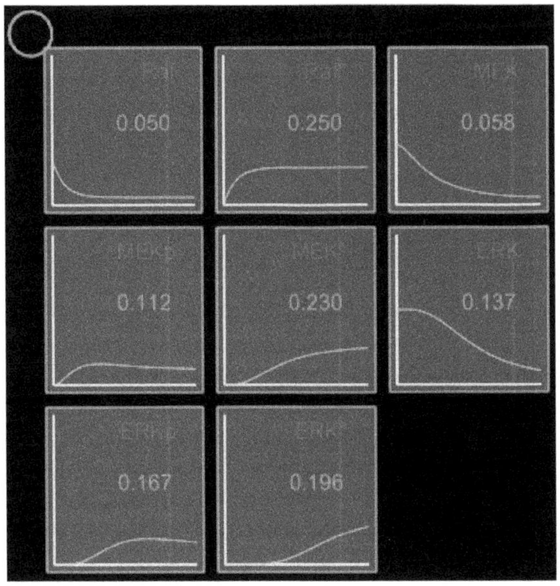

Figure 6. The latest output charts of the MAP Kinase cascade pathway. The red vertical line is moving with time to show the concentration at a certain time. Also, the curves are plotted in advance.

Tangible Input

It is hard to make a decision of when to use tangibles, and when to use more direct manipulation with finger touches. As the interaction surface supports both the tracking of tangible objects and finger touches, we frequently encountered decisions regarding when to prefer one method of interaction to the other. With tangibles, only the person holding the tangible has the control of the tangible's corresponding digital component, whereas finger touches allow all users an equal chance to manipulate the media on the tabletop. Tangibles thereby lead to scenarios with more centralized control of the simulation, and (perhaps) fewer accidental modifications.

A limitation to the current set of tangibles is that they occasionally block the view of the digital content on the tabletop. Since the orientation of a tangible can be determined, the orientation of digital content can be adjusted to face the user. The current build of the application uses tangibles for all major interactions, which include: modifying molecule concentrations, adding molecules to the network, positioning the graphs of the ODE, and starting and stopping the reaction simulation.

One tangible we use is modeled after the dials on old VCR remote controllers (see Figure 7). When a user rotates the VCR dial clockwise, video playback speeds up. The more she rotates, the greater the speed. When the user releases the dial, it returns to the initial state and plays the video in a normal speed. Likewise, a counter-clockwise rotation rewinds the video. The dial in Pathways operates similarly. Only instead of manipulating time, it adjusts the initial concentration of a molecule (see Figure 8). When a user releases the dial in Pathways, the dial returns to its balance state and the corresponding number stops changing.

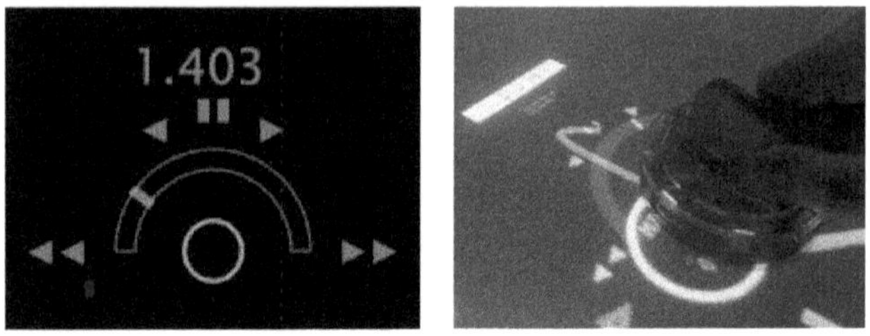

Figure 7. The left image is the digital content when a physical dial is pointing at about 10 o'clock. Turning in this direction decreases the number. In the right photo, a user increases the number by spinning the dial toward "▸", which is the symbol of "*forward*".

User Scenario

When a user comes to Pathways, she can either load a pre-defined metabolic network into the simulation environment, or start from a blank slate. The user creates the elements of the metabolic pathway using both physical and graphical widgets. By stamping the molecule widget onto the tabletop, she creates a molecule. Following the stamping, a virtual keyboard appears and prompts the user for the name and initial concentration of the molecule. After creating several molecules, she uses either her finger or a stylus to draw lines between molecules, thus creating a reaction network. Now that the network is constructed, she can run the simulation. To start the simulation, she simply places the simulation widget onto the surface.

FEEDBACK

As this is a system designed to support scientific discovery in a complex area, the available user base is very low (around 10 researchers) and their needs are diverse, so it is difficult to do formal evaluations to find out the efficiency of different visualizations. We have conducted a series of user feedback sessions with individual researchers, and we are using this feedback to develop a new prototype. We expect many cycles of this iteration process before a final prototype is reached. Here we present the initial feedback on the current prototype.

A PhD student from Lab G (G10) attended the early demonstration of the project and gave us feedback based on the first prototype. One of the most important points he raised was the need for graphs. Since the researchers' current practice largely depends on the output charts, they cannot understand the reaction without the graph. Even though one of our goals was to replace the equations and output charts with visualization of the reactions and molecules, at this point, the researchers' thinking relies heavily on the output charts. This user really liked the animation of iFBA mentioned earlier and suggested using the same visualization in Pathways. This involves using the reaction stroke width to indicate the reaction speed, and showing the simulation in different playback speeds. Also, system biologists work with output charts with different initial condition sets. Comparison of charts to show different setups and outputs is necessary for them to work effectively. He also mentioned that there are several types of modeling methods, each generating different ODEs. Thus, it will be helpful to show the ODEs.

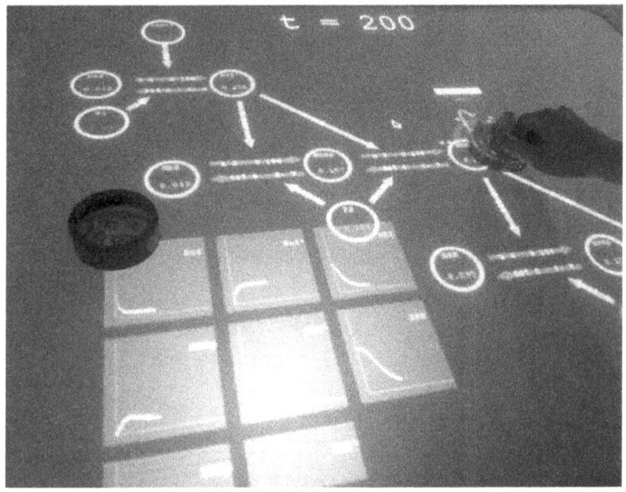

Figure 8. An overview of the running Pathways. A counter is shown above the pathway. A user is manipulating the concentration of a molecule.

G4, a system biologist whose concentration has been in modeling biological systems for many years felt that the glimmering dots inside the molecules distracted him when he tried to read the numbers. He recognized the biochemical reaction immediately and suggested showing more complicated structure. Since the current one is too simple, he had no interest in discovering anything from it. He mentioned that the lack of equations or chemical formulas in the visualization made him feel insecure. He'd like to enter the equations by himself and let the computer generate the graph. G4 mentioned that he has other visualization tools available in his lab, but most researchers do not use them. He doubted whether they would use this novel system. Even though he did not think Pathways would be good for exploration, he thought it would be an ideal platform for demonstration and educational purposes.

C7, a member from another Lab G, attended the latest demonstration of Pathways. He was especially interested in connecting MAP Kinase cascade, a subset to MAPK/ERK, to the pathway. He could read the information from the charts, but could not relate this information to the entire pathway. He wanted to understand how changing the concentration of one molecule affected the entire system. On the other hand, he also wanted to see how changing a larger pathway impacted a smaller region of it. He said a lot of the time his work is to find out the model based on the experiment results, namely the output charts. However, instead of continuous curves, the charts are often composed of discrete points, which make modeling difficult. He particularly hopes to see a tool that helps him simplify the task. C7 also mentioned the importance of being able to see and compare different points of time in a simulation. Graphs help with this, however we believe this information could also be incorporated into the representation of the pathway itself. G6, another member from Lab G, wanted to be able to change the topology of the pathways. Moving the nodes and edges of a graph around was important for her to connect the model in her mind.

CHALLENGES

Within our lab, the system has been iterated several times to find out the most appropriate representation of the simulation and the most straightforward interaction techniques. The feedback from the respondents indicated several challenges in developing such a visualization.

A Comprehensible Representation

Since there is no standard for drawing a pathway, every researcher has a different method. Sometimes a researcher chooses the representation based on the modeling method. For example, sometimes intermediates are critical under one modeling method, but are ignored in another modeling method. Also, researchers like to work with a graph that matches their mental model. Two researchers may use the same modeling method and visual representation, but the way they organize the pathway can be very different.

The Appropriate Visualization

To make the molecule look organic and life-like, we embedded animations into the simulation. The molecules move randomly in a small confined area. Also, the shape of the molecule morphs with time. The speed of the movement and magnitude of the morph are affected by the concentration of the molecule. We particularly exaggerate this effect for users to see the maximum and minimum values of the visualization. We discussed alternative methods to visualize concentration changes, such as varying the color of the molecule or the thickness of the molecule border. But these techniques make subtle changes hard to notice.

One important topic in information visualization is to maintain graphical integrity.[20] For example, in a bar chart, if the height ratio of three bars are 1:2:3, the ratio of the underlying data values should be 1:2:3. Using animations in visualization can help users understand the overall distribution of the data, but it does not show the details, unless additional features are added. The animations may need to be exaggerated to emphasize the effect; this can cause the user to misinterpret the data. Several of the respondents suggested changing the circle sizes of molecules to signify the concentration changes. However, this changing of a two-dimensional area is not a good mapping for the one-dimensional concentration data.

Tabletop Interaction

It is difficult to design tangible interactions controlling physical objects that map to digital contents. Systems biologists largely rely on pen and paper. The goal is to create an interface that allows them to continue their regular productive tasks more effectively. Even though there is research showing that tabletop interfaces are effective collaborative tools, some users feel awkward when they first approach the table. Moving an object on a digital surface to reveal further information is uncommon in real life. So is moving an object with one finger. We expect the popularity of multi-touch mobile devices will cause users to grow accustomed to this type of interface in the coming years.

ONGOING CHANGES

The objective of Pathways is to help systems biology researchers find the best parameter set for each molecule, so that the data for the whole pathway fits the experimental data. This optimization is currently supported somewhat, as the user can explore the parameter space by manipulating multiple values simultaneously using the tangible user interface. A separate visualization needs to be added, to indicate when an optimized network model is found, and this will help to improve the accuracy, reliability and quality of the model.

Our original plan was to generate a dynamic graph that followed a set of physical rules. In this graph, when a node is pulled away, the elastic force will bring it back. A node is connected to another by an invisible spring. However, one user wants the functionality to change the topology of pathways. The ongoing improvement is to build a graph that adheres to specific physical laws, while allowing topology to be adjustable by users.

Charts are very important to systems biologists. The charts have evolved from a single chart with multiple curves to multiple charts and then to multiple charts with baselines that highlight the value. A newer version of charts is now being implemented for each molecule.

Since every biologist has a different way of modeling, the new Pathways interface should be customizable. The system will offer an interface for users to customize the network model by providing a variety of options, such as changing colors of nodes, grouping certain molecules and visualizing with different layouts. Also, users' personal settings and modeling data should be stored separately and be accessible from multiple locations. Controlling parameters will reflect in the simulation in real-time, and the updated results will be visualized with multiple graphs showing the history of parameter changes. Users will be able to compare and analyze based on time differences, which will also be projected as an animation within the representation of the pathway itself.

For the purpose of discovery, Pathways needs to provide more statistical and computational tools for researchers to analyze the network model. On the other hand, for educational purposes, the system needs to focus on providing a simple intuitive interface and graphical expressions. This will help students get interested in the system, and provide a better understanding of network models.

Other than using tangible objects, finger gestures are another option for controlling the network model, and manipulating it in an intuitive and efficient way. The system currently provides different interfaces and options when there is more than one person using Pathways. For educational purposes, the system can track which person controlled a parameter, and its log files provide a history of data manipulation.

DISCUSSION

Two of the design challenges we face are: what are the appropriate visualization and kinesthetic manipulations of the pathway for a researcher trying to fit a model? And what is the right data, and form of data, to present so that a fit can be achieved using the visualization? In our current prototype, based on the users' preference, we chose to show the concentration values in the visualization, using different representations. However, it is possible that the change of reaction speeds might be a more effective means for them to comprehend the data, such that a fit can be achieved.

More generally, what is the relationship between the fitting process and the representations, and also the visual and kinesthetic manipulations? There is very little known about the cognitive principles and processes underlying modeling, and even less on how visual and motor manipulations contribute to discovery using simulations [1, 13]. We hope that the development and use of the Pathways interface will help shed light on these cognitive principles and processes, and thus pave the way for more sophisticated kinesthetic interfaces that support discovery.

ACKNOWLEDGMENTS

We gratefully acknowledge the support of National Science Foundation REESE grant DRL097394084 and a research collaboration grant from Steelcase Inc. in conducting this research.

REFERENCES

1. Chandrasekharan, S. 2009. Building to discover: a common coding model. *Cognitive Science*. 33, 6 (2009), 1059-1086.
2. Cooper, S. et al. 2010. Predicting protein structures with a multiplayer online game. *Nature*. 466, 7307 (2010), 756-760.
3. Covert, M.W. et al. 2008. Integrating metabolic, transcriptional regulatory and signal transduction models in Escherichia coli. *Bioinformatics*. 24, 18 (2008), 2044.
4. Davis, R. 2002. Sketch understanding in design: Overview of work at the MIT AI lab. *Sketch Understanding, Papers from the 2002 AAAI Spring Symposium* (2002), 24–31.
5. Havre, S. et al. 2002. Themeriver: Visualizing thematic changes in large document collections. *IEEE transactions on visualization and computer graphics*. (2002), 9-20.
6. Hu, Z. et al. 2005. VisANT: data-integrating visual framework for biological networks and modules. *Nucleic acids research*. 33, suppl 2 (2005), W352.
7. Kaltenbrunner, M. and Bencina, R. 2007. reacTIVision: a computer-vision framework for table-based tangible interaction. *Proc. TEI '07, (*2007), 69-74.
8. Karp, P.D. et al. 2010. Pathway Tools version 13.0: integrated software for pathway/genome informatics and systems biology. *Briefings in bioinformatics*. 11, 1 (2010), 40.
9. KEGG PATHWAY: Metabolic pathways - Reference pathway: *http://www.genome.jp/kegg-bin/show_pathway?query=&map=map01100&scale=0.71&show_description=show&multi_query=*. Accessed: 2011-04-29.
10. Kobayashi, K. et al. 2003. A tangible interface for IP network simulation. *CHI '03 extended abstracts on Human factors in computing systems* (2003), 800-801.
11. Mazalek, A. et al. 2009. Architales: physical/digital co-design of an interactive story table. *Proc. of TEI '09*, (2009), 241-248.
12. MT4j - Multitouch For Java: *http://www.mt4j.org/mediawiki/index.php/Main_Page*. Accessed: 2011-04-29.
13. Nersessian, N.J. 2008. *Creating scientific concepts*. The MIT Press.
14. Patten, J. and Ishii, H. 2007. Mechanical constraints as computational constraints in tabletop tangible interfaces. *Proc. of CHI (*2007), 809-818.
15. Patten, J. et al. 2001. Sensetable: a wireless object tracking platform for tangible user interfaces. *Proc. of CHI* '01, (2001), 253-260.
16. PhET: Free online physics, chemistry, biology, earth science and math simulations: *http://phet.colorado.edu/*. Accessed: 2011-04-29.
17. Plaisant, C. et al. 1996. LifeLines: visualizing personal histories. *Proc. of CHI '96* ,(1996), 221-227.
18. Shannon, P. et al. 2003. Cytoscape: a software environment for integrated models of biomolecular interaction networks. *Genome research*. 13, 11 (2003), 2498.
19. The DOT Language: *http://www.graphviz.org/doc/info/lang.html*. Accessed: 2011-04-30.
20. Tufte, E.R. and Howard, G. 1983. *The visual display of quantitative information*. Graphics press Cheshire, CT.

An Artistic Dialogue with the Artificial

David Norton, Derrall Heath, Dan Ventura
MIND Lab
Computer Science Department
Brigham Young University
Provo, Utah
USA
dnorton@byu.edu, dheath@byu.edu, ventura@cs.byu.edu

ABSTRACT
In conjunction with Brigham Young University's Visual Arts program, we conducted a study centered around a system designed to be an artificial artist, in order to synthesize the ideas of visual artists and computer scientists. Participants from both disciplines designed activities that imposed the limitations of the artificial system on their fellow participants. These activities sparked discussion and insight into the nature of the creative process and how it can be better emulated in artificial systems. We present our system and several of the activities designed around it and discuss the synergistic results.

Author Keywords
creative process, art, collaboration, evolutionary system

ACM Classification Keywords
I.2.m [Artificial Intelligence]: Miscellaneous; K.3.1 [Computers and Education]: Computer Uses in Education — collaborative learning

General Terms
Design, Documentation, Experimentation, Human Factors

INTRODUCTION
In order to instigate a dialogue, a group of college art students was presented with a series of anonymous images and asked to comment on the creativity and value of the images. The images ranged from Van Gogh's *Starry Night* to Malevich's *Red Square* to a fourteen year old student's meticulous reproduction of *Starry Night*. They included a painting titled *Purple Haze* by Rumba the Wonder Horse, a digital image from the Mandelbrot set, and a phase contrast micrograph of *Trichodina pediculus*. They also included three images each produced by one of the digital artists: AARON [5], The Painting Fool [1], and DARCI [7]. The students knew the work of Van Gogh and Malevich. They could immediately spot the fraud of the *Starry Night* reproduction. They marveled at the mathematical beauty of the Mandelbrot set and phase contrast micrograph. None of them knew the works of Rumba the Wonder Horse, or the three digital artists—while intrigued, they did not know how to appreciate these works. From these students' perspective, they could not properly attribute creativity without understanding the process behind the creation.

C&C'11, November 36, 2011, Atlanta, Georgia, USA.

This exercise inaugurated a four month study designed to create synergism between the (apparently disparate) disciplines. With the collaboration of students and faculty from Brigham Young University's Visual Arts department, we designed the study to explore the process of creation in the visual arts. Our interest in the collaboration was to learn how to better emulate the human process of creation in our digital artist, DARCI. For the participating art students, it was an opportunity to explore their own personal approaches to creation and why they do what they do when they create.

The centerpiece of the study was DARCI (Digital ARtist Communicating Intention) a computer system designed to create original images through processes perceived as creative. We facilitate the perception of creativity by giving the system a name and referring to DARCI as a she. *She* is central to our research in the budding field of computational creativity. Computational creativity is a branch of artificial intelligence focusing on emulating human creativity in computer systems. One of the goals of this field is to automate tasks that one would say require creativity to perform such as mathematical deduction, the creation of art and music, and storytelling. Another goal of the field is to better understand creativity so that we may identify, foster, and augment the creative process in society.

DARCI presently does not produce wholly original images; rather, using a variety of image processing filters, she renders provided images so that they will reflect an accompanying description, currently limited to adjectives (see Figure 1 for example). In accordance with Colton's arguments concerning *appreciation* [2], this process requires that DARCI be able to evaluate the degree to which an image matches a list of adjectives. She is able to make this assessment by learning to associate image features with individual adjectives via supervised machine learning. In other words, the data used to train DARCI is created by teachers—humans.

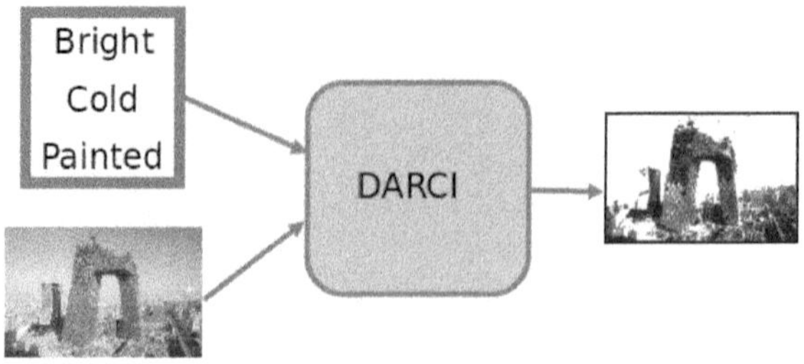

Figure 1. Example of DARCI in action.

The opportunity to teach DARCI is open to the public with no restrictions through a persistent public website. What this amounts to, is that DARCI's interpretation of images is an unpredictable amalgamation of human sentiment and the machine learning algorithms at play behind the curtain. Effectively, DARCI presents a unique interpretation of the social culture surrounding her development—arguably the role of an artist.

Clearly, DARCI is limited by constraints far more restrictive than her human counterparts; at the same time, these constraints provide a unique viewpoint. During the study, we engaged in activities designed to explore the constraints of DARCI from an artistic perspective in an attempt to stimulate introspection about the process of creating art in the participants while helping us improve DARCI. The study culminated in *Fitness Function*, an interactive art show, hosted by Brigham Young University's Visual Arts Department, in which DARCI acted as the sole juror for any-and-all submissions made on site.

This paper will explore the insights gained from simulating current computationally creative systems with social activities. We will begin by detailing the processes by which DARCI currently learns and creates, and observe the constraints imposed by these processes. We will then describe the activities, designed by both artists and computer scientists, that were employed during the study to foster an understanding of DARCI's limitations and provoke discussions about creativity. We will illustrate how these activities sparked insights into the creative process by those participating in the study. We will also outline how these insights will be used to redesign DARCI and improve her capacity to be perceived as a creative agent. Finally, we will describe the art show, *Fitness Function*, and the response it received from those who participated in it.

DARCI

An important component of creativity is appreciation, or the ability to evaluate one's own created artifacts [2]. In order for DARCI to appreciate art, she must first acquire some basic understanding of art. For example, in order for DARCI to appreciate an image that is bright and cold, DARCI must first understand the concepts 'bright' and 'cold'. To do this, DARCI must learn to associate images with descriptions. We teach DARCI to associate images with descriptions by providing her with hundreds of images, each labeled with adjectives that describe it. We also provide negative labels, or adjectives that the images are not. DARCI considers low level features of each image that deal with light, color, texture and shape. These image features are then associated with the provided adjectives through a collection of artificial neural networks [6]. The more examples of happy and non-happy images that are provided, the better DARCI is able to understand what it means for an image to be happy and be able to evaluate how happy an image is. We collect labeled images for DARCI through a website that allows people to label images with adjectives (http://darci.cs.byu.edu). The user is presented with a random image from DARCI's database and the user is asked to provide adjectives that describe that image. Additionally, there is a section of the website in which DARCI attempts to label an image with adjectives herself and the user can correct DARCI by tagging the adjectives that are incorrect, thus providing negative labels.

Once she has sufficiently learned enough adjectives, the next step for DARCI is to modify an image to match a list of adjectives. DARCI has a large set of image filters, similar to what would be found in software like Photoshop, which are capable of modifying images. DARCI uses genetic algorithms to explore different image filter combinations and to learn how to use these filters to modify images to convey the meaning of each adjective [7]. Genetic algorithms have often been described as a creative process due to their purposeful, yet unpredictable nature [4].

Genetic algorithms are governed by a subroutine called a *fitness function* that evaluates each artifact. The fitness function for DARCI generates a single score that measures how well a set of filters modifies an image to match the provided adjectives. This fitness function is the output of the artificial neural networks that have been learning image-to-adjective associations. For example, if DARCI were given a photograph and the adjectives 'bright' and 'happy', then DARCI would begin the creation process by trying out random sets of image filters on the photograph. For each set of image filters, DARCI would score how 'happy' and 'bright' the resulting image is using the artificial neural networks. The sets of filters with the lowest scores would be discarded, while DARCI would keep the sets of filters with the highest scores. DARCI would then alter some of these filters (*mutation*) and even try recombining the best sets of filters (*crossover*). In this way DARCI is continually searching for the set of filters that would modify the photograph to be the most 'happy' and 'bright'. This process continues for many iterations, after which DARCI applies the best set of image filters found and outputs the modified image. A high level overview of DARCI can be seen in Figure 2.

DARCI is a simplified model of a complex process and hence has several important limitations. For example, DARCI's language is limited to lists of adjectives. Her percepts are limited to low-level image features and her ability to modify images is limited to a finite set of image filters. DARCI has no social context or past experience from which to draw analogies and insights. Finally, DARCI's feedback consists of a single metric with no context. These limitations will be discussed in greater detail throughout the paper.

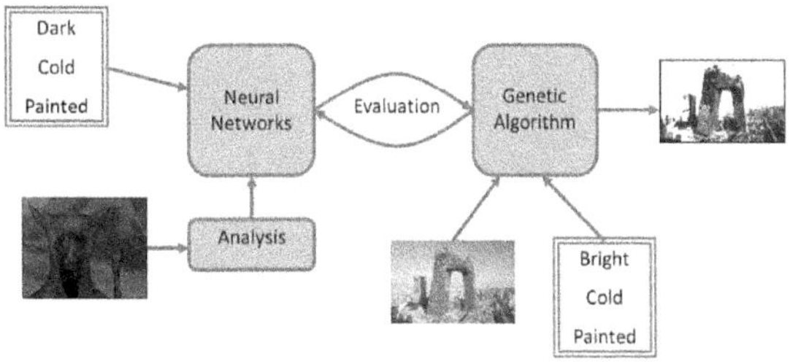

Figure 2. Overview of DARCI's artifact creation process.

ARTIST INTERPRETATIONS

We began the study by introducing the participants to DARCI. Soon after that, still early in the study, we asked several of the artists to come up with activities for the rest of the participants that they felt represented the processes underlying DARCI as they understood her. This was not only to solidify their understanding of DARCI, but also to help the atists begin to think about their own processes of creating art. The artists came up with activities that highlighted many of DARCI's aforementioned limitations. This section contains a description and analysis of three of the activities that the artists devised.

Copy of a Copy

Copy of a copy was based on the simple premise that as information is transferred, it degrades. The participants were divided into four groups. Each group created a black-and-white picture as a team using only pencil and ink. There were no other rules. Once each team had finished their pictures, they found a copy machine on campus and made a copy of the picture. They then made a copy of the copy. They proceeded to copy each copy for fifty iterations. The groups then convened to show their results and discuss what happened.

As expected, the quality of each copy deteriorated to the point that the original image could no longer be recognized. Some groups experimented with different patterns or shade strengths. While the fidelity of each copy decreased, interesting artifacts would sometimes occur due to the way the original images were drawn. The participants decided that from an artistic perspective the degradation, to a point, was not always a negative thing.

This activity was designed by an individual who was concerned that as DARCI was taught adjectives, the quality of her learning would be suspect. Said another way, since both DARCI's percepts and the communication between teacher and DARCI are not perfect, there will always be a degradation of information. This individual assumed that DARCI was meant to reflect the opinion of her teachers. After this activity, the general consensus was that this imperfection in learning was, in fact, a good thing and not unlike a human teacher-student interaction. The flaws in communication are part of what allow the novel to emerge. This idea was explored throughout the study and the many activities we participated in; but this activity set the tone.

Rotating Artists

This activity had participants creating collaborative drawings all using the same medium, pencil. An 18 x 24 inch sheet of paper was set up on a drawing board for each individual. Each sheet was associated with a random adjective. Then each person was assigned a random rule restricting the mechanics of their drawing. These rules included requirements such as "draw with your off hand", "draw from over the top of the paper", "draw with your teeth", etc. The participants were randomly assigned a sheet of paper to start on. They were instructed to begin a drawing that fit the adjective assigned to the sheet of paper. After five minutes, the participants rotated to another sheet of paper. They were instructed to continue the previous individual's drawing using the adjective connected to the sheet. Participants continued to rotate until everyone had contributed to every drawing. Individuals were required to use their restriction on every other rotation. Finally, when all of the drawings were completed, the participants were split into three groups and each group created a collage out of one third of the drawings.

This activity simulated DARCI on several levels. First, participants were given a task similar to DARCI's primary function: they were required to create an image to fit an adjective. Second, participants were given hardware restrictions, their drawing rule and use of only pencils. This was an attempt to constrain them in the way that DARCI is constrained to digital media using only filters. The restriction is not identical but it did force individuals to create without their complete faculties, giving them something to think about. Finally, there were two attempts to specifically simulate the way DARCI generates her artefacts. The first was in rotating people from drawing to drawing. The second was in cutting up the drawings and combining them in some form of collage. These activities were attempts to copy the crossover and mutation mechanisms used in the genetic algorithm driving DARCI's image creation. Mutation is an iterative mechanism not unlike the incremental alterations contributed to each drawing by new artists. Crossover does combine features from multiple solutions as the collages did. However, unlike actual genetic algorithms, there was no evaluation of the changes made at each step and no decision based on these evaluations as to how to proceed. Also, the goal of the activity differed from DARCI's in that the participants were creating a wholly original image rather than modifying a source.

This was the first activity of the study to directly simulate DARCI's processes. As such, it began to bridge the gap between the understanding of the artists and that of the computer scientists.

Systems

In this activity the designer attempted to more accurately simulate DARCI's genetic algorithm based on the discussion deconstructing *Rotating Artists*. In addition, the designer added some style by presenting the activity as if those participating were themselves machines. *Systems* was divided into two sessions called *System 1* and *System 2* respectively. Each participant was given a unique *Ink Hardware*, a tool for

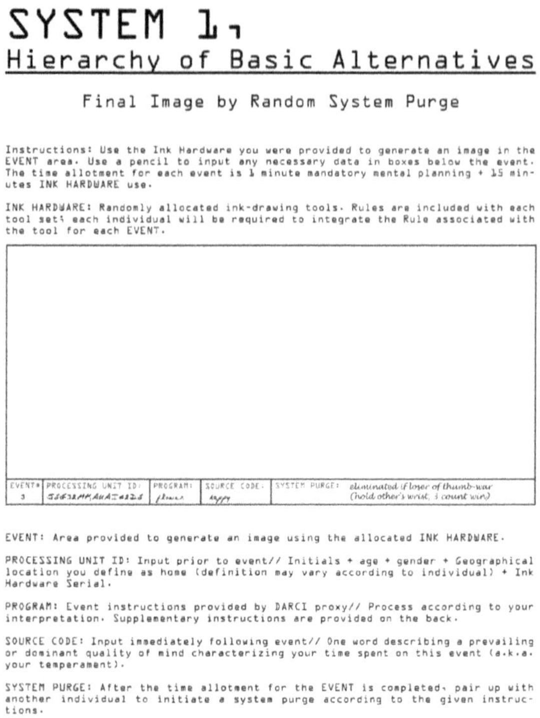

SYSTEM 1,
Hierarchy of Basic Alternatives

Final Image by Random System Purge

Instructions: Use the Ink Hardware you were provided to generate an image in the EVENT area. Use a pencil to input any necessary data in boxes below the event. The time allotment for each event is 1 minute mandatory mental planning + 15 minutes INK HARDWARE use.

INK HARDWARE: Randomly allocated ink-drawing tools. Rules are included with each tool set; each individual will be required to integrate the Rule associated with the tool for each EVENT.

EVENT#	PROCESSING UNIT ID:	PROGRAM:	SOURCE CODE:	SYSTEM PURGE: eliminated if loser of thumb-war (hold other's wrist, 3 count win)
3	JJF32MMAUAI#22.5	flower	happy	

EVENT: Area provided to generate an image using the allocated INK HARDWARE.

PROCESSING UNIT ID: Input prior to event// Initials + age + gender + Geographical location you define as home (definition may vary according to individual) + Ink Hardware Serial.

PROGRAM: Event instructions provided by DARCI proxy// Process according to your interpretation. Supplementary instructions are provided on the back.

SOURCE CODE: Input immediately following event// One word describing a prevailing or dominant quality of mind characterizing your time spent on this event (a.k.a. your temperament).

SYSTEM PURGE: After the time allotment for the EVENT is completed, pair up with another individual to initiate a system purge according to the given instructions.

Figure 3. The instructions for *System 1* as presented to participants.

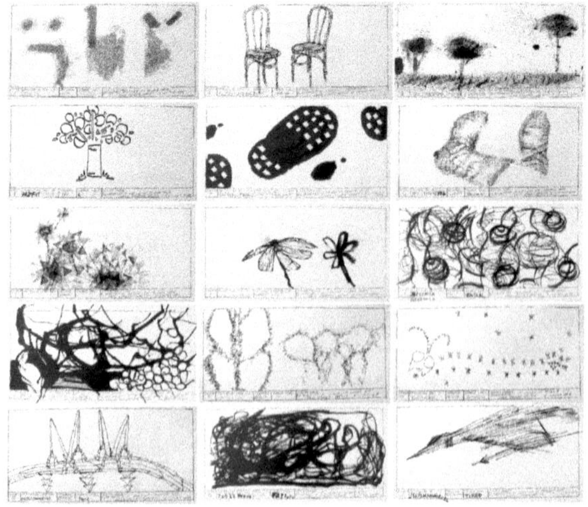

Figure 4. The results of the first round of *System 1*.

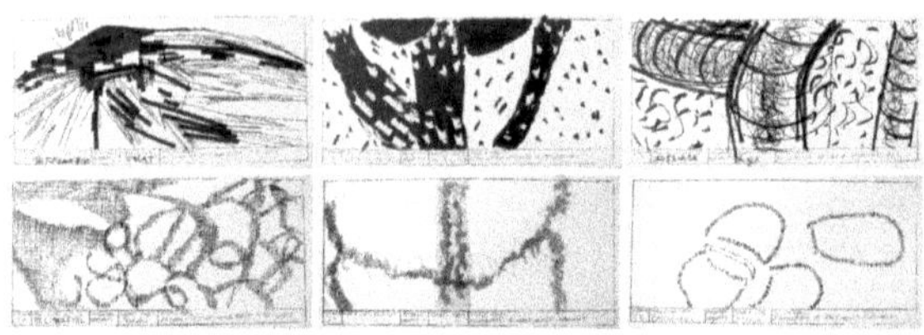

Figure 5. The results of the second round of *System 1*.

applying ink on paper (i.e. various pens, ink blots, an eye dropper, etc.). The participants were then presented with the instructions shown in Figure 3 and each given a card similar to the one in the instructions. Basically, within sixteen minutes, each participant created an image of the noun listed under *Program* using their "hardware". They then wrote a word that described their experience under *Source Code*. Finally, they paired up with another random participant and performed the *System Purge* to determine which individual would progress in *System 1* and which would be eliminated and move on to *System 2*. Those that progressed within *System 1* got a new card with a *Program* to modify the eliminated participant's art in some way. Individuals continued to pair up and *System Purge* until there was only one person left who then created the final image.

The results of the four rounds of elimination that occurred in *System 1* are shown in Figures 4-7(a) respectively. The final image is shown in Figure 7(b). This activity simulated the generational progression of DARCI's genetic algorithm. Each generation, the "optimal" images would move on to compete in the next generation. Furthermore, each generation was built off of the previous one. While an analogue for crossover was not present, one for mutation was. The significant difference between *System 1* and DARCI's genetic algorithm was that the criteria for success in an image was not directly correlated with the quality of the image. The winner of each *System Purge* was determined by either winning a thumb war, having the fewest siblings, being born furthest from the activity location, or wearing the most articles of clothing, depending on the round. Typically, such an indirect evaluation criteria is not ideal in genetic algorithms. However, it can have unforeseen and fascinating implications (maybe people with strong thumbs make better artists).

As participants were eliminated, they moved on to *System 2* (see Figure 8). *System 2* was essentially a group project where each panel iterated on the previous one. People were assigned a panel to complete in the order they were eliminated from *System 1* and then by birth date for individuals eliminated simultaneously. Each panel was supposed to reflect the predetermined *Program* and the previous panel. Participants could use whatever *Ink Hardware* was available at the time they started their panel. This system explored the concept of evolution at a high level. Mutation occurred in the sense that individuals iterated upon one another's work. The progress of the panels was aided by an evolutionary theme

Figure 6. The results of the third round of *System 1*.

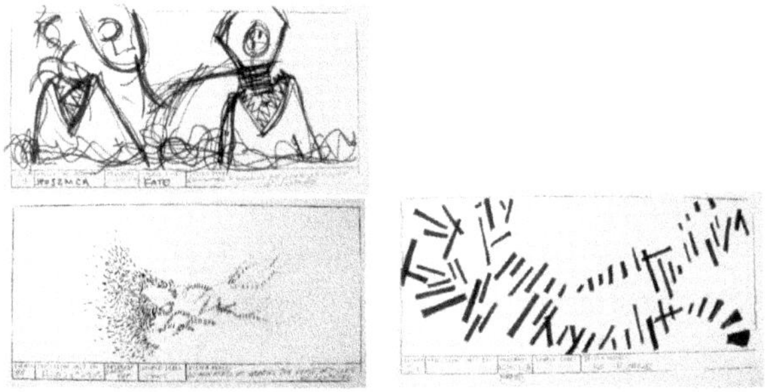

(a) fourth round results (b) final image

Figure 7. Fourth round and final image results for *System 1*.

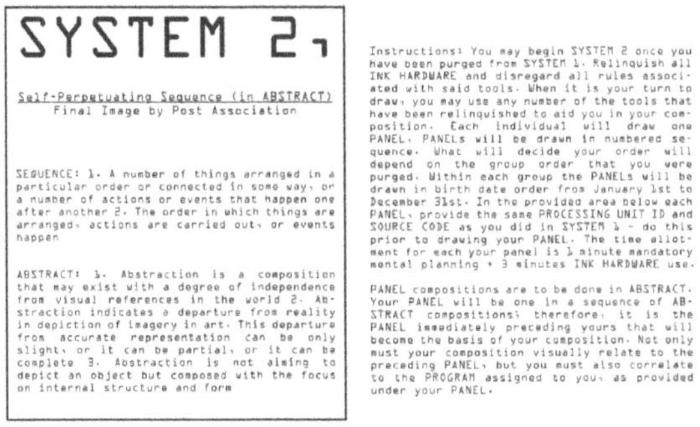

SYSTEM 2.

Self-Perpetuating Sequence (in ABSTRACT)
Final Image by Post Association

SEQUENCE: 1. A number of things arranged in a particular order or connected in some way, or a number of actions or events that happen one after another 2. The order in which things are arranged, actions are carried out, or events happen

ABSTRACT: 1. Abstraction is a composition that may exist with a degree of independence from visual references in the world 2. Abstraction indicates a departure from reality in depiction of imagery in art. This departure from accurate representation can be only slight, or it can be partial, or it can be complete 3. Abstraction is not aiming to depict an object but composed with the focus on internal structure and form

Instructions: You may begin SYSTEM 2 once you have been purged from SYSTEM 1. Relinquish all INK HARDWARE and disregard all rules associated with said tools. When it is your turn to draw, you may use any number of the tools that have been relinquished to aid you in your composition. Each individual will draw one PANEL. PANELs will be drawn in numbered sequence. What will decide your order will depend on the group order that you were purged. Within each group the PANELs will be drawn in birth date order from January 1st to December 31st. In the provided area below each PANEL, provide the same PROCESSING UNIT ID and SOURCE CODE as you did in SYSTEM 1 - do this prior to drawing your PANEL. The time allotment for each your panel is 1 minute mandatory mental planning + 3 minutes INK HARDWARE use.

PANEL compositions are to be done in ABSTRACT. Your PANEL will be one in a sequence of ABSTRACT compositions; therefore, it is the PANEL immediately preceding yours that will become the basis of your composition. Not only must your composition visually relate to the preceding PANEL, but you must also correlate to the PROGRAM assigned to you, as provided under your PANEL.

Figure 8. The instructions for *System 2* as presented to participants.

in the *Program* titles. The *Program* themes progressed in the following order: birth, adaptation, bewilderment, fear of other, conflict, power, unification, stress, pain, relief, disbelief. The result of *System 2* can be seen in Figure 9. While open to interpretation, the *Program* themes hint at a message about the process of merging ostensibly conflicting viewpoints: say that of visual arts and that of computer science. With this in mind, *Systems* not only demonstrated an artistic interpretation of DARCI's creative process, but also acted as a metaphor for the study as a whole.

COMPUTER SCIENTIST INTERPRETATIONS

When an artist creates art, what is going on in their head? Said another way, given the artist's inputs, what determines the output? In this context, the input includes feelings, education, training, genetics, the weather, day-to-day senses—everything that one experiences. The output is the art. Some process occurs that transforms these inputs into artifacts. The activities that we designed were aimed at trying to understand this process. The first activity, *Bromerly*, was aimed at exploring the process of learning associations and expressing them in art. The second, *Celebrities Crossover*, was aimed at exploring the idea that meaning is not universal. The third activity, *External Evaluation*, was aimed at exploring the evaluation of art from both the creator's and the critic's perspectives.

Bromerly

When we, as humans, hear adjectives like 'happy', 'scary', or 'red', we have a lifetime of experiences and examples to

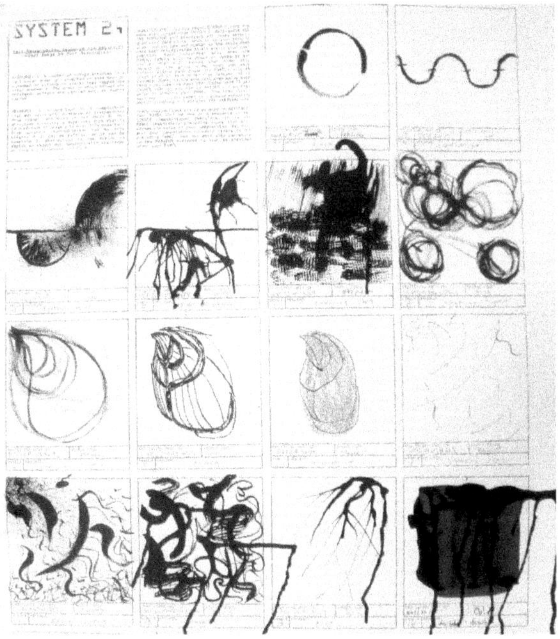

Figure 9. The results of *System 2*.

help us understand what these words mean. These adjectives fit into a cultural and environmental context that influences how we interpret them. DARCI has none of these advantages. When DARCI learns a new adjective like 'gloomy', she has no past experience to draw upon, and she has no cultural influences to help define it. All DARCI has are the example images of 'gloomy' and 'not gloomy' that are given to her.

An activity was designed for the human artists to simulate DARCI's processes and limitations as much as possible. The goal was to see how they would compare to DARCI, to determine what their creative processes would be like in a restricted setting, and to discover improvements for DARCI. Three fake adjectives were invented that have no reference to any other word, and have no background or cultural meaning. These adjectives are 'orfly', 'bromerly', and 'flamping'. Unbeknownst to the human artists in the study, these adjectives actually represented a real adjective that DARCI knew fairly well. Orfly meant weird, bromerly meant blocky, and flamping meant lonely. The artists were then provided with the same example images for each adjective that DARCI was trained on (both positive and negative examples).

The participating artists were split into three groups. Each group was given one of the fake adjectives and the example images for that adjective. The artists spent several minutes looking over the provided images to learn as best they could what the fake adjectives meant. Each artist was then given their own source image and instructed to create something based off the source image that reflected the adjective that they just learned. Essentially they had to communicate the meaning of their adjective through their creation. Some of the resulting images along with their sources can be seen in Figure 10. After everyone was done, all the paintings

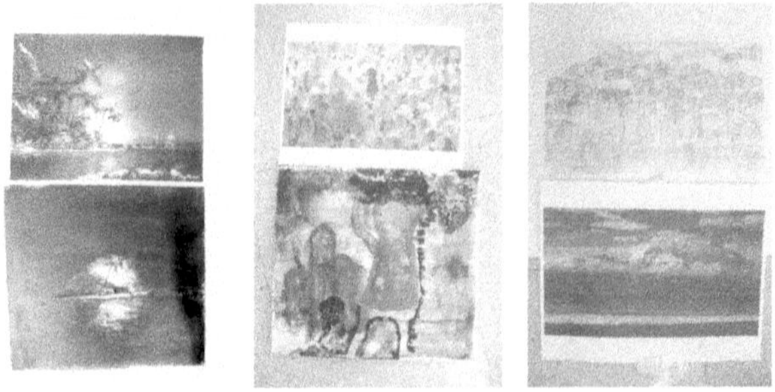

(a) flamping (b) orfly (c) bromerly

Figure 10. Three example images (with their sources) created during the Bromerly activity. One example of each fake adjective is presented. Flamping means lonely, orfly means weird, and bromerly means blocky.

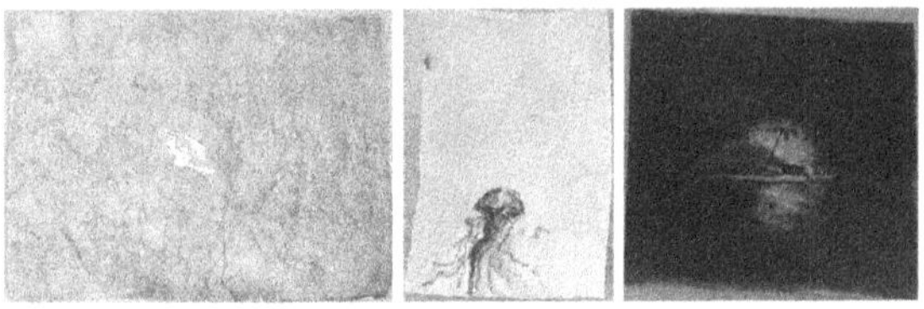

Figure 11. The cluster of flamping (lonely) images.

were put together. A random group of college students, not involved with the study, was then brought in to divide the paintings into three groups. These people had no knowledge of the activity or how they were supposed to group the paintings. The volunteers were able to group the paintings of the same adjectives together with the exception of one painting. The grouping results can be seen in Figures 11-13.

Although unable to specifically define their adjective, the artists were able to identify certain image features or qualities that they associated with their adjective. For example, they were able to tell that bromerly (blocky) images tended to have hard geometric lines, tended to be very structural, and tended to have a lot of divided space. They could tell that orfly (weird) images often had exaggerated curvy shapes and had some distinct peculiarity. They could also tell that flamping (lonely) images were usually dark and had a singular focus. The artists were then able to incorporate these characteristics into their own paintings. During the grouping phase, the people doing the grouping were able to pick up on these features and successfully group similar paintings together, while only miss-classifying one painting. This notion of evaluating the paintings by grouping led to a paper currently in submission that explores the use of clustering algorithms to evaluate DARCI's artifacts.

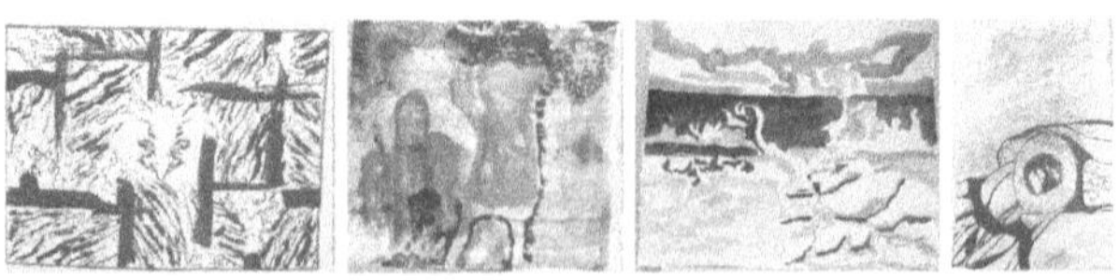

Figure 12. The cluster of orfly (weird) images. The far left image should have been clustered with bromerly (blocky).

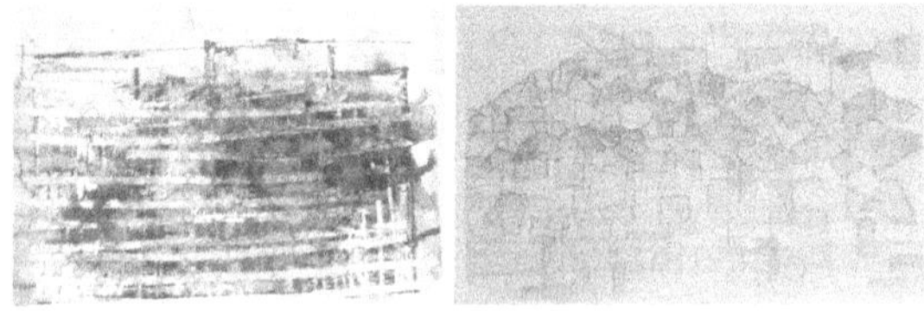

Figure 13. The cluster of bromerly (blocky) images.

A notable difference between DARCI and the human artists was how quickly humans were able to learn the adjective with so few example images. This is not surprising considering how sophisticated human vision is. DARCI needs hundreds of example images and can only see explicitly specified low level image features, while the human artists were able to quickly identify and extract the useful image features and then convey those features into their own paintings. Taking note of the way the human artists examined the example images and identified the important image features has provided us with useful insights into the type of image features DARCI needs to extract.

Through this activity, the artists gained a better understanding of how DARCI learns adjectives with the limitations that she has. The artists found it very interesting to learn a new word with only images rather than linguistically. They mentioned that when most words are heard, an associated image usually comes into people's minds. For example, if someone hears the word 'chair', an image of a chair pops into their mind. It may be a different type of chair for each person, but some kind of image pops into their head.

> "When I say chair, everybody thinks of a chair in their mind. They see that image, it might be a different chair. I just think that the images are the words."

They also said that using visuals to convey the mean of a word is less ambiguous than using other words to explain the meaning because those other words have different meaning and connotations for different people, while images are more concrete.

> "It is easier for us to get it visually than through words, words are very ambiguous. ... I usually have to see something visually to remember it."

In order to provide a more direct comparison with DARCI, several artists were asked to learn additional fake adjectives and then, using only image filters found in Photoshop, modify a source image to reflect multiple adjectives. Restricting the artists to Photoshop ensured that they were limited to the same tools that DARCI has to modify an image. We had DARCI do the same task with the same adjectives and same source images. The results can be seen in Figures 14-16. The artists were again able to quickly identify the distinctive image features that they associated with their adjectives. Some artists were unfamiliar with Photoshop and spent time trying different image filters to learn how they would affect the source image. They would then find the ones that modified the source image to best reflect their understanding of

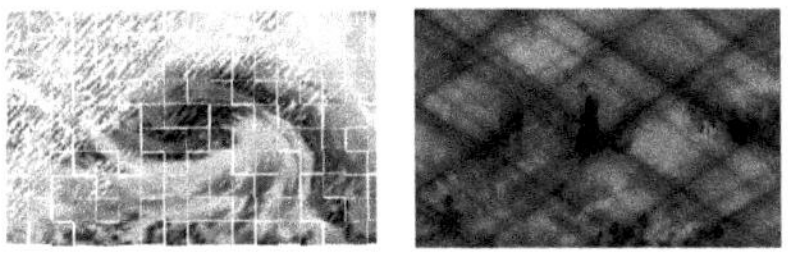

(a) human (b) DARCI

Figure 14. Images produced by a human and DARCI from the same source image for the combination of the adjectives bromerly (blocky), blemistic (majestic), and diambic (avian).

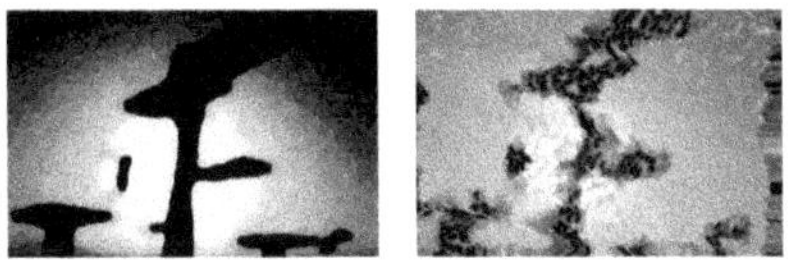

(a) human (b) DARCI

Figure 15. Images produced by a human and DARCI from the same source image for the combination of the adjectives flamping (lonely) and orfly (weird).

the adjectives. This process that they described is very similar to the genetic algorithm process DARCI uses to learn the filters to modify images. Additionally, these results are consistent with prior research that shows that DARCI is capable of producing images comparable to human artists under similar constraints [7].

Celebrities Crossover

This activity was structured around the party game *Celebrities*. In this game, players secretly write the names of several people or characters (fictional or not, famous or not, made up on the spot or not) on about 40 pieces of paper. The players are divided into two teams. Each team takes 30 second turns by having one of its members describe the characters on the pieces of paper while the other members try to guess the character. Every correct guess scores the team a point. This continues until all of the characters have been guessed. This process is repeated for two more rounds using the same set of characters and same teams but with different rules. During the second round, players can only use a single word to describe the character. On the third and final round, players can only use gestures to describe the characters. Since the same characters are used every round, as the game progresses, players develop unique associations to aid in describing these characters. Often these associations have nothing to do with a character at all, but stem from players attempting to describe characters they don't know as fast as possible. These frequently bizarre associations get picked up by everyone in the game (both teams) and can even become memes within the group that played the game together.

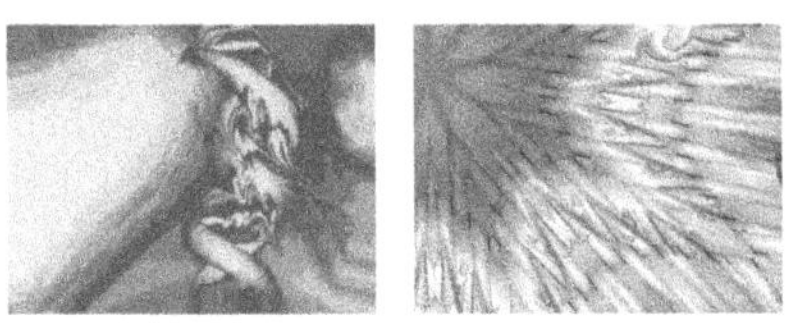

(a) human (b) DARCI

Figure 16. Images produced by a human and DARCI from the same source image for the combination of the adjectives orfly (weird), blemistic (majestic), and diambic (avian).

The study participants were divided into two groups (with two teams in each group). Each group played *Celebrities* with the exact same character names, but physically separated from each other. Thus, two divergent sets of character associations were allowed to develop. Once the groups had completed their games, one team from each group was transplanted into the other group. Each of the resulting groups then played a revised version of *Celebrities*. The new version of the game was no longer a team game; instead, it was everyone for themselves. The participant with the most points from each group would be the winner. The rules for the game were the same as round two from *Celebrities* (meaning that participants could only say a single word or use gestures) except that each participant was performing for everyone else in the group instead of teammates. Each individual that correctly guessed a character was awarded a point; the person performing only received points if the player who correctly guessed the character came from a different group than their original one. If this happened, the performing player was awarded 3 points. This forced the participants to deliberately avoid the associations they had formed previously, while developing new ones that would give everyone playing the same chance of guessing correctly.

In semiotics, the association between a sign and that to which the sign refers denotes meaning. An important aspect of visual arts is the ability of the artist to convey meaning to an audience through their art. Thus, the image that an artist produces would be the sign that is conveying the meaning that the artist intends. We designed this activity to stress the idea that not every culture associates signs with the same meanings. In this context, the term culture can refer to social groups of any scope, including an individual. When an artist creates a piece of work, to what extent is the artist communicating meaning? Is the artist only communicating to those that share the same associations as intended in an artifact? Do artists make an effort to communicate outside their personal semiotic domains [3]? We intended for this activity to force those participating to ask themselves these questions. In answering these questions, we hoped to learn the extent to which the communication of meaning would need to be emulated in DARCI for her to be accepted as an artist.

In *Celebrities*, the signs are the gestures or single words, and the meanings are the character names. With DARCI, the signs are the feature vectors that she extracts from an image, and the meanings are adjectives. Since the feature vectors represent DARCI's percepts of an image, we suggest that DARCI's signs are effectively the images themselves. In *Celebrities Crossover*, each group forms its own semiotic domain for the set of character names. When the groups cross-pollinate, they are required to communicate outside these newly formed semiotic domains. In our experience, this involved relying upon alternative associations that existed prior to the activity—in other words experience outside the activity's restricted gesture/word based symbolism.

One shortcoming of DARCI that was brought to our attention by these observations was that currently, DARCI has no associations besides the image-adjective relationship. This means that she is unable to use experiences external to these associations to communicate with an audience outside her personal semiotic domain. Another shortcoming we discovered was that, even within the image-adjective relationships, DARCI is only able to model a single semiotic domain. This domain represents a function of all of the opinions of people who have trained DARCI weighted by how much time they have spent with her. While the associations this creates may be interesting, there is no attempt to cater to a specific audience. We are redesigning DARCI so that she will be able to model each individual that trains her in addition to a general model. This will allow her to cater to specific individuals when commissioned—essentially communicating within that person's semiotic domain for image-adjective associations. Whether DARCI should cater to individuals is another question; but, at least having the capability to communicate more effectively is something we are interested in.

Referring to *Celebrities Crossover*, the following comment was made by a participating artist:

> "I was so fascinated by the associations that we made. Dan said he didn't think it was a big deal that we made "incorrect" (insane, irrational...) associations, but does DARCI make associations that are incorrect? Does anything she do come out of random associations or is all of her information supplied by us? What happens if the associations she makes are incorrect? Maybe nothing. Maybe it doesn't matter."

Another artist replied with:

> "The associations being created are not always expected. They may not be the prophesied outcomes. But that does not make them incorrect. Each association has been built upon an individuals [sic] experiences. So for that individual the association is alive and correct. Even if it is not the association that was predicted."

This discussion illustrates some ideas that were brought to the participant's attention as they pondered the activity. Whether or not these ideas are actually valid in the domain of visual arts is irrelevant. What's important is that the participants are thinking about the process of creation—their process of creation.

Abstracted Feedback

As described previously, DARCI uses genetic algorithms to learn what set of image filters will modify an image to reflect a certain adjective. This genetic algorithm uses a fitness function to guide the exploration. For example, if DARCI was trying to make an image fiery, then DARCI would try several sets of image filters. The modified images would then each get a numerical score from the fitness function. This score tells DARCI how fiery each image is. This is just a single number—it does not tell DARCI anything about how or why it is or isn't fiery. All DARCI knows is that the higher the number the better. DARCI can then take the highest scoring sets of image filters and perform crossover and mutation on them to search for even higher scoring sets of image filters.

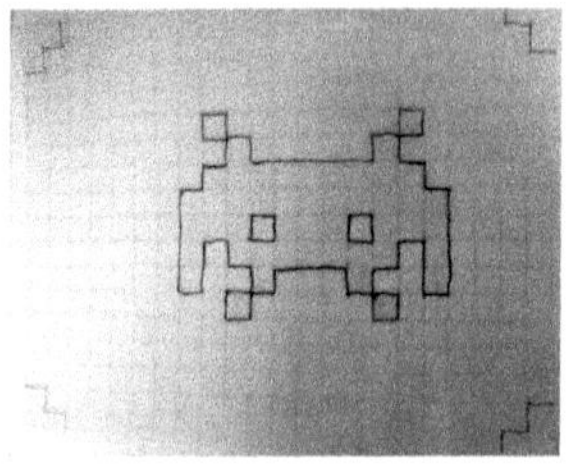

Figure 17. The template used to evaluate the objective group.

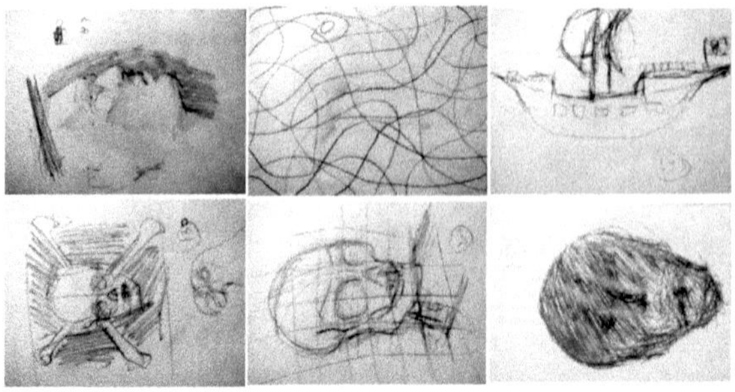

Figure 18. Examples of drawings created by the group evaluated subjectively based on how scary their images were. Drawings are chronologically ordered from top left to bottom right.

An activity was designed to give human artists this same limitation in feedback in order to see how they would perform, and to see what their thought processes would be. Each person was given a quarter sheet of paper and had to draw a picture that matched a specific criterion. To start with, no one had any idea what that criterion was. The only direction they were given was that their drawing would be scored based on some criterion unknown to them and they had to try to maximize their score. After each person submitted a drawing, the drawings were each given a numerical score. The drawings were handed back with their score, and each person could view the returned drawings and try to figure out why one drawing scored higher than another. Each person then submitted another drawing in order to increase their score. This process was repeated for several iterations.

The participating artists were split into two groups each with different criteria. The first group had a purposefully subjective criterion for which they had to draw a scary image. The drawings were each given a score based subjectively on how scary the human evaluators thought the drawing was. The second group's criterion was more objective. They had to draw a specific shape with the correct size and location on the paper. Human evaluators scored each drawing on how well it matched a specific template (seen in Figure 17) by holding the template up to the drawing and counting how many square regions on the template overlapped with the drawing. Example drawings from group 1 and group 2 can be seen in Figures 18 and 19 respectively.

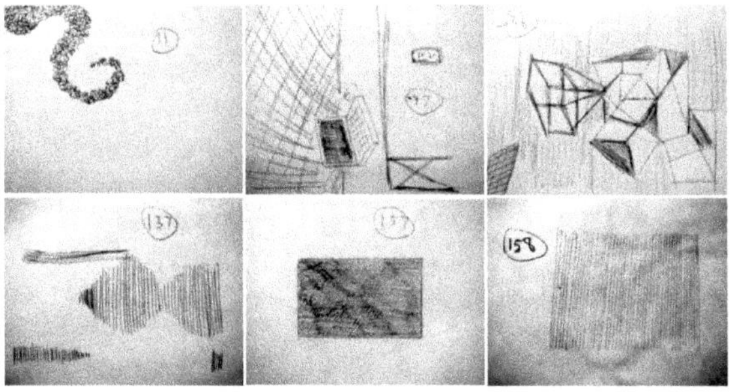

Figure 19. Examples of drawings created by the group evaluated objectively based on how closely their images fit a grid template. Drawings are chronologically ordered from top left to bottom right.

The artists got frustrated quickly when they would put time and effort into a drawing and then receive a low score and not know why. The first group at first submitted a very wide range of drawings. Eventually, someone drew a pirate ship which bumped up their score considerably. The others in the group keyed in on this higher score and all started drawing pirate related things. Soon every artist in group 1 converged to drawings of skulls. The second group was never able to get the shape completely right, they converged to a drawing of a shaded square. They did, however, converge roughly to the correct size and location on the paper.

This activity proved to be difficult and frustrating for the artists. To successfully submit a high-scoring drawing required a lot of time, persistence, and patience. This activity helped the artists understand how DARCI has to deal with limited feedback. It quickly generated a discussion on how art is evaluated in the real world. Many of the artists who had submitted their artwork to various art exhibits admitted that they were usually oblivious to the requirements of a particular art show. They would just submit all of their best work and hope something got in. This discussion developed into the idea for the art exhibit *Fitness Function*.

FITNESS FUNCTION

Fitness Function is an interactive art exhibit where DARCI acts as the sole juror for pieces submitted throughout the show. The exhibit begins with an empty wall that gets filled with art that DARCI selects from submitted work. DARCI is set up in the exhibit with a simple interface for submitting images via USB sticks. Participating patrons provide their name, email, the title of the piece, and the image itself and then DARCI scores the image between 0 and 100 using the neural networks mentioned previously. Images that receive a score of 70 or higher are printed for the artist to hang on the wall, and images that receive a score of 90 or higher receive a jury award. Artists can submit as many images as they want and anyone is eligible.

With the collaboration of Brigham Young University's Visual Arts department, we set up *Fitness Function* in the Harris Fine Arts Center to operate between March 19th and 30th, 2010, with a closing reception on the 31st. Advertisements for the exhibit were spread throughout campus via school website, posters, fliers, and word of mouth.

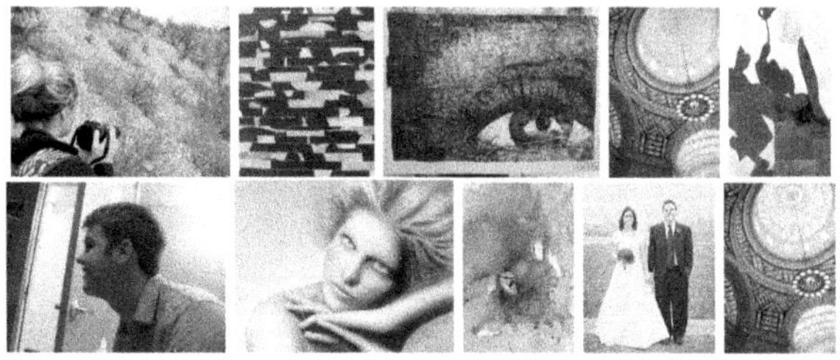

Figure 20. The ten images that received jury awards at *Fitness Function*.

We used a model of DARCI trained exclusively by the participants in our study. Just as potential images created by DARCI's own genetic algorithms are evaluated based on how closely they match particular adjectives (described earlier), the images submitted by participants of *Fitness Function* were evaluated based on how closely their images matched a set of secret adjectives that we chose for the exhibit. The adjectives we chose were 'phantasmagoric' and a special artificial adjective that we created for the purpose of *Fitness Function*. The special adjective was DARCI's prediction of whether a piece would be accepted to Brigham Young University's Museum of Art. In other words, the adjective was 'museum-of-artsy'. So that the artists involved in our study could participate, the adjective 'phantasmagoric' was kept secret from them; they weren't even told about the existence of 'museum-of-artsy'.

By the end of the exhibit, 93 people had submitted 787 images. 145 of these images were accepted, and 10 of those received a jury award at the closing reception. The jury award winners are shown in Figure 20. A website documenting the show can be found at http://darci.cs.byu.edu/fitnessfunction/.

As indicated by the comment book in the exhibit, word of mouth, personal observations, and the nature of submissions, people's reactions to the exhibit varied significantly. Some felt pride and vindication due to the acceptance of their art: "I MADE IT IN! YEAH!". Some felt frustration: "Fun and frustrating at the same time. More like a game to try and figure out than serious." Others took it as a personal challenge. One individual submitted 106 images, clearly experimenting with lighting, image quality, and other less conventional alterations (Figure 21). Thirty-eight of his images were accepted. As the last entry in the comment book he wrote, "IT WAS FUN WHILE IT LASTED DARCI." Whatever their opinion, people couldn't help but personify DARCI: "An interesting project, however, it seems that DARCI is very opinionated in her ratings. From a look at the wall, she has some rather odd tastes."

In this exhibit DARCI represents a metaphor for all kinds of external evaluation criteria to which an artist is subject, whether implicitly, explicitly, consciously, or unconsciously. We wanted to challenge people's notions of evaluation. How does one decide that they have succeeded with a piece of art? Does one only esteem a work if it is valued by others; if it can get into an art show? What if one's art gets a high score from a machine? That was quite significant for some peo-

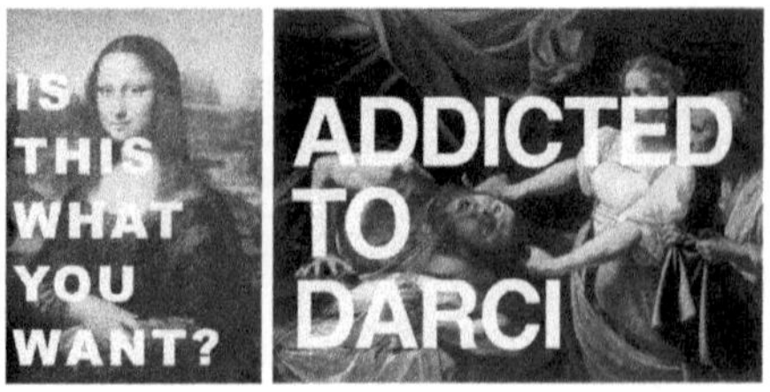

Figure 21. Two sample submissions from a witty artist.

ple. The ability to evaluate artifacts on some level is critical in any act of creativity, and from this exhibit we learned that people at least perceive that DARCI has an opinion (i.e. that DARCI is capable of evaluation). The perception of creativity has been argued to *be* creativity [2]. If this is the case, then shows like *Fitness Function* are a step in the right direction for indentifying arguably creative systems.

CONCLUSIONS

During the study, the question was raised: "does DARCI think?" The computer scientists responded with "if we can describe it, we can program a computer to do it." This quote encapsulates the computer science viewpoint and our motivation for the study. If we can formalize the process of thinking, then a computer can be programmed to think. If we can formalize what it means to be creative, then a computer can be programmed to be creative. The activities in the study were designed to elicit personal introspection on one's creative process in the hopes of shining light on that elusive process. By focusing the activities on DARCI's limitations, we were able to help those participating in the study isolate the thoughts and actions behind their creations.

As illustrated in the previous sections, we were able to gain some insight for our system, DARCI, through the activities we designed and the discussions that followed: the degradation of information associated with learning is acceptable, clustering algorithms can be used in the evaluation of artifacts, more realistic image feature extraction is vital, the creation of perceptual associations is important (perhaps in all creative systems), genetic algorithms do appear to emulate part of the creative process, the creation of unique relationships is acceptable and useful, being able to create relationships across multiple senses is necessary to communicate across semiotic domains, and finally the external evaluation of one's work is significant in the creation process.

Throughout the study, participants were encouraged to contribute to a blog titled Art[ificial] (http://computationalcreativity.blogspot.com/). This blog was designed for participants to leave their thoughts on the activities and discussions we engaged in during the study. Consider the following entry:

> "Today I was thinking of interpretation. I interpret a lot of things. I think that's a good word to put to my process of taking a lot of input and making an output that I feel will have significance in a realm beyond my personal self. I am interpreting emotions, thought processes/concepts, words, into a visual language. Other words I think might be synonymous are 'translating,' or 'encoding.' Often times I have heard the word 'feel' used in critiques, or have thought it to myself, where something simply feels consistent, or right, or something feels like it doesn't belong. It is a way of interpreting things across different areas, from visual to emotional, or visual to psychological—a synesthesia of emotion, subconscious, and physical senses.
>
> I read some interesting articles about synesthesia and creative processes, and I think that is something significant to art making—the ability to have ideas cross over from one realm to another, or one language to another, while still maintaining a certain degree of integrity or self sufficiency."

This thought sums up the nature and purpose of the study—the synthesis of artistic and scientific interpretations for the goal of understanding the process of creation.

ACKNOWLEDGMENTS

We thank Professor Joseph Ostraff and his VASTU 480/680 students for the fruitful collaboration.
This material is based upon work supported by the National Science Foundation under Grant No. IIS-0856089.

REFERENCES

1. The painting fool. http://thepaintingfool.com/.

2. S. Colton. Creativity versus the perception of creativity in computational systems. *Creative Intelligent Systems: Papers from the AAAI Spring Symposium*, pages 14–20, 2008.

3. J. P. Gee. *What Video Games Have to Teach Us About Learning and Literacy*. New York: Palgrave Macmillan, 2003.

4. J. S. Gero. Creativity, emergence, and evolution in design. *Knowledge-Based Systems*, 9:435–448, 1996.

5. P. McCorduck. *AARON's Code: Meta-Art, Artificial Intelligence, and the Work of Harold Cohen*. W. H. Freeman & Co., 1991.

6. D. Norton, D. Heath, and D. Ventura. Establishing appreciation in a creative system. *Proceedings of the International Conference on Computational Creativity*, pages 26–35, 2010.

7. D. Norton, D. Heath, and D. Ventura. Autonomously creating quality images. *Proceedings of the International Conference on Computational Creativity*, pages 10–15, 2011.

Creative Gadget Design in Fictions: Generalized Planning in Analogical Spaces

Boyang Li and Mark O. Riedl
School of Interactive Computing
Georgia Institute of Technology
{boyangli, riedl}@gatech.edu

ABSTRACT

Science-fiction and fantasy stories often contain objects never envisioned previously. Inventing gadgets like lightsabers or mythical creatures like griffins is a creative task. Traditional computational storytelling systems are limited in their expressivity because they cannot create new types of objects or gadgets. The Japanese manga series *Doraemon* exemplifies the role of new and creative gadgets in creating fun and successful stories. We surveyed five volumes of *Doraemon* and identified 9 cognitive strategies of gadget creation, unified in a 5-step process. We present an algorithm to create new types of gadgets in the context of story generation. The algorithm is a combination of partial-order planning and analogical reasoning. Although *Doraemon* is our motivating example, we can also generate gadgets commonly seen in other science fictions and fairy tales.

Author Keywords

Story generation, fictional gadget, computational creativity

ACM Classification Keywords

H.4.m [Information Systems Applications]: Miscellaneous; J.5 [Arts and Humanities]: Literature

General Terms

Algorithms, Design.

INTRODUCTION

This paper attempts to investigate and simulate a major creative capability exhibited by human storytellers: the ability to create imaginary objects. Many science fictions, fantasies, and fairy tales contain imaginary objects that do not exist in our world. These objects usually have special powers, supposedly due to futuristic technologies or magic, which allow them to accomplish impossible deeds. Lightsabers in *Star Wars* and the magic mirror in *Snow White* are two famous examples. These objects contribute significantly to the fun of reading and sometimes dictate story development. The "gadget story" is proposed as one of the four subgenres of science fiction [10]. The cognitive construction of such objects, which we call *gadgets*, is a creative act that we attempt to imitate with an Artificial Intelligence (AI).

C&C'11, November 3–6, 2011, Atlanta, Georgia, USA.

Simulating the human ability to write stories has long been an objective of AI, and some storytelling systems are considered as creative [5, 11]. However, almost all storytelling systems require a pre-specified micro-world which defines all characters, objects, places, and their inter-relationships. A few systems can modify this configuration to a limited extent [14, 19, 24]. We are not aware of storytelling systems that can create new types of objects previously unknown. In contrast, human authors' ability to perform this imaginative task is well-known, as we can see from examples as disparate as *Star Wars*, *Snow White*, and *Doraemon*.

The hugely successful, 45-volume Japanese manga *Doraemon* is often considered as a Japanese cultural icon and one of the most prominent illustrations of the human ability to imagine new objects. Doraemon is a cat-like robot coming from the future to accompany and help a primary school student, Nobita. The repeated theme of the series is that Doraemon helps Nobita to cope with problems such as exams and bullies by using high-tech gadgets indistinguishable from magic. However, in the end they usually backfire and cause unexpected consequences, emphasizing the importance of self-reliance. Dream-fulfilling gadgets that solve intractable problem are the highlights of *Doraemon* [18]. In this paper, we focus on *Doraemon* as an example of creative use of gadgets in fiction.

In an attempt to reverse engineer the creative processes of *Doraemon*'s creator, we surveyed five volumes of the manga. From an information-processing viewpoint, we identified 9 techniques that appear to be used by the *Doraemon* authors to create gadgets. These techniques are unified into a 5-step process. We then present an algorithm for generating gadgets based on our taxonomy, utilizing a combination of planning, analogical reasoning, and knowledge of everyday objects and tools to create gadgets serving narrative purposes. The algorithm extends partial-order planning to systematically explore in space of analogies. We show our algorithm can reproduce gadgets in *Doraemon*. To our best knowledge, this is the first attempt at the generation of novel gadgets as part of AI storytelling.

For an artifact to be considered creative, Boden [1] asserts it must be (a) valuable, useful or entertaining, (b) significantly different from artifacts known or created previously, and (c) not easily predicted by consumers of the artifact. Our algorithm generates gadgets that are different from any known objects and achieve narrative goals other objects cannot ordinarily achieve. Hence, we believe the process is creative. Our algorithm combines aspects of combinational and transformational creativity since it can combine multiple objects and transforms rules of the fictional world in which the story happens.

BACKGROUND AND RELATED WORK

Following cognitive research on narrative comprehension, we model a story as a sequence of events that happen in and transform a fictional world. Cognitive science reveals that readers build mental models of narratives, which capture events described by stories. It is found that people naturally segment continuous narratives such as texts and movies into discrete event structures [27]. Furthermore, people can perceive events of different granularities organized in hierarchies, where a large event can include several small events [28]. Causality and temporality between events are also important constituents of mental models of narratives, directly affecting comprehension (cf. [27, 29]). Causal relationships between events allow readers to make inferences about narratives and missing causal links can hinder comprehension [20].

A corresponding AI formalism that captures a sequence of events as well as temporal and causal relationships between them is a partial-order plan. In story generation, a plan may be used to imitate mental models of stories and make inferences about readers' perception of stories. This leads to the development of story planners [9, 12, 14, 15, 26]. Story planners require both an initial state and a goal situation to be specified as inputs before generation takes place. The initial state describes the world before the story happens, and the goal situation describes changes the events caused when the story ends. The planning algorithm generates a plan as a feasible path linking the beginning and the end of the story. Traditional story planners have limited expressivity because they have to accept both a given beginning and a given outcome.

From a narratological perspective, Ryan [16] considers comprehension of stories as reconstruction of fictional worlds. Ryan makes two observations. First, readers learn about the fictional world bit by bit throughout the story, rather than everything at the beginning. Second, readers generally assume aspects not mentioned in the story to depart minimally from our world.

One implication of readers learning bit by bit throughout the story is that they are usually happy to believe that facts learned later existed all along. For example, when the story describes a lightsaber for the first time, readers can easily accept that this apparently novel technology existed in the fictional world the entire time. This implies that, with proper justification, we can introduce facts and novel objects later in the story without complete loss of believability. This observation motivates story planners that dynamically assert facts in the story world. Riedl and Young [14] proposed a story generation technique that starts out with a pre-defined micro-world, but allows some of the details of the world to be retroactively modified to suite the narrative arc. From a narratological perspective, their system can be considered to start from a set of possible worlds and later settle on one where the best story can be developed. The idea is later generalized [19, 24]. Our work on gadget generation complements these techniques for world-altering during storytelling. The world-altering story planning techniques described above can adjust relationships between objects and attributes of objects, and instantiate new objects of known types. These techniques, however, cannot create new types of objects. The work presented in this paper directly addresses the problem of creating an object of previously unknown type.

The second of Ryan's observations, the theory of minimal departure, suggests that readers re-use existing knowledge to interpret newly encountered fictional worlds. For example, we are willing to assume most characters in movies and novels pay at restaurants, even when such details are often omitted. In AI terminology, when the reader learns that a person eats at a restaurant , they bring into the fictional world the knowledge frame of restaurant visits, which includes paying. Based on this observation, we believe the connection between a common object that people are familiar with and the unfamiliar gadget is crucial for the understanding of a gadget. When the gadget is analogous to a common object, old knowledge can shed light on the new, which allows the new gadget to be easily understood and accepted. For instance, since we understand a lightsaber is analogous to a sword, we can accept that a lightsaber deflects upon hitting another lightsaber blade, even though physics indicates two beams of laser would actually pass through each other. Take another example from the *Doraemon* manga, a piece of toast bestowing the power of memorization on its user (Volume 2 Story 1, abbreviated as D2.1 thereafter). Although the analogy between the gadget and a toast cannot completely explain how to use the gadget, it provides some hints; readers can easily understand using the toast gadget involves eating it. We believe that for imaginary gadgets, such analogies are crucial for its comprehension and intuitive appeal. A good analogy can enhance the intuitive appeal of the gadget. Gadget generation in this paper focuses on finding the correct common object and modifies it to make a gadget while preserving the analogy between the two.

To reason about analogies between the common object and the gadget, we draw from the research on analogical reasoning. Several AI programs, such as SME [2], ACME [8], and Sapper [22, 23] attempted to simulate the human ability to recognize analogies. An analogy maps between two conceptual spaces including entities with attributes and interrelationships. SME distinguishes between the mapping between surface properties (such as color and size) and relations (such as causality or inequality). Mappings of only relations are considered as true analogies, whereas mappings of only surface properties are superficial and mappings of both are literal similarities. Nonetheless, other researchers [8, 22, 23] utilize both properties and relations in analogical mapping. Since most mappings are not perfect, we consider both surface and relational features contribute to intuitive appeal of analogies. Most relevant to our work, Sapper utilizes both types of features, and allows analogies to be built incrementally via the incremental rule. This well fits into the refinement search paradigm of partial-order planning.

STRATEGIES OF NOVEL GADGET DESIGN

As fictional gadgets exist only in the imagination of the author and the reader, it is often impossible to provide a detailed scientific account for their mechanisms. No one ever read HAL's code or understood how a time machine works, but it does not make them less happy reading those stories. This differentiates design of fictional gadgets from design in the real world, where a working mechanism must be designed for any product. Computational systems that automate the design task have been investigated (cf. [6]). The most similar to our work are systems that utilize analogy in design, such as [13] and [7].

For a gadget to be accepted by readers, it must be comprehensible. In our opinion, to comprehend a gadget is to be able to recognize it and to make predictions about it; the understanding consists of its appearance and behavior. We consider anyone who knows how to use a phone to transmit voice as "understanding" a phone, even though they may not understand the underlying physics. Hence, we propose that to generate a gadget is to generate a reasonable behavior for it and its corresponding appearance. The appearance should intuitively match the behavior. For example, a gadget that can fly is likely to have wings or propellers. However, the coupling between the appearance and the behavior is not the focus of this paper.

Across all 45 volumes, it is estimated that *Doraemon* contains about a thousand gadgets [18]. We closely analyzed the first five volumes of *Doraemon* for a total of 87 stories and attempted to deconstruct the process of gadget creation. Consequently, we identified 9 concrete strategies of gadget design. Several exclusion criteria are applied in our study. We disregard gadgets that interact with time (e.g. time machines) since such interactions may result in logical inconsistencies problematic for AI systems. We ignore stories where multiple gadgets are used in combination and none is described well enough for our analysis. We further exclude gadgets creating scientific simulations and virtual reality (e.g. the virtual reality skiing field in D2.15), or directly taken from fairytales and obviously existing ideas, such as Aladdin's lamp (D1.15) and Cupid's bow and arrows (D3.12). After these exclusions, we identified 60 gadgets from the five volumes, and found that the 9 strategies proposed here can explain 55 or 91.6% of these gadgets.

Next, we describe specific strategies with examples from the manga. However, as with many cognitive phenomena, gadget creation is a fluid and organic process. Strategies may have fuzzy boundaries and can be used in combination. The main aim here is to illustrate different techniques rather than providing a strict taxonomy.

Strategy I: Default Form Factors

The simplest strategy is to use default form factors for certain types of functions. Robots (D2.2), hand puppets (D3.9) and dolls (D2.6) are used when the gadget is supposed to exhibit human behaviors, for example, to love our protagonist, to be a life guide, or to tell hidden desires. Gadgets that alter mental states, such as temperament (D5.1), are sometimes portrayed as pills. When other strategies fail to generate gadgets, a default form like a micro-computer may be used. Examples include gadgets that perform facial plastic surgeries (D4.7) and make dim sum (D2.13). The appearances and behaviors of the gadgets do not deviate much from the original objects. Robots can be turned on or off, and pills are directly swallowed.

Strategy II: Symbolized Abilities

Some characters are exemplars of their unique abilities. Sherlock Holmes's ability to reason and Superman's ability to fly are very well known. In addition, these characters are also typically associated with and identified by some personal items, such as Holmes's cap and pipe and Superman's red and blue suit. Hence, a conceptual slippage (cf. [23]) may associate iconic personal items with special abilities. Such associations are employed to create gadgets. D3.7 features a Superman Costume Set that allows the wearer to fly at a low altitude. D3.4 features a Holmes Mystery Solver Set, including a cap, a pipe, a magnifying glass and a walking stick, which helps the user to explain seemingly mysterious events and find culprits. D5.15 features a black belt, a symbol of Judo masters. The wearer of the belt gets the ability to throw away anyone touching her. This strategy relies crucially on finding the conceptual association between the personal item, its owner, and a special ability.

Strategy III: Typical Components of Typical Scenes

Sometimes a particular ability can be conceptually associated with a typical scene. For example, ghost stories often contain an image of flickering lights, or will-o'-the-wisps in darkness. Thus, a gadget that makes ghost story come true (D2.3) can adopt the form of a lamp that looks like a will-o'-the-wisp. As another example, a garden-under-moonlight scene may involve fragrant flowers, singing crickets and bright moonlight. Not surprisingly, a gadget that simulates the sound of crickets appears as a flower (D4.6). This strategy seems to work by first imagining a typical scene associated with the function, and extract a component from the typical scene.

Strategy IV: Decoraters and Decoratees

Another association employed by the author of *Doraemon* is between an object and the one it decorates. Examples include personal accessories or clothes and corresponding body parts. In the Holmes Mystery Solver Set (D3.4), the cap enhances the ability to reason since the cap sits upon the head where reasoning happens. D1.10 features a lipstick that grants its wearer the ability to say extremely pleasant compliments. A slightly different example is Gravity Paint (D5.2). Walls painted with it generate gravity and work like floors, i.e. allowing people to stay on them without falling. This strategy requires little additional transformation after the initial prototype is retrieved. The intuitive appeal of gadgets generated relies on the "decorating" relationship.

Strategy V: Reversed Use of Models

When a model represents a certain aspect of the real world, modifying the model can be imagined to affect the real world. The practice of inserting needles into voodoo dolls suggests a long historic trace behind this thought. D4.1 features a camera producing dolls very much the same as voodoo dolls. D3.2 contains a wrist watch that, when tweaked, changes the actual date. D3.11 features a camera that reverses the ordinary picture taking procedure. You can change someone's dress by putting a picture of the desired dress in the camera and pressing the shutter towards her. When the camera is not loaded with a picture, however, all her clothes will disappear.

A similar example of causality reversal appears in D4.17. The gadget is a revolver used to play Russian roulette. In the original Russian roulette, one needs good luck to survive. In the story, the revolver contains bullets of good and bad luck. She who takes a bullet will become extremely luck or unlucky for a short period.

Strategy VI: Substituting Operands

Strategy VI allows a known tool to operate on things it cannot ordinarily operate on. The flu-transmitting phone (D2.14) transmits flu instead of voice. The friend remote control (D4.9) controls people, not home appliances. D1.9 features a pair of scissors that can cut one's shadow off, which can then work as a slave. Other than the operand, behaviors of these gadgets (e.g. cutting, transmitting, controlling) usually do not change significantly from the prototype object. It seems to us that the new operand should bear resemblance to the old, which would justify the substitution. Both flu virus and voice are invisible to the naked eye and can spread in space. A shadow may look as thin as paper.

Strategy VII: Combining Multiple Tools

From flying cars to lightsabers, combining different things is a great source of inspiration for gadgets. Many mythical creatures are also combinations of common animals. The Pegasus is a horse combined with wings of a bird. A griffin is an eagle plus a lion. The memory toast (D2.1) is an exemplar from the *Doraemon* manga. The gadget helps people to memorize things on a book page. First, put a memory toast on that page, and the printings will be transferred from the page onto the toast. After that, eat the toast, and you will have precise memory of anything on that page. This gadget seems to be a combination of silly putty, which provides the printing transfer, and a toast, which provides the edibility. The alarm clock in D3.5 is a robot whose body and head are replaced by a clock.

Strategy VIII: Relaxing Preconditions or Constraints

Tools in the real world have constraints we may wish to remove or relax. A telescope cannot see through a wall. A pencil cannot write by itself but needs someone to write with it. This strategy modifies or removes these constraints from the original object. If we remove the precondition that two rooms connected by a door must be adjacent in space, we create one of the most well-known gadgets in *Doraemon*: the Anywhere Door, walking across which can bring the user anywhere within a 10-lightyear radius. The smart pencil (D1.11) writes right answers to exam questions by itself. A mailbox in D2.17 predicts the reply to your letter before it is sent, thereby removing a constraint of time. Telescopes can see through walls in D4.11 and into the future in D4.10.

Strategy IX: Extending or Reversing Effects

Sometimes a gadget looks like an ordinary object and is also used in a similar manner, but it can create extraordinary effects. Though the effects are extraordinary, they are usually not arbitrary. In *Doraemon*, effects of ordinary objects are often replaced by something similar to the original effects but better. Body cream is usually used to alleviate the harsh feeling of winter. D1.14 enhances this ability to create a cream gadget that reverses the feeling of temperature. When one wears the cream, winter feels like summer. Ringing a bell is often a signal for gathering. The bell in D2.4 can summon people to play with you while in dreams. Sometimes the new effects are reversals of the old. A mirror tells the truth in Snow White, but in D2.8 it tells lies.

The Generalized Process

A general gadget generation process unifying these strategies is shown in Figure 1, with each step numbered. Real-world design usually starts with a desired function and seeks a structure to realize it [4]. Similarly, in the first step our process starts with a given function, and retrieves an object from all known objects as a gadget prototype. Steps 2 and 3 generate a behavior and an appearance for the gadget respectively. Our approach to generating the behavior and appearance of the gadget is to reuse corresponding components of the prototype object directly and/or adapt aspects of the prototype to suit the function. The fourth step indicates mutual influences between the usage and appearance, reflecting the fact that the gadget can be iteratively refined. The fifth step indicates that the appearance or behavior may prompt a retrieval of additional prototype objects. For example, if during the generation of the behavior we realize the gadget should be able to fly, we can decide to retrieve an airplane and transplant its wings onto our gadget. Steps 1-3 are major

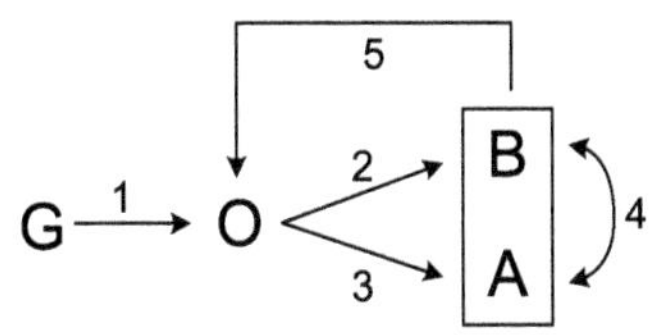

F = desired function O = prototype object
A = appearance of gadget B = behavior of gadget
→ = transformation / derivation

Figure 1. The process for gadget generation.

steps, which are performed each time a gadget is produced. In contrast, steps 4-5 are "maintenance" steps, reflecting that gadget generation often can go back-and-forth or circuitously rather than always straightforward. In summary, gadget generation is the generation of an appearance and a behavior for the gadget, mediated by one or more analogies with known objects and tools.

Gabora [3] notes that creative problem solving often involves alternation between an associative phase, where possible or similar solutions are retrieved, and an analytic phase, where products of the first phase is amended to meet quality and realistic constraints. Here, the prototype retrieval step corresponds to the associative phase. The subsequent goal-driven analytic phase attempts to fill any causal gaps and minimize unnatural human behavior during interaction with the gadget. If any problems arise during the analytic phase, the associate phase can be restarted.

The gadget generation process generalizes strategies I-IX presented before. Strategy I makes use of default prototype objects, which supply default appearance and behavior for certain functions. Strategies II-V focus on the association between the desired function and the prototype object and often perform little subsequent adaptation. These strategies utilize focused retrieval. Strategy IV, for instance, retrieves only those prototype objects that decorate another object or organ related to the function. Strategies VI-IX perform substantial adaptation after the retrieval and may be applicable to a wider type of prototype objects. Strategy V, for example, modifies the prototype object by reversing causes and effects.

The gadget generation process includes different tasks, each relying on different types of computation and knowledge. The retrieval of prototype objects relies crucially on efficient memory organization. Once an object is retrieved for strategies II-V, little to no subsequent transformation is needed. Strategies VI-IX require careful analysis and transformation of a series of causes and effects in the prototype to produce a coherent description of how the gadgets interact with the world. Generating the appearance of gadgets is different from the previous two tasks and concerns the relationship between behaviors and structures that enable them. The generation of visual appearance of novel gadgets is left for future work.

In this paper, we focus on the functional aspect of gadgets and implement mainly Step 2, with some consideration for Step 1. In the next section, we propose an algorithm that first retrieves a prototype object and then transforms it to produce gadgets similar to those generated by Strategies VI and VII. Strategies VI is supported by the ability to transform known actions analogically to create new action. Strategy VII is supported by iterative merging of multiple prototype frames. Analogical transformation can also handle special cases of Strategy IX when the new effect is analogous, but not opposite, to the old effect. Efficient memory organization and appearance generation are left for future work. Although the efficiency of the algorithm can be negatively affected without efficient retrievals of known objects, we believe in a divide-and-conquer approach and currently use a simple retrieval method as a surrogate.

GADGET STORY GENERATION

We formulate the gadget generation problem as follows: find a new type of object that, when used by a character in the story, causes the desired change in the story world. We should be able to describe the object, or gadget, in sufficient details that it can be appreicated and believed by readers. In order to maintain the believability of gadgets, our system use common objects as prototypes for gadgets and prefers to minimize modifications to prototypes. Our algorithm creates a new object type through a combination of analogical mapping of elements from the prototype to the gadget and planning to fill in additional details.

Following Young [26], there has been a growing trend of modeling a story as a partial-order plan (e.g. [9, 12, 14, 15]), where generating a story is equivalent to solving a planning problem with aesthetic constraints. In our work gadget generation is a computational process that augments story planning by automatically producing a new type of device that can be incorporated into the story. The story planner provides a narrative goal and the gadget generation process produces a plausible gadget that, when used, changes the world to achieve the goal. In the next sections, we provide a general background on AI planning and then describe our representation for gadgets and the algorithm for producing them using a combination of planning and analogical mapping.

AI Planning Background

Planning produces a sound plan, or a sequence of actions that guarantees to achieve a goal situation from an initial world. The goal situation and the initial world are two sets of first-order logic expressions or predicates. An action has preconditions and effects, also expressed as predicates. Before an action can occur, its preconditions must be true. After the action occurred, its effects become true. A sound plan properly links a series of actions so that the goal conditions are achieved by effects of some actions – whose preconditions are in turn achieved by earlier actions – and preconditions of the earliest actions are in the initial state. Actions take objects and/or characters as parameters. Objects belong to hierarchically organized types. For example, the object `my-car` belongs to the type `Car`, which is a subtype of `Vehicle`.

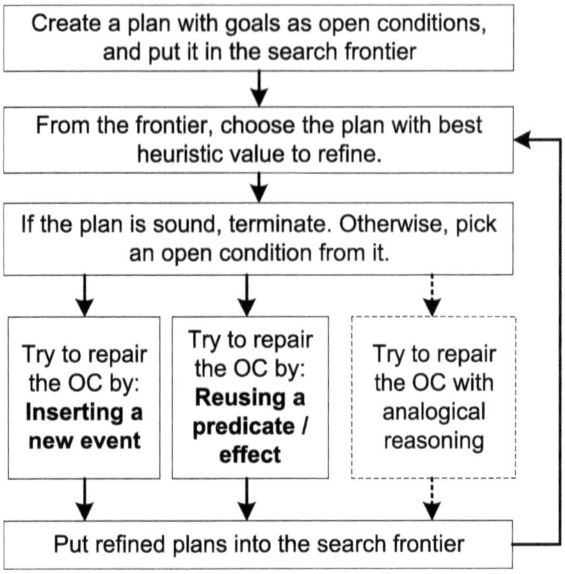

Figure 2. A brief outline of partial-order planning.

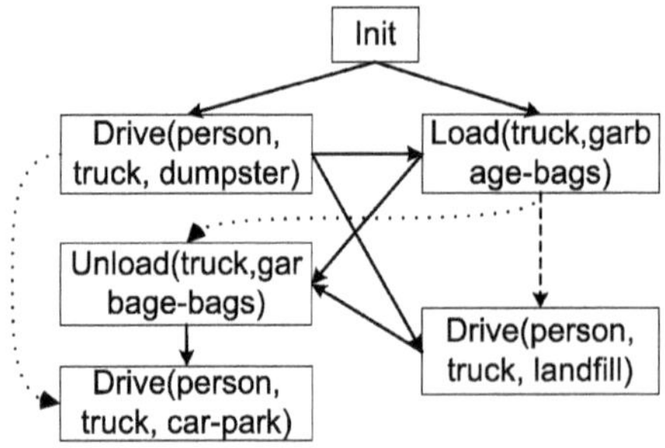

Frame-level variable/type: person/Person, truck/Truck garbage-bags/Bagged-Trash landfill/Landfill car-park/ Land-Location dumpster/Land-Location

Figure 3. The usage frame of a garbage truck.

Partial-order planning (POP) is primarily concerned with selecting correct actions from an action library, giving them correct parameters and inserting them into the plan to achieve open conditions. An open condition (OC) is a precondition of an action or a goal predicate not yet achieved. An OC can be achieved (or in POP terms, *repaired*) with an identical effect from an action. The action may be an existent action in the plan or newly inserted into the plan for the purpose. In addition, an OC can be achieved with an identical predicate in the initial state. A repair operation produces a refined plan, where a matching predicate (either from the initial state or an effect) is linked to the OC with a *causal link*. Note that if an action is inserted during the repair, it may bring in new preconditions which become new OCs. When there are multiple possible ways to repair an OC (e.g., different actions with the same effect), each will yield a refined plan, which are put into the search frontier. A heuristic function estimates the quality of a plan and number of further refinements it needs to reach a sound plan. From the search frontier, the plan with the best heuristic value is selected as the candidate for the next iteration of OC repairs. The process continues until a sound plan containing no open conditions is found on the frontier. See Weld [25] for more details of partial-order planning, such as causal threats. The POP algorithm is outlined in Figure 2 as a flowchart. In gadget generation, we extend POP by employing analogical reasoning to repair OCs, as indicated by the dotted box in Figure 2.

Usage Frames

We represent the gadget's behavior as a plan describing how the gadget interacts with its user and the world during a typical use. This plan is called a *usage frame*. It portrays a typical scenario of the gadget being used, including actions that typically happen right before and after its use. In the story plan, a usage frame is summarized as a single meta-action, forming an action hierarchy. Such a hierarchy supports flexible description of gadgets in different media.

As an example, Figure 3 shows the usage frame for a garbage truck. The truck is first driven to the dumpster to collect bagged trash, and then to the landfill to unload it, and finally returned to the car park. Solid arrows denote causal links. Dashed arrows denote temporal links, which indicate orderings of actions. Dotted arrows in the frame denote *closure actions*, which restore the world to a normal or routine state after other actions change it. Closure actions are not necessary for a gadget's intended purpose, but they complete the frame and may improve story coherence. Here, the action where the truck unloads garbage is a closure action, which "closes" the actions where garbage is loaded so that the truck is usable again.

Usage frames deviate slightly from the general plan data structure in that we use a set of variables, called *frame variables,* instead of objects. All actions in usage frame take frame variables as parameters. This allows us to identify parameters of different actions to *co-resolve* (i.e. bind to the same object) without committing until the gadget is used in the story. Values of frame variables depend on how the gadget is used in the story. We also find it convenient to distinguish between actions performed by a human and those performed by machines, tools, or natural occurrences.

Computing Analogies

An key aspect of gadget's believability and appeal is the resemblance between the gadget's usage frame and an usage frame of an ordinary object. Analogy is critical in both retrieving the ordinary object and in subsequent transformation. We employ Sapper [22, 23] as the analogy making engine. Representing knowledge in a semantic network, Sapper lays dormant bridges between concepts that share enough properties or participate in same relations. When we determine if two concepts are analogous, dormant bridges may be activated to support the analogies. We can make analogies between object types, predicates, and actions, but not across categories. All known object types, predicates and actions are stored in the semantic network. Objects types are considered analogous if they share properties or are involved in relations of the same type. Analogies between predicates and actions are supported by analogies or matches between corresponding parameters. Semantic roles, such as subject, object, etc., of each parameter in predicates and actions are annotated to facilitate mapping. Furthermore, we utilize the notion of *spatial signatures* [21] to capture similarities between predicates and actions. Spatial signatures capture the embodied understanding of verbs as movement patterns, which can reveal hidden connections between actions. For instance, climbing a staircase and a rise in social status both imply upward movements. Thus, a metaphor can be created between them. Two predicates or actions with matching spatial signatures and analogous corresponding parameters will be considered highly analogous. All these comparisons are incorporated in Sapper's activation spreading process. The basic idea in transformation is that if two object types, predicates, or actions are analogous enough then they can stand in place for one another in a creative domain.

Initiating Gadget Generation

As a partial-order planning story generator iteratively establishes open conditions, it may invoke gadget generation when a gadget is deemed the best option to achieve an open condition p in the story, which becomes the narrative goal of the gadget. There are three reasons to generate a gadget to achieve a goal. First, the goal may be impossible or too difficult to achieve without assistance of a gadget (e.g. stopping the rain). Second, the goal may require unpleasant actions or significant time commitments from the protagonist, such as housework, that the character in question generally wants to avoid. The third reason is the lack of reliable means to achieve an improbable goal, such as winning a lottery. Admittedly, a story planner can create coincidences without considering probabilities. However, two many coincidences can damage the believability of a story. A gadget which makes the improbable happen can believably justify an unlikely outcome and rescue the story.

After the gadget usage frame is completed, it is summarized into a single "use gadget" meta-action and put in the story. At this time, frame variables will be assigned to objects and characters in the story in a way that is consistent with the usage of the gadget and the larger story context. If a new narrative goal needs to be achieved by gadgets when one gadget already exists in the story, the existing gadget can be adapted to satisfy a new narrative goal, or a new gadget can be generated. As a special case, when a precondition of a "use gadget" meta-action initiates gadget generation, an additional prototype will be retrieved to merge with the existing gadget. This paper omits details and assumes a story generation system capable of selecting the open conditions to be achieved by gadgets.

Retrieving a Prototype

Prototypes are *a priori* known object types from our ontological hierarchy. Prototypes become the basis from which we create new gadgets. Usage frames of these objects are stored and indexed by predicates they are typically employed to achieve. When gadget generation is initiated to achieve a narrative goal p, the system searches for known tools that achieve a predicate analogous to p. Saunders and Gero [17] propose that an artifact is usually considered the most creative when it is neither too similar nor too dissimilar to what we already know. Following that, an object whose effect is optimally moderately analogous to p is first attempted as the prototype for the new gadget. The algorithm may backtrack and try a different tool.

Constructing the Gadget Frame

To construct a usage frame for a new gadget, we extend POP with new methods, informed by the usage frame of the retrieved prototype object, to achieve open conditions. The gadget usage frame starts as an empty usage frame – an empty plan – with an empty initial state and the narrative goal p being the only open condition. Gadget generation incrementally repairs open conditions by trying each of the methods, putting the resulted usage frames into the search frontier, and starting the next round of repairs with the usage frame having the best heuristic value. In the next few sections, we introduce the newly proposed methods to repair open conditions during gadget generation.

Analogical reasoning and partial-order planning are unified in the idea called projection. Projection provides a tactic to achieve open conditions by copying an element from the prototype usage frame – either an action or a predicate in the initial state – and inserting it into the new gadget usage frame either literally or through analogical transformations. A literal projection simply copies an element over. An analogous projection transforms the projected element based on analogies between the two frames before copying it over. In order to keep the resemblance between the gadget and the prototype, we prefer literal projections to analogous projections. When an action or a predicate is projected, all referenced frame arguments are also copied over into the gadget frame. Each element can only be projected once. Table 1 lists all projection methods alongside traditional methods gadget generation takes from POP [25] and the Initial State Revision story planner [14].

Projection allows the gadget usage frame to imitate the prototype usage frame and achieves its own goals at the same time. Given an open condition in the gadget frame, we first attempt to find the same condition or an analogous condition in the prototype frame. If such a condition is found, the gadget frame tries to imitate the way the prototype frame achieves the original open condition. As mentioned previously, the condition could have been achieved by an action's effect or a predicate in the initial state. In the former case, we attempt to project the action. In the latter, we attempt to project the predicate into the initial state of the gadget frame. In both cases, literal projections are attempted before analogous projections as literal projections provide closer imitation of the prototype.

	Projection		Traditional
	Literal	**Analogous**	
Insert an New Action	Copy an action from prototype frame to gadget frame	A. Analogically transform an action from the prototype frame B. Select an analogous action from the action library	Insert an action directly (same as POP [25])
Modifying the Initial State	Copy an predicate from prototype frame to gadget frame	Analogically transform a predicate from the prototype frame	Insert a predicate to gadget frame directly (similar to ISR [14])

Table 1. Traditional and project methods that insert actions and modify the initial state.

Projecting and Inserting Actions

In order to achieve an open condition *c*, a literal projection copies an action with the effect *c* from the prototype frame into the gadget frame. However, often we cannot find such an action in the prototype frame, and we will attempt an analogous projection. Analogous projection empowers partial-order planning to systematically explore in the space of analogies.

The first method of analogous projection is to transform an action in the prototype frame based on analogies in order to produce a new action that achieves *c*. We call this analogical transformation. As mentioned earlier, an action takes parameters of predefined types. Take, for example, an action from a telephone usage frame: `Transmit(voice?, person1?, person2?)`, which transmits voice between two people. A question mark denotes a parameter. Paratermized actions can be applied in different situations (e.g. transmitting voices between different people). This action has one effect `close-by(voice?, person2?)`. `voice?` is of type `Voice` and `person1?` and `person2?` are of the type `Person`. Suppose the stories requires us to create a gadget that transmits flu viruses, and one open condition in the gadget frame is `close-by(virus?, person2?)` where `virus?` is of type `Virus`. Normally, the transmit action cannot take parameters of the type `Virus`. Analogical transformation creates a new action that can do so based on the analogy between flu viruses and voice. Hence, after the transformation we are able to achieve the desired open condition. In order to keep intuitive appeal of the gadget and prevent nonsensical actions, analogical transformation is only allowed when the actor of the action is not human. Even though a stone may look like a cookie, a person cannot eat the stone like a cookie. On the other hand, it is reasonable if a high-tech or magical gadget interacts with this stone as if it is a cookie. The heuristic value, or the desirability of an analogical transformation is positively correlated to the analogies used during the transformation.

If analogical transformation is not applicable due to our restriction on actors, we can apply the third analogous projection. Suppose an action A_p in the gadget frame has an effect c_p, which is analogous to our open condition *c*. To keep the resemblance between the gadget and the prototype, we look for another action A_g from the action library that is analogous to A_p and has the effect *c*.

If any of the above three projection methods succeeds, an action with the effect *c* will be inserted into the gadget frame, achieving the desired open condition. However, if none is applicable, we can still use the conventional POP method that inserts any action from the action library that achieves *c* into the gadget frame. This final method does not imitate the prototype and has lower preference.

Projecting and Inserting Predicates into Initial States

An open condition *c* in the gadget frame can also be achieved by a predicate in the initial state. Similar to actions, we first try to perform a literal projection, i.e. copy the same predicate *c* which exists in the initial state of the prototype frame directly into the gadget frame. If such a predicate does not exist, we then try to perform an analogous projection. If a predicate c_p in the prototype frame is analogous to *c*, we can insert c into the gadget frame. This is possible because we consider *c* as resulted from a analogical transformation of c_p. Finally, we may directly insert *c* into the initial state of the gadget frame directly. This is similar to the functionality in the Initial State Revision story planner [14]. In fact, all three methods produce the same refined usage frame where *c* is inserted into the initial state. However, frames produced by the three methods have decreasing heuristic values because they differ in degree of imitation. The first method preserves the most of the prototype frame, while the last method does not imitate the prototype frame at all.

Other Methods to Repair Open Conditions

Besides the projection methods introduced above, our algorithm is also capable for reusing effects of actions and predicates in the initial state, just like traditional POP. In addition, we may also assume an open condition is resolved by the "power of the gadget". For example, the requirement that direct line of sight can be removed from a telescope, resulting in a gadget that can see through walls. Whether this method is used is controlled by rules capturing the human author's intuition about when this should be allowed and what gadget powers can accomplish. We reckon that overusing this method may remove too many open conditions, break analogy between gadgets and common objects and hurt believability. Its use may be domain-specific. Currently, we only use it to remove any knowledge requirement of gadgets because gadgets in *Doraemon* rarely need complex skills or knowledge.

Closing and Summarizing the Gadget

When all open conditions in the gadget frame are established, we add closure actions and summarize the frame. If a corresponding initiating action has been projected, the closure action is projected into the gadget frame with the same projection method. This may create new flaws in the gadget frame. However, since the narrative goal will be achieved before the closure actions take effect, adding closure actions is optional. If the cost becomes too high, the algorithm can choose to ignore closure actions.

The summarization generates a "use gadget" meta-action from the gadget frame to insert into the story plan. Its preconditions include all predicates from the gadget frame's initial state, and effects are accumulated from the effects of all actions in the gadget frame. Frame arguments become parameter variables of the meta-action. The meta-action can then be used to achieve narrative goals of the same type as the usage frame.

EXAMPLES

Our algorithm can generate some highly complex gadgets, including some from the *Doraemon* manga, such as a truck collecting rain clouds and the flu-transmitting phone (D2.14). Due to limited space, we show how these gadgets can be created schematically with major decisions during their generation.

The first example is a truck that collects rain cloud to stop the rain. The initiating narrative goal in the story is `not(at(rain-cloud, sky))`. The system compares this condition with all known tools, and finds that a garbage truck can achieve an analogous effect: `not(at(garbage-bags, dumpster))`. The usage frame of garbage truck (shown in Figure 3) is retrieved as the prototype. The analogies between rain cloud and bagged garbage and between sky and dumpster are made at this time. Based on the analogies, we analogously project the action `Load(truck, garbage-bags)` from the truck frame to create a new action `Load(truck, rain-cloud)`.The algorithm choose not to project `Drive(person, truck, dumpster)` to the gadget frame. Although `dumpster` is considered analogous to `sky`, the analogy is rather stretched, so the analogical transformation yields a low heuristic value and we prefer not to project. After we repair remaining open conditions of this action by revising the initial state, gadget planning completes.

Later, the story generator realizes that it cannot find a way to deliver the cloud-collecting truck to the sky where the clouds are – that is, `at(truck, sky)` cannot be achieved. The cloud-collecting truck is blended with the prototype frame of an airplane to give it the ability to fly. The final gadget frame is in Figure 4, showing the result of the double-blend.

In the next example, a flu-phone gadget is built to achieve the narrative goal `infected-by(bob, flu)`. In words, the flu is transferred from one person to another via phone. A

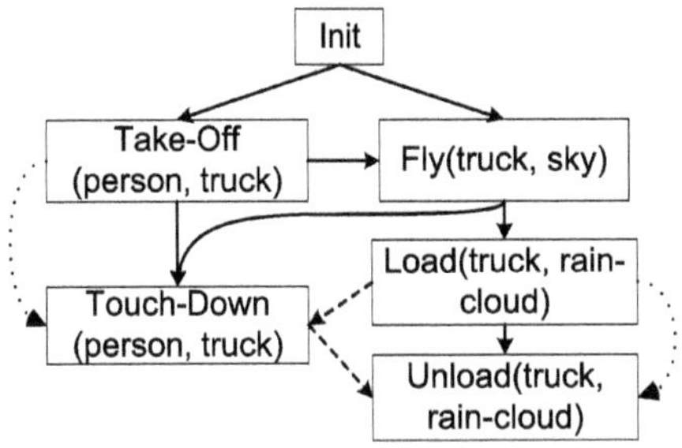

Figure 4. The final usage frame of the flying cloud-collecting truck.

telephone frame is retrieved based on the analogy between the flu virus and voice, and the analogy between understanding voices and being infected by viruses. These analogies allow us to modify effects of the main transmission action of the telephone frame. The action `Speak(person?, voice?)` is projected from the telephone prototype frame to `Cough(person?, virus?))`. As the actor of `Speak` is a person, analogical transformation is not applicable. This projection is done by finding an analogous action from the action library.

CONCLUSIONS AND FUTURE WORK

Based on our survey of the *Doraemon* manga, we have identified a general process for generating novel gadgets in fictions, which unifies nine different strategies. The process first retrieves one or more known objects, then adapts and combines them to generate a typical behavior for the gadget. After that, an appearance is generated to match the behavior. In this paper, we implement mainly two strategies of gadget generation: Strategies VI and VII, with special cases of Strategy IX. We present an extended planning algorithm that generates a usage frame of the gadget. The algorithm is a planning process using analogically generalized actions and is informed by other known plans. Analogically generalized actions expand the space of plans that can be generated. Known plans, when used as guidance, focus planning on the parts of the expanded space that are more reasonable and intuitively appealing. Our algorithm can generate complex gadgets, including some from *Doraemon* and other science fictions as well as mythical creatures. Future work will address performance issues of the algorithm and other steps and strategies in the gadget generation process.

Our algorithm can be considered as creative from multiple perspectives. We generate an unknown gadget, which serves narrative purposes, satisfying the novel and useful criteria [1] and the notion of c-creativity [11]. As the need arises in the story, gadgets are created on the fly and expand the spaces of stories that can be generated. Boden [1] classifies this as transformational creativity. Combining multiple known objects to create a new gadget fits the category of combinational creativity. Gero [4] defines innovative design as assigning variables with values outside their typical ranges and creative design as introducing new variables. Binding variables analogously may be considered as innovative, whereas a combination of two objects takes variables from both, and is hence creative design.

Our work suggests that a goal-driven analogy making process is a viable approach for computational creativity. Fictional gadgets are vivid illustrations of the importance of human imagination in writing stories. Any progress in the field of computational storytelling will require advances in computational creativity, of which the algorithm in this paper can be considered one such example.

ACKNOWLEDGMENT

This paper is based upon work supported by the National Science Foundation under Grant No. IIS-1002748.

REFERENCES

1. Boden, M. A. Computer Models of Creativity. *AI Magazine*, 30, 3 (2009), 23-34.
2. Falkenhainer, B., Forbus, K. D. and Gentner, D. The structure-mapping engine: Algorithm and examples. *Artificial Intelligence*, 41, 1 (1989), 1-63.
3. Gabora, L. Revenge of the 'neurds': Characterizing creative thought in terms of the structure and dynamics of memory. *Creativity Research Journal*, 22, 1 (2010), 1-13.
4. Gero, J. S. Design Prototypes: A knowledge representation schema for design. *AI Magazine*, 11, 4 (1990), 26-36.
5. Gervás, P. Computational approaches to storytelling and creativity. *AI Magazine*, 30, 3 (2009), 49-62.
6. Goel, A. K. Design, analogy, and creativity. *IEEE Expert*, 12, 3 (1997), 62-70.
7. Helms, M., Vattam, S. and Goel, A. Compound analogies, or how to make a surfboard disappear. Proc. CogSci 2008 (2008).
8. Holyoak, K. J. and Thagard, P. Analogical mapping by constraint satisfaction. *Cognitive Science*, 13 (1989).
9. Li, B. and Riedl, M. O. An offline planning approach to game plotline adaptation. *Proc. AIIDE'10* (2010).
10. Malmgren, C. D. Worlds Apart: Narratology of Science Fiction. Indiana University Press, 1991.
11. Pérez y Pérez, R. and Sharples, M. Three computer-based models of storytelling: BRUTUS, MINSTREL and MEXICA. *Knowledge-Based Systems*, 17, 1 (2004), 15-29.
12. Porteous, P. and Cavazza, M. Controlling narrative generation with planning trajectories: The role of constraints. *Proc. ICIDS'09* (2009).
13. Qian, L. and Gero, J. S. A design support system using analogy. *Proc. AID '92* (1992), 795-813.
14. Riedl, M. O. and Young, R. M. Story planning as exploratory creativity: Techniques for explanding the narrative search space. *Computational Creativity*, 24, 3 (2006), 303-323.
15. Riedl, M. O. and Young, R. M. Narrative planning: Balancing plot and character. *Journal of Artificial Intelligence Research*, 39 (2010), 217-268.
16. Ryan, M.-L. *Possible worlds, artificial intelligence, and narrative theory*. Indiana University Press, 1991.
17. Saunders, R. and Gero, J. Curious agents and situated design evaluations. *AI for Engineering, Design, Analysis, and Manufacturing*, 18, 2 (2004), 153-161.
18. Schilling, M. Doraemon: Making dreams come true. *Japan Quarterly*, 40, 4 (1993), 405-417.
19. Swartjes, I. M. T. and Theune, M. *Late commitment: virtual story characters that can frame their world.* Technical Report TR-CTIT-09-18, University of Twente, Enschede, Netherlands, 2009.
20. Trabasso, T. and van den Broek, P. Causal Thinking and the Representation of Narrative Events. *Journal of Memory and Language*, 24, 5 (1985), 612-630.
21. Veale, T. and Keane, M. T. Conceptual Scaffolding: A spatially founded meaning representation for metaphor comprehension. *Computational Intelligence*, 8, 3 (1992).
22. Veale, T. and Keane, M. T. Metaphor and memory: Symbolic and connectionist. issues in metaphor comprehension. *Proc. ECAI 1994 Workshop on Neural and Symbolic Integration* (1994).
23. Veale, T. and O'Donoghue, D. Computation and Blending, *Cognitive Linguistics*, 11, 3/4 (2000), 253-281.
24. Ware, S. G. and Young, R. M. Rethinking traditional planning assumptions to facilitate narrative generation. *Proc. INT3* (2010).
25. Weld, D. An Introduction to least commitment planning. *AI Magazine*, 15, 4 (1994), 27-61.
26. Young, R. M. Notes on the use of plan structures in the creation of interactive plot. *Proc. INT1* (1999).
27. Zacks, J. M., Speer, N. K. and Reynolds, J. R. Segmentation in reading and film comprehension. *Journal of Experimental Psychology: General*, 138, 2 (2009), 307-327.
28. Zacks, J. M. and Tversky, B. Event structure in perception and conception. *Psychological Bulletin*, 127 (2001), 3-21.
29. Zwann, R. A., Magliano, J. P. and Graesser, A. C. Dimensions of situational model construction in narrative comprehension. *Journal of Experimental Psychology: General*, 21, 2 (1995), 386-397.

Performing Places

Colombine Gardair, Patrick G.T. Healey
Queen Mary University of London
Interaction, Media and Communication Research Group
London, UK
{colombineg, Pat.Healey}@eecs.qmul.ac.uk

Martin Welton
Queen Mary University of London
Department of Drama
London, UK
m.welton@qmul.ac.uk

ABSTRACT
Street performers use carefully designed interactions to: create their performance space, build their audience, and elicit payment. Two of the key transformations a performer must achieve are (1) to transform a public space into a distinctive performance place that passers-by acknowledge as such; and (2) to turn a crowd of passers-by into an audience. In this ethnographic study of street shows we analyse the specific practicalities of creating a performance place within a public space. We propose that performers design their actions in ways that help passers-by and audience members identify them as part of a performance. We investigate how passers-by display their recognition that a performance is being created, becoming watchers before being audience members. We explore various techniques performers use for place-construction and demonstrate that in each case, while objects themselves may be important in attracting initial attention, it is only through interaction that they are successful in actual building of a performance place.

Author Keywords
Street performance, audience, space, place, human interactions.

ACM Classification Keywords
H.5.m. Information interfaces and presentation (e.g., HCI): Miscellaneous.

General Terms
Design, Experimentation, Measurement.

INTRODUCTION
Different types of actions are performed everyday in public places. Not all of them are designed for an audience to watch. People perform private actions and hope to go unnoticed – a woman adjusting her outfit in the reflection of a shop window. Others display their actions to a small group of familiar people – a group of friend juggling with a football in a park. Street performers, however, design their actions to be public, to be watched by whoever so desires.

Figure 1. A street performer (Mark) doing a chainsaw-juggling act.

Objects, like actions, produce different effects on people depending on the context they are used in. Passers-by and audiences react and construct the meaning of the street performer's objects and actions. For example, a chainsaw displayed in the middle of a street is an unexpected object and prompts people to look for an account of why it is here. The performer's actions around the chainsaw suggest that it will be part of a performance, hence making it a performance tool. The same goes of actions. A juggler who rehearses his juggling technique in the middle of a park does not necessarily design his actions for an audience. If a crowd gathers and people watch and respond to his routine, the juggler will probably adapt his actions as he takes into account those watching him. Having said that, the same juggler may decide to juggle with the purpose of attracting an audience. Consequently, he must design his routine in ways that are specific. For example, the juggler may take out his juggling material differently if he intends to rehearse privately or if he puts on a public show. He may use purpose-designed gestures such as showing his material to the audience, demonstrating the potential dangerousness of an object, building audience expectations by emphasising the difficulty of what he is about to perform, etc. He may also direct his gaze and speech towards the surrounding people and try to elicit responses from them.

C&C'11, November 3–6, 2011, Atlanta, Georgia, USA.

Using video recordings of street shows, we analyse how performers and audiences collaboratively create a performance space that is acknowledge by all. By carefully designing their actions, performers stand out from the rest of the crowd. Using weird looking objects and specific techniques they attract the attention of passers-by. In return, passers-by adapt their body orientation to display that they recognise the space as becoming a performance one.

CONSTRUCTING PERFORMANCE PLACES

Some studies in social sciences, especially in the fields of Conversation Analysis (CA) have looked at specific aspects of audience responses during an event. These include – but are not limited to – the analysis of applause [1, 2, 9] and the analysis of laughter [3, 7]. These studies are not interested in performance in particular but look at any situation involving an audience, from political speeches to classrooms settings to stand-up comedies. Most of them however focus on interactions between the performer (or speaker) and the audience and are oblivious of interactions amongst the audience (although see [4]). Research shows that audience responses occur according to specific rules often comparable to the patterns found in normal conversation. We explore the idea that the interactional organisation of street performance can be usefully analysed by reference to the organisation of ordinary conversational interactions. In particular, the ways in which people orient to the physical configuration of conversational participants as constituting a special kind of social space.

People's body orientations define spaces in which they are more likely to interact. The study of how passers-by orient to each other's and to performance should inform how the space changes its social status. This change of status echoes Harrisson and Dourish's distinction of *space* and *place* [8, 5]. *Space* refers to the physical characteristics of the three-dimensional environment, while *place* refers to its social use. Although this conception of place has been widely used, surprisingly little work has directly analysed the specific practicalities of constructing a place in space. We are interested in understanding how performers create a performance stage in a public street. Objects, actions and people can be *in place* or *out of place* and can fall in and out of that category depending of the normal social understanding of the place [8]. For example someone dressed as a clown in the middle of the street could be considered *out of place* but would become *in place* if this street were turned into a performance place.

In social encounters, people often group themselves into set patterns. Kendon [10] terms an F-formation the pattern that "arises whenever two or more people sustain a spatial and orientational relationship in which the space between them is one to which they have equal, direct and exclusive access". This type of formation emerges for example in freestanding conversational groups. It has the capacity to draw a separation between the interaction itself and what is occurring outside of it, while focusing the attention of the participant on the interactional situation. The participants, who constantly rearrange their physical position and orientation, dynamically maintain the formation. If a new participant enters the formation, or if another leaves it, the arrangement is modified in consequence, ensuring equal access to the space. People who are not part of it acknowledge the space delineated by the F-formation: they avoid crossing it or, if necessary, tend to duck or behave in ways which make manifest the socially marked or 'intrusive' character of crossing the shared space. Performance spaces appear to share many characteristics of F-formations.

Participants use specific orientation of the different segments of their body to maintain the formation. Body torques are ``divergent orientations of the body sectors above and below the neck and waist, respectively" [10]. These postural configurations are displays of engagement towards multiple courses of action. A torque occurs when the upper body orientation, usually led by the eyes, followed by the head, and eventually the shoulders, deviates from the lower body orientation, starting from the feet up to the hips. This orientation of the upper body indicates that a side activity is being inserted in, or is interrupting, the main activity in which the individual is already engaged.

Schegloff [11] and Kendon [10] claim that the lower part of the body is generally oriented towards the main activity while the upper part of the body can be orientated towards lower priority activities. Body torques are unstable postures of the body, they are prone to re-alignment. Body torques define a ranking of the engagement in the different activities and resolve in two ways: (1) the upper body re-aligns with the lower body, which indicates the ranking of the activities does not change; (2) the lower body orientation shifts to align with the upper body orientation, displaying a re- ranking of priorities. The activity that was previously considered as a side activity becomes the primary course of action. Behaviours such as body torques can be usefully applied, we argue, to the kinds of mass co-present interactions involved in street performance.

Wile's survey of performance spaces [12] observes that a common design feature of these spaces is to place the audience in a position where their body is oriented towards a common point, usually the performance. Consequently, transforming a street into a performance place will involve changes in the body orientation of the participants. Passers-by who walk up and down the street will have to stop and orient their body from facing towards their destination to facing towards the performance.

In street performance, most of the performers actions are done in front of the audience. There is little way to escape backstage in order to prepare for the act. Street performers must achieve the audiences' recognition that they are distinguishing between some things that are a) part of the 'official' performance, some that are b) commentary on that (or build up to it in some explicit and designedly performative way) and some that are c) actually not designedly 'performative' in the sense of being done to obtain this recognition.

Goffman's schematic analysis of how people design their behaviour for others [6] claims that individuals design their actions according to the impression of themselves they want to project onto others. To foster that impression, an individual manages three regions of interaction. (1) The *front region* is a shared space to which the individual and his ``audience'' both have a legitimate access. There, actions are designed to maintain social standards. (2) The *back region* or backstage is the space where all the support activities necessary for maintaining the impression of the front region goes on. Intrusion from the ``audience'' should not occur in this space. (3) The *outside region* comprises all that is happening outside the two previous regions.

This study presents some of the strategies used for the construction of a performance place. First, using a series of example, the passers-by body orientation are analysed in response to the performer's action. We show that (1) people use body torques to display their level of engagement with the performance; and (2) audience members are sensitive to each other's orientation. Second, we examine the techniques used by performers to direct the passers-by attention towards their performance. We show that, while the tools used by the performer may be important in attracting initial attention, it is only when constituted as performative through the interaction that they are successful in actual building of a performance place.

THE STUDY

Covent Garden

London offers numerous places for street performance, some of which are world famous. This privileged situation makes the street performances of London an extremely relevant object of study. Covent Garden was selected for this study as one of London's most popular sites for street entertainment.

Covent Garden is a busy leisure area in Central London. At the heart of the West End, Covent Garden is surrounded by UK main theatres and cinemas, and is itself home to the Royal Opera House. Covent Garden is designed as an Italian style piazza: a large square dominated by a church on one end, surrounded by noble mansions with colonnades, and usually host to a market and a busy social life. The central market building is packed with shops, bars and restaurants. In the surrounding pedestrian streets, performers entertain shoppers all year long.

Covent Garden is the only licensed area in London for street performance. The Council has established regulations to prevent too much congestion in this busy area. In James Street, the main thoroughfare between the subway station and the piazza, a maximum of five performances are allowed at any time. These pitches (the term used by performers to describe a performance spot) are subjected to noise and music restriction rules and are forbidden to 'circle' performances. The Council defines 'circle' performances as shows ``in which a crowd is encouraged to gather around, rather than view the performance in passing"[1]. Living statues and budding musicians are the most commonly found artists on James Street pitches. The East side of the piazza is regulated in a similar way and offers two additional pitches.

Three pitches are subjected to more permissive rules about amplification and type of performance, but must be auditioned for. Two are located within the market building; one of the pitches is solely for classical musicians. Acrobatics and variety shows can be held in the other market pitch or on the outdoors pitch located on the West Piazza, in front of portico of the church. There, performers are allowed to actively gather a crowd.

Methods

This study looks exclusively at the performances on the West Piazza pitch. This pitch is the biggest and most popular one in the area, if not in London. The crowd gathering around a performance can number up to two hundred people. Shows performed there are mainly acrobatic acts including tightrope walking, handstand, juggling and unicycle ridding

The material consists of video recordings, observations and informal chats with regular street performers. A total of thirteen performances were recorded using three cameras. Two cameras are positioned facing the audience; one records the performer from behind and follows him whenever possible (the performer sometimes goes off screen); the other captures a fixed portion of the audience. A third camera gives a fixed above view of the performance area. For transcription ease, sound is recorded separately using a voice recorder placed in front of the performer's loudspeaker. The method used was fully audited by the Queen Mary University of London research ethics committee

In order to illustrate the transitions in the status of the place, a sequence of short vignettes are presented below. As a means to present a variety of tools, shows that start with different techniques and are successful in the establishment of a performance place compose this selection. We selected four different shows, based on the diversity of techniques at hand, and performed a detailed analysis of the first few minutes of those shows. The start point of the analysis is the arrival of the performer on the pitch. For each section, the performer's speech is transcribed as well as audible

---

[1] From the "Central Covent Garden: Management Guidelines", accessible online: http://www3.westminster.gov.uk/docstores/publications_store/westend/Managemen t-guidelines-Covent-Garden.pdf.

audience contributions. To analyse body torques, head and body orientations of selected individuals are coded in EUDICO Linguistic Annotator (ELAN)[2]. More generally, the analyse is based on careful observation of the recordings, numerous replays at various speeds, often frame by frame, with and without playing the soundtrack.

Two of the shows feature the same performer (Mark). This is unintentional and is due to the variety of the data at our disposal. Mark performs a unicycle riding and chainsaw juggling show. We use extracts from two different performances of his show to analyse how the production of loud sounds and the display of unexpected object in the middle of the street serve to attract attention towards the performance space. A third show demonstrates the use of space-delimiting objects such as ropes. At the top of a telescopic ladder, Sam, the performer, juggles three clubs with a sword down his throat. The last performance selected is an escapologist performance. During his show, Paul escapes from chains while restrained with a straitjacket. We use this show to illustrate how performers display their actions in ways that are specific to the needs of a performance.

FROM PASSER-BY TO AUDIENCE MEMBER

Street performers and passers-by collaboratively work towards the creation of an audience. Performers need to first attract passers-by attention and then engage them into stopping and watching. In this section we show through two examples that passers-by display their attention and willingness to engage as an audience through torques of their body.

Example 1: from passer-by to watcher

In a first show, Mark starts by setting up his microphone. The first sounds it emits resemble a white noise or a hushing sound (``shh shh"). It is closely followed by a second succession of hushes (``shh shh shh shh") and a succession of hellos (``hello hello hello"). During the whole sequence, Mark is bent over his sound system. He initiates a raising motion on the third ``hello" and stands facing the audience. Then he says ``hello" another time before commenting on a baby he hears cry.

Prima facie, the succession of hellos can be interpreted as a purely functional sequence used to test that the microphone is working. However, before the sound got amplified, Mark was already hushing to test the microphone. This suggests that the "shh" "shh" are the primary testing sounds. Consequently, the switch to "hello" is designed for a different purpose: to attract the attention of the surrounding people. The performer's change in posture and body orientation is consistent with this suggestion. By raising and taking an audience facing position, Mark is designing the hellos as address to a neo-audience.

The second piece of interactional evidence that the shift from "shh" to "hello" is a device for engaging people rather than just testing equipment is provided by the way this transition is integrated with the responses of the passers-by. Until sounds are emitted, people have walked past the performer as he is installing his material and have paid very little attention to him. They have either shown no change of orientation from any section of the body, or just given a glance, i.e. performed a rapid orientation of the head only in direction of the object and back to its original orientation. The glance could be attributed to many elements, such as the presence of a trunk, a unicycle and a chainsaw in the middle of a street, or the presence of cameras.

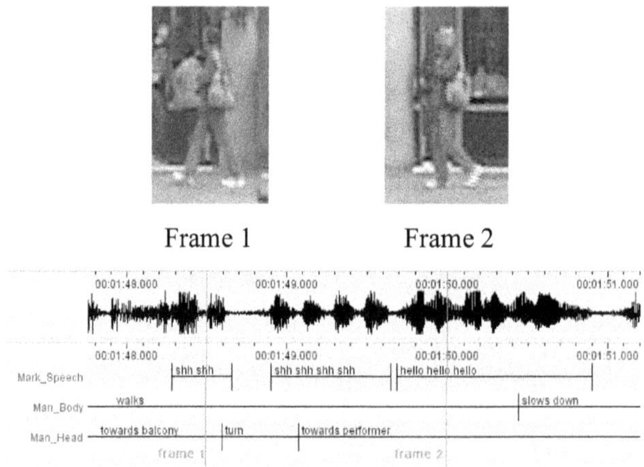

Figure 2. Change of orientation of a man in response to sounds produced by the performer.

The man in Figure 2 enters the camera's field of view directing his attention towards the balcony above him. His head is oriented away from the camera with an upward inclination. On the first ``shh shh" his head abruptly turns towards the camera, in direction of the origin of the sound, while he keeps walking at the same pace. This fast change of head orientation demonstrates a shift of attention from the scene on the balcony to the event that triggered the sound. His walk slows down on the second succession of hushes, nearly coming to a halt towards the end of the series of hellos. He regains his initial pace after he has turned his head away from the sounds, and oriented it in direction of the balcony above him. This reset to the initial position shows the man's interest remains in what is happening on the balcony.

The head and shoulders of the man are the only segments which orientation changed throughout the scene. We argue that such body engagement, along with the decrease in pace, shows a form of early assessment of the potential interest of the performance. However, at no point does the man change his initial course of action to realign to a new

[2] ELAN is a free video and audio annotation software developed by the Max Planck Institute for Psycholinguistics. It allows for synchronization of several media files in one analysis. It can be downloaded from http://www.lat-mpi.eu/tools/elan/.

activity. The next example shows how passers-by display their willingness to engage as an audience through a complete re-orientation of the body.

Example 2: from passer-by to audience member

In a second show, Mark begins with starting a chainsaw. Prior to the scene the chainsaw has been on display in the middle of the road (see Figure 3). Once again, passers-by have either show no interest or glanced. In this section we discuss how two of the first passers-by stop to watch: a man and a boy wearing light-blue shirts and entering the scene from the left-hand side of the camera (Figure 4(a)).

Figure 3. Mark's material as he first displays it.

Mark has been trying to start his chainsaw for ten seconds when the boy and the man appear in the camera's field of view. The chainsaw is making a repetitive clapping noise as Mark is pulling the cord (about once every 0.6 second). For the first three seconds the boy and the man appear to be engaged in a conversation, and display no evident sign of paying attention to what is going on around them. They are walking, their body oriented towards their destination, their shoulders are aligned with their hips and their heads slightly turned towards each other. The torque of their body is not very marked, suggesting that they are acknowledging each other's presence but are mainly engaged in their motion.

As Mark stops to pull the cord of his chainsaw for 2.5 seconds the man turns his head towards the performer accompanied by a slight rotation of his shoulders (Figure 4(b)). This movement is initiated 0.6 second after the first missing pull, probably in response to a noticeable change in the background noise. After one second, he resets his head and shoulders in their original position. The man then orients his body towards the left (Figure 4(c)), indicating he is about to change direction to turn towards the market. At that moment Mark's chainsaw makes a purring slightly longer than all the previous ones. The man turns his head towards the performer, followed by his shoulder, his trunk, his hips and his right foot and stands having performed a rotation of 45 degree to the right. It is only when the chainsaw is properly running that the man re-orients his lower body, completing his 90-degree rotation and now facing the performer (Figure 4(f)). His right foot that he brings backward next to the left one, resolving the body torque, and anchoring him in a stable standing position, drives this re-alignment.

(a) (b) (c) (d) (e) (f)

Figure 4. Evolution of the posture of two passers-by (a man and a boy) through time.

Unlike the man, the boy's movement to re-orient his body and face the performer is initiated by the positioning of his feet. The boy has been looking in direction of the performer since soon after entering the camera's field of view. His head is oriented towards the performer while his body remains in alignment with his initial goal of walking. He rapidly performs a rotation of 90 degrees to the right starting with orienting his right foot, followed by the left one. His hips, torso and finally shoulders (Figures 4(d) and 4(e)) soon after come in alignment. He comes to a halt fully facing the performer.

In the case of the boy, feet initiate the gesture. For the man, the completion takes longer and is initiated by the head leading the shoulders, the torso and finally the feet. We propose that this difference in rapidity and lead segment signify a different initial level of engagement with the performance. The boy appears eager to watch the performance while the man ponders the question of carrying his original goal versus watching the performance. Although there is no evidence in this example of direct interaction between the man and the boy leading to the man's decision, the following examples show that people often coordinate with each in their decision to stop and watch.

COORDINATION OF POTENTIAL AUDIENCE MEMBERS

Passers-by are often present as part of a social group. They arrive as a couple, a family, a group of friends, etc. Most of the time, groups do not split and either all members stop and watch or they all carry on with their primary occupation. We observe that the decision to stop and watch is taken collectively with little verbal interaction. People are sensitive to each other's body orientation and carry out very subtle negotiations. Using two examples, we examine the ways in which, within a group, its members maintain its cohesion through body orientation and collectively become audience members.

Example 3: two girls

Example 3 is extracted from the same show at the same moment as Example 1. Before any sound is heard, Girl1 (on the right of the images in Figure 5) is coming down the step facing backwards while Girl2 (on the left of the images) attempts to kick a pigeon with her left leg as she comes down the step. At the first ``shh shh" Girl1 immediately turns her head towards the origin of the sound, shifting her attention away from controlling her backward descent and onto the origin of the sound. Girl2 who was looking at Girl1, stops walking and turns her head in the same direction as Girl1. In the meantime, Girl1 has turned her body around, now facing forward. She starts walking, followed by Girl2. Girl1 says ``hoo" in response to Marks hellos, triggering Girl2 to look in her direction. It is unclear if Girl2 addresses Girl1 at this moment, but Girl1 adjusts her orientation to walk in direction of the performer. Throughout the episode, the performer did not directly interact with the girls.

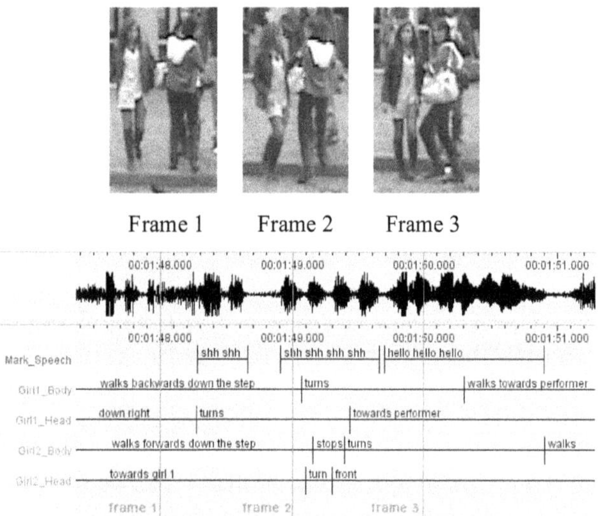

Figure 5. Change of orientation of two girls in response to sounds produced by the performer. Girl1 is on the right hand side of the image, Girl2 on the left hand side.

The sound coming out of the microphone initiates a body torque for both the man (Example 1) and Girl1. However, the man resolves his torque by resuming to his initial course of action while the Girl1 re-orient towards the performance. This difference can be attributed to how each of them perceives the interaction. On the one hand, the first girl's response to the performer's ``hello" shows that she considers herself a direct recipient of the interaction. The man, on the other hand, acts as a side participant. This difference of status in the interaction directly impacts their likelihood to become members of the audience and is reflected by their body orientation. Girl2's engagement with the performance directly results from her interaction with Girl1.

Example 4: a couple

Our fourth example is extracted from Paul's show. Paul has been trying, with no success, to get people to stop and watch by standing on a trunk on the side of the street and verbally addressing passers-by. He has just decided to change his technique, and to play some music while he sets up his material in the middle of the street.

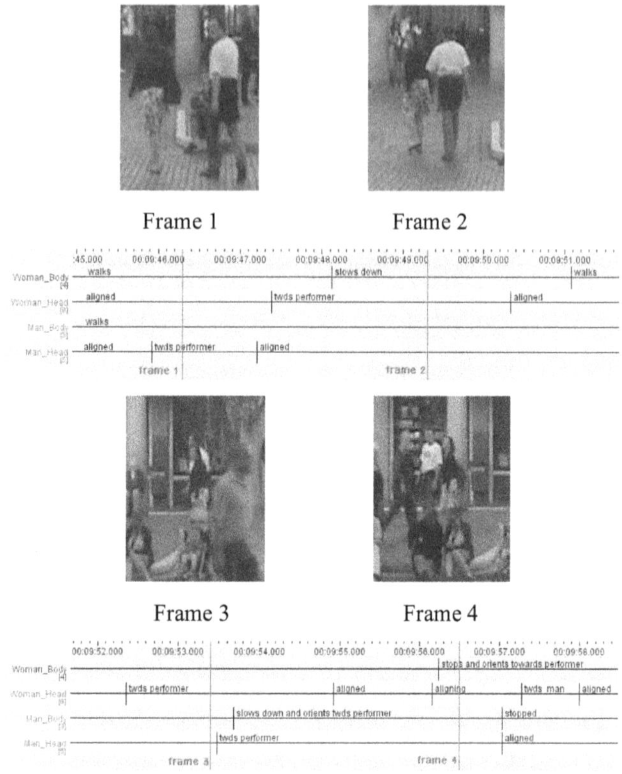

Figure 6. A couple who stops and watch Paul's warm-up routine. Frames 1 to 4 show the evolution of the couple's orientation. The transcripts represent the orientation of the man and the woman's head and body throughout the sequence.

The couple featured in Figure 6 enters the scene as music starts playing, without paying any attention to the performer. The man first turns his head towards the performer after he has moved his trunk (Frame 1). This head turn might come in response to the banging noise made by the trunk as it hits the ground. The woman then too orients her head towards the performer (Frame 2). We believe this movement to occur in response to her partner's. Unlike him, she slows down and keeps her head orientation for nearly twice as long, signifying a greater interest towards the performance. After resetting to her primary course of action, she looks again towards the performer (Frame 3), movement that triggers her partner to slow down and look again. They then both align their entire body towards the performance and stop to watch.

ALIGNING WITH OTHER AUDIENCE MEMBERS

As well as sensitivity to other group members, passers-by react to people who are already part of the audience. The next example reveals that new audience members position themselves in alignment with those already there. Space-defining objects have, in fact, little effect. This finding is of prime importance since it uncovers the utmost importance of audience interactions in shaping performance spaces.

Example 5: overrated ropes

Sam starts his show with laying out two ropes, one on each side of the space, across the street. On Figure 8 he is finishing to lay out the second rope. Two persons are seated on the floor on the inner-side of the rope (see Figure 8 (a)). They have most likely been watching the previous show and have not moved since. The effect of Sam laying the rope on the ground is immediate. As soon as Sam has dropped the extremity of the cord, the person closest to the rope initiates a standing motion closely followed by the other one. They both rise, walk to the other side of the rope, and sit side by side just behind the rope, facing the stage area (see Figure 8(b)). The entire sequence has occurred without Sam directly addressing them or looking at them.

(a) Before (b) After

Figure 7. Position of two persons just (a) before and (b) after the performers lays his rope.

During the next 2 minutes, Sam finishes to set up his material without interacting with the crowd. Most of this time, he is turning his back to the people watching. For these two minutes, the number of people sitting or standing behind the ropes remains unchanged and is exclusively constituted of groups of people who where present before the ropes were laid. However, once the performer starts interacting with the crowd, both through speech and through performing tricks, a crowd of newcomers starts forming. The new people who arrive don't seem to pay any particular attention to the ropes themselves. On the side where the two persons moved just behind the ropes, newcomers sit next to them, positioning themselves behind the rope, in a straight line parallel to the rope. On the other side though, a first group of three individuals sit about a meter away from the rope, forming a line with a 45-degree angle from the rope. The people who arrive next align themselves with them, leaving a gap between them and the rope. The gap is only filled when the performer asks the audience to come closer.

Performers consider ropes an important tool. Ropes are thought to give the passers-by an indication of where to position themselves, and what space not to cross. However, our data show that people's sensitivity to ropes mainly exists if they are present when the performer is laying them. In other cases, individuals are sensitive to the orientation of other audience members. They orient and position themselves accordingly.

PERFORMER'S TECHNIQUES

We have examined some of the interactional techniques passers-by use as they start to become audience members. Although newcomers are sensitive to existing audience members, how do performers attract the first ones? This last section investigates some of the successful performer's techniques.

Performative Objects

We discussed in Example 2 that before Mark interacts with the chainsaw, the presence of the chainsaw only generates changes in the head orientation of passers-by. The rest of their body remains in its initial orientation and the course of action is not modified. Before he starts the chainsaw, Marks stands just behind it and gestures his arms. His elbows are raised at shoulder height on each side of his body, his wrists are in extension with his palms opened flat in front of him, and he extends and flexes his forearms in front of him repetitively. He initially uses both arms simultaneously, while looking at passers-by. This specific gesture does not produce any noticeable effect on passers- by. The only interesting performer-audience interaction at that moment occurs when a woman crosses the space with her head oriented towards Mark. Mark notices it as his head start following her move. He orients his gesture toward her using only the arm closer to her. However, he does not succeed in getting her to stop.

Once Mark starts to interact with the chainsaw, his attention is completely focused on getting the chainsaw running by pulling the cord. He is bent towards the chainsaw and his head is oriented towards the ground. He is not looking at passers-by anymore. However, some passers-by start showing a different type of response: they initiate a body torque.

As soon as the chainsaw is running Mark rises, with the running chainsaw in his right hand, and direct his attention back to the passers-by. He browses the passers-by with a right-to-left head movement. He then resumes the extension-flexion arm gesture described before, using his left arm only. This time, the gesture produces an effect on some passers-by. Those who have stopped in the middle of the space and are watching (like the man and the boy in Example 2) move backwards and position themselves in alignment with the people already seated on the kerb.

Mark's pushing away arm gesture explicitly constructs the chainsaw as a potentially dangerous—hence exciting—object. Without the chainsaw running, the gesture itself fails to produce any effect among passers-by. The fact that he is checking who is looking at his gesture, and orients it accordingly, constitutes an evidence of the gesture being designed for a specific type of passers-by. Those passers-by are the one who might be willing to stop and watch, and therefore potential audience members. With the chainsaw running, the gesture doubles up as an audience-shaping tool. It implicitly invites passers-by who have stopped to watch to gather with the rest of the audience.

Performative Actions

Paul is trying to get people to stop and watch. He is standing on his trunk surprisingly positioned on the side of the street. Most performers position their trunk, suitcase or any other piece of equipment further away in the middle of the street. For nearly three minutes he remains standing on his trunk, addressing passers-by as they pass, asking them if they want to watch his show. The transcript in Figure 7 presents a 40 second extract of these three minutes. During these 40 seconds, Paul addresses three different passers-by. Passer-by 2 is the only one who engages in a verbal exchange with the performer. The issue of the interaction is not that hoped for by the performer since Passer-by 2 does not stop. During the whole interaction Passer-by 2 carries on walking. As he passes the performer, he re-orients his body in order to keep eye contact with the performer, performing a half-turn on himself. He finishes the interaction walking backwards but not stopping.

So far, Paul's position as a performer is not established clearly. Even though he is speaking with a microphone and standing on a trunk, his position, his tone of voice and his gestures are not different from that of someone who would have stepped onto something to amuse a small group of friends. As a result, he is not succeeding in getting people to stop and watch. Passers-by orient their head towards him, one even engage in a short conversation with him, but keeps his primary course of action unchanged. Maintaining his course of action even leads him to have to walk backwards in order to keep interacting with the performer.

After three minutes of similar attempts, Paul changes his technique. He gets down of his trunk and comments: ``I'm just gonna make a bit of noise first. See if we can attract a bit more of an audience and then we'll get started with more stuff." He then starts playing some music. The music itself does not create any change of reaction among the passers-by crossing the space. He then moves his trunk towards the middle of the street. He stands next to it and performs a series of movements. He jumps from one foot to the other six times, circles his arms on each side of his body twice, opens and closes them in front of him three times, shrugs his shoulders once and finally bends, keeping his legs straight to touch his toes. He performs this routine facing the audience and making staged glances. The glances are made with an exaggerated rotation of the neck as to display to the passers-by that he is looking at them. The routine resembles an athlete warm-up routine, but the way it is designed makes it performative. The number of repetition of his movements is too small to have any real use as a warm-up and the speed of the motion is exaggerated. Additional, his constant checking of people looking at his routine makes explicit the fact that it is designed to be watch. During the 30 seconds that it takes him to complete this series of actions, four people have stopped to watch and within a minute an additional 10 people are watching.

```
Paul:          When you're a street performer
               you don't have a stage or an
               audience ready you've gotta kind
               of like make them all happen so
               I'm gonna try and do that.
               ((to Passer-by 1)) Hello sir!
                     (3.5)
               So here we go. Let's see if we
               can get some people to stop. Hmm
               ((to Passer-by 2)) Hello Sir!
               Would you like to see my show?
Passer-by 2:   (                    )
Paul:          OK all right.
Passer-by 2:   I'm on my way
Paul:          (What?)
Passer-by 2:   I'm on my way to (       )
Paul:          OK   fair   enough.   I   think
               everything over there is closed
               though.
Passer-by 2:   (                    )
Paul:          OK fair enough. Fair enough.
               Funny. Right OK so uh... All
               right.
               ((to Passer-by 3)) Stop! Watch
               the show!
                     (1.0)
               Stop!
                     (1.0)
               Stop!
                     (1.4)
               No keep walking.
```

Figure 8. Transcript of Paul's attempt to stop passers-by and watch his show.

The way Paul performs his actions directly impacts the responses he gets from passers-by. When designing his actions to be recognised by other people present, as he does with his warm-up like routine, he is successful at gathering a crowd. However, when his actions are performed casually, without emphasizing the performative aspects through staged glances and gestures, he fails at building an audience.

DISCUSSION

Throughout this series of examples, performers use various objects to construct their performance space. This includes 'out-of-place' objects like a chainsaw or a dustbin in the middle of the street. More often it includes objects that are recognisable as performance 'props' e.g. a unicycle or juggling clubs. The performers also attempt to delineate the physical boundaries of the performance place by exploiting elements of the physical space such as the kerb and the church façade and by laying out ropes.

The recognition that the performer intends to display these elements of the physical environment as performative is achieved through the work he does in integrating them into interactions with actual and potential audience members. We have presented evidence that although some of these elements might in themselves attract the attention of passers-by, they are only successful at building a performance space when specifically constituted as performative through interaction. A dustbin in the middle of the road is not itself 'performative' it could equally be 'accidental'. The emphasis put on objects and props is directly linked to the nature of the performances reported in this paper. Other types of street performances will probably rely on a different set of techniques; however, interaction is likely to be a central concern for all performers who try to achieve the recognition of their action as performance.

Importantly, the work the performer does is to embed these elements in interactions that establish their performative character. This is manifested in the way that passers-by and audience members orient to each other's and the performer's actions. Conversely, they show little sensitivity to objects as such. We propose that it is the performers interactions with others that enable them to construct objects and actions as performative in order to encourage individuals to stop and watch.

Weird looking or unexpected objects per se do not fulfill the task of changing the primary course of action of passers-by. They need to be interacted with to be constructed as performative objects. In most shows, the transition where passers-by go from just orienting their head towards the action without changing their course of action, and the moment when they start orienting their full body towards the action is very noticeable. In a time frame of about two minutes, one can observe significant changes of activities on the piazza. At the beginning of the sequence, passers-by carry individual courses of action. It is possible to identify small groups interacting together, such as families, couples or groups of friends, but there is no general orientation pattern that links these groups together. At the end of the sequence, it is possible to identify two different types of activity: the people who are watching the show and those who are not. The first group displays three main characteristics: (1) they are all oriented towards a same point, usually the performer's space, (2) they are distinguishable by their motion: they show a form of synchrony in clapping, laughing and changing orientation, and (3) they orient to each others as members of an audience.

Ropes have a particular status as they have the support function of shaping the space. Unlike a chainsaw or a unicycle, they will not be part of an act. Performers claims ropes make a difference in the gathering of the crowd and in the way individuals position themselves. In fact, even with the help of ropes, the performer must interact with the passers-by in order to gather a crowd. Sometimes in summer, people do not need active encouragement to gather due to the high density of tourist. But even then, people are more sensitive to other audience members than to ropes. This is a key point for a wider argument about the way audiences form. The fact that individuals orient and position themselves in response to the physical position of other members of the audience—and not just to the performer or the physical layout—is quite salient.

Occupying the centre of the space, exaggerating gestures while oriented towards the crowd and looking at people are all techniques to which passers-by are responsive. They are constitutive of the construction of actions as performative. The construction of actions as performative is a first necessary step towards the establishment of a performance place. For a performance place to be fully established, in addition to be constructed and displayed as performative, it must be recognised by the crowd as performative.

A street performance routine can be broken down into a succession of goals that the performer aims to achieve. In order to get money, performers must gather a crowd and engage the people within it as audience members. Before that, they need to achieve the recognition of their actions as a performance, which in turn, help transform the public street into a performance space. The techniques performers use to achieve these goals and the order in which they use them is specific to each performance and depends on the performer's script as well as the particular interactional situation.

Due to the public character of the event, all activities, whether they are preparation of the performance, commentary on the performance or the performance per se, are managed in the front region. As a result, preparative activities such as laying out props and creating the performance space are staged. Street performers rarely have access to a back region hidden from their audience. They solve this issue by designing back region actions in ways that display their private or non-performative quality. For example performers can choose to turn their back to the audience or to not look in their direction for extended periods of time. Performers sometimes ask their audience to produce loud noises for no apparent reason, or, they explicitly collude with the people present to help them gather others. This is one example of concrete evidence that the rate of response matters: passers-by are attracted by shows receiving the highest rate of responses. As a consequence, part of the performance is designed for the outside region.

This paper focused on the first problem to be solved in street performances and the techniques used to solve it such as display of props, use of sound amplification and individual addresses to passers-by. Arguably, these techniques constitute a sort of pre-performance: the performers are working on setting up their material and no performance space is yet established. Further work will investigate how, through eliciting loud responses and using specific types of addresses, performers create a sense of community within the gathered crowd. We hypothesise that, ultimately, the creation of a specific social group—the audience, and the mutual recognition of its members, is key to the rate of audience responses and the elicitation of payment.

ACKNOWLEDGEMENTS

We thank the management of the Covent Garden market, the Punch & Judy and St Paul's church for allowing us to film on their premises. We also thank Mark, Paul, Sam and all the performers who made this study possible.

REFERENCES

1. Atkinson, J. M. (1984b). Public speaking and audience responses: some techniques for inviting applause. In Atkinson, J. M. and Heritage, J., editors, Structures of Social Action. Cambridge University Press.
2. Bull, P. (2006). Invited and uninvited applause in political speeches. BritishJournal of SocialPsychology, 45:563–578.
3. Clayman, S. E. (1992). Caveat orator: audience disaffiliation in the 1988 presidential debates. Quaterly Journal of Speech, 78:33–60.
4. Clayman, S. E. (1993). Booing: The anatomy of a disaffiliative response. American SociologicalReview, 58(1):110–130.
5. P. Dourish. Re-space-ing place: “place” and “space” ten years on. In ACM Conf. Computer-Supported Cooperative Work CSCW’06, Banff, Alberta, Canada, 2006.
6. Goffman, E. (1990 [1959]). The Presentation of Self in Everyday Life. Pinguin Books, London, reprint edition.
7. Greatbatch, D. and Clark, T. (2003). Displaying group cohesiveness: Humour and laughter in the public lectures of management gurus. Human Relations, 56(12):1515–1544.
8. Harrison, S. and Dourish, P. (1996). Re-place-ing space: The roles of space and place in collaborative systems. In ACM Conf. Computer-Supported Cooperative WorkCSCW’96, pages 67–76, Boston, MA. New York: ACM.
9. Heritage, J. and Greatbatch, D. (1986). Generating applause: A study of rhetoric and response at party political conferences. The American Journal of Sociology, 92(1):110–157.Conger., S., and Loch, K.D. (eds.). Ethics and computer use. *Commun. ACM 38*, 12 (entire issue).
10. Kendon, A. (1990). Spatial organization in social encounters: the F-formation system. In Conducting interaction: Patterns of behavior in focused encounters. Cambridge University Press.
11. Schegloff, E. A. (1998). Body torque. Social Research, 65(3).

Post-it Note Art: Evaluating Public Creativity at a User Generated Art Installation

Anijo Mathew
IIT Institute of Design
350 N. Lasalle St, Chicago, IL 60654, USA
anijo@id.iit.edu

Yvonne Rogers, Peter Lloyd
The Open University
Milton Keynes, MK7 6AA, UK
y.rogers@open.ac.uk, p.lloyd@open.ac.uk

ABSTRACT
As computing increasingly deals with our lived experiences in complex social ecologies such as urban and public environments, designers are challenged with new methods and ways of appropriating computation and experience around public creativity. Public creativity deals with interactions in public interactive installations that are not task-based queries of information but social constructions of user generated and collaborative content. In this paper, we present an analytic framework to evaluate such interactions in public installations. We then present a study where we designed, installed and evaluated a user generated art installation through the lens of this framework.

Author Keywords
design, engagement, public creativity, collective creativity

ACM Classification Keywords
H5.m. Information interfaces and presentation (e.g., HCI): Miscellaneous.

General Terms:
Design, Human Factors, Theory

INTRODUCTION
Interactive public installations are now commonplace and have become part of the fabric of our daily living. Mergers of physical and digital infrastructure mean that more information can be embedded in to seemingly everyday objects and places, resulting in new meaning and creative experiences for users. These experiences are often situated in particular spatial, social, and cultural contexts which provide the ground for both specific (in the moment) and extended (over time) user interaction with these installations. As new tools and technologies for social interaction start to permeate spatial constructs, expectations from public about interactive installations too will change. Shirky and others [1, 21, 22] claim that new tools of "social media" create unprecedented opportunities to create, share, cooperate, and take collective action, introducing a differentiating factor in the way information is processed in society - erstwhile consumers of information are now also producers of information.

Gee [11] tells us why this shift in balance happens:

1. It is easier today for everyday people not only to consume media but also to produce it themselves. The general public – not only experts –, can produce content as much as they consume, using relatively simple tools and services.
2. Digital tools are also changing the balance of participation and spectatorship. People are no longer restricted to the role of the spectator. As participants, they can (and often do) participate in what used to be creative practices reserved for professionals. The ability to produce information and the tools to produce and access sourced information are now readily available. Information is not fixed; being aggregated and constructed upon. So much so that it is often possible to take a single information source and watch it change over time because of content generated by users.
3. Digital tools are changing the nature of groups, social formations, and power. Prior to our current digital tools, it was hard to start and sustain a group. Today, with social networking sites like Twitter, Flickr, Facebook, and digital devices like mobile phones, it is easier than ever to form and join groups, even for short-term purposes. Without the requirement of formal structure, groups [or what McLuhan [14] would call "tribes"] can organize bottom up around specific topics or interest areas through constant communication and feedback.

Soon public installations will include interfaces which build upon constructed experiences, collective co-creation of content, and the transformation of this content in near real time. Or in other words, respond to *public creativity*. In this paper, public creativity is defined as social constructions of user generated and collaborative content at public interfaces. It is an extension of collective (group) creativity where the creativity comes from aggregated construction of user generated content *in public spaces*. As the balance shifts from consumption to production within our social structure, new lenses and metrics will also be needed to study users and user behavior, especially as they engage in public creativity. We describe one such lens – an analytic framework, and the results of its use in the study of an interactive user generated art installation in a public setting. The framework brings together several prior research findings in public engagement into one analytic composition, providing criteria by which user researchers can examine public creativity and derive insights from such engagements.

BACKGROUND

Public installations that are built as part of the physical environment are "neutral"; they only come into being and awareness when *individuals* form stable and enduring representations of their experiences through embodied interaction [2]. Such experiential systems are often viewed from a phenomenological perspective [9, 12]; an emergent paradigm which treats interaction not as a form of information processing but as a form of meaning making in which the artifact and its context at all levels are mutually defining and subject to multiple interpretations [20]. This perspective does not exist *a priori* as a series of abstract categories, but emerges through people's actions and activities, practice and experience in locational space [6]. Furthermore, it is constructed from an aggregated point of view – several people coming together to construct a collaborative experience. Traditional HCI methods which focus on the design of systems that convey a specific and clear interpretation of what they are for and how they should be used and experienced [20] are inappropriate for designing user experiences in such contexts. As a consequence, designers have been ill-equipped when designing for public creativity in interactive public spaces and user researchers lack the tools to evaluate interactions in such spaces.

An Analytic Framework

Several researchers have attempted to look at user behavior around interactive and reactive art installations using theories of embodied engagement. Such observations are either in the form of studies of installations designed by the researchers [4, 5, 13, 18, 19] or studies of engagement with existing installations [3, 4, 8]. While such discrete observations can be used as effective tools to evaluate some aspects of interactive installations they do not provide a comprehensive metric to evaluate rich interactions and engagements that emerge from public creativity.

To address this gap, we combined a number of disparate observations from an extensive review of the literature, based on research of behaviors at public installations, into a single analytic framework. The ensuing framework comprises a set of criteria, drawn from based on how they can influence public creativity in interactive installations. These criteria were categorized into three phases of user engagement at a public interface.

Criteria pertaining to perception

The first phase is *perception*, when the user/participant first comes in contact with the installation/interface. At this time, the user creates an initial understanding about both the installation and the social ecosystem that surrounds the installation.

An important distinction for initial perception of public installations comes from the early work of Cornock and Edmonds [7]. In this research, the authors describe the various ways in which (art) installations might be perceived by users:

1. *Static:* The installation is perceived (almost always) in a static state by the viewer. There is no interaction between the installation and the person viewing it.
2. *Dynamic-passive:* The installation has internal programming that allows it to change or be modified. While the art itself is dynamic, the viewer continues to be a passive observer and cannot impact the change or the modification of the art piece.
3. *Dynamic-interactive:* In this context, the human actor plays an active role in the modification of the installation or the environment it is set in.
4. *Dynamic-interactive (varying):* In such systems, the installation grows or evolves based on the manipulations of the actors on the installation or the environment.

Evaluation Apprehension

In their urban experiment, the RedNose game, O'Hara et al. [17] found that most people who interact (or wish to interact) with the public installations feel an *evaluation apprehension* or a fear of their behavior being judged by others in the vicinity witnessing the behavior. Brignull and Rogers [5] also observed this behavior and claim that such *social embarrassment* can be a key factor in determining whether people will interact with a public display in front of an audience.

Thresholds of Activity

A key attribute of public installations is how people interpret the installation within the context it is placed. Not all contexts convey the same level of interaction. O'Hara et al. [17], for example, point to different zones of interaction around the installation where they noticed that activities of audience members can range from passive viewing to active engagement depending on where they were located around the installation.

Brignull and Rogers [5] characterize these activity zones into three thresholds of activity:

1. *Peripheral awareness threshold:* People will nearly always judge the interaction from a broad perspective as they move through the space in which the installation is located. In general, people in these activity spaces are peripherally aware of the installation's presence but do not intend to interact.

2. *Focal awareness threshold:* People in these activity zones are engaged in socializing activities associated with the display – talking about, gesturing to and watching the installation being used. At this point, users may give the installation attention and try to learn more about it.
3. *Direct interaction activities:* In this activity space, an individual (or a group acting cooperatively) act upon the installation or may have indirect influence in another performer or user's interactions with the installation.

Criteria pertaining to Interaction

The second phase is *interaction*, which starts when the user has the intention or actually moves in to interact with the installation. When this happens, the following behaviors can be seen:

The Honey Pot Effect

Brignull and Rogers [5] describe an important aspect of interactive installations in public areas, known as the *honey pot effect.* This is the progressive increase in the number of people in the immediate vicinity of the installation as performers or other users start to interact with the installation. Even when people are not interacting, the honey pot effect creates a sociable 'buzz' around the installation that allows them to evaluate the system or at least show that they are interested. People standing in this space are often *potential* users looking for cues that will help them in their own interaction with the system.

Spectator Experience

Another significant taxonomy of interaction has been presented by Reeves et al. [19]. They evaluated the performer-spectator experience in interactive installations, deconstructing public interaction into two core attributes:

1. *Manipulations:* Manipulations are the actions carried out by the primary user of the interface or in their words, *the 'performer.'* Manipulations are often physical actions of the performer that lead to a transformation in the interactive installation.
2. *Effects:* While manipulations are a property of the performer or the user, effects are a property of the installation. Effects may take the form of images, graphics and sounds or the physical actuation leading to transformations of the physical attributes of the installation and/or objects in its environment, and/or the environment itself.

Strategies of Use

When larger groups of people interact with a public installation, they develop strategies of use based on the social context that the installation is situated in. Such strategies of use are developed irrespective of the relationship of one user to another. This is an important behavioral trait because the interaction at a public installation is an embodied act, complete with all the characteristics of social use. Peltonen et al. [18], observed that users may adopt *personas* and take turns at playing one or even all of these roles – depending on circumstances. Roles that they observed included that of a *teacher–apprentice* where one or more person took on the role of an experienced or technologically savvy user, and went on to explain the features of the application, assisting the other members of the group when needed.

Criteria pertaining to Engagement

Engagement is the final phase in the trajectory of interaction. This is the phase when the user moves from interaction into a deeper understanding of or a dialogue with the installation or other actors in the engagement. Bilda and Edmonds [4] describe the trajectory of user engagement as comprising three elements which shape a user's passage into engagement:

1. *User intent:* User of an interactive installation will have intent in using the system. This intention (in performing an action) can be identified from the user's *specific purpose* (fun, pleasure, curiosity etc.) in performing the action. The intent of use comes from the user's prior knowledge of other such interactions s/he has performed.
2. *User expectation:* In addition to the intent with which users approach interactive systems, they also expect an outcome or goal from the interaction. User *intent* is related to the experience of the user, his/her construction of all prior experiences. It is derived from an interaction perspective. User *expectation* is related to the participant's expectations from computing systems and his/her knowledge of computing systems. It is derived from an interface perspective.
3. *User dialogue (engagement):* In most interactions, users are able to determine if their manipulations with the system has had the necessary effect if the expected result is achieved. However, in ambiguous and abstract systems such as interactive art, this may not be an appropriate judge of whether an action is successful. User dialogue/engagement is derived from the installation's ability to act as a lever for unintended results like connections with other actors or reflection on the progress of content, both of which are important for public creativity.

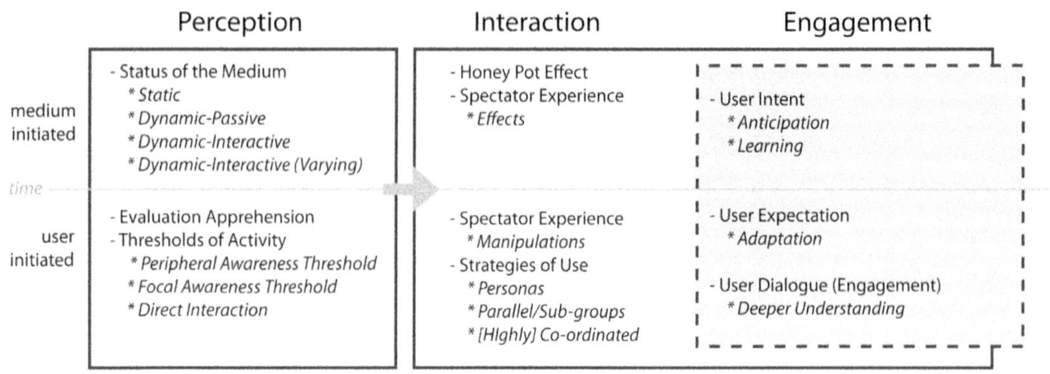

Figure 1. The analytic framework showing the trajectory of user engagement

Figure 1 presents the analytic framework combining all the criteria of evaluation categorized in terms of the three phases of engagement. Each of the criteria in the different phases can be further subdivided into two: some are medium-initiated while others are user-initiated. Medium-initiated behaviors come from the basic construct of the medium/installation itself. An example is the *status of the medium* which is a characteristic feature of the design of the medium. User initiated behaviors are derived from the user's actual use of the installation. An example of this is *strategies of use* – it is the users who determine how they will engage with the system and is often dependent on the socio-cultural structure of the audience that is at the installation at that point in time.

EVALUATING THE FRAMEWORK

In order to evaluate the framework, we decided to focus on public art. Public art invites audiences to engage through interaction and, in so doing, participate in the realization of the work itself [4]. Experience of art is driven by perception, and involves, in addition to an active engagement, the ability to reflect through interaction on the spot and at a later time [10, 15]. Noë [15] claims that art can be used as an instrument for phenomenological investigation but to do so, investigators must understand characteristic features of the installation. The first of these characteristics, according to Noë, is *environmental*, i.e. where an installation is located will determine how users perceive and interact with that installation.

We spent considerable time in the design of a prototype installation, such that its situation and construction would enable us to employ the analytical framework. The installation was also designed to pull from existing contextual cues in where it is located.. It is important to note that this is a preliminary study where we are interested in understanding user behavior. We made a conscious decision to *echo* technology in the design of the installation instead of designing a computer-based system. The intention is to separate the interface from the interaction, or in other words simulate the interface to focus on the contextual behaviors generated around a social creative interaction.

Situating the installation

The installation was housed in the main reception area of the IIT Institute of Design. It must be noted that the prototype was deliberately placed in a "public" area of the school, where it was accessible to students, faculty and visitors including potential collaborators, corporate/industrial/research partners, and potential student applicants. The installation titled "Post-it note Art" asked users to add content one post-it note at a time such that over time, through collaboration and social interaction, a larger composition would evolve.

The installation is composed of two parts (see Figure 2) – a box, made of black foamcore, serving as a placeholder for content creation; and the screen, constructed from white foamcore with a light grid pattern, which serves as a placeholder for content aggregation and display. In our design the box fulfills multiple purposes: it is a place to hold post-it note packs and pens; it is a place where users can create content; and it is also a visual focal point in a high traffic zone, indicating a change in the normal environment and a call to interact. The screen, on the other hand is designed to act as an aggregator of information, where people could build up new information, add on to existing information, or simply transform what is already there. Designed to resonate an actual visual display, the screen was hung on the wall. Very faint grid lines on the screen suggest that post-it notes can be positioned on the screen using the grid pattern. The space in between the box and the screen was intentionally maintained to allow for people to gather and discuss what was happening on the screen.

Interaction at the installation is very simple. A potential user can come up to the box, pick up one of the post-it notes, and draw, or write, or construct a pattern using the provided pens. This user can peel the post-it and post it on the screen. They can do this in response to something that is already there or to start a whole new thread of activity.

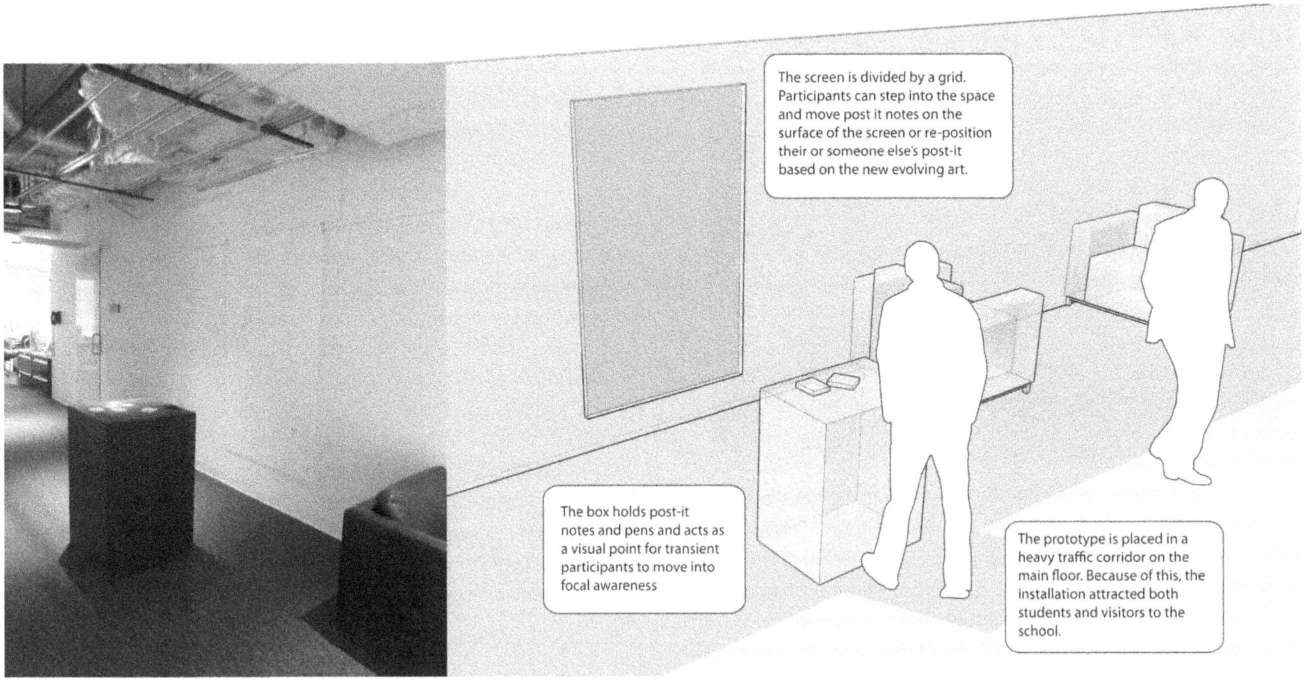

Figure 2. Design schematic and photograph of the prototype installation placed in context

Lacking in perspicuity

Noë [15] points out that art should be designed to be *lacking in perspicuity,* i.e., you cannot understand everything about the installation in one glance, and to be understood it must be explored. Through such explorations, observers are able to construct individual representations which enable meaning making and reflection. Likewise, in our design, no specific instructions were provided as to what to do or how to interact with the installation. Instead two signs were placed in the space; one said "Post-it collaborative art" and the other was a disclaimer note which said "You are being watched." Any formal construction of intent or goal was intentionally left to the user to work out. We did this to determine if the contextual position of a public installation implies to users the purpose of its existence. In other words, users will evaluate public installations from its construction and context to form a representation of what must be done. Moreover, we hypothesized that as the aggregated content and the gradual build up of information at the installation "grew" it would allow the users to develop their own understanding of what has to be done over what the designer was trying to accomplish.

Base level assumptions about the design

We made a few assumptions about the design of the installation:

1. It is contextual – the school has a history of using post-its for various design purposes. Moreover as students, faculty, and most visitors are used to prototypical research projects in the building, the interaction models should be largely familiar to the target population.
2. It is social – the installation invites people to interact at a social level by reading and changing/adding to what others have left behind.
3. It is collective and incremental – people will build on the work of others. There is no correct answer and so, interpretations are personal, subjective and constructed over time.
4. It is interactive - people will interact with the information, change it if they want (it is constructed of post-it notes after all). Even though, it only resonates interactive technology, analog interaction at the installation can be translated into digital space eventually.
5. It is episodic yet continuous - the direct interaction with the installation is episodic however the overall experience continues over time. People will come back to find out what others did; how others expanded their sketch; and since it is a tight community even talk to others to find out why they did what they did.

User evaluation

User evaluation was conducted at two levels:

At the level of contextual behavior

Since we are seeking to understand composite behavior of users and patterns of engagement, we decided to do a "fly-on-the-wall" observation study. To do this we set up a small non-intrusive webcam with a motion detector system which captured a series of low resolution stop motion photos (see Figure 3) every time someone moved or interacted with

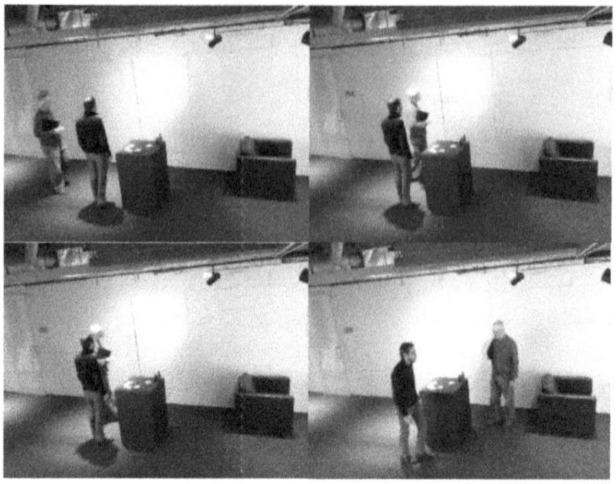

Figure 3. Examples of stop motion photos from camera

installation. The area of capture was slightly larger than the installation in order to observe the movement of passerbys and the behavior of individuals and groups in nearby spaces. The analytical framework was used to evaluate the behaviors observed. In addition, we also looked for new behaviors that could supplement or deviate from these criteria.

At the level of content generation.

We were primarily interested in the broad implications of the public setting and how users aggregate content in public spaces. Thus our observations at the content level focused on how behavior affects content and how existing content affected behavior. To evaluate this, we photographed the screen at periodic intervals (see Figure 4) – to see how content developed and to look for patterns of behavior.

OBSERVATIONS

Over a period of three weeks, we observed in the range of 40 people passing by per day. Not all of these converted into actual interaction. Any move from peripheral awareness to focal awareness was counted as an interaction. On average, 10-15 unique instances of interaction per day were observed. These figures include the congregation of groups where large numbers of people may accumulate around the installation. The numbers also increased on days when visitors came into the space. In general, a visitor was more likely to move into focal awareness (but not necessarily direct interaction) than a regular passer-by.

Figure 4. Example of content progression on the screen

In the following sections we highlight some of the behavior we observed through the lens of the analytical framework:

At the level of contextual behavior

Individual interactions

Many interactions at the installation were individual; passer-bys stopped to watch the *manipulations* of the actors in direct interaction but did not move forward to interact. Given that the prototype was placed in a main passageway, casual stopping by were common. Some people would stop periodically to see how the content had changed without actually modifying the content. This indicates strong *thresholds of activity* being set up around the installation (see Figure 5). People in peripheral awareness threshold seldom moved into focal awareness, and people in focal awareness seldom moved into direct interaction. However when interaction did occur, it was often people in focal awareness moving into direct interaction. The transition from peripheral awareness to focal awareness is the most difficult threshold to cross.

Beyond the individual

When group interaction happened, it was almost always preceded by a *honey pot effect*. Groups of people would assemble in the space in front of the installation to try and figure out the *manipulations and effects* of interacting with the system. An inevitable result of the *honey pot effect* was that one member of the group would move into interact with the installation. This often resulted in others discussing that specific interaction; leading to others in the group moving into interact as well. In most cases, we observed that transition from focal awareness to direct interaction was much more likely to happen if the *honey pot effect* preceded the interaction. On several occasions we also observed *teacher-apprentice* models being set up in groups of people – experienced users explained to new passers-by the installation, (their perception of) expectations, *manipulations* required to interact with the system, and the *effects* of these manipulations. We also observed that such

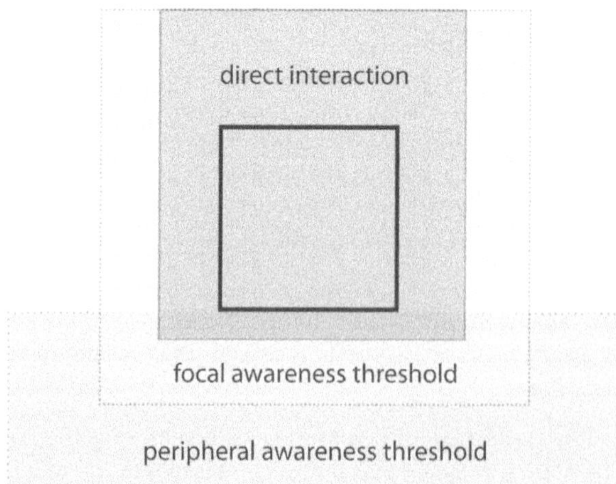

Figure 5. Thresholds of activity around the prototype

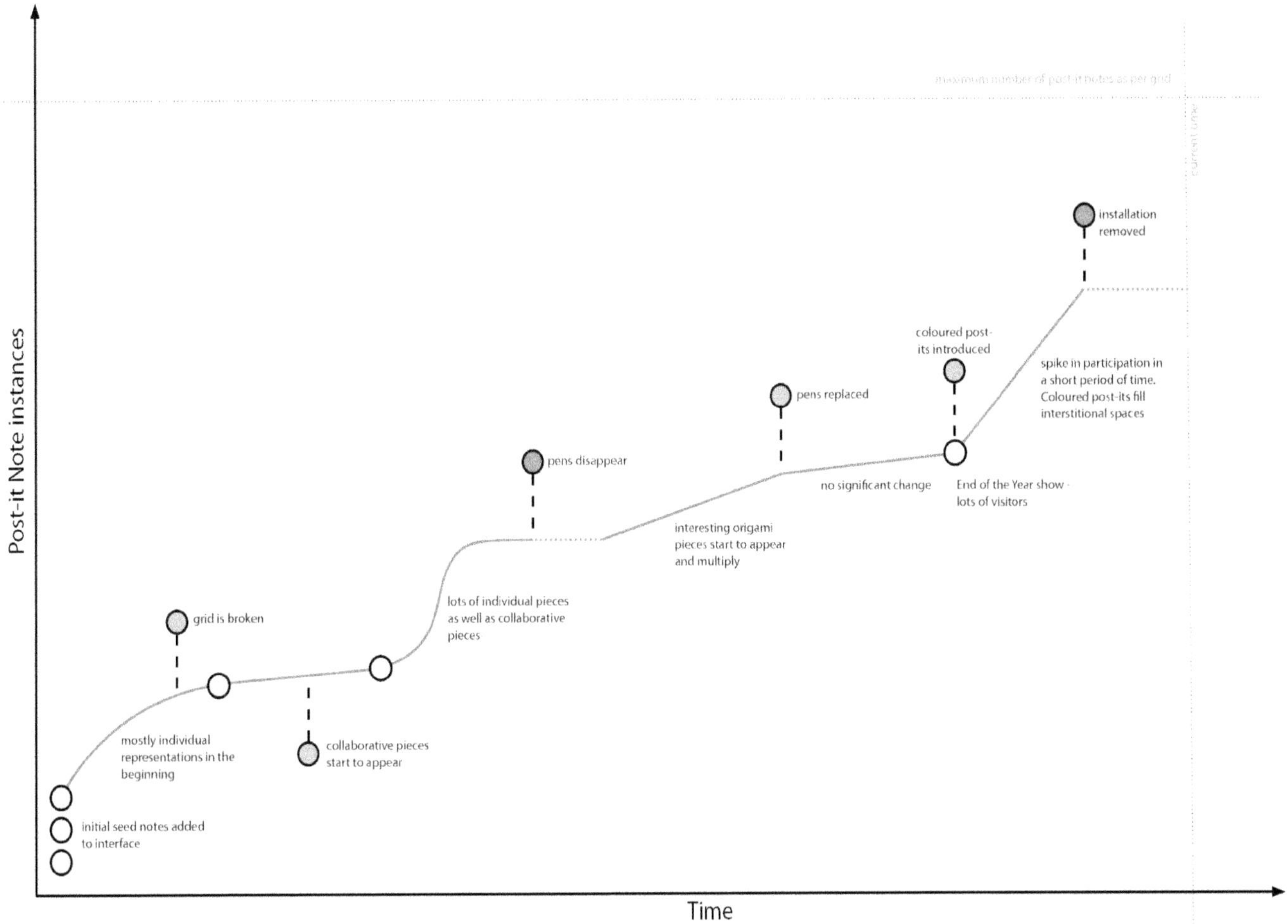

Figure 6. Plotting the change in user generated content at the installation [showing significant milestones]

role playing often occurred outside of *honey pots* or just before a *honey pot* formed.

The honey pot effect manifests itself when more than one person congregates and attempts to understand the installation or the *manipulations* and *effects* of the interaction. Such a social grouping also helps users to ascertain the level of *social embarrassment* among the current peer group, and the degree of transaction required through social interaction. Because such an evaluation happens before actual engagement, the *honey pot effect* is a strong signifier of actors moving in from *focal awareness* to *direct interaction* with the installation. It also indicates when one person has crossed this threshold, others will soon follow suit.

Interpretation of situation

People clearly understood the installation's position as an art installation project. In one instance, we observed a group of people getting together to use the box as a place to discuss. During this time, they did nothing to affect the installation. Sometime later they realized that they were hindering activity at the installation and moved away to another spot to work.

At the level of content generation

Interpretation of context

We observed that users would often look for clues in the environment as to how to use the interface. Contextual cues such as the situation of the installation in conjunction with explicit messages (such as the limited signage) helped users to construct an image of how the installation should be interacted with. When users found these cues and messages to be lacking, they would look for signals within the content itself – to figure out what others had done before. This was evident because for a short period of time, no content was generated. This changed when we added a couple of post-it notes as "seed" content. Signals could also be in the form of *manipulations* of a user currently interacting with the installation or derived from content already generated before the person arrived. Such signals sometimes influenced users' to follow existing patterns of use; but more often than not it allowed them to construct their own representations of what should be done and deviate from existing patterns.

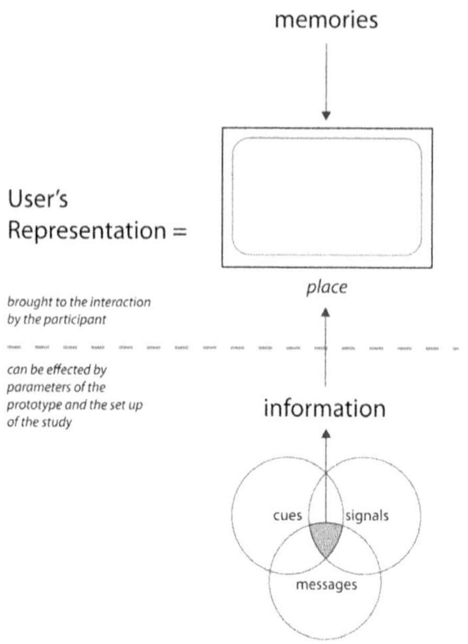

Figure 7. Cues, Messages and Signals in the construction of a user's mental model

Consistency of content activity

The first instances of content were mostly individual – very often artful renderings, sketches, cartoony representations of contextual elements. There were also some written pieces – speech bubbles or artful representation of type. However, over time collaborative pieces started to appear and multiply. Some of these pieces were collaborative completion of artistic renderings which indicated a lot of time was spent on content generation. Most were quick sketchy extensions of previous sketches. Some content pieces were clearly intended as generator pieces (intended to start a thread) while others were clearly continuation pieces (continuing an existing thread) or stand-alone pieces. Not all generator pieces were continued – several generator pieces were not followed up on many parts of the screen. We also noticed that some users would come back at regular intervals to see if others had added to their initial input. The grid was almost rigorously followed but post-its breaking the grid appeared periodically. While a few post-its changed position, it is difficult to say if this was done by the post-it note generator or someone else. But in general users seldom changed, destroyed, or added on to a post-it note someone else had created. If they wanted to make a change or comment, they chose to use a new grid position altogether.

Reaction to changes

Figure 6 charts important events that took place during the study. Two significant events that we noted were:

a. Pens disappear: At a certain point, all the pens disappeared. For a short period of time this meant that there was no activity on the screen. Passer-bys would look for pens and not finding any, would walk away. As a result of not having anything to write with people started creating 'origami' pieces with the post-it notes.. The first origami pieces were experiments but soon they multiplied until a majority of the new content was origami based. Pens were re-introduced after some time and it was interesting to note that origami pieces continued to appear as did other posts which did not use the pens.

b. Color post-it notes were introduced following a period of inactivity.. This also coincided with the End of Year show at the school which represented an increased number of visitors. At this time, there was a spike in the number of pieces that were added to the screen but no relative change in the type of content that was generated. Color post-its were mostly used to fill interstitial spaces – often the color of the post-its determined its position rather than the content on the post-it.

INSIGHTS

In this section we analyse our findings with respect to how designers might conceive of installations that address public creativity.

Ownership in User Generated Content

We observed several behaviors which suggest that in a social installation (especially one designed for public creativity) people respect ownership. In our installation we observed that users in general refrained from changing, mutating, or re-positioning post-its that were placed by someone else. New post-its were added next to others, post-its may comment on other post-its but we never saw users deface or add any graffiti to existing content. This showed that (at least within this particular context) people viewed post-its as belonging to or authored by someone. This kind of authorship suggests a line of communication is being established; changing content generated by someone else is a negative behavior, akin to interrupting when someone is talking.

Cues, Messages, and Signals

Another insight from this study was the role of cues, messages, and signals in a user's understanding of spatial installations; especially those installations that do not provide specific and clear interpretation of what they are for and how they should be used and experienced. Differentiating contextual information into these three categories will allow not only researchers to understand how users develop a model of interaction, but also for designers to design for new models of interaction.

Cues – Within spatial installations, users look for contextual cues to understand an installation and develop *user intent*. These cues can be spatial (where an installation is located) or experiential (how the installation is situated within a particular location). A brick out of place in a pile of bricks in a construction site presents completely different cues to the user as same installation is placed in a museum.

In the case of our installation the position of the screen and the box, its location in space, and the grid lines on the screen formed cues that users used to comprehend the system. The missing pens proved to be a cue to users to get more creative about how content could be generated.

Messages – When users have processed contextual cues, they look for explicit messages to supplement their interpretations. Messages are direct information that are provided to the users by the interface. The more messages that are provided, the less interpretive the system becomes. Messages may be in the form of explicit information (such as instructions) or in the form of example interactions (such as automatic replays). In the case of our installation, the information on the wall, and the seed post-it notes formed the messages. Messages in tandem with experiences also enable users to construct or re-construct *user expectations*. The introduction of color post-it notes was a message that they did not have to depend on single color post-its to construct their art and that they could use the color of the post-it to add to the art.

Signals – In the lack of messages, users look for signals from a variety of sources to determine how to approach an installation. Norman refers to these as social signifiers [16], suggesting that we use such signifiers to construct models in real life. Signals may come from existing patterns of use; signals may also be in the form of *manipulations* of other actors and the *effects* of the system in reaction. Users may depend on others to explain the system to them, or appropriate a direction from interacting with others in a *honey pot*. In the case of our installation, the first origami posts suggested to users that it was alright to create posts, without using pens. We also saw new ways of creating posts such as using a coffee cup stain.

In sum, a user's representation of public creativity can be described as a combination of memories working in tandem with cues, messages, and signals (see Figure 7). The former is brought to the interaction by the user, while the latter is affected by the parameters of the installation. When users locate these two factors within the context of place (in which the installation is located) they construct a representation of what the installation is for and how they will interact with the interface.

EMPLOYING THE FRAMEWORK

We suggest that designers use our framework as a conceptual lens when developing an installation rather than as direct input for their work. In other words, the framework is intended as *scaffolding* for generating public creativity installations, not as a replacement for a designer's intuition or artistic conception. In our own study, we were able to derive several insights for developing the installation by simply using the framework as metrics for evaluating each decision made through the design process. The framework is also designed to be expandable. We plan to include new insights such as cues, messages, and signals into the body of the framework in future iterations. From a designer's point of view, broad categorization of what to observe should be what remains as the basis of the framework; specific criteria of behaviors can be added or removed depending on the specific nature of the study.

Analyzing behaviors from the lenses of the different criteria within the analytic framework - perception, interaction, and engagement – will allow designers to look for specific behaviors and determine how they affect other behaviors in the space. In our study, we found that the criteria in each of the phases influenced each other. For example, *thresholds of activity* around the installations had impact on *honey pot effect* and *spectator use;* user understanding of *status of the medium* influenced *user intent* and *expectation*; and getting over *evaluation apprehension* informed the user on what to *expect* and how to *adapt* to the system.

CONCLUSION

In this paper, we introduce the concept of public creativity as creativity which comes from aggregated construction of user generated content in public spaces. We evaluated user behavior at a user generated content installation through the lens of an analytic framework. From the observations we were able to derive specific insights that are useful for designers of public creativity. While the observations are specific to the context and construction of a study, the overall insights are more general and can be transferred to other designs of this nature in the future.

Designers of public installations can use the framework as scaffolding for their own design process. At an implementation scale, the framework should help designers evaluate the different factors which go into public creative installation. In conclusion, we have shown how our conceptual framework, comprising a comprehensive set of criteria derived from the literature on public installations, can inform the development of novel user-generated social installations, leading to new insights into public creativity.

REFERENCES

1. Anderson, C. *The Long Tail: Why the Future of Business is Selling Less of More*. Hyperion, 2006.
2. Auburn, T. and Barnes, R. Producing place: A neo-Schutzian perspective on the 'psychology of place'. *Journal of Environmental Psychology*, 26, 1 2006), 38-50.
3. Benford, S., Giannachi, G., Koleva, B. and Rodden, T. *From Interaction to Trajectories: Designing Coherent Journeys Through User Experiences*. ACM, Boston, MA, 2009.
4. Bilda, Z., Edmonds, E. and Candy, L. Designing for creative engagement. *Design Studies*, 29, 6 2008), 525-540.
5. Brignull, H. and Rogers, Y. Enticing people to interact with large public displays in public spaces.*Interact 2003* (2003). Ios Pr Inc, 17

6. Ciolfi, L. and Bannon, L. Space, Place and the Design of Technologically-Enhanced Physical Environments. *Spaces, Spatiality and Technology*, 2005), 217-232.
7. Cornock, S. and Edmonds, E. The Creative Process Where the Artist Is Amplified or Superseded by the Computer. *Visual Art, Mathematics and Computers: Selections from the Journal Leonardo*, 1979),
8. Dalsgaard, P. and Hansen, L. K. Performing perception - staging aesthetics of interaction. *ACM Trans. Comput.-Hum. Interact.*, 15, 3 2008), 1-33.
9. Dourish, P. *Where the Action Is: The Foundations of Embodied Interaction*. The MIT Press, 2004.
10. Edmonds, E., Muller, L. and Connell, M. On creative engagement. *Visual Communication*, 5, 3 2006), 307-307.
11. Gee, J. P. Digital Media and Learning as an Emerging Field, Part I: How We Got Here. *International Journal of Learning*, 1, 2 2009), 13-23.
12. Harrison, S., Tatar, D. and Sengers, P. The Three Paradigms of HCI.*CHI '07 extended abstracts on Human factors in computing systems* (San Jose, CA, 2007). ACM,
13. Hornecker, E. "I don't understand it either, but it is cool"-visitor interactions with a multi-touch table in a museum.*TABLETOP 2008. 3rd IEEE International Workshop on Horizontal Interactive Human Computer Systems, 2008.* (2008). IEEE, 113-120
14. McLuhan, M. *Understanding Media: The Extensions of Man: Critical Edition*. Gingko Press, 1964/2003.
15. Noë, A. Experience and experiment in art. *Journal of Consciousness Studies, 7*, 8, 9 2000), 123-136.
16. Norman, D. A. Signifiers, not affordances. *interactions*, 15, 6 2008), 18-19.
17. O'Hara, K., Glancy, M. and Robertshaw, S. *Understanding collective play in an urban screen game*. ACM, San Diego, CA, USA, 2008.
18. Peltonen, P., Kurvinen, E., Salovaara, A., Jacucci, G., Ilmonen, T., Evans, J., Oulasvirta, A. and Saarikko, P. It's Mine, Don't Touch!: interactions at a large multi-touch display in a city centre.*CHI 2008, 26th Annual SIGCHI conference on Human factors in computing systems* (Florence, Italy, 2008). ACM, 1285-1294
19. Reeves, S., Benford, S., O'Malley, C. and Fraser, M. Designing the spectator experience. *Proceedings of the SIGCHI conference on Human factors in computing systems*, 2005), 741-750.
20. Sengers, P. and Gaver, B. Staying open to interpretation: engaging multiple meanings in design and evaluation.*Proceedings of the 6th conference on Designing Interactive systems* (University Park, PA, USA, 2006). ACM, 99-108
21. Shirky, C. *Cognitive Surplus: Creativity and Generosity in a Connected Age*. Penguin Press HC, 2010.
22. Shirky, C. *Here Comes Everybody: The Power of Organizing Without Organizations*. Penguin Two, 2009.

An Information-Processing Account of Creative Analogies in Biologically Inspired Design

Ashok K. Goel, Swaroop Vattam, Michael Helms, & Bryan Wiltgen
Design & Intelligence Laboratory, and Center for Biologically Inspired Design
Georgia Institute of Technology, Atlanta, Georgia 30332, USA.
{goel, svattam, mhelms3, bwiltgen}@cc.gatech.edu

ABSTRACT

Biologically inspired design perhaps is one of the most important movements in engineering design. The paradigm espouses use of analogies to biology in generating conceptual designs for new technologies. In this paper, we briefly summarize some empirical findings about biologically inspired design, and then develop an information-processing theory of creative analogies in biologically inspired design. We also compare our theory with similar theories. In addition, we examine how biologically inspired design is fundamentally different from other design paradigms.

Author Keywords

Analogy, Biologically Inspired Design, Biomimetics, Creativity, Innovation, Task Analysis, Task Models.

ACM Classification Keywords

J.6 Computer-aided engineering: Computer-aided design

General Terms

Design

INTRODUCTION

Biologically inspired design [5,13,23,26] perhaps is one of the most important movements in engineering design. The paradigm espouses use of analogies to biology in generating conceptual designs for new technologies. This paradigm has inspired many designers in the history of design, such as Leonardo da Vinci, the Wright brothers, etc. But it is only over the last generation that the paradigm has become a movement, pulled by the growing need for environmentally sustainable design and pushed by the desire for creativity and innovation in design. The design of blades of windmill turbine mimicking the designs of tubercles on flippers of humpback whales is one example of biologically inspired design [2,12]. As seen in Figure 1, the tubercles are large bumps on the leading edges of the flippers, which create even, fast-moving channels of water flowing over them. The whales thus can move through the water at sharper angles and turn tighter corners than if their flippers were smooth. When applied to wind turbine blades, they improve lift and reduce drag, improving the energy efficiency of the turbine [7].

Note that the design of biologically inspired energy-efficient wind turbine blades illustrates both sustainable design as well as creative design. However, although biologically inspired design is rapidly growing as a design movement, its practice is *ad hoc*, with little systemization of either biological knowledge from a design perspective, or of the processes of biologically inspired design. Transformation of the promising paradigm of biologically inspired design into a principled methodology requires development of theories of biologically inspired design, e.g. [27].

Theories of biologically inspired design can be of many types and take many forms. Vincent et al. [27], for example, describe a theory of biological designs in terms of material, energy, information, structure, substance, space and time. Their analysis suggests that while biological systems at some spatio-temporal scales often use information for achieving many functions, technological systems at the same scales typically use energy for similar functions. In contrast, our goal is to develop *an information-processing theory* of biologically inspired design. Information-processing theories themselves can be

Figure 1. Two examples of humpback whale flippers, adapted from [3,4]. The structure of the flippers inspired an improved windmill turbine design.

C&C'11, November 3–6, 2011, Atlanta, Georgia, USA.

of several types. Some information-processing theories propose cognitive models of specific tasks such as problem solving and decision-making. Newell & Simon [21], for example, describe particular memory, inference and attention processes of human problem solving. In contrast, we seek to conduct a cognitive task analysis (e.g., [10]) and describe a task model of biologically inspired design based on the analysis. A task model describes the processes, knowledge and representations that result in the accomplishment of open-ended tasks such as design (e.g., [16]). Further, an information-processing theory of biologically inspired design may describe the behaviors of an individual designer, the interactions among a team of designers, or the behaviors of a design team viewed as a unit. Although in general we are interested in all three levels of aggregation, in this particular paper we focus on interdisciplinary design teams of biologists and engineers viewed as units.

To summarize, then, our goal in this paper is to develop a task model of cross-domain analogies from biology to engineering in the conceptual phase of biologically inspired engineering design. Through this work, we wish to contribute to the relatively small but growing body of literature (e.g., [17,18,20,24,28]) that investigates biologically inspired design from an information-processing perspective. We view this work as a step in the broader agenda of developing (1) a design methodology that promotes systematization of biologically inspired design, (2) pedagogical techniques for fostering education and training in biological inspired design, and (3) interactive technologies that facilitate the work of individuals and teams engaged in biologically inspired design.

In this paper, first we briefly summarize some empirical findings about biologically inspired design. Then we conduct a task analysis and develop a task model of creative analogies in biologically inspired design. Next, we compare our theory with the two best-known information-processing theories of biologically inspired design. Finally, we examine if and how biologically inspired design is fundamentally different from other design paradigms.

RESEARCH CONTEXT AND METHODOLOGY

Since 2006, we have observed ME/ISyE/MSE/PTFe/BIOL 4740, a yearly, interdisciplinary, project-based undergraduate class taught by jointly biology and engineering faculty at Georgia Institute of Technology, in which mostly senior-level design students work in small teams of 4-5 on design projects. The class is composed of students from biology, biomedical engineering, industrial design, industrial engineering, mechanical engineering, and a variety of other disciplines. The projects involve identification of a design problem of interest to the team and conceptualization of a biologically inspired solution to the identified problem [30].

Although it changes slightly every year, the class is consistently structured around lectures, found object exercises, journal entries, and one or more design projects (usually a single project that lasts the entire term). Most lectures focused on exposing the designers to existing biologically inspired design case studies. Other lectures were devoted to the design processes involved in biologically inspired design work: reframing engineering problems in biological terms, functional analysis of a problem, optimization, and the use of analogy in design. Some lectures posed problems for the students to solve in small group exercises.

The focal point of our data collection was the design projects. Each design project grouped an interdisciplinary team of 4-5 students together. Each team had at least one student with a biology background and a few from different engineering disciplines. Each team identified a problem that could be addressed by a biologically inspired solution, explored a number of solution alternatives, and developed a final solution design based on one or more biologically inspired designs.

In this paper, we analyze two such design projects from the Fall 2010 section of the course: the SNAP project and the NOLA4NOLA project. The same design team within the class conducted both projects, and each consisted of about a month-long design episode. We report on this team because one of the authors (Wiltgen) performed a participatory ethnography of the class in Fall 2010, and the course instructor assigned him to be a member of this team during that study. Through participating in the team's design activities, we were able to gain insight into the particulars of this team's designs and design processes. Although we report in detail only on this team, our analysis of these two projects will illustrate how a rich task model is required to encapsulate the variety of design processes that occur within biologically inspired design. We refer the reader to [25] for additional examples of projects in this class context.

The SNAP Project

In this project, the students first selected a set of biological organisms, did research to understand those organisms, and then were asked to find a human-related problem that the functionality of one or more of those organisms could help solve. SNAP, which stands for Shrimp-inspired Non-harmful Attack Prevention, was directed at preventing shark attacks off the coast of the United States without harming the sharks. The students designed an underwater sound-based shark repellant device inspired by the snapping shrimp [22], a small shrimp with the ability to create loud, underwater sound waves using one of its claws. The device worked by emitting sounds, generated by the same mechanism that the snapping shrimp uses to emit sound, but at a frequency that sharks dislike. By placing a line of these devices between human beach-goers and shark populations, the design team envisioned creating something akin to an "invisible fence," a field that would repel sharks without harming them.

The NOLA4NOLA Project

For this project, the students were first asked to come up with a set of human-related problems, decide upon and investigate a single one of those problems, and then to find organisms whose functionality could help solve that problem—the opposite methodology of the first project. The goal of the NOLA4NOLA project, which stands for Novel Optimized Levee Architecture for New Orleans, Louisiana, was to prevent another disaster like 2005's Hurricane Katrina by strengthening the levee system in New Orleans. The design team identified several modalities of failure for the levees in New Orleans, such as scouring, overtopping, and joint cracking, and devised biologically inspired solutions for each. For example, the team designed a better joint system for concrete levees inspired by the iron snail [29] that would be resistant to incoming water forces by being multi-layered like the snail's shell.

BIOLOGICALLY INSPIRED DESIGN: A TASK ANALYSIS

In this section we analyze a set of tasks that we have observed in biologically inspired design.

Cross-Domain Analogies

By definition, biologically inspired design engages cross-domain analogies, e.g., analogies from biology to engineering. Although we have observed that extended episodes of biologically inspired design involve both within domain and cross-domain analogies [24], it is the essentialness of cross-domain analogies that defines it.

Problem-Solution Co-Evolution

Conceptual design in biologically inspired design undergoes problem-solution co-evolution as described by Maher et al. [19] and Dorst & Cross [11]. That is, the design process iterates between defining and refining the problem and the solution, with both influencing each other. As a solution (S) is developed and evaluated for a given problem (P), it reveals additional issues, spawning a new conceptualization of the problem (P+1). The process continues with the development of a new solution (S+1) and will iterate until a final solution is decided upon, which in our examples was driven primarily by instructor-mandated deadlines.

For example, the original design problem of the SNAP project was simply to prevent coastal shark attacks. Inspired by the snapping shrimp, the team designed a decoy-like device that would attract the sharks to a location away from human population using sound. However, the team discovered new problems upon evaluation of the idea, such as durability of the decoy if sharks were going to attack it instead of humans. The overall problem then evolved to account for these newly identified issues (e.g., that one must prevent shark attacks with a design that doesn't get eaten by sharks), resulting in a changed solution from a shark-attracting to a shark-repelling device.

Problem Decomposition and Multifunctional Design

A central challenge in biologically inspired design is how to leverage biological knowledge in service of an engineering problem. At the heart of this problem is how to understand and represent the engineering problem and biological solutions such that analogical transfer is facilitated, allowing for the development of a design solution. Functional decomposition of the problem and biological solution is one such method to overcome this challenge.

When developing these decompositions, each function can be used as a cue to retrieve known solutions that achieve that function, thus expanding the number of alternative solutions. Solutions are transferred to the current problem, and aggregated to generate the overall solution. We show how an analysis of snapping shrimp provided inspiration for prevent shark attacks in Figure 2.

Here both the natural solution and the problem have been decomposed into functions until a level is reached where functions overlap and a crossover can occur. In this example, the ability of the snapping shrimp to defend itself

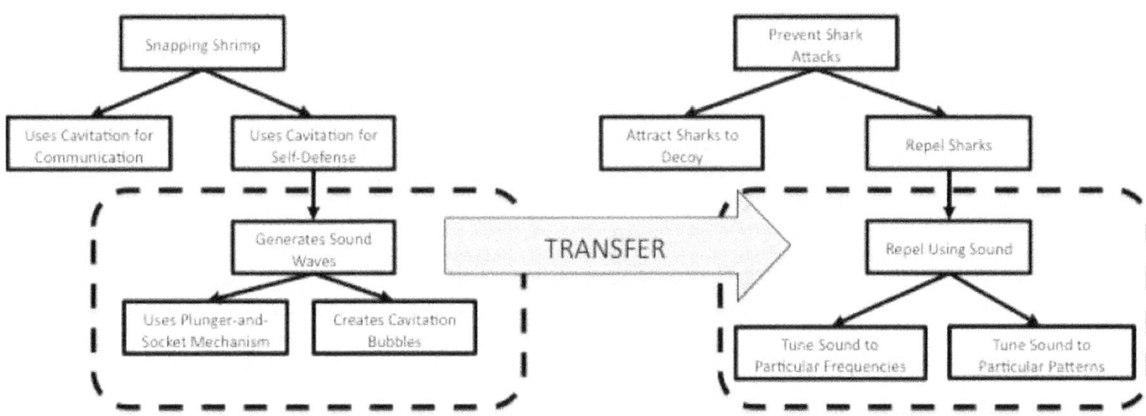

Figure 2. The functional decomposition of the snapping shrimp's ability to defend itself with cavitation was constructed in parallel to similar analyses of the design challenge of preventing shark attacks. By decomposing the biological solution and the problem, the designers were inspired by way the snapping shrimp defends itself to prevent shark attacks on humans by generating shark-repelling sounds and patterns using cavitation.

using sound was an inspiration for a sound-based shark repellent device.

Memory Processes and Compound Analogies

We have found that biologically inspired design often involves compound analogies in which a new design concept is generated by composing the results of multiple cross-domain analogies [17, 24]. This process of compound analogical design relies on an opportunistic interaction between two processes: problem decomposition and memory. Of course, that designers decompose a large, complex design problem into smaller, simpler problems is not a new finding. Equally unsurprising is the fact that designers retrieve and use analogies to generate new designs. However, an interesting aspect of biologically inspired design that we noted was how these two processes interacted and influenced each other, resulting in generation of a compound solution: the overall solution is obtained by combining solutions to different parts of the problem where the solution to each part is derived from a different (biological) analog retrieved from memory.

For example, in the NOLA4NOLA project (see Figure 3), the design goal was to strengthen levees against floods. During their research, the designers identified four sub-problems that were related to levee failure: scour (the eroding of soil by water), regional failure (local levee failures causing whole regions to flood), levee joint cracking (water forces breaking through the joints between levee sub-structures), and foundation destruction (water undermining the foundation of non-earthen levees). The team could not identify a single solution that would overcome all four of these sub-problems, so the final design solution incorporated (1) foundation strengthening underground structures inspired by riparian buffers and *Bacillus pasteurii* bacteria, (2) multi-layered, force-resistant structures to improve the levee walls and joints inspired by the iron snail, and (3) overall levee placement inspired by *Polyrachis sokolova* ant nests, which prevent complete flooding by localizing failure points. Note that Figure 3 only displays how analogical design followed for scour and cracking sub-problems.

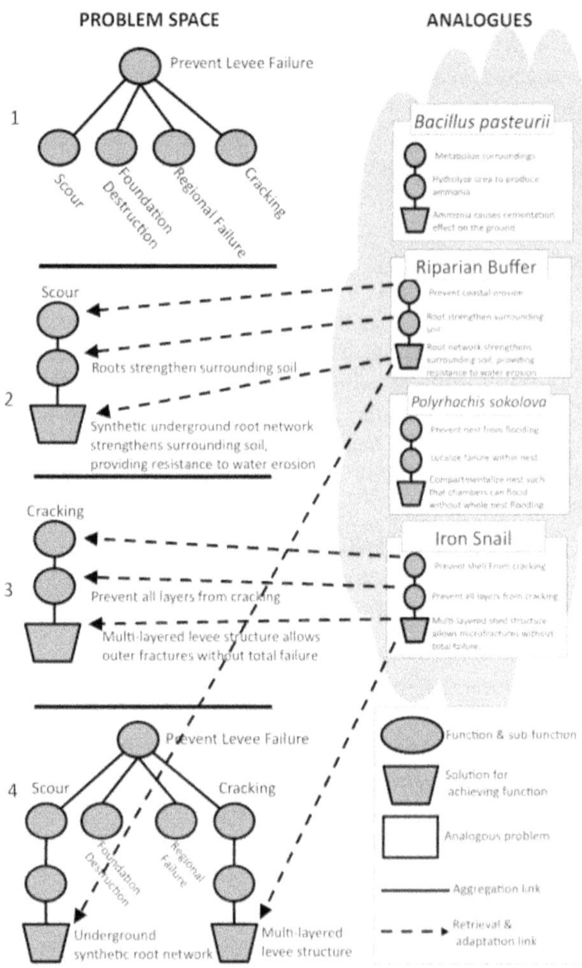

Figure 3. Design trajectory of the NOLA4NOLA project, which exemplifies compound analogical design. Note that only two of the four analogies made by designers are shown.

Problem-Driven and Solution-Based Processes

We observed the existence of two high-level processes for biologically inspired design based on two different starting points – *problem-driven* and *solution-based* [17,24,28]. As depicted in Figure 4(a), in a problem-driven approach, designers identify a problem that forms the starting point for subsequent problem solving. They usually formulate their problem in functional terms (e.g., stopping a bullet). In order to find biological sources for inspiration, designers "biologize" the given problem, i.e., they abstract and reframe the function in more broadly applicable biological terms (e.g., what characteristics do organisms have that enable them to prevent, withstand and heal damage due to impact?). Designers use a number of strategies for finding biological sources relevant to the design problem at hand based on the "biologized" question, and then they research the biological sources in greater detail. Important principles and mechanisms that are applicable to the target problem are then extracted to a solution-neutral abstraction and applied to arrive at a trial design solution.

The NOLA4NOLA project is an example of the problem-driven process. The design team began with the general problem of preventing levee failure, "biologized" their problem (e.g., "protect against incoming forces" and "prevent erosion"), and then conducted a solution search. The search returned such organisms as the iron snail and riparian buffers. Principles were extracted from these solutions (hierarchical, multilayered structures and dense underground networks, respectively), which were then applied to the design problem.

On the other hand, in the solution-based approach, as depicted in Figure 4(b), designers begin with a biological source of interest. The designers understand (or research) their biological source to a sufficient depth to support the extraction of deep principles from it. Then they find human

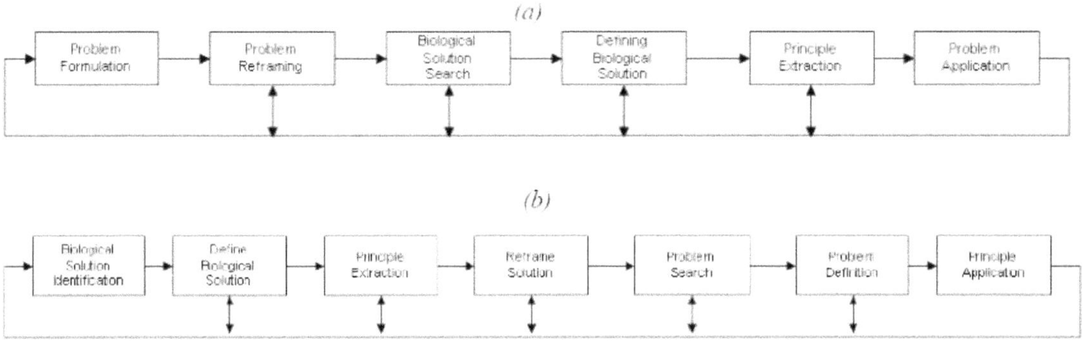

Figure 4. Observed biologically inspired design processes. (a) Problem-driven process. (b) Solution-based process.

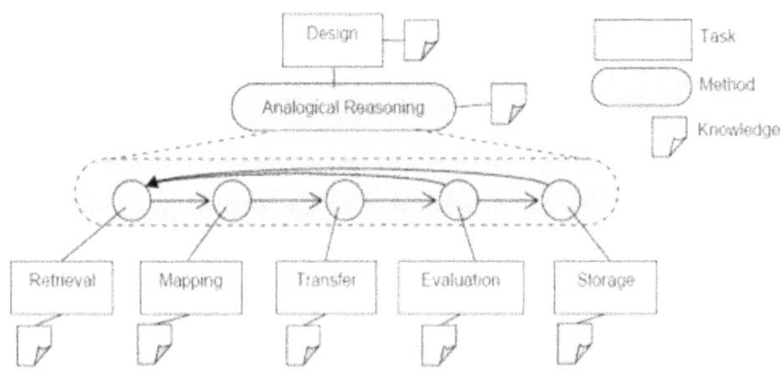

Figure 5. A generic model of analogical design.

problems to which the principle can be applied. Finally they apply the principle to develop a design solution to the identified problem.

The SNAP project is an example of the solution-based approach. The team began with knowledge of the snapping shrimp. From that organism, they extracted the principle of cavitation as a means to both defend oneself and to create sound. Next, the team sought out human problems to utilize the principle, whereby the retrieved shark attacks. By applying their knowledge of cavitation along with its functional use in defense and sound-generation, the team designed a device that repelled sharks in defense of humans using sounds generated by cavitation bubbles.

BIOLOGICALLY INSPIRED DESIGN: A TASK MODEL

In this section, we first summarize a generic task model of analogical design. We will then elaborate this generic model to incorporate the findings presented in the previous section to obtain a task model of biologically inspired design.

Figure 5 illustrates a generic information-processing theory of analogical design (based on [15]) that is consistent with information-processing theories of analogical reasoning in general (such as [14]). The overall *task* is design (see Figure 5). This is accomplished by using the *method* of analogical reasoning. The analogical design method sets up further *subtasks* like retrieval of a source analogue, mapping and transfer of relevant knowledge across source and target to obtain the new solution, and evaluation and storage of the new solution. Each subtask (e.g. retrieval) might, in turn, be accomplished by one of several methods (e.g. feature-based similarity matching for retrieval). *Knowledge*, here, refers to the knowledge inputs and outputs associated with the processing of each task, subtask or a method. For example, the knowledge associated with the subtask of transfer includes what may get transferred between the source and the target design situations; this can include, among others, elements of a previous design like components and relationships between components.

Our task model of biologically inspired design is based on the above generic theory of analogical design, but will extend the generic theory to incorporate the two key findings from our study described above: (i) problem-driven and solution-based design and (ii) compound analogies.

Incorporating Problem-Driven and Solution-Based Analogies

Earlier we identified two processes followed by designers engaged in biologically inspired design, suggesting two *methods* for the *task* of biologically inspired design: the problem-driven and solution-based methods. These methods should incorporate tasks that were noted in their respective processes, depicted in Figure 4. See Figure 6 for an updated task model that incorporates problem-driven and solution-based methods. The problem-driven method incorporates the design subtasks: problem formulation, problem reframing, biological solution search, defining biological solution, principle extraction and principle application. Similarly, the solution-based method incorporates the design subtasks: defining biological solution, principle extraction, solution reframing, problem search, problem definition, and principle application.

As one might expect, there are correspondences between many of the subtasks in the generic analogical design theory and the subtasks in our task model of biologically inspired design processes (see Figure 7). For example, the "biological solution search" in the problem-driven method and "problem search" task in the solution-based method corresponds to the "retrieval" subtask in the generic analogical design theory. The aggregate of "defining biological solution," "principle extraction" and "principle

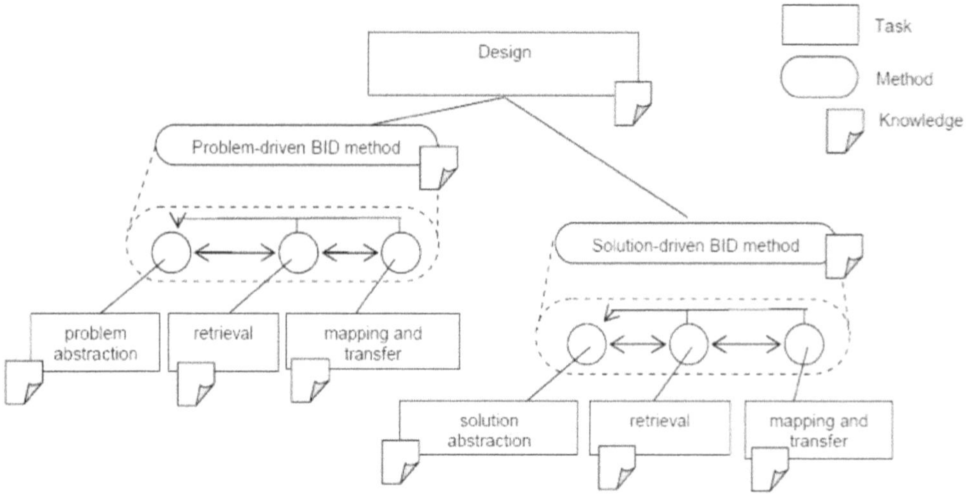

Figure 6. A generic task model of biologically inspired design after incorporating the two processes of problem-driven and solution-based design.

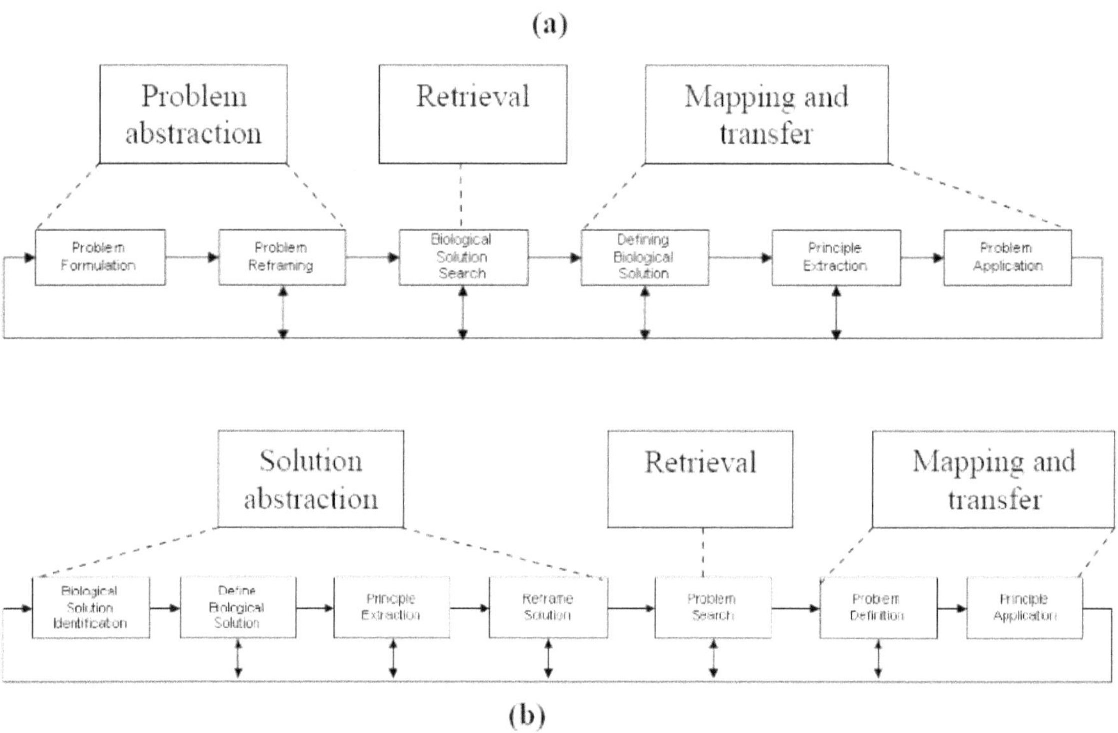

Figure 7. Correspondences between (a) problem-driven and (b) solution-based processes and the generic task model of biologically inspired design.

application" subtasks in the problem-driven method corresponds to the "mapping" and "transfer" subtasks; similarly, the aggregate of "problem definition" and "principle application" tasks results in mapping and transfer between source and target design situations.

On the other hand, there are elements of our observed biologically inspired design processes that are not addressed by the general analogical design theory. There is a set of subtasks that are considered preparatory to the subtasks of retrieval, mapping and transfer that follow. These include "problem abstraction" and "solution abstraction," which are pre-pended to the problem-driven and solution-based processes respectively.

Incorporating Compound Analogies

The second aspect of our observations that our task model must account for is the notion of compound analogy. Above we described compound analogy in the context of biologically inspired design and provided two examples.

Our observations also suggest a pattern of occurrence as far as compound analogy is concerned. In this pattern, compound analogy occurred as a result of the evaluation of initial design solution. First, the designers retrieved and transferred a biological source to propose an initial solution to the design problem at hand. For example, in the NOLA4NOLA project mentioned above, the team determined that multiple sub-problems caused the levees to fail in New Orleans (scour, joint cracking, etc.). After transferring one biological source to generate a design (e.g., transferring the complex underground network principle from riparian buffers to design a synthetic underground root network), the team evaluated their design and realized it was not sufficient to cover all the sub-problems. Addressing these additional problems became a design sub-problem in itself, for which they underwent another cycle of biologically inspired design to obtain a sub-solution. For example, they transferred the principle of multi-layered structures from the iron snail and redesigned the concrete levees to be multi-layered to solve the sub-problem of joint cracking. This sub-solution is incorporated into the initial solution to obtain a more complete solution. The process continued until all design challenges were met.

Incorporating compound analogy expands the task model of biologically inspired design model into the one shown in Figure 8. Here, S1 represents the initial solution obtained. The new subtask "evaluate" is added to both problem- and solution-based methods evaluates this initial solution. If a partial failure occurs, a new biologically inspired design subtask is added to address this failure as a new design sub problem. This in turn suggests a new sub solution S2. The subtask "compose" composes S1 and S2 to obtain a more complete solution to the original problem. For expediency, it is assumed here that subtask execution for compound analogy is sequential, represented by one-way arrows between the circles denoting the evaluation, designing and composition. The actual process may in fact involve more complex interactions.

COMPARATIVE ANALYSIS

In this section we will compare our task model of biologically inspired design with existing information-processing theories in terms of the four issues that we identified as being important for biologically inspired design: (i) making cross-domain analogies, (ii) accounting for the two processes of biologically inspired design, viz. problem-driven and solution-based design, (iii) problem decomposition, and (iv) compound analogy. We will show that while all current theories provide some theoretical coverage with respect to the above issues, none account for all four of these characteristics.

Design Spiral

Perhaps one of the most popular processes used for biologically inspired design is the Biomimicry Guild's "Design Spiral" [6]. The Design Spiral is a prescriptive theory for an iterative design process, where each design iteration informs the next. The basic idea of design spiral has been around in the design literature for some time (e.g., [8] in the domain of software design).

Within an iteration, the Design Spiral sub-divides biologically inspired design into six steps [6]: Identify, Interpret, Discover, Abstract, Emulate, and Evaluate. Each step has a set of prescribed actions associated with it. For example, the designer is advised in the Interpret step to

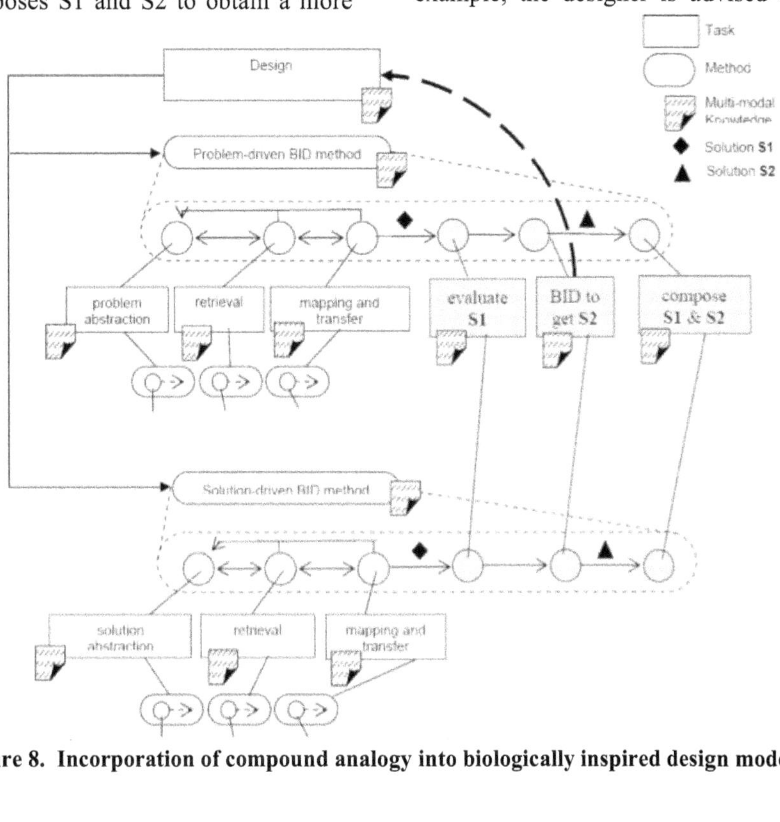

Figure 8. Incorporation of compound analogy into biologically inspired design model.

"[t]ranslate the design function into functions carried out in nature. Ask 'How does Nature do this function?' 'How does Nature NOT do this function?'"

A comparison between our task model and the Design Spiral reveals the following similarities and differences:

- The Design Spiral is a prescriptive theory for biologically inspired design, presumably derived from best practices in other kinds of design. In contrast, our model is a descriptive theory that is based on *in situ* observations of biologically inspired design.
- Like our model, the Design Spiral characterizes biologically inspired design as an iterative process. The Design Spiral implies that one should pursue an entire iteration before beginning a new iteration (e.g., to return to Identify, one must go through all Interpret, Discover, etc. steps), whereas our model suggests that one could interrupt the process at any point to return to an earlier phase of design.
- The Design Spiral is problem-driven. The Identify and initial step assumes the designer begins with a design problem or desired function. Our model accounts for both problem-driven and solution-based design processes.
- The Design Spiral is silent on compound analogy *per se*, whereas our model explicitly accounts for this phenomenon. However, the iterative nature of the Design Spiral suggests that compound analogies may be possible within the framework.

Design Matrices

BioTRIZ [27] is a recent and preliminary information-processing theory of biologically inspired design derived from the earlier theory of engineering invention known as TRIZ [1]. The TRIZ theory begins with a repository of design cases with known solutions, where each case is indexed by contradictions that arose in the original design situation. For example, consider a case in the repository that represents the design of an airplane wing. In this case the designer faces the contradiction of obtaining a material that is both strong and light-weight, and solves it using a solution, say S_1. This case is then indexed by the contradiction "strong yet light-weight material." Additionally, if the particular solution S_1 belongs to a more general way of resolving contradictions of a particular kind, it may be categorized as a generic abstraction, such as "use porous materials (to resolve the contradiction of strong yet light-weight material)". TRIZ posits the existence of forty such generic ways of resolving conflicts, called inventive principles. The inventive principles were extracted by dropping the domain specifics and retaining the essence of how a particular class of contradictions is solved, so we can imagine each principle pointing to numerous cases (potentially belonging to different domains) in which that principle was used to resolve a conflict.

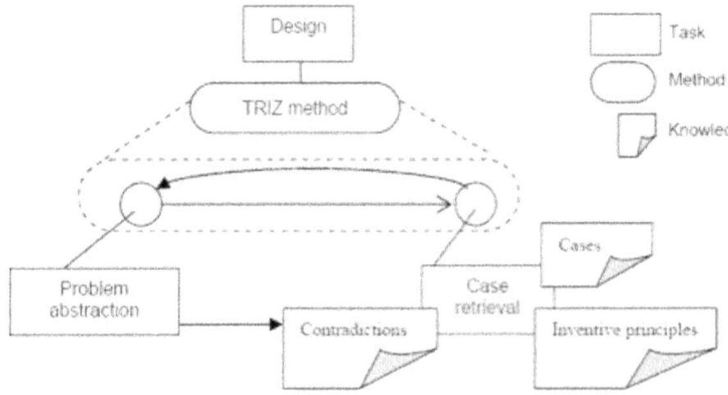

Figure 9. A model of TRIZ.

When the designer is presented with a design problem, she reformulates the problem to identify certain key contradictions in the requirements of the design. For each contradiction, she is reminded of a general inventive principle that is applicable for resolving that conflict. In addition to suggesting the essence of a solution for resolving that conflict, the inventive principle also points to a number of cases in which that general principle was instantiated. These cases can originate from domains different from the one in which the designer is currently working. TRIZ however does not address the issue of how transfer occurs [9]: "Then the creative skills of the designer are dedicated to interpret these models with their industrial realities in order to build a concrete given solution."

Although TRIZ facilitates cross-domain design, it was developed primarily to work within engineering. Therefore, Vincent et al. [27] developed a modified version of TRIZ called BioTRIZ specifically for biologically inspired design. The primary difference between the two theories is a change in the features that compose the contradiction matrix. Whereas TRIZ defines 39 features with which to determine contradictions and index into innovative principles, BioTRIZ abstracts to six "operational fields": substance, structure, space, time, energy, and information. The authors claim that these fields better characterize biological systems.

A comparison of Figures 8 and 9 reveals the following similarities and differences between BioTRIZ and our task model of biologically inspired design:

- BioTRIZ is a prescriptive theory of biologically inspired design, derived from best practices in engineering design. In contrast, our task model is a descriptive theory based on *in situ* observations of biologically inspired design in our classroom context.
- BioTRIZ provides an account for cross-domain case retrieval, but it does not address the issue of mapping and transfer.
- BioTRIZ is problem-driven. It does not address the question of how, given a design solution, one can find and solve other interesting problems that this solution is applicable to. Our task model accounts for both problem-driven and solution-based design.

IS BIOLOGICALLY INSPIRED DESIGN DIFFERENT?

This brings us to the question of if and how biologically inspired design is different from other kinds of creative design, or, put another way, what precisely makes it a new design paradigm? Note that the question is not whether or not biology and technology are different. As Vincent et al. [27] note, "biology and technology solve problems in design in rather different ways." French [13] makes a detailed analysis of the similarities and differences between biology and technological systems. Instead, the question here is whether or not the information *processes* of biologically inspired design are different from other kinds of creative and innovative design.

The design spiral and the design matrix theories of biologically inspired design certainly can be, and have been, applied to many kinds of design. In fact, the TRIZ design matrix theory arose out of engineering inventions, and it has been applied to many kinds of design. Similarly, the design spiral is used extensively in software design. Thus, according to the design spiral and the TRIZ design matrix theories, the processes of biologically inspired design are fundamentally the same as that of other kinds of creative design.

However, our task analysis offers some insights into what makes biological inspiration a new design paradigm from an information processing or cognitive perspective. Firstly, biologically inspired design is by definition based on cross-domain analogies. While other creative design can also sometimes engage in cross-domain analogies, and while biologically inspired design also engages within domain analogies, there are not many other kinds of design that are by definition based on cross-domain analogies. Secondly, many biologically inspired designs often entail compound analogies. Once again other kinds of creative design sometimes engage in compound analogies as well, but this seems to be a stronger characteristic of biologically inspired design. Finally, and perhaps most importantly, biologically inspired design engages in two very different creative design processes, namely, problem-driven and solution-based design. Insofar as we know, there are at present few theories of solution-based analogies in other kinds of creative design. Solution-based design appears to be another definitional characteristic of biologically inspired design.

CONCLUSIONS

In this paper, we first presented a task analysis of biologically inspired design based on our empirical observations of its practice. (1) Biologically inspired design by definition engages cross-domain analogies. (2) Problems and solutions in biologically inspired design co-evolve. (3) Problem decomposition is a fundamental process of biologically inspired design. (4) Biologically inspired design often involves compound analogies, entailing a complex interplay between the processes of problem decomposition and the processes of analogical retrieval from memory. (5) Biologically inspired design entails two distinct but related processes: problem-driven analogies and solution-based analogies.

We then described a task model of biologically inspired design. Due to lack of space, our description of the task model focused on only two results of our task analysis: that biologically inspired design involves compound analogies, and that biologically inspired entails both problem-driven and solution-based design. Insofar as we know, our task model of biologically inspired design is novel and unique.

Next, we compared our task model with the two best-known information-processing theories of biologically inspired design in the field: the design spiral and the design matrix TRIZ. Both the design spiral and the design matrix models address cross-domain analogies and admit problem decomposition. We can also see how the design spiral can admit problem-solution co-evolution and how the design matrix can admit compound analogies. However, both the design spiral and the design matrix are limited to problem-driven analogies; neither address solution-based analogies.

Finally, we analyzed what makes biologically inspired design a new design paradigm, and, in particular, how the process of biologically inspired design differs from other kinds of design. The design spiral and the design matrix theories view the process as fundamentally the same. In contrast, our task model of biologically inspired design suggests that it differs from other kinds of design in the use of cross-domain analogies, the use of compound analogies, and the use of both problem-driven and solution-based analogies. We are presently investigating the methodological, technological and pedagogical implications of our task model of creative analogies in biologically inspired design.

ACKNOWLEDGMENTS

We are grateful to the instructors and students of the ME/ISyE/MSE/PTFe/BIOL 4740 class from 2006 through 2010, especially Prof. Jeannette Yen, the prime coordinator and instructor of the class, and the design team that developed the SNAP and NOLA4NOLA projects. We thank the US National Science Foundation for its support of this research through an NSF CreativeIT Grant (#0855916) entitled "Computational Tools for Enhancing Creativity in Biologically Inspired Engineering Design."

REFERENCES

1. Altshuller, G. (1984). *Creativity as an exact science*. Gordon and Branch Publishers, Luxembourg.
2. Ashley, S. (2004) Bumpy flying. Scalloped flippers of whales could reshape wings. *Scientific American*, 291(2):18, 20.
3. Baird, "Mike" Michael L. (2011) flickr.bairdphotos.com http://www.flickr.com/photos/mikebaird/5906968596/. Last retrieved on August 13, 2011.
4. Baird, "Mike" Michael L. (2011) flickr.bairdphotos.com http://www.flickr.com/photos/mikebaird/5915321634/. Last retrieved on August 13, 2011.

5. Benyus, J. (1997) *Biomimicry: Innovation Inspired by Nature*. New York: William Morrow.

6. Biomimicry Institute (2009). Biomimicry: A Tool for Innovation. http://www.biomimicryinstitute.org/about-us/biomimicry-a-tool-for-innovation.html. Last retrieved on April 25, 2011.

7. Biomimicry Institute (2011). Energy. http://www.biomimicryinstitute.org/case-studies/case-studies/energy.html. Last retrieved on April 28, 2011.

8. Boehm, Barry W. (1988). A Spiral Model of Software Development and Enhancement. *IEEE Computer*, 21(5), pp. 61-72.

9. Cavallucci, D. (2002). TRIZ, the Altshullerian approach to solving innovative problems. In Chakrabarti, A. (Ed.), *Engineering design synthesis: understanding, approaches, and tools*. London: Springer.

10. Crandall, B., Klein, G., and Hoffman, R. (2006). *Working minds: A practitioner's guide to cognitive task analysis*. MIT Press.

11. Dorst, K., Cross, N. (2001). Creativity in the design process: co-evolution of problem-solution. *Design Studies*, 22, pp. 425-437.

12. Fish F., & Battle J. (1995). Hydrodynamic design of the humpback whale flipper. *Journal of Morphology*, 225:51–60.

13. French, M. (1994) *Invention and evolution: design in nature and engineering.* 2nd edition. Cambridge University Press, 1988.

14. Gentner, D, Holyoak, K., & Kokinov, B. (2001) *The Analogical Mind: Perspectives from Cognitive Science,* MIT Press.

15. Goel, A., & Bhatta, S. (2004) Use of Design Patterns in Analogy-Based Design. *Advanced Engineering Informatics*, 18(2):85-94, April 2004.

16. Goel, A., & Chandrasekaran, B. (1992) Case-Based Design: A Task Analysis. In *Artificial Intelligence Approaches to Engineering Design, Volume II: Innovative Design*, C. Tong and D. Sriram (editors), pp. 165-184, San Diego: Academic Press, 1992.

17. Helms, M., Vattam, S., & Goel, A. (2009) Biologically Inspired Design: Process and Products, *Design Studies*, 30(5):606-622.

18. Linsey, J., Wood, K., Markman, A. (2008). Modality and representation in analogy. *AI for Engineering, Design, and Manufacturing*, 22:85-100.

19. Maher, ML, Poon, J., & Boulanger, S. (1996). Formalising design exploration as co-evolution: a combined gene approach. In *Advances in Formal Design Methods for CAD*. Gero, J. (ed.). Chapman & Hall, pp. 3-30.

20. Mak, T., & Shu, L., (2008). Using descriptions of biological phenomena for idea generation, *Research in Engineering Design*, 19/1:21-28.

21. Newell, A., & Simon, H. (1972) *Human Problem Solving*. Prentice-Hall.

22. Ritzmann, R. (1974). Mechanisms for the Snapping Behavior of Two Alpheid Shrimp, *Alpheus californiensis* and *Alpheus heterochelis*. Journal of Comparative Physiology, 95, p. 217-236.

23. Shu, L., Ueda, K., Chiu I., & Cheong, H. (2011). Biologically Inspired Design, CIRP Annals, Manufacturing Technology.

24. Vattam, S., Helms, M., & Goel, A. (2010) A Content Account of Creative Analogies in Biologically Inspired Design. *AI for Engineering Design, Analysis and Manufacturing, Special Issue on Biologically Inspired Design* , 24: 467-481.

25. Vattam, S. S., Helms, M., & Goel, A. K. (2010). Biologically Inspired Design: A Macrocognitive Account. In Procs. ASME 2010 International Design Engineering Technical Conferences & Computers and Information in Engineering Conference (IDETC/CIE 2010). August 15-18, 2010, Montreal, Quebec, Canada.

26. Vincent, J., & Mann, D. (2002) Systematic Transfer from Biology to Engineering. *Philosophical Transactions of the Royal Soceity of London*, 360: 159-173.

27. Vincent J., Bogatyreva O., Bogatyrev N., Bowyer A, Pahl A. (2006) Biomimetics: its practice and theory. *Journal of the Royal Society Interface*, 3, 471–482.

28. Wilson, J., Rosen, D., Nelson, B, & Yen, J. (2010) The Effects of Biological Examples in Idea Generation. *Design Studies*, 31(2): 169-186.

29. Yao, H., Dao, M., Imholt, T., Huang, J., Wheeler, K., Bonilla, A., Suresh, S., & Ortiz, C. (2010). Protection mechanisms of the iron-plated armor of a deep-sea hydrothermal vent gastropod. In *Proc. of the National Academy of Sciences (PNAS),* 107(3), pp. 987-992.

30. Yen, J., Helms, M., Vattam, S., & Goel, A. (2010) Evaluating biological systems for their potential in engineering design. In *Procs. 3rd International Conference on Bionics Engineering, Zhuhai*, China.

Understanding Repair as a Creative Process of Everyday Design

Leah Maestri
School of Interactive Arts and Technology
Simon Fraser University
2400 Central City
Surrey, B.C. Canada
Leahm@sfu.ca

Ron Wakkary
School of Interactive Arts and Technology
Simon Fraser University
2400 Central City
Surrey, B.C. Canada
rwakkary@sfu.ca

ABSTRACT

This paper presents the findings from an exploratory study that looks at how creativity plays a role in the repair and reuse of objects in the home. We are interested in a particular form of creativity that manifests in the everyday – what John Dewey [8] describes as a constant *doing* and *undergoing,* as we actively adjust to everyday situations. The goal of this study is to show evidence of repair as not only an act of restoration, but also as an act of creativity that entails the repurposing and resourcing of objects. This study is part of a larger research initiative known as the Everyday Design, where it is believed that everyone is a designer and that design is an ongoing activity that includes the repair, modification, and appropriation of design objects and systems. Furthermore, this study serves as baseline research for future investigations in how to inform the design of technologies whose lifecycle can be extended for various contexts of use through repair.

Author Keywords

Repair, reuse, everyday design, creativity, appropriation.

ACM Classification Keywords

H.5.m. Information interfaces and presentation (e.g., HCI): Miscellaneous.

General Terms

Design, theory.

INTRODUCTION

This paper reports on a qualitative study that looks at understanding how creativity plays a role in the everyday repair of objects in the home. We see creativity as a phenomenon that occurs throughout our daily lives. We describe creativity as *resourceful* and *adaptive* actions that lead to unique design situations and systems. The goal of this research is to reconstruct the notion of *repair* as a creative process that serves an important role in the multiple lives of objects in the home.

C&C'11, November 3–6, 2011, Atlanta, Georgia, USA.

This study is part of the larger study of Everyday Design. The aim of this research is to re-construct the "user" as an 'everyday designer,' or someone who creatively 'designs' systems in by re-appropriating artifacts through *design-in-use* [27]. We believe that by understanding the evolution of artifacts and systems through the lens of repair (as a process of *design-in-use*), we can then begin to inform the design of interactive technologies that can be reused and appropriated to fit a variety of changing contexts and needs.

Understanding everyday repair in the home has relevant implications for interaction design, as we explore the fundamental barriers of objects' physical attributes that either *compel* or *prohibit* the repair, reuse and/or appropriation of everyday technologies. We set out to answer the following three questions:

1. Is repair a creative process?
2. In what way does repair relate to appropriation?
3. How do acts of appropriation and repair fit within the context of Everyday Design – specifically as aspects/dimensions of design-in-use?

This paper outlines the current status of the project, as we describe the methods of our data collection (via a web survey) and the analysis of 30 responses. We describe our two methods of analysis. The first method entailed the development of an open-coding rubric for defining various states of repair, reuse and 'digitality' of the broken objects submitted. Our second method included an affinity analysis where patterns of repaired objects, particularly their physical attributes, were defined as part of an initial design framework for facilitating creative repair and appropriation. We conclude with a discussion of what implications this research has for the design of technology, and what challenges this poses for the interaction design community.

RELATED RESEARCH

There are several different areas of research that focus on understanding the reuse of objects to inform sustainable design practices. There are few, however, that focus on understanding repair as a creative process for informing the design of more reusable and repurposeful technologies in the home.

Current research on repair is written in more general terms within the emerging discourse of Sustainable Interaction design (SID) [4]. Odom et al. look at why people keep certain objects as 'heirlooms' [17]. Huang et al. explore why people dispose, recycle and/or reuse technologies prone to obsolescence such as mobile phones [12]. These papers have made significant contributions in providing foundational theories for the development of sustainable design frameworks.

Work by Jung et al. looks at the materiality of digital artifacts with the aim of developing a taxonomy of digital material *qualities* for informing the design of technologies [15]. Here the authors also highlight the need to look more closely at the notion of *reconfigurability* – where technologies' software and hardware components can be easily broken down and assembled for different purposes of use through the addition and transformation of parts.

Industrial design initiatives look at designing for *disassembly* or *remanufacturing,* where manufactured objects are conceptualized with the end of their lifecycle in mind [18,21,23]. Frameworks related to remanufacturing include best practices around how to inform products' material design for facilitating transportation and disassembly processes [21]. Other frameworks look to inform business strategies by analyzing the rate of products technological innovation and their expected end of lifecycle [18].

Also related is Leah Buechley's work in understanding the role of DIY culture in the reuse and appropriation of technologies [5]. Buechley's research looks at *customization* as a key aspect of DIY culture, but also focuses on reuse and creativity as inherent characteristics of DIY practices. The goal of this workshop is to understand how thinking within Do-it-yourself communities can facilitate HCI design practices.

A key objective of our research is to understand repair as a creative practice that is strongly related to acts of appropriation. Designing for appropriation has become an emerging issue within the disciplines of interaction design and HCI. Literature pertaining to appropriation is found primarily within the contexts of the workplace [3,6,9] and the home [7,24,25]. Theories of designing for appropriation have also been discussed using ideas proposed by Heidegger, as well as in Activity Theory related frameworks like Instrumental genesis [16].

The arts have also been referenced as a realm in which acts of appropriation occur due to avant-gardism and the artist's pursuit of *authenticity* and *authorship* [10]. Senger, Höök and Gaver discuss the notion of *multiple interpretations* as a means of facilitating appropriation. They posit that *ambiguity* can compel more dynamic forms of interaction that go beyond usability and more towards explorative and creative activity [10,13,20].

Darinka Aguirre's work looks at applying the concept of *design for repurposing* as "an evolved design strategy that could help ease the negative environmental impacts in today's world." [1] This research proposes two checklists for informing small to large-scale businesses production processes. These frameworks serve as guidelines for best practices around the use of non-hazardous materials, as well as informing the design of affordances that lend themselves to repurposing.

Our own work under the rubric of Everyday Design has looked at the appropriation of artifacts and systems in the home, where we describe these processes as fundamental aspects of design-in-use [27]. We will discuss the parallels between the everyday design framework and the findings from this study further on in the paper. In the following section we outline our methods for data collection and data analysis.

METHODS

Data collection took place in the form of a qualitative survey that was distributed via email and Facebook. The goal of the survey was to gain insights into the processes by which people repair broken objects, as well as understand the reasons for why certain objects are kept and repaired. Another aspect of this study looked at uncovering the different kinds of values people attributed to objects that are broken, kept and repaired. Participants ranged from ages 20-67 years of age, with a range of different occupations including university students, a lawyer, designers, musicians, teachers, a dental hygienist, and a stay-at-home mom.

The survey population was composed of 50% female and 50% male participants, most of which were between ages 20-29. A total of p=30 responses were submitted with each participant including anywhere between 1-7 examples of repaired and/or broken objects from their home. The total number of objects submitted was n=87. Some of the responses were too vague to give a proper assessment, thus the total objects used in our data analysis came to 74.

The survey took place in two phases; the first phase asked participants the following three questions:

1. Do you have something that is broken but not thrown away?
2. Do you have something that is broken which you have repaired and is now more valuable (monetary or sentimental) and/or functions better than before?
3. Do you have something that is broken which you are still using or reusing in a new way?

Participants were also asked to include pictures of their broken items wherever possible. Photos were used as part of the analysis to determine the objects repair, type (mechanical or digital) and reuse (we will discuss this further in the following section.) The second phase of the survey included follow up emails with participants in an attempt to elicit further information about how and why their objects were or weren't repaired.

The data collected from the survey responses was categorized into two sets. The first set quantified object types and the instances of repair present in each type. These were based on their *degree of repairability* and *degree of digitality,* and *degree of reusability*. The second data set is comprised of value-themes that resulted from an affinity analysis of the participants' submissions. The following two sections will describe each data set and the methods used to analyze them.

Defining Repairability, Digitality and Reusability Through Open-Coding

The first phase of data analysis entailed the development of an open code rubric for categorizing the repair of each object. The open-code included the following categories: *degree of repairability*, *degree of digitality* and the *degree of reusability*. Values for each of the three categories were developed through an iterative process lead by the principal researchers. In order to validate the rubric, two inter-raters assessed all 74 objects using the values defined in each category – first independently and then together to check for any discrepancies. Discrepancies between the open-codes were discussed until an overall agreement was reached.

For degree of repairability, objects were rated as one of the following values: (1) This object is not repaired and not usable; (2) This object is not repaired and is partially usable; (3) There is an attempt to repair this object and it is not usable; (4) There is an attempt to repair this object and it is partially usable; and lastly (5) This object is repaired and is fully usable.

Distinctions of all the objects' type, or *degree of digitality*, were defined, as we were particularly interested in finding examples of repaired digital objects and the processes that lead to their repair. An object's type was determined based on the following values: (1) This object is mechanical - it has no digital mechanisms; (2) This object has both mechanical and digital mechanisms; and finally (3) This object is digital - it only has digital mechanisms.

Objects were then assessed for their *degree of reusability* under the following rubric: (1) This object is no longer usable; (2) This object is used as it is originally intended/designed; and (3) This object is used with new intentions/functions.

By using this rubric, we set out to answer the following questions:

1. Are there visible differences amongst objects repaired versus those unrepaired? Reused or not reused? Repurposed or not repurposed?
2. What can any emerging patterns from the open-coding scheme say about creativity as part of everyday repair?

We describe the results our analysis in the following section.

Open-code Analysis: Results

Based on the open-coding scheme, we defined 64 objects as mechanical, 8 as digital and 2 as a combination of both mechanical and digital parts.

Out of the total digital objects submitted, 63% were assessed as "*not repaired, not usable*." These objects had completely stopped working and could not perform their intended function. The remaining 27% were deemed to be "*not repaired, partially usable;*" these technologies had parts of their hardware broken, but their software parts were still fully functioning.

Out of the total number of mechanical objects, 11% were assessed as *"not repaired, not usable,"* 28% were *"not repaired, still usable,"* 6% were *"repaired, not usable,"* 6% were *"repaired, partially usable,"* and lastly, 48% were *"repaired, fully usable."* Objects where no repairs were made and were no longer functional usually entailed electrical breaks that were beyond the participants' knowledge to fix. Objects where attempts of repair were made but still remained broken fell under the same circumstances where professional knowledge was required. Mechanical objects that were repaired to partial or full usability were simple in their material nature and thus easy to disassemble and put back together.

A particularly interesting outcome of the open-code analysis was the results for the instances of *reuse* of digital objects and mechanical objects. Out of the total digital objects, none of them were reused or repurposed. Conversely, out of all the mechanical objects, 56% were reused as they were originally intended (after their repair), and 31% were repurposed (as an outcome of repair). The implications of reuse in mechanical objects are discussed in more detail in our description of key attributes of repairable objects (See *Affinity Analysis*.)

In summary, it is somewhat unsurprising that a lower number of digital objects were repaired compared to those that were mechanical. This comparison gives evidence of a much larger phenomenon where not only mechanical objects are found to be more 'repairable' than digital objects, they also lend themselves to be more reusable. As an example, four participants described keeping their 'broken' iPods without any attempt to repair or reuse them in a different manner. It can be assumed that this is mainly due to the materials used in their manufacturing process (including hardware and software), which are difficult and often impossible to alter in any way. The value in comparing mechanical and digital objects' degrees of repairability and reusability gives evidence of the need for interaction design to reconsider how digital objects are designed for instances of repair, which can lead to reuse and creative repurposing.

Affinity Analysis: Emerging Attributes of Repairable Objects

What do the findings from the open coding analysis mean for the repair of digital technologies? How can we make sense of the vast difference between digital and mechanical objects and their repairability? Or more pointedly, what can we learn from the creative repair of mechanical objects for informing the design of more reusable digital technologies? To try and answer these questions, we conducted an affinity analysis inspired by Huang and Truong's work in [12].

The affinity analysis entailed a thorough inspection of all 30 surveys where descriptions of broken objects and the process by which they were repaired were identified. These were used as direct quotes and were clustered into similar themed categories through the use of inductive open-coding. The pictures included by the participants also informed the development of these categories. We focused our analysis on the material qualities of the objects' hardware and their *influence* on repair and reuse. Three key material attributes of repair emerged from the analysis. They are described as follows:

1. ***Flexible materials*** – the ability of an object's parts to bend, twist and warp to accommodate its intended functions or entirely new ones.
2. ***Substitutable materials*** – the capacity of an object to be disassembled for the replacement of broken parts. These parts can be either made for it (standardized components), or jerry-rigged from other objects.
3. ***Salvageable materials*** – the ability to salvage broken items in order to create an entirely new structure or system. This has similar qualities to *flexible materials* but focuses more on the reclamation of parts for new contexts of use.

We believe these attributes can facilitate the creativity inherent in everyday design systems based on our observations of repair particular to mechanical objects. We discuss this further on in the paper (see *Discussion*). In the following section we describe each of the three material attributes and provide examples from the surveys.

Flexible Materials

Flexible materials are best described as an object's material ability to bend, twist and warp into new dimensions. The following examples all have some form of flexibility that have allowed their owners the ability to maintain their functionality, or repurpose them into something entirely new.

P19 gives an example of how he fixed the strap of his laptop bag by easily tying the ends together:

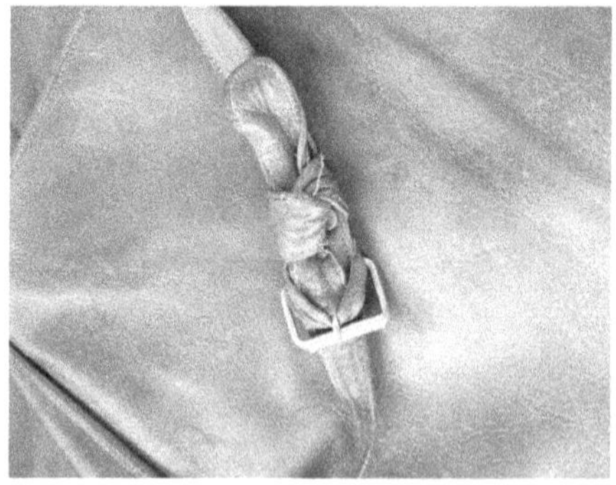

Figure 1. P19's shoulder bag with fixed strap

P19: *"The strap on my laptop bag is broken: the buckle continually comes undone and falls open (meaning the bag falls off my shoulder). It's been like that for at least a year. I 'fixed' it by tying a big knot in the strap above the buckle. So I haven't properly repaired it but the quick fix was good enough that it's lasted for a long time (even though the knot is kind of uncomfortable). I've been meaning to replace or repair the strap, but haven't gotten around to it."*

Flexible materials also allow for easy repurposing of the object entirely. P27 describes how she repurposed her necklace in two novel ways:

P27: *"[An] item that is broken and has new use as of recent is a leather necklace my baby cousin made me a few years ago. The 'pendant' part of it is a string of leather that has been twisted in a circle – kind of like a stove element – and the strap is just a simple long leather strap. The strap broke so now I'm using the strap to hold my curtains open. I glued a small safety pin behind the pendant and now it's a button (I collect buttons).*

In an example submitted by P22, she describes the repair of her old climbing rope by transforming it into a doormat:

P22: *"I have an old climbing rope that could be labeled as 'broken'. It's not suitable as a safety device while climbing anymore but I have woven it into a door mat/ rug and love it once again. (Though it is a very expensive rug). A lot of climbers turn their old ropes into rugs, I would assume that's because you invest a lot into that piece of equipment, both monetarily as well as in trust and care to make sure it functions properly. [...] So I knew to make it into a rug from talking to other climbers about gear and caring for/ retiring it. Also it does function quite well as a rug. I think it would be nicer as a middle-of-the-room large area rug than a doormat (its not the easiest thing to clean/ shake out without needing to tinker with the shape a bit) and it does feel good on bare feet."*

The climbing rope is an exemplar of the simple properties flexible objects have, which allow their owners to easily alter (and creatively resource) their physical properties into forms that could serve their needs in alternative ways.

Figure 2. P22's climbing rope transformed into a doormat.

These examples highlight the ease with which people creatively reuse and repurpose their broken objects based on the flexibility inherent in the objects themselves. The materials found in these objects are typical, everyday resources that have a certain familiarity of use. Consequently, foreseeing solutions to their repair and/or other possible uses come almost as second nature through their design-in-use.

Substitutable Materials

Objects whose parts were easily substitutable facilitated repair by replacing and re-attaching other parts. In the examples that follow, each participant discusses how they were able to repair their objects resourcing other artifacts and systems with similar material qualities. P6 describes the repair of her sunglasses lens as the following:

P6: *[I repaired] my favorite pair of sunglasses that I got for $5. It was missing a screw at the time of purchase so I took a screw from another pair of sunglasses (as I didn't mind breaking it for this pair), and now it is all in one piece. I wear it whenever it's sunny while driving, even if it's not summer anymore. [...] I took the screw from the brown ones at the top to put together the red ones. Unfortunately, the hinge of the red ones recently broke, and I really love this pair so I'm hoping to find one that's similar to screw on - or maybe go to a repair shop.*

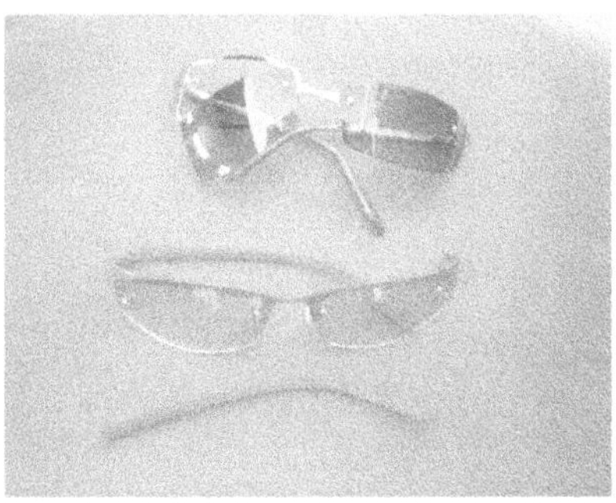

Figure 3. P6's sunglasses repaired with a similar sunglasses' screw.

P6's repair is a common example of the substitutable qualities of common items such as screws, hooks and other adhesives. However, in the next examples P11 and P15 used alternative everyday materials for repairing their objects. These examples demonstrate the use of unobvious materials as resources for creative repair. Note that the flexibility of the materials used were easily adapted to serve the same functionality of the objects' broken parts.

A couple of years ago, P11 and her boyfriend were given a juicer as a housewarming gift. The juicer came broken; the waste collector had a crack in it and was rendered unusable. P11 explains that instead of replacing the juicer altogether, her boyfriend came up with an entirely new solution that proved more effective than the original waste collector.

P11: *The "waste collector" for our juicer broke, so [my boyfriend] put a plastic bag in its place to catch all the fruit spit-outs. It actually works pretty slick because we can just pull the bag off and toss it, without any clean up! I guess he originally tried to use the broken waste collector [only a man!] and shockingly it didn't work-- threw fruit chunks out all over the place. That's where the plastic bag idea came into his head. He did mention that it's great because it requires no clean up, and was nice and easy. The machine/unit part of the juicer has clamps that would attach the waste collector [you'd unattach it for washing purposes], so he just clamped the bag down in its place. Works like a dream.*

Figure 4. P11's juicer with new garbage bag waste collector.

P15 had a similar situation with his popcorn machine where the metal cover (also used for melting butter) went missing. He devised a solution that he describes as follows:

P15: *I have an old popcorn popper that I've had forever. It originally came with a little metal dish to melt butter in. The idea was that as the popcorn pops, the hot air runs under the dish and melts the butter. That dish has been missing for years. Instead, I have a sheet of aluminum foil over the hole where the dish goes. (If you don't cover the dish, the popcorn shoots out the hole and gets all over the kitchen.) In one sense, it's now less functional, since I have to melt the butter in the microwave. In another sense, I've fixed a safety problem: The dish would get darn hot, and I* *remember burning my fingers on it when I was little. I also don't remember why I decided to use tin foil on the popcorn popper. I remember trying to make popcorn once without the butter tray, and popcorn got all over the kitchen. Aluminum foil might have been the first thing I tried.*

Figure 5. P15's popcorn popper with aluminum foil butter-dish replacement.

In both P11's and P15's repairs, we can see that their solutions take on characteristics that are similar to their broken counter-parts. The plastic bag is easily attached to the juicer and performs the same 'container' functions of the original waste collector. Similarly, P15's addition of his own aluminum foil cover takes on the same form as the missing butter dish.

A necessary aspect of substitutable materials is the simplicity of the object's form and function. As observed in the open-coding analysis, virtually all the digital objects had fairly rigid and complex structures making any kind of alteration impossible. There are still considerable challenges to facilitating the everyday repair of technologies whose software and hardware mechanisms are designed with built-in obsolescence. We submit, however, that designing with substitutable parts in mind is a viable place to start informing design practices.

In the following section we describe salvageable materials as a third attribute common to repairable objects. We describe salvageability as a key aspect for the creative repurposing of a broken object, and the degree to which its reuse depends on the presence of both flexible and substitutable parts.

Salvageable Materials

Many of the broken objects we observed were salvaged based on their perceived potential for reuse. An object's reclamation often resulted in the transformation of an object's physical properties towards new functionality – or creative repurposing. In the following examples, we make light of objects whose parts were transformed to create entirely new uses. We focus on the material attributes these objects embodied in facilitating their repair and inevitably, their appropriation.

P13 gives an example of a broken hockey stick in which its state of disrepair is used to function as two window stoppers:

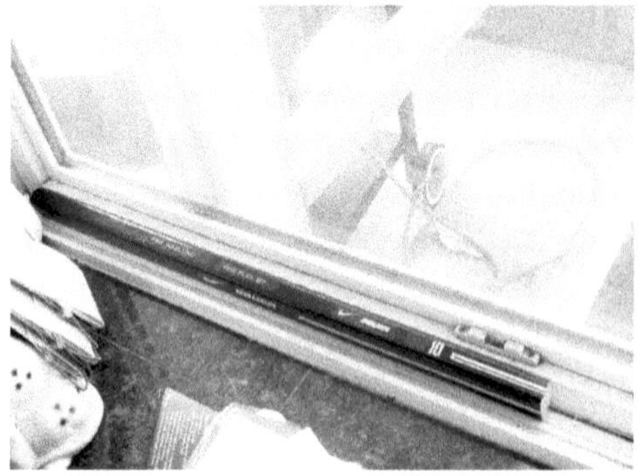

Figure 6. P13's broken hockey stick used as window stoppers.

P13: *"I had a cracked hockey stick, which I cut into two, removing the cracked portion, to use as window stoppers for my own room window and my sister's, because our plastic built-in window "stoppers" broke. (Window "stopper" used to prevent a window from opening fully). I felt the hockey stick graphics were stylish to use as a window "stopper", then just any old piece of wood."*

In this case, the material structure of P13's broken hockey stick was seen as an effective solution for replacing his broken window stoppers. Both the simplicity of the hockey stick's form, as well as the structure of the windowsill itself allowed the two to comply with each other, thus creating an entirely new system. This illustrates the need for designing objects that are simple in their material nature in order to facilitate their reclamation for new contexts of use.

Similar to P13's hockey stick is P15's salvaged piece of plywood that his roommate cut too short when building a part of his desk. Instead of throwing the 'broken' piece of plywood out, P15 found another use for it:

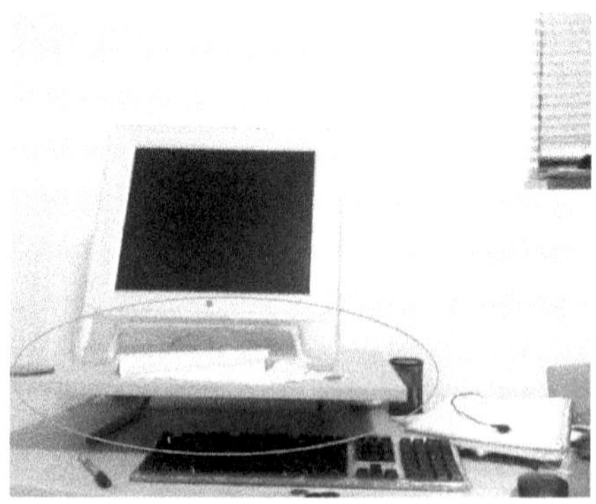

Figure 7. P15's mis-cut piece of plywood reclaimed as a monitor stand.

P15: *"When my roommate got his desk, he went to Home Depot to get some plywood to make a keyboard tray, but he cut the plywood too small and couldn't use it. We kept the board around for months, for no particular reason. Then I* *got a monitor riser for my desk. Except my monitor has an enormous footprint and didn't fit on the riser. I ended up putting the mis-cut plywood between my monitor and the riser, and now the monitor is at the right height. (You can see the feet of the riser underneath the plywood.)"*

The fact that P15 and his roommate had kept the piece of plywood around for 'no apparent reason' speaks to its implicit potential for future use. Again, we attribute this to the simple qualities of its form and the ease with which it substituted the monitor riser in its new context of use.

In summary, the emphasis we wish to draw from the examples shown is the need for flexible, substitutable, and salvageable materials in order to facilitate the creative processes inherent in repair. Furthermore, we stress the need for simplicity as an x-factor in the design of objects' physical materials – it is in the simplicity of form and function that the proposed attributes of repair hinge upon and that without, everyday repairs would less likely occur.

REPAIR, MODIFICATION OR APPROPRIATION?

Through the course of our analysis, we came across various examples of objects that didn't seem to fit the conventional sense of the term 'broken.' Objects that were considered 'repaired' also seemed to border on the line of being a modification. The example of the mis-cut piece of plywood had us reconsider broken to entail either of the following scenarios: (1) an object that is physically impaired (i.e. cracks, tears, dents, etc.), or (2) an object that no longer meets its *expected* functionality.

To illustrate our point further, we use P8's example of his 'broken' staircase and how some house renovations rendered it as an unusable space in his house:

P8: *I have a staircase that's been closed off and I wanted to use it as storage [...] It used to be a functional staircase, but a new floor was added at the top of the staircase, blocking it off. So as a staircase, it no longer functions, and as a storage space, it's very difficult to use. So, sure, I could see [the staircase] as being 'broken.' [...] A little creative re-engineering later, I re-built some Ikea storage units to work in the staircase.*

Was P8's staircase transformation into a storage space a repair or modification? Does a space actually break? At what point do we consider an object (or space) broken if only part of its functionality no longer works? Are the alterations of an unusable but fully intact object/space mean it's just been modified and not repaired? Are these situations then what we know as appropriation?

P8 considered his staircase 'broken' because it no longer functioned as a usable pathway for accessing the top floor to his apartment. We can also see the same issue with the mis-cut plywood – it was deemed broken because it could no longer fulfill its intended purpose as a keyboard tray. If a lack of functionality were a primary delineator for something being broken, would P15's monitor riser be considered broken since it could not hold his computer monitor? Is the addition of the plywood its appropriation and the addition to the riser a modification?

Figure 8. P8's 'broken' staircase reconfigured into storage space.

Given these questions, we believe there are strong correlations between repair and the appropriation of objects in the home. More specifically, we see the impairment of objects as an instigator of creativity that prompts home dwellers to think about alternative uses for their broken or unusable objects.

In the following section, we discuss these considerations within the larger context of our everyday design framework and how our proposed attributes of repair can contribute to our current research within Everyday design and its connection to appropriation.

DISCUSSION

Repair and Everyday Design

We see creative repair having direct parallels with previous observations from our Everyday Design studies [26,27,28]. As mentioned earlier, we describe "users" as a type of designer - someone who remakes and modifies artifacts and systems through the process of *design-in-use*. We argue that repair is also a form of design-in-use as people often explore alternative uses for objects that are deemed unusable or broken.

We recognize emerging synergies between the attributes of repair proposed in this paper and the everyday design frameworks previously published in [26,27,28]. In these papers we describe patterns of everyday design as acts of creativity and highlight the influence social dynamics have on the incremental adaptations of everyday design systems through *materiality* and *substitutability*. We will describe these parallels using the three key aspects of everyday design; these include *resourcefulness*, *adaptation*, and *quality)*, and the notion of *materiality-substitutability* as a key factor for facilitating the social needs of everyday design systems in the home.

In [27] we described *resourcefulness* as the appropriation of artifacts and systems for serving new purposes in the home. We see flexible, substitutable and salvageable materials as key considerations that facilitate acts of resourcefulness. Resourceful behavior can be seen in the repair of P6's sunglasses, as she used another pair's screws to fix them. We also see resourceful behavior with P11's waste collector replacement using a plastic bag for her juicer, and with P15's use of aluminum foil to properly cover his popcorn popper. P15's reuse of his roommate's broken piece of plywood was also resourced as a platform for his monitor riser. What we wish to highlight here is that the need for repair often prompts resourceful actions that lead to creative outcomes that are unique in order to fit individuals' needs and situations.

In terms of *adaptation*, we see various manifestations of adapted objects in situations where parts of broken objects are changed and altered to serve new needs. This is particularly obvious with P22's climbing rope rug and P13's transformed hockey stick into a "window-stopper." Again, these adaptations are made possible through simple functional and physical properties of systems and artifacts.

We also see repair as a process of quality assurance that through design-in-use, compels people to explore and understand an object's materiality and its potential for reuse. *Quality* can be seen most prominently in examples where substitutions and reclamations were made with broken objects. As we describe in [26], *materiality-substitutability* as a necessary factor that extends the use of artifacts and systems by resourcing other objects and adapting them based on their simple functionality. We see this in the example of P11's use of a plastic bag for catching all the excess fruit parts from her juicer. This solution not only repaired the situation with the cracked waste collector, it also simplified the process of cleaning up. We can assume this system has a high degree of quality given P11's continual use of plastic bags when using her juicer.

Quality of an everyday design system, however, is subject to constant change and thus the success of a repair is always under scrutiny. We see quality as an integral part of repair, as people continually assess the degree to which they had met their own expectations, as well as those of others. A lack of quality perceived within a system can often lead to one of two scenarios; the object's disposal (as seen mostly with digital objects), or the adaptation of its broken parts through creative repair.

Given the conceptual overlaps between repair and the everyday design framework, we wish to reconstruct the notion of repair as a type of modification, and as a fundamental part of appropriation. More specifically, we see repair as a higher level of creativity that directly contributes further insights into the process of everyday design in the home. We recognize there's still more work to be done in making the distinctions clear between repair and appropriation. We intend to investigate these ideas further in future work. Ultimately, we hope this research offers provocative insights to current discourses around designing for appropriation and the inherent creativity of everyday designers.

Implications for Interaction Design

The physical attributes proposed in this paper help to describe the relationship between the creative actions of people imposed on the objects they use, and how the physical attributes of these objects facilitate their design-in-use – particularly in instances where repair is a consideration. As for the repair of digital technologies (or lack there of) that was evidenced by our open-code analysis, we see this as a prominent consideration for interaction design. Our analysis suggests that the simple nature of mechanical objects enable repair, though the presence of electronics and computational mechanisms in digital objects add further complexity that make adaptations and resourcefulness difficult. We advocate that designers use the framework of resourcefulness, adaptation and quality as a tool for anticipating a technology's design-in-use, coupled with the framework of physical attributes of repair for facilitating the appropriations made to systems in the home from a material standpoint. We can already learn from current DIY initiatives – particularly with "repair-hacks" who actively find ways of jerry-rigging technology towards new uses.

We see resourcefulness in the repair of more electronic-based objects that are made possible through the use of other flexible objects. As one example, an old expired credit card is used as reinforcements to repair this person's broken headphones (see *Figure 9)*. This person uses electrical tape as an adhesive for strengthening the overall structure. The headphones' are easily repaired using everyday materials like plastic form credit cards and tape. [19]

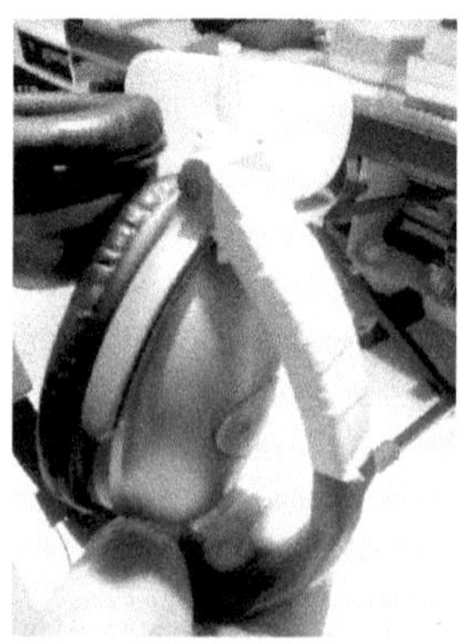

Figure 9: Headphone repair using expired credit cards and electrical tape.
(https://picasaweb.google.com/dmaranan/Jerryrigging?feat=flashalbum#5566932613349931330)

Adaptations of digital technologies are also prevalent in DIY communities. Binaebi Akah discusses the need for people to modify their technologies based on personal identity and through acts of appropriation [2]. She references the *Steampunk* movement as an example of how people make use of the steampunk aesthetic for presenting their personal identity through their technologies. We see glimpses of flexible and substitutable materials present in many of these modifications, which allow everyday people the ability to personalize their technologies based on their own preferences. In the example below, Jake von Slatt modified an old LCD display and keyboard to express the steampunk aesthetic [22].

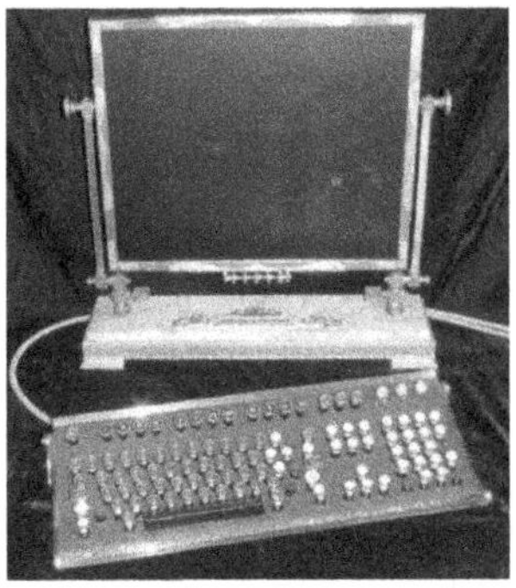

Figure 10 This steampunk keyboard and monitor is made at the Steampunk Workshop (http://steampunkworkshop.com/lcd.shtml). Photo by Irish Typepad from flickr (http://www.flickr.com/photos/irisheyes/2505570986/#/photos/irisheyes/2505570986/lightbox/)

Lastly, *Hack A Day* (hackaday.com) is a blog dedicated to presenting various repaired and reused technologies of those who actively seek ways of repurposing them. We see seeking improvements in quality as an integral part of such communities, as people share how they've salvaged old electronics by finding other accessible parts that improve the way they work. As an example, this hack demonstrates an easy way of utilizing an old alarm clock LCD by using common electronic circuits and arduino (see *Figure 11*) [11]. The programming allows these readily available displays to be used in many new ways.

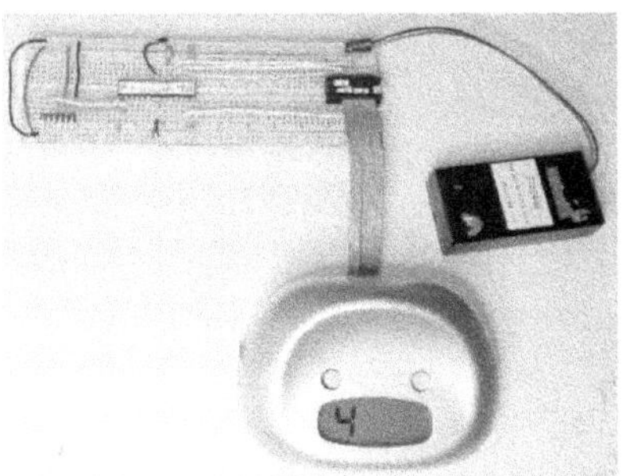

Figure 11: Repaired Alarm clock LCD using arduino and electronic wires. (http://hackaday.com/2011/02/10/driving-a-salvaged-lcd/)

In summary, there are clear directions for future investigations based on the findings presented in this paper. More research is needed for navigating through the challenges of implementing our proposed attributes of repair when designing complex digital technologies. We hope to continue our explorations by finding more examples of repaired and reused digital technologies in the home that can contribute further insights to the current list of repairable physical attributes. As a potential direction, we see the benefit in conducting ethnographic methods for observing the processes of repair in the home over a longer period of time and accounting for other factors that either instigate repair, or prevent it altogether.

CONCLUSION

This study demonstrates the need to consider repair as creative activity in the use, and reuse, of objects in the home. Based on the data collected in the surveys, it is clear that we can learn a lot from the material qualities of mechanical objects – specifically when considering the benefits of their inherent simplicity. Further research in this area can move us towards a framework of design that accommodates for creativity in situations where repair is needed – a scenario that is inevitable once the life of a technology ends.

In this paper we give evidence of the barriers to repairing digital technologies. We see the potential in considering how everyday designers operate as creative agents in the multiple 'lives' of objects – particularly in situations where repair entails the creative re-design of objects through resourceful and adaptive actions to meet new needs. This study also offers a different perspective on what we define as broken given the fine line between something that is no longer useful, or no longer usable. This has significant implications for interaction design, as designers accommodate for situations where repair is a viable option when it comes to the "end" of a technology's lifecycle – whether it means the end of its intended usefulness, or when its use may be appropriated in other ways.

Lastly, we see the need to incorporate flexible, substitutable and reclaimable attributes as key aspects of material use in the design of digital technologies, as inspired by our observations of mechanical objects and the ease with which our participants repaired and creatively reused them. We see this as a useful starting point and intend to investigate these factors further in future work.

ACKNOWLEDGMENTS

We'd like to thank GRAND-NCE for supporting this research initiative. We also thank the Everyday Design team for their contributions and support.

REFERENCES

1. Aguirre, D. How to Design for Repurposing. In *Design for Repurposing*. Retrieved April 17, 2011, from http://www.designforrepurposing.com/

2. Akah, B. and Bardzell, S. Empowering products: personal identity through the act of appropriation. In Proc. Ext. Abstracts CHI EA 2010. ACM, New York, NY, USA, 4021-4026.
3. Balka, E. and Wagner, I. Making things work: dimensions of configurability as appropriation work. In Proc. CSCW '06, (2006). ACM, New York, NY, USA, 229-238.
4. Blevis, E. Sustainable interaction design: invention & disposal, renewal & reuse. In Proc, CHI '07, (2007). ACM, New York, NY, USA, 503-512.
5. Buechley, L., Rosner, D.K., Paulos, E., Williams, A. DIY for CHI: methods, communities, and values of reuse and customization. In Proc. Ext. Abstracts CHI EA, 2009, Boston, MA, USA
6. Bossen, C. and Dalsgaard, P. Conceptualization and appropriation: the evolving use of a collaborative knowledge management system. In Proc. CC '05, (2005) Olav W. Bertelsen, Niels Olof Bouvin, Peter G. Krogh, and Morten Kyng (Eds.). ACM, New York, NY, USA, 99-108.
7. Crabtree, A. and Rodden, T. Domestic routines and design for the home. CSCW, 13. 2004, 191-220.
8. Dewey, J. (1934). Art as experience. New York: Minton Balch.
9. Dourish, P. The Appropriation of Interactive Technologies: Some Lessons from Placeless Documents. CSCW, 12, 4 (2003), 465-490.
10. Gaver, W., Beaver, J., and Benford, S. Ambiguity as a resource for design. In Proc. CHI '03, (2003). ACM, New York, NY, USA, 233-240.
11. Hack a Day. Retrieved April 21, 2011, from: http://hackaday.com/2011/02/10/driving-a-salvaged-lcd/
12. Huang, E., and Truong, K. Breaking the disposable technology paradigm: opportunities for sustainable interaction design for mobile phones. In Proc. CHI '08, 2008. ACM, New York, NY, USA, 323-332.
13. Höök, K. Designing familiar open surfaces. In Proc. NordiCHI '06, (2006), Anders Morch, Konrad Morgan, Tone Bratteteig, Gautam Ghosh, and Dag Svanaes (Eds.).
14. Huh, J., Nathan, L. P ., Silberman, S., Blevis, E., Tomlinson, B., Sengers, P., and Busse, D. Examining appropriation, re-use, and maintenance for sustainability. In Proc. Ext. Abstracts CHI EA 2010. ACM, 2010, 4457-4460.
15. Jung, H., Blevis, E., Stolterman, E. (unpublished). Conceptualizations of the Materiality of Digital Artifacts and their Implications for Sustainable Interaction Design. University of Indiana.
16. Kaptelinin, V. and Nardi, B.A. 2009. Acting with Technology: Activity Theory and Interaction Design. The MIT Press.
17. Odom, W., Pierce, J., Stolterman, E., and Blevis, E. Understanding why we preserve some things and discard others in the context of interaction design. In Proc. CHI '09, (2009). ACM, New York, NY, USA, 1053-1062.
18. Östlin, J., Sundin, E., Björkman, M. (2009) Product Life-cycle Implications for Remanufacturing Strategies. J. Clean. Prod. 17: 999-1009.
19. Maranan, D. Jerryrigging. Retrieved April 21, 2011, from: https://picasaweb.google.com/dmaranan/Jerryrigging?feat=flashalbum#5566932613349931330
20. Sengers, P., and Gaver, B., 2006. Staying open to interpretation: engaging multiple meanings in design and evaluation. In Proc. DIS '06, (2006). ACM, New York, NY, USA, 99-108.
21. Shu, L., Flowers, W. Considering remanufacture and other end-of-life options in selection of fastening and joining methods. In Proc. IEEE '95, (1995). Orlando, FL, USA, 75–80.
22. Slatt, Jake Von, Steampunk Workshop. Retrieved April 21 from: http://steampunkworkshop.com/lcd.shtml
23. Takeuchi, S. and Saitou, K. Design for product embedded disassembly. In Proc. IDETC/CIE ASME '95, (2005), California, USA.
24. Taylor, A.S. and Swan, L., Artful systems in the home. In Proc. CHI 2005, (2005), 641-650.
25. Tolmie, P., Pycock, J., Diggins, T., MacLean, A. and Karsenty, A., Unremarkable computing. In Proc. CHI'02, (2002), ACM Press, 399-406.
26. Wakkary, R., Maestri, L., Four Factors of Change – Adaptations of Everyday Design, CHI '11 (2011), ACM Press – in print.
27. Wakkary, R., and Maestri, L. 2007. The resourcefulness of everyday design. In Proc. C&C '07, (2007). ACM, New York, NY, USA, 163-172.
28. Wakkary, R., Tanenbaum, K., A Sustainable Identity: The Creativity of an Everyday Designer, In Proc. CHI '09, (2009), Boston, ACM Press, pp. 365-374.

Traces in Creative Spaces

Jelle van Dijk
Research Centre Technology and Innovation,
Utrecht University of Applied Sciences
P.O. Box 182, 3500AD Utrecht, Netherlands
jelle.vandijk@hu.nl
+31 6 23156597

Gerrit Willem Vos
Department of Industrial Design
Eindhoven University of Technology
P.O. Box 513, 5600MB Eindhoven, Netherlands
g.w.vos@student.tue.nl
+31 6 13380099

ABSTRACT
We organized one-week 'IncompanyLabs' (i.e. on site co-design activities) at three different creative companies, seeking opportunities for an embodied interactive media tool to support creative sessions. Our concept TRACES is an interactive floor guiding the creation of shared insights and supporting taking the step from individual thinking to group-level integration. User explorations with a Wizard-of-Oz prototype revealed directions for improving the interaction quality and indicated how a system like TRACES could act as a 'scaffold' for discussion.

ACM Classification Keywords
H.1.2. Models and Principles: User/Machine Systems
H.5.2. User Interfaces: Theory and methods, Prototyping

General Terms:
Design, Human Factors, Theory

Authors' Keywords:
Embodied, Situated Cognition, Movement, Interaction, Shared Understanding, Creativity, Traces

INTRODUCTION
Increasingly, companies are developing dedicated physical spaces with the purpose of facilitating creative sessions for clients. These sessions aim to produce new design opportunities, solutions for organizational problems, or simply new creative input from company employees. Since the majority of these participants are inexperienced with creative sessions, professional facilitators guide the creative process with the aid of various methods, tools and the space itself in order to spur the creative process. Typically, a creative process is characterized as a process by which people associatively build on each other's contributions by generating new ideas, to get outside of the mind's beaten track, or, as one says, to think 'out of the box' [6].

C&C'11, November 3–6, 2011, Atlanta, Georgia, USA.

Shared insight
Apart from being creatively stimulated, during these sessions people typically also gradually develop a deeper understanding of the original design challenge. Research has shown that a deeper understanding of the problem *co-evolves* with generation and evaluation of proposals for solving it [3]. Ideally, as individual participants question and learn from each other, people's understanding of the design challenge will gradually merge into a robust, group-level insight. However, this does not always happen, since people easily misunderstand one another, or incorrectly believe that they are talking about the same thing, or have difficulty in 'letting go' their own line of thought in service of the group process [5]

Scaffolding in creative sessions
Inspired by the theory of embodied situated cognition [2,4], we hold that the formation of shared insight is supported by continuous interactions with (adaptations and re-organizations of), physical elements in the environment. In the typical creative session this involves post-its, sketches, diagrams on the whiteboard, and personal notes. These creations on physical materials are what we call the 'traces' people leave behind as a result of the creative process. Traces are not only 'results', outcomes of a process; they are also used as 'things to think with' [5], that is, they function as 'cognitive scaffolds' [2]. For instance, in deictic referencing, one may point to a sketch or post-it and use words such as 'that one' and 'over there'. As a result, much of the implicit knowledge needed for shared understanding need not be made explicit. One can simply 'see' what the other person means.

In short, our concept proposal aims to support communication and the development of shared insight offering new ways of creating 'traces' and using them as cognitive scaffolds.

INCOMPANY LABS
We organized three one-week IncompanyLabs, which entailed empirical studies *in situ* at three different companies involved in the project. Each of these companies have access to their own creative spaces and facilitate creative sessions for their clients. We held interviews with facilitators, observed creative sessions and held co-design workshops.

Fig. 1. Participants of a co-design workshop reflecting on the 'live-sketched' storyboards

In each week we developed a concept which we discussed as a lo-fi prototype with company employees in an acting-out activity. Acting outs were live sketched by an artist into a storyboard which was then discussed by employees and designers in the same meeting.

Being 'on site' for a week proved beneficial for getting in touch with end-users and creating a good feel of the everyday affairs in the context of practice. Meanwhile, we sought to link principles of embodied theory to our observations of practice, and from those links create concepts. Since we had researcher-designer double roles, our design activities were not separated from analyzing the practice and assessing user experiences. Interpreting, communicating, creating and evaluating ideas were all intertwined and mutually informing [7]. Our guiding rule was to ground the emerging concept both in the theory *and* in the context of practice, in parallel.

Fig. 2. Participants of a co-design workshop working with one of the concepts that entails an interactive floor.

Results of the InCompanyLabs

We asked how shared insight is formed in practice, and what role do physical 'traces' and the space itself play in that process. We summarize our results below:

- Participants may lose 'commitment' to the process, going from small subgroups to plenary sessions. In subgroups individual people are recognized and feel free to contribute individual ideas on post-its. Later on it is difficult committing oneself to plenary conclusions, especially if these are represented by conclusions written by a facilitator on a flip-chart for a 'passive' audience.
- Facilitators attempt to control the session's evolution but also express the wish to let the session evolve 'bottom up' without too much interference. Giving people something to *do* seems to help participants into taking an active role in the session's evolution.
  Quote: "I sometimes just give them a marker and tell them to write down their thoughts and ideas, that should get them involved."

Fig. 3. What is important in these post-its to take with during the session? What should be 'stored'?

- There is a paradox of wanting to save all physical traces (e.g. by taking pictures) for fear of losing an important insight along the way, while people already say they know they are never going to look into these materials later on.
- For participants the activities of sorting out and integrating all the physical materials could be very beneficial for creating integrated insight, however, the facilitator alone mostly does this physical activity of 'wrapping up'. Participants are active during generation of ideas, and more passive during the 'converging' steps of the process.
- Facilitators are afraid that participants will not keep the 'spirit' of the session alive after the session has ended. Quote: "When people step into their car, they are already thinking about their next appointments." Personal transformation of people should happen in the session itself, because it is less likely to occur afterwards.

THE CONCEPT: TRACES

Based on three early concepts of the Incompany Labs we created TRACES, an interactive floor that invites participants to be actively involved in showing and discussing with others ones own insights, gathered during the session. TRACES stimulates an active dialog between participants, but acknowledges as a starting point their individual thoughts and commitments. The central floor of the creative space acts as a medium to convey and visualize the thought processes of the individual, as well as the emerging insights (the session's 'results') on the group level.

How it works

Each participant is asked to take photos of all physical materials that were created and proved useful in the earlier phases, like sketches, diagrams, post-its, objects, or even people. These 'traces', which support the participant's thought process, serve as a representation of ones current 'view' on the session. When stepping on to the central meeting floor, a circle with 'your' traces is projected around you, enabling you to walk around with them.

Fig. 4. Interact with your own personal traces using your feet

One interacts using ones feet (Fig. 4). Stepping on to a trace lets you move them around, or throw them away. That way, participants can re-arrange, adjust, or sort out, their traces before stepping into the discussion. The traces provide a first eye-catcher and aid in visualizing people's viewpoints. Participants are able to give traces to each other, or build up a shared set on the ground. For this purpose, a shared workspace can be created to enable the integration of multiple viewpoints (Fig. 5).

Fig. 5. Integrate ideas in a shared workspace.

People in a conversation can link to a physical placeholder by sliding traces onto it, (Fig. 6), which forms the start of working from personal ideas towards shared insights.

Fig. 6. Placeholders become carriers of group insights

EXPLORATIVE USER STUDY

An explorative user study was set up to gain an understanding about the photos on the floor that act as a trace, supports the creation of shared insights, and how participants would experience the interaction. For this purpose a Wizard-of-Oz prototype was created which enabled participants to experience working with circles of traces on the floor, while being free to 'invent' interactions and elements in the interface.

Fig. 7. Participants of the user study discussing their 'traces' during a brainstorm.

The participants, three groups of four engineering students and/or researchers working on a similar design project, were asked to work individually for 10 minutes on a real design problem they currently faced in their projects. During this session they received digital cameras with which they could create personal 'traces' of the problems, ideas or insights that had emerged in this session and which would later on be used in the user study. This way the topic to be discussed with help from the prototype was valid and interesting enough to start a discussion.

Observations of use

Throughout the user study there were several recurring trends and interaction patterns, which we summarize here:

- Participants work from an individual workspace to a shared workspace. The circles were used as an individual space for organizing ones traces and bringing them into focus for the others to see. From this individual space, personal traces were added to a shared workspace in between the participants where they were integrated into a 'collage' that became a scaffold of a discussion or shared insight.
- Resizing a trace on the floor altered its meaning in the discussion. Participants would make a trace bigger or smaller to bring it in and out of focus, or define its importance amongst multiple traces. Enlarged traces became a representation of the discussion or shared insight it stood for, while smaller traces became carriers of detailed, or 'extra', information.

- Participants would use either their own traces or those of others to refer to during discussions. A trace would be brought into focus or pointed at to illustrate an argument they were currently having.
- Participants showed commitment to personal traces in their workspace and awareness about others being able to see their 'thoughts'. Adding a trace to the shared workspace was well deliberated and discussed, each of the participants showing an active approach to the discussion.
- Participants showed a strong need for 'parking' traces that were part of a shared insight created. Quote: "Perhaps it is a good idea to lock these ideas in place". The meaning of a trace changes when combined with others. They become a trace of a new discussion or insight.

DISCUSSION AND CONCLUSION

We have created TRACES, a concept for an interactive floor by means of which people can be more actively engaged with the 'traces' of their own creative activities, especially during the 'integration' phase. TRACES promises to support a higher personal commitment by participants towards group-level insights than in traditional settings. It may at first seem to be a more individually oriented tool and less supporting 'group-level' processes, but this is precisely what we aim for: using TRACES, people start from an individual perspective (to which they *are* committed), and by means of multiple local interactions with other individuals they slowly work towards group-level insights, grounding the new insights in their original ideas.

Our hypothesis is that this activity creates stronger commitment then when one is passively staring at a *powerpoint* show with 'the main conclusions', presented by a facilitator. On a side note, this process of multiple local interactions from which new insight gradually emerges is actually rather similar to our own research-through-design process in which we have intertwined generative design activities and analysis by reflection iteratively [cf. 7].

TRACES supports this process by making use of people's own 'cognitive scaffolds' and invites them not only to create materials during idea generation but also to actively use these materials during the integration phase. The idea is that shared insights develop gradually while the group discussion is 'scaffolded' by people's embodied interactions with their own 'traces'. Over time, local interactions between people, scaffolded by the traces on the floor, will produce new, long-term traces locked to physical placeholders, representing group-level insights, scaffolding the creation of shared results to which all participants have actively contributed and to which they feel committed.

In the end, TRACES promises to by-pass the need to store 'results' in an offline, static report, since the active reworking and re-organizing of ones traces will already bring about the necessary personal transformation in the participants during the session itself. Instead of focusing on the results of a session as an object to take home, TRACES allows for the session itself to be the main result.

NEXT STEPS

In this paper we presented a work-in-progress which is the outcome of several IncompanyLabs. The prototype represents a physical hypothesis that is the outcome of this research, but also forms the start for a second project, currently in progress. As a first result, we created a working system with six multiple beamers, creating a large floor for interaction, as well as stable, real-time tracking of individual people using the *Microsoft Kinect* system. The main steps that will be taken next in this project are:

- Testing of the basic concept in an experimental setting. Different aspects of the concept will be tested by letting multiple groups work in a creative session with two different conditions: with a working prototype versus no/adjusted prototype (control condition).
- Improving and detailing of the interaction design by taking directions for improvement from the user study into account.

ACKNOWLEDGMENTS

We like to thank Martijn van de Wiel, Van Berlo, YOUMEET, LEF, Sippe Duisters, Sijme Geurts, Remko van der Lugt and Kees Overbeeke. This research was funded by a CELL grant from the Dutch Ministry of Economic Affairs

REFERENCES

1. Cross, N., *Developments in Design Methodology,* Chichester: John Wiley (1984).
2. Clark, A., *Being there: Putting brain, body and world together again.* Cambridge, MA: MIT Press. (1997)
3. Dorst, K., On the problem of design problems-problem solving and design expertise, *Journal of Design Research*, 4(3), (2004).
4. Kirsh, D., Thinking with external representations. *AI & Society*, 25, (2010) 441-454.
5. Kleinsmann, M., Valkenburg, R., and Buijs, J.. Why do(n't) actors in collaborative design understand each other? An empirical study towards a better understanding of collaborative design. In *CoDesign*, 5(1), (2007), 1-15
6. Osborn, A.F. *Applied Imagination.* New York: Scribner's. 3d ed. (1963)
7. Schön, D.A., *The reflective practitioner - how professionals think in action.* New York: Basic Books. (1983).

Enduring Interaction: An Approach to Analysis and Design of Animated Gestural Interfaces in Creative Computing Systems

Kenny K. N. Chow
School of Design
The Hong Kong Polytechnic University
sdknchow@polyu.edu.hk

D. Fox Harrell
Comparative Media Studies Program
Computer Science and AI Laboratory
Massachusetts Institute of Technology
fox.harrell@mit.edu

ABSTRACT

This paper provides an interdisciplinary reflection on the nature meaning-making involving users and animated gestural interfaces. In particular, we propose a new model for analysis of creative computing systems incorporating gestural input into dynamically animated interfaces. Our contributions are based on a theoretical framework synthesizing embodied cognition approaches in cognitive science, phenomenology in philosophy, and user interface design in computing. We introduce the term *enduring interaction* to refer to the phenomenon of bodily and conceptually engaging interaction within constantly changing computational environments. Our construct centralizes the issue of how users' motor-sensory experiences inform their construction of meaning in the design of interactive systems. We argue that *creative computing systems*, a class of artifacts including types of hobbyist websites, video games, and computer-based artworks, require a new design perspective quite distinct from user-centric interface design approaches focused on productivity-oriented applications. Using examples including outcomes of the Gestural Narrative and Interactive Expression (GeNIE) project (Harrell, PI; Chow and Erik Loyer collaborators) along with existing prevalent, exceptional, or historically significant artifacts, we articulate a continuum of various kinds of engagement, showing design implications of our perspective, enabling users to use gestural interaction (through multi-touch and gyroscope/accelerometer-based input devices) to result in narratively salient, evocative, and even intimate interaction mechanisms in interactive narrative environments.

Keywords

interface design, embodied cognition, phenomenology, digital media, gestural interfaces

ACM Classification Keywords

J.5 Computer Applications: ARTS AND HUMANITIES.

General Terms: Design, Theory.

C&C'11, November 3–6, 2011, Atlanta, Georgia, USA.

1. INTRODUCTION

"Do you wish to continue reading the paper?" asks a character in an interactive narrative game. You, the player, have four discrete choices to choose from: (1) "yes," (2) "no," (3) "is it a technical paper?" or (4) "is creativity a significant focus of the paper?" Your discrete choice, selected by mouse-click, will result in a discrete response by the system, continuing a conversation. It is a feedback loop involving a turn-based exchange. Now, imagine instead a system in which the same question is asked, but in response you rest your hand on a multi-touch screen. As the character asks questions, you might continuously slide your finger up and down, puppeteering your own character's nodding head to indicate a "yes" response. Or you might use your finger to draw a '^' shape, raising a character's eyebrow to express skepticism, followed by your performance of a pinch-in motion using your fingers to result in your character's mood becoming more withdrawn. The computer-controlled character's facial expression *continuously changes in response to your actions*.

Imagine now, a computer hang-gliding simulator in which you must hold a mobile gaming device with a built in gyroscope ahead of you. Without thinking about what commands to use, you gently tilt the device from the left to the right, signaling shifting of your character's weight rightward, causing the hang-glider to bear into the simulated easterly wind. Seamlessly, continuously, you are *deploying a now habituated movement in response to the computational environment at hand*: the hang-glider has drifted in the direction you intended.

In each of these imagined scenarios, a type of habituated gestural interaction was scaled appropriately to the device in hand. The interface also required response to a continuously changing animated environment. We call this phenomenon, to be defined in Section 3 below, ***enduring interaction***, and argue that accounting for such phenomena is important as recent gestural interface systems grow increasingly robust.

With increased popular deployment of gestural interfaces in systems such as the Nintendo Wii, Microsoft Kinect for Xbox 360, mobile phones with multi-touch screens and built-in gyroscopes and accelerometers, and laptop computers equipped with touchpads, it has become apparent that computational media objects engage users not just in sensory perception, but also in increasing degrees of motor-based bodily interaction. A user whose attention is absorbed in engagement with audio-visual content, for example in a game where one must perform dance-like moves at certain rhythmic intervals, is also driven to take timely action and to react promptly because the artifact invites user participation meanwhile continuing to show a concert-like animated visual presentation. The body of the user is engaged continuously, in terms of attention – like being captivated in a theater performance, and also alternately, in terms of action – like participating in a tennis game.

Furthermore, while there are some accounts focused on usability of such interfaces, there are few accounts of such interfaces for creative computational media that have expressive aims such as hobbyist websites, video games, and computer-based artworks. We turn to an interdisciplinary framework, primarily based on embodied cognition perspectives from cognitive science, phenomenology in philosophy, in addition to user-interface design in computing, to better understand enduring interaction and to suggest new design strategies for systems employing this interaction paradigm, particularly creative computing systems. This paper develops and synthesizes theoretical models from Chow's Ph.D. dissertation work on embodied cognition approaches to animation, Chow and Harrell's work on the same, and recent results of the National Endowment for the Humanities (NEH)-funded Gestural Narrative and Interactive Expression (GeNIE) project (Harrell, Principal Investigator; Chow and Erik Loyer collaborators).

In this paper, we describe processes of expressive meaning-making involving significant motor-sensory interaction. Section 2 provides further motivation for our theoretical framework and grounds our argument in a synthesis of existing theories. In Section 3, we focus on specific ways that bodily motion and temporality are central to these analyses. With emphases on motility and temporality, we explain the idea of *enduring interaction* as a continuum of degrees of interface engagement varying in these two major parameters in Section 4.

2. THEORETICAL FRAMEWORK

When engaging in enduring interaction, the user makes meaning through simultaneous engagement of sensory and motor apparatuses with the system. On the sensory side, the user understands animated visual images at both immediate (perceptual) and metaphorical (conceptual) levels through what we call material-based imagination [1]. On the motor side, as we argue in this paper, the user also makes *conceptual* meaning through performing bodily motor action. A common example is a user running his or her fingers over a touchpad and seeing pages scrolling in a window as a result. That user might be provoked to imagine the scrolling process as reminiscent of panning a camera over the document. The two sides conjoin in a motor-sensory feedback loop, constituting conceptually meaningful interaction between the user and the system. Based upon this loop, users can imaginatively elaborate new meanings from the experience at hand.

Indeed, everyday experiences that provide a basis for imaginative elaboration involve our bodies in motor-sensory connections. For example, a lifestyle application on a tablet computer displaying a digital pond presents fish that do not only swim around, but also respond to user stimuli like pointing or touching – metaphorically suggesting that the fish are alive. This sense that the fish are alive is an imaginative elaboration of the perception of the fish as merely dynamic animated CGI artifacts. Understanding similar motor-sensory loops in familiar human environments where we similarly see artifacts as lively can help in understanding and designing how users engage in creative and expressive systems. The theoretical framework in this section informs our understanding of such systems.

2.1 Meaning between Bodies and Environments: Feedback and Affordances

Various motor-sensory loops exist in interaction between users and systems in different scenarios. When riding a bike, typing on a keyboard, playing computer games with the gamepad, or using other motion-sensing input devices, a user has to engage part or all of the body in "controlling" the machine and "sensing" the feedback. When these actions become conventionalized and second nature, the interaction mechanisms are similar to general cases in which living creatures deploy extensions of the body as control mechanisms. For example, consider a sparrowhawk subtly adjusting its wings to change its trajectory in order to swerve in response to an updraft of wind and nearby building. Our use of interface objects can become so second-nature that they effectively become extensions of our bodies like the birds wingtip feathers.

Quite a few scholars have paid attention to the similarities in interaction mechanisms between engineered systems and physical environments. Norbert Wiener is credited with introducing the term "cybernetics" for the study of control and communication theories in animals and machines [2] (p.19). His awareness of the value of attending to people's ongoing interactions with objects in their environments reminds us that observation of the natural environments and their inhabitants is informative to designing interactive systems because of the forgotten commonalities between two sets of environments. Recall the first time that one attentively uses the mouse to drag a file icon onto a folder icon in a GUI environment. The users keeps moving the mouse while tracking the moving file icon on the display until it reaches the folder. This motor-sensory phenomenon is reminiscent of our physical experience of sliding a paper across a table in an office. We need to "see" something being "moved" from one location to another. In the GUI environment, after being quite attentive during an initial experience, a user no longer notices details of the action after many repetitions. Current users are quite accustomed to operating a wide array of input devices and interpreting sensory feedback from these systems, much like the way our bodies get used to physical environments. Digitally mediated environments absorb the body no less than the physical environment.

In addition, J. J. Gibson's theory of affordances also calls attention to a vital link between bodies and environments. Gibson coined the term "affordance" to mean those environmental features that support what actors can do. Gibson believes that these properties in an environment, whether natural or the artificial (in fact Gibson dismisses this dichotomy in environments as in [3] (p. 130)), are usually directly perceivable, without requiring much learning (p. 143). This idea inspired Donald Norman's asserting that in designing interfaces affordances should be made perceivable and noticeable to users [4] (pp. 22-23). How? As Gibson puts it, "affordances are properties taken with reference to the observer" (p. 143). A property that is "commensurate with the body of the observer" is "more easily picked up." Therefore, Gibson's idea reminds us that accounting for relative scales between bodies and environments should be a more central concern in interaction and interface design. This idea of human-scale embodiment, as we shall show in Section 3.1, applies to not only spatial concerns, but also temporal.

2.2 Meaning in Tools: Dourish's Embodied Interaction

With an awareness of the role of the body in designing interactive systems, Paul Dourish advocates an approach to interaction design grounded in the idea of embodiment. Dourish draws upon notions from phenomenology, particularly Martin Heidegger's "being-in-the-world," to interpret embodiment as people's engagement in the world in order to make meaning of it [5] (p. 126). For Dourish, engagement includes both physical and social interactions. Therefore, to create embodied interactive systems he suggests making use of people's "familiarity" with the mundane everyday world, including practical experiences with physical objects and communication skills in social communities. His book delineates several high-level principles to achieve this goal.

By embodiment, Dourish seems to mean largely the embodiment of tools in the working environment. This bias toward utilitarian situations may originate from Heidegger. As in his well-known hammer analogy describing that a carpenter would only see a hammer available for his tasks (what he calls "ready-to-hand"), Heidegger presupposed a "work-world" in his pronounced dictum [6] (p. 233). It follows that Dourish's proposal also emphasizes the practical and functional meaning of everyday world objects and tools. Although this meaning of "everyday experience" with objects is in line with the major notion of phenomenological embodiment [7] (p. 36), we believe that Dourish's approach can be complimented by approaches that focus to an even greater degree on the body that uses those objects. Our approach focuses less on systems oriented toward productivity (though our ideas apply in those cases too), instead primarily addressing culturally-oriented creative systems. Instead of tools, we also address creative computing systems whose aims are expressive, aesthetic, and/or playful.

2.3 Meaning in Bodies: Merleau-Ponty on Motility

Maurice Merleau-Ponty asserted that the "body is our general medium for having a world" through motor habit [8] (p. 146). Based on Gelb and Goldstein's empirical studies of brain-impaired patients, Merleau-Ponty describes two types of bodily movement, namely "greifen," meaning "to seize," and "zeigen," as "to show" (p. 123). The former refers to concrete movements toward some existing objects, while the latter refers to abstract movements not relevant to any actual situation, but dependent upon one's imagination. For example, an impaired patient may be able to touch her or his forehead because of a mosquito bite, but not able to point to it without preparatory movement. A typical subject can perform a hand-to-forehead salute, but the patient cannot do so without placing himself in an actual situation that calls for it. The patient cannot enter into the situation if forced to only imagine it. This helps to reveal the fact that unimpaired people have turned most abstract movements, like pointing or other gestures, into situated motor habits. Merleau-Ponty believes that it is our body that actually absorbs meaning, in the form of bodily experience (pp. 146-147). In Hubert Dreyfus's words, our body gets involved through practice and acquires bodily skills [9].

Merleau-Ponty posited that what is impaired in the patient is the "power of laying out a past in order to move toward(s) a future." He called this the "intentional arc," which is our disposition, attitude, and *aboutness* toward something (pp. 135-136). The intentional arc exists in both space and time and works beneath the level of conscious conceptualization. Through repeated practice, we enrich our repertoire of actions within the intentional arc [9]. It is the way we acquire bodily skills and build motor habits. Our bodies "absorb" motor knowledge and take care of our everyday motion [9]. Therefore, a typical subject can perform seemingly imaginary abstract movements based on the intentional arc as easily as concrete movements at the immediate cognitive level. This *motility*, as Merleau-Ponty puts it, reveals our consciousness as "not a matter of 'I think that' but of 'I can'" move toward something [8](p. 137). In other words, bodily motion performed in space and time embodies one's intention. This dictum underpins the notion of enduring interaction.

3. ENDURING INTERACTION: MOTIVE INPUT AND ENDURING ENVIRONMENT

The theoretical framework above has been meant to reinforce the importance of attending to issues of embodiment in meaning construction using devices for gestural interfaces. Specific important points that motivate the need for our concept of enduring interaction include that:

- relative scales between our bodies and environments matter not only in physical interaction with the world, but interaction with digital devices,
- meaning is embodied not just in the ways we use tools, but also in how our bodies act upon expressive artifacts like devices for entertainment media,
- our bodies can turn any movements into motor habits that reveal our intentionality toward things.

In this section, we shall further show that meaning is best embodied in movement taking place in an animated computational environment and time frame that closely matches our bodily and perceptual scales.

In creative computational media, this goal can be achieved by mobilizing two sides of the motor-sensory connection: (1) user input contains *motion components that are significant to user intention*; and (2) this user input is in *response to a continuously changing environment*. We call the paradigm of interaction mechanisms consisting of these two mobilized qualities ***enduring interaction*** in contrast to the discrete, conversational style of alternating computer-human interaction, like the classical command-line interface, or the conventional point-and-click mouse-based input mechanisms found in many GUIs.

HCI research has offered an approach called enactive interaction, which is related to ours. Yet, there are also significant differences between the concept of enduring interaction and the concept of enactive interaction. What the terms share is a concept of interface design that centralizes motor and perceptual actions and responses between users and computers. Enactive interface research explores new kinds of interfaces representing a paradigm shift in HCI from symbolic, iconic knowledge representation toward more motor-sensory-oriented forms. [10] The diffence between the terms is that rather than addressing a broad, over-arching agenda, the term enduring interaction has a more narrow focus in an emergent domain – creative computing systems. These types of system often require specific attention to the embodiment of intentionality and temporality.

3.1 Motive Input: Spatiotemporal Embodiment of User Intention

The two types of bodily action mentioned by Merleau-Ponty aid in articulating commonly assumed general divide between mechanisms of user input in HCI, (1) point-and-click (or related types if discrete, command oriented input) versus (2) on-going gestural input. The former corresponds to "grasping," whereas the latter "showing." Our aim is not to detract from conventional point-and-click mechanisms, indeed they can be usefully deployed as shown by various examples provided by Ben Shneiderman's idea of direct manipulation. As Shneiderman puts it, the primary goal of direct manipulation is to bring human-computer activity back to the level of early stages of Jean Piaget's theory of child development, in which children comprehend largely through physical actions. Interfaces based on this principle should be easier for children, not to mention adults, to use [11]. That is to say, direct manipulation requires not much learning and just demands users of the innate capabilities of concrete movements.

On the other hand, the concept of gestural interfaces en vogue in HCI often envisions users performing abstract movements with their empty hands, such as pointing. Early research on gestural input includes Richard Bolt's interface combining finger-pointing and speech-ordering [12], Alan Wexelblat's feature-based approach [13], and others. These research works built upon rigorous reviews of gesture taxonomy and non-verbal human communication.

However, we argue against any hard distinction between the two types of motor input in human-computer interaction. Repeated use of any input mechanisms in digital environments would enrich, to use the terminology of Merleau-Ponty cited above, our "intentional arcs," turning any possible movement into a motor habit. For example, double-clicking a mouse button is a learned (and arbitrary) *gesture* at first, but repeated exercising turns it into a meaningful *habitual action* embodying a user's intention to confirm. Hence, stringently separating gestural input from other more discrete types of motor input might not lead us toward tighter motor-sensory connection and more embodied meaning in interactive systems. Instead, distinctions should be drawn based on whether a given type of motor input contains meaningful (intentional with respect to the computational environment) motion components related to our intentional arc. That is whether the gestural input it a type of situated, embodied, and evocative motion.

Consider the jog dial of a video tape recorder (VTR). When a user spins the dial, the motion, including speed and direction, conveys his or her intention of going forward or backward at variable speed. This kind of motion has already been borrowed as a gesture of hurry in live performance, in which the spinning speed roughly reflects the hurriedness! (Figure 1) Similar motion-based signals can be applied to computer interaction as well, such as circling on the touchpad to browse through a huge image database. Therefore, we call for a specific kind of motor input, called *motive input*, in which motion embodies the intentional arc in space and time with meaning and information. In other words, many types of bodily motion, with repeated use and practice, will be spatiotemporal embodiment of intention.

When one performs a bodily action, body parts such as hands or fingers, move in different directions quickly or slowly, continuously in time, carrying and conveying one's various intentions. We believe interactive systems can be designed for tighter motor-sensory links and potential for more evocative meaning-making by taking these spatiotemporal bodily scales into consideration.

Figure 1: Use of the jog dial of a VTR

3.2 Enduring Environment: Temporal Embodiment of System Behavior

Since Merleau-Ponty's work discussed above, other thinkers have focused on how our bodies interact with worldly situations. Cognitive scientists George Lakoff and and Mark Johnson believe that bodily interaction comprises the basis for much of both everyday and higher level, conceptual thought. They assert that most of our early-acquired cognitive models are based on motor-sensory experiences of the world, called image schemas. For example, we encounter artifacts such as tubs containing water as infants, so we might also project a container metaphor onto abstract concepts, as when we understand a tribe as living "in" the forest [7] (p. 36). The theory of image schemas is a powerful tool for us to understand how we reason based on spatial logic. However, although image schemas are based on motor-sensory actions, which necessarily carry both spatial and temporal dimensions, many examples seem to emphasize spatial relations while downplaying temporality. As is well discussed in the cognitive linguistics literature, because time is an abstract concept, we are used to spatializing time metaphorically. When we say the "flow" of time, we may mean seeing time as a moving object (e.g., a river) from a static observer's viewpoint. In short, we conceive of time in a source-path-goal schema in which we situate our body. It seems that our inclination to reason spatially is a result of the body's spatial existence in the world. However, the body also inhabits time. As Merleau-Ponty puts it, "I belong to space and time, my body combines with them and includes them" [8](p. 140). In this paper we emphasize aspects of the notion of embodiment involving the concept of time.

Merleau-Ponty tends to dismiss the river metaphor of time, saying that time is "not like a river, not a flowing substance" and "it is not the past that pushes the present, nor the present that pushes the future, into being" [8] (p. 411). Merleau-Ponty's doubt regarding the more-or-less ongoing linear ordering of past, present, and future echoes Gilles Deleuze's cinematic philosophy. Deleuze theorizes a perspective of time in his two famous volumes about cinema. On one hand, his work points out that human natural perception introduces "halts" or "fixed points" in our everyday lives [14] (pp. 22-23). We tend to "immobilize" the continuous flow of life, slowing down the intense "flux" of data, in order to think [15] (p. 149). Hence, we see time as connections of those fixed points within an ordered whole. This model is best illustrated by the use of storyboards in filmmaking or in interface design, where they are often called "wireframes." To an interface designer, a wireframe helps understand the connection between input and feedback. In such media, time is just a sequence of alternating stimuli and responses. In other words, humans usually experience time as a discrete order of events based on our natural perception.

On the other hand, Deleuze reminds us "cinematographic perception works continuously," meaning that the camera does not naturally encode these discrete events [13] (pp. 22- 23). His major theses include the notions of the "movement image" and the "time image." The movement image refers to the kind of cinematic images enabled by the moving camera and/or montage, a type of image in which movement is not just about individual changes of an object in space, but is also related to variation or change in the whole [13] (pp. 8-9). Each movement, as Claire Colebrook explains, is "not just a change of place within a whole but a becoming in which the movement is a transformation of the body which moves" [16] (p. 45). For example, a static camera can just capture a fixed camera view of an object changing in the frame, while a moving camera together with shot juxtaposition can show the object's movement actually transforming the whole surrounding holistically. Here, change is individual movement with the whole as background, and transformation refers to the change in state, or "becoming," of the whole environment. The moving camera, together with montage, reveals relative movements simultaneously happening in the whole.

The idea of the "becoming" whole, Deleuze believes, is "to change constantly, or to give rise of something new, in short, to endure" [13] (p. 9). Deleuze uses this common cinematic phenomena to reveal that time is not alternating sections of sensory perception, but constantly changing wholes involving concurrent segments of varying saliency and attention. We add that cinema makes this "becoming" perceptible to humans, that is, scales it appropriately to the human body and human perception.

We believe that cinema, with its hundred years of history, has shaped recent perception of time in creative computational media, making it different from the natural "stimulus-response" mechanism [14] (p. 149). In such media, the ordered perception of time corresponds to the common discrete, conversational style of interaction. For instance, a classical command-line interface introduces "halts," breaking the engagement into ordered, discrete, and alternate segments of input and feedback.

Today's creative computing system can present powerfully evocative meanings by invoking a sense of the "becoming" whole in spatiotemporally embodied interaction. This means that users are engaged in interfaces that highlight perceivable continuity and variation. Hence, we argue, in creative computing systems the idea of embodiment must be reconsidered from the perspective of engagement in a holistically transformative and partially responsive world.

Many expressive interactive creative computing artifacts need to project an illusion of a constantly changing environment, or an *enduring* environment. Such systems simultaneously respond users' motive input while continuing to vary their output.

One exemplar of enduring environments is John Conway's well-known *Game of Life*. The "game" is a two-dimensional cellular automaton in which the cells live, die, and reproduce according to pre-defined rules based on the neighboring cells. The running of the game often looks like an animated work featuring vivid patterns that are constantly changing. Meanwhile, a user is always free to interfere with the growth of cells by putting extra cells in the two-dimensional grid. This motor input is motion-sensitive, because to add cells the user just runs the mouse-cursor, or finger in case of the touchpad or touch screens, across the grid (in some cases clicking is required, other implementations work based on mouse-over).

At the motor-sensory level, the piece is a generative and interactive animation. At the metaphorical level, it projects an image of life, which is constantly changing on the whole because of its rules, and is always differing in various parts because of its openness to intervention. The interaction between the user's motion-based motor action and the animated images of the whole cell habitat exemplify spatiotemporally perceptible embodiment in a "grid" of "becoming." Similar enduring environments make computer interaction more reminiscent of our everyday life experiences. Our notion of enduring interaction becomes a lens for expressing several aspects of why many people find the *Game of Life* to be so compelling to watch and use.

In summary, the necessary conditions of an enduring interaction mechanism include two sides of the motor-sensory feedback loop:

- *Motive Input*: The motion qualities of user input represent user intention, effecting significantly on system output;
- *Enduring Environment*: The system still presents continuous variation on the whole, even without any user input. Meanwhile, motive user input it would show differing output in specific parts in response.

We believe computational artifacts with enduring interaction interfaces hold the potential to make creative computing systems, and even more utilitarian systems, more familiar, intimate, and close to human users in light of our typically situated, enculturated performance of gestures in the world.

4. ILLUSTRATIVE ANALYSES: MECHANISMS OF ENGAGEMENT

Toward creation of human-computer interaction that is more evocative and intimate to human users, we require a new model derived from spatiotemporal embodiment of meaning, including motive input and an enduring environment. We introduce a continuum of mechanisms from the least to the most engaging (see Figure 2):

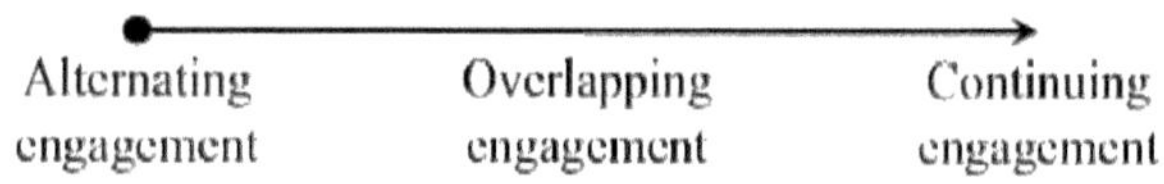

Figure 2: A continuum of Engagement

This continuum provides a model for designing interfaces in non-productivity applications or creative computing systems. To illustrate, we first analyze interaction mechanisms of some existing artifacts, including both mechanical and digital ones. We then discuss how this continuum is manifested in the authors' on-going interactive narrative project GeNIE. The GeNIE project aims to formulate computational models for gesture-based interactive narrative systems and to enable development of multimedia narratives exploring and demonstrating expressive non-verbal digital interaction. The developing computational narrative platform GeNIE is inspired by accounts of how other media represent embodied expressive affordances such as Henry Louis Gates Jr's notion of the "speakerly text" in literary theory [17], William Labov's sociolinguistic narrative model, studies of gestural interaction such as referenced in Subsection 3.1 above, and modes of multi-touch interaction currently implemented on the iOS platform.

Authors using the GeNIE system must produce formal descriptions of nonlinear narratives in XML format, gestural input functions, and sets of sprite images in order to generate instances of interactive narrative as iPhone or iPad applications. The multi-touch-screen device allows users to perform gestural or motive input to the narrative application while perceiving non-verbal expression (such as smiling, frowning, crossing arms, or extending arms) of the characters in the narrative. The gestural interaction within a GeNIE work constitutes an embodied form of using input intimately tied to the meaningful trajectory of the narrative. This section will refer to the design and implementation of the non-verbal interaction in a sample narrative *Rainbus Ecstatic*, which features a girl's bus journey and poignant dialogue with a stranger augmented with gestures and facial expressions. Below we use this system to exemplify the three types of engagement listed at the start of this section.

4.1 Alternating Engagement

Alternating engagement mainly refers to a conversational style of interaction with artifacts or machines. The mechanism, like verbal dialogue, involves discrete sections of motor input and sensory feedback taking turns alternately. The ordered connection of these sections is the "immobilized" and "fixed" nature of the environment. The use of mechanical typewriters is a typical example. The typewriter responds to each key tap by the typist with a corresponding character strike in sequential order. When a typist performs any one stroke without waiting for the feedback of the preceding tap's completion a jam occurs. In other words, the input and feedback sections cannot overlap. This mechanical constraint leads to strictly alternate sections, resulting in the defining characteristic of alternating engagement. Moreover, alternating engagement involves no motive input. In typing a text, motion qualities like the direction from which the finger hit a key or the speed of reaching a key could have no significant effect on the outlook of the printed text.

The phenomenon of alternating engagement seems to be a result of the mechanics of the apparatus, yet this type of engagement should not be thought of only limited to mechanical artifacts. In fact, examples can be found in digital environments as well, including the command-line environment of MS-DOS or early text-based adventure games, and the point-and-click mechanism in most graphical user interfaces. In these cases, a system always takes a user input, whether it is a tap of the "return" key or a mouse click on a button, and then responds accordingly. The system does not immediately process the next input until it completes the current output. If no input arrives after output, it waits indefinitely. Clearly the alternating pattern is a matter of design conventions, not physics as in the typewriter example.

Alternating engagement can also be seen in gesture-based interaction. In the sample narrative *Rainbus Ecstatic* from the GeNIE project, user input is largely gestural, quite different from conventional mouse click or finger tap input. A user causes the girl protagonist to explicitly express her feeling, represented as "external state" variables, through facial expressions like smile or frown (Figure 3). Drawing a "U" shape results in a smile; an inverted results in a frown. However, the corresponding engagement is alternating because the system must wait for the end of drawing before it recognizes the shape. For shape or icon recognition, the input and output section intrinsically cannot overlap. In the implementation of the GeNIE system, the recognition of input starts after a touch ends, not during a touch moves, determining the type of engagement. To a user of *Rainbus Ecstatic*, it is like giving a command to the protagonist, who then acts accordingly. The interaction does not spatiotemporally embody her or his intention.

4.2 Overlapping Engagement

Overlapping engagement differs from alternating in that user input sections seem to overlap with system output sections. An artifact accepts users' motive input, the motion data of which affects output instantaneously. This process results in an illusion of continuous response. A user is simultaneously engaged in performing motor action and perceiving sensory feedback. Some machine interfaces provide good examples. As mentioned, professional VTRs with jog dials allow users to control video playback by rotating the knob. The motion components of the dial affect how the medium is presented. A clockwise spin results in fast-forward, whereas a counter-clockwise spin rewinds the tape. The faster it spins, the faster the tape plays. The case is similar to the mechanics of a zoetrope. The direction of rotating the zoetrope determines the direction of the animation seen through the slits. These machines accept motive input and enable overlapping engagement.

Figure 3: Iconographic gestural input and facial feedback in *Rainbus Ecstatic*: Drawing a "U" shape results in a smile while an inverted one a frown.

Yet, these machine interfaces present just a partially enduring environment. Although the motor input in the zoetrope or the jog dial is motion-sensitive, a delay of user input could slow down the "becoming" of the output. In case of the zoetrope, the viewer needs to keep spinning the apparatus in order to see the animated effect. The spinning speed determines what the viewer exactly sees through the slits. If the viewer defers the motor action, the animation would slow down and finally halt. Similar to the alternating cases, these interfaces would also wait indefinitely for user input, resulting in an environment not constantly changing and less engaging.

In this regard, many so-called immersive computer interfaces entail similar moderately engaging interaction. These kinds of immersive interfaces, whether 2- or 3D, are ones in which users can navigate by moving the mouse, swiping on the touch screen, or moving fingers on the touchpad. The most classical examples include the interfaces of many first-person shooting games, like *Doom*, in which the player moves the mouse left or right to look around, forward to walk, backward to retreat. Multimedia websites enabled by technologies such as Quicktime VR or Flash often present interactive panoramic views or menus allowing visitors to pan the views or menus left or right with the mouse (e.g., *Out My Window*, an interactive documentary by Katerina Cizek [18]).

Meanwhile, many hand-held devices or tablet computers let users run their fingers on the touch screen to scroll through screens or some large-than-screen canvas. Users of the Mac OS X system are able to scroll a web page or a long document up or down by moving two fingers on the touchpad. Many of the above systems even implement an inertia effect making users feel like physically panning a viewing camera or move a canvas. The direction, speed and even frequency of users' motive input cause immediate visual feedback on the screen. Users are engaged in motor action and sensory perception simultaneously. While the motor-sensory feedback is comparable to that in the jog dial of VTR machines or the zoetrope, these computer interfaces, although evocative, inevitably cease to vary if there is no input.

In *Rainbus Ecstatic*, users can also be engaged in motive input and sensory feedback simultaneously. One can make the girl protagonist express her view by running fingers on the touch screen. Swiping up and down causes the girl to nod, showing agreement to her exchanger. Swiping left and right causes the girl to shake head, meaning dismissal. Furthermore, one can let the girl leak her stance implicitly, being either defiant or submissive, which are represented by "internal state" variables. Pinching out inclines the girl toward an open and receptive posture, while pinching in toward a closed and introverted one (Figure 4a & 4b). Here the gestural interaction in *Rainbus Ecstatic* enables overlapping engagement. The girl is animated in real time to respond to users' motive input. The animation takes place during a touch moves in case of swipe or pinch. When the user swipes fast, the girl nods or shakes vigorously. If the user keeps pinching in and out, the girl changes pose frequently. The user experiences a sense of performing gestures, not only his or her own finger gestures, but also the girl's body gestures, resulting in spatiotemporal embodiment of the user's intention in the virtual story world.

Figure 4a (above): Motive input and gestural feedback in *Rainbus Ecstatic*; swiping up and down makes nodding

Figure 4b (above): Motive input and gestural feedback in *Rainbus Ecstatic*; pinching in or out makes the girl cross or extend her arms.

4.3 Continuing Engagement

Lastly, continuing engagement describes those systems showing ceaseless transformation, with or without user input. This kind of engagement is continuing in that the whole environment continues to change autonomously at all times. Simultaneously, a user's motive input, at any time might trigger particular variation that would carry on. This "becoming" whole is persistent and divergent. A good analogy is the tea-serving mechanical doll of Edo-period Japan called a karakuri. After winding it up, the automaton paces slowly with a cup of tea to approach its user. When it bows, the gesture cues the user to pick up the teacup. If the user does so, it waits for the return of the cup; otherwise, it turns away, and comes back after a while. Winding it up notwithstanding (which is a type of alternating engagement), the doll is geared to follow its internal rules continuously. The doll might react to its audience's timely motor action or wander around. In short, it behaves differently in different occasions and engages its audience in continuing and differing happenings.

In computational media, examples of this kind of continuing engagement are emerging. One example is the greeting front page *SnowDays* at Popularfront.com [19]. The page displays an outdoor view of snow falling (Figure 5). The downward drifting flakes vary in shape because they are actually other web visitors' individual submissions. A visitor may create a customized snowflake using a simple interactive cutting tool and attaching a message. Once the visitor submits the flake, it is added to a database and now falls in the scene, constituting part of the "becoming" whole. Using a touchpad, a visitor can run a finger across it to "catch" a falling flake and check out the details and the attached message. Yet one has to take timely action, otherwise the target may fall out of the window frame. The mechanism here is a simple example of motive input. This is because direction and speed of finger motion still embody one's intention toward a snowflake. Furthermore, while a flake is held by a visitor, new flakes from others are still continuously added to the database and may enter the scene at any time. At times, a visitor may choose to do nothing but watch as the scene keeps snowing while the background color changes with the time of day. The whole environment is undergoing enduring change no matter regardless of whether the user oversees all flakes or performs close-up actions.

Figure 5: A snapshot of *SnowDays* at Popularfront.com

Another good example is the water-level interface of the Japanese mobile phone N702iS. The interface displays computer-generated images of water that react to user action in real time. When a user tilts the phone, the direction, speed, and frequency of the user's hand motions determine how the water dynamically flows on the screen, yielding an illusion of a water-filled cell phone (Figure 6). Shaking more vigorously leads to other effects like turning off an incoming call. That means the user input is motion-sensitive and embodies the user's intention. Meanwhile, because the water level actually represents the battery level, even when there is no user action, the water level drops very gradually according to the battery consumption. This subtle, but persistent, change inside the virtual container reflects an enduring environment. All in all, the reactive and transformative water image constitutes another example of a "becoming" whole, continuously engaging the user.

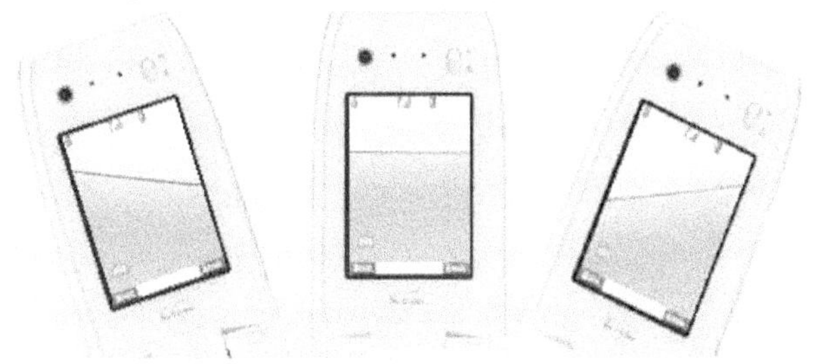

Figure 6: The interface of the mobile phone N702iS showing computer-generated imagery of water reactive to user action

In GeNIE, whether to make the story environment continue to change without user input is a matter of aesthetic choice. The narrative *Rainbus Ecstatic* features an uncanny dialogue between the girl and a stranger. After the stranger utters something, the story cannot advance without the girl's response; otherwise it would become just the stranger's monologue. On the other hand, we can implement time-sensitive triggers to create an illusion that the story world still evolves without user input. For example, the time of day may change, the stranger may get off the bus, and another one could get on. The story environment in these cases would change in the absence of dialogue. The goal of such additions would be to implement an enduring environment without contradicting the aesthetic or logic of the intended narrative. Continuum of engagement is not rule of thumb, but rather an important type of phenomenon to consider in the goal of achieving engaging interaction.

In summary, continuing engagement includes both motive input and enduring environments. Overlapping engagement generally involves the former but lacks the latter. If both vital components are missing, an interactive system likely belongs to examples of alternating engagement. A brief look at the examples we raised reveals that the continuum from alternating to continuing aligns with the inclination from tool-based to toy-like artifacts.

5. CONCLUSION AND IMPLICATIONS

In this paper, we have provided a model of enduring interaction that calls attention to important phenomena regarding animated gestural interfaces, with a focus on creative computing applications. Furthermore, in our account a continuum of engagement, we have proposed perspectives useful for designing interfaces for non-productivity-oriented, or creative computing systems. Our approach is mainly grounded in theories of embodied cognition, bolstered by Merleau-Ponty's phenomenological work on motility and Deleuze's cinematic philosophy. The resultant theoretical framework provides a valuable lens for considering animated gestural interfaces since it centralizes two essential components of our everyday lives, namely bodily motion and temporality at a human scale. This lens helps to focus on two issues, motive user input and enduring environment, useful for building embodied, evocative, and engaging interfaces. Through an array of illustrative examples corresponding to a continuum of types of nuanced user engagement with both mechanical and digital devices, we have proposed emerging design orientation in creative computing applications. An orientation that moves away from tools or instruments toward types of interfaces more reminiscent of users' everyday life experiences that involve reactivity, continuity, and divergence.

We believe that the type of engaging interfaces that we propose reflect a phenomenon of "soft anthropomorphism," alternative to the debatable aim of artificial intelligence research to develop agents that fully anthropomorphize the computer by emulating human behavior, rather than *human experience*. By "soft," we mean that idea of enduring interaction represents a step toward making computers holistically "human-familiar," rather than stringently "human-like." This perspective can inform design of creative computing systems that are bodily familiar and cognitively intimate, in other words systems that enable types of engagement close in scale to humans' embodied experiences. Finally, our approach suggests a change of focus from utilitarian issues such as ease-of use regarding types of interaction. Rather, we advocate *an approach centralizing embodied meaning-making* in the study and design of computational media interaction. It is an approach potentially relevant to both everyday work activities and to creative computing systems aimed at enabling expression of, and insight regarding, the nature of the human condition.

REFERENCES

1. Chow, K. K. N. and Harrell, D. F. "Material-Based Imagination: Embodied Cognition in Animated Images," *Proceedings of the 2009 Digital Arts and Culture Conference*, Irvine, 2009.
2. Wiener, N. *Cybernetics : or, control and communication in the animal and the machine*. M.I.T. Press, New York, 1961.
3. Gibson, J. J. *The ecological approach to visual perception*. L. Erlbaum, Hillsdale, N.J., 1986.
4. Norman, D. A. *The Psychology of Everyday Things*. Basic Books Inc., New York, 1988.
5. Dourish, P. *Where the Action Is: The Foundations of Embedded Interaction*. MIT Press, Cambridge, 2001.
6. Moran, D. *Introduction to phenomenology*. Routledge, London, 2000.
7. Lakoff, G. and Johnson, M. *Philosophy in the flesh : the embodied mind and its challenge to Western thought*. Basic Books, New York, 1999.
8. Merleau-Ponty, M. *Phenomenology of perception*. Routledge & Kegan Paul, London, 1962.
9. Dreyfus, H. L., Wrathall, M. A. and ebrary Inc. *A companion to phenomenology and existentialism*. Blackwell Pub., Oxford, 2006.
10. *Enactive network - Enactive Interfaces*. www.enactivenetwork.org/index.php?8/objectives, 2007 (accessed August 7, 2011).
11. Shneiderman, B. *Direct Manipulation: A Step beyond Programming Languages*. MIT Press, Cambridge, 2003 [1983].
12. Bolt, R. A. *"Put-That-There": Voice and Gesture at the Graphics Interface*. ACM Press, New York, 1980.
13. Wexelblat, A. *A feature-based approach to continuous-gesture analysis*. Massachusetts Institute of Technology, 1994.
14. Deleuze, G. *Cinema*. University of Minnesota, Minneapolis, 1986.
15. Colebrook, C. *Understanding Deleuze*. Allen & Unwin, Crows Nest, NSW, 2002.
16. Colebrook, C. *Gilles Deleuze*. Routledge, London ; New York, 2002.
17. Gates Jr., H. L. *The Signifying Monkey: A Theory of African-American Literary Criticism*. Oxford, New York, 1988.
18. Cizek, K. *Out My Window*. National Film Board of Canada/Interactive, 2010.
19. *Snowdays*. snowdays.popularfront.com (accessed August 7, 2011)

Music One Participates In

Atau Tanaka
Culture Lab
Newcastle University
atau.tanaka@ncl.ac.uk

ABSTRACT
Digital music has undergone fundamental shifts – it has gone real time, it has become interactive, it has become miniaturized, and completely democratized. I'll map out my personal trajectory in this time to look at broader evolutions in the field with sensors, networks, and mobility. These are not just technological changes, but changes that bring about shifts in musical approaches. Form factors change, analogue is reconciled with digital, and new directions in Open Source and DIY culture continue to challenge our assumptions on what it means to be an artist, composer, performer, participant, in these evolving musical/technological landscapes.

Author Keywords
Interactive music, sensor instruments, participatory art

ACM Classification Keywords
J.5. Computer Applications: Music.

General Terms
Experimentation, Performance, Theory

PLAYING, LISTENING, MUSICKING

Content created by users is a public affair. In the cultural field of music, this includes diverse activities of listening, sharing, editing, recording. Jacques Attali predicts that music will become a network of *composition*, where people actively participate in music-as-process, as a form of collective play [3]. Christopher Small coined the term, *musicking*, to describe music as a social act [11]. This sets a context of participation for acts of sound making practice - how can composers, authors, and artists conceive of new forms of music where the listener enters into the process of co-creation?

In such a dynamic of participatory creativity, traditional distinctions between musicians (composers, performers) and audiences, or, for that matter, between musicians and non-musicians become less clear. Conventional musical training and skills, while still useful, are no longer an absolute requirement: each participant, regardless of level of training, is able to produce something they could call and enjoy as "music". [4]

C&C'11, November 3–6, 2011, Atlanta, Georgia, USA.
ACM 978-1-4503-0820-5/11/11.

Barthes [5] divides music into two categories: the music one listens to and the music one plays to. The former occurs when people engage passively to the sound representation by listening. The latter occurs when people subjectively engage in the creation of sound, where listening has a subordinate role. In recent sound making practice, the boundary between the two increasingly blurred. People subjectively engage with sound representations through listening and simultaneously engage with the creation of sound. Each person is a listener of others, and a performer to others. We describe this practice as "the music one participates in."

THE LADDER OF CITIZEN PARTICIPATION

Arnstein [2] defines eight levels of citizen participation, from 'manipulation' to 'citizen control.' We adapt this ladder of participation to sound making practice. We explore three broad levels of participation, from 'non-participation', through 'tokenism', to 'citizen power' by which people obtain decision-making majority, or full creative power.

We consider the meaning of participation by looking at the roles of people in sound making practice. While this includes familiar roles such as composer, conductor, or performer (i.e. artist), in contemporary sound making practice they have gradually shifted. We see a shift of focus from the individual who once passively received sound representations to actively being involved in sound-making as participants.

In the area of contemporary art, Bishop describes the social dimension of participation in art practices that strive to collapse the distinction between performer and audience [6]. She observes three motivating agendas: 1: activation to create subjects to determine their own social and political reality in a work, 2: authorship to cede control of a work entailing aesthetic benefits of greater risk and unpredictability, and 3: community as the social bond through a collective elaboration of meaning.

In order to map these sociological notions of participation to the open-ended potential of music noted by Attali, Barthes, and Small, the sustainability of musical communities and methods for encouraging participation become crucial. We adapt Arnstein's three levels of participation to explore different means of participation in sound making practice. We are interested in understanding and supporting how people engage socially with music. Instead of directly proposing new modes of musical production, we propose ways of looking at emergent creative situations that may lead to new forms of musical engagement.

THE MULTIPLE MEANINGS OF PERFORMANCE

We unpick the multiple meanings of the word, performance, as they are used in arts and engineering disciplines:

- Performance as a form of artistic expression
- Performance as a form of systems optimization

We add to this a third, social science perspective on the word performance, drawn from the work of Turner [Ref] and Goffman [8]. With this, we consider a body of interactive music work.

Sensor instruments have been used in traditional musical ensemble performance. My own practice in this area dates to the early 1990s with the trio, Sensorband, [7] and continues in the 2000s with live sound/image performance with another trio, Sensors_Sonics_Sights [10]. In the most recent group, we use of a consumer electronics device (Apple's iPhone) as gestural musical instrument. The familiarity of the device becomes a form of participation in decoding otherwise unfamiliar computer-based electronic sound [12].

Interactive installations place interactive instruments in gallery settings. This creates hybrid instruments for performance and exhibition and invites play by novice gallery viewers at the same time the instrument is used in concert performance at the exhibition opening. The instrument described, Global String [15], is designed to respond organically these different levels of play, and in this way can be said to resemble a traditional instrument such as a piano, which, unmodified can provide musical satisfaction to novices as well as virtuosi. This approach differs from the programmatic level of difficulty that can be set in video games and computer-based tasks.

Musical approaches to locative media art extend musical interaction beyond the stage and outside the gallery. Net_Dérive used early 3G and GPS hardware in a wearable computing harness to create an updated, digital rendition of the Situationist games of the *dérive* [14]. Three participants would explore the neighborhood around a gallery, where the trajectories of their walk were aggregated, visualized, and sonified, and streamed back to create an abstract soundscape that at once reflected and directed their collective walk. The Chiptune Marching Band takes the mobile telephone away from the notion of mobile music, and creates a participatory dynamic with DIY electronics workshop and ad-hoc street performance intervention [1].

ACKNOWLEDGMENTS

The notions of musical participation were developed with Kazuhiro Jo and have previously been published as [9].

REFERENCES

1. Allen, J., Galani, A., and Jo, K. An Ecology of Practice: Chiptune Marching Band. In Proc. *Creativity & Cognition*, (2009), 347-348.
2. Arnstein, S. R. A Ladder of Citizen Participation. *Journal of the American Institute of Planners 35*, 4 (1969), 216-224.
3. Attali, J. *Noise: The Political Economy of Music*. Trans. B. Massumi, University of Minnesota Press, Minneapoplis, MN, USA, 1985.
4. Auslander, P. Fluxus Art-Amusement: The Music of the Future? [revised and expanded version], *Contours of the Theatrical Avant-Garde: Performance and Textuality*, ed. James Harding. University of Michigan Press, Ann Arbor, MI, USA, 2000.
5. Barthes, R. Musica pratica, In *Image-Music-Text*, Hill and Wang, New York (1977), 149-154.
6. Bishop, C. *Participation: Documents of Contemporary Art*. MIT Press, Cambridge, MA, USA, 2006.
7. Bongers, B. An interview with Sensorband. *Computer Music Journal 22*, (1998), 13-24.
8. Goffman, E. *The Presentation of Self in Everyday Life*. Doubleday, New York, NY, USA, 1959.
9. Jo, Kazuhiro and Tanaka, A. The Music Participates In. In F. Schroeder (ed.) *Performing Technology: User Content and the New Digital Media*. Cambridge Scholars Publishing, Newcastle upon Tyne, UK, (2009), 34-50.
10. Sensors_Sonics_Sights. http://www.ataut.net/site/S-S-S.
11. Small, C. *Musicking: The meanings of performing and listening*. University Press of New England, Hanover, NH, USA, 1998.
12. Tanaka, A. Mapping Out Instruments, Affordances, and Mobiles. In *Proc. New Interfaces for Musical Expression (NIME),* (2010), 88-93.
13. Tanaka, A. Sensor-Based Musical Instruments and Interactive Music. In R. Dean (ed.) *The Oxford Handbook of Computer Music*. Oxford University Press, Oxford, UK, (2009) 233-257.
14. Tanaka, A. and Gemeinboeck. P. Net_Dérive: Conceiving and Producing a Locative Media Artwork. In Goggin, G. and Hjorth, L. (eds.) *Mobile Technologies: From Telecommunications to Media*. Routledge, London, UK, (2008), 174-186.
15. Tanaka, A. and Bongers, B. Global String: A Musical Instrument for Hybrid Space. In *Proceedings of cast01: Living in Mixed Realities*. Fraunhofer IMK, St. Augustin, Germany, (2001), 177-181.
16. Turner, V. *Dramas, Fields and Metaphors: Symbolic Action in Human Society*. Cornell University Press, Ithaca, NY, USA, 1974.

Temporal Integration of Interactive Technology in Dance: Creative Process Impacts

Celine Latulipe, David Wilson and Berto Gonzalez
HCILab
University of North Carolina at Charlotte
{clatulip, davils, agonza32}@uncc.edu

Sybil Huskey and Melissa Word
Department of Dance
University of North Carolina at Charlotte
{sdhuskey, mword}@uncc.edu

ABSTRACT
Interdisciplinary projects bridging technology and the arts face challenges across many dimensions. In this paper, we reflect on the issue of temporal constraints on integrations of interactive technology within dance production. We describe lessons learned and illustrate practical impacts on stakeholders, creative process and outcomes from over three years of experience in developing dance productions at our university. Specifically, we reflect on perceptions of how the timing of the technology integrations impacted the creativity of the stakeholders involved. We separate results that are idiosyncratic to our project and highlight those that we expect are more generally applicable to other art and technology projects. Finally, we provide a set of temporal integration considerations that others can use to assess when it is best to integrate technology into an arts project.

Author Keywords
interdisciplinary integration, arts, creativity, dance, temporal effects

ACM Classification Keywords
J.5 Computer Applications: Arts and Humanities—*Performing Arts*

General Terms
Human Factors.

INTRODUCTION
There are long-term research projects that cross many disciplinary boundaries, and how the inter-disciplinary integration occurs varies according to the needs of the component disciplines. In performing arts productions that involve technology, the question of temporal integration arises. Performing arts productions are complex and temporally driven. Because of the deadline imposed by 'opening night' there is a clear temporal process that is followed to move the production to opening night readiness. We liken the performance production process to the flowering of a plant: for the most exciting bloom, all of the necessary elements have to be provided at the right time.

The goal of a dance production, as with any other art, is the creative exploration of an idea. Within dance, this exploration takes place through the choices made regarding choreographic expression, musical accompaniment, costuming, lighting, scenic elements, and props [8, 16, 14, 7]. Moreover, for our project and others, these choices also consider interactive technology. A single dance production is thus a pinpoint in a large, multi-dimensional space of possible design choices. Each of these dimensions may itself have multiple facets: what to use, how to use it, and when to bring it into the production process. While choreography is the cornerstone of the dance production and a rehearsal schedule anchors the process timeline, the other production elements can vary in the timing of their integration into the process.

The production process in dance is a generative dialogue between the varying 'actors' of movement, sound, lighting, props, costuming, scenic elements and digital effects, though not all of these actors play a role in every dance. The dance production 'conversation' that takes place between all of these 'actors' is determined by the timing of entry of each — if the accompanying soundtrack or orchestra is brought in towards the end of a dance production, it has a more limited ability to impact the choreographic development. If props are available for use at the beginning of the process, they are more likely to be well-integrated into the choreography. Thus, the timing of entry of different elements into an arts production impacts the creative process in significant ways. We call these phenomena 'temporal integration effects' and in this paper we focus on the temporal integration effects of technology on dance.

At UNC Charlotte, the Dance.Draw project has been integrating technology and dance over the past three years. Our interdisciplinary team has been involved in six different dance production cycles, integrating various technologies, at various stages, into dance productions [10, 12, 11]. The different technology integrations have focused on sensing dancer movement to drive interactive visualizations that

C&C'11, November 3–6, 2011, Atlanta, Georgia, USA.

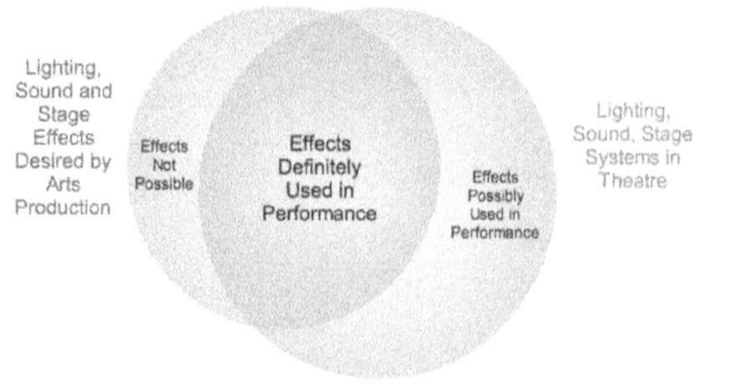

Figure 1. The use of built-in technology systems in a theater space constrains what is possible for a temporal arts production, and the production can only make use of what is available.

are projected as part of the choreography. In this paper we address the question: If technology is to be integrated into an arts production and play an important role, during which part of the production process should the technology enter? We do not attempt to provide a *correct* answer, as that will vary between projects and circumstances. Rather, we reflect on the impact of bringing in technology at various points in the production process, based on our experience in dance production. We show that the timing of the technology integration has considerable impacts on the creative process, and we expect that these lessons learned will be useful to others.

This paper is structured as follows: first we discuss previous work in the study of art and technology integration, highlighting the temporal aspects. Next, we describe our experiences in our interdisciplinary dance project outlining the impacts of the timing of the technology integration for each production cycle. These experiences have been gathered through a combination of design team reflection, interviews with choreographers and post-performance focus groups with dancers. Based on our experiences and lessons learned, we develop a set of general considerations for the temporal integration of technology that we expect will be relevant to other researchers, artists and technologists considering such cross-disciplinary work.

BACKGROUND

Technology Integration in Traditional Dance Processes

To say that bringing digital interactive effects into dance is the 'introduction of technology' belies the incredible amount of technology that is already in use in current performing arts processes. Much of modern stage mechanics, such as the effects used in shows by Cirque de Soleil or in Broadway productions, is incredible in its technological sophistication. Even in productions that are on a smaller scale with limited budget and thus less commercially successful, there is still a significant amount of technology at work in operating sound systems and sound effects, lighting systems and lighting effects and in staging mechanisms. What is common about all of these systems is that they are 'situated technologies' that live in a theater space. Because of their permanent installation, the artistic productions that use these spaces *adapt to* these technological systems. In this sense, the production integrates itself to work with the effects that can be provided by the built-in lighting, sound and stage systems. This concept is illustrated by the diagram in Figure 1.

These situated technologies prescribe the timing of their integration with the arts production: when the piece moves from a rehearsal space onto the stage, these technologies are integrated into the production. While the production crew (lighting designer, scenic designer, sound designer) may have visited the piece in rehearsal ahead of time to see the production and plan the effects, the majority of this type of technological integration happens once the piece moves into the theater. In most cases, this means that there is only a week or two in which to convert the theoretically planned effects into actual working effects. The fixed timeline for integration of traditional theater technologies is an important consideration for temporal integration of less conventional digital effects: it is very stressful to leave all of the technological integration to the last week or two of a production cycle. This also means that the choreographer or director may have difficulty visualizing the final production effects early on in the cycle, and this could have a negative impact on decision making.

Interactive Technologies in Dance

There is a significant amount of work, both within academia and in the professional dance world, that involves the integration of interactive, reactive or non-active multimedia technology in dance productions [5, 6, 13]. This is the subdomain that is of special interest to us and that is causing excitement in dance communities world-wide, as seen by the very active communities on sites such as dance-tech.net. Various research groups have been working on ways to capture the movement of dancers and turn that movement into digital interaction [9, 1]. While there have been interesting reports on this work, none have focused attention on the temporal aspects of technological integration in the dance production process. There has also been significant work in the creativity research community about the integration of art and technology in general, such as the work by Edmonds and Candy [4]. However, to our knowledge there has not been a thorough, methodical investigation of the effects of the temporality of technology integration into the arts in general or dance in particular.

TEMPORAL INTEGRATION EXPERIENCES

In this section we describe our experiences integrating interactive technologies into six different dance production cycles, and we highlight some of the lessons learned. All of these productions took place within a university setting, though some productions traveled beyond the university. A chart that illustrates the temporal integration of various elements of a dance production across these six different production cycles is shown in Figure 8.

Exquisite Interaction

In our pilot production, which we called "Exquisite Interaction," the technology used was wireless gyroscopic computer mice, which the dancers held in their hands as they danced. The motion data from these mice were transmitted

Figure 2. Project pilot performance.

to a central laptop and used to control a projected visualization. From the very first rehearsal with the three dancers, the technology was used and worked well. The main visualization used was ready immediately and another visualization was added during the very short three week production period before the first performance. The pilot dance was performed at three different venues, and there was no specialized lighting or other theatrical effects in use. The soundtrack was chosen before the first rehearsal. The dance was three minutes long and the choreography was developed in response to the technology, highlighting the fact that the dancers were carrying the mice and trying to demonstrate that the dancers were controlling the visualizations by using the mice. Because the dancers were carrying mice, the costuming did not need to be adapted or specialized to handle the technology, and so the costuming was simply designed to enhance the movement and spirit of the dance. Figure 2 shows an image from the pilot performance.

Lesson: Existing technology integration can be the idea of the performance and drive the entire creative process.

A Mischief of *Mus musculus*

The production, "A Mischief of *Mus musculus*," involved technologists, an artist, a choreographer and six dancers, and was an 11-minute, pure movement piece (see Figure 3). In this case, the technology was the same as in the pilot – dancers held wireless gyroscopic mice in their hands while they danced, but they also made use of the mouse buttons to actuate particular visualizations. In addition, the dancers handed the mice off to each other throughout the dance, as three pairs of mice were used by six dancers. A visual artist was hired to develop more aesthetic visualizations, still making use of the movement data from the mice carried by the dancers. While the visual artist had some coding experience, a significant portion of the technologist's time was devoted to coding visualizations throughout the production cycle in order to fulfill the artistic vision. Thus, in this case, the choreography and the visualizations were developed in tandem. Some of the choreography that was developed inspired the artist to design new visuals and some artist-created visuals inspired new choreography. The visual artist and the technologists needed to be present at all rehearsals in order for this tandem development to work, and much time was devoted to trying out different movement sections with different visualizations. The development process mainly followed a chronological ordering, in which the choreography and the visuals for the first part of the dance were designed first, and then the choreography and visuals for the next part of the dance were designed, etc. However, most rehearsals involved a 'visual show-and-tell' that allowed the visual artist and the technologist to show previews of interactive visualizations that were being worked on for future sections of the dance, in order to get feedback and know which ideas were worth pursuing.

Lesson: Tandem development of interactive visualizations and choreography requires the continual presence of all stakeholders at rehearsals.

"A Mischief of *Mus musculus*" was the first production to be performed in a formal dance concert setting. This was the technology team's first experience with the stage-readiness aspects of a dance concert setting. A costumer was used to create costumes especially designed for this piece, but the costumes did not require any special technology accommodation features. This meant that costuming ran as a separate, parallel production activity, with the costumer attending one or two early rehearsals and then worked on her own or in out-of-rehearsal sessions with the choreographer and individual dancers. Lighted display boxes were used to highlight the mice on stage before initial pick-up by dancers, but were not used as part of the dance movement. In addition, there was a 30 minute delay between opening the house for patrons and the start of the performance. Because the mice would go into a 'sleep mode' after a certain period of inactivity, it was necessary to have a stage technician ensure they were in an active state just prior to the start of the piece.

The technology used was not impacted by moving from the rehearsal space to the theater in terms of stage spacing or prop usage. However, this was our first encounter with formal theater lighting, and given that the main component of our technology is communication of kinetics through projected visuals, the impact of stage lighting on projected visuals was very important. It is typical in stage performances for a set of lighting cues to be developed for each scene, section, or movement phrase during a process called 'lighting cue-to-cue'. A typical five minute dance may have 10 different lighting cues. When projected visuals are a part of the performance, it is necessary to adjust each lighting cue to ensure that the projections are visible and not washed out. Typically, the lower the lighting, the more vibrant the projections. However, it is not usually possible to have very low lighting levels as dancers need to be able to see and be seen. Seeing is particularly important for dancers — it is very dangerous for dancers to spin or move quickly in the dark, as they become easily disoriented without the ability to focus on a visible anchor point. This could easily lead to injuries. Thus, the integration of projected visuals with stage lighting requires fine-tuning the trade-off between safe lighting levels and visible projections. Given that most choreographic pieces in a university setting have only one or two hours in which to do lighting cue-to-cue, this is a very difficult and stressful part of the technological integration. In our production, we made use of a good, research-quality projector in the dance studio, and then made use of a much more powerful, performance-quality Christie projector that is built into the theater space. This required calibrating the visualization brightness and colors to work with the Christie pro-

Figure 3. "A Mischief of *Mus musculus*" performance.

jector, and this had to be done before the lighting cue-to-cue could proceed. It is important to note that once cue-to-cue occurs, it is highly impractical to make any changes to visual effects, other than fine-tuning. Thus all visual interactive effects had to be completed before moving into the final production space.

An interesting event occurred during this production, that was disappointing, but proved to be educational: on the final performance day, the Christie projector in the performance venue stopped working just before the dance was about to be performed for a packed theater of 300 patrons. The technology team did not realize the projector had stopped functioning until the dance had begun and the projector shutter would not open. To their credit, the dancers performed as if everything was fine, and most audience members were unaware that there was any issue. This highlights an interesting issue: as with any performance element (lighting, sound, etc.), decisions sometimes have to be made about whether a performance should go forward if a particular system is not functioning. Given that technological systems are fallible, we have learned that it is wise to have a backup plan or a decision made about whether the performance should go ahead if the interactive technology fails.

Lesson: Decide ahead of time whether a performance should run if the technology fails, and who should make that call.

Whispering to Ophiuchus

The third production, "Whispering to Ophiuchus" was significantly different from the first two productions in almost every aspect (see Figure 4). Our technology team expanded and our hardware technologist developed a set of wired 3D accelerometer sensors that each dancer could wear at their wrists. These sensors sat at the wrists, with wires that ran up the dancers' arms and down their torsos, connecting to a battery and wireless transmitter pack worn at the sternum. This technology required specially designed costuming to secure, stabilize, and hide the instrumentation. The production process for "Whispering to Ophiuchus" was a massive parallel effort, with choreography, artistic storyline, musical score, hardware, interactive visualizations, costumes, scenic design and props all being developed simultaneously. This was a significantly more ambitious piece, totaling 22 minutes in length, with seven dancers performing. The piece was a modern, narrative dance, based on a myth about the thirteenth constellation of the zodiac. The complexity of the narrative demanded scenic pieces and props including ramps, an altar, a vessel, platforms, glass bowls, ribbons and a chair.

A single working prototype of the technology the dancers wore was developed before the production cycle began, but complete technical instrumentation needed to be constructed for each of the seven dancers involved. This meant that at the beginning of the production cycle the technology was not completely ready. This lead to a number of temporal integration issues. One of the technology issues that couldn't be dealt with until multiple dancer packs were in use was networking the sensors. The visualizations and choreography were meant to be developed in tandem, as had been the case in the previous production. However, the visualizations were dependent on the hardware technology, and while they could be developed, they could not be tested until the hardware was completely in place. This meant that the development of visuals lagged behind the development of the choreography. The impact of this was that the choreography was set by the time the hardware was in place and the visuals could be tested. This meant that visuals which didn't work as anticipated had to be reworked, but there was no opportunity for the choreography to change in response to the visuals because of the looming performance deadline. In this case, the visuals were reworked more to suit the hardware and to suit the narrative storyline than to suit the choreography, leading to some visuals that didn't necessarily enhance the kinetic connection with the dancers.

Another issue that arose because of the late introduction of the hardware was that the dancers were not wearing the instrumentation initially, and they learned much of the choreographic material without wearing the technology. The technology setup was somewhat cumbersome for the dancers to wear and it impacted the quality of their dancing when worn during later rehearsals. While the dancing did improve with the worn technology, the choreographers noted that it did not reach the level of the choreography as originally developed.

As with the previous production, there were particular issues that arose when moving this piece from the rehearsal studio onto the stage. Some of the choreography could not really be tried and set until the ramps and platform were in place on stage, and so the tracking/sensing technology used in those parts of the performance could not be tested until that time. In addition, the wireless networking required by the accelerometer setups was affected by electronic noise in the theater, where there is a lot of built-in technology. In an initial rehearsal on stage, the tracking did not work adequately because of networking issues. Due to this issue, in combination with the fact that the dancers performed better when not wearing the technology, we decided to run the performances using logged motion data from the dancers. This was disappointing, but it highlighted the importance of the timing of technology integration. With complicated technical systems, the systems need to be in place and used from the beginning of the production cycle, and more time needs to be allotted to moving the technology into the stage space.

Lesson: Late integration of technology at best limits creative conversation and at worst may degrade creative outcomes.

Figure 4. "Whispering to Ophiuchus" performance.

Figure 5. "Bodies/Antibodies" performance.

Bodies/Antibodies

The fourth production, "Bodies/Antibodies," was different yet again (see Figure 5). This was a restaging and expansion of a student-choreographed dance based on the concept of community, in this case, the community of cells in the human body. In this dance, we began synthesizing sensors. The student choreographer was an undergraduate research assistant on the project who was aware of the project goals and the technology we were using. We used the wireless gyroscopic mice employed in earlier productions, but this time they were embedded in a padded pocket sewn into the sports bra part of the costume worn by dancers. In addition, wireless, self-contained versions of the accelerometers (called 'blue boxes') were deployed and worn by the dancers in pockets located in the forearm of the costume. The software used data from both the mice and accelerometers from each dancer as input for the interactive visualizations. While the initial choreography was set, the dance was lengthened from an original 5 minutes to 11 minutes, so a significant portion of new material was developed. When the dance was originally staged it was not performed with any interactive (or non-interactive) technology enhancements. Because the existing choreography was designed to narrate a biological phenomenon, the visuals in this dance were designed in reaction to the choreography and the phenomenon. However, there was still some adaptation of choreography to fit the technology. For example, there were significant sections of floor work in the original choreography that required the dancers to press their whole front torsos against the stage. This had to be adapted in order not to have the dancers pressing the mice embedded in the front of their torsos against the floor, both because there was a fear of hurting the dancers and a fear of damaging the technology. In addition, in this dance, the performers responded to the technology explicitly, watching a visualization of cell division and dividing themselves in response. This was clearly a change from the original choreography and arose serendipitously during one of the many rehearsals involving the technology.

Lesson: Using technology throughout the rehearsal cycle can give rise to serendipitous opportunities for exploration.

"Bodies/Antibodies" was performed in various venues but not in a formal theatre setting, thus a singular lighting level always sufficed for performance. The dance had no scenic pieces or props, and so the main concern was setting a lighting level in each performance venue that would allow the dancers to see and be seen and ensure that the visuals were not washed out. A similar constraint occurred as in "Whispering to Ophiuchus," in that not all of the self-contained wireless sensor boxes were complete at the beginning of the production. However, having learned how important it is for the dancers to accommodate the technology as early as possible, we used empty blue boxes for some of the dancers while the real blue boxes were being completed.

An Instance Of...

The fifth production in the project was a shorter dance that was modular in nature, consisting of a trio that could be deconstructed into three solos or various duets. The modular, flexible nature of this choreography led to the dance being titled, "An Instance of ..." (see Figure 6). The technology consisted of synthesizing audio feed data with the blue box sensors. The dancers wore the blue box sensors in sweatbands at their ankles and could trigger changes in visualizations by stomping that foot, allowing 'personalization' of the visualizations by any of the three dancers at any time. The dancers wore performance-quality radio mics, which consisted of a wireless transmitter worn at the hip, with a wire mic that was threaded through the back of the costume and up to the head, with the end of the mic sitting at the hairline. The temporal integration of visualizations and choreography was significantly different in this piece. The piece was choreographed collaboratively over a summer by four different people, with the official production cycle beginning in the fall. Thus, the choreography was developed before any software visualizations were created. The conceptual theme behind the dance evolved slowly and continued to evolve throughout the process. When the software visualizations were developed in the early fall, they were designed to react to the sounds the dancers were making with their bodies.

One of the interesting temporal issues that arose in this production was related to the evolving theme of the dance. The costumer was initially called in to see the choreography and developed a costuming concept based on the cello music that accompanied the piece and the types of movements she observed. However, one of the changes that took place during the production cycle was the decision to have the dancers wear iPod Shuffles so that only they would hear the cello sound-track, allowing the audience members to focus on the body sounds of the dancers and the visualizations created by those sounds. In order to make this relationship clear to the audience, the waveform of the cello soundtrack was projected below the dancer-generated visuals, and it was decided that the iPod Shuffles and ear buds should be evident and not hidden under costuming. This change did not work with the existing costuming, resulting in a full costume redesign at some expense to the project and inconvenience to the costumer. To adapt to this new conceptual structure the

Figure 6. "An Instance of ..." performance.

Figure 7. "The Angled Angels Assembly" performance.

choreography also had to be reworked somewhat. However, this particular set of choreographic movements had been designed to be modular and flexible, and did prove to be very flexible in adapting to these conceptual changes.

Lesson: Even when technology is integrated early, changes in the way the technology is used can cause issues for other elements of the production.

When this piece was moved from the rehearsal studio to the stage, the Christie projector in the theater was not operational. Thus, our research quality projector had to be used in the very large theater space, which meant that the visualizations were not as bright as expected. This led to extra time being needed to light the dance, again to try to deal with the tradeoff between visuals being washed out and the dancers being able to see and be seen. In addition, it was necessary to fine-tune and adjust the audio levels from the microphones the dancers wore. It was critical to the piece that the audience be able to hear the breathing, stomping and other percussive sounds made by the dancers, amplified through the sound system in the theater, especially since the audience was not hearing the soundtrack that the performers were dancing to. However, care was needed to ensure that audio feedback didn't occur, and so this required extra time in the stage-readiness phase.

The Angled Angels Assembly

Our more recent production (see Figure 7), titled "The Angled Angels Assembly," used an overhead fish-eye lens camera, and software developed to track the positions of the dancers using a combination of background subtraction and K-means clustering. With this piece, the hardware technology was ready and in place at the beginning of the production cycle and about 60% of the visualizations had been developed before the production cycle began. Another 20% of the interactive visualizations were developed in the first month of the production, with the remaining being added and fine-tuned throughout the rehearsal process. In particular, the order of the different visualizations and the transitions between them were the main tasks performed by the software team during the production cycle. The original 14 minutes of choreography was divided into three distinct sections. Because there were two choreographers working on this piece, the movement material was developed, taught and cleaned in an overlapping, non-chronological manner. For example, a sequence in the third section would be developed and taught while material in section one was being cleaned. Given that the choreography was not developed ahead of the production cycle, the existence of the majority of the visualizations at the beginning was helpful to the production process while contributing a context within which the choreographers could evolve the content for the piece.

However, the introduction of this new technology did pose some temporal challenges. The choreographers needed every possible minute of rehearsal to develop, teach and clean the material, and so fine-tuning and testing the tracking of the overhead camera took away valuable time from this process. There were times when the technology could have used more exploration, testing and fine-tuning, but that time had to be sacrificed in order to get through the choreographic development. Similarly, there were times when choreographic development time was sacrificed in order to figure out how to best make use of the particular tracking algorithm.

The inclusion of various lengths of 3-inch wide black elastic as props was suggested by the strong horizontal line imagery of the initial visualizations. The use of the elastic added a third dimension to the 2-dimensional visualizations, allowing the elastic to reflect the lines and right-angled geometric shapes seen on the screen. The elastic props were used in each of the three sections, providing interesting choreographic tools and serving as one of the bridges between the physical dancing and the visualizations. The addition of this prop only occurred because the visualizations pre-existed; there would not have been time to incorporate them in response to a visualization development later in the process.

Lesson: Early technology integration allows for the inspiration, design and deployment of relevant props.

Finally, the use of an overhead camera required additional technical rehearsal time when the piece moved from the rehearsal studio to the stage. The camera had to be installed, tested and adjusted to get it at the right height to maximize stage coverage. It was critical that this installation and testing be done ahead of the spacing rehearsal, so that the spacing adjustments could take into account the visualizations and the visual field of the camera.

DISCUSSION

Figure 8 shows a temporal integration comparison across all six of our productions, aligned to the all-important opening night deadline. There are clear patterns that emerge, some of which are independent of the technology. For example, the three choreographic phases of development, teaching/learning and cleaning always occur in that order with some level of overlap. Similarly, lighting is always set in the final week before performance, when the piece moves

Temporal Spanning of Elements of Dance Productions

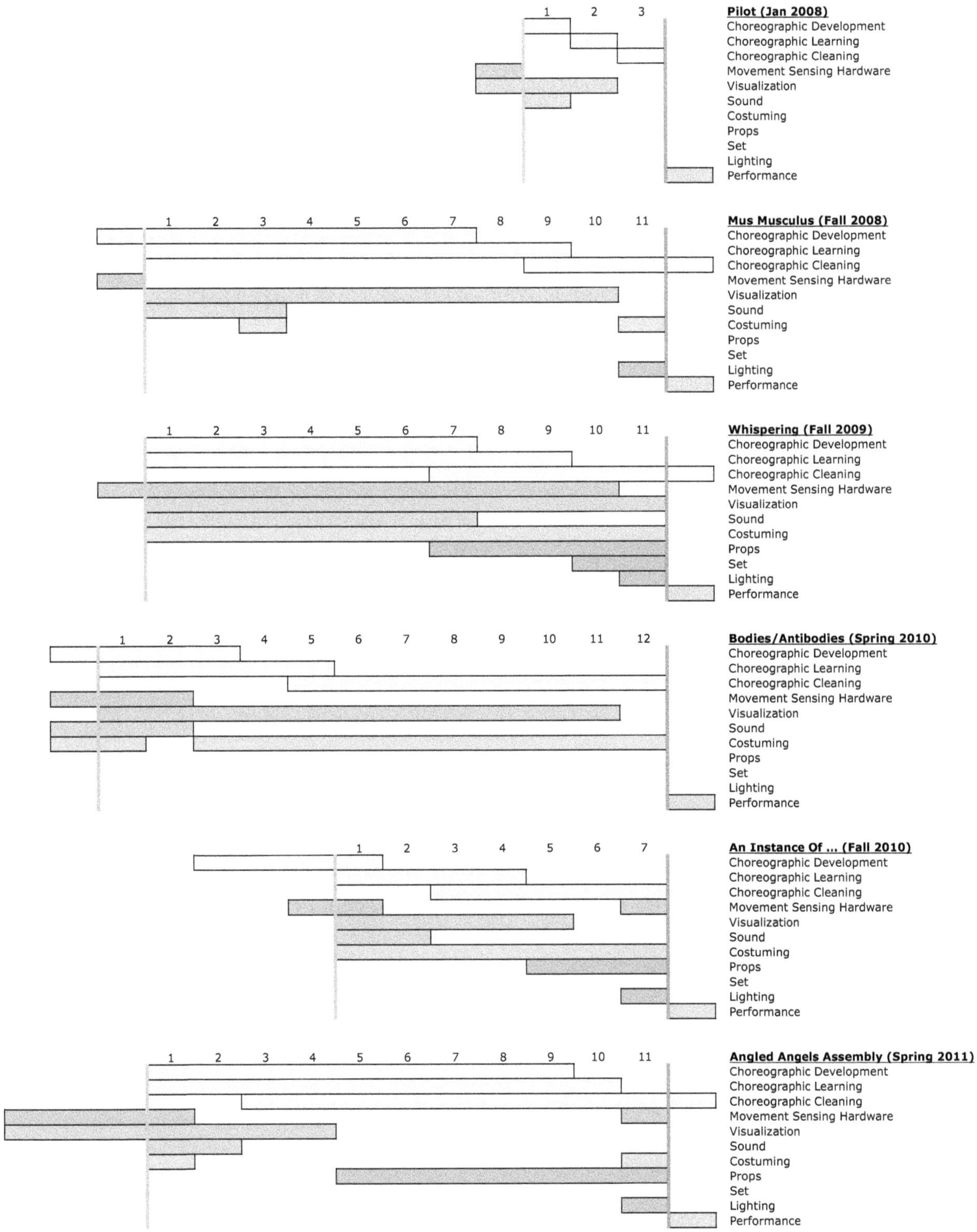

Figure 8. The temporal integration of production elements into six dance production cycles (numbers represent weeks), with hardware shown in purple and interactive visualizations shown in pink. The green vertical line designates the beginning of the formal rehearsal schedule, while the red line designates the end of rehearsal and the beginning of the formal performances.

from the rehearsal studio to the stage. Costuming typically occurs outside of the rehearsal space and parallel to the process, with the costumer attending an early rehearsal in order to plan costuming, followed by subsequent design meetings with the choreographer and fittings with the dancers. Dress rehearsals occur in the final week before performance. When special modified costumes are required in order to house technological sensors, markers or devices, the costuming schedule changes and the costumes need to be available throughout the production cycle, as seen in the "Whispering to Ophiuchus" and "Bodies/Antibodies" productions.

It is interesting to note the variation across productions in level of parallelism of various elements. This gives a visual sense of how much time was allotted in which the choreographic development and the interactive visual effects development could impact each other. What is also striking is that the "Whispering to Ophiuchus" performance had a high level of parallel activity across almost all elements of the production, and this was certainly the most stressful production for all stakeholders. This is an example of trying to do too much at once, and the stakeholders agree that from a process perspective, this was our least successful production.

Deadlines

Most projects thrive on deadlines, but in performance disciplines the deadlines completely drive the work. Stage time is often scheduled more than a year in advance, well before the performance team is put together. For performance productions, opening night is a hard-stop deadline. Production managers, theater directors and choreographers work backwards from that date, scheduling what needs to be done by what date in order for everything to be ready.

Team Participation in Rehearsals

Both the number of team members attending rehearsals and the frequency of that attendance had direct impact on the choreographic process. The more people attending the more likely it was that multiple side conversations about different aspects of the work would occur. The more conversations, the more difficult it was for the choreographer and dancers to concentrate. In the first few productions there was also an issue of the dancers feeling as though they were being 'watched' by the large technology team, and that was uncomfortable for some of the dancers. When the visualizations and hardware were being developed throughout the process it was necessary to have technologists at all rehearsals, but we learned that it was possible to minimize the size of the technology team present. In the most recent production, "The Angled Angels Assembly," where the hardware was ready to use immediately and the interactive visuals were largely developed ahead of time, two technologists attended each of the early rehearsals. Later in this cycle, it was not necessary for the technologists to be at every rehearsal, as by that time the visualizations were set. This successfully minimized disruption and distraction.

Unused Resources

It is common for movement sequences to be developed for a piece and then not used. This is a typical aspect of the choreographic selection and editing process. The same is true for interactive elements. In productions where the interactive visualizations were being developed throughout the production cycle, there were instances of choreographic movements being discarded or adapted to work with the new visualizations. In "The Angled Angels Assembly" no choreography that was created for the visualizations went unused, but some general movement sequences created early were discarded by the choreographers. There were also visualizations developed before the production cycle and early in the production cycle that were subsequently discarded, as they did not work with the choreographic concept, or they demanded too much visual attention. Similarly, in "An Instance of...", costumes developed early in the production cycle were not used and were replaced with new costumes to better fit the evolved theme and technological focus. Thus, elements developed earlier are more likely to be discarded or changed, while elements introduced later are designed to fit what exists and are therefore less likely to be discarded or require reworking.

Physical Impedance

Every technology that is used to create interactive dance will have some impact on the choreography. It is especially true that if dancers are going to be required to wear some type of technology (sensors, markers, devices), this technology needs to be in place early so that dancers can adapt to wearing it. There are a variety of reasons: the dancers need to become accustomed to the worn technology so that it becomes a 'part of their bodies'. Also, depending on where the technology is worn or held on the body, it may impact the choreographic vocabulary. For example, in our productions in which dancers were required to hold mice, the choreography could not include any floor work, since the dancers would not be able to brace themselves. Similarly, there could not be any risky leaps, because the dancers would not be able to brace themselves in case of a fall. It is not possible to integrate technology that would require this type of choreographic adaptation late in the production cycle.

Impacts on Choreography

Every type of sensing or technological tracking of dancers will have some impact on the choreography. For example, an instrumented floor will define a space in which dance movements that activate the technology can take place. A camera-based tracking system will similarly define a 'viewable' space in which the dancers can be successfully tracked. These types of technologies then have the same type of impact as stage size does in traditional dance. In normal dance productions, spacing takes place when the production moves from rehearsal studio to the performance stage, typically a week or two before opening night in academia. The choreographers know the final stage dimensions ahead of time and can sometimes tape off those dimensions in the rehearsal space so that the performers can practice adapting to the actual stage size. This can also be done for technological interventions that affect spacing.

Other technological interventions may impact the dancers' movements more directly. Having dancers wear equipment impacts the types of movements made and the level of energy employed. Thus, it is imperative that the technology to be worn is ready at the beginning of the production cycle and is available to be worn at every rehearsal. In our early productions that involved dancers holding wireless mice, the choreography had to be designed around the dancers holding the mice, since they were not hidden. Dancers need to get comfortable with the weight and feel of the equipment and learn how the devices handle after performing and sweating.

Costuming

In cases where the technology being integrated is worn by the performers, or where the costumes worn affect how the technology works, the temporal integration needs to take into account the costuming schedule. Costumes are typically conceptualized early but created mid-way through the production cycle, tailored towards the end of the production cycle and used in the dress rehearsals in the final week before the show. The costumer is usually present at one or two early rehearsals to get a sense of the choreographic concept and vocabulary and discuss costuming ideas with the choreographer. If the costumes need special features in order to accommodate sensors or techno-props, it is imperative that this is known early, at the costume conceptualization phase, since not only will the costumes need to be fitted, but they will also need to be tested with the technology, early enough to make adjustments for the technology if necessary. As an example of what can go wrong in costuming technology, multiple layers of costuming can inhibit wireless data transfer from sensors worn under the costume. Additionally, adding extra layers of costuming to hide technology can elevate core body temperatures, making the dancers uncomfortable. Determining early on what the parameters are for adequately hiding technology while ensuring the technology still works, and is comfortable for the dancers, is important.

In the "Whispering to Ophiuchus" production, where dancers were wearing wired wrist sensors with battery packs on their torsos, all hidden under their costumes, the gadgetry had to be designed so as to limit the discomfort experienced by the dancers. Getting the dancers into the worn gadgetry was time-consuming at each rehearsal (taking away from actual movement rehearsal time), but was necessary to help the dancers feel comfortable dancing while wearing the technology. The choreographer noted that in rehearsals when the technology was not worn, the dancers performed more articulately. The choreographer felt that with time that could improve, but that this particular technology setup was cumbersome enough that the performance would always be slightly hindered by it. This suggests that more cumbersome technology worn by performers may actually require a longer production cycle, and certainly requires that the technology and costuming be ready to use at the beginning of the cycle.

Academic versus Professional Dance Settings

While the experience we have reported on here has taken place within the academic context, one of the authors has extensive experience working with professional dance companies. The biggest difference is that professional dance companies have longer rehearsal hours in general, which means there is more time for experimentation. They also have significantly more time when moving from rehearsal space to the stage. However, new and experimental works often have less time. Some bigger dance companies have constant access to their own stage, which makes some of the issues we discuss here less salient. Professional dance companies also employ professional dancers who are able to create, learn and retain material more quickly, which allows more time for technology interfacing. However, the timing of the introduction of the interactive technology (both hardware and software) and how that impacts choreography or vice-versa is still quite salient.

Collaborative Production Software

Integrating interactive technologies into a dance performance is one way to bring technology into dance, but there are other aspects of technological integration. For example, there have been efforts to enable 3D choreographic modeling through software such as LifeForms [2, 3]. We have also developed a software tool that is aimed at allowing out-of-studio collaboration for the dance rehearsal process [15]. The use of collaboration software to enhance the process is relevant to this paper in that such systems may be able to mitigate some of the issues we have uncovered, where the integration of interactive technologies requires more rehearsal time or more time when moving to the stage.

TEMPORAL INTEGRATION CONSIDERATIONS

In this section, we present a list of considerations (and the potential impacts of these considerations) when planning a project that integrates technology into dance or perfomance in general.

Hardware Integration Does the technology being used involve hardware setup in the space or on the performers? Hardware is probably the most critical component that needs to be in place at the beginning of a production cycle. The dependencies, in terms of setup, costuming, tracking and testing all point to the necessity of having hardware in place before production begins.

Interaction Design Is the technology interactive, in that it responds to the performers and/or the performers respond to it? The best temporal integration for the design of interactive elements varies according to how that development takes place. If the dancers are to respond through the choreography to the digital elements, then the digital elements need to be in place early. If the digital elements are to respond to the dancers, then the choreography needs to be set and the digital elements can be designed in response. In the most compelling designs the interaction is bidirectional and requires tandem development.

Costuming Does the technology require being hidden, or alternatively, being exposed, by the costuming of the performers? There are issues of safety, comfort, and aesthetics that come into play when embedding technology into costumes. It is our experience that costuming takes time, and that dancers need significant rehearsal time to adjust to costumes that embed technology, thus embedding tech in costumes needs to be done very early in the process.

Lighting and Projection Systems Will the interactive technology performance make use of projections? There is a trade-off between being able to see the dancers, allowing the dancers to be able to see well enough to be safe, and the projected visuals being washed out by lighting. Since the actual stage lighting cannot be tested until the work is moved to the stage, scheduling additional technical rehearsal time for a piece with projections is often essential. Computers running visuals should be calibrated with the theater projector early on. We have found it useful to test the projector before each performance, as projection settings are sometimes reset or altered by others.

Sound Does sound play an important interactive role? If so, extra time is needed when the piece is moved to the stage in order to test and understand the acoustics in the stage space. Sound systems in rehearsal studios are typically very limited compared to those in professional venues.

Rehearsal Participation What is the appropriate team balance for rehearsals? Managing the team such that a small number of technology team members are at rehearsals and only when necessary, appears to be the best temporal integration strategy to ensure minimum disruption.

CONCLUSION

We have presented our experiences with integrating technology into six different dance productions at UNC Charlotte over the past three years. This has provided us valuable experience with a variety of models for the temporal integrations that employ different hardware and software systems for the creation of interactive dances. We have found that the timing of the introduction of the technology has salient effects on the dance production as a whole and on the choreography in particular. We have created a list of temporal integration considerations which will be very useful to others attempting to integrate interactive technology into dance.

ACKNOWLEDGEMENTS

We would like to acknowledge other Dance.Draw team members and past contributors: Erin Carroll, Vikash Singh, Adam Harris, Art Carroll, Mike Wirth, Nathan Nifong, Danielle Lottridge, Caroline Deeprose and Jordan Stevens. This work was supported by NSF CreativeIT (IIS-0855882).

REFERENCES

1. R. Aylward and J. Paradiso. Sensemble: a wireless, compact, multi-user sensor system for interactive dance. In *Proceedings of the 2006 conference on New interfaces for musical expression*, page 139. IRCAMCentre Pompidou, 2006.
2. T. Calvert. Animating dance. In *Proceedings of Graphics Interface 2007 (GI'07)*, pages 1–2, New York, NY, 2007. ACM.
3. T. W. Calvert, A. Bruderlin, S. Mah, T. Schiphorst, and C. Welman. The evolution of an interface for choreographers. In *Proceedings of the INTERACT '93 and CHI '93 conference on Human factors in computing systems*, pages 115–122, New York, NY, USA, 1993. ACM.
4. L. Candy and E. Edmonds. *Explorations in Art and Technology*. Springer-Verlag, 2002.
5. K. de Spain. Dance and technology: A pas de deux for post-humans. *Dance Research Journal*, 32(1):2–17, 2000.
6. K. Farley. Digital dance theatre: The marriage of computers, choreography and techno/human reactivity. *Body, Space and Technology*, 3(1):39–46, 2002.
7. R. Grove, C. Stevens, and S. McKechnie, editors. *Thinking in Four Dimensions: Creativity and Cognition in Contemporary Dance*. Melbourne University Press, 2004.
8. J. Hanna. *To Dance is Human: A Theory of Nonverbal Communication*. University of Texas Press, 1979.
9. J. James, T. Ingalls, G. Qian, L. Olsen, D. Whiteley, S. Wong, and T. Rikakis. Movement-based interactive dance performance. In *Proceedings of the 14th Annual ACM international Conference on Multimedia*, pages 470–480, New York, NY, 2006.
10. C. Latulipe, E. Carroll, and D. Lottridge. Evaluating longitudinal projects combining technology with temporal arts. In *CHI '11: Proceedings of the 29th International Conference on Human Factors in Computing Systems*, pages 1835–1844. ACM, 2011.
11. C. Latulipe and S. Huskey. Dance.Draw: Exquisite interaction. In *People and Computers XXII: Proceedings of HCI 2008*, pages 47–51. British Computer Society, 2008.
12. C. Latulipe, D. Wilson, S. Huskey, M. Word, A. Carroll, E. Carroll, B. Gonzalez, V. Singh, M. Wirth, and D. Lottridge. Exploring the design space in technology-augmented dance. In *CHI EA '10: Proceedings of the 28th of the international conference extended abstracts on Human factors in computing systems*, pages 2995–3000, 2010.
13. W. S. Meador, T. J. Rogers, K. O'Neal, E. Kurt, and C. Cunningham. Mixing dance realities: collaborative development of live-motion capture in a performing arts environment. *Comput. Entertain.*, 2(2):12–12, 2004.
14. R. Mitchell and M. Gallaher. Embodying music: Matching music and dance in memory. *Music Perception*, 19, 2001.
15. V. Singh, C. Latulipe, E. Carroll, and D. Lottridge. The choreographer's notebook – a video annotation system for dancers and choreographers. In *To appear in: Proceedings of the 2011 Conference on Creativity & Cognition*, C&C '11, 2011.
16. C. Stevens, S. Malloch, S. McKechnie, and N. Steven. Choreographic cognition: The time-course and phenomenology of creating a dance. *Pragmatics & Cognition*, 11, 2003.

A Scale Model of Mixed Reality

Evan Barba
Georgia Institute of Technology
Atlanta, GA 30332
ebarba3@gatech.edu

Blair MacIntyre
Georgia Institute of Technology
Atlanta, GA 30332
blair.macintyre@cc.gatech.edu

ABSTRACT
Augmented Reality (AR) is becoming more interesting to a variety of research communities beyond the small group of researchers that have traditionally studied AR technology. From its earliest years, AR has been presented as a subset of Mixed Reality (MR), and both have been conceived of in terms of the technologies they use. However, while the definition of AR has been fixed for a number of years, MR is much more ambiguous. Through a re-examination of the accepted definition of AR, we derive a new definition of MR that centers on human experience rather than technology. Then, through discussion of a number of paradigmatic examples that fit this new definition, we generate a classification system for MR experiences based on the concept of *spatial scale* and its associated cognitive processes. Finally, we discuss how this new "scale model" of MR helps to identify key concepts that can be used in the design process of future MR experiences.

Author Keywords
Mixed Reality, Augmented Reality, Multi-scale Design.

ACM Classification Keywords
H5.1. Artificial, augmented, and virtual realities.

General Terms
Human factors, Design

INTRODUCTION

Motivation
Mixed Reality (MR) technologies are at an important crossroads in the evolution of MR as a new medium. These experiences, which blend the physical and virtual worlds, have sparked the imaginations of many technology enthusiasts in the cultural mainstream, and are receiving new attention from researchers in communities outside the core technical community that has traditionally done MR related research. We have already seen a substantial increase in the number and kind of MR experiences available to the general public, and as professionals, students, and hobbyists all begin to engage with these technologies we can expect this trend to continue.

C&C'11, November 3–6, 2011, Atlanta, Georgia, USA.

Such growth is a healthy and necessary step in the evolution of new media, and has historical precedent in the adoption of other media forms associated with film, television, and the web, as examples [4,17]. Because MR is in its adolescence, there is still much to be learned about how elements of physical and virtual realities can be combined, and what the effects of these combinations might be. This fact, along with the lack of examples that might prejudice designers toward specific uses of the medium, places the imagination and creativity of MR designers at the forefront. As researchers, we therefore have a rare opportunity to examine how these designers conceive of MR and its possibilities, and to understand the cognitive processes that shape and constrain the creation of artifacts within this emerging and complex medium.

Approach
Models provide a way of comparing and contrasting different systems and applications, a language for talking about the experiences these systems enable, and help form the questions and interpretations that guide research and design. The current model of MR experiences is rooted in its history as a collection of technologies. However, as MR begins to play a larger role in mediating human experience, those experiences must become more central to our conception of MR than the technologies involved.

As a first step toward this change, we advance a more tightly constrained definition of MR that helps to remove some of the ambiguity in the current use of the term, and allows us to specify a collection of artifacts and experiences that we believe is representative of the current state of MR development. These examples, which are the products of various cognitive and creative processes, embody much of their designers' own mental models of how mixed realities should look and function. Through an analysis of the ways these examples approach the construction of mixed or "hybrid" space, we identify the concept of *spatial scale* as a central, and largely unconscious, component of MR experiences. We further ground the discussion of spatial scale in the cognitive science literature on the topic and advance a new model of MR with spatial scale as its organizing principle. Finally, we show how our model can be used to classify and organize MR experiences apart from the technologies they employ, and discuss how it can be operationalized in MR design and research.

Background
Augmented Reality (AR) has been conceived of as subclass MR. We wish to preserve this relationship and use it as a

starting point for our analysis. According to Milgram and Kishino [27] MR is best conceived of as a continuum between the two extremes of purely physical reality and completely virtual reality. While many MR researchers acknowledge the importance of this foundational work, recent advances have also highlighted a number of its shortcomings. Most notably, Milgram and Kishino's description of MR (primarily through discussion of examples rather than explicit criteria) is rooted in the notion that all MR experiences are most importantly characterized by their method of "display," which is usually visual, although sometimes auditory. However, MR experiences involve a number of cognitive capacities beyond the visual perception of a scene. These range from lower-level sensorimotor processes that manage interaction in the combined physical-virtual space, up to the higher order representational and symbolic processes associated with learning, memory, and meaning-making. None of these can be adequately accounted for in Milgram and Kishino's conception, and are increasingly central in discussions of MR.

Mann's related notion of Mediated Reality (also abbreviated MR) involves many of the same technological systems, and is also conceived of as a superclass of AR [23]. Mann's motivation is somewhat more humanistic and revolves around the idea of "agency." He suggests using Mediated Reality systems to filter the perception of reality with virtual information, based on the user's desires and needs. Although Mann is more engaged with the in-situ cognitive processes of the user, his notion of Mediated Reality also maintains a primary focus on the visual comprehension of reality through a display.

More recent computer-mediated experiences challenge these display-centric conceptions of MR. Mobile and geo-located applications for navigation, entertainment, and informal learning, routinely use virtual information to enhance the experience of physical reality. Although visual elements are often included, these experiences also use "embodied" elements of physical reality, like orientation and motion, as control inputs into the virtual world. Likewise, the increasing predominance of interactive systems (like billboards and kiosks) embedded in the physical environment, provide access to the world of information at an unprecedented scale. While neither entirely consistent with Milgram and Kishino's conception of MR, nor Mann's idea of Mediated Reality, these applications and systems mix virtual information from a variety of sources and mediate our experience and perception of physical reality.

OUR DEFINITION OF MIXED REALITY

The conception of MR must be broadened to include the perception and apprehension of hybrid realities as more than simply visual if we wish to adapt our knowledge of previous MR systems to the changing landscape of computer-mediated experiences. Yet, for any notion of MR to be useful, we must also keep those features of the traditional conceptions that set these experiences apart from other applications of technology. Otherwise, any definition will be so overly encompassing that the mere presence "virtuality" in any capacity will create an "MR experience," and essentially render the term meaningless. The central questions surrounding the role of virtual representations in the experience of physical space should still be at the core of MR research. However, we must also recognize that the answers to these questions can only be partially found in MR's technical apparatus. To answer them fully, researchers must also understand the user's cognitive apparatus, which is forged by culture and experience, colored by context, and bound in the body.

A complete discussion of how we arrived at our working definition of MR is not possible in the space available here, nor is it necessarily important. However some discussion is necessary, as we need to introduce a number of concepts relevant to the core of our model. The sections below are intended to communicate these core concepts as briefly and thoroughly as possible.

We have found it helpful to begin with the clear, precise and well-accepted definition of AR, introduced by Azuma [1]. Reconsidering this definition of AR for the broader class of MR accomplishes a number of goals. Most importantly, it gives us a vocabulary that we can use to explain the issues we considered while attempting to create a working definition of MR that encompasses a diversity of applications and future directions for research, while also allowing us to engage with a broader notion of human experience.

AR as Defined

Azuma specifies three criteria for an AR system:

1. Combines the real and virtual
2. Interactive in real time
3. Registered in 3D

Mapping Physical and Virtual

The first of Azuma's criteria, combining the real and virtual, is the most basic element of all MR experiences, and is straightforward on its surface. Unfortunately, specific definitions of "real" and "virtual" are hard to come by, leaving the boundaries of MR open to interpretation. To avoid getting into an extended philosophical discussion we consider "real" to be synonymous with "physical," and related to objects and environments that can be perceived without any technological mediation. Virtual elements then, are simply those elements that exist primarily as information, and can only be accessed through information and communications technologies (ICTs). Usually, this requires some mode of representation of the information that puts it into a form that can be perceived and understood by a user.

The question of how physical and virtual elements are combined is the subject of Milgram and Kishino's continuum. At one end of the spectrum, virtual elements are added visually into a physical scene, creating the familiar configuration of AR. At the other end of the spectrum, physical elements are placed into a virtual scene, creating the less well-known concept of Augmented Virtuality (AV). As is the case with any continuum, there are varying degrees of combining physical and virtual elements that constitute the middle of the spectrum. This conception suggests the notion that hybrid realities are created through process of "mapping" [21] or "blending" [12]. In the case of AR, virtual elements are mapped into physical reality, and in the case of AV, physical elements are mapped into a virtual reality. The notion of mapping is a very familiar one to cognitive scientists, many of whom consider it central to analogical and metaphorical reasoning processes [13]. This idea works as a bridge between these two disciplines and allows us to frame and interrogate issues of cognition within the realm of MR experiences while maintaining our focus on the combination of real and virtual elements.

Embodied Interaction

The second criterion, that AR be interactive in real time, involves two ideas that need to be expanded when considering MR, "interaction" and "real time." The analysis of interactions between people and technology is the central object of study for Human-Computer Interaction (HCI) research. That discipline has recently broadened its scope, including larger social and cultural issues surrounding the integration of computers into society [19] and examining computing as it occurs in a variety of contexts [29]; MR research must follow suit. Practically, this means treating MR technologies as part of a larger socio-technical system that both affects, and is affected by, human experience in a multitude of ways.

Engaging with the newly revised practices and frameworks in HCI research, therefore seems integral to a less techno-centric understanding of MR. While HCI offers many theories and frameworks to choose from, we focus primarily on the idea of "embodiment," identified by Dourish [11], as it already has close ties to the notion of "embodied cognition" that is well established in cognitive science research and intimately connected with the idea of metaphorical mapping already discussed. However, we recognize that there are synonyms and related concepts that also encapsulate this notion with slight nuances, such as the anthropological notion of "participation" [30], and the discourse surrounding "situated-ness" in both cognitive science and HCI [31]. More discussion of these terms and their relative differences and similarities is warranted, but impossible here, and so we simply chose what we felt was the most familiar one for most readers.

Real Time(s)

In addition to the concept of "interaction," the second part of Azuma's second criterion, "real time," also needs to be expanded when considering MR more broadly. Where Azuma intended for the term to denote immediate, observable changes in the state of the system, much as the term is used in HCI, a broader conception might allow for systems whose changes occur over extended time periods. Time, of course, operates on a number of scales ranging from the imperceptibly small computations of a microprocessor, to the imperceptibly large changes of geologic time. These are all "real" time frames. Although the extreme ends of this continuum might not be relevant to MR (or any mediated) experiences, a range of interaction times on the order of seconds, minutes, hours, or months, which are directly perceptible in human experience, must all be considered in a broader conception of MR.

Registered Frames of Reference

The final criterion, 3D registration, is perhaps the most constitutive of AR experiences. While most computer systems combine real and virtual elements that users interact with in real time frames, most are not registered in 3D. Because this idea is so integral to AR we must tread carefully as we try to expand it to include other kinds of MR experiences.

At the most general level, 3D registration marks AR technology as being primarily spatial, and this spatial element is something we want to carry with us into the more general MR domain. 3D registration is a 3-dimensional version of "image registration," which refers to the process of combining multiple images taken in different coordinate systems (typically different cameras, lenses, or positions) into one unified coordinate system (see [10,35] for a complete discussion). In the case of AR, instead of 2D images, we are typically discussing 3D spaces and models, and while all the objects being registered need not be 3D objects themselves, the final space does need to appear as if it is rendered in 3D (even if it is then projected onto a 2D screen). This is somewhat confusing for novices, and this part of Azuma's definition reflects the underlying techno-centric view that has been pervasive in AR research.

There is another way of conceiving of registration that, while no less complicated, is perhaps more intuitive. The essence of registration is that data from one or more *frames of reference* are mapped into one unified frame of reference. This can be done either by transforming one to fit the other, or by transforming both into a third, hybrid frame. Essentially, this is a more abstract way of describing the mapping or blending of the real and virtual that was discussed above; these terms are also the ones often used to describe stages or techniques of 2D or 3D registration.

Typically, when talking about registration, *frames of reference* are taken to be synonymous with *coordinate systems*. This is a mathematical interpretation of the term, and is appropriate given the mathematical operations needed to register two objects into one frame of reference. However, frames of reference can be understood more broadly as elements of cognition (particularly spatial cognition) and reveal themselves in linguistic and cognitive artifacts as well as mathematics. Adopting this larger view of frames of reference allows us to both expand our understanding of registration from AR into MR and to maintain its prominence in the definition of these systems.

The application of frames of reference as a cognitive mechanism for interpreting action is largely owed to Bateson [2], who noted that "framing" was the means by which play behaviors are distinguished from identical non-play behaviors. In Bateson's conception, establishing "play" as the frame of reference colors the interpretation and meaning of all actions and behaviors that follow. A typical example is found in the play of dogs. When dogs play, their actions are the same as when they are fighting. Yet, once a play frame is established, these actions are not interpreted as threatening. Not surprisingly, framing has also been studied in regard to MR gaming and performance [4], and so application of this concept to MR experience more broadly, is not without precedent. Additionally, the sociologist Erving Goffman, takes the notion of framing one step further in his development of "frame analysis" [15], and applies it to a wider range of human activities outside of play, specifically to "everyday life," [14]. He suggests, like Bateson, that framing is a foundational cognitive process responsible for organizing experience into meaningful categories.

Framing also comes into play in the work of Lakoff and Johnson [15], whose arguments for the fundamental role of metaphor in human thinking form the cornerstone of the theory of embodied cognition. In their conception, humans form "image schemas" through bodily experience that serve as the basis for understanding new experiences and abstract concepts. During the process of "mapping" a source domain (such as an image schema) is used to determine how the structure and relationships in the target domain are interpreted. Different aspects of the target domain will be emphasized or hidden, depending on the source domain used. In the often-cited examples of LOVE IS WAR and LOVE IS A JOURNEY different source domains are used to generate different models of the target domain (love). In this way the source acts to frame the interpretation of the target.

A Working Definition of MR

At this point we can give a reasonable working definition of Mixed Reality grounded in the very clear and concise definition of AR given by Azuma. From this discussion we could summarize MR as having the following elements:

- mapped
- embodied
- spatial
- temporal
- framed

For those who prefer a more traditional definition we might say:

Mixed Reality maps physical and virtual elements into a hybrid frame of reference that mediates interactions in time and space.

While neither form is perfect, they both accomplish the important goal of allowing us to consider different types of human experiences, either with or without technology, as part of the family of MR experiences. This larger collection of examples can now be systematically organized and used to illustrate our model of MR.

SPATIAL SCALE AS A MODEL

When using Milgram and Kishino's taxonomy one can classify MR experiences based on similarities in the technologies used. For example, handheld, head-mounted, or GPS based MR might all serve as categories. However, because we wish to remove technology as the basis for classification we must provide some other way of grouping MR experiences together. One alternative might be classification according to application domain. This would mean grouping experiences and systems into categories like "maintenance," "medical," or "tourism." Such a system might be useful in some cases, but it ignores the fact that interactions might be different depending on the task within the domain. For example, stitching a wound is more similar to sewing a button than it is to treating diabetes. This suggests that we need a framework that allows us to classify MR systems based on the kinds of interactions and experiences that they afford. The following sections of this paper aim to do just that. Using the concept of *spatial scale* as a lens, we extract the important commonalities in some archetypal MR experiences, and raise some specific questions about how these experiences work that have not been part of the discussion of MR up to this point.

The idea that scale, meaning "a relational system of general size categories," plays an integral role in the human experiences of space is not a new one. It is however, not one that is often discussed. The next section will serve as a brief introduction to work in this area, which is primarily at the intersection of the cognitive sciences, geography, and architecture, but also, as we demonstrate, applicable to interactions with technology. The essence of our argument is that mapping the physical and virtual into a single frame of reference can occur at any scale, and that classifying particular MR experiences according to the scale at which this mapping occurs provides a basis for understanding the cognitive processes involved in MR experiences.

Multiple Scales of Spatial Experience

Spatial cognition has been a vibrant area of research for quite some time, and overlaps a number of related disciplines from the obvious, like geography and architecture, to the less obvious such as media studies [34] and anthropology [30]. Spatial scale represents only one approach to understanding spatial cognition, but it is a valuable one for understanding MR experiences because it is premised on the idea that people use different cognitive abilities (especially internal representations) to understand space at different scales [16].

Many of the rudiments of what might be termed *scale cognition* can be found in the seminal work of Lynch [22], who describes observer's internal "images" of cities. The first explicit application of scale in spatial cognition, however, comes from Ittelson [22]. Ittleson noted the importance of understanding "environmental" cognition as distinct from the object space typically studied by psychologists up to that point. The distinction he draws is an embodied one; that is, it relies on the relationship of the physical body of the subject to the space being studied. Small-scale spaces are small relative to the body and can therefore be perceived in their entirety from one perspective; they are also usually manipulable. In contrast, large-scale spaces, or "environments," are larger than a human subject and therefore require movement and locomotion to comprehend completely. Due to their large size and limited view, environments also require the internal cognitive summation or integration of multiple views over time.

Deriving Our Framework

Building on Ittelson's work, many cognitive psychologists have posited various schemes to create more nuanced distinctions between and within the categories of large-scale and small-scale spaces. Similarly, geographers have also taken up this question of how spatial cognition is influenced by and dependent on scale, as the representation and perception of spaces is fundamental to their work. The model of spatial scales we use here is based primarily on the one proposed by Montello [18], and is depicted in Figure 1.

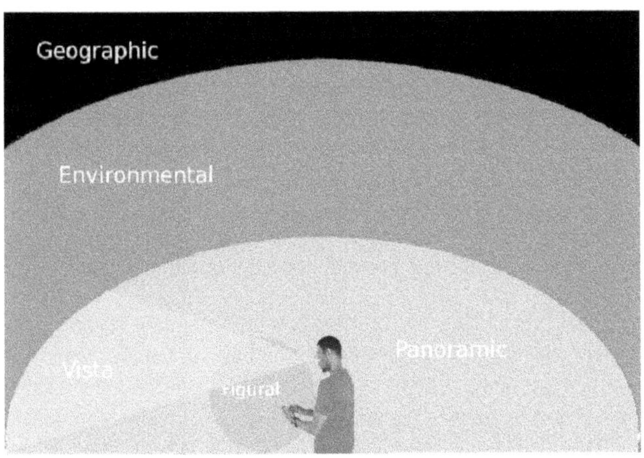

Figure 1. Our model of spatial scales.

Montello's framework consists of four categories of scale, making it among the simpler conceptions. What makes it most compelling for our purposes though, is that each of his scales can be correlated to specific positions, movements, and actions of the human body; making it entirely consistent with the focus on embodied experience running throughout our argument. However, Montello's conception does have one major weakness that needs to be addressed before we apply it. The immediacy of visual experience, and its importance in AR, requires that we add a fifth kind of space (panoramic), although the four original spatial scales are still maintained. Montello describes each of his scales as follows:

Figural Space - Objects less than or equal to the size to the human body, can be apprehended without locomotion, can be subdivided into *object* (3D) and *pictoral* (2D) spaces.

Vista Space – As large or larger than the human body, can be visually apprehended from a single place without locomotion.

Environmental Space – Larger than the human body, too large or obscured to be apprehended without locomotion and therefore requires the integration or summation of information over time.

Geographical Space – Larger than the human body, cannot be directly (physically) experienced and, therefore, must be represented figurally in a map or model.

Figural Space

At the lowest level, the figural scale, the space can be viewed in its entirely and is experienced through the act of manipulation. A further point about figural scale representations comes in regard to maps. As noted in his description of geographic scale, the only way to perceive geographic space is through some figural scale representation. This can be either a map (2D) or a model (3D). Because these representations involve two distinct scales (a larger scale space projected into a smaller scale space) and are the only way to perceive environmental and geographic spaces in their entirety, they play an important role in the experiences of larger scale spaces.

Vista and Panoramic Space

The next scale, what Montello refers to as vista space, needs further elaboration. We have relabeled this scale "panoramic" and reserved the term "vista" for a subspace that is essentially a currently visible slice of the panoramic space, as can be seen in Figure 1 above. However, this was not solely our invention. In [28], the geographers, Scott Freundschuh and Max Egenhofer summarize and examine 20 different models of spatial scale, including Montello's, and derive the category of "panoramic" space based on elements common to many of these conceptions. The scale of panoramic space is identical to Montello's vista scale; however, for our application to MR, conceiving of vista as a subspace is more productive for two reasons. First, as we have continued to note, AR is largely visual in nature and while panoramic spaces and vista spaces are of the same scale, panoramic spaces are not visible in their entirety from any orientation. Instead, to experience a panoramic space an observer must rotate their body or head to "scan" the world, effectively integrating numerous views together. Yet, at any given time, only a segment of this space is visible. We need a term to describe this currently visible space, and a "vista" serves this purpose nicely. Second, "panorama" is a specific MR technique that can be used to create a virtual space that surrounds the user, but is independent of his position (only rotation or orientation matters). This makes the adoption of panoramic space as a category even more apt, as it correlates exactly to a known MR technique. It is also noteworthy that, in that same survey, the authors also acknowledge the special "bi-spatial" quality of maps and give "map space" its own category in their model.

Environmental Space

Where figural and panoramic spaces can both be comprehended from one position, Environmental spaces require locomotion to experience them, and that is their defining characteristic. What panoramic and environmental spaces have in common, however, is that both surround the human body and therefore require the integration of spatial information over time. As observed by Ittleson, people interact differently in these spaces, compared to figural spaces, and call upon different skills to do so. The implication here is that different cognitive faculties, internal representations and mental models for example, are required at different scales. Furthermore, where embodied cognition suggests that internal models are at least partially the result of unconscious processes associated with positioning and moving the body in space, the individual actions of *manipulation*, *scanning*, and *locomotion* are likely to activate different internal models.

Geographic (Global) Space

Because geographic scale experiences cannot be experienced directly, one might be inclined to believe that they are less relevant for MR. However, the earlier discussion of frames of reference makes the idea of geographic scale MR experiences a bit more tangible. A geographic scale space provides a frame of reference for the scales below it (just as an environment frames a panorama). The act of blending a virtual and physical frame at this scale creates a hybrid frame of reference. Exactly what kind of experience this might create is explored further below. For now though, in recognition of the top-level framing quality of geographic scale, we will re-label this type of space *Global Space,* a conception that brings it closer to the idea of a "global variable" found in computer programming that is accessible from any scope (or scale) below it.

SCALE IN MR APPLICATIONS

The following sections discuss some exemplars of MR experiences and applications at each of the various scales with particular attention to the external representations they employ and how these relate to internal representations derived from embodied experience. This list is far from exhaustive as the number and kind of these experiences is growing rapidly. However, the examples discussed here are some of the most commonly cited examples of AR and MR experiences. By highlighting how each of these experiences leverages spatial scale, we aim to demonstrate how this framework can be used to organize any experience that fits our definition of MR.

Figural Scale MR Experiences

The figural scale of MR experiences is currently the most well explored area of MR. The simple reason for this is that the most widely available and easiest to use technology up to this point has relied on the use of easily trackable fiducial markers to correctly register virtual content into the world. These markers themselves are figural scale objects, and so the virtual objects and 3D worlds mapped onto them are naturally figural scale as well. In many of these examples, an entire virtual environment is mapped into the figural space.

Levelhead

Figure 2. Levelhead.

The game "Levelhead," developed by Julian Oliver, uses some particularly interesting applications of scale. In this game, which is described by the creator as, "A 3D Spatial Memory Game," the player must twist and tilt a cube to move an animated character from a predefined "entrance" to an "exit." It is essentially a 3D maze. Each face of the cube represents a single room that has a number of doorways for entering and exiting, as well as a number of obstacles such as walls and stairs. Although the original version uses just one cube with six rooms, later versions use three cubes for a total of eighteen rooms, creating a more complex puzzle. What makes the game novel is that AR technology is used to "map" the various 3D rooms onto the individual faces of the cube, creating the appearance that each face of the cube corresponds to an entirely different and overlapping volumetric space.

Viewing this MR experience through the lens of spatial scale we can see first that the experience has all the elements that we would expect at the figural scale. The entire AR world is contained on a tabletop and therefore viewable from a single position, and the mode of interaction is manipulation; the player rotates and tilts the cube on the tabletop. The most interesting aspect of Levelhead though is the choice of representations it uses. While the experience occurs at the figural scale, the representations used on the faces of the cubes are at the panoramic scale when imagined from the perspective of the player's avatar. Similarly, the 3D environment of Levelhead is a summation of these panoramas; a collection of rooms with relationships between them that require locomotion of the avatar in order to perceive them as a whole. Thus, solving the puzzle requires the player to construct an internal representation that connects these various spaces together, an internal representation of environmental space. Such a representation is often referred to as a *cognitive map* [8,16,33].

Levelhead is also a "map," (although "model" is more technically correct) in the sense that it is a projection of a larger scale space, the panoramic scale of the rooms, into a smaller scale space, the volume of the cube. Levelhead could easily have been accomplished with purely figural representations. However, Oliver's choice to use the metaphor of navigating through a building taps into other cognitive abilities related to experiences of space at different scales. One possible strategy for navigating Levelhead would be for the player to internally adopt the perspective of the avatar and imagine walking through the maze in the first person. Although no study of Levelhead has been done to determine if this strategy is used, perspective-taking is considered one possible "mediating variable" in the coordination of action across spatial scales [11].

Tversky [32] identifies three distinct perspectives adopted by research subjects asked to take a researcher on a verbal tour of their apartments. These perspectives, *survey*, *gaze*, and *route*, also correspond to the figural, panoramic and environmental scales. Knowing how, when, and why participants in MR experiences adopt these different perspectives and what tasks each are suited for would be tremendously valuable for MR research. As Levelhead demonstrates, these choices affect the kinds of strategies users employ when interacting with these systems and could enhance certain aspects of MR experiences. The choice to incorporate spatial scales in Levelhead was, most likely, not consciously based on any cognitive theory. What is more likely, is that Oliver was attempting to tap into an unconscious and embodied understanding of space, which suggests that scale cognition is something innate and natural and can make its way into the design process implicitly.

Panoramic Scale MR Experiences

The Artvertiser

Figure 3. The Artvertiser.

Another of Julian Oliver's projects, The Artvertiser, created in collaboration with Clara Boj, and Diego Diaz is a good example of a panoramic AR experience. A user views the hybrid space through a device that resembles a high-tech pair of binoculars. A computer in the device uses a computer vision algorithm to detect the sharp corners and rectangles that typically define a billboard or poster advertisement. Once an advertisement is within view, the system selects an image from an onboard database and inserts it over the advertisement. The Artvertiser was created as a way to give consumers more control over their environment. As the authors claim, it transforms the "read-only" spaces of billboards into "read-write" spaces. While the political ramifications of this are interesting, and the potential to "rent your eyes" to artists and advertisers is a compelling business model, it also has interesting implications when analyzed in terms of scale.

The Artvertiser is a panoramic scale AR application, as the entire experience can be viewed from one location and the primary means of observing the space is through "scanning." However, it is actually only a vista experience, because the virtual content is limited to what is currently in view, it is not immersive. Perhaps standing in the center of Times Square and scanning around with the device would create the impression that one is surrounded by virtual content; yet, the underlying technology of The Artvertiser only selects bounded segments of the surrounding space as isolated areas for augmentation. One never has the impression that a single augmentation extends beyond the current view, the virtual space of The Artvertiser is discrete and much more like the fiducial marker tracking described in the section above. Yet, the idea that content from one view might be conceptually related to content in another view is very much still a possibility for The Artvertiser and systems like it. The Artvertiser underscores the already observed [7,20] fact that the role of *boundaries* in MR experiences is an important one. How users recognize what is, and is not, part of an MR experience; how relationships between disjoint areas or representations are connected; and how these experiences are engaged and disengaged, turned off and on, need to be considered when creating immersive interactive MR experiences.

Although they occur at the same spatial scale, "panoramas" created with a different technology, the Argon AR Browser[1], offer a truer panoramic scale experience than The Artvertiser, and hint at how this experience might be successfully deployed. Panoramas created with this system are essentially a collection of perspective-adjusted images placed to form a box (akin to the skybox used in video game design) around the user. As Figure 4 illustrates, these spaces are continuous areas of virtual content that completely surround the user, and require scanning to perceive completely. Of course only a vista can be viewed

[1] http://www.argon.gatech.edu/

at one time, and only through a small "window" created by the screen of a handheld device. Yet, the lack of boundaries that mark the beginning and end of the virtual space create a more continuous and immersive panoramic scale experience. Figure 4 is taken from a MR tour of a college campus and the role of the panorama shown here is to provide a "virtual tour stop" that allows the user to experience a space that they would otherwise not have access to on the physical tour, the inside of the football stadium. Creatively manipulating these kinds of immersive panoramas in different contexts seems to be a wide-open area for both research and design.

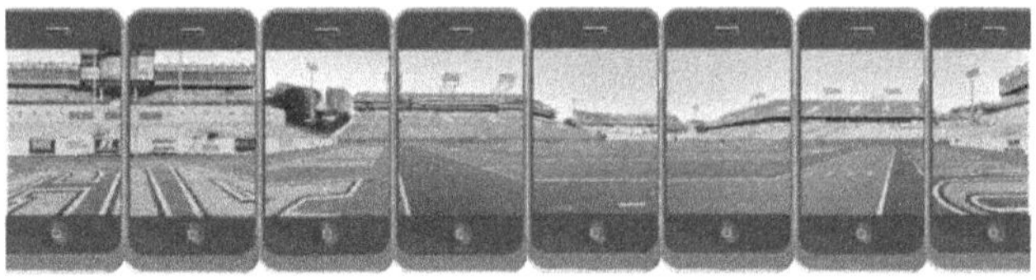

Figure 4. Handheld Panorama.

Environmental Scale MR Experiences

Human beings are only capable of seeing what is in directly in front of them, objects and places that are out of view exist only in memory as symbols and sense impressions. This implies that AR is only possible in figural and vista spaces where the entire space is perceptible from one vantage point. Regardless of whether content persists visually, it is still a component of the user's experience of the space, as part of their internal representation of that space, and is available again with a glance in the right direction. Because larger scale experiences combine the physical and virtual in ways that are not wholly visual the emphasis naturally shifts to methods and techniques needed to construct coherent internal representations of the hybrid spaces.

Can You See Me Now?

Figure 5. Can You See Me Now?

The game Can You See Me Now? (CYSMN) [3] is a good example of an environmental scale MR experience. In the game, which is essentially a game of "tag," online players access a virtual model of a real city, although the usable playspace is limited to a 500x1000 meter area. Online players can move through the model using the keyboard. "Runners" in the physical world move throughout the real city and their GPS locations are updated in real time within the virtual model so online players can see the location of the runners chasing them. Likewise, runners have an interactive map on their handheld device that shows their location and that of the players they are chasing.

Although CYSMN involves representations at numerous scales, (runners can stop and look around to get a panoramic view, or look at the figural space of their handheld), the mapping of virtual and physical spaces, occurs at the environmental scale. The physical environment of the runners and the virtual environment of the online players are registered to create a hybrid space that frames the actions of both. This hybrid space exists only as an internal representation, a cognitive map, in the minds of the players and runners. Externally, only fragments of relevant information are perceptible. An avatar represents the runner's position in the online virtual world, and the GPS coordinates represent the location of the online player in the real world. Apart from suggesting that MR environments can exist as shared representations across a number of individuals, CYSMN also brings up issues surrounding what bits of information from higher scales can and should be represented in lower scales. Deciding what forms these should take, and understanding how they are coordinated together to facilitate the creation of good cognitive maps, is going to be of paramount importance for understanding and building future environmental scale MR experiences.

In work that reflects on a number of these environmental scale MR experiences [5,6] that "[...] extend over space and time and involve multiple roles and interfaces," Benford et al. introduce the notion of "Trajectories of Interaction" as a theoretical construct. They describe three classes of trajectories, *canonical*, *participant*, and *historic*. A canonical trajectory defines a path through the experience that the designers intend (or at least suggest) for users to follow. The participant trajectory, refers to the actual path that the participant took through the experience, and the historic trajectory describes the result of retrospectively recombining segments of the participant's experience to create an alternate timeline of the events. While an in depth discussion of these is not possible here, they do present interesting possibilities as a metric for evaluating and comparing individual experiences of environmental scale MR, and as a starting point for understanding the mental processes involved in the generation of cognitive maps.

Geographic (Global) Scale Experiences

Due to huge expanses of space and large amounts of time, geographic space cannot be directly experienced. Like environmental scale spaces we can only view geographic spaces as maps, projected into a smaller scale. The possibility of geographic scale MR experiences though, is an interesting one. As mentioned above, applying the notion of frames of reference that is built into our definition of MR makes the idea of global scale MR more tangible. One example might be Alternate Reality Games (ARGs). These games, discussed in detail by McGonigal [25,26], create alternate contexts for the experience of everyday reality. Essentially, ARGs add virtual content to our everyday physical world by creating a narrative structure that works to recontextualize everyday experiences and objects. Physical environments are not altered, however the experience of them is, by giving them new significance in the virtual narrative of the game. ARGs can last for months, and are played simultaneously by many people separated over large distances (across continents, for example). These large distances and time-spans are the hallmarks of geographic scale spaces. Global scale MR then, would seem to require creating a virtual frame of reference that colors and shapes experience at the lower scales.

For McGonigal, the element of these games that sets them apart from other kinds of ubiquitous games, is their "immersive" nature. For her, immersion refers to the degree to which the play frame permeates the everyday life of the players. This is a different idea than the sensory-based notion of immersion found in traditional MR literature. Reconciling these two conceptions, which still have much in common, is likely to be a productive line of inquiry for future MR research.

Multi-scale MR Experiences

As compelling as MR experiences at individual scales can be, experiences that map at multiple scales offer unique emergent opportunities for design. One of the particular opportunities within multi-scale design is the ability to make the relationship between scales meaningful. One project, which grew out of an MR design studio we held in spring 2011, demonstrates this quite elegantly.

Figure 6. Diagrams of "Space in the Artist's Memory."

"Space in Artist's Memory" (Figure 6) by Chanju Lee, is an art installation designed to tell the universal story of the cycle of life. The installation depicts the artist in her youth and as an adult with a family, as well as her young children who allow her to experience being young again through their eyes. To communicate this eternal and universal cycle, Lee uses a painting mounted on the wall of the gallery and a small dollhouse in one corner. Users can view either the painting or the dollhouse through their handheld device. The painting depicts the artist and her home as they currently are, however the accompanying AR imagery contains animations that show the artist's children running to the small house in the distance. This house is also represented physically in the space as a dollhouse painted with abstract images depicting a number of the artist's childhood memories. When the dollhouse is viewed with the device, the AR content animates the artist as a child walking through the dollhouse as if it were her childhood home, and has the dreamlike quality of memory.

There was no discussion of spatial scale in this class, and the project was largely conceived before the semester even began, which makes it all the more remarkable that the student designed the project using scale so explicitly. Each scale space represents time in this project. The present is panoramic scale (a vista), while the past and potential future is the figural scale. The association between these two, accomplished through the juxtaposition, is one of continual movement and transformation. Where each scale represents a particular time period, the connection between the two represents the flow of time, both linearly and circularly. We think this project, although incomplete at the time of this writing, is a particularly elegant approach to coordinating and transitioning between scales in meaningful ways, and one that reveals the depth of spatial scale as universal cognitive construct and its power as a model of MR.

IMPLICATIONS FOR DESIGN

Although space does not allow for a thorough discussion of how our scale model might be used in the design of MR experiences, there are nonetheless a few concepts worth mentioning in addition to those discussed already, and which we hope to expound upon further in future work. Obviously, the notion of *scale transitions* mentioned above has great potential. In multi-scale experiences how, when, and why users might switch between representations of the mixed reality at different scales is an important consideration. How to make these transitions clear and understandable is a basic concern, but adding additional meaning is an excellent opportunity for creative decision-making. Furthermore, this concept seems closely related to the notion of the "coordination of representations" originally observed by Hutchins as integral to Distributed Cognition [17]. Although his original formulation, in regard to the "fix cycle" used to chart the course of a ship, focuses on coordination of various representations across media we believe the notion describes the coordination representations across scales equally well, and warrants further analysis.

A second relevant concept has to do with *scale matching*. When creating an MR experience it is important to recognize the scale at which the task occurs and then chose the appropriate design elements (technology, representations, etc.) accordingly. For example, navigation in the physical world is largely an environmental scale task (although vistas and figural maps can play a role), a user must move through an environment from one place to another. Creating a mixed reality that requires manipulating small objects, pins on a map for example, might place too much emphasis on the figural scale at the expense of actually completing the environmental scale task. Understanding what scale a task is at, and what strategies and technologies are best suited to that scale can potentially identify good and bad design choices early on in the design process.

REFERENCES

1. Azuma, R.T. A Survey of Augmented Reality. *Media 4*, August (1997), 355-385.
2. Bateson, G. *Steps to an Ecology of Mind*. Jason Aronson Inc., (1973).
3. Benford, S., Crabtree, A., Flintham, M., et al. Can you see me now? *ACM Transactions on Computer-Human Interaction 13*, 1 (2006), 100-133.
4. Benford, S., Crabtree, A., Reeves, S., Flintham, M., Drozd, A., and Sheridan, J. The Frame of the Game: Blurring the Boundary between Fiction and Reality in Mobile Experiences. *Interfaces*, (2006).
5. Benford, S., Giannachi, G., Koleva, B., and Rodden, T. From Interaction to Trajectories : Designing Coherent Journeys Through User Experiences. (2009), 709-718.
6. Benford, S. and Giannachi, G. Temporal trajectories in shared interactive narratives. *Proceeding of the twenty-sixth annual CHI conference on Human factors in computing systems - CHI '08*, (2008), 73.
7. Benford, S., Greenhalgh, C., Reynard, G., Brown, C., and Koleva, B. Understanding and constructing shared spaces with mixed-reality boundaries. *ACM Transactions on Computer-Human Interaction 5*, 3 (1998), 185-223.
8. Billinghurst, M. and Weghorst, S. The use of sketch maps to measure cognitive maps of virtual environments. *Proceedings Virtual Reality Annual International Symposium '95*, (1995), 40-47.
9. Bolter, J.D. and Grusin, R. *Remediation: Understanding New Media*. The MIT Press, 2000.
10. Brown, L.G. A survey of image registration techniques. *ACM Computing Surveys 24*, 4 (1992), 325-376.
11. Dourish, P. *Where the action is*. MIT Press, 2001.
12. Fauconnier, G. and Turner, M. *The Way We Think*. Basic Books, 2002.
13. Gentner, D., Holyoak, K.J., and Kokinov, B.N. *The analogical mind: Perspectives from cognitive science*. MIT Press, 2001.
14. Goffman, E. *Presentation of Self in Everyday Life*. Doubleday & Company, INC., New York NY, 1959.
15. Goffman, E. *Frame Analysis*. Harper and Row, 1974.
16. Hegarty, M., Montello, D., Richardson, A., Ishikawa, T., and Lovelace, K. Spatial abilities at different scales: Individual differences in aptitude-test performance and spatial-layout learning. *Intelligence 34*, 2 (2006), 151-176.
17. Hutchins, E. *Cognition in the Wild (Bradford Books)*. The MIT Press, 1996.
18. Ittelson, W. Perception of the large-scale environment. *Transactions of the New York Academy of Sciences*, (1970).
19. Kling, R. Social Analyses of Computing: Theoretical Perspectives in Recent Empirical Research. *ACM Computing Surveys 12*, 1 (1980), 61-110.
20. Koleva, B., Schnädelbach, H., Benford, S., and Greenhalgh, C. Developing mixed reality boundaries. *Proceedings of DARE 2000 on Designing augmented reality environments - DARE '00*, (2000), 155-156.
21. Lakoff, G. and Johnson, M. *Metaphors We Live By*. University of Chicago Press, 1980.
22. Lynch, K. *The Image of the City*. The MIT Press, 1960.
23. Mann, S.N. Mediated Reality. *Technical Report 260. MIT Media Lab, Perceptual Computing Group*, (1994).
24. Manovich, L. *The Language of New Media (Leonardo Books)*. The MIT Press, 2002.
25. Mcgonigal, J.E. This might be a game: ubiquitous play and performance at the turn of the twenty-first century. *Construction 54*, (2006), 258.
26. McGonigal, J. A Real Little Game : The Performance of Belief in Pervasive Play. *Network*, (2003), 0.
27. Milgram, P. and Kishino, F. A Taxonomy of Mixed Reality Visual Displays. *IEICE Trans. on Information Systems*. Vol. E77-D,12 (1994), 1-15.
28. Montello, D. Scale and multiple psychologies of Space. In *Spatial Information Theory: A Theoretical Basis for GIS*. Springer Vering Lecture Notes in Computer Science 716, Berlin, 1993.
29. Nardi, B.A. Context and consciousness: Activity theory and human-computer interaction. In MIT Press., Cambridge, MA, 1996.
30. Shore, B. *Culture in mind*. Oxford University Press, 1996.
31. Suchman, L. *Plans and Situated Actions*. Cambridge University Press, 1987.
32. Tversky, B. Narratives of Space, Time, and Life. *Mind and Language 19*, 4 (2004), 380-392.
33. Tversky, B. Spatial Cognition: Embodied and Situated. (2008).
34. Warf, B. and Arias, S. *The Spatial Turn: Interdisciplinary Perspectives*. Routledge, 2009.
35. Zitova, B. Image registration methods: a survey. *Image and Vision Computing 21*, 11 (2003), 977-1000.

Audience Empathy: A Phenomenological Method for Mediated Performance

Greg Corness, Kristin Carlson and Thecla Schiphorst
gcorness@sfu.ca, kca59@sfu.ca, thecla@sfu.ca
School of Interactive Arts and Technology, Simon Fraser University
250-13450 102nd Avenue, Surrey, BC, Canada, V3T0A3

ABSTRACT
This research investigates audience experience of empathy with a performer during a digitally mediated performance. Theatrical performance necessitates social interaction between performers and audience. We present a performance-based study that explores audience awareness of performer's kinaesthetic activity in 2 ways: by isolating the audience's *senses* (visual, auditory, and kinaesthetic) and by focusing audience perception through defamiliarization. By positioning the performer behind the audience: in their 'backspace', we focus the audience's attention to the performer in an unfamiliar way. We describe two research contributions to the study of audience empathic experience during performance. The first is the development of a phenomenological interview method designed for extracting empirical evaluations of experience of audience members in a performance scenario. The second is a descriptive model for a poetics of reception. Our model is based on an empathetic audience-performer relationship that includes 3 components of audience awareness: contextual, interpersonal, and sense-based. Our research contributions are of particular benefit to performances involving digital media, and can provide insight into audience experience of empathy.

Author Keywords
Kinesthetic Empathy, Dance, Audience Perception, Phenomenological Methods, Performance Technology

ACM Classification Keywords
J.5 Arts and Humanities

General Terms
Human Factors, Measurement, Theory, Experimentation

INTRODUCTION

Research in audience-performer connection often focuses on three elements: performative, choreographic and support of design qualities (sound, set, lighting, media etc.). These elements are presented as the foundation to building a connection with a *passive* audience with the goal of eliciting an interpretive and affective response from the audience [12]. Other research considers an audience member's kinesthetic perception as an integral part of their connection with the performer [29]. In both cases the increased use of media on stage has challenged the audience's traditional relationship to the performer both physically and conceptually [2][7]. Projections utilizing live and pre-recorded media alter representations of space and time thereby shifting the audiences' relationship to a performer. We are interested in *how* a deeper understanding of the audience's experience of perceiving performance can support the development of a *poetics of reception* for the use of media onstage. In the presence of media, performance remains a social interaction involving an empathetic connection between audience and performer. We explore this empathetic connection by applying phenomenological methods for extracting and analyzing data. An intimate, mediated performance environment was designed in conjunction with an 'experimental choreography' [18]. The performance design enabled us to defamiliarize [28] the audience's perception of the performer by placing the performer in the audience's 'backspace' (Figure 1). We developed phenomenological interview methods based on Petitmengin's research into intuitive experience [22][23] as a starting point for our investigation into audience perception of contemporary dance performance. Our analysis of audience interviews resembles a grounded theory approach in so far as we

Figure 1. Audience experience of perception supports *poetics of reception*

construct our models of audience experience from themes that emerged directly from data gathered from our study of audience experience. These models provide the basis for our articulation of a poetics of reception. We demonstrate how this research design provides a rigorous and descriptive method for exploring experience in performance.

BACKGROUND

Traditionally, western performance practice focuses the audience's experience on visual and auditory sensations in front of them through the use of the proscenium arch [26]. Some contemporary approaches to performance expand the proscenium arch model by positioning the performance within the audience space. Such approaches take advantage of the human ability to simultaneously perceive action arising from multiple directions including the space behind the self [26]. Theatre and dance works have explored human's perceptive ability in attempts to enhance the feeling of immersion within performance, enabling connection with the performers. Works such as John Jasperse's 'Just Two Dancers' and 'Prone' employ audience-performers proximity and nontraditional seating arrangements where portions of the performance can only be viewed through personal mirrors or from a ceiling of mylar [15][16]. These works are designed to explore the audience's perception and expectations, challenging them to become aware of how they construct meaning. We propose that a greater understanding of the audience's kinesthetic experience can provide insight into how the audience is forming a connection with performers and constructing their understanding of the work.

Interpersonal Connection

As humans, we are both subject and object in the world [20] and we mature by constructing meaning through embodied sensory experience [31][17]. The fundamental understanding that our experience in the world is related (as subject and object) to others suggests that audience-performer connection is, at least partly, interpersonal. This view of connection is paralleled by research in neuroscience on mirror neurons. Mirror neurons are largely found in the pre-motor area of the brain and are triggered by watching goal-oriented actions in others. It is suggested that the firing of these neurons provides the viewer with a low level kinesthetic response parallel to the performer, and is therefore associated with empathy and social learning [10]. In recent years researchers exploring audience empathetic response to performers have borrowed from emerging discoveries in neuroscience by considering the role mirror neurons play in creating empathic connection [24]. This research is ongoing yet reveals the growing view that audience-performer connection is founded in intersubjective human relationships.

Discussions on audience-performer connection have also considered social interaction. Goffman's view that humans perform versions of themselves in different situations has been applied to understanding the performer's role [2]. Underlying Goffman's theory is the suggestion that humans in a social interaction are reading the performance of others in order to understand, interact and connect. The context of an audience-performer relationship can then be understood as a layer akin to this fundamental human interaction. The audience is engaged in an act of social perception [1] in order to construct a connection with the performer.

Media in Performance

Digital media challenges traditional assumptions of the audience's role and position in a performance through the use of interactive technologies and live media feeds [7]. The role of the body as both perceiver and perceived can be easily manipulated through the use of media. The manipulation can both distort and enhance the fundamental process of understanding through the body. Aspects of the audience's perception such as time, proximity, and perspective can easily be shifted through the use of digital media. As digital media becomes more pervasive it is necessary to consider the role that the body's presence has on audience's experience and their perceived connection to the performer(s). Paul Sermon's work 'Telematic Dreaming' illustrates how media can transport both audience and performer to a shared space. Although performers are separated by physical distance, an intimate connection and closeness is experienced [19]. In her discussion of 'Telematic Dreaming', Kozel notes that both the performer and audience remain keenly aware of their interpersonal and social perception throughout this interaction [19].

Researching Experience

Audience members are not often conscious of the cognitive processes they enact when perceiving a performer. This social connection involves body cues that produce an empathetic and embodied experience. In order to examine audience experience fully, there is a need to develop a method for accentuating audience's awareness and facilitating description of their experience as articulately as possible. We have developed a phenomenological approach that is consistent with research on experience undertaken in Cognitive Science by Depraz [5], Varela [30][31] and Petitmengin [22][23], Design for Interactive Art within Human-Computer Interaction by Schiphorst [27] and in Dance by Kozel [19] and Fraleigh [9]. We recognize that audience experience contains uniquely individual elements in response to a performance; yet an analysis of similarities and differences between audience members can lead to a general model of audience experience.

RESEARCH DESIGN

For this study we have defamiliarized the audience's experience by placing the dancer behind them. Their visual focus was directed to the screen directly in front of them in order to view the performance. The proscenium arch style performance has largely conditioned audiences to attend to performances through their visual and auditory senses. By placing the performer behind, yet in physical proximity to the audience we engage additional senses such as audience's kinesthetic awareness. Social perception of others involves several senses working simultaneously and in combination [21][1]. It may be viewed as a tool constructed through human evolution as social beings. By manipulating senses we disrupt the use bringing conscious awareness to the tool [14]. Through an iterative experiential design process, we found that temporally shifting the visual and auditory senses of the audience member disrupted audience perception of the performer enough to bring attention to individual senses. The iterative design process applied to this study involved the first person experience of the authors as well as selected participants experiencing the environment. The goal was to develop an environment in which the viewer reported a high degree of sensation in their "backspace" and a heightened attention to the dancer's activities behind them. In preliminary tests, we found this manipulation of sensory experience encouraged audience members to become aware of their cognitive process while remaining continuously attentive to their experience.

The final study environment emphasized the sensation of *backspace* thereby creating unique potential for audience-performer connection. The term *backspace* is borrowed from the field of dance and is defined as the sensation of perceiving objects and actions behind one's self [21]. The experience is often attributed to heightened sensation beyond sight or sound. Although it may be described as a feeling, the experience generally involves several senses. The combination of senses promotes a non-visual and dynamic sense of space, facilitating an imagined sensation of movement [8]. Our study engages *backspace* by placing the dancer and audience on the same floor, in close enough proximity to affect personal space (Figure 2). These factors combined to contribute to the type and magnitude of kinesthetic experience we could expect the audience member to have.

Figure 2. Dancer contributing to construction of kinaesthetic experience in audience backspace

Design of Space

The research-performance incorporates four approaches for focusing the audience's awareness of their backspace. First, the research-performance was designed as an intimate individual experience. Second, the audience is seated facing a rear projection screen. The performance space is situated directly behind the audience (in their 'backspace') and shares the same sprung dance floor (see Figure 3). This design heightens awareness of physical phenomena produced by the dancer such as the floor vibration, air flow, and breath and contributes to the sensation of backspace for the audience. Third, a camera is placed at a distance to the side of the audience. The feed from this camera is projected on the screen in front of the audience. The placement of the camera ensures that the visual stimulus and the physical stimulus are separated. The separation of sensory stimulus is further enhanced by continually altering the length of delay in the camera feed. Fourth, the auditory experience is provided through headphones. Microphones placed on the

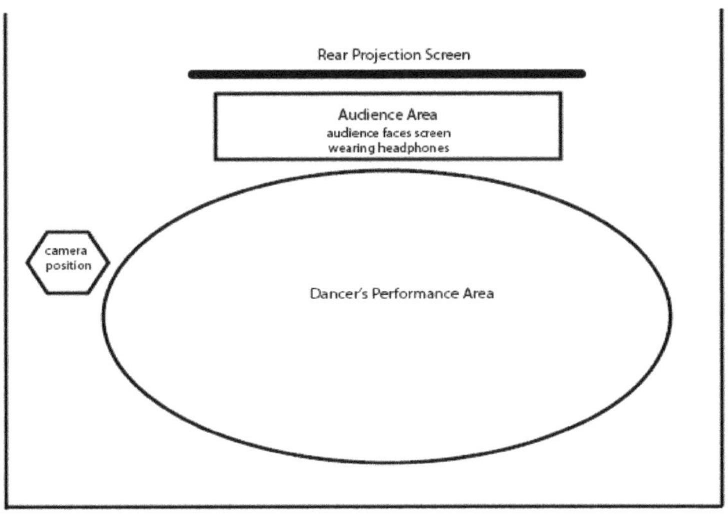

Figure 3. Technical Drawing of Stage Design

headphones worn by the audience provide an individualized spatialized audio feed for each audience member. The audio feeds are delayed independently from the video feed.

Design of Movement

We developed our research tool by exploring movement with dynamic changes in effort, sound, level and speed. Priority was placed on movements that explored the illusion of closeness and performer attention to the audience. Movements were also explored for their use in creating *'markers'* from which the audience could, in theory, recall their experience. The design of this 'experimental choreography' [18] aided us in isolating the experience of audience-performer sensation from the experience of constructing an interpretive understanding of a fully developed choreographic work. The final version was performed as a structured improvisation. The performer was aware of the percussive nature of their movements, their physical proximity to the audience and camera, as well as their mediated visual representation on the screen. Considering these components allowed the performer to make movement choices based on the temporal difference of the media event from the physical event.

Design of Procedure

The performance design enabled us to conduct the research as sessions with individual audience members. The protocol used for each session was developed iteratively during preliminary sessions. The final protocol consisted of the participant experiencing a 10 minute structured improvised dance piece followed by an open interview focused on facilitating their description of the experience. During the dance, the environment progressed through four stages: 1. from presenting a synchronized audio feed with no video image, 2. with a synchronized audio and video feed, 3. with a synchronized audio and a delayed video feed and finally 4. with both the audio and video feeds being delayed separately (See Figure 4).

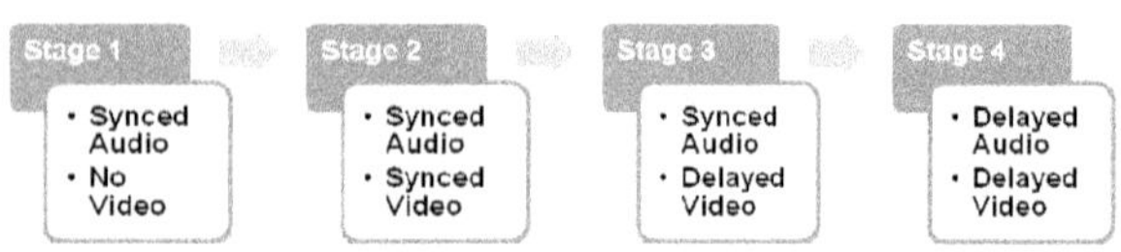

Figure 4. Stages of Study Progression with Dancer Always Present

Each stage included the dancer performing behind the audience member (in their backspace). The progression of stages gave the audience a contextual foundation of the experience to guide their understanding through the continual shifting complexity of the environment.

Execution of Procedure

Over the course of this study we interviewed 9 participants about their experience of the 'Illusion of Togetherness' performance. The participants came from a diverse mix of backgrounds including computer science, cultural studies and performing arts. Of these participants, 5 were male and 4 were female. Most participants had some exposure to the performing arts, though the exposure varied greatly. During the interviews the researchers' own first-person experience helped to provide an intersubjective understanding of the audiences' experience. This process allows us to triangulate the data between several sources thereby improving the validity of our findings.

DATA COLLECTION

Background

The focus of this study is the audience's perceived connection to the performer, which is a personal experience. In researching experience, there is the challenge that subjects may not have the practiced skills of self-reflection [5] or the vocabulary [12] to adequately articulate their experience. Methods have been developed in the domain of cognitive science that attempt to address this difficulty. In these methods the researcher acts as a facilitator to help the subject articulate their experience. As facilitator, the researcher uses their own experience and knowledge of the phenomena to help the subject fully explore their experience. Care is taken to construct questions using the subject's own words so as to not lead or influence their answers. The interviewer helps the audience member achieve a mental state of re-living the experience in part by focusing questions on the physical sensations being experienced during a particular moment. The interviewer can then ask questions focused on *how* the audience member perceives sensations in this re-lived moment, encouraging a contemplative reflection on their experience. This reflection facilitates descriptions of their process and avoids interpretations of their experience from an objective stance. [23]. Such interviewing techniques aim to help the participant achieve an authentic reflection that mimics the practiced reflection achieved in first person phenomenological description [5][19].

Adapting the Data Collection Method

In applying this interviewing technique to our performance research, we recognized that the cognitive research it had been designed for focused on short task oriented experiences or critical moments within longer general experiences [23]. We expected that the audience's experience of connection with a dancer could similarly be tethered to a moment with in the longer performance. In the work done by Petitmengin [23], *'markers'* in the form of statements by the researcher or environmental elements were used to help guide subjects back into a state of *re-living*. We explored using choreographic elements in a similar way but found during preliminary sessions that these moments did not resonate with the participants as moments of interest. We therefore adapted the procedure by structuring the manipulation of the media into four stages as described above (see Figure 4). We found that the progression of the media manipulation framed the audience ability to structure, remember and identify moments to refer back to and re-experience. Audience members were able to recall the adding or manipulating of the audio or visual material. We also found that the beginnings and ends of the stages provided points of known identifiable physical sensation such as seeing the video or hearing sound not linked with the video. These moments provided points that the researcher could use to guide the audience member back into re-living the experience. We developed this structure through comparative studies between sessions employing structured and unstructured manipulation of the media using first and second person methods.

Interview Process

Each participant experienced the performance alone as a single audience member. Directly after experiencing the performance they were interviewed on their experience. Each interview was structured with a set opening, then using open-ended questioning to facilitate the audience member's description of their experience. Each interview lasted 30 to 60 minutes. When the audience members' descriptions started to get short or repeated what they had said before, the researcher made an assessment as to whether the interview should be drawn to a close. To ensure that the experience was fully explored and that unexamined material was kept to a minimum the audience member was asked if the discussion had missed any other part of the experience that they wanted to talk about.

The interviews started with a quick explanation of how questions would be asked and opened with the same general question.

> **Researcher**: So what we want to do is help you place yourself back into that experience and tease apart how you were sensing the dancer.
> Was there a moment you really felt a connection with the dancer?

From this general question the interviewer followed the lead of the audience member. Care was taken to phrase new questions using words used by the audience member. These questions were focused on encouraging the participant to re examine their description and see if there was any more to the experience then they first described.

> **P1**: I tried to figure out how the dancer moved and then tried to see the image on the screen and tried to figure out the distance that she was moving …
> **Researcher**: And how did you try to figure out how the dancer was moving?
> **P1**: I tried to figure it out by seeing what she was doing and by listening to the sounds and noticing the delay but there was some problems … its kind of no delay

In the above example the researcher clarifies that the audience member is not just using their eyes but is also aware of other senses such as sound. This example also illustrates the use of "how" questioning, where questions are phrased to ask how the audience member perceived or sensed the experience. In this example the audience member realizes through the questioning that there was a problem with the sound that is worth mentioning. This form of questioning focuses the audience member on describing the physical sensations and mental process of the experience, avoiding rational explanations for the experience.

Data Analysis

Our method for analyzing of the phenomenological data borrows from Grounded Theory in so far as the themes used in the analysis were derived from the data itself. The interview of each audience member was transcribed and analyzed to construct an individual model of the experience in connecting with the dancer.

We began the analysis by separating the descriptions into senses. Each comment was flagged with the sensation it reference.

> **P3**: But I tried to see something interesting from the screen but I couldn't really find more engagement here.

The above example was flagged as a comment on visual sensation due to the reference to seeing. In the case that audience members used ambiguous terms such as *felt*, the context of the comment and the researcher's personal experience was used to derive a flag. This process was used to distinguish between statements of physical movement such as floor vibration and 'felt' empathetic connection. Both researchers independently carried out their own analysis of the interview data. The independent analysis by the two researchers helped provide increased validity.

The intentional nature of each comment was also considered. In general, comments can be divided into two types of intentions: descriptive and explanatory. With descriptive comments the audience member had the intention to describe the experience in terms of an action or state. In the above example the descriptive flag of "trying to make connection" was used since there is a reference to *trying to see something interesting* and *find more engagement*. This is an example of an action statement. Other descriptive statements might comment on a state of confusion or a progression of time.

The second intention, explanatory, often focused on providing explanations of assumption or beliefs. As Petitmengin suggests [22][23], we found that these statements provided little insight to the audience member's experience but were valuable in determining a context for the experience that they provided through their more descriptive comments.

An iterative process (described below) was used in the analysis involving categorization, comparison and reassessment of experience descriptions. This allowed the individual models and general model to be developed concurrently while being compared for validity.

General Model

The first stage of model construction was to compile the re-occurring themes of individual audience members to construct an *Individual Thematic Model* for each member, what Pentimengin referrers to as a *Synchronic Model* [22]. We developed a general vocabulary through these comparisons. Non re-occurring themes were also noted on topics such as sensing, understanding, awareness of presence and connection. The Individual Thematic models were compared in order to construct a *General Thematic model* of the experience. From these connections we constructed several categories that encompassed the comments of all the participants. These were: Safety, trust, empathy, assumed role, disparity, re-assessment, comparison, confusion, and synesthesia (connection between senses).

Temporal Model

Once the Individual and General Thematic models were constructed, we looked at the interview data again considering time signifiers. Some comments made by the participants referred to time or a sequencing of sensations.

> **P6**: Interestingly I think I was more aware of the chair early on and because it was a new kind of experience?

As discussed earlier, in preliminary studies we found that audience members had difficulty remembering when experiences occurred. For this reason the performance had been structured in four sections: Stage 1 dancer behind the audience/ sound synchronized with dancer's movements/ no projection on the screen, Stage 2 video projection and audio streams synchronized with the dancer's movements, Stage 3 audio stream synchronized with the dancer/ video stream delayed, Stage 4 audio and video streams delayed (see Figure 4). These sections could be referred to or identified by the researcher or participant to help give an indicator for when in the piece an experience occurred.

The researcher could also use this structure to help guide the participant to examine sensations that lead up to or came out of an experience.

> **Researcher:** So it seemed it was in sync to begin with – then what happened after?
>
> **P6:** I started to notice that she wasn't directly reflected by the mirror so when the dancer was on this side of the screen she wasn't on that side and I started to notice the inconsistencies of the sound, of the feet moving, of the jumps – things like that.

By analyzing the data in this manner a *Temporal Model* for each participant was constructed. After an *Individual Temporal model* was constructed for each audience member a comparison was made between individuals to construct a *General Temporal model*.

Through the construction of the Temporal model, a connection between the categories identified in the individual Thematic models emerged. We saw that audience members' comments on their assumed role, disparity in their understanding or assumptions, and their re-assessment of their understanding was associated with their process for constructing a *new role* or understanding of the performance. Similarly, their comments on awareness of personal safety, their trust in the performer's intention and authenticity, and their empathetic connection with the dancer's embodied state were associated in a process of developing an empathetic knowledge of the dancer. Finally, their comparison between senses, their connecting of senses and confusion when senses did not align was part of their process for balancing their priority in the senses. Through this analysis the interplay between the Thematic model and the temporal model became apparent. Relationships between comments could be identified as developments and shifts within elements that were equal parts in the audience's perception of connecting with a performer.

RESULTS

General Findings

It became apparent during the research that connecting with the dancer was a primary goal of most of the participants. This was a goal initiated by the audience members themselves with out the suggestion of the researchers. Additionally, each participant had a personal idea of what this connection would be. In comparing the individual temporal and thematic models, a single model for a poetics of reception emerged which incorporated three separate but interdependent components of awareness: contextual, interpersonal and physical (see Figure 5).

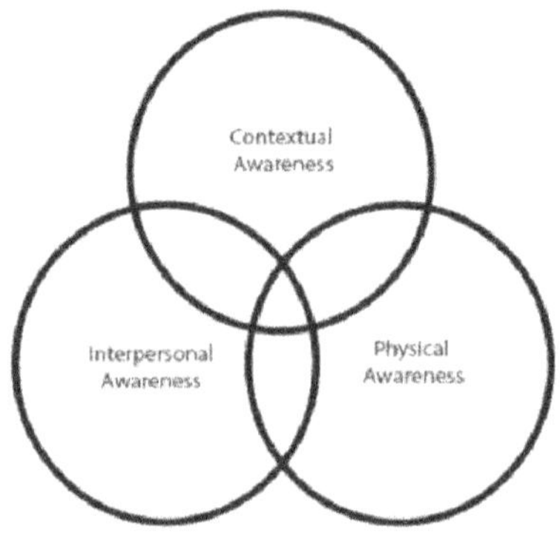

Figure 5. General Model of Connection

These components were identified through our analysis of the audience member's descriptions. The process for this was the identifying of connections between the emerging themes in the Thematic model forming three categories

1. Safety, trust, empathic knowledge [interpersonal]
2. Assumed role, disparity, re-assessment, construction of understanding [contextual]
3. Sensory comparison, confusion, synesthesia, and priority of senses [physical]

By considering the context and time that these comments were made through a temporal model, we were able to synthesize the data into the three overarching categories. These categories could be described as *components of audience's general awarenesses*. The three components may be viewed themselves as kinds of awareness: Contextual awareness, Interpersonal awareness, and Physical awareness. These describe the component of an audience member's awareness that focuses on their social perception, general context, and their physical sensations. The presence of each is evident in the following two comments.

> **P6:** 'I experienced it with the addition of each of the things you were doing as they progressed, so I was very aware of that going on. When it started I thought, wow,

> she is behind me and that is unusual and there is nothing on the screen. I found myself very aware of the noises coming behind me and in my peripheral vision and the floor moving, those were the only impressions I had. And then the image was in front of me so that combined with the peripheral vision and the floor bouncing and feeling that in my seat was suddenly very effective, and a very different experience. Then I tried to figure out if she was mimicking or repeating what was on the screen and at times it felt that you were opposite of what I saw on the screen. But I just felt strangely aware of her in two parts.'

> **P8:** 'I'm not quite sure what was happening in the beginning because I have the screen quite close to me. I have this moving image at the same time someone is at my back, and when I watch the image – I'm not sure if it's the sounds from behind me or if it's in front of me so I kind of just don't know exactly what is happening. I have feeling that she is running circles sometimes but I'm not sure if it is my illusion or is a reflection in my glasses.'

We suggest that a dynamic interplay between these three basic components of awarenesses can be used as a model for the audience's perception of connection with a performer. This general model relates to other models of audience understanding of performance by considering the audience's awareness of the performance context. This *Contextual Awareness* includes the understanding of the performance form and the expectations involved. But our model also includes a temporal aspect to this awareness. We found that comments made by the audience members indicated an assumption of what their role would be for a dance performance. When the environment did not afford them the perspective they expected, such as not being able to see the dancer, they described experiencing a disparity between what they wanted and what was being offered. This sensation then led to a re-assessing of their role, most often re-considering how they understood dance, what a performance is and if this environment was a performance. This re-assessment constructed a new understanding of the situation, which was then put into question again when the performance progressed. This process reoccurred throughout the performance whenever this component of their awareness was challenged, directly or by association to the other components (discussed later in this paper).

In the *Interpersonal Awareness*, audience members commented first on a feeling of questioning their safety, leading to questions of trust and finally to empathy. This related to research in non-verbal social gestures [1] but also illustrates a dynamic or temporal aspect. It is interesting to note that participants moved throughout these stages at different rates. It is noteworthy that *determining level of safety* was noted by most participants as an initial response to having the dancer positioned behind them. Those who did not comment on a safety concern, when asked, indicated that their contextual understanding (that this is a research project) assured them they did not need to be worried, suggesting they had thought about it and passed through this stage before the performance began and had already made it part of the contextual awareness.

Participant's comments on their physical awareness indicated there was a sequencing aspect to comparing sensations over time. For example comparing what was heard to have happened with what was seen to have happened created confusion as a result of the temporal disparity between events. But the most significant finding was not a progression as much as a prioritizing. Comments made by the audience members show that each individual had a preferred sense through which they perceived the performance. If disparity was perceived between the preferred sense and what was expected, or between the preferred sense and more then one other sense, the audience member would comment on shifting their awareness to another sense. Several comments indicated that when two or more senses aligned to give the same perception of the performance, these senses were given priority over other senses for constructing an understanding of the performance. Due to the way we constructed the performance environment, this priority was always in flux and audience members commented on constantly needing to reconstruct new understandings of the performance. This finding suggests that constant re-prioritizing is common for most performances. In normal conditions the new prioritized sense remains identical to the last, so audience member is not aware of this dynamic process.

Detailed Connection Model

In "The Illusion of Togetherness" we concentrated on the audience's sensual experience in order to explore their process of perceiving a connection with a performer. By viewing the audience-performer relationship as an inter-subjective human experience, we highlight how the audience's previous assumptions and expectations interact with their current sensations to create the perception of a performer's presence. We propose a model that extends earlier research in audience-performer connection that had focused on interpretation and connection with the piece as a whole [12]. Our model attempts to go beyond the rational act of interpretation to consider the dynamic experience of being and being with, the empathetic audience-performer connection. The dynamic relationship between the components (described earlier) lay at the foundation of our model. Though each component is independent, each affects how the others are perceived. Within each of the three components of awareness: contextual, sensual and interpersonal there is one part that represents an acceptance or knowledge (see Figure 6). We suggest that a stronger connection is perceived in experiences when one or more parts in the three elements represent a state of accepted knowledge.

We support this claim from experiences described by the audience/participants. We found in our study that audience members were sensitive to the *effort* of the performer, claiming the dancer was always felt as 'present'. They made several references to being aware of the performer 'going through something'; even when they were not able to visually see the events or articulate a specific gesture of narrative understanding. All these comments illustrate *empathetic knowledge*. Audience members also mentioned not feeling a need or desire to identify the detailed movement the dancer was executing behind them, since they could not directly witness it. But in the same statement, they explained that their curiosity was on the kinesthetic awareness of the dancer's physical journey rather than the visual representation. Such comments illustrate a *prioritizing* of the kinesthetic sense. One participant described letting go of any expectation of rational meaning and focusing on just the experience of kinesthetic connection with the body behind him, *constructing a new role* for the experience. These comments also imply that thematic understanding was not part of the relationship, and illustrate the desire to connect with the performer as a human first before an association of interpretation can be made.

The knowledge illustrated in these comments is understood as forming the connection made with the physical presence of the performer. However, our question remained of how that connection was made. A special element in the connection was the sensation of *breath*. Several participants mentioned *feeling* the dancer's breath. When asked to elaborate it became apparent that they were talking about an empathetic sensation of breath. These comments are significant in two ways. The first is the significance of breath as an indicator of the presence and intentional indicator of those around us, especially in intimate situations. But perhaps more importantly, and surprisingly, it illustrates the necessity of sensations working together to create a connection to the presence of the dancer. Our analysis shows that audience members built an understanding and connection when they could align single senses with other senses and with their current beliefs, creating concrete knowledge in that situation. Sensations were trusted to be real more when the sensations were experienced together and could connect to create knowledge. As the phases of the experience shifted so did their method for connecting.

DISCUSSION

In any performance the audience is presented with a variety of sensations. Throughout the performance experience they make decisions as to what to pay attention to and what to ignore [6]. The model we have constructed from our analysis of audience participants addresses this phenomenon by acknowledging the dynamic nature of experiencing connection. Research in social presence in virtual reality has suggested a similar dynamic nature to social presence [13]. Based on our analysis, we view audience-performer connection as being constantly re-constructed moment to moment from the sensations presented. As has been suggested by Argyle in his seminal work *Social Interaction* [1] non-verbal cues are used by people as part of their social perception. Our analysis of participant's responses has allowed us to expand on the work of Argyle by considering kinesthetic empathy as a component of audience performer relationship. In our analysis of participant's responses we found that kinesthetic perception provided an empathetic relationship as part of the audience's experience. As discussed in the results section, an interpersonal connection was noticed in comments on feeling the effort of the dancer and most notably feeling the breath of the dancer. This connection between performer and audience through breath is to our knowledge rarely discussed in the literature though it has significant relevance to all the performing arts and has anecdotal backing and recently possible scientific backing in the form of mirror neuron research.

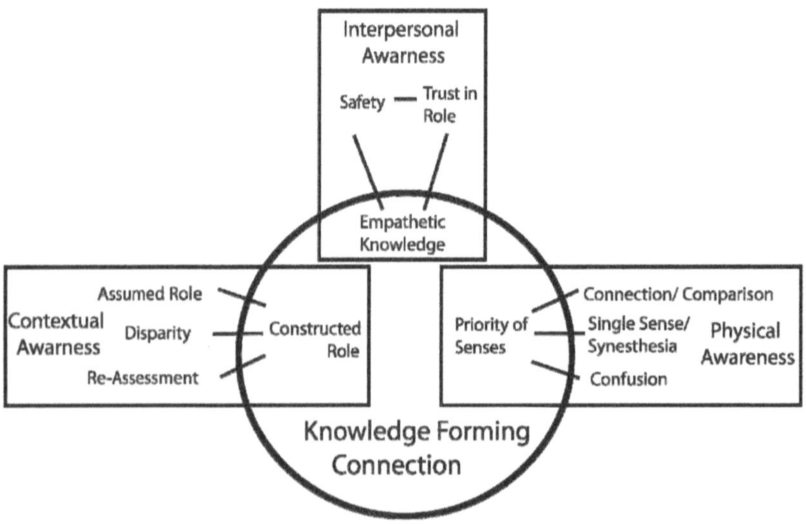

Figure 6. How Knowledge Combines to Form Connection

The empathetic connection illustrated by our audience participants also referenced the notion of personal safety. This was of some surprise since the participants were made aware that this was a performance context. Still even those with some prior knowledge of the dancer mentioned the sensation of nervousness at having some one moving behind them. We therefore believe this is a normal, though often unconscious, concern for audience members, which can be observed when audiences are wary of being asked to participate in a performance.

The elements of interpersonal awareness and physical awareness combine with contextual awareness. The audience constructs expectations and roles depending on what they perceive in the environment. The notion of participants constructing contextual understanding to change their behaviour in an environment is well research both in sociology interaction and virtual reality [1][13]. This work contains parallel concepts to what we have referred to as *Contextual Awareness*. However, largely overlooked in these discussions is what sense to use or trust. Often it is assumed that the audience experiences a performer leaving the stage and then appearing on a screen, as the performer walking *into* the screen space. In our study, the audience experienced seeing the dancer on the screen in front of them, while perceiving the sound as if from in front and *continuing to have a perception of the dancer behind.* In these moments a variety of understandings were reported. What is most noteworthy is that the confusion or disparity between the context awareness, physical awareness and interpersonal awareness consistently led to a weakened connection that forced a restructuring of the relationship between the three elements. Earlier work by Argyle has demonstrated how participants given conflicting stimuli within a social interaction ignore the sense they see as conflicting [1]. Our work has suggested that the sense that is ignored can be manipulated. Our audience participants mentioned that synchronized senses were often taken as more reliable over senses that were perceived without supporting sensory activity. The simultaneous and corroborating senses were then used to re-assess and reconstruct the understanding of the performance environment. It is through this re-assessment and reconstruction that our research contributes and has significant relevance to media performance. Based on our proposed model, we suggest that media can either distract or override the connection with a live performer but it can also create new connections and awareness by shifting the attention of the senses and bring greater attention to audience understanding of their sensory context. A similar shift can also direct attention to the physical environment or even construct a counterpart between the physical and the media environments, such as when participants were 'feeling' two or three performers in the space.

CONCLUSION

The goal of this study was to investigate audience experience of empathy with a performer during a digitally mediated performance. Through building a model of audience experience of connecting with a dancer, we have moved towards a poetics of reception as it applies to mediated performance environments. We suggest that such a poetics can acknowledge the intersubjective and social connection between the audience and the performer. It can also consider the dynamic interplay between components of our awareness. Our model expands the current understanding of audience-performer connection by considering the audience's empathetic connection with the performer as the basis for their connection with the performance piece. We illustrate how audience experience of connecting with a performer is founded on the interplay between our Contextual, Interpersonal and Physical awareness. The model presented illustrates the dynamic nature of this connection and suggests methods for developing and manipulating an intersubjective connection in media and augmented reality performances.

In presenting this study we have demonstrated the use of a research method for investigating experience in a performance context. This method involves three stages. First we constructed a performance environment that defamiliarized the audience's experience of the performance. This stage helps bring the audiences awareness to their experience, highlighting sensations that in normal circumstances might go unnoticed. Second we developed a Phenomenological interviewing technique that facilitates audience participants in reflecting on their experience. Through this process, audience participants become more articulate in describing their experience. Final we demonstrated a method for analyzing the interview data. This method has its roots in both Phenomenological methods and Grounded Theory. The key is that it attempts to remain faithful to the audience's own description of their experience while building a model of that experience that acknowledges the experience of others. The demonstrated research method provides a level of depth and clarity that is necessary for the investigation of empathetic experience in performance.

REFERENCES

1. Argyle, Michael (1969), Social Interaction, London: Methuen and Company.
2. Auslander, Philip (2000), *Liveness, Mediatization, and Intermedial Performance*, Degrés: Revue de synthèse à orientation sémiologique.101: 1-12.
3. Auslander, Philip (2006), "Musical Personae", The Drama Review, 50. 1 (Spring, 2006) pp.100-119.
4. Birringer, Johannes (1999), 'Contemporary Performance/Technology', Theatre Journal 51.4: 361-81.
5. Depraz, Nathalie. Varela, Francisco. Vermersch, Pierre (2002), *On Becoming Aware*. Amsterdam: John Benjamins Publishing Company.
6. Dix, Alan. Sheridan, Jennifer. Reeves, Stuart. Benford, Steve. & O'Malley, Claire (2006), 'Formalising Performative Interaction', *Proceedings of DSVIS'2005*,

Newcastle, UK, 13-15 July 2005, Springer, LNCS 3941, pp 15-25.

7. Dixon, Steve (2007), *Digital Performance*, London: MIT Press.
8. Fabius, Jeroen (2009), 'Seeing the Body Move'. *Contemporary Choreography: A Critical Reader*. London.
9. Fraleigh, Sondra. Hanstein, Penelope. (1999) *Researching Dance: Evolving Modes of Inquiry*, Pittsburgh: University of Pittsburgh Press.
10. Gallese, Vittorio (2001), 'The "Share Manifold" Hypothesis: From Mirror Neurons to Empathy.' *Journal of Consciousness Studies* 8.5-7 pp.33-50.
11. Gibson, James J. (1966), *The Senses Considered as Perceptual Systems.* Boston: Houghton Mifflin Company.
12. Glass, Renee (2005), 'Observer Response to Contemporary Dance', *Thinking in Four Dimensions*. Melbourne: Melbourne University Press.
13. Heeter, Carrie (2003), 'Reflections on Real Presence by a Virtual Person', *Presence,* 12:4, pp. 335-345.
14. Heidegger, Martin (1976), *Basic Writings.* San Francisco: Harper Collings.
15. Jasperse, John (2003), *Just Two Dancers.* http://www.johnjasperse.org Last Accessed August 20, 2010.
16. Jasperse, John (2005), *Prone.* http://www.johnjasperse.org Last Accessed August 20, 2010.
17. Johnson, Mark (1987), *The Body in the Mind: The Bodily Basis of Meaning, Imagination and Reason.* Chicago: University of Chicago Press.
18. Jola, Corinne (2010), 'Research and Choreography'. *The Neurocognition of Dance.* New York, NY: Psychology Press.
19. Kozel, Susan (2007), *Closer: Performance, Technologies, Phenomenology.* Boston: MIT Press.
20. Merleau-Ponty, Maurice (1962), *Phenomenology of Perception*. Trans. Colin Smith. London: Routledge.
21. Pallant, Cheryl (2006), *Contact Improvisation: An Introduction to a Vitalizing Dance Form.* London, England: McFarland & Company, Inc. Publishers.
22. Petitmengin, Claire (1999), 'The intuitive experience', in *The View from Within: First-Person Approaches to the Study of Consciousness*, a special issue of the *Journal of Consciousness Studies*, 6 (2–3), pp. 43–77.
23. Petitmengin, Claire (2006), 'Describing one's subjective experience in the second person: An interview method for the science of consciousness', *PCS*, 5: 229-269.
24. Rokotnitz, Naomi (2008), '"Too for gone in disgust" Mirror Neurons and the Manipulation of Embodied Responses in The Libertine', *Configurations*, 16:3 pp. 399-426.
25. Sartre, Jean-Paul (2004), 'Existentialism'. *Basic Writings of Existentialism.* Ed. G. Marino, New York: Random House.
26. Schechner, Richard (1977), *Performance Theory*. New York: Routledge.
27. Schiphorst, Thecla. (2011), 'Self-evidence: applying somatic connoisseurship to experience design.' *Proceedings of the 2011 annual conference extended abstracts on Human factors in computing systems. CHI EA '11* Vancouver, BC, :ACM (pp 145-160).
28. Shklovskij, Viktor. "Art as Technique." Literary Theory: An Anthology. Ed. Julie Rivkin and Michael Ryan. Malden: Blackwell Publishing Ltd, 1998.
29. Smyth, Mary M. (1984), 'Kinesthetic Communication in Dance', *Dance Research Journal* University of Illinois Press16/2 (fall) pp.19-22.
30. Varela, Francisco J. & Shear, Jonathan (1999), 'First-person Methodologies: What, Why, How?', *JCS*, 6: 1-14.
31. Varela, Francisco J., Thompson, Evan & Rosch, Eleanor (1991), *The Embodied Mind*, Cambridge, MA: The MIT Press.

Tech Break Up: A Research Method for Understanding People's Attachment to their Technology

Elizabeth Gerber
Northwestern University
Evanston, IL USA
egerber@northwestern.edu

ABSTRACT
Tech Break Up is an early stage research method that enables researchers to gain insights into ways in which people are attached to technology through improvised "break-ups." Informants verbally reflect on and formally end their relationships with technology that they previously used. The method was used in a study to understand peoples' relationship to technologies that enable creative work and reasons and moments for change in the relationship. This paper provides an overview of the method and its execution. The study reveals three primary factors of detachment for technologies that support creative work: changing self-identity, creative process, and creative ability. This case study suggests that the Tech Break Up Method can provide insights into product attachment to inform the design of new technology while simultaneously providing informants with an immediate positive experience through direct emotional expression to technology.

Author Keywords
Emotion, User Research, Methods, Design, Product Attachment.

ACM Classification Keywords
H.5.2. Information interfaces and presentation: User Interfaces

General Terms
Design

INTRODUCTION
People relate to technology as they relate to people [20]. Just as relationships with people can be emotional, so can relationships with technology. Such emotions influence people's perceptions of a technology, including its usability and functionality [17, 27].

Figure 1. People develop attachments to technologies used to support creative work. Technologies include digital (computers) and non-digital technologies (post-it notes).

The design research community advocates understanding these emotional relationships [5, 17] to improve the usability and functionality of product as well as to increase the lifespan of product use [30]. Product attachment theory explains how people develop emotional attachments to their products through a process of meaning making and identity construction [30]. People invest psychic energy into their products and develop attachment through repeated use over time [2].

Attachment is defined by the strength of the emotional attachment a consumer experiences to a product [23]. Such attachment is to the product rather to the brand [23]. When attached, people may be more likely to repair and less likely to replace when a product no longer functions [11, 24].

Studies of attachment to consumer products such as lamps, clocks, cars, and ornaments, reveal a number of factors that may influence product attachment [23]. Some are inherent in the product, such as its utility, market value, and reliability. Others are more dependent on the perceptions of the specific user, including the extent to which the product supports the user's identity and roles, its ability to make a person independent from others and give control, the goals it symbolizes, the enjoyment it activates, and the memories it triggers [23, 24, 30].

Different factors may influence product attachment at different times. In a study of attachment to cars, researchers found that enjoyment was particularly important for attachment to new products whereas as memories were important for attachment to older products [24]. While attachment tends to decrease after the first year, product attachment is highest for products owned for more than 20 years [23]. If the product is beyond repair, people may continue to hold onto the product if the attachment remains strong. This suggests that product utility is not a necessary condition for product attachment [23]. Each new study reveals a more nuanced understanding of how contextual and product specific features influence product attachment to different products over time. Understanding these relationships can support designers as they create new technologies with increased functionality, usability, and life-span.

Research Methods to Understand Product Attachment

Observation, Interviews, and Surveys

Historically, researchers use traditional design research methods such as observation, interviews, and surveys to understand product attachment to specific technologies [30]. Observations allow researchers to observe behavioral interactions with technologies in context during a discrete period of time. Interviews and surveys allow researchers to ask questions about specific observed interactions and gather additional information about the users and their feelings, values, preferences, and beliefs about the technologies in question [19].

In a study of the relationship between product attachment and personalization for bicycles, researchers approached Dutch students on their university campus and asked them to complete a survey [16]. The survey was concerned with the energy that students invested in altering the appearance of their bicycle, the extent to which their bike expressed who they were, and their attachment to their bicycle. The students rated the extent to which they agreed or disagreed with statements such as "My bicycle fits my identity," (self-expression), "I have devoted much time to altering the appearance of my bicycle" (energy invested), and "I am very attached to my bicycle" (product attachment). This survey-based study revealed that product personalization requires energy investment and informs the degree of self-expression which positively affects product attachment [16]. While such traditional research methods reveal factors that influence product attachment to existing technologies, designers seek new research methods to understand how to use the existing context to inspire and inform the design of new technologies [30].

Research Through Design

When designing new technologies with a product attachment perspective, designers have taken a research through design approach. In this approach, designers observe people in context with working prototypes to understand behavioral interactions and attachments [31]. As an example, Zimmerman and colleagues explored how role identity and control influence product attachment for children and parents when designing a new clock to encourage children to stay in bed until an appropriate wake-up time. While designing prototypes, they learned that parents have a strong attachment to the physical books they read to their children at bedtime and associate book reading with the role of a good parent. They also learned that children have a strong desire for control during bedtime routines. To encourage parent attachment to the clock, they placed the interaction with the clock at the same time as book reading, when parents are most engaged in their "good parent role." To encourage children's attachment to the clock, they designed the clock's wake up music to be programmable by children. By taking a research through design approach, this design team used an existing and specific context to which people were attached to design a new technology.

Role-Playing

While informative and inspiring, the research through design method requires prototyping capability and such capability is not always available at early stages in the design process. When such capability is not available, researchers may rely on role-play to understand product attachment to new, not yet designed technologies. In an attempt to understand emotion and attachment through direct observation, designers simulate an experience such as traveling on a plane and ask informants to hold simple props as substitutes for future tools while spontaneously navigating the travel experience. Informants communicate their needs, emotions, and possible uses for the props as they act [12]. While role-playing reveals ways in which future interactions may be designed, this technique may require extensive resources of time and space. Additionally, the technique requires informants who are willing to engage in extended dramatic performances. Finally, emotions about the context and props are imagined and based on future intentions rather than based on actual experience. As such, the emotions expressed may be less accurate.

While the traditional research methods such as observation, interviews, and surveys, and more experimental methods such as research through design and role-playing, provide ways of gathering information about people's past and future product attachments, the emotional expression is not necessarily directed at the technology with which the person has a "relationship." Such indirect expression potentially reveals less about the character and strength of attachment to a specific product. Further, the current methods ask informants' to calmly rate and reflect on their relationships with certain technologies or encourage controlled experimentation or role-play with new technologies. Given the importance of strongly felt emotions in product attachment, *how might design researchers elicit stronger emotional expression into the reflective research task?* In an effort to discover new research methods that elicit stronger emotional attachment, let us consider how professional writers capture and communicate strong emotional attachments to technology.

Eliciting Strong Emotional Expression

Understanding that people relate to technology as they relate to people [20], writers write love and hate letters to express their emotions to products, services, and people. The letters are addressed to "entities unlikely to respond" and based on actual experiences with these entities. The letters rely on the traditional structure of a personal letter. Each letter opens with a salutation, presents a thesis about the relationship, defends the thesis throughout the letter, and concludes with new terms of the relationship. In a letter to his SonicCare Electric Toothbrush [29], a writer begins

> *Dear SonicCare Electric Toohbrush, I admit, I was always skeptical of your much-heralded tooth-cleansing prowess.*

The letter continues with evidence that of the toothbrush's limitations. The author concludes with a termination of the relationship.

> *You and your $10 replacement brushes are hereby demoted to electric grout scrubber.*

Just as people communicate strong emotions with each other, this artistic endeavor suggests that people can communicate strong emotions to the technology in their lives. In a letter to Facebook, a writer expresses frustration with Facebook's suggestions to befriend people when she writes [15]

> *Cease your incessant suggestions and leave me to wallow, lonely and in peace.*

The language is not only strong but descriptive. In a letter to his cubicle, a writer expresses anger with himself when questioning his cubicle [7]. He writes,

> *If I hate you so much, why do I spend the waking hours of my prime locked in this terrible relationship?*

With disappointment, the writer allows himself to ask a question as if in a two-way conversation with his cubicle. In a letter to TacoBell CrunchWrap Supreme, a writer expresses love in her letter [18]:

> *I had no idea how deeply I had fallen for you until the terrible day came when you were no longer available. I stood in line, waiting patiently for you like I'd always done. But when I said your name, the cashier responded, callously, "Limited-time item, sorry." My eyes burned like fire sauce as I fought to keep back tears. I didn't even have time to say goodbye!.... Darling, I missed you, and I promise I will never take you for granted again. Please don't ever leave me. I'm nothing without you.*

The letter reveals strong emotion and the details about the context of the relationship.

Because of the familiarity of letter writing as a form of emotional expression, the format is appropriate for revealing product attachment/detachment. *Yet, are all people capable of composing such well-written and emotionally expressive letters to objects unlikely to respond?*

While playful and even tending towards the absurd, these letters reveal through humor and product personification insights about potential product or service improvements. Indeed, design consultancies have recently begun exploring this approach to understand people's emotional relationships to product and services [8]. By asking people to write and recite breakup letters to products and services in an hour plus long workshop, the researchers hoped to understand the emotional connection between people and products; and to differentiate between what they call the "warmer values" and "colder values" of a product (such as "speed, size, and slick styling") [8]. In the workshop, people wrote letters to a variety of services and products such as Starbucks and single cup coffee makers. Participants read the letters out loud to the other conference participants.

This initial recent work suggests that a broader audience is capable of writing emotionally expressive letters and that such letters can express emotional attachment to products and services. Such written expressions, however, ignores the key theoretical insights of Media Richness Theory, which suggest that personal, even face-to-face communications are generally more effective for communication of emotionally laden, equivocal issues than leaner, less rich media such as writing [4]. The myriad visual, vocal, aural, and tactile cues of face-to-face interaction enable this richer communication [4]. Richer communication may reveal greater detail about emotion and product attachment.

To realize the promise of this new method for exploring emotional attachment to products and services, we introduce the Tech Break Up method. The method leads informants to verbalize actual memories of technology love and loss and change, by personifying the technology in the break-up narrative. This brief improvised activity allows informants to describe the most salient factors explaining attachment (and subsequent detachment) to a technology and provides nuanced insights into informants' emotional needs and desires. The brevity of the activity emphasizes the most memorable and meaningful connections in the relationship. Verbal and visual cues in "face-to-face" communication with the technology emphasize these connections.

TECH BREAK UP METHOD

The Tech Break Up method reveals strong emotional relationships to technology through improvised conversations directly with technology. The method was developed in a study to understand peoples' relationship to technologies that enable creative work and reasons and moments for change in the relationship. The study focused on creative work as researchers find a strong link between creativity and emotion [i.e. 1] and thus people may have strong emotions about technology that supports their creative work. Further, despite the proliferation of technologies to support creative work, few researchers have taken a product attachment perspective in their design and such an approach may reveal new opportunities [21].

In addition to revealing insights for designers, the Tech Break Up method provides psychological benefits for participants. Research in psychology finds that the expression of strong emotions leads to physical and mental health. Interpersonal expression is most effective, however written expression of emotion about past and current traumas is beneficial when interpersonal expression is not viable [25] .

We describe the characteristics and execution, of the method and present observations of product attachment as well as observations about the method more generally.

Recruitment

Fifteen design professionals and students (8 women) were recruited from a Midwestern city to participate in the study. No participants had formal acting experience. Participants were recruited through a snowball technique in which each informant asked a friend to participate in the study after participating in the study.

Process

Upon entry into the research lab, informants were briefed about the purpose of the study – to understand attachments to technology that supports creative work. Following the one-minute brief, they were asked to consider a technology they were no longer using and to think about this technology as if it were a person with whom they had effectively "broken up with." Participants were then given one minute to mentally prepare a "break up letter" including the thoughts they wanted to share directly with the technology. After briefly preparing, the informant sat down in a chair positioned three feet from a video camera, the approximate position in a human-to-human break up conversation. They were asked to address the camera as if it was the technology with whom they were breaking up and told to begin the conversation when they felt ready (see figure 2). Participants took between 5 to 30 seconds to begin.

They were told they would have up to three minutes to communicate their feelings to the technology, however in reality informants were allowed as much time as they needed. A short time limit was set to encourage informants to focus on the key moments of the relationship and to encourage them to stay in character over time. The camera was turned on when they began speaking and turned off when they were finished. Upon completion, participants were asked about their experience preparing and performing the break-up. If alone, the participants were dismissed from the lab. If in the lab with others, with permission they were invited to stay.

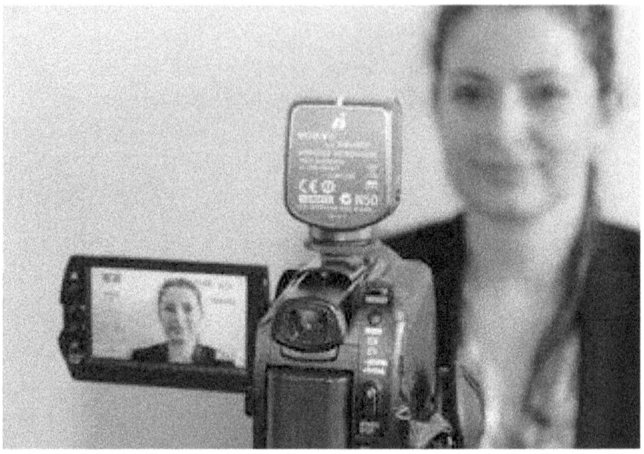

Figure 2. Informant performing a Tech Break Up in the laboratory.

Data, Analysis and Documentation

Informants spoke for 30 seconds to 4 minutes resulting in a total of 19 minutes of video recordings. Each recording was separated into clips representing different types of statements, including salutations, reasons for initial relationship, moment of change, reasons for change, and sign-off. Segments that included reasons for initial relationship, moments of change, and reasons for change were summarized and affinity diagrams were created to reveal factors informing technology detachment.

A three-minute video was created to reveal the breakup story arc and highlight examples of participants' performances, however examination of all data was necessary for understanding product attachment to technologies to support creative work.

FINDINGS

People broadly interpreted technology as tools to support behavior. Examples of technologies ranged from non-digital technologies such as Post-it notes and LEGOs to more digital technologies such as iPads (See Figure 1). All technologies were used for more than one year, with the average use length of use being three years. No products were used for 20 years.

Although not instructed to do so, most informants began with a description how the relationship started, how it grew, and why it ended. A design professional spoke directly with her design logbook offering the following explanation:

> *When we first got together during grad school, I loved spending time with you. I carefully decorated your outside cover with interesting-looking magazine clippings, and lovingly doodled in your margins. I was new to the concept of formalized creativity training, and flush with the promise that something innovative could be born from your blank, white, lineless pages.*
>
> *Looking back, it's obvious that much of the time I spent with you was wasted. I assumed that the more time I spent sketching and doodling, the more interesting my ideas would become. I didn't yet realize that interacting and collaborating with other humans would get me further than holing myself up in my loft space with you. You became an unhealthy obsession for me.*
>
> *After school, I dropped you, hard. I guess it was burn-out. I've never really gone back, though someday maybe I will. Don't get me wrong – I think you and I can still have a good thing. Just don't expect my undivided love and attention.*

Informants tended to start with what one participant called "the great moments". Leaning into the camera, a design professional explained,

> *Blog, when we first met...you were always there for me.*

The informants regularly addressed the technology by name throughout the break up when emphasizing critical points in the relationship. The language used to describe the relationship resembled language people might use to describe their relationship with other people.

Yet, all language was not based on people to people relationships. A design student happily complimented the technology he used to draw using technology relevant adjectives.

> *You were simple and useful.*

Such adjectives can be directly translated to the design of new technology for creative work.

Looking up as if remembering their moments together with fondness, a design student recalled what the technology, building blocks, in this case, allowed him to do,

> *I built giant structures with you – mazes, cars.*

He concluded with a sigh. These "great moments" were followed by the moment of change, often including a new recognition. A professional nodded her head signaling her regret as she described her relationship as "unhealthy obsession" and "wasted time." Informants then went on to describe the decline of the relationship, the detachments. A participant looked down, apparently searching for the right words to express his disappointment in the relationship. Another participant raised his voice and pointed his finger at the technology in accusation saying,

> *You are too over-powerful. You are too overbearing.*

The dialogues typically concluded with a story of replacement. With a quiet voice, a professional confessed,

> *Facebook has kind of replaced you.*

The break-ups included both verbal and visual cues of emotional attachments to technologies including sighs and downward glances of disappointment.

The Tech Break Up method case study revealed insights into how people became detached from technology and suggests that the method can be used as an easy and fast way for users to communicate strong emotions around product use and designers and researchers to learn from them. The familiar format of person to person communication supported easy expression of emotion. Dramatic performances were brief and based on familiar rather than imagined relationships.

REASONS FOR DETACHMENT

Like relationships with people, relationships with technologies have a beginning and a build-up period. Over time, these relationships may continue or deteriorate [13]. The study revealed two primary reasons for the deterioration of relationships with technologies: changing self-identity and changing creative process.

Changing Self-Identity

People understood technology as an extension of the self [14]. A professional designer said the following to her blog:

> *You became my identity. Instead of crying, Blog, I would go to you. I would sit down at the keyboard and I would write it up.*

As self-identity changed, informants detached from their technologies. Most informants reported a tipping point. The professional designer described above explained how the blog revealed too much of herself to strangers she did not know, and consequently switched to Facebook as a way of expressing herself exclusively to her friends. A design student described that back when he was "analytical" using grid paper worked well but as his creative identity strengthened, the grid paper began to hold him back. Now, he said,

> *I want to be intuitive. I want to be creative.*

Consistent with past research, product attachment to technologies is informed by the user's identity and roles [23, 24, 30]. As roles creative identity changes, attachment to technology that support creative work may also change. Strong relationships with technology may be most likely to undergo change during professional development when identity is actively being formed. To encourage product attachment, designers may consider how new technologies are introduced during times of professional transformation.

Changing Creative Process

In addition to changing identity, creative process also changed people's relationships to technology. People detached from technology due to changes in their creative process such as increased collaboration with others, increased standards of performance, and the desire to do less commercial work.

A professional designer broke up with her logbook when she realized that her intimate relationship with the product was limiting her creative ability. She was interested in involving more people in her creative process. With frustration and disappointment, she confessed to her logbook.

> *I didn't yet realize that interacting and collaborating with other humans would get me further than holing myself up in my loft space with you.*

A design student increased his standards of performance after gaining experience in a summer internship. He complained to his Post-it notes, saying,

> *I think quality matters. I'm no longer satisfied with one-liners.*

He acknowledged his change of standards and the technology's limitation in meeting his standards as a reason for ending the relationship.

As one of the professional designers became less interested in doing creative commercial work, her relationship with her technology changed. She describes the influence of external factors on the relationship saying,

> *The whole commercialization of you, Blog. It started kinda [sic] killing my creativity.*

Consistent with past research, product attachment is supported by the goals the technology symbolizes [23, 24, 30]. Over time, the goals of the technology and the goals of the users became misaligned. Just as people's goals may diverge in person-to-person relationships, so might they diverge in technology-to-person relationships. When designing new open-source technologies online, designers may consider how the need to commercialize such products to earn a profit may change early adopters attachment to the technologies.

Changing ability

In addition to changing creativity identity and process, informants described how they became detached from technology as their abilities changed and the utility of the product remained the same. A design student says that he no longer plays around with children's building toys because he is able and wanting to "design real things now."

When breaking up with his iPad, a design professional accused the technology of being designed to limit the user's control and thus the utility of the technology:

> *You want to be in control of everything.*

As his programming skills increased, he wanted to use the technology in a new way. At the conclusion of his break up, he tells his iPad that it will be given to his 5-year-old daughter. Consistent with existing research, the ability to make a person independent from others and give control is a reason for product attachment [23, 24, 30]. This finding suggests that taking away control may be a reason for product detachment. When designing new technologies for creative work, designers may consider how technologies can be changed or upgraded to meet the users' changing ability. Game designers who scaffold increasing levels of difficulty into the games they design understand the importance of designing for increasing skill ability [9].

EXPLAINING DETACHMENT

Women tended to reveal the technology replacement with guilt whereas men tended to be confident in their replacement. Women blamed themselves when breaking up, explaining, "It's not you, it's me," and, "You were everything to me." Men tended to place blame on the technology explaining, "You are too overpowering, too overbearing," and "You're not enough." Such gender differences reflect orientations toward conflict and emotional endings. Designers may consider such explanations when designing tutorials to support new technologies when users may feel vulnerable or angry with a product.

PROMISES OF THE TECH BREAK UPS METHOD

Tech Break Ups elicited confessions of strong emotional attachments that people once had to technologies. The early research method compelled informants to briefly reflect on and communicate the high and low points of their past relationships with technology and tipping points for terminating the relationship. Informants presented strong emotions about particular features of the technologies. At the same time that it provided useful data, expectations of participants is minimal compared to other experimental methods and the procedure was a satisfying experience for the participants.

Further, preparation time was intentionally brief so as to encourage informants to remember the most emotionally salient events. In pilot testing, we learned that when given more time, informants expended effort on the witty expression of emotion and were more concerned about their ability to "act" well. The brief time appeared to encourage greater expression of raw emotion.

Participant experience

Participants devoted minimal time (less than 5 minutes total) in the study and therefore expectations for compensation were minimal and significant less than what might be required of using the other research methods describes such as interviews or research through design. Because of the short duration of the task, recruiting participants with high levels of commitment and interest in the project was not necessary as it is for other user research techniques that require at least one hour of commitment. If design research techniques have wide spread appeal, the diversity of participants increases. A technique that requires creative writing skills such as composing break up letters [8], may eliminate participation. While I anticipated video recording might inhibit participation, only one person declined participation due to discomfort improvising while being filmed. Watching others complete the task built comfort for the more shy participants. Further the short, improvised duration of the conversation normalized pauses and discomforts associated with breaking up.

Although design research methods tend to focus on the quality of the data and efficiency with which the data is retrieved, the Tech Break Up method highlights the possibility of designing enjoyable research practices for informants. All of the informants described their satisfaction at the conclusion of the procedure. This is consistent with psychologists' finding that emotional expression promotes psychological well-being [25]. A professional designer described the experience as "cathartic," another shared the following with the experimenter:

> *I didn't realize how attached I still was. What a relief to formalize the break-up.*

The research method also stimulated thoughts about other products and services with which informants had "broken up," revealing to them the transitory nature of their relationship with technology. A student designer shared the following reflection with the experimenter the next day:

> *I never thought of breaking up. It was thought provoking. I talked to my roommate after about breaking up with toys and how you want to be careful about who to give them to because they still mean something to you even though you no longer play with them.*

Finally, while some participants chose to sit alone in the lab when breaking-up with their technology, others felt comfortable having peers in the room to observe during recording. All participants were eager to see the recordings of other people's break-ups upon completion. Perhaps the voyeuristic nature of overhearing a break up enhanced the satisfaction with the method.

Because the language and structure of person-to-person break-ups are familiar, participants were able to role-play easily without extensive preparation. Further, they could express strong emotions with less inhibition because of the short improvised format.

DISCUSSION

Objects have been described as "props" that support people's presentation of self [10], as a companion to help people think [26], and helping to achieve life goals [3]. Similarly, this study found that detachment to technology was often the result of changing self-identity, creative process, and ability. The findings reinforce the way in which we conceive of technology as part of the self. And yet, as the self changes, so must the technologies associated with past creations of self.

Viewing relationships with technology as we view people-to-people relationships may further inspire and inform the design of new technologies. This perspective may be increasingly important for designers as utility and ease of use become standard features of design and emotional connection with technology in our professional and personal lives is increasingly desired. Additionally as the population and consumption of technology increases, understanding ways to expand product lifespan is increasingly important. As such, we need research methods that help to inform and extend these relationships. This work is an attempt to meet the growing demand among designers and the consumers for whom they design.

FUTURE WORK

This study suggests future investigation into new methods for understanding product attachment. Given that people interact with technology as they interact with people [20], we intend to explore other popular communication media such as telephoning, emailing, and texting. While these media are less rich mediums, they allow for inclusion of a larger population. The use of such media are also consistent with growing efforts to conduct research and engage the "crowd" in creative work [6]. Further we intend to compare Tech Break-Ups directly with written love letters and interviews to understand the differences in the quality of information gathered and experience of the participants. We also intend to consider the role of emotional intelligence, the set of skills hypothesized to contribute to accurate appraisal and expression of emotion in oneself and others and regulation and use of emotion to plan and motivate [22], as well as reasons for participation in the research method. While researchers have emphasized the functionality, ease, and usefulness of research methods for researchers, few have considered the experience of the participant. As companies increasingly rely on user involvement in product development process, it is important to design research methods that users enjoy [28].

Finally, future work may investigate the role of culture on research methods that reveal emotional attachment. While self-disclosure is increasingly normative in the United States, such methods may need to be modified for cultures that do not support such self-disclosure.

CONCLUSION

Increasingly, we are interested in designing technologies that are not only functional and easy to use, but also emotionally engaging. Thus, we eagerly search for new ways to understand the people for whom we design and the way in which they are emotionally connected. We can review behavioral theory and conduct field work to gain a grounded and empathetic perspective on the use, yet new methods are needed to reveal new insights [30].

The Tech Break Up method quickly and relatively easily provided grounded insights to inform the design of new technology that supported creative work while simultaneously providing informants with an immediate positive emotional experience.

ACKNOWLEDGMENTS

I am grateful to my colleagues and peers in the design community for their contributions to this research, whether through example or critique. Specifically, I am grateful to Caitlin Martin Kennedy who produced the video compilation and to Ron Wakkery and the three anonymous reviewers for their helpful insights.

REFERENCES

1. Amabile, T., Barsade, S., Mueller, J. and Staw, B. Affect and Creativity at Work. *Administrative Science Quarterly*, *50*. 367-403.
2. Belk, R.W. Possessions and the Extended Self. *Journal of Consumer Research*, *15* (2). 139-168.
3. Czikszentmihalyi, M. and Rochber-Halton, E. *The Meaning of Things: Symbols and the Self.* Cambridge University Press, Cambridge, UK, 1981.
4. Daft, R.L. and Lengel, R.H. Information richness: a new approach to managerial behavior and organizational design. in Cummings, L.L. and Staw, B.M. eds. *Research in Organizational Behavior*, JAI Press, Homewood, IL, 1984, 191-233.
5. Desmet, P., Hekkert, P. and Jacobs, J. When a car makes you smile: Development and application of an instrument to measure product emotions. in Hoch, S. and Meyer, R. eds. *Advances in Consumer Resarch*, 2000, 111-117.
6. Dontcheva, M., Gerber, E. and Lewis, S. Crowdsourcing and Creativity. ACM ed. *CHI 2011: Crowdsourcing Workshop*, ACM Press, Vancouver, B. C., 2011.
7. Easley, J. An Open Letter to My Cubicle *An Open Letter to Entities or People Unlikely to Respond*, McSweeneys Publishing, San Francisco, 2010.
8. Enga, A. and Diana, C. Finding Love in Everyday Objects: How a Product's Personality Connects with Women *7th International Conference on Design & Emotion*, Chicago, IL, 2010.
9. Gee, J. Learning by design: Good video games as learning machines. *Interactive Educational Multimedia*, *8*. 15-23.
10. Goffman, E. *The Presentation of Self in Everyday Life.* Doubleday, Garden City, NY, 1959.
11. Govers, P.C.M. and Mugge, R., "I love my Jeep, because it's tough like me," the effect of product-personality congruence on product attachment. in *Proceedings on Design and Emotion*, (2004), Design and Emotion Society.
12. Kuutti, K., Iacucci, G. and Iacucci, C. Acting to Know: Improving Creativity in the Design of Mobile Services by Using Performances. *Proceedings of Creativity and Cognition.*
13. Levinger, G. *Development and change.* W. H. Freeman and Company, New York, 1983.
14. McLuhan, M. *The Medium is the Message.* John Wiley, New York, 1967.
15. Mes, D. An Open Letter to Facebook *Open Letters to People or Entities Who Are Unlikely to Respond*, McSweeneys Publishing, San Francisco, 2010.
16. Mugge, R., Schifferstein, H. and Schoormans, J., Personalizing Product Appearance: The Effect on Product Attachment. in *Design and Emotion*, (Ankara, Turkey, 2004), Design and Emotion Society.
17. Norman, D.A. *Emotional Design: why we love (or hate) everyday things.* Basic Books, New York, NY, 2004.
18. Paris, R. An Open (Love) Letter to Taco Bell's CrunchWrap Supreme, McSweeneys, San Francisco, 2006.
19. Plowman, T. Ethnography and Critical Design Practice. in Laurel, B. ed. *Design Research: Methods and Perspectives*, The MIT Press, Cambridge, Mass, 2003, 30-40.
20. Reeves, B. and Nass, C. *The media equation: how people treat computers, television, and new media like real people and places.* Cambridge University Press, New York, NY, 1996.
21. Resnick, M., Myers, B., Nakakoji, K., Shneiderman, B., Pausch, R., Selker, T. and Eisenberg, M. Design Principles for Tools to Support Creative Thinking *NSF Workshop Report on Creativity Support Tools*,

National Science Foundation, Washington DC, 2005, 25-36.

22. Salovey, P. and Mayer, J. Emotional Intelligence. *Imagination, Cognition, and Personality*, *9* (3). 185-211.
23. Schifferstein, H. Consumer-product attachment: Measurement and design implications. *International Journal of Design*.
24. Schifferstein, H., Mugge, R. and Hekkert, P. Designing consumer-product attachment. in McDonagh, D., Hekkert, P., Van Erp, J. and Gyi, D. eds. *Designing consumer-product attachment*, Taylor & Francis, London, 2004, 327-331.
25. Smyth, J. Writen Emotional Expression: Effect Sizes, Outcome Types, and Moderating Variables. *Journal of Consulting and Clinical Psychology*, *66* (1). 174-184.
26. Turkle, S. *Evocative Objects: Things We Think With*. MIT Press, Cambridge, MA, 2007.
27. Velazquez, M. and Gul, E., Exploring the factors affecting emotion elicitation. in *7th International Conference on Design & Emotion*, (Chicago, IL, 2010), Design & Emotion Society.
28. von Hippel, E. *Sources of Innovation*. Oxford University Press, New York, 1988.
29. Whitehead, J. An Open Letter to My Sonicare Electric Toothbrush *Open Letters to People or Entities Who Are Unlikely to Respond*, McSweeney's Publishing, San Francisco, 2005.
30. Zimmerman, J., Designing for the Self: Making Products that Help People Become the Person they Desire to Be. in *CHI 2009*, (Boston, MA, 2009), ACM
31. Zimmerman, J., Forlizzi, J. and Evenson, S., Research through design as a method for interaction design research. in *CHI*, (San Jose, 2007), ACM Press, 493-502.

Formally Modeling Pretend Object Play

Alexander Zook
School of Interactive Computing
Georgia Institute of Technology
a.zook@gatech.edu

Brian Magerko
School of Literature, Communication, and Culture
Georgia Institute of Technology
magerko@gatech.edu

Mark Riedl
School of Interactive Computing
Georgia Institute of Technology
riedl@gatech.edu

ABSTRACT

We address the problem of building computational agents that are capable of play. Existing research has examined the forms, characteristics, and processes involved in various kinds of play at a high level. However, this research does not provide a unified framework at a level of detail sufficient for building computational agents that can play. As a step toward addressing this gap we synthesize diverse research on pretend play to recognize important components of pretend play agents. We also develop a formal model of one key component of pretend play, pretend object play, and present a computational implementation of this model. Our work provides initial criteria for the content and processes necessary for pretend play agents.

Author Keywords

play, games, creativity, artificial intelligence

ACM Classification Keywords

I.2.0 [Artificial Intelligence] General---Cognitive simulation; I.2.1 [Artificial Intelligence] Applications and Expert Systems---Games

General Terms

Design, Algorithms

INTRODUCTION

What knowledge and processes are necessary for building an agent that can play? Existing play research has examined diverse aspects of play, including the forms, characteristics, and processes involved in a variety of kinds of play. Pretend play is an exemplar of everyday creativity – the generation of creative output by normal individuals in mundane contexts [3]. Yet play research to date falls short of providing a unified model of play at a level of detail sufficient for building computational agents. Understanding play at the computational level can drive more detailed explanations of play, connect play to other domains of human activity, particularly creativity, and enable technologies that leverage these detailed models in supporting human play and creativity.

C&C'11, November 3–6, 2011, Atlanta, Georgia, USA.

Creativity research has typically focused on the generation of novel or innovative artifacts such as music, paintings, architectural designs, or engineered artifacts by high-performing individuals. Yet both children and adults routinely engage in related creative processes when playing. During play activities individuals incorporate knowledge from multiple domains to co-construct interesting experiences or products [7,16,25,32,36]. Players devise and enact amusing stories, build kingdoms in sand, and conjure imaginary playmates.

Play and playful activities are also known to contribute to important everyday skills: emotional expression and regulation, self-exploration and social comparison, group dynamics and problem solving, training for social roles, and divergent thinking [27]. Unstructured activities and self-structured activities in particular have been found to benefit cognition and education [18,23,28]. Play appears to involve fundamental processes that contribute to a variety of human behaviors.

Playful behavior is closely connected to creative activity. Play involves many features of central importance to creative cognition and interaction, including: evolving and highly contextual processes, interactions and negotiations among multiple individuals, open-ended frames for interaction, and the interaction among real and pretend frames. The process of play requires highly contextualized cognitive processes responding to a constantly evolving frame of activity, rather than working within a predefined and fixed space [31]. During play multiple individuals are continually required to negotiate the terms of the activity with one another, rather than working solely within their own mental framework. These negotiations result in open-ended frames for the play activity that are constantly co-created. A central aspect of play interactions and the evolving play activity is the interplay between the real-world space and the pretend domain being used. Interacting individuals must continually communicate and reason about both levels of an activity, rather than escaping to a purely conceptual domain.

Despite the known benefits of play the number of spaces and opportunities for free, unstructured play has diminished. The extent to which children are allowed to freely explore in urban areas without supervision has consistently decreased over the last several decades [15]. In response several movements have attempted to mitigate these limitations or leverage the benefits of play, including play therapy for adults and children, construction of playgrounds, and the incorporation of more self-directed and less structured forms of activities into educational systems [23]. All attempts to leverage play to enhance flexibility and the ability to effectively handle novel experiences have been based on high-level frameworks of play activity.

Understanding play is particularly important since artificially intelligent agents are increasingly part of the everyday world of human interactions. Researchers in social robotics have begun to explore how robots can interact with humans and other robots in socially appropriate and meaningful ways [1]. Examples range from the emotional modeling and affective communication explored by Breazeal's *Kismet* robot [4,5,6] to the RoboticsLab's development of more autonomous and adaptive robots with the *Maggie* robot [34]. Play research can complement these efforts by examining the key cognitive and behavioral processes involved in free-form interaction and make-believe. Understanding play computationally can enable the development of agents that playfully interact both with humans and other agents, complementing existing efforts to increase access to playful interactions.

Play research to date has established the high-level theoretical and conceptual models of play mentioned above. The play scholar Sutton-Smith, in his comprehensive review of the play literature, has argued the next step to understanding play will be the development of detailed processual accounts of play [36]. Processual accounts must push into providing detailed models of the cognitive, social, and affective processes involved in play. Without such models we cannot understand how play relates to such a diversity of human activities. Further, computational agents that engage in play require exactly this level of detail in process and content to be realized.

We propose the development of *computational play* to formally understand the processes and content of play through the lens of computation. Computational play focuses on creating detailed models of play activities that are grounded in theoretical and empirical research on play and human cognition. Developing such models can address the knowledge and processes used in play, benefiting play research and enabling the creation of playful agents. Play research can be extended to understand the underlying aspects that unify diverse forms of play and link play to other domains of human activity. Computational agents can be used to leverage the many benefits of play.

We present two primary contributions in this work. First, we unify diverse research on play and cognition in the category of pretend play to identify its key representations and processes. Second, we develop a formal model of pretend object play, a necessary component of pretend play, as a first step toward formally grounding this framework.

We develop these contributions as follows. We first synthesize play research on ontologies, definitions, and core processes of play to develop the key content and processes involved in pretend play. We argue that pretend play provides a domain to examine situated and dynamic creative cognition, connecting play to the processes of analogy and conceptual blending. In order to ground these high-level models we next focus on a key component of pretend play, the pretend use of objects. We develop a formal model of pretend object play and present a computational implementation of this model. We conclude by outlining additional developments needed to develop a formal model of pretend play.

SYNTHESIZING PRETEND PLAY

In this section we synthesize play research toward a unifying framework for pretend play agents. Pretend play is characterized by dual representations of the real and pretend domains of interest. Pretend domains contain knowledge about particular themes, scripts, and rules for activities. The pretend and real domains are connected and blended together in play, with these combinations balancing constraints of coherence against free-form change. Communicating about both pretend and real domains simultaneously requires the process of metacommunication.

Play Ontologies

Many researchers have examined the various kinds of play activities and organized these by their primary characteristics. Sutton-Smith organized play activities into several categories based on the existing play literature [36]:

- mind or subjective play (e.g. imagination)
- solitary play (e.g. collecting objects)
- playful behaviors (e.g. pranks)
- informal social play (e.g. joking, parties)
- vicarious audience play (e.g. spectator sports)
- performance play (e.g. performing music)
- celebrations and festivals (e.g. Mardi Gras)
- contests (games and sports) (e.g. athletics, casinos)
- risky/deep play (e.g. caving)

Brown and Vaughan [7] recognized nine major categories of play derived from their research:

- attunement – mother-infant connection formation
- body play and movement – moving in the world
- object play – manipulating objects
- rough and tumble play – e.g. playful wrestling
- belonging play – developing social connections
- celebratory play
- pretend play – creating one's own sense of the world

- storytelling play – conveying a sense of the world to others
- creative play – realizing an envisioned change in oneself or the world

Among these we focus on pretend play as an exemplar of the creative processes involved in play. Pretend play corresponds roughly to Sutton-Smith's mind play and Brown and Vaughan's pretend play.

Pretend play – also known as fantasy play, sociodramatic play, or symbolic play – is play that involves constructing and enacting scripts and roles that children draw from life experiences and media sources such as fairy tales, books, and television [26]. Children socially interact and communicate with peers during the dramatic enactment and co-construction. Pretend play involves many of the commonly recognized instances of creativity in play, ranging from imaginary friends to playful re-enactments and alterations of popular media stories. While understanding pretend play will not unify all forms of play, the emphasis on interaction makes this domain particularly conducive to the development of interactive play agents.

Play Definitions

Definitions of play recognize play as involving both pretend and real domains. These definitions have emphasized an important duality between structure and freedom in play. As such, pretend play agents will need models of these two domains and the process of balancing freedom and constraint involved in pretend play.

The cultural historian Huizinga provided one of the earliest definitions of play, emphasizing its social manifestations [17]. He defined play as: outside normal life; non-serious, but absorbing; not involving material interest; bounded in time and space; including fixed rules and an orderly manner; promoting formation of social groupings surrounded with secrecy; and having groups that stress their difference from the normal world. These criteria were based on his focus on play as underlying the formation of human culture.

The sociologist Caillois [8] agreed with Huizinga's emphasis on the social aspects of play, but disagreed with his narrow focus on mystery and ritual. Caillois sought to ground a definition of play in understanding the difference between acting a role and enacting a situation. This distinction captures the difference of the *as if* attitude of theatre, where roles are played, and the *for real* attitude of sports, where games are enacted. Caillois found play has six primary traits, being:

- free – not obligatory
- separate – limited in time and space
- uncertain – leaving uncertainty in outcomes
- unproductive – not yielding goods
- governed by rules – having special regulations
- make-believe – requiring awareness of a second reality

Using this definition of play, Caillois expounded on a model of games using two dimensions: the rubric of the game and the attitude taken towards the game. Game rubrics consisted of the categories of competition (*agôn*), chance (*alea*), pretend (*mimicry*) and vertigo (*ilinx*). Games of competition and chance both seek equality among players, with the former differentiating players by skill and the latter by luck. Pretend games seek to convince an audience of something. Vertigo games are based around the pleasure of disorientation, such as in roller-coaster rides. Each of these rubrics can be approached either with a rule-based (*ludus*) or improvisational (*paidia*) attitude. Ludus emphasizes the concrete game being played, strict adherence to rules, and explicit structure. Paidia instead focuses on personal experience, the more abstract fantasy realm being used, and spontaneous change. Caillois sought to organize play by both the structure of the activity and the particular attitude taken towards it.

Fromberg's [13] review of early childhood play research found children's play is:

- symbolic – representing reality in "as-if" or "what-if" terms
- meaningful – in connecting or relating experiences
- active – in children doing things, including imagining
- pleasurable – even if children are seriously engaged in the activity
- voluntary
- intrinsically motivated – regardless of drive by curiosity, mastery, affiliation, or others
- rule-governed – whether implicitly or explicitly expressed
- episodic – in having emerging and shifting goals that children develop spontaneously

As in Huizinga and Caillois's definitions, Fromberg recognizes the importance of structure (rule-governed) and freedom (symbolic, voluntary, intrinsically motivated).

A common thread among play, creativity, and cognition research is the nature-nurture or innate-learned distinction. In psychology, this relates to the extent to which a given behavior or trait can be explained by fixed innate aspects or changing and developed features. Play definitions fall along a similar spectrum ranging from fixed and predetermined (nature, innate) to flexible and acquired (nurture, learned). In play this spectrum manifests as extending from fixed games to open-ended play or improvisation.

Structured perspectives on play emphasize the scripted and rule-based nature of play. Huizinga, Caillois, and Fromberg all see play as involving orderly processes or episodes and also recognize rules that govern play activities. Caillois's ludus and games of competition and chance emphasize highly structured forms of play based strictly in conventionalized rules. These structures parallel Boden's emphasis on an accepted set of generative structures that bound a creative domain [3]. Pretend play agents will need the ability to recognize and enforce rule structures based on a given activity. These must include both explicitly declared game rules as well as implicit conventions of play including social and cultural context.

Play also involves open-ended, improvisational aspects. Huizinga, Caillois, and Fromberg all recognize play as free or intrinsically motivated. Freedom in these accounts is based on play involving a separate domain or frame outside the context of normal activity. Caillois's paidia and games of pretend and vertigo all emphasize play as not fully tethered to external constraints and circumstances, working within a subjective, make-believe realm or loosening connections to the physical realm. Both Caillois and Fromberg emphasize play as symbolic. Play is free and creative by working with an additional mental domain that is not simply the physical space of activity. Activities are fluid in using make-believe to manipulate an ongoing activity, drawing from other domains of knowledge. Fauconnier and Turner's conceptual blending describes the similar process of combining domains for creative results [10,11]. Thus, pretend play requires the capacity for modeling a separate make-believe domain that maintains some connections to the real domain and some connections to other make-believe content.

Metacommunication, Analogy and Blending

While the above definitions recognize the dual domains of pretend and real in play, they do not give detailed accounts of the behavioral or cognitive processes involved in relating these domains and communicating about these relations to other players. Pretend play agents require models of the specific content of make-believe domains and the processes of connecting, combining, and communicating about these domains.

Pretend Domain Content

Empirical research on children and adults at play provides the types of content that comprise the make-believe domain. Both Sawyer [32] and Horst et al. [16] have found that children at play engage in a process of appropriating elements of their surrounding media culture for development of their play activities. Children borrow major themes, roles and narratives from television, fairy tales and other sources. Real-life activities are also incorporated into play as loose scripts. In addition, rules based on analog and digital games are used to structure play activities. Sutton-Smith found that 90% of children's descriptions of play with toys focused on pretending, personal narratives and dialogues in play, rather than the specific characteristics of the toys themselves [35]. Children thus selectively borrow and modify content from their everyday life and media environment to suit their ends, and draw from many sources when constructing any given activity. In the context of creativity research this work provides examples of the processes involved in combining, exploring and modifying conceptual domains [3]. Pretend play agents thus need models of outside domains of content to inform their make-believe frames. These outside domains should provide knowledge of themes, event scripts, and rule structures.

Metacommunication

Players constantly draw from outside domains to add structure and content to their ongoing activity, communicating these changes to one another. The central process of navigating between the pretend and real aspects of play is *metacommunication*. The cyberneticist and anthropologist Bateson [2] found play activities constantly involve communication at two levels: the real-world activity and the pretend domain being used. Metacommunication is the process of communicating at both of these levels simultaneously to regulate interaction. This involves both communicating about a real-world action and communicating about that communication to connect it to a pretend domain. When a dog nips another dog on the ear during play it communicates the real-world action of nipping and metacommunicates the pretend action of biting.

Sawyer [31] notes that play actions are more properly understood as being *metapragmatic*. In linguistics, communication uses language to denote aspects of the world, referring to the direct meaning of a word or expression. Pragmatics involves use of language at the level of framing or contextualizing communication. Communication involves relatively fixed and shared meanings, while pragmatics emphasizes fluid and contextual meanings. Metacommunication refers to content of an activity, while metapragmatics refers to the frame of an activity or conversation. Metapragmatics and metacommunication are the means by which agents can arrive at a shared understanding of a given situation, here a pretend scenario [14]. Metacommunication underlies the processes of understanding given objects within a play session, while metapragmatics investigates the ongoing changes made to the framing of that session. Sutton-Smith describes this distinction as the difference between play – manipulating the content of a given activity – and *metaplay* – manipulating the structure of an activity itself [36]. Playful creativity can involve both of these domains and pretend play agents will need the ability to manipulate both the content and frame of a play activity.

Sawyer [31] has provided an empirically grounded formulation of the pretend play process as improvisation. He grounds this formulation in two key concepts: *indexical presuppositions* and *indexical entailments*. Indexes are signs that require an association between the sign and its object. Sawyer examines speech acts in play that are indexical in referring to aspects of the play context, such as recognizing a shared topic. For example, a play interaction can have the context, or frame, of playing house. Indexical presuppositions refer to accepted frame aspects of an ongoing interaction. A child may draw on a presupposed setting or role, such as a country home or being a mother. Indexical entailments are statements that convey a potential direction for an interaction. Children may propose new relations among their characters such as one player being a mother with another player as her baby. Over the course of a play session all players constantly balance between the given structure of indexical presuppositions and changes to that structure possible with indexical entailments. Thus, a child enacting a mother must balance between enacting the motherly role while proposing new activities to play out, such as feeding her baby or cooking.

Indexical presuppositions and entailments can serve as the elements agents use when communicating to one another during a play activity regarding the content and frame of the activity. These do not specify, however, the process of interrelating the pretend and real domains. When an agent pretends that a cardboard tube is a sword it must simultaneously reason about properties of the real cardboard tube, pretend sword, and the relation between them within the context of the play activity. This reasoning must be used to drive actions that in turn convey information regarding all these same aspects. A model of pretend play requires an account of how an individual maps between the real and pretend frames and reasons about their relationship.

Analogy

Recognizing and making analogies involves comparing the conceptual structure of two domains. Analogical reasoning can enable pretend play agents to find connections between a real and pretend domain. In making or recognizing an analogy an agent must build a mapping between the conceptual structures of two domains in order to interpret one domain in terms of the other. Two computational models of analogy are SME [9] and MAC/FAC [12]. SME is based on recognizing matched systems of relations among concepts, emphasizing shared structure over particular features. It models the process of building a mapping between two given concepts. For example, SME maps from the solar system to an atom by recognizing their similar processes of revolving objects and forces of attraction. The mapping pairs the sun to the nucleus of the atom and planets to the electrons of the atom. MAC/FAC extends the SME model by incorporating a model of retrieval of potential analogies using a simplified, non-structural filtering process, before using a full structure-mapping process to evaluate the quality of resulting analogies.

Conceptual Blending

Conceptual blending accounts for the unconscious process of combining features and relations of concepts to yield novel concepts [11]. Pretend play leverages conceptual blending when reasoning about objects that mix features of the real and pretend contexts of an activity. Conceptual blending theory starts from given conceptual spaces consisting of features and structures and explains the constraints and processes involved in combining these spaces to yield novel results. Specifically, two (or more) input conceptual spaces are linked via a third generic space used to map among these spaces. Components of these spaces are selectively mapped into a resulting fourth blended space. Reasoning within the blend space can be propagated back to the input spaces.

As an example, a modern boat, *Great America II*, sailing from San Francisco to Boston in 1993 was compared to a historical one, *Northern Light*, which made the same trip in 1853 [10]. Observers at one point noted: "At this point, *Great America II* is 4.5 days ahead of *Northern Light*." To make this comparison a blend with both boats occupying a shared space starting at the same time is constructed. Based on this blend, inferences about the relative positions of the boats can be made and mapped back to the input space of the *Great America II*'s current trip to infer its lead in time.

Veale's SAPPER [37] is based on a bridge-building model of structure mapping that recognizes local regularities of structure and bridges these elements. The most elaborate local model of similarity serves as an anchor for mapping between the domains, with additional consistent mappings being folded into this structure. The final structure represents a blended result. SAPPER's process of matching, selecting a best match, and extending that match by adding in additional relevant features can ground the process of blending the real and pretend domains for the purpose of pretend play. The Riu system has used a similar process to model imaginative remembering using memories structured using force-dynamic models, supporting the viability of this approach for navigating imagined and real domains [38].

PRETEND OBJECT PLAY

The research above synthesizes key aspects of pretend play that hold across many concrete domains needed for pretend play agents. We have drawn from several studies of pretend play with objects to formulate an account of this particular pretend play activity at a sufficient level of detail for building a computational model.

Pretend Object Play Research

Pretend object play is the process of using real-world objects as substitutes for pretend objects as part of a pretend scenario, a core component of pretend play activities [25]. Modeling pretend object play requires specifying how objects are represented when making substitutions and the substitution process of relating and reasoning about the pretend object referenced and the real object used.

Object Representation

Sawyers and Carrick [33] note that four levels of object substitution occur in children's pretend play: functional, high-level prototypical, low-level prototypical, and insubstantial. *Functional* substitution is the use of an object in its intended or real-world manner. An example is using a real pen as a pretend pen. *High-level prototypical* substitution is the use of a real-world object that closely resembles the desired pretend object, such as using a replica sword as a pretend sword. *Low-level prototypical* substitution involves referring to a pretend object with a real object that does not closely resemble it, such as using a cardboard tube for a pretend sword. *Insubstantial* substitution involves communicating through words or gesture about pretend objects without real object proxies. An example is miming the presence of a sword by shaping one's hands as if holding a handle and acting out sword-swinging motions.

Both Sutton-Smith's research on toys and Sawyers and Carrick's research on pretend players found low-level prototypical substitutions to be the most common in play activities, aligning with Montessori schooling techniques that find such objects most conducive to creative play [23,33,35]. Our model focuses on low-level prototypical substitutions in our agent model. High-level prototypical and functional substitutions both de-emphasize the processes involved in reasoning about the relations of the pretend and real domains by narrowing any distinction between these realms. Insubstantial substitutions instead emphasize the properties of gestures and verbal communication, losing the grounding role of particular objects as props. By modeling low-level prototypical object substitutions we intend to explore how agents work within the joint real and pretend domains.

We represent objects by combining insights from Rosch's [29] work on cognitive models of categorization and Lakoff and Johnson's [20] work on mental representations used in metaphors. Rosch found humans employ a graded model of categorization of objects, seeing members of categories as more or less central to a group. Drawing from this insight, we represent objects using a set of *fuzzy attributes*. Fuzzy set theory relaxes the assumption of binary membership values used by classical set theory, instead allowing real-valued degree-of-membership values [19]. Intuitively this captures the common-sense notion that cognitive models of objects classify them as being more or less members of many categories, rather than being exclusively limited to disjoint sets [21]. Fuzzy modeling techniques have been used to support agents capable of interacting with humans in improvisational domains [24] as well as for machine reasoning about numerical data [22]. As an example, a sword has a 0.8 (on a [0-1] scale) degree-of-membership (DOM) value for stabbing, as swords are prototypical objects used for stabbing. Swords have only a 0.3 DOM value for size, reflecting their relative smallness compared to humans. Note that all real dimensions are scaled to have 0.5 DOM values as representing "human-scale" dimensions.

The set of attributes we have chosen is derived from Lakoff and Johnson's work on the properties of objects used to drive metaphorical understanding [20]. Lakoff and Johnson argue that humans understand objects in terms of four sets of *interactional properties*. Interactional properties are sets of properties of objects derived from interacting with these objects, rather than abstract concepts not grounded in the real world. Lakoff and Johnson term such sets of properties *dimensions*, in recognition of their shared features. The four dimensions of interactional properties are: (1) perceptual, (2) functional, (3) motor-activity, and (4) purposive properties. *Perceptual properties* capture perceived features of objects. Perceptual properties include the size of an object, its color, and shape. *Functional properties* capture uses of objects as mechanisms or means towards ends. For example, chairs function to allow sitting while guns perform shooting. *Motor-activity* properties capture ways in which the object can be readily manipulated. Motor-activity properties include ease of gripping an object, object flexibility, and object brittleness. *Purposive properties* involve the ends towards which objects are applied. For example, a blanket may be used to keep warm, conceal an object, or to bundle objects together for carrying.

Based on Sawyers and Carrick's findings that children typically rely on resemblance of physical properties of objects when using them for low-prototypicality substitution we do not represent functional properties of the real objects being used. This captures the notion that most low-prototypicality objects are used for their appearance, ease of physical use and possibly their normal purposes, with less attention paid to specific mechanisms of operation. Most low-prototypicality objects, such as sticks, rulers, or pens, have sufficiently simple and lacking functional mechanisms that these mechanisms are less relevant to object representations. Modeling objects using Lakoff and Johnson's scheme provides principle types of attributes to use when modeling the pretend object substitution process.

Object Substitution Process

Sawyer's [30] study of communication processes used in pretend play in a preschool classroom provide details on the object substitution process. He found that play communication occurs at one of four play frame levels:

1. *in character, in frame*
2. *in character, blended frame*
3. *out of character, blended frame*
4. *out of character, out of frame*

In character, in frame communication (level 1) involves using the voice of an enacted play character and making no reference to the play frame. In character, blended frame communication (level 2) uses a character voice but makes some reference to real-world objects or events not part of the play frame. An example is asking "Jennifer, is this our baby?" where Jennifer is the name of a real-world person while the baby is pretended. Out of character, blended frame communication (level 3) involves directing others (that is, not acting as a character) while still referring to objects or events that relate to the play activity. Finally, out of character, out of frame communication (level 4) does not make any reference to the play frame or act as a character within that frame.

Sawyer's aggregated results over all observed communication interactions found children on typically used a framing level of 2 or 3. This reflects children primarily working in character and mainly referencing pretend objects while still occasionally acting to provide out of character directions to other players or using references to real-world objects and events. We model this level of play reference as the layering of a pretend frame atop an existing physical frame. Agents reason about this mixed frame by blending the real and pretend objects used in object substitution. This draws from the descriptions of pretend play given by the children studied by Sawyers and Carrick and the use of metapragmatic communication found by Sawyer [31,33].

Pretend Object Play Model

We model pretend object play as the layering of a pretend domain onto a real domain, deriving a blended space for use in communication and reasoning. Agents must map between these domains in both directions. First, when an agent has a desired pretend object it must search the local environment to find a suitable real substitute, and then understand how this substitute can be used as the pretend object. Second, when one agent observes another agent manipulating a real object, it must find an appropriate pretend object to match the given selection of a real object, again basing its interpretation on the pretend context. Our model captures the process of representing and mapping between objects in these domains while respecting the constraints and features specific to both domains.

Real and pretend domains impose differing constraints on pretend object play. The real domain captures knowledge about the workings of real world objects and constraints imposed by those objects on actors for their activities. These constraints enforce real-world physical limitations such as not being able to pretend a heavy object is substantially lighter than it is, or a rigid object is more flexible than it is. The pretend domain captures the pretend objects of interest. These objects impose constraints on any mapping between the spaces through their distinctive features, such as a pretend sword (typically) being treated as threatening, or used for stabbing. Pretend constraints captures norms of interpretation any player must respect when using a given object in a pretend scenario. Pretending an object is a sword entails assuming others will consider it sharp and used for actions such as stabbing or slashing. Mapping between real and pretend domains involves three primary processes: (1) filtering objects; (2) evaluating object similarity; (3) blending objects.

Pretend To Real Mapping

During pretend play an agent may have a desired pretend object that it seeks to map onto an available real object. To do so, the agent first filters the set of real objects in its environment. Using a given set of constraining attributes and a threshold for attribute violation does this. Constraining attributes relate to the needs of a particular play context, encoding information such as the need for an object to have perceptual features of a certain kind or for the object to be manipulated in particular ways. Each constraining attribute of each pretend object is checked and the object is rejected if any of its attributes violates these constraints by an amount greater than or equal to the threshold. Computationally, constraints are differences between real and pretend object attribute values. As an example, a pretend sword with a 0.4 DOM value for weight would violate a threshold of 0.2 DOM difference when compared to a real log with a 0.7 DOM value for weight as a constraint. That is, a log is too heavy to be used as this specific pretend sword. Note that we have fixed the context of pretend play to human-scale domains, making all physical attributes of objects related to the category of human everyday interactions.

All remaining pretend objects are next evaluated for their similarity to the given real object. Our computational implementation currently uses a simple Euclidean distance

Table 1: Objects

	size	length	width	weight	sharpness	grippable	bendability	stabbing	slashing
cardboard tube	0.3	0.4	0.2	0.1	0.1	0.8	0.0	0.1	0.1
umbrella	0.3	0.4	0.2	0.2	0.1	1.0	0.3	0.2	0.1
pen	0.1	0.1	0.1	0.1	0.3	1.0	0.1	0.7	0.0
broom	0.5	0.5	0.1	0.2	0.1	0.7	0.1	0.3	0.1
mace	0.3	0.3	0.3	0.4	0.1	0.9	0	0.0	0.0
dagger	0.1	0.1	0.1	0.1	0.9	1.0	0	1.0	0.7
spear	0.6	0.6	0.2	0.5	0.8	0.7	0.5	1.0	0.1
sword	0.4	0.4	0.2	0.4	0.9	1.0	0	1.0	1.0
broom-sword	0.5	0.5	0.1	0.2	0.1	0.7	0.1	0.3	1.0

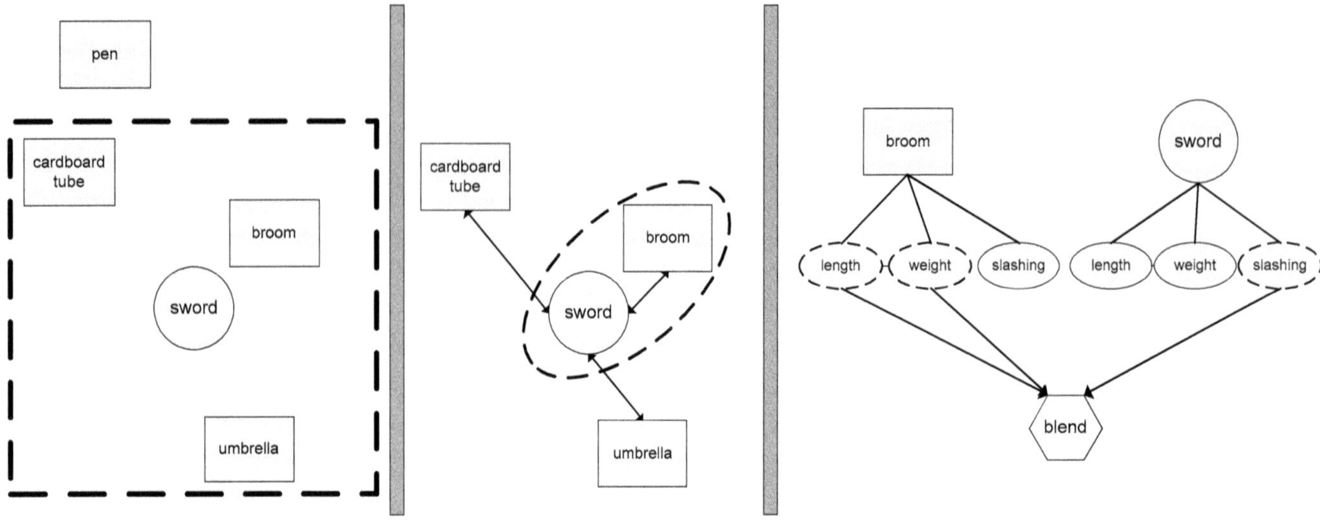

Figure 1: Blending a pretend sword with a real broom. Dashed lines indicate selections made by the agent. Double-headed arrows indicate distance comparisons, single-headed arrows indicate mapping values, and lines indicate attributes of an object. Three steps of the model are shown schematically: filtering objects based on constraints (left), selecting objects based on similarity (center), and blending real objects with iconic values of pretend objects (right).

metric using all attributes of both objects. This approach is based on prior work on computational modeling of prototypes [22]. The real object with the least distance to the desired pretend object is selected for use in the object substitution.

Blending occurs by mapping *iconic* attributes of the pretend object onto the real object. The real object attributes are used by default based on our model of layering the pretend on top of the real domain. Iconic attributes of the pretend object are those attributes that distinguish the pretend object from all other potential pretend objects within its category. Specifically, iconic attributes of an object have values that are the most different from all other objects in the set according to that attribute. Our algorithm calculates iconicity as the sum of Euclidean distances of a pretend object's attribute DOM from the DOM of all other pretend objects for that attribute. Iconicity values are normalized

Third, the agent blends the real and pretend objects for the purposes of reasoning. As before, the real object is used as a baseline to capture the process of layering the pretend domain upon the real. Iconic values of the pretend object are mapped onto the blended object and used as the final result.

within categories of objects and an attribute is considered iconic for an object if it is within a given range from the maximum value. The blending process finds all iconic values of the pretend object and maps these onto the blended object, replacing the physical object attribute values. This allows the final blended object to retain the constraints of its real form while allowing an agent to reason about the pretend features of the object.

Real To Pretend Mapping

Observing the use of a real object in a play context, an agent must find the potential pretend object being represented and understand how it relates to the current play activity. This process also occurs when an agent observes some real object in the environment and seeks to give it a pretend instantiation.

First, the agent filters out all pretend objects based on a set of constraints and a threshold for constraint violation. As above constraints reflect the physical limitations of the domain and are used to reduce the space of potential pretend object candidates.

Second, the agent calculates the similarity of the real object to all remaining pretend objects. This process uses the same Euclidean distance minimization process as above and results in a maximally similar real object.

Example: Pretend Sword

As an example, consider an agent attempting to map an imaginary sword to a real object among an available cardboard tube, umbrella, pen, and broom (Figure 1 and Table 1). First, the agent focuses on the constraining attributes of overall size, length, width, and thickness of the real objects, using a threshold of an absolute difference of 0.2 (Figure 1, left). The agent rejects the pen for being too short and too small (both differences of 0.3) to be used as a pretend sword.

Second, the agent evaluates the similarity between each remaining real object and the pretend sword (Figure 1, center). Distance to objects is calculated as the sum of the Euclidean distances of all attributes. The normalized inverse of this quantity determines similarity. According to this measurement the broom is most similar to a sword (1.0 similarity), followed by the umbrella (0.55) and then cardboard tube (0).

Third, the agent evaluates each attribute of the sword to determine its iconic attributes. Each pretend object is compared to all other pretend objects along a particular attribute. The iconicity value for that attribute for that object is calculated as the sum of the Euclidean distances of that objects attribute value from all other objects. For example, the sword's iconicity for its slashing attribute is calculated as:

$$(1.0 - 0.0)^2 + (1.0 - 0.7)^2 + (1.0 - 0.1)^2 = 1.9$$

After normalizing iconicity values across all objects this becomes a value of 1.0. The sword is iconic for being most typically used for slashing among the pretend objects. Among all attributes this is the only iconic value of the sword.

Finally, the agent produces a blended object that integrates both the real broom with the pretend sword (Figure 1, right). The blended sword matches the real broom on all attributes except the sword's iconic slashing attribute. The result is a broom-sword blend that functions for slashing.

Discussion and Future Work

We have presented a synthesis of research on pretend play in order to identify the key features necessary for implementing computational play agents. Pretend play involves navigating dual real and pretend domains while working on a blended level that takes elements from both domains. Pretend domains include information about themes, scripts, and rules to guide activities based on everyday experiences and the surrounding media environment. Navigation between the pretend and real domains involves constructing a blended frame using analogical and conceptual blending processes. This frame is continually manipulated using metacommunicative and metapragmatic processes that balance coherence with existing indexical presuppositions and open-ended change using indexical entailments. Pretend object play grounds representation and process features of this model in graded category representations and analogical and blending processes.

Our model of pretend object play requires human evaluation. The metrics for similarity and iconicity both are designed to be relatively insensitive to the exact details of the attribute data they are given as they serve only to impose an ordering on objects. Evaluation of the model will require gathering human data for attribute values and specific objects used in play categories. As estimations of similarity are context-dependent this data collection will need to be grounded in a particular play domain and particular real-world setting. Additionally, we also need to collect human data on the constraints of relevance to physical mappings.

Further specifying the pretend play model as a whole requires greater specification of the processes involved in selecting and using play contexts and interacting between pretending agents. We have assumed a given pretend context for our pretend object play model. During pretend play many contexts are found and integrated in real time. How do agents select a pretend domain, such as a fairy tale world, to use in pretend play? What content from these domains do players use and how do they select it? When using a particular play frame, how do players draw multiple objects or stories from them and integrate them? Research on play has already found narratives, pretend worlds, and digital game rules are appropriated, but has left unspecified how this process occurs. As many pretend domains are integrated in most pretend play sessions, how are these additional domains selected and combined? Conceptual blending and analogy are likely involved in the appropriation process, but the details of their guiding constraints and considerations remain unclear.

Future research also needs to specify the constraints of particular real world play contexts. Play behavior differs between playgrounds and indoors, as well as when playing with siblings, friends or relative strangers. Incorporating play agents into real-world applications will require further investigation of the social and cultural constraints that frame pretend play in these domains. Additional extensions of this work must model the metapragmatic processes of recognizing and incorporating such frames into activities during the course of the activities themselves.

Pretend play interactions use metapragmatics to negotiate the ongoing play activity. What content is conveyed using these statements? Indexical presuppositions and entailments provide an initial framework for how agents communicate about these appropriations. However, Sawyer notes the need to understand the relation between these statement types and the content they convey [31]. What is the nature of the indexical presuppositions and indexical entailments that players use in terms of their content and selection? How do players make decisions about the balance between existing structure and open-ended freedom? Such processes are central to enabling coherent play experiences and will be requisite for any agent that interacts with human players if it is to keep them engaged in playful activity and drive players to reap the benefits of play.

REFERENCES

1. Bartneck, C. and Forlizzi, J. A design-centred framework for social human-robot interaction. *Robot and Human Interactive Communication, 2004. ROMAN 2004. 13th IEEE International Workshop on*, (2004), 591–594.
2. Bateson, G. A Theory of Play and Fantasy. In *Steps to an ecology of mind*. Chandler Pub. Co., San Francisco, CA, 1972, 177–193.
3. Boden, M.A. Computer models of creativity. *AI Magazine 30*, 2009, 23-35.

4. Breazeal, C. and Scassellati, B. Infant-like social interactions between a robot and a human caregiver. *Adaptive Behavior 8*, 1 (2000), 49.

5. Breazeal, C. Toward sociable robots. *Robotics and Autonomous Systems 42*, 3-4 (2003), 167–175.

6. Breazeal, C. Social interactions in HRI: The robot view. *Systems, Man, and Cybernetics, Part C: Applications and Reviews, IEEE Transactions on 34*, 2 (2004), 181–186.

7. Brown, S.L. and Vaughan, C.C. *Play: How it shapes the brain, opens the imagination, and invigorates the soul.* Avery Pub Group, 2009.

8. Caillois, R. *Man, play, and games*. University of Illinois Press, Urbana, 2001.

9. Falkenhainer, B. and Dedre, K.D.F. The structure-mapping engine: Algorithm and examples. *Artificial intelligence 41*, 1 (1989), 1–63.

10. Fauconnier, G. and Turner, M. Conceptual integration networks. *Cognitive Science: A Multidisciplinary Journal 22*, 2 (1998), 133–187.

11. Fauconnier, G. and Turner, M. *The way we think: Conceptual blending and the mind's hidden complexities*. Basic Books, 2003.

12. Forbus, K.D., Gentner, D., and Law, K. MAC/FAC: A model of similarity-based retrieval. *Cognitive Science 19*, 2 (1995), 141–205.

13. Fromberg, D.P. A review of research on play. In *The early childhood curriculum: Current findings in theory and practice*. 1999, 27–53.

14. Fuller, D. and Magerko, B. Shared mental models in improvisational performance. *Proceedings of the Intelligent Narrative Technologies III Workshop*, (2010), 1–6.

15. Gaster, S. Urban Children's Access to their Neighborhood. *Environment and Behavior 23*, 1 (1991), 70.

16. Horst, P.G.L., Mahendran, D., Martinez, K., et al. *Hanging Out, Messing Around, Geeking Out: Living and Learning with New Media.* Cambridge: MIT Press, Forthcoming.

17. Huizinga, J. *Homo Ludens: A Study of the Play-Element in Culture*. Taylor & Francis, 2003.

18. Jenkins, H. Complete freedom of movement: Video games as gendered play spaces. *From barbie to mortal kombat: Gender and computer games*, (1998).

19. Kosko, B. *Fuzzy thinking: The new science of fuzzy logic*. 1993.

20. Lakoff, G. and Johnson, M. *Metaphors we live by: With a new afterword.* Chicago: The University of Chicago Press, 2003.

21. Lakoff, G. *Women, fire, and dangerous things: What categories reveal about the mind.* University of Chicago press, 1987.

22. Lesot, M.J. Similarity, typicality and fuzzy prototypes for numerical data. *6th European Congress on Systems Science, Workshop on Similarity and resemblance*, (2005).

23. Lillard, A. and Else-Quest, N. The Early Years: Evaluating Montessori. *Science 313*, 5795 (2006), 1893–1894.

24. Magerko, B., Fiesler, C., and Baumer, A. Fuzzy Micro-Agents for Interactive Narrative. *Proceedings of the Sixth Annual AI and Interactive Digital Entertainment Conference*, (2010).

25. Morgenthaler, S.K. The meanings in play with objects. In *Play from birth to twelve and beyond: contexts, perspectives, and meanings*. 1998, 359–367.

26. Nourot, P.M. Sociodramatic play: Pretending together. In *Play from birth to twelve and beyond: contexts, perspectives, and meanings*. 1998, 378–391.

27. Power, T.G. *Play and exploration in children and animals*. 2000.

28. Proyer, R.T. Being playful and smart? The relations of adult playfulness with psychometric and self-estimated intelligence and academic performance. *Learning and Individual Differences*, (2011).

29. Rosch, E. Principles of categorization. In *Concepts: core readings*. 1999, 189–206.

30. Sawyer, R.K. Levels of Analysis in Pretend Play

Discourse: Metacommunication in Conversational Routines. *Play and educational theory and practice*, (2003).

31. Sawyer, R.K. *Pretend play as improvisation□: conversation in the preschool classroom*. L. Erlbaum Associates, Mahwah N.J., 1997.

32. Sawyer, R.K. Improvisation and Narrative. *Narrative Inquiry 12*, 2 (2002), 319–349.

33. Sawyers, J.K. and Carrick, N. Symbolic play through the eyes and words of children. *Play and educational theory and practice*, (2003), 159.

34. Scheeff, M., Pinto, J., Rahardja, K., Snibbe, S., and Tow, R. Experiences with Sparky, a social robot. *Socially Intelligent Agents*, (2002), 173–180.

35. Sutton-Smith, B. The role of toys in the instigation of playful creativity. *Creativity Research Journal 5*, 1 (1992), 3–11.

36. Sutton-Smith, B. *The ambiguity of play*. Harvard University Press, Cambridge Mass., 2001.

37. Veale, T. and Donoghue, D.O. Computation and blending. *Cognitive Linguistics 11*, 3/4 (2000), 253–282.

38. Zhu, J. Story and Text Generation through Computational Analogy in the Riu System. (2010).

NOOT: A Tool for Sharing Moments of Reflection during Creative Meetings

Jelle van Dijk, Jirka van der Roest, Remko van der Lugt
Research Centre Technology and Innovation
Utrecht University of Applied Sciences
P.O. Box 182, 3500 AD, Utrecht, Netherlands
jelle.vandijk@hu.nl
+31 6 23156597

Kees Overbeeke
Department of Industrial Design
Eindhoven University of Technology
P.O. Box 513, 5600 MB, Netherlands
c.j.overbeeke@tue.nl

ABSTRACT
We present a fully working prototype of NOOT, an interactive tangible system which supports (sharing of) moments of reflection during brainstorms. We discuss the iterative design process, informed by *embodied situated cognition* theory and by user studies in context using various versions of the prototype. Apart from a potentially useful product, NOOT served as a research-tool showing how physical materials and social interactions *scaffold* people's sense-making efforts, and how technology might fit in to support this process.

ACM Classification Keywords:
H.1.2. Models and Principles: User/Machine Systems
H.5.2. User Interfaces: Theory and methods, Prototyping

General Terms:
Design, Human Factors, Theory

Authors' Keywords:
Embodied situated cognition, interactive systems, design, sense-making, reflection, creativity, audio, tangible

INTRODUCTION
In several iterations we developed NOOT [5][6][18], a system of tangible, interactive 'clips'. By activating a clip for the first time one creates a time-tag in a live recording of, and during, a *creative group meeting* (aka *brainstorm* [16]). Clips can be positioned anywhere in the room, clipped onto sticky-notes, put on the whiteboard, or on other objects, so as to provide a spatial, physical context to the audio tags. By re-activating a clip, the system plays back the conversation participants were having when that clip was first tagged.

Apart from being a potentially useful product, NOOT served as a research-tool by means of which we investigated in what ways *sense-making* activities during creative meetings are *embodied* and *situated* [12].

C&C'11, November 3–6, 2011, Atlanta, Georgia, USA.

Figure 1. A brainstorm in our 'ConceptSpace'.

We will first introduce the theory and then the design concept.

Sense-making in creative meetings
Creative meetings are group events in which people together take on a challenge, or problem, and by means of several activities collaboratively create opportunities or solutions. Sometimes meetings are highly regularized, as in a classical brainstorm with a professional facilitator [16]. But one may also think of an *ad hoc* get together of team-members aiming to tackle a particular problem in a project. Three phenomena interest us in particular:

1. Participants dynamically switch back and forth between individual and socially shared activities.
2. The *generation* of solutions often *co-develops* with the (further) *analysis* of the original challenge [8].
3. Talking and thinking are supported by the use of various materials: a growing physical record of the thought process in physical space. (Think of sticky-notes, personal notes, flip-charts, sketches and models on the whiteboard, quick prototypes in cardboard, screen projection, etc…).

Within this mesh of materials and activities, we ask how each participant tries to make sense of other people's contributions, and how the group as a whole develops a better sense of the design challenge. As said, this latter process is not restricted to the so-called 'problem definition phase' which often takes place at the beginning of a session. Understanding the problem co-develops [8,19] with exploring solutions, e.g. during idea generation, integrating, prototyping and 'pitching' concepts. Presumably it goes on during coffee-breaks, or even after the session has ended (driving home, reflecting on the day). As one participant remarked: 'Only when I had to present our solution to the others did I really start to understand the complexity of it all'.

Instead of stimulating 'creativity' and 'out of the box' thinking per se, we focus on how people gradually try to get a better grip on the challenge. To get a feel for it, think of those moments where you completely misunderstood another person (but only realized much later), or where you tried to recall something 'very important' someone said earlier (but failed to remember); or when you realized the problem was not as simple as it looked, and you felt that some 'underlying issue' needed to be resolved first (even though you couldn't quite put your finger on it yet).

Cognitive scaffolding

In contrast to traditional theories that place the locus of cognition inside the head, the theory of *embodied, situated cognition* explains how internal processes and embodied actions in the material and social environment all work in concert to create cognition. (For introductions see [1],[3],[4]). Here we focus on *cognitive scaffolding* [3][13]. Cognitive scaffolding refers to the way elements in the environment can be 'things to think with' [13,11].

Figure 2. Deictic referencing during a design session at Van Berlo Design, our partner company in this project

For example, two people in a brainstorm may use a sketch in order to support their talking while using *deictic references* (i.e. pointing to the sketch and using phrases like 'this one' and 'over there' [4]). Using the sketch as a scaffold, much of the implicit knowledge needed for shared understanding need not be made explicit: one can simply show/see (figure 2).

The *activity* of creating a sketch, or the organization of items in space may also function as a scaffold: each action is quick 'trial', its result directly available, which may then guide further action [1,4]. Thus, physically organizing sticky-notes into groups on the wall is a way of 'organizing ones thoughts' [19] and a sketch grows interactively as the idea is formed ([14], figure 3).

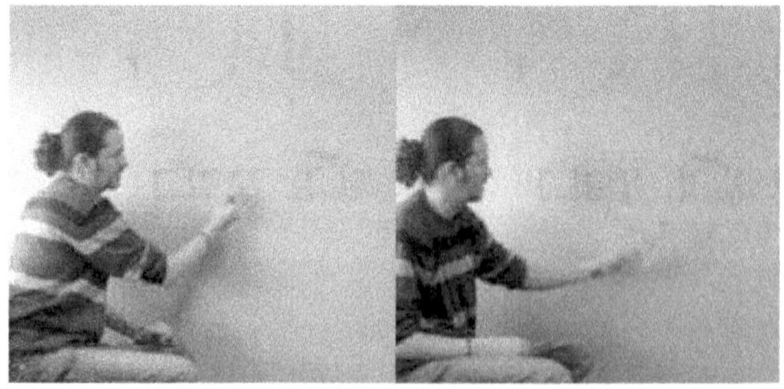

Figure 3. Sketching as a scaffold for sense-making.

Finally, making changes in the environment is often a form of 'epistemic action' [13]: People re-organize the world such that it better suits the task and their means for solving it. For example, it is easier to find a sticky-note if one first lays them out in groups, then if one searches in one junky pile.

The examples may sound familiar, but it is not always easy to predict how people use the environment as a scaffold. Scaffolding may involve local, idiosyncratic couplings that serve the thoughts of *that* person in *that* situation at *that* moment only [3]. As a result of ongoing interaction with the environment, pragmatic, locally effective strategies emerge that are objectively speaking not necessarily the most 'rational' or 'optimal' way of doing things, precisely because people will make do with what happens to be available in a given situation [4]. Some consequences of this for design are discussed in [9].

DESIGN & RESEARCH QUESTION

Our goal is to gain insight in 1) how cognitive scaffolding is part of people's sense-making efforts in the creative space, and 2) how digital technology might support this process in a natural, coherent way. The examples above show how people use spatial arrangements of items to guide their thoughts. Our initial goal was to create interaction with digital media that could support such existing practice. As we will explain below, our project converged on the role of *digital audio recordings* and how audio-playback of earlier moments in a session could come to function as a scaffold for sense-making.

We will first describe our research-through-design approach. We then present NOOT's various iterations, and how conceptual analysis and results of user studies shaped our understanding. We end by revisiting the role of digital technology from the perspective of embodied and situated cognition.

APPROACH

Our approach was guided by three basic principles:

1. *Grounding in theory*: At each major design decision, we discussed whether and how the concept fitted the theory of embodied situated cognition. The prototype

is our 'physical hypothesis': our operationalization of the theory in the context of practice.

2. *Grounding in practice:* We continuously contrasted our design proposals with observations of creative meetings, either with or without our prototype. We also organized two *co-design* workshops with 12 stakeholder parties (professional facilitators, designers and owners of creative facilities).
3. *Evaluate on the basis of people's behavior, rather than their opinion.* Embodied couplings evolve 'in action', in (subconscious) ways that may not be open to post-hoc verbal accounts by the user himself [22]. Our empirical point of departure is therefore always what people *actually do* (including natural talk).

Following these three principles, we argue, the design process is also a research process into how cognitive scaffolding supports sense-making in the creative space. Through a discussion of the evolution of NOOT we will now present our findings.

THE EVOLUTION OF NOOT

Figure 4: First generation NOOT clip, placed on a whiteboard

First generation NOOT

The first NOOT consists of a system of tangible clips with wireless transmitters and central system that continuously recorded audio. The clips can be attached to sticky-notes or sketches and spatially arranged in the creative space, e.g. on the whiteboard (each contains a magnet; figure 4) Attaching the clip to a piece of paper sends a signal to the computer, which creates a time-tag in the audio recording. Pushing the button on the clip activates playback, via central speakers, of a 20 second sample, starting 10 seconds before the time-tag. With NOOT one can tag a fragment of conversation *about* a certain sticky-note and physically couple it *to* that sticky-note [5].

Initial motivation

Observing several brainstorms, we noticed that participants talk a lot, offering rich experiences or reasoning, but write down only very little. People write down some words on a sticky-note, but the *talk* contained the real insight, not the words on the note. At the end of a session, all that was left was the sticky-notes and the meaning of the stories behind them would be quickly forgotten. In other words, the physical record created in the session did not function very well as a 'storage medium' for the content [2]. Linking back to the theory, our reasoning was that the physical record nonetheless serves a powerful function, not by 'storing' insights for later, but by 'scaffolding' communication and sense-making during the session. The sticky-note worked as a conversational 'anchor', constraining and guiding the ongoing conversation, inviting people to show, explain, ask questions, 'keep in mind', recall, relate, and so on.

The concept

We decided to *augment* the scaffolding of the physical record with digital audio. As we saw it, NOOT offers 'audio-context' for physical materials such as sticky-notes, helping these materials to function as cognitive scaffolds for a bit longer, since the audio-fragment would help people recall the original idea [5].

User study

We observed three creative meetings during the creation of the concept and did a qualitative evaluation using a Wizard of Oz prototype in 4 sessions, asking people to freely recount ideas a week later, either with our without an audio-sample. First results suggested that with audio-context, ideas were remembered in more detail. Results remained inconclusive mainly because NOOT proved a 'strange' new thing, the 'clip' didn't work very handy, and people were somewhat hesitant in using the device. We needed a more user-friendly 'clip' and observations over a longer period. That is, we needed a new prototype.

Second generation NOOT

We developed a second prototype (figure 5) that was reliably working and could be tested in the creative space for a longer period of time. Inserting paper was more easy this time, but clips increased in size comparable to hockey-pucks (because of *Arduino* board & batteries). And we had only eight clips.

Studying the use of NOOT in practice

We videotaped six student teams using NOOT in a brainstorm session of one hour each. Sessions were part of educational design projects for an external client and not organized specifically for the test.

Figure 5. Second generation NOOT in context, wireless radio inside each clip. Audio playback from central speakers.

Each session figured the same overall design case, but with different student teams. Since we wanted to see how a person would 'get used' to NOOT over a longer period of time we decided to focus on the facilitator, a colleague in our centre, who guided all sessions. We also observed participants, but 'through the eyes' of the facilitator, who was gradually developing a sense of how to use NOOT, based on his experience with the prototype and on his professional expertise. The facilitator was in a way our 'informant' into the context of practice, serving the role both of a user and of a participant-observer [6].

We performed a grounded theory analysis [20] on three types of data: 1) video recordings of each session, 2) interviews with the facilitator between sessions and short interviews with participants 3) the physical record of the session (sticky-notes, whiteboard, etc…).

Results

Over the sessions, the facilitator (F) evolved a certain routine for using NOOT. This became our basis for revisiting the function of NOOT in the context of cognitive scaffolding. The routine consists of three steps:

Step 1. Marking the Moment (figure 6, top)

- *Opportunity for marking.* F steps back from the group and observes. An opportunity arises.
- *Prepare to mark.* F grabs a clip and an empty paper. F waits with both items in hand.
- *Marking the moment.* F puts the paper in the clip at a carefully chosen moment in the conversation

Step 2: Position (figure 6, bottom)

- F positions the clip on a suitable place in the space, e.g. on the table or on the whiteboard.

Step 3: Playback (figure 7)

- *Activating playback.* F presses the replay button.
- *Listening:* Participants stop talking and listen.

Figure 6. Top: Opportunity for Marking (l); Mark the moment (r). Bottom: Position on object (l); on wall (r).

Figure 7. Activating playback on one of the clips

A changing use of NOOT

Originally we saw NOOT as a natural extension of writing a sticky-note: one comes up with an idea, writes it down on a sticky, and then one attaches a clip to the sticky-note, linking 'talk' to 'text'. Analyzing our data we saw a different way in which NOOT is related to physical materials. F did not use clips while actively engaged in a conversation. He used NOOT upon stepping *outside* of the action, in a moment of reflective listening. This routine evolved with experience. In the beginning, F would talk a lot about the audio and the fact that NOOT created a fixed sample of 20 seconds. He was busy "trying to get the *right* piece of talk [i.e. in which a particular idea was explained by a participant] *into* the 20 second sample". This was a frustrating and conscious effort we had not intended. In later sessions he let go of this goal. F would listen to the group's discussion, and in the middle of an engaging conversation he would simply mark a moment of 'interesting conversation'. Taking a clip in hand caused a particular focus: F would become sensitive to upcoming opportunities for making a 'good mark'.

NOOT was not used by F the way we had designed it. Instead of clipping to an existing sticky or sketch, F would use a clip and an empty sheet of paper to 'mark a moment'. Only *after* that he would write a label which referred to the audio content, instead of the audio being a context for what was already on the paper. Putting the clip in a physical context would happen afterwards, when he *positioned* the clip with label in the space (figure 6).

We slowly began to see that the biggest value of NOOT is not to augment the existing physical record with audio, but to create new opportunities for scaffolding by putting digital audio in a physical, 'actionable' context. Grabbing a clip means one takes on a different role: one listens on a more reflective level. Marking a moment with NOOT invites short moments of reflection, of 'taking a step back', which is already valuable even without playback.

Playback

Still, the biggest problem was playback. It was not used often, and when it was used, it often disturbed the conversation rather than supporting it. Based on interviews and observations we offer three reasons why.

Firstly, participants did not see the immediate value of playback during a session, saying they 'still remembered everything'. (This could be disputed, but it is how people experience it). Participants saw NOOT as a fancy memo-recorder to record and store 'ones ideas' for later. Since the sticky-notes were still functioning as scaffolds for the ideas, people didn't see the added value of adding audio. We will return to this issue in the general discussion.

Secondly, the system did not invite 'experimenting with'. The main reason for this is that audio was centrally played from the speakers. Activating playback quickly becomes an obtrusive act people will not easily perform. There was no way of privately listening to – and growing accustomed to - the recordings. People did not get a chance to experience its value first-hand.

Thirdly, in order to 'tune into' a piece of conversation one needs to be attentive. One cannot listen to more than one person speaking at the same time. This is different from certain kinds of visual patterns or sound that can be peripheral and still not disturbing. When one person suddenly decides to play a clip, other participants might not be ready for listening. A related problem was that playback simply started 10 seconds before the time-tag, regardless of the content. One could not scroll back or forth to find a meaningful bit of the speech that could be used to 'step into' the conversation.

THIRD GENERATION NOOT

In the third iteration we made substantial changes based on the following premises:

- Taking a clip means 'marking a moment', not 'record a fixed sample'. The clip should function as a physical link to one time-point in the entire audio-recording.
- Marking a moment is a short moment of reflection. One is –if only briefly - a passive listener to an ongoing conversation. The user is not herself actively engaged in the conversation.
- It should be possible for individuals to 'experiment' with playback in unobtrusively, just as one can gloss over the writings on the wall without disturbing other people. By experimenting participants get the chance to find how NOOT may provide scaffolds for them.
- The limited number of clips and their large size also inhibited its use. Ideally here are many small clips available at all times (like whiteboard magnets or pens) allowing for the creation of a large web of tangible entry-points to the audio-record in space.

Figure 8. The final NOOT prototype. From left to right: audio-playback, a clip on a sticky-note, the dispenser tray and the central computer. Physical design by *Van Berlo*

Final design

In the previous version clips were very large and expensive due to all the technology inside. We decided to take out all technology, leaving only a small RFID tag for identification, and a magnet. This way we can create many clips for a low price. This meant we had to create two new devices: a 'dispenser tray' which provided the 'audio time tagging' functionality and an audio-playback device, both connected wirelessly to the central computer (figure 8). Taking a clip from the tray causes the time-tag to be placed in the audio (figure 9). Holding the playback device close to a clip causes it to start playing the audio from the time-tag onwards, in 'individual listening mode' (figure 10). To encourage 'playing around with', the playback device has a large wheel on top that allows scrolling back and forth through the audio. When one has found 'that one bit' one was looking for (or another interesting bit one happens to hear), one may ask the attention of other participants and push a button, which activates a 'play out loud' mode. When one scrolls to a starting point one feels comfortable with and stops playback, the clip will remain linked to that new point in time (the software also stores all old time-tags as well).

DISCUSSION

In this last iteration, we have further concretized cognitive scaffolding for sense-making. Following up on the previous study, NOOT provides a physical invitation to create personal, reflective moments. We now discuss how this works out in final prototype.

Marking the moment

Taking a NOOT means creating a mini-moment of reflection, in which one acknowledges: '*I* find *this* moment interesting, I might want to revisit it later and think some more about it.' This can be of great value for creating deeper insight into the problem at hand [19].

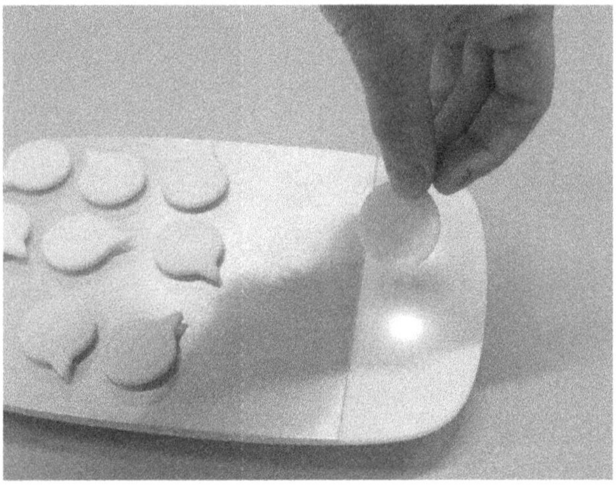

Figure 9. Marking a moment by taking a clip from the tray

Without NOOT, one would have to make a 'mental' note or make one on paper. Mental notes are easily forgotten, and a written note means being explicit about what one is thinking about. Sometimes this is disturbing: one feels that there is 'something' – but one wants to postpone further analysis for later, exactly because things are happening fast and one does *not* want to miss out on the group action. Using NOOT one does not have to be explicit about *what* the moment is about, only *that* it is a 'noteworthy' moment.

Cognitive scaffolding and reflection

Each clip becomes as one 'point of access' to the complete, audio recording. This idea of 'entry-points' is strengthened by the possibility for the user to scroll, from the time-tag, all the way through the entire audio recording. In effect, NOOT maps the temporal domain of recorded audio (the history of what has been discussed so far) onto the spatial, physical world, by which it becomes open for embodied actions in the here and now [7]. By coupling audio-moments to the physical space, NOOT puts these moments within a concrete field of action-possibilities These actions (taking a NOOT, marking a moment, listening privately to a moment in the session-history, presenting a moment to others, discussing the moment) may then lead to new perceptions and insights. This is how we see the way that NOOT links digital audio to the process of cognitive scaffolding for sense-making. In particular, we hold, it invites reflection *in*- as well as *on* action, following the terminology of Donald Schön [19]. Reflection-in-action: when one marks a moment, 'in the heath of the moment', and there is no time to think further. Reflection-on-action: at a later moment, when current affairs in combination with the visible availability of existing NOOT-clips in the space invite one to take up the audio-playback device and return to that previous moment in order to reflect on it some more.

Creating couplings

Positioning 'moments' in space is different from graphical representations of time (as in a conventional user interface). To see why, consider that one could, if one wanted, use NOOT to create a symbolic representation like a timeline, positioning all clips on the whiteboard from left to right. NOOT offers much more freedom; all kinds of ad hoc, local, idiosyncratic ways of spatially organizing clips are possible. User can therefore create their own particular ways of using the system. For example, one may position audio-moments (by way of the physical clip) on a prototype that was being discussed at that moment, or on the sketch that was referred to at that moment, or on some meaningful point in a mind-map, or

Figure 10. Privately listening and scrolling through audio

next to an object symbolizing that moment, or in front of oneself on the table ("here are *my* moments"), or in the very corner where people where having the discussion that was tagged, or even right on the person that was speaking.

Social scaffolding

One aspect of embodiment that emerged quite strongly in this study is that the 'social' aspect of situated cognition [21,9] is strongly connected to the role that material objects and spatial elements have in cognition [13,11,4]. In the literature, 'material' situatedness and 'social' situatedness are both acknowledged but sometimes discussed as separate processes [e.g. 4]. In our concept we see that all interaction with the audio: marking the moment, positioning the clip in space, listening privately to the audio, is always clearly visible to the other members of the group, since they involve intentional actions with hand-sized objects (the dispenser, the tray, the clips) in a shared space. This means that quiet, personal moments of reflection now become socially *accountable* [9 p.79]: I see you 'marking this moment', which may cause me to have a moment of reflection as well: 'What might be interesting about this moment?' One might say that NOOT creates 'deictic references' towards moments of personal reflection: Using NOOT, I explicitly show others that I am experiencing a moment of reflection, and later on we can all literally 'point to' that earlier moment of reflection (i.e. the clip), and use that to work on a shared understanding. Even if I have forgotten about one of 'my clips', someone else experimenting with the playback device may stumble upon it and ask who tagged that clip and why. In this way, NOOT not only services personal reflection but also sharing moments of thought in the social sense, which may aid in the group's ongoing attempt at creating a better understanding of the design challenge.

Some questions regarding the classical information-processing function of digital technology

In closing, we would like to offer some speculations on how NOOT shows a re-conceptualization of the role of digital technology for an embodied, situated process like brainstorming. At the start, the fact that so little of what was being said got 'stored' in the physical record quickly lead us to abandon ideas like a "digital sticky-note" or "interactive whiteboards". We focused on the conversation instead. This first concept still retained something of a 'storage device': saving 'important bits' of the conversation for later, which was also how users and facilitators will first talk about NOOT. When introduced to the concept, people see NOOT as a kind of memo-recorder, in which to 'store good ideas'. Facilitators quickly express the need to 'store all results' and then 'make them available very quickly and easily' after a session.

We doubt whether the audio will often be used after the session, especially if it is framed as a kind of database in which all 'results' are stored. The word 'result' is an ambiguous term. People will say "I've got the results", holding a pile of flip-charts under their arm. Participants photograph all materials, 'so as not to forget anything', but rarely look at the photo's afterwards (figure 11). Participants and facilitators were aware of this problem, saying things like: 'Of course, nobody is going to read the report'. *during* a session. The insight is not in what is written on the sticky-note so much as it is in the activity it supports.

Figure 11. A facilitator photographing 'the results'.

This is to be expected given the thesis that physical materials do not in and of themselves 'store' the actual insight generated in a session, but function mostly as cognitive scaffolds facilitating 'insightful activities'.

The ability for 'live' playback during a session was our first step away from seeing digital technology as a means for the 'storage' of the 'results' of the thought process in a session, towards thinking about how recording technology could actually support the ongoing cognitive process *as it was happening*. The next step was to acknowledge that audio playback functions as its own kind of scaffold (instead of 'stretching' the scaffolding power of a sticky-note). As we tried to argue, NOOT invites moments of reflection and sharing these moments with others.

Our view of the role of digital technology within embodied, situated practices, then, is that it offers new kinds of couplings between people's action-possibilities and digital processes [7], which in turn invite and support, in real-time, certain kinds of sense-making *activities*. This is an altogether different role than the recording, representing and storing the *outcomes* of such activities (results, facts, data, conclusions), as is the case in traditional information technologies.

FURTHER DIRECTIONS

Our next goal is to conduct a qualitative, longitudinal study in which we will try out the new NOOT for a longer period of time (several weeks), at Van Berlo company. Our main question concerns the actual effect of playback on the group's understanding of the design challenge.

CONCLUSION

In three iterations we developed a tangible interactive prototype called NOOT that served as a research tool into the role of cognitive scaffolding for sense-making processes in the context of creative meetings. By means of the iterative design and the user research results we provided a concrete operationalization of the way the theory works out in practice. In this way we hope to have added to a better understanding of how embodied situated cognition may play a role in sense-making processes during brainstorms. We ended with speculations on the changing role of digital technology, away from information processing and towards creating real-time couplings between ongoing human activities and digital information.

ACKNOWLEDGMENTS

We thank Van Berlo (Edouard Messager, Sjoerd Hoyink) for the physical design and fruitful discussions. This research was supported by a CELL grant from the Dutch Ministry of Economic Affairs. We also thank Janneke Sluijs and Marnick Menting.

REFERENCES

1. Anderson, M.L. Embodied cognition: a field-guide. Artificial Intelligence, 149 (1) (2003) 91-130.
2. Brouwer, C.E. and Van Dijk, J. Brainstorming: Talk and the representation of ideas and insights. Proc. of PINC11 (2011).
3. Clancey, W. J. *Situated cognition: On human knowledge and computer representation.* Cambridge, MA: Cambridge University Press. (1997)
4. Clark, A. *Being there: Putting brain, body and world together again.* Cambridge, MA: MIT Press. (1997)
5. Dijk, J. van, Lugt, R. van der & Overbeeke, C.J. Let's take this conversation outside: supporting embodied embedded memory. *Proc of DPPI'09*, Compiegne, France. (2009)
6. Dijk, J. van & Brouwer, C.E. Making sense of brainstorms: Some NOOTs to reflect on. *Proc of PINC'11*, Sonderborg, Danmark. (2011) 11-14.
7. Djajadiningrat, J.P., Wensveen, S.A.G., Frens, J.W. and Overbeeke, C.J. Tangible products: redressing the balance between appearance and action. Personal and Ubiquitous Computing, 8(5), (2004) 294-309.
8. Dorst, K. & Cross, N. (2001) Creativity in the design process: Co-evolution of problem-solution. *Design studies, 22*, 425-437.
9. Dourish, P. Where the Action Is: The Foundations of Embodied Interaction. Cambridge, MA: MIT Press. (2001)
10. Fish J. & Scrivener, S. Amplifying the mind's eye: sketching and visual cognition. Leonardo, 23 (1), (1990) 117-126.
11. Hutchins, E.. Cognition in the wild. Cambridge: MIT Press (1995)
12. De Jaegher, H. and Di Paolo, E. Participatory sense-making: An enactive approach to social cognition. Phenomenology and the Cognitive Sciences, 6(4), (2007) 485-507
13. Kirsh, D. Thinking with external representations. AI & Society, 25, (2010) 441-454
14. Lugt, van der, R. How sketching can affect the idea generation process in design group meetings. Design Studies. 26(2) (2005). 101-122.
15. Merleau-Ponty, M. *Phenomenology of perception.* New York: Routledge, (1962).
16. Osborn, A.F. Applied Imagination. New York: Scribner's. 3e ed. (1963)
17. Robertson, T. Cooperative Work and Lived Cognition: A Taxonomy of Embodied Actions. In: Proc Fifth ECCSCW Dordrecht: Kluwer Academic Publishers (1997), 205-220.
18. Sluijs, J.M. & Dijk, J. van. NOOT: A tangible interaction tool supporting memory in creative practices. Presented at CHI-NL09, Leiden, Netherlands. (2009)
19. Schön, D.A. The reflective practitioner - how professionals think in action. New York: Basic Books. (1983)
20. Strauss, A. and Corbin, J. Basics of qualitative research. Grounded theory, procedures and techniques. Sage: London. (1990)
21. Suchman, L. Plans and Situated Actions. Cambridge: University Press. (1987)
22. Wegner, D.M. The illusion of conscious will. Cambridge (MA): MIT Press. (2002)

Designing Reality-Based Interfaces for Creative Group Work

Florian Geyer, Ulrike Pfeil, Anita Höchtl, Jochen Budzinski, Harald Reiterer
Human-Computer Interaction Group, University of Konstanz
Universitätsstraße 10, 78457 Konstanz, Germany
{firstname.lastname}@uni-konstanz.de

ABSTRACT
Using affinity diagramming as an example, we investigate reality-based interfaces for supporting creative group work. Based on an observational study grounded in the reality-based interaction framework, we identified power vs. reality tradeoffs that can be addressed to find a close fit to embodied practice. Using this knowledge, we designed and implemented a digital workspace for supporting affinity diagramming. Its hybrid interaction techniques combine digital pen & paper with an interactive table and tangible tokens. An additional vertical display is used to support reflection-in-action and for enhancing discussion and coordination. A preliminary user study confirmed the applicability of our tradeoffs and the general acceptance of the tool design.

Author Keywords
Creative group work, affinity diagramming, reality-based interaction, digital pen & paper, hybrid interactive surfaces

ACM Classification Keywords
H.5.3 Group and Organization Interfaces: collaborative computing, computer supported cooperative work

General Terms
Design, documentation, experimentation, theory

INTRODUCTION
During early phases of design processes, designers often closely collaborate on design problems and design solutions. Especially during idea generation and evaluation activities, cooperation can lead to more creative ideas and better solutions [22]. The most effective cooperation between designers frequently takes place in traditional co-located sessions in combination with structured methods and techniques that moderate the influences of social factors [7]. The use of technology in such group sessions is often considered harmful since using desktop-based digital tools would isolate participants, leading to a breakdown of communication that is vital for a shared understanding in the group [18,19]. Rigid interaction modalities may further impose limitations on crucial characteristics of design practice, like the workflow of design methods, coordination and communication as well as embodiment of thought. As long as digital tools do not consider and actively support these aspects, they will hardly be adopted for use in practice.

As a result, designers often use traditional media for group sessions. By using physical artifacts and by harnessing the spatial properties of the environment, they can make use of rich forms of expression like body language, facial expressions and the immediacy of verbal communication that are crucial for expressing their creativity [21]. Thereby, physical artifacts serve as boundary objects and as a collective memory for facilitating discussion. In design studio environments, the physical space in the room itself is an important tool that allows organizing information in an informal and fluent way [20]. Design sketches for example can easily be shared on large whiteboards or spread out on tables for comparison and discussion with other designers. While these aspects facilitate efficient cooperation in face-to-face sessions, they also lead to challenges concerning the documentation and sharing of results in digital repositories, which is often desired during the course of a design project. Due to the dynamic nature of creative work, organizing and archiving individual contributions in a formal structure is an awkward task that often fails and therefore impedes the reuse of design knowledge in later phases of the design process. Furthermore, by solely relying on physical material, designers cannot benefit from the power of digital tools that could be used to augment ideation and synthesis by providing additional information or by enabling reuse, sharing or analytical functionalities. Both strength and limitations of embodied practice point to the need for an integration of computational functionality with physical tools for better supporting creative group work.

It is only recently that ubiquitous computing technologies which blend in with the physical environment promise a better integration of technology in co-located collaborative work. Interactive surfaces, like tabletops or wall-size displays, closely resemble real-world work surfaces. Multi-touch interfaces can provide multi-user workspaces, allow for equal participation of users and thus may improve group awareness compared to desktop computing [3]. Nonetheless, they may also stimulate engaging and playful explorations by simulating the physicality of the real-world. Tangible user interfaces (TUIs) allow for combining digital information with the affordances and qualities of physical artifacts. They may also be actively used to democratize interactions [9]. Hybrid interactive surfaces [14] combine direct-manipulative interfaces like multi-touch tabletops with TUIs and therefore

C&C'11, November 3–6, 2011, Atlanta, Georgia, USA.

provide a large design space that should be further explored in the context of creative group work.

Theoretical frameworks such as Reality-based Interaction (RBI) provide guidance on how to utilize this huge design space for designing user interfaces that build upon the knowledge and experiences of people in the "real world" [10,11]. RBI is based on the assumptions that people's interactions in the real world are highly practiced and robust and thus require little effort to learn and perform. In the design of reality-based interfaces, designers and researchers therefore should consider a "power vs. reality tradeoff", with the goal "to give up reality only explicitly and only in return for increasing power" [10]. A wisely chosen balance between the power of the interface and its level of reality enables the digital tool to go beyond the possibilities of the real world. We argue that by investigating embodied practice in creative group work using RBI, we can identify critical tradeoffs between reality and computational power. By carefully considering these tradeoffs in the design of digital tools, we may overcome the described limitations of creative practice and provide additional benefits through computational power. Consequently, we seek to answer following research question:

RQ: Can we design reality-based tools that preserve the original workflow and embodied practice of creative group work but also enable additional functionality?

To answer this question we chose to study a specific collaborative design method in order to identify crucial characteristics of embodied practice with a real-world example. Using this data, we seek to identify tradeoffs that allow augmenting practice without changing crucial characteristics of the original workflow. Based on this, we may then design and implement reality-based interfaces to examine the effects of these tradeoffs.

RELATED WORK

Our work extends related research in computing environments for co-located creative group work. A range of researchers have presented promising approaches for supporting design sessions with tangible user interfaces and interactive surfaces.

An influential tangible approach was introduced with *The Designer's Outpost* [15]. This digital tool introduced paper-based interaction concepts in the context of collaborative web site design. It combines physical sticky notes with an interactive whiteboard system. By using overhead image capture, notes can be combined with digital ink annotations for creating hybrid website diagrams. The system thereby bridges physical and digital representations to support the documentation and sharing of results. Yet, the system lacks efficient multi-user support and is only suitable for a limited number of physical artifacts. *Pictionaire* [6] also uses overhead image capture and projection to combine physical artifacts with digital annotations on a hybrid tabletop system. The system thereby supports the sharing and discussion of digital and physical design artifacts within idea-generation activities. It also provides digital containers for creating storyboards from captured or retrieved images.

Researchers have also shown that interactive surfaces and multi-display environments can be used to support creative group work. i-LAND [18] combines interactive surfaces, like tables, walls and mobile devices, for supporting fluent creative collaboration and for easing the transfer of information across devices. But, it focuses on the design of an adequate technical infrastructure instead of addressing specific tasks or support for established workflows. *BrainStorm* [8] combines multiple pen-operated displays to support creative problem solving processes. Digital notes can be created on an interactive table and transferred to a wall projection for discussion and clustering. Thereby, it provides stylus-based interaction techniques for creating, sharing and clustering of digital notes. Though, it does not add supplementary functionalities to significantly augment practice and supports only dyadic groups. *The Designer's Environment* [5] supports the KJ creativity method with multimodal interaction techniques for grouping and linking digital notes on a tabletop system. Handwritten digital notes are sent to the table from multiple tablet PCs. Text recognition is used on the tablets for retrieving images from the web according to the content of notes. The system however primarily focuses on novel multimodal interaction techniques for grouping digital notes rather than workflow support or support for tangible media. *TeamStorm* [4] combines multiple Tablet PCs with an interactive whiteboard interface for collaborative sketching sessions. Sketches can be transferred from mobile devices to the whiteboard for coordinating discussion in the group and for enhancing reflection activities. The system shows how technology can be effectively used to support social interactions across digital artifacts. However, like many of the presented systems, it replaces physical practice, thereby requiring the exclusive use of digital modalities.

Many of the described approaches share our goal to integrate technology into physical design practice. Some systems may also be partly classified as reality-based interfaces. However, many design decisions were made implicitly, without stating the tradeoffs to physical practice, existing workflows or their impact on the embodiment of actions. Consequently, we seek to make our tradeoffs between physical practice and digital tool support more explicit than other researchers.

ANALYSIS

In the following we will describe a detailed analysis of embodied practice using a structured observation of a specific real-world example. The knowledge gained from this analysis is to be used for identifying potential tradeoffs.

Theoretical Framework

The RBI framework [11] provides the theoretical foundation for our approach because we consider its themes adequate for identifying crucial characteristics of embodied design practice. In an initial description of RBI, Jacob et al. provide general guidance on how to deal with the tradeoff between power and reality [10]. In a following paper [11], they further refine their definition of reality and distinguish between four themes of reality-based interaction that should be considered when designing interfaces, namely: naïve

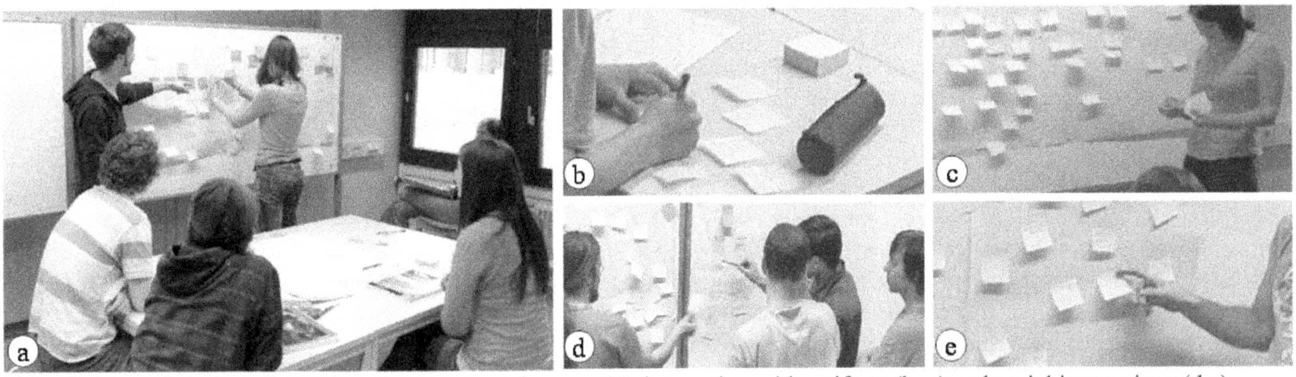

Figure 1. Our study focused on the use of workspaces (a), interaction with artifacts (b, c) and social interactions (d,e).

physics (NP), body awareness and skills (BAS), environment awareness and skills (EAS), as well as social awareness and skills (SAS). NP considers people's knowledge about the physical world, like gravity, friction and relative scale. These characteristics may be simulated by using physical metaphors such as multi-touch manipulations or TUIs. BAS describes people's knowledge and experiences of working and thinking with their bodies. Interactive systems may therefore also consider whole-body interaction as interaction modality. EAS includes the navigation and manipulation of the physical environment as well as the orientation and spatial understanding in the environment. These aspects may be considered when designing digital work surfaces or objects. SAS deals with people's interactions and communication amongst each other, including group dynamics in collaborative work and the exchange of artifacts among group members. TUIs are an example for interfaces that may augment this theme.

Technique Selection

Creative professionals hardly work in group situations without a formal structure or workflow [7]. A wide variety of methods and techniques provide control over social factors and group coordination. Hence, we decided to focus our investigation on one representative example for creative group work that includes a methodic workflow. Affinity Diagramming [1] is a collaborative design method applied early in the design process for analyzing a design problem or to create first design solutions. It is typically practiced with pen & paper and a shared surface such as a whiteboard or a large wall. Beyer & Holtzblatt [1] explicitly recommend traditional media for practicing affinity diagramming. The technique consists of three main phases: 1) generating (participants individually create content on sticky notes), 2) sharing (participants present and collect notes), and 3) structuring (participants arrange notes into meaningful categories). These basic phases (ideation, sharing and evaluation) can be considered typical for a range of collaborative design methods that have the goal to achieve a shared understanding of design problems or design solutions [7]. While other methods may employ other contents and design artifacts, affinity diagramming is explicitly limited to words, sketches or short sentences on small sticky notes to stimulate diversity in ideation phases. During convergent phases, shared understanding is further promoted by the collaborative task to make sense out of a large number of artifacts. Due to the high frequency of actions that are enforced by the use of small artifacts, this technique is especially suited for a quantitative analysis.

Observation

By analyzing individual interactions with the environment (EAS), communication with group members (SAS), embodied interactions (BAS) and the use of physical artifacts (NP), we strive to identify aspects of affinity diagramming practice that should be preserved and issues that may benefit from computational power. Therefore, we observed three groups of students (4-6 each, N=15) practicing affinity diagramming within a hands-on session in context of an interaction design course. The work environment was based on a horizontal (table) and a vertical (whiteboard) work surface (see Fig. 1,a). We further supplied colored sticky notes and pens. After an introduction to the technique and a design problem, the students carried out the design technique independently. The group sessions were videotaped and lasted between 1.5 and 2 hours. In addition, each group session was observed by a researcher who made notes of the group's activities. Based on the procedures of interaction analysis [13] and qualitative content analysis, separate categories within the four themes of RBI were inductively developed for coding the videos. Doing so, multiple iterations were conducted before the code scheme was considered to be saturated and sufficiently described the data set. Two sub-sets of video-data (one part covering the two phases of generating and presenting notes and one part covering the phase of sorting notes on the whiteboard) were coded by two independent researchers. In order to do so, the video was separated into chunks and both coders were then asked to code the chunks into categories. Coding was not exclusive to the categories, which means that one chunk could also be coded into multiple categories. An inter-coder reliability analysis revealed a Cohen's Kappa of 0.86, which was considered to be satisfactory. The whole data-set was then coded by one researcher.

Overall, three categories describing participants' interactions with the environment (EAS) were derived from the most frequent coded events across the design sessions. We distinguished between participants focusing their attention on the table, the whiteboard as well as on other individuals. The frequency of these actions is given in Figure 2 for each of the three categories. The values describe the percentage of the time the video was coded into the categories for each of the three phases. In the first phase, participants primarily worked in individual workspaces on the table (86%, see Fig. 1,b). In the third phase, individual attention was mainly distributed between other participants (18%) and the whiteboard (74%). Phase two was characterized by transitions between these workspaces. All groups used the whiteboard as a shared workspace during convergent activities. However, participants made use of their individual workspaces throughout the sessions. We also observed rapid changes of attention between individual and shared workspace as well as between different participants during the third phase. Through a qualitative analysis, we found that when engaging in actions during convergent activities, the view on the vertical surface was frequently blocked by members of the group, thereby limiting access and visibility to the other participants (see Fig. 1,d).

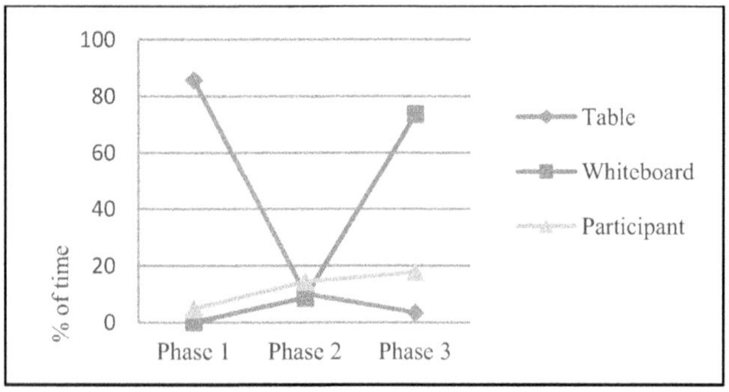

Figure 2. Coding results for EAS

Participants' social interactions (SAS) were investigated based on the kind of communication that they engaged in with other members. This included discussion, presentation as well as silence. While participants mostly worked quietly in the first phase (96%), the second phase was characterized by the presentation of artifacts (16%) and short discussions (5%). The third phase was dominated by extensive discussions (22%). Thereby, we observed alternations between detailed discussion of specific artifacts (see Fig. 1, e) and group coordination that required an overview over all artifacts.

Concerning physical and bodily interactions (NP and BAS), four categories were identified that describe these key interactions within the design sessions (see Fig. 3). In the first phase, each participant spent on average 60% of the time creating content and 56% on sorting notes within an individual workspace on the table (see Fig. 1, b). Based on overlapping data within these categories, we could identify that creation of content is tightly coupled with sorting actions in a personal workspace. Our qualitative analysis revealed that participants were utilizing the personal workspace for preparing contents for presentation or to search for inspiration by reflecting on created contents. Nevertheless, we could also observe that the pre-sorting behavior led to physical restrictions during the transfer of artifacts between workspaces due to the physical distance between these surfaces. For example, participants used mobile piles in their hands (see Fig. 1, c) to keep their artifacts in order when presenting (36%) or to collect notes during discussion (7%). Both the second phase and the third phase were accompanied with sorting actions on the whiteboard (~13%). Due to the small size of artifacts and their spatial distribution on the whiteboard, we could observe mutual blocking when participants were engaging in parallel actions at the partly very crowded whiteboard (see Fig. 1, d). We also observed that participants frequently used their bodies (e.g. fingers and arms) for deictic gestures to emphasize the focus of discussion to other participants (see Fig. 1, e). Overall, sorting notes into categories required mutual understanding and consensus in the group.

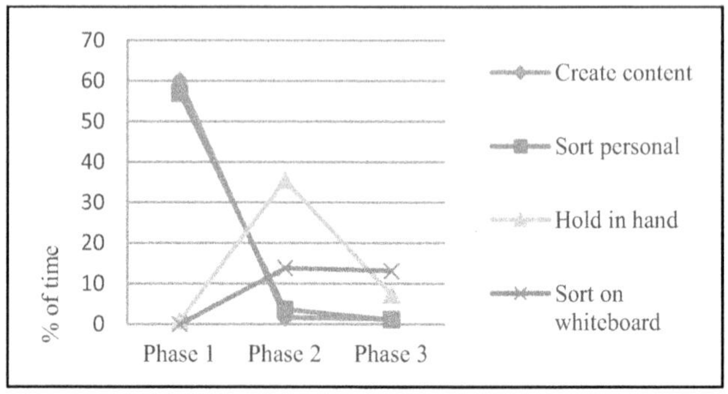

Figure 3. Coding results for NP and BAS

Power vs. Reality Tradeoffs

Based on the results of our study we examined potential power vs. reality tradeoffs. The goal of this investigation was to identify characteristics that should be preserved because they are considered crucial to the effectiveness and efficiency of the design method (Reality). At the same time, we thought about potential divergences from reality that may allow augmenting typical tasks (Power).

Physical Workspace vs. Digital Workspace

We believe that the design of the physical work environment has implications for group awareness and social factors like production blocking (EAS). Work surfaces were appropriated due to their differences in accessibility of artifacts and available display space. This finding is supported by studies from Vyas et al. [20,21], that describe the appropriation of physical surfaces in professional design studios. The authors report that horizontal surfaces mainly serve as a space for *action*, while vertical surfaces are useful for *reflection* during convergent activities. Physical blocking is likelier to occur on vertical surfaces (see Fig. 1, d), while overview on multiple artifacts is limited on horizontal surfaces. Thus, we argue that both types of surfaces should be preserved, but may be enhanced through computational power to increase visibility and accessibility.

Within convergent phases, we observed alternations between manipulations and reflection and between detailed discussions of artifacts and coordination activities that required an overview on all created artifacts (SAS). These findings are in line with reflective practice as described by Schön [17]. Though, we also found that this behavior may lead to coordination and communication issues when dealing with a large number of artifacts during discussion. At some points, participants had problems following discussion due to rapid shifts of attention or because some artifacts on the shared work surface were blocked by other participants. Therefore, we argue that this activity should be actively supported to aid participants to "think what they are doing while they are doing it" [17].

From our analysis we also discovered that individual workspaces are essential for preserving the workflow of the design technique because they moderate social factors like evaluation apprehension by providing a semi-private retreat from the group. This conclusion is in line with findings reported by Warr & O'Neill [22]. Other social factors like production blocking and free riding are partly addressed by the workflow of the design technique itself (SAS). Conversely, we discovered issues with the transfer of artifacts between workspaces throughout the sessions. Consequently, we argue that individual workspaces should be preserved, while the transfer could be improved with computational functionality.

A possible solution to these tradeoffs could be a digital workspace that replicates the physical properties for action and reflection activities, but at the same time provides additional features to enhance equal access and group awareness, thereby fostering shared understanding in the group.

Physical Artifacts vs. Digital Artifacts

We observed that physical artifacts are especially useful during individual *divergent* activities, where a large number of different artifacts are created in rapid cycles. Participants used paper notes efficiently within tightly coupled alternations between individual creation and reflection (NP). This is in line with results from a study reported by Cook & Bailey [2] on the use of paper in professional design practice. The authors conclude that paper is highly appreciated due to its unique physical affordances that support both fluent access and flexible handling. They also emphasize the usefulness of paper in face-to-face collaborations. However, we found issues with the transfer of physical artifacts between workspaces and their visibility and accessibility during *convergent* phases (BAS). This is partly due to the small size of the artifacts and their spatial distribution. Nevertheless, this may influence group awareness and coordination.

A possible solution to these tradeoffs could be to employ hybrid artifacts that have both a physical and digital representation. The physical representation could be used within individual divergent activities, while the digital representation may offer improved visibility (e.g. magnification) and improved accessibility (e.g. parallel access). Digital representations would also allow for more advanced functionalities, like duplication, semi-automatic grouping and associations with additional or analytic information that may improve ideation or reflection activities. Still, the transformation between these representations needs to be smooth to minimize the costs of this transition. At the same time, digital representations should mimic the affordances of physical artifacts as closely as possible to allow for embodied interactions like deictic gestures that are important forms of expression.

Tradeoff Decisions

We summarize our analysis with following specific tradeoff decisions: T1: preserve the physical workspace setting; T2: preserve individual ideation and reflection with physical artifacts; T3: support the handling of digital artifacts during convergent activities; T4: augment collaborative actions with more equal access and better visibility of artifacts; and T5: augment reflection activities for improving coordination and group awareness.

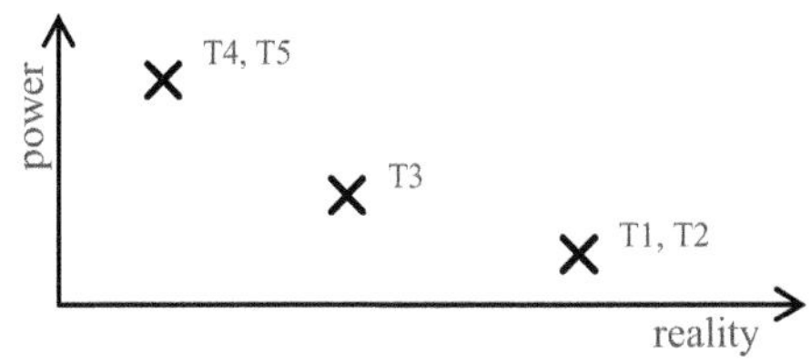

Figure 4. Tradeoffs along the power vs. reality continuum

Figure 4 visualizes these tradeoffs along the power vs. reality spectrum [10]. While T1 and T2 strive to *preserve* reality as closely as possible, they hardly add power to the interface. Nonetheless, these are necessary to ensure our goal to preserve the original workflow of the design technique. T3 departs from closely imitating reality in order to *support* convergent activities through the use of digital artifacts. However, the goal should be to transfer important characteristics of physical artifacts and sacrifice less important characteristics for computational power. T4 and T5 add digital features that are not possible in the real world. They significantly depart from reality by offering "super powers" [11]. The challenge is to design these tradeoffs in a way that does not negatively influence T1 and T2. Therefore, T1 and T2 have priority and T4 and T5 should be designed in a way that *augments* rather than changes.

DESIGN

We translated our tradeoffs into specific designs in order to test whether they can be successfully implemented by using ubiquitous computing technologies. Because T1 and T2 were given priority, we decided to design an adequate workspace first, before designing interaction techniques for the other tradeoffs in a second step. Doing so, we wanted to make sure that T3 to T5 do not conflict with the basic workflow and that the interaction techniques complement the workspace setting.

Workspace Design

With the aim of preserving the physical workspace setting (T1), we decided to keep the basic layout of one horizontal and one vertical work surface. But, these are to be replicated by using interactive displays. This design decision will allow using dynamic visualizations of digital representations of artifacts, which is the key to multiple other tradeoffs (T3,T4,T5). Figure 5 shows the final workspace design, which is based on a large interactive table for collaboratively interacting with artifacts and a very high-resolution wall display. The table is to be used for interacting with digital

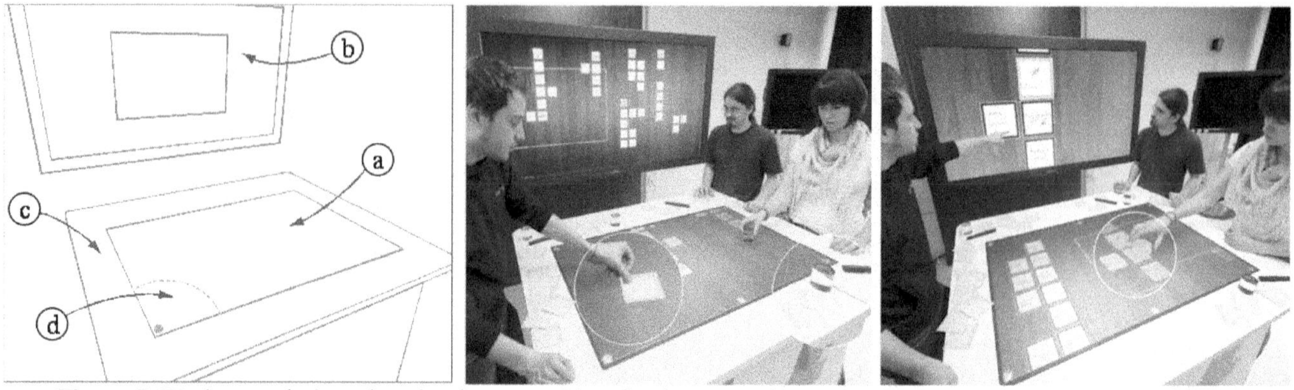

Figure 5. Workspace design: shared action space (a), reflection space (b), personal spaces (c) and transfer spaces (d).

artifacts (*shared action space,* see Fig. 5, a), while the vertical display is to be used for reflection (*shared reflection space,* see Fig. 5, b). Thereby, we seek to preserve the benefits of both types of surfaces, but concentrate manipulations on a horizontal surface that is equally accessible to all participants. Because the vertical display cannot be blocked, it improves the visibility of artifacts. However, this decision either requires a transfer of artifacts from the *action space* to the *reflection space* or a virtual workspace across these displays. Because we want to minimize the effort of transferring artifacts, we decided for the latter by implementing the possibility of providing different "views" onto a virtual workspace that spans across the displays. Thereby, the table only displays a magnified region (*detail view*) of the whole workspace, which is shown on the vertical display (context view, see Fig. 5, center). Consequently, the same digital representation of a note is available on both displays. The workspace can be navigated via panning gestures on the table. A *focus box* on the vertical display visualizes the view that is currently displayed on the table (see Fig. 5, b). The coupled vertical display can also be used for dynamic views on selected artifacts during phases of discussion (see Fig. 5, right).

Since we seek to preserve individual work with physical artifacts (T2), we decided to employ digital pen & paper for supporting individual ideation and reflection activities. Therefore, the table offers individual workspaces on its non-interactive rim (*personal spaces,* see Fig. 5, c). By providing small paper notes and multiple digital pens we can preserve the ability for individuals to create and reflect upon their contributions in a natural way. At the same time, we gain the ability to integrate further computational power for adding power to the interface. For additional functionalities (T4,T5), we later also added optional personalized interactive areas at the corners of the table (*transfer spaces,* see Fig. 5, d). These interactive zones can be accessed on demand by pressing buttons in each corner of the table. They provide the possibility for personalized interactions within the shared workspace.

Interaction Techniques

Based on our workspace design, we designed hybrid interaction techniques to support the basic workflow of affinity diagramming through *copying*, *clustering*, *piling*, and *collecting* (T1,T2,T3). Additional functionalities that augment physical practice were integrated with interaction techniques for *highlighting*, *focusing*, *searching*, and *image retrieval* (T4,T5).

Copying

Within the first phase of the technique, participants work quietly in their individual workspaces. However, when presenting their notes in the second phase, they need to transfer their contents into the shared workspace. Since our shared workspace is digital, a conversion between the physical and a digital representation is necessary. To simplify this transition physical notes can be copied to the shared workspace by placing them on the interactive table (see Fig. 2, center). A digital representation of the physical note appears within the virtual workspace (on both displays), while the physical copy is kept in the personal workspace. Users may manipulate their notes later on by writing or crossing out words on the physical note. These manipulations are synchronized with the digital copy. When placing a note onto the table that was already copied into the workspace, it is not duplicated but moved to this new location instead. Overall, this technique allows the sharing of artifacts with minimized transfer costs while still preserving the ability to reflect upon all individual contents in the personal workspace throughout the session. It also enables rapid switching between the personal and the shared workspace.

Clustering and Piling

During convergent activities, notes can be discussed and organized into meaningful arrangements. Once copied into the shared workspace, digital notes can be dragged, rotated and flicked by using typical multi-touch manipulations on the interactive table. It is also possible to change the color of notes or to delete notes. To facilitate the collaborative organization of notes into groups we included a simple clustering algorithm that automatically aligns and associates notes when released close to each other (see Fig. 6, a,b,c). Piles of notes can be created by releasing notes on top other notes. Clusters and piles can be moved by dragging them with multiple fingers (see Fig. 6, d,e,f). We designed these interaction techniques with the goal to imitate collaborative sorting actions at the whiteboard as closely as possible through multi-touch manipulations (T3). However, we traded some of the flexibility that is provided by paper artifacts against the possibilities introduced with digital representations. Yet, since all user action is focused on a horizontal surface, which is accessible to all participants, this might lead to more equal access and increased awareness of actions within the group.

Figure 6. Clustering: alignment, association and dragging.

Collecting

When collecting notes or clusters from arbitrary locations within the shared workspace, it is a tedious task to move them individually via touch and panning manipulations across longer distances in the virtual workspace. In physical practice, notes can be collected into mobile piles (see Fig. 1, c). We replicate this ability by providing multiple two-sided tangible objects called "collector tokens" (see Fig. 7). By placing the colored side of this token on a digital note, it becomes selected (see Fig. 7, a). By turning over the token and placing it on the table with the blank side, selected notes are moved to this new location (see Fig. 7, b). This technique allows converting physical movement into virtual movement by preserving some of the original physical characteristics (T3).

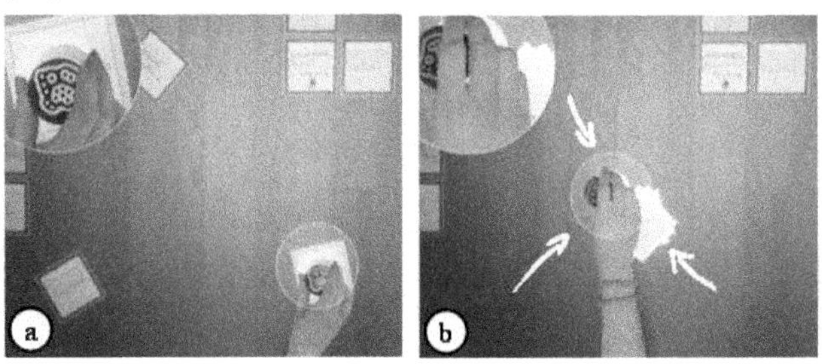

Figure 7. Collecting: selecting (a) and piling (b).

Highlighting

During discussion, deictic references on notes are often used as a form of communication and for coordination in the group (see Fig. 1, d,e). We augment these interactions by providing additional functionality. When touching digital notes, they are highlighted around their border with a glowing effect. Each highlight fades out after five seconds. This fading is also visible on the context display and thus can be used for deictic gestures across displays. When clustering notes, the fading glow implicitly communicates a history of actions that may help participants to remember the current focus of discussion if they got lost in the process. Therefore, this interaction technique focuses on promoting the chance for individual reflection and on fostering group awareness (T4,T5).

Focusing

Similarly, a physical "focus token" can be used to focus on a specific region within the virtual workspace during discussion (see Fig. 5, right). By placing this token onto the table, a region within the virtual workspace is selected for a detailed view on the vertical display. By turning the token (see Fig. 8, a), the users can increase or decrease the zoom-factor of the magnified view on the vertical display. By lifting the token from the table, the original view is restored. This interaction technique aims at improving group awareness and coordination. Because all other artifacts are temporarily hidden when using the token (except the immediate surroundings on the table), this technique is a powerful tool that allows placing focus on selected artifacts in order to moderate discussion and reflection (T5). It also minimizes physical movements and mutual blocking. However, particular dominant members of the group may also use this tool for gatekeeping.

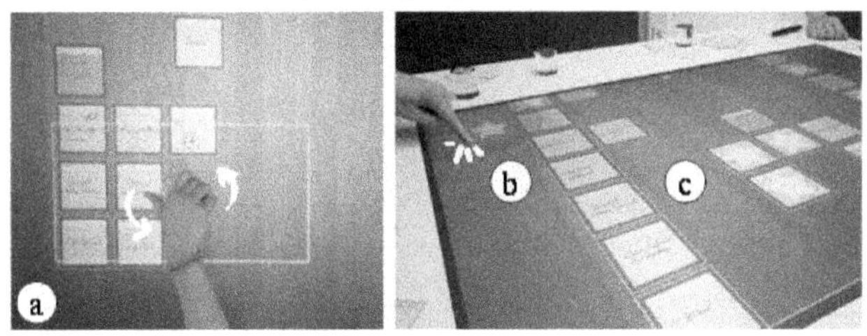

Figure 8. Focusing (a) and searching (b,c).

Searching

We integrated a lightweight search function based on the author of a note that is identified through digital pen IDs. By tapping personal symbols that are available in the *transfer spaces* at the corners of the table (see Fig. 8, b), the notes created by the corresponding user are marked with that symbol (see Fig. 8, c). This allows participants to look up the responsible author of a particular issue or idea during discussion. It also allows analyzing participants contributions to certain clusters and thus may provide information about consensus in the group (T5). This search function may introduce positive effects by reducing free riding, but may also have negative effects by increasing evaluation apprehension [22]. However, since notes are anonymous throughout the session and identity is only revealed on demand, this technique may stimulate individual contributions without putting too much pressure on participants.

Image Retrieval

When presenting ideas and issues it can be helpful to add additional information to make a clear point. Therefore, we added image retrieval functionality based on the content of notes. When placing notes into the *transfer spaces* at the corners of the table, five images that are related to the words on the note are retrieved from the web and displayed around the physical note (see Fig. 9). Users may then drag digital images along with a copy of the physical note into the shared workspace (see Fig. 9, a,b). Images in the workspace can be clustered along with digital notes. Hence, they can also be used to visually point out important clusters by adding representative images. This technique may have a positive influence on fixation effects because the selection of images can be used to further open up divergent activities (T5). Instead of using images from the web, this technique may also be used to augment notes with other data from custom design knowledge repositories.

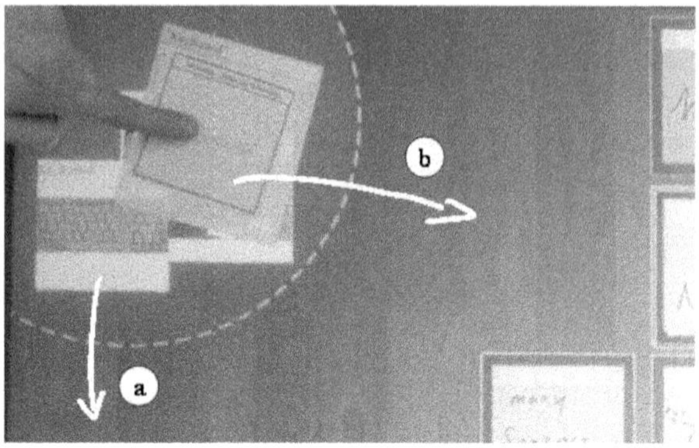

Figure 9. Adding images (a) along with notes (b).

Implementation

Our tool runs on a custom-built interactive table that measures 128cm x 157cm x 105cm. The non-interactive rim (20cm) was designed by considering guidelines for supporting leaning, personal workspaces and for avoiding involuntary interaction. The graphics are rear-projected with a WUXGA projector (1900px x 1200px). Multi-touch and object recognition is provided with IR illumination and three tiled XGA cameras (1024px x 768px). The vertical display measures 76cm x 162cm and features 4K resolution (4096px x 2160px). The software runs on two networked workstations with MS Windows 7. The interface is implemented using the ZOIL framework that integrates WPF multi-touch controls with distributed user interface synchronization and zooming functionality [12]. The size of the virtual workspace displayed on the vertical display can be adapted and therefore offers space for a very large number of artifacts. However, when increasing the space for artifacts, their representations on the vertical display become smaller and the effort for navigation on the table increases. We use ReacTIVision[1] for marker tracking and Squidy [16] for finger tracking. Data from Anoto's ADP-301 digital pens is received via Bluetooth by using the Anoto streaming API[2]. Text recognition is implemented using MS Windows 7 SDK. We use the Yahoo image search service for retrieving digital pictures from the web. All interface components are stored in a database system, thus allowing distributed access for later reuse of session results or for continuing sessions. Consequently, we also designed a client application that can be used on workstations. It allows for exploring created diagrams in a zoomable user interface and also enables data export.

[1] http://reactivision.sourceforge.net/

[2] http://www.anoto.com

USER STUDY

We conducted a preliminary user study with four groups of students (3-4 participants each, N=13) to investigate whether our tradeoff decisions were successfully implemented and how they might affect the workflow of the original technique. The goal of this study was not to measure the usability or efficiency of the interface itself. Rather we aimed to investigate general applicability and whether our tool successfully supports embodied practice (see Research Question). We invited the same students that took part in our initial study. Therefore, each participant already had experience in applying the affinity diagramming technique. All participants were graduate students in the area of interaction design. The average age was 25.8 years, ranging from 23 to 32. All had previous experiences using multi-touch devices. Participants were introduced to the functionality by one researcher who demonstrated the interaction techniques. Then they were given a design problem to solve collaboratively. Each session lasted about one hour. We observed the behavior of participants with two researchers and two video cameras. Moreover, participants filled out questionnaires before and after the sessions in order to assess their general perception of the tool design. Finally, a semi-structured interview was conducted in which participants were asked about their experiences with specific interaction techniques.

One of the key decisions we made was to preserve the physical workspace setting and thus provide a horizontal (table) as well as a vertical (wall display) surface (T1) as well as keeping the division into shared and personal spaces to allow for individual ideation and reflection (T2). However, to add power, we alternated the functionalities of these work surfaces in order to *ease the transfer* between them and to allow for a *smoother iteration between action and reflection.* Results of our questionnaires show that participants highly appreciated the table for collaborative manipulations, while stating that the vertical display supports reflection on the process. This included to identify isolate notes or to evaluate the structure of the diagrams like the size of clusters and the hierarchy of notes. Thereby, participants did not encounter any complications with the hybrid representation (physical/digital) of the same notes during the session. In contrast, participants discovered great potential in the reuse of the physical artifacts after the ideation phase. For example, some kept browsing through their physical notes long after they had been digitalized in order to get inspiration for further ideas. Likewise, we observed that one group used multiple physical notes in order to move digital representations into clusters (see Fig. 10, left). Considering the personal workspaces, we found that participants efficiently used the rim of the table to create and sort their notes into sequences or piles. Nevertheless, we think the experience could be improved by providing a slightly larger rim for supporting more refined spatial arrangements. Participants also did not encounter any difficulties in transferring physical notes onto the table. This interaction was mostly performed smoothly, even for pre-sorted collections of notes. *Overall, we could not identify any violations of the original workflow or*

Figure 10. User Study: hybrid use of artifacts (left), simultaneous interaction (center), resulting diagram (right)

embodied practice with T1 and T2. Conversely, we could preserve important characteristics of the physical workspace whilst also enabling additional functionalities.

Our goal with T3 was to *support the handling of digital artifacts* within convergent activities. During our study, participants encountered no difficulties with clustering and piling digital artifacts on the table. The style of our multi-touch interaction techniques seems to be a close enough fit to participant's experiences with interacting with physical artifacts. Although it was possible for all group members to work on the table concurrently, we observed that simultaneous interactions were mostly negotiated in the group before they were executed, similar to the behavior we observed in real practice. This may be due to the fact that interactions of multiple users may still interfere with each other, e.g. when one participant tries to move the current view on the table and other users seek to work on clustering notes (see Fig. 10, center). Participants generally appreciated the automatic alignment and association of notes into clusters. However, due to inaccurate finger tracking, very quickly dragging clusters over a long distance on the table sometimes led to the interaction being interrupted. With regard to the collector token, we found that participants only rarely made use of it. They rather seemed to be quite emerged in the activity of interacting with the notes through multi-touch. This was further strengthened by the fact that the tokens were not essential for completing the session as the number of artifacts remained rather small. Therefore, a future study should investigate the usefulness of these physical tools in more detail. Nevertheless, we conclude that in our preliminary study, *the implementation of T3 did successfully support the original workflow of the design technique*.

We aimed to augment collaborative actions by *improving equal access and visibility of artifacts* with T4. In the beginning of the sessions, all participants focused primarily on the table because we constrained interaction onto this work surface. None of the participants stated that this had negative effects on their individual contributions to the process. Towards the end of the sessions, reflection became more important and participants more often worked with the context view. This tendency was further strengthened by the fact that none of the four diagrams fitted onto the table view and thus the context display was indispensible in order to gain a comprehensive overview over the diagram. Hence, it becomes even more important when dealing with a larger number of artifacts, a larger virtual workspace and more complex diagrams during more extensive design sessions. Participants did not express the need for the ability to manipulate contents directly on the vertical display. As a result, the vertical display did not get blocked in any of the sessions, thereby offering continuous visibility of artifacts to all participants. Hence, our study showed that *T4 successfully constrained the space for interaction while improving the visibility of artifacts*. However, a more detailed study may focus on measuring the potential benefits of T4 for accessibility and group awareness.

Our goal with T5 was to *augment reflection activities for improving coordination and group awareness*. Therefore, we implemented a focus token and the ability to search for notes based on the author. We also included the capability to retrieve images based on the content of notes. In our study, the focus token was primarily used for detailed explorations of notes that included a sketch or for focusing on images. We argue that due to the exceptionally high resolution of the vertical display that makes text readable from a larger distance and the ability to remotely highlight notes by touch, it was not required for notes that contain text only. The search function was hardly used during the sessions, but at the end of sessions. This might be due to the fact that it is hidden in the transfer spaces and is only available on demand. When we asked participants, some stated that it is most useful at the end of sessions or when reusing the diagram at later times because it might help to remember the process. This confirms our design decision to provide on demand access only in order to prevent negative effects on the workflow. The picture retrieval functionality was very well perceived among participants. We found that rather than searching for further inspiration, participants primarily tried to find pictures that helped to clarify the content of their notes. All pictures were eventually added to clusters (see Fig. 10, right). One participant stated that including pictures might help to quickly communicate the basic content of the clusters. Overall, the functionality clearly triggered lively discussions among participants. However, we found that it might slightly change the workflow of the affinity diagramming session when used by untrained people. In one group, it led to an early transfer of physical notes into the shared workspace as participants were curious to work with the pictures and thus placed their notes onto the table right after writing on them instead of waiting until their turn for presentation. In this case, the pictures also encouraged participants to transfer each note individually instead of digitalizing them in pre-sorted clusters. Yet, this is likelier to occur with inexperienced first-time users that are curious about the interface itself. Consequently, a future study should measure the effects on the workflow with a longitudinal approach. Overall, we can summarize that *interaction techniques within T5 generally did not conflict with the workflow of affinity diagramming* whilst providing additional functionality at the same time.

CONCLUSION

In this paper we presented our approach for designing reality-based interfaces for creative group work. Based on an observational study of the design technique affinity diagramming, we decided on specific tradeoffs to preserve embodied practice and for adding computational power. On the basis of these tradeoffs, we designed a workspace that integrates an interactive table and tangible tools with a vertical display. A preliminary user study showed that by combining this workspace with digital pen & paper and multi-touch interaction, we can still preserve the basic workflow of the design technique. The study also indicates that an additional vertical display may be used for supporting reflection-in-action and for enhancing the visibility of artifacts. Regarding our research question, we may conclude that we were able to preserve the general workflow by still adding some power with a digital tool. However, a more focused longitudinal user study with creative professionals and more extensive design sessions should be applied to measure the potential benefits that are introduced with the tradeoffs. Nevertheless, we argue that our approach represents a unique example for supporting important aspects of collaborative creativity with reality-based interfaces. At the moment, our system is limited to a maximum of five users due to the size of the table and available rim space. We are currently improving it by adding more power to our clustering functionalities and by providing a larger rim space. The general workspace design and some of the described interaction techniques can be adapted to other design techniques that share the phases of ideation, presentation and discussion. Therefore, in future work, we will also focus on extending the basic interaction model with other paper-based artifacts for supporting sketching techniques or creativity workshops.

ACKNOWLEDGEMENTS

This research is funded by the German Research Foundation DFG (Deutsche Forschungsgemeinschaft) under grant number RE 1843/3-1.

REFERENCES

1. Beyer, H. & Holtzblatt, K.: Contextual design: defining customer-centered systems. Morgan Kaufmann. San Francisco. (1998)
2. Cook, D. J. & Bailey, B. P.: Designers' use of paper and the implications for informal tools. In Proceedings of OZCHI'05. ACM Press. (2005)
3. Dourish, P. and Bellotti, V.: Awareness and coordination in shared workspaces. In Proceedings of CSCW '92, ACM Press, 107-114. (1992)
4. Hailpern, J., Hinterbichler, E., Leppert, C., Cook, D. & Bailey, B. P.: TEAM STORM: demonstrating an interaction model for working with multiple ideas during creative group work. In Proceedings of C&C'07. ACM Press. 193-202. (2007)
5. Tse, E., Greenberg, S., Shen, C., Forlines, C. & Kodama, R.: Exploring true multi-user multimodal interaction over a digital table. In Proceedings of DIS'08. ACM Press. 109-118. (2008)
6. Hartmann, B., Morris M.R., Benko H. & Wilson, A.D.: Pictionaire: supporting collaborative design work by integrating physical and digital artifacts. In Proceedings of CSCW'10. ACM Press. 421–424. (2010)
7. Herring, S. R., Jones, B. R. & Bailey, B. P.: Idea generation techniques among creative professionals. In Proceedings of HICSS'09. IEEE. 1-10. (2009)
8. Hilliges, O., Terrenghi, L., Boring, S., Kim, D., Ritcher, H. & Butz, A.: Designing for collaborative creative problem solving. In Proceedings of C&C'07. ACM Press. 137-146. (2007)
9. Hornecker, E.: Understanding the benefits of graspable interfaces for cooperative use. Cooperative Systems Design: A Challenge of the Mobility Age. IOS Press. 71 -87. (2002)
10. Jacob, R. J.K., Girouard, A., Hirshfield, L. M., Horn, M. S., Shaer, O., Solovey, E. T. & Zigelbaum, J.: Reality-based interaction: unifying the new generation of interaction styles. In CHI'07 EA. ACM Press. 2465-2470. (2007)
11. Jacob, R. J.K., Girouard, A., Hirshfield, L. M., Horn, M. S., Shaer, O., Solovey, E. T. & Zigelbaum, J.: Reality-based interaction: a framework for post-WIMP interfaces. In Proceedings of CHI '08. ACM Press. 201-210. (2008)
12. Jetter, H.-C., Gerken, J., Zöllner, M. & Reiterer, H.: Model-based design and prototyping of interactive spaces for information interaction. Proceedings of HCSE'10. Springer. 22-37. (2010)
13. Jordan, B. & Henderson, A.: Interaction analysis: foundations and practice. The Journal of the Learning Sciences. Vol. 4(1). 39-103. (1995)
14. Kirk, D., Sellen, A., Taylor, S., Villar, N. & Izadi, S.: Putting the physical into the digital: issues in designing hybrid inter-active surfaces. In Proceedings of BCS HCI'09. 35-44. (2009)
15. Klemmer, S.R., Newman, M.W., Farrell, R., Bilezikjian, M. & Landay, J.A.: The Designers' Outpost: A tangible interface for collaborative web site design. In Proceedings of UIST'01. ACM Press. 1-10. (2001)
16. König, W. A., Rädle R. & Reiterer, H.: Interactive design of multimodal user interfaces - reducing technical and visual complexity. Journal on Multimodal User Interfaces. Vol. 3(3). Springer. 197-213. (2010)
17. Schön, D. A.: The reflective practitioner: How professionals think in action. Basic Books. (1983)
18. Streitz, N. A., Geißler, J., Holmer, T., Konomi, S., Müller-Tomfelde, C., Reischl, W., Rexroth, P., Seitz, P. & Steinmetz, R.: i-LAND: An interactive landscape for creativity and inno-vation. In Proceedings of CHI'99, ACM Press, 120-127.(1999)
19. Terry, M. & Mynatt, E. D.: Recognizing creative needs in user interface design. In Proceedings of C&C'02. ACM Press. 38-44. (2002)
20. Vyas, D., Van Der Veer, G., Heylen, D. & Nijholt, A.: Space as a resource in creative design practices. In Proceedings of INTERACT'09. Springer. 169–172. (2009)
21. Vyas, D., Heylen, D., Nijholt, A. & Van Der Veer, G.: Collaborative practices that support creativity in design. In Proceedings of ECSCW'09. Springer. 151-170. (2009)
22. Warr, A. & O'Neill, E.: Understanding design as a social creative process. In Proceedings of C&C'05. ACM Press. 118-127. (2005)

Creative Personal Projects of the Elderly as Active Engagements with Interactive Media Technology

Anu Kankainen, Vilma Lehtinen
Helsinki Institute for Information Technology HIIT / Aalto University
P.O. Box 19215, 00076 Aalto, Finland
firstname.lastname@hiit.fi

ABSTRACT
Interactive media technologies are increasingly designed to support an active life among senior citizens and not solely to diminish the effects of physical and cognitive decline. One aspect of active life in one's old age is engagement in creative "personal projects," such as new hobbies and reflection on past events. To our knowledge, research has not yet explicitly focused on the role of creative personal projects in senior citizens' media use. In our analysis of media diaries and contextual interviews with seven seniors, we focus on how interactive media technologies are involved in these projects. Proceeding from our findings, we provide suggestions on how to enhance creative personal projects with interactive media technology design.

Author Keywords
Seniors, media use, personal projects, user experience, interactive media technology design, everyday creativity.

ACM Classification Keywords
H.5.m. Information interfaces and presentation (e.g., HCI): Miscellaneous.

General Terms
Human Factors

INTRODUCTION
The image of older people as computer-illiterate, and solely a target of health-related technologies such as monitoring devices, is rapidly changing. The elderly are seen as avid users of media technologies, and technologies are designed to support an active life [17]. As well as contributing to general well-being, the design efforts targeting the aging baby-boomer generations in industrialized nations are contributing to a rapidly growing market. The elderly are an established target group for interactive media design. Its role in their lives has been studied quite comprehensively in both quantitative and qualitative studies, such as Hernandez-Encuentra et al. [6], Jones & Fox [9], Lindley et al. [17] and Salovaara et al. [27].

C&C'11, November 3–6, 2011, Atlanta, Georgia, USA.

With this study we point to an aspect of later life that has not, to our knowledge, been examined explicitly by those aiming to design media technology for the elderly: personal projects in which the elderly engage. Luborsky, in his studies of retirement [20, 21], approaches engagement in personal projects such as new hobbies and interests as a way of coping with the changes retirement involves. Through these projects, elderly people reflect on their past life and renegotiate their social positions. Since these projects can be regarded as creative by default, we consider this concept to have great potential to inform design efforts for supporting creativity in one's later years.

In this paper, we identify aspects of creative personal projects that people pursue in later life. We look at these in relation to media usage, in order to support designers addressing this stage in life. Also, for anyone interested in aspects of media use by the elderly, this paper provides an analysis of the topic from a fresh viewpoint. In our analysis of media diaries and contextual interviews with seven senior citizens concerning the role of media technologies in their daily activities, we identified a number of creative personal projects in seniors' day-to-day life: documenting and reflecting on one's life and that of one's family; collecting media content; choosing, recommending, and sharing media content; organizing social events; creating small presents to others; following special topics via multiple channels; and playing games.

We suggest design directions, based on our findings, for interactive media technologies that enhance day-to-day creativity among the elderly. Our study indicates that creative personal projects have a significant role in older people's everyday life. Elderly people invest time and money in these projects, and the projects enhance social activities that they value highly. Therefore, we think that addressing creative personal projects in interactive media design not only provides new design opportunities but might also have great impact on life in one's old age.

BACKGROUND
We position our study in the discussions on how to support the positive developments that can take place also in later life, including creative activities. First, we back up our viewpoint with Laslett's [13, 14, 15] views of retirement as a "third age." To these we connect Luborsky's [20, 21] ideas of personal projects. After this, we go through studies

in human–computer interaction (HCI) that address designs that can be seen as supporting creative personal projects in the third age. By doing this, we aim to grasp a picture of what might be missing from the existing understanding of the role of interactive media technology in creative personal projects in later life.

The Third Age and Creative Personal Projects

According to Laslett's [13, 14, 15] ideas of retirement as a third age, aging should not be seen as inevitable physical and cognitive decline and isolation from social life. Instead, it should be regarded as another phase of life, one characterized by development, activity, and growth as much as earlier stages in life are. These positive developments are not absent from the life of people experiencing physical, cognitive, or economic deficiencies either. However, Gilleard and Higgs [5] remind us that active later life depends on socio-economic factors, which are bound to societal and cultural changes. These include, according to Gilleard and Higgs [ibid.], increased material wealth and personal freedom, changing patterns of work, and widened consumption opportunities accompanied with a sense of increased personal insecurity.

In accordance with Gilleard and Higgs, we consider that, in any case, Laslett identified a cultural phenomenon increasingly taking over in industrialized countries. Life after retirement is seen as an opportunity for individual growth and expression of personal lifestyles. We believe that senior citizens' media use enacts the qualities of the third age as a cultural and societal phenomenon. In our discussion below, we do not limit the definition of the third age by a certain year in life but define it through certain characteristics. It is associated with changes in social roles because of retirement and children, if any, having moved away.

Some other characteristics people of this age may share include using the increased amount of free time available for getting involved with new interests and hobbies, interacting with grandchildren and/or old friends, and reflecting on one's life [1, 13, 14, 15]. Luborsky [20, 21] claims that these kinds of personal projects people pursue are ways to cope with the losses inherent in later life. He approaches these not as pathological efforts of older people to make themselves useful but, instead, as creative acts. Personal projects are meaningful for seniors in their negotiation of changed relationships to themselves as well as surrounding society.

As Luborsky [20, 21] states, these projects may involve reflections on one's past life as a way to orient oneself in relation to it, and organizing it for retirement. Luborsky [20] himself refers to this with the concept of life review, comparable to the "active remembering" discussed by Myerhoff [22, 23]. Price [25] studied women pursuing personal projects in their third age and found that taking advantage of one's professional skills and acquiring new ones, and meeting people aligned around one's personal interests, are functional means of adjusting to the transitions retirement involves. These studies provide us with a view of elderly life as active engagement in personal projects that support old persons' new relationship to self and others. In our study, we aim to map the role of interactive media technologies in these efforts.

Interactive Media Technology for Creative Personal Projects

Reviewing studies of elderly people's use of communication technologies, Lindley et al. [17] noted that design work within the field of HCI has increasingly been directed to supporting the positive developments in later life. These include interaction with grandchildren, time with old friends, new interests and hobbies, and the wisdom derived from experiences in life, as well as the recognition of losses. To our knowledge, design work has not directly addressed the details of interactive media technologies' use in creative personal projects in the third age. We consider this approach to be needed, since identifying and acknowledging the meaning of interactive media technology for the projects aids in the design of technologies taking into account the demands that engagement in the projects poses.

The concept of interactivity is central in our approach. Without interactivity, the projects could be neither creative nor personal or social. However, "interactivity" is still a buzzword used to describe all kinds of digital media products and services and requires elaboration. Our attempt here is not to define interactivity but to point out some key aspects of it that are relevant for our study. Quiring [26] provides a good overview of academic discussion of the concept of interactivity. He identifies three viewpoints: interactivity as an attribute of technological systems, of communication process, and of user perceptions.

From the technological standpoint, interactivity is related, to, for example, responsiveness, real-time nature, options for selection and modification of content, temporal independence, and sensory complexity. As a communication process, interactivity may mean, for example, exchange, dialogue, control, and two-way communication. In turn, from the user perception angle, interactivity is related to perceived responsiveness; perceived navigation; perceived speed; sensory activation; and sensations of playfulness, connectedness, proximity, and presence.

Quiring [ibid.] conducted his own study of interactivity by letting German users state what they associate with the term "interactivity." His results indicate that users associate the term most with issues of the social and individual, such as what they could accomplish by using media, in terms of self-development, social influence, and social relationships. In our study as well, self-development and social relationships were key motivations for the personal creative projects that seniors work on. However, we also see that, for example, options for selection and modification of content, which Quiring [ibid.] considers to be technological aspects of interactivity, are important in the personal and creative projects enhanced by interactive media.

Interactive media technology has, by definition, great potential to support reflection on one's past life, orientation to a new social position, and concentration on topics for which it was hard to find time earlier. Previous research in the field of HCI points toward a variety of interactive media technology devices and applications that could be taken advantage of in the creative personal projects of the elderly. The designs are not necessarily targeted solely at the elderly, but they are inspirational to look at, as people engage in creative personal projects earlier in life too.

Examples of interactive media technology developed particularly for seniors for memory organization and storytelling include tabletop photo sharing, as in the work of Apted et al. [2] and Donaldson et al. [4]. Intergenerational sharing of stories and organizing has been studied and supported by a tabletop interface developed by Kirk et al. [11]. Another example is the MagicBox, a tangible device for interaction with grandchildren through play [32]. Storytelling has also been extended to relate life histories to historical events, as shown by Schutt [28]. All these media support engaging in creative personal projects. With this study, we aim at further supporting the efforts of designing interactive media technology for engaging in these projects.

Our approach is aligned with those HCI studies that reflect on "thirdageism," looking at the possibility of technology supporting the positive developments and growth that characterize the third age, such as creative projects, rather than focusing on minimizing the effects of physical and cognitive decline on technology usage. We consider the viewpoint that life after retirement is a third age, and that personal projects as an aspect thereof provide a good framework for looking at interactive media use in this phase of life. With our study, we aim to add to these discussions an analysis of how interactive media technology is engaged in the creative personal projects.

METHODS

In this section, we describe our motivation and the accordant methods we used to conduct our study, which we believe offers a fresh viewpoint on interactive media design for the creative personal projects of the elderly. First, the participants in the study are introduced, then the data collection methods are described. Finally, we explain our data analysis approach.

Participants

In total, seven senior citizens participated in our study, in the capital area of Helsinki, Finland, in spring 2010. They were 68–82-year-old retired persons who lived alone or with their spouses. Two of them were men, and five were women. They all had used computers and the Internet at least occasionally at home or in a community center for seniors. All of them had cellular phones. They did not have severe physical illnesses, and they were active socially.

Our sample is suitable for in-depth qualitative research. We admit that it and, hence, our findings are bounded by a socio-economic background in a middle-class neighborhood. However, we consider there to be certain benefits in limiting the participants to a certain locality and to people who know each other. This allows us to understand in more depth the meaning of place and social circles for the use of interactive media technology in personal projects. We do not aim at statistical generalizations; instead, we wanted to gain an in-depth understanding of seniors' media practices and fully comprehend the nature of personal projects and motivations for them. As selection criteria for our participants we used the following: 1) They lived in the same part of town in Helsinki. Locality is an important success factor where media are concerned, and we wanted to explore how that manifests itself in the participants' media practices. 2) Most of the participants knew each other. They had a long history together, starting in high school. We wanted to explore how this social interaction was present in their media practices.

Diaries and Contextual Interviews

Both one-week diaries and contextual interviews were used as qualitative user research methods. All participants were first met face to face for explanation of the background of our study, agreement on the schedule, and instruction in filling in the diaries. After that, they completed the diary for one week, and at the end of the week, the researchers visited them at home for contextual interviews.

For the diary, the participants were asked to mark, for every morning, afternoon, and evening, at least one media moment they'd had either in the course of the day or, preferably, in that part of the day. We let them define "media" themselves. We instructed them to think about media in broad terms, ranging from mobile and e-mail communication to newspapers and movies. Moreover, they were asked to describe the media moment itself, what they did before and after it, whether they shared or wanted to share that moment with somebody, and how that moment could be even better. After one week of using the diaries, the participants were interviewed about the diary content in conjunction with contextual interviews.

During the contextual interviews, the participants were asked to show the researchers media equipment and media items they used at home. When regarding each item, they were asked also to show how they interact with it and what kinds of services or content they used with it. During this showing and telling, the researchers asked motivation-related questions and also sought ideas for future services. Besides conducting the interviews, the researchers observed what the participants did during that half-day visit in general.

Data-driven Approach

We conducted our analysis with a data-driven approach inspired by grounded theory [29]. When going through the qualitative data for the first time, we discovered that the participants often mentioned "personal projects" in the diaries and interviews. We found that interesting and began seeking literature that would support this finding. We were encouraged by the supporting literature and started to analyze the data systematically in order to find more information about these projects. From the data we sought indications of media practices that had some kind of continuum in the participants' everyday life – the projects that they worked on whenever they had time to do so. After all the creative personal projects had been identified from the data, we started to classify them into certain thematic groups. Through this, we discovered the project themes described in the following sections. The themes are presented in the order in which the researchers considered them to be meaningful for the people participating in the study. Meaningfulness refers to the extent to which the projects were part of daily activities, how much the elderly themselves brought them up in the interviews, and how we interpreted the projects as supporting their active social life.

GENERAL OBSERVATIONS ON MEDIA PRACTICES AMONG THE ELDERLY

In general, the seniors had time to concentrate on their media moments. These moments were relatively long and interruptions-free, unlike those of working people. Therefore, exploring and creating media content that takes time was suitable for them. The participants seemed interested in digital services but faced usability challenges even with their cell phones, and, therefore, most of them were not among the first to adopt new services. However, technical skills did vary among the participants in our study. Even though many of them were socially very active, they considered social media not to be for them. They still preferred face-to-face meetings, postcards, letters, phone calls, and (for some) e-mail for keeping in touch with friends and relatives. One could say that their media practices represent the traditional way of consuming media. Their daily rhythm is determined somewhat by broadcast times and not vice versa. However, digiboxes have made it possible to consume TV content whenever suitable for them.

If usability problems could be solved with interactive media technologies, interactive media could have a remarkable role in enhancing seniors' creativity through the special projects. We saw some indications of what easy-to-use technology can be at its best, as part of special projects: a lady who had no particular technical background was working on printed photo collages that she gave as gifts to her friends once in a while. At home, she had a PC laptop with wireless Internet connection. When she was showing us how she copied and shared digital images with it, she constantly repeated that she is very frustrated with the laptop and with establishing the Internet connection. After that, we went to a physical photo shop, where she wanted to print out her latest digital images with a machine with a touchscreen. She edited the pictures with the machine before printing and was smiling the whole time while doing so. She was very happy with this process, unlike with her laptop at home.

THE PERSONAL PROJECTS DISCOVERED

This section describes in more detail the personal and creative projects the elderly people were working on during our study.

Documenting and Reflecting on Personal and Family Life

Our findings are in line with those of Karahasanovic et al. [9] indicating that, particularly for elderly people, collective memory seems to be among the motivations for working on one's own content. In our study, those senior citizens who had children wanted to leave behind some memories from their lives for coming generations. Combining their own media content and storytelling in digital form inspired them to engage in their special projects. A senior lady had received printed pictures from her childhood from relatives. She had started to scan them in to digital format and was planning to make a book with text and pictures for her daughter. The picture in Figure 1 shows this lady staying with her siblings and mother somewhere out of town during the war in order to be safe from bombings.

Most of the participants had taken pictures, and some of them video material, showing meaningful happenings throughout their family life. They also had pictures from their childhood. Moreover, they had experienced the transition from physical pictures to digital pictures, and some of them were occupied by projects involving scanning their printed pictures and saving them in digital form.

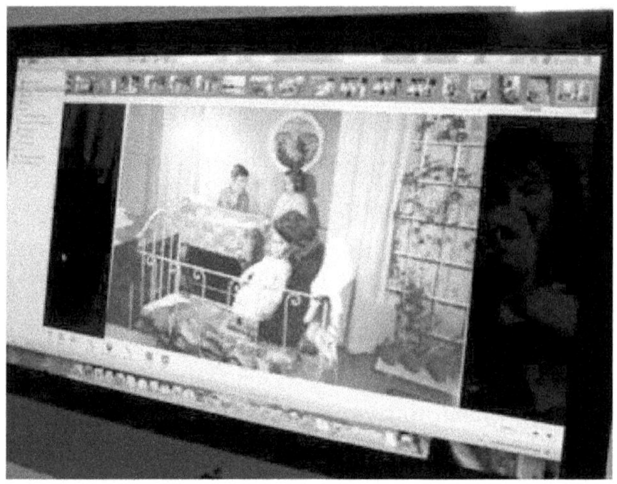

Figure 1: Organizing personal memories for future generations

Since the participants had so much material, they were concerned about how they could select the items that are most meaningful and perhaps even delete those that they figure their children and grandchildren would not appreciate. In general, they felt that there was too much material and it would need more sorting, deletion, and annotation than they had time for. The seniors were also concerned about where they could save all the material they had processed so that it really was saved and would be accessible for later generations many years from now. The solution they were using was to print out the material in book format.

Figure 2: Collecting media for moments with grandchildren

Collecting Media Content

The participants had stored professional media content for decades and were still sharing it with their relatives and family. Some of the stored content was related to meaningful moments with children and grandchildren. As seen in Figure 2, a senior lady had kept all of the Donald Duck magazines that her children were reading years ago. Now she is sorting them for grandchildren who visit her often.

Figure 3: Storing content for reflecting on earlier times in life

Some of the stored content was related to reflections on one's personal life. One senior lady had saved a magazine story clipping, as seen in Figure 3, already for 40 years. It is a poem of children who gather to decide what to do with the property of their deceased parents. It had had a great impact on this older lady. She still sometimes wanted to talk about it with her friends, and she also asked the researchers to read it aloud. At the time of the study, the material was in physical format only. Collecting professional media content became creative work with time, since the content was sought and selected for storage according to its relevance to personal experiences. In this way, it became a part of storytelling in face-to-face meetings.

Choosing, Recommending, and Sharing Media Content

Another type of special project that included social interaction was related to making choices on what media content to consume on the basis of one's own and one's social network's interests. This included recommendation and lending of professional media content to others. For example, a senior gentleman met with former classmates once a month in a certain cafe. In the meeting, they discussed interesting books, among other topics. They recommended books to each other, and sometimes someone brought an interesting book with him and lent it to a friend. Reading a book and sharing thoughts with others about the topics in the book fueled these people's creative thinking and social interactions. They considered making choices about what to read to be a creative and social process that was directed by their interests and those of friends and other reference groups. Another good example is a senior lady who was an active visitor to the library but also was reading books that her sister lent her. She selected the library books according to reviews in a local newspaper or recommendations by the librarian, who knew her interests very well. Making choices about what to read was, in itself, a creative personal project for her.

Figure 4: Mixing media content to create small presents

Creating Small Presents for Each Other

Many of the people who participated in our study were working on projects to create gifts for friends that incorporated media the givers had created themselves. In Figure 4, we see a scrapbook made for a friend by a senior lady. Printed digital pictures have been attached to an old advertising catalog. The participant took lots of pictures on social occasions and printed them in a photo booth for scrapbooks that she worked on in her garden in summertime or when watching TV. Moreover, the participants had received similar gifts from their relatives and friends, such as handmade paper calendars with family pictures and a photo album with pictures from times in a holiday home. These projects were highly creative, and it seemed that the process of making gifts was as important as actually giving the gift. Also the receivers took it well that the gifts looked rough and self-made. They appreciated the time invested in making the gifts, and the outcome was not that important.

Organizing Social Events

The seniors who participated in our study emphasized several times the importance of face-to-face interactions with family members and friends. They followed face-to-face events that matched their interests and got ideas for doing things together from media. For most of them, it was important to be creative in planning their weekly schedule. There were several diary entries describing how participants had heard on the radio, or read in a newspaper, about some exhibition or a certain place and thus become inspired to go there with friends. It seems that getting ideas from media to do things together was some kind of everyday special project for many of them. They also kept an eye on bulletin boards in meaningful places such as the senior center and registered for interesting events. Figure 5 shows a bulletin-board announcement at a senior center advertising a visit to a chocolate factory, with the opportunity to register. The bulletin board was full of such event announcements, and others could see who would take part in the event.

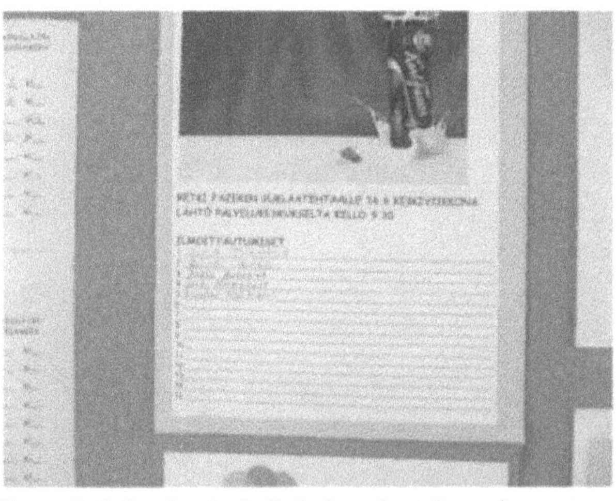

Figure 5: Following the bulletin boards at the senior center

Besides events organized by others, the participants were active in organizing social events themselves. Organizing social events was sometimes considered a special project. For example, a senior gentleman used several communication channels (but not social media) for contacting his former army friends in order to invite them to a party. He was coordinating this with a friend, and they had also planned the agenda for this festive event together. Another example worthy of mention involved an older lady who was actively inviting her friends to a play in which her daughter was acting (see Figure 6). She had printed out an advertisement of the theatre event from the Internet and distributed these printouts to her friends when meeting them face to face. She had also motivated her friends to attend by gathering groups that would go to see the play together on a certain date at a prearranged time.

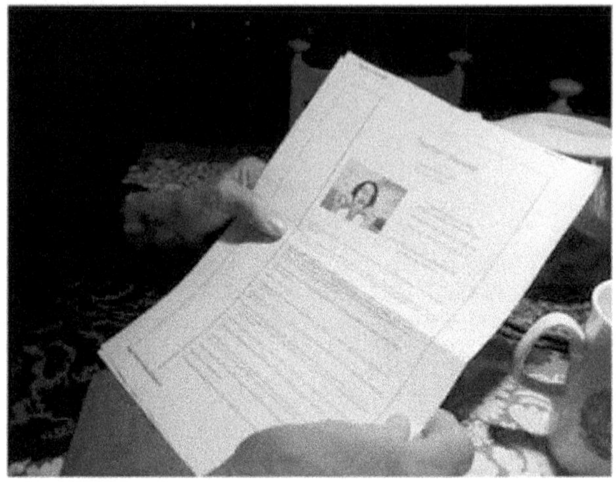

Figure 6: Inviting friends to events

Following Special Topics from Multiple Channels

Many of the people who participated in our study had one or two special topics that they had been interested in for several years already. Some of the topics were related to working life (such as engineering), a hobby (e.g., history, gardening, or cooking), or their childhood (such as news from one's childhood hometown). In particular, those topics that were related to a participant's hobbies were linked to some creative activities as well. The seniors followed those special topics by means of several media channels (TV, radio, magazines, newspapers, and/or books) and collected material concerning them as well. They were also interested in sharing their "expertise" in the subject with others, mainly when meeting face to face.

Playing Games

Not all but some of our participants reported in their diaries that they played non-digital games. Some of the playing could be considered a creative personal project, such as completing all crossword puzzles in weekly magazines or playing board and card games with friends regularly. Even though this finding is weak in our research material, we want to bring it up as a potential future area of application for interactive media technologies among the elderly.

DESIGN DRIVERS

In high-level concept design, it is useful to start by defining a design driver – a product or service idea. It is typically a brief description of new properties or novel applications of the product or service that the marketplace seems to be missing. Design drivers determine design opportunities and provide suggestions for solutions [12]. Studying the use of the product or service is often a starting point for creation of new concept ideas. To form the design drivers proposed here, we examine our findings on current practices of the elderly in light of previous research conducted in the social sciences. We identified aspects of creative personal projects of the elderly, and the role of interactive media in these. In our analysis, we brought up the view of later life as a third age, an active phase of life that entails processes of coming to terms with one's past life and adjusting to a new social role.

Our analysis added to previous research on third-age life by showing in detail how interactive media technologies are used in this reflection and adjustment. The concept of a creative personal project helped us to find aspects of interactive media use by the elderly that had not been addressed in earlier studies of the topic. Some of these aspects, such as the organization and sharing of media content, are already acknowledged in efforts to design for creativity in later life. In addition, however, we found elements that had not been pointed out explicitly, such as gift-giving and following of special topics of interest.

In the following discussion, we describe our conclusions concerning the aspects of the projects we identified, and we consider them from the standpoint of how interactive media technology design could enhance these creative personal projects. Also, we consider the current developments in interactive media design in order to explicate the potential of these developments in supporting the creative personal projects. The design drivers presented below are assumed to serve as "themes" for design of novel interactive media products and services for elderly people.

Organizing Media Content Proactively and Collaboratively

The seniors were highly motivated to work on projects to create comprehensive stories of their life for future generations. However, they faced time-consuming obstacles since their material needed so much preparatory work before the actual storytelling could commence. Apted et al. [2], Donaldson et al. [4], and Kirk et al. [11] are good examples of supporting the organization of personally made media. We suggest further that the design of future interactive media tools and services should make it possible to do some proactive work at the time when material is collected – e.g., tagging the captured media right away before saving for later projects. Earlier studies also acknowledge the importance of collaboration with family members and friends when one engages in creative special projects. Similarly, we suggest that collaboration could be a way of making life reflection projects more effortless.

Using Shared Access to Professional Media Content

When the participants spoke about their life to us, the researchers, they often also referred to something historical that had happened in their community, in Finland, or internationally in order to offer a larger framework for their stories. We saw that they often possessed physical, professional media content related to these events. Suggestions to support the mixing of physical and digital memories have been offered by, for example, West et al. [33] and Petrelli and Whittaker [24]. For the creative personal projects of the elderly, in addition to mixing of physical and digital, we call for support for the ability to take advantage of professional media content across a large span of time.

Schutt's [28] Small Histories is an illustrative example of how to combine online media content to create and share life stories. For supporting creative special projects in the third age, its idea of creating and sharing life histories with online content needs to be extended to non-digital media formats, and to content from media corporations. This requires support for organization of the material collected, as well as open digital online archives by the corporations owning the media content. Besides easing the project work, storytelling could become richer if seniors could combine their own content with media reserves owned by media corporations.

Collecting meaningful media content for later reflection and sharing raises at least two design drivers: enhancing the ability to 1) copy parts of magazines or books according to one's interests and 2) share them in face-to-face meetings with others. This could be possible with tablets, but it also requires a good place to store parts of media products or complete series of magazines, books, etc. The development of cloud services could provide support for safely storing and sharing material for creative special projects. Moreover, one could provide enhanced access to storage with different devices in different use contexts (such as a big screen at home or a center for the elderly, or a portable screen in a cafeteria).

Sharing Personal Media Preferences

For our participants, sharing recommendations on media content, such as books, was a way to fuel social interaction and focus on special topics of interest. Previous research on elderly people's use of interactive media technologies has addressed primarily the sharing of their homemade media content. We call for interactive media technologies that support recommending and possibly sharing commercial media content as well, especially physical media.

Online recommendation systems have gained great attention (see, e.g. Bernstein [3]), with the motivation often being to reduce the effort of finding interesting information, through the aid of one's online social network. From our study, we see that in the creative personal projects of the elderly, the media content recommended was not limited to online content but stretched across format boundaries and spanned media brands. Neither was it limited to the latest blog feeds; it covered a large time span for both literary classics and global news.

One clear design driver enhancing recommendations among friends and relatives regarding media content is to provide a possibility of keeping and annotating a personal history of reading / other kinds of consumption, including physical material. This should be complemented by the option of sharing the annotated history with others digitally or in face-to-face meetings. In addition, the history could suggest what to recommend to a certain friend according to his or her preferences. This kind of recommending could also lead to lending one's content to others.

Making Digital Gifts Meaningful

Personally made media content appeared important for our participants, particularly when they were creating gifts for their friends and relatives. We interpret this to be due to the importance they placed on showing the dedication and effort in making the gift. There is a vast body of research on how interactive media content is appropriated in gift-giving, at least by younger generations (see, e.g., Håkansson [7] and Taylor [30]). These studies could be exploited in designing interactive media for creative personal projects of the elderly, since we can see that gift-giving can be interpreted as a creative personal project that supports social interaction as well.

In view of our findings, we want to highlight the importance of the creative process of making the gift. This process should be visible in the end result as well. The biggest design opportunities that we can identify include, first, making the process of creating media gifts enjoyable and rewarding for the maker and, second, enhancing gift-making in such a way that the results indicate how much effort and thinking the maker has put into it, for the gift to become valuable for the receiver – for example, to enhance making of such digital gifts as can become a visible part of the receiver's everyday activities, such as the calendars with family photos that our participants shared.

Organizing Social Events with Group-oriented Social Media

Face-to-face interaction with close social relations was a significant part of media technology's use for pursuing creative personal projects in the third age. Organizing social events required that the elderly be able to combine professional and their original media in a creative way, for marketing their own events and organizing them into groups that one belongs to. Afterward they often also shared memories of the events. Sharing information on interesting events is familiar from social network services. This could be an opportunity for older generations as well, but previous research has identified the absence of seniors from social media [9]. A study by Lehtinen et al. [16] has explained this with the negative image that, for example, social networking services have among seniors, as a medium of hectic self-promotion to an uncontrollable audience.

The opportunity to share media content could be taken advantage of with enhanced privacy and publicness management, which takes groupwise sharing as its primary principle. This could as well facilitate the organizing of social events with a defined set of people. As a special challenge for taking advantage of interactive media technologies in the creative projects of the elderly, we identify again the mixing of commercial and original media. The opportunity to mix these would support creating alluring invitations, and facilitating the organization and sharing of both digital and physical material from the events.

Following Topics of Interest across Media Brand Boundaries

In the pursuit of following special topics of interest as well, we identify the mixing of digital and physical media content, both professional and original. Previous research on seeking information online, such as that of Torrey et al. [31] on hobby crafting, provides valuable suggestions for designing information seeking technologies to support the creative personal projects of the elderly. Similarly to recommending and sharing media content, we found that, for our participants, engaging in following particular topics involves mixing of media context in relation to both its format and its producer. This is probably due to the large time span that the life experience of the elderly brings in. We see that, in addition to the borders between physical and digital content, traditional media brand limits should be crossed in order for digital media services to be developed that would help in following specific topics more easily. For following topics of interest, platforms for editing, storing, and sharing the content provided by different media companies would be needed to support these efforts.

Supporting Creativity with Playability

Designing interactive games that could enhance seniors' creativity in a project-oriented manner is something that is absent from the discussion of the elderly and games. As IJesselsteijn et al. [8] point out, one can cite at least four reasons elderly people might wish to play digital games in the future: relaxation and entertainment, socializing with others, sharpening one's mind, and engaging the whole body. We would like to add to that list the motivation to be creative in social contexts.

CONCLUSIONS

Usability of interactive media is a fundamental requirement for making creative personal projects enjoyable and is needed if the process is to be valued as much as its outcome is. Rather than usability, we wanted to pay attention to how interactive media are able to support the engagement in creative personal projects of the elderly. In summary, documenting and reflecting on one's life; collecting, choosing, recommending, and sharing media content; making gifts; organizing social events; and playing games are the aspects of creative personal projects in which we identified interactive media technology as playing a role.

Previous research on interactive media technologies in creative personal projects, of any generation, can be exploited to enhance the pursuit of these projects by the elderly. We have pinpointed some aspects of creative personal projects of the elderly that we see as still absent from interactive media technology design.

Table 1: Projects discovered, supporting research, and design drivers

Projects Discovered	Previous Supporting Research	Design Drivers
Documenting and reflecting on personal and family life	Studies on memory organization, storytelling, and intergenerational sharing: Apted et al. [2], Donaldson [4], Kirk [11], Petrelli and Whittaker [24], West et al. [33]	• Support co-creation • Simplify the organization of the material one has created • **Give shared access to professional media content** • Provide interfaces for mixing physical and digital content
Collecting media content	Life stories with online content: Schutt [28]	
Choosing, recommending, and sharing media content	Online recommendation systems: Bernstein [3]	• Develop annotated personal **media preferences** – especially for **physical content with a large time span**
Creating small presents to each other	Digital media as gift-giving: Taylor and Harper [28], Håkansson [7]	• Support the creative process of making the gift, and the visibility of the gift-making effort
Organizing social events	Seniors' use of social media: Lindley et al. [18], Lehtinen et al. [16]	• Enhance the **mix of professional and personally made media** to create alluring event invitations • Use group-oriented social media to support the organization of events
Following special topics via multiple channels	Information-seeking online: Torrey et al. [8]	• Make it easy to **aggregate content across brand boundaries**
Playing games	Digital games for the elderly: Ijstellstein [8]	• Support creativity and playability with creative games

These include the mixing of commercial content and media content created personally, the vast time span of the media content to be shared, sharing of commercial media content, creation of digital products in which the creative effort can be seen, and connection of playability to creative projects. To conclude, we present a table (Table 1) that illustrates the creative personal projects discovered, the previous research that we find supporting the design drivers, our design drivers, and (in bold) the design gaps identified. These gaps we encourage designers to work on, to support creative personal projects of the elderly with interactive media design.

ACKNOWLEDGMENTS
The study was conducted as part of the Next Media research program, funded by Tekes, Alma Media, Idean, Seed Digital Media, and Undo. We are grateful for our participants, without whom the study would not have been possible, and to project researchers Jaana Piirainen and Mikko Prami, who participated in gathering the research material. We also thank Antti Salovaara and the anonymous reviewers, for their valuable comments.

REFERENCES

1. Adams, R.G., Blieszner, R., de Vries, B. 2000. Definitions of friendship in the third age: Age, gender, and study location effects. *Journal of Aging Studies, 14,* 1, 117–133.
2. Apted, T., Kay, J., Quigley, A. 2006. Tabletop sharing of digital photographs for the elderly. *Proc. CHI'06.*
3. Bernstein, M., Marcus, A., Karger, D. & Miller, R. Enhancing directed content sharing on the web. *Proc. CHI'10.* 971–980.
4. Donaldson, J., Evnin, J., Saxena, S. 2005. ECHOES: encouraging companionship, home organization, and entertainment in seniors. *Proc. CHI'05.* 2084–2088.
5. Gilleard, C., Higgs, P. 2002. The third age: class, cohort or generation? *Ageing & Society, 22,* 369–382.
6. Hernandez-Encuentra, E., Pousada, M., Gomez-Zuniga, B. 2009. ICT and older people: beyond usability. *Educational Gerontology, 35,* 3, 226–45.
7. Håkansson, M., Rost, M., Holmquist, L. 2007. Gifts from friends and strangers: A study of mobile music sharing. *Proc. ECSCW'07.*
8. IJsselsteijn, W., Nap, H.H., de Kort, Y. 2007. Digital game design for elderly users. *Proc. FuturePlay'07*, 17–22.
9. Jones, S. & Fox, S. 2009. *Generations Online in 2009.* Pew Foundation, Washington, D.C.
10. Karahasanovic, A., Brandtzaeg, P.B., Heim, J., Luders, M., Lotte Vermeir, L., Pierson, J., Lievens, B., Vanattenhoven, J. & Jans, G. 2009. Co-creation and

user-generated content – elderly people's user requirements. *Computers in Human Behavior, 25*, 655–678.

11. Kirk, D., Izadi, S., Sellen, A., Taylor, S., Banks, R., Hilliges, O. 2010. Opening up the family archive. *Proc. CSCW'10*, 261–270.

12. Lawson, B. 1990. *How designers think - the design process demystified.* 2nd edition. Butterworth Architecture, London.

13. Laslett, P. The emergence of the third age. 1987. *Ageing and Society, 7*, 133–160.

14. Laslett, P. 1991. *A Fresh Map of Life: The emergence of the third age.* Harvard University Press.

15. Laslett, P. 1996. *A Fresh Map of Life.* 2nd edition. Macmillan, Basingstoke, Hampshire.

16. Lehtinen, V., Näsänen, J., Sarvas, R.: A little silly and empty-headed: older adults' understandings of social networking sites. *Proc. HCI 2009.*

17. Lindley, S., Harper, R., Sellen, A. 2008. Designing for elders: Exploring the complexity of relationships in later life. *Proc. HCI 2008*, 77–86.

18. Lindley, S., Harper, R., Sellen, A. 2009. Desiring to be in Touch in a Changing Communications Landscape: Attitudes of Older Adults. *Proc. CHI'09.*

19. Lowenthal, M.F., Robinson, B. 1976. Social networks and isolation. In R. Binstock & E. Shanas (eds.) *Handbook of Aging and the Social Sciences.* Van Nostrand Rheinhold, New York, NY.

20. Luborsky, M. 1993. The romance with personal meaning in gerontology: cultural aspects of life themes. *The Gerontologist 33,* 4, 445–452.

21. Luborsky, M. 1994. The retirement process: Making the person and cultural meanings malleable. *Medical Anthropology Quarterly, 8,* 4, 411–429.

22. Myerhoff, B. 1978. *Number Our Days.* Dutton, New York.

23. Myerhoff, B. 1984. Rites and Signs of Ripening: The intertwining of ritual, ritual time and growing older. In *Age and Anthropological Theory*, 305–330. Cornell University Press, Ithaca, NY.

24. Petrelli, D. & Whittaker, S. 2010. Family memories in the home: contrasting physical and digital mementos. *Personal and Ubiquitous Computing, 14*, 153–169.

25. Price, C. A. 2003. Professional women's retirement adjustment: the experience of reestablishing order. *Journal of Aging Studies, 17*, 341–355.

26. Quiring, O. 2009. What do users associate with "interactivity"? A qualitative study on user schemata. *New Media and Society, 11*, 6, 899–920.

27. Salovaara, A. Lehmuskallio, A., Hedman, A., Valkonen, P., Näsänen, J. 2010. Information technologies and transitions in the lives of 55-65-year-olds: The case of colliding life interests. *International Journal of Human-Computer Studies, 68,* 11, 803–821.

28. Schutt, S. 2007. Spinning stories: the development of the small histories project as an online facilitator of multiple life stories. *Proc. Creativity & Cognition'07*, 91–98.

29. Strauss, A. & Corbin, J. 1990. *Basics of Qualitative Research.* Sage, Newbury Park.

30. Taylor, A. & Harper, R. 2002. Age-old practices in the 'new world': a study of gift-giving between teenage mobile phone users. *Proc. CHI'02.*

31. Torrey, C., Churchill, E. & McDonald, D. 2009. Learning how: the search for craft knowledge on the internet. *Proc. CHI'09.* 1371–1380.

32. Vetere, F., Davis, H., Gibbs, M., Howard, S. 2009. The Magic Box and Collage: Responding to the challenge of distributed intergenerational play. *International Journal of Human-Computer Studies 67*, 2, 165–178.

33. West, D., Quigley, A., Kay, J. 2007. MEMENTO: a digital-psychical scrapbook for memory sharing. *Personal and Ubiquitous Computing, 11*, 313–328.

Computing Harmony with PerLogicArt: Perceptual Logic Inspired Collaborative Art

Nicholas Davis, Ellen Yi-Luen Do
School of Interactive Computing
Georgia Institute of Technology
Atlanta, GA 30308 USA
{ndavis35, ellendo} @gatech.edu

Pramod Gupta, Shruti Gupta
School of Computer Science
Georgia Institute of Technology
Atlanta, GA 30308 USA
{pramodgupta, gupta.shruti} @gatech.edu

ABSTRACT
This paper proposes a new model of perception called Perceptual Logic and applies it to the domain of art to understand artistic style. We describe style in terms of affordances, or ways in which an artist can interact with and contribute to an artwork. Different types of Perceptual Logic are found to influence the perceived affordances of an artwork. We present a computational collaborative art program called PERLOGICART that uses a computational model of Perceptual Logic to learn an artist's style through collaboration. The research is conducted using a practice-based method— we are working on building an interactive tool to support the making of artworks and the understanding of the creative process at the same time. PERLOGICART is a compelling interactive artwork as well as a valuable research tool that records and categorizes the creative process in a systematic manner.

Author Keywords
Creative Process, Artistic Style, Practice-Based Research, Computational Art

ACM Classification Keywords
H.5.m. Information interfaces and presentation (e.g., HCI): Miscellaneous.

General Terms
Design, Theory

INTRODUCTION
In this paper, we outline a new approach for understanding artistic style by enabling a computer to learn from artists through collaboration. We present the theoretical framework and initial implementation of PERLOGICART, a collaborative sketching interface that records user input and generates a response based on the computational model of the user's artistic style. Our research agenda is practice-based in nature [16], meaning that we aim to develop useful tools for artists while at the same time gaining insight into the creative process. Adopting this research method enables the implementation details of PERLOGICART to remain fluid and sensitive to research findings. The contribution of this paper is a novel model of perception called Perceptual Logic, and a description of the implementation of PERLOGICART, which stands for Perceptual Logic based Interactive Collaborative Artwork.

The development of New Media Art, and specifically interactive art, introduces a new way to conduct creativity research. Traditional creativity research methods such as protocol analysis provide valuable insight into the creative process, but these approaches run the risk of altering the creative process [18] or collecting inaccurate reports [7]. With interactive art and creativity support tools in general, computers can monitor and record nuanced details about how artists engage their medium throughout their creative process while making an actual artwork. However, these computer programs do not know what this data signifies, how to group it, or what conclusions can be drawn from it. The wealth of research findings from rigorous protocol analyses can be applied to craft intelligent computational algorithms that systematically gather and structure data generated during the creative process in meaningful ways. The current paper works toward that goal by synthesizing research from creative cognition, design creativity, and new media arts to build an interactive artwork that creatively engages an artist while simultaneously gathering data about his or her artistic style.

Research on creativity has a variety of viewpoints ranging from the psychological traits of creative individuals [15], the cognitive mechanisms underlying the creative process [8], and the socio-cultural significance of the objects that are produced through creative acts [5]. These paradigms coalesce into three distinct approaches that study creative people, processes or products. The theory proposed in this paper takes a creative cognition approach by trying to understand the cognitive mechanisms underlying the creative process. In particular, we contribute a theoretical framework that describes style as a critical and organizing principle that propels the artistic creative process.

Our hypothesis is that there are two types of considerations in art, namely visual harmony and conceptual harmony. During the creative process, attention will be focused at some point on a continuum varying from visual forms to the conceptual whole of a piece, and these considerations will afford different artistic choices. We propose a cognitive mechanism called *Perceptual Logic* that determines which type of artistic contributions will create visual or conceptual harmony. Perceptual Logic is not a formal logic, but rather a learned and often implicit perceptually based rule system that determines what artistic combinations make sense for an individual.

In the remainder of this paper, we will first consider other approaches to studying style and provide some background information on generative and interactive art. Next, we will describe the theoretical framework for our cognitive model of artistic style, and then describe its implementation in PERLOGICART. We will then explain how artists could use such a program. The future work section will outline final implementation details, evaluation strategies, and experimental paradigms for PERLOGICART. Finally, we will conclude by summarizing Perceptual Logic.

BACKGROUND

The development of generative and interactive art has introduced a wide variety of research questions relating to creativity. Here, we review some of the basic developments in the field and explain how they relate to our research.

Computational Art

Generative art uses computational algorithms to create visually pleasing images. Harold Cohen was among the first to program a computer to make art [20]. His program Aaron is comprised of a set of rules, parameters, and a certain amount of randomness used to develop visual form. Random numbers are frequently used in generative art to instill a sense of indetermination into the code so that no two images the program creates will be alike. Although the rules of the program are hard coded, the random interjections have the potential to create emergent behavior, which results in surprising compositions.

It is interesting to note that observers often remarked that Aaron's art looked strikingly similar to Cohen's [20]. Cohen's visual style was implicitly translated into the code base of Aaron. Although Cohen never intended for Aaron to mimic his style, he couldn't help the similarity because the aesthetic judgment that Cohen developed as an artist seeped into the rule structure guiding his program.

Greenfield's Computational Aesthetics project [7] explored the notion that computers can learn an individual's aesthetic preference. In his approach, users were presented with multiple iterations of an evolutionary art program and asked their preference, and this data was used to construct an aesthetic preference to guide the generative algorithm.

The current project builds upon this notion of generative art and takes an interesting twist to explore new ways for defining the rules of a generative art system. Our program, PERLOGICART, does not explicitly define rules that dictate how it generates art, but rather we define a process by which the system can learn a model of an artist's style. The generative rules of the program will be based on the model of artistic style produced through collaborative art making, which defines our program as a hybrid generative-interactive art program.

Interactive art is a genre of art in which the audience plays an active role in shaping the artwork. PERLOGICART is an example of dynamic interactive art [4], which means that the input of the audience/artist will trigger a response by the program. However, these responses are not one size fits all, and each artist will train a customized model that reflects his or her aesthetic preferences.

Creativity Support Tools

Willis & Hina [17] present work that focuses on supporting idea generation in the early phase of creative sketching. They argued that studying the actual process of drawing gives more information about creativity than merely studying the final product. Their creativity support tool, Alchemy is designed to help expand and stimulate creative ideas in the early phases of a sketch. Alchemy encourages users to visually explore a range of ideas and possibilities by morphing early lines into many different object-like shapes and simulates continuous exploration.

By introducing structures that may resemble conceptual forms, Alchemy strives to stimulate news kinds of creative discoveries through conceptual association and re-combination, two important properties of creative cognition [8]. Alchemy supports the generative component of creative cognition, namely idea generation [8]. Creativity support tools can also support the explorative aspect of creativity, which is a more in depth analysis of one solution [8].

Boden's [1] computational model of creativity claims that creativity can be defined as manipulations in and of a computational search space with rules defined by a given domain. Combinatorial creativity refers to employing rules in this search space in novel ways to come up with new combinations, while transformational creativity describes radically restructuring this search space so that new operations are possible. In transformational creativity, one changes the rules of the game, so to speak, which enables new ways of seeing and interpreting familiar items. The Alchemy approach to creativity support encourages transformational creativity by expanding the search through presenting lines in a novel format. With PerLogicArt, we aim to support both combinatorial and transformational creativity by interpreting artistic contributions through a visual and conceptual perspective, which will yield separate analyses.

RELATED WORK

Artists tend to exhibit a recognizable style. Artists, art historians, and art enthusiasts have intuitively felt this notion for a long time. Recently, Gabora established this intuition scientifically by showing that individuals that were thoroughly familiar with an artist were able to correctly attribute authorship to unknown art works [9]. Furthermore, style was shown to exist across mediums—visual artworks produced by writers were recognized based on participants' familiarity with their writings [9]. Her experiments reveal that artists exhibit an underlying aesthetic sense that guides their interaction with different kinds of materials, which generates an objectively recognizable style. Gabora's work showed that the notion of artistic style is in fact scientifically valid, but the question still remains as to what exactly constitutes style.

Many theories consider style in terms of the features of products that distinguish them as a recognizable exemplar of a particular style [19]. These approaches consider style as a recognizable element in the world, but not so much as a fundamental aspect of creativity. On this view, stylistic decisions are aesthetic choices made after the functional requirements for a product are satisfied. However, when considering art, one has to take a substantially different stance because there is not usually a functional requirement for art, but rather style might be a requirement in itself. By considering and theorizing about artistic style, we may begin to gain a new insight into the role that style plays in the creative process.

Creative Cognition

Our investigation of artistic style entails understanding the cognitive mechanisms responsible for the observed aesthetic preference. There are various strands of creativity research that propose two ways of seeing and interpreting the world. Style depends on perception and conception, and considering this research will help lay the groundwork for our model of artistic style.

Perceptual Modes

Design creativity and sketching research has put forth a perceptual spectrum ranging from what is termed *seeing-as* to what has been called *seeing that* [14]. *Seeing-as* refers to interpreting a set of lines on the page as a figure that is only present in the imagination, and using the sketch as a form of 'interactive imagery' or 'sketch-thinking' [14] to explore that mental figure. *Seeing-that* describes a situation in which a designer uses the visual features of a drawing to make structural inferences that pertain to reality, such as the function of a door and the implications of its size relative to the room. Suwa & Tversky build upon this seeing-as/seeing-that distinction when they studied the way in which architects see and interpret sketches [21]. They found that expert architects were better at 'reading' a sketch, which means that they were able to surmise a greater amount of functional details based on visual information. Reading off non-visual elements from perceptual qualities corresponds to *seeing that* a relationship exists between the visual properties of a sketch and the functional properties of that element in reality. The second major finding was that expert architects employ a recognizable attention shifting strategy in which they work on one area in depth, generating a wealth of non-visual interpretation, and then shift their focus to another region of the drawing [21]. When a shift in attention occurs, there is a spike in the generation of non-visual information.

Architects acquire a visual lexicon of geometric shapes and develop a form-function association that provides insight as to the purpose and meaning those shapes can have in physical reality [21], which represents the seeing-that form of perception. Sketches can also be re-interpreted from a conceptual point of view to see visual elements *as* some other entity. Perception can either focus on the visual or conceptual components of a sketch, and this focus influences how that sketch will be perceived.

Cognitive Modes

There is a large body of creativity research that proposes two cognitive modes that constitute creative cognition. These modes have been called convergent and divergent thinking [15], vertical and horizontal thinking or transformations [13, 21], explorative and generative [8], and analytic and associative [10]. All of these terms describe thinking as deep and focused in one domain or broad and shallowly focus on many domains, respectively. Gabora makes an important contribution to this discussion when she points out that the shape of a creative thought pattern (deep or wide) corresponds to the kind of memory retrieval that activity is using [10]. She describes analytic and associative cognitive modes in terms of activation functions in neural networks. The degree to which one focuses on a particular topic or task increases the 'spikiness' of the memory activation function, meaning that more detailed information related to the task at hand will be retrieved, such as causal and procedural information. Conversely, when attention is defocused, there is a 'flat' activation function, meaning that many disparate domains will be considered, possibly increasing happenstance or serendipitous combinations that lead to creative solutions to problems.

Gabora proposes the honing theory of creativity, which describes the creative process as a cycle between focused analytic cognitive activity and defocused associative thought [10]. According to this theory, insights found through associative thought are often vague and somewhat impractical, and these insights have to be refined and honed using the analytic framework of the problem context.

DEFINING ARTISTIC STYLE

By synthesizing a diverse range of creativity research, we have identified a growing consensus in the field that there are two modes of perception and cognition. The two modes of perception have been termed seeing-as and seeing that. Seeing as is an associative type of perception in which visual forms are interpreted and manipulated in terms of an associated mental figure, and seeing-that 'reads-off' functional relationships from visual elements. This suggests that perception is dynamically shaped by the cognitive

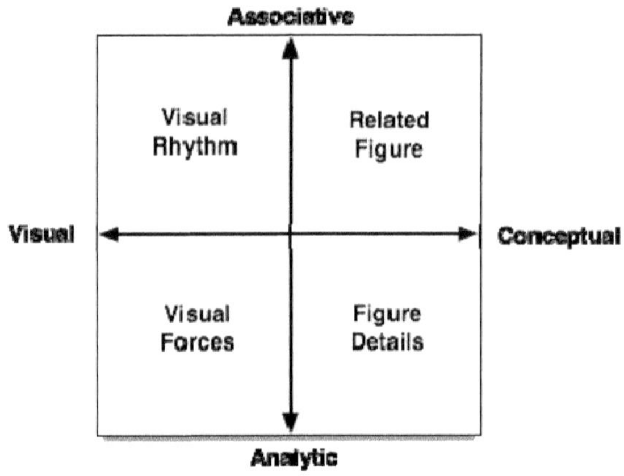

Figure 1: Axes of Perceptual Logic

mode and visual elements that one focuses on. We combine these two modes of perception and cognition to construct the Axes of Perceptual Logic depicted in Figure 1.

Figure 1 shows how the modes of cognition and modes of perception combine to form what we refer to as the two *Axes of Perceptual Logic*. The situated, embodied, dynamic (SED) framework in cognitive science has found that perception and conception are largely interrelated and mutually influential [3]. Perception is not a passive reception of sense data, but rather an interpretation of the world in terms of one's relation to it. As Gibson put forth in his ecological theory of perception, objects in the world are perceived in terms of how they can be used and interacted with [12]. Gibson found that objects are perceived in terms of their affordances, or the way in which humans can manipulate and use that object. The SED framework makes an important contribution to the notion of object affordances by proposing that affordances change based on one's current conceptions [3]. Perceived affordance of an object are relative to the desire one currently holds [2, 3]. For example, if one needs to change a light bulb, a chair becomes a kind of ladder. Perception is an active process of interpreting the world relative one's current cognitive state [3].

The Logic of Lines

Art is intentional, and as a result, the lines, shapes, and colors that are put on a page are guided by a system. The hypothesis that we put forth is that the Axes of Perceptual Logic represent the different ways in which an art object can be considered. There is a visual and conceptual harmony that can be thought of in terms of associative and analytic means.

Visual harmony determines the line and shape configurations that create a sense of balance. Conceptual harmony integrates concepts and figures from memory to achieve a conceptual cohesion in an artwork. At any given point, one can either choose to focus on the visual forms or the conceptual whole of the piece, and these considerations will have different kinds of evaluation criteria. The Perceptual Logic by which each of these artistic components is evaluated varies dynamically based upon where on the Axes of Perceptual Logic one's focus is currently situated.

A short case study will help to clarify how perceptual logic varies as a function of position on the axes of dynamic perception. The case study will analyze one of the authors' abstract drawings shown in Figure 2.

Visual-Associative

From the outset, the drawing was perceived in terms of the visual elements of the drawing. Within that, there are situations in which associative lines were made, such as the sets of parallel lines throughout the piece. These parallel lines satisfy a type of visual rhythm that stems from an association of similar visual forms.

Visual-Analytic

On the other hand, the triangular lines at the bottom of the drawing suggest a consideration of visual analysis in terms of lines being included in a broader shape. The interior lines are contained and cannot permeate the borders of their container. These lines were made following a rule that can be described as visual containment. In the visual-analytic type of perception, perceptual logic develops into what can

Figure 2: Example of visual harmony (geometric consistency) and conceptual harmony (emergent face) in abstract art

be called a visual physics. For example, lines can become barriers, have a gravitational pull, and embody other kinds of visual forces, which intermingle to form the visual-analytic type of Perceptual Logic. When situated at this point on the Axes of Perceptual Logic, valid and harmonious line placements are determined according to an individually unique set of visual-analytic criteria.

For example, in this piece the majority of the intersecting lines have a nearly 90-degree angle of intersection, exemplifying a special kind of bounding barrier rule that can be translated as: lines have enough visual force to 'overcome' a barrier if they approach it from 90-degrees. In this way, a drawing builds up a set of internal visual forces that serve to guide the placement of lines. The idea of visual forces and visual thinking was first introduced by Arnheim [1] when he proposed that certain shapes and configurations have a psychological effect on the viewer that can be measured through the degree of tension that is created.

Conceptual-Associative
On the conceptual side, a consciously attributed theme, figure, or object, is derived through association or analysis. Associative figures can originate in the mind or be triggered by associating a figure with a group of lines that appear on the page. Figures, such as faces, can be integrated into the drawing. Once a group of lines has been associated with a face, the artist can then take steps to actively shape that group of lines into a face. Now that the individual is thinking of a face, it could happen that a related object comes into their mind, and they begin to associate other objects such as a body, a hat, or other face related elements into the drawing. On the conceptual side of the Axes of Perceptual Logic, lines are determined based on the figural elements of a concept. In this drawing, the artist began to see a face and turned lines into eyes and a nose near the center of the piece.

Conceptual-Analytic
Once a figure has been identified, that figure can be considered from an analytic point of view to identify areas of the drawing that can be recruited to help represent that face. In this drawing, the face became a theme and goal of the piece, and lines are interpreted in terms of that face, just like the seeing-as phenomenon Suwa & Tversky report [21]. The circle that is above the triangle at the bottom of the drawing became a chin, and circular figures on either side of the head became ears. When considering an artwork from the conceptual-analytic point of view, Perceptual Logic strives to transform visual elements into shapes that will support the figure that has become the conceptual goal of the piece.

The Perceptual Logic that guides visual and conceptual contribution varies, and as a result may disturb the equilibrium in one or the other based on the type of contribution the artist is currently focusing on. The lines that create the face may violate some of the visual forces developed in the piece. The individual may choose to temporarily disregard visual harmony to pursue the face because it has become a priority. The degree to which an individual balances visual and conceptual harmony in different situations contributes to his or her style. For example, one artist may always privilege the visual over conceptual, which would result in largely abstract artworks. Other artists may strictly follow their conceptual framework, which would result in a photo-realistic representational art pieces.

To maintain aesthetic equilibrium, the artist cycles between these visual and conceptual aspects of a work gradually refining and expanding on the creative product. Maintaining aesthetic equilibrium is an artistic application of the honing theory of creativity [10]. Visual and conceptual contributions have to be honed according to the Perceptual Logic of the other domains. Tensions between the two equilibriums spark creative exploration. Thinking about aesthetic equilibrium in terms of style and creativity has interesting implications.

Aesthetic Equilibrium
Visual and conceptual harmonies both have an equilibrium that represent their balanced steady state in which the artist's preference for formal or figural harmony are satisfied, respectively. Both of these equilibriums can be disturbed by contributions from the other. Once equilibrium is perturbed, methods for regaining harmony become a catalyst for creativity. The interaction and competition among visual and conceptual harmony creates a dynamic tension that drives creativity in a way that is unique to each individual artist.

Creating harmony from disharmony is fundamentally different than continuing harmony. Instead of merely *elaborating* on more visually harmonious lines according to an internalized set of Perceptual Logic, an artist has to creatively adapt to a situation and find a solution. When an artist works to come back from disequilibrium, the individual must solve a perceptually based logic puzzle to figure out methods to transform conceptually guided lines into a visually harmonious whole, or vice versa. Solving this logic puzzle can be viewed as a mental exercise in Perceptual Logic and a way to train and improve Perceptual Logic by expanding the horizons of one's style. In Figure 2, the artist incorporated the central features of face into the drawing, and then had to re-establish harmony by integrating those elements into the piece according to his principles of visual harmony.

Integrating figural elements, such as the face, can serve as catalysts in the creative process. Conceptually derived lines have the potential to disturb a visual equilibrium. In returning to equilibrium, Perceptual Logic is applied to new circumstances, which creates novel shape combinations and offers new opportunity for creative exploration. The converse is also true, if conceptual harmony is dominating a work (i.e. it is largely representational), changes that are purely aesthetic may challenge the conceptual harmony and enable the artist to see new ways of expressing objects. There are therefore two types of artistic contributions:

- **Elaborative**: Contributions that abide by the prevailing set of Perceptual Logic and serve to further the sense of harmony and balance.
- **Catalytic**: Contributions that introduce elements from a competing Perceptual Logic system and therefore create a sense of disharmony and tension that can be resolved.

Perceptual Logic suggests that art may be affordance-based in the sense that visual combinations afford certain kinds of contributions based on the way in which they are perceived. The embodiment theory claims that perception is for action, meaning that we perceive our environment in terms of how we can interact with it [22]. The same is true for art. An artist sees a piece of work in terms of how they can contribute to it. Perception varies based on one's mode of cognition (associative vs. analytic) [10] and the object of thought (visual vs. conceptual) [21]. Perceptual Logic is dynamically determined based on the type of perception one is engaged in. Putting this all together, we can begin to see art as an embodied and meaningful activity in which certain artistic actions are more or less successful at creating a sense of aesthetic equilibrium. Each artist has a slightly different pattern of perception, leading to a unique Perceptual Logic, which generates identifiable styles.

Thus far, we have described how Perceptual Logic is a guiding mechanism that determines how visual and conceptual configurations achieve a subjective sense of harmony and balance. Next, we will describe an approach to compute visual and conceptual harmony and learn a computational model of style through collaborative art making.

PERLOGICART PROGRAM

Translating Perceptual Logic into a computational model requires defining the components of visual and conceptual harmony and a method of controlling the influence of each module. The visual component will analyze shapes to determine features, relations, and patterns among an input shape and a response shape. The conceptual component will compare the input and response to a database of images using basic computer vision algorithms to determine if figures are emerging. In the current proof of concept implementation, we have only developed the visual component of the system. However, we have included the conceptual component in the computational model of style that is guiding the overall implementation strategy. In this section, we will first outline the general architecture, and then explain the two phases of the program, training and drawing, and provide example outputs of each phase.

The visual component of PERLOGICART has been separated into *features, relations, and patterns* to begin to understand the visual component of Perceptual Logic. This approach references the architecture of Covlan [6], a computational visual language that breaks down images into visual elements (rectangle, circle, arrow, line, and curve), visual concepts (location, size, thickness, speed, direction, length, distance, angle, and direction), and visual relations (touching, above-below, and right-of-left-of). At this point in the implementation cycle, we have some features and relations in place, but these are subject to change as we experiment with artists to determine which relationships best capture their Perceptual Logic.

At this point, *features* consist of shape, size, position and orientation. *Relations* compare shapes together by considering aspects like intersecting, parallel, right-of, left-of, above, below, and inside. *Patterns* are groups of relations, such as stripes, grid, radiating from, and contain. Features and relations deal with the visual-associative aspect of visual harmony, while patterns represent the visual-analytic component and begin to approximate the visual forces in the Axes of Perceptual Logic. The implementation details are intentionally loose and flexible so that interesting research findings can inform the system's development in the spirit of practice-based research. Figure 3 shows the PERLOGICART system architecture.

Phase One: Learning Artistic Style

The first phase of this project resembles an experiment in which confounding variables are controlled and one variable is tweaked to examine its impact on the dependent variable, which in this case is the artist's Perceptual Logic. The confounding variables are artistic features such as color and freehand lines, which surely contribute substantially to an artist's style, but our project is going to begin with the most rudimentary artistic features and this framework can be extended to incorporate increasingly complex artistic interactions as the project continues.

To develop the foundation for modeling artistic style, we are going to have the artist draw geometric shapes in response to a predefined geometric shape shown on the screen. One could argue that this is not an example of art,

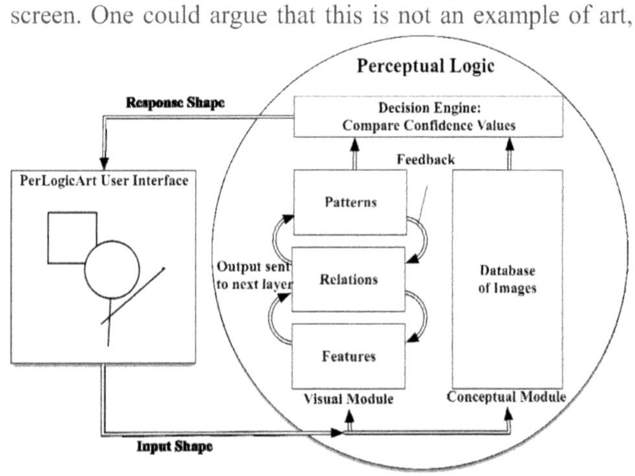

Figure 3: PerLogicArt Architecture

but we contend that it is the most basic artistic scenario possible, namely determining the placement of lines on a page. By simplifying the context in which the artist is situated and presenting him or her with a predefined set of inputs, we can examine the response to determine whether there are any significant correlations between the features, relations, and patterns of their artistic responses.

In phase one, the user interface is collecting data from the artist. This data includes the name of the artist that will be associated with the artistic model of style that is built up. This name will be added to a list of artistic styles that the program has on file. In training mode, the computer creates a shape on the screen to which user responds by drawing a new shape of its own. At this point, the shapes have been simplified to lines in order to demonstrate the framework. The computer's input lines are light and the user's response lines are dark black. See Figure 4 for a demonstration of instances of training phases for two different users A and B. Figure 4A shows that the user A responds with mostly short lines, while Figure 4B shows the user B responds with large lines. The program is recording other properties, such as angle, distance, and position, but length is the most apparent feature.

The responses generated by the user are used to train the various parameters of the feature, relation and pattern layers using the Randomized Weighted Majority Learning Algorithm. In this procedure, an input is tested for a set of expected results or values to compute a statistical probability (between zero and one) that represents the likelihood of a result or value being valid for a randomly chosen input. For example, using the user's responses, we can learn which of the relations (intersection, parallel, etc.) are most dominant in that user's artistic style.

The Randomized Weighted Majority Learning Algorithm is especially suitable to our case since it is an online learning algorithm and can be used to further train the model even in the drawing phase using the feedback loop as shown in Figure 3.

In every parameter, there is also an unknown element added to allow for new attributes to be added later on. The unknown element enables flexibility in the system that lets it handle input that is completely novel.

After all the user responses have been parsed, each layer returns a list of probabilities that correspond to how confident it is that particular data points match its pre-encoded values. Each list is stored as a file and passed to the next phase of program.

With reference to Figure 4, the Perceptual Logic model trained from the responses of user A prefers short lines, while the model trained from the responses of user B prefers longer lines (other aspects of style are also computed, but length is easily observable). See Figure 5 for two examples PerLogicArtworks created by the models generated for users A and B.

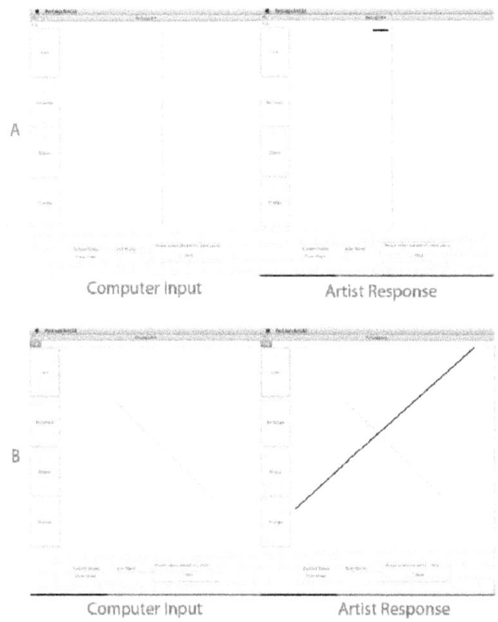

Figure 4: PerLogicArt Training Phase

Phase Two: Using Learned Style to Collaboratively Generate Art

In phase two, the model trained for a user in phase one is available for creating collaborative art. An artist can pick any of these models to collaborate with and begin drawing. The user interface for drawing will be similar to the first with a limited set of geometric shapes and a drawing canvas. The main difference with this UI is that lines that are added stay on the page like a real sketch.

After the artist draws a shape, the system records the shape that was used and the initial and final mouse positions and creates a shape object with this information. The input data is passed on to the model, which has a similar layered structure as the first phase, namely features, relations and patterns. The only difference being that the output of these layers is aggregated to create a shape that can be drawn to the screen, such as a line or a square. The artist's input is first given to the feature class where it is analyzed and a response shape is generated based on the model parameters trained in the first phase. Note that this generated shape is just a starting suggestion for the response and not the final response because the feature class doesn't have any information as to how lines interact, only correlations and averages between mutual occurrences. It will know things such as long lines tend to occur with other long lines, or circles tend to occur with lines. It will not know relations or patterns that occur in a drawing. The shape generated by the feature class is passed to the pattern class, which analyzes its relationship with the user input and compares it to the relations that this artist tends to use. If the feature class has provided a bad suggestion, the relation layer will reject the suggestion and provide a critique and a suggested solution. The critique will consist of an explanation as to why these shapes do not go well together by citing some dominant relation or lack thereof. The feature class learns from this critique and adjusts the parameter weights of the model using the Randomized Weighted Majority Learning Algorithm. The feature layer then generates a better suggestion and passes it to the relation layer. If the relation layer agrees with the new shape, it will pass it to the pattern layer.

A similar cycle happens between the pattern and relation layers. The pattern layer looks at more of the global picture and looks to see how this particular relation compares to the other relations emerging in the piece. If the group of relations demonstrates a significant resemblance to a certain pattern that is contained in its examples, then the pattern layer outputs the suggested shape to a decision engine. This output has a confidence value associated with it that corresponds to the degree to which the patterns layer is sure that the particular shape matches the artistic style. Normally, the decision engine would compare the confidence value from the visual module with the confidence layer from the conceptual model to determine what shape to draw, but the conceptual module is not implemented yet, so the decision engine takes the shape from the pattern layer and draws it to the screen as the computer's response in the collaborative drawing.

Creative Experience

There are two motivations for this project. The first is to create a computational model of artistic style, and the second is to use this model as the generative mechanism in a computational collaborative art program. The collaborative art program would be the first of its kind that is based on the style of individual artists. This has several exciting implications. In this section, we will outline the types of creative experiences that will be possible with this technology.

Generate with PerLogicArt: Once the system has learned at least one artistic style by collaborating with an artist, PerLogicArt will be able to generate artworks on its own based on the style of the artist. Furthermore, with multiple artistic styles, the system could generate a collaborative artwork between two or more of its computational models of style. What would happen if you mixed Picasso's style with Van Gogh's? Another interesting prospect in the generative application is that the audience would be able to watch as the program composed a drawing. The temporal display of an artwork may facilitate a newfound understanding of a particular artist by watching how they create.

Simulate with PerLogicArt: The generative mode could be turned on or off based on the artist's current goals. If the artist wanted to test how a certain contribution may affect the rest of the PerLogicArtwork, s/he could add a line and then simulate one possible trajectory the drawing could take by turning the generative mode on. When generative mode is on, the system adds all lines according to the style that is selected. Experimenting with simulation mode

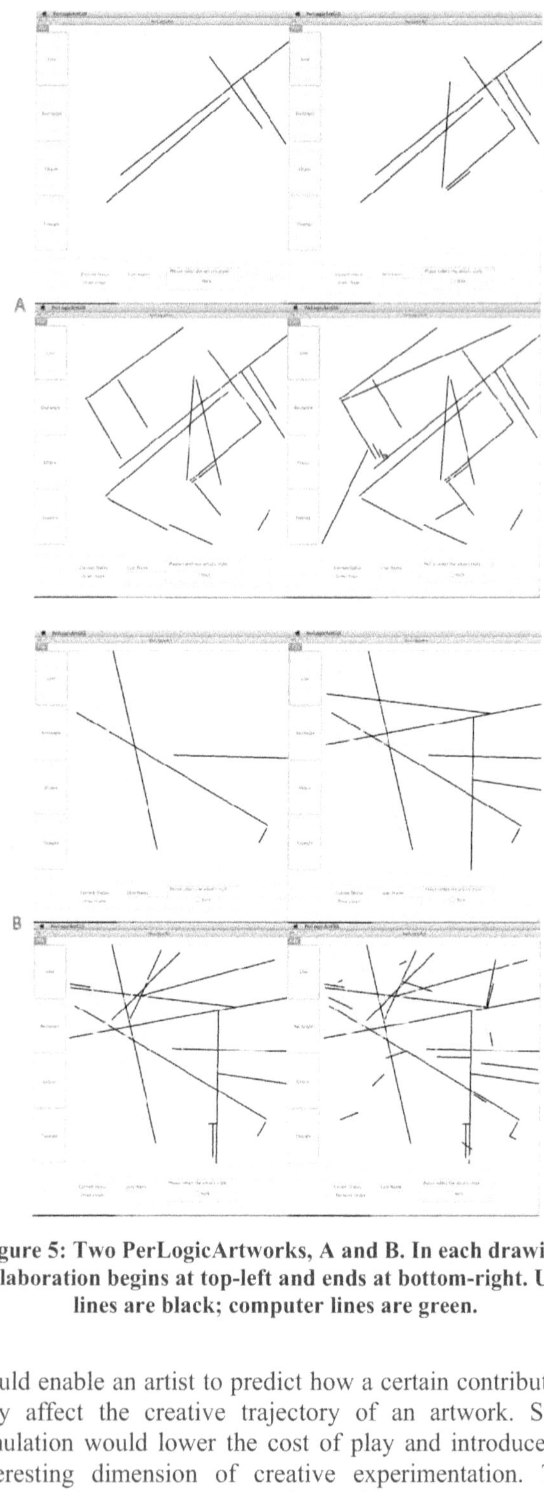

Figure 5: Two PerLogicArtworks, A and B. In each drawing, collaboration begins at top-left and ends at bottom-right. User lines are black; computer lines are green.

would enable an artist to predict how a certain contribution may affect the creative trajectory of an artwork. Such simulation would lower the cost of play and introduce an interesting dimension of creative experimentation. The process of creating an artwork would become an art in itself, and artists would have the option of seeing how different inputs alter the structure of their PerLogicArtwork.

Collaborate with PerLogicArt: This is the basic collaborative mode in which the artist draws a line, and then the program draws a line, and so on. Self-collaboration is one potential application of the program, but there are other more interesting collaborative possibilities as well. Computational models of style can be constructed for many individuals and these can all be used concurrently in a PerLogicArtwork. For example, an artist could train the program on many of his friends, and subsequently construct a collaborative artwork with contributions form the artistic styles of all of his friends. Each individual would be represented by a different color line to identify contributions.

Learn with PerLogicArt: One traditional method of learning how to do art is to imitate the style of expert artists. PerLogicArt enables aspiring artists to actually collaborate with these styles rather than passively copying them. With the ability to learn multiple artists' style, we could theoretically learn the style of high profile artists. Art students would then be able to make collaborative drawings with extremely skilled and iconic artists' styles. The user would be able to watch the order and process by which an artist may create an artwork, as well as collaborate with well-known artists.

FUTURE WORK

This proof of concept implementation was successful in indicating the explanatory and pragmatic potential of using Perceptual Logic to model artistic style. Future work will commence in three directions: detailed implementation, evaluation, and experimentation. To fully implement the program, each of the three layers have to be fully constructed, and the conceptual module must be added. Formative evaluations will help guide this work.

Evaluation

There are two ways to evaluate the system. The first approach is to test the model of artistic style by comparing the artist's lines to the model. After the training phase is complete, a few additional query-response pairs can be sent to the drawing phase of the program to test the efficacy of the computational model of style. The user's response will be passed to the relations layer as-if it was constructed by the feature layer. Typically, the feature layer comes up with the initial shape suggestion and the relation layer evaluates the suggestion. By sending user input directly to the relation layer, the program will evaluate how well it thinks the user's test lines satisfy the model of artistic style. This evaluation technique essentially tricks the system into evaluating itself. The relation layer will analyze the data and either accept or reject what it believes to be the suggestion coming from the feature layer. If it rejects the user's test line, it will provide the rules that it violated, and this discrepancy will help tweak the implementation details to more accurately model artistic style.

There is a second and equally valuable way to evaluate the system. The computational model of style will be deemed successful if the artist feels that contributions from the computer were harmonious. To evaluate harmony, the program can draw its response line and ask the user to rate how much they like this line on a scale from 1-10. The results of these evaluations may serve to help tweak the weightings in each layer as well as suggest new relations and patterns to make the program more robust.

Experimentation

PerLogicArt provides an experimental platform with which to empirically study the creative process, artistic style, and computational collaborative art. The first impressions of interacting with the system are promising. Creating PerLogicArtworks is a compelling experience. Furthermore, the lines contributed by the computer have a deeper significance than lines created strictly in an algorithmic manner. The user is able to attribute some amount of human intentionality to the lines because s/he knows that the justification for these lines came from a real artist. Such an interaction design paves the way for qualitative studies of how computational collaborative art influences the creative process. Do individuals creating PerLogicArtworks with the style of other artists feel a sense of co-presence with that artist they are 'collaborating' with?

As a creativity research tool, PerLogicArt collects a wealth of information about the creative process without disturbing it. From this, we plan to create an index of the creative process in a tool called CreatEx that will provide information about the temporal dynamics of the creativity by using information visualization techniques on PerLogicArt data.

CONCLUSIONS

This paper had two goals, namely to present a novel model of perception called Perceptual Logic, and to describe the initial implementation of a computational model of Perceptual Logic in a collaborative art program called PerLogicArt.

We synthesized cognitive science and creativity research to propose a novel model of perception that describes how perception changes based on intention and applied this model to art. There are two factors that determine how perception varies, and these are the mode of cognition (associative vs. analytic) and the object of attention (visual vs. conceptual). Charting these two dimensions in space yields what we have termed the Axes of Perceptual Logic. It is two-dimensional representation corresponding to how an artwork (or object) is perceived, namely from an associative or analytic point of view and whether that person is attending to the visual or conceptual qualities of the piece.

The way in which an artwork is perceived determines where one is located on the Axes of Perceptual Logic, which in turn influences the affordances that are perceived and recognized in an artwork. We propose an affordance-based view of style where certain artistic contributions are more or less 'logical' based on the degree to which they satisfy either a visual or conceptual harmony.

Visual and conceptual harmonies have an aesthetic equilibrium. Based on one's position on the Axes of Perceptual Logic, lines on the page afford certain artistic contributions that elaborate the harmony of one of these systems. However, artistic contributions that create harmony in one system may create tension in the other. Altering the way in which the artwork is perceived and applying the resultant Perceptual Logic can resolve this tension. Applying Perceptual Logic to resolve tension amounts to solving a perceptually based logic puzzle, which acts as a catalyst for creativity by changing the set of affordances typically associated with either the visual or conceptual system. The interaction and interrelation of the two systems of harmony represent the unique style of an individual.

We've demonstrated a successful proof of concept implementation of a computational model of Perceptual Logic in PERLOGICART, which is a computational collaborative art program that learns artistic style by creating collaborative artworks. Such a program offers exciting opportunities as an interactive artwork, creativity support tool, and creativity research platform.

ACKNOWLEDGMENTS

We would like to thank the artist Nicholas Davis for allowing us to use his drawing in this paper.

REFERENCES

1. Arnheim, R. *Visual thinking*. University of California Press, Berkeley, 1969.
2. Boden, M. The Creative Mind: Myths and Mechanisms. London, Basic Books, 1990.
3. Beer, R. Dynamical systems and embedded cognition. In K. Frankish and W. Ramsey, eds., *The Cambridge Handbook of Artificial Intelligence*. Cambridge Univ Press, Cambridge, In Press.
4. Candy, L. and Edmonds, E. Interaction in Art and Technology. *Crossings: eJournal of Art and Technology 2*, 1 (2002), No Pagination.
5. Csikszentmihalyi, M. Implications of a Systems Perspective for the Study of Creativity. In Sternberg, R.J. ed. *Handbook of Creativity,* Cambridge University Press, Cambridge, 1999, 313-336
6. Davies, J. and Goel, a. Transfer of problem-solving strategy using Covlan. *Journal of Visual Languages & Computing 18*, 2 (2007), 149-164.
7. Ericsson, K. A., & Simon, H. A. *Protocol Analysis*. Cambridge, MIT Press, 1984.
8. Finke, R. A., Ward, T.B., Smith, S.M., *Creative Cognition*. MIT Press, Cambridge, 1992.
9. Gabora, L. Recognizability of Individual Creative Style Within and Across Domains: Preliminary Studies The Recognizability of Creative Style. *Proceedings of the Annual Meeting of the Cognitive Science Society*, (2010), 1-6.
10. Gabora, L. Revenge of the "Neurds": Characterizing Creative Thought in Terms of the Structure and Dynamics of Memory. *Creativity Research Journal 22*, 1 (2010), 1–13.
11. Gary R. Greenfield. 2005. Computational aesthetics as a tool for creativity. In *Proceedings of the fifth conference on Creativity & Cognition* (New York, NY, USA, 2005), ACM, 232-235.
12. Gibson, J.J. *The ecological approach to visual perception*. Lawrence Earlbaum, Hillsdale, 1979.
13. Goel, V. *Sketches of Thought*. Cambridge, MIT Press, 1995.
14. Goldschmidt, G. The Dialectics of Sketching. *Creativity research journal 4*, 2 (1991), 123–143.
15. Guilford, J.P. Creativity, *American Psychologists 5*, (1950), 444-454.
16. Jennings, P. and Giaccardi, E. Creativity Support Tools for and by the New Media Arts Community. NSF Workshop Report on Creativity Support Tools, (2005), 12–14.
17. Karl D.D. Willis and Jacob Hina. 2009. Alchemy: experiments in interactive drawing, creativity, & serendipity. In *Proceeding of the seventh ACM conference on Creativity and cognition* (New York, NY, USA, 2009). ACM, 441-442.
18. Lloyd, P., Lawson, B., & Scott, P. (1995). Can concurrent verbalization reveal design cognition? *Design Studies*, 16(2), (1995), 237-259.
19. Stacey, M. Psychological challenges for the analysis of style. *Ai Edam 20*, 03 (2006), 167-184.
20. McCorduck, P. 1991. *Aaron's Code*. W. H. Freeman & Co., New York, NY, USA.
21. Suwa, M. and Tversky, B. What do architects and students perceive in their design sketches? A protocol analysis. *Design Studies 18*, 4 (1997), 385-403.
22. Varela, F.J., Thompson, E., Rosch, E., *The Embodied Mind*. MIT Press, Cambridge.

Artists & Designers: An Experiment in Data Visualization

Sara Diamond
Ontario College of Art & Design University (OCAD U)
sdiamond@ocad.ca

ABSTRACT

OCAD University's strategic plan *Living in the Age of Imagination* places a priority on focusing the lenses of art, design and media on contemporary issues and practices outside of the traditional boundaries of art and design. This has resulted in a myriad of innovative curriculum and research initiatives of specific relevance to HCI. For example in concert with led partner York University, the University of Toronto and a set of industrial partners OCAD University has created the Centre for Innovation in Information Visualization and Data Driven Design (CIV/DDD), a research hub for the development of next-generation data visualization techniques and their underlying information processing and communication technologies (ICT). This centre is the focus of this talk. The idea was that by bringing an unprecedented number of interdisciplinary artists, designers, media makers, humanist analysts and social scientists into the research partnership we would develop new paradigms of data enquiry, user-centered visualization models, and information processing and display technologies.

Author Key Words
Data Visualization; Aesthetics; Design; Art; User-Driven Design; Metaphor; User-Centered Design

ACM Classification Keywords
Computer Applications Arts and Humanities

General Terms
Algorithms; Design; Theory

The Organization of Research along the Design Research Axis

Design research is fundamentally engaged with advancing knowledge about the nature of data driven research and related design practices. Design is integrated into the thematic and technical research in order to provide effective visualization solutions for large-scale data sets, discover new ways of representing these, approach technology design from the user perspective and discover new design approaches to presenting visualizations within emerging technologies. We argue that technical solutions (data mining in volumetric visualizations or with emergent algorithms, cloud computing, model-based scientific visualization tools, display technology capacities, and the functionality of annotation tools) are bound up in design decision, that is what the end users require to be displayed and the degree of interaction that they require.

C&C'11, November 3–6, 2011, Atlanta, Georgia, USA.
ACM 978-1-4503-0820-5/11/11.

Design methodology researchers are developing protocols for participatory and usability testing. It contributes to current dialogues about visualization aesthetics. It explores the appropriate use of 2D or 3D visualizations, or even the use of other and in closely related research, whether visualization should be immersive or interactive, or both immersive and interactive. It will consider the means through which scientifically accurate visualizations can be created, or abstract synthetic visualizations. It will consider the impacts of specific cultural understandings to chosen structures and metaphors. It will examine when generic tools are appropriate and when interfaces or even tools should be designed for specific users. It will consider whether certain metaphors lead more effectively to discovery. It will combine with cognitive science and HCI research to organize user feedback and eventually, usability testing. Several themes within the design research are of specific relevance to this conference:

Design and Affect—Tools and Usability Testing

In Affective Computing Picard (1998) draws connections between emotions and insight. She notes that mood influences 'evaluative judgment' and 'information retrieval'. Affective computing research has a significant potential application within visualization design. However, engaging the body and mind in emotional and feeling ways creates, "the design challenge [of] how to deploy new representations in such a way that they influence wider groups of people" (2007, 162). Fishwick et al. (2005) and Tractinsky and Zmiri (2005) also recognize the importance of analyzing emotion in order to provide graphics tools. Analysis of users' response to various metaphors and navigation strategies will include analysis of affect and related aesthetics. Tools will extract and measure the emotion within data; and emotion expressed by users of the data. Sub-tools, such as annotation tools, could make use of affective expressions or the analysis of affect to be expressive or graffiti-like. Potential links between affect and discovery will be drawn from this research.

Data Driven versus User-Driven Design/ Participatory Design

Specific technologies are fundamental to allowing data-driven design to occur—it is designers who will create the interfaces that allow users to have close proximity to the data structures. While data analysis and visualization require the creation of an appropriate metaphor, and hence always introduce subjectivity, there are two directions from which design researchers derive metaphors and navigation processes. A user-based, ethnographic approach is increasingly common within information visualization. Yet Spangler, Kreulen and Newswanger (2007, 786) propose a role for the computer, as 'facilitator, neutral observer'. The Centre hypothesizes that a less intuitive visualization approach, induced through data-driven analysis, could make a significant contribution to the visualization of informational contents and affective structures in narrative texts, and could help guard against one of the dangers of user-driven design (Greenberg & Buxton, 2008) - namely, that questions and metaphors simply recapitulate existing knowledge. Yet the user-driven approach does allow for the dynamic management of visualization metaphors and underlying data structures, facilitating understanding within the context or culture of the users. Hence our research systematically compares differences between data-driven and user-driven design, in order to provide a qualitative analysis of the two approaches, and to outline strategies for blending best practices of the two methods for purposes of visualizing narrative patterns. These questions will be posed by design researchers within each of the thematic user groups.

What are Visualization Aesthetics?

Aesthetics structure experiences in formal perceptual ways and provide interpretive tools with which to construct meanings. Aesthetics from the arts are as bound up in an understanding of perception as cognitive science is. Recognizing the value of visual culture to visualization, design and arts-based knowledge and research on information design will.

Research strength in aesthetic theory and applications allow the CIV/DDD to treat visualization as communication, albeit strongly tied to science; hence requiring knowledge of visual representation, cognition and the ways that design choices influence viewers. Visualization tools will use devices and metaphors drawn from realism, to abstraction, to narrative. The effectiveness of different aesthetics will be tested for the same data set by using distinct designs. Lee (2007) argues that user interface design must integrate form and function, rather than accept a timeworn polarization that privileges function. Common data structures and metaphors will be catalogued and tested. Research at the centre will contribute to the growing field of visual analytics and to qualities of data aesthetics and feed back into the success of technology research and the capacity of the user groups to successfully deploy tools.

Method and Conclusion

The research method allows testing and comparison of visualization methodologies. Data is assembled and extracted → Effective algorithms are produced to represent data qualities over time; to represent data qualities over dimensions; to represent change, as appropriate → Data analysis is used to create a pattern-recognition system and a structure→ Analyze the qualities in data that can be represented and choose a metaphor→Protocols for participatory design in relation to data-driven inquiry and visualization are developed and tested for group→Participatory design exercises with user groups (as above)→Aesthetics are developed and tested that fit the structures and patterns→Data-led visualizations of extracted features/patterns occur→User-led visualizations of features, and aesthetics occurs, comparing data sets→Effective means are sought to create interaction with the data as represented→ Modeling methods for complex phenomena across different data sets are applied (social media, biological, physics) →Visualization tools are created that allow the analysis of differentiated data sets and these are compared for similarities and differences→Results are contrasted and compared results→Use and usability testing is undertaken for tools→ Selection, adaptation; development of analysis tools→Visualization tools tested with commercialization partners.

Art, design methods and aesthetics are analyzed and the findings shared to better understand the impacts of the integrated design, computation approach and user approach.

FOOTNOTES

1. Fishwick, P., Diehl, S., Prophet, J. & Lowgren. J. (2005) Perspectives on Aesthetic Computing. *Leonardo*. vol. 38, pp. 133-41.
2. Fry, B. (2008) *Visualizing Data: Exploring and Explaining Data with the Processing Environment.* Sebastopol, CA: O'Reilly Media Inc.
3. Greenberg, S. and Buxton, B. (2008) Usability Evaluation Considered Harmful (Some of the Time). *CHI 2008 Proceedings*, April 5-10, Florence. Florence: ACM, pp. 111-120.
4. Ireland, C. (2003) Qualitative Methods: From Boring to Brilliant In: Laurel, B., ed. *Design Research: Methods and Perspectives* Cambridge, MA: MIT Press, pp. 23-29.
5. Kosara, R. (2007) Visualization Criticism – The Missing Link Between Information Visualization and Art, *Proceedings of the 11th International Conference on Information Visualisation* (IV), 2007, North Carolina: IV, pp. 631–636.
6. Lee, C. (2007) *HCI and Aesthetics: The Future of User Interface Design* [Internet] Available from <www.carrielee.net> pp. 1-4. [Accessed January, 2009]
7. Tractinsky, N. and Zmiri, D. (2005) Exploring Attributes of Skins as Potential Antecedents of Emotion in HCI, In: Fishwick. P, ed. *Aesthetic Computing* Cambridge, MA: MIT Press, pp. 1-28.

The Choreographer's Notebook - A Video Annotation System for Dancers and Choreographers

Vikash Singh, Celine Latulipe, Erin Carroll
HCILab
University of North Carolina at Charlotte
{vsingh7, clatulip, e.carroll}@uncc.edu

Danielle Lottridge
Department of Communication
Stanford University
lottridg@stanford.edu

ABSTRACT
We present a collaborative tool for choreographers and dancers, the Choreographer's Notebook, which allows multimodal annotation of rehearsal videos during the dance production process. The dance production process is a creative process in which exploration and expression are paramount and we describe issues we have observed over four different dance production cycles. The Choreographer's Notebook addresses the recurring problem of scarcity of rehearsal time and space, which is a limiting factor for exploration and expression. The tool is a web-based video application that enables choreographers to provide multimodal, context-sensitive instructions and feedback to the dancers outside of formal rehearsal time. The novelty of this tool is its ability to provide a multimodal collaborative video-based workflow. This article also presents a thorough ethnographic investigation of the dance production process and results from the use of the Choreographer's Notebook as an artifact within that process.

Author Keywords
Dance, Choreography, Video Annotation, Picture-in-Picture, multi-modal communication, collaborative creativity

ACM Classification Keywords
H.4 Information Systems Applications: Miscellaneous

General Terms
Human Factors

INTRODUCTION
Dance production is a very creative process and requires exploration of a variety of movement expressions through many trial and error cycles. This creative process starts with an idea and goes through different stages (development, learning, cleaning) leading up to the final performances. The process depends heavily on dance rehearsals and one of the major constraints in this creative process is the availability of studio/rehearsal time. The scarcity of time in rehearsal studios limits the amount of exploration that is possible. The lack of useful tools in a contemporary dance production to assist the choreographers and other stakeholders to efficiently utilize the available studio/rehearsal time is a major concern.

This paper proceeds as follows: first we describe our observations of the dance production and rehearsal process, and highlight a number of salient issues as well as our assessment of opportunities for technological interventions. Second, we discuss related work in video annotation systems and in integrating technology into the dance production process. Next, we present the Choreographer's Notebook, detailing the interaction and how it is designed to facilitate the dance production process. The Choreographer's Notebook has been used in various dance productions at our institution, and so in the Results section we give initial responses to the system from the choreographers and dancers. Finally, we conclude with a summary and plans for future work.

THE DANCE PRODUCTION PROCESS
As part of a long-term interdisciplinary dance and technology project at our institution [20], we have had the opportunity to observe a number of different casts of dancers and choreographers work through complete production cycles. This ethnographic approach to studying the dance production process involved members of our team participating in and observing dance rehearsals and performances, typically for 2-5 hours per week and as much as 15 hours per week during performance weeks. In the following paragraphs we present our observations from this experience, generalized into the typical stages in a dance production process.

Process Stages
The dance production process typically involves the following stages: choreographic development, choreographic learning, cleaning, stage readiness, performance. We describe our observations of the activity during these stages, based on dance productions at our educational institution.

Choreographic Development

The first stage in the dance production process may be long or short, depending on whether the choreographer is developing a completely new piece of choreography or adapting or re-staging an existing piece of choreography. Though the choreographer may have some ideas about dance movements from the very beginning of the project, usually they start working on development of movements through experimentation and innovation with dancers as soon as possible. If the choreographer is developing completely new material, this is a long process. While the work is going on in the dance studio, there is also much work going on in the mind of the choreographer while away from the studio. The development of movement phrases and sections of the dance is done over time, sometimes in serial order, sometimes out of order. As parts of the choreographic material are set, this development process may overlap with the next phase, where the cast of dancers learns the material.

Although a dance piece is based mainly on a choreographer's vision, communication and interaction among all the people involved is a major part of the choreographic development process. Choreographers shape their vision in dance studios where they develop definite movements that dancers will learn. In a more exploratory creation, a choreographer may involve his/her dancers in a process of shared investigation through improvisation.

If a choreographer is adapting an existing piece of choreography, the length of development time will depend on the magnitude of the changes being made to the existing material, as well as the familiarity of the choreographer with the material. If a choreographer is adapting or re-staging their own work, they will be more familiar with the material than if they are re-staging another choreographer's work. If the choreographer is simply re-staging a piece and there is no adaptation being made, the development process may be skipped altogether.

Choreographic Learning

Once the choreography is set, the dancers must learn the material. It is sometimes the case that choreographers develop material for specific dancers that they have already hired (in which case those dancers work with the choreographer to develop the material, and learn it while it is being developed). In most university dance productions, the material is developed independent of the dancers and the dancers are selected after the material is set. Sometimes advanced or especially talented dancers are recruited early to help the choreographer explore and experiment with the material.

During the learning phase, dancers are taught the choreography, a few minutes at a time. As they master more and more of the dance, they continue to rehearse what they have learned. Dancers' muscle memory is taken advantage of by constant repetition of movement. If the dancers are learning existing material, they often take advantage of videos of previous productions to learn the movements, playing the videos in slow motion.

If the material is new, the option of watching videos is not available. However, it is typical for choreographers to videotape parts of rehearsals where material has been set. These videos are then reviewed at the end of the rehearsal or the beginning of the next rehearsal, with the choreographer using the video to point out problems or corrections. This is critical for the dancers, since they are able to see a third-person's view of themselves in the space and in relation to the other performers. This allows them to better understand their part in the piece as a whole, and their spatial, positional relationship to other dancers.

Choreographic Cleaning

Once the dancers have learned the material, the rehearsals turn to movement cleaning and detailing, adding subtle nuances and intentions to the gestures. The choreographer works to make sure each individual dancer is executing the movements as they were intended and then ensures that the relationships between and among dancers is clear in terms of the spatial and temporal aspects of the movement as well as the specific physical articulation. For instance, the choreographer will work to make a unison section flawless by addressing differences in timing, directional facing, height level of arms or legs, etc. Likewise, the choreographer will pay attention to everything from proper technical execution of the movements (is the dancer's leg fully stretched or is her body alignment precise?) to more subtle aspects of internal intent of the gesture (is the focus correctly projected or is the movement quality commensurate with the feeling to be conveyed)? Choreographers typically record rehearsal videos during this stage and much time is spent discussing the fine details of every second of the dance (while watching the videos), in order to perfect these subtleties. In dance pieces with multiple dancers, a choreographer will spend time working with the group as a whole, working with small groups and working with individual dancers.

Stage Readiness

In the week or two leading up to the scheduled performances, the dance production goes through a process of stage readiness. The dance, which is rehearsed in a rehearsal studio, is put on the stage for *spacing*. This allows the choreographer to see the piece on the stage and make adjustments to take advantage of the width/depth and wing size of the stage. The next step in stage-readiness is called *lighting cue-to-cue*, where lighting effects are set and fine-tuned for each phase of the dance piece. After this, there will be a few *tech rehearsals* where the piece is rehearsed on stage with lighting and any stage effects that are required. The final steps of stage-readiness involve *dress rehearsals*, where dancers are in full costume and makeup, and lighting and stage effects are employed. The final dress rehearsal typically happens the evening before opening night.

Performance

During the days in which performances happen, the dancers engage in warm-ups, makeup and costume, and then perform. We have observed that the choreographer's work is done at this stage, and although the choreographer usually attends opening night, he or she may not attend the rest of the performances. The production does not change after the final dress rehearsal, although every performance is unique, even for the most well-trained dancers.

Post-Performance

Our observations of educational dance productions have shown that there is little to no activity in the production process that occurs after the final performance. The activity of 'striking the stage', i.e. removing all stage props, lighting, lifting of the marley dance floor, etc. takes place immediately after final curtain call and the student performers are expected to help with this. This is quite different from professional dance productions, in which the hired stage crew takes care of strike. Beyond this activity, there may be an informal cast party, but there are no formal meetings or other activities. In the dance productions we have been involved with, we have introduced the concept of post-performance focus groups as a debriefing method, and this practice has become quite popular with the dancers.

It is evident that the dance production process depends heavily on rehearsals. Rehearsals not only help in refinement of movements but also in many cases help the choreographer to revisit and redefine their vision for the piece. The dance production process for a dance piece at a university usually spans 2-3 months, framed by the semester. In commercial dance companies, the process may span 3-6 months but will typically involve many more rehearsal hours per week. In the next session we highlight some of the issues that we observed in the dance production process.

Production issues

Our main focus is the rehearsal, given its importance in the dance production process. Choreographers face two major problems in arranging rehearsals, related to availability of time and space. They require not only dancers' time (and must work around their schedules) but also access to a dance studio. Choreographers often have a very tight budget, and if not carefully planned, paying the dancers and paying for the rehearsal space can quickly put a project over budget.

Rehearsal Space and Time

A rehearsal space is generally a dance studio which has a sprung marley floor, mirrors on the walls and ballet bars. Rehearsal space is critical in the phases of the dance production process from choreographic development to cleaning. Though some large private dance companies have their own rehearsal space, most small and mid-size dance companies cannot afford their own rehearsal space and must rent. In cities where rehearsal spaces are limited in number, high demand makes the rehearsal spaces very expensive. In the Manhattan area, a 1000 square foot dance studio, costs $100-400 per hour. A typical rehearsal may last 3-4 hours and a professional production generally has rehearsals daily for months before the show is staged. Clearly this can be a very expensive process and choreographers will want to make the most of this expensive time.

In educational settings studio space is part of the infrastructure, and so does not have to be rented. However, it is shared amongst different choreographers and productions, and so access is scarce. At our institution, a choreographer typically has rehearsal space available for only 3-6 hours per week for each production.

A dance performance involves many people including dancers and technicians. They are often involved in more than one project at a time and hence gathering everyone together at the same time for a rehearsal can be challenging. In private dance companies, full-time dancers may be salaried, but many dancers will be paid hourly. Technicians and other support staff (rehearsal assistants, costumers) may also be hourly workers, adding to the hourly expense of a rehearsal.

The scarcity of space and time is a prevalent concern that impacts the quality of a production in both the commercial and university dance environments. Thus, it is very important to utilize these spaces and the time of the dancers judiciously and for everyone involved in a production to make the best use of the rehearsal time. For dancers and choreographers, the best use of time in a dance studio with a sprung marley floor and mirrored walls involves actual dancing. However, in our observations of dance productions, we have seen significant amounts of time spent in discussion and critique, rather than in practicing and refining movement. Consider the following scenario, which is typical of many rehearsals we observed:

> The dancers and choreographer arrive at rehearsal and warm up with stretches. The choreographer then pulls out a television cart and hooks up a camera that was used to record a run-through of the piece at the last rehearsal. The dancers sit on the floor in a circle, watching the video, with notebooks out. The choreographer continually pauses the video to talk about something that she would like changed or something that is not quite working. Sometimes the choreographer will rewind a portion of the video so the dancers can watch it again. The dancers take notes in their notebooks, based on what the choreographer tells them, but also based on their own observations of movements that they want to work on improving. The dancers occasionally stop the choreographer and ask questions about something they see on the video. When they have finished watching the video, the choreographer may also give general comments about overall issues in performance that she wants the dancers to think about. After this, the dancers do a formal warm-up and begin to rehearse.

The process described above is typical and may take anywhere from 15 minutes to a full hour. While the discussion that occurs during this time period is obviously very important to the dance production process, it could just as easily take place in a conference room. So, while this is an effective use of dancer and choreographer's time, it is not an efficient use of the dance studio space.

Stage Readiness Issues

While studio rehearsal time is expensive, it pales in comparison to stage time. While a few large dance companies may have their own performance stage, it is much more typical for dance companies to arrange for stage space at other venues. Stages are often fully utilized, and it is common for dance productions to have initial access to the actual performance stage only a week or two before the first performance. During the stage readiness phase, lighting, stage effects and props must be put into place, tested and refined. The amount of time available for this process is extremely limited, and we have observed that there is often a feeling that the production is short-changed at this stage, because there is not enough time to fully explore lighting effects, sound level variations and stage effect possibilities.

BACKGROUND

The use of computing technology has not been applied to some of the major issues of dance production that we discussed earlier. We noticed that computing technology is almost absent in the process of rehearsal and fine tuning. We propose that the effective use of computing technology can enhance the rehearsal process so that more time during rehearsals can be dedicated to movement. This could lead to a decrease in the time needed in the rehearsal studio space (therefore saving money and freeing up the space for others to use) or to an increase in the quality of the dance production because more rehearsal time is actually spent developing, learning and perfecting movement. Based on the issues described here, we developed the Choreographer's Notebook, to allow choreographers and dancers to communicate online, using rehearsal videos as the main artifact for discussion.

Choreography and Computing

Merce Cunnigham was among the first to introduce computing to choreography by using animated stick figures to plan choreography [16]. A system of dance notations called Labanotation, similar to music notations, was developed by choreographers in the 1990s which is now widely used in North America [22]. Schiphorst and Calvert developed an interface based on Laban movements that allowed choreographers to visually compose pieces in space and time [23]. Calvert developed Life Forms software (later DanceForms) that Cunningham used for dance productions [14]. In recent years software like Poser (Curious Labs), Motion Builder (Alias) and 3dsMax (AutoCad) have offered features for human figure animation, however, not all of them are customized for dance purposes. Troika Ranch, a well-known interactive dance company, use their custom designed Isadora software for managing interactive dance performances [3].

Choreographers have also used computer graphics and interactive technologies in live performances, which are generally pre-programmed and sometimes reflect the movement of dancers using sensors. A team at Purdue University produced a dance performance which looked into issues related to the collaborative design of live-motion capture and multi-image projection in dance [21]. The Dance.Draw project has investigated IT support in creative dance design and the use of wearable sensors on dancers to generate live projected visuals [20]. Dance-tech.net is an online platform that showcases the work of a community of dancers and choreographers embracing technology with varying levels of assistance [24].

Video Interfaces and Annotation Support

The Choreographer's Notebook is an application that supports multi-modal annotation of a video. Video annotations, similar in concept to notes in the margin of a book, are metadata associated with video content. Annotations are anchored to a point in the timeline of a video but are stored externally. Annotations are a good platform for asynchronous collaboration as different users can insert annotations for the same video content across multiple sessions separated in time. Furthermore, annotations enhance the end-user experience when they are displayed in-context (at the anchor point where they were made).

Video annotation interfaces to facilitate communication between different stakeholders has been explored by different groups in the past decade. Many interfaces were developed to support multimedia annotation as educational tools for the distance learning market, such as the Classroom 2000 project [9] and the Microsoft Research Annotation System [11]. The 'WACTool' supports P2P capabilities that allow user collaboration and content sharing using voice and digital ink comments over individual frames of a video [15]. 'Project Pad' is a standalone web application for adding text notes to media clips and sharing those notes with others [2]. 'Video Image Annotation' tool is a Windows application that provides an interface to manually annotate a video with text [6]. 'VideoANT' is a web-based video annotation application developed for e-learning, to annotate videos with time point markers and text [18]. 'Advene' allows people to design and exchange videos with annotations [10]. 'Anvil' is another tool that allows annotation of audiovisual material by inserting time-anchored comments and gesture elements [19].

There are many video-based interfaces with text annotation that are commercially available. Youtube allows user to annotate videos they upload, while others can see the annotation [7]. 'BubblePLY' is a web application that allows users to annotate remote videos hosted on other websites such as Youtube. Users can add text, drawing, pre-defined clipart, subtitles etc. on a remote video to create bubbles (annotated videos) and can edit their own bubbles [1]. 'veotag' [4] and 'viddler' [5] also support annotations of video content. Sports and News broadcast domains have also seen a significant amount of work dealing with video annotations [8, 13, 12].

The applications discussed typically support annotations in only one form (mostly text) and lack multimodal capabilities (Figure 1). While the majority of interfaces developed share similarities with the Choreographer's Notebook, none support fine-grained access and navigational control, multimodal annotation grouping, rich annotation positioning and user-based color coding. All of the applications discussed allow some form of video annotation but none of them comprehensively address the issues of collaboratively working on a creative temporal project, such as dance. In the dance

Tool	Modalities supported	Context-based navigation	FIle archival system	User Collaboration		Web-based
				Synchronous	Asynchronous	
BubblePly	text + digital ink	No	No	No	No	Yes
YouTube	text	No	No	No	Yes	Yes
veotag	text	No	No	No	No	Yes
viddler	text + video	No	No	No	Yes	Yes
WACTool	text + digital ink + audio	No	No	Yes	Yes (p2p)	No
videoANT	text	Yes	No	No	Yes	Yes
Project Pad	text	No	No	No	Yes (Allows Notes sharing)	Yes
Anvil	text	No	No	Yes	No	No
Advene	text + pre-defined shapes	Yes	No	No	Yes (Allows file exchange)	No
Choreographer's Notebook	*text + digital ink + video*	*Yes*	*Yes*	*Yes (minimal)*	*Yes*	*Yes*

Figure 1. Comparison of features of existing video annotation systems that supports multiple user collaboration on a single video.

production process, we observed that choreographers were using video cameras to record the rehearsals. Then, all participants would sit on the studio floor and discuss and critique the rehearsal, watching the video on a small TV. However, the VCR playback restricted their ability to navigate the rehearsal video. This observation led us to believe that a digital video interface with annotation support would ease the rehearsal process. Any tool targeted towards these issues should:

- Support various modalities of annotations including text, digital ink and video.
- Allow for the synchronized video playback with annotated comments.
- Have a simple interface for users with varying degrees of technological expertise.
- Provide an archival system of video.
- Promote collaboration and facilitate discussion among all stakeholders.
- Provide context-related video navigational tools.

THE CHOREOGRAPHER'S NOTEBOOK

The Choreographer's Notebook (Figure 4) is a tool designed to address the scarcity of rehearsal space and time in the dance production process. It is a web-based application that allows users to annotate a rehearsal video using a variety of modalities including text, digital ink and video. The application also supports visual indexing of annotations and a rich navigational control for inserting and editing video annotations. Annotations are anchored to a point in the timeline of a video, but are stored externally in a separate file. They enable synchronous collaboration as multiple users can login and work simultaneously, as well as asynchronous collaboration as different users can insert annotations across multiple sessions separated in time. Furthermore, annotations enhance the end-user experience when they are displayed in context (at the cue-point where they were made). The application also provides a self-documenting archival system which captures not only the choreographic movements but also the choreographer's intent for the dance. This documentation is important because it provides finer details of a dance without any extra cost to the choreographer.

Architecture

An overall architecture of the Choreographer's Notebook is shown in Figure 2. The Choreographer's Notebook is implemented in the Adobe Flex framework and works in all major web browsers, supporting mp4 and flv video files. After logging in, users can load videos, play them and insert an annotations. The application sends the text, digital ink drawings or video annotations to a MySQL database via PHP. Text is stored as a string while digital ink drawings are stored as a snapshot of the transparent canvas on which the drawing was made. Video comments are stored as an .flv file in a separate folder. Information is then retrieved by the Choreographer's Notebook as annotations from the MySQL database. The annotations are first retrieved as a proxy XML feed, which is written dynamically using PHP, and then are rendered in the application.

Interface

When the application is loaded, the user must first login as rehearsal videos are not publicly available. Each user is assigned a username and password and has a color assigned to them so that each user's comments are color-coded. A choreographer can upload a rehearsal video and post her comments in the form of text, digital sketches or video com-

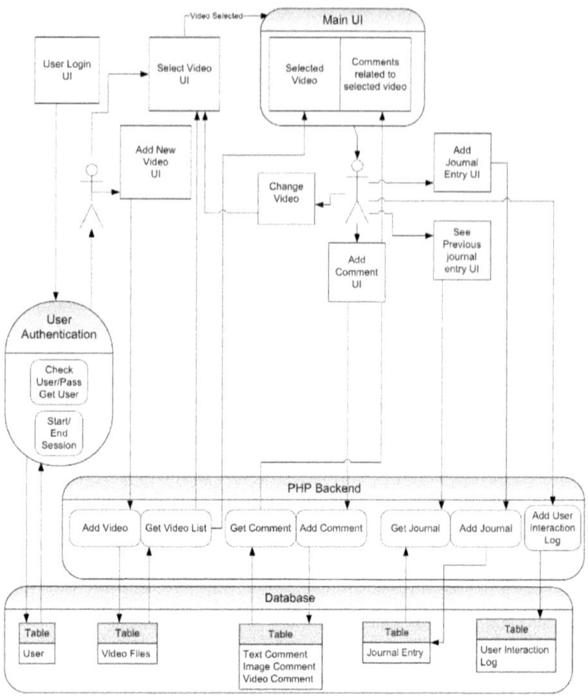

Figure 2. Choreographer's Notebook architecture.

ments. Dancers can then log in, analyze their rehearsal performance and read comments posted by the choreographers in context. If the comments are related to their dance movements they can review them to refine their movements and respond with video, ink or text comments. Dancers are able to add comments about their own movements or about the movements of other dancers. However, in practice, we observed that the dancers did not use the commenting system to comment on other dancers. They did add comments to ask questions of the choreographer or to self-critique their own dancing.

Uploading/Selecting Videos

After signing in, a user can upload a new video or open an existing video. If the user opens an existing video the application opens the "main screen", which shows the video and comments posted to that video by any user. The main screen consists of a large video window on the left with a timeline scrubber, a control bar beneath it and a comment data-grid on the right (Figure 4).

Inserting Comments

On the main screen, comments can be inserted on the video timeline in three different modalities by clicking the 'Add Comment' button. Once a user chooses to insert a comment, he can choose between text, sketch or video or any combination of these three modalities. Sketch commenting currently supports multi-color sketching with two different pen widths. The user has the option of clearing the canvas if she is not satisfied with her sketch (Figure 4). Video commenting (Figure 7) requires a web-cam to capture the video comment of the user. Once a comment is submitted, it is

Figure 3. UI for selecting a video file to open. This UI provides an archive of all the videos.

added to the data-grid and a cue-point marker (a color-coded circle) appears over the video timeline showing the position of the inserted comment in the video.

Exploring and Editing Comments

Each user's comments are color-coded, which helps in visual identification of comments while navigating (Figure 4). Posted comments can be explored three different ways. A user can click on any comment in the data-grid or on a colored circle (cue-point marker in Figure 6) on the video timeline. This seeks the video play-head to the cue-point and pauses the video. Comments related to that cue-point are then overlaid on the main video. This feature delivers comments in context, which makes it easy for dancers to correlate comments with their movements. The third way for a user to explore comments is by watching the video while the 'Show All Comments' checkbox is checked. In this interaction, the video plays through, pausing at all comment points to display each comment. Users can click in the data-grid to edit or delete their own comments.

Journaling

Choreographers and dancers sometimes keep a journal documenting notes on their progress and ideas and images to be explored. In some production processes journal is an explicit aspect of the development [17]. The Choreographer's Notebook supports a journal feature which can be used by choreographers or dancers to record and review private thoughts about the dance. A user can access this feature anytime while using the application, once logged in, and journal entries cannot be seen by other users.

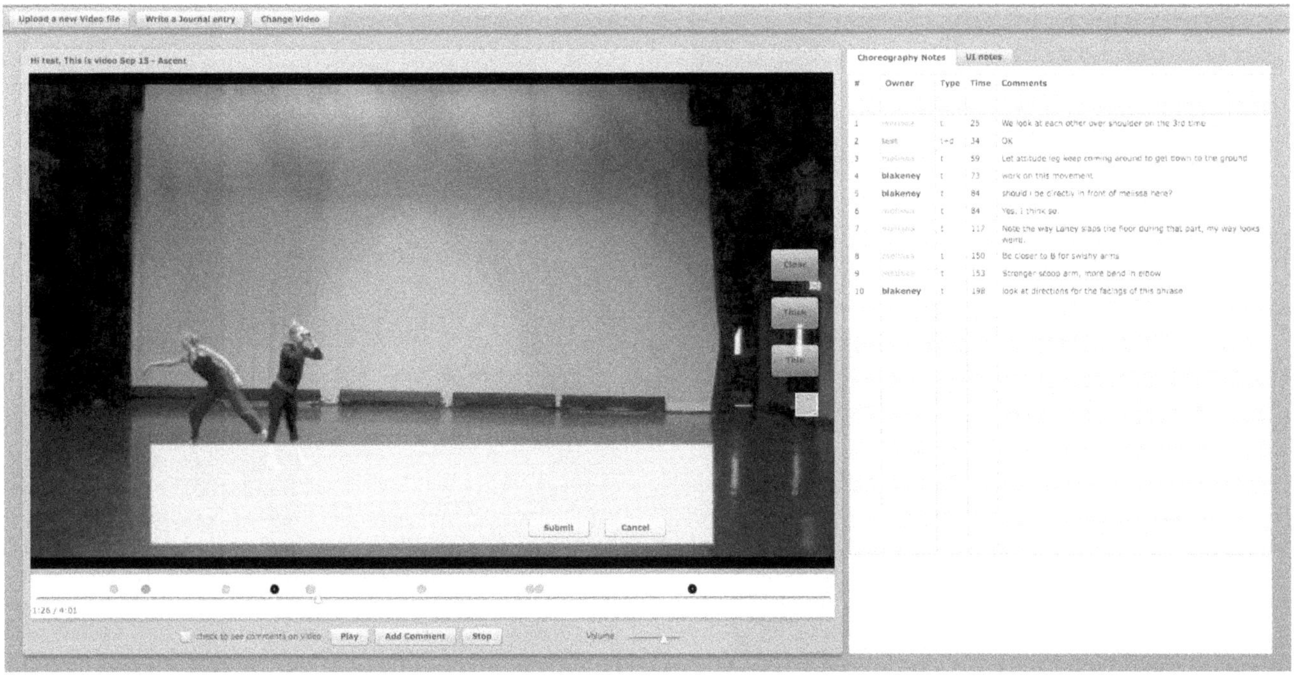

Figure 4. The Choreographer's Notebook main screen showing video panel and comments

Figure 5. Sketch overlaid on the video panel with the choreographer's comments.

EVALUATION

The development of the Choreographer's Notebook has been and continues to be an iterative process. It has evolved over four different dance productions based on input from all stakeholders. The choreographers and the dancers have remained enthusiastic about this application and have provided us with valuable feedback. Two choreographers and more than 25 dancers have used the Choreographer's Notebook during four production cycles. To evaluate whether the tool enabled more creative exploration and enhanced the quality of the creative process, we have conducted three focus groups with dancers and two interviews with choreographers. We asked:

- How did you use the Choreographer's Notebook?
- When/where/why did you use it?
- How did using it affect dance rehearsals?
- Would you want to use it again? Why/Why not?

For any application it is important to understand how the application was actually used in practice [25]. Hence we also implemented an instrumentation module in the application to track the usage pattern of different types of users. We categorized all users in two different groups called 'the dancers' and 'the choreographers'. We recorded total time spent by different users in each session as well as their usage of different features in the application. We also tracked the commands used, high-level user interface events and the time of the day when the application was used. The log data provided insights into the usage behavior of different groups.

Results

The usage pattern of the choreographers and the dancers was very different in nature. While the choreographers spent significant time critically reviewing recorded video, frequently making comments on dancers' positions and movements, the dancers spent most of their time navigating through posted comments. The choreographers spent significantly more time in each session than the dancers. Choreographer1 logged into the system three times per week and spent an average of 62 minutes in each session and Choreographer2 spent about 40 minutes per session three times per week. The dancers spent an average time ranging from 8 minutes to 26 minutes per session. The rehearsals were scheduled twice a week in the evening and the choreographers generally made it a point to post their comments before noon

Figure 6. A close-up of the control bar showing video controls and timeline cue-point markers for navigation.

Figure 7. Video-in-video commenting.

the next day to provide enough time for the dancers to go through the posted comments before the next rehearsal. The dancers exhibited a wide range of usage time. Some of the dancers preferred to go through the annotated video late at night while others used the application to review the last rehearsal an hour or two before the next rehearsal. Though the application was designed to be fairly democratic in nature, allowing everyone to post comments, we noticed that most of the comments came from the choreographers and the dancers used the commenting feature mainly to ask questions about their own movements. While using the Choreographer's Notebook, the choreographers mostly used text commenting to communicate their remarks to the dancers in comparison to the other modalities which were used less frequently.

The focus groups and interviews provided qualitative feedback. All stakeholders found the Choreographer's Notebook very useful and said that it helped them in the choreographic learning and cleaning process. They used it often in their leisure time as well as just before coming to the rehearsal. One dancer said that, "It was actually nice that you could integrate a dance rehearsal into the rest of your life. It became part of my routine, my computer routine, like gmail, school email, Facebook and Choreographer's Notebook." Awareness of the fact that their rehearsal was being recorded helped them to remain in what the choreographer referred to as "performance mode". One dancer noted that, "... it made me feel more in my character and in my story." One choreographer liked the ability to watch a rehearsal video whenever she needed to. She said, "... I was kind of multi-tasking, drinking morning coffee and reading the Choreographer's Notebook." She also liked the ability to jump from scene to scene while annotating, which she was unable to do with her VCR. While video players are old technology, we note that this older technology is still common in the under-funded arts world. Even where choreographers may be using DVDs, most DVD players do not allow easy scrubbing through video.

Both choreographers and dancers felt that using the Choreographer's Notebook allowed them to devote more time to actual dancing in the dance studio and that this had positive impacts on the quality of the final performance. Sometimes they also projected the commented video during rehearsal and used it as a rehearsal tool. Some of the dancers asked for permission to use the Choreographer's Notebook for their own work in their choreography classes. The two choreographers we interviewed have asked to continue using the tool. We also noted that during performance week of one production, the choreographer used the tool to celebrate the work of the dancers by posting many positive comments about each night's performance. The choreographer noted that there is never time for standard video review during performance week, but the Choreographer's Notebook allowed this.

In the Spring of 2011 a guest lighting designer also used the tool to view the production from outside of the country, demonstrating the use of the tool to enable remote, asynchronous collaboration. The lighting designer used the tool to familiarize himself with the dance, which helped him to plan lighting effects in advance of actually visiting the university.

DISCUSSION

Interviews and focus groups brought out some exciting themes which are contextual as well as behavioral. The over-arching context of use of the Choreographer's Notebook was high expectations for excellence and responsiveness. The choreographers felt that the dancers who used the application could be 'trusted'. During the rehearsal process, there existed a tension of how best to utilize rehearsal time. The choreographers wanted to take advantage of viewing rehearsal video as a group, but on the other hand didn't want to spend a lot of time just sitting and watching video during rehearsal time. Choreographers noted that as dancers had already done their home-work (watching videos with comments), it took less time in group discussion and so they were able to spend more time dancing.

Choreographers also noted that filming rehearsals and putting them on the Choreographer's Notebook made dancers step up their performance by dancing at 100% during rehearsals. This was remarkable because dancing at 100% is an important quality for professional dancers and important to foster in students. For example, dancers made mistakes work; they did not stop and request to start again. Instead, they dealt with the mistake to the best of their ability. This is a critical skill that is important to teach and the application provided an excellent platform for promoting that.

Dance Critiquing Process

One of the major themes which emerged from the focus group studies and the interviews was the change in the dance critiquing process because of the use of this application. The Choreographer's Notebook greatly modified the traditional critiquing and correction process. Before Choreographer's Notebook, the practice was for choreographers to quickly scribble down notes while the dancers danced. Sometimes these notes could be difficult to read, and it was also difficult to know what part of the dance the notes referred to. Imagine the difficulty in taking detailed notes while watching a continuous string of dozens of movements, each lasting only a few seconds. The Choreographer's Notebook supplemented this process by providing the choreographer a 'pause-able' and 'scrub-able' video, and a commenting feature to make clean and clear annotations. Sometimes when watching one part of the video, it reminded the choreographer to make a note at another point in the dance. This is an important behavior that could not be supported without video annotation. The choreographers noted that watching and annotating a 22 minute long dance video took approximately two hours. This is illustrative of the wealth of feedback and critique that is missed when commenting on dance in real-time. This application enabled the choreographer to decide that only main critiques were made during rehearsal, while details were saved until later. As in the traditional critiquing process, the choreographers attempted to manage the psychosocial and emotional burden of critique. They made sure they critiqued all dancers, so that no one was singled out. Some dance-related tasks were clearly appropriate to be computerized and/or done at home, and others were best communicated in rehearsal. For example, the Choreographer's Notebook was very helpful in highlighting spatial relational aspects that involved multiple bodies, like matching arm angles. Watching this feedback was beneficial in terms of instantly communicating the problem and necessary adjustment(s).

SUMMARY AND FUTURE WORK

The Choreographers Notebook has proven to be instrumental in augmenting the creative process of dance productions. Not only has it helped to create a workflow that increased the efficiency of rehearsal time, but it also provided choreographers and dancers a platform where they could collaborate and critically analyze their progress. The qualitative analysis further shows that the tools usage increased the time available for actual dancing during the rehearsals which had a positive impact on the quality of the final performances.

There are limitations to address and features to add. The dancers and choreographers would like comment threading and more powerful navigation mechanisms to help them review short segments of a video on a loop. We are currently working on the second version of the Choreographer's Notebook, which will make this application accessible on mobile devices such as smart-phones and tablets. We want to make the application available for the choreographers at rehearsal so that they can easily add comment markers while watching rehearsal. It is also important to note that dancers have their own critical eye. An open research question is how do dancers watch an annotated video, versus one that has not been annotated? Would it be beneficial to encourage or require dancers to watch the video with and without annotations? We are also interested in exploring the socio-technical impact of this tool. The Choreographer's Notebook can be further expanded in the future to enable creative exploration of elements such as lighting and interactive effects. This would expand the creative participation to include other stakeholders such as lighting directors, stage managers and interactive technologists. We will continue this interdisciplinary work and plan to test the application in other performance domains.

ACKNOWLEDGEMENTS

We would like to thank our dancers and choreographers for providing valuable feedback. This work is supported by an NSF CreativeIT grant.

REFERENCES

1. Plymedia - bubbleply. http://www.plymedia.com/products/bubbleply/bubbleply.aspx [Last accessed: 04/19/2011].

2. Project pad - home page. http://dewey.at.northwestern.edu/ppad2/ [Last accessed: 04/19/2011].

3. TroikaTronix - isadora. http://www.troikatronix.com/isadora.html [Last accessed: 04/19/2011].

4. veotag. http://www.veotag.com/whatis/[Last accessed: 04/19/2011].

5. Viddler. http://www.viddler.com/[Last accessed: 04/19/2011].

6. Video image annotation tool-informatics and telematics institute (CERTH-ITI). http://mklab.iti.gr/via/[Last accessed: 04/19/2011].

7. YouTube - broadcast yourself. http://www.youtube.com/t/annotations_about [Last accessed: 04/19/2011].

8. Click-it: Interactive television highlighter for sports action replay. In *Proceedings of the 14th International Conference on Pattern Recognition-Volume 2 - Volume 2*, ICPR '98, pages 1484–, Washington, DC, USA, 1998. IEEE Computer Society.

9. G. D. Abowd, C. G. Atkeson, A. Feinstein, C. Hmelo, R. Kooper, S. Long, N. Sawhney, and M. Tani. Teaching and learning as multimedia authoring: the classroom 2000 project. In *MULTIMEDIA '96: Proceedings of the fourth ACM international conference on Multimedia*, pages 187–198, New York, NY, USA, 1996. ACM.

10. O. Aubert and Y. Prié. Advene: an open-source framework for integrating and visualising audiovisual

metadata. In *Proceedings of the 15th international conference on Multimedia*, MULTIMEDIA '07, pages 1005–1008, New York, NY, USA, 2007. ACM.

11. D. Bargeron, A. Gupta, J. Grudin, and E. Sanocki. Annotations for streaming video on the web. In *CHI '99: CHI '99 extended abstracts on Human factors in computing systems*, pages 278–279, New York, NY, USA, 1999. ACM.

12. M. Beetz, N. von Hoyningen-Huene, B. Kirchlechner, S. Gedikli, F. Siles, M. Durus, and M. Lames. ASpoGAMo: Automated Sports Game Analysis Models. *International Journal of Computer Science in Sport*, 8(1), 2009.

13. D. C. A. Bulterman, P. Cesar, and A. J. Jansen. An architecture for viewer-side enrichment of tv content. In *Proceedings of the 14th annual ACM international conference on Multimedia*, MULTIMEDIA '06, pages 651–654, New York, NY, USA, 2006. ACM.

14. T. W. Calvert, A. Bruderlin, S. Mah, T. Schiphorst, and C. Welman. The evolution of an interface for choreographers. In *CHI '93: Proceedings of the INTERACT '93 and CHI '93 conference on Human factors in computing systems*, pages 115–122, New York, NY, USA, 1993. ACM.

15. R. G. Cattelan, C. Teixeira, R. Goularte, and M. D. G. C. Pimentel. Watch-and-comment as a paradigm toward ubiquitous interactive video editing. *ACM Transactions on Multimedia Computing, Communications, and Applications (TOMCCAP)*, 4:28:128:24, Nov. 2008. ACM ID: 1412201.

16. M. Cunningham. *Changes: Notes on Choreography*. Something Else Press, New York, NY, USA, 1969.

17. R. Grove. *Thinking in four dimensions : creativity and cognition in contemporary dance*. Melbourne University, Carlton Vic., 2004.

18. B. Hosack, C. Miller, and D. Ernst. Videoant: Extending video beyond content delivery through annotation. In T. Bastiaens, J. Dron, and C. Xin, editors, *Proceedings of World Conference on E-Learning in Corporate, Government, Healthcare, and Higher Education 2009*, pages 1654–1658, Vancouver, Canada, October 2009. AACE.

19. M. Kipp. Anvil - A Generic Annotation Tool for Multimodal Dialogue. In *Proceedings of the 7th European Conference on Speech Communication and Technology (Eurospeech)*, pages 1367–1370, Aalborg, Sept. 2001.

20. C. Latulipe, D. Wilson, S. Huskey, M. Word, A. Carroll, E. Carroll, B. Gonzalez, V. Singh, M. Wirth, and D. Lottridge. Exploring the design space in technology-augmented dance. In *CHI EA '10: Proceedings of the 28th of the international conference extended abstracts on Human factors in computing systems*, pages 2995–3000, New York, NY, USA, 2010. ACM.

21. W. S. Meador, T. J. Rogers, K. O'Neal, E. Kurt, and C. Cunningham. Mixing dance realities - collaborative development of live-motion capture in a performing arts environment. *Computers in Entertainment (CIE)*, 2:1212, Apr. 2004. ACM ID: 1008233.

22. J. Newlove. *Laban for Actors and Dancers: Putting Laban's Movement Theory Into Practice: A Step-by-Step Guide*. Routledge, 1 edition, Aug. 1993.

23. T. Schiphorst, T. Calvert, C. Lee, C. Welman, and S. Gaudet. Tools for interaction with the creative process of composition. In *Proceedings of the SIGCHI conference on Human factors in computing systems: Empowering people*, pages 167–174, Seattle, Washington, United States, 1990. ACM.

24. M. B. Solano. dance-tech.net/producer. `http://www.dance-tech.net/` [Last accessed: 04/19/2011].

25. M. Terry, M. Kay, B. V. Vugt, B. Slack, and T. Park. Ingimp: introducing instrumentation to an end-user open source application. In *CHI '08: Proceeding of the twenty-sixth annual SIGCHI conference on Human factors in computing systems*, pages 607–616, New York, NY, USA, 2008. ACM.

Distributed Creative Cognition In Digital Filmmaking

Nicholas Davis, Boyang Li, Brian O'Neill, Mark Riedl
School of Interactive Computing
Georgia Institute of Technology
Atlanta, GA 30308 USA
{ndavis35, boyangli, boneill, riedl}@gatech.edu

Michael Nitsche
School of LCC/ Digital Media
Georgia Institute of Technology
Atlanta, GA 30308 USA
michael.nitsche@gatech.edu

ABSTRACT
This paper reports on an empirical study that uses a Grounded Theory approach to investigate the creative practices of Machinima filmmakers. Machinima is a new digital film production technique that uses the 3D graphics and real time rendering capability of video game engines to create films. In contrast to practices used in traditional film production, we've found that Machinima filmmakers explore and evaluate ideas in real time. These filmmakers generate vague and underspecified mental images, which are then explored and refined using the real time rendering capabilities of game engines. The game engine assists the filmmaker to fill in indeterminate details, which allows creative exploration of scenes through playfully experimenting with parameters such as camera angle and position, lighting, and character position. Creative exploration distributes the cognitive task of evaluation between the human user and the Machinima tool to enable evaluation through exploring possible scene configurations.

Author Keywords
Creativity, Digital Filmmaking, Creative Cognition

ACM Classification Keywords
J.5 Arts and Humanities: Fine Arts

General Terms
Experimentation, Design

INTRODUCTION
This paper reports on an empirical investigation of the creative practices of a relatively new digital filmmaking technique called *Machinima*. Machinima is a digital film production technique that uses the 3D graphics and real time rendering capability of video game engines to create films. It has been defined as "animated filmmaking within a real-time virtual 3D environment" [12]. Machinima filmmakers, or *machinimators*, are able to script character actions and camera sequences to create a visually robust animated film with relative ease. The genre has become so popular in recent years that many computer games, such as *The Sims*, *The Movies*, and *Grand Theft Auto* are released with tools and interfaces to provide fine-grained control of their 3D game engines to create Machinima. Likewise, more generic game engines including Epic's *Unreal* engine, Valve's *Source* engine, and Crytek's *CryEngine* ship with improved Machinima production tools and editors. Machinima gradually evolved from a technical and esoteric manipulation of video game engine code to more user-friendly and widely accessible graphic user interfaces designed exclusively for making films [13]. This has led to specific Machinima engines that completely focus on the cinematic elements and reduce the gameplay mechanics, as is the case with *Moviestorm* and *iClone*.

C&C'11, November 3–6, 2011, Atlanta, Georgia, USA.

Currently, little is known about how these new techniques have affected the creative process of machinimators. We conducted a study of the creative practices of five expert machinimators through a qualitative methodology called Grounded Theory. Using this approach, we interviewed experts and coded transcripts in an iterative process that exposed common creative practices.

The contribution of this paper is a novel model, *Distributed Exploratory Visualization* that describes the creative practices of Machinima digital filmmaking. Our analysis indicates that the real time rendering capabilities of Machinima tools enable filmmakers to distribute part of their creative process onto these tools by creatively exploring and evaluating images through active manipulation. Consequently, our model elaborates on the concept of Distributed Creative Cognition [6] by blending the generation and exploration cycle of the Geneplore [2] account of creativity with the basic premise of distributed cognition [5]. Distributed Cognition proposes that humans offload cognitive work onto technology to coordinate action, and Distributed Creative Cognition proposes that humans offload cognitive work in during creative ideation.

In the remainder of this paper, we first consider the development of Machinima and its role as a medium. Next, we will describe our study and summarize our results. In the discussion, we will define Distributed Creative Cognition in detail. We will then reflect on our findings and offer some design recommendations based on the technological strengths and limitations of current Machinima tools. Finally, we conclude with a summary of our contributions and findings.

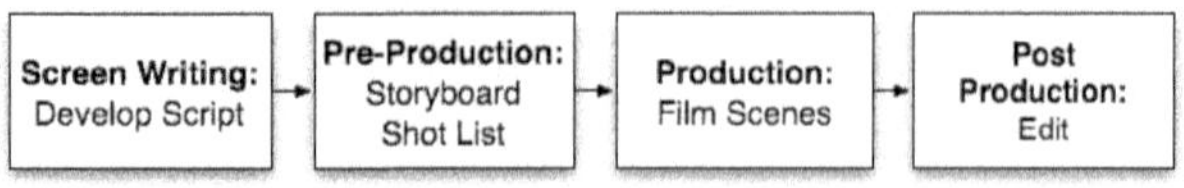

Figure 1: Traditional Film Process

BACKGROUND

Historically, the technological development of Machinima has been traced back to the early hacker and demoscene [19] and the practice of game modding and demo recording. Lowood traces the history of Machinima and identifies the video game *DOOM* as being a critical catalyst in its development [10]. Id Software, developers of the *DOOM* engine, allowed gamers to make modifications, or 'mods' of the main game. A community of practice evolved as hackers shared their experiences and manipulations [1]. This included manipulations of so-called demo files that allowed players to record and play back gameplay in the game engine. Using these demos, players started making recordings to demonstrate their skills, which eventually led to the narrative based Machinima productions that many people are aware of today.

Early on Machinima was recognized as an emergent form of play [15] and artistic practice that evolved from a game-like activity. Game companies realized the potential in crafting a cinematic piece from a gameplay-based engine. *Stunt Island* (1992) – a pioneer engine for Machinima creation – offered little more than a staging ground for virtual stunts that could be "filmed" from a range of variable perspectives and shared with other players. The game's very design makes the distinction between "play" and "filmmaking" difficult. In parallel, players seem to easily move between both worlds. Many of the first Machinima production groups evolved from player communities, such as the ILL Clan or The Rangers, who are credited with the first narrative Machinima. The concept of video game play as a creative practice evolved as games became more accepted as cultural artifacts; examples include play as sport and performance [1, 11, 14]. While the growing role of Machinima as evolving art form in a community of practice is noted, little research is available regarding *how* the specific conditions of Machinima support new forms of creativity.

Because the history of Machinima is closely tied to game engine development like the evolution of their visual capabilities and available editors, one can learn from work on tool development, that reflects the evolution of expressive range in Machinima [7]. But a technologically deterministic approach like this lacks an analysis of the underlying cognitive effects at work during the production of a Machinima movie. Without denying the role of technology, tools, and Machinima as a socio-cultural phenomenon, this paper focuses on those neglected aspects.

Machinima differs from traditional uses of Computer Graphic Imagery (CGI) animation in film. CGI animation in film mirrors the traditional filmmaking process of extensive planning and production to deliver a final moving image. In CGI, the rendering process can take a very long time and mistakes are costly. Consequently, in CGI and other traditional film techniques, a process called *storyboarding* is used to plan out films. Storyboarding is the use of descriptive drawings and sketches that depict how shots in a scene should appear. A storyboard helps to optimize the production process as it includes which characters are in a shot, as well as camera perspective and shot distance, which define which part of the film set need to be prepared. To minimize the final cost of rendering, scenes have to be planned in detail, which leads to a linear production cycle like that represented in Figure 1.

Large film productions using Computer Generated Imagery (CGI) have used Machinima as a method of rapid and low-cost pre-visualization [9, 15]. As a pre-visualization tool, Machinima is a cheap way to quickly evaluate scene configurations and technical decisions before full CGI rendering is committed to. Developing CGI movies is a high cost and time consuming activity. Machinima provides an interactive, robust, and rapid pre-visualization tool that minimizes the risk during the actual production. As such a tool, Machinima provides a new form of film pre-production that combines playful exploration with shot planning [15]. But for a pure machinimators, this process constitutes not a phase of pre-production but the core creative activity. Machinimators work continuously on the final render image as they re-adjust their visuals. This constitutes a principle difference in production. We argue that this difference is reflected in the creative engagement.

RELATED WORK

Distributed Exploratory Visualization builds off two key cognitive models: Distributed Cognition and the Geneplore model for creative cognition.

Distributed Cognition considers cognition as a feature of the larger context in which humans exist, including environmental conditions, socio-cultural practices, and technological artifacts [5]. Cognition is embodied and situated [19], which means that thought and action are dynamically coordinated through interaction with one's environment. This ability is leveraged when humans restructure their environment to aid cognition, such as spatially arranging important notes so they are immediately visible. In this example, a memory task is restructured into a visual representation, changing the nature of the task from remembering to interpreting a spatial representation. In this way, representations are propagated through different mediums to facilitate and optimize cognition [5].

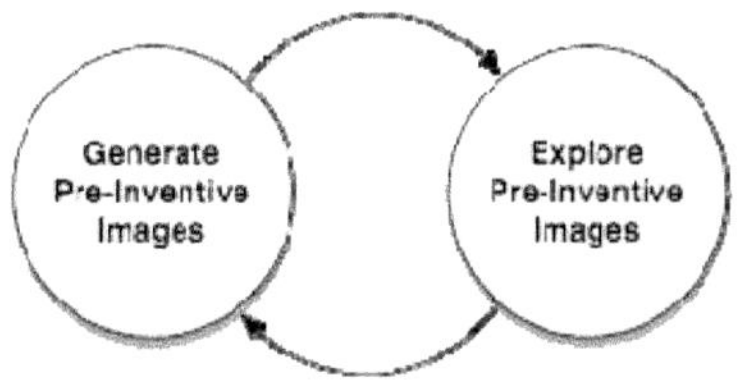

Figure 2: Geneplore Model of Creativity

Kerne and Koh [6] developed the *Distributed Creative Cognition* framework to describe creative cognition as a system distributed among social collaboration, tool use, and mental operations. These researchers used distributed creative cognition to analyze a creativity support tool called combinFormation [6]. With this tool, users construct and manipulate a composition space containing visual images generated through iterative searches and semantic grouping procedures. The system employs an intelligent online search to find items to stimulate new ideas. The researchers conclude "the mixed-initiative capabilities of procedural generation and human manipulability of visual information representation in the composition space support distributed creative cognition and situated creative learning" [6]. Users report being able to make new connections and think about concepts in different ways after being able to see and manipulate concepts in their composition space. Distributed Creative Cognition does not provide a specific account for the cognitive processes underlying creative thinking.

Finke et al. [2] developed the creative cognition approach to study cognitive mechanisms underlying creative process. The Geneplore model of creative cognition describes creativity in two basic phases where individuals generate vague ideas and refine these mental constructs through exploration. In the generation phase, the creative thinker generates what Finke et al. refer to as pre-inventive structures, which include visual patterns, object forms, mental blends, category exemplars, mental models, and verbal combinations. Pre-inventive structures are explored through specific mental operations in the next phase.

The Geneplore model proposes that creative cognition cycles between these two phases to gradually refine the initial pre-inventive structure (See Figure 2). As one explores the pre-inventive structure, the initial idea is updated, and the cycle continues until a satisfactory result is reached. Below we will argue that machinimators report a similar process whereby they generate vague mental images and gradually refine these images by exploring them using their Machinima tools.

However, Geneplore does not account for the fact that, for machinimators, a large portion of the creative process is distributed between the system and the self. For example, concepts and ideas are explored through the capabilities of the tool, which provide additional information with which to make informed evaluations. To remedy this shortcoming, a new framework is proposed that considers creative cognition as distributed across mental operations and the technological tools used throughout the creative process.

STUDY DESIGN

In our study, we used qualitative data collection methods to perform an exploratory study about the creative practices of machinimators. We conducted five semi-structured interviews with professional level machinimators lasting approximately one hour each. We define a professional machinimator as one who has had a significant impact on the Machinima community, including film awards from the community, important roles in organizing community events, publishing books, and holding classes and workshops. A questionnaire was distributed before the main interview to control for experience. The questionnaire addressed issues such as how many films they had released, how many hours per week they spend per week making films, and how long they have been a filmmaker.

The interviews were conducted over Skype in all but one case where the participant was present in person. The first half of the interview centered on the general creative processes and motivations for developing Machinima films. These questions included details about creative experiences before Machinima, the Machinima environment they typically use and limitations they often face, and the planning and preparation process used when creating films. This section was meant to identify the overall creative strategy of the individual and understand their intentions for making movies. What do they hope to achieve and how do they achieve this goal? How does the technology shape their efforts?

In the remainder of the interview, we conducted a film walkthrough of one of the participant's films using desktop sharing technology. During a walkthrough, the interviewer and director both watched the movie, and the director explained what he or she was thinking in each of the scenes. The movie was paused at times to provide opportunities to elaborate on certain elements. The filmmaker would point out any technical difficulties s/he had with the tools in trying to make specific scenes. We were particularly interested in the technical means employed to achieve a sense of narrative and emotion in their films. Technical methods in consideration included how the filmmakers used scriptwriting, storyboarding, camera, lighting, sound design, set design, staging and directing performance, editing, and special effects to achieve their goals. All interviews were video recorded.

Because of the lack of empirical work on the creative practices of machinimators, it was important to conduct an exploratory study to accurately assess the creative processes of these digital filmmakers, which included their often rather varied attitudes and interpretations of the tools they use. We analyzed the transcript data using Grounded Theory [3], which is a flexible and robust approach to data-driven theory building. Grounded Theory encourages iterative hypothesis generation and adaptive data collection methods that are updated based on new research questions. In this approach, analysis coincides with data collection, and transcript data is coded into categories. The features and relations of these categories help form hypotheses to systematically explain the data.

As interview data were analyzed, we introduced new questions into the subsequent interviews to gather more data about hypotheses emerging in our Grounded Theory, while other questions were eliminated due to irrelevance. Questions that were introduced include those about specific filmmaking skills and strategies for developing films, such as: What aspect of filmmaking are you most confident in? How do you handle a problem in a domain with which you are inexperienced? What are your favorite and least favorite aspects of making movies with Machinima? How much of the story do you typically have worked out before you start, and in what form does it exist (i.e. mentally, story board, text, etc.)? These questions helped us understand the creative process of machinimators in relation to the specific toolsets they use.

Grounded Theory originated as a method in sociology to provide a systematic and uniform approach to study qualitative data. The human centered movement in Computer Science has recognized the inherent power of such a method in understanding how users engage with technology. For example, Grinter et al. [4] used Grounded Theory to understand the social and technical dynamic of software development teams. Grounded Theory yields an explanatory framework that serves to elucidate central features of the domain in question. It has become especially relevant to Human Computer Interaction and its related disciplines that investigate how users interact with systems. Findings from Grounded Theory can lead to design recommendations that support naturalistic interaction.

RESULTS

The results of the study are organized around four categories that emerged as central to Machinima filmmaking. These categories are (1) mental images, (2) creation, (3) exploration, and (4) evaluation. The remainder of this section will go into detail explaining each of these categories, cross-referenced with the data collected from the interviews. To ensure the anonymity of filmmakers, we have coded the filmmakers with letters A-E.

Mental Images

The content of mental images used to create films vary depending on the current intention, creative practice, and task of the filmmaker. The most basic dimensions along which mental images vary are their level of abstraction and the extent of their precision. The visualizations of filmmakers contain different levels of narrative abstraction that vary along a spectrum ranging from the most abstract global structure of narrative events, to less abstract individual scenes, and finally to concrete features in those scenes. The content of the mental image in each of these layers of abstraction can be more or less determinate. A machinimators might have a clear image regarding the setting and lighting of a shot but that image might lack details in staging and framing, for example. Precision varies along a spectrum from none, to a vague requirement, and finally to a more precise object or element that is fully represented in the mental image.

Examples from each of these two dimensions will help elucidate the distinction. The most abstract types of mental images are those that pertain to the entire narrative. Usually developed in the beginning of the creative process, these ideations may include some sort of notion about the order of critical narrative events and the overall aesthetic style for the movie. Filmmaker A, for example, defines a general notion for a kind of style s/he wants for the movie:

> A: I remember seeing some videos of *Unreal 2003* and some of the stuff there looked just photorealistic to me back in the day. But still I felt like that never really translated to animation, and so very early on I decided that it would be really important to have a layer of abstraction

Filmmaker A has certain parameters for the way s/he wants the film to appear, but these are rather vague. In reality, s/he defines what *not* to do rather than explicitly stating what to do. This is an example of an abstract mental image that provides a set of guidelines of imagistic requirements rather than one specific value. The director goes on to describe the process by which s/he started working:

> A: It's not that I actually wrote it down. It's just that I had this thing in my idea, and I had an idea, and I had some pictures in my head, and I just started working.

The environment in which the machinimator is working can also influence aesthetic style. Oftentimes, directors want to the push the capabilities of a game engine and impress their audience.

> B: The entire series was constructed from the start because I knew I wanted to make a fancy film from the Neverwinter Nights engine as an experienced Machinima creator.

> C: Shadows hadn't really been used this way in Moviestorm before this movie as far as I know...I just thought that was artistically quite nice, and it was a bit more creative than just having the camera on the main characters.

These aesthetic motivations set up an overarching aesthetic priority that is applicable to the entire narrative. However, this priority does not mean one specific thing; it is a vague notion of a general way they want the movie to look.

Mental images of a particular scene are less abstract than overarching narrative images. Filmmaker C describes a method for approaching the production of a scene:

> C: For the scene I will sometimes have in my mind like the money shot basically. There will be one particular point in the scene I want the camera to be low looking up and a close up of the guy's face and it's going to

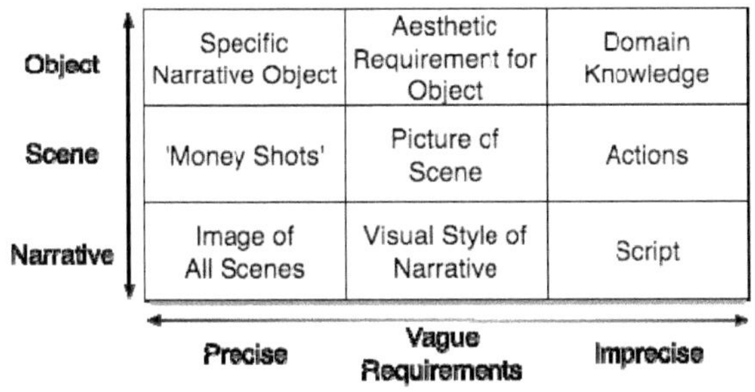

Figure 3: Properties of Mental Images

> zoom behind him and we'll see someone come through the door, so I'll have it in my mind quite clearly that there's going to be certain angles and scenes that I'll be looking to play out, but I don't, I certainly don't draw it on paper or anything like that because I'm not really terribly good at drawing.

In the filmmaker's mental image, s/he is focused on an individual scene with a relatively high level of precision because s/he is actually picturing individual shots and what is included in those shots. The most concrete type of mental image is that which is focused on individual objects in a scene, and even this type of mental image can have imprecision. For example, filmmaker D became concerned about the lighting in a particular room, which led to the inclusion of a candle in the room.

> D: Something that's always bugged me about TV in particular... somebody would turn off the lights and you'd see these other lights come on because obviously they can't have it pitch black, so there's these other lights that don't emanate from anywhere, its just the set lighting kicking in. Even when I was a kid I jarred by that...it just reminds you you're on a set...I wanted to have very little lighting in this set where lighting was very important to what I was going to convey. I wanted the light to have a source, and I figured after what just happened in this room, the guy is not going to have all the lights on, he's not going to have all the lamps turned on, but there has to be light coming from somewhere, so the candle is just what was available and seemed like the good way to go.

In this case, the individual's mental image consisted of a vague requirement for one concrete aspect of a scene, namely the lighting. There was a certain way that D wanted the lighting in particular to behave. The mental image contained a guideline of what a solution should look like, and after checking what was "available" in the game; a candle was deemed a proper solution.

Figure 3 depicts how the properties of mental images vary along the dimensions of narrative abstraction and precision. When mental images are precise, they deal with concrete visual qualities, while the imprecise end of the spectrum are visually barren and corresponds more to the verbal and procedural information specified in the story.

Creation Practices

The capabilities of the video game engine do not always align with the desires of the machinimator. As a result, they often face technical difficulties in trying to craft elements of their film. These problems can arise from limitations in the tool itself, or a lack of knowledge about either the tool or film practices.

The game engines used to create Machinima films are often poorly documented. Online forums have grown up around each of the game engines, but the knowledge generated on these forums is fragmented and incomplete.

> E: Knowledge can be a funny thing within the Machinima community because it will be that half the people will know something and the other half don't. And the half that know it don't know that the other half don't. It just seems normal and natural to them. And that's a feature of being self-taught...if you are self-taught you don't know what the bases are, and you don't know if you've missed them.

The fragmented knowledge can be traced in part to the way in which problems are solved during Machinima creation. If the solution to a problem is unclear, directors translate that problem to a domain they do know in order to solve it. This is accomplished through what has been referred to as a 'work-around' or 'hack.' Depending on the background of a director, s/he will revert to familiar techniques to try to solve unfamiliar problems.

> A: Whenever I encountered a creative decision problem, usually my first approach was: can I somehow work around it with the camera? Like can I hide it? Can I create [or] do editing in a way that conveys that?

It often turns out that these workarounds help overcome glitches or bugs in the video game engine itself. For example, character animations sometimes refuse to execute properly, resulting in characters moving through solid objects. As a result, the director will have to direct the camera away from the action at that point in order to hide the bug. Although each of these scenarios represents an individual case, the filmmakers have generated heuristics for approaching technical difficulties, and these methods usually rely on a familiar skill based on their knowledge of the 3D engine that is applied in a creative manner.

Exploratory Practices

The Machinima environment is used as a tool to experiment with and play with different ideas because of the real time rendering capabilities of the game engine.

> E: One of the really appealing things about Machinima is that you can experiment quickly...you don't have to wait to see what you've done in many things.

Being able to explore scenes encourages a sense of play, which impacts the overall creative practices of these directors. From the outset, the directors have a playful attitude in which they experiment and explore in order to develop their ideas. This is in sharp contrast with the practice of storyboarding in conventional filmmaking. Storyboarding is the use of descriptive drawings and sketches that depict how shots in a scene should appear. Filmmaker C describes how he plays around and experiments with different ideas for sets in the beginning of his process as a replacement for storyboarding:

> C: I don't storyboard it really, although…before I've got the script I've got an idea as to what the film is about, I'll quite often play around in the software and build a few tests, sets sometimes. Usually, in fact, they don't make it into the final movie, but they let me play around if I've got an idea for how I want to use new textures or a different lighting, or a different way maybe of framing shots with the camera. I'll play around and from that I'll get an idea of what's going to be possible in the movie.

Exploring scenes in this way has the potential to facilitate emergent creativity. The game engine allows one to see the scene in a way that cannot be imagined. There is no way for the mind to actively hold all the details of a scene in a conscious image [8] and perform the kind of movements that the Machinima tools do. Thus, filmmakers often make creative discoveries by exploring the scenes in real time.

> E: The way that the camera pans in under that beer tap, again, that was just a happy coincidence because originally the camera wasn't there… it was when I was building this set and I was getting the other beer tap ready I suddenly caught an angle, and I just thought that beer tap looks fantastic with the light just on one side around the actually pump and it just looked really good. So that gave me an idea that actually what I should do is start off close up around the tap and then move down the bar to show the characters… had I story boarded this in any detail I probably wouldn't have had this shot because it wouldn't have occurred to me. Its more like having built this set its kind of like I'm now starting to look around the set that I've built and think of how I might actually use it.

Filmmakers C and E explored the set to refine their ideas of how the scene should appear. The sets provide a good mechanism by which to simulate different possibilities for the final film and in production quality. It is used as a tool to think. One may even say that they are using the game engine as a kind of temporal sketching mechanism to work out visual concepts and moving image ideas.

Evaluation Practices

Exploring scenes in real time also enables directors to evaluate these explorations in real time. Cinematic ideas such as camera movements and cuts can be rapidly tested and evaluated on the screen. It is very beneficial to the creative practices of these individuals to receive immediate feedback on the decisions they make in the Machinima environment.

> E: I always find being able to see something is very useful…the kind of what you see is what you get is one of the things I really like about Machinima. That's kind of different from the classic CGI where you have to imagine what you're going to get…Being able to adjust things in real time, so you can just move something and change it, so you can see what the difference is, that seems to be a theme for me, in the most popular tools that people use.

Explorative evaluation of this nature can reveal tensions that require solutions. Broadly speaking, tension can come from an aesthetic or narrative discrepancy between what appears in the picture in the mind and what appears on the screen. Filmmaker C describes how the set that was created as a reference to the original *A Clockwork Orange* (1971) does not align with the narrative s/he has crafted:

> C: The reveal of the characters, of this gang, wasn't working at all. In *A Clockwork Orange* …the opening scene…we see them in this nightclub and…the camera pulls back and we meet Alex and so I was trying to an extent recreate that without it being a direct copy and so I had this nightclub and I had all of the characters and lots of space in it, and I just thought, ya know what, In this dystopian world I'm working in, which isn't the same as… *A Clockwork Orange*, you wouldn't have nightclubs you would have little run down grotty little places…I think I felt *as I watched what I was working with it just didn't fit with the story* and so that was the source of my dissatisfaction. So it didn't matter what sort of camera pans and zooms or whatever I did, I just wasn't getting the result I was happy with, and so I just thought I just tore it up and started again with this new bar.

This example elucidates a situation in which there are both narrative and aesthetic discrepancies. At the scene level, the author has a clear idea that s/he wants the set to look like the bar scene from *A Clockwork Orange*. When the scene image was only present in his/her mind, s/he was not able to realize it conflicted with the goals of his/her narrative. However, s/he realized there was a problem once the scene was built because s/he was able to look around the final virtual set, evaluate it and realize that 'it just didn't fit with the story.'

C employs the typical creative exploration techniques of playful manipulation to try to overcome what s/he thinks is an aesthetic discrepancy. 'Hacks' and manipulations, such as tweaking the camera pans and zooms, can help to work-around aesthetic discrepancies. However, in this case s/he noticed the more fundamental problem once the entire set was built. The problem was a narrative discrepancy between the set and the overarching narrative. It was only after s/he he 'watched what [s/he] was working with' that it became apparent that there was an actual narrative discrepancy. Even after this was realized, there was a

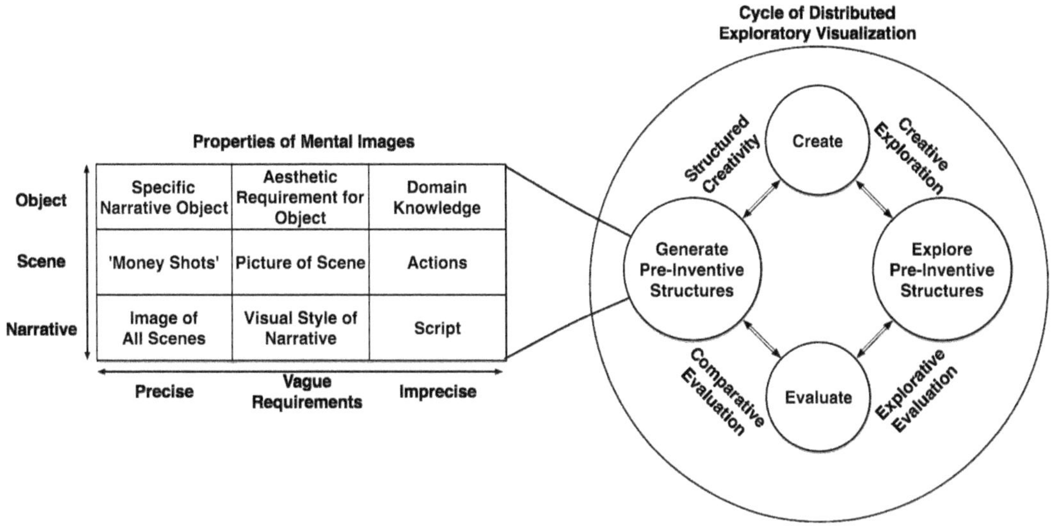

Figure 4: Distributed Exploratory Visualization in Machinima Filmmaking

general reluctance to restart the entire set because so much time and effort had already been invested in this set.

DISTRIBUTED EXPLORATORY VISUALIZATION

Machinima offers immediate feedback on any creative choice made. This distinguishes it from other forms of traditional filmmaking. The real time rendering offered in Machinima supports distributed creative cognition by encouraging ideas to be developed through exploration and evaluation inside the tool. The data reveal a cyclical pattern in the creative process of machinimators in which they generate vague mental images and explore those images by playing and experimenting with their tools.

Psychological theories of the creative process, such as Wallas' Stage Model [21] of creativity (preparation, incubation, illumination, and verification) do not account for the technologically mediated aspect of creativity this study reveals. Specifically, the data reveal a cyclical pattern in the creative process of machinimators in which they generate vague mental images and explore those images by playing and experimenting with their tools. We explain our results through a new framework Distributed Exploratory Visualization, which elaborates on distributed creative cognition [6] with an account of creative cognition inspired by the Geneplore model [2]. Our model is unique in that we consider a practice-based and emergent creative process in a pragmatic context.

Our findings show that the immediate feedback and rendering offered through video game engines has made on-the-fly evaluation more practical than elaborate pre-planning. In Machinima, we see evidence of situated cognition and action, whereby plans are dynamically developed and updated on the fly [17]. In this context, situated action leads to serendipitous creative discoveries.

Instead of planning scenes out in detailed sketches, machinimators describe a process in which they begin their projects by developing a script and creating mental images of scenes and refine them throughout the production. Machinima software supports this creative process because the indeterminate features in the mental image can be defined by playfully exploring the scene. The filmmaker may rapidly navigate through the scene using various camera positions and angles, lighting, and staging. In fact, the fluidity with which scenes are explored has led to creative discoveries that may have been overlooked if scenes were explicitly defined in storyboards. In other words, ambiguity has led to an increase in creative potential, which agrees with an assertion in creative cognition that states that ambiguity in pre-inventive structures often promotes creativity [2].

Mental images are cyclically generated and explored by playfully engaging the video game engine. In this context, the Machinima tool can be used to think about and elaborate vague images generated in the mind of the filmmaker. It is not necessary to painstakingly articulate each detail before a scene is shot. Thanks to affordable real time 3D engines, more effort can be spent evaluating the aesthetic value of a final scene configuration. Moving around the scene and interacting with lighting and camera settings can provide additional resources to help evaluate the aesthetic quality and narrative accuracy of elements in a scene. As a result, real time play and on-the-fly decision making have become central elements to the creative practices of successful machinimators.

The Geneplore model of creative cognition accounts for the generation and exploration component of creativity, but it does not consider how creating things in the real world affects the creative process. As a result, the Geneplore model has been expanded to consider the distributed properties of creativity. Filmmaking requires the use of external representation, and in Machinima we see a scaffolding of tools to rapidly generate and test various permutations of scene configurations. To account for the importance of externalizing mental content and evaluating that content, two additional components have been added to the Geneplore model: creation and evaluation.

Our model, Distributed Exploratory Visualization, has four central processes, structured creativity, creative exploration, explorative evaluation, and comparative evaluation (see Figure 4). Each of these processes will now be presented in detail.

Structured creativity

Structured creativity is the creation of elements in the Machinima environment based on the director's envisioned outcome. It is a goal-directed activity that strives to make the images on the screen match the image in the head of the author. The system has rules and limitations that constrain which objects can be created and how those objects will act within a scene. Additionally, the author may be lacking the knowledge or skill required to achieve some goal. In this stage the author uses the resources available to him/her to create an object based on a desired goal. Difficulties in this phase are typically technical in nature and are often solved through a work-around.

> D: When I engaged the animation to have him turn around and open that door…it did this weird thing where his body like twisted and went down through the floor, just a bizarre bug, and I couldn't fix it without scrapping the whole scene, so I decided ok I'm just going to start in just a little bit tight, and I'm going to let the sound tell the story of him opening the door, and the mind fills in that gap, and it ended up working out just fine.

Instead of directly solving the technical difficulty, the problem was translated into the domain of camera and sound, and D employed a solution that would implicitly achieve the same narrative effect.

Creative Exploration

Creative Exploration occurs after some form of an object has been created in the Machinima environment. Although the Machinima environment can be restrictive in some respects, such as a limited array of objects and animations, it is incredibly rich in others, such as texture details, nuanced lighting schemes, a robust physics engine, and many camera angles. These tools can be adopted to help the object in consideration match the intended goal of the user.

> C: If I'm not getting the results on screen that I want then I'll start playing around with the lighting…because you can totally change the feeling of a scene by repositioning the lighting, changing the intensity of lighting, adding multiple light sources

This part of the creative process is distributed between the mind of the individual and their interaction with the tool. New ideas can emerge while playing around with the configurations of a scene. While creatively exploring the possibilities offered by the tool, directors may actually make creative discoveries, such as new camera angles or a new use for a familiar feature. For example, A discovered an emergent feature in the game engine *Unreal Tournament* that ended up significantly impacting the rest of the movie:

> A: I noticed that with the particle system in *Unreal Tournament*, and this was going a long way in my future work…you can attach it to a moving object, so that the particles stay static but the object moves, so basically what you do is that you have the object paint its way down.

Exploring the physics engine enabled a creative discovery that would have been overlooked if the process were not flexible and open to creative exploration. The same is true when D created a set and discovered a new camera angle by looking around in the scene. Creative discoveries are made possible because the filmmaker's creative process balances vague requirements and creative explorations that refine and add to mental images.

Explorative Evaluation

Explorative evaluation is an evaluative process in which the real time rendering capabilities of the system are used to navigate through a scene to gain additional information, therefore helping to make a more informed evaluation. Mental images can only contain so much detail [8]. However, when the scene is visually present, the filmmaker is able to gain useful information that provides a clear idea about how the final image is going to look.

> E: The actual messing about when you're in it, the creative play element, where you can immediately see what you've done and whether it works or not. I think a lot of people really find that is one of the biggest things that really appeal to them about this way of working. You don't have to wait and see what you've done in many things.

Whereas creative exploration had the intention of experimenting with the tool in order to create, explorative evaluation uses camera angles and positions to navigate in a scene and to gather more information for evaluation of the aesthetics of the image. The immediate feedback offered through Machinima tools enables rapid evaluation.

Comparative Evaluation

Comparative evaluation is a different type of evaluation in which the current object is compared to mental images residing on different levels of narrative abstraction. It is largely a mental activity, but it draws upon the information gathered through explorative evaluation. An element created in the virtual studio may be aesthetically appealing, but it could very well conflict with the overall goal of the scene or narrative, like when C created an entire set only to find out it did not match his narrative.

DESIGN RECOMMENDATIONS

The Distributed Exploratory Visualization model describes how machinimators rely on their tools to creatively explore, evaluate, and refine vague mental images. As such,

Machinima tools should strive to keep the cost of creative exploration and explorative evaluation as low as possible. The cost of exploration and evaluation is proportional to the amount of time reqiured to create an element in the Machinima environment because something has to be created on the screen before it can be explored and evaluated. The quality of the evaluation increases with the detail of the object being created.

When creating an element, evaluation tends to be focused on the aesthetics of the element itself, rather than how it relates to the larger narrative. This is especially true in long creation tasks such as sets and custom objects and animations. In these cases, a significant amount of time elapses before the element can be explored and compared to overall narrative. For example, Filmmaker C had to build an entire set before s/he realized it did not mesh with the feeling of his narrative.

The cost of creating a scene should be kept as low as possible to encourage rapid production and a low cost of complete restart in the early stages of the creation process. Machinima productions often use pre-build scenes provided by the game developer, but the cost of creating an entire scene can be very high. Committing time and resources to scene fabrication prevents a filmmaker from wanting to throw a scene away even though it simply does not work, and it also prevents rapid evaluation because the majority of a scene has to be built in order to accurately and effectively evaluate it. A system that aims to support creativity in digital filmmaking should offer possibilities to help rapidly and automatically prototype a very rough sketch of a scene. The user should be able to set some parameters to generate a rough scene very quickly so as to encourage evaluation early on in the creation process for a particular item.

The different types of mental images, namely those focused on the narrative, scene, or individual object, are connected in interesting ways. Narratives are composed of many scenes, which have a pluarity of objects within them; each layer is interconnected and depends on the next. Scenes and objects are ealuated with respect to the overall narrative, but these aspects sometimes require a multi-step process to create because they contain many pieces. Multi-step processes that do not provide immediate exploration and evaluation are more likely to cause a narrative discrepancy. It is not that multi-piece elements (such as scenes or complex objects) are more likely to conflict with narrative structure, but rather that more work has to be done on these objects before they can be evaluated with respect to the global structure of the narrative, which means that mistakes are not realized until late in the creation process. In terms of Distributed Exploratory Visualization, these multi-step creation processes require more time for the 'create' part of the cycle because each element that is created contains other components that also have to be created, and so on, as seen in Figure 5.

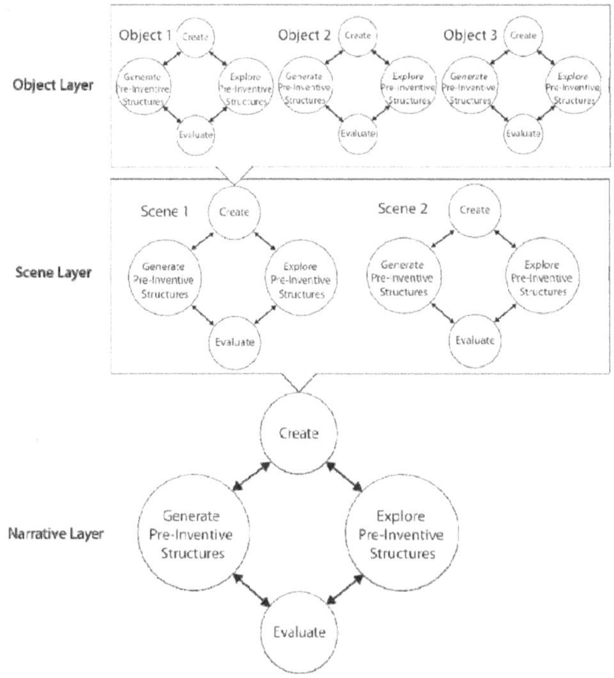

Figure 5: How layers of narrative abstraction affect Distributed Exploratory Visualization

Intra-layer problems are usually aesthetic discrepancies between a desired mental image and the image present on the screen. These problems can typically be resolved through technical means such as the workaround solutions generated through creative exploration and subsequently evaluated through exploration. However, inter-layer problems are more serious and can represent a conflict with the narrative, which can be harder to detect and also harder to resolve. The chances of having a narrative discrepancy increase when an object cannot be evaluated early in the cycle to determine whether the idea aligns with the goals of the overall narrative. The multi-step creative process described above plays one part in this, but there may also be another contributing factor.

The mental images at the narrative level have no actual representation in physical reality besides in the scenes or the script in most Machinima production. There is no high level visual breakdown of the scenes. Traditional film production techniques use storyboards to visually define the structure of a film, and they can also be used as an evaluation reference throughout film production. Real time manipulation has replaced this function and revolutionized the creative process of digital filmmaking, but in the process, it may have also contributed to the discrepancy of narrative abstraction. This issue could be resolved through a high level virtual sketch of the narrative structure that includes support for multi-modal scene description, image manipulation, and creative exploration.

Machinimators describe the prime benefit of the medium as the immediate feedback and real time support for decision-making. Therefore, the most important design recommendations are those that maximize the relevance of immediate feedback. This can be accomplished through lowering the cost of exploration and increasing the fluidity of evaluating different narrative layers.

CONCLUSIONS

Based on a Grounded Theory analysis of the data collected during our interviews with expert machinimators, we have presented a critical reading of some creative practices at work during Machinima development. Modifying Geneplore's approach, we have developed a model of Distributed Exploratory Visualization. Within this process, player/ producers craft the final features of the film by constantly exploring and evaluating their interaction with the game system.

Whether the individual feature was planned or emergent, elements added to the scene are evaluated by exploring how they interact with the rest of the scene. Evaluation is intermixed with creation – mental imagery with digital crafting (in this case 3D modeling). As the filmmaker explores the scene, new perspectives and ways of interpreting the scene evolve. These new interpretations of the scene alter the pre-inventive structure, which in turn changes the parameters by which elements are evaluated. Distributed creative cognition illustrates the way in which creative exploration and explorative evaluation are intimately connected.

Following our research with machinimators, we see a close connection to Machinima's unique capabilities that support this creative cycle and can trace this cycle to an expanded version of the Geneplore model. This form of playful creative exploration of the final artifact through digital technology can be seen as a form of digital crafting. As Machinima provides this exploration for the moving image, it serves as a unique example platform for creativity in digital filmmaking that can and should inform traditional filmmaking.

ACKNOWLEDGMENTS

This work was supported by the National Science Foundation under Grant No. IIS-1002748. We would also like to thank the machinimators for their time and insights.

REFERENCES

1. Cameron, D. and Carroll, J. Encoding liveness: Performance and real-time rendering in Machinima. *Proceeding of DiGRA 2005 Conference: Changing Views-Worlds in Play*, (2009), 1-9.
2. Finke, R. A., Ward, T.B., Smith, S.M., *Creative Cognition.* MIT Press, Cambridge, 1992.
3. Glaser, B. Strauss, A., *The Discovery of Grounded Theory,* Aldine Transaction, New Brunswich, 1967.
4. Grinter, R.E. Decomposition: Putting It All Back Together Again. *ACM Conference on Computer Supported Cooperative Work*, (1998), 393-402.
5. Hutchins, E., *Cognition in the Wild.* MIT Press, Cambridge, 1996.
6. Kerne, A. and Koh, E. Representing Collections as Compositions to support distributed creative cognition and situated creative learning. *New Review of Hypermedia and Multimedia 13*, 2 (2007), 135-162.
7. Kirschner, Friedrich "Toward a Machinima Production Studio" in: The Machinima Reader, eds. Henry Lowood and Michael Nitsche (MIT Press: Cambridge, MA 2011), 53-71.
8. Kosslyn, S. M., *Image and Mind*, Harvard University Press, Cambridge, 1980.
9. Lehane, Scott. July 2001. "Unrealcity: ILM Creates Artificial Cities for Artificial Intelligence." Film and Video 18(7).
10. Lowood, H. Found Technology: Players as Innovators in the Making of Machinima. *Digital Media*, (2008).
11. Lowood, Henry. 2007. High-Performance Play: The Making of Machinima. In *Videogames and Art*, edited by G. Mitchell and A. Clarke. Bristol, UK: Intellect Books.
12. Marino, Paul. *3D Game-Based Filmmaking: The Art of Machinima*. Scottsdale: ParaglyphAnderson, 2004.
13. Nitsche, Michael, 'Film live: And Excursion into Machinima' in: Developing Interactive Narrative Content: sagas_sagasnet_reader, ed. by Brunhild Bushoff (Munich: High Text, 2005), 210-243Conger., S., and Loch, K.D. (eds.). Ethics and computer use. *Commun. ACM 38*, 12 (entire issue).
14. Nitsche, Michael. 'Games as Structures for Mediated Performances,' in *Logic and Structure of the Computer Game*, ed. by Stephan Guenzel, Michael Liebe, and Dieter Mersch (Potsdam: University Press, 2010).
15. Nitsche, Michael. "Experiments in the Use of Game Technology for Pre-Visualization," in *Proceedings of Futureplay 2008*. Eds. Bill Kapralos, Mike Katchabaw, and Jay Rajnovich. New York: ACM, 2008. 160-66.
16. Salen, Katie. 2002. Telefragging Monster Movies. In *Game On. The History and Culture of Videogames*, edited by L. King. London: Laurence King Publ.
17. Suchman, L. *Human Machine Reconfigurations: Plans and Situated Actions.* Cambridge University Press, Cambridge, 2007.
18. Suwa, M. and Tversky, B. What do architects and students perceive in their design sketches? A protocol analysis. *Design Studies 18*, 4 (1997), 385-403.
19. Tasajärvi, Lassi. 2004. *Demoscene. The Art of Real-Time.* Helsinki: evenlake studios.
20. Varela, F.J., Thompson, E., Rosch, E., *The Embodied Mind.* MIT Press, Cambridge, 1993.
21. Wallas, G. *The art of thought.* New York, Harcout, Brace, and World, 1926.

Using Semantic Similarity to Predict Angle and Distance of Objects in Images

Sterling Somers
Institute of Cognitive Science, Carleton University
1125 Colonel By Drive, Ottawa, ON K1S 6B6 Canada
sterling@sterlingsomers.com

Jonathan Gagné
Dept. Systems Design Engineering
University of Waterloo
200 University Ave West
Waterloo, ON N2L 3G1 Canada
jgagne@engmail.uwaterloo.ca

Cesar Astudillo
Universidad de Talca
Facultad de Ingeniería
Departamento de Ciencias de la Computación, Km. 1
Camino a los Niches, Curico, Chile
castudillo@utalca.cl

Jim Davies
Institute of Cognitive Science, Carleton University
1125 Colonel By Drive, Ottawa, ON K1S 6B6 Canada
jim@jimdavies.org

ABSTRACT
A presentation of an Artificial Intelligence (AI) called Visuo that stores and guesses quantitative visual-spatial magnitudes (e.g., sizes of objects). In this analysis, Visuo is used to store polar (angle and distance) relationships between objects in images. It uses a database of tagged images as its memory and approximates unexperienced magnitudes by analogy with semantically related concepts. This shows the transferring of information from high semantically related concepts yielding significantly higher accuracy in angle and distance estimations over using medium or low semantically similar items.

Author Keywords
Creativity, imagination, visualization, analogy.

ACM Classification Keywords
I.2.0 General---Cognitive simulation

I.6.4 Model Validation and Analysis.

General Terms
Theory.

INTRODUCTION
Human visual imagination is an incredibly complex cognitive phenomenon. Imagining a scene draws on our memory to populate the scene with relevant scene objects in varying fidelity. Recent evidence suggests further that the same brain regions involved in vision are also involved in visual imagination, suggesting that we in fact, in some sense, see the products of our own mind [5, 7]. When imagining a scene intended to mimic the real world, the creative process has to produce objects of an appropriate colour, size, *et cetera* to fit the intended context of the scene. Imagined scenes are populated with the right kinds of objects for the intended context. Furthermore, how objects in an imagined scene relate to each other spatially is typically determined realistically. For example, when imagining a bird in the sky, such a scene might also involve secondary objects such as trees, the ground, the sun, among others. All elements included in the scene will have spatial relationships to each other. In an image of such a scene, the bird in the sky will be an appropriate angle and distance from the trees, while the trees will be an appropriate angle and distance from the sky and the ground, and on it continues until all objects are spatially related to each other.

Our theory is that visual imagination exploits regularities in experience. When we imagine a realistic scene, the visual-spatial properties of that scene end up being the way they seem because that is how they occur to us through our experience. Grass is on the ground, trees are above the ground, and the sky is above the trees; and that is how we experience them. When we take photographs, these regularities get stored digitially (see Figure 1). We propose that an AI designed to perform human-like imagination can exploit the visual-spatial information contained in digital photographs to inform the visualization of imagined scenes.

There are times, however, when we might want to imagine a scene containing objects in contexts we have never experienced them in. Extrapolating from the example above, perhaps the imagined bird in the scene is a raven. Although you have never seen one outside of a bird identification guide, you know, more or less, what a raven looks like. You might know that crows, which are often seen, are very similar to ravens. Could an analogy relating ravens to crows be used to fill in the details of our imagined scene with the raven? Apart from looking similar, crows are likely to have similar spatial relationships to trees and the other elements of the scene. Would the same likely hold true if the analogous object was less similar? Would any bird have similar spatial relationships? Would any animal?

C&C'11, November 3–6, 2011, Atlanta, Georgia, USA.

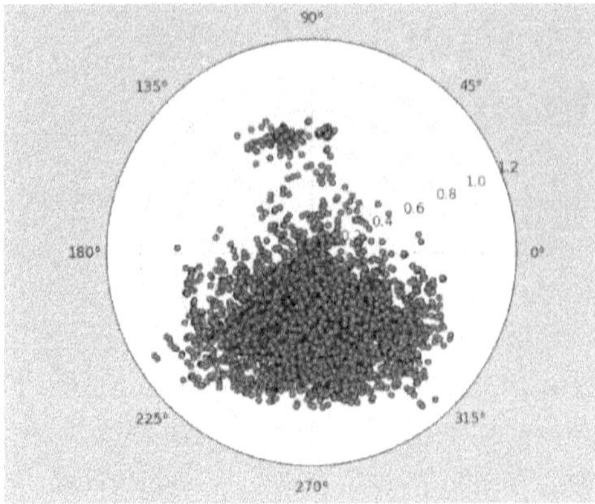

Figure 1. 'tree-grass'. To interpret this picture, consider the centre to represent 'tree'. Each dot represents an instance of the relationship between 'tree' and 'grass' in our image database. As expected, the grass appears below trees in most cases.

This paper presents an extension to a Python program, Visuo, intended to model visual-spatial instantiation [2,5]. Shown already to predict sizes of analogous objects when using size modifying adjectives (e.g., 'large'), for the present work, Visuo has been extended to store angles and distances. This paper will provide an answer to the above questions by evaluating Visuo's storage of angle and distance relationships between two objects of high, medium, and low semantic similarity. We hypothesize that the spatial relationships between items of high semantic similarity will approximate a target relationship with greater accuracy than those of medium or low semantic similarity.

VISUO

Visuo is a program written in Python intended to be a model of memory for quantitative data, and as a model for re-instantiating quantitative information from known priors as well as using analogy to instantiate quantitative information for cases that have not been experienced. For example, Visuo has been shown to predict the size of target objects, such as *large raven*, when it had information on *raven* sizes but not the target *large raven*. Having data on the size of one object, say all ravens, data on a semantically similar object, say the size of crows, and data on the size of the same semantically similar object with a linguistic modifier, such as *large crow,* Visuo was able to predict the size of a *large raven* [2].

Visuo implements two phases: a training phase and a visualization phase. While previous papers have addressed both phases, this paper is primarily concerned with the training phase and comparing the results thereof. While we have developed a method for instantiating spatial relationships, this method remains largely untested. Therefore, our discussion of theory will be limited to the assumptions and processes of the training phase.

Visuo is trained by reading text files with numerous entries. In this particular application of Visuo, the text file describes spatial relationship data (angle and distance) between object pairs. For example, a single entry could be for the spatial relationship of a raven to a tree, consisting of a description, "raven <relationship> tree"; a value for angle, "angle=27.45"; and a value for the distance between the two items, "distance=200.43". Each entry read by Visuo is called an 'experience,' Angles are measured in degrees and distances are percentages of a picture divided by 100. For example, the distance of 200.43 is approximately 2% of an image away. All angles and distances used to train Visuo were taken from images of uniform size.

Training

Visuo implements two types of memory: episodic memory and semantic memory. Exemplars, Visuo's implementation of episodic memories, represent memories of objects occurring at a specific place and time [12]. As Visuo's episodic memory is not involved in the present analysis, we will concentrate on its semantic memory.

Semantic Memories are memories of general concepts abstracted from specific instances [11]. When Visuo experiences a relationship for the first time both an episodic and a semantic memory are formed. With every following instance of the same general relationship, new episodic memories are formed, and the semantic memory is modified, with the new information being incorporated with the old. Semantic memories in Visuo are called prototypes.

Distribution of Fuzzy Set Membership

While Visuo experiences precise quantitative values, the precision is not stored in semantic memory. Behavioural data show that people represent with graded membership in categories [9]. To account for this, each perceptual detector in Visuo represents using fuzzy-set perceptual categories. In fuzzy set theory, the membership of an instance in a given set is described with a fuzzy membership value ranging from 0 (clearly not in the set) to 1 (clearly a member of the set). In the present analysis, Visuo employs a category set for distance and a category set for angle. For a relevant example, a *crisp* input of "10" becomes a vector of membership values in for a set of *fuzzy* number categories [4]. We will describe what exactly these numbers are in the following subsections.

Every crisp number gets distributed as a member of all fuzzy number categories to *some degree.* Membership degrees are represented by a real number between 0 and 1. For example, a crisp number 10 would have a high membership in a fuzzy number set 8, and a lower membership in a fuzzy number sets for 2 and 15. *Fuzzification* is the process of transforming a crisp number to a fuzzy number. A separate distribution is created for each distance and angle pair.

Representation of Distance

Dehaene, et al. [3] provides evidence that people naturally (without educational intervention) represent distance logarithmically. Therefore, Visuo uses a 15 point, approximate logarithmic scale (0, 2, 5, 10, 20, 35, 65, 100, 160, 150, 400, 600, 900, 1350, 1800) as categories for distances. The fuzzy categories have overlapping ranges and input values will be distributed across relevant categories. For example, a distance of 10 (1% of a picture in distance) would be represented as the vector (0.0, 0.0, 0.67, 1.00, 0.33, 0.0, ...). Each value in that vector represents a membership in the fuzzy number set described above.

Representation of Angle

Huttenlocher, Hedges, and Duncan [10] provide evidence for the use of polar coordinates (angle and distance) as well as angular categories in object location estimation. Visuo uses a 16-point scale with 22.5-degree intervals for estimating angle (180, 157.5, 135, 112.5, 90, 67.5, 45, 22.5, 0, -22.5, -45, -67.5, -90, -112.5, -135, -157.5). Similarly, the fuzzy angular categories have overlapping ranges, with values distributed across relevant categories. For example, an angle of 45 degrees is represented by the vector (0, 0, 0, 0, 0, 0.5, 1.0, 0.5, 0, ...). Each value represents degree of membership in the fuzzy number sets (e.g., 0.5 membership in 22.5-degrees set).

Incorporating New Data

Visuo creates a prototype for each tag pair (e.g., tree-grass). For each novel prototype experienced, Visuo creates a fuzzy distribution for distance and a fuzzy distribution for angle. Instead of creating a new vector for angle and distance, for each repeated tag pair, Visuo incorporates the new data into the old. When a new example of a previously experience tag pair is observed, each fuzzy membership number in the distribution is replaced by a recursive average:

$$v_{avg} = \frac{(n * v_{old}) + v_{new}}{n + 1}$$

where v_{old} is the previous value, v_{new} is the new value, and n is the number of experiences. Following the calculation of v_{avg}, the count n is increased by one. For each fuzzy number in the vector, the prototype represents the mean value of the membership for exemplars for the corresponding fuzzy number. In this way, the prototype represents and average of all experiences. For example, there would be a prototype storing a distribution representing all of the angles ever experienced between a tree and grass.

Inferring Missing Data Through Analogy

While Visuo uses prototypes to instantiate visual descriptions of scenes, it need not rely on exact matches in memory of the intended visualization.

When data is missing from Visuo's experience, it will use analogy (in this case, semantic similarity) to approximate the desired data. For example, in the database used in the present analysis (see below), there is no instance of a raven above grass in Visuo's experience. If Visuo is asked to visualize a raven above grass, instead of reporting that no data is available, it will find the closest semantically related item to one of the targets and use that data as an approximation. Visuo uses the Wu-Palmer similarity measure [14] as implemented in NLTK version [1] of WordNet [8]. The Wu-Palmer similarity measure is squared to help bias for similarity.

EVALUATION

Data

The Peekaboom [13] image database is a database with point clouds and tags for elements in the images. We used approximately 50,000 images from the Peekaboom database and mined approximately 200,000 unique spatial relationships, for both angle and distance between tagged item pairs. We used the centroids of the point clouds as an indicator of the location of each tagged element. The database uses images from the internet, including photographs, advertisements, drawings, etc. It was not filtered.

Of the ~200,000 unique spatial relationships (tag pairs), we chose to work with the 100 pairs with the largest number of instances to maximize the number of data points per tag pair. These top 100 spatial relationships are called the target pairs. Of each target pair, the first tag is the static tag and the second the dynamic tag. To determine semantic relatedness, the static tag remained the same and the dynamic tag was replaced. For example, with the pair *grass-raven*, 'grass' would be the static element while a suitable match, based on semantic similarity, would be found for 'raven'. Using the data from our database, 'crow' has the highest similarity to raven and the prototype of *grass-crow* would be used as the source concept for the analogy.

After selecting the target pairs, three test replacements for the dynamic targets were found and sorted into groups of **high** (Wu-Palmer similarity^2 0.7 – 0.9), **medium** (Wu-Palmer similarity^2 0.34 – 0.69), and **low** (Wu-Palmer similarity^2 0 – 0.33) similarity. The new targets were selected to maximize the degree to which they represented their group: maximizing similarity for the high group, maximizing closeness to the middle for the medium group, and as dissimilar as possible for the low group. A minimum of 25 data points was required for replacement tags to be included.

	Mean Membership Difference, High Semantic Similarity	Mean Membership Difference, Medium Semantic Similarity	Mean Membership Difference, Low Semantic Similarity
Distance Membership	0.0377	0.0685	0.0971
Angle Membership	0.0634	0.0924	0.1159

Table 1. Mean fuzzy membership difference for high, medium, and low semantic similarity groups.

Procedure

For each of the 100 target pairs, Visuo was trained on all the pairs and the vectors for angle and distance for each pair were stored in text files. The training was conducted across two different computers, utilizing 2 CPUs on each computer. Due to a file-reading error resultant from the attempted concurrent use of a single database file, 1 target pair was excluded from the present analysis. Thus, a total of 99 target pairs, resulted in 4 (target, high, medium, and low) × 99 = 396 training sessions. Each training session produced one distribution for angle and one distribution for distance, resulting in 792 distributions.

If our hypothesis is correct, the predicted angles and distances between the elements of each target pair should be closest to the actual angles and distances when analogizing from the high-similarity group, and furthest when analogizing from the low-similarity group. The medium-similarity group's accuracy should fall somewhere in between.

Results

Angle

The high-angle group was a significantly better approximation than the medium-angle group (Wilcoxon test, $z = -10.77$, $p < .01$, $r = -1.08$). The low-angle group was also significantly worse than the medium-angle group ($z = -8.34$, $p < .01$, $r = -0.84$). The high-angle group was also significantly better than the low-angle group ($z = -18.62$, $p < .01$, $r = -1.87$).

For statistical analysis, data was grouped on a per-test-pair basis. For each test pair, categories for distance were coded 1-15, allowing us to group each logarithmic distance category for each test pair. Likewise, categories for angle were coded 1-16, categorizing the angle categories. Because the present analysis is aimed at testing how well pairs in the different groups approximate the target pairs, differences between the target and high, target and medium, and target and low pairs were calculated. Figure 2 illustrates a comparison for target, high, medium, and low groups for one sample target pair. Table 1 contains a summary of the mean differences across membership vectors for all 99 item pairs. While the mean differences may seem small, recall that the 0-1 range is distributed across 15 items and 16 items for distance and angle, respectively. For perspective, the average membership for the target pair in the angle group is 0.125 and the average membership for the target pair in the distance group is 0.130. An average difference of 0.1159 (see Table 1) is larger than it might initially appear without this perspective. As shown in Table 1, the mean membership decreases (increasing difference) as semantic similarity decreases.

Distance

Wilcoxon tests between the high-distance group and the medium-distance group revealed that the high group was significantly more accurate than the medium group, ($z = -10.73$, $p < .01$, $r = 1.08$). The low-distance group was also significantly less accurate than the medium-distance group, ($z = -7.43$, $p < .01$, $r = 0.75$). The high-distance group was also significantly more accurate than the low-distance group ($z = -15.96$, $p < .01$, $r = 1.67$).

Discussion

The results above are very encouraging as a preliminary analysis into the use of analogy to supplement spatial relationship data. Moreover, they are particularly promising when one considers the sources of error and variance.

The first source of error comes directly from our data. Due to the nature of the Peekaboom data collection (point cloud creation), the point clouds around the elements in a picture are inexact. Furthermore, the outside boundary (convex

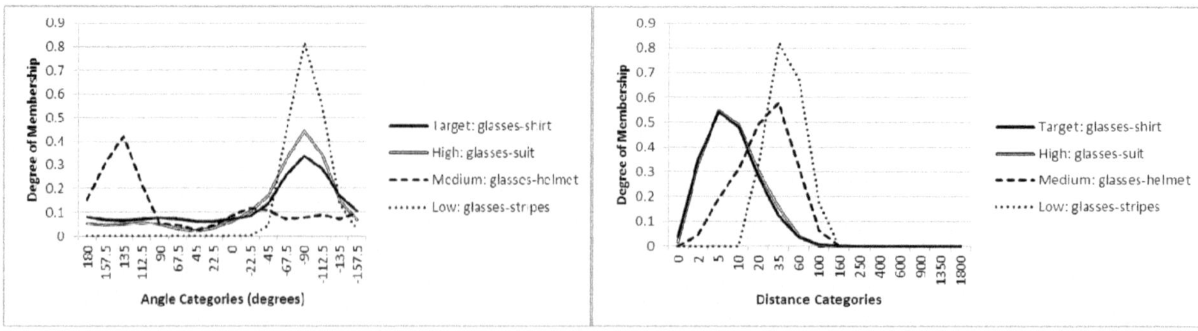

Figure 2. Angle (left) and distance (right) vector comparison for target pair *glasses-shirt*.

hull) of point cloud may not perfectly outline the tagged object it is meant to identify. These point clouds were used to calculate a centroid and therefore, the larger the error in the point cloud, the larger the error in the centroid.

Secondly, due to availability of data, there was a good deal of variance in the precise similarity values within a group. For example, there are instances where tag pairs that have a high degree of semantically similar are at the lower bound of the high category and medium semantically similar items are at the upper bound of the medium category, which results in items with similar semantic similarities to the dynamic target. Although our results suggest that this source of variance is acceptable in the present analysis, future work will address this issue to maximize semantic similarity. In this future analysis, we would expect a close approximation of the target group by items restricted to some minimum semantic similarity. That said, there are still a number of data filtering issues yet to resolve.

One issue yet to resolve is the use of centroids as specifying an object's location. Using centroids is a simple approach in determining an object's location but can be misleading in terms of data extraction. For instance, in an image where a bird appears in the sky, the centroids become meaningless as the sky surrounds the bird. More complex relationships such as 'in' will require specific detectors that go beyond angle and distance.

CONCLUSION

Human visual imagination is an important and largely unaddressed problem in the cognitive sciences. While creating computer programs that can combine multiple experiences to produce imagination-like scenes presents an intriguing software engineering problem space, creating programs that can create scenes in novel and realistic ways goes beyond that and begins to explore the nature of creativity. Our running theme throughout this paper has been to advocate the use of analogy to apply semantically related data to visualizations otherwise impossible for an AI to instantiate. While one AI approach to our problem space is to get larger and larger databases, we aim to adopt more human-like solutions.

We have shown in this paper that using high semantic similarity is a plausible candidate for analogical visual-spatial reasoning. By showing that high semantic similar items more closely approximate angle and distance data than do medium or low semantic similar items, we have given reason to investigate this use of analogy further. For instance, an appropriate next step would be to determine what minimal degree of similarity is required for analogous relationships to reliably approximate their targets. Furthermore, qualitative analyses on the distributions such as the ones in Figure 1 has suggested that there is perhaps some form of categorizing possible for the spatial relationships as some distributions seem ideal for visualization, while other distributions appear flat.

The work that has been presented here represents a module in a much larger project of simulating visual imagination. As discussed in the introduction, knowing how elements in a novel image should be organized spatially is an essential step in having AIs capable of producing realistic scenes. Also part of our aim is to explain how human imagination works. It is our hope that by implementing a model of imagination, that the model can act as a tool for guiding the scientific inquiry into the nature of human imagination.

Visuo, we expect, will be at the heart of our imagination model. Visuo itself represents a theory about how we learn certain concepts and relationships, and how we store and retrieve quantitative data. Visuo does not explicitly make rule-based concepts such as 'trees are always above the grass.' Instead, rules that capture the regularities of experience emerge as an average of experience. The cluster of dots in Figure 1, for example, provide compelling qualitative evidence that at least some concepts might emerge that way. That some method of storing and retrieving quantitative data is required for visual imagination is obvious, whether the theory behind Visuo holds is yet to be seen. While in the present study we have validated the approach of using semantic similarity to supplement a database, we are also carrying psychological experiments to determine if humans use similar approaches when approximating data.

REFERENCES

1. Bird, S. and Loper, E. NLTK: The Natural Language Toolkit. *Proceedings of the ACL demonstration session*, (Barcelona, Spain, 2004), Association for Computational Linguistics, 214-217.
2. Davies, J. and Gagné, J. Estimating quantitative magnitudes using semantic similarity. *Twenty-Fourth Conference of the American Association for Artificial Intelligence workshop on Visual Representations and Reasoning* (Atlanta, GA, 2010), 14-19.
3. Dehaene, S., Izard, V., Spelke, E., and Pica, P. Log or Linear? Distinct Intuitions of the Number Scale in Western and Amazonian Indigenous Cultures. *Science, 320* (5880) 1217-1220.
4. Dubois, D. and Prade, H. Fuzzy numbers: an overview. in J.C. Bezdek *Analysis of Fuzzy Information Vol. I: Mathematics and Logic*, CRC Press Boca Raton, 1987, 3-39.
5. Gagné, J. and Davies, J. Visuo: A model of visuospatial instantiation of quantitative magnitudes. *Knowledge Engineering Review. Special Issue on Visual Reasoning*, forthcoming.
6. Kosslyn, S. M. Image and Brain: The Resolution of the Imagery Debate. MIT Press, Cambridge, 1994.
7. Miyawaki, Y., Uchida, H., Yamashita, O., Sato, M., Morito, Y., Tanabe, H. C., Norihiro, S. and Kamatani, Y. Visual image reconstruction from human brain

activity: A modular decoding approach. *Neuron, 60* (5), 915-929.

8. Fellbaum, C. *WordNet: An Electronic Lexical Database.* MIT Press, Cambridge, 1998.
9. Hampton, J. A. Typicality, Graded Membership, and Vagueness. *Cognitive Science, 31* (3), 355-384
10. Huttenlocher, J., Hedges, L. V., and Duncan, S. Categories and Particulars: Prototype Effects in Estimating Spatial Location. *Psychology Review, 98* (3), 352-376.
11. Rosch, E.H. Natural categories. *Cognitive Psychology, 4* (3), 328-350.
12. Tulving, E. Précis of Elements of Episodic Memory. *Behavioral and Brain Sciences, 7,* 223–268
13. Von Ahn, L., Liu, R. and Blum, M. Peekaboom: A Game for Locating Objects In Images. *Computer-Human Interaction Conference*, (Montréal, Canada, 2006) 55-64.
14. Wu, Z. and Palmer, M. Verb semantics and lexical selection. *32nd Annual Meeting of the Association for Computational Linguistics*, (Las Cruces, New Mexico, 1994), 133-138.

Understanding Exploratory Creativity in a Visual Domain

Kyle E. Jennings,[1,2] Dean Keith Simonton,[2] and Stephen E. Palmer[1]
Departments of Psychology
University of California, Berkeley (1)
University of California, Davis (2)
kejennings@ucdavis.edu, dksimonton@ucdavis.edu, palmer@cogsci.berkeley.edu

ABSTRACT

This paper describes a computerized aesthetic composition task that is based on a "creativity as search" metaphor. The technique collects detailed, moment-to-moment data about people's search behavior, which can help open the "black box" that separates independent variables that influence creativity from their outcomes. We first describe the technique and provide a detailed theoretical framework. Then, we discuss how the technique is typically applied, describe several in-progress studies, and present some preliminary results. Finally, we discuss relations to other work, limitations, and future directions. We argue that this technique and the research that it enables will facilitate a deeper understanding of the creative process, become a valued tool for creativity researchers, and contribute to methodological and theoretical advances in how creativity is studied and understood.

Author Keywords

creativity, search, optimization, experimental methods

ACM Classification Keywords

J.4 Computer Applications: Social and Behavioral Sciences—*Psychology*

General Terms

Experimentation, Measurement, Theory

BACKGROUND

The creative process can be thought of as the search for an ideal solution to a problem. One way to understand creativity is to understand this search process. This paper describes an under-development research technique that is based on the "creativity as search" metaphor. By capturing detailed information about the moment-to-moment progress of a person's creative search, this technique can both test models of creativity as search, and enable more detailed studies of common phenomena in the creativity literature.

C&C'11, November 3–6, 2011, Atlanta, Georgia, USA.

Search can either be seen as finding a path from a starting state to a valid end state, or as finding the best (or nearly best) solution from among many others. The former case, which we call *path* search, is relevant when the desired outcome is known but the way to reach it (the path) is not (e.g., proving a mathematical theorem), and has been studied extensively [19, 20, 22]. The latter case, which we call *place* search, applies when the desired outcome (the place) is unclear but the means for achieving it are relatively straightforward, such as when an artist arranges a still life or composes a photograph. Particularly given that the creativity of artists depends more on these early decisions than on the execution of these decisions [10], this research focuses on how people select the desired outcome from among competing alternatives.

In open-ended domains like the arts, choosing what outcome (or solution) to pursue is seldom a simple matter of deciding among a few choices. Instead, the set of possibilities is too vast to be considered simultaneously, meaning that searchers must iteratively consider subsets of the space. How people control this iterative process can be called a *search strategy*, and includes considerations such as how people move from one subset to another, and how people evaluate each solution. Though search strategies might be an important determinant of how creative the final solution is, they are not directly observable. However, if the options under consideration at each stage can at least partially be observed, it becomes possible to trace how people move through the space of possibilities over time. This *search trajectory* offers clues as to what kind of search strategy people use.

We have developed an experimental paradigm that can efficiently capture detailed information about people's search trajectories in a visual domain. Using this technique, we aim to determine:

- what can be learned about people's search strategies from their search trajectories; and,
- whether differences in solution creativity can be traced to differences in search strategies.

We also aim to apply our technique to better understand broader questions, such as how personality and situations affect people's creative processes. Our technique should help open the creative process "black box" that sits between the independent and dependent variables in much of this research.

NEED FOR A NEW INSTRUMENT

Satisfying the above aims requires a research method that can track people's search trajectories. Because studies of personality and situational influences require large samples, this method must be economical to apply. Existing methods cannot satisfy both of these requirements [15], leading to the development of the present technique.

Structure of Present Technique

Our technique centers around a computerized aesthetic composition task. In this task, participants see a picture with several three-dimensional objects. They can manipulate the picture by changing the placement of the camera or the light source, both of which are on fixed orbits around the objects (see Figure 1). The moment-to-moment positions of the camera and light constitute the search trajectory. Because the objects reflect and refract the light, the task is more complex than it first appears (see Figure 2 for examples). Though we will eventually add more control dimensions, the current two-dimensional trajectories are easily plotted, which is helpful as we check our quantiative metrics against our visual intuitions.

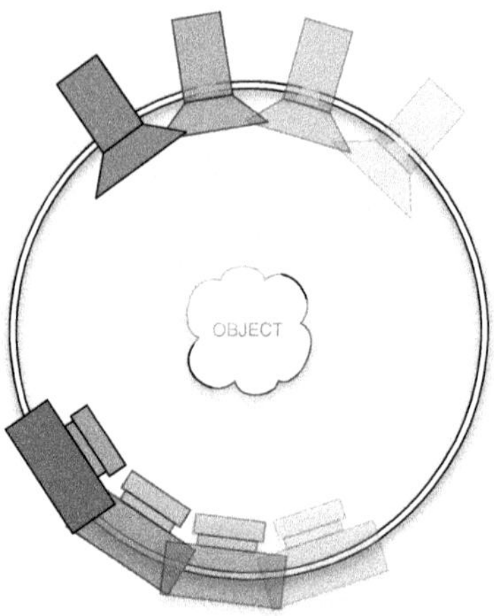

Figure 1. Illustration of camera and light configuration.

Relation to Creativity

Our task is similar to what an artist or photographer must do when composing a still life painting or photograph. Just as paintings and photographs will vary in their creativity, our participants' final images will vary in their creativity. While our task is not as open-ended as its real-world analog, participants still have latitude in how they interpret the goal (e.g., what "harmonious" or "artistic" means in the context of the scene), and in how diligently they search for an ideal configuration. We believe that our task encompasses more of the creative process than insight or divergent thinking tasks, and that the loss in ecological validity relative to tasks used with holistic assessment or protocol analysis is outweighed by the gains in precision, consistency, and accuracy.

THEORETICAL MODEL: OPENING THE BLACK BOX

A great deal of creativity research can be thought of as inputting a problem into a creative process "black box" and analyzing the final solution. Our tool expands this chain to encompass *problem* → *creative process* → *search trajectory* → *solution*. However, the process that produces the trajectory is still unknown. In order to make inferences about the process, we will first expand our model of the problem, and then consider the nature of the process more thoroughly. (See Figure 4 for the complete model.)

Search Landscapes and Landscape Topology

Our software allows transitions to adjacent camera and light positions, but not large jumps. Therefore, we can imagine the search process using the metaphor of a hiker traversing mountainous terrain, which we will call a *(search) landscape*. The hiker's longitude and latitude correspond to the camera and light angle of the current view, and the hiker's elevation corresponds to how well the resulting image satisfies the search goal. Finding the best camera and light angles becomes analagous to finding the highest point on the landscape. However, dense fog limits visiblity and the hiker has no map, making nearby elevation changes the only way to navigate.

Landscape Fogginess and Blind Variation

Using the landscape metaphor, consider how problem structure will influence strategy choice. Suppose that the landscape is covered in such thick fog that there is zero visibility. In this case, the hiker must actually move to a new position in order to determine the landscape's shape. Which direction to travel would largely be a matter of guesswork, leading to many false starts and a meandering trajectory. If instead the fog were very light, the hiker could move deliberately toward higher terrain, resulting in a more direct trajectory.

The above two strategies vary in how "blind" or "sighted" their transitions are, a distinction introduced by Campbell [6] and further elaborated by Simonton [26, 27, 29] and others [21, 23, 31]. Countering the idea that creators always move deliberately toward their final solution, this *Blind Variation and Selective Retention* (BVSR) theory suggests that human creators often make progress by blind trial and error.[1] Domains differ in how much "blindness" there is to the creative process, which may be inversely related to how constrained the domain is [28]. Artistic domains, which are much less constrained than scientific or engineering domains, are likely to involve a lot of blindness. For example, studies of Picasso's sketches for his painting *Guernica* show that they do not move monotonically toward the final painting [8], suggesting a trial and error component to his method.

Several things affect the "fog", and hence expected variational blindness, in our experimental task. Scenes may vary in how much images at nearby perspectives or nearby light angles resemble each other, or in how easy it is for participants to imagine how the image would look from a different perspective without actually seeing it. Even if it is

[1]Blindness is different than randomness. A variation process is blind if a desirable variation has as much chance of being produced as an undesirable variation. Thus, both "brute force" processes (trying each variation in order, as in a radar sweep), and purely random processes are blind, but not all blind processes are random. [30]

Figure 2. A variety of views from our most commonly-used scene.

easy to imagine the image itself, people may have a harder time evaluating an imagined image when given one goal (e.g., "harmonious") than another (e.g., "aesthetically composed"). We can also reduce fogginess via the software interface by providing previews of images at adjacent camera and light angles.

Landscape Ruggedness and Blind Retention

BVSR theory assumes that creators make variations blindly, but that desirable variations are selected deliberately. This may not be an optimal strategy, as illustrated by the landscapes in Figure 3. In the landscape on the left, the hiker can simply move uphill and be confident that the point where every adjacent step goes downhill is the best. In the landscape on the right, a hiker using this strategy might stop at the top of a molehill (called a local maximum) rather than the tallest mountain (the global maximum). We will use the term *rugged* to describe a landscape with many local maxima. How rugged a landscape is depends on the structure of the problem itself. A simple problem easily reveals the path to the best outcome and plays no tricks, whereas a hard problem tempts people toward decent outcomes, but hides the best outcomes.[2]

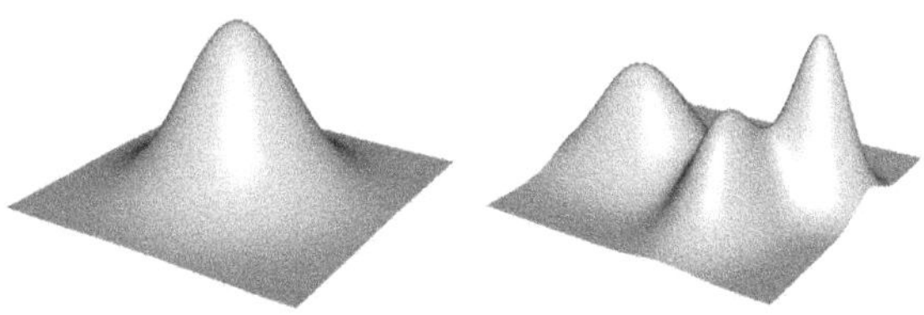

Figure 3. Smooth (left) and rugged (right) landscapes.

To understand how creators might move past local maxima, we can look at numerical optimization algorithms in computer science. Many optimization problems have numerous local maxima. Whereas algorithms that are guaranteed to find the global maximum are often prohibitively slow (not just mildly—their execution time grows exponentially with the problem size), several strategies have been devised for moving past inferior local maxima and toward higher maxima. Most of these strategies, known as *metaheuristics*, work by adjusting the algorithm's balance between *diversification* (exploring a broad range of solutions) and *intensification* (incrementally improving the current solution) [4].

Campbell's theory of blind variation and selective retention assumed that only the variation process was blind. However, metaheuristics work by making blind retentions as well. That is, they sometimes retain changes that make the solution worse, the aim being to facilitate movement away from a local maximum and toward a higher maximum. (These decisions are blind since the downhill moves are not guaranteed to lead toward higher maxima.) We expect to find similar dynamics in human creative search, allowing us to broaden Campbell's theory to encompass both blind variation and blind retention.

Inclusion of Landscapes in the Model

Knowing the structure of the search landscape helps us make stronger inferences about people's search strategies. We can measure landscape fogginess on a per-participant basis by having participants rate a target image, and then predict their ratings for (unseen) adjacent images. These predictions can be compared to actual ratings, collected later. We can also assess landscape ruggedness using a broad sampling of ratings from each participant.

We can now expand our model to include landscapes (see Figure 4). We first note that problem structure depends on the search interface, the goal, and the scene, all of which affect the ruggedness and fogginess of the search landscape, and all of which we control. These features of the search landscape, as well as the interface itself, should influence the search strategy that people choose, which should be reflected both in the search trajectory and the solution. We have good visibility into the search trajectory and partial visibility into the search landscape, and control the three aspects of the problem itself. This knowledge expands our ability to understand search trajectories, and to reverse engineer the remaining black box of search strategy.

Translating Goals to Criteria

Our model thus far assumes that people are able to directly and reliably evaluate the particular objective that we give

[2]The distinction between a rugged and smooth landscape is similar to Perkins' [24] distinction between reasonable problems and unreasonable problems, though Perkins' work deals with path searches (as in Newell and Simon, et al.) instead of place searches, as we are discussing here.

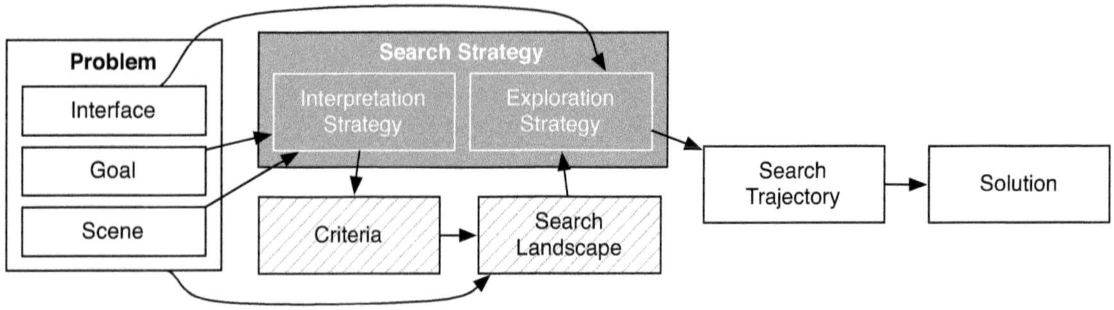

Figure 4. Illustration of theoretical model used in this research.

them. While this may be true with very concrete objectives (e.g., finding the brightest image), the objectives we more typically use are much more open-ended (e.g., finding the most artistic, harmonious, or captivating image), which means that the participant must decide how he or she wishes to interpret the objective. We call the high-level objectives that we give our participants *goals*, and refer to the concrete translation of goals into features of the scene as *criteria*. The criteria that people use are likely to vary across individuals, and even to evolve during the course of each individual's search.

To accommodate criteria, we expand our model in two ways. First, we note that people's search strategies will have two components: an *interpretation strategy*, which is how people translate goals into criteria, and an *exploration strategy*, which is how people move through the search landscape. Second, we note that we can ask people to describe their criteria in order to better understand both kinds of strategies. This is reflected in Figure 4. Thus, people engaged in our task are actually completing a dual-space search, encompassing a criterion space (how the goal is interpreted) and a solution space (the specific views of the scene). This is analogous to models of scientific problem solving [18] and permits creativity both in how the goal is interpreted, and in the specific solution that is found.

People's criteria help determine the shape of the landscape, and hence the difficulty of their search over solution space. One way that difficulty can increase is via conflicts between criteria. For instance, people may wish to find bright, symmetric images, but the structure of the scene may be such that the brightest images have a glare that detracts from the perceived symmetry. Such conflicts may emerge because the dimensions that people can control (camera and light angle) are irregularly related to the dimensions that people use to evaluate the image (e.g., symmetry and brightness). The difference between *control* and *evaluation* dimensions is analogous to the difference in genetics between *genotypes* (the genetic code for an individual) and *phenotypes* (characteristics affecting fitness). In genetics, *epistasis* refers to interactions among genes that lead to, say, the suppression of one gene's effect by the presence of the other. Just as epistasis complicates the course of evolution [17] we believe that our participants' task will be made more difficult via interactions and conflicts between control and evaluation dimensions. These interactions should complicate the search problem by introducing local maxima into the landscape [17, 1].

Model Summary

To restate our model (see Figure 4):

- We provide participants with a **problem**, which consists of a **goal** to be satisfied, the **scene** that they will use, and an **interface** that constrains what information is available and what kinds of changes can be made
- We can directly measure people's **solution** (their final image), as well as the detailed **search trajectory** that got them there
- We can partially measure **criteria** and **landscape**—partial because we may not be able to measure these things in their entirety, and may not be able to measure all changes to these things throughout the search
- From this information, we hope to make inferences about people's search strategies, which includes their **interpretation strategy** and their **exploration strategy**

Guiding our efforts to understand these strategies is the view that landscape **fogginess** and **ruggedness** affect the strategies that people use, which we believe will incorporate degrees of both **blind variation** and **blind retention**. Finally, an important determinant of landscape ruggedness is the degree of **epistasis** that exists due to the choice of criteria.

TYPICAL EXPERIMENTAL SETUP

Our typical experiment involves an exploration phase, a criteria description phase, and a landscape rating phase. The exploration phase comes first so that participants are unfamiliar with the scene as they attempt to achieve the given goal. The criteria description and landscape rating phases usually occur in the order listed, though in principle they could be reversed.

Exploration Phase

In a typical experiment, participants are introduced to the setup of the scene using a diagram like that shown in Figure 1. Then, participants become acquainted with the exploration interface using a trial scene. Following the trial, participants are given their goal and explore the target scene.

We have used various scenes. As each consists of a potentially infinite number of variations, we naturally must choose a subset. Our first experiment [15] used every combination of 90 evenly-spaced camera and light angles. We have used smaller subsets in other experiments, for two practical reasons. First, we have conducted some studies online, which limits how many pre-rendered images we can use (for instance, a low-resolution, 10 by 10 subset of our main scene requires seven megabytes). Second, in some experiments we later get ratings of all images in the scene, again placing an upper limit on the total number of images we can include.

We have used two kinds of exploration interfaces. The single-image interface presents one view of the scene, which participants can change by adjusting the camera and light angle through some control mechanism. In our first experiment [15], the controls were virtual "dials" that were manipulated with the mouse. Because this interface made people reluctant to switch between varying camera and light angle, subsequent experiments have presented a compass rose, where the north-south axis controls camera or light, the east-west axis controls light or camera, and the diagonal axes control both. This interface encourages more switching between dimensions, but is only suitable for smaller subsets. Recently, we have created a hardware controller with two physical dials that we hope will encourage frequent switching between dimensions (Figure 5). The controller also has up and down buttons, which we will eventually use to control a "zoom" dimension.

Figure 5. Hardware controller.

Our grid interface presents a three by three array of images. The center image is the current image, and the surrounding images are a single step difference in camera and/or light angle. In some cases, the adjacent images are obscured until clicked on. Participants then select a new "current" image by double-clicking one of the variations. This allows us to explicitly measure how people explore the neighborhood of the current position in the landscape.

Criteria Description Phase

At present, we measure criteria by asking participants to write open-ended descriptions of how they interpreted the goal. We encourage people to be concrete, referring to the camera and light angles, as well as the objects and visual features of the scene. To assist them in this description process, a slide show of a representative subset of the scene plays on the side of the screen as they are writing. We typically require participants to spend at least two minutes on this process. We also plan to develop a standardized, Likert-type questionnaire containing the most common criteria that people have mentioned in other studies.

Landscape Rating Phase

To measure the coutours of the search landscape (the elevation of each position, in our hiking analogy), we again have two techniques. Our first technique is to ask participants to rate a standard subset of images from the much larger set that is available (e.g., a 5 by 5 subset). In studies where participants are limited to a small subset of the space, we can get ratings of the entire space. Typically, participants are first shown a movie that cycles through all of the images in the subset for one second each, with smooth transitions in between. When practical, participants rate all of the images twice, in two different random orders. This allows us to estimate how reliably people can make the ratings, which we have found varies across goals.

Sometimes we may wish to have more detailed ratings for specific regions of the space. For instance, in our first experiment, we tabulated the amount of time each participant spent in various regions of the space, and determined the ten most visited regions. Then, participants were asked to rank and then rate each of these ten images. This technique allows us to look for features such as local maxima in the most relevant regions of the space. Our software can analyze people's search trajectories and select the appropriate images during the course of the experiment.

Technical Details

Our software is either written in the Processing language (for laboratory applications), or for modern web browsers using the jQuery library and an XML and PHP backend. Our hardware interface is based on an Arduino microcontroller. Analysis, including automated analyses done during the experiment, are performed using the R statistical software. Our stimuli are rendered using POVRay.

ANALYSIS TECHNIQUES

Our technique offers the mixed blessing of incredibly detailed data. This section provides a sampling of our ongoing efforts to develop a standardized analysis approach.

What is "Creative"?

Researchers generally define something as creative if it is both "novel" (meaning statistically rare) and "appropriate" (meaning that it adequately addresses the problem at hand). For each scene-goal combination that we use, we can measure novelty by keeping track of the relative frequency of different final points across studies. For appropriateness, creativity researchers generally use a permissive standard of only excluding outright inappropriate responses (e.g., answering "strawberries" when listing things that are blue). In our case, we can safely conclude that common solutions are unlikely to be inappropriate. For uncommon solutions, we have raters who are blind to study conditions determine whether the solution satisfies the given goal, and ask them to be open to metaphorical or unusual interpretations of the goal. Only if a solution fails by this standard will we exclude it. This being done, we operationalize creativity as statistical unusualness relative to norms that we are accumulating.

Characterizing Trajectories

At present, we characterize trajectories with aggregate metrics, such as the proportion of space explored, the average rate of exploration, the proportion of explored space that was revisited, the number of times that the trajectory doubles back (an indication of uncertainty), and so on. We also plan to use multivariate time series analysis in order to look at things such as changes in rate over time, which may indicate diversification and intensification. We are also examining how spatial trajectories are analyzed in zoology and other disciplines.

Coding Criteria Descriptions

We have developed a detailed coding language for translating open-ended criteria descriptions into standardized, embedded propositions. For instance "I liked images where the cone reflected on the sphere" would be translated as:

```
PRESENCE of[REFLECTION
     of[Scene/Objects/Cone]
     on[Scene/Objects/Sphere]] is(+)
```

In words, this translates to "the presence of a reflection of the cone on the sphere is good". We are developing a software tool to facilitate detailed analyses of these propositional representations. Our aim is to use this language to build a comprehensive map of the criterion space that people are exploring, as well as techniques for characterizing movement through this space. This effort is related to separate work we have begun on characterizing idea generation as movement through a semantic space [14].

Analyzing Landscape Ratings

We analyze landscape ratings with three objectives. First, we aim to see how reliably people can rate different goals, which we currently operationalize as the correlation between the two sets of ratings we typically collect. Second, we aim to see how consistently different people rate the same goal, which we currently measure with the Intraclass Correlation Coefficient [25]. Third, we are interested in how different one person's ratings are from other people's ratings, which we operationalize as the correlation between that person's ratings and the average ratings across all participants. We are also exploring more sophisticated measures that recognize differences in reliability across goals [3].

EARLY RESULTS

Our work on this project fits within four categories:

- Connecting Goal and Scene to Criteria, Trajectory, and Solution — this work will test the predicted connections between the observable parts of our model
- Modeling Exploration Strategies — here the goal is to "reverse engineer" people's exploration strategies using a combination of behavioral research and computer simulations
- Characterizing Interpretation Strategies — this aspect involves characterizing the nature of criteria change through the course of exploration, which will suggest questions for future research into interpretation strategies
- Application to Common Phenomena — here we apply the technique to common findings from the creativity literature (e.g., [11, 13, 2, 7])

Details of an earlier experiment can be found in [15]. In this section, we will discuss ongoing work and future plans in each of these areas.

Connecting Goal and Scene to Criteria, Trajectory, and Solution

There are many questions that can be explored by focusing just on the observable parts of the model (that is, without reverse engineering search strategies). This approach includes mapping how different goals are translated into criteria, determining how criteria affect search landscape topology, looking for specific landscape features such as ruggedness and epistasis, looking for evidence of diversification and intensification in trajectories, and connecting differences in outcome creativity to trajectory features, landscapes, and criteria choice.

Currently, we are analyzing data from a study that asked 40 participants to consider different goals and to (1) rate how well each of 25 images satisified that goal and (2) describe their criteria. We chose six different goals (including being "bright", which is more accurately a criterion in our nomenclature, and serves as a control) that are meant to vary the subjectivity of the goal and the complexity of the resulting criteria (see Table 1). We also varied whether people looked at our standard, "complex" scene (Figure 2), or a "simple" scene where the objects were opaque and less reflective. Table 1 shows the correlations among the averaged effectiveness ratings of the image subset for the different goals, and Table 2 shows the averaged test-retest correlation, intraclass correlation coefficient, and averaged spatial auto-correlation for the six goals over the simple and complex landscape.

	(1)	(2)	(3)	(4)	(5)	(6)
1. bright	.97	.51	-.73	.54	-.72	.23
2. aesthetic	.61	.90	-.01	.77	-.68	.77
3. artistic	.59	.55	-.10	.05	.47	.13
4. captivating	.95	.76	.70	.71	-.57	.55
5. convoluted	-.36	-.76	-.20	-.46	.64	-.70
6. harmonious	.37	.85	.19	.49	-.86	.91

Table 1. Correlations of averaged goal ratings with respect to different goals. Entries above the diagonal are for the simple scene, entries below the diagonal are for the complex scene, and entries on the diagnoal are correlations across the simple and complex scenes for the same goal.

Perhaps unsurprisingly, bright is universally the most reliable and agreed-upon goal, and results in the smoothest land-

		Bright	Aesthetic	Artistic	Captivating	Convoluted	Harmonious
Test-Retest	Simple	.91	.64	.36	.59	.49	.64
	Complex	.84	.67	.44	.63	.54	.74
ICC	Simple	.86	.08	.06	.00	.08	.14
	Complex	.72	.14	.02	.19	.10	.13
Spatial Corr.	Simple	.78	.28	.07	.28	-.01	.18
	Complex	.72	.23	-.02	.49	.14	.26

Table 2. Landscape statistics for different goals.

scapes. The other goals vary greatly in their reliability and smoothness, as well as in how distinct they are from each other. Interestingly, the simple landscape does not necessarily lead to more reliable ratings or smoother landscapes, which may in part be due to uncertainty about how to interpret some goals when the objects are all opaque. For instance, "convoluted" has a clear meaning in the complex scene, where the glass cone produces very distorted images, but may be harder to apply to the simple scene. We have coded the open-ended criteria descriptions from this study, and are currently analyzing them.

After we have created and validated a closed-form questionnaire for eliciting people's criteria, we plan to conduct a large-scale study to test the causal pathways implied by Figure 4. For instance, we expect to find that the originality of a person's solution is related to how different that person's search landscape is from the norm, which should itself be related to how unusual the person's criteria are.

Modeling Exploration Strategies

In our typical experiments, we expect both that criteria will differ across individuals, and that each person's criteria will evolve over the course of the search. This makes it difficult to reverse engineer exploration strategies in great detail. However, relatively objective criteria (e.g., brightest, most symmetric) show less evidence of change and are judged more consistently across participants. This allows us to use standardized ratings over the entire landscape to better understand each step of a trajectory. Though using objective criteria may limit creativity, it enables us to make stronger inferences about exploration strategies, which will provide a baseline for understanding how people approach more open-ended goals.

So far, our research has used the exploration interface that presents the current image and its eight neighbors. In such a setup, people's behavior can be described by the following algorithm:

$x \leftarrow$ random starting point
while stopping criteria not met **do**
  $N \leftarrow$ neighborhood of x
  $x \leftarrow$ select point from $N \cup \{x\}$
end while

Our goal is to understand how people choose a neighborhood, select the next image, and decide to stop. We ran two experiments designed to test whether people use a "hill climbing" strategy, meaning the greedy strategy of always selecting the best image in the neighborhood and stopping when the current image is better than all neighbors. In these experiments, the entire neighborhood was visible at all times. In our first experiment ($N = 24$), people looked for both the brightest and darkest images (order counterbalanced). Compared to simulations using a hill climbing algorithm, people's path lengths were longer, though their solutions fit with a hill climbing approach. We also found a great deal of variability in path length, but reasonable within-subjects consistency across searches ($r = .47$). We hypothesized that people were using a hill climbing algorithm, but evaluated images with error and varied in the size of neighborhood they considered. In the second experiment ($N = 24$), we first simulated a search for the most symmetric and asymmetric images, using algorithms that considered various neighborhood sizes, and made evaluations with error proportional to the variability of pilot ratings of each image's symmetry. The experiment's results matched the simulations in most regards, but we found that while our simulations predicted longer paths for the asymmetric goal than the symmetric goal (because the former was harder to evaluate), our data showed the opposite. We are running a follow-up experiment that requires participants to click on images in the neighborhood to expose them, which will explicitly test our hypotheses about variable neighborhood size and allow us to model stopping criteria.

Our plan is to continue modeling search strategies based on data from the grid interface, and then to begin modeling search strategies based on data from the single-image interface. We also plan to test searches with multiple criteria, and then to expand in the direction of searches using more open-ended criteria.

Characterizing Interpretation Strategies

We are presently collecting data for a study where participants rate an image subset on four goals (bright, aesthetic, artistic, and captivating) on two consecutive days. On both days, participants rate the images in two random orders. The purpose of this study is to disentangle the unreliability of individual ratings from actual changes in how people evaluate the goals over time. By gauging the temporal stability of these goals, we can better understand how large a role interpretation strategies play in people's exploration processes.

Moving forward, we plan to use a variety of methods (e.g., think-aloud, surprise interruptions) to capture criteria change over the course of exploration. Our aim is to discover triggers and indicators of criteria change, and then to conduct studies that induce change.

Application to Common Phenomena

Replicating common phenemena from the creativity literature serves two purposes. First, it establishes that our technique does indeed allow room for the sort of creativity that has been studied in previous research. Second, our technique can be used to expand understanding of how various known influences on creativity have their effects.

One early result in the divergent thinking literature is that simply telling people to "be creative" on a creativity test will increase their scores [11]. We ran a study ($N = 189$) where we manipulated the instructions (control and "be creative") and goal (finding the most "aesthetically composed" or "artistic" image). We found that while instructions had no effect in the "aesthetically composed" condition, the "be creative" instructions significantly increased creativity in the "artistic" condition (see Figure 6). We are planning follow-up work to better understand this dissociation.

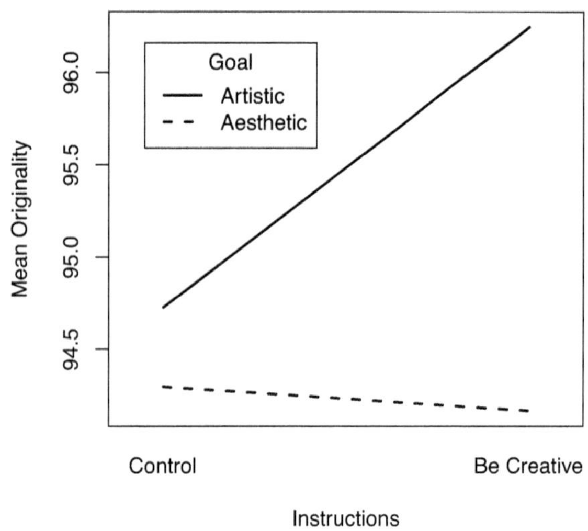

Figure 6. Results for "be creative" study.

Moving forward, we plan to explore other independent variables, such as positive affect [13] and intrinsic motivation [2]. We also expect to find more interesting connections between personality and search strategies, both with high-level predictors such as the Big Five [16], and with more specific individual differences like latent inhibition [7].

GENERAL DISCUSSION

Relation to Other Work

We are not the first to view creativity as a search process. As already mentioned, Simon and colleagues have done extensive work on what we call path search, wherein the task is to reach a predetermined solution (or class of solutions) to a problem (e.g., [20]). However, this work has been criticized for neglecting problem identification or framing (see, e.g., [5, 24]), which we address in part by considering criteria change. Also, the earlier work focuses on formal domains such as math and science, whereas we focus on a visual, aesthetic domain.

Finke, Ward, and Smith [9] conducted extensive research culminating in what they called the geneplore model (for generate and explore). Their work focused on how people's creative processes involve generating so-called "preinventive forms", and then exploring the possible desirable outcomes that can arise from combining these forms. Though their approach is both as comprehensive and less constrained than ours, their methodology is time-intensive to apply, and they do not offer as detailed a theory of how people coordinate their cognitive processes as we aim to produce.

Outside of the creativity literature, Hills, Todd, and Goldstone [12] have drawn connections between foraging behavior in animals and both spatial and conceptual foraging behavior in humans. We believe that their work has useful connections to ours, but see foraging, for which the goal is to accumulate resources, and optimization, for which the goal is to maximize an objective function, as entailing different normative considerations.

Our work is also relevant to work in computational creativity, which encompasses both computer simulations of creative cognition and creative societies, and programming creative artificial intelligence. As we better integrate our work with theories from computer science, we hope to be able to build stronger connections between psychology and computational creativity research.

Limitations

We acknowledge that our technique taps into a restricted form of creativity. Though broader in scope than some techniques (e.g., insight tasks), it is certainly more constrained than others (e.g., holistic assessement), and vulnerable to the criticism that our participants—who, after all, are selecting one from among many pre-rendered images—are not in fact making anything new. We therefore acknowledge that this task only taps exploratory creativity, and not transformational creativity [5], though we are sympathetic to the argument that exploratory creativity isn't necessarily easy [32]. We also acknowledge that while our task may be an externally valid proxy for some kinds of creativity (e.g., still-life photography) and may generalize to less constrained aesthetic tasks, it may not be an appropriate model for scientific or engineering creativity.

Despite these limitations, we believe that our work moves in several useful directions. First, we note that divergent thinking tasks, perhaps the most popular index of creativity, only tap a small part of the creative process and often lack external validity. Despite this, they have contributed a great deal of useful information about the influences on creativity, and continue to be valued for their practicality. Second, we believe that our technique's limitations are outweighed by the depth of real-time information that can be gathered about people's search behavior. We have constrained our participants so that we can automatically collect tractible, quantitative data. Once we have refined our analyses, we can expand the task dimensions that participants can control. In a similar vein, we hope that this technique will help create a broader approach to studying the entire creative process, which can then be extended to any sort of problem in which movement through solution space can be tracked in real-time, and the outcome is a single solution.

CONCLUSIONS

We hope that our work will lead to a more comprehensive understanding of how problem structure and search strategies affect creative outcomes. In so doing, we hope to help connect the theoretical work in psychology (BVSR theory) and computer science (metaheuristic optimization) that underlies our approach. As our technique matures, we also look forward to sharing our tools with other researchers, who will no doubt apply them to questions that we cannot anticipate.

ACKNOWLEDGEMENTS

The authors acknowledge Matthew Peters and Melissa Lim for contributions to data coding and software (respectively), to Rosa Pogessi, Rodica Damian, and Palmer and Simonton Lab research assistants for logistical assistance, and the hundreds of research participants who provided the data.

REFERENCES

1. L. Altenberg. NK fitness landscapes. In T. Back, D. Fogel, and Z. Michalewicz, editors, *The Handbook of Evolutionary Computation*, chapter B2.7.2. Institue of Physics Press, 1996.
2. T. Amabile. *Creativity in Context*. Westview Press, Boulder, CO, 1996.
3. H. X. Barnhart, J. Song, and M. J. Haber. Assessing intra, inter and total agreement with replicated readings. *Statistics in Medicine*, 24:1371–1384, 2005.
4. C. Blum and A. Roli. Metaheuristics in combinatorial optimization: Overview and conceptual comparison. *ACM Computing Surveys*, 35(3):268–308, 2003.
5. M. A. Boden. *The Creative Mind: Myths and Mechanisms*. BasicBooks, New York, 1991.
6. D. T. Campbell. Blind variation and selective retention in creative thought as in other knowledge processes. *Psychological Review*, 67:380–400, 1960.
7. S. H. Carson, J. B. Peterson, and D. M. Higgins. Decreased latent inhibition is associated with increased creative achievement in high-functioning individuals. *Journal of Personality and Social Psychology*, 85(3):499–506, 2003.
8. R. I. Damian and D. K. Simonton. From past to future art: The creative impact of Picasso's 1935 *Minotauromachy* on his 1937 *Guernica*. *Psychology of Aesthetics, Creativity, and the Arts*, March 21 2011. Advance online publication. doi: 10.1037/a0023017.
9. R. A. Finke, T. B. Ward, and S. M. Smith. *Creative Cognition: Theory, Research, and Applications*. MIT Press, Cambridge, MA, 1992.
10. J. W. Getzels and M. Csikszentmihalyi. *The Creative Vision: A Longitudinal Study of Problem Finding in Art*. John Wiley & Sons, New York, 1976.
11. D. M. Harrington. Effects of explicit instructions to "be creative" on the psychological meaning of divergent thinking test scores. *Journal of Personality*, 43:434–454, 1975.
12. T. T. Hills, P. M. Todd, and R. L. Goldstone. Search in external and internal spaces. *Psychological Science*, 19(8):802–808, 2008.
13. A. M. Isen, K. A. Daubman, and G. P. Nowicki. Positive affect facilitates creative problem solving. *Journal of Personality and Social Psychology*, 52:1122–1131, 1987.
14. K. E. Jennings. Early results with faceted classification of "alternate uses" test responses. In *C&C '09: Proceeding of the seventh ACM conference on Creativity and Cognition*, pages 383–384, New York, NY, USA, 2009. ACM.
15. K. E. Jennings. Search strategies and the creative process. In *First International Conference on Computational Creativity*, pages 130–139, Lisbon, Portugal, 2010.
16. O. P. John and S. Srivastava. The big-five trait taxonomy: History, measurement, and theoretical perspectives. In L. A. Pervin and O. P. John, editors, *Handbook of personality: Theory and research*, pages 102–139. Guilford Press, New York, 2 edition, 1999.
17. S. A. Kauffman. *The Origins of Order: Self-Organization and Selection in Evolution*. Oxford University Press, New York, 1993.
18. D. Klahr and K. Dunbar. Dual space search during scientific reasoning. *Cognitive Science*, 12:1–55, 1988.
19. D. Klahr and H. A. Simon. Studies of scientific creativity: Complementary approaches and convergent findings. *Psychological Bulletin*, 125:524–543, 1999.
20. P. Langley, H. A. Simon, G. L. Bradshaw, and J. M. Zythow. *Scientific discovery*. MIT Press, Cambridge, MA, 1987.
21. C. Martindale. *The clockwork muse: The predictability of artistic styles*. Basic Books, New York, 1990.
22. A. Newell and H. A. Simon. *Human problem solving*. Prentice-Hall, Englewood Cliffs, NJ, 1972.
23. T. Nickles. Evolutionary models of innovation and the meno problem. In L. V. Shavinina, editor, *The international handbook on innovation*, pages 54–78. Elsevier Science, New York, 2003.
24. D. Perkins. *The Eureka Effect: The Art and Logic of Breakthrough Thinking*. W. W. Norton, New York, 2000.

25. P. E. Shrout and J. L. Fleiss. Intraclass correlations: Uses in assessing rater reliability. *Psychological Bulletin*, 86(2):420–428, 1979.

26. D. K. Simonton. Scientific creativity as constrained stochastic behavior: The integration of the product, person, and process perspectives. *Psychological Bulletin*, 129(4):475–494, 2003.

27. D. K. Simonton. *Creativity in science: Chance, logic, genius, and zeitgeist.* Cambridge University Press, Cambridge, 2004.

28. D. K. Simonton. Creativity as a Darwinian phenomenon: The blind-variation and selective-retention model. In M. Krausz, D. Dutton, and K. Bardsley, editors, *The idea of creativity*, pages 63–81. Brill, Leiden, Netherlands, 2nd edition, 2009.

29. D. K. Simonton. Creativity as blind-variation and selective-retention: Constrained combinatorial models of exceptional creativity. *Physics of Life Reviews*, 7:156–179, 2010.

30. D. K. Simonton. Creativity and discovery as *blind* variation: Campbell's (1960) BVSR model after the half-century mark. *Review of General Psychology*, 2011–In press.

31. B. M. Staw. An evolutionary approach to creativity and innovations. In M. A. West and J. L. Farr, editors, *Innovation and creativity at work: Psychological and organizational strategies*, pages 287–308. Wiley, New York, 1990.

32. G. A. Wiggins. A preliminary framework for description, analysis and comparison of creative systems. *Knowledge-Based Systems*, 19:449–458, 2006.

The HCI Researcher as Artist and Designer: Approaches to Creativity and Distance

Viveka Weiley and **Ernest Edmonds**
Creativity and Cognition Studios, Centre for Human Centred Technology Design (HCTD)
University of Technology, Sydney. P.O. Box 123, Broadway, NSW 2007, Australia
www.viveka.id.au | www.ernestedmonds.com | www.creativityandcognition.com.au

ABSTRACT

We first describe the process of working on creative problems using three different but related approaches: Art, Design and Human Computer Interaction research. We present case studies of two interactive artworks; *Magic Hopscotch* and *Cities Tango: Melbourne/Sydney*, and explain how engagement with those works has informed our further practice in art, design and HCI.

We consider how HCI research can influence art and design, and how art and design can influence HCI research, thereby *making some kinds of decisions more explicit*, supporting *stronger hypothesis generation* and crucially *enriching evaluation methods* for creativity support tools.

Categories and Subject Descriptors

H.5.2 User Interfaces: Theory and methods

General Terms

Design, Human Factors, Experimentation, Theory.

Keywords

Art, Design, Geographically Distributed Collaboration, Place, HCI, Creativity Support Tools, Mixed Reality.

INTRODUCTION

Three Approaches to Creativity and Distance

The two authors of this paper both practice as artists, designers and human-computer interaction researchers; and in each practice concentrate on interactive systems and creativity. In this we are not alone: many in the field of creativity research apply different modes of enquiry to their core subject of interest.

The Creativity and Cognition conference series was instituted to bring together artists and scientists around these subjects, that they might inform each other's work. In some cases however the artist and scientist are already unified in one person; it is only that they must separate their personae when presenting their work to others.

When describing our work we tend to fall into the prescribed modes of each discipline, writing about artistic intent, or problem-solving, or scenarios and observations. Each mode (of work, and of reflection) has strengths that it can bring to bear; conversely each has much that is unsaid, unconsidered or assumed.

In this paper we describe our approaches to a single research area across art, design and HCI projects. We investigate how each approach informs the other; how what is passed over in one discipline can be at the heart of another; and how the approaches can be synthesised as a research undertaking. In particular we discuss how art and design practice can contribute to HCI research, by making some kinds of decisions more explicit, by supporting stronger hypothesis generation, and by enriching evaluation methods.

The projects described are at the intersection of creativity, place and distance. Research questions included: How can we overcome the barriers of distance to collaborative creativity and shared experience through technical means? Can we create a shared Place between two locations, and if we can, how should that Place best be articulated?

Implications and complications of bridging cultures

The distance from art to HCI research may not quite be the gulf of cultures described by CP Snow [19]. HCI research does at least partake of the phenomenological view; as an intersubjective enquiry it engages with the human perspective of art. Design could even be positioned as a further bridge between them, sharing the techniques and aesthetic concerns of art though in a more instrumentalised form. It has also been argued that research in interactive art can inform the research agenda of HCI [10].

C&C'11, November 3–6, 2011, Atlanta, Georgia, USA.

Nonetheless, from a scientific perspective the methods of the artist may seem to lack rigour. The persistent advantage that these methods confer, however, is the room they give to divergent thinking. Artistic goals need not be explicit, and so are allowed to shift in response to the trajectory of the practice itself, and the phenomena that emerge from its interaction with participants.

In a practice-based research context where the aim is for each work to inform later work in a cycle of practice, interpretation and theory [9], this trajectory can seem to have an inexorable course. However this course need not be reductive; the cycle will bring up complications as well as implications.

Further, the cycle is only one of many intertwingling [16] matrices of information. Creative work takes place in a social context [9] so it is influenced by the work and responses of others. As creative works do not take notice of the genres or disciplines in which we seek to place them [5], these influences will cross those lines as well.

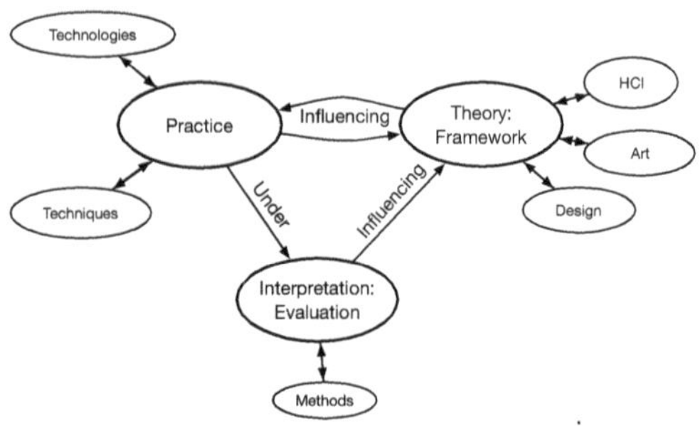

Figure 1. Elaboration of Edmonds & Candy 2009

When the practitioner is active in other disciplines, some of this line crossing may become more explicit within the practice.

ARTISTIC EXCURSIONS INTO SPACE AND PLACE

As artists, we separately exhibited experimental interactive works in Beta_Space. This site was conceived as a living laboratory within the Powerhouse Museum, Sydney and curated by Deborah Turnbull from the Creativity and Cognition Studios at the University of Technology, Sydney. The experimental works were titled *Magic Hopscotch* and *Cities Tango: Sydney, Melbourne.* As an example of the transformations that terminology undergoes when it crosses disciplines, it should be noted that in the artistic context, "experimental" simply means any art practice that explores new ideas. It does not refer to the experimental method as it is understood in the sciences; hypotheses are not necessarily made or tested, controls are not established, and conclusions are entirely and intentionally subject to interpretation.

While each work was situated in Beta_Space, each also had a second simultaneous location. *Magic Hopscotch* took participants into a forest behind Kinkakuji, the golden temple in Kyoto. The Beta_Space version of *Cities Tango* was connected to another version of itself installed on a public screen in Melbourne's Federation Square.

Magic Hopscotch

This work began with the intention to investigate virtual place, and thence proceeded in response to the site, its use and the user population. To the artist (the first author of this paper), a user-centred design methodology grounded in HCI research is the natural starting point for any interactive system.

Initial site observations indicated that many visitors to the museum are school children, and that they universally ignore the detailed instructions that accompany many interactive artworks, instead proceeding to jump about in the hope of triggering a response. To accommodate this a mode of interaction familiar and welcoming to children was sought. In discussion with collaborators the traditional hopscotch court emerged as an ideal candidate; children know how to play hopscotch without instruction; in Australia every schoolchild has been exposed to the game, with standardisation in primary school playgrounds beginning in the 1950s [13]. The game has a built-in turn-taking mechanism and consistent sequence [1], and with its terminal semi-circular "square" often labeled "home" or "sky blue" the game is already structured around a journey toward an imaginary place.

Figure 2. The Artist's Children Playing Hopscotch

Figure 3. Images from Magic Hopscotch as Installed

Figure 4. Magic Hopscotch as Experienced

In the work as installed, participants first see a room with an image of itself on a wall-sized screen at the end of a hopscotch court marked on the floor with reflective tape; this court serves as an attractor [7], indicating to children that this is a space intended for them. As players jump on the numbered squares in turn, a forest grows in the image of the room, until at SKY BLUE the forest fills the room entirely. In the work as experienced, the images, response and experience of the magical journey evoked imaginative explorations, with players inviting each other into stories and games that they were constructing about that journey. The artist was irresistibly reminded of Maurice Sendak's *Where the Wild Things Are* [17], in which a disobedient boy is sent to his bedroom, which is then transformed into a magical world. The children who interacted with Magic Hopscotch joyfully engaged with the work, using it as a starting point for their own transformations and inventions. "*I'm in a forest!*" became "*come on, let's be forest creatures in another world!*" [from observation transcripts].

In the process of defining how Magic Hopscotch would be realised, the artist embraced the philosophy expressed in *White Noise* [8] - "Clarity follows from starting with the unembellished concrete truth and building upon it using a careful economy of means". This artistic philosophy reflects an engineer's love of the elegant solution, and also supports a user-centred design process, as it allows the artist to devise a system that can be tested with as few variables as possible. The question of how the user is represented in the work serves as an example. 3D computer-generated avatars were prototyped, as well as a mediated video silhouette inspired by Myron Krueger's VIDEOPLACE [14]. In the installed work however the user was not shown on the screen at all; instead they were represented only by their effect on the world on the screen, with their primary self-identification remaining in their own bodies. Instead, considerable effort was directed toward eliminating lag produced by the sensor and processing systems, in order to ensure immediate feedback in response to user actions. This follows Krueger's creed that in interactive art "response is the medium" [14], and so a more responsive system is truer to that medium. This creed concords with the interaction design principle that feedback should be given by a system in accordance with the psychological expectations of the user; for example that in an interaction that is analogous to conversation with a human (such as waiting for confirmation of a command) the delay should be no more than two seconds in order to mimic human conversational pace, and responses to control activations (analogous to moving a key or switch) should be given within 0.1 second [15].

Numerous rough prototypes [20] were rapidly generated and tested with the artist's children, for example to confirm when we had met the responsiveness threshold that corresponded with the psychological expectations of jumping into an imaginary forest.

Magic Hopscotch was installed in Beta_Space from 23rd June until 13th August 2008. During this period we conducted structured qualitative observations of engagements with the work. We recorded players' stories, remarks and suggestions and observed that the stripped back, responsive version of the work afforded bodily engagement with the interaction and sparked creative response. Many interactions were recorded, but no quantification of the observations was attempted.

Cities Tango: Sydney, Melbourne

In contrast to *Magic Hopscotch*, qualitative evaluations of works in the *Tango* series were reported quantitatively, alongside comments, having been gathered in structured interviews [10]. As the purpose for this enquiry was to inform later work in the series the questions were focused on matters of specific use to that practice, such as their likelihood of engaging the work were it to be placed in a gallery rather than public context [10].

Figure 5. Cities Tango: Sydney, Melbourne.

For this iteration of the work, communities in Sydney and Melbourne interacted with one another. *Cities Tango: Sydney, Melbourne* linked the Powerhouse Museum with Federation Square. In each city the work collected images from the screen location and reacted to them. The analysed information also influenced the work's behaviour in the other city. Changing colour stripes were interleaved with segments of images of the remote location at different times of the day and mixed with real time snapshots of people at the remote site.

The work grew out of two distinct long standing interests. One was human communication through technology and the other was interactive generative art. The former was part of an artistic exploration that began in 1972 and developed into a long series of HCI studies of co-operative work. For example, the question of what bandwidth, and how little 'noise', was needed for a feeling of communication to be facilitated was investigated. The second interest had its origins in the early 1980s and was part of the development of the design of time-based abstract structures that explored various aspects of human perception. Perceptual colour models, for example, were part of this design concern, looking at the perception of change and colour distance.

Cities Tango: Sydney, Melbourne formed part of a series of works; it was preceded by *Tango Tangle*, a single site work [2], and was followed by a work joining Melbourne to Berlin and most recently by *Cities Tango: between Belfast and Sydney* [10].

As part of an ongoing series of experimental interactive works the *Tango* installations are involved in the practice, interpretation and theory cycle.

However it is worth noting resonances from HCI research. The influential connected video experiment Portholes [6] installed to connect Xerox PARC in Palo Alto, USA with EuroPARC in Cambridge, UK is a seminal work in this instance, and is relevant today.

For example, compare these observations:

Cross-site visits are a particular source of sightings. For instance, a PARC visitor to EuroPARC was amused to notice a EuroPARC visitor to PARC using her "home" workstation to demonstrate software. [6]

It created a small stir, for example, when people in the Sydney gallery recognised Ernest Edmonds appearing on their display. He was, of course, in Belfast. [10]

CONCLUSIONS

The two experimental artworks we have described contain illustrative points of similarity and difference.

First, each contained an enquiry into the nature of mediated place. *Magic Hopscotch* investigated whether it is necessary to create an immersive virtual environment in order to engage participants in an experience of transformative place. The work became an existence proof of the opposing hypothesis: that it is possible to have such an experience while consciously inhabiting the real and virtual worlds simultaneously. *Cities Tango: Sydney, Melbourne*, continued an exploration into the power of time-based abstraction in creating a place for human communication.

Second, evaluation methods differed markedly. Both proceeded from the experiences of participants, but then diverged. The *Magic Hopscotch* observations were embodied in a sheaf of anecdotes, whereas the *Cities Tango: Sydney, Melbourne* interviews were further condensed down to quantitative analysis. The latter method may be more amenable to becoming part of the larger HCI research corpus, to be built upon by other researchers.

The most salient similarity however comes from looking at the works in the broader context of the authors' art, design and HCI research practice. Both works were directly informed by the artists' previous work in HCI research, and both materially influenced their subsequent art, research and design work.

Opportunities from Crossing Disciplines

HCI Research Influencing Art and Design:

Interaction designers have learnt to adopt lessons from HCI research; some seek out research findings in order to apply them in their work, and others join in as they see the new techniques being used successfully by their peers. Interactive artists are less eager, despite the usefulness of ideas such as attractors and feedback, quite possibly because much HCI research assumes that the goal of any interactive work is efficient task performance; whereas in art that is unlikely to be a central concern. Difficult engagements, thoughtful response and intentional complication are often part of an artistic goal. However other ways to look at HCI exist; for example Csikszentmihalyi's [4] theory of *Flow* recognises rising challenge as a positive for maintaining creative engagement with a task. Artists in collaboration with HCI researchers should be able to develop other such models that can be applied to the concerns of art.

Art and Design Influencing HCI research:

The explorations of place described above have influenced the direction of an ongoing HCI research project by the first author, but in ways that are difficult to convey in a traditional HCI context.

In particular, the demonstration that mixed-reality systems can engage users without requiring them to abandon their connection to their real environments, as immersive virtual worlds attempt to do, has influenced the design of subsequent projects. When reporting on HCI projects however, the reasons for underlying design decisions are commonly ignored. We conclude that these implicit decisions should instead be elucidated.

Making Some Kinds of Decisions More Explicit

The first author's HCI research project, for example, began as a problem-solving activity. A series of interviews and observations conducted in creative workplaces revealed a need for shared socio-technical environments to link geographically distributed workgroups. A widely proposed solution is to build immersive virtual environments. However the reason for considering that approach is not well documented in the papers that report on the work: they begin with the problem and then jump to the approach taken. It seems reasonable to prioritise results over ideation. However a result is that only the convergent thinking is documented; the divergent is valuable too, and ignoring that documentation leads to unstated assumptions. The ease with which participants dealt with being in two places at once in *Cities Tango*, and also in the mixed reality environment of *Magic Hopscotch* challenges the necessity for creativity-supporting virtual environments to be immersive. This experience inspired the first author to re-investigate media spaces like Portholes and others from the same era such as RAVE and Hydra [3], and then to begin sketches and prototypes for mixed-reality media space systems.

Supporting Stronger Hypothesis Generation

This kind of hypothesis generation is the product of divergent thinking and informed intuition, not of a rigorous or quantifiable process. As such it would be simpler to report on the testing of the hypothesis without elaborating on how it came about. However the description of this process, as well as the later process of refining the hypothesis through design practice, **does in fact warrant examination**. If we formally discuss our methods of coming to hypotheses, including the influences from beyond the discipline at hand, we can strengthen those methods.

Enriching Evaluation Methods

A commonly used HCI research method is to set up two similar systems in a controlled setting, in order to examine the factor that is varied between the systems. There are unspoken design choices in experimental HCI projects. Why measure these two options, instead of others? Why ignore execution? Why always test on naive users? All these questions should be asked. Still, this technique is meaningful when applied to problems that are largely solved, but for which some particular elements can be usefully refined. It is less useful when examining novel systems, or as Greenberg and Buxton [12] argue, with expert users; or when evaluating creativity, which is especially difficult to pin down over the brief time scales of this sort of experiment.

Deeper longitudinal studies using ethnographic methods have had more success, but new evaluation techniques "applicable to ill-defined, open-ended problems" are still needed [11]. We propose that the reflective practice of artists and designers can be built upon to help develop new evaluation methods for HCI. In the broader context, artistic works are assessed first by curators and then by the public for their aesthetic, social and historical value. However it is also possible for the practitioner to establish their own evaluation methods and criteria in order to reflect more fully on their practice and guide their research.

These methods are practice-based: for example in art and design a new technique can be considered to be useful if a large number of practitioners adopt it in their practice, and a new theory is considered useful if it can be expressed through an improved practice.

Combining Approaches

If we are to combine the approaches of these three disciplines, we must be willing to acknowledge the congruence between the problems that each addresses and their methods for doing so. We can also experiment with adapting their techniques. Try applying the experimental method to art - repeat a work by another artist, to see what's different when the work exists within a different socio-technical environment. Try applying artistic methods to HCI research, in an acknowledgement that execution matters. By considering the problems of the other fields as our own and collaborating in cross-disciplinary groups where the different problems can be simultaneously addressed, we can work towards a true and useful rapprochement.

REFERENCES

1. Bauer, L. & Bauer, W. *New Zealand playground language project*, School of Linguistics and Applied Language Studies, Victoria U. of Wellington, N.Z. 2002.
2. Bilda, Z., Edmonds, E. A., and Turnbull, D. Interactive Experience in a Public Context, in *Proceedings of Creativity and Cognition 2007.* ACM Press, New York, NY, pp 243-244.
3. Bly, S., Harrison, S. & Irwin, S. Media spaces: bringing people together in a video, audio, and computing environment, in *Communications of the ACM*, vol. 36, no. 1, 1993, ACM Press, New York, NY, pp. 28-46.
4. Csikszentmihalyi, M. *Creativity: Flow and the Psychology of Discovery and Invention*, Harper Perennial, NY, New York, 1996.
5. Dahlgren, P. Prismatic Television, in *Television and the Public Sphere: Citizenship, Democracy and the Media*, Sage, pp. 2-45, 1995.
6. Dourish, P. & Bly, S. Portholes: supporting awareness in a distributed work group, in *CHI '92 – Proceedings of the SIGCHI conference on Human factors in computing systems*, ACM, New York, NY.
7. Edmonds, E. On creative engagement with interactive art, in *Proceedings of the 3rd international Conference on Computer Graphics and interactive Techniques in Australasia and South East Asia*, GRAPHITE '05. ACM, New York, NY, 297-297.
8. Edmonds, E. White Noise: the Question of Economy, *White Noise*, Edmonds and Stubbs (eds), ACMI, Melbourne Australia, 2005.
9. Edmonds, E., Candy, L., Cox, G., Eisenstein, J., Fischer, G., Hughes, B. & Hewett, T. 'Individual and/versus social creativity (panel session)', *Proceedings of the 3rd Conference on Creativity & Cognition*, C&C '99, Loughborough, United Kingdom, October 11 - 13, 1999, ACM Press, NY, 36-39.
10. Edmonds, E. A. and Franco, F. From Communication Game to Cities Tango, in *Proceedings of Computational Aesthetics*, BCS, London, June 2010.
11. Fischer, G. Challenges for Future Research Activities and Projects focused on "Software Tools and Socio-Technical Environments to Enhance Creativity in *NSF Workshop Report on Creativity Support Tools, International Journal of Human-Computer Interaction*, 20(2), 61-77, 2006.
12. Greenberg, S. & Buxton, B. Usability Considered Harmful (Some of the Time), in *Proc. of the 2008 ACM Conference on Human Factors in Computing Systems*, CHI'08, 111-120.
13. Howard, D. Australian "Hoppy" (Hopscotch)', *Western Folklore*, Vol. 17, No. 3. (July 1958), 163-175.
14. Krueger, M, 'Responsive Environments', *AFIPS 46 National Computer Conference Proceedings*, 1977, 423-433.
15. Miller, R.B. Response time in man-computer conversational transactions, in *Proceedings of Fall Joint Computer Conference*, 1968, 267-277.
16. Nelson, T. *Computer Lib/Dream Machines* (Rev. ed.), Tempus Books of Microsoft Press, Redmond, WA, 1987.
17. Sendak, M. *Where the Wild Things Are*, Harper and Row, 1963.
18. Shneiderman, B. *Designing the User Interface: Strategies for Effective Human-Computer Interaction.* Addison-Wesley Longman Publishing Co., Inc., Boston, MA, USA, 1986.
19. Snow, C. P. *The two cultures, and a second look : an expanded version of The two cultures and the scientific revolution*, Cambridge University Press, 1963.
20. Wong, Y. Rough and Ready Prototypes: Lessons from Graphic Design', *Human Factors in Computing Systems*: CHI '92 Conference, Posters and Short Talks, ACM, NY, New York, 83-84.

Design and Evaluation of Creative and Emotional Motion

Kaori Yamada
Department of Mechanical Engineering
Kobe University
1-1 Rokkodai, Nada, Kobe 6578501, Japan
k.yamada@stu.kobe-u.ac.jp

Toshiharu Taura
Department of Mechanical Engineering
Kobe University
1-1 Rokkodai, Nada, Kobe 6578501, Japan
taura@kobe-u.ac.jp

Yukari Nagai
School of Knowledge Science
Japan Advanced Institute of Science and Technology
1-1 Asahidai, Nomi, Ishikawa 9231292, Japan
ynagai@jaist.ac.jp

ABSTRACT
In this study, we propose a method for the design of a creative and emotional motion. Our work is based on the hypothesis that a creative motion that is beyond the ordinary human imagination can produce emotional impressions that resonate with deep feeling. The proposed method involves computer implementation of motion blending, movement analogous to natural objects, rhythmic emphasis, movement of the entire design object, and sound-related effect. Using a computer system we constructed, we conducted two experiments that confirmed both our hypothesis and the effectiveness of our methodology.

Keywords
Motion Design, Sound, Creativity, Emotion

ACM Classification Keywords
J.5 ARTS AND HUMANITIES: Performing arts (e.g., dance, music).

General Terms
Design

INTRODUCTION
The most significant ambition in design is to create objects that resonate with deep-seated human feelings [7]. In this study, we attempt to establish a method for the design of a creative and emotional motion that resonates with such feelings.

Because design in recent years has turned its focus toward forms and shapes, the output of the field has limited itself to such parameters. However, as so many mediums of expression have become available in today's information society, fields of design have widened their scope to include dynamic expression. In this study, we attempt to enhance the design of objects using motion. Humans have innovated a great variety of motion behaviors both for their own bodies and for products ranging from vehicles to robots to two-dimensional animated figures. However, the conventional methods of generating these behaviors are always based upon visual or physical impressions created by the designer.

Compare this to another field of dynamic expression, music. In this field, instruments are created to facilitate the capacity of the creators to innovate. It is arguable that musical instruments themselves trigger (or at least impact) the human feelings that people express via their music. We must note here that music differs from natural sound in that it is an artificial creation of humans, and that we can be deeply impressed by music that evokes feelings that are beyond the ordinary human imagination.

Humans receive emotional impressions not only from natural objects but from artifacts as well. We are deeply impressed by artifacts such as pictures or music just as we are impressed by nature, albeit in slightly different ways. (Here, the term "emotional impression" suggests an active impression of the subject as something that touches the depths of human feeling, while the unadorned term "impression" suggests a passive or static impression.)

We assume that "creative" expression that is beyond the ordinary human imagination can produce such an emotional impression upon us (hereafter, the term "creative" is used to imply the notion of "that which is beyond ordinary human imagination"). This idea constitutes our research hypothesis. We then develop a method with which to design such a creative and emotional motion to investigate the validity of the hypothesis.

In order to receive emotional impressions, relatively normal functioning capacity of the visual and auditory senses is essential. For example, paintings and architecture appeal to the eye, while music and poetry appeal to the ear. Video arts, such as animation or movies, input a high degree of stimulus information to both our visual and auditory perception. Many studies have addressed the dynamics of human impressions that are received via the visual and/or auditory senses, highlighting their great significance.

In this study we develop a method for the design of a "creative" and "emotional" motion by focusing on the causal relationship between a creative motion that is beyond the ordinary human imagination and emotional impressions that resonate with deep feeling. However, any motion that is beyond the ordinary human imagination is thought to inspire emotional impressions. In this study, we attempt to generate a creative motion by starting with the motion of a natural object and transforming and elaborating it.

To verify our hypothesis and the effectiveness of our methodology, we constructed a computer system which is expected to trigger (or at least impact) the human feelings that people express like musical instruments. The system had two components: one to investigate the effect of extending the motion itself beyond the ordinary human imagination by emphasizing its rhythmic features, and the other to investigate the effect of auditory stimulation on the emotional impressions of motion through the addition of sound.

This study is conducted by focusing on a motion that may be applied to something such as a moving logo, which we use as an example, because such a motion can be designed in the laboratory and its validity can be confirmed by experiment. We anticipate that these kinds of moving corporate logos will soon become widespread on the internet.

PROPOSAL AND METHOD

The purpose of this study is to develop a method of designing a creative and emotional motion based on our definitions of the terms and our hypothesis that such a motion can more produce emotional impressions that resonate with deep feeling.

First, we develop a method of designing the proposed creative motion. Next, we construct computer systems that implement the proposed method in order to verify our hypothesis.

METHOD FOR DESIGN

We developed a method of designing a creative and emotional motion by extending the principles set forth in our previous works [12] [13].

Analogy with Natural Objects

Humans have evolved within the natural environment and are thought to have images of nature imprinted in their minds. Indeed, humans have created many artifacts that are based on or suggested by natural objects, and their motions are both unique and charming [1]. For example, research in the field of biologically inspired design has pointed out motions that were developed through the application of analogous biological phenomena [11]. It is for this reason that we use natural objects as a source for the design of a creative and emotional motion that extends beyond the ordinary human imagination and resonates with deep feeling. This method can thus be considered a process of analogy.

Blending of Motions

However, a motion that is generated solely by applying such an analogy to natural objects cannot be said to extend beyond the human imagination. On the other hand, according to studies of design creativity, concept blending is crucial to the creative generation of concepts [6]. Concept blending is based not on analogy but on the combination of two input concepts to yield a third concept. While a blended concept inherits part of its structures from the input concepts, it also expected to include emergent structures of its own. In this study, we apply the notion of concept blending to the design of a creative and emotional motion, and we develop a method of blending the motions generated by analogy with natural objects in order to generate a more creative motion.

Emphasis on Rhythmic Features

In order to generate a more creative motion that extends far beyond the human imagination, we attempted to emphasize the rhythmic features of motion, that is, the changes in the number of angles of joints and in the angular velocities. Rhythm in music involves the interrelationship between the accented (strong) beat and the unaccented (weak) beat [2]. Incidentally, accents that are produced by stress (dynamics) imply the dynamic intensification of a beat, that is, an emphasis implied through the use of a louder sound. For example, in Western musical literature, p (piano) means "soft," while f (forte) means "loud." Based on these considerations in the field of music, we attempted to emphasize the rhythmic features of a motion by increasing or reducing its frequency. Using this method, we anticipated that motions that extend far beyond the human imagination could be designed.

Based on the considerations stated above, we developed a method of designing a creative and emotional motion that incorporates an analogy with natural objects, the blending of motions, and an emphasis on rhythmic features (hereafter called "Rhythmic Feature-based Motion Blending" (RFMBlending)).

The method used for the calculation of RFMBlending is given below. First, we obtain the motions of natural objects as a source for a creative and emotional motion (base motion). The rhythmic features are extracted by conducting a frequency analysis of each obtained motion. Regarding this analysis, we decided to use wavelet analysis because it can process both the phasing and frequential characteristics in the same operation [3]. The wavelet coefficients obtained from wavelet analysis are then used as the rhythmic features of motion. Let $\omega_1(t)$ be the Tth rhythmic feature (wavelet coefficient) of natural object1. The emphasized rhythmic feature is then defined by the following equation (1):

$$\omega_1(t) = \begin{cases} m_1\omega_1(t) & (p_1 \le |\omega_1(t)|) \\ \omega_1(t) & (q_1 < |\omega_1(t)| < p_1) \\ n_1\omega_1(t) & (|\omega_1(t)| \le q_1) \end{cases} \quad (1)$$

Here, p_1 and q_1 are the thresholds for emphasis of a rhythmic feature, with $m_1 \ge 1$, and $n_1 \le 1$. This emphasis makes a large motion larger and a small motion smaller. The rhythmic feature of the motion of another natural object is emphasized in the same way. The two rhythmic features are then blended together. The operation of blending rhythmic features is defined in equation (2). Here, R_1 and R_2 are the rhythmic features of the motion of natural object1 and natural object2 respectively, and C_1 and C_2 are the weights for the rhythmic features of natural objects 1 and 2.

$$R_{blending}(t) = C_1 R_1(\omega_1(t)) + C_2 R_2(\omega_2(t)) \quad (2)$$

Inverse wavelet transform is performed on the blended rhythmic features so that a new motion is created.

Movement of the Entire Design Target

RFMBlending was implemented for the design target, which consisted of a number of joints, and the motion of the design target was affected by changing the angles of the joints in the design target. Although the motion of the design target is expected to be creative and emotional in itself, we assume that it could be even more so if the entire design target also moves in space (external motion), in addition to the motion of the design target itself (internal motion); such motion expands the possibilities for free and dynamic motion in general. In this study, the motion of a natural object was also used as a model for the movement of the entire design target. Motion capture was used to obtain characteristics of motion by the natural objects in question.

Design of the Sound to be Played with the Motion

In order to investigate the effect that the auditory sense has upon the emotional impressions created by motion, we designed a sound to accompany the designed motion. To do so, we focused on three basic elements of sound: tone color, loudness, and pitch.

Tone Color

Differences in tone produce different impressions [5]. In our addition of the designed sound, we attempted to avoid giving any impression that might be specific to an emotional context. Hence we used beeps, represented by a square wave sound and often implemented in computers. Usage of a square wave sound made it possible to capture the loudness of a sound as the amplitude of its wave and pitch of a sound as the wave's frequency.

Loudness

In music, rhythm consists of duration and timing. Our aim was to synchronize the rhythm of the sound with the rhythm of the motion. Therefore, if the rhythmic feature of a motion exceeded a predefined threshold, the sound was amplified. A larger motion would thus be accompanied by a louder sound, and a smaller motion would be accompanied by a softer sound or no sound.

Pitch

In this study, the sound was not composed in order to create a beautiful melody. Our intention was for the pitch of the sound to change in correspondence with the motion. Since the rhythmic feature of the motion was obtained by changing the number of joint angles and the angular velocities, the pitch of the sound would then be changed according to the velocity of the terminus of the design target. We expected that this method would give the sound greater synchronicity with the motion.

Based on these considerations, we developed a method of designing the sound to be played with the motion. First, the loudness of the sound was determined according to the blended rhythmic feature obtained using equation (2).

$$s_i(t) = \begin{cases} 1 & (p_s > |R_{blending\,i}(t)|) \\ 0 & (p_s \le |R_{blending\,i}(t)|) \end{cases} \quad (3)$$

$$S(t) = \sum_i s_i(t) \quad (4)$$

Here, i is the number of joints, $R_{blending\,i}(t)$ is the rhythmic feature of the ith joint at time t, and p_s is the threshold of the rhythmic feature of the motion for the sound. In equation (4), S(t) is the number of joints whose rhythmic feature exceeds the threshold. The loudness of the sound is determined according to S(t).

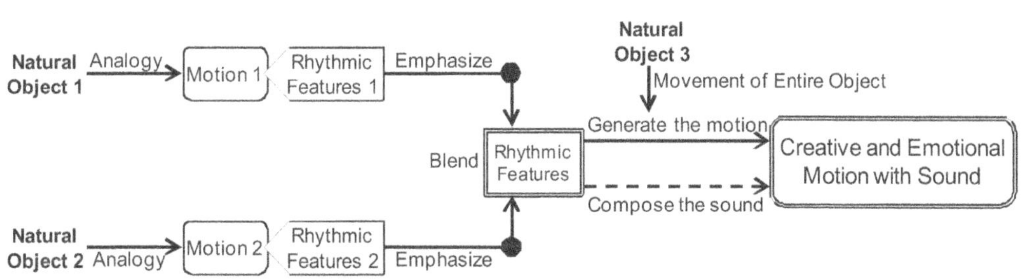

Figure 1. Outline of proposed method.

Next, the frequency of sound f(t) is determined by the following equation (5):

$$f(t) = f_c + v(t) \quad (5)$$

Here, f_c is the bias to be added in order to make the sound audible to the human ear, and v(t) is the magnitude of the velocity of the terminus of the target.

An outline of the proposed method is shown in Figure 1.

PROCEDURE

Based on the method described above, two computer systems for designing a creative and emotional motion were developed. The procedures that comprise these systems can be summarized in the following steps: one system is comprised of Step1) to Step7), while the other system is comprised of Step1) to Step11).

Step1) Obtain the angle $\theta(t)$ in sequential order by selecting each of the 4 joints of a natural object as a characteristic point.

Step2) Calculate the angular velocity $\dot{\theta}(t)$ of each joint from the changes in its angles.

Step3) Perform wavelet analysis for the angular velocity calculated in Step2. In this study, we used Daubechies8 wavelets as wavelet prototype functions, since these wavelets are widely used. The wavelet coefficients obtained in Step3 are used as the rhythmic features.

Step4) The rhythmic features are emphasized using equation (1). In the process of emphasis, designers can determine *p, q, m* and *n* according to their individual criteria.

Steps 1 to 4 are performed on each joint of the natural object.

Step5) The rhythmic features of two natural objects that were emphasized in Step4 are blended using equation (2). Here too, motion designers can decide the weights for each rhythmic feature according to their individual criteria.

Step6) Inverse wavelet transform is performed on the blended rhythmic features of each joint $R_{blending}(\omega(t))$, and angular velocities $\dot{\theta}_{blending}(t)$ are obtained. The angle $\theta_{blending}(t)$ of each joint is calculated from its angular velocity.

Step7) The motion is created by transforming the angle of each joint to that of the design target.

Step8) Capture a certain position (x_p, y_p) of the natural object in order to obtain the movement of the entire natural object and transfer it to the original position of the design target (x_0, y_0).

Step9) The loudness of the sound is determined according to the blended rhythmic features of each joint $R_{blending}(\omega(t))$ using equation (3).

Step10) The pitch of the sound is determined using equation (5) from the velocity of the end of the design target.

Step11) Combine the sound with the motion that was created in Step8.

We developed a computer system that could perform the steps described above. This system was implemented on Windows XP/Vista, and it was developed in Microsoft Visual C++ using a numerical library GSL (the GNU Scientific Library) [4] and GLUT (the OpenGL Utility Toolkit) [9] to represent the designed motion in 3D graphics. In addition, OpenCV (Open Computer Vision Library) [8] was used for the capturing of motion.

EXPERIMENT 1

Experiment1 was performed to investigate the effect of extending the motion itself beyond the ordinary human imagination by emphasizing the rhythmic features of the motion using RFMBlending [14]. In this experiment, three types of motion were created that differed in the way they emphasized rhythmic features.

Designing a Creative and Emotional Motion Using RFMBlending

Selected characteristic motions of frogs and snakes were used as the base objects for analogy, since they both have unique ways of moving that people tend to recognize easily. We chose the arms of a virtual robot in CG as a design target. In order to design a motion that would be beyond human imagination, and we set no limitations on the disposition of the robot's arms, for example, that would neither limit the joint angle nor prevent a collision. The types of rhythmic features that were emphasized are listed in Table 1. Here, the determinations of p and q were calculated beforehand from the average of each rhythmic feature of each joint in Step3. The weights for each rhythmic feature C1:C2 were determined as 1:1. Motion 1-I was expected to enhance a large motion by making it larger, while Motion 1-II was expected to diminish a small motion by making it smaller. Motion 1-III emphasized no rhythmic features.

	Motion1-I	Motion1-II	Motion1-III
p m	top25% 4.0	–	
q n	–	bottom25% 0.25	

Table 1. Types of Motions.

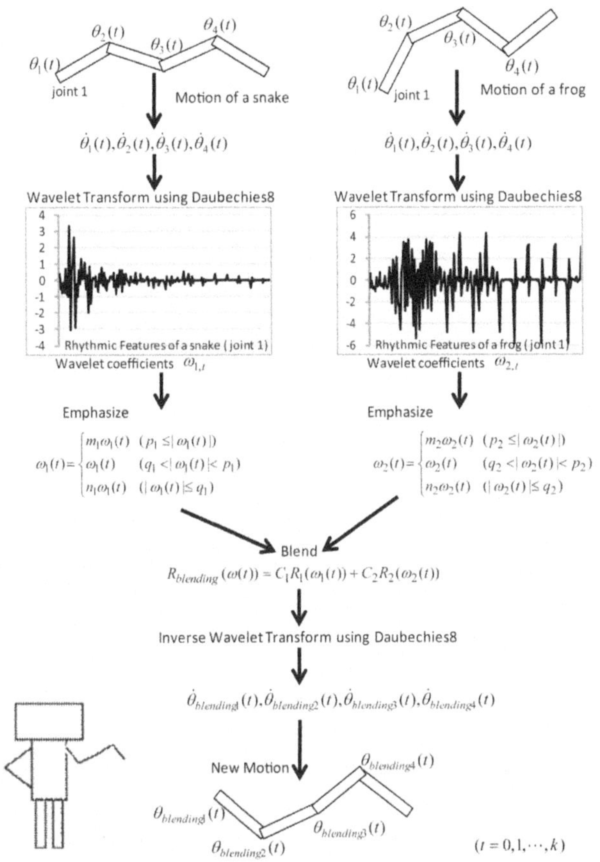

Figure 2. Procedure of generating motion for Experiment 1.

The procedure for creating motion is shown in Figure 2. Step1 to Step7 are performed to create the motion for Experiment1. The examples of newly designed motion are shown in Figure 3 (a) to (c), which show these motions in a time sequence with 2-second intervals. The arms of both the bodies were design targets.

Evaluation of Created Motions

The Semantic Differential (SD) method[10] was used to evaluate the motions in this experiment. In this method, subjects are asked to evaluate their impressions by identifying the value of the pre-defined scale on the answer form. In this experiment, the motions were evaluated according to 10 terms on a seven-point scale. The terms are presented in Figure 4. Twelve subjects participated in the evaluation. After being shown three motions, they were asked to evaluate them. The subjects were college students and graduate students aged 21–24. In order to eliminate the possible effect of the order of presentation, six of the subjects evaluated Motion 1-I first, Motion 1-III second, and Motion 1-II last, while the others evaluated Motion 1-II first, Motion 1-III second, and Motion 1-I last.

An SD profile obtained from Experiment1 is shown in Figure 4. The points in the figure show the average of all subjects for each term for each motion. In the figure, we can see that the following five terms elicited a significantly different response to Motion 1-I (a large motion enhanced to become larger) versus Motion 1-III (no feature

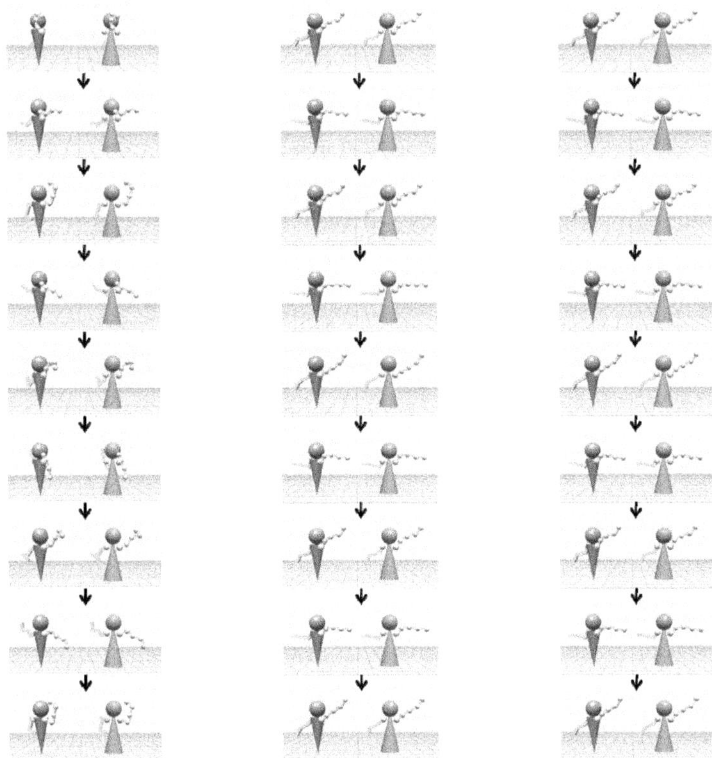

(a) Motion 1-I (b) Motion 1-II (c) Motion 1-III

Figure 3. Example of motions created in Experiment 1.
(Although Motion 1-II and Motion 1-III appear very similar here, they look different in an actual motion)

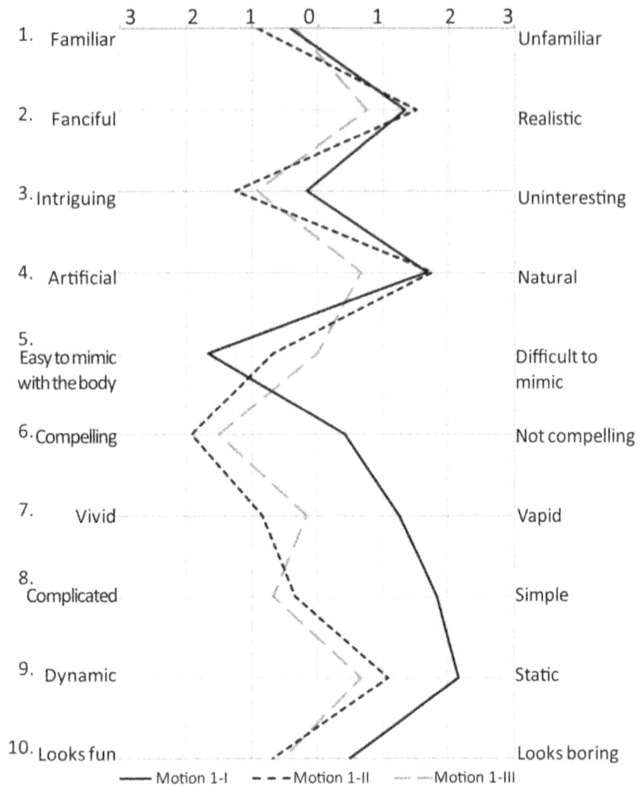

Figure 4. SD profile obtained from the evaluation of Experiment 1.

emphasized): term 5, "Easy to mimic with the body – Difficult to mimic" ($F(2, 200) = 4.74$, $p < .01$); term 6, "Compelling – Not compelling" ($F(2, 200) = 10.53$, $p < .01$); term 7, "Vivid – Vapid" ($F(2, 200) = 4.74$, $p < .01$); term 8, "Complicated – Simple" ($F(2, 200) = 12.52$, $p < .01$); and term 9, "Dynamic – Static" ($F(2, 200) = 4.07$, $p < .01$). Furthermore, the following three terms elicited a significantly different response to Motion 1-I versus Motion 1-II (a small motion diminished to become smaller): term 6, "Compelling – Not compelling" ($F(2, 200) = 10.53$, $p < .01$); term 7 "Vivid – Vapid" ($F(2, 200) = 4.74$, $p < .01$); and term 8, "Complicated – Simple" ($F(2, 200) = 4.74$, $p < .01$). On the other hand, the values of Motion 1-I and Motion 1-II were close to one another for the following two terms: term 2, "Fanciful – Realistic" and term 4, "Artificial – Natural," while both of these values were different from the value obtained for Motion 1-III.

In the SD profile shown in Figure 4, a significant difference can be found between the motions for terms 5, 6, 7, 8, and 9. Among these motions, term 5, "Easy to mimic with the body – Difficult to mimic" and term 8, "Complicated – Simple" are assumed to be related to creative expression that extends beyond the ordinary human imagination. On the other hand, term 6, "Compelling – Not compelling"; term 7, "Vivid – Vapid"; and term 9, "Dynamic – Static" are assumed to be related to an emotional impression that resonates with deep feeling. These results demonstrate that there is a tendency for motions that extend beyond the ordinary human imagination to produce emotional impressions, thus confirming of our hypothesis.

p	Top 25%
m	2.0
p_s	Top 50%
f_c	220

Table 2. Types of Motions.

EXPERIMENT 2

Experiment2 was performed to investigate the cooperative effect that the auditory sense has on the emotional impressions of motion; this was done by adding sound to the motion. By focusing on how sound extends the impression beyond the human imagination and how it further imparts an emotional impression to the motion, we can better assess the relationship between the human imagination and the emotional efficacy of a motion; this assessment is then used to verify our hypothesis.

Designing Creative and Emotional Motion using RFMBlending with Sound

As in Experiment 1, the motions of frogs and snakes were used as base objects for analogy. For the movement of the entire design target, the motion of a plant leaf was used. In order to investigate the effect of the sound alone, an abstract object (ten linked spheres) was used as the design target. In order to design a motion beyond the human imagination, we set no limitations on the condition of the design target. The parameters used to create the motion are listed in Table 2. Here, the determinations of p and p_s were calculated beforehand from the average of each rhythmic feature of each joint in Step3. The weights for each rhythmic feature C1:C2 were determined as 1:1.

The procedure for creating motion with sound is shown in Figure 5. The examples of created motion that were obtained in Experiment2 are shown in Figure 6, which shows these motions in a time sequence with 2-second intervals. Motion 2-I is motion with sound, while Motion 2-II is motion without sound. The motion in Motion 2-I is the same as that in Motion 2-II.

Evaluation of Created Motions

The motions were evaluated using the SD method in order to investigate how the sound extends the impression beyond the human imagination and how it further imparts an emotional impression to the motion. Fourteen subjects participated in the evaluation. After two motions (with sound and without sound) were shown, the subjects were asked to evaluate them according to 8 terms on a seven-point scale.

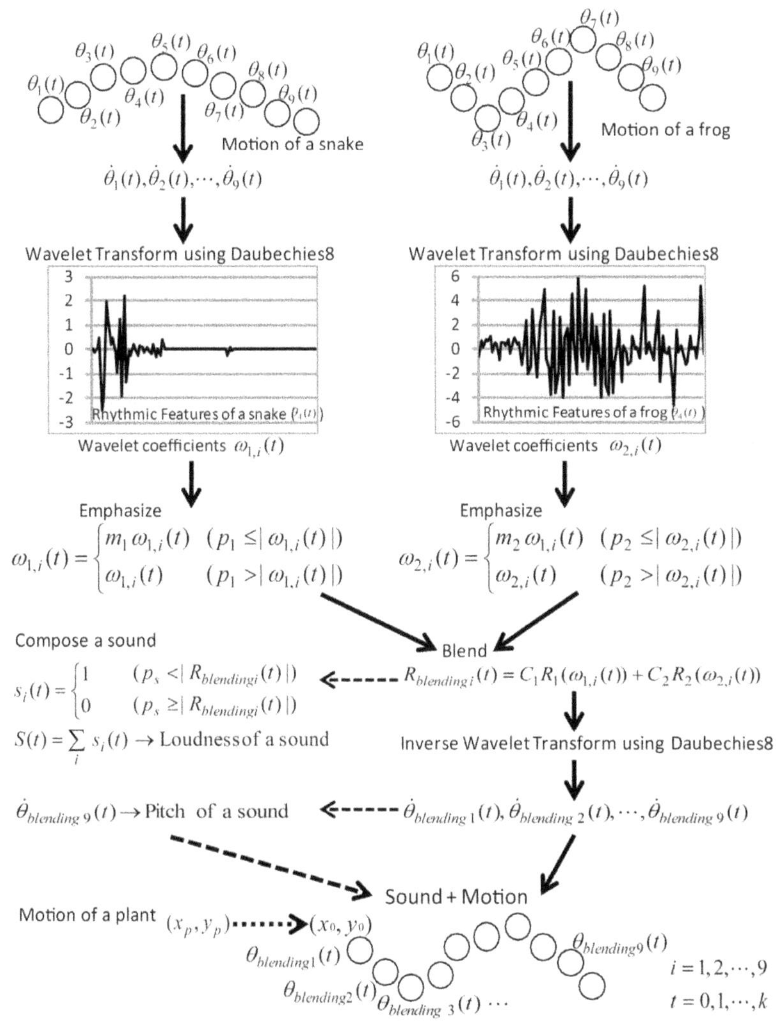

Figure 5. Procedure of generating motion with sound for Experiment 2.

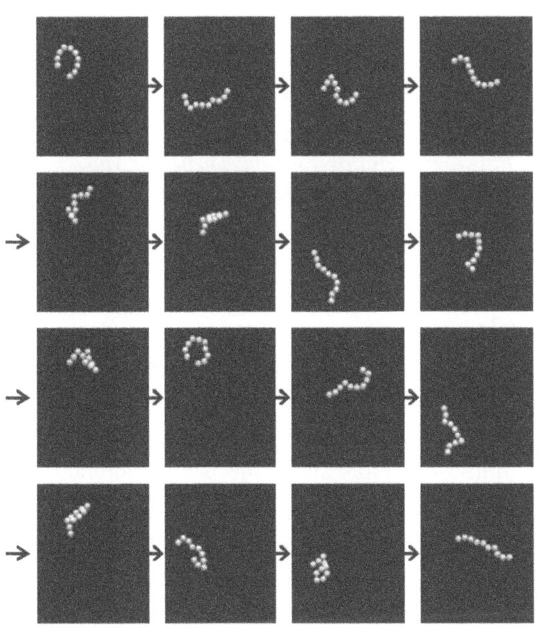

Figure 6. Example of motions created in Experiment 2.

The evaluation terms are presented in Figure 7. The subjects were college students (aged 19–21). In order to eliminate the possible effect of the order of presentation, seven of the subjects evaluated Motion 2-I first and Motion 2-II second, while the others evaluated Motion 2-II first and Motion 2-I second.

An SD profile obtained from the experiment is shown in Figure 7. The points in the figure show the average of all subjects for each term for each motion. In the figure, we can see that the following terms elicited a significant (or marginal) difference between Motion 2-I (motion with sound) and Motion 2-II (motion without sound): term 1, "Fanciful – Realistic" ($F(1, 96) = 2.93$, $p < .1.0$); term 4, "Looks fun – Looks boring" ($F(1, 96) = 7.51$, $P < .05$), term 5, "Intriguing – Uninteresting" ($F(1, 96) = 2.93$, $p < .01$); and term 8, "Compelling – Not compelling" ($F(1, 96) = 10.9$, $p < .05$).

The SD profile shown in Figure 7 shows that a significant (or marginal) difference was found between the motions for terms 1, 4, 5, and 8. Among these motions, term 1, "Fanciful – Realistic" is assumed to be related to creative

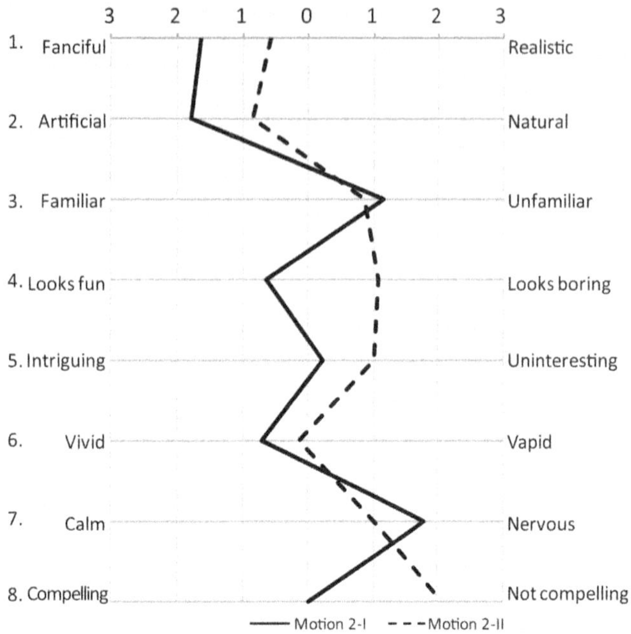

Figure 7. SD profile obtained from the evaluation of Experiment 2.

expression that extends beyond the ordinary human imagination. On the other hand, term 4, "Looks fun – Looks boring," term 5, "Intriguing – Uninteresting," and term 8, "Compelling – Not compelling" are assumed to be related to an emotional impression that resonates with deep feeling. These results demonstrate that there is a tendency for motions that extend beyond the ordinary human imagination to give more emotional impressions, thus confirming the validity of our hypothesis.

CONCLUSION AND FUTURE WORKS

In this study, we developed a method for the design of a creative and emotional motion. This work was based on the hypothesis that a creative motion that is beyond the ordinary human imagination can produce emotional impressions that resonate with deep feeling. The proposed method involves computer implementation of motion blending, movement analogous to natural objects, rhythmic emphasis, movement of the entire design object, and sound-related effect. Using a computer system we constructed, we conducted two experiments that confirmed both our hypothesis and the effectiveness of our methodology.

The results of both experiments showed a tendency for motion that extends beyond the ordinary human imagination to be imbued with more effective emotional impressions, confirming the validity of our hypothesis.

These results imply that the methods employed to emphasize the rhythmic features of the motion and to add sound to it make the motions more creative and emotional according to our definitions of the terms.

However, not just any motion that extends beyond the ordinary human imagination could produce emotional impressions. The method developed in this study involves two strategies that may at first glance seem contradictory: one is to use natural objects as a source, and the other is to elaborate them so that they extend beyond the ordinary human imagination. We believe that these seemingly contradictory strategies are effective for designing a truly creative and emotional motion. However, we have yet to understand the reasoning behind the efficacy of these strategies, nor have we clarified how we might innovate another method for designing such a motion. These issues must be addressed in future works.

Even though our discussion has been limited to the method developed in this study, a number of issues remain to be clarified. For example, in this study, we chose frogs and snakes as sources for natural objects. Furthermore, we created only one type of movement for the entire target design, and one type of sound. We must assume that the validity of our hypothesis depends on the source of the motion employed and the means by which it is enhanced. More case studies would be necessary in order to more thoroughly investigate our method of designing a creative and emotional motion.

REFERENCES

1. Chakrabarti, A., Sarkar, P., Leelavathamma, B., and Nataraju, B.S. A functional representation for aiding biomimetic and artificial inspiration of new ideas. *Artificial Intelligence for Engineering Design, Analysis and Manufacturing, 19,* 2 (2005), 113-132.
2. Cooper, G.W., and Meyer, L.B. *The Rhythmic Structure of Music.* University of Chicago Press, Chicago, 1960.
3. Daubechies, I. *Ten Lectures on Wavelets.* Society for Industrial Mathematics, Philadelphia, 1992.
4. GNU Scientific Library. http://www.gnu.org/software/gsl/.
5. Hermann, V.H. *On the Sensations of Tone as a Physiological Basis for the Theory of Music.* Longmans Green and Co., London, 1885.
6. Nagai, Y., Taura. T., and Mukai, F. Concept blending and dissimilarity: Factors for creative concept generation process, *Design Studies, 30,* 6 (2009), 648-675.
7. Norman, D.A. *Emotional Design: Why We Love (or Hate) Everyday Things.* Basic Books, New York, 2003.
8. Open Computer Vision Library. Available at http://sourceforge.net/projects/opencvlibrary/.
9. OpenGL Utility Toolkit. Available at http://www.opengl.org/resources/libraries/glut/.
10. Osgood, C.E., Suci G.J., and Tannenbaum, P.H. *The measurement of meaning.* University of Illinois Press, Urbana, 1957.

11. Swaroop, V., Michael, H., and Ashok, K.G. Biologically-Inspired Innovation in Engineering Design: A Cognitive Study, *Technical Report, Graphics, Visualization and Usability Center* (2007), Georgia Institute of Technology, GIT-GVU-07-07.

12. Taura, T., and Nagai, Y. Designing of Emotional and Creative Motion. *Emotional Engineering: Service Development* (2010), edited by Shuichi Fukuda, Springer-Verlag, 377-388.

13. Tsujimoto, K., Miura, S., Tsumaya, A., Nagai, Y., Chakrabarti, A., and Taura, T. A Method for Creative Behavioral Design Based on Analogy and Blending from Natural Things. *Proceedings of ASME 2008 International Design Engineering Technical Conference and Computers and Information in Engineering Conference* (2008), on CD-ROM.

14. Yamada, K., Taura, T., and Nagai, Y. Design of Emotional and Creative Motion by Focusing on Rhythmic Features. *Design Creativity 2010* (2010), Springer-Verlag, 139-146.

Design Space Exploration in Parametric Systems: Analyzing Effects of Goal Specificity and Method Specificity on Design Solutions

Naghmi Shireen **Halil I. Erhan** **Rodolfo Sánchez** **Jelena Popovic** **Robert Woodbury** **Bernhard E. Riecke**

School of Interactive Arts and Technology, Simon Fraser University
250-13450 102nd Avenue, Surrey, BC, Canada, V3T 0A3
{nshireen, herhan, rsanchez, jpopovic, rw, ber1}@sfu.ca

ABSTRACT

In this paper, the effects of design-task specificity level on design space exploration are studied. An experiment was conducted to study the effects of goals and methods on design process and design solutions by 16 individual designers, who performed two design tasks under different combination of design goal and method specifications. Protocol analysis and outcome-based analysis were carried out. The results of the outcome-based analysis reveal that the *quality* of the design solutions can greatly be affected by goal specificity level of a design task, whereas in case of *quantity*, *novelty* and *designer's self satisfaction level*, the effects are insignificant. None of these metrics showed significant influence of method specificity levels of a design task. The process-based analysis on the other hand, reveals some interesting search behaviors in parametric systems, which are then used to explain the possible reasons for insignificance in quantitative data.

Author Keywords

Design space exploration, parametric systems, design outcomes

ACM Classification Keywords

H.5.m. Information interfaces and presentation (e.g., HCI): Miscellaneous.

General Terms

Design, Experimentation, Theory, Performance, Measurement.

INTRODUCTION

Design is a goal-oriented process. It entails purposes and methods to achieve those purposes [2, 6, 10, 23]; together they define a boundary for design space exploration [27, 33]. Parametric systems, which recently have received wider attention across various design domains, have influenced design search behavior [36]. These systems provide designers with generative capabilities and model-making tools that can be used to explore alternatives and their variations through parametric changes [35]. In other words, they build models to explore solutions computationally while keeping the design logic consistent. In addition, through parametric dependencies, goals can become an integral part of the solution space.

In this study, we attempt to understand how design task specifications in parametric systems affect designers' solution search, and how they determine the outcome of the alternative solutions. Our major research question is to find if there exists any correlation between alternative solutions generated in parametric system and task specificity level in terms of goals and methods. This paper is part of a larger study that aims to understand design space exploration in parametric CAD systems when design goals and available parametric modeling methods are constrained; however, here the focus is mostly on design outcomes, and we measured the effects of design task specificity level on designer's satisfaction level; quantity, quality and novelty of design solutions produced.

We believe this topic needs further attention, for there are several approaches addressing the influence of task specifications on design, and they can be substantially different from each other. For example, while Shneiderman [25] suggests providing a semi-structured but orderly process to improve discovery and innovation in design processes, Akers [1] suggests that explorative-backtracking (which is but one strategy for design space exploration) happens only when there is a freedom to explore design alternatives, i.e., when the goal specificity is low. On the other hand Fricke [16, 17] claims that the more precise the problem statement given, the less time designers take in framing the problem hence they can produce a wider range of solution concepts. These approaches need to be tested further to determine how design task specifications affect design search patterns while developing alternative solutions and subsequently affect the design output.

We aim that the results from this study will contribute in (a) developing a descriptive model focusing on task specificity and method specificity effects on design exploration using parametric systems; (b) designing of effective user interfaces for design alternatives; and

(c) helping designers to adapt or develop new use patterns in parametric systems when they are searching for alternatives.

LITERATURE BACKGROUND

The effects of task specificity on the effectiveness of the design exploration process in parametric systems can be measured by *process-based analysis* through protocol studies [2, 14, 30] or *outcome-based analysis* [18, 22, 25]. In this paper, however, a combination of both outcome-based and process-based evaluation was adapted. Both approaches are needed because (a) the value of a productive design generation phase is often evident in the quality of the solutions [19] that should assure finding a "*satisficing design*" [27, 28]; (b) discovery of activity patterns can be achieved by process analysis of design space exploration that can then be adopted to improve software interface design. Outcome-based analysis was mostly used for the verification of the hypotheses, while process-based analysis was used to see if there exist any patterns in design space exploration and to understand and explain why one hypothesis was verified and not others.

Design Outcome: What to Measure

We examined several design outcome evaluation metrics measuring creativity, innovation, flexibility, variety, novelty, feasibility, quality and quantity of alternatives produced. However, for objectivity and simplicity for this study we chose the metrics proposed by Shah et al. [24] which are widely accepted in various design domains [20]. The metrics measures effectiveness of design generation process and comprise of four properties: *quantity, quality, variety and novelty*. Out of these four metrics quality, novelty and quantity are applied in our study. Variety was also considered initially, but after the end of the study, we found out that most of the designers produced only one design solution for a given design task. This was not enough to measure variety. Instead, we asked participants to rate their satisfaction-level with the solutions they generated. This was considered important to measure, as it could reveal the designer's preference of specificity-level of goal and method as they search for design solutions.

Number of Alternatives Generated

Classical literature on design confirms that generating alternative solutions is one of the most important stages of design [3, 4, 12]. According to Shah, Vargas-Hernandez and Smith [24] "quantity" can be defined as total number of *ideas* generated. It can also be understood as a measure of total number of global solutions [22], where global solutions refer to a set of one or more ideas generated against same design problem. The rationale for this measurement is that generating more ideas increases the chance of better ideas.

Novelty

Novelty is a measure of how unusual and unexpected an idea is when compared with other ideas [24]. Being a relative term it can be measured on different levels; against the whole world of ideas or a group of ideas generated with a design process. A solution may be considered novel on personal, societal or historical levels [24], each at different scales. This metric has also been studied by many other authors [3] for its significance and influence. Some authors related this measure of newness in ideas with innovation [25].

Quality

Quality as defined by Shah et al. [24] is the measure of the feasibility of an idea and how closely it meets design specifications. Measuring quality of a design is challenging. For objectivity and simplicity, some authors [22, 24] have tried to parse it to quantifiable attributes. When ideas are generated at a conceptual level, quality is largely related to the feasibility of an idea [22, 24].

Designer satisfaction level

Fundamentally, designer satisfaction with a solution is a chief measure of design outcomes [3, 8, 27, 28] – designers apply such evaluations routinely in their work. Satisfaction is inherently composite—it can be based on several variables such as complying with specifications and requirements, meeting cost constraints or any of the various "-ilities" (buildability, serviceability etc.). We chose to measure satisfaction as a single coarse Likert scale, accepting that this hides the actual composition of a designer's evaluation. The purpose of measuring satisfaction level is to probe the effects of goal specificity and method specificity level on designer's satisfaction with the generated solutions.

HYPOTHESIS

The objective of the study is to measure and explain the effects of task specifications on design process and design outcomes. The experimental hypotheses are as follows:

H1: There exist a relation between the *design task specificity level* (IV) and *number of alternatives* produced (DV) using a parametric CAD system by a sample designer group (MV) with advance or intermediate expertise levels in using the system.

H2: There exist a relation between the *design task specificity level* (IV) and the *quality* of designs produced (DV) using a parametric CAD system by a sample designer group (MV) with advanced or intermediate expertise levels in using the system.

H3: There exists a relation between the *design task specificity level* (IV) and the *novelty* of design alternatives (DV) produced using a parametric CAD system by a sample designer group (MV) with advance or intermediate expertise levels in using the system.

H4: There exists a relation between the *design task specificity level* (IV) and the *designer's satisfaction level* for design alternatives (DV) produced using a parametric CAD system by a sample designer group (MV) with advance or intermediate expertise levels in using the system.

RESEARCH METHODOLOGY

Research Design

In order to analyze the effects of goal specificity and method specificity on the design space exploration process using parametric design systems, a 2-by-2 task taxonomy proposed by Akers [1] was adapted with two specificity levels (high and low) of design goals and design methods. (Figure 1) The study tests each combination of goal and method and applies both outcome-based and process-based evaluations for analysis. Comparisons were made to identify similar patterns that might be observed among individuals.

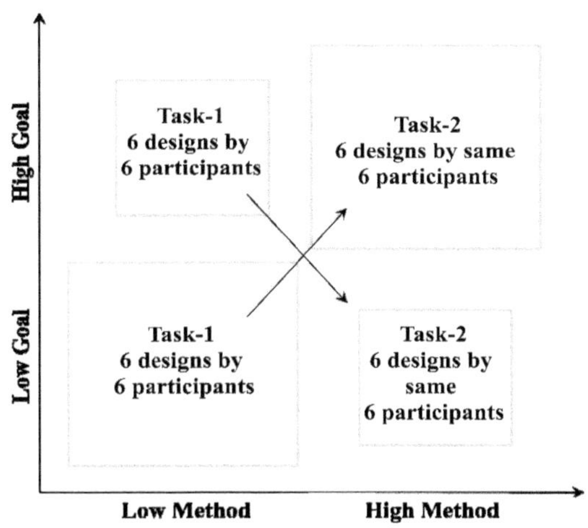

Figure 1 – Order of participants (Experimental group)

Sampling Design

The target population comprises designers with *SolidWorks* [29] experience. Upper-division undergraduate and graduate students of the School of Interactive Arts and Technology at Simon Fraser University were invited to participate in the experiment. The undergrad students had taken an advanced design course using *SolidWorks*. The graduate students had design backgrounds and were intermediate or advanced *SolidWorks* users.

The experiment ran over a three weeks period, yielding a sample size of 16, sufficient for ANOVA. Out of these 16 participants, 12 were assigned to the treatment group and 4 to a control group.

Pre-experimental Survey

Although we invited students who had *SolidWorks* experience before by successfully completing an upper-division course, a pre-experiment survey was conducted to ensure that the sample population had a suitable background. It was designed to confirm that all participants had a design background and intermediate or advanced level *Solidworks* experience. A questionnaire was used to prescreen the participants based on their self-reported confidence level in using *SolidWorks*. The questions included whether they had any design experience if so, how much and in what field. In addition, they were asked to rate their experience in various parametric software on a 5-level Likert scale where '1' represented "Novice" and '5' represented "Expert". We used the above information largely to interpret outliers in the collected data. Only one participant showed inconsistency with the expertise level chosen. This participant attempted to use online help in the beginning of the experiment. We eliminated this participant's data from the evaluation.

The pilot experiment

Before starting the experiment, we performed a pilot test using similar design problems and the same media we gave to all participants. We found the average time used to design all possible solutions under both conditions was about 50 minutes and the number of alternatives produced, on average, was 2.5. Using this as a guideline, we then came up with the maximum time expected for the experiment to be 60 minutes.

Experimental Design

Confounding Variables

It is necessary to identify the confounding variables that possibly could affect the design space exploration process. In this section, we discuss these variables one by one and how we attempted to control them.

Human Factor

Designer's personality, for example, mood, motivation and experience with the related design problems and expertise in parametric design tools, are some of the variables that influence the designer's search for alternatives. Three strategies were adopted to control this confound. In addition to the pre-experiment survey, a $30 gift card honorarium was offered to all participants as well as the possibility of winning a $30, $50 or $100 gift card for the best overall designs. This was chosen to increase the motivation level of participants. Furthermore, each designer was asked to perform two design tasks randomly under two different goal and method specificity levels.

Type of the Design problem

Each participant completed two design tasks. In order to reduce learning effects, we constructed two different design problems with similar design typology and complexity: a bus stop and a beach changing room. Although these design tasks are slightly different with respect to detailed requirements, e.g. one structure requires privacy for use, while other demands visibility for upcoming bus; they are highly similar structurally, as they both are temporary-use structures and comprise similar architectural elements.

Environment variables

In order to reduce the effects of tools and design environment, all designers were asked to use the same parametric design software (*SolidWorks*) and each session was conducted in the same location, seating and computers and with controlled ambient light and temperature. The time of day could not have been controlled and was set to be convenient for the participants.

Grouping of Participants
Participants were grouped to perform tasks in one of the combinations of the three factors: design problem (bus stop or changing room), goal specificity level (High or Low) and method specificity level (High or Low). Participants were grouped into two groups: a first-group with 12 participants for experimental analysis and a second-group with four participants as a control group. This allowed us to test the plausibility of alternative explanations that could account for the study results. The major reason to use a control group was to detect and measure any effects of design task design problem with minimum design specifications. An example for low and high goal specificity level for changing room is shown (Table 3).

Whereas, in case of method specificity level, at the low level participants were given no constraint on the method they use and at the high level they were introduced to three parametric design patterns [36]: *ClearNames* refers to a series of clear and meaningful names to identify objects and features throughout the model. *Jig* suggests users build abstract frameworks that can later be embedded with more details while maintaining the base structure intact. Lastly, *Increment* structures parametric changes to occur in the model through explicit sequences of related values and functions. An example of how low and high method specified design tasks were given to the participants is shown in Table 3.

No. of participants (Experimental Group)	Task 1			Task 2		
	Goal	**Method**	**Design Problem**	**Goal**	**Method**	**Design Problem**
3	Low	Low	Bus Stop	High	High	Changing Room
3	Low	Low	Changing Room	High	High	Bus Stop
3	High	Low	Bus Stop	Low	High	Changing Room
3	High	Low	Changing Room	Low	High	Bus Stop
12						

Table 1 - Distribution of participants in experimental group

No. of participants (Control Group)	Task 1			Task 2		
	Goal	**Method**	**Design Problem**	**Goal**	**Method**	**Design Problem**
1	Low	Low	Bus Stop	Low	Low	Changing Room
1	High	High	Changing Room	High	High	Bus Stop
1	Low	High	Changing Room	Low	High	Bus Stop
1	High	Low	Bus Stop	High	Low	Changing Room
4						

Table 2 – Distribution of participants in control group

order. Participants in the control group were assigned the same goal and method specifications under both conditions; the only changing condition was type of design task (bus stop or changing room).

Participants were randomly assigned to either of the groups. The distribution of the participants along with the randomization of design conditions, under which they were analyzed, is shown in Table 1 and Table 2.

Order of Participants
In case of goal specificity level, out of the 12 participants, 6 were randomly assigned low goal design tasks for their first session and high goal for their second session. Whereas, remaining six were given high goal deign task for the first session. In method specifications, all 12 participants were assigned low methods for their first session. The reason was that before high method specificity design task, the participants were taught parametric design patterns to use during their exploration for alternatives. (Figure 1)

Goal and Method Specificity
The goals were assigned mostly on the basis of design requirements. A low-goal design task in our study refers to

Outcome-based Evaluation

Number of Alternatives Generated
In this paper we use the term "number of alternatives" to represent the quantity of design outcomes. During the design of the study, the authors unanimously decided that this would be the total number of solutions indicated by a designer as an "alternative solution". Otherwise, interpretation of the solutions during encoding as 'alternative' could introduce bias without using any metrics. So far, we haven't seen a metric presented in the literature.

Low Goal-Low Method	Propose two person free standing changing room for Vancouver beaches
Low Goal-High Method	Propose a two person free standing changing room for Vancouver beaches. When designing try to use the Increment, Jig and ClearNames design patterns.
High Goal-Low Method	Propose a two person free standing changing room for Vancouver beaches. Make sure your design is between 1.50 – 2.00m long, 1.20 – 1.50m wide and 2.30 – 2.50m tall. The design should also include a wind proof roof, provide privacy to the user while maintaining proper natural ventilation, and be securely and easily fixed to the underlying surface.
High Goal-High Method	Propose a two person free standing changing room for Vancouver beaches. Make sure your design is between 1.50 – 2.00m long, 1.20 – 1.50m wide and 2.30 – 2.50 tall. The design should also include a wind proof roof, provide privacy to the user while maintaining proper natural ventilation, and be securely and easily fixed to the underlying surface. When designing try to use the Increment, Jig and ClearNames design patterns.

Table 3 - Description of design tasks with respect to levels of "Goal" and "Method" specifications

m	**Attributes (*f*, *weights*)**	$S = 1$	$S = 3$	$S = 5$
1	Type of structure (0.15)	Solid Wall and Roof	Column and beam	Others
2	Geometry (0.15)	Square or rectangular	Deformed square or rectangle	Others
3	Added purpose (0.1)	No purpose	One purpose	2+
4	Privacy(0.1)	Door / full coverage	Partial coverage / zigzag Entrance	Others
5	Fixable to base surface (0.1)	Weight / bolts	Cables	Others
6	Light (0.1)	Artificial light	Natural light	Others
7	Natural ventilation(0.1)	Artificial	Upper and lower windows / Louvers	Others
8	Roof drainage (0.1)	Flat roof for snow and rain drainage	Slanted or curved roof	Others
9	Materials (0.1)	Steel / Concrete / Wood / Glass	Cloth / Plastic / Rubber /	Others

Table 4 – List of attributes and weights for calculating "Novelty" score for beach changing room

Novelty

Two methods were adopted for calculating novelty scores for each design. First one is the *a priori* method proposed by Shah et al. [24]. It is used where a universe of ideas for comparison is subjectively defined for each function or attribute, and at each stage [24]. It is given preference over *post facto* approach, as in *a priori* method attributes are defined before analyzing any data to avoid bias. Please note that, in this study, all designs were analyzed only at a conceptual level, befitting the time constraints on the experiment. To do the analysis, the design problem was first decomposed into a set of key functions or characteristics, and a weight was given to each function prior to data collection (Table 4). Each function was then described in terms of how novelty for that function can be fulfilled in any design solution. It was again decided prior to data collection that what would be considered novel and a weight was assigned accordingly (Table 4).

Overall novelty for each idea was then computed from the formula [24];

$$Novelty = \sum_{j=1}^{m} f_j \sum_{k=1}^{n} S_{jk} P_k$$

Where, m is the total number of functions/attributes, f is the weight assigned to each function with respect to its importance. S is the sub novelty score for each function, P is the weight assigned to each stage, and n is the total number of stages analyzed. As in our study only one stage (conceptual level) was used so, P was ignored.

In our second method, a jury of three design professionals was asked to grade each design for novelty in their ideas on the conceptual level. All three professionals were selected on the basis of their educational background in architecture and expertise in design education. All of them have minimum seven years of education and two to four years of professional design experience. They were asked to rate each design for novelty by comparing it within the group. It was considered important to compare the designs with each other to see which specificity level of goal and method helps in producing more novel outputs.

Quality

Quality is a construct requiring a carefully designed analysis technique. As when we talk about measuring "how close a design comes to meet the design specifications" [24] both explicit and implicit design requirements must be considered. Explicit requirements occur directly in the design problem. Implicit requirements may be just as firm, but are taken as givens. For example, if a person is asked to design a chair, then it is an implicit requirement that a chair will have a base to bear load and will provide a place to sit. Keeping this in mind, while using Shah's [24] measuring formula for quality, various implicit attributes were selected as shown in the Table 5. Weights were given to each attribute such that if one attribute is satisfied fully, it was given a maximum score of 5 and was then multiplied by its weight. Adding all together gives a total score for quality.

m	Attributes	Weight (f)	Max. Score(S)	Stage (k)
1	Privacy	0.14	5	1
2	Size	0.14	5	1
3	Wind proof roof	0.14	5	1
4	Securely fixed to surface or other structure	0.14	5	1
5	Light	0.14	5	1
6	Natural ventilation	0.14	5	1
7	Roof drainage	0.14	5	1
	SUM OF WEIGHTS	1		

Table 5 – List of attributes and weights for calculating "Quality" score for beach changing room

To avoid inter-rater bias, three researchers together calculated the scores for quality for each design, according to the set rules discussed above, and weights specified in the table. Again, like novelty, each design was analyzed for quality at a single conceptual stage. In case of a designer presenting two or more alternatives as a solution, an average score was calculated. The final score was calculated by the formula as stated by Shah et al. [24];

$$Quality = \sum_{j=1}^{m} f_j \sum_{k=1}^{n} S_{jk} P_k \Big/ n * \sum_{j=1}^{m} f_j$$

Where, m is the total number of attributes/functions, n is the total number of stages (which is 1 in our case, conceptual stage). S is the score for each attribute against each design and f is the weight of that attribute. P is the weight for stage k.

Designer satisfaction level

Designers were asked for their self satisfaction with the proposed design solutions under each condition. They were asked to rate their satisfaction level on a 5 level Likert scale where 1 represented least satisfaction level and 5 represented highly satisfactory design solution.

Process based evaluation

Data collection

To record the design process, each participant's computer screen was videotaped during the experiment. These videos provided authors with insight into designers' intentions through a chain of iterated actions, along with the design completion time. In addition to these videos, designers were asked to save screen shots whenever they believe they have accomplished a sub-goal task during their design process. The sub-goal could either be a designer's self specified goal or a goal explicitly stated inside a design problem. Such moments in a process were named *design states.*

A post-experiment survey asked participants their satisfaction level with the design outcomes, as well as their preference for specificity level of design goals and methods.

Data encoding

After the successful collection of screen captures, videos and *SolidWorks* files; data was reviewed, encoded by three encoders and was transformed into design trees. It was noticed that some of the participants did not save screen shots to depict design states. According to the post experimental survey, they forgot to do so, while searching for design solutions. So a new strategy was adopted to define design states. Various signals were decided by the authors to call for a design state, which included: saving a file, prolonged interface actions (zooming/rotating) and opening a new file or part. According to these signals, design trees were prepared, analyzed and compared for significant patterns.

RESULTS

Outcome-Based Analysis

The data collected was analyzed using a factorial design ANOVA with two between-subjects factors (Goal and Method specificity levels). Each of the dependent variable mentioned was analyzed individually. In this section, the results from the analysis are discussed one by one.

Quality

This analysis revealed a significant main effect for goal specificity level, $F(1, 20) = 6.16$; $p = 0.022$. The sample means are displayed in Figure 2. Tukey's HSD test showed that participants in the high-goal specificity condition scored significantly higher on quality than participants in the low goal specificity condition ($p < 0.05$).The main effect for method specificity level was not significant, $F(1, 20) = 0.79$; $p = 0.38$. The interaction between goal and method specificity level was also not significant, $F(1, 20) = 0.08$; $p = 0.77$.

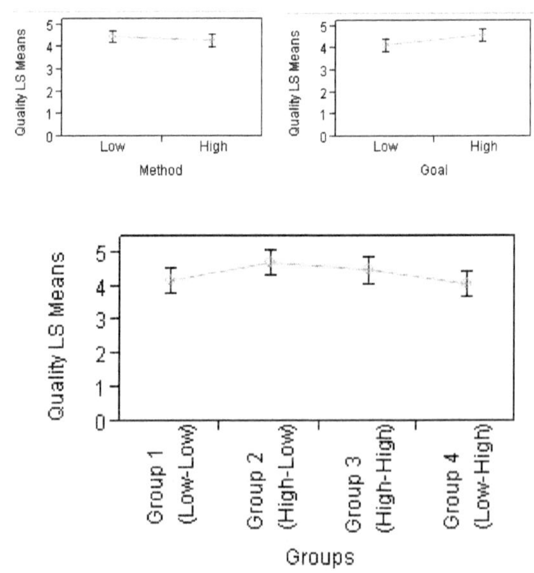

Figure 2 – Comparison of "Quality" score between groups

The results were also compared among four groups made according to each combination of goal and method. The line graph in Figure 2 shows that participants score highest under high-goal and low-method specification design task compared to all other groups. In the figure, *High-Low* means high-goal and low-method respectively.

Quality Score by Professionals

To our surprise, the quality scores given by professionals were insignificant for both goal specificity and method specificity, F (1, 20) = 0.09; p = 0.766, and F(1,20) = 0.09; p= 0.766 respectively. Figure 3, shows the distribution of quality grades assigned by professionals, across groups.

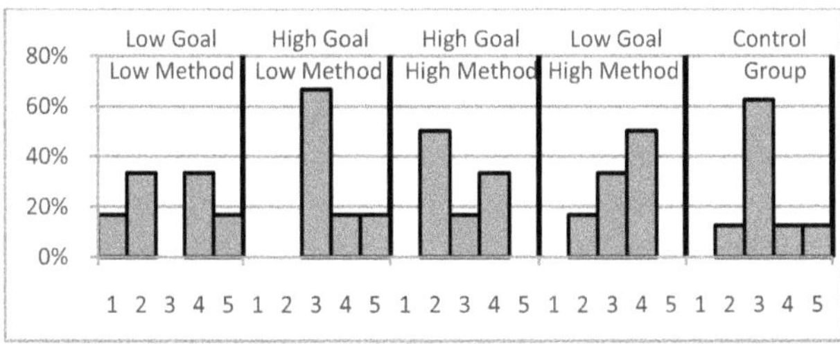

Figure 3 – Normalized distribution of *Quality* scores by professionals in each group on a Likert scale of 1 to 5

Novelty

This analysis did not reveal any significant main effect. Neither for goal specificity level, $F(1, 20) = 1.42$; $p = 0.25$, nor for method specificity level, $F(1, 20) = 1.46$; $p = 0.24$. The interaction between goal and method specificity level was also not significant, $F(1, 20) = 1.88$; $p = 0.18$.

Again the results were compared among four groups made according to each combination of goals and methods. The line graph in Figure 4, shows that mean novelty scores under low-goals high-methods is higher compared to all other groups, where group 4(Low-High) scores highest; *Low-High* means low-goal and high-method respectively.

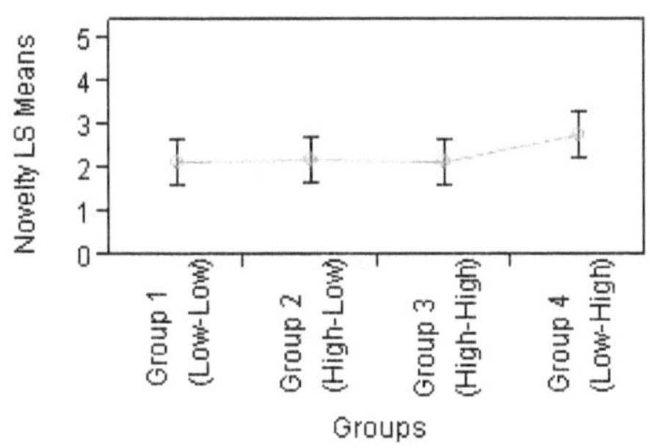

Figure 4 – comparison of "Novelty" score between groups

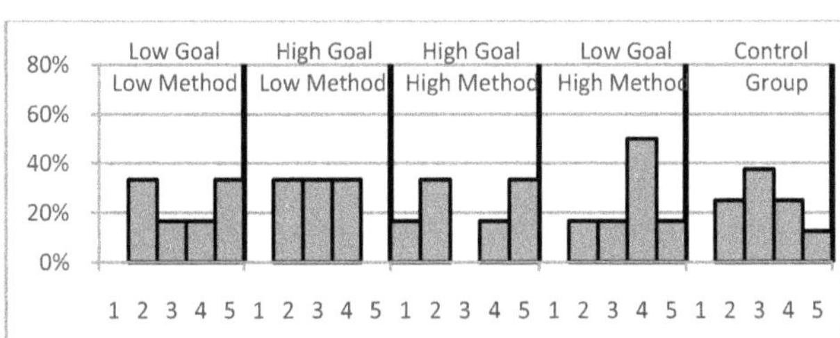

Figure 5 – Normalized distribution of *Novelty* scores by professionals in each group on a Likert scale of 1 to 5

Novelty Score by Professionals

The novelty scores given by professionals like quality scores were insignificant as well, for both goal specificity and method specificity, F (1, 20) = 0.08; p = 0.77, and F(1,20) = 0.21; p= 0.65 respectively. (Figure 5)

Number of Alternatives

This analysis did not reveal any significant main effect either. Neither for goal specificity level, F (1, 20) = 0.33; $p = 0.57$, nor for method specificity level, $F(1, 20) = 0.58$; $p = 0.45$. The interaction between goal and method specificity level was also not significant, F (1, 20) = 0.0366; $p = 0.85$.

Results when compared among groups show that the mean value for number of alternatives is highest for the group performing low-goal and low-method design task (Figure 6) but is neither significant nor large.

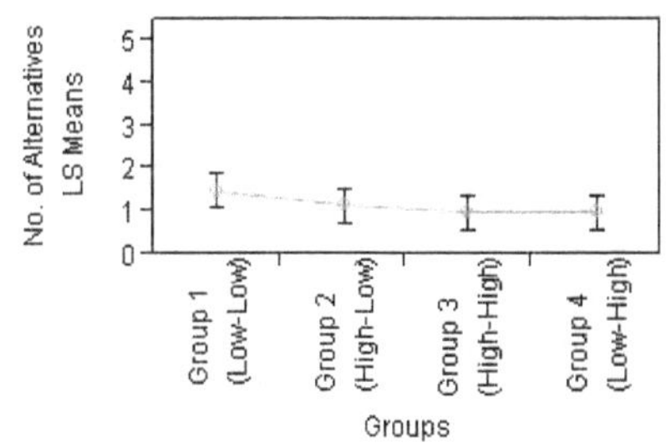

Figure 6 – Comparison of "No. of Alternatives" between groups

Designer's Satisfaction Level

The results for satisfaction level are non-significant again (Figure 7), but it was observed that the mean value for the satisfaction level was higher when the design task given to designers was set with high goals and low method specifications.

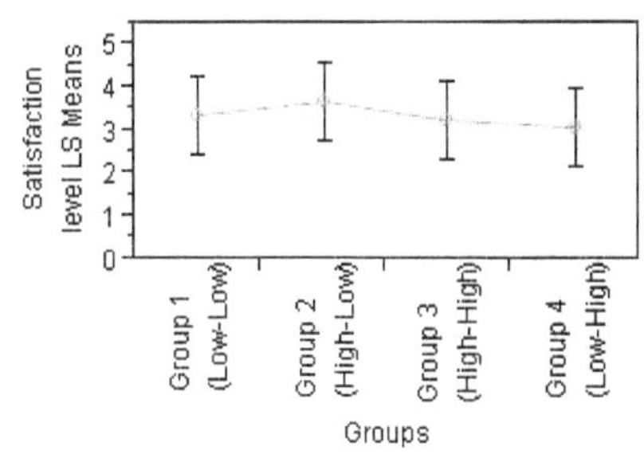

Figure 7 – Comparison of "Satisfaction level" between groups

Process Based Analysis

Except for the quality of design solutions, the results from the quantitative analysis of design outcomes were mostly insignificant, therefore, it was considered necessary to give an alternative explanation through process-based analysis. We structured our analysis using the classical literature on design problem solving [27, 28] and designer's search behavior/pattern [10, 12, 23].

Design Goals

We observed that Akin's [2, 3] act of "redefining design problems", persists even more strongly in parametric design patterns. As designers move ahead in design space, they keep on redefining goals and constraints even though the problem could have been considered well-defined [30]. Designers exercise this freedom of changing goals and constraints, as the understanding of the problem develops and the definition of the solution proceeds [14]. This pattern in design is consistent with 'opportunistic' strategy. The same pattern was observed among all participants, which could be the possible reason behind the significance of quality scores against goal specificity in this experiment.

It was observed that in parametric systems, most of the designers first set a rough framework of ideas with ill-defined problem goals and constraints, and as they proceed, they take the liberty of going back at any stage for alterations. Such backtracking events were sometimes observed to be explorative, and sometimes to refine details (if designer had already reached a satisfactory design solution). In both cases, designers were observed to be defining goals and sub-goals repetitively.

According to design literature on designer's behavior, it is the evaluation of the solution that is important, not the analysis of the problem [14]. This strategy was observed in many design processes, when designers reached a certain design state where they took some time to think either to proceed or to go back and make alterations. It was observed that instead of going through design goals or requirements one by one in an orderly strategic manner, designers preferred making decisions depending upon the current scenario after analyzing the partial solution.

An evidence of co-evolution of solution and problem [10] was also observed when designers develop intermediate solutions to help understand the problem formulation. They move back and forth in problem space and solution space with intermediate partial structuring of sometimes problem and sometimes solution [12].

Design Methods

According to literature on design search, designers are reasonably efficient whenever they adopt systematic and logical approaches, while designers produce mediocre or poor design solutions when they act unsystematically [16, 17]. But according to our analysis, the reason for no correlation in methods is not that there was no systematic approach in their process, instead parametric systems allowed backtracking at and to any stage of the design process to make changes. We found that none of the designers followed a strategic methodology in terms of sequencing such actions. One thing which was quite evident in all design processes was introducing parametric dependencies through equations and smart dimensions as a way of recording design constructs or intent while proceeding towards a satisfactory solution. Designers were able to backtrack at any moment of design process and add such dependencies. This opportunity has given designers a freedom not to adopt any strategic plan of actions. This may partially explain some of the lack of significance in the quantitative data.

Satisfaction level

Designers satisfice rather than optimize [28]. The criteria by which a designer decides that a design is satisfactory are complex, including explicit, implicit, external and internal. In the study, designers who were unable to accomplish their pre-conceived goals rated their work at a low level of satisfaction, even though their solution was considered "better" by the evaluators compared to solutions by other designers or by the same designer.

Number of Alternatives

It was observed that due to the use of parametric systems, the final solution proposed by most of the designers was a single solution, yet there is an evidence of variations and alternatives at the process level. During the experiment all designers tried alternatives by using one of the following strategies: by changing parameters, by improving details in an already built model-part through backtracking or by saving instances of already built parts through design tables (a feature - provided inside *SolidWorks* for creating alternative solutions for a model part).

Although the quantitative analysis shows no significance in terms of number of alternatives saved by designers, there is a clear evidence of alternative solutions tried during the process. These alternatives were part of the design process but were not saved, and hence no record for them was seen in the final design solutions.

DISCUSSION

The reasons behind the insignificance of quantitative data has already been discussed and explained in process-based analysis, still there is a need to discuss some issues which might have affected the results and hence the insignificance. One of the major issues could be the fact that all designers were asked to perform two design tasks in the time span of two hours (max.), this limited time frame plus the fatigue might have influenced the results for the second task.

Secondly in the high-method design task, designers were asked to use three parametric design patterns, in their design process. But most of the designers, while searching for solutions, either forgot to incorporate those patterns or they chose not to use them, considering them less important with respect to the design solution they had in their minds. This variability in use of patterns can be the major reason behind non-significance in method specificity level. In retrospect, we likely asked subjects to apply patterns too early in the process. Woodbury [36] points out that patterns are most appropriate when model-making requires a divide-and-conquer strategy, that is when models become complex. The relative simplicity of the models produced may simply have not been amenable to patterns.

Goal	Method	No. of Observations	Mean (Quality)	Mean (Novelty)	Mean (Satisfaction level)	Mean (No_ of Alternatives)
Low	Low	6	4.21	2.16	3.33	**1.50**
Low	High	6	4.10	**2.82**	3.08	1.00
High	Low	6	**4.72**	2.21	**3.67**	1.17
High	High	6	4.50	2.17	3.25	1.00
Control Group		8	4.45	2.5	2.625	1.00

Table 6 – Overall results comparing the mean values of each dependant variable against both "Goal" and "Method"

CONCLUSION

The outcome-based analysis of an experiment with designers exposed to different design goal and method specificity levels allowed us to measure the effects of these design task specificities on the design process and ultimately the design solutions generated. These effects were measured by an outcome-based analysis technique, and the alternative explanation for those effects was made through process-based evaluation.

Although most of the quantitative results were insignificant in order to make a claim, still depending upon the differences in mean values (Table 6) and descriptive explanation of results from protocol analysis, a thought should be given to what level of goal and method specificity should be provided to designers, to gather what sort of design outcomes, while exploring design space in parametric systems. Here are some speculative thoughts.

- When quantity of the solutions is sought, then designer might be given low specifications for both design goals and design methods.
- When more feasible and quality-wise better output is sought, then designers might be triggered with high goals and low method specifications.
- When higher novelty in design solutions is sought, then design task with low goal but high method specifications might be formed.
- When higher satisfaction level is sought, then a design task might be formulated with low goal specificity and high method specificity level.

Besides these conclusions, there is a need for further analysis of data, and perhaps running the experiment one more time with more participants in all task specificities; and with reduced confounding variables, such as, fatigue and individual expertise level in using parametric design patterns. Furthermore, as this study analyzed design outcomes only on conceptual level, further investigation should include analysis at embodiment and detail levels.

ACKNOWLEDGMENTS

We thank Dr. Thomas M. Loughin for his help on statistical analysis, Dr. Brian Fisher and Dr. David Botta for their comments and contributions in experimental design. We also thank Jawad Ahmed Tahir, Asma Khalid and Mariyam Kashani for their contributions as experts in grading the design solutions.

This work was partially supported through the Canadian Networks of Centers of Excellence program through the Graphics, Animation and New Media Network.

REFERENCES

1. Akers, D.L., Backtracking Events as Indicators of Software Usability Problems. (2010) *(PhD Dissertation)*. Department of Computer Science, Stanford University.
2. Akin Ö, How do Architects Design? *Artificial Intelligence and Pattern Recognition in Computer Aided Design, (1978)* J C Latombe (ed), IFIP, New York
3. Akin Ö and Lin C. Design Protocol Data and Novel Design Decisions *DesignStudies (1995)*16(2): 211-236
4. Akin, Ö. and Sen, R. Navigation within a structured search space in layout problems. *Environment and Planning B: Planning and Design,* 23, (1996) pp. 421-442.
5. Akin, Ö. & Akin, C., On the process of creativity in puzzles, inventions, and designs. *Automation in Construction,* 7(2-3), 123-138. (1998)
6. Chandrasekaran, B., Design Problem Solving: A Task Analysis. *AI Magazine,* (1990)11(4), pp. 59-71.
7. Christiaans H and Dorst C., Cognitive Models in Industrial Design Engineering: a protocol study, *Design Theory and Methodology - DTM92,* D L Taylor and D A Stauffer (ed), (1992) American Society of Mechanical Engineers, New York
8. Cross N., Creativity in Design: analyzing and modeling the creative leap *Leonardo (1997)* **30**(4): 311-317
9. Cross N., Natural Intelligence in Design *Design Studies (1999)* **20**(1): 25-39

10. Cross N and Dorst K Co-evolution of Problem and Solution Spaces in Creative Design: observations from an empirical study, *Computational Models of Creative Design IV(1998)* , J Gero and M L Maher (ed), University of Sydney, NSW, Australia
11. Cross N., Christiaans H and Dorst K. Design Expertise Amongst Student Designers *Journal of Art and Design Education(1994)* **13**(1): 39-56
12. Cross N Christiaans H and Dorst K (ed) Analysing Design Activity, John Wiley & Sons, Chichester, UK(1996)
13. Cross, N. Expertise in design: an overview. *Design Studies* (2004), *25*(5), 427–441.
14. Cross, N. Design cognition: Results from protocol and other empirical studies of design activity. Chapter 5 in *Design Knowing and Learning: Cognition in DesignEducation*(2001). Eastman, C., McCracken, M., and Newstetter, M. (eds.). Elsevier Science, 79-103.
15. Eisentraut, R. Styles of problem solving and their influence on the design process. *Design Studies*(1999) , Vol. 20-5, pp. 431-437
16. Fricke G., Empirical Investigations of Successful Approaches When Dealing With Differently Précised Design Problems *International Conference on Engineering Design (1993) ICED93*, Heurista, Zürich
17. Fricke G Successful Individual Approaches in Engineering Design *Research in Engineering Design(1996)* 8: 151-165
18. Jeff Wt Kan, Gero, J.S, Can An Objective Measurement Of Design Protocols Reflect The Quality Of A Design Outcome? *International Conference On Engineering Design*,(2007) ICED'0728.
19. Kurtoglu, T., Campbell, M. I., & Linsey, J. S. An experimental study on the effects of a computational design tool on concept generation. *Design Studies* (2009), 30(6), 676-703.
20. Linsey, J. S., Tseng, I., Fu, K., Cagan, J., Wood, K. L., & Schunn, C. A Study of Design Fixation, Its Mitigation and Perception in Engineering Design Faculty. *Journal of Mechanical Design,*(2010). 132(4)
21. López-Mesa, B., & Thompson, G. On the significance of cognitive style and the selection of appropriate design methods. *Journal of Engineering Design*(2006)17(4), 371.
22. López-Mesa, B., Mulet, E., Vidal, R., & Thompson, G. Effects of additional stimuli on idea-finding in design teams. *Journal of Engineering Design (2011).*, *22*(1), 31.
23. Motta E., Zdrahal Z. The Trouble with What: Issues in method-independent task specifications. *In Proceedings of the 9th Banff Knowledge Acquisition for Knowledge-Based Systems Workshop (1995)*(B.R.Gaines and M.Musen eds.). pp. 30-1 - 30- 17.
24. Shah, J.J., N. Vargas-Hernández and S.M. Smith, Metrics for measuring ideation effectiveness, *Design Studies* (2003) Vol 24, pp. 111–134.
25. Shneiderman, B., Creativity support tools: accelerating discovery and innovation. *Communications of the ACM* (2007), 50, 20–32.
26. Shneiderman, B. The Eyes Have It: A Task by Data Type Taxonomy for Information Visualizations. *Proc. IEEE Visual Languages*: 336-343(1996).
27. Simon, H. A., The Sciences of the Artificial,(1999b), (3rd rev. ed.) MIT, Cambridge, MA. (First published in 1969)
28. Simon, H. The structure of ill-structured problems. *Artificial Intelligence(1973)*, 4:181-203
29. SolidWorks (Version 2010), (Software), USA , Dassault Systèmes SolidWorks Corp, 2010.
30. Thomas J C and Carroll J M., The Psychological Study of Design *Design Studies(1979)***1**(1): 5-11
31. Ullman D G Dietterich T G et al., A Model of the Mechanical Design Process Based on Empirical Data *A I in Engineering Design and Manufacturing(1988)*: 33-52
32. Visser W (1990) More or Less Following a Plan During Design: opportunistic deviations in specification *I J Man-Machine Studies* 33: 247-278
33. Visser, W., The Cognitive Artifacts of Designing, *Lawrence Erlbaum associates*, New Jersey, London.(2006)
34. Woodbury, R. F., & Burrow, A. L. Whither Design Space? AI EDAM (2006), 20(02), 63-82.
35. Woodbury, R., Datta, S., & Burrow, A. Erasure in design space exploration. *Artificial Intelligence in Design (2000), 521–544.*
36. Woodbury, Robert. *Elements of Parametric Design.* (2010) 1st ed. Routledge

Exploring the Sensitivity to Representation of an Evolutionary Algorithm for the Design of Shapes

Andrés Gómez de Silva Garza
Computer Engineering Department
Instituto Tecnológico Autónomo de México (ITAM)
Río Hondo #1, Colonia Progreso-Tizapán, 01080—México, D.F., Mexico
+52 55 5628 4000 ext. 3644
agomez@itam.mx

ABSTRACT
Evolutionary algorithms have been used in many ways for design tasks and other creative endeavors. The choice of representation in these evolutionary algorithms influences the way in which the operators used by a given evolutionary algorithm need to be implemented. In this paper, I explore the way in which it also influences the performance of the algorithm, both from the point of view of the reliability and speed of the algorithms as well as from the point of view of the designs generated by them.

Keywords
Evolutionary algorithms, genotype representation, phenotype representation

ACM Classification Keywords
D.m. Miscellaneous.

General Terms
Algorithms.

INTRODUCTION
Evolutionary algorithms (EA's) are general-purpose search methods that evolve the potential solutions to a search problem in their populations through a series of generations until at least one of the solutions satisfies a convergence criterion [9]. As such, they have often been applied to the solution of design problems and related tasks. Two compendia of examples can be found in [2] and [3]. Design is evolutionary in the sense that, most of the time, new designs are not completely novel. Rather, the features of new designs can usually be traced back to one or several previously-existing designs from which they originated and were adapted. Viewed at this level of abstraction, EA's represent an appropriate computational metaphor for the general way in which technology progresses in human societies.

One of the important design decisions behind EA's is the choice of representation for the genotypes and/or phenotypes used by the algorithm. This choice can have a critical impact on the range of possible solutions supported by the algorithm (the solution space) and the way in which the evolutionary operators that guide the algorithm need to be implemented. This paper describes a set of experiments designed to observe the impact that such a choice has on the performance of an EA.

The paper begins by giving a brief overview of a generic EA's functioning. The specific EA used for the experiments described in this paper, including its design domain, is then discussed, together with two alternate knowledge representation schemes. Then two experiments that were performed to observe the effect of these alternate representations are presented, together with their results. Finally, some conclusions are drawn about an EA's sensitivity to the choice of representation.

EVOLUTIONARY ALGORITHMS
In general, an EA contains a population of potential solutions whose make-up is often initialized randomly. Each individual solution in the population is evaluated according to some criteria related to the type of problem that is being solved with the EA, and assigned a fitness value. A series of evolutionary operators, typically including at least crossover and mutation, are applied to the individuals in the population in order to generate new potential solutions. These new potential solutions are evaluated using the same fitness function as the previous ones, and the best solutions (usually taken from both the set of old and the set of new solutions) are kept in the population. This process continues cyclically, through a series of evolutionary generations, until some convergence criterion is reached. Because only the best of the solutions that have been seen are kept between one generation and the next, the average fitness value, *i.e.*, the average quality, of the population as a whole monotonically increases throughout the process. This is the computational equivalent of the "survival of the fittest" principle from biological evolution.

The convergence criterion is often the appearance, in the population, of the first potential solution whose fitness value surpasses a given threshold value (supposing that higher fitness values represent better quality solutions—in some EA's the opposite is true, in which case it would be the first solution to have a fitness value that goes below a given threshold value). Other possible convergence criteria could be that all the potential solutions in the population surpass a given threshold value, that the average fitness value of the population as a whole surpasses a given threshold value, or that a certain maximum acceptable number of evolutionary generations have passed.

The individuals in an EA's population are described by their genotypes, typically a linear sequence of genes. The semantics of these genes, and of the way they are put together and are interpreted, varies from EA to EA and domain to domain. Some EA's represent each individual in two ways, as genotypes and as phenotypes. This reflects the distinction that is made in biological genetics between the way in which an individual is characterized by its genetic material (genotype) and the way in which that genetic material ends up manifesting itself through the individual's physical appearance and/or behavior (phenotype). When such a distinction is made by an EA, it is the phenotype that is evaluated by the fitness function, and methods for mapping genotypes to phenotypes have to be implemented.

The genetic operators perform adaptations to the genotypes of the individuals in an EA's population. The most basic form of the crossover operator takes two parent genotypes as input, randomly chooses a crossover point for them, splits them into two pieces at that point, and produces two offspring genotypes as output by splicing together the opposite pieces taken from the two parents. That is, one offspring consists of the first part of the first parent concatenated with the second part of the second parent, whereas the other offspring consists of the first part of the second parent concatenated with the second part of the first parent. Figure 1 illustrates the functioning of the crossover operator graphically.

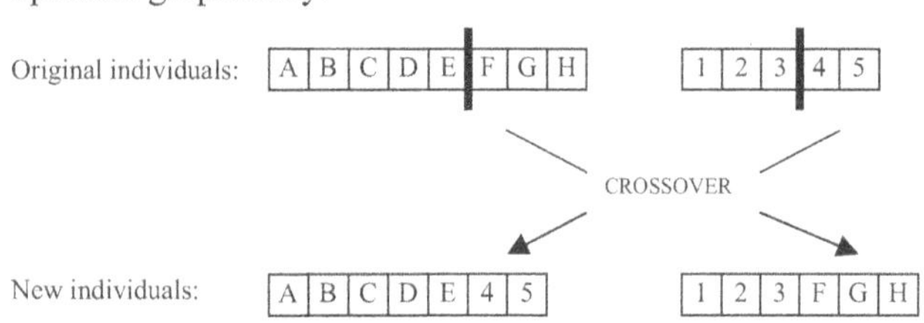

Figure 1. A graphical illustration of the genetic crossover operator.

The most basic form of the mutation operator takes one parent genotype as input and changes one of its genetic characteristics by randomly deciding which one to change and randomly choosing a new value for it, producing one resulting offspring genotype as output. Figure 2 illustrates the functioning of the mutation operator graphically. Note that both crossover and mutation operate "blindly," without paying attention to the semantics of the genotypes they operate on, and thus are very generic operators that do not depend on the implementation domain, *i.e.*, on the type of individual that is described by the genotypes in an EA's population. The individuals in the population may represent paintings, car designs, airplane wing profiles, or footwear sole cross-sections, just to give a few examples of creative design domains for which an EA may be used.

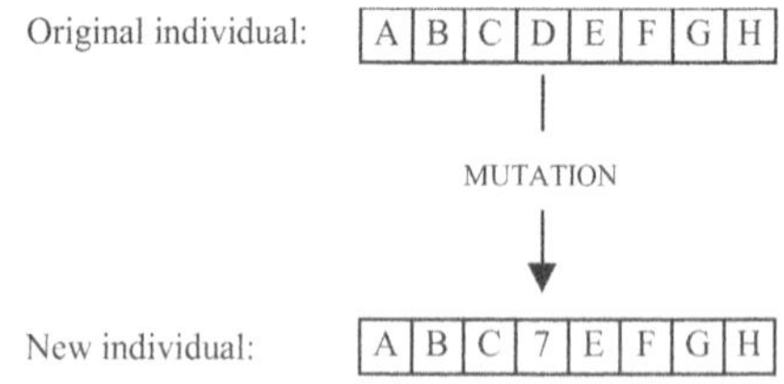

Figure 2. A graphical illustration of the genetic mutation operator

DOMAIN AND REPRESENTATIONS

The EA used in the experiments described in this paper is called ShEvolver (a contraction of "shape evolver"). Its domain is the evolution of shapes that consist of configurations of colored unit squares. This kind of domain and algorithm can be used, for example, for the design of bathroom tile patterns, though for the purposes of this paper (experimenting with ShEvolver and observing its performance under different conditions) this is not really important.

Representation R1

Some EA's used for design tasks, such as that described in [11], interpret genes to be actions, and a genotype thus represents a sequence of actions which, if performed, end up producing a design (phenotype). The idea behind this duality is that, by having a design described at two levels of abstraction, using genetic operators at one of the levels, but evaluating the results at the other level, the EA is more likely to produce unexpected results. Since creativity involves producing things that are both new and useful [4], but also unexpected [8], this seems like a good idea. On the other hand, it has been argued in [6] that greater fidelity between EA's and natural evolution (such as making the distinction between genotypes and phenotypes in an EA and making it operate at the two levels of abstraction) does not necessarily produce better quality in the results.

Using these ideas in ShEvolver's domain, one representation (R1) can involve genes that perform a "move-and-place" action: each gene involves moving from an initial location, by a distance of one unit square, in a certain direction to a destination location, and placing a unit square of a particular color there. Both the direction and the color are encoded into the specific value (allele) of a given gene. The sequence of genes that form a genotype are interpreted such that the starting location of a given gene is the end location, where a unit square of a given color was placed, of the previous gene in the sequence. The exception, of course, is the first gene, which has no previous gene (its starting location is arbitrary, and does not affect the end result, as it begins on a "blank canvas"). After interpreting an entire genotype as a series of move-and-place actions as described above, we end up producing on the "canvas" a shape made up of colored unit squares, *i.e.*, a phenotype.

In ShEvolver's Representation R1 there are eight valid directions of movement that can be encoded in a gene: to the right, to the left, down, up, and four diagonal movements. These are illustrated in Figure 3, which ignores color for simplicity.

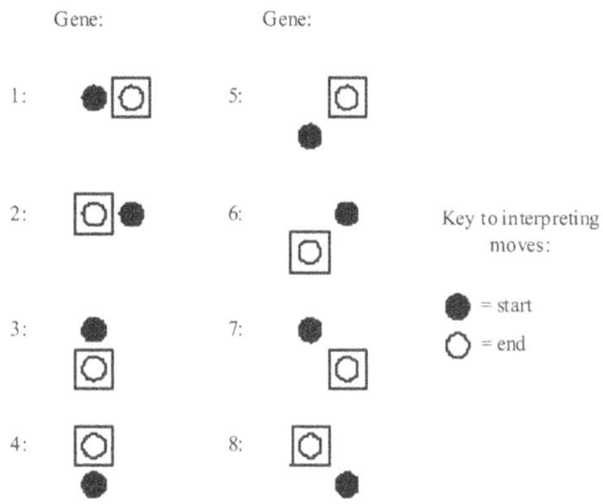

Figure 3. Eight valid directions of movement in R1.

Each of the eight movements ends up placing a unit square of one of four colors (red, blue, green, and white) in its destination location. Thus, there is a total of 32 possible distinct gene values (alleles) in ShEvolver's R1. Note that this type of representation implies that a given shape can be produced in several ways (*i.e.*, its production can be described by several alternate genotypes). For instance, a shape consisting of two side-by-side unit squares of a given color can be produced by a sequence of two right-ward moves (of that color), or by two left-ward moves (of that color), or by two right-ward moves followed by one left-ward move (of that color), or any number of other possibilities. This last example also shows that, when decoding the moves described in a genotype (*i.e.*, when interpreting the genotype as a phenotype), a unit square of a given color may be placed over a unit square that had already been placed in a particular location by a previous move. When this occurs, ShEvolver assumes that the actual color of the shape's unit square in that location is the color specified by the final gene that placed a colored square there. The genotypes are read from left to right when performing this decoding process (genotype-to-phenotype mapping).

Figure 4 illustrates some shapes that cannot, and also some shapes that can, be created when using R1 as a representation scheme. For simplicity, in the figure color is ignored and the numerical values assigned in Figure 3 to the eight possible directions of movement are used as stand-ins for the possible gene values in the genotypes that are shown to the right of the shapes in the second column (which represent genotypes that may produce the shapes shown).

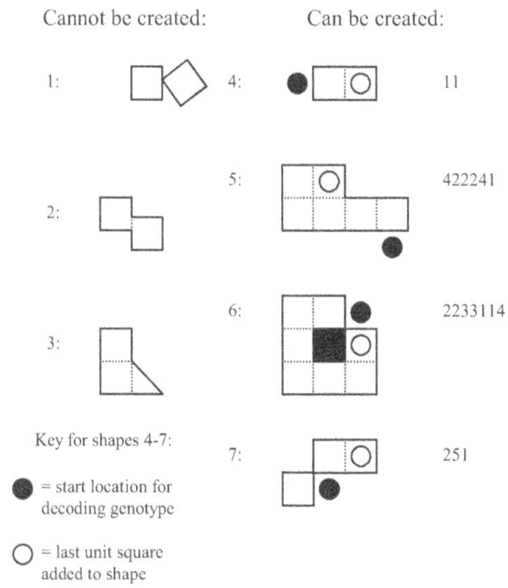

Figure 4. Some shapes that cannot, and some that can, be produced using R1.

Representation R2

Some EA's used for design tasks, such as that described in [10], interpret genes to be direct encodings (descriptions) of the features of designs, instead of actions that, when performed, produce a design with certain features. A genotype, which groups together all of the genes of an individual, is thus a full description of all the features of a given design (phenotype). In this scenario, the mapping between genotypes and phenotypes is more straightforward than in the previous one, as there is a one-to-one correspondence between the value of each gene and some characteristic of the phenotype it partially describes. Some EA's of this type don't even distinguish between genotypes and phenotypes, applying both the evolutionary operators and the fitness evaluation process to the same set of data.

Using these ideas in ShEvolver's domain, a different representation (R2) to the one described previously can involve genes that are associated with a given position within a grid. The possible values for those genes are the colors that a unit square placed on that position might have, including a value that represents the absence of a unit square in that position. Figure 5 illustrates a possible genotype and its equivalent phenotype in ShEvolver using R2 as a representation scheme. In the figure, only white and red unit squares appear in the shape, though ShEvolver permits more colors, as mentioned previously. The grid positions that are shown empty in the genotype denote positions to which no unit square of any color belongs in the represented shape. Note that in this kind of representation there is only one genotype that can describe any one particular phenotype.

Genotype:

```
wr r r
 r ww w
rwrwr r
  w w
```

Phenotype:

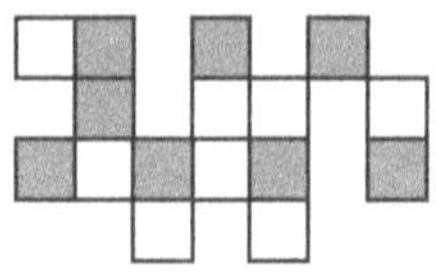

Figure 5. A genotype and its equivalent phenotype in R2.

When, as in R2, a genotype is not a linear sequence of genes, there are two possibilities. One is to transform the genotype into a linear version in order to use the "traditional" (linear) versions of the crossover and mutation operators in the EA. In ShEvolver's case we could take, for example, the different rows of R2's bi-dimensional genotype and concatenate them to each other to transform it into a linear genotype. But this would give an "unfair" advantage to the rows (which wouldn't be broken up) over the columns (which would be broken up and their constituent parts separated into disjoint regions of the genotype). The second possibility is to implement different versions of the crossover and mutation operators that take into account the non-linearity of the genotype.

In ShEvolver's R2, a matrix version of the crossover operator has been implemented that takes two parent genotypes as input, separates out a sub-region of the same shape and dimensions from each of the two parent genotypes, and exchanges the genes contained in these sub-regions between the two genotypes. Thus crossover involves randomly selecting a crossover region rather than a crossover point in each of the two parent genotypes. The offspring genotypes are formed through the exchange of the genetic material in the two regions. The crossover region is always a rectangular "hole" in ShEvolver, unlike the irregularly-shaped holes used in a similar context by [7]. Figure 6 illustrates a matrix-genotype version of the crossover operator as implemented in ShEvolver.

The mutation operator in ShEvolver's R2 representation scheme implies changing the color of the unit square in a randomly-selected position within the genotype. This includes the possibility of making a given unit square disappear (changing its value from any of the four valid colors to "non-existent") and the possibility of making a unit square of a given color appear within a genotype in a position where there wasn't one before.

EXPERIMENTAL DESIGN

Given the two representation schemes used in ShEvolver described above, R1 and R2, two experiments were set up. The size of the population, the number of new genotypes produced through crossover and mutation at each evolutionary generation, and other similar EA parameters remained fixed in both experiments. The convergence criterion used in both experiments was chosen to be the appearance in the population of at least one solution with a fitness value of at least 85%, or the reaching of 500 evolutionary generations, whichever comes first. The limit of 500 evolutionary generations is designed to halt the EA when no individual with a fitness of at least 85% is found within a reasonable amount of time, instead of permitting the EA to continue potentially forever, with the possibility of never converging. In both experiments the population of the EA was initialized randomly.

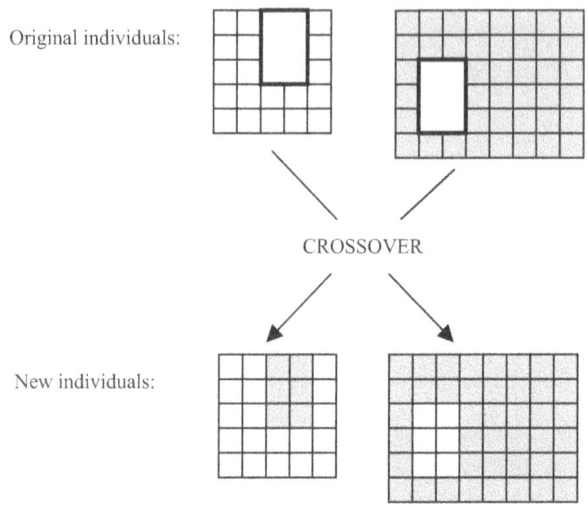

Figure 6. A graphical illustration of the genetic crossover operator operating on matrix genotypes.

In both experiments the fitness function consisted of a linear combination of two evaluation criteria, *c1* and *c2*. Each of these evaluation criteria was used to evaluate a phenotype *p*, assigning to it a fitness value that falls between 0 and 1, where 0 is worst and 1 is best, and both criteria were given the same weight. Thus, if *c1(p)* is the fitness value of phenotype *p* when evaluating it by using *c1*, and *c2(p)* is its fitness value when evaluating it using *c2*, then the global, normalized, fitness value *F* for *p* is calculated as:

$$F(p)=c1(p)+c2(p)/2.$$

Experiment E1

In the first experiment (E1), *c1* was chosen to be a measure of the degree of vertical symmetry of a shape. This reflective symmetry with respect to the central vertical axis of a shape is measured without regards to the colors that unit squares may have. What is measured is the existence of pairs of unit squares, within a given row of the phenotype, that are equidistant from the central vertical axis of the phenotype. This is done for all the rows in the phenotype, and the final degree of vertical symmetry is calculated by dividing the total number of such pairs by the total number of comparisons, where each comparison stems from either a unit square that does have a symmetrical "twin" on the other side of the central vertical axis, or a unit square that doesn't have such a "twin."

In E1, *c2* was chosen to be an indication of whether the height and width of the phenotype both fall within certain threshold values: 15 unit squares as a minimum and 35 unit squares as a maximum. In this evaluation criterion, the fitness value is always 0 (either the width or the height, or both, violate the threshold constraints) or 1 (both the width and the height of the phenotype fall within the acceptable limits).

Experiment E1 consisted of running ShEvolver 50 times with the parameter settings described above, each time running two versions of the EA "in parallel." The first parallel version had a population of genotypes represented using R1, and thus used the "traditional" linear versions of the crossover and mutation operators. The second parallel version started out with an initial population of individuals that had identical phenotypes to those used in the first parallel version, but whose genotypes were represented using R2, and thus the matrix versions of the crossover and mutation operators were used. This means that, while it would be ideal for the two parallel versions to differ in only one aspect, the representation used, they also differ in the way the crossover and mutation operators are implemented. The reason for this is the fact that the implementation of the genetic operators depends on the genotype representation scheme used. But this is not as problematic as it might seem: because the two aspects cannot be decoupled, it would be equivalent to attribute any interesting results obtained from the experiment to the different representations as it would be to attribute them to the different ways in which the genetic operators were implemented. The purpose of running ShEvolver 50 times was to be able to filter out any unusual results that may have been due to the random nature of many of the decision points in an EA, such as the initial makeup of its population or the selection of crossover points, and instead be able to observe general trends in the overall set of results.

Results of Experiment E1

Table 1 shows the evolutionary generation at which convergence was reached for each of the 50 runs (labeled 0-49) of E1, both for the version of ShEvolver that was using R1 as a representation scheme and for the version that was using R2.

The data that is included in Table 1 permits us to measure two aspects related to the performance of ShEvolver's EA: reliability and speed. The reliability of an EA is the percentage of times that convergence occurred because an acceptable fitness value had been reached, as opposed to occurring because the EA was halted due to reaching an unsatisfactorily high number of evolutionary generations. The speed of an EA is the average number of EA generations needed for the EA to converge.

Table 1. Convergence results for 50 runs of experiment E1:

Run:	Convergence R1:	Convergence R2:	Run:	Convergence R1:	Convergence R2:
0	22	219	25	21	500
1	27	500	26	33	500
2	29	500	27	36	500
3	19	500	28	24	500
4	20	500	29	26	500
5	33	500	30	56	500
6	18	500	31	19	256
7	25	500	32	49	500
8	19	500	33	23	500
9	28	500	34	12	500
10	43	500	35	18	500
11	25	500	36	16	500
12	21	425	37	22	500
13	28	500	38	22	500
14	23	500	39	15	500
15	24	500	40	28	500
16	38	500	41	37	500
17	18	500	42	19	500
18	24	275	43	24	200
19	16	500	44	25	500
20	25	500	45	26	500
21	27	500	46	20	500
22	21	500	47	14	500
23	17	500	48	33	500
24	20	500	49	27	500

As can be seen in Table 1, the version of ShEvolver that was using R1 converged 100% of the time, with, on average, convergence occurring after 25.1 evolutionary generations. On the other hand, the version of ShEvolver that was using R2 converged only five times in the 50 runs, *i.e.*, 10% of the time, and on those five occasions when the EA was not halted after 500 generations, convergence occurred on average after 275 evolutionary generations.

Table 1 shows that, from the point of view of both reliability and average speed of convergence, R1 seems to be a "better" representation than R2 according to Experiment E1. From the point of view of the phenotypes produced, R1 and R2 tend to generate qualitatively different shapes. Figure 7 shows a typical phenotype (viewed in its symbolic form rather than using actual colored unit squares) produced at the end of one of the 50 runs when using R1, whereas Figure 8 shows a typical phenotype (viewed in the same way) produced at the end of one of the 50 runs when using R2.

```
     wb
      br  gg
      rgrbrwg
       wbwgbw
       ggw wrb
      r wwbgww
    b bbbggrrbw
   wwr wrrwwwbrbbww
 brrrbrrgrbrbbwggrbb
wbb rrrbrrwwrrrr rbr
wggwggwrwrbrrwwrrgbw
  rrwbgwggrwwwbr
 w rw r bww bgrw
  rrrbwbgbgwbb bg
   rwgrbwbbwrbwbb
   rgrbww  w ww
        w     w
```

Figure 7. A typical phenotype produced when using R1 in Experiment E1.

```
 w  b r rrb  gwgrwb
 r       bw  wb      brb
rwb  b wbw rr  wg g
    bg  gr    w r  rr
 r w      gb r  b  b   r
    r   b     wg  w   r
   g      rrb     w ww
gr              gbb   b
 r   wg  br   g rrg w
    gr    r      b g  b
 gw        wrb  g bw w
 bg    b rr bwr wrgw b
g   r  b   w b     g b
   gw  w    w b b  gb
  b r      rb         r
  r
```

Figure 8. A typical phenotype produced when using R2 in Experiment E1.

When comparing the phenotypes in Figures 7 and 8, we can see that the phenotypes produced when using R1 tend to be more compact shapes that only have a tendency to be vertically symmetric (as required by one of the evaluation criteria used in the fitness function). The phenotypes produced when using R2 tend to be shapes with more "holes" in them, and tend to exhibit, though not always, some degree of symmetry around the horizontal axis as well as the vertical one, even though horizontal symmetry was never specified as a requirement in the fitness function. This phenomenon probably emerges as a result of the bi-dimensional crossover operator used and the fact that genotypes and phenotypes are much more similar to each other in both their form and their semantics in R2 than in R1. So from the point of view of the phenotypes (designs) produced, the results obtained by using R1 and R2 are quite different, and which one of the representations is "better" to use depends on whether we are interested more in phenotypes that look like the one shown in Figure 7 or like the one shown in Figure 8.

Experiment E2

In the second experiment (E2), *c1* was chosen, as in E1, to be a measure of the degree of vertical symmetry of a shape. In E2, *c2* was chosen, as in E1, to be an indication of whether the height and width of the phenotype both fall within certain threshold values, but the limits were slightly modified compared to E1. Now 5 unit squares were set as the minimum acceptable height/width and 15 unit squares as the maximum acceptable height/width of shapes. The purpose of E2 is to see whether a slight change in the fitness function, which has an indirect influence on the phenotypes, if not necessarily the genotypes, of the solutions that tend to be produced by an EA, causes any differences in the performance of the EA.

Experiment E2, like E1, consisted of running ShEvolver 50 times with the same parameter settings described above, again each time running two parallel versions of the EA. The first parallel version had a population of genotypes represented using R1, and thus used the "traditional" linear versions of the crossover and mutation operators. The second parallel version started out with an initial population of individuals that had identical phenotypes to those used in the first parallel version, but whose genotypes were represented using R2, and thus used the matrix versions of the crossover and mutation operators.

Results of Experiment E2

Table 2 shows the evolutionary generation at which convergence was reached for each of the 50 runs (labeled 0-49) of E2, both for the version of ShEvolver that was using R1 as a representation scheme and for the version that was using R2.

As can be seen in Table 2, the version of ShEvolver that was using R1 converged 100% of the time, with, on average, convergence occurring after 6.88 evolutionary generations, which is faster than in E1. On the other hand, the version of ShEvolver that was using R2 converged 43 times in the 50 runs, *i.e.*, 86% of the time, much more often than in E1. On those occasions when the EA was not halted after 500 generations, convergence occurred sometimes very quickly (after 1 or 3 generations, for instance), and on average after 54.65 evolutionary generations, faster than in E1.

Table 2. Convergence results for 50 runs of experiment E2:

Run:	Convergence R1:	Convergence R2:	Run:	Convergence R1:	Convergence R2:
0	4	3	25	17	100
1	9	58	26	7	149
2	7	9	27	1	5
3	7	12	28	7	1
4	8	105	29	10	200
5	5	500	30	5	90
6	5	5	31	6	119
7	11	500	32	5	500
8	13	500	33	9	126
9	6	500	34	4	8
10	6	78	35	1	6
11	5	8	36	10	4
12	10	295	37	7	500
13	8	17	38	9	20
14	5	7	39	7	38
15	3	1	40	11	6
16	6	18	41	8	142
17	4	155	42	8	14
18	5	19	43	7	6
19	5	171	44	8	9
20	4	293	45	6	19
21	8	8	46	7	27
22	10	10	47	1	1
23	11	57	48	6	3
24	9	194	49	3	500

From the point of view of both reliability and average speed of convergence, R1 seems to be a "better" representation than R2 in Experiment E2. However, the gap has narrowed compared to what it was in E1, and the best runs for R2 were better than the best ones for R1 as far as their speed of convergence. From the point of view of the phenotypes produced, both R1 and R2 tend to generate similar shapes. Figure 9 shows a typical phenotype produced at the end of one of the 50 runs when using R1, whereas Figure 10 shows a typical phenotype produced at the end of one of the 50 runs when using R2.

When comparing the phenotypes in Figures 9 and 10, we can see that they are qualitatively similar. The large numbers of "holes" in the phenotypes produced when using R2 that were observed in Experiment E1 have diminished considerably, thus making these phenotypes appear much more like those produced when using R1. This is probably due to the smaller dimensions allowed for the phenotypes in E2 compared to E1, which don't "encourage" the appearance of too many holes. There is also less of a tendency in E2 when using R2 to produce phenotypes that exhibit some degree of symmetry around the horizontal axis as well as the vertical one, unlike what was observed in Experiment E1.

```
  w
 rwrw
rwrgg
rrwwrw
 w  b
w
```

Figure 9. A typical phenotype produced when using R1 in Experiment E2.

```
 r   w
gbw rg
b b brg
rbrrbwr
r brbg
  grw
```

Figure 10. A typical phenotype produced when using R2 in Experiment E2.

SUMMARY AND DISCUSSION

In ShEvolver, an EA used for evolving shapes that consist of configurations of colored unit squares, two representation schemes were implemented, each with its own, appropriate, set of genetic crossover and mutation operators. In the first representation scheme, R1, genotypes encode actions which, if performed, end up producing shapes (designs, phenotypes). In the second representation scheme, R2, genotypes directly encode characteristics of shapes.

In a first experiment, E1, ShEvolver was run 50 times, each time running in parallel two versions, both starting out with the same initial population of shapes. The first version used R1 as its representation scheme, with its corresponding versions of the genetic operators, and the second version used R2, with its corresponding genetic operators. Three performance measures were used to evaluate and compare the two versions. The first performance measure was reliability: the percentage of times that convergence was reached due to finding an acceptable solution (whose fitness value was sufficiently high) in the population, rather than due to reaching a maximum allowable number of evolutionary generations without finding such an acceptable solution. The second performance measure was speed: the average number of evolutionary generations that the EA passed through before converging. The third performance measure was the qualitative nature of the solutions found by the EA.

The result of E1 was that, despite the only difference being the representation scheme used, the two versions of ShEvolver vary greatly in all three performance measures. The version using R1 was superior in the first two performance measures, both in absolute terms and on average. The third performance measure is qualitative, so choosing between the results given by R1 or R2 depends on what type of solution one prefers for a given application. In the experiment he types of results obtained when using R1 looked quite different from those obtained when using R2. A preliminary conclusion from these observations is that the performance of an EA is extremely sensitive to the representation used.

In a second experiment, E2, the same scenario was repeated, with a slight tweak: one of the criteria taken into account in the EA's fitness function was adjusted so that the dimensions of evolved solutions that were deemed to be acceptable were now smaller than in E1. The rest of the EA parameters remained the same, and the same performance measures were used to compare the results of the version using R1 with those of the version using R2.

The result of E2 was that the version using R1 was better than that using R2 according to the first performance measure (reliability), but nowhere near as superior as in E1. The version using R1 was also better on average than that using R2 according to the second performance measure (speed of convergence), but the best measures for R2 were actually better than the best measures for R1 due to a greater variance in the results obtained with R2. The third performance measure (quality of solutions) found no significant differences between the designs produced when using R1 compared to those produced when using R2. A preliminary conclusion from these observations, in isolation from those of E1, would be that the performance of an EA is somewhat sensitive to the representation used, but not according to all performance measures, and not to a large degree.

Given the very small difference between the experimental set-ups of E1 and E2, it is surprising that the conclusions obtained from E1 and E2 in isolation are so different from each other. Put together, the global conclusion is that in general the performance of an EA is very sensitive both to the representation used and to a number of other factors indirectly related to representation, specifically in this case a slight variation in the fitness function used. A very small tweak in the representation (or related factors) can cause quite large differences in performance, though it won't always.

There is a long history of experimental comparisons of EA's. Some researchers (for instance [1]) have focused on measuring the reliability and relative speed of convergence of alternative EA's, which are two of the performance measures we have used. Other researchers (for example [5]) have focused on measuring the robustness of the different alternative EA's applied to a wide variety of fitness function types, which is something we haven't done. But in each of these cases the multiple alternatives being compared differ in algorithmic aspects. They do not leave the evolutionary algorithm alone and vary the genotype representation scheme in order to create the alternatives to compare and evaluate, which is what we have done.

Research papers that describe EA's that have been implemented to solve specific problems tend to indicate the values of crossover and mutation rates, population sizes, and other EA parameters, and describe the genotype representation used. The final values chosen for crossover and mutation rates are generally given and explained (the explanation usually being that they arise from performing some preliminary experiments and observing the performance of the EA with different values for these parameters until the "best" values, or combinations of values, are found). On the other hand, the genotype representation used by the EA is usually merely described, without any explanation about why it is an appropriate representation or whether alternative representations might be feasible or were tested. This leads us to suspect that in most cases alternative representations may not have even been considered, and that the representation that was used was chosen merely because it was the first one that came to mind to the researcher involved in the project, or because it has worked in the past for the same or other researchers (whether the application domain was similar or not), or because the researcher is comfortable with it, or other such possibilities.

However, as we have seen with our experiments, the performance of an EA can vary greatly when even minor variations in the representation (or related aspects of an EA) are considered. What this indicates is that, when using an EA, making a few preliminary trials that evaluate alternate knowledge representation schemes might enable the construction of more robust, more efficient, more reliable EA's, capable of producing better solutions (depending on one's particular needs). If, instead, an EA is simply endowed with whatever the first representation scheme that comes to mind is, without even thinking about alternative representations, there is no guarantee that one has achieved the "best" possible EA for that particular domain.

ACKNOWLEDGMENTS

This work has been supported by Asociación Mexicana de Cultura, A.C.

REFERENCES

1. Bäck, T. *Evolutionary Algorithms in Theory and Practice*. Oxford University Press, Oxford, 1996.

2. Bentley, P. (ed.). *Evolutionary Design by Computers*. Morgan Kaufmann, San Francisco CA, 1999.

3. Bentley, P., and Corne, D.W. (eds.). *Creative Evolutionary Systems*. Morgan Kaufmann, San Francisco, 2002.

4. Boden, M. *The Creative Mind: Myths and Mechanisms*. Routledge, London, 2003.

5. Coello Coello, C.A., Van Veldhuizen, D.A., and Lamont, G.B. *Evolutionary Algorithms for Solving Multi-Objective Problems*. Kluwer, New York NY, 2002.

6. Fogel, D.B. Phenotypes, Genotypes, and Operators in Evolutionary Computation, in *Proceedings of the Second IEEE International Conference on Evolutionary Computation* (Perth Australia, December 1995), IEEE Press, 193-198.

7. Kane, C., and Schoenauer, M. Topological Optimum Design Using Genetic Algorithms. *Control and Cybernetics 25*, 5 (1996).

8. Kim, M.J., and Maher, M.L. Creative Design and Spatial Cognition in a Tangible User Interface, in *Computational and Cognitive Models of Creative Design VI* (Heron Island Australia, December 2005), University of Sydney, 233-250.

9. Mitchell, M. *An Introduction to Genetic Algorithms*. MIT Press, Cambridge MA, 1998.

10. Noonan, L., and Flanagan, C. An Effective Network Processor Design Framework Using Multi-Objective Evolutionary Algorithms and Object Oriented Techniques to Optimise the Intel IXP1200 Network Processor, in *Proceedings of the ACM/IEEE Symposium on Architecture for Networking and Communications Systems* (San Jose CA, December 2006), IEEE Press, 103-112.

11. Rosenman, M. Case-Based Evolutionary Design. *Artificial Intelligence for Engineering Design, Analysis, and Manufacturing 14* (2000), 17-29.

Shared Mental Models in Improvisational Theatre

Daniel Fuller
School of Literature, Communication, and Culture
Georgia Institute of Technology
686 Cherry St., Atlanta, GA
dfuller3@gatech.edu

Brian Magerko
School of Literature, Communication, and Culture
Georgia Institute of Technology
686 Cherry St., Atlanta, GA
magerko@gatech.edu

ABSTRACT
This article presents our currents findings from an empirical study of the cognition employed by performers in improvisational theatre. Improvised theatrical performance is an activity in which one or more individuals create a dramatic or comedic performance in real-time and is an interesting example of creative, real-time, collaborative problem solving. Unlike other forms of creative problem solving, improvisers are constrained from explicitly coordinating with the other improvisers on stage or revising their decisions after the fact. This article focuses on the means by which a group of improvisers converge on a shared understanding (i.e. a shared mental model) of what a scene is about and how it should proceed. We present our findings on how improvisers build shared mental models during a performance and discuss our applications of these findings to the design and development of improvisational intelligent agents.

Keywords
Improvisation, cognition, theatre, intelligent agents, mental models

ACM Classification Keywords
I.2.0 General: Cognitive simulation.

General Terms
Theory.

INTRODUCTION
Theatrical performance is an activity in which one or more individuals create a dramatic or comedic performance in real-time. It involves intricate orchestration of emotional expressions, communication, interaction strategies, and problem-solving, all of which can place varying levels of cognitive demands on the performers depending on the degree of improvisation in a particular performance setting.

There is a spectrum of spontaneity in theatrical acting, from completely predetermined (e.g. heavily scripted acting) to completely non-predetermined (e.g. children at play). In the middle of the spectrum one will find the genre of theatre called *improv* [8, 9, 22]. Improv is a remarkable example of creative group performance because (a) the creation process of narrative content is completely in real-time, (b) there is no explicit coordination between the improvisers, and (c) the constraints on a performance typically follow the form of a set of game rules plus audience suggestions (called *short form* improv).

While there have been studies of improvisation and cognition in other art forms [16, 21, 25], these studies have relied mainly on observational techniques coupled with applying music theory to describe what happens on stage. Little work has been done to elicit data at the level of goals and knowledge (as opposed to fMRI research [11], for instance) on the decision making processes of improvisers [15, 16] and no work, to our knowledge, has been done on cognition within the domain of improvisational theatre[1]. Therefore, our goal is to fill in the gaps of our understanding of creativity and improvisation through the study of improvisational theatre and by better understanding the knowledge and processes employed by improvisers, to build computational improvisation agents that represent our formal findings on studying humans.

Many of the standard approaches to data collection in artistic domains must be adapted to theatre because of the real-time, dynamic, and group collaborative nature of performance. Our current work has focused on methodologies from (a) observational study [1], (b) concurrent verbal protocols, (c) group interview, and (d) semi-structured interview. We invited improvisers to perform a scene while we filmed, after which we replayed the footage to each individual improviser while interviewing him in regards to his thought processes during the performance. We followed up these individual interviews by interviewing the entire group at once, seeking further insight into their thought processes from a different perspective. Our current findings are based on close analysis of the video recordings of these interviews and performances. The terminology we use to describe the findings of this study is derived by comparing our data to relevant existing works. Where we found an absence of terminology to describe phenomena, we invented our own.

C&C'11, November 3–6, 2011, Atlanta, Georgia, USA.

[1] Sawyer's studies of theatrical improvisation from an ethno-linguistic stance are the only previous large scale study of the domain [20].

Thus, rather than approaching our study with a specific vocabulary in mind, we first gathered data and then borrowed and invented the necessary terminology to describe what we observed. For more information on the details of this methodology, see [13].

The key contributions of this work are:

The identification of (a) cognitive processes underlying improvisation, and (b) knowledge employed in improvisation, through a variety of studies involving human improvisers. Improv performance utilizes rich, diverse, and constrained cognitive processes that are not well understood. In this article, we focus on shared mental models and the processes by which performers, in conditions in which they are not able to explicitly communicate or coordinate, are able to converge on a shared understanding.

SHARED MENTAL MODELS

A major recurring theme in our analysis of improv performances is of the construction of shared mental models by performers. Shared mental models are an extension of the concept of mental models (i.e., "organized knowledge structures for an individual" [3, 19]) to the notion of shared knowledge between individuals in a group. For our purposes, mental models are any underlying assumptions held by an improviser. Therefore, shared mental models are "knowledge structures held by members of a team," or in other words, assumptions (i.e. mental models) held by a group such that "members think about a phenomenon in a similar manner" [10].

Shared mental models are heavily related to concepts in other fields, such as "grounding" in discourse studies, which also deals with navigating and correcting misunderstandings [4, 23]. Amongst all of these related ideas, we consider "shared mental models" to be the most appropriate concept for our work on group improvisation because of its association with team decision-making and problem solving [3, 10, 14]. Work on grounding, on the other hand, provides useful secondary terminology for understanding the specific techniques used to construct these shared mental models.

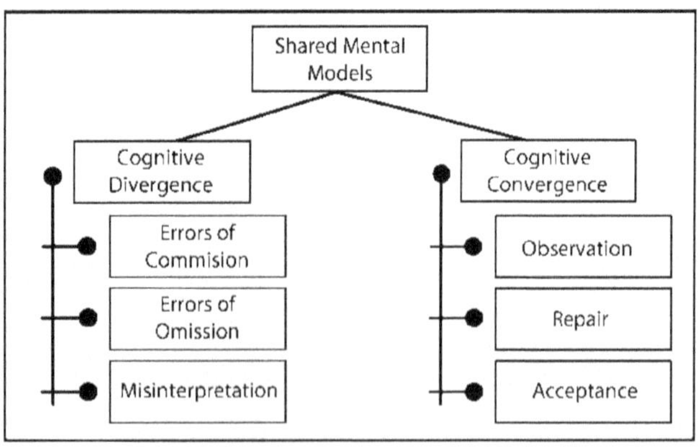

Figure 1: Divergence and Convergence

SHARED MENTAL MODELS IN IMPROVISATION

Since improv performances lack a script or other predetermined plan, there are inevitably moments during performances that improvisers describe as "not being on the same page." This phenomenon is the result of an initial absence of shared mental models. Improvisers share little knowledge about a scene before beginning it–they typically know only the functional and content constraints and little to nothing about the plot, character definitions, or what the focus of the scene will be. This phenomenon of "not being on the same page" is *cognitive divergence*, a disagreement of mental models. The term is borrowed from Levesque et al's work on cognitive divergence and shared mental models in software development project teams and is implicit in other similar works in the field of organizational psychology [10]. For instance, Mohammed and Ringseis use the terms "cognitive diversity" and "dissensus" to describe the same phenomenon in their discussion of group decision-making [19].

Divergences are inevitable: every new element or change to a scene has the potential to cause a conflict between mental models. Therefore, how improvisers navigate these divergences when they occur is central to the progression and development of any improv scene. This process is *cognitive convergence*, the opposite of cognitive divergence. Cognitive convergence in a group repairs cognitive divergences and develops a group understanding, i.e. a *shared mental model*.

The ultimate goal of cognitive convergence is *cognitive consensus*, the state of agreement of assumptions (that is, mental models) between two or more improvisers [18, 19]. Cognitive consensus is directly tied to the concept of shared mental models. When a divergence is transformed into a shared mental model, cognitive consensus is achieved. The presence of cognitive consensus means that the process of cognitive convergence succeeded.

Creating shared mental models involves a constant process of cognitive divergence, convergence, and consensus of mental models (see Fig. 1). Sometimes this process is instantaneous, but other times it requires significantly more effort. Specific to improv is how shared mental models are often created without explicit means (e.g. explicitly stating one's own mental model) due to the performative nature of being on stage; every act on stage is done within the context of performing a scene. Instead, indirect techniques are used to navigate divergences in real-time as they occur, correcting mistakes without disrupting the narrative flow of a performance. This process of constructing mental models in performance is explored below within the specific domain of improvisational theatre, which we have determined has its own contextual variations on what divergences can exist and how they are dealt with by improvisers.

COGNITIVE DIVERGENCE

Causes of Cognitive Divergences

Cognitive divergence occurs whenever two or more mental models disagree (i.e. diverge). Divergences may occur because of errors of *commission, omission,* and *sensory misinterpretation* (see Figure 1). These three phenomena are *how* divergences may occur. Detailed later are the types or divergences, or *what* information the divergence concerns.

Errors of Commission

An error of commission occurs when an improviser portrays a model that another improviser misinterprets. An example is a scene in which an improviser was pretending to rake leaves, but a second improviser interpreted that action as sweeping, resulting in a misinterpretation of the meaning of the first improviser's actions.

Errors of Omission

An error of commission occurs when an improviser portrays a model that another improviser does not understand. For example, in one scene an improviser mentioned "queso," but a second improviser became confused because he did not know what "queso" (Spanish for "cheese") was. The omission is due to the first improviser's reference to knowledge that the other did not have.

Sensory Misinterpretation

An error of sensory misinterpretation occurs when an improviser portrays a model which another improviser mishears. For example, one improviser mentioned "pitchers" but a second improviser heard "pictures," leading to two entirely different interpretations of the setting of the scene ("baseball game" and "movie theatre").

Types of Cognitive Divergences in Improv

There are several types of divergences in improvisation depending on what type of information diverges: character, environmental, future-oriented, external knowledge, theoretical, methodological, moral, actor, audience, sensory, and repair divergences. Many of these are adapted from Mitroff and Emshoff's list of types of assumptions [17], which was based on studying business management. The original list is inadequate for describing the specific domain of improvisation (excluding, for instance, divergences relevant to a narrative). Therefore, we have expanded the original list based on our own observations to include several more items. The mechanics behind each type of divergence is explained in detail below.

Character Divergence

A *character divergence* is a disagreement concerning the attributes, relationships, history, goals, or emotions of a persona in the scene, which is distinct from the improviser's actual identities. For example, in one scene in which a male improviser portrays a female character, his co-performer became convinced that the former was portraying a male character, commenting later "I thought you were a very effeminate man."

It is important to note that character divergence is one of the types of divergences that can exist implicitly in the rules of the scene. In the improv game *Party Quirks*, the rules dictate that one improviser plays the role of a party host does not know the quirks (i.e. character attributes) of any of the other improvisers, who each play guests at his party. The host has to correctly guess the quirks of each guest in order to complete the game. This creates several inherent divergences between the host and the guests.

Environmental Divergence

An *environmental divergence* is a disagreement concerning locations, objects, or the attributes of locations or objects in the scene. One scene progressed almost entirely to the end with one improviser thinking he was in an office break room while the other two believing that they were in a coffee shop.

Environmental divergence is the other type of divergence that can exist implicitly in the rules of the scene. In the improv game *Blind Scene*, the rules specifically dictate that one of the improvisers does not know the initial setting or premise. There can be other types of implicit divergences, but character and environmental are the most common.

Future-Oriented Divergence

Future-oriented divergences are about the direction of the development of the story. As opposed to disagreements about the current state of an improv scene, this type of divergence involves different ideas about what will happen next. One improviser noticed this happening in a scene that alternated control of the story between several improvisers: "I kind of had a different idea of what might happen next and then [another improviser] will come in and say something."

External Knowledge Divergence

An *external knowledge divergence* is a disagreement about a reference to cultural knowledge from the "real world" (i.e. beyond the context of the scene). An external knowledge divergence might arise simply because one of the improvisers involved does not know anything about the referent. The earlier example of confusion over the word "queso" is an external knowledge divergence.

Theoretical and Methodological Divergences

Our study confirmed the existence of both theoretical and methodological divergences, both of which have been studied previously (although we interpreted a relevant mapping to the domain of improv). A *theoretical divergence* [17-19] is a disagreement concerning the broad nature of improvisation and its practice as it relates to the current scene. A *methodological divergence* [17-19], on the other hand, is a disagreement concerning the methods, procedures, or conventions of a specific improv game. While these two types of divergences may seem similar, methodological divergences differ from theoretical divergences in terms of scope. Both types may refer to improvisational techniques, but their context is different. Theoretical divergences relate to improvisational theory as a whole, while methodological divergences relate to the specific game being played in the scene.

One improviser introduced elements of "negativity" to a scene while the second improviser was motivated to maintain a positive attitude in the scene, explaining later that his "goal was to be positive because conflict's easy. We do that all the time, and we talked about it in our Wednesday rehearsal. This weekend we should try as much as we can in every scene that we can to be positive." A theoretical divergence resulted when the first improviser did not behave in accordance with the discussion from rehearsal while the second one did.

In a scene of *Party Quirks*, the party host began to welcome a second party guest to the stage before she had guessed the quirk of the first party guest (refer to the section on Character Divergence above for the rules of this game). This action worried one of the other improvisers, who said that "I did get concerned at this point…'cause [another improviser] looked at me and was like 'isn't she supposed to guess before the next person comes in?'" The party host, on the other hand, explained, "I didn't realize that. I thought that it was ok to come back to the person." The conflict of opinions on how to play *Party Quirks* resulted in a brief methodological divergence. The divergence was not theoretical because it specifically concerned the game *Party Quirks*.

Interpersonal and Moral Divergence

An *interpersonal divergence* is a disagreement concerning what is an appropriate way for improvisers to interact with each other [17-19]. The key factor of interpersonal divergences is trust. This is related to, but not the same thing as, *moral divergence*, which is a disagreement concerning what is appropriate for public performance [17-19]. Instead of issues of trust and personal space, a moral divergence involves issues such as taboo topics, drinking alcohol on stage, or swearing in front of a young audience.

In one scene, an improviser ended up kissing another improviser on the cheek even though they had never performed together before. The second improviser commented "I've never met her before and I mean later on I think she kisses me on the cheek or somethin' which is kinda like one of those things that you don't really expect when you don't know somebody." The second improviser's surprise at the forward actions of the first improviser is an example of interpersonal divergence.

In a different scene, the story eventually became about Jesus being a "pimp", which disappointed one of the improvisers who had to act it out:

> I had no idea it was going to go into Jesus, you know? But at the point that it did go to Jesus, here's a few things that I try to stay away from when I do improv: politics and religion…because you don't know who the hell you are going to offend.

In this case, the improviser had different ideas than his scene partners about what was appropriate, resulting in a moral divergence.

Actor and Audience Divergence

One of our key findings from the study is a form of divergence that we call *actor divergence*. Actor Divergence is a disagreement concerning the mental model of another improviser. It is a divergence of assumptions about assumptions. Actor divergences occur in addition to any other divergences. In one game of *Party Quirks*, a party guest drew the wrong conclusions about the party host's assumptions. The guest thought that the host had just figured out the quirk of another party guest ("someone who is invisible"). As the improviser explains, "I thought [he] knew who she was." Believing that the host had figured out the quirk of the first party guest, the improviser decided to enter the scene as the second party guest. As it turns out, the host had not actually figured out the first guest's quirk. In this example, there was a character divergence between the host and the invisible guest and an actor divergence between the host and the second guest.

Another key finding from the study is *audience divergence*, defined as a disagreement between an improviser's mental model and his perception of the collective mental model of the audience. It deals with what an improviser perceives the audience understands. It is an assumption about assumptions, similar to an *actor divergence*. An audience divergence need not confirm the audience's point of view in order to exist. It is impossible to gather data on what an entire audience was thinking during a performance, but it is adequate that the improviser *perceived* the divergence. In their mind, there is a divergence.

The improv game *Three Sheets* is one of a category of improv games called *knowledge disparity games* that explicitly create divergences as part of their rules. In this game, each improviser has a sheet taped to their back describing one aspect of the scene's frame, visible only to the other improvisers. Over the course of the game, consensus about the frame must be reached. In one scene of this game, an improviser made a guess that the audience incorrectly confirmed:

> "So I was like, "Oh, maybe missionaries!" So when I said we're on a mission, people started clapping and [snaps] doing all that kind of stuff, so I was like, "Oh, we're missionaries!" But that wasn't it, and I was like, "What the hell are we?"

The improviser perceived the audience feedback as a sign that his guess was correct, but he soon realized that his guess was wrong, making it seem as if the audience led him astray.

There are several conditions when an improviser might perceive an audience divergence. The first three are cases we have observed so far while the last case is an anticipated condition that we have yet to observe directly. The first case is when the improviser believes that the audience does not understand what has just happened. For example, one improviser repeated that an imaginary object in the scene was a Barbie car in order to remind his fellow improviser and the audience of the fact.

The second case is when the improviser believes that the audience will not understand what is about to happen. In a scene of *Three Sheets*, one improviser gave a clue that he knew his fellow improviser would understand even if the audience did not:

> "I knew that he was going to get that so that's why I said it… Even thought the audience didn't get it, people were like [makes a confused face], nobody reacted to that, but he got, I knew he was going to get it so, whatever."

The third case is if the improviser realizes that the audience does not find his behavior appropriate (also a *moral divergence*). A good example of this was mentioned earlier: the improviser who was worried about offending the audience when the scene became a story about Jesus being a pimp.

The fourth and final case is when the improviser believes that the audience does not have the correct social context for what is going on (as might be the case with "in-jokes").

Sensory Divergence

A *sensory divergence* (defined by us) occurs when one improviser does not notice or hear information communicated by another improviser. As one improviser reports: "There was a moment where I did not understand something that [he] said, and so I almost asked him…I almost was just like 'What? What did you just say?' 'Cause I didn't hear him…" A sensory divergence can simultaneously be another type of divergence based on the content of the information that the second improviser attempted to communicate. If the "something" that the improviser did not hear had been about the location of the scene, an environmental divergence might have developed from the sensory divergence.

Repair Divergence

A *repair divergence* (defined by us) occurs when one improviser uses a *repair* technique (discussed more in the next section) that another improviser does not perceive as a repair technique. A repair divergence can also be about the nature of a repair technique. One scene of *Party Quirks* escalated into a group of three party guests all giving clues for each other about their quirks. During this, the party host could not discern which clues were intended for which guests, resulting in several repair divergences.

COGNITIVE CONVERGENCE

Once one or more improvisers recognize that a divergence exists, improvisers must correct it in order to achieve cognitive consensus. This begins the process of cognitive convergence. However, it is possible that some improvisers will not even realize that a divergence has occurred. In one performance, three improvisers played out an entire scene of romantic tension while each believed different facts about the relationships and even the gender of everyone else. The problem was a lack of *observation*, the usual first step of cognitive convergence [18, 19]. As Mohammed and Ringseis point out, "[o]ne of the first steps in the development of cognitive consensus is the simple recognition that differences exist among group members, not just with regard to decision preferences, but also with regard to assumptions and interpretations underlying the issues"[19]. Based on this description, observation is an improviser's perception of a divergence. Since observation is a *perception*, it does not matter whether or not the divergence actually exists. It still occurs within the mind of the improviser.

Once an improviser observes a divergence, he or she can attempt to correct it (initiating the process of *repair*). One of the interesting points of our study is that we found instances in which observation was not a necessary precondition for an attempt at correction. We identified instances in which improvisers try to correct divergences that they *anticipate* without even waiting to see if they have occurred. In general, however, we found that cognitive convergence usually takes place in three steps: observation, repair, and acceptance (see Figure 1).

Repair

Regardless of whether a divergence is observed or merely anticipated, any attempt to reconcile a divergence is a *repair*. The term "repair" is one of several terms we adapted from literature on discourse theory. A repair is made in order to correct (potential) misunderstandings [4, 23]. In improv, repairs are the techniques used by improvisers to move toward cognitive consensus. There are several specific techniques that improvisers use to accomplish this purpose. Repair techniques can be influenced by the constraints of a particular improv scene. For instance, improvisers in *knowledge disparity games* may employ multiple techniques for giving information to others.

All repair techniques have an intended target, making them either *other-oriented* or *self-oriented*. Other-oriented techniques attempt to affect someone else's mental model. These techniques are *presentation* and *clarification* [19],[4],[23]. Improvisers use self-oriented techniques to help themselves get on the same page with someone else's mental model. These techniques, inspired by Traum's work on representing common ground in discourse [23], are *clarification requests*, *deferment*, *verification*, and *blind offers*.

Presentation

The foremost repair technique is *presentation*, which is a demonstration of what an improviser believes to be true [4, 23]. In other words, presentation introduces new information that relates to an individual's mental model. In knowledge disparity games such as *Party Quirks*, presentation typically manifests as a "hint." The idea of presentation is borrowed from Clark and Schaefer [4], who use the phrase "Presentation Phase" to describe the part of a conversation when someone makes an assertion for someone else to consider.

Presentation is other-oriented in intent. However, in knowledge disparity games especially, improvisers sometimes make presentations on behalf of someone else. In one game of *Party Quirks*, the first party guest had the quirk "someone who is invisible." Late in the scene, another party guest tried to help the host realize the first guest's quirk by mentioning "H.G. Wells," who wrote the book *The Invisible Man*.

In the context of a performance space, there is a special type of presentation that improvisers refer to as *side-support*. Side-support is when an improviser who is offstage temporarily intrudes upon the scene in order to make a contribution (such as a presentation). Side-support can also be a type of clarification (see the next section).

Clarification

Clarification is another other-oriented repair technique used by improvisers to correct any misunderstandings or misinterpretations of information that has already been communicated. It is different from presentation in that it does not introduce any *new* concepts (unless those new concepts are meant to clarify old ones). The idea of clarification is taken from Mohammed and Ringseis, who discusses it as a part of the process of achieving consensus:

> "Through listening to other members clarify ideas and provide rationales for their interpretations, members may proceed from understanding the different perspectives of others to accepting the legitimacy of alternative points of view" [19].

There are three main types of clarification: actor, audience, and side-support. *Actor clarification* is clarification directed towards a fellow improviser. Similar to presentation, sometimes an actor clarification can be made on behalf of another improviser's mental model. *Audience clarification* is simply a clarification directed towards the audience. *Side-support clarification* is the same as side-support presentations except that the intrusion is made to clarify rather than to introduce new information.

For each type of clarification, there are two sub-types: *anticipated* and *perceived*. A perceived clarification is one that an improviser makes in order to correct a divergence that he observes directly. An anticipated clarification, on the other hand, attempts to address a potential divergence. For example, one improviser clarified that somebody was *literally* Jesus because she believed that it was ambiguous whether he was Jesus or just some guy named Ron pretending to be Jesus. Even though she did not observe a divergence, she made the clarification to correct any divergences that might have arisen from the ambiguity of the situation. Anticipated clarifications are evidence that observation is not always a prerequisite for repair.

Another common technique we identified in our study, which we call *reverse scaffolding*, involves the performer giving subtle hints at the onset of the scene and increasing the clarity of his hints over time. The term "scaffolding" comes from educational science. Scaffolding is a technique employed by educators in which they give a large amount of guidance to a learner early on in a learning experience and then "fade" the amount of support of the student as the student gains mastery [6]. *Reverse scaffolding* is therefore our term for the use of subtle hints early on and increasingly heavy-handed hinting over time.

The purpose of reverse scaffolding is to avoid the other performer quickly reaching cognitive consensus in a knowledge disparity game and thus ending the scene prematurely. This technique directly influences the content of a repair technique, leading a given repair to intentionally convey more or less information depending on the situation.

Another noteworthy phenomenon is the use of *reincorporation* (i.e. referring to past concepts or events from a performance) as a tool for clarification. As mentioned earlier, one improviser mentioned a Barbie car a second time after another improviser seemed to forget what the object was. The first improviser explained later that he didn't want the audience to think that they (the improvisers) had forgotten what it (the Barbie car) was, making this an example of both *actor clarification* and *audience clarification*.

Deferment

The first type of self-oriented repair technique that we have identified is *deferment*. It is a deliberate choice to wait and listen for more information, hoping that consensus will occur with time. Deferment is unique among all repair techniques in that it is a choice to be passive rather than actively engage another improviser (a quality that otherwise defines repair requests).

Clarification Request

The remainder of the self-oriented repairs fall under the category of the *repair request* (called "request repair" by Traum [23] when referring to discourse), in which an improviser engages with other improvisers in order to elicit additional information that can be used to develop cognitive consensus.

The first type of repair request is the *clarification request*, a term invented to combine the meanings of clarification [19] and request repair [23]. A clarification request is when an improviser explicitly asks for help because he does not understand something. An improviser might say "What do you mean?" "I have no idea what you're talking about," or "Somebody help me out here!" This technique is sometimes directed towards the audience and usually "breaks the fourth wall" or "breaks the scene" (i.e. interrupting the narrative flow).

Improvisers tend to use other repair techniques instead of clarification requests. From a non-performance point of view, directly asking for help is the most efficient way to receive help. However, it seems that improvisers consider such behavior undesirable, perhaps because it throws off the performance and interrupts flow of the scene. As some improvisers have reported, there are sometimes more important things than just "being right." Reverse scaffolding, as mentioned earlier, is another example of prioritizing other factors over correctness. This phenomenon is why knowledge disparity games are more than just guessing games. Otherwise, improvisers would be much more aggressive about getting the right answer right away.

Verification

When an improviser has an idea of what another improviser's mental model *might* be, he often communicates his impression to his scene partner(s) in order to verify it. This is *verification*, a self-oriented repair technique. The term is borrowed from Traum [23], who describes it as "a repetition or reformulation of what has just been said." In knowledge disparity games, verification usually takes the form of a "guess."

Verification is not always an exact formulation of what an improviser believes. It can also manifest as a statement that is related to a belief that an improviser wants to test for accuracy (i.e. wants to *verify*). For example, when one improviser thought that he and his scene partners might be preachers, he did not ask "Are we preachers?" but instead commented "Preach the people!" In a different scene, an improviser made the verification "I could get Ghost Hunters in here" instead of just guessing that someone was a ghost. This method of verification seems to be the typical application of the technique. The motivation is unclear, but perhaps improvisers make these verifications because they are less disruptive to the scene and integrate better with narrative flow.

Blind Offer

A *blind offer* (related to the canonical improv *offer*, which is when an improviser presents a new potential contribution to a scene) is the final self-oriented repair technique. Improvisers use this term to describe when they intentionally introduce new, vague, and poorly-defined information. The purpose of this action is for the improviser's scene partner(s) to take the information and expand upon it, using the blind offer as an opportunity to present or clarify their mental model(s). In one scene of *Party Quirks*, an improviser playing the party host mentions "gifts" to a party guest and implies that she might have brought some gifts for him. He later identified his comment as a blind offer, explaining:

> "If she says 'Oh yeah! Actually I got you—' and she could actually give me a clue at this point…I could open it up, and she could say 'It's a whatever' and that would be clue as to what I'm supposed to be guessing."

Acknowledgement Request

Sometimes an improviser will suspect that cognitive consensus exists between himself and another improviser, but evidence of the consensus is not immediately obvious. In such cases, the improviser might make an *acknowledgment request,* indicating to his scene partner(s) that he desires a sign of consensus (i.e. acknowledgment). The term is a modified version of Traum's "request ack" [23], which Traum describes as a "[s]ignal for other to acknowledge." In one scene of *Party Quirks*, this technique manifested very explicitly when one of the party guests asks "Do you really know who I am? …You do? Please tell me! Please tell me!" At that point in the scene, the scene had continued for several minutes without the party host guessing the quirk of the last guest. However, the host acted as if he knew, he just hadn't said the quirk aloud. Because of this, the guest acted the way she did: "I'm like 'Spit it out! I know you know! Come on, you're so close!'"

Assessment

Most repair attempts end with *assessment*. Assessment is an improviser's evaluation of whether or not an other-oriented repair was successful. According to Clark, "The route by which A and B reach [mutual understanding] depends on the partner's initial assessment of his understanding" [4]. Assessment can either reveal that a repair was successful and that cognitive consensus was achieved, or that a repair was unsuccessful and that another repair needs to be made. For example, one improviser tried to communicate the idea of "Mormans" to another by mentioning bikes and t-shirts. The first improviser quickly realized (i.e. assessed) that this statement confused the second improviser, so he came up with different clues to communicate the same information. Before an assessment can be made, however, the recipient of the repair must *accept* the repair (unless he simply did not notice it).

Acceptance

After an attempted repair, there are two possibilities. The first is that the repair fails or goes unnoticed such that the divergence continues or a new one takes its place. The other possibility is that the repair is met with *acceptance* [4, 18, 19, 23]. Clark and Schaefer also identify this dichotomy:

> "Almost every time a speaker starts a new turn, he or she either (a) accepts what the last speaker has just said or (b) initiates a repair of the problem they ran into in accepting it" [4].

Acceptance, however, does not necessarily equate to cognitive consensus. Acceptance is merely an intentional response to a repair attempt.

Perceived Cognitive Consensus

Ideally, the type of acceptance that occurs is always cognitive consensus, the state of agreement between mental models (i.e. the existence of a shared mental model). Cognitive consensus is "similarity among group members regarding how key matters are conceptualized" [19]. This similarity of mental models is the ultimate goal of the process of cognitive convergence. However, even among cognitive consensus there are variations that are less desirable. When an improviser accepts his *perception* of another improviser's mental model, *perceived cognitive consensus* occurs. Perceived cognitive consensus results in the change of an improviser's mental model, but this change is not always correct. An improviser might incorrectly accept what he perceives to be true, which then leads to further divergences. In contrast, groups may arrive at a decision without reaching a commonality in how issues are framed (e.g., [5]). For example, [24] contrasts *operational* consensus (group members agree upon decisions but do not share underlying beliefs) with *perceptual* consensus (group members experience a commonality of representations).

An example of perceived cognitive consensus is one scene in which an improviser had to figure out whom he and his fellow improvisers were supposed to be (a fact that his fellow improvisers and the audience knew but that he did not). The improviser eventually decided that the "who" must be "missionaries." After the audience seemed to confirm his guess, the improviser assumed that he was correct. At this point, he achieved perceived cognitive consensus. Soon afterwards, however, he realized that he was wrong and that "missionaries" was not the correct answer (it was actually "Mormons"), proving that perceived cognitive consensus is not always accurate.

True Cognitive Consensus

The ideal form of consensus is *true cognitive consensus*. True cognitive consensus is when an improviser correctly accepts another improviser's mental model. It is different from perceived cognitive consensus because the consensus necessarily exists. It can only be identified through unanimous confirmation by all the improvisers originally involved in the divergence (a phenomenon we capture in our group interview data). Cognitive consensus, however, can be partial: it does not necessarily mean that *all* mental models will be identical. Instead, it means that at least two mental models that used to be different have become the same. In the same scene as the last example, a different improviser had to guess the goal of the scene. He eventually figured out that it had to do with "dragons." While the correct answer was "converting dragons," the improviser still achieved partial cognitive consensus by understanding part of the whole. However, a divergence still existed in regards to "converting."

Sometimes acceptance is followed by *acknowledgment* [4, 23]. Acknowledgement is an improviser's confirmation that he is on the same page as someone else. It is often accompanied by a form of cognitive consensus. Traum explains that acknowledgment serves to "[d]emonstrate or claim understanding of previous material" [23]. The manifestation of acknowledgment can be as simple as "yeah," "ok," or even just a nod or meaningful eye contact. Improv differs from the standard forms of communication that Clark and Traum discuss because acceptance frequently does not involve acknowledgement because the act of acceptance might be construed as breaking out of character. However, even though improvisers can often understand each other without needing to say anything, sometimes acknowledgment is necessary for all parties involved in a divergence to achieve complete consensus,. Furthermore, even acknowledgment can occur mistakenly. Just because an improviser says that he understands does not mean that he necessarily does (as might occur with perceived cognitive consensus).

Groupthink

Not all forms of acceptance are desirable. *Groupthink*, for example, is when an improviser accepts someone else's strongly-portrayed mental model without ever contributing his own personal creativity [2, 7]. Groupthink was originally conceived by Janis to describe a psychological phenomenon on a much larger level [7]. Many aspects of it, such as "pressures for uniformity," are still relevant to improvisational theatre. Groupthink often leads to passive mimicry and usually a less "entertaining" scene. It can result from laziness, lack of experience, the perceived unimportance of one's own ideas and assumptions, or from an overzealous desire to prevent divergence. Instead of making offers (i.e. actions that are potential contributions to a scene), groupthink repeats offers. It is a lack of individual thought. Unlike the improv technique of doing "yes, and" (i.e., accepting what another improviser has done and adding to it), which contribute to a scene while seeking consensus, groupthink neither contributes to the scene nor seeks understanding.

According to interviews with our subjects, a phenomenon that we can match to groupthink is identified as the "easy way out." Therefore, the biggest distinction of groupthink from other techniques is the negative connotation that it carries. While consensus is good, groupthink is bad because it limits the ability of a group to explore the full range of possibilities for a scene. As Mohammed and Ringseis point out, "because one of the benefits of the group context is the harnessing of multiple perspectives, cognitive consensus can become a liability when the uniqueness of individual contributions is lost" [19].

It is important to distinguish between groupthink and a common non-groupthink technique employed by improvisers in knowledge disparity games called "yes-anding." Improvisers who do not possess certain knowledge due to the constraints of the game may agree with everything their scene partner says and does. However, yes-anding is a natural and acceptable way to discover knowledge that the improviser does not posses. The distinguishing factor is whether or not the improviser is *contributing* and whether or not he is *seeking to understand* the mental model of his scene partner(s). If he is doing both of these things, then he is not using groupthink.

Rejection

Sometimes consensus is deliberately avoided. Such is the case with *rejection*, the decision not to repair a divergence [23]. Improvisers choose rejection for many reasons. The improviser might be stubborn and unwilling to admit that he is wrong. An improviser also might be indifferent or he might get frustrated and give up. Some improvisers even go so far as to allow a divergence to persist for comedic effect because they think the audience will find it funny. Along similar lines, other improvisers might decide that a certain divergence makes for a more "interesting" scene. In one unusual case, an improviser decided not to repair a divergence because he did not perceive repairing it as important. He saw his role in the scene as the person who was supposed to constantly move the scene forward, so he figured that trying to correct the divergence would cause difficulties and impede him in his greater purpose.

Summary

After the acceptance phase, the entire cycle of cognitive divergence and convergence repeats. Ideally, the repetition of the process will eventually result in the development of a shared mental model among the improvisers onstage. However, sometimes divergences persist and cognitive consensus never occurs before a scene comes to an end. Meanwhile, as the scene continues, new divergences might arise. Resolving one divergence sometimes is more urgent than resolving another. While some shared mental models will develop, others will never exist. We have not empirically derived a relationship between consensus and scene quality, but informally there seems to be a strong connection between the expertise of the performers in the scene and how long it takes them to reach consensus.

Mental models underlie everything that happens in a scene. Since improv involves the perpetual invention and contribution of new information to a scene, there is a constant potential for errors of commission, omission, or misinterpretation regarding that information. Because of this, understanding how to create shared mental models and navigate those errors is especially important. The process of cognitive convergence allows improvisers to deal with their mistakes and reach an understanding, using shared mental models as the foundation for their construction of a collaborative scene.

Figure 2: The Party Quirks Agent in Action

THE NEXT STEP: PARTY QUIRKS AGENT

Given the importance of shared mental models to the process of improvisation, our next step has been to construct an intelligent agent that models the process of cognitive convergence. Doing so allows us to evaluate the strength of our representation and to determine mechanically how the techniques performed by real improvisers map into actions that a machine can understand and perform.

In order to scope this phase of the project, we limited our domain to a single improv game: *Party Quirks*. The structure of *Party Quirks* lends itself well to this domain because of the built-in constraints. The purpose of the game is to resolve a divergence that is introduced at the very beginning (the host guessing the secret identity, such as "a pirate," of each of the party guests). It serves as a convenient starting point for implementing our framework as most, if not all, improv games involve some aspect of building shared mental models. This particular game is also advantageous since it typically does not involve the construction of complex stories, which would make any modeling efforts much more difficult without first understanding how to computationally represent the construction of shared mental models. The details of this implementation are described in [12].

SUMMARY

The resulting work from our empirical study of theatrical improvisation has lead us to a better understanding of the special role that shared mental models take in the performance of improvised scenes and the details for what actors do on stage to identify, address, and asses cognitive divergences. This supports Sawyer's observation that *collaborative emergence* is essential to improvisation [20] while providing the details of the process necessary to build formal computational models of it. What is special about improvisation and shared mental models is that the communication and coordination that might take place in non-performative group problem solving domains, such as a design task in a studio, cannot commonly take place on stage. In improv theatre, *the coordination is the performance* and, therefore, all attempts at reaching shared mental models must be done so within the context of the performance. This makes understanding the specific observations, knowledge, and actions improvisers employ on stage all the more important in the pursuit of formally understanding improvisation in theatre. This work also points to the kinds of reasoning and ambiguous knowledge that is reasoned about continuously in creative acts. Furthermore, the creation of improvisational agents has helped us better formalize our findings as we engage in the process of theorizing and building agents, which in turn helps us ask better questions for future studies or reinterpret our data in a clearer way so that we can build more complex agents in the future.

REFERENCES

1. Bakeman, R., and J.M. Gottman, *Observing interaction: An introduction to sequential analysis*, Cambridge Univ Pr, 1997.
2. Baron, R.S. So right it's wrong: Groupthink and the ubiquitous nature of polarized group decision making. *Advances in experimental social psychology*, vol. 37, 2005, p. 219–253.

3. Cannon-Bowers, J.A., Salas, E., and Converse, S. "Shared mental models in expert team decision-making," *Environmental Effects of Cognitive Abilities*, 2001, p. 221–245.

4. Clark, H.H., and Schaefer, E.F. Contributing to discourse. *Cognitive Science: A Multidisciplinary Journal*, vol. 13, 1989, p. 259–294.

5. Donnellon, A., Gray, B., and Bougon, M.G. Communication, meaning, and organized action. *Administrative Science Quarterly*, vol. 31, 1986, p. 43–55.

6. Jackson, S.L., Krajcik, J., and Soloway, E. The design of guided learner-adaptable scaffolding in interactive learning environments. *Proceedings of the SIGCHI conference on Human factors in computing systems*, 1998, p. 187–194.

7. Janis, I.L. *Victims of groupthink: A psychological study of foreign-policy decisions and fiascoes*, Houghton Mifflin Boston, 1972.

8. Johnstone, K. *Impro for Storytellers*, Routledge, 1999.

9. Johnstone, K. *Impro: Improvisation and the Theatre*, Routledge, 1987

10. Levesque, L.L., Wilson, J.M., and Wholey, D.R. Cognitive divergence and shared mental models in software development project teams. *Journal of Organizational Behavior*, vol. 22, 2001, pp. 135-144.

11. Limb, C.J., and Braun, A.R. Neural substrates of spontaneous musical performance: an FMRI study of jazz improvisation. *PLoS One*, vol. 3, 2008, p. e1679.

12. Magerko, B., Dohogne, P., and DeLeon, C. Employing Fuzzy Concepts for Digital Improvisational Theatre. In *Proceedings of the Seventh Annual International Artificial Intelligence and Interactive Digital Entertainment Conference* (Palto Alto CA, 2011), AAAI Press.

13. Magerko, B., Manzoul, W., Riedl, M., Baumer, A., Fuller, D., Luther, K., and Pearce, C. An Empirical Study of Cognition and Theatrical Improvisation. In *Proceedings of ACM Conference on Creativity and Cognition* (Berkely CA, 2009).

14. Mathieu, J.E., Heffner, T.S., Goodwin, G.F., Salas, E., and Cannon-Bowers, J.A. The influence of shared mental models on team process and performance. *Journal of Applied Psychology*, vol. 85, 2000, pp. 273-283.

15. Mendonça, D.J., and Wallace, W.A. A cognitive model of improvisation in emergency management. *Systems, Man and Cybernetics, Part A: Systems and Humans, IEEE Transactions on*, vol. 37, 2007, p. 547–561.

16. Mendonça, D.J., and Wallace, W.A. Cognition in Jazz Improvisation: An Exploratory Study. Chicago, IL: 2004.

17. Mitroff, I.I., and Emshoff, J.R. On strategic assumption-making: a dialectical approach to policy and planning. *Academy of Management Review*, vol. 4, 1979, p. 1–12.

18. Mohammed, S. Toward an Understanding of Cognitive Consensus in a Group Decision-Making Context. *Journal of Applied Behavioral Science*, vol. 37, Dec. 2001, pp. 408-425.

19. Mohammed, S., and Ringseis, E. Cognitive Diversity and Consensus in Group Decision Making: The Role of Inputs, Processes, and Outcomes. *Organizational Behavior and Human Decision Processes*, vol. 85, Jul. 2001, pp. 310-335.

20. Sawyer, R.K. *Improvised dialogues: Emergence and creativity in conversation*, Ablex Publishing Corporation, 2003.

21. 19.Seddon, F.A. Modes of Communication During Jazz Improvisation. *British Journal of Music Education*, vol. 22, 2005, pp. 47-61.

22. Spolin, V. Improvisation for the theater: A handbook of teaching and directing techniques, Northwestern Univ Pr, 1963.

23. Traum, "Computational models of grounding in collaborative systems," *working notes of AAAI Fall Symposium on Psychological Models of Communication*, 1999, p. 124–131.

24. Vertzberger, Y. *The world in their minds: Information processing, cognition, and perception in foreign policy decisionmaking*, Stanford Univ Pr, 1990.

25. Yokochi, S., and Okada, T. Creative Cognitive Process of Art Making: A Field Study of a Traditional Chinese Ink Painter. *Creativity Research Journal*, vol. 17, 2005, pp. 241-255.

The Rise of Personal Fabrication

Catarina Mota
Universidade Nova de Lisboa (FCSH-UNL)
Avenida de Berna, 26-C, 1069-061 Lisbon, Portugal
New York University (ITP-NYU)
721 Broadway, 4FL, New York, NY 10003, USA
catarina@openmaterials.org

ABSTRACT
In recent years we have been witnessing the first stages of a democratization of manufacturing, a trend that promises to revolutionize the means of design, production and distribution of material goods and give rise to a new class of creators and producers. A disruptive technology and several cultural and economic driving forces are leading to what has already been called a new industrial revolution: public access to digital fabrication tools, software and databases of blueprints; a tech Do-It-Yourself movement; and a growing desire amongst individuals to shape and personalize the material goods they consume. This paper is an overview of the current state of personal digital fabrication and the trends that are shaping it.

Author Keywords
Digital fabrication, do-it-yourself, democratizing creativity, democratizing innovation, distributed production.

ACM Classification Keywords
A.1 Introductory and survey: General literature.

General Terms
Design, Experimentation, Human Factors.

THE PROMISE OF DIGITAL FABRICATORS

In his 2005 book *FAB*, Neil Gershenfeld [9] describes a not too distant future in which everyone will have a personal fabricator, a machine capable of producing not only material objects but also other machines: "Like the earlier transition from mainframes to PCs, the capabilities of machine tools will become accessible to ordinary people in the form of personal fabricators (PFs). This time around, though, the implications are likely to be even greater because what's being personalized is our physical world of atoms rather than the computer's digital world of bits."

This democratization of manufacturing,—which has already been termed industrial revolution 2 [21], a manufacturing revolution [23] and the next industrial revolution [2]—is based on the fact that, after one century of mass production and consumption, a growing number of individuals now has access to sophisticated production tools and the knowledge to manufacture objects for artistic, personal or commercial purposes.

Digital fabrication tools turn bits into atoms, i.e. they create material objects from digital designs. A computer-aided design (CAD) model is fed into a fabricator which then builds its physical instance from a stock material. Laser cutters, computer-numeric controlled (CNC) mills, and 3D printers are amongst the most practical and versatile of these tools. While laser cutters and CNC mills create parts by cutting sheets of wood, acrylic, metal, cardboard and other flat stock, 3D printers build the objects up by depositing and binding successive layers of materials such as thermoplastics, ceramics and powdered metals.

One of the major advantages of these technologies is that, unlike mass manufacturing tools, they make possible the production of many or just a few one-of-a-kind parts at the same cost as a series of identical items[1]. Besides this general-purpose flexibility, the additive nature of 3D printing wastes almost no stock material and, in some instances, allows the fabrication in one single piece of objects which would otherwise have to be manufactured in several parts and then assembled.

Laser cutters, 3D printers and CNC mills can make objects out of a range of plastics, wood, glass, ceramic slips, wax, resins, leather, and metals (including titanium), but most digital fabricators provide the ability to make parts from only one type of material at a time and no single of these machines can yet create a finished complex device, such as a cell phone, in one swoop. Likewise, the speed at which 3D printers can currently manufacture products is not yet comparable to those of traditional mass production techniques such as injection molding.

Nevertheless, in the last few years the capabilities of digital fabrication tools have been increasing as their cost decreases. While in 2001 the cheapest 3D printer available in the market was priced at $45,000, personal 3D printers now cost

C&C'11, November 3–6, 2011, Atlanta, Georgia, USA.

[1] Unlike mass manufacturing machines, digital fabrication technologies require no tooling, i.e. the changing of accessories and cutting tools of a machine each time something different needs to be made.

between $1000 and $10,000, making them accessible to individuals and small organizations. Similarly, laser cutters and CNC mills have also become more affordable as manufacturers started commercializing smaller models at prices that are within the reach of schools, small businesses and local production shops.

There are now significant indicators that digital fabrication can and will likely play an important role on the emergence of lightweight factories and the expansion of micro production and mass customization (a combination of mass production processes with individual customization) [10] [11] [16]. This has already given rise to an array of new businesses producing on-demand, customizable products ranging from iPhone stands, jewelry and toys to machine parts and prosthetic limb cases [23]. But another profound transformation will occur if and when these technologies start to infiltrate individual practices on a large scale. In order to consider this possibility let us start by noting that a widespread adoption of personal digital fabrication will depend on tools, designs and motivation. Whereas access to tools and designs for production are the essential material conditions, motivation to use them is the elusive last link without which the previous two could be rendered meaningless.

THE NEW FACTORIES

If until 2007 it was extremely difficult for an individual to turn an idea into a material product, nowadays the panorama has radically changed with the introduction and expansion of online fabrication services, distributed manufacturing networks, local production shops, and personal 3D printers. Taken together these ventures are providing a wider distribution of digital fabrication technologies and giving a growing number of creators the possibility to produce and circulate goods outside of the centralized manufacturing model.

Online Fabrication Services

Online fabrication services cater to the consumer looking for a custom product, the independent designer or artist seeking small scale production and distribution of her designs, and the hobbyist in need of prototypes or parts.

Services such as Shapeways, Ponoko, i.materialize and Sculpteo provide on-demand 3D printing and laser cutting services to individuals. In addition to upload-to-make (customers upload a digital design and receive the corresponding physical object in the mail a few days later), Shapeways and Ponoko also offer community marketplaces where creators can sell their designs and fabricated objects directly to the public, web-based platforms for product customization, databases of Creative Commons[2] (CC) licensed designs and, in the case of Ponoko, a request-to-make area where buyers can crowdsource[3] a custom product by asking the community of creators to design and make it (buyer posts a request with a description and creators submit bids to design/make it).

Even though they're barely three years old, online fabrication services have grown substantially not only in terms of the number of bureaus, but also in what concerns the variety of their offering. Ponoko, for example, started by providing only laser cutting services to its customers, but in the second half of 2010 added 3D printing, new materials, and also electronics through a partnership with Sparkfun, thus getting one step closer to becoming a multifunctional public factory.

Distributed Manufacturing Networks

Distributed manufacturing networks such as 100kGarages, CloudFab and MakerFactory connect designers with manufacturing tools, allowing creators to get their concepts produced locally and providing tool owners with a new stream of revenue. Users of these online services can find local shops and equipment operators through maps and lists or by posting a request for a specific job and then selecting from the bids submitted by equipment owners.

Other types of infrastructures are starting to emerge in the form of grid manufacturing structures. MakerBot Industries, a manufacturer of open source personal fabricators, is currently setting up its first BotFarm, a cluster of networked 3D printers. Even though still embryonic, such a structure suggests the possibility of fully distributed grid manufacturing systems which would make use of 3D printers located in several points of the globe.

Local Production Shops

Local production shops are still taking their first steps, but there are already a few meaningful examples in place:

TechShops, self described as "a Kinko's for makers, or a Xerox PARC for the rest of us," are membership-based workshops that provide members with access to an enormous array of fabrication tools as well as instructions to make whatever they wish, regardless of skill level. There are currently six TechShops across the US, with several more in the planning stage.

Fab Labs, a program of the MIT's Center for Bits and Atoms, are workshops equipped with essential fabrication tools with the goal of providing communities around them with the means to create smart devices for themselves. There are currently over 50 Fab Labs in 16 countries, with many more on the planning stage.

Hackerspaces are community-operated physical spaces where people of diverse backgrounds—usually with common interests in science, technology, and digital art, but not necessarily with formal training in these areas—meet to work, collaborate, and socialize. Even though physical

[2] A non-profit organization dedicated to developing and supporting a legal infrastructure for the sharing of knowledge and content.

[3] A distributed problem-solving and production method.

infrastructure and material resources are important aspects of these community laboratories, hackerspaces are above all centers for peer learning, collaborative problem solving, and community building. Unlike TechShops and Fab Labs, hackerspaces emerge directly out of local communities and are all completely independent from each other—even though there is loose network of hackerspaces. This means that the tools available vary greatly from one collective to the other but, due to the drop in cost of digital fabrication technologies, the number of spaces equipped with laser cutters and/or 3D printers is growing. The world map on hackerspaces.org currently registers around 500 hackerspaces worldwide.

Personal 3D Printers

At the same time as professional 3D printers are becoming increasingly sophisticated, a new type of tool is emerging and taking its place in the digital fabrication techno-system: the personal 3D printer, a device small enough to fit in the home or office, low-cost enough to be within the reach of the average individual consumer, and simple enough to be operated by someone with no technical skills.

In February 2004, Adrian Bowyer, professor at the University of Bath in the UK, and his graduate student Ed Sells, announced the RepRap project [3], a research effort dedicated to creating a self-replicating[4], highly affordable, personal 3D printer. RepRap was from the start developed as open source—a method of production in which all of the product's source materials and blueprints are made publicly available, allowing anyone to contribute to its development—and was immediately joined by several engineers and programers, both amateur and professionals, around the world.

To achieve its goals and allow distributed development, RepRap's 3D printers have since been designed as a combination of rapid manufactured parts and inexpensive and readily available hardware. Seven years after the project's launch, and even though sourcing the materials and assembling the machine is still far from being a trivial task, RepRap 3D printers have improved radically in terms of overall reliability, volume, and precision, resulting in plastic objects that now closely approximate end-use products.

Given the open source nature of the project, all that is necessary to become a RepRap operator and developer is being able to source and acquire the materials and then assemble them into a functional machine. According to a 2010 survey conducted by Erik De Bruijn [4], "most people who become involved in the RepRap project and adopt the technology have done so fairly recently. The adoption rate increases so fast that new adopters outnumber all those who joined more than 6 months ago. (…) Regression-fitting this growth curve yields a duplication of the community every 6 months and a 10 fold growth every 20 months."[5]

In late 2008, the difficulty in sourcing the materials required to build a RepRap 3D printer led some developers to the idea of creating kits. It also became apparent that several improvements could be made to the technology by temporarily putting aside the goal of self-replication and dedicating more resources to the project. New RepRap-derived 3D printers and the kits to build them were not only an important step towards expanding the adopter and developer community but also created a business opportunity. From this emerged Bits from Bytes and MakerBot Industries, two startups dedicated to developing and commercializing RepRap-derived open source kits and machines at consumer prices—ranging between $950 (MakerBot) and $3,900 (Bits from Bytes). In July 2010, the Chinese company PP3DP launched the proprietary, fully assembled, desktop 3D printer UP! retailing for $2,990. And in March 2011, Ultimaker entered the market with its reprap-based personal 3D printer selling for approximately $1,700.

While RepRap 3D printers use thermoplastics as stock material, two other open source projects appeared in subsequent years that allow 3D printing of objects from pastes and edibles. That's the case of the syringe-based Fab@Home which 3D prints with anything that can be squirted (eg. silicone, epoxy, cheese, chocolate, frosting, clay, playdoh, plaster, etc.) and also of CandyFab, a machine that creates edible three-dimensional objects from sugar. Other open source projects dedicated to creating laser cutters or CNC mills have also arisen in recent years and include BuildLog, DIYLilCNC, and Bluumax CNC.

During 2009 and 2010, some of the more prominent and established additive manufacturing companies, such as Stratasys, 3D Systems and Solido, also launched smaller and lower priced tools, capable of working with plastics and resins, marketed as personal 3D printers and costing between $10,000 and $17,000.

Access to 3D printing tools is thus following along a path similar to that of document printers. On the one hand the large, professional machines are now accessible to the public mostly through online fabrication services. On the other hand, we're seeing the emergence of personal 3D printers which, just like their small 2D counterparts, are geared towards the home and office. Naturally, there are noticeable differences between the capabilities of professional and personal 3D printers. While the professional machines can produce complex objects out of a wide range of materials, the personal versions are constrained by size and cost, i.e the

[4] It should be noted that its latest model, Mendel, is currently capable of producing only its plastic parts, i.e. the brackets that hold the machine's structure together.

[5] De Bruijn's survey encompasses operators and developers of all open source 3D printers, including those directly associated with the RepRap project but also RepRap-derived 3D printers such as the ones developed by MakerBot Industries and Bits from Bytes.

need to be small and affordable enough. This translates into smaller prints, but also influences speed, resolution, overall quality, and the variety and types of materials (while multiple types of plastics are a given, printing with metals and glass is still not possible with the desktop-sized 3D printers).

Despite the progress of the last years, there are still a few technical barriers to overcome before a widespread adoption of personal digital fabrication can become possible, namely:

Materials

Most personal 3D printers produce objects from a variety of plastics, but even a quick glance around tells us that the majority of products in homes and offices are made out of a combination of different materials. There are already many useful things that can be created from plastics and progress is being made towards introducing additional materials. But in order for these technologies to become so practical that a large number of homes and offices will consider it worthwhile having one, they will need to not only be able to manufacture with diverse materials but also to combine them in one single print. Meanwhile, syringe-based extruders, which work with any paste-like material, offer a still not fully explored flexibility and are already being used for food preparation and decoration [17].

Fumes and Dust

Small CNC mills cut a wider variety of stock materials, but are not as clean as 3D printers, i.e. they produce dust and shards, making them excellent garage tools but inappropriate for homes. Laser cutters also require fume extraction devices and air compressors which are often loud and bulky. For these reasons, laser cutters are not commonly used at home and are usually kept in a separate room in the workplace. It should also be noted that, while smaller laser cutters are already priced within the reach of schools, small shops and hackerspaces, they are not yet affordable enough for individuals.

Interface and Speed

All the digital fabrication tools described above still require some technical knowledge to operate and are very far from the fictional Star Trek replicator which was capable of materializing objects and edibles at a voice command. Also, 3D printers, while highly flexible in terms of what they can make, are still not very fast. Printing an object takes time and while a plastic whistle can be printed in as little as 10 minutes, a mount for an iPhone may take one or two hours to produce. Naturally, as the technology becomes more reliable and with additions such as MakerBot's automated build platform (which allows the manufacturing of series of different or similar items with no human intervention in between prints), operators can leave the machine unattended as it prints, but they will still have to wait for the finished objects to be finalized and ejected.

The current state of personal 3D printers has often been compared with the early days of personal computers [9] with its relatively small community of developers working in hackerspaces and garages around the world. But, despite the technology's current limitations, this is clearly starting to change. As described above, between 2009 and 2011 new developers and manufacturers of low cost personal 3D printers appeared in the market, resulting not only in more research and development, but also in an increasing number of digital fabrication tools in the hands of individuals. As De Bruijn [5] points out, since each adopter of an open source 3D printer is also a potential developer, the growth in the number of adopters also translates into improvements in the technology. In turn, cheaper, better and easier to operate 3D printers tend to draw new adopters and developers. Because of this, in the same two years, these machines went from producing mostly mangled plastic objects vaguely resembling shot glasses to being able to generate prints as complex as a Gothic Cathedral model.

Just as with computers 40 years ago, it might now be difficult to imagine these digital fabrication tools being operated by anyone other than engineers or technically inclined hobbyists. But, following in the footsteps of PCs, personal 3D printers are now taking the leap from a technology requiring specialized skills to something the average individual can operate. This shift is illustrated by the fact that between early 2009 and late 2010 the under $4000 personal 3D printers available in the market went from being just a combination of bill of materials plus plans (the user sources the materials and assembles the machine), to kits plus instructions (the user assembles the machine but all the materials are provided), to fully assembled machines (user just needs to know how to operate and maintain it). With important improvements, additions and new models being introduced at a fast rate, personal 3D printers are rapidly transitioning from a tech hobby to a functional technology accessible to all.

FROM BITS TO ATOMS AND BACK

Professional CAD software is extremely complex. Even though the best of these applications are very powerful, the time and effort required to become a skilled CAD user is non-trivial. Nevertheless, just as it happened with digital imaging applications which were once too complex for the average user, simple and free modeling applications are now available and even include versions for portable devices.

Public databases of blueprints also play an important role in providing both designers and non-designers with blueprints for fabrication. Thingiverse.com is today the most prominent example of such a database. This online 'universe of things' consists in a repository of mostly open and free digital designs for physical objects, i.e, models that can be downloaded and then materialized using fabrication tools such as 3D printers, laser cutters and CNC mills. As of mid 2011, Thingiverse contained over 8000 models (contributed both by highly skilled designers and beginners, some of which are children and adolescents) and included a little bit of everything from kitchenware, toys and jewelry to machine parts, electronics, architectural models, and eye glass frames.

The open licenses under which most of these designs are published allow the website's users to not only download and fabricate the objects but also to alter and combine them. Currently, Thingiverse is expanding rapidly not just with new models but also with an increasing number of derivatives and mashups (the mix of different designs and content to create a new derivative work).

While Thingiverse was created specifically for open and free sharing of designs, Shapeways Shops and Ponoko's Showroom are examples of also user-populated databases with commercial purposes, where artists and designers can sell their creations while giving buyers the opportunity to customize the models using simple software. Thus we have now platforms for free sharing of designs which users must then fabricate by their own means and also online marketplaces where customizable objects and designs are available for purchase.

At the same time as digital fabrication technologies are getting better and cheaper, thus becoming accessible to a wider number and range of individuals and businesses, so is 3D scanning technology advancing. In parallel with developments in professional 3D scanners, a few new open source and/or inexpensive versions—some of which run on smart phones—were made available in 2010. Also noteworthy is the case of Microsoft's Kinect. Initially launched by Microsoft in late 2010 as a hands-free game controller, the Kinect was soon adapted by users for several other applications, including 3D scanning. Once again, these developments seem to indicate a progression of the technology towards becoming efficient and affordable enough for anyone to own and operate. Therefore, in addition to designing and acquiring 3D models for fabrication, we are now also able to turn physical objects and the human body [8] into digital data.

MAKERS

Signals pointing towards a democratization of manufacturing begin to cluster around 2007 [18]. Why was it so? The technology had already been mature enough for some time and dreams of personal factories had been around for many years. What then made several people throughout the world realize the time was ripe for online fabrication services and personal 3D printers? The answer lies mostly in a cultural trend: a renaissance of the Do-It-Yourself (DIY) movement with a hi-tech facet.

DIY is commonly used to describe the act of creating, producing, modifying or repairing something that lies outside of one's professional expertise. It's based on a notion of self-reliance and self-improvement through the acquisition of new knowledge and skills. The term is used across many fields of activity from home improvement and repair to all areas of creative endeavor.

The DIY stance can be traced back to the 1900s Arts and Crafts Movement and in the U.S. it evolved from cost saving home improvement activities of 1940s and 1950s into a creative act of rebellion against mass production, consumerism, planned obsolescence and waste. Even though many different cultures, motivations and goals intersect within this practice, Amy Spencer [22], author of *DIY: The Rise of Lo-Fi Culture*, points out the core aspect common to all of them: "the DIY movement is about using anything you can get your hands on to shape your own cultural entity: your own version of whatever you think is missing in mainstream culture. You can produce your own zine, record an album, publish your own book - the enduring appeal of this movement is that anyone can be an artist or creator. The point is to get involved."

The 21st century DIY movement has now extended its practices to include both on and off line technologies. In *Rise of the Expert Amateur*, a large-scale study of DIY communities, Kuznetsov and Paulos [12] point out that in the last decades, the combination of social computing, online sharing tools, and other collaboration technologies has led to a renewed interest and wider adoption of DIY cultures and practices, namely through facilitated access to and affordability of tools, as well as the emergence of new sharing mechanisms. Further on in the study the authors [12] elaborate: "Recent breakthroughs in technology afford sharing such that anyone can quickly document and showcase their DIY projects to a large audience. An emerging body of tools allows enthusiasts to collaboratively critique, brainstorm and troubleshoot their work, often in real-time (...). This accessibility and decentralization has enabled large communities to form around the transfer of DIY information, attracting individuals who are curious, passionate and/or heavily involved in DIY work."

A subset of the DIY community, namely those involved in creating/modifying hardware and/or technologically enhanced arts and crafts, has become know as the maker community. The word maker refers here to Make magazine, a combination of website and quarterly book that celebrates "your right to tweak, hack, and bend any technology to your own will" [1] by showcasing DIY projects and tutorials to build or modify technologies ranging from personal gadgets to cars. On its first issue, Dale Doherty [6], editor of the magazine, writes: "More than consumers of technology, we are makers, adapting technology to our needs and integrating it into our lives. (...) Think of how many devices each of us interacts with on a regular basis today. And that's only the beginning. Neil Gershenfeld (...) writes in his book *When Things Start to Think* that 'personal computing has not gone far enough; it lets us shape our digital environment but not our physical environment.' In other words, technology that allows us to create complex things will soon become as affordable as the technology we used to create and manage data. We are just beginning to see the impact of technology in our personal lives."

Thus, starting in 2005 and with Make magazine at its center, a community of tech DIYers began to gather around an emerging identity, that of the maker. In addition to using web platforms to share tutorials (instructions for humans) in websites such as Instructables.com, makers are also sharing, remixing and mashingup ready-to-make files (instructions for machines) in web communities like Thingiverse. As Lipson and Kurman [13] note, "Personal manufacturing technologies are accelerated by the online communities of people who create electronic blueprints, those who build and fix machines, and consumers. Similar to the already well-known online community of open source software enthusiasts, communities are a critical part of the personal manufacturing revolution since little formal training and tech support exists. Online colleagues offer one another help, teamwork and encouragement."

Among these makers are the users of online fabrication services and Fab Labs, the members of TechShops and Hackerspaces, the adopters and developers of personal 3D printers, the creators, sharers and mashupers of digital designs for physical objects, the sellers and buyers of the new fabricated-on-demand customizable goods. While these pioneers are still a minority of the population, they may be what Eric Von Hippel [25] terms lead users: early adopters of products and practices that will eventually become widespread and customary.

FACTORIES AT HOME

From the trends and signals described above we can thus infer that, even if not yet fully matured, the digital and physical tools are in place and available to the public. We also know that a fringe of the population is already acquiring and/or using these technologies for personal and micro production. In addition, recent articles in mainstream U.S. publications such as The New York Times, The Wall Street Journal and The Economist have not only contributed to a growth in the number of adopters, but also drawn attention to this confluence of trends and the promise it carries to revolutionize the creation, production and distribution of material goods. Amongst the many difficult questions this potential disruption raises, there is one that is pivotal for a mass adoption of personal fabrication: what will we want to fabricate ourselves?

In Factory@Home, a report commissioned by the U.S. Office of Science and Technology Policy, Lipson and Kurman [13] write: "A number of converging forces will promote personal manufacturing from a fringe technology used by pioneers and hobbyists, to an everyday tool for mainstream consumers and businesses. Within a few years, personal manufacturing technologies will be commonplace in small businesses and schools. Within a decade or two, every household and office will own their own machine. Within a generation, you will have a hard time explaining to your grandchildren how you were able to live without your own fabber, when you actually had to buy ready made things online, and wait a long 24 hours before they showed up in your mailbox."

For now, adopters of personal digital fabrication fall into two, often overlapping, categories: the technical hobbyists, excited about the technology itself and eager to push it forward, and the artists, designers and makers who are mostly interested in what they can create with them (sculptures, consumer products, parts for DIY projects). These are the technology's lead users. But what applications will make a large number of others want to own and/or use a digital fabricator just as they now own and use laptops? What will compel them to get home, turn on their computer, check their email and set their 3D printer or laser cutter to fabricate something? What's that something that no one else can offer or that costs too much to acquire?

The motivation for personal fabrication that has been most often put forward is a growing desire for personalized products [10] [13]. According to a survey conducted by the Institute For The Future [10], "a self-motivating, self-educating, and self-organizing sector of society is emerging that may define an alternative economy. This sector tends to seek out customized or alternative goods, services, and entertainment—preferring to have a more active hand in shaping their own goods, environments, and experiences in conjunction with relatively small groups of like-minded people."

The production of affordable objects tailored to fit perfectly one's specific needs is certainly a powerful trend that is changing the manufacturing world. This has already given rise to a series of small manufacturing businesses, often times one-person factories, offering made to order and customized products. Large and medium manufacturers should follow shortly. For commercial manufacturers, whatever their size, the world is indeed about to change. [11] [16]

But, when it comes to personal fabrication, i.e. making something oneself, we must ask: in what circumstances will it be more advantageous for a large number of people to use their own personal fabricator, or a digital fabrication service, instead of ordering something from a designer/manufacturer who will customize it to the client's specifications at an affordable price? Even when personal fabricators become capable of making something as complex as a cell phone, they will still need to supplied with stock materials. How many different materials and components, and in what quantities, will homes and offices need to acquire and store in order to be able to manufacture a variety of goods that justifies having the digital fabricator in the first place?

Disruptive technologies, once put in the hands of enough users, tend to take a life of their own and very few would say, as Ken Olsen did in 1977 about computers, 'there is no reason anyone would want a digital fabricator in their home' (in fact, the author of this paper does have a personal 3D printer on her desk, printing away as she writes this). But, just as in the late 1970s, it's now extremely difficult to predict which technologies will be massively adopted and what they will be used for. For now, here are some factors that might influence a widespread adoption of personal fabricators:

Creative Remixes and Mashups
While it might be easier for many to simply order a gadget accessory from a professional manufacturer, it is very likely that some will want a version that combines different models they've seen on their friends or on shop windows[6]. Remixing and mashingup are already common practices when it comes to photos, videos and music and there are now indicators that this cultural practice is spilling over into the production of some material goods, as illustrated by a rising object mashup trend on Thingiverse. When the acts of remixing and mashingup are of a creative and playful nature, they are usually undertaken by oneself. Once the design is finished, it can be manufactured on a personal fabricator, in the color of its creator's choice, or at a local fabrication shop.

Problem Fixers
It has happened to everyone. Suddenly a small plastic part of a dish washer breaks. The rest of the machine still works perfectly, but the manufacturer can't provide that one part that is necessary to repair it. Or one of the legs on a kitchen table is too short and none of wedges available in the market fit it properly. Or a dish drying rack needs to be raised just a few millimeters so the water can drain properly. While the number of businesses allowing buyers to customize what they acquire will very likely grow, these types of things are still too small and specific for any one manufacturer to address. Access to simple CAD software and a personal digital fabricator allow someone to design, mashup or remix a model tailored to their unique needs and manufacture these little problem fixers that can't be acquired from stores.

Kits Are Cheaper Than Assembled Goods
For the same reason that furniture manufacturer and retailed IKEA is able to sell cheaper goods by making them available unassembled, it might also be less expensive to obtain the blueprints, raw materials and components, probably in the form of a kit, and have one's own fabricator produce the various parts for a product which we would then assemble ourselves. That is, until personal fabricators become capable of printing a complex object already fully assembled.

Turnaround Time
Even if it takes a 3D printer one hour or two to fabricate an iPhone stand, that is still significantly less than waiting one or more days for it to arrive in the mail. As personal digital fabrication tools grow faster and more efficient this might become an increasingly important motivation to have a fabricator at home or in the office. One example shared by a Thingiverse user illustrates this perfectly. Marty McGuire [15] had just moved into a new town. Even though he was able to buy a shower curtain at the local drugstore, they were all out of rings. While pondering the possibility of taking a bath instead, McGuire remembered that he owns a personal 3D printer. He quickly designed and printed some shower curtain rings and had his shower. But it doesn't end there, McGuire made his ring model parametric, so that it can be adapted to fit other curtain rods, and posted the model on Thingiverse for anyone to download and modify for free.

[6] Which raises complex intellectual property issues that will not be address here.

THE FUTURE?
As beautifully illustrated by the Nueve Ojos' *Full Printed* animation [20], the scenario now being debated in numerous blogs and conversations but also on the mass media is that, in a not so distant future, we will all be manufacturing exactly what we want, when and where we want it. Naturally, this vision has such profound implications that are just as difficult to foresee as the future of the personal computer was in the 1970s. What we have at the moment is a series of questions posed by this scenario:

What Happens to Safety, Environmental and Quality Regulations?
While the manufacturing industry is currently subject to regulations concerning the safety, quality and environmental impact of the goods they produce, how can these be applied to the objects individuals fabricate themselves? Who is liable if someone gets injured by one of these home-made objects? It is very likely that these regulations, and mostly the burden of ensuring safety, will still lie on the providers of digital fabricators, materials and blueprints—while alterations or misuses on the part of the users will be their own responsibility—just as it now happens with home appliances and other such devices. Nevertheless, depending on the uses we make of these technologies, it is very likely that the current legislation may quickly be made obsolete by the new practices.

More Sustainable or a New Source of Waste?
Digital fabrication tools can turn out to be either a much more sustainable form of production or the generators of an enormous amount of additional refuse. On the one hand, additive fabrication technologies waste almost no stock material and don't require molds. Also, if we can have exactly the products we want, tailored to our needs, and the ability to easily repair and repurpose most of these objects, chances are that most products' life cycles will be greatly extended. The ability to have something manufactured only when and where it's needed would also considerably decrease fuel consumption, pollution and surplus waste. On the other hand, precisely the fact that products can be made at the push of a button may lead us to regard them as disposable and easily replaceable, thus decreasing the product's life cycle and greatly increasing the amount of waste.

What About Intellectual Property?
What happens when everyone has access to fabricators and 3D scanners and parametrized models for nearly everything circulate freely on the web? In November 2010, Michael Weinberg [26], from Public Knowledge, published an article, titled *It Will Be Awesome If They Don't Screw It Up: 3D printing, intellectual property and the fight over the next*

great disruptive technology, in which he describes the complex legal implications of these trends and technologies.

While copyright court battles over music, movie and book file sharing still rage, and the advocates of open source and free culture continue their fight for increased openness and less restrictive intellectual property laws, practice is simply outdating the law. Everywhere individuals and groups are choosing to give away their creations for free, to build on each others' work, to open, adapt and repurpose the goods they acquire, and to share all this knowledge and accompanying blueprints through the internet. This has been poignantly expressed by Allan Ecker [7], blogger for Thingiverse, on a post dated May 13, 2009: "The Creative Commons, when applied to machinery, to parts and equipment and tools and toys, will serve as an alternate understanding, and a 'made law' that will let designers leverage the power of personal fabrication to improve the world, by improving the way things are made."

CONCLUSION

In this hi-tech revival of the pre-industrial era of artisan production—but now enabled and exponentiated by the most powerful many-to-many network the world has ever known—we are able to not only manufacture products at home but also instantly share our creations with everyone else. A whistle designed in Germany can be held in the hands of someone else in New York City in as little as 15 minutes [19]; we can be 3D scanned in under five minutes and our likeness published and 3D printed a few hours later [8]; a replacement part can be fabricated for a few cents, avoiding a repair which would otherwise cost hundreds of dollars [14].

In addition to the profound repercussions these technologies will likely have on the manufacturing industry [11] [16], the democratization they enable promises to unleash creativity and innovation at a level comparable to those brought about by the personal computer and the internet. As Von Hippel [25] points out, "User-centered innovation processes offer great advantages over the manufacturer-centric innovation development systems that have been the mainstay of commerce for hundreds of years. Users that innovate[7] can develop exactly what they want, rather than relying on manufacturers to act as their (often very imperfect) agents. Moreover, individual users do not have to develop everything they need on their own: they can benefit from innovations developed and freely shared by others."

Access to tools capable of turning digital designs into physical objects, coupled with the ease with which digital files can and are being modified and circulated, is bringing a third dimension to the practices of sharing, mashup and remix, and giving everyone the opportunity to not only reinvent and shape the world of bits, but also the world of atoms. The next decade will tell if indeed, as Doherty [6] suggests, more than consumers, we are makers.

[7] In a 2010 study comparing businesses and household sector innovation in consumer products, Von Hippel, De Jong and Flowers [24] found that "6.2% of UK consumers - 2.9 million individuals - have engaged in consumer product innovation during the prior 3 years. In aggregate, consumers' annual product development expenditures are 2.3 times larger than the annual consumer product R&D expenditures of all firms in the UK combined."

ACKNOWLEDGMENTS

Thank you to Tom Igoe and Art Kleiner, professors at ITP-NYU, for the wisdom with which they helped me think through this complex and rapidly evolving landscape.

This research was conducted in the context of the digital media doctoral program of the UT Austin|Portugal protocol and funded by a fellowship from FCT-MCTES.

REFERENCES

1. About Make. http://makezine.com/about
2. Anderson, C. In the Next Industrial Revolution, Atoms are the New Bits. In *Wired*, 2 (2010), 58 - 67.
3. Bowyer, A. Wealth Without Money. (2006). http://www.reprap.org/wiki/BackgroundPage
4. De Bruijn, E. On the Viability of Open Source Development Model for the Design of Physical Objects. (2010). http://thesis.erikdebruijn.nl/master/MScThesis-ErikDeBruijn-2010.pdf
5. De Bruijn, E. Self-replicating Devices: The statistics. (2010). http://blog.erikdebruijn.nl/archives/145-Self-replicating-devices-the- statistics.html
6. Doherty, D. The Making of Make. In *Make*, 1, (2005), 7.
7. Ecker, A. Thingiverse & The Creative Commons. (2009). http://blog.thingiverse.com/2009/05/13/thingiverse-the-creative-commons
8. Ethan. New York Notables. (2011). http://www.makerbot.com/blog/2011/06/13/new-york-notables/
9. Gershenfeld, N. *Fab: The coming revolution on your desktop—from personal computers to personal fabrication.* Basic Books, New York, 2005, 59-62 (kindle ed. Locs.)
10. Institute for the Future. Manufacturing: Do It Yourself? (2009). http://www.iftf.org/node/2786
11. Karlgaard, R. 3D Printing Will Revive American Manufacturing. (2011). http://blogs.forbes.com/richkarlgaard/2011/06/23/3d-printing-will-revive-american-manufacturing/
12. Kuznetsov, S. and Paulos E. Rise of the Expert Amateur: DIY projects, communities, and cultures. In *Proceedings of the 6th Nordic Conference on Human-Computer Interaction: Extending Boundaries* (NordiCHI '10). ACM (2010), 295-304.

13. Lipson., H., and Kurman, M. Factory@Home: The emerging economy of of personal manufacturing. (2010). http://www.mae.cornell.edu/lipson/factoryathome.pdf

14. Makerblock. Justifying a 3D Printer. (2011). http://www.makerbot.com/blog/2011/07/21/justifying-a-3d-printer/

15. McGuire, M. Shower Curtain Hook. http://www.thingiverse.com/thing:3465

16. Mills, M. Manufacturing, 3D Printing and What China Knows About the Emerging American Century. (2011). http://blogs.forbes.com/markpmills/2011/07/05/manufacturing-3d-printing-and-what-china-knows-about-the-emerging-american-century/

17. Moskvitch, K. Printer Produces Personalized 3D Chocolate. (2011). http://www.bbc.co.uk/news/technology-14030720

18. Mota, C. Timeline of the Democratization of Manufacturing. (2011). http://timeglider.com/app/viewer.php?uid=line_c7dabf30a753afe36ddd17b25a0d03c1

19. Norton, Q. Is the Makerbot a Hacker-friendly Version of My Little Cupcake or a Harbinger of a Major Sea Change? (2011). http://www.maximumpc.com/article/features/inside_makerbot_future_3d_printing?page=0,1

20. Nueve Ojos. Full Printed. (2010). http://vimeo.com/12768578

21. Pettis, B. Industrial Revolution 2. (2009). http://www.brepettis.com/blog/2009/9/24/industrial-revolution-2.html

22. Spencer, A. *DIY: The rise of lo-fi culture.* Marion Boyars Publishers, London, 2008, 11.

23. Vance, A. 3D Printing Spurs a Manufacturing Revolution. (2010). http://www.nytimes.com/2010/09/14/technology/14print.html?_r=1

24. Von Hippel, E., De Jong, J. and Flowers, S. Comparing Business and Household Sector Innovation in Consumer Products: Findings from a Representative Study in the UK. (2010). http://ssrn.com/abstract=1683503

25. Von Hippel, E. *Democratizing Innovation.* The MIT Press, Cambridge, 2005.

26. Weinberg, M. It Will Be Awesome If They Don't Screw It Up: 3D printing, intellectual property and the fight over the next great disruptive technology. (2010). http://www.publicknowledge.org/files/docs/3DPrintingPaperPublicKnowledge.pdf

Finding the Odd One Out: A Fractal Analogical Approach

Keith McGregor and Ashok Goel
Design & Intelligence Laboratory, School of Interactive Computing
Georgia Institute of Technology, Atlanta, GA 30332, USA
keith.mcgreggor@gatech.edu, goel@cc.gatech.edu

ABSTRACT

The Odd One Out test of intelligence consists of 3x3 matrix reasoning problems organized in 20 levels of difficulty. Addressing problems on this test appears to require integration of multiple cognitive abilities usually associated with creativity, including visual encoding, similarity assessment, pattern detection, and analogical transfer. We describe a novel fractal technique for addressing visual analogy problems on the Odd One Out test. In our technique, the relationship between images is encoded fractally, capturing inherent self-similarity. The technique starts at a high level of resolution, but, if that is not sufficient to resolve ambiguity, it automatically adjusts itself to the right level of resolution for addressing a given problem. Similarly, the technique automatically starts with searching for similarity between simpler relationships, but, if that is not sufficient to resolve ambiguity, it automatically searches for similarity between higher-order relationships. We present preliminary results from applying the fractal technique on a representative subset of the problems from the Odd One Out test.

Keywords

Computational creativity, visual representations, analogical reasoning and inference, psychometrics

ACM Classification Keywords

I.2.4. Knowledge Representation Formalisms and Methods

General Terms

Algorithms, Theory

CREATIVITY, ANALOGY AND COGNITION

There is little agreement in the literature on a definition of creativity. Most definitions characterize creativity in terms of its products. Sternberg & Lubart [18], among many others, have defined the products of creativity as "novel'' and "useful." Maher [15], among others, has characterized them as "surprising" in addition to novel and useful. In the arts, creative products are sometimes characterized as novel and surprising to the receiver, if not also to the producer.

In contrast, we have chosen to focus on the information processes of creativity. Here, there is remarkable agreement on two of the core information processes of creativity, viz., analogical thinking and visual thinking. For example, Clement [20], Goel [26], Hofstadter [29], Holyoak & Thagard [30], Nersessian [33], and Vattam, Helms & Goel [36], all have emphasized the central role of analogical thinking in human creativity in domains ranging from calligraphy to design to science. Similarly, Arnheim [13], Ferguson [14], Goldschmidt [27], and Stafford [17], among others, have focused on the key role of visual thinking in creativity in art, design and science. Indeed, many creativity researchers have investigated visual analogies, i.e., analogies based on visual knowledge, as a fundamental construct in creative information processes, (e.g., Casakin & Goldschmidt [19]; Croft & Thagard [21]; Davies, Goel & Nersessian [22]; Davies, Goel & Yaner [23]; Yaner & Goel [34][35]).

Visual analogies are common on standardized intelligence tests that measure personality, aptitude, knowledge, creativity, and academic achievement, such as the Miller's Geometric Analogies test, the Wechsler's intelligence test [11], and the Raven's Progressive Matrices test [9]. Some tests of intelligence, such as the Wechsler's, contain a mix of verbal and visual questions. Others, such as the Raven's Progressive Matrices test, consist of purely visual analogy problems. Yet, because of its high correlation with other measures of general intelligence, the Raven's test has acquired a position of centrality in psychometrics. There is general agreement that addressing the matrix reasoning problems on tests such as Raven's requires integration of multiple abilities including visual encoding, pattern detection, rule integration, similarity assessment, analogical transfer, and problem solving.

Research on "computational psychometrics" dates at least as far back as Evan's Analogy program [4], Recently, Bringsjord & Schimanski [2] have proposed psychometric AI, i.e., AI that can pass psychometric tests of intelligence, as a possible mechanism for measuring and comparing AI. Most computational models of the Raven's test rely on propositional representations of the visual inputs [2][3] [8]. Hunt [7] gave a theoretical account of the information processing demands of certain problems from the Raven's test, in which he proposed that two qualitatively different solution algorithms—"Gestalt," which uses imagistic representations and perceptually based operations, and "Analytic," which uses feature-based representations and logical operations—could yield identical results on at least portions of the test. However, the algorithms were never implemented.

Given that the inputs and outputs of all problems on the Raven's test are visual, recently there have been have some attempts at building computational models based on purely visual representations and reasoning [31][32]. For example, in [32], we described a fractal technique for addressing problems on the Raven's test.

The recently developed Odd One Out test of intelligence [5] was algorithmically designed to examine brain activity while solving problems at various levels of difficulty. It consists of 3x3 matrix reasoning problems organized in 20 levels of difficulty. Like the Raven's test, addressing the Odd One Out test requires multiple abilities ranging from visual encoding to pattern detection, from rule invocation to problem solving, from similarity assessment to analogical transfer. Unlike the Raven's test, the Odd One Out test seeks to discover dissimilarity, an ability at the core of attention and visual search.

In this paper, we present preliminary results from applying a novel analogical perspective of our fractal technique onto a representative subset of the problems from the Odd One Out test. Like our prior work on Raven's [31], our technique here uses fractal representations of the problems on the test. However, from the cognitive perspective, two of the advantages of our new fractal technique are that (1) the technique starts at high level of resolution, but, if that is not sufficient to resolve ambiguity, it automatically adjusts itself to the right level of resolution for addressing a given problem, and (2) the technique automatically starts with searching for similarity between simpler relationships, but, if that is not sufficient to resolve ambiguity, it automatically searches for similarity between higher-order relationships.

VISUAL ANALOGIES AND FRACTALS

The main goal of our work is to evaluate whether visual analogy problems may be solved using purely imagistic representations, without converting the images into propositional descriptions during any part of the reasoning process. We use fractal representations, which encode transformations between images, as our primary non-propositional imagistic representation. The representation is imagistic (or analogical) in that it has a structural correspondence with the images it represents.

Analogies are based on similarity and repetition. Fractal descriptions capture self-similarity and repetition at multiple scales. Thus, we believe fractal representations to be a good choice for addressing analogy problems. Our fractal technique is grounded in the mathematical theory of general fractals [9] and specifically of fractal image compression [1].

We are unaware of any previous work on using fractal representations to address either geometric analogy problems of any kind or other intelligence test problems. However, there has been some work in computer graphics on image analogies for texture synthesis in image rendering. Hertzmann et al. [6] describe a technique that abstracted a textural filter between an image A and a filtered rendering A′ and then applied it to generate the desired image B′ from a different image B. The technique uses a Gaussian pyramid technique to construct a multi-scale image and then determines features for individual pixels in this image by examining luminance distributions in pixel neighborhoods.

Both the class of problems we address and the fractal technique we have designed differ entirely from those of Hertzmann, et al. We explicitly represent each image fractally and use this representation to determine its transfer. As a result, the underlying pixels, while significant in determining initial matching, become irrelevant for transfer; our method determines similarity between two images via derived feature sets indicative of both geometric and colorimetric properties.

FRACTAL REPRESENTATIONS

Consider the general form of an analogy problem as being A : B :: C : D. One can interpret this visually as shown in the example in Figure 1.

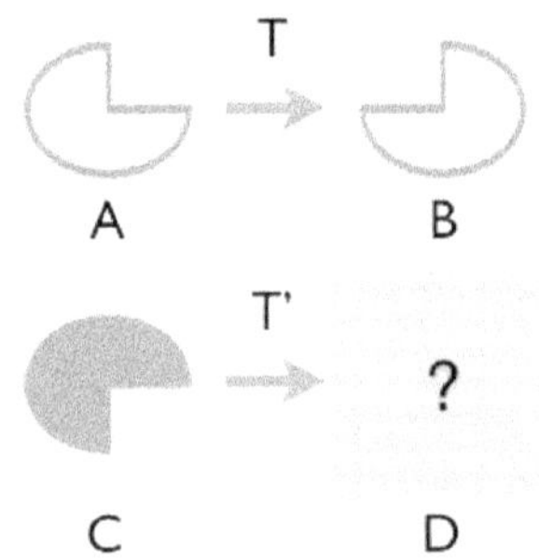

Figure 1. An Example of Visual Analogy.

For visual analogy, we can presume each of these analogy elements to be a single image. Some unknown transformation T can be said to transform image A into image B, and likewise, some unknown transformation T′ transforms image C into the unknown answer image.

Analogy, Similarity, and Features

The central analogy in such a visual problem may then be imagined as requiring that T is analogous to T′; that is, the answer will be whichever image D yields the most analogous transformation. That T and T are analogous may be construed as meaning that T is in some fashion similar to T. The nature of this similarity may be determined by a number of means, many of which associate visual or geometric features to points in a coordinate space, and compute similarity as a distance metric [11]. Tversky developed an alternate approach by considering objects as collections of features, and similarity as a feature-matching process [11]. Using fractal representations, we shall define the most analogous transform T′ as that which shares the largest number of fractal features with the original transform T.

Mathematical Basis

The mathematical derivation of fractal image representation expressly depends upon the notion of real world images, i.e. images that are two dimensional and continuous [1]. There are two key observations:

1. All naturally occurring images one perceives appear to have similar, repeating patterns; and
2. No matter how closely one examines the real world, one will find instances of similar structures and repeating patterns.

These observations suggest that it is possible to describe the real world in terms other than those of shapes or traditional graphical elements—in particular, terms which capture the observed similarity and repetition alone.

Computationally, determining fractal representation of an image requires the use of the fractal encoding algorithm. The collage theorem [1] at the heart of the fractal encoding algorithm can be stated concisely:

> *For any particular real world image D, there exists a finite set of affine transformations T which, if applied repeatedly and indefinitely to any other real world image S, will result in the convergence of S into D.*

Although in practice one may begin with a particular source image and a particular destination image and derive the encoding from them, it is important to keep in mind that once the finite set of transformations T has been discovered, it may be applied to any source image, and will converge onto the particular destination image. The collage theorem defines fractal encoding as an iterated function system [1].

The Fractal Encoding Algorithm

Given an image D, the fractal encoding algorithm seeks to discover the set of transformations *T*. The algorithm is considered "fractal" for two reasons: first, the affine transformations chosen are generally contractive, which leads to convergence, and second, the convergence of S into D can be shown to be the mathematical equivalent of considering D to be an attractor [1].

Partition D into a set of smaller images $\{d_1, d_2, d_3, \ldots\}$.

For each image d_i:

- Examine the entire source image S for an equivalent image fragment s_i such that an affine transformation of s_i will likely result in d_i.
- Collect all such transforms into a set of candidates C.
- Select from the set C that transform which most minimally achieves its work, according to some predetermined metric.
- Let T_i be the representation of the chosen transformation associated with d_i.

The set $T = \{T_1, T_2, T_3, \ldots\}$ is the fractal encoding of the image D.

Algorithm 1. Fractal Encoding

The steps for encoding an image D in terms of another image S are shown in Algorithm 1. The partitioning of D into smaller images can be achieved through a variety of methods. In our present implementation, we merely choose to subdivide D in a regular, gridded fashion. Alternatives could include irregular subdivisions, partitioning according to some inherent colorimetric basis, or levels of detail.

We note that the fractal encoding of the transformation from a particular source image S into a destination image D is tightly coupled with the partitioning P of the destination image D. Thus, a stronger specification of the fractal encoding T may be thought of as a function:

$$T(S, D, P) = \{T_1, T_2, T_3, \ldots\}$$

where the cardinality of the resulting set is determined solely by the partitioning P.

Searching and Encoding

As mentioned, a chosen partitioning scheme P extracts a set of smaller images d_i from the destination image D. In turn, the entire source image S is examined for a fragment which most closely matches that fragment d_i. The matching is performed by first transforming di, as described below, and then comparing photometric (or pixel) values. A simple Euclidean distance metric is used for the photometric similarity between the two fragments.

The search over the source image S for a matching fragment is exhaustive, in that each possible correspondence s_i is considered regardless of its prior use in other discovered transforms. By allowing for such reuse, the encoding algorithm captures the important notion of repetition, one of the two key observations driving fractal encoding.

Similitude Transformations

For each potential correspondence, the transformation of d_i via a restricted set of similitude transformations is considered. A similitude transformation is a composition of a dilation, orthonormal transformation, and translation. Our implementation presently examines each potential correspondence under eight transformations, which correspond to the dihedral group D4, the symmetry group of a square.

We fix our dilation at a value of either 1.0 or 0.5, depending upon whether the source and target image are dissimilar or identical, respectively. The translation is found as a consequence of the search algorithm.

Fractal Codes

Once a transformation has been chosen for a fragment of the destination image, we construct a compact representation of that transformation called a fractal code. A fractal code T_i is a six-tuple:

$$T_i = < <o_x,o_y>,<d_x,d_y>, k, s, c, Op >$$

With each member of the tuple defined as follows:

$<o_x,o_y>$ is the origin of the source fragment;

$<d_x,d_y>$ is the origin of the destination fragment d_i;

$k \in$ { I,HF,VF,R90,R180,R270, RXY, RNXY }, one of the eight D4 transformations;

s is the block sized used in the given partitioning;

$c \in [-255, 255]$ indicates the overall color shift to be used uniformly to all elements in the block; and

Op is the pixel-level operation to be used when combining the color shift c onto pixels in the destination fragment d_i.

A fractal code thus collects the spatial and photometric properties necessary to transform a portion of a source image into a destination.

Arbitrary selection of source

Note that the choice of source image S is arbitrary. Indeed, the image D can be fractally encoded in terms of itself, by substituting D for S in the algorithm. Although one might expect that this substitution would result in a trivial encoding (in which all fractal codes correspond to an identity transform), in practice this is not the case, for we want a fractal encoding of D to converge upon D regardless of chosen initial image. For this reason, the size of source fragments considered is taken to be twice the dimensional size of the destination fragment, resulting in a contractive affine transform. Similarly, color shifts are made to contract. This contraction, enforced by setting the dilation of spatial transformations at 0.5, provides the second of the key observations which drive fractal encoding, that similarity and repetition occur at differing scales.

Arbitrary nature of the encoding

The cardinality of the resulting set of fractal codes which constitute the fractal encoding is determined solely by the partitioning of the destination image. However, that partitioning may be traversed in any order during the matching step of the encoding algorithm. Similarly, once discovered, the individual codes may be applied in any order at all, so long as all of the codes are applied in any particular iteration, to satisfy the constraint of the Collage Theorem.

The fractal encoding algorithm, while computationally expensive in its exhaustive search, transforms any real world image into a much smaller set of fractal codes, which form, in essence, an instruction set for reconstituting the image.

Determining Fractal Features

The fractal representation of an image is an unordered set of specific similitude transformations, i.e. a set of fractal codes, which compactly describe the geometric alteration and colorization of fragments of the source image that will collage to form the destination image. While it is tempting to treat contiguous subsets of these fractal codes as features, we note that their derivation does not follow strictly Cartesian notions (e.g. adjacent material in the destination might arise from strongly non-adjacent source material). Accordingly, we consider each of these fractal codes independently, and construct candidate fractal features from the individual codes themselves.

Each fractal code yields a small set of features, formed by constructing subsets of the underlying six-tuple. These features are determined in a fashion to encourage both position-, affine-, and colorimetric-agnosticism, as well as specificity. Our algorithm creates features from fractal codes by constructing almost all possible subsets of each of the six members of the fractal code's tuple (we ignore singleton sets as well as taking the entire tuple as a set). Thus, in the present implementation of our algorithm, we generate C(6,2)+C(6,3)+C(6,4)+C(6,5) = 106 distinct features for each fractal code, where C(n, m) refers to the combination formula ("from n objects, choose m").

Mutuality

The analogical relationship between source and destination images may be seen as mutual. That is, the source is to the destination as the destination is to the source. However, the fractal representation which entails encoding is decidedly one-way (e.g. from the source to the destination). To capture the bidirectional, mutual nature of the analogy between source and destination, we now introduce the notion of a mutual fractal representation.

Let us call the representation of the fractal transformation from image A to image B as T_{AB}, as shown in Figure 2. Correspondingly, we would label the inverse representation as T_{BA}.

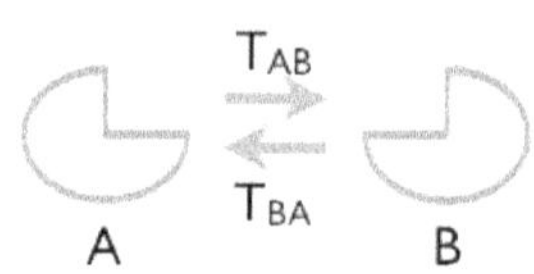

Figure 2. Mutual relationships.

We shall define the mutual analogical relationship between A and B by the symbol M_{AB}, given by this equation:

$$M_{AB} = T_{AB} \cup T_{BA}$$

By exploiting the set-theoretic nature of T_{AB} and T_{BA} to express M_{AB} as a union, we afford the mutual analogical representation the complete expressivity and utility of the fractal representation.

Thus, we have the necessary apparatus for reasoning analogically about the relationships between images, dependent upon only features which describe the visual similarity present in those images.

THE ODD ONE OUT PROBLEMS

The recently developed Odd One Out test of intelligence [5] was algorithmically designed to examine brain activity while solving problems at various levels of difficulty. It consists of 3x3 matrix reasoning problems organized in 20 levels of difficulty. In the test, a participant must decide which of the nine abstract figures in the matrix does not belong (the so-called "Odd One Out"). Figure 3 shows a sampling of the problems, illustrating the nature of the task, and several levels of complexity.

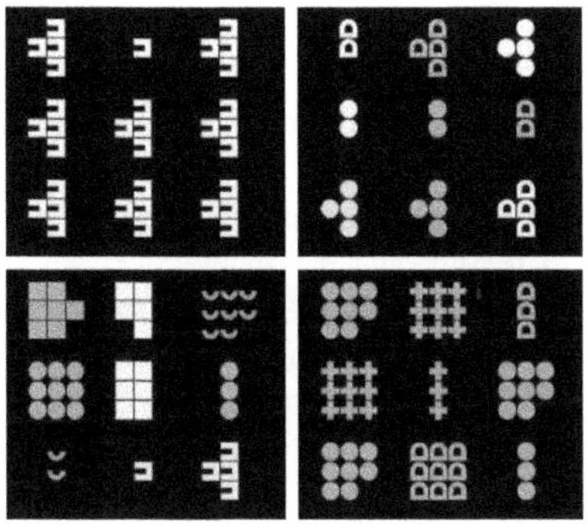

Figure 3. Odd One Out problems.

From the computational perspective, one drawback of computationally modeling a visual analogy task such as the Raven's test is that the algorithm for generating the problems on the test is not known; human examiners generate the test problems based on historical and empirical data. In contrast, problems on the Odd One Out test are generated using a complex set of algorithms [5]. Thus, many tens of thousands of novel problems may be generated.

FINDING THE ODD ONE OUT, FRACTALLY

We now present our algorithm for tackling the Odd One Out problem, using the mutual fractal representation as a basis for visual reasoning. The algorithm consists of three phases: segmentation, representation, and reasoning.

The segmentation phase.

First, we must segment the problem image P into its nine constituent subimages, I_1 through I_9. In the present implementation, the problems are given as a 478x405 pixel JPEG image, in the RGB color space. The subimages are arrayed in a 3x3 grid within the problem image. At this resolution, we have found that each subimage fits well within a 96x96 pixel image, as may be seen in Figure 4.

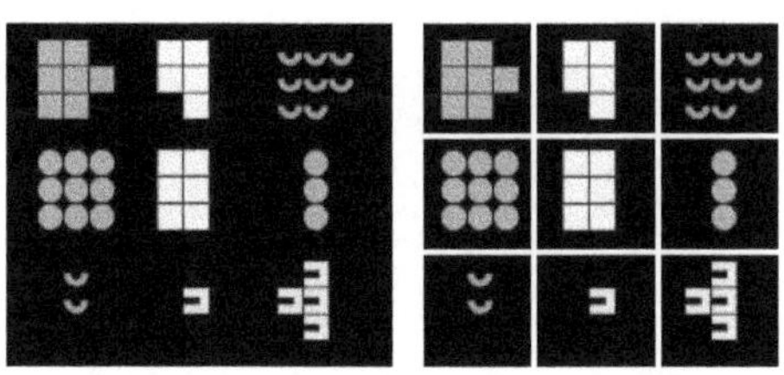

Figure 4. Segmentation of an Odd One Out problem

We note that each subimage is readily discernible from the general background of the problem image (which is black). Apart from this segmentation of the problem image, we undertake no further ad-hoc analysis of either the problem image or the resulting subimages.

The representation phase.

We now must transform the problem into the domain of fractal representations. Given the nine subimages, we group subimages into pairs, such that each subimage is paired once with the other eight subimages. Thus, we form 36 distinct pairings. We then calculate the mutual fractal representation M_{ij} for each pair of subimages I_i and I_j. We determine the fractal transformation from I_i to I_j in the manner described in [32], then form the union of the sets of codes from the forward and backward fractal transformation to construct the new set which is M_{ij}.

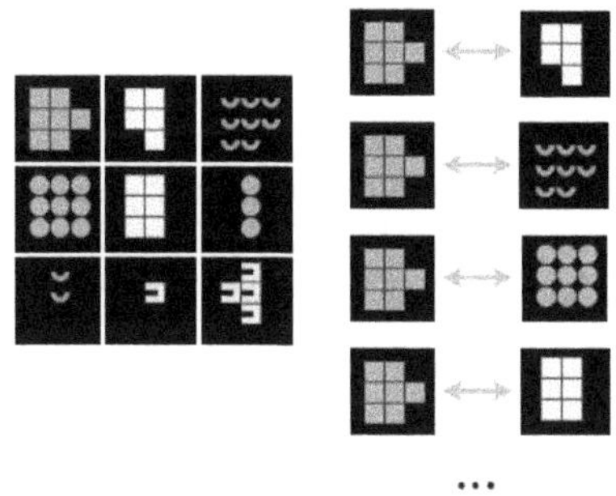

Figure 5. Pairing Subimages

The block partitioning we use initially is identical to the largest possible block size (in this case, 96x96), but subsequent recalculation of M_{ij} may be necessary using finer block partitioning (as proscribed in the reasoning phase). For the present implementation, we will conduct the finer partitioning by using uniform subdivision of the images into block sizes of 48x48, 24x24, 12x12, 6x6, and 3x3 pixels, upon demand.

Extended Mutuality

At this phase, we note that the mutual fractal representation of the pairings may be employed to determine similar mutual representations of triplets or quadruplets of images. As a notational convention, and in our present implementation, we construct these additional representations for triplets (M_{ijk}) and quadruplets (M_{ijkl}) in this manner:

$$M_{ijk} = M_{ij} \cup M_{jk} \cup M_{ik}$$

$$M_{ijkl} = M_{ijk} \cup M_{ikl} \cup M_{jkl} \cup M_{ijl}$$

The reasoning phase.

We shall determine the odd one out solely from the mutual fractal representations, without reference or consideration to the original imagery. We start by considering groupings of representations, beginning with pairings, and, if necessary, advance to consider other groupings.

Reconciling Multiple Analogical Relationships

For a chosen set of groupings, G, we must determine how similar each member is to each of its fellow members. To do this, we first derive the features present in each member, as described above, and then calculate a measure of similarity as a comparison of the number of fractal features shared between each pair member [11].

We desire a metric of similarity which is normalized with respect to the number of features under consideration, and where the value 0.0 means entirely dissimilar and the value

1.0 means entirely similar. Accordingly, in our present implementation, we use the ratio model of similarity as described in [11]. According to the ratio model, the measure of similarity S between two representations A and B is calculated thusly:

$$S(A,B) = f(A \cap B) / [f(A \cap B) + \alpha f(A-B) + \beta f(B-A)]$$

where $f(X)$ is the number of features in the set X. The weights α and β may be varied to favor features found in one or the other considered set, but not in both. Tversky notes that the ratio model for matching features generalizes several set-theoretical models of similarity proposed in the psychology literature, depending upon which values one chooses for the weights. We have chosen to set $\alpha = \beta = 1$, to favor features from neither image more so than the other.

Relationship Space

As we perform this calculation for each pair A and B taken from the grouping G, we determine for each member of G a set of similarity values. We consider the similarity of each analogical relationship as a value upon an axis in a large "relationship space." The dimensionality of this space is determined by the size of the grouping: for pairings, the space is 36 dimensional; for triplets, the space is 84 dimensional; for quadruplets, the space is 126 dimensional.

Treating Maximal Similarity as Distance

To arrive at a scalar similarity score for each member of the group G, we first construct a vector in this multidimensional relationship space and then determine its length, using a Euclidean distance formula. The longer the vector, the more similar two members are; the shorter the vector, the more dissimilar two members are. As the Odd One Out problem seeks to determine, literally, "the odd one out," we seek to find the shortest vector, as an indicator of dissimilarity.

Distribution of Similarity

We have determined a score for the grouping G, but have not yet arrived at individual scores for the subimages. To determine the subimage scoring, we distribute the similarity equally among the participating subimages. For each of the nine subimages, a score is generated which is proportional to its participation in the similarity of the grouping's similarity vectors. If a subimage is one of the two images in a pairing, as an example, then the subimage's similarity score receives one half of the pairing's calculated similarity score.

Once all of the similarity scores of the grouping have been distributed to the subimages, the similarity score for each subimage is known. It is then a trivial matter to identify which one among the subimages has the lowest similarity score. As it turns out, this is not yet sufficient for solving the problem, as ambiguity may be present.

Ambiguity

Similarity scores for the subimages may vary widely. If the score for any subimage is unambiguously smaller than that of any other subimage, then the subimage is deemed "the odd one out." By smaller, we mean that numerically the score will be deemed as least similar as it approaches 0. By unambiguous, we mean that there is no more than one score which is less than a prescribed value epsilon (e), which we may vary as a tuning mechanism for the algorithm, and which we see as a useful yet coarse approximation of the boundary between the similar and the dissimilar in feature space. In practice, we calculate the deviation of each similarity measure from the average of all such measures, and use confidence intervals (as calculated from the standard deviation) as a means for indicating ambiguity.

Iteration

However, if the scoring is inconclusive, then further examination is warranted. There are two readily available mechanisms at the algorithms disposal: to modify the grouping such that larger sets of subimages are considered simultaneously (from pairs to triplets, or from triplets to quadruplets), or to recalculate the fractal representations using a finer partitioning. In our present implementation, we attempt bumping up the elements considered simultaneously as a first measure. If after reaching a grouping based upon quadruplets the scoring remains inconclusive, then we consider that the initial representation level was too coarse, and rerun the algorithm using ever finer partitions for the mutual fractal representation. If, after altering our considerations of groupings and examining the images at the finest level of resolution the scores prove inconclusive, the algorithm quits, leaving the answer unknown.

Example

We now present an example of the algorithm at work. Figure 7 shows one problem from the Odd One Out test, selected for its illustrative power, and not for its difficulty. We do note that the answer to this particular problem may be at once obvious to the reader.

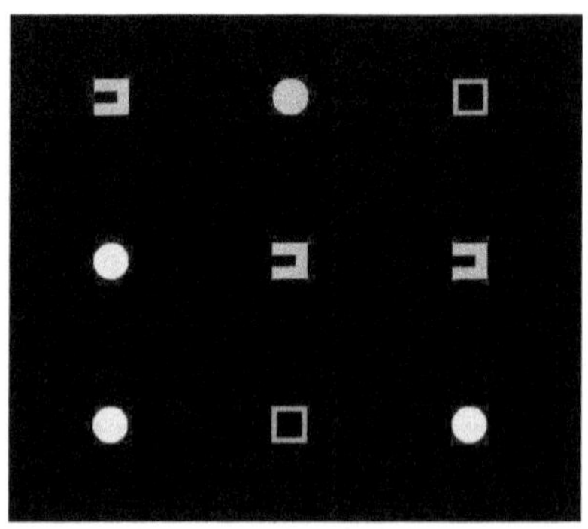

Figure 7. An example problem from the Odd One Out test.

The algorithm begins by segmenting the image into the nine subimages. For convenience, let us label the images A through I, advancing horizontally and then vertically, with A in the upper left corner, and I in the lower right, as shown in Figure 8. Once segmented, fractal representations are formed for each possible pairing of the subimages, for a total of 36 distinct representations. The initial partitioning of the subimages for fractal encoding shall be at the coarsest possible level, 96x96 pixels.

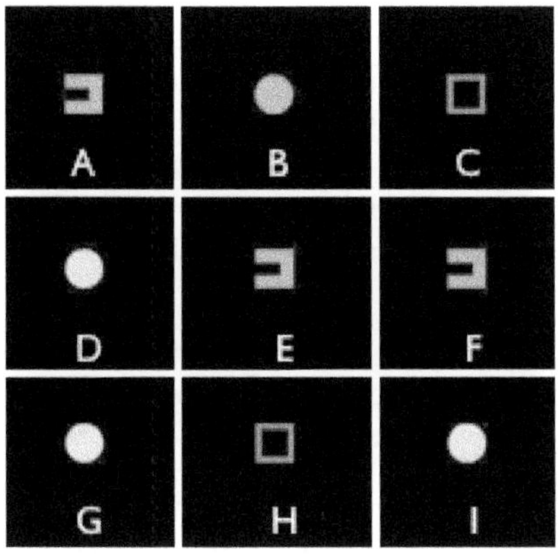

Figure 8. The example, segmented and labelled

In this example, it is quite clear to the reader that there are pairings which are identical (e.g. {A,E}, {E, F}, {A, F}, {C, H}, {D, G}, {D, I}, and {G, I}). The fractal representation of each of these pairings, at this coarsest level of partitioning (96x96) will yield the Identity transformation, with zero photometric correction. Thus the similarity between these particular transform pairs will be 1.0. These pairings we shall deem therefore to be perfectly analogous. However, not all of the representations will be similar. For example, the pairing of subimage C to any image other than subimage H will result in a substantially different fractal encoding than the {C,H} pairing.

For each subimage, we calculate the similarities of all eight possible pairings of that subimage against all other unique pairings. We next construct a similarity vector in 36-space for each pairing.

We derive the length of the 36-tuple similarity vector, normalize the result, and distribute this value to each of the subimages involved in the pairing by summing. In this example, the length of the similarity vector for the pairing {A,B} is found to be 4.55, we divide by 6 (the length of a 36-tuple with all entries 1.0), for a value of 0.7583. This value is added to the current summation for subimages A and B. At the close of this process, each subimage will have a score, representing the distributed similarity scores for all of the pairings in which it played a part.

The algorithm then examines the set of scores for all of the subimage, looking for ambiguity. Our present implementation defines ambiguity as the data having more than one item which deviates from the mean by a value greater than the standard deviation of the data. If this holds true, then the result is deemed ambiguous.

96x96		
0.727	0.727	0.674
0.716	0.727	0.727
0.716	0.674	0.716
μ : 0.711, σ : 0.022		

48x48		
0.534	0.413	0.468
0.510	0.534	0.534
0.510	0.468	0.510
μ : 0.499, σ : 0.041		

Table 1. Similarity scores for 96x96 and 48x48 partitions.

Table 1 illustrates the ambiguity found in using a 96x96 partitioning of the subimages, with two values having a deviation of 1.713σ. Thus, the algorithm must proceed to a finer partitioning in order to produce an unambiguous answer. A subsequent iteration, using a 48x48 partitioning, produces a single unambiguous result, with a deviation of 2.117σ. Accordingly, subimage B is selected as the Odd One Out.

PRELIMINARY RESULTS

At present, we have run our algorithm against a typical assortment of problems of the Odd One Out. We selected 44 problems randomly from a span of difficulty from the very easiest (level one) up to quite difficult (level 15). The example problem presented in Figure 7 is a level 11 problem.

We restricted the algorithm to attend only to pairings of subimages, and to progress to no further refinement of partitioning than 24x24, in order to fully exercise the strategic shifting in partitioning, to assess the similarity calculations, and to judge the effect of mutuality, at a tradeoff in execution time.

We have discovered that the algorithm either reaches a unambiguous decision which is the correct answer, or discovers sufficient ambiguity to force a transition to the next level of detail in the partitioning. Amongst the 44 problems in our preliminary set, we note that the algorithm does not answer incorrectly in an unambiguous fashion.

Our preliminary results show that, at least for some problems in our sample, having the algorithm proceed past the partitioning at which an unambiguous answer is obtained may result in additional ambiguity. While this is an artifact of our preliminary run (to continue past a decisive point), the reoccurrence of ambiguity leads us to speculate upon the potential emergence of a sufficient level of detail arising as a consequence of the fractal representation itself. We are unaware of any other visual reasoning technique with such a property.

We do note that there appear to be Odd One Out problems for which considering pairs of subimages shall prove inconclusive (that is, at all available levels of detail, the results will be found to be ambiguous). It is this set of problems which we believe implies that a shift in grouping (from pairs to triplets, or from triplets to quadruplets) must be undertaken to reach an unambiguous answer.

DISCUSSION

We have described a fractal technique for addressing visual analogy problems on the Odd One Out test of intelligence. The technique provides a precise characterization of ambiguity in answering problems on the test. For a sample of 44 problems ranging in difficulty from level 1 to level 15, whenever the fractal technique provided an unambiguous answer, that answer was correct. When the fractal representation at a given scale results in an ambiguous answer to an Odd One Out problem, our algorithm automatically shifts to a finer level of resolution, and continues this refinement step until it reaches an unambiguous answer. If the answer remains ambiguous through all of the possible levels of resolution, then our algorithm shifts toward considering groups of triplets, and then quadruplets, working through each grouping from coarsest to finest resolution as necessary.

Our efforts thus far, while intriguing, are very preliminary, and our observations are based upon consistent results as seen from the small yet representative sample of Odd One Out problems. Presently, we are running our algorithm on the balance of the ~3,000 problems at our disposal.

Fractal representations are analogical in that they have a structural correspondence with the images they represent. Like other representations, fractal representation support inference and composition. As we mentioned in the introduction, we have earlier used a different fractal technique to address a subset of problems on Raven's Standard Progressive Matrices Test [31][32]. That work, and the algorithm and preliminary results presented here, suggests a degree of generality to fractal representations for addressing visual analogy problems.

The distinction between reasoning analogically and reasoning based upon similarity is a measure of the depth and nature of the features considered. With the fractal representation, we have developed a cognitive strategy which admits correspondence comparisons across a spectrum of visual features. While this may be most easily characterized as similarity metrics, we believe that the conjunction of spatial and photometric fractal features capture, in a new and novel way, analogical relationships between and within those features traditionally associated with images. We suggest that the Odd One Out problems, by their nature, allow an exploration of analogical reasoning by way of novelty discovery. The fractal approach affords a means of noting this novelty without resorting to rule induction or identification.

CONCLUSION

Analogy often is viewed as central to intelligence [4]. Analogies are based on similarity and repetition. Fractals capture self-similarity and repetition at multiple scales. Thus, the fractal representation adds the powerful idea of self-similarity to analogies.

The fractal representation captures detail at multiple scales. In doing so, it sanctions an iterative problem solving strategy. The twin advantages of the strategy are (1) to start at high level of resolution, but, if that is not sufficient to resolve ambiguity, to automatically adjust to the right level of resolution for addressing a given problem, and (2) to start searching for similarity between simpler relationships, but, if that is not sufficient to resolve ambiguity, to automatically search for similarity between progressively higher-order relationships.

Cognitively, this is an illustration of what Davis, et al [37] referred to as the deep, theoretic manner in which representation and reasoning are intertwined.

ACKNOWLEDGEMENTS

We are grateful to Dr. Adam Hampshire at the Cambridge University MRC Cognition and Brain Science Unit (http://www.cambridgebrainsciences.com/about-us/) for generously sharing nearly 3000 Odd One Out problems with us. All illustrations of Odd One Out problems in this paper have been adapted from his work. We should note however that we neither sought nor received Dr. Hampshire's algorithm for generating the odd one out problems. Thus, insofar as our fractal technique is considered, Odd One Out is a "blind" test of novelty detection in creativity, and we alone are responsible for any errors. We also thank Maithilee Kunda and Agata Rozga as well as our other colleagues in the Design & Intelligence Laboratory (http://www.dilab.gatech.edu/) for many discussions that benefited this work.

REFERENCES

1. Barnsley, M., & Hurd, L. 1992. Fractal Image Compression. Boston, MA: A.K. Peters.
2. Bringsjord, S., & Schimanski, B. 2003. What is artificial intelligence? Psychometric AI as an answer. IJCAI, 18, 887–893.
3. Carpenter, P. A., Just, M. A., & Shell, P. What one intelligence test measures: A theoretical account of the processing in the Raven Progressive Matrices Test. Psychological Review 97 (3): 404-431. (1990)
4. Evans, T. 1968. A program for the solution of a class of geometric-analogy intelligence-test questions. In M. Minsky (Ed.), Semantic Information Processing (pp. 271-353). Cambridge, MA: MIT Press.
5. Hampshire, A. 2010 The Odd One Out Test of Intelligence. <http://www.cambridgebrainsciences.com/browse/reasoning/test/oddoneout>
6. Hertzmann, A., Jacobs, C. E., Oliver, N., Curless, B., & Salesin, D. 2001. Image analogies. In SIGGRAPH (pp. 327–340).

7. Hunt, E. 1974. Quote the raven? Nevermore! In L. Gregg (Ed.), Knowledge and cognition (pp. 129–158). Hillsdale, NJ: Erlbaum.

8. Lovett, A., Forbus, K., & Usher, J. 2007. Analogy with qualitative spatial representations can simulate solving Raven's Progressive Matrices. Proc. 29th Annual Conf. Cognitive Science Society (pp. 449-454).

9. Mandelbrot, B. 1982. The fractal geometry of nature. San Francisco: W.H. Freeman.

10. Raven, J., Raven, J. C., & Court, J. H. 1998. Manual for Raven's Progressive Matrices and Vocabulary Scales. San Antonio, TX: Harcourt Assessment.

11. Tversky, A. 1977. Features of similarity. Psychological Review, 84(4), 327-352.

12. Wechsler, D. (1939). Wechsler-Bellevue intelligence scale. New York: The Psychological Corporation.

13. Arnheim, R. (1969) Visual Thinking. University of California Press.

14. Ferguson, E.S. (1992) Engineering and the Mind's Eye. MIT Press.

15. Maher, M.L. (2010) Understanding Creativity Through Computation. Invited Talk to the Creativity, Computation and Cognition Seminar Series, Georgia Institute of Technology, Sep. 29, 2010.

16. Polya, G. (1957) How to Solve It: A New Aspect of Mathematical Method, 2nd edition, Doubleday.

17. Stafford, B. (2001) Visual Analogy: Consciousness as the Art of Connecting. MIT Press.

18. Sternberg, R., & Lubart, T. (1999) The Concept of Creativity: Prospects and Paradigms. In Handbook of Creativity, R. Sternberg (editor), Cambridge University Press.

19. Casakin, H., & Goldschmidt, G. Expertise and the Use of Visual Analogy: Implications for Design Education. Design Studies, 20(2): 153-179, 1999.

20. Clement, J. Creative Model Construction in Scientists and Students: The Role of Imagery, Analogy, and Mental Simulation. Dordrecht: Springer. (2008)

21. Croft, D., & Thagard, P. 2002. Dynamic imagery: A computational model of motion and visual analogy. In L. Magnani & N. J. Nersessian (Eds.), Model-based reasoning: Science, technology, values (pp. 259-274).

22. Davies, J., Goel, A., & Nersessian, N. 2009. A Computational Model of Visual Analogies in Design. Journal of Cognitive Systems Research, Special Issue on Analogies - Integrating Cognitive Abilities, 10:204-215.

23. Davies, J., Goel, A., & Yaner, P. 2008. Proteus: A theory of visual analogies in problem solving. Knowledge-Based Systems, 21, 636–654.

24. Davies, J., Nersessian, N., & Goel, A.K. Visual Models in Analogical Problem Solving. Foundations of Science, 10(1):133-152, 2005. (2005)

25. Evans, T. 1968. A program for the solution of a class of geometric-analogy intelligence-test questions. In M. Minsky (Ed.), Semantic Information Processing (pp. 271-353). Cambridge, MA: MIT Press.

26. Goel, A. K. Design, Analogy, and Creativity. IEEE Expert 12(3): 62-70. (1997)

27. Goldschmidt, G. (2001). Visual analogy – A strategy for design reasoning and learning. In Eastman, Newsletter, & McCracken (Eds.), Design knowing and learning: Cognition in design education (pp. 199–219). New York: Elsevier.

28. Gross, M. D., & Do, E. Y. 2000. Drawing on the Back of an Envelope: A framework for interacting with application programs by freehand drawing. Computers & Graphics, 24(6), 835-849.

29. Hofstadter, D., & Fluid Analogies Research Group (Eds.). 1995. Fluid concepts & creative analogies: Computer models of the fundamental mechanisms of thought. New York: Basic Books.

30. Holyoak, K., & Thagard, P. Mental Leaps: Analogy in Creative Thought. Cambridge, MA: MIT Press. (1995)

31. Kunda, M., McGreggor, K. & Goel, A. Taking a Look (Literally!) at the Raven's Intelligence Test: Two Visual Solution Strategies. In Proc. 32nd Annual Meeting of the Cognitive Science Society, Portland, August 2010.

32. McGreggor, K., Kunda, M., & Goel, A. 2011. Fractal Analogies: Preliminary Results from the Raven's Test of Intelligence. In Proc. International Conference on Computational Creativity, Mexico City, Mexico, April 27-29.

33. Nersessian, N. Creating Scientific Concepts. Cambridge, MA: MIT Press. (2008)

34. Yaner, P. W., & Goel, A. K. 2006. Visual analogy: Viewing analogical retrieval and mapping as constraint satisfaction problems. Applied Intelligence, 25(1), 91–105.

35. Yaner, P., & Goel, A. (2008) From Design Drawings to Structural Models by Compositional Analogy. International Journal of AI in Engineering Design, Analysis and Manufacturing, Special Issue on Multimodal Design, 22(2): 117-128.

36. Vattam, S., Helms, M., & Goel, A. (2010) A Content Account of Creative Analogies in Biologically Inspired Design. AI for Engineering Design, Analysis and Manufacturing, Special Issue on Biologically Inspired Design , 24: 467-481.

37. Davis, R., Shrobe H., and Szolovits, P. "What is a Knowledge Representation?" AI Magazine 14.1 (1993):17-33.

An Agent-based Model of the Cognitive Mechanisms Underlying the Origins of Creative Cultural Evolution

Liane Gabora
Department of Psychology
University of British Columbia
Okanagan campus, 3333 University Way
Kelowna BC, V1V 1V7, Canada
250-807-9849
liane.gabora@ubc.ca

Maryam Saberi
School of Interactive Art and Technology
Simon Fraser University
Surrey BC, V3T 0A3, Canada
778-868-5159
msaberi@sfu.ca

ABSTRACT

Human culture is uniquely cumulative and open-ended. Using a computational model of cultural evolution in which neural network based agents evolve ideas for actions through invention and imitation, we tested the hypothesis that this is due to the capacity for recursive recall. We compared runs in which agents were limited to single-step actions to runs in which they used recursive recall to chain simple actions into complex ones. Chaining resulted in higher cultural diversity, open-ended generation of novelty, and no ceiling on the mean fitness of actions. Both chaining and no-chaining runs exhibited convergence on optimal actions, but without chaining this set was static while with chaining it was ever-changing. Chaining increased the ability to capitalize on the capacity for learning. These findings show that the recursive recall hypothesis provides a computationally plausible explanation of why humans alone have evolved the cultural means to transform this planet.

Author Keywords

EVOC; Homo erectus; action; agent-based model; creativity; cultural diversity; cultural evolution; gesture; innovation; invention; mimetic; origin of culture; recursive recall, self-triggered recall and rehearsal loop

ACM Classification Keywords

Primary Classification: J.4 SOCIAL AND BEHAVIORAL SCIENCES: Subjects: Psychology and Sociology; Additional Classification: J.5 ARTS AND HUMANITIES I.2 ARTIFICIAL INTELLIGENCE I.2.6 Learning; I.2.11 Distributed Artificial Intelligence

General Terms

Algorithms, Experimentation, Theory, Verification

INTRODUCTION

How did humans come to be so creative? No other species has transformed this planet to anything near the degree that our species has. We now have the technology at our disposal to design computer models that enable us to investigate how our remarkable creativity came about. Humans are not only creative; we put our own spin on the inventions of others, such that new inventions build cumulatively on previous ones. This cumulative cultural change is referred to as the *ratchet effect* (Tomasello, Kruger, & Ratner, 1993), and it has been suggested that it is uniquely human (Donald, 1998).

This paper uses an agent-based simulation to address the question of what enabled humans to be creative enough that cumulative, open-ended cultural evolution could take hold and flourish. Our approach is motivated by the view that there is a distinct difference between (1) culture as a system involving transmission of chance innovations, which is observed in several species, and (2) culture as a process involving the accumulation and differentiation of strategic innovations, which is unique to our species. Only (2) constitutes a genuine evolutionary process, for to achieve descent with adaptive modification it is necessary that change be cumulative.

A POSSIBLE MECHANISM FOR THE ORIGIN OF CULTURAL EVOLUTION

The minds of our earliest ancestors, *Homo habilis,* have been referred to as *episodic* because there is no evidence that their experience deviated from the present moment of concrete sensory perceptions (Donald, 1991). They were able to encode perceptions of events in memory, and recall them in the presence of a reminder or cue, but had little voluntary access to memories without environmental cues. They were therefore unable to voluntarily shape, modify, or practice skills and actions, and unable to invent or refine complex gestures or means of communicating.

Homo erectus lived between approximately 1.8 and 0.3 million years ago. The size of the *Homo erectus* brain was approximately 1,000 cc, about 25% larger than that of *Homo habilis*, at least twice as large as the brains of living great apes, and 75% the cranial capacity of modern humans (Aiello, 1996; Ruff et al., 1997). This period is widely referred to as the beginnings of cumulative culture. *Homo erectus* exhibited many indications of enhanced intelligence, creativity, and ability to adapt to their

C&C'11, November 3–6, 2011, Atlanta, Georgia, USA.

environment, including sophisticated, task-specific stone handaxes, complex stable seasonal home bases, and long-distance hunting strategies involving large game, and migration out of Africa.

This period marks the onset of the archaeological record and it is thought to be the beginnings of human culture. It is widely believed that this cultural transition reflects an underlying transition in cognitive or social abilities. Some have suggested that they owe their achievements to onset of *theory of mind* (Mithen, 1998) or the capacity to imitate (Dugatkin, 2001). However, there is evidence that other species possess theory of mind and the capacity to imitate (Heyes, 1998), yet do not compare to modern humans in intelligence and cultural complexity.

Evolutionary psychologists have suggested that the intelligence and cultural complexity of the *Homo* line can be attributed to the onset of *massive modularity* (Buss, 1999, 2004; Barkow, Cosmides, &Tooby, 1992). However, although the mind exhibits an intermediate degree of functional and anatomical modularity, neuroscience has not revealed vast numbers of hardwired, encapsulated, task-specific modules; indeed, the brain has been shown to be more highly subject to environmental influence than was previously believed (Buller, 2005; Byrne, 2000; Wexler, 2006).

Donald (1991) proposed that with the enlarged cranial capacity of *Homo erectus*, the human mind underwent the first of three transitions by which it—along with the cultural matrix in which it is embedded—evolved from the ancestral, pre-human condition. This transition is characterized by a shift from an *episodic* to a *mimetic mode* of cognitive functioning, made possible by onset of the capacity for voluntary retrieval of stored memories, independent of environmental cues. Donald refers to this as a *self-triggered recall and rehearsal loop*. Self-triggered recall enabled information to be processed recursively, and reprocessed with respect to different contexts or perspectives. Self-triggered recall allowed our ancestor to access memories voluntarily and thereby act out[1] events that occurred in the past or that might occur in the future. Thus not only could the mimetic mind temporarily escape the here and now, but by miming or gesture, it could communicate similar escapes in other minds. The capacity to mime thus ushered forth what is referred to as a *mimetic* form of cognition and brought about a transition to the mimetic stage of human culture. The self-triggered recall and rehearsal loop also enabled our ancestors to engage in a stream of thought. One thought or idea evokes another, revised version of it, which evokes yet another, and so forth recursively. In this way, attention is directed away from the external world toward one's internal model of it. Finally, self-triggered recall allowed for voluntary rehearsal and refinement of actions, enabling systematic evaluation and improvement of skills and motor acts.

The recursive recall hypothesis is difficult to test directly, for if correct it would leave no detectable trace. It is, however, possible to computationally model how the onset of the capacity for recursive recall would affect the effectiveness, diversity, and open-endedness of ideas generated in an artificial society.

THE MODEL

We tested Donald's hypothesis using an agent-based computational model of culture referred to as 'EVOlution of Culture', abbreviated EVOC (Gabora, 2008b, 2008c; Gabora & Leijnen, 2009; Leijnen & Gabora, 2009). EVOC has been used to address such questions as (1) how does the presence of leaders or barriers to the diffusion of ideas affect cultural evolution dynamics, (2) what is the effect of the ratio of creators to imitators in a society, and (3) what is the impact of locally clustering the creators. It is an elaboration of Meme and Variations, or MAV (Gabora, 1994, 1995), the earliest computer program to model culture as an evolutionary process in its own right (as opposed to modeling the interplay of cultural and biological evolution).The approach was inspired by Holland's (1975) genetic algorithm, or GA. The GA is a search technique that finds solutions to complex problems by generating a 'population' of candidate solutions through processes akin to mutation and recombination, selecting the best, and repeating until a satisfactory solution is found. The goal here was to distil the underlying logic of not biological evolution but cultural evolution, i.e. the process by which ideas adapt and build on one another in the minds of interacting individuals. In cultural evolution, the generation of novelty takes place through invention instead of through mutation and recombination as in biological evolution, and the differential replication of novelty takes place through imitation, instead of through reproduction with inheritance as in biological evolution (Gabora, 1996). EVOC (as did MAV) uses neural network based agents that could (1) invent new ideas by modifying previously learned ones, (2) evaluate ideas, (3) implement ideas as actions, and (4) imitate ideas implemented by neighbors. Agents do not evolve in a biological sense—they neither die nor have offspring—but do in a cultural sense, by generating and sharing ideas for actions. EVOC (like MAV) successfully models how 'descent with modification' occurs in a cultural context. The approach can thus be contrasted with computer models of how individual learning affects biological evolution (Best, 1999, 2006; Higgs, 2000; Hinton & Nowlan, 1987; Hutchins & Hazelhurst, 1991).

EVOC consists of an artificial society of neural network based agents in a two-dimensional grid-cell world. It is written in Joone, an object oriented programming environment, using an open source neural network library written in Java. We now summarize the key components of the agents and the world they inhabit.

[1] The term *mimetic* is derived from "mime," which means "to act out."

THE AGENTS

Agents consist of (1) a neural network, which encodes ideas for actions and detects trends in what constitutes a fit action, and (2) a body, which implements actions. The core of an agent is an auto associative neural network, as shown in Figure 1. The network learns ideas for actions. An idea is a pattern consisting of six elements that dictate the placement of the six body parts. Learning and training of the neural network is as per Gabora (1995).

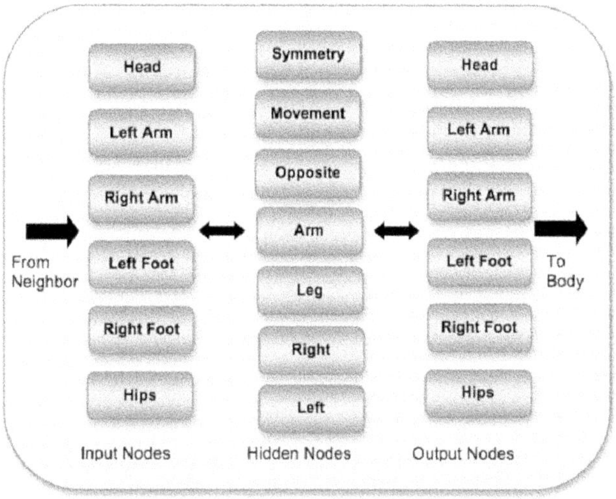

Figure 1. The core of an agent is an autoassociative neural network composed of six input nodes and six corresponding output nodes that represent concepts of body parts (LEFT ARM, RIGHT ARM, LEFT LEG, RIGHT LEG, HEAD, and HIPS), and seven hidden nodes that represent more abstract concepts (LEFT, RIGHT, ARM, LEG, SYMMETRY, MOVEMENT and OPPOSITE). Input nodes and output nodes are connected to hidden nodes of which they are instances (e.g. RIGHT ARM is connected to RIGHT.) Activation of any input node activates the MOVEMENT hidden node. Same-direction activation of symmetrical input nodes (e.g. positive activation—which represents upward motion—of both arms) activates the SYMMETRY node. Sequential opposite movement of an ARM activates the OPPOSITE node. This hidden node was newly added to this version of the program to implement the chaining of actions to form multi-step actions. The hidden nodes are used to bias invention using learned trends about what constitutes a fit action.

In EVOC, the neural network can also be turned off to compare results with a data structure that cannot detect trends, and thus invents ideas merely at random. If the fitness of an action is evaluated to be higher than that of any action learned thus far, it is copied from the input/output nodes of the neural network that represent concepts of body parts to a six digit array that contains representations of actual body parts, referred to as the body. Since it is useful to know how many agents are doing essentially the same thing, when node activations are translated into limb movement they are threshold such that there are only three possibilities for each limb: stationary, up, or down. Six limbs with three possible positions each gives a total of 729 possible actions. Only the action that is currently implemented by an agent's body can be observed and imitated by other agents.

THE ARTIFICIAL WORLD

MAV allowed only worlds that were square and toroidal, or 'wrap-around' (such that agents at the left border that attempt to move further left appear on the right border). In EVOC the world can assume any shape, and be as sparsely or densely populated as required, with agents placed in any configuration. EVOC also allows for the creation of complete or semi-permeable permanent or eroding borders that decrease the probability of imitation along a frontier (although this was not used in the experiments reported here).

INCORPORATION OF COGNITIVEPHENOMENA

The neural network can be turned off to compare neural network results with those obtained using a database that cannot learn trends, and thus invents ideas at random. The following cultural evolution parameters can also be turned off or on (in some cases to varying degrees).

Imitation

Fit actions diffuse through the society when agents copy neighbors' actions. During imitation, the input is the action implemented by a neighbor. The process of finding a neighbor to imitate works through a form of lazy (non-greedy) search. An imitating agent randomly scans its neighbors, and adopts the first action that is fitter than the action it is currently implementing. If it does not find a neighbor that is executing a fitter action than its own current action, it continues to execute the current action.

Invention

Agents generate new actions by modifying their initial action or an action that has been invented previously or acquired through imitation. During invention, the pattern of activation on the output nodes is fed back to the input nodes, and invention is biased according to the activations of the SYMMETRY, MOVEMENT, and OPPOSITE hidden nodes. (Were this not the case there would be no benefit to using a neural network.) The extent to which the generation of novelty is biased by past experience is referred to as the *learning rate*. To invent a new idea, for each node of the idea currently represented on the input layer of the neural network, the agent makes a probabilistic decision as to whether the position of that body part will change, and if it does, the direction of change is stochastically biased according to the learning rate. If the new idea has a higher fitness than the currently implemented idea, the agent learns and implements the action specified by that idea. (See Gabora, 1995 for further details.)

Learning

Invention makes use of the ability to detect, learn, and respond adaptively to trends. Since a new action (or, in invention, a new idea for an action) is not learned unless it is fitter than the currently implemented action, new actions provide valuable information about what constitutes an effective idea. Thus knowledge acquired through the evaluation of previous actions is translated into educated guesses about what constitutes a successful action, and this is accomplished by updating the learning rate.

There are two learnable trends. The first concerns the overall level of activity involved in successful actions. Learning this trend can bias the generation of new ideas in favor of either more movement or less. Each body part starts out at a stationary rest position, and with an equal probability of changing to movement in one direction or the other. If the fitter action codes for more movement, increase the probability of movement of each body part. Do the opposite if the fitter action codes for less movement. If movement is generally beneficial, increase the probability that new actions involve movement of more body parts.

This trend is based on the assumption that movement in general (regardless of which particular body part is moving) can be beneficial or detrimental. This seems like a useful generalization since movement of any body part uses energy and increases the likelihood of being detected. It is implemented as follows:

a_{m1} = movement node activation for current action

a_{m2} = movement node activation for new action

$p(im)_I$= probability of increased movement at body part i

$p(dm)_I$= probability of decreased movement at body part i

IF $(a_{m2}>a_{m1})$

THEN $p(im)_I$= MAX(1.0, $p(im)_I$ + 0.1)

ELSE IF $(a_{m2}<a_{m1})$

THEN $p(im)_I$= MIN(0.0, $p(im)_I$ - 0.1)

$p(dm)_I = 1 - p(im)_i$

The second learnable trend is: if successful actions tend to be symmetrical (e.g. left arm moves to the right and right arm moves to the left), the probability increases that new actions are symmetrical. (See Gabora 1995 for details.) This generalization is biologically sensible, since many useful actions (e.g. walking) entail movement of limbs in opposite directions, while others (e.g. pushing) entail movement of limbs in the same direction. However, the reason for implementing a preference for symmetrical limb coordination is not to produce a biologically realistic model of motor control but to provide a systematic rationale for associating different actions with a graded distribution of fitness values.

The preference for symmetrical limb coordination is implemented in a manner analogous to that of the first rule. Of particular relevance to the current investigation, if multi-step actions involving one limb moving sequentially one direction and then the other are beneficial, the probability of inventing such actions increases.

In summary, each action is associated with a measure of its effectiveness, and generalizations about what seems to work and what does not are translated into guidelines for what action to take.

Evaluation

Before committing to implementing an idea as an action, agents can assess how successful the action would be if it were implemented. They evaluate the effectiveness of their actions according to how well they satisfy needs using a pre-defined equation that rewards actions that make use of trends detected by the SYMMETRY, MOVEMENT, and OPPOSITE hidden nodes. A successful action is one in which all body parts except the head are moving, and limb movement is asymmetrical. (Thus if the left arm is moving up, the right arm is moving down, and vice versa.) For the experiments reported here with chaining turned off, where total body movement, m, is calculated by adding the number of active body parts, and m_h is head movement, the fitness, F_{nc}, is calculated as follows:

s_a = 1 if arms are moving symmetrically; 0 otherwise

s_l = 1 if legs are moving symmetrically; 0 otherwise

m_h = 1 if head is stationary; 0 otherwise

$F_{nc} = m + 1.5(s_a + s_l) + 2(1 - m_h)$

This gives a fitness function with a maximum value of ten, because while movement of the head contributes positively to the first term (which represents overall movement) it contributes negatively to the third term (which represents head stability). This corresponds to a relatively realistic action with respect to the need to attract the attention of, and maintain eye contact with others including a potential mate.

Since there are two optimal movements for the hips, one optimal movement for the head (or in this case, a lack of movement), two optimal arm combinations, and two optimal leg combinations, there are eight different optimal actions. In previous versions of the program that did not allow for chained actions, once an agent converged on one of the eight optimal actions (out of the possible 729 actions), it implemented that action for the rest of the run. Therefore, once all agents had found one or another of the optimal actions, the mean fitness of actions across the society plateaus, and the set of implemented actions became fixed.

Chaining

Chaining, which is new to this version of the program, gives agents the opportunity to execute multi-step actions. For the experiments reported here with chaining turned on, if in the first step of an action an agent was moving at least one of its arms, it executes a second step, which again involves up to six body parts. If, in the first step, the agent moved one arm in one direction, and in the second step it moved the same arm in the opposite direction, it has the opportunity to execute a three-step action. And so on. The agent is allowed to execute an arbitrarily long action so long as it continues to move the same arm in the opposite direction to the direction it moved previously. Once it does not do so, the chained action comes to an end. The longer it moves, the higher the fitness of this multi-step chained action. Where n is the number of chained actions, the fitness, F_c, is calculated as follows:

$$F_c = F_{nc} + (n - 1)$$

The fitness function with chaining provides a simple means of simulating the capacity for recursive recall.

We omit a detailed explanation of EVOC options that were not used in the experiments reported here, such as broadcasting, which allows the action of a leader to be visible to not just immediate neighbors, but all agents, thereby simulating the effects of media (Gabora, 2008a,b; Leijnen & Gabora, 2010).

A TYPICAL RUN

Each iteration, every agent has the opportunity to (1) acquire an idea for a new action, either by imitation, copying a neighbor, or by invention, creating one anew, (2) update the knowledge-based operators, and (3) implement a new action. To invent a new idea, for each node of the idea currently represented on the input/output layer of the neural network, the agent makes a probabilistic decision as to whether change will take place, and if it does, the direction of change is stochastically biased by the knowledge-based operators. If the new idea has a higher fitness than the currently implemented idea, the agent learns and implements the action specified by that idea. To acquire an idea through imitation, an agent randomly chooses one of its neighbors, and evaluates the fitness of the action the neighbor is implementing. If its own action is fitter than that of the neighbor, it chooses another neighbor, until it has either observed all of its immediate neighbors, or found one with a fitter action. If no fitter action is found, the agent does nothing. Otherwise, the neighbor's action is copied to the input layer, learned, and implemented.

Fitness of actions starts out low because initially all agents are immobile. Soon some agent invents an action that has a higher fitness than doing nothing, and this action gets imitated, so fitness increases. Fitness increases further as other ideas get invented, assessed, implemented as actions, and spread through imitation. The diversity of actions initially increases due to the proliferation of new ideas, and then decreases as agents hone in on the fittest actions.

THE GRAPHIC USER INTERFACE

The graphic user interface (GUI) makes use of the open source charting project, JFreeChart, enabling variables to be user defined at run time, and results to become visible as the program runs. The topmost output panel, shown in Figure 2, is provided to give the reader a sense of how the program works.

EXPERIMENTS

In previous versions of EVOC, that did not allow chaining, there were only a fixed number of possible actions, and once all agents converged on optimal actions, cultural change ground to a halt. We hypothesized that if agents were able to chain actions together to form arbitrarily long actions, fitness would not stop increasing, and the agents would not converge on the same fixed set of actions.

For these experiments the artificial world was a toroidal lattice with 100 nodes, each occupied by a single, stationary agent. We used a von Neumann neighborhood structure, (agents only interacted with their four adjacent neighbors).

All graphs plot averages of ten runs, with an invention to imitation ratio of 1:1, and a rate of conceptual change of 1/6. (Since there are six body parts this means approximately one body part movement per step of an action). All agents were stationary at the start of a run.

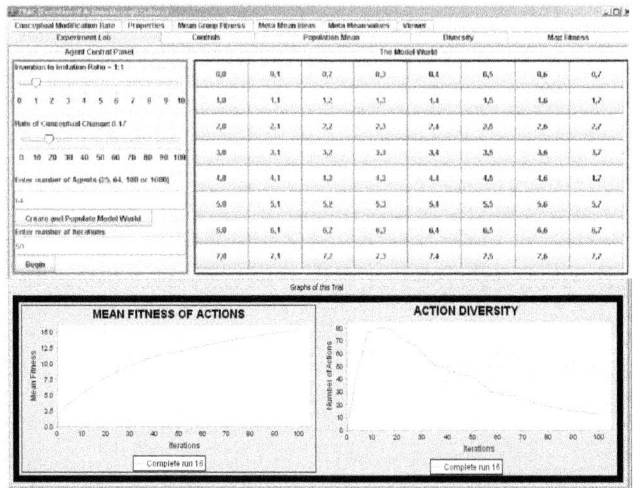

Figure 2. Output panel of GUI. At the upper left one specifies the Invention to Imitation Ratio. This is the probability that a given agent, on a given iteration, invents a new idea for an action, versus the probability that it imitates a neighbor's action. Below it is Rate of Conceptual Change, where one specifies the degree to which a newly invented idea differs from the one it was based on. Below that is Number of Agents, which allows the user to specify the size of the artificial society. Below that is where one specifies Number of Iterations, i.e. the duration of a run. Agents can be accessed individually by clicking the appropriate cell in the grid on the upper right. This enables one to see such details as the action currently implemented by that agent, or the fitness of that action. The graphs at the bottom plot the mean idea fitness and diversity of ideas. Tabs shown at the top give access to other output panels.

Effect of Chaining on Fitness of Actions

Figure 3 shows the results of comparing how the capacity to recursively chain actions together affects the mean fitness of actions across the artificial society over the duration of a run.

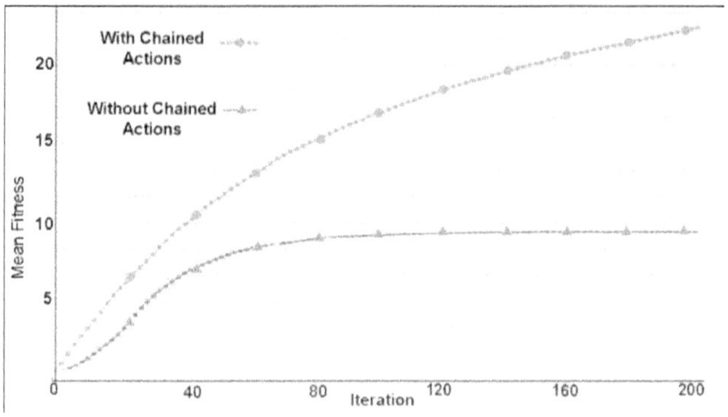

Figure 3. Mean fitness of actions in the artificial society with chaining versus without chaining.

The capacity to chain together simple actions to form more complex ones increases the mean fitness of actions across the artificial society. This is most evident in the later phase of a run. Without chaining, agents converge on optimal actions, and the mean fitness of action reaches a plateau. With chaining, however, there is no ceiling on the mean fitness of actions. By the 100th iteration it reached almost 15, indicating a high incidence of chaining.

Effect of Chaining on Diversity of Actions

Figure 3 shows the results of comparing how the capacity to recursively chain actions together affects the mean fitness of actions across the artificial society over the duration of a run.

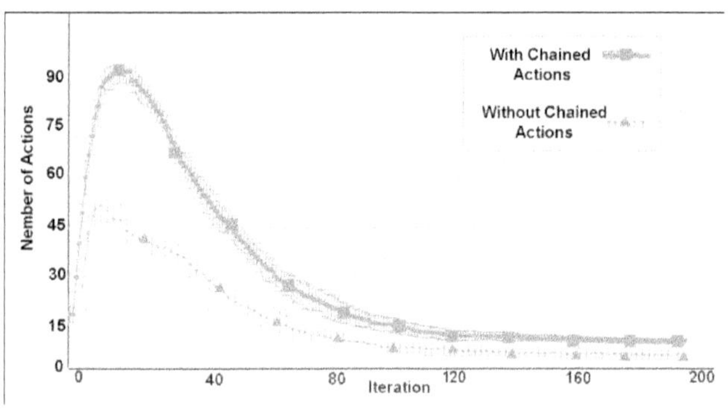

Figure 4. Mean number of different actions in the artificial society with chaining (continuous line) versus without chaining (dashed line).

Chaining also increases the diversity of actions. This is most evident in the early phase of a run before agents begin to converge on optimal actions, though it remains the case throughout the duration of a run. Interestingly, although in both cases there is convergence on optimal actions, without chained actions, this is a static set (thus mean fitness plateaus) whereas with chained actions the set of optimal actions is always changing, as increasingly fit actions are found (thus mean fitness keeps increasing).

The Effect of Chaining on Learning

Recall that agents have the capacity to learn trends from past experiences (using the knowledge-based operators), and thereby bias the generation of novelty in directions that have a greater than chance probability of being fruitful. Results obtained previously with this kind of computer model of cultural evolution showed that learning increases the mean fitness of actions throughout the duration of a run (Gabora, 1995). Since chaining provides more opportunities to capitalize on the capacity to learn, we hypothesized that chaining would accentuate the impact of learning on the mean fitness of actions across the artificial society. Figure 5 compares the effect of chaining with knowledge-based operators turned on (agents are able to learn) versus when they are turned off (agents are unable to learn).

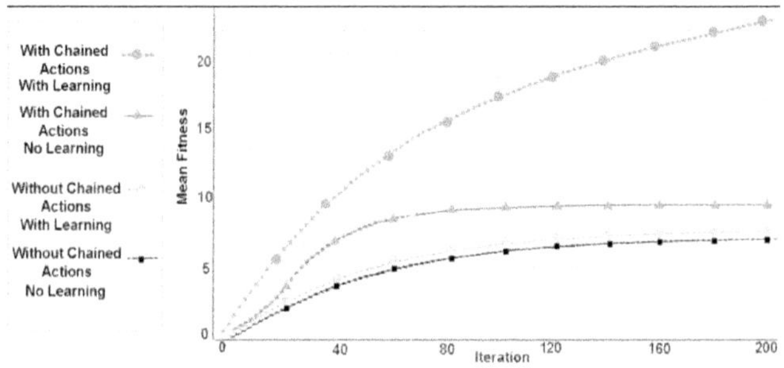

Figure 5. Mean fitness of actions in the artificial society with both chained actions and learning (top), with just chained actions (second from the top) with just learning (second from the bottom), and with neither chained actions nor learning (bottom).

This hypothesis was confirmed. Since waving an arm back and forth increased activation of the OPPOSITE hidden node, agents learned to generate increasingly longer moves throughout the duration of a run. When agents are given the capacity to chain together simple actions to form more complex ones, the increase in mean fitness of actions throughout the duration of a run is more pronounced, indicating that the society as a whole benefits much more from learning.

Discussion

Many species possess what could be called culture, but human culture is unique in that ideas build on each other cumulatively; indeed culture is widely thought to be an evolutionary process (e.g. Bentley, Ormerod, & Batty, 2011; Cavalli-Sforza & Feldman, 1981; Gabora, 1996, 2008; Hartley, 2009;Mesoudi, Whiten & Laland, 2004, 2006; Whiten, Hinde, Laland, & Stringer, 2011). Using an agent based computer model of cultural evolution, we obtained support for the hypothesis that the onset of cumulative, open-ended cultural evolution can be attributed to the evolution of a self-triggered recall and rehearsal loop, enabling the recursive chaining of thoughts and actions.

Our results suggest that it is the capacity for recursive recall that makes possible the open-endedness of some computational models of language evolution (*e.g.* Kirby, 2001). Note that in the chaining versus no chaining conditions the size of the neural network is the same, but how it is *used* differs. This suggests that it was not larger brain size *per se* that initiated the onset of cumulative culture, but that larger brain size enabled episodes to be encoded in more detail, allowing more routes for reminding and recall, thereby facilitating the ability to recursively re-describe information stored in memory (Karmiloff-Smith, 1992), thereby tailor it to the situation at hand.

By demonstrating that onset of the capacity for recursive recall constitutes a viable explanation for how cultural change became cumulative and open-ended, we believe that this research is a pivotal step forward in the development of a scientific theory of cultural evolution. Nevertheless, the model is simplified, and caution must be taken applying such results to the real world. The agents can be said to have the goal of optimizing the fitness of their actions, but they do not have values, norms, or social bonds remotely like ours. The goal behind a computational model such as EVOC, however, is to extract the skeleton of a process as complex as cultural evolution and investigate questions that are difficult to investigate by other means. To our knowledge, this is the only experimental test of, and tentative support for, the hypothesis that the capacity for self-triggered recall of thoughts and recursive execution of actions played a key role in ratcheting the kind of cumulative, open-ended novelty and cultural complexity that surrounds us. Despite that evolved cultural complexity essentially defines our humanness, we know of no other computational modeling support for this or any other competing hypothesis concerning how the transition from episodic to mimetic cognition came about.

Future work will focus on simulating more complex forms of recursive recall that would require a larger neural network, and corroborating findings obtained with the model with archaeological and anthropological evidence. Another direction of future research involves using EVOC to investigate competing hypotheses concerning what cognitive mechanism could have given rise to the explosive cultural transition in the Middle-Upper Paleolithic (Klein, 1999; Leaky, 1984).

ACKNOWLEDGMENTS

We would like to acknowledge grants to the first author from the *Social Sciences and Humanities Research Council of Canada* and the Concerted Research Program of the *Fund for Scientific Research, Belgium*.

REFERENCES

1. Aiello, L. C. Hominine pre-adaptations for language and cognition. In P. Mellars & K. Gibson (Eds.), *Modeling the early human mind*, Cambridge, UK: McDonald Institute Monographs (1996), 89–99.
2. Barkow, J. H., Cosmides, L., & Tooby, J., Eds. *The Adapted Mind: Evolutionary Psychology and the Generation of Culture*. New York: Oxford University Press, 1992.
3. Bentley, R. A., Ormerod, P., & Batty, M. Evolving social influence in large populations. *Behavioral Ecology and Sociobiology, 65* (2011), 537–546.
4. Best, M. How culture can guide evolution: An inquiry into gene/meme enhancement and opposition. *Adaptive Behavior, 7*, 3 (1999), 289–293.
5. Best, M. Adaptive value within natural language discourse. *Interaction Studies, 7*, 1(2006), 1-15.
6. Buller, D. J. *Adapting minds*. Cambridge, MA: MIT Press, 2005.
7. Buss, D. M. *Evolutionary Psychology: The New Science of the Mind*. Boston, MA: Pearson, 1999/2004.
8. Byrne, R. W., & Russon, A. E. Learning by imitation: A hierarchical approach. *Behavioral and Brain Sciences, 21*(1998), 667–721.
9. Cavalli-Sforza, L. L., & Feldman, M. W. *Cultural transmission and evolution: A quantitative approach*. Princeton: Princeton University Press, 1981.
10. Cloak, F. T. Jr. Is a cultural ethology possible? *Human Ecology, 3*(1975), 161-182.
11. Donald, M. Hominid enculturation and cognitive evolution. In C. Renfrew & C. Scarre (Eds.), *Cognition and Material Culture: The Archaeology of Symbolic Storage*. McDonald Institute Monographs (1998), 7–17.
12. Donald, M. *Origins of the Modern Mind: Three Stages in the Evolution of Culture and Cognition*. Cambridge, MA: Harvard University Press, 1991.
13. Dugatkin, L. A. *Imitation Factor: Imitation in Animals and the Origin of Human Culture*. New York: Free Press, 2001.
14. Gabora, L. A computer model of the evolution of culture. In R. Brooks & P. Maes (Eds.) *Proceedings of the 4th International Conference on Artificial Life*, July 4-6,Boston, MA, 1994.
15. Gabora, L. Meme and Variations: A computer model of cultural evolution. In L. Nadel & D. Stein (Eds.) 1993 *Lectures in Complex Systems*. Reading, MA: Addison-Wesley (1995), 471–486.
16. Gabora, L. A day in the life of a meme. *Philosophica, 57*, (1996), 901-938.
17. Gabora, L. EVOC: A computer model of cultural evolution. In V. Sloutsky, B. Love & K. McRae (Eds.), *Proceedings of the 30th Annual Meeting of the Cognitive Science Society*, Sheridan Publishing (2008a), 1466-1471.
18. Gabora, L. Modeling cultural dynamics. *In Proceedings of the Association for the Advancement of Artificial Intelligence (AAAI) Fall Symposium 1: Adaptive Agents in a Cultural Context*, Menlo Park, CA: AAAI Press (2008b), 18-25.

19. Gabora, L., Leijnen, S., & von Ghyczy, T. The relationship between creativity, imitation, and cultural diversity. *International Journal of Software and Informatics*, (in press).

20. Hartley, J. From cultural studies to cultural science. *Cult. Science, 2* (2009), 1-16.

21. Higgs, P. G. The mimetic transition: a simulation study of the evolution of learning by imitation. *Proceedings of the Royal Society B: Biological Sciences, 267*, 1450(2000), 1355–1361.

22. Heyes, C. M. Theory of mind in nonhuman primates. *Behavioral and Brain Sciences, 211*(1998), 104–134.

23. Hinton, G. E. & Nowlan, S. J. How learning can guide evolution. *Complex Systems*, *1*(1987), 495–502.

24. Holland, J. K. *Adaptation in Natural and Artificial Systems*. Ann Arbor, MI: University of Michigan Press, 1975.

25. Hutchins, E. & Hazelhurst, B. Learning in the cultural process. In Langton, C., Taylor, J., Farmer, D., &Rasmussen, S. (Eds.) *Artificial Life II*. Redwood City, CA: Addison-Wesley, 1991.

26. Kirby, S. Spontaneous evolution of linguistic Structure—An iterated learning model of the emergence of regularity and irregularity. *IEEE Transactions on Evolutionary Computation, 5*, 2(2001), 102-110.

27. Leijnen, S., & Gabora, L. How creative should creators be to optimize the evolution of ideas? A computational model. *Electronic Proceedings in Theoretical Computer Science, 9*(2009), 108-119.

28. Mesoudi, A., Whiten, A., & Laland, K. Toward a unified science of cultural evolution. *Evolution 58*, 1(2004),1-11.

29. Mesoudi, A., Whiten, A., & Laland, K. Toward a unified science of cultural evolution. *Behavioral and Brain Sciences, 29*(2006), 329-383.

30. Mithen, S. (Ed.). *Creativity in Human Evolution and Prehistory*. London, UK: Routledge, 1998.

31. Ruff, C., Trinkaus, E., & Holliday, T. Body mass and encephalization in Pleistocene Homo. *Nature, 387* (1997), 173–176.

32. Tomasello, M., Kruger, A. C., & Ratner, H. H. Cultural learning. *Behavioral and Brain Sciences*, *16*(1993), 495–552.

33. Wexler, B. *Brain and Culture: Neurobiology, Ideology and Social Change*. New York: Bradford Books, 2006.

34. Whiten, A., Hinde, R. A., Laland, K. N., Stringer, C. B. Culture evolves. *Philosophical Transactions of the Royal Society B, 366*(2011), 938–948.

Social Discovery Framework: Building Capacity and Seeking Solutions

Ben Shneiderman
Department of Computer Science & Human-Computer Interaction Lab
University of Maryland, College Park, MD, USA
Email: ben@cs.umd.edu Twitter: @benbendc

ABSTRACT
While journalists often portray discovery as the thrilling insight of a brilliant individual, many discoveries require years of work by competing and collaborating teams. Often large amounts of foundational work are necessary and dialogs among participants help clarify goals. The Social Discovery Framework suggests that (1) there are important processes in building capacity and then seeking solutions and (2) those that initiate requests are often as important as those who seek solutions. The implications of the Social Discovery Framework are that improved social tools to build capacity, initiate requests, and support dialog would accelerate the discovery process as much as the more visible tools for individuals seeking solutions.

Author Keywords
Social discovery, user interfaces, creativity support tools, collaboration, search, crowdsourcing, collective intelligence, community

ACM Classification Keywords
H.5.m. Information interfaces and presentation (e.g., HCI): Miscellaneous.

General Terms
Design

INTRODUCTION
Creativity in the arts and discovery in the sciences have common sources. Innovative artists, performers, entrepreneurs, technologists, and scientists often enact similar processes such as the often described: preparation, incubation, illumination, and verification [2,3].

However, these individual efforts are often embedded in much larger social processes that stimulate discovery over periods of months or years. Often precursors to discovery are necessary to create the capacity by way of data, theories, tools, and much more. Crude lenses were necessary before Galileo could think of grinding lenses to construct his telescope, which enabled him to see the moons of Jupiter. Tycho Brahe's diligent data collection laid the basis for Kepler's elegant theories. Similarly, transistors had to be developed before printed circuit boards could give way to integrated circuits that enable modern laptop computers. More than a hundred molecular biologists co-authored the key paper on DNA structure and thousands of physicists worked to develop the Large Hadron Collider.

While many researchers have studied large-scale collaborations that lead to discovery, a clearer framework about how social discovery operates is needed. Such a framework would guide designers of desktop, web-based, mobile, or cloud-based tools to support rich dialogs over weeks and months [1].

SOCIAL DISCOVERY FRAMEWORK
The proposed Social Discovery Framework (Table 1) is oriented around information gathering that leads to breakthrough discoveries [9]. Biologists are collecting data by way of the Encyclopedia of Life (www.eol.org), while museum professionals are gathering annotations through the Steve Museum Project (www.steve.museum). These and thousands of other tagging, reviewing, data collecting projects (www.citizensciencealliance.org) are being joined by crowdsourcing efforts using Amazon's Mechanical Turk or volunteer associations [9].

Social Discovery	Create Capacity	Seek Solutions
Initiate Requests	Assemble thesauri Collate catalogs Aggregate info Curate collections	Ask questions Offer challenge Desire collaboration Seek experts
Provide Responses	Tag/taxonomize Comment/annotate Rank/rate/review Summarize	Give answers Respond to challenge Discuss alternatives Offer advice

Table 1: The Social Discovery Framework describes the two stages of work: creating capacity and seeking solutions. These are carried out by a dialog between those who initiate requests and those who provide responses over a period of weeks and months.

C&C'11, November 3–6, 2011, Atlanta, Georgia, USA.
ACM 978-1-4503-0820-5/11/11.

The two aspects of creating capacity are those who initiate the requests and those who provide responses. Typically a small number of people will initiate requests, but they may be affiliated with prominent organizations that have the capacity to reach many people and the respectability that will generate responses. For example, the Encyclopedia of Life is organized by the Smithsonian Institution, thereby encouraging thousands of citizen scientists and nature enthusiasts to contribute photos and related information. Those who initiate requests may have a dialog about how best to make requests and what recognition or reward to provide for active contributors. Those who respond to requests may be part of intermediate organizations that have agreed to contribute or they may be individuals.

For some discoveries, the volume of capacity creating contributions may be huge, either in numbers of contributors or size of data. Then when challenges are proposed, those who seek solutions may have a large dataset to work from. Another example, from a commercial source was the Netflix Prize (www.netflixprize.com). The 100M customer ratings provided the database that challenged developers to find an improved prediction algorithm, then the thousands of solution seekers competed to find a 10% improvement over the existing algorithm to win the $1M prize. The leaderboard showed daily progress of competing teams, but finally a collaboration among leading teams won the prize. Their description of their solution techniques advanced research in recommender algorithms and other areas.

Interest in social discovery mechanisms is growing rapidly as government and industry turn to challenges and crowdsourcing techniques [7]. The U.S. government website www.challenge.gov lists more than 100 challenges with monetary prizes for solutions. The capacity and rules for agencies to run challenges was spelled out in a 12-page memorandum [5], in which the benefits included "Capture the public imagination and change the public's perception of what is possible." The commitment to supporting scientific discovery was reinforced with a later memorandum [6]: "Scientific discovery, technological breakthroughs, and innovation are major engines for expanding the frontiers of human knowledge and are indispensable for promoting sustainable economic growth, improving the health of the population, moving toward a clean energy future, addressing global climate change challenges, managing competing demands on the environment, and safeguarding our national security."

Business interest in social discovery has also grown with the success of commercial websites such as www.innocentive.com, whose white paper spells out the effective strategies and dangers of social discovery [4].

CONCLUSION

Social discovery has long been identified as a powerful force. The Social Discovery Framework suggests four categories to dramatically improve tools for mass collaboration. Designing tools to create capacity and seek solutions is an emerging challenge for those who seek to accelerate discovery. Similar challenges exist in creating social mechanisms that elicit dialogs from knowledge domain experts as they formulate requests and provide responses.

REFERENCES

1. Chi, E. H., Munson, S., Fischer, G., Vieweg, S. and Parr, C., Advancing the design of technology-mediated social participation systems, *IEEE Computer* **43**(11) (2010), 29–35.
2. Fischer, G. Distances and diversity: Sources for social creativity. *Proc. Conf. Creativity and Cognition*, ACM Press, New York (2005), 128–136.
3. Fischer, G. and Giaccardi, E., Sustaining social creativity, *Communications of the ACM* **50**(12) (2007), 28-29.
4. Innocentive, Inc., Solving The World's Toughest Challenges in Grand Fashion, (2011), available at www.innocentive.com
5. Orszag. P., Guidance on the Use of Challenges and Prizes to Promote Open Government (March 8, 2010), http://www.whitehouse.gov/sites/default/files/omb/assets/memoranda_2010/m10-11.pdf
6. Orszag, P., Science and Technology Priorities for the FY 2012 Budget, (July 21, 2010), http://www.whitehouse.gov/sites/default/files/omb/assets/memoranda_2010/m10-30.pdf
7. Quinn, A. J. and Bederson, B. B., Human Computation: A survey and taxonomy of a growing field, *Proc. CHI 2011 Annual Conference on Human Factors in Computing Systems*, ACM Press, New York (2011), 1403-1412.
8. Shneiderman, B., Creativity support tools: accelerating discovery and innovation, *Communications of the ACM* **50**(12) (2007), 20–32.
9. Shneiderman, B., Social discovery in an information abundant world: Designing to create capacity and seek solutions, *Information Services & Use* (to appear, 2011).

Creative Ecologies in Action: Technology and the Workshop-as-artwork

Jamie Allen
School of Arts and Cultures-Digital Media
Culture Lab
Newcastle University
jamie@heavyside.net

Rachel Clarke
School of Computing Science
Culture Lab
Newcastle University
r.clarke@ncl.ac.uk

Areti Galani
International Centre for Cultural and Heritage Studies
Newcastle University
areti.galani@ncl.ac.uk

Kamila Wajda
Digital Media in Education
University of Bremen
kwajda@informatik.uni-bremen.de

ABSTRACT
A shift is occurring, particularly evident in art-and-technology practice, in which the artist-led-workshop is transformed into an distinct and distinguishable artistic form. Resulting from, and contributing to, the new access and relationships people have to information, creative culture, materials and like-interested individuals, the "workshop-as-artwork" is herein proposed and outlined. As a set of multiple artistic (material), social and learning agent interactions, thinking this new form as an ecology has shown benefits in terms of the aims and design of these new works, as well as their thinking, planning and execution. Further, from the artist-interventionist point of view, positing the workshop-as-artwork and ecological thinking seeks to update notions of legacy, consequence and significance for the art-and-technology practitioner and his or her audience.

Particular attention is given to the links made between the workshop-as-artwork to other historical art forms, the potentials for these structures to provide a means of rendering technologies more convivial, as well as understanding the participative and performative interactions possible within such a form. We conclude with a set of reflections on the artistic context of this work, and possible directions and prospects arising from the "workshop-as-artwork."

Author Keywords
Artist, workshop, ecology, community, DIY.

ACM Classification Keywords
J.5. Arts and Humanities: Arts, fine and performing

General Terms
Design, Documentation, Experimentation, Human Factors

INTRODUCTION
Within traditional artistic communities, the artist-led-workshop is often regarded as a somewhat subsidiary format for the presentation of ideas, in contrast to papers or artworks. To the organiser (of conferences) or curator (of festivals and exhibitions), the workshop can be an inexpensive, if perfunctory way of declaring and developing attention to "practice," while lowering the resource commitments inherent to supporting artworks and/or publications. For the artist-instigator, the "delivery" of technology-based workshops can serve tactical agendas to "engage with communities of users," clouding the potential and import of artistic, social and pedagogical (in the broadest sense) objectives. The design of content-rich, meaningful and thoughtfully presented workshop-as-artworks have great potential to transform social settings and transcend these cynicism.

"Workshopping" now forms a large part of the art-and-technology practitioner's activities. As such the value in repositioning this sort of activity as an artistic "form" seems apparent. Not only does such a shift in thinking allow for a developed discourse and a review of the value of these activities, but it can serve to create a vehicle for understanding the conditions of co-created, creative meaning which take place when all involved are invited to become "part of an artwork."

C&C'11, November 3–6, 2011, Atlanta, Georgia, USA.
ACM 978-1-4503-0820-5/11/11.

THE WORKSHOP-AS-ARTWORK
The authors have designed, executed and documented a series of workshop-as-artwork events in art-and-technology festivals, conferences and as part of curriculum-based artistic activities for young people. All of the workshops had as common denominator a sensitivity related to alternative energy sources, and the use of electronic hardware as enablers for personal creative expression in social, public spaces. Each of the workshops, titled Transmisol, Chiptune Marching Band and Sundroids, respectively developed a link to an art-historical material practice or form. Transmisol elaborated ideas from an arena known as Transmission Arts, Chiptune Marching Band developed linked to public music performance and public Happenings, and Sundroids evolved from interests in autonomously-powered Kinetic Art systems. It is important to note that these art-historical reference points were tapped not as an appeal to traditionalist forms, but for their potential to be re-thought in terms of Open Work and convivial/constructionist ideals.

Transmisol
Transmisol is a 3-day workshop-as-artwork that first took place in Mexico City in the summer of 2008. The event was developed as a collaboration between artist Geraldine Juarez and Jamie Allen, partially inspired by the work of Tetsuo Kogawa (author of the "Micro Radio Manifesto"). Participants at the initial event were a group of young people aged 18-20 who were attending the Transitio Festival, a week-long new media and electronic arts event. The Transmisol group was invited to make a set of solar-powered MP3-player and radio transmitter devices, which

were to be installed in public space as a distributed exhibition.

Chiptune Marching Band (CTMB)

CTMB is a series of workshop-performances, inviting attendees to learn, build and perform together while engaging with localised energy generation and a public sound performance. CTMB workshops have been hosted by Maker Faire UK, Pixelache Helsinki, Bent Festival NY, NK House Berlin and Creativity & Cognition (all in 2009) , among others, all with 7-20 participants at a time. The workshop-as-artwork was developed by Jo Kazuhiro and Jamie Allen, with further ideas for user contribution and feedback contributed by Areti Galani. CTMB is designed as a 3-hour event, during which participants build a small sensor-driven sound making circuit (oscillator), powered by an alternative energy source (hand-crank generator). At the end of the march, participants take their instrument home, along with a self-addressed stamped postcard, to be used to report back to the Band as to what has become of their instrument in the weeks following the event itself. Many characteristics suggesting the potential of the workshop-as-artwork were suggested via CMTB.

Sundroids

Sundroids is a workshop-as-artwork using solar robotics to create a set of autonomous kinetic sculptural works for and from the countryside environment of Northeastern England. The workshops held thus far have all taken place at Harehope Quarry, a sustainability co-operative and outdoor creative educational facility in rural County Durham, UK. They were delivered in collaboration with secondary schools in the North East of England (Spring 2010), for young people aged 13 to 14. The sessions explore site-specific and kinetic art through the use of found materials on-site and small solar powered motor circuits. Art-practice inspiration came through the work of artists like Jean Tinguely and Arthur Ganson as art-and-technology practice. Participants personalised their collected materials through elaboration with handmade structures (for which bits of wood, tape and glue were provided), which they animated via their solar powered motors. The day culminated in a showcase of autonomous kinetic sculptures, which participants presented to one another, outdoors. Sundroids was designed to emphasise an improvisatory and contingent approach to materials, aesthetics and the run of the event.

Artistic Context

Why conceptualise these events as workshop-as-artworks? We might liken the workshop-as-artwork to a kind of technological knitting circle, in which the common reference point of a set of technologies, and being part of an artwork/event, become a partial solution to the mutual knowledge problem that can make ad-lib and ad-hoc community formation cumbersome and time consuming. In attempts to understand this sociality, we have found positioning these events as distinct artistic forms helpful, as this structure seems to capture the polyvocal, dialogical and ecological messiness which recognises multiple forces at play in any given situation, without feeling overly systematised or technological (as terms like "system," "complex," or "network," seem to do). The workshop-as-artwork gives artists, artist-initiators, educators and the general public a way to discuss these diverse event structures outside of the language of "audience," "users," and "creator." It is true that each represents a framework devised and somewhat prescribed by an initiating person or artist, but with further reflection of notions of Lifelike Art [1] and conviviality suggests a hybrid form which is minimally assertive of its creators' intentions (This has been further explored in subsequent loosely-organised performative workshop "structures" organised by the authors).

Insights Into Practice

What workshop-as-artworks demonstrate is a complicated mesh of limitations and support structures, established by a number of situated and related elements, which participants choose to navigate or subvert in their own individual and collective ways. Some of the challenges in discussing such creative ecologies in action in relation to workshops such as Sundroids is how best to capture, document and analyse these structures, as spurious and constantly evolving to respond to the changing dynamics of any given situation. In the instances described herein, participants' responses were captured through interviews and observations, which sought to measure their personal autonomy and creativity through their sculptures and their personal descriptions of their sculptures. These evaluations did not, however, take account of the artist-facilitator (as participants), but only participants (as artists). The workshop-as-artwork partially addresses the situation, concerns and impetus of the artist-instigator working with creative ecologicals forms.

How might the art-and-technology workshop, as a particularly contemporary fusion of real-world technologies, learning potentials, and creative possibilities be even further restructured as a more radical improvisation, Happening, or performance? Could pedagogic and artistic goals be a driver of new institutional conventions, cultural forms and everyday interactions which create expanses like those imagined by Kaprow and Illich? Claire Bishop develops the idea of a collaborative/ relational work which is not judged solely on its moral ("bringing people together") or instrumental ("teaching people to solder") merit. Instead she suggests that "practices need to be thought of in terms other than their ameliorative consequences; they should also question the very terms of these ameliorative assumptions." [2] As words like "laboratory" and "workshop" now comfortably replace words like "gallery" and "exhibit" as a description of artistic forms and venues, the workshop-as-artwork provides a framework for just the kind of questioning Bishop suggests.

ACKNOWLEDGMENTS

Culture Lab, SiDE, Harehope Quarry, K. Ladha, J. Davoll, T. Schofield, W. Schrimshaw, S. Dales, K. Chen.

REFERENCES

1 Kaprow, A. (1996). Essays on the Blurring of Art and Life. Kelly, J., Kaprow, A. (Eds.), U. of California. p.201.

2. Roche, J. (2006). Crawford., H., 'Artistic Bedfellows.' University Press of America. p. 202.

Toward a Dynamic Dramaturgy: An Art of Presentation in Interactive Storytelling

Jason B. Alonso, Angela Chang, David Robert, Cynthia Breazeal
MIT Media Lab
{jalonso,anjchang,lifeform,cynthiab}@media.mit.edu

ABSTRACT
In interactive storytelling systems, we see common challenges of artistic expression that pertains to presentation, standing apart from narrative structure. We believe this expression can be achieved computationally, which is a core challenge in using procedurally-generated worlds in interactive storytelling. This computational expression so is what we call *dynamic dramaturgy*. We intend dynamic dramaturgy as a complement to interactive narrative systems, particularly drama management, and as a fundamentally distinct task from plot-level narrative construction, yet it is still a basic medium for artistic expression by an author. It is, in effect, an art of presentation in interactive storytelling.

ACM Classification Keywords
H.5.1 Information Interfaces and Presentation: Multimedia Information Systems—*Artificial, augmented, and virtual realities*

General Terms
Theory

INTRODUCTION
We see procedural world building in interactive storytelling (as in [5, 6]) as a nascent approach with rich narrative potential. There remains significant challenges, however, in making a procedural world a viable medium for storytelling rather than just a medium for simulation-style gaming. One of the chief questions is, "given dynamically-created resources, possibly entire characters, how are the resources choreographed into compelling, interactive dramatic action?" Another important question, and the focus of our work, is "given a plot and the resources to execute it, how can the experience be presented with regard to its dramatic meaning?"

This latter question has its roots in all forms of storytelling, interactive and otherwise. In a video game, what is the camera angle that most effectively and dramatically communicates the meaning of a scene? On a theater stage, how can the lights be manipulated to show isolation, tension, or even love? In a text adventure, what choice of words can be used to shape the way a moment is perceived? In each of these cases, we see a challenge of artistic expression that stands apart from the narrative structure. We believe this expression can be achieved computationally. To do so is what we call *dynamic dramaturgy*.

Despite the many possible implications of the word "dramaturgy," we define *dynamic dramaturgy* to be the algorithmic construction of an interactive experience to achieve a dramatic objective for a prescribed narrative. We intend dynamic dramaturgy as a complement to interactive narrative systems, particularly drama management, and as a fundamentally distinct task from plot-level narrative construction. It is, in effect, an art of presentation in interactive storytelling.

THEORY
We take the view that the telling of a story can (and often should) be treated separately from the story itself. This view is not new. R. Michael Young discussed story and discourse as a "bipartite model" of narrative generation, using Mimesis as his basis for an example [8].

As such, we propose an architecture composed largely of two parts: a narrative engine (especially a drama manager) interacts with a presentation engine. The job of the presentation engine is to provide *dramaturgical handles* through which the narrative engine can communicate authorial intent to the human player. The presentation engine is also responsible for handling and interpreting player interaction, feeding relevant information back to the narrative engine. The presentation engine thus takes on a role analogous to a theater director: it interprets authorial intent, from both the dramatist (a human author or the narrative engine as proxy for a human author) and itself and selects the presentation most effective for communicating that intent.

What interface should our presentation engine present to the narrative engine? This interface is composed of *dramaturgical handles*, affordances[3] that, in addition to allowing the character-level manipulations motivated by Aristotle, expose semantics that can cue non-character presentation activities, like perspective choice and lighting. We claim that the following is a list of suitable handles, though not necessarily exhaustive:

- *Importance* (of a character, thing, activity, or scene): this allows for dynamic cinematography to emphasize the target element.

C&C'11, November 3–6, 2011, Atlanta, Georgia, USA.
ACM 978-1-4503-0820-5/11/11.

- *Mood* (of a scene): this allows for the choice of ambient sounds, background people and animals (happy couples vs. funeral procession, blue jays vs. crows, etc), weather, and other ambient properties.
- *Mood* (of a character): including ideas like "isolation," this allows for animation-level decisions like choice of gait and path planning (showing various levels of affinity for ambient elements)
- *Relationship* (between a character and another character or thing): taken with *Mood*, the OCC model of emotion, with some adjustments[1], can be used to motivate character expression and posture toward other elements.
- *Perspective* (of a scene): largely driving cinematography and sound design, this allows for the dramatic emphasis of how things and events should be perceived.

It is this last point, *Perspective*, that we make an early attempt at demonstrating. Later in this paper, we discuss our implementation of "point-of-view kits," which are a proof-of-concept that at least the *Perspective* handle can scale dynamically with the world.

UNPARKED PERSPECTIVES

Historically, interactive storytelling engines have adopted various narrative unfolding devices from literature and film[7]. In some cases, alternating between different character perspectives as the story develops allows users to access the different characters' thoughts and experiences[4]. We call this pattern "interleaved perspectives."

Our example system, Unparked Perspectives, extends the notion of interleaved perspectives to include all of the contents of the environment or secondary world as characters with their respective unique perspectives. In our system, the user (or drama manager) can dynamically blend the current story perspective with that of any other character or prop. The ability to fluidly shift to any perspective within the world's object catalog enriches the story possibilities thus providing more robust options for transmedia storytelling authors[2].

In Unparked Perspectives, the viewer clicks on any story element and triggers a dramatic response from the system A simple park-scene is rendered using a combination of realtime 3D and 2D procedural animation techniques. The scene is populated with two main characters: Lady Tofu and Tofu Sir, along with several omniscient trees and two park benches (see Figure 1).

Each time the drama manager adds (instances) a story element (character or prop) to the world's catalog and instances that object into the rendered story world, a kit is automatically generated to enable the object's participation in the presentation engine. The kit consists of the 3D geometry model, a description of the model's visual appearance, and an asset library of animated behaviors and associated dialog sound files. Most notably, each instanced object defines a personal perspective by instancing a camera whose location serves as a waypoint anchor for the 3D perspective planning module.

Figure 1. World objects and their instanced POV kits camera as it relates to the object of interest

DISCUSSION

As an exploration into creating a scalable system for future storytelling, our proposed architecture succeeds at providing a broader palette of creative options. Though our larger vision of dynamic dramaturgy has yet to be tested in earnest, we have presented a test system, Unparked Perspectives, with a minimalist story that shows that at least one of our proposed dramaturgical handles can be manipulated computationally.

REFERENCES

1. C. Bartneck. Integrating the OCC Model of Emotions in Embodied Characters, 2002.
2. G. A. Long. Transmedia Storytelling: Business, Aesthetics and Production at the Jim Henson Company. Master's thesis, Comparative Media Studies Program, Massachusetts Institute of Technology, May 2008.
3. M. Mateas. Expressive AI: A Semiotic Analysis of Machinic Affordances. In *Proceedings of the 3rd Conference on Computational Semiotics and New Media*, University of Teeside, UK, 2003.
4. A. Mazalek, G. Davenport, and H. Ishii. Tangible viewpoints: a physical approach to multimedia stories. In *Proceedings of the tenth ACM international conference on Multimedia*, MULTIMEDIA '02, pages 153–160, New York, NY, USA, 2002. ACM.
5. Mojang AB. Minecraft. Minecraft web site, 2011. `http://www.minecraft.net/`.
6. Re-Logic. Terraria. Terraria web site, 2011. `http://www.terraria.org/`.
7. C. Strohecker, K. M. Brooks, and L. Friedlander. Tired of Giving In: An Experiment in Narrative Unfolding. Technical Report 99-16, MERL — A Mitsubishi Electric Research Laboratory, Cambridge, MA, 1999.
8. R. M. Young. Story and Discourse: A Bipartite Model of Narrative Generation in Virtual Worlds. *Interaction Studies: Social Behaviour and Communication in Biological and Artificial Systems*, 8(2):177–208, 2007.

Embroidered Confessions: An Interactive Quilt of the Secrets of Strangers

Julynn Benedetti
MFA, Design + Technology, Parsons The New School for Design
66 Fifth Avenue, New York, NY 10011, USA
benej568@newschool.edu

ABSTRACT
The condition of anonymity creates a private space within a public space as a person feels the freedom to act without attribution. This phenomenon holds true in both physical and digital spaces. People feel free to post their most intimate secrets on the Internet with the belief that their confessions are ephemeral and intangible. In reality, this data is perpetually archived and cached on distant servers. A disconnect exists between the perception of the transitory quality of digital data and the truth of its enduring existence. Through the weaving of the stories and secrets of strangers from the Internet into a material artifact, *Embroidered Confessions* represents the physical manifestation of the duality of digital information.

Author Keywords
Craft and Technology, Tangible Interface, Secrets

ACM Classification Keywords
K.4.m Computing Milieux: Computers & Society—Misc, J.5. Computer Applications: Arts & Humanities--Fine arts

General Terms
Design, Experimentation, Human Factors

INTRODUCTION & AUDIENCE
Embroidered Confessions is an installation that curates, archives, and physically embodies secrets that exist solely in digital form. Collections of found secrets from the Internet are accessed through embroidered Quick Reference (QR) codes that have been integrated into a quilt. A QR code, in its seemingly random clusters and formations, visually evoke the wrong side of a piece of embroidery. Turn an embroidered pillow inside out and there emerges a different pattern of bumps and clusters of thread than the ordered pattern of artwork on the "right" side. A QR code is a visual secret manifested in a physical object that evokes tradition and craft, but also must be decoded in an interaction that is technologically dissonant yet visually congruent. *Embroidered Confessions* is a commentary on the duality of digital information: the perception of its fleeting nature and the reality of its enduring existence.

C&C'11, November 3–6, 2011, Atlanta, Georgia, USA.
ACM 978-1-4503-0820-5/11/11.

IMPETUS
Embroidered Confessions is more than a physical manifestation of digital secrets; it is also an embodiment of and allusion to a series of myths about confession and revelation that exist across many cultures. Most people are familiar with the story of King Midas and his golden touch, but Midas also plays a prominent role in the tale "The Musical Contest of Pan and Apollo" from Ovid's *Metamorphoses*.

In this myth, the gods Pan and Apollo compete in a musical contest. All judges, with the exception of King Midas, choose Apollo as the clear winner. Apollo becomes angry with Midas for his poor judgment and uncouth taste in music, and punishes him by turning his ears into those of an ass. Midas, embarrassed by these ears, covers them at all times and manages to hide them from everyone, except his barber. The barber is so overwhelmed by keeping Midas's shameful secret, that, on the advice of a wise man, he digs a shallow hole in the banks of a river, whispers the secret inside of it, and then covers it back up with mud. Later, a grove of reeds grows in the bank and betrays the secret that the barber planted.

If the Internet is the bank of the river in which people deposit their secrets, *Embroidered Confessions* is the resultant reeds that sprout as the physical relic of secrets planted on the web. The language of the reeds must be translated, just as QR codes must be decoded, in order to understand the secrets that lie encrypted in the artifact. The quilt is a physical reminder of the immortality of musings, indiscreet personal disclosures, and heart felt declarations that exist and are archived in the digital stratosphere.

Figure 1. Embroidered QR code encrypted with a secret

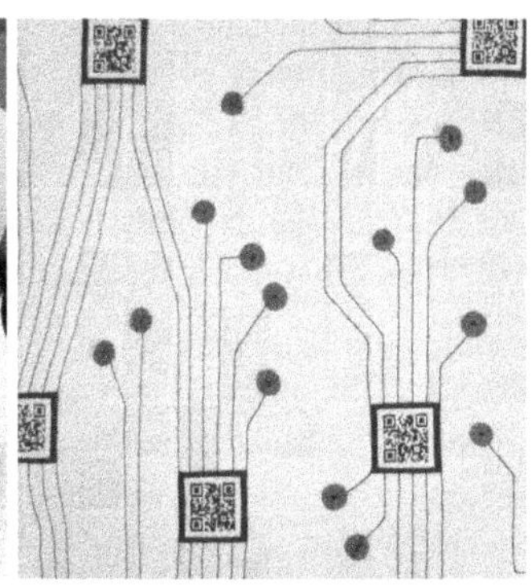

Figure 2. The quilt design evokes both a circuit board as well as the reeds that sprout as a result of planted secrets.

DOMAINS & PRECEDENTS

Anonymity

There are many peculiarities of interaction that occur because of the compact nature of urban spaces. Personal distances between strangers are compressed, or suspended, due to more constricted configurations of space [3]. The boundary between private and public space becomes blurred as people are forced to eavesdrop, overhearing intimate details about the lives of others.

The anonymity and forced interactions of city life share parallels with anonymous interactions on the web. People behave in a similar manner whether surrounded by strangers on the street or on the Internet. People speak loudly on their cell phones while walking down the street, while others post anonymous, highly personal declarations of love on Craigslist. Being surrounded by strangers provides a sense of anonymity despite the openness of both physical and digital spaces.

Psychology of Secrets

Why do people keep secrets? The most common answer is the fear of social rejection and damage to relationships. This explains why people confess under condition of anonymity. If a secret is told to strangers, there is no impact to existing relationships.

In addition to the psychological, there may also be a physiological reason behind confession. Subjects of a study were asked if they had a secret unknown to anyone else. Some were asked to either write about the secret in a journal entry or talk about their secret into a tape recorder. The control group had no outlet for secrets. The study found that those who confessed their secret visited their doctor less frequently in the subsequent six months than the control group. [2]. Expression and confession are important to both psychological and physiological health, even if the act involved an inanimate object that provided no feedback.

Secret-Telling in Myths

In addition to the story of King Midas, other myths across history center around confession to inanimate objects. A legend in Kyrgyzstan tells of another rich ruler, the king of the Ossounes. This king is also afflicted by shamefully long ears and betrayed by his barber. In this version, however, the barber confesses to a well. Forgetting to close the lid after confessing, the well overflows, flooding the palace and adjacent lands. This is the fabled origin of the Issyk-Kul, a lake that never freezes despite its high altitude [4].

"Maon and the Willow" is yet another tale that borrows heavily from the previous stories. In this Celtic myth, the object of the barber's confession is a willow tree. A harpist, needing to mend his instrument, uses the branches from the willow. When he plays in front of the royal court, the harp betrays the king's secret [6]. The fact that these myths occur across cultures and throughout time is a testament to the very human compulsion to reveal secrets.

Craft & Technology

An important inspiration for *Embroidered Confessions* came from Janine Antoni's *Slumber*. In this performance piece, Antoni slept overnight in a gallery with an electroencephalograph machine recording her rapid eye movement cycles. During the day, this data was woven into a pattern that formed the blanket she slept under at night [1]. The translation of electronic data to an everyday object creates a new context in which to experience information. Her blanket suggests intimacy, warmth, and a state of unconscious dreaming. The *Embroidered Confessions* quilt is also generated from very intimate gestures, the sharing of secrets, an act usually reserved for close friends.

CONCLUSION

The Internet is the modern-day equivalent to the hole in the bank of the river dug by King Midas's barber. It is the inanimate object to which users confess their darkest secrets, believing they are protected by the anonymity and intangibility of digital communications on the Internet. However, everything published on the Internet, from Google searches to Facebook status updates to blog posts, becomes part of a permanent archive. As a result of this endless recording of information, anonymity in the digital age is an illusion, and communications shared on the Internet have real, lasting impact [5].

Embroidered Confessions embodies the enduring life span of these digital communications by giving it a physical form. The act of curating and preserving digital data in an artifact emphasizes the reality and permanency that communications and behaviors on the Internet possess.

ACKNOWLEDGMENTS

Faculty advisors include Katherine Moriwaki, Andrew Zornoza, Scott Pobiner, Louisa Campbell, and Melanie Crean. Thanks also to Janet Benedetti and Annette Metz for their help and expertise in materials and quilt construction.

REFERENCES

1. Antoni, Janine. *Slumber*, installation and performance, MASS MoCA, North Adams, MA, 1993.
2. Kelly, Anita, The psychology of secrets, New York: Kluwer Academic/Plenum, 2002.
3. Lawson, Bryan. The language of space. Oxford; Boston: Architectural Press, 2001.
4. Maillart, Ella, Turkestan solo: a journey through Central Asia. Translated by John Rodker. London: Tauris Parke Paperbacks, pp 48-49, 1934.
5. Mayer-Schonberger, Viktor. Delete: the virtue of forgetting in the digital age. Princeton, Princeton University Press, 2009.
6. Rolleston, T.W., Myths and Legends of the Celtic Race. New York: Cosimo, pp 154-155, 1911.

Towards Supporting Creative Design: Analysis of the Use of the TRENDS System according to Designers' Expertise

Nathalie Bonnardel
Research Centre in Psychology of Cognition, Language and Emotion (PsyCLE, EA 3273)
Aix-Marseille University
& University Institute of France (I.U.F)
Nathalie.Bonnardel@univ-provence.fr

Carole Bouchard
Laboratoire Conception de Produits et Innovation (LCPI, EA 3927)
Arts et Métiers ParisTech
carole.bouchard@ensam.eu

ABSTRACT
Towards the end of favoring the emergence of new ideas in design situations, we first characterize cognitive processes involved in creative design and we describe a new computational system, called TRENDS, which aims at helping designers find inspirational material. Then, we present an exploratory study that contributes to a better understanding of the use of this system for performing a creative task, according to the users' level of expertise in design. The obtained results allow us to point out differences of use by novices and experienced designers and, on these bases, to suggest complementary support depending on the designers' level of expertise.

Author Keywords
Design, creativity, expertise, images, inspirational processes, design support environment.

ACM Classification Keywords
H.5.2. Information interfaces and presentation: User-centered design.

General Terms
Design, Experimentation, Human Factors.

INTRODUCTION

Design activities occur in many areas, ranging from technical to more artistic domains. Whatever the domain, final product designs should have some innovative aspects in order to be attractive for customers or future users. Thus, it is a constant challenge for designers to introduce creativity in each design project they work on as well as to satisfy constraints about the object to be designed [1]. Therefore, design science is becoming oriented towards the development of computer-based tools that aim to support designers to achieve creative design solutions. In line with this objective, we first characterize main cognitive mechanisms involved in creative design activities and we describe a computational system, called TRENDS, which aims at helping designers find inspirational material. Then, we present an exploratory study that contributes to a better understanding of the use of this system for performing a creative task, according to the users' level of expertise in design.

C&C'11, November 3–6, 2011, Atlanta, Georgia, USA.
ACM 978-1-4503-0820-5/11/11.

CHARACTERISTICS OF CREATIVE DESIGN

From a cognitive point of view, a first characteristic of design activities is that the designers' mental representation is, initially, only incomplete and imprecise. It is throughout the design problem-solving process that designers can complete their mental representations [4]. According to the A-CM – Analogy and Constraint Management – model [1], two main cognitive processes continuously interact during the design activity, which can have opposite effects in line with divergent and convergent thinking:

- *analogy-making*, which may lead designers to extend or "open up" their research space of ideas and thus lead to creative design ideas;
- the *management of constraints*, which orients design problem solving by allowing designers to both progressively delimit their research space, take into consideration different points of view and assess design options, until they find a satisfying design solution.

Such cognitive processes contribute to reach a design solution that satisfies two main criteria in the case of creative design: to be new and adapted to the context [1].
Previous results, obtained in experimental situations, and without any interaction with a computational system, showed that designers need to access to various sources of inspiration to be able to extend their research space of ideas [2]. Therefore, we argue that it should be possible to favour creative design activities by introducing, through the use of a computational system, some diversity in the retrieved material taken into account by designers.

THE TRENDS SYSTEM

The development of the TRENDS system (see Figure 1) was funded by the European Commission (research contract FP6 IST 2005 27916). This system aims to facilitate the early design process by providing designers with inspirational materials. It works with a database of 2 millions of images covering more than 350 websites. Accessing to such inspirational materials is based on a hybrid semantic search of text and images, which was formalized through the *Conjoint Trends Analysis method* [3]. Especially, semantic adjectives used in the design world allow the user to query with a single word and to retrieve images related to the words defining it. For example, querying *elegant* will search for images referring to *elegant, style, refined, nice, beautiful, classy, tasteful...*

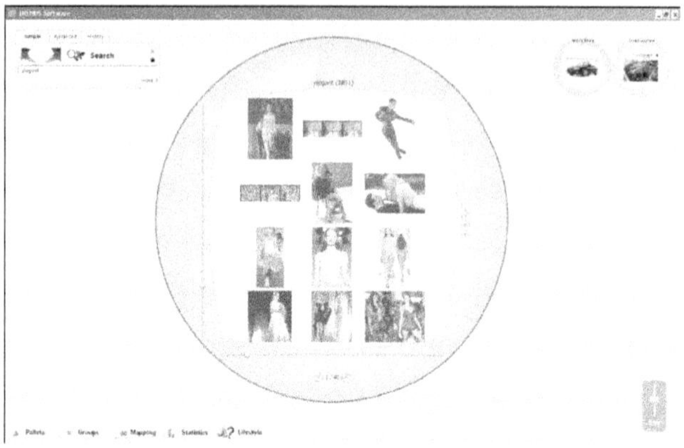

Figure 1: TRENDS software presenting results of a semantic search with the keyword "elegant".

ANALYSIS OF THE USE OF TRENDS ACCORDING TO THE LEVEL OF EXPERTISE IN DESIGN

Method

30 students participated in this experiment: 15 of them, called "novices", were in their 3rd year at the university and had no experience in design whereas 15 other participants, called "experienced", were in their 3rd year in a school of design.

These participants were asked to imagine that they were employed, as a designer, in a society in charge of the design of new cars. Firstly, they were provided with a design brief (or schedule of conditions) that specifies constraints about the car they have to design (*e.g.*, unconventional, fun) as well as about the future client (*e.g.*, urban, international). Then, the TRENDS system was presented to them as well as its main functionalities.

The experiment itself consisted in two phases: (1) a phase of search of images with the computational system (during half an hour) on the basis of key-words expressed by the participants, (2) a design phase during which the participants had to design the new car while thinking aloud (without limitation of time).

Results

Concerning the 1st experimental phase, the results show that the experienced designers produced more key-words than novices but that the number of images they gathered on the TRENDS system was about the same: around 3 images, whatever the participants' level of expertise (see Figure 2).

Concerning the 2nd experimental phase, we analyzed both the number and nature of objects evoked by the participants, which could serve as sources of inspiration for designing the new car. Two "judges" categorized these objects-sources of inspiration as corresponding to either intra-domain sources (which belonged to the same conceptual domain as the object to be designed, i.e. the car domain) or inter-domain sources (which belonged to other conceptual domains). The results show that, although both groups of participants evoke more intra-domain sources than inter-domain ones, experienced designers evoked significantly more inter-domain sources of inspiration than novices ($F(1,26) = 5.13$, $p = .03$; see Figure 3).

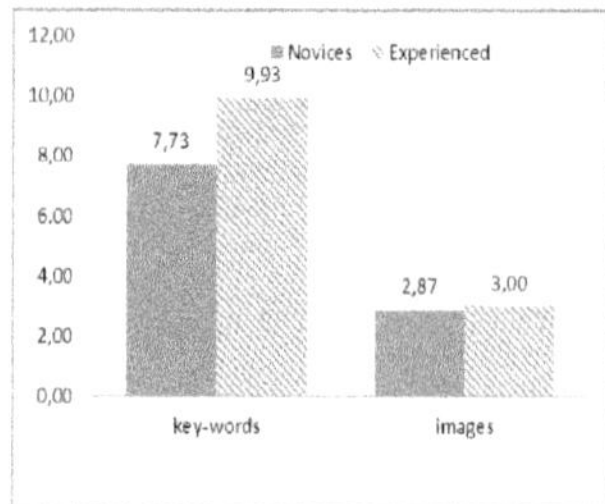

Figure 2: Mean number of key -words and images according to users' expertise in design.

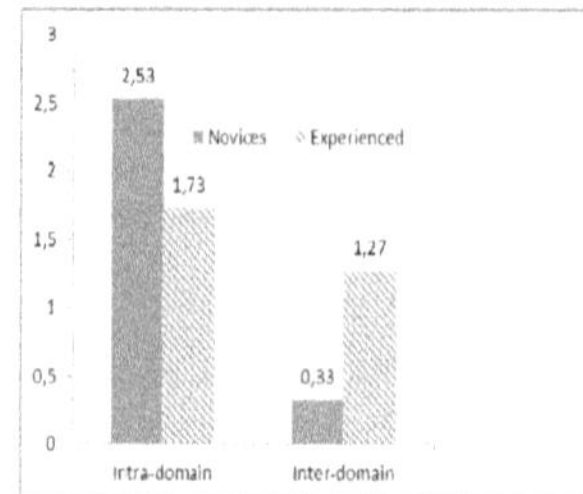

Figure 3: Mean number of intra- and inter-domain sources of inspiration according to expertise.

Discussion

Whatever the designers' level of expertise, participants in this study were able to generate key-words to search for images on the TRENDS system, which corresponds to the main functionality of this system. In addition, we observed that, independently of the number of key-words they produced, all participants selected a similar number of images, which is around 3. It could be an optimal number of images designers can focus on during the design task. This number of images could allow participants to dispatch their attentional resources for both reflecting on the object to be designed, analyzing features of these images to potentially perform analogical transfer to the design problem at hand, and drawing sketches representing their design solutions. We also noticed that the sources of inspiration taken into consideration by novices were mainly intra-domain whereas experienced designers were more able to refer to both intra- and inter-domain sources. Thus, additional kinds of support consisting, for instance, in explanations, exercises or a specific training could be proposed to novices to allow them to exploit analogies with inter-domain objects and, thus, benefit from the variety of images that they can obtain by using the TRENDS system.

REFERENCES

1. Bonnardel, N. Towards understanding and supporting creativity in design: Analogies in a constrained cognitive environment. *Knowledge-Based Systems, 13* (2000), 505-513.
2. Bonnardel, N., and Marmèche, E. Evocation processes by novice and expert designers: Towards stimulating analogical thinking. *Creativity and Innovation Management, 13,* 3 (2004), 176-186.
3. Bouchard, C., Omhover, J.F., Mougenot, C., Aoussat, A., and Westerman, S. TRENDS, a content-based information retrieval system for designers, *Proceedings of Design Computing and Cognition - DCC08* (Atlanta, June 2008), Springer, 593-611.
4. Simon, H.A. Problem forming, problem finding and problem solving in design. In A. Collen & W. Gasparski (Eds), *Design & Systems.*Transaction Publishers, New Brunswick, 1995, 245-257.

Social User Generated Content's Effect on Creativity in Educational Games

Acey Boyce, Katie Doran, Antoine Campbell, Shaun Pickford, Dustin Culler, and Tiffany Barnes
Department of Computer Science
University of North Carolina at Charlotte
9201 University City Blvd., Charlotte, NC, USA
Tiffany.Barnes@uncc.edu

ABSTRACT
BeadLoom Game (BLG) is an educational puzzle game developed by adding game elements to a free-play educational tool called the Virtual Bead Loom (VBL). To motivate students who prefer the creative freedom of VBL, we added Custom Puzzle mode to BLG so players can create, share, and rate user-generated puzzles. We compare VBL and BLG Custom Puzzles to show that this mode increases the creativity and complexity of student work.

Author Keywords
Game development, education, motivation

ACM Classification Keywords
K.3.2 Computers and education: Computer and information science education. – Computer science education.

General Terms
Design, Human Factors

INTRODUCTION AND RELATED WORK
The Virtual Bead Loom (VBL) [csdt.rpi.edu] helps students learn Cartesian coordinates, geometry, and symmetry while creating virtual bead art. The BeadLoom Game (BLG) is a game version of VBL that adds the computing concepts of iteration and layering, and has more replayability than VBL [3]. The new Custom Puzzle mode allows players to publish, rate, and comment on, playable custom puzzles, with over 200 puzzles created in 3 months [1]. In this poster we investigate the impact this socially collaborative custom puzzle mode has on the overall creativity and complexity of player designs by comparing student VBL creations with custom BLG puzzles.

BEADLOOM GAME
BeadLoom Game is a puzzle game where players recreate a target bead design, or puzzle, in the fewest moves possible. Each puzzle is a 41 x 41 target bead pattern and a move is using one of the six different bead-placing functions. The point, line, rectangle, and triangle functions require students to specify one to three points to draw the given shape. The Linear and Triangle Iteration functions are more advanced, using iteration to place beads algorithmically. These algorithms are based on creating a pattern in one row, and repeating and modifying it in subsequent rows. Thus, the linear and triangle iteration tools provide a unique graphical demonstration of nested loops, a notoriously difficult concept for beginning programmers to understand The Linear Iteration function begins with a straight line of beads of a given length at a given point. In the next row, in a specified direction, the row is repeated, but is shifted by adding or subtracting a given number of beads from each side of the line. This process is repeated for the given number of lines total. This visually introduces players to the concept of iteration while exposing them to new patterns and ways to draw half circles and slopped edges. The Triangle Iteration function is similar but adds the same number of beads to each side every so many iterations creating isosceles triangles. Writing a program to do this function is quite complex, requiring several nested loops.

BeadLoom Game uses layering: when beads are placed on top of one another you see only the top bead. This principle can be used to minimize moves in BLG, and players quickly use this idea to make backgrounds like a blue sky first. However, nontraditional uses like drawing the American Flag using one solid red rectangle and add the white stripes on top, takes longer for players to learn.

The new Custom Puzzle mode allows: 1) publishing custom puzzles online, 2) custom puzzle play and leaderboards, and 3) a custom puzzle showcase with rating and commenting. Puzzle creators are motivated to make visually appealing, complex designs to encourage repeated attempts and rating. Since the first page of the showcase shows the highest-rated designs and has the most traffic, getting designs on this page is an honor and a strong motivator. Comments can be used to share tips and tricks on creative solutions to these puzzles, which is especially helpful since these puzzles do not come with a predetermined ideal solution. The Custom Puzzle Mode is a strong motivating force for creative players, raising these students' play times [1]. As we show here, BLG Custom Puzzles are more creative and complex than the designs made by students using VBL.

EXPERIMENTAL METHOD
VBL examples were gathered from a five-day summer camp with 20 middle school students. The first day students did a 30 minute VBL walkthrough and then had an hour to create their own designs, which could only be saved with

C&C'11, November 3–6, 2011, Atlanta, Georgia, USA.
ACM 978-1-4503-0820-5/11/11.

screenshots. Each day students had 30 minutes of free play time, and many chose VBL.

Custom Puzzle examples were gathered from a five one-hour outreach sessions during a local middle school computing class. Day 1 was like the camp, with a VBL walkthrough and 30 minutes to make original designs. On Days 2-4, a new feature was introduced first and students could choose which features to use for the second 30 minutes. The features were: none (VBL), target puzzles (BLG), custom mode (BLG-Custom), and high scores (BLG-Scores). On Day 5, the students chose among all the features for the full hour. Both the camp and the class were given URLs where they could access the game and tools at home.

Five BLG experts rated 54 VBL and BLG designs on 7-point Likert scales for creativity and complexity. Experts were chosen based on previous work developing or using the BLG in outreach. Creativity was defined the originality of content and implementation, and complexity was the difficulty of finding the ideal solution. Designs were chosen from creative students who spent the most time making designs. BLG experts were needed because the creativity and complexity of a design is not apparent on first glance. For example, making a circle smooth requires creativity and complex tool use. Experts were blind to student identities or VBL/BLG use.

RESULTS

Standard deviations suggest that agreement across raters was acceptable. The BLG average creativity score (M=4.51, SD=0.91, N = 28) was significantly greater than that for VBL (M = 3.75, SD = 1.25, N = 26) using two sample t-test for unequal variances, t(46) = 2.57, p <= .014. The BLG mean complexity score (M = 4.1, SD = 0.91, N = 28) was significantly higher than that for VBL (M = 3.36, SD = 1.24, N = 26) using two sample t-test for unequal variances, t(46) = 2.46, p <= .018. Pearson product moment correlations yielded a coefficient of .90, indicating that as complexity of the designs increased, so did their creativity.

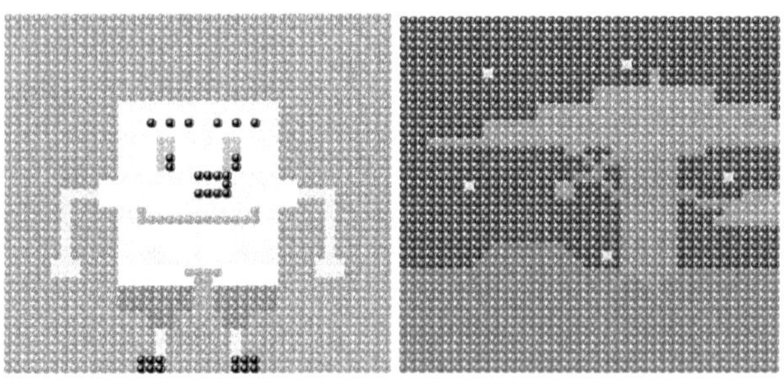

Figure 1: "Spongebob" & "Tree" of VBL Group

Although the VBL group had no formal way of sharing designs, they often showed each other their designs. If a design was particularly nice, other students would recreate the same design for themselves. For example, this group had a larger number of traditional concentric square designs. In BLG-Custom, many students would try to make a "better" version of a popular design, or spun off new designs in the same theme. One student created a basic Christmas tree, and more complex trees then emerged.

In VBL, sharing occurs but is most often in the form of mimicry. The BLG showcase allows students to share themes and design elements, while the rating system inspires competitive incremental improvements. This interaction is completely absent from VBL.

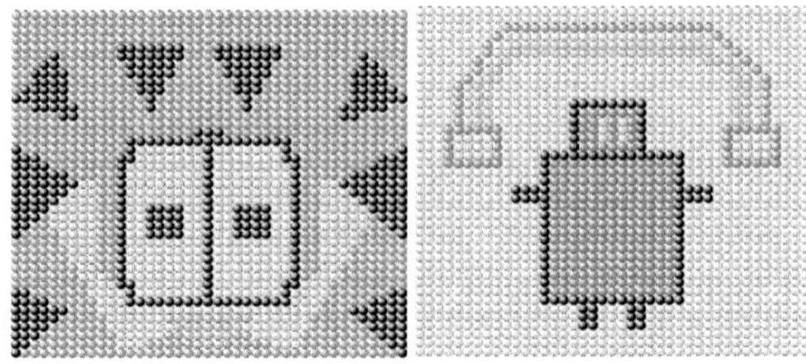

Figure 2: "Garfield" & "Robo Rainbow" of BLG Group

CONCLUSION

Custom Puzzle designs had significantly higher ratings in both creativity and complexity. These results suggest that the social experience around puzzle creation fosters creative exploration and greater design complexity. The high correlation between creativity and complexity does not tell us if complexity increases lead to increases in creativity or if creativity increases lead to more complexity, but it does suggest that the Custom Puzzle Mode affects both. BLG rewards complexity through interaction and rankings, which could enhance creativity. Or, perhaps the Custom Puzzle Mode directly fosters creative puzzle design by providing inspiring examples.

Adding user generated content to an educational game can enhance appeal and creativity while making a game more replayable. Creating game modes to encourage learning while contributing new content improves learning gains and appeals to creative and competitive players [1]. All players then master the intended material whether creating or solving puzzles.

ACKNOWLEDGMENTS

This work was partially supported by NSF grants CNS-0634342 CNS-0739216, CNS 0540523, and IIS-0757521.

REFERENCES

[1] Boyce, A, A. Campbell, S. Pickford, D. Culler, T. Barnes (2011). Experimental Evaluation of BeadLoom Game: How Adding Game Elements to an Educational Tool Improves Motivation and Learning. ACM ITiCSE 2011.

[2] Boyce, A, K. Doran, A. Campbell, S. Pickford, D. Culler, T. Barnes (2011). BeadLoom Game: Adding Competitive, User Generated, and Social Features to Increase Motivation. ACM FDG 2011.

Creativity and Conducting: Handle in the CAIRA Project

Selmer Bringsjord • Colin Kuebler • Joshua Taylor • Griffin Milsap • Sean Austin
Jonas Braasch • Pauline Oliveros • Doug Van Nort • Adam Rosenkrantz • Kasia Hayden
Selmer.Bringsjord@gmail.com • kueblc@rpi.edu • tayloj@rpi.edu • milsag@rpi.edu • austis@rpi.edu
braasj@rpi.edu • paulineo@deeplistening.org • dvnt.sea@gmail.com • amrmecheng@gmail.com • kasiahayden@gmail.com
Department of Cognitive Science • Department of Computer Science
The Rensselaer AI & Reasoning (RAIR) Lab
Rensselaer Polytechnic Institute (RPI)
Troy, NY 12180, USA

ABSTRACT
After providing some context via (i) earlier work on literary creativity carried out by Bringsjord et al., and (ii) an account of creativity espoused by Cope, which stands in rather direct opposition to Bringsjord's account, we summarize our nascent attempt to engineer an artificial conductor: Handle. Handle is a microcosmic version of part of a larger, much more ambitious system: CAIRA. Both are under development courtesy of a three-year CreativeIT grant from the National Science Foundation (PI Braasch, Co-PIs Oliveros & Bringsjord).

Author Keywords
Creativity, music, conducting, AI, computation, modeling

ACM Classification Keywords
I.2.0 Artificial Intelligence: Cognitive simulation

General Terms
Experimentation, Performance, Theory

PRIOR WORK
In earlier work, Bringsjord, joined by Ferrucci, argues that while machines can't be *genuinely* creative, at least in the literary sphere they can nonetheless be engineered to *seem* to be creative (2000). This two-part position is partly philosophical in nature (based as it is upon *a priori* reasoning), and partly engineeringish (based as it is upon producing a computational artifact capable of generating compelling short-short stories (Brutus.1). On the philosophical side, in order for a machine to be genuinely creative (*creative*$_B$), it would need to pass the so-called "Lovelace Test" (LT), which essentially means that what the machine does cannot be anticipated by the designer of this machine (Bringsjord, Bello & Ferrucci 2001). On the engineering side, it is enough for the storytelling machine to trick human readers, in Turing-testing-style, into believing that the stories produced by this machine were produced by creative humans (*creativity*$_T$).

COPE'S ACCOUNT OF CREATIVITY
But how does Cope define creativity? An explicit answer is supplied in his seminal *Computer Models of Musical Creativity*, where he tells us that for him creativity is "[t]he initialization of connections between two or more multifaceted things, ideas, or phenomena hitherto not otherwise considered actively connected" (Cope 2005, 11). Immediately after giving this latitudinarian definition, Cope provides a series of examples of his brand of creativity (*creativity*$_C$) in action. The first of these examples is an endgame chess puzzle that a modern chess program would have no trouble with; another is a simple card trick. But his last example is the solving of the following somewhat more interesting puzzle:

> "I have three sons whose ages I want you to ascertain from the following clues. Stop me when you know their ages. One, the sum of their ages is thirteen. Two, the product of their ages is the same as your age. Three, my oldest-in-years son weighs sixty-one pounds."
>
> "Stop," says the second man, "I know their ages."
>
> What are their ages?

Under the assumptions that: (i) the second man is an adult, and hence—in our culture—at least 21 years of age; (ii) the second man couldn't deduce the answer after the second clue; and (iii) the second man knows his own age,[1] it is possible to provide an outright proof that the correct answer is 2, 2, and 9. In an informal nutshell here, the reasoning runs as follows: Of the permutations of three numbers n, m, and k that sum to 13 and have a product that's at least 21, the only two that produce the same product (36) are: 1, 6, 6 and 2, 2, 9. Since in the former case there is no oldest, we are left with the latter as the only possibility.

Since, using standard formalisms in logic-based AI (Bringsjord 2008), we have engineered a machine able to find and certify a formal proof of the argument just given, it's clear that a theorem-prover-based program able to solve this problem would not be creative$_B$. The reason is that the designer of such a computer program wouldn't be genuinely surprised in the least when a formal proof expressing the argument is found; Bringsjord is an example. In addition, such a program wouldn't be creative$_T$, for the simple reason that cracking such puzzles is precisely the kind of thing humans *expect* computers to be able to do, while humans, save for a select few trained in formal logic, have quite a bit of trouble with such puzzles (Bringsjord & Yang 2003).

[1] The truth is that a number of other premises are required (pertaining to the nature of arithmetic!), but we leave this aside in the interest of brevity.

C&C'11, November 3–6, 2011, Atlanta, Georgia, USA.
ACM 978-1-4503-0820-5/11/11.

BRUTALLY QUICK OVERVIEW OF CAIRA

CAIRA is an-at-least-creative$_T$ artificially-intuitive and reasoning agent, designed and implemented in the context of ensemble music improvisation. Creative musical works are often a product of deliberative or spontaneous processes intuited by musicians. In most—if not all—cases, it is a combination of both. Our new AI system demonstrates creative musicianship that is based on reasoning/logic *and* spontaneity; our aim, in fact, is to better understand the relationship between both modes in the creative process. Using logic-based reasoning, the agent will be able to self-reflect upon its actions, based on integrated formal knowledge. CAIRA is intended to be embedded in an ensemble of musicians, or to communicate with an individual human performer. It can also be configured as a multi-agent system. It can analyze acoustic environments and respond by producing its own sound, or conduct music via a multi-modal display. CAIRA will first specialize in classic avant-garde music. In this genre, a composition or improvisation often consists of a sequence of textures that meet different verbal criteria (e.g., "rhythmic, dense, and atonal," or "very sparse but melodic"). The architecture of CAIRA is summed up in the following figure.

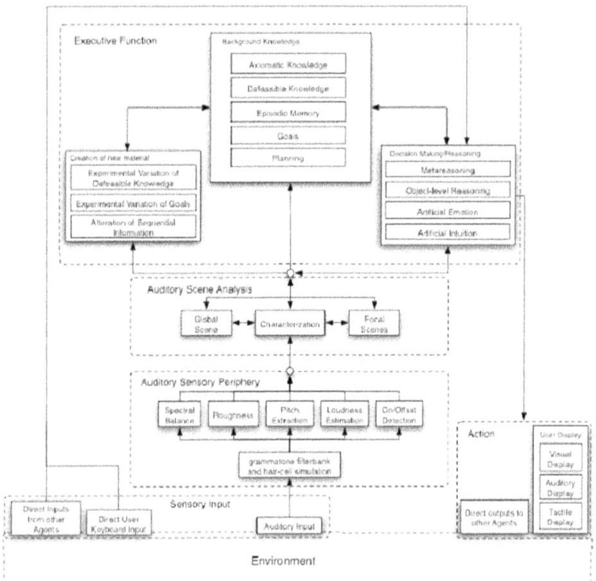

SUPER-QUICK OVERVIEW OF HANDLE

Handle is a microcosmic version of the non-generative logic-based parts of CAIRA, allowing for initial focus and testing of these parts. (These parts fall within the "Executive Function" of CAIRA in the overall architecture.) This focus is achieved in the absence of sophisticated live musical performance by *groups* of musicians. While prior work on the part of Bringsjord and Ferrucci demonstrated that machine *literary* creativity can be engineered on the basis of formal logic, the use of computational formal logic to perceive and reason over *music* as it is produced in real time by groups of accomplished musicians is more demanding. Can a computing machine "understand" the analysis of music and reason from that analysis to the prods issued by a great conductor, themselves issued in real time so as to improve the performance in question? While we are confident the answer is Yes, the only way to provide via engineering an existence proof of this affirmative answer is to start humbly, and gradually scale up. Accordingly, while CAIRA allows for groups of human or machine musicians to play music of any type, Handle.1 is based on a single pianist playing a short piece, and specifically on the understanding and "conducting" of this playing. A streamlined description of the composite architecture that includes the basic structure of Handle is shown in the following figure.

Composite Architecture (v1)

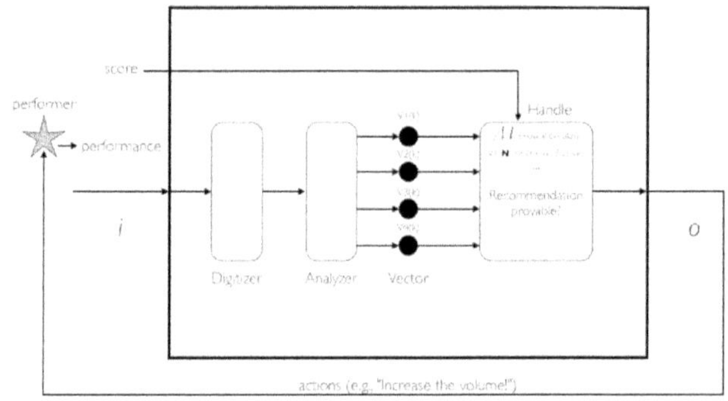

DEMONSTRATION

Handle 1.3 will be demonstrated in Atlanta at the conference. One demonstration will be based on a Beethoven piano sonata, and will feature real-time analysis of the sonata and—within Handle proper—reasoning on the strength of automated theorem proving over what this analysis provides. Currently, Handle 1.1 is capable of extracting key audio features used to construct formalized proofs 32 times per second, providing real time feedback for the performer.

ACKNOWLEDGMENTS

We thank the NSF for sponsorship of our research and development.

REFERENCES

1. Bringsjord, S. (2008) "The Logicist Manifesto: At Long Last Let Logic-Based Artificial Intelligence Become a Field Unto Itself" *Journal of Applied Logic* **6.4**: 502–525.
2. Bringsjord, S. & Ferrucci, D. (2000) *Artificial Intelligence and Literary Creativity: Inside the Mind of Brutus.1, A Storytelling Machine* (Mahwah, NJ: Erlbaum).
3. Bringsjord, S., Bello, P. & Ferrucci, D. (2001) "Creativity, the Turing Test, and the (Better) Lovelace Test" *Minds & Machines* **11**: 3–27.
4. Bringsjord, S. & Yang, Y. (2003) "The Problems that Generate the Rationality Debate are Too Easy, Given What our Economy Now Demands" Behavioral and Brain Sciences **26.4**: 528–530.
5. Cope, D. (2005) Computer Models of Musical Creativity (Cambridge, MA: MIT Press).
6. Russell, S. & Norvig, P. (2002) *Artificial Intelligence: A Modern Approach* 2nd edition (Prentice-Hall).

Capturing 'In The Moment' Creativity Through Data Triangulation

Erin A. Carroll
HCILab
University of North Carolina at Charlotte
Charlotte, NC, USA
e.carroll@uncc.edu

Celine Latulipe
HCILab
University of North Carolina at Charlotte
Charlotte, NC, USA
clatulip@uncc.edu

ABSTRACT
We present a first attempt at capturing 'in the moment' creativity (ITMC) through a triangulation self-report techniques, external judges, and physiological measures. In our study, participants were asked to sketch for 30 minutes while wearing GSR and EEG; then they retrospectively self-reported their creativity using a custom interface. External judges were also utilized to rate when participants were creative. Our initial results indicate high reliability for self-reporting ITMC, consensus between judges and participants, and that physiological measures trended according to the expectations from research. Our work sets the stage for more extensive research that makes use of temporal measures of creativity.

Author Keywords
creativity, self-report, physiology, GSR, EEG

ACM Classification Keywords
H.5.2 Information Interfaces and Presentation: User Interfaces—*Theory and methods*

General Terms
Human Factors

INTRODUCTION
One of the main challenges in evaluating creativity support tools (CSTs) is that we are not able to measure when a person is actually being creative. Many studies in physiological creativity have taken the stand that creativity is being measured provided that the task is creative or the participant is classified as a 'creative' person [6]. However, it seems evident that in the course of working on a creative activity, there would be ups and down: periods of intense creativity and periods of very little creativity. In this work, we make a first attempt at capturing 'in the moment' creativity (ITMC), which we hope will eventually lead to a level of granularity that allows us to study the temporal, creative work process.

C&C'11, November 3–6, 2011, Atlanta, Georgia, USA.
ACM 978-1-4503-0820-5/11/11.

BACKGROUND
Perhaps the most common approach to measuring creativity are survey metrics – such surveys typically ask about creative attitudes or about past creative behaviors and activities. Self-report is a limitation of using surveys, but these tools are cost efficient and easy to administrate. There's also a long history of using external judges to rate the creative product of other people's work [5]. Sometimes judges are given elaborate definitions of creativity, whereas other times, no definition is provided. Amabile [1] argued for this approach because allowing people to use their own definition helped them to be more consistent and gave more reliable results. One of the main criticisms of expert judgements is that they lack discriminate validity in that judges are not able to discriminate creativity from other similar constructs [5].

Significant research also exists linking creativity and physiology. Typically, these studies look at the relationship between cortical arousal and creativity. The commonly reported findings are that creative people have higher overall cortical arousal, but when they're engaged in a creative task, they exhibit *lower* arousal than non-creative people. It is hypothesized that this occurs because creative people are able to defocus their attention, whereas non-creative people may focus their attention more and thus spike their arousal [6]. Other accepted positions are that creative people have higher variability in cortical arousal when engaged in a creative task and also that creative people use more of both brain hemispheres compared to non-creative people. These results lead us to believe that physiological measurements may be beneficial for studying ITMC.

EXPERIMENT
Sketching Activity
We conducted an experiment with 11 participants to investigate whether people were able to self-report ITMC and whether there was a relationship between self-reported ITMC and physiological measurements. Each participant sketched for about 30 minutes using a digital tool and graphics tablet. While sketching, physiological measurements were captured, which included galvanic skin response (GSR) with Affectiva Q sensor [7] and electroencephalography (EEG) with Emotiv EPOC [3]. Their sketching activity was screen recorded and when they were finished, they were asked to watch this recording through a custom interface. The self-report ITMC application allowed them to retrospectively identify when they were being creative. As they

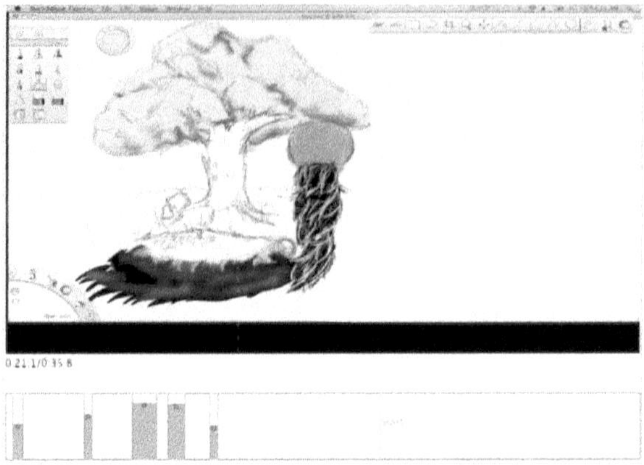

Figure 1. Custom video playback application for self-reporting ITMC. Participants assess their creativity by watching their screen recording inside the application, while using keystrokes to indicate when their creativity begins and ends. Each rectangle represents creative time periods. After identifying creative time periods, participants adjust the level of creativity using the knob inside of each rectangle.

watched the video, they were instructed to push a keystroke when they were being creative in the video and to push the same keystroke again when their creativity had ended. After the segment had been selected, a pink visual rating scale appeared. They were told to adjust the rating scale to account for how creative they felt during that segment. This process was repeated many times throughout the video in order to capture and rate all creative moments. They were not instructed on how often they should indicate creativity.

Throughout the study, several surveys were also given: the Creative Behavior Inventory (CBI) [4] to classify how creative our participants were; the Creativity Support Index (CSI) [2] to evaluate the sketching tool; and a post experiment survey to assess how comfortable and accurate participants felt when self-reporting their ITMC.

External Judges

Procedure

We used three external judges to access the validity of the participant's self-reported ITMC. We had them watch the sketching videos of each participant using the same custom application. Similar to Amabile [1], we did not give our participants any definition of creativity, however, we did specify that we were interested in people's creative process, rather than a judgment of the end product. We also discussed creativity vs. technical skills and that the judges should try to ignore the skill level when judging the creative process.

PRELIMINARY RESULTS

External Judges

We wanted to see high reliability between judges, and this was assessed by computing the Intra-Correlation Coefficients (ICCs) between all of our judges' creativity ratings across all participants as a measure of inter-rater reliability. We focused on the ICC measure for average ratings across judges, which is the reliability of taking the average of all three judges' ratings (ICC Average). We found positive results with the average of all ICC Averages being 0.61, indicating high reliability. We also looked at the reliability between judges and our participants, by computing ICCs between the average ratings of our judges and the ratings for each participants. We used ICC Single, which is the reliability of just one of the measures (opposed to the average); we found a weaker correlation at 0.24.

Physiological Measurements

We also investigated the relationship between arousal and creativity. In our preliminary analysis, we looked at autonomic nervous system (ANS) arousal as measured through GSR. We found that people who were more creative – quantified as scoring in the top 30% on the CBI survey– had higher levels of ANS arousal, than people with lower levels of creativity, but this difference was not significant. We also anticipated that highly creative people would have lower levels of arousal during highly creative moments. We found a negative correlation between GSR from creative moments and high scores on the CBI, but unfortunately it was weak and not significant ($r=-1.7$, $p>.05$). It is worth noting that many studies in physiological creativity report these trends but do not always find statistical significance. Our analysis of the EEG data is currently in progress.

SUMMARY AND FUTURE WORK

We found support for measuring ITMC through our data triangulation techniques. Our next step is to focus on analyzing the EEG data.

ACKNOWLEDGEMENTS

This work was funded by an NSF CreativeIT grant (#IIS-0855882).

REFERENCES

1. Amabile, T., Goldfarb, P., and Brackfield, S. Social influences on creativity: Evaluation, coaction, and surveillance. *Creativity Research Journal 3* (1990), 6–21.
2. Carroll, E. A., Latulipe, C., Fung, R., and Terry, M. Creativity factor evaluation: Towards a standardized survey metric for creativity support. In *Proceedings of ACM Creativity & Cognition* (2009).
3. Emotiv. http://www.emotiv.com.
4. Hocevar, D. Intelligence, divergent thinking, and creativity. *Intelligence 4* (1980), 25–40.
5. Hocevar, D. Measurement of creativity: Review and critique. *Journal of Personality Assessment 45*, 5 (463 1981), 450.
6. Martindale, C. *Handbook of Creativity*. Cambridge University Press, 1999, ch. Biological Bases of Creativity.
7. Poh, M., Swenson, N., and Picard, R. A wearable sensor for unobtrusive, long-term assessment of electrodermal activity. *IEEE Transactions on Biomedical Engineering 57*, 5 (May 2010), 1243–1252.

A Computer System Aiming to Stimulate Creativity for Narrative

Yun-Tai Chang
Master's Program in Digital Content and Technologies
National Chengchi University
Taipei 11605 Taiwan (R.O.C)
98462002@nccu.edu.tw

Sheng-Chih Chen
Master's Program in Digital Content and Technologies
National Chengchi University
Taipei 11605 Taiwan (R.O.C)
scchen@nccu.edu.tw

Tsai-Yen Li
Computer Science Department
National Chengchi University
Taipei 11605 Taiwan (R.O.C)
li@nccu.edu.tw

ABSTRACT

The goal of our research is to develop a computer system based on the concept of pictures-and-attributed-notes (PAN) aiming to stimulate creativity and imagination when users create a story. We have conducted an experiment and used the *Conceptual*, *Operational*, *Perceptional* and *Evaluation* (COPE) coding system to analyze the process of creating a story with the aid of computer system. The preliminary results revealed that the computer system based on PAN can stimulate user's creativity during the process of story creation.

Author Keywords

Creativity, Cognition, Computer-aided system, Narrative

ACM Classification Keywords

H.1.2. Information interfaces and presentation (e.g., HCI): user/machine Systems — human information processing. H.5.2. Information interfaces and presentation (e.g., HCI): user interfaces — training, help and documentation.

General Terms: Human Factors

INTRODUCTION INTRODUCTION

A good storyteller usually needs good inspiration during the story construction process. McKim [3] proposed seeing-imaging-drawing as a framework of visual thinking, which explained that visual thinking can stimulate creativity. Therefore, it is crucial to provide visual objects to enhance creativity. Rabiger [4] proposed a method to systematize the stimulating materials, called CLOSAT CARD. The storytellers write down their interpretation of a picture through six attribute elements: *character*, *location*, *object*, *situation*, *act* and *theme*. These cards are collected regularly and used when they need inspiration for writing a story. It is a helpful method to collect, store up, review and classify our imagination when we see a picture. Liu [2] reassembled a shape to provide different shapes for users, so their creativity can be stimulated through seeing more variables. This study tries to use Liu's method to reproduce more elements. But it is difficult for computer to automatically generate pictures and texts. Therefore, we propose to develop a computer-aided storytelling system, named PAN (Pictures-Attributed-Notes), aiming to stimulate users' imagination by providing pictures and attributed notes in the form of CLOSAT. In view of the preceding research purpose, the major research issue to be addressed here is as follows: How does a user create a story with the PAN system? To understand more details of the creation process, we used content analysis by adopting the *Conceptual*, *Operational*, *Perceptional* and *Evaluation* (COPE) coding system [1] and adapted sub-categories for narrative creation. By analyzing the creation process, we can contribute to the understanding of how to stimulate creativity in the creation of a story.

C&C'11, November 3–6, 2011, Atlanta, Georgia, USA.
ACM 978-1-4503-0820-5/11/11.

IMPLEMENTING THE PAN SYSTEM

The PAN system has been designed based on the Genex framework, proposed by Shneiderman [5]. The interactions between the user and the system are depicted in Fig.1. The user interface of the system consists of three main panels: *idea exploring*, *data buffer*, and *story writing area*. The goal of the idea exploring panel is showing data and giving the user stimulations when s/he is exploring. When s/he finds an interesting data item, s/he can put it into the data buffer panel for subsequent use. The user reads and generates new ideas in both two panels. Then s/he begins to arrange data, organize his/her thinking, elaborate and write down the story in the story writing panel. When developing a story, the user may go back to the idea exploring panel if s/he needs a new idea or to the data buffer panel for recalling her previous thinking. The relationship of the three panels becomes a loop through user's activity. Fig.2 shows a snapshot of the user interface of the PAN system. Since we want participants to focus on exploring data in the beginning, the idea exploring panel is maximized when a new session starts.

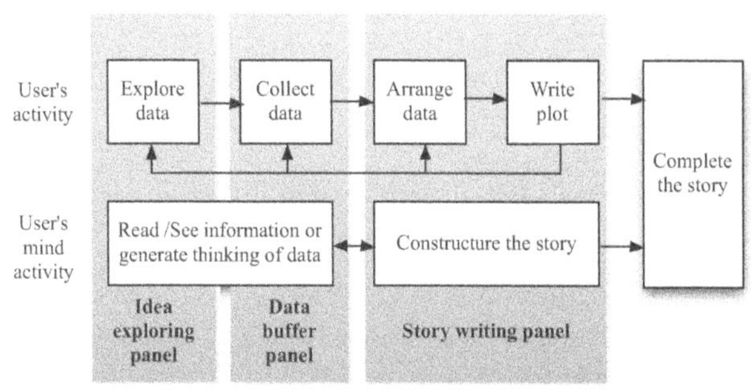

Fig.1. The interaction between the system and the user.

Fig.2. A snapshot of the user interface.

EXPERIMENTS

The initial sample consisted of only one participant, whose background is communication. The system showed 50 picture cards and the related attributed notes. The participant was asked to write a tale in about an hour. Immediately after the participant finished the task, she was asked to do protocol analysis.

RESULTS

The participant spent around one hour to create a story and used 18 pictures she picked up for the story. Then we used the COPE coding system to analyze the user's protocol data as shown in Table 1. The operational field occurred most often among all the fields because the participant explore and see the picture/text cards often to complete her story.

Conceptual	Operational	Perceptual	Evaluation
94	127	42	71

Table 1. Numbers of actions in each category.

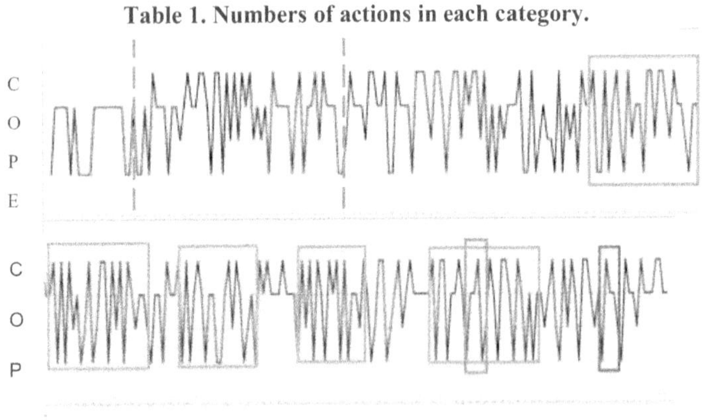

Fig. 3. Action sequence pattern in the story creating process.

Fig. 3 shows typical action sequences in the story creating process of the participant. The dotted lines divide it into 3 sessions: 1) finding what kind of elements to use, 2) viewing the elements, and 3) starting to write a story. The red rectangles in Fig. 3 are shocks composed of conceptual and evaluation actions. They occurred when the participant tried to find ideas to develop her story. During the process, she repeatedly produced thinking (C), evaluated it (E), and sometimes explored pictures (O) to generate new ideas. Following we are going to elaborate the two patterns of the creation process of the participant.

Evaluation-Conceptual-Operational (ECO) Pattern

There are many ECO patterns (blue rectangle as a representation) in the process. When the participant evaluated a picture (E) and decided to use it (E➔C), she usually dragged it directly to the story writing area, or wrote new sentences for the story (E➔C➔O). Another similar pattern with different actions happened when the participant evaluated her thinking (E), decided to use it (E➔C), and then searched pictures to find a picture represent this thinking, or revised her story (E➔C➔O).

Operational-Conceptual-Evaluation (OCE) Pattern

The OCE pattern is also common in the creating process as shown in the green rectangle in Fig. 3. The participant explored her thinking (O), decided to use it or produced a new idea (O➔C), and then appraised how to use it (O➔C➔E). When she was revising her story (O), she may recall her memory (O➔C) and then evaluated it (O➔C➔E).Another serial actions of OCE pattern are when the participant saw a picture (O) and decided to use it (O➔C), she would evaluate the idea of the picture (O➔C➔E).

The OCE pattern can mix with the ECO pattern becomes OCECO pattern. Because after the evaluation, sometimes the participant might choose another thinking as her element (O➔C➔E➔C) and then revised her story or searched pictures for using (O➔C➔E➔C➔O).

DISCUSSION

In our research, we have designed a system based on the pictures-and-attributed-notes (PAN) framework and observed the story creating process. After analyzing the creating process by COPE, we found that the process could be divided into 3 sessions and discovered the ECO and OCE patterns. In general, the preliminary experiment allows us to observe that the participant diverged and converged her thinking with our system. This matched the design goal of the system based on PAN.

REFERENCES

1. Chen, S.C., *Analysis of the use of computer media by expert and novice designers.* The International Journal of Design Computing, 2002. **3**.
2. Liu, Y.-T., *Creativity or novelty?: Cognitive-computational versus social-cultural.* Design Studies, 2000. **21**(3): p. 261-276.
3. McKim, R.H., *Experiences in Visual Thinking*1980: Brooks/Cole Publishing Company.
4. Rabiger, M., *Developing story ideas*2000, Boston, Mass. : Focal Press.
5. Shneiderman, B., *Creating creativity: user interfaces for supporting innovation.* ACM Trans. Comput.-Hum. Interact., 2000. **7**(1): p. 114-138.

MusEEGk: Design of a BCMI

Yee Chieh (Denise) Chew
Georgia Institute of Technology
85 Fifth St. NW
Atlanta, GA 30332
ychew@gatech.edu

Eric Caspary
Georgia Institute of Technology
85 Fifth St. NW
Atlanta, GA 30332
caspary.eric@gmail.com

ABSTRACT
We present a novel integration of a brain-computer interface (BCI) with a music step sequencer. Previous BCIs that utilize EEG data to form music provide users little control over the final composition or do not provide enough feedback. Our interface allows a user to create and modify a melody in real time and provides continuous aural and visual feedback to the user, thus affording a controllable means to achieve creative expression.

Keywords
Brain-Computer Interface, P300 Evoked Potential, Music composition

ACM Classification Keywords
H5.5. Information interfaces and presentation (e.g., HCI): Sound and Music Computing

General Terms
Design, Experimentation

INTRODUCTION
A brain-computer interface (BCI) is a tool that translates neural signals into a digital output. This output can allow users to control an interface or objects in their environment. BCIs for creative expression include using BCIs to paint images [6] or draw shapes [3]. Following in that vein of creativity, we designed and implemented a BCI that can be used for musical composition and performance.

Brain Computer Musical Interface (BCMI) research has been lacking in real-time user control. So far, BCMIs have produced devices where the music output is one of two things: a modulation of a pre-recorded piece or an algorithmically generated composition. There has been only one study that the authors are aware of that allows the user direct control over the output (discussed below), and none of the interfaces allow for real-time composition with continuous visual and aural feedback. Creating a reliable musical BCI will be an important step, not only for the community of musicians, but also for the realm of assistive technology.

C&C'11, November 3–6, 2011, Atlanta, Georgia, USA.
ACM 978-1-4503-0820-5/11/11.

BACKGROUND AND RELATED WORK
The most common method of measurement used by researchers looking at BCIs is electroencephalography (EEG). EEG measures electric fields produced by neurons through the use of electrodes that are placed on the scalp.

One method that researchers can employ to control a BCI combines EEG with Hjorth analysis and results in a system that is able to derive a musical piece by using a subject's brainwaves [5]. However, because this study attempts to "guess" at a musical piece, the subject has little control over the final piece that is produced. Another method used in BCI research– and the method used in this paper - is based on the P300 response. The P300 is an event-related potential (ERP) – a brain signal that occurs in response to an external stimuli. In a pilot study, researchers attempted to create a BCMI by using the P300 response to choose sequential notes from a matrix [1].

Affording the user discrete selection of individual notes is a concrete step toward building a flexible BCMI, but can be cumbersome if an individual has to compose a song by only selecting one note at a time and stringing them all together at the end. Additionally, audio feedback in this experiment was given when a note was selected and at the end of the experiment. The individual would not hear the melody of the song until after the composition was over.

P300 Based Music Composition
Our aim for MusEEGk is to create a composition program that has both a low threshold and a high ceiling. This phrase, sometimes used to describe a property of new musical interfaces or instruments, means to have a low entry/learning curve for beginners while at the same time having a high ceiling for mastery. With that in mind, we designed MusEEGk with the goal of having a system that was expressive, transparent, and flexible.

Expressive
One of our goals when designing MusEEGk was to allow for a freeform composition interface that provides constant as well as consistent feedback to the user. To do this we decided to use a traditional musical step sequencer. A step sequencer was chosen as the composition mechanism because, since selection is slow compared to a mouse click, having a system that loops allows the composition to feel longer and more complete. MusEEGk functions exactly like a traditional step sequencer, only on a slightly smaller scale. The bottom row is designated Middle C, with each

successive row one note above the previous row's note until the top row (exactly one octave above Middle C).

Transparent

The issue of interface comprehensibility revolves around the ability of the user to understand what is happening in the system and how they go about influencing the system. Users must be able to see all available actions and interpret whether or not the action taken had the desired effect. Figure 1 shows the display that our participants see. The left matrix is used for note selection and the right matrix displays and plays the selected notes. Notes that are selected are highlighted in pink and available notes are the default blue color. The selected notes remain highlighted in pink until either the session ends or the user decides to deselect that note. There is a 1:1 mapping of notes between the selection matrix and the sequencer matrix, and each note on both matrices are labeled for faster recognition.

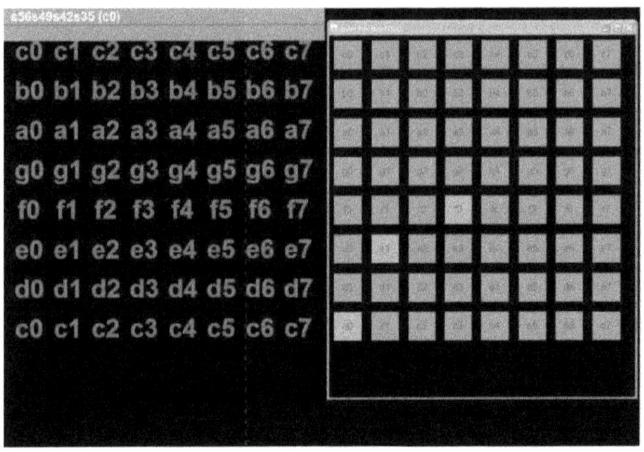

Figure 1: The left matrix (BCI2000) is used for selection of notes while the right matrix (Clojure) displays notes selected.

Flexible

Unlike in traditional interfaces, BCIs must be much more resilient to inaccurate or unintended actions. The high occurrence of such errors might lead to multiple sequential mistakes. BCI inferences should be designed to not only limit the frequency of errors, or provide means of undoing errors, but also mitigate any frustration or user anxiety that arises from errors.

In MusEEGk, the main flexibility component is the ability to deselect notes. This function allows users to undo mistakes – unintended selections by the interface or the user – and inject variety into their compositions. Furthermore, mistakes can be undone during the start of any selection period and is independent of any actions that come before. Unlike a traditional P300 speller, users of MusEEGk can choose to ignore mistakes initially and go back to correct them at a later time without long periods of forced backtracking.

EEG & Music Processing

For real-time processing of EEG data, we used BCI2000 [7]. Audio events were handled by a SuperCollider synthesis server [4] which we control via the open source Overtone music toolkit. We render the step sequencer via a wrapper around the Processing visualization library. For sound synthesis, we used the SuperCollider synthesis engine [4]. The audio loop runs at a tempo of 110 beats per minute, allowing for approximately three loops during a single note selection. Visualizations were created using the Processing graphical library, and interaction with SuperCollider was handled by the Overtone library. MusEEGk is written in Clojure [2].

This interface was tested on twenty-one participants who were given approximately six minutes to create a composition of their choice. Post-experiment questionnaires rating the task difficulty, task enjoyment, and tune enjoyment as well as comments on the interface were collected. Results showed that the task was not difficult, that it was enjoyable, and that users generally enjoyed the tune they created. This suggests that MusEEGk is a viable design for a brain-computer music composition interface that can be used for creative expression. Future work will look at enhancing the user experience by allowing more customization of sounds and tempo as well as including the addition of a start/stop button.

ACKNOWLEDGEMENTS

The authors would like to thank Melody Moore Jackson, Parag Chordia, and Ellen Do for their advice and support throughout this project.

REFERENCES

1. Grierson, M. Composing with Brainwaves: Minimal Trial P300 Recognition as an Indication of Subjective Preference for the Control of a Musical Instrument. Proceedings of the ICMC, (2008).
2. Hickey, R. The Clojure programming language. ACM Press, New York, New York, USA, 2008.
3. Mappus, R., Venkatesh, G., Shastry, C., Israeli, A., and Moore, M.M. An fNIR Based BMI for Letter Construction Using Continuous Control. Extended Abstracts from the Conference on Human Factors in Computing Systems (CHI), (2009).
4. Mccartney, J. SuperCollider : a new real time synthesis language. 4-7.
5. Miranda, E.R. and Brouse, A. Toward direct brain-computer musical interfaces. New Interfaces For Musical Expression, (2005).
6. Rapoport, E.D., Nishimura, E.M., Zadra, J.R., et al. Engaging, Non-Invasive Brain-Computer Interfaces (BCIs) for Improving Training Effectiveness & Enabling Creative Expression. Human Factors and Ergonomics Society Annual Meeting Proceedings, Human Factors and Ergonomics Society, (2008).
7. Schalk, G., McFarland, D.J., Hinterberger, T., Birbaumer, N., and Wolpaw, J.R. BCI2000: a general-purpose brain-computer interface (BCI) system. IEEE transactions on bio-medical engineering 51, 6 (2004), 1034-43.

Influence of Design Tools on Conceptually Driven Processes

Amod Damle
University of Wisconsin
Stevens Point
B 246, 2001 4th Avenue
adamle@uwsp.edu

Trudi Miller
University of Wisconsin
Stevens Point
B 246, 2001 4th Avenue
Trudi.Miller@uwsp.edu

ABSTRACT
Design thinking literature suggests that design tools can influence early design activities in a bottom-up, data-driven manner. This study suggests that design tools can influence design thinking in a top-down manner and cause designers prematurely to fixate on the details of a design solution. Further, such fixation can take place before a designer actually utilizes these features to produce a sketch.

ACM Classification Keywords
DJ.4 Computer Applications: SOCIAL AND BEHAVIORAL SCIENCES

General Terms
Experimentation, Theory

INTRODUCTION
The perception of partially developed external drawings aids the process of generating novel design solutions [4]. The influence of external sketches on the generation of design solutions can be characterized as a bottom-up or data-driven process [6]. Some design tools influence such bottom-up processes by making it more or less difficult for designers to produce partially developed, tentative drawings [3]. Unlike bottom-up processes, top-down or conceptually determined processes are driven by a designer's knowledge of a design problem and can occur prior to the generation of external sketches.

Previous research indicates that design environments can act as external representations and influence conceptually driven processes involved in solving a design problem. For example, Damle and Smith [2] and Damle [1] found that the availability and utilization of multiple colors to develop a sketch created a perceptual and cognitive discontinuity and caused designers to adopt a depth-first strategy. The term "depth-first" refers to a design strategy that involves adding details to the individual components of a design before attending to its overall form. The authors explain the findings using a model that attributes the utilization of a depth-first strategy to perceptual grouping as discussed by Gestalt psychologists.

Gestalt psychologists demonstrate that our perceptual system groups visual elements based on their similarity or proximity and separates them from the surrounding area [5]. The surrounding area is perceived as ground while the perceptual cluster forms the figure. We attend to the grouped entities in a focused manner and ignore what falls in the background. Color is known to be a strong stimulus for triggering Gestalt-like grouping of elements into discrete categories [7]. Damle and Smith [2] and Damle [1] argued that the availability of colors compelled the participants to segregate the basic components of their designs by rendering each component in a different color. Segregation of components through color variation caused participants to attend to the components in a focused manner and ignore the overall form. Although the authors suggest that the availability of colors influenced designers to adopt a depth-first strategy, their experiments do not allow us to determine whether or not such behavior can be attributed to top-down processes alone. In other words, the viewing of a multicolored sketch could have triggered data-driven processes and caused designers to adopt a depth-first strategy. The current study was designed to verify whether or not the mere idea of using multiple colors could influence design thinking in a top-down manner.

C&C'11, November 3–6, 2011, Atlanta, Georgia, USA.
ACM 978-1-4503-0820-5/11/11.

METHODS
Forty-five design students enrolled in a 16-week prototyping course were randomly assigned to two groups.

Task description
Group one, the multi-color group, was provided with a *MS Word* document containing the instructions shown below (Figure 1).

> You have been provided with an ink pen that allows you to draw in four different colors: Yellow, red, black, and blue.
>
> Imagine creating a detailed line drawing of a table lamp using this pen. Type the imagined sequence of actions that you might perform in order to complete the drawing.

Figure 1: Instruction given to the multi-color group

Group two, the single-color group, was provided with a slightly different set of instructions seen in Figure 2.

> You have been provided with an ink pen. Imagine creating a detailed line drawing of a table lamp using this pen.
>
> Type the imagined sequence of actions that you might perform in order to complete the drawing.

Figure 2: Instruction given to the single-color group

Hypothesis

The research focused on whether the idea of having access to multiple colors could influence designers to adopt a depth-first strategy even at the stage before actually perceiving and utilizing multiple colors to develop a sketch.

Data analysis

Two independent coders not involved with any other aspect of this study coded the data. It was said that the participants had adopted a depth-first strategy if their reports indicated that they wanted to outline a component and add details to it before sketching the outline of the next component. If the participants mentioned that they wanted to embellish the outline of a component with a decorative pattern, tone, shade and light, or the rendering of a specific material, it was said that they were adding details to the component. The data were analyzed using the Fisher's exact test. Additionally, the obtained data were analyzed using hierarchical logistic regression analysis with color and gender as two independent variables.

RESULTS

Interrater reliability for the raters was found to be Kappa = 0.97, 95% CI (0.93,1) suggesting that the two coders were in almost perfect agreement with one another. Nineteen out of 21 participants (90.47%) from the multi-color group indicated that they would use multiple colors to develop their sketch. One out of 24 participants from the single-color group indicated that he wanted to draw the outline of a component and add details before sketching the outline of the next component. Six out of 21 participants from the multi-color group did the same. A statistically significant p value of 0.03 was obtained from a 2-tailed Fisher's exact test. Hierarchical logistic regression analysis showed that the availability of multiple colors had a significant effect ($p=.058$) on the number of participants reporting that they utilized a depth-first strategy. This variable was positively correlated to the observed scores ($b=2.155$, standard error= 1.136, Nagelkerke $R^2 = .207$). Gender ($b= .602$, standard error= 1.194, $p=0.614$, Nagelkerke $R^2 = .028$) did not have significant effect on the number of participants adopting a depth-first strategy.

DISCUSSION

The current findings suggest that the availability of multiple colors can influence designers to adopt a depth-first strategy. For example, one of the participants from the multi-color group mentioned that she would outline the base of the lamp and fill it with the color blue. She would make the base look three-dimensional by adding highlights. She would then draw the outlines of the remaining components and complete them one at a time. The multi-color group was asked to imagine drawing a sketch with a pen that could produce four different colors. As a result, the multi-color group's design strategy cannot be attributed to the perception or utilization of colors. The findings suggest that it was the idea of utilizing colors that caused cognitive discontinuities and made the problem representation more modular. This study indicates that a design environment itself can act as an external representation prior to the creation of a sketch and shape the representation of a design problem. The mental representation of a design problem subsequently influences the development of a sketch. Given the small sample size, one needs to be cautious in generalizing the current findings. Additionally, the results could have been different if the participants were art students. Art students receive explicit instructions to attend to the overall form of an object during the preliminary stages of drawing or painting. As a result, they could have ignored the presence of colors and instead sketched the overall form of the lamp using only one color.

REFERENCES

1. Damle, A. Utilizing monochromatic design views to avoid a premature fixation on design solutions. *Human Factors*, *52*. pp. 28-40.
2. Damle, A. and Smith, P. Biasing cognitive processes during design: the effects of color. *Design Studies*, *30*. pp. 521-540.
3. Fish, J. and Scrivener, S. Amplifying the minds eye: sketching and visual cognition. *LEONARDO*, *23*. pp. 117-126.
4. Goel, V. *Sketches of thought*. MIT Press, Cambridge, MA, 1995.
5. Kohler, W. *Gestalt Psychology, an introduction to new concepts in modern psychology*. Liverlight, New York, 1947.
6. Scrivener, S., Ball, L. and Tseng, W. Uncertainty and sketching behavior. *Design Studies*, *21*. pp. 465-481.
7. Triesman, A. Perceptual Grouping and Attention in Visual Search for Features and for Objects. *Journal of Experimental Psychology: Human Perception and Performance*, *8*. pp. 194-214.

Correlation between Coherent Heart Rate Variability and Divergent Thinking

Gina Deininger
University of Wales Institute, Cardiff
Cardiff, CF5 2YB, UK
gideininger@uwic.ac.uk

Gareth Loudon
University of Wales Institute, Cardiff
Cardiff, CF5 2YB, UK
gloudon@uwic.ac.uk

ABSTRACT

In this paper, a new quantitative method is proposed for measuring the unconscious mind in the incubation stage of the creative process. The method uses Heart Rate Variability (HRV) as a measure of the emotional and mental state of the participants. The creative process is measured quantitatively by the degree of divergent thinking shown by participants during a study of idea generation. The aim of the study is to see if there is a correlation between coherent HRV and divergent thinking.

Authors' Keywords

Conscious, unconscious, creativity, divergent thinking, HRV, coherence.

ACM Classification Keywords

J.4 Social and Behavioral Sciences.

General Terms

Experimentation, Measurement and Performance.

INTRODUCTION

In the 1920s, Wallas [8] proposed four stages to creative thinking. These were: preparation (the stage of investigation); incubation (the stage in which one is not consciously thinking about the problem); illumination (the spontaneous insight); and verification (where the insight is consciously verified and applied).

In the 1950s, Guilford [3] proposed traits of creativity that included divergent thinking, where divergent thinking was defined as the exploration of many possible answers rather than thinking toward one right answer (convergent thinking).

Wallas suggested that during the incubation stage "voluntary abstention from conscious thought from any particular problem may, itself, take two forms: the period of abstention may be spent either in conscious mental work on other problems, or in a relaxation from all conscious mental work".

In 2006, Dijksterhuis and Meurs [2] explored the relationship between incubation and divergent thinking by running a comparative study of "different modes of thought and the generation of creative and original ideas". The result of their study showed that a period of non-conscious thinking (using a method spent on conscious mental work on another problem) led to higher divergent thinking.

The aim of this study is to replicate the work of Dijksterhuis and Meurs [2] but instead explore Wallas's second form of incubation, i.e. "relaxation from all conscious mental work" in relation to divergent thinking.

BACKGROUND

The authors have previously run a series of creativity workshops with undergraduate and postgraduate students exploring the role of the conscious and unconscious mind in the context of product design and innovation. This involved monitoring their mental and physiological states during the creative process using Heart Rate Variability (HRV) as a key indicator.

HRV has been shown to be one of the promising methods for measuring Autonomic Nervous System (ANS) activity [5]. In addition, there is evidence to suggest that there is a close relationship between HRV and neural activity in the frontal midline area of the brain [4] and that there is a link between emotional states and HRV [6]. HRV has the additional advantage over Electroencephalography (EEG) recording because of its simplicity of use and reliability.

During the creativity workshops participants were asked to undertake a design challenge. Whilst observing the participants in the incubation stage (of the creative process) it was found that there was a change in the pattern of the HRV signal from a random signal to a more periodic (orderly) oscillation.

This effect of the change in HRV pattern from random to more orderly was also shown in studies by Tiller et al. [7] who used the measure of coherence to quantify this changing HRV pattern in looking at emotional states.

This led to the idea of replicating the study of Dijksterhuis and Meurs using Wallas's mental relaxation form of incubation (in the creative process) and using the HRV coherence measure as an indicator of mental relaxation to see if there is a correlation between HRV coherence and divergent thinking.

METHODOLOGY

Overview of the experiment

The methodology followed closely the methodology used by Dijksterhuis and Meurs in Experiment 1 of their study conducted in 2006 [2]. As in their experiment, participants

C&C'11, November 3–6, 2011, Atlanta, Georgia, USA.
ACM 978-1-4503-0820-5/11/11.

were instructed to generate new names for pasta. As before, five examples were given of existing pasta names and all examples ended with the letter "i".

It was shown in the study conducted by Dijksterhuis & Meurs that conscious thought led to more generated pasta names that end with an "i" (converging items), whereas unconscious thought generated more names that did not end with an "i" (diverging items) .

Participants and Design

48 undergraduate students from the University of Wales Institute, Cardiff were recruited to participate in this experiment. They were randomly assigned to one of three conditions (as was the case in the experiment by Dijksterhuis and Meurs): an immediate generation condition, a conscious thought condition, and an unconscious thought condition, with 16 students per condition.

Procedure and Materials

During the experiment, participants worked in a separate room and instructions for the exercise were given in printed format. The experiment was introduced as being an experiment on Enquiry Based Learning and participants were asked to generate new names for pasta.

In the instruction, five examples of existing pasta names were listed, all ending with the letter "i". The participants were hooked up to a monitoring device that recorded their HRV. After participants read the instructions, they were randomly allocated to one of the three conditions.

In the immediate generation condition, they were immediately asked to list new pasta names. They were given one minute to complete this task. In the conscious thought condition, participants were given three minutes to think about new pasta names before they were given one minute to list new names. In the unconscious thought condition, participants were first told of the task but then asked to generate the pasta names sometime later and that they should first 'chill out by watching the monitor in front of them for a few minutes'. These participants would then watch a three minute software program [1] on a monitor (that has been shown to help increase HRV coherence) before they were given the one minute to list the pasta names.

The Coherence Coach program [1] by HeartMath was used to assist the participants to move into a 'relaxed mental state' as defined by Wallas as the second form of the unconscious thought condition necessary for the incubation period of creativity. The task was introduced to participants as a chance to 'chill out' whilst waiting to begin the task.

RESULTS

Table 1 shows the mean number of pasta names created by the participants for each condition that ended in the letter "i" (converging items) and those that did not (diverging items).

	Immediate	Conscious thought	Unconscious thought
Converging	4.7	3.5	2.2
Diverging	2.3	1.8	2.6

Table 1. Mean number of convergent and divergent items.

Table 2 shows the percentage of diverging items created compared to the total number of items created.

Immediate	Conscious thought	Unconscious thought
35%	31%	50%

Table 2. Percentage of divergent items created.

Therefore the results matched those of Dijksterhuis and Meurs where unconscious thinkers (but through mental relaxation this time) diverged more than participants in the other two conditions. However there was no clear, direct correlation between the HRV coherence values and divergent thinking, across the conditions. This area therefore needs further study and analysis.

REFERENCES

1. Coherence Coach. Retrieved April 24, 2011, from Institute of HeartMath: http://store.heartmath.org/cd-roms/coherence-coach-cd
2. Dijksterhuis, A. and Meurs, T. Where creativity resides: The generative power of unconscious thought, *Consciousness and Cognition,* 15 (2006), 135–146.
3. Guilford, J.P. Traits of Creativity in Anderson, H.H. (ed.), *Creativity and its Cultivation*, Harper, 1959, 142-161.
4. Kubota, Y., Sato, W., Toichi, M., Murai, T., Okada, T.,Hayashi, A. and Sengoku, A. Frontal midline theta rhythm is correlated with cardiac autonomic activities during the performance of an attention demanding meditation procedure, *Cognitive Brain Research*, 11 (2001) 281–287.
5. Malik, M. Heart Rate Variability: Standards of Measurement, Physiological Interpretation, and Clinical Use: Task Force of The European Society of Cardiology and the North American Society for Pacing and Electrophysiology, *Annals of Noninvasive Electrocardiology,* Volume 1, Issue 2 (April 1996), 151–181.
6. McCraty, R., Atkinson, M., Tiller, W.A., Rein, G. and Watkins, A.D. The Effects of Emotions on Short-Term Power Spectral Analysis of Heart Rate Variability, *American Journal of Cardiology*. 1995; 76 (14): 1089-1093.
7. Tiller, W.A., McCraty, R. and Atkinson, M. Cardiac Coherence: A New, Noninvasive Measure of Autonomic Nervous System Order. *Alternative Therapies in Health and Medicine,* 1996;2 (1): 52-65.
8. Wallas, G. *The Art of Thought*, Jonathan Cape, 1926, 79-96.

Phenomenologies of Practice: The Artist in Virtual Worlds

Dr Denise Doyle
School of Art and Design
University of Wolverhampton
Wolverhampton, WV1 1SB UK
+44 1902 322443
D.Doyle@wlv.ac.uk

ABSTRACT

In the field of art and technology engagement with virtual worlds as spaces for creative practice challenges and enhances our understanding of the phenomena of imagining. The experience of creating in technology-mediated spaces (through an avatar form) brings the phenomenological experience of the body into the act of creating itself. Ways of explaining this creative process and its relationship to imaginative experience highlights a phenomenology of practice *of artists working in this realm. This article considers the implications of the methodological approaches that have been chosen in an inter-disciplinary context and the case for investigating artistic and imaginative experience through adapting phenomenological research methods. It presents the results of the analysis and provides an account of the method of Imaginative Variation and its adaptation for use in new contexts.*

Author Keywords

Phenomenology of Practice, Creativity, Technology, Imaginative Variation, Second Life, Avatar Body.

ACM Classification Keywords

Computing Methodologies

General Terms: Experimentation, Human Factors

INTRODUCTION

According to Edward Casey 'imagination (in Western thought) is not securely situated in regard to such decidedly different acts as sensory perception and conceptual thinking' [2]. Perhaps this is because 'imagining is easy enough to enact as experience, but it is extremely difficult to capture in midair for the purposes of scrutiny and examination' [2]. This paper considers the importance of investigating imaginative experience in relation to the process of artistic creativity through adapting phenomenological research methods and discusses the ways in which the 'virtuality' of the space and the art created have impacted on the analysis of what is termed here as the *phenomenology of practice* of artists working in virtual space.

C&C'11, November 3–6, 2011, Atlanta, Georgia, USA.
ACM 978-1-4503-0820-5/11/11.

Since it's inception eight years ago artists have been exploring the virtual space of *Second Life* where the act of creating is already mediated through technology. The *Kritical Works in SL* exhibitions were presented during 2008 and 2009 on Kriti Island (that acts as a laboratory space for ongoing artistic and imaginative practice research in *Second Life*). As an artist-researcher a strategy was to create a presence on the platform and invite others to participate. Following the realisation of the exhibitions, interviews were conducted with six of the participating artists and analysed for the artist's insight in the context of creating immersive and interactive experiences in the *Second Life* space.

THE METHOD OF IMAGINATIVE VARIATION

Moustakas observes that 'the uncovering of the essences, the focusing on pure possibilities, is central in the Imaginative Variation process' [4]. The principle key structural themes within this method draw on what 'we imagine [as] possible structures of time, space, materiality, causality, and relationship to self and to others' and that through this method 'countless possibilities emerge that are intimately connected with the essences and meanings of an experience' [4]. In turn the essences and meanings of an experience are reduced to key elements that are identified at the stage of being tested as an invariant constituent. Consideration was given to how reductive this particular method of Imaginative Variation should be in attempting to understand *a phenomenology of practice* in avatar-mediated online space that may equally suggest an individual variance of experience. However, Imaginative Variation appeared to be a most notable method in which to understand experiences such as time, space, and materiality.

The Van Kaam method, as presented by Moustakas, was followed through from (1) horizonalization, the listing of every expression relevant to the experience; (2) reduction and elimination, to reveal the horizon of experience; (3) the clustering of the invariant constituents into thematic labels which represent the core themes of the experience; and (4) final validation, that the core themes are expressed explicitly or are compatible with the interview itself [4]. The final four steps of the Imaginative Variation method presented by Moustakas were modified slightly for final presentation within the mixed-method approach of the research. Typically, a full study such as this would be with twelve to fifteen co-participants and a final textual-structural description of the whole group would be created (this being the overall outcome of the research). However, in this study, the method was used to inform a broader study of the artist and the artist's work in avatar-mediated space.

A PHENOMENOLOGY OF PRACTICE: 'REAL BUT NOT REAL'

In the final step of the Imaginative Variation method the research brings together the experience of all of the participants (in this case the six artists working in the *Second Life* space) and is presented in what is described as a Textural-Structural description of the variations and essence of the experience. In this phenomenological account of the experience a poetics of writing is fashioned to enable the possibility of Bachelard's phenomenological reverberation [1].

Textural-structural description of the artist group

The artists' experience of time and space in *Second Life* was one of an increased and heightened awareness, whether that was in simply reflecting the experience of the physical world or conversely being set free of the constraints of the laws of the physical world. There was a freedom associated with the 'timelessness' of the space, of 'not being handcuffed to a situation', rather 'being unlocked from time'; of having the opportunity of 'being in a different space and time' and 'to be set free in the space'. Space is invariably experienced as one that does follow the logic of the physical world and this is only reinforced by the 3D nature of the grid itself. There is a sense of the known and there is something comfortable about the logic of the space. An artist comments that:

> *Second Life* does have that kind of traditional perspective sensibility to it. And the way that things represent in the space is very much according to traditional perspective visualisation and it feels very comfortable in that sense [3].

Conversely, the space is also experienced as a lived space and evokes other experiences such as the experience of a mirrored or other world, or a world that both evokes and reflects the experience of dream states, one that is 'half clear and true and half a story that is made up'. The playfulness of the space was experienced by a number of the artists, and for some it felt like 'a big toy sand box' or like being in 'a theme park'. Closely linked to the experience of space is the sense of embodiment in the space and the ways in which the artists developed and engaged with their avatar(s). The intense sense of immersion through the embodiment of the avatar was a common experience amongst the artists. For some, the avatar is a way of being 'in two spaces at once', or to experience an aspect of themselves 'in concurrent time'. For another the avatar is an extension 'of myself that allows me to be in a different space and time'. Some artists experienced a playfulness and desire to explore their own identity through the avatar, and for others embodying the persona of another person (whether real or imagined) made them feel like they were 'a different person'. Sometimes a sense of immateriality in the space reinforced the materiality of the physical world, and inversely, at times a sense of materiality of virtual space itself was suggested. This tension is expressed in the 'lack of physicality', or a 'stepping away from reality', and 'an almost physical way of creating the imaginary and the impossible'. This 'tangible imagination world' all challenged the artists' sense of what it means to experience the material. At the centre of the responses to *Second Life*, of this 'hyper-real place', and what is expressed above in the vividness of the imaginative experience, is a 'freer and more expressive space' in order to be mentally 'set free in the space'.

CONCLUSIONS

Adapting existing phenomenological methods (a particular approach taken in this research) was a strategy that uncovered the true richness of the interview material. Using this method of analysis on the data brought into focus another layer of the artist's experience of practice in the space. In writing a phenomenological account of the artists' experience of creative practice in *Second Life*, a richness and variety of experience was able to be included in the final textural-structural description. The opportunity to play with time and space were seen as an important aspect of the potential of the space for creative investigation and there was a freedom associated with this loosening of time-space relationships. The heightened experience of the imagination was consistently seen as something difficult to describe. This almost physical, almost tangible, was a particularly interesting expression used by some of the artists. This points to the phenomenological experience of the imagination and the opportunities that arise in technology-mediated space for the experience and understanding of creative practice and the extent to which the body, and in turn the avatar-mediated body, informs those creative and imaginative processes.

REFERENCES

1. BACHELARD, G. *The Poetics of Space.* Beacon Press, Boston, 1994. Originally published in 1958. Translated by M. Jolas.
2. CASEY, E. *Imagining: A Phenomenological Study.* Indiana University Press, Bloomington & Indianapolis, 2000.
3. DOYLE, D. *Art and the Emergent Imagination in Avatar-Mediated Online Space.* PhD THESIS. SMARTlab, University of East London, 2010.
4. MOUSTAKAS, C. *Phenomenological Research Methods,* SAGE Publications, Thousand Oaks, California, 1994.

Creative Strategies in Artists' and Engineers' Approaches to Technology Development: First Results of a Case Study

Jill Fantauzzacoffin
Department of Digital Media
Georgia Institute of Technology
Atlanta, Georgia USA
jill@gatech.edu

Juan D. Rogers
School of Public Policy
Georgia Institute of Technology
Atlanta, Georgia USA
jdrogers@gatech.edu

Jay David Bolter
Department of Digital Media
Georgia Institute of Technology
Atlanta, Georgia USA
jay.bolter@lcc.gatech.edu

ABSTRACT

In this paper we present early findings from our comparative case study of the work practices of artists and engineers independently developing similar technologies. We describe two patterns of creative strategies: *teleological* and *stochastic*. We also draw a connection between these creative strategies and our subjects' negotiation of the uncertainty inherent in the creative process.

Author Keywords: Creativity, innovation, art, engineering.

ACM Classification Keywords: H5.m. Information interfaces and presentation (e.g., HCI): Miscellaneous.

General Terms: Theory, Design.

INTRODUCTION

While engineering is the assumed path to technology development, increasingly throughout the 1990s and 2000s artists working with high technologies have been developing novel technologies and novel applications of technologies [1]. We have designed and are carrying out a comparative case study that identifies artists and engineers (or engineering teams) working separately but developing similar technologies. We focus on describing and illustrating the work practices of the artists and engineers within these comparative cases in order to establish evidence-based articulations, or vocabularies, to advance the understandings of creative practice particularly with respect to technological innovation in the arts and engineering. In this paper we present some of our early findings.

STUDY METHODOLOGY

The artists and engineers in our study are paired into comparative dyads based on their development of similar technologies. Our subjects are pursuing these projects on their own accord in the course of their professional work without orchestration for study or academic purposes. We collect data on our subjects' work practices through observation, documentation of work artifacts, and semi-structured interviews over the course of six months. We are currently studying two single-artist/engineering team dyads and one artist/computer science team dyad. We are not studying the work of every individual on a team. Instead we focus on the lead engineer or artist and augment our understanding by also studying the work of one of their co-workers, if applicable.

Case studies are often used to study "real life" phenomena in depth in order to understand complex relationships and mechanisms in detail. As is well established in the literature of qualitative methodologies [2, 3], the generalization of a case study does not proceed to the prediction of attributes of a population in the way that a statistical study would. We will not be reporting outcomes such as "The majority of engineers work in this way, and the majority of artists developing technologies work in that way." Instead, we give name to and articulate phenomena in play during our subjects' creative work as we witness it. We do not expect to generalize these results to the entire population, but to use our concentrated lens to articulate phenomena that occur within these arenas of creativity and innovation. The advantage of theory developed from case studies is that it is grounded in rich, well-developed evidence.

PREVIOUS WORK

This work is indebted to previous research and documentation, including documentation of artists' and engineers' collaborations for E.A.T. (Experiments in Art and Technology) beginning in the 1960s [4], chronicles of the Xerox PARC artists-in-residence program in the 1990s [5], Linda Candy and Ernest Edmonds' studies of collaborative digital arts projects in the COSTART program [6], Jill Scott's Swiss Artists-in-Labs ethnographies [7, 8], as well as multiple articles from the Creativity and Cognition conferences and throughout the forty years of the *Leonardo* corpus [9].

FINDINGS

We found that studying the parallel processes of artists and engineers conceptually bound together through similar projects and technologies throws the work processes and design decisions of each group into relief. We have identified two distinct patterns to the creative strategies observed in our two artist/engineering team dyads. We characterize the engineering teams' overall creative strategy as *teleological* and the artists' creative strategy as *stochastic.*

Teleology is a central concept in philosophy. A process is teleological when its end acts as a final cause that directs its development. The final cause can be thought of as a predetermined purpose, target, or end state toward which the piece develops. In the cases we studied, this final cause was determined during the initial stages of work and was

C&C'11, November 3–6, 2011, Atlanta, Georgia, USA.
ACM 978-1-4503-0820-5/11/11.

projected forward as either a final form of a technology or a set of requirements to be met by the technology. The engineers worked toward this target while constantly checking the emergent work against that target as a reference, iteratively refining it to match that final cause. Thus the concept of the invention and/or the project requirements served not as a beginning point, but as a terminal reference. As the engineers faced intermediate problems and resolved them, they came to deeper and more detailed understandings of that final cause.

Stochastic processes are probabilistic processes with non-deterministic outcomes. In comparison with the teleological creative strategy, which determines the final cause early in the process and manages each step in reference to the final cause, the stochastic creative strategies we witnessed in the work of our artists proceeded as a random walk with transitions from one step to another as the process unfolded. Here the term 'random' has a precise definition, meaning not that the process is arbitrary or aimless, but that it is not possible to precisely predict the outcome. The trajectory of the random walk consisted of successive decision points. At each decision point the artist conjured multiple paths. A subset of these paths were taken to achieve convergence to a design.

Processes within processes

Our characterization of the creative strategies of the engineers and artists in our study are not absolute. For example, we found interesting bursts of stochastic strategy emerge during the fabrication stage of one of our engineering teams under study. When materials and equipment did not produce an anticipated result, novel fabrication methods had to be devised and even improvised. This led to a stochastic sequence of events which in turn led to an aha moment that ultimately expanded the applications to which the technology could be put. This in turn enabled the technology to reach additional markets.

Relationship to uncertainty

We can interpret the teleological and stochastic creative strategies we witnessed as ways to negotiate the uncertainty of the creative process. A teleological strategy has many advantages including coordinating project work among individuals within a team and ensuring that criteria such as the public safety, reliability, efficiency, cost effectiveness, and improving quality of life are met. We found that in our cases, it was also a way to manage the uncertainty of the creative process. This is expressed by a lead engineer when describing his design methodology:

The detailed analysis adopted in arriving at the {anonymized} design minimizes the risks associated with the success of the project. All the performance requirements {anonymized} can be met by the design and the fabrication technologies are well-proven in the {anonymized} industry further improving the chances of success.

Project stabilization and predictability were priorities of the engineering teams we studied. A teleological creative strategy is one way to cultivate this stabilization through minimizing uncertainty. For our engineering subjects, it was important not to deviate from the project plan. It was a priority to constrain the path toward the final cause.

The artists in our study negotiated the uncertainty of the creative process by maintaining internal criteria of authenticity. Staying true to their own individual sense of the project's integrity allowed them to negotiate the vagaries of the stochastic creative process with as little negative impact as possible on their well-being. One artist expressed this in the following way:

When I talk about the project as being well-formed, I feel like I'm able to coherently project into the future what my personal goals for the project are. It's something I can trust. So instead of a project taking me on a wild ride, I feel like I have a better relationship to it.

While the engineers in our cases used a teleological creative strategy to ensure that they met external criteria such as public accountability, budgets, or timelines, it was important for the artists in our cases that their projects maintained an internally-determined authenticity. Staying true to this internal compass allowed them to endure the uncertainty of the stochastic process in a healthy way.

CONCLUSION

Through the careful and in-depth comparison of work practices between artists and engineers developing similar technologies, we have constructed and characterized two creative strategies, teleological and stochastic, described here. It would be a mistake to take away from this paper that we are saying that all engineering processes are teleological and all art processes are stochastic. The main contribution of this paper is to give us a vocabulary to discuss patterns of creative strategies and to understand future cases, as well as to articulate the relationship between these creative strategies and the negotiation of the uncertainty inherent in the creative process.

ACKNOWLEDGMENTS

This research is funded by NSF CreativeIT grant 1002820.

REFERENCES

1. Artsactive.net:patents available at http://www.artsactive.net/en/resources/patents.
2. Yin, R.K. *Case Study Research: Design and Methods*. Thousand Oaks, California: Sage Publications. 2008.
3. Miles, M.B. and Huberman, A.M. *Qualitative Data Analysis*. Thousand Oaks, California: Sage Publications. 1994.
4. Experiments in Art and Technology (E.A.T.), Klüver, B., Martin, J., and Rose, B., eds. *Pavilion*. New York: E.P. Dutton and Co. 1972.
5. Harris, C., ed. *Art and Innovation: The Xerox PARC Artist-in-Residence Program*. Cambridge, MA: The MIT Press. 1999.
6. Candy, L. and Edmonds, E. *Explorations in Art and Technology*. London: Springer-Verlag. 2002.
7. Scott, J., ed. *Artists-in-Labs: Processes of Inquiry*. Wien: Springer-Verlag. 2006.
8. Scott, J., ed. *Artists-in-Labs: Networking in the Margins*. Wien: Springer-Verlag. 2010.
9. *Leonardo, the journal of the International Society for the Arts, Sciences and Technology*. Cambridge, Massachusetts: MIT Press.

Beyond Participation: Empowerment, Control and Ownership in Youth-Led Collaborative Design

Lalya Gaye
Culture Lab Newcastle
Newcastle University
Newcastle Upon Tyne, UK
lalya.gaye@ncl.ac.uk

Atau Tanaka
Culture Lab Newcastle
Newcastle University
Newcastle Upon Tyne, UK
atau.tanaka@ncl.ac.uk

ABSTRACT

We describe a collaborative design project with a group of young people in which an interactive educational information pack for teenagers was implemented. Instead of just providing input to a design project, the young people initiated, controlled and partially implemented the project themselves, with the support of an interdisciplinary research team. Here we present this approach to participatory design research, describe the design process and show that initiative, control, and hands-on engagement in youth-led collaborative design, can bring to the young people a strong sense of ownership and empowerment.

Author Keywords

Participatory design, initiative, DIY, control, ownership, empowerment, youth, interactivity, engagement.

ACM Classification Keywords

H.5.2. Information interfaces and presentation (e.g., HCI): User Interfaces: User-Centered Design.

General Terms

Design, Experimentation, Human Factors, Management.

INTRODUCTION

In many participatory design (PD) research projects, the impetus of the project comes from the researchers themselves, not from the other participants: design researchers are often the ones who initiate the project, and retain control and ownership over its outcome, especially in projects involving children or young people. The power relationship this brings up can sometimes stray from the initial objectives of PD [1] and miss opportunities to empower participants, as well as weaken the project's sustainability and long-term innovation: What happens once the collaboration stops? Once researchers have moved on to another project, are participants able to take on a prototype's development to push it further or adapt it to changes of circumstances? How dependent are the participants on the researchers or other stakeholders in terms of being able to actually use the developed system, prototype or artefact in the real world? In the project described in this paper, we explored turning around the power balance in such a way that the "participants" themselves would be the ones taking the first initiative, having most control over decision-making in the design process, and retaining ownership over results – thus putting the researcher in the position of a facilitator, a contributor… or a participant. For this we applied the notion of youth-led innovation [2, 4] and used a DIY (Do-It-Yourself) approach where participants develop and implement their project themselves and take it to the direction of their choice; our role being that of facilitators. This relates closest to the work of Druin in terms of direct engagement of children as researchers into a design research project (e.g. [3]) but differs in the power balance between researchers and participants – equally distributed in Druin's work, and mainly retained by the young people in ours.

Here we describe this case study in which this power-balance between researchers and young people was reversed, and show that initiative-taking, having control over the decision-making and partially implementing the project themselves can have a strong impact on the sense of ownership and sense of empowerment for the young people at the core of project.

CASE STUDY

The project described in this paper was a collaboration between our research lab and a youth-work organization (Regional Youth Work Unit) – more specifically with their Youth Advisory Board, which included young people aged 15 to 18. The project consisted of developing an interactive information pack that the young people wanted to implement but did not know how to. The concept – which was brought by the young people themselves – was to provide concise and information about future educational paths for 14-19 year-olds enrolled in English schools and encourage dialogue between the young people and their carers (parents or tutors) about their aspirations and educational goals, in a playful and engaging manner. The young people had a very clear vision of how they wanted the information pack to be used, about its user experience and strongly believed in the importance of making this pack

C&C'11, November 3–6, 2011, Atlanta, Georgia, USA.
ACM 978-1-4503-0820-5/11/11.

easily accessible for a majority of young people in the region and in making its use playful and interactive.

The resulting prototype became a CD-ROM – for reasons of socio-economical accessibility – that contained the information in a form similar to a website. It was coded in html in order to enable the young people to easily update, maintain and sustain the textual content themselves after the end of the project, and also had animations coded in flash. The prototype consisted of three sections: 1) an 'About' section describing the purpose of the pack and the young people's aspiration for doing this project; 2) a 'Get to Know Me' interactive game for a young person and their carer(s) focused on the subjects of ambitions and interests; 3) a 'World of Possibilities' part that would then enable users to navigate through their available educational options.

In order to facilitate the design of this prototype we gathered an interdisciplinary team of experts and worked with the young people during weekly design sessions of two hours over period of 2 months. In these sessions, the young people developed most of the prototype, and our role was to assist them in designing and implementing it. A set of rules and goals for collaboration inspired by the DIY ethos had been put in place: a) The young people would be implementing the project themselves (to the limit of their ability), and we would mostly guide them in the process; b) They would be the ones having the final say in decision-making moments; the final judges in evaluating the success of the resulting prototype and would retain intellectual property and legal ownership over the resulting product; c) The process would aim at enabling them to maintain, update and sustain the prototype themselves at the end of the collaboration; d) The aim of the process was to implement the envisioned interactive information pack, not strive for innovative design with user input.

The sessions consisted of periods of plenary discussion and decision-making, and periods of focused design work in separate groups. The young people grouped themselves according to their interests in graphic design, game interaction, user experience design, textual content or programming, and were tutored by us. The composition of these groups was however fluid and open rather than fixed, and all groups worked in parallel, most of the time in the same room. Important components of the work sessions facilitation were to make sure there was enough turn-taking in conversations, that the opinions of less vocal young people would be heard, that goals that had been set could be realistically met with the timeframe and skills at hand, and to manage the time devoted to each design activity.

OBSERVATIONS AND OUTCOME

Interesting observations made during the sessions were that some young people were more hands-on in the process than others who assumed more on higher-level management roles; that shy people came to contribute as much as loud ones; and that sessions were very informal in tone and language. Trust had been established in such a way that the young people did not fear to say what they had in mind.

After implementing the prototype, our research team conducted an group interview-based evaluation of the impact of the design process format on the sense of ownership and empowerment of the young people involved in the project, and whether it had met their expectations. This showed through complete control over decision-making in the design process, the resulting prototype very much corresponded to what the young people had initially envisioned and was very positively received. They also felt a strong sense of ownership over the project's outcome, individually and as a group, and through working on it had gained significant amounts of knowledge in web-design and project management, which would be useful for them in keeping the prototype up-to-date, and even applicable in other projects. In terms of collaboration among the different stakeholders of the project, the young people largely found it to be successful due mutual trust and respect, enthusiasm, and being considered equals to adults in the project.

CONCLUSIONS AND FUTURE WORK

We have described a case study in which we applied notions of youth initiative and DIY hands-on engagement in the design process. This approach had led to a strong sense of ownership and empowerment in the young people involved in the project. Our next step will be to help the young people set-up a youth-led user study of the prototype in a real-world setting, and study the long-term sustainability of the project in how the young people themselves will take it further.

ACKNOWLEGMENTS

This project is funded by the British EPSRC through the SiDE project. We wish to thank RYWU, in particular the young people from YAB and Neil Burke; the rest of the facilitator team (Steven Ronnie, Andrzej Wojtas, and Simon Honeywell); and Ranald Richardson, Joëlle Bitton and Andreia Cavaco for valuable feedback.

REFERENCES

1. Bjerknes, G., Ehn, P., Kyng, M., and Nygaard, K. (1987) *Computers and Democracy: A Scandinavian Challenge*. Gower Pub Co.
2. Bragg, S., England, A. C., and Partnerships, C. (2007) Consulting Young People: A Review of the Literature: a Report for Creative Partnerships. Arts Council England
3. Druin, A. (1999) Cooperative inquiry: Developing New Technologies for Children with Children. *Proc. CHI'99*.
4. Sebba, J., Griffiths, V., Luckrock, B., Hunt, F., Robinson, C., and Flowers, S. (2009) Youth-led Innovation: Enhancing the Skills and Capacity of the Next Generation of Innovators. NESTA

The Taste of Criticism: Enhancing Feedback for Creativity

Georgi V Georgiev
School of Knowledge Science, Japan Advanced Institute of Science and Technology
Nomi, Ishikawa, Japan
georgiev@jaist.ac.jp

Yukari Nagai
School of Knowledge Science, Japan Advanced Institute of Science and Technology
Nomi, Ishikawa, Japan
ynagai@jaist.ac.jp

ABSTRACT
Criticism is important for cultivating creativity. In this paper, we propose a method to enhance feedback to creators of creative works. We separate the explicit evaluation from the implicit evaluation. We pay particular attention to cases in which the viewer expresses a positive evaluation of a work but the actual implicit evaluation is rather negative. In such cases, the feedback of the implicit criticism is important for creativity. We describe a prototype system designed to deliver such feedback to the creator. The feedback interface is represented by the taste of green tea, directly delivered to the creator, thus motivating the creator.

Author Keywords
Feedback system, creator, implicit evaluation, impressions.

ACM Classification Keywords
H.4.m. Information Systems Applications: Miscellaneous; H.5.m. Information Interfaces and Presentation: Miscellaneous.

General Terms
Design, Experimentation, Languages.

CRITICISM FOR CREATIVITY
In order to cultivate creativity in any field, critical feedback is important. Creative and critical thinking are two sides of the same coin [4]. However, strong criticisms do not usually reach the creators. This study is based on the idea that true critical evaluation can be detected in the comments of *viewers* and delivered confidentially to the *creator*. In this study, we use the term *creator*, which refers to the designer, artist, or author of the work being discussed. Constructive criticism is necessary for enhancing creativity [1] and for the further improvement of a work. Critical evaluation plays a common role in many areas where technical appreciation is not the only aspect being evaluated. For example, in the domain of the arts, the typical evaluation mechanism is to evaluate works based on criticism from professional groups and expert critics in a particular field. Creators sometimes have difficulty accepting criticism. Fear of negative criticism is a common problem, which often negatively affects the work and thus, creativity [1]. Moreover, no matter how well the creator is prepared to accept them, deep criticisms can be unacceptable to a creator. In the field of design, critical evaluation is based on criticisms by non-experts (users) rather than experts, and analysis of the content of criticism is essential to detect the true evaluation [2]. The real motivation effects of evaluation are often hidden, even from the evaluator; however, creators' designs can benefit from such feedback. In other words, despite the differences in critique in the art, design and other creative fields, critical evaluation fosters creativity. It is necessary to extract and provide *feedback* from the meanings hidden behind superficial evaluation (Figure 1). However, harsh criticism can cause tremendous stress in its recipient. Therefore, it is necessary to devise a method to communicate such evaluations. A *system* for providing such feedback would allow criticism without the risk of damaging relationships, because its meaning would be undisclosed to others.

C&C'11, November 3–6, 2011, Atlanta, Georgia, USA.
ACM 978-1-4503-0820-5/11/11.

STUDY
We pay attention on cases where the viewer expresses a positive opinion regarding a work but their actual opinion is rather negative (Figure 1). In such cases, the feedback of the actual opinion is important for creativity. Hence, the main question is how to enhance creativity through criticism without damaging it. In this study, we propose a prototype system to enhance feedback to creators of creative works based on the implicit evaluations of the viewer (usually, but not restricted to, art or design works). The *goal* of this study is to detect the deeper criticism or appraisal within an explicit evaluation and provide a proper interface to relay that criticism or appraisal to the creator without disclosing it to others. When proposing a method for providing critical feedback, we considered embodied and mediated feedback. As for the *method* of analysis and evaluation, we explore the associations behind each impression (verbalization) given by a person who interacted with a created work. Associations are the stimulus words used to evoke these explicit impressions.

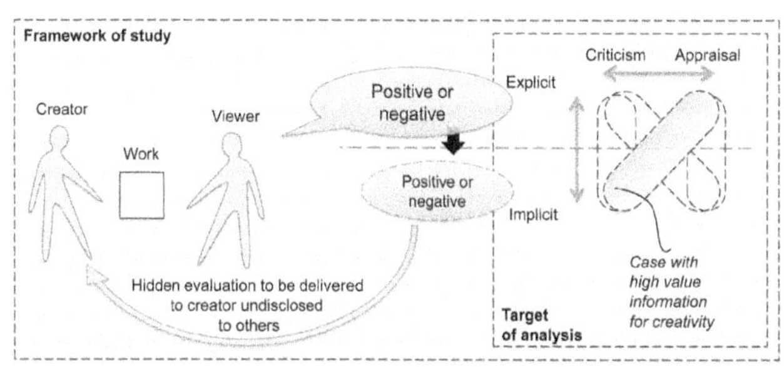

Figure 1. Framework of study and target of analysis.

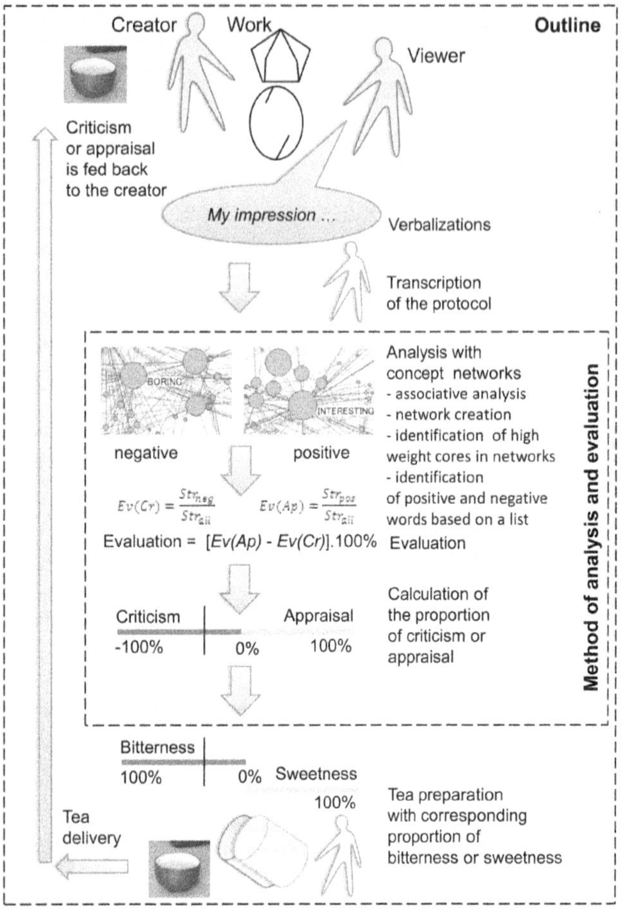

Figure 2. Outline of the prototype system and method.

Case	Implicit evaluations		Delivered feedback by tea (aver.)
	Criticism	Appraisal	
Paper lamp	–50% e.g. "burn"	-	(–)50% (bitterness)
Paper lamp	-	100% "comfort."	(+)100% (sweetness)
Stained glass lamp 1	-	100% "grace"	(+)100% (sweetness)
Stained glass lamp 2	–66.7% "alarm"	-	(–)70% (bitterness)

Table 1. Implicit evaluations and feedback in four cases.

We employ a concept network-based methodology to identify these implicit association words, which lie beneath the superficial impressions of a work [3]. The words obtained in this analysis are mapped in concept networks and separated into words with negative and positive meanings (Figure 2), based on a list of words created by experts. We considered the *weight* of the positive and negative words in the concept network as an indicator of the strength of the criticism and appraisal. Delivering such feedback to a creator with numbers or visualizations is not expected to be effective without compromising their feelings. In order to deliver criticism undisclosed to others that was likely to be accepted, we developed a system in which criticism is represented by specific tastes—*tea interface*. Negative criticism was conveyed by giving the creator bitter taste (green tea catechins (GTC)) and positive criticism was conveyed through sweetness (Figure 2), serving our purpose for embodied and mediated feedback. We use a tea blended for amount of bitterness/sweetness, averaged at 10%. The addition of taste does not affect the heath of the creator and remains undisclosed to the viewer.

To examine the proposed identification method for the critical evaluation, we conducted a four case *experimental study* with non-experts in the field (Table 1). For example, the data subset obtained in the first case was: Ev=[(0/0.0048)–(0.0024/0.0048)].100=–50%. All explicit evaluations were classified as positive by the creator. The creator, after tasting the evaluation of own works, could recognize and compare the evaluations.

DISCUSSION AND CONCLUSIONS

This study describes a method to enhance feedback to creators of creative works in order to convey implicit feedback, to ultimately enhance further creativity. The study analyses implicit criticisms based on experimental results. The identified and evaluated implicit information is represented by an embodied and mediated interface—green tea. The proposed system requires the creator to literally taste the criticism their work receives. If the evaluation is positive, the creator is provided with sweetened tea. Conversely, if the evaluation is negative, the creator is provided with bitter-tasting tea. The true intent of viewer evaluation is confidently delivered, contributing to the creator's self-evaluation and intrinsic motivation. We showed the results of evaluations of four works, which resulted in different degrees of criticisms. The feedback system allowed creators to discern differences between explicit and implicit evaluations—possibly fueling further creativity. Future plans aim at improvements and investigating the effects on creators.

REFERENCES

1. Amabile, T.M. How to kill creativity. *Harvard business review 76,* September-October (1998), 76-87.
2. Gwilt, I., Georgiev, G.V. and Nagai, Y. Fabrications of Natural and Artificial: A Case Study of Enhancing Users' Impressions. *1st Int. Conf. on Design Creativity (ICDC2010),* (2010).
3. Nagai, Y., Georgiev, G.V. and Zhou, F. A methodology to analyze in-depth impressions of design on the basis of concept networks, *Journal of Design Research 9,* 1 (2011), 44-64.
4. Runco, M.A. Critical thinking. In Runco, M.A. and Pritzker S.R. (Eds.), *Encyclopedia of Creativity 1,* Academic press, San Diego, CA, USA, 1999, 449-453.

Do HCI Researchers Use Computers?

Gunnar Harboe
University of Zürich
Binzmühlestrasse 14, 8050 Zürich, Switzerland
harboe@ifi.uzh.ch

ABSTRACT

Doing scientific research involves creative and complex forms of thinking. This paper examines the effect that information and computer technology (ICT) has on research practice. I present a bibliographic study that examines the role of ICT as a research tool in the field of human–computer interaction (HCI) through an analysis of 79 CHI papers, identifying five themes in their references to ICT. Among recent ICT developments, the internet is found to have had the greatest effect on research methods.

Author Keywords

science, technology, HCI, scientometrics

ACM Classification Keywords

K.4.m. Computers and Society: Miscellaneous

General Terms

Human Factors

INTRODUCTION

Scientific research requires advanced cognitive processes and creative imagination [5], involving "the processes of human thinking in some of its most creative and complex forms." [4] Throughout scientific history, technology has played an important role in the research process. What impact might it thereby have on what scientists do and how they think?

Because HCI researchers are trained to observe and understand human needs, to imagine how computer technology might address them, and to design and implement those systems, one might expect that they would be the first to create and take advantage of computer tools in their own research. We will see if this is the case.

Does Technology Influence Science?

The old linear model of technology development held that science makes discoveries and technology applies those discoveries. [1] Accordingly, science is of paramount importance to technology, but any effect of technology on science is unaccounted for.

However, some ways in which technology may influence science are: enabling new scientific instruments, providing practical problems that motivate scientific advances, and supplying analogies for understanding problems.

C&C'11, November 3–6, 2011, Atlanta, Georgia, USA.
ACM 978-1-4503-0820-5/11/11.

The *law of the instrument* ("it is tempting, if the only tool you have is a hammer, to treat everything as if it were a nail" [7]) asserts that the tools you have available influence what you consider to be worthwhile problems and how you go about solving them. This insight suggests that available technologies determine what kind of research gets done, and what activities are considered research.

More detailed analyses of the impact of technology range from the *technological imperative* ("technology [is] an exogenous force which determines or strongly constrains the behavior of individuals and organizations") to social constructivist and emergent perspectives that emphasize how social structures determine the role of technology. [6]

In any case, we can distinguish *incremental changes* where technology simplifies or speeds up methods that were already used, and *qualitative changes* where it leads to the creation of new research methods. The impact of ICT on research varies between fields, [3] and I therefore examine one particular field, HCI, as a case study.

STUDY

I investigated the use of ICT in HCI research through a document analysis where I looked at 79 full papers from the CHI conference every 5 years from 1990 to 2010, and open-coded [8] the references to ICT I found in them.

I examined the five most highly cited papers and ten other randomly selected full papers from each conference. For 2010 and 2005 I examined the "best paper" nominees instead of/in addition to highly cited papers.

Finally I tagged each paper with multiple overlapping codes. To validate the codes, another researcher separately coded five of the papers. There was agreement in the coding except for the application of one particular code, and the coding scheme was subsequently refined.

Some limitations of this method are immediately obvious. Nevertheless, I believe the approach is useful as an exploratory investigation, to form some initial impressions and hypotheses about the evolving role of ICT in HCI research, and to identify possible patterns and questions for further inquiry.

The results (Table 1) show that by far the most common way ICT is involved in HCI research is as the subject of the research. However, only a minority of papers (too small to identify trends over time or paper type) report actually employing ICT tools specifically for research.

Research Subject	**(69)**	
proto-probe	(37)	*A system that prototypes and evaluates a design concept*
existing system	(30)	*Research on an existing system*
prototype	(11)	*A system that prototypes a design concept, without evaluation*
Research Tools	**(15)**	
experimental probe	(15)	*A system to run an experiment, not to be studied for itself*
analysis tool	(1)	*A system to support the analysis and interpretation of research data*
Standard Methods	**(29)**	
statistical analysis	(24)	*Data analyzed using statistics software*
log analysis	(22)	*A system stores a log of data, which are then analyzed*
Adapted for Online	**(14)**	
online recruiting	(8)	*Participants recruited via online communication (web, email, ...)*
online survey	(5)	*An online survey or questionnaire administered remotely*
web scrape	(5)	*Content to populate a system with data collected from an online source*
online test	(4)	*A user test or experiment administered remotely online*
online interview	(3)	*An interview conducted via online communication (IM, videochat, ...)*
web deployment	(2)	*A prototype system deployed online to a wide user base*
New Data Sources	**(7)**	
message analysis	(3)	*Computer-mediated messages collected and analyzed*
social network study	(3)	*Study of social data from an online social network*
user media analysis	(2)	*Media created or collected by a participant analyzed (photos, videos, ...)*
experience sampling	(1)	*Data collected digitally through experience sampling*
Miscellaneous	**(4)**	
video capture	(2)	*Video recorded in ways not possible with analog recording*
recorded interactions	(2)	*User interactions recorded and later played back for use in tests*

Table 1: Categories of references to information and computer technology in the papers analyzed, with number of papers in which the category appears and explanation of the category.

Use of experimental probes, log analysis and statistical analysis is fairly common, and represents standard, long-established methods. The remaining codes refer to somehow novel research methods that have been enabled by ICT. The biggest cluster of these utilize the internet. They are generally incremental modifications of well-established approaches.

A modification to an old method that is dramatic enough to qualify as a qualitative shift is *research in the large* [2]: the ability to deploy a prototype system online to potentially astronomic numbers of users.

Computer connectivity has also generated new collections of data that may be analyzed. A small number of studies in the sample examined communications between users on online forums, took advantage of people's online social networks to run group studies, or examined user-created media like photos and videos.

Finally, I only found one paper in the sample that described creating an ICT tool to support or assist in the study analysis, and there were no reported tools to assist scientific creativity. This may be an opportunity for improvement.

In summary, conservative methods of experimental instrumentation, logging and statistical analysis dominate, but new ways of doing research enabled mainly by the internet have been applied effectively in a few studies. The technologies changing research today and in the near future could include smart phones, social network sites and microblogging. Given the many and intimate links between technology and science, there should be a multitude of ways for technology to augment and amplify scientific creativity and cognition.

ACKNOWLEDGMENTS

I would like to thank Elaine M. Huang for help with the coding and input on the ideas of this research.

REFERENCES

1. Barnes, B. The science-technology relationship: A model and a query. *Social studies of science*, (1982).
2. Cramer, H. et al. Research in the large. *Ext. Abs, Proc. UbiComp*, (2010).
3. Heimeriks, G. and Vasileiadou, E. Changes or transition? Analysing the use of ICTs in the sciences. *Social Science Information 47*, 1 (2008), 5.
4. Klahr, D. and Simon, H.A. Studies of scientific discovery: Complementary approaches and convergent findings. *Psychological Bulletin 125*, 5 (1999), 524.
5. Magno, C. Assessing the Relationship of Scientific Thinking, Self-regulation in Research, and Creativity in a Measurement Model. *International Journal 6*, 1.
6. Markus, M.L. and Robey, D. Information technology and organizational change: causal structure in theory and research. *Management science*, (1988), 583–598.
7. Maslow, A.H. *The psychology of science: A reconnaissance*. Harper & Row, 1966.
8. Strauss, A.L. and Corbin, J.M. *Basics of qualitative research: Techniques and procedures for developing grounded theory*. Sage Publications, Inc, 1998.

Measuring Creative Impact with Web-based Data

Richard W. Hass, Ph.D.
University of Delaware
Department of Psychology
Newark, DE 19716 USA
rhass@psych.udel.edu

ABSTRACT

This paper reviews a method of collecting creative-impact data utilizing the All Music Guide (AMG, www.allmusic.com) database. This type of data is suitable for quantitative analysis and has been used to test cognitive-psychological hypotheses about the creative process. Implications are discussed.

ACM Classification Keywords

J.4 Social and Behavioral Sciences: Psychology; J.5 Arts and Humanities: Music

General Terms

Measurement, Standardization, Theory

Author Keywords

Creativity, Creative Impact, Musical Composition

INTRODUCTION

Creativity has often been operationalized in psychological research in terms of the impact that a creative product has on a domain, culture, or society at large [2,12] but impact-related phenomena are nearly impossible to observe in a laboratory. As an alternative, so-called historiometric methods have been developed to measure creative impact throughout the careers of historically important creators. Historiometric data are quantitative data constructed from any kind of psychologically-significant archival data [9]. Examples of such data include information in public records (e.g., copyright dates, sales figures, auction values), as well as any data pertaining to recognition of creative achievement (e.g., awards or textbook citations).

Historiometric analysis has been successful in the examination of creativity in classical music [8,9,12], science [3,11], and the arts [4]. Until now, there has been no attempt to compare text-based historiometric data, used in older analysis, with database historiometric data available via the Internet. This paper will outline the advantages to using electronic databases and wikis like All Music Guide (AMG, www.allmusic.com) for collecting historiometric data. A review of text-based methods is out of the scope of this paper but can be found elsewhere [3,4,9,11].

MEASURING CREATIVE IMPACT OF POP SONGS

Recently Hass and Weisberg [5] conducted a variant of historiometric analysis (the quantitative case study method [12]) that focused on the careers of two popular-music composers: Irving Berlin and Cole Porter. We found that tabulating the number of times each song from Berlin's and Porter's body of work was covered by another artist and appeared on an album in the AMG database served as a valid measure of creative impact that was well correlated with other text-based measures. Since then AMG data has been tabulated for a number of American popular songwriters [c.f. 6] and continues to provide an important source of information of creative-impact data.[1] The following sections outline the advantages and limitations of the methodology.

Advantages

There are two main advantages to collecting AMG data. First, since AMG qualifies as a wiki, the criteria for inclusion of a work in the database are unbiased and transparent. That allows for reliable and standardized assessments of all composers, not just those deemed important by a reference-book author. The only criterion for a commercial album's inclusion in the database is that it is a valid representation of an artist's work (i.e. no bootlegs or unauthorized recordings). For example, a search for Cole Porter's "Night and Day" returns a list of all commercial albums containing the song, recorded by any artist since the publication of the song—a cumulative measure of impact. In other words, AMG data are not merely snapshots taken at the time of publication of a particular reference work.

AMG also has a search function for composers who, unlike Porter, performed their own work (e.g. John Lennon and Paul McCartney). For example, one can search the AMG database for the name "John Lennon" and AMG will return an artist profile. Part of the profile is a tab labeled "songs composed by", which applies a filter such that a list of songs composed by John Lennon but *not* performed by Lennon or the Beatles is populated. Use of that filter avoids the inflation of cover counts that might result from tabulating Lennon songs that appear on Beatles releases. Thus, songwriters like Lennon can be treated in the same

[1] The cover-count data are analogous to citation counts, a valid and reliable measure of impact of scientific theories and inventions [c.f., 3,11], and to the consensual assessment technique [1]. That is, the choice to cover a song made by a bandleader or the choice to include a previously recorded song on an anthology made by a record producer is analogous to the choice made by an author citing another author's work, or the choice made by a committee to recognize achievement.

C&C'11, November 3–6, 2011, Atlanta, Georgia, USA.
ACM 978-1-4503-0820-5/11/11.

fashion that Porter was treated, thus ensuring standardized procedures for all kinds of popular-music composers. A forthcoming publication will present the results of a non-linear trend analysis of Lennon's and McCartney's careers using AMG data.

Second, AMG specifically allows measurement on a ratio scale (integers). That is, the data are frequencies and, as such, are fit for statistical procedures commonly employed to analyze laboratory data. This is advantageous since the distribution of impact ratings is highly skewed for popular songs. As in experimental studies, skewed data can be made fit for parametric statistical analysis via a number of data transformations. For example, a forthcoming publication will utilize square-root-transformed impact ratings for approximately 800 songs from The Great American Songbook for the purpose of quantifying the relationship between impact and melodic originality.

Limitations

First, the data collection process, though supported by web-based software, is manual. That is, in order to accurately tabulate cover-counts, each album must be counted manually and entered into a spreadsheet. In addition, once the data have been tabulated two control measures must be implemented. Broadway composers like Porter, issued their songs as parts of musicals, and the songs often are available on a series of full-cast recordings of the show, which also populate the AMG database. In order to ensure those recordings do not inflate the cover-counts, the number of cast-album recordings must be subtracted from each song's cover count.

A related limitation involves the influence of historical time on cover counts. Preliminary analysis of AMG cover counts from the careers of the Beatles, David Bowie, Bob Dylan, and the Rolling Stones revealed that cover counts monotonically declined from the 1980s to the present day. A special transformation can be employed as a remedy though it too requires an extra step: cover counts must be weighted in terms of the number of years the song has been commercially available. In a forthcoming analysis of the Beatles, Bowie, Dylan, and the Rolling Stones, all raw cover counts subjected to the transformation, mathematically eliminating the years-available effect.

Finally, cover counts only represent the impact of a particular song on the domain of popular music and do not provide direct measures of cognitive, social, or emotional influences on the creative process. However, the results of existing AMG studies, using career age as a predictor of impact, provided positive evidence for a cognitive phenomenon—the ten-year rule—in the careers of Porter and Berlin [5] as well as songwriting teams like the Gershwins and Rodgers and Hart [6]. Forthcoming publications will focus on cognitive and social correlates of the impact ratings and will allow for more direct conclusions about the creative process.

GENERAL IMPLICATIONS

Wiki databases like AMG provide the opportunity to quantify creative-impact in more accurate and dynamic ways than text-based reference sources. AMG data is reliable, valid, and allows for standardized data collection across a variety of individual cases. Methods are being developed to directly identify the music-psychological correlates of the AMG impact ratings, and to investigate other psychological evidence of the creative process [c.f., 7]. The results of such future work will be valuable in obtaining a more complete psychological understanding of the creative process and will be beneficial to music education.

ACKNOWLEDGMENTS

Special thanks go to Robert Weisberg for laying the groundwork for this paper.

REFERENCES

1. Amabile, T. (1982). Social psychology of creativity: A consensual assessment technique. *Journal of Personality and Social Psychology*, 43, 997-1013.
2. Csikszentmihalyi, M. (1999). Implications of a systems perspective for the study of creativity. In R. J. Sternberg (ed.), *Handbook of creativity* (pp. 313-335). Cambridge: Cambridge University Press.
3. Feist, G. J. (1993). A structural model of scientific eminence. *American Psychologist, 4*, 366-377.
4. Galenson, D. (2005). *Old masters and young geniuses: Two life cycles of artistic creativity*. Princeton, NJ: Princeton University Press.
5. Hass, R.W. & Weisberg, R.W. (2009). Career development in American popular songwriters: A test of the equal odds rule. *Creativity Research Journal, 21*, 183-190.
6. Hass, R. W., Weisberg, R. W., & Choi, J. (2010). Quantitative case studies in musical composition: The development of creativity in popular-songwriting teams. *Psychology of Music, 38*, 463-479.
7. Hass, R. W., Weisberg, R. W., Kwok, S. (in review). The musical expertise of Cole Porter: A quantitative case study. *Psychology of Aesthetics, Creativity, and the Arts.*
8. Kozbelt, A. (2004). Reexamining the equal-odds rule in classical composers. In J.P Frois, P. Andrade & J.F. Marques (Eds.), *Art and Science: Proceedings of the XVII Congress of the International Association of Empirical Aesthetics* (p. 540-543).
9. Kozbelt, A. (in press). Age and aesthetic significance in classical music: A multi-level reanalysis of Halsey's (1976) ratings. *Empirical Studies of the Arts.*
10. Simonton, D. K. (1977). Creative productivity, age, and stress: A biographical time-series analysis of 10 classical composers. *Journal of Personality and Social Psychology, 35*, 791-804.
11. Simonton, D. K. (2003). Scientific creativity as constrained stochastic behavior: The integration of product, person, and process perspectives. *Psychological Bulletin, 129*, 475-494.
12. Weisberg, R.W. (2006). *Creativity: Understanding innovation in problem solving, science, invention and the arts.* New York: John Wiley and Sons.

Creativity Barometer: An Approach for Continuing Micro Surveys to Explore the Dynamics of Organization's Creativity Climates

Angela Carell
angela.carell@rub.de

Thomas Herrmann
thomas.herrmann@rub.de

Jan Nierhoff
nierhoff@iaw.rub.de

Universität of Bochum
Universitätsstraße 150
44780 Bochum, Germany

ABSTRACT

An approach has been designed for computer-supported micro surveys which measure dynamic changes of an organization's creativity climate. Employees are unobtrusively prompted to occasionally answer single questions. The main challenges are to ensure acceptance and to maintain a high participation. This is done by guaranteeing anonymity, avoiding perturbation and distraction, giving valuable feedback, and including aspects of entertainment.

Author Keywords

Creativity climate, employee survey, micro survey

ACM Classification Keywords

H.5.3. Group and Organization Interfaces

General Terms

Human Factors, Measurement

INTRODUCTION

Innovative companies must be aware of the creativity climate – the "...stimulants and obstacles to creativity in organizational work environments [1]". In the past, several survey instruments for measuring this climate of organizations and to encourage organizational change have been developed and tested (e.g. KEYS: Assessing the Climate for Creativity, [1]; TCI, Team Climate Inventory, [3]). But due to the increase of economic pressure, these instruments turn out to be insufficient: Fast economical changes force organizations to change and adapt their processes, products or services in less time and foreshorten the periods in between these changes. A very high workload and uncertainty about one's own employment could be the results and are main obstacles for creativity [2]. This causes difficulties for those companies which have to rely on their innovativeness and therefore on the creativity of their employees.

To enable organizations to timely counteract unpropitious developments, we see the need to overcome the limitation of one time a year surveys. For example [5] examined in a meta-analysis that the time between preparing a survey and presenting the results lasts eight months on average. Approaches and instruments of dynamic surveys have to be developed. Also, they have to shift from single or occasional surveys to continuing micro surveys, which are able to monitor and feedback the current creativity climate of a company or a team.

C&C'11, November 3–6, 2011, Atlanta, Georgia, USA.
ACM 978-1-4503-0820-5/11/11.

The Creativity Barometer provides immediate feedback by repetitively prompting the employees to give their opinion. By continuously evaluating the given answers, the employees can observe the development of their own attitude and mood and they can comprehend how their colleagues perceive the creativity climate. Moreover, aggregated data are provided for both, the management and the employees. Traditionally implemented employee surveys (whether online or offline) are not able to meet theses affordances.

This article presents the main features of the Creativity Barometer, a prototype for computer-supported micro surveys. It measures and reflects the creativity climate constantly and unobtrusively. We describe the challenges as well as our suggestions to meet them. The prototype is currently in operation in six companies with four more following soon. First results will be available by August 2011. We have designed a highly adaptive solution which can be easily modified and applied to different organizations or to certain events such as conferences.

CHALLENGES, SOLUTIONS AND PROTOTYPICAL IMPLEMENTATION

A tool for continuing surveys has to motivate the employees to participate and to acquire their acceptance. One central requirement is to guarantee complete anonymity if needed. Online surveys are conceived to provide anonymity. Therefore, our tool, the Creativity Barometer, is implemented as a web service and so this advantage of online surveys directly applies to the project.

The main challenge regarding the continuous character of the survey is to maintain a high participation rate over a long period of time. Answering the questions may be perceived troubling if the questions disturb the workflow or if the prompts for answering a question are presented at an unfavorable point of time. Because of the repetition of the questions the news value decreases quickly, which could be a negative influence on the participants acceptance and motivation. To face all these challenges the Creativity Barometer is based on the three following principles:

None-obtrusiveness and self determination - The participants are enabled to answer the questions very fast without getting distracted from their workflow. We are testing several approaches to this problem by identifying typical short idle phases during work when employees are usually bored since they have to wait for something: Referring to these situations, we provide popups during the booting process of the computer, access to the survey via a terminal located at the coffee kitchen, a mobile device, or a modified screensaver. The participants can freely decide when and where they answer questions. The only restriction is that they have to complete a given amount of the questionnaire within a predefined timespan or else their answers cannot be regarded in the evaluation of that survey cycle without distorting the results (e.g. a minimum of three answers in four weeks regarding the category *autonomy*). This survey cycles help synchronizing the feedback to whole groups (e.g. teams or departments) and enable us to reflect a company's creativity climate at fixed points of time. To retain a satisfying participation rate within the given freedom of decision, several awareness-raising activities are applied (e.g. email reminder, calendar entries or home screen widgets) to prompt the employees and to offer them multiple occasions to answer the questions.

Short actions – Every prompt being displayed to the employee only requests the answer to one single question. The phrasing of the question is as simple as possible so it can be easily understood. The employee only has to choose his answer on a scale of 1 to 7. Picking one option is usually connected with the activation of an additional function of the computer or the mobile device, such as opening a certain webpage or unlocking an application.

Entertainment and stimuli – It is for sure the best motivator if the participants enjoy using the Creativity Barometer. Ways to achieve this are a fetching experience design, different ways to answer questions that are rich in variety (e.g. mini games, photos, drawings…) and community features. Additionally the tool offers content that aims at stimulating the participants' creativity and thereby acts as a first, small intervention on the lowest level.

Confidence and transparency via continuous reflection – The employees should not get the feeling of being monitored by the survey. The Creativity Barometer approaches this requirement on two levels: Confidence has to be created on the organizational level. The Creativity Barometer is not a tool that judges the creativity of individual employees. Instead it reflects the corporate culture. It is an instrument of organizational development, which empowers the employees to actively change the environment they work in for the better. Transparency is achieved by the openness of information. There is no data that is exclusive to persons in leading positions. The results of the whole company and of any group are reflected to every employee. Additionally personal results are reflected. Striking differences between the own and the group results are highlighted. The Creativity Barometer also confronts the users with information about their behavior of answering. Apart from data about the current answering cycle, notifications that an users way of answering differs much from the average way of answering is given to the participants (e.g. very high/ low answering rate or long spans of time between logins at the service)

THE SET OF ITEMS

The Items which we use in the Creativity Barometer derive mainly from well-known and tested instruments, for example from [1] and [3]. They are categorized in 7 components like *encouraging leadership, pursuit of ideas, autonomy or freedom, pressure, team spirit, vision, and challenging work.* A typical example, which has to be rated, is: "Ideas which have been created in our team, are pursued by our company." Typically there are around 40 items for a company. Moreover, we combined creativity-related questions with a health-related perspective and included nine questions of the Salutogenese Concept developed by [4]. The underlying assumption of this approach is that creativity and health are highly intertwined and influence each other. Incidentally, the Creativity Barometer allows us to test this hypothesis. The data provided will enable us to run a variety of analyses which help individuals and teams as well as the management to understand their situation and the development of the creativity climate.

TECHNICAL IMPLEMENTATION

The Creativity Barometer is implemented as a Web service which can be consumed by a wide array of different devices such as…. Possible clients may be desktop applications, web applications, smartphone apps or widgets integrated in third party websites. This also enables the participants to use the service independent of time and location and makes it possible to develop micro applications that only serve the purpose of answering questions en passant.

REFERENCES

[1] Amabile, T. et. al. (1996). Assessing the work environment for creativity. *Academy of Management Journal* **39** (5), 1154-1184.

[2] Amabile, T. & Conti, R. (1999). Changes in the work environment for creativity during downsizing. *Academy of Management Journal*, 630--640.

[3] Anderson, N. & West, M. (1998). Measuring climate for work group innovation: development and validation of the team climate inventory. Journal of organizational behavior 19(3), 235-258.

[4] Antonovski, A. (1979). Health, stress and coping: New perspectives on mental and physical well-beeing. San Fransisco: Jossey-Bass

[5] Hossiep, R. & Frieg, P. (2008). Der Einsatz von Mitarbeiterbefragungen in Deutschland, Österreich und der Schweiz. [The Use of Employee Surveys in Germany, Austria and Switzerland] *Planung & Analyse, 6(2008)*, 55-59. [Only in German]

Improvisational Theater for Computing Scientists

Raquell Holmes
University of Connecticut Health Center
263 Farmington Ave
Farmington, CT 06030
860-679-7519
rholmes@uchc.edu

ABSTRACT

Computing disciplines integrate computing and another discipline. In the field of computational biology this often includes mathematics, physics, biology and computing. To better understand the qualitative character of learning, collaboration and creativity in computational biology, a pilot study was initiated to determine if training in improvisational theater affects computing scientists' ability to be creative in their research. In this work we provide introductory improvisational theater training to students and researchers along the computational biology continuum. We are developing a better understanding of the creative character of computational biology education and research. Our evaluation suggests participants recognize that interpersonal relationships affect learning and creativity; and reexamine their notions of learning and creativity.

Author Keywords: Improvisation, interdisciplinary, collaboration, environment

ACM Classification Keywords: J.5 Arts and Humanities

General Terms: Experimentation, Human Factors

INTRODUCTION

Educational practices rarely teach students and prospective science researchers to develop their creativity or an understanding of creative process in science. This work builds on the premises that learning and creativity are social in nature [3,7], that creativity can be fostered, and that the understanding and practice of research as an improvisational performance creates a context in which scientists may be able to continuously transform how they see and do science.

Improvisation creates a performance that is collaborative and unscripted. While best known in the context of jazz music or theater, improvisation is present in a host of wider settings. In areas including teaching, engineering and design, it has been introduced as a catalyst for developing teams, brainstorming and enhancing creativity [1, 2, 4, 6]. Creativity in this context is identified as the ability to produce numerous or novel suggestions.

C&C'11, November 3–6, 2011, Atlanta, Georgia, USA.
ACM 978-1-4503-0820-5/11/11.

At the same time that previous work highlights the Instrumental benefits of improvisation, authors express the significance of seeing the process and environment as itself improvisational and creative. We find here the interesting dialectic of humans creating as participants (actors) the social context (scene) in which they are able to be creative.

Backdrop

Over the past ten years, graduate programs that integrate computer science, applied mathematics and a variety of biological disciplines have been established around the country. These are being followed steadily by undergraduate programs and courses offered by faculty from different disciplinary backgrounds who themselves are new to the field. Thus, the approaches to teaching computation and computational thinking within computational biology [8] are still fluid. This provides a rich opportunity for creative processes to contribute to the overall development of the curriculum including the possibility of explicit inclusion of creative practices within the curriculum as a pedagogical approach.

IMPROV WORKSHOPS FOR SCIENTISTS

In the past two years, experimental workshops have introduced ~200 students, staff and faculty in the field of computational biology to improvisational theater. These workshops create an opportunity for participants to stretch and develop muscles in active listening, building a group and the central tenet of improv, "Yes, and".

A warm up exercise that builds group awareness involves everyone walking around the room without speaking. At any time a person can choose to stop. Once a person stops, the whole group stops. The group moves again when the first person who stopped begins to move again. The initial movements of the group are slow and jerky. Early in the exercise, individuals might explore controlling or tricking the group with quick stop and start moves. But, over time as the group continues to focus on moving together, it develops an awareness and rhythm. The grouping of individuals becomes visible as an ensemble.

In our everyday work scientists are taught to be precise in our words, accurate in our data and knowledgeable in our field. Yet, a cultural environment of negation and challenge creates a stressful, anxious, non-creative environment. The improvisation workshops create a context in which each contribution -- phrase, motion, thought -- is accepted and built upon. Each offer can be used to create a social environment in which the scientists can meander through their world in new ways.

Topic Related Exercises

Computational biologists participated in a 2 day workshop to define creativity in their field and train in improvisation. Freed from the constraints of "having to be right" and "look smart", they were able to play with ideas in biology and computing. Together they created new exercises to explore computational biology related concepts. After learning a number of exercises [5], they combined games for others to play with computational biology.

FishBowl: During or after a lecture or seminar, phrases or words are written on index cards. These are then used to start the game *I am a tree*. Here is the example that was performed by graduate students and faculty:

Student 1 chooses a random card and walks to the front of the room (stage). Student 1: I am a bug (hunches over with hands under chin). Faculty: I am a computer screen (stands nearby with arms arched up and around the student). Student: I am a debugger (standing behind bug, extended arms, opening and closing).

This version of *FishBowl* and *I am a tree*, was tried in an undergraduate course on mathematical modeling of biological systems. This lab course of 20 students, primarily juniors and seniors, used their responses to the course as material for the *FishBowl*. Comments from students after the improv lab included: "I was surprised by how creative we are." "It was harder doing content related improv." "It was easier because I had a lot of material to draw on." "I was surprised by what we put together."

Current Evaluation and Analysis Instruments

Surveys and interviews of workshop participants were used as a mixed-method evaluation to develop indicators for 1) individual creativity 2) the understanding of the role of creativity in research and learning and 3) the current conditions for collaboration in the field. Are there changes in creativity due to participation in an improvisational theater workshop? How do we measure them?

A pre- and post- Likert-scale survey was implemented immediately before and after improvisation workshops. For creativity, the participants were asked to rate on a scale of strongly agree to strongly disagree such statements as "I am comfortable with uncertainty," "I am a good listener," and "I wish I had more imagination or originality." Collaboration statements included: "I receive sufficient input on my work to advance," "I value collaboration with coworkers," and "Most of the progress I experience at work stems from discussions with co-workers." The results averaged across the pool showed no apparently significant change in participant perception of their individual creativity and collaborative conditions.

Yet in semi- structured interviews held 5-8 weeks after the 2-day workshop, participants expressed having a new relationship to aspects of science and scientific communication. Of the 8 participants interviewed, the following classes of statements were made:

a: Participant becomes aware of creative components of science (4 participants, 8 occurrences); b: Participant becomes reflective about communication (5 participants, 6 occurrences); c: Research seminar reveals a science communication hierarchy (5 participants, 6 occurrences); d: Research seminar contrasts with environment of improv (6 participants, 8 occurrences).

CONCLUSIONS

We have yet to discover if the improvisation workshops support advances in learning, particularly in computational biology, that would be measurable on traditional exams. Yet, we find that the improvisation workshops begin a practice and dialog that engages computing scientists in reflecting on the possibility of new interactions in the scientific workspace.

ACKNOWLEDGMENTS

Thanks to: Sarah Hug, University of Colorado, Boulder for evaluation and feedback; Carrie Lobman and Lois Holzman, East Side Institute, for training; Uri Alon, Weizmann Institute, for organizing the first workshop for computational biologists; and the large number of students, postdocs and colleagues who provide feedback on the significance of our socio-cultural environment for our personal and scientific endeavors. Supported by NSF Award # 1002878

REFERENCES

1. Gerber, E. Improvisation Principles and Techniques for Design, in *Proceedings of CHI '07* (New York NY,2007), ACM Press, 1069-1072.
2. Gerber, E. Using improvisation to enhance the effectiveness of brainstorming, in *Proceedings CHI '09* (Boston MA, April 2009), ACM Press.
3. Holzman, L. *Vygotsky at Work and Play*. Psychology Press, East Sussex London, 2009.
4. Kuutti, K., Iacucci, G., Iacucci, C. Acting to Know: Improving Creativity in the Design of Mobile Services by Using Performances, in *Proceedings C&C '02* (New York NY, 2002), ACM Press, 95-102.
5. Lobman, C., and Lundquist, M. *Unscripted Learning: Using Improv Activities Across the K-8 Curriculum.* Teachers College Press, New York NY, 2007.
6. Sawyer, R.K. Creative teaching: Collaborative discussion as disciplined improvisation. *Educational Researcher 33*, 2 (March 2004), 12-20.
7. Vygotsky, L. *Mind in Society: The development of higher psychological processes.* Harvard University Press, Cambridge MA, 1978.
8. Wing, J.M. Computational Thinking. *Communications of the ACM 49, 3 (March 2006), 33*

User Roles in Asynchronous Distributed Collaborative Idea Generation

Sara Jones, Anni Poulsen, Neil Maiden and Konstantinos Zachos
Centre for Creativity in Professional Practice
City University London, UK
saraj@soi.city.ac.uk, anni@annipoulsen.com, cc559@soi.city.ac.uk, kzachos@soi.city.ac.uk

ABSTRACT
This paper presents the findings of an exploratory study within a real-life context that investigates participant behaviour and emergent user roles in asynchronous distributed collaborative idea generation by a defined community of users. In the study, a high-fidelity prototype of an online virtual ideas room was built and used by a Community of Interest consisting of representatives from 10 different voluntary organisations spread across Denmark. The study revealed five user roles, which the authors propose that future asynchronous distributed collaborative idea generation platforms should consider.

Author Keywords
Collaborative creativity, user behaviour, distributed collaborative idea generation, Community of Interest.

ACM Classification Keywords
H.5.3 [Information Interfaces and Presentation] Group and Organization Interfaces---asynchronous interaction, collaborative computing, web-based interaction.

General Terms
Experimentation, Human Factors

INTRODUCTION
Collaborative idea generation has been embraced by large companies such as British Telecom [1] as an effective way of generating new ideas, and a number of open innovation platforms are already available. This paper describes the behaviour of a community of individuals using an online platform to collaboratively develop new ideas for problem solution, and in particular, identifies different user roles that emerge within the community.

CASE STUDY
A high-fidelity prototype of our system, called The Ideas Room, was built using an installation of the core Wordpress combined with a number of plug-ins altered to meet our requirements and a new Wordpress template designed specifically for The Ideas Room (figure 1). The prototype was designed to allow distributed participants from a defined Community of Interest [2] to contribute, build on and discuss ideas to solve submitted problem statements. Following recommendations in the literature, our platform was designed to support facilitation [3], and follow rules outlined by Osborn (cited in [4]) as follows: criticism was ruled out; freewheeling was welcome; quantity was wanted; and combination and improvement were sought.

To maximize ecological validity, our study of The TRoom was conducted in a natural setting with members of a real Community of Interest with real motivation to solve common problems. A convenience sample of 11 representatives from 10 different Danish voluntary organisations participated in the study. They were distributed over 3 age groups: 26-39=3, 40-59=5 and 60-74=3.

To initiate the study, two problem statements were collected from each participant and posted in The Ideas Room. Participants were then invited to generate new ideas to solve these problems. The study ran for a period of 24 consecutive days. All participants were informed that they should decide when, how and the frequency at which they wished to participate in that time period. During the study, facilitation was limited to leaving encouraging responses to the contributions to solving the problems and incubation exercises. In order to encourage participation, weekly summary emails of the number of ideas generated were also sent to the participants.

RESULTS
A total of 165 ideas were generated during the study period. This equates to an average 15 ideas per participant (SD=18.5). 65 of the total 165 ideas were accredited as the source of new ideas, equating to 39% of all ideas providing inspiration for one or more new ideas.

A total of 307 comments were made in The Ideas Room during the study, of which 64 were encouraging comments from the facilitator. The remaining 243 comments equate to an average of 22.1 comments per participant (SD=22.5) and 1.5 comments per idea.

C&C'11, November 3–6, 2011, Atlanta, Georgia, USA.
ACM 978-1-4503-0820-5/11/11.

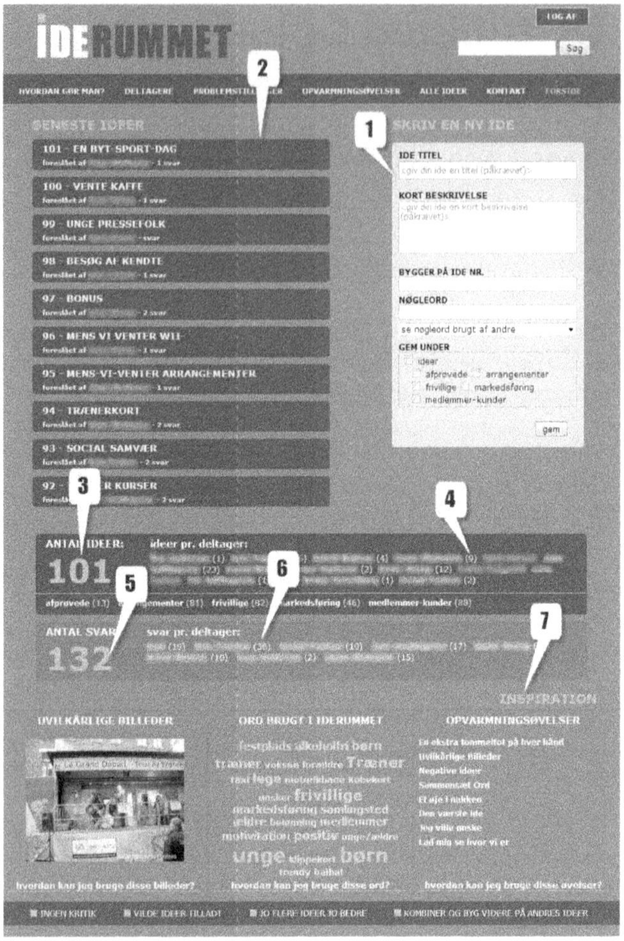

Figure 1. Screenshot of The Ideas Room (original in Danish): 1. Form for posting ideas; 2. List of ideas; 3. Number of ideas generated; 4. Number of ideas by participant; 5. Number of comments left to ideas; 6. Number of comments by participant; 7. Incubation exercises.

193 unique visits were paid to The Ideas Room during the evaluation, equating to an average of 17.5 unique visits per participant during the entire study period (SD=17.3) and ranging from 2 visits from two of the participants to 48 visits from another. The total time spent on The Ideas Room during the evaluation period was 55:03:52 hours, equating to an average 5:00:21 hours per participant (SD=4:18:22) and ranging from 0:45:51 hours by one participant to 13:05:44 by another.

USER ROLES

Four major activities were possible in The Ideas Room: log in to The Ideas Room; submit ideas in relation to problem statements; provide feedback to ideas in the form of comments or by marking ideas as new ideas; and download ideas. When analysing each participant's activity, different patterns of behaviour emerged, and 5 different user roles were identified to characterize these patterns. Table 1 below shows these user roles and their characteristics in terms of the activities they typically engaged in.

User Role	Login	Ideas	Feedback	Download
Contributor				
Encourager				
Social Loafer				
Harvester				
Absentee				

Table 1. User Role Characteristics

In summary, of the 13 people who consented to participate in The Ideas Room, we judged that 2 were mainly Encouragers, 4 were Contributors and Encouragers, 2 were Social Loafers, 1 was a Harvester, 2 were Absentees and 2 did not participate enough to be classified.

CONCLUSIONS AND FUTURE WORK

While the data from our case study is not sufficient to conclude the external validity of the distribution of participants across the above user roles, we propose that any platform supporting distributed collaborative idea generation within a defined community should consider these user roles in order to ensure as effective a collaboration as possible, and should help steer all participants towards the roles of Contributor and Encourager. Measures that may help ensure that all users participate, and hence avoid Absentees include: holding a synchronous launch event, and asking users to activate their accounts and enter their own problem statements. Measures for moving participants from Social Loafers to Contributors may include: asking participants to take turns in facilitating, and introduction of a visible reward system for different kinds of contribution. The effectiveness of measures such as these needs to be investigated in future work.

REFERENCES

1. Bross, M. (2008). *Innovation at the Speed of Life.* http://www.btplc.com/Innovation/Journal/BTIJ/current/HTMLArticles/Volume01/03Innovation/Default.aspx
2. Fischer, G. (2001). Communities of interest: Learning through the Interaction of multiple knowledge systems. *24th Annual Information Systems Research Seminar In Scandinavia (IRIS24).* pp. 1–14. Ulvik, Norway.
3. Gerber, E. (2009). Using Improvisation to Enhance the Effectiveness of Brainstorming. *Proceedings of the 27th International Conference on Human Factors in Computing Systems.* New York: ACM, pp.97-104
4. Putman, V.L., Paulus, P.B. (2009), Brainstorming, Brainstorming Rules and Decision Making. *Journal of Creative Behavior*, Vol 43(1), 2009, pp. 23-39.

Study of Affective Communication Method in Tactile Hand Gesture Feedback

Hae Youn Joung
College of Architecture, School of Industrial Design, Georgia Institute of Technology
247 4th St Atlanta, GA 30332, USA
joannejoung@gatech.edu

Ellen Yi-Luen Do
College of Architecture & School of Interactive Computing, Georgia Institute of Technology
828 W. Peachtree St. NW, GA 30332, USA
ellendo@gatech.edu

ABSTRACT

We are interested in the usability of haptic hand gestures in emotional online communication. To investigate how different emotions are associated with different tactile hand gestures, we built a tactile user interface device to record parameters of hand gestures exerted on it such as the hand gesture intensity, temporal frequency, spatial frequency and pattern correlation to be used as the source of information to access emotions. We observed the behavioral aspects of tactile hand gestures used for emotional interaction through the sensory input device and analyzed the data using a model-based analysis tool. The obtained gestures are categorized into the groups defined by the tactile signal parameters. Based on the findings of this research, we show a possibility that the tactile hand gesture-to-emotion map can be used to enable affective on-line communication. We are applying the relationships between tactile hand gestures and emotions to emotional online communication devices.

Author Keywords

Tactile hand gesture analysis, human computer interaction, affective communication, tangible interaction and tactile stimulation

ACM Classification Keywords

H.5.2 Information Interfaces and Presentation (e.g., HCI): User Interfaces

General Terms

Human factors, measurement and theory

INTRODUCTION

To enable on-line communication that approximates a face-to-face interaction, human computer interaction (HCI) and affective computing researchers have converted emotional messages into the form of text, voice, and video [Dourish, 2001; Fagerberg et al., 2003; Moen, 2006]. They have also employed various sensory modalities that enable affective online communication through interactive media. Recently, researchers have developed a wearable tactile interface that attempts to encourage humans to share their emotions through online digital communication methods. These emotional communication techniques, however, require an explicit process of conversion from emotions to predefined formats such as human-computer languages and symbols. In contrast, tactile hand gestures are a natural and intuitive way to express personal emotions and situations [Russell, 1890]. Therefore, this research focuses on the study of tactile hand gestures for the use in affective online communication. This research is performed to determine how emotions affect the motion of tactile hand gestures and how we can code different emotions with tactile hand gestures in devices for online communication.

C&C'11, November 3–6, 2011, Atlanta, Georgia, USA.
ACM 978-1-4503-0820-5/11/11.

APPROACH

We focus on the relationship between human emotions and their corresponding tactile hand gestures, specifically on those performed with fingers. This research aims to show that different emotions are associated with different tactile hand gestures, and therefore, the findings of this research can be used to create online emotional communication devices that approximate the use of natural tactile hand gestures in face-to-face communication.

Type of emotions

We identified eight essential emotional states for the subjects in our research to perform based on Russell's dimensional model, also known as the circumflex model of affect. In this model, Russell provides the mental map of how emotions are distributed in a two-dimensional system of coordinates where the y-axis is the degree of arousal and the x-axis is the valence and categorizes emotions in terms of pleasure and arousal.

Model of Tactile Hand Gestures

To define the types of tactile hand gesture, we propose a new model that consists of four tactile signal properties: (1) Intensity: the degree of contact pressure, (2) Temporal frequency: the number of occurrences of contact per unit time, (3) Spatial frequency: the number of occurrences of contact per unit distance, and (4) Pattern correlation: the vector correlation between input gestures and the geometric patterns such as circle, cross, line, etc.

Mapping between emotions and tactile hand gesture

In the experiment we observed participants performing each of the eight emotional situations and found statistically significant data that demonstrated a possibility of tactile hand gestures communication in online environment.

Results of experiment

The user research using the wearable tactile sensor device provides us evidence of the relationship between tactile hand gestures and emotions. By performing analysis of variance (ANOVA) of the recorded tactile data we found correlation between the signal properties of tactile gestures and the emotional states.

The balanced one-way ANOVA of the obtained tactile gesture sample data was performed for the signal properties: (a) intensity; (b) temporal frequency; (c) spatial frequency; and (d) pattern correlation. Very small p values for all the four signal properties that are obtained from ANOVA ($p(a) = 2.08e\text{-}82$, $p(b) = 1.76e\text{-}111$, $p(c) = 4.88e\text{-}13$, $p(d) = 3.99e\text{-}4$) indicate that at least one emotional sample mean is significantly different from the other emotional sample means. The type of emotion whose sample mean is significantly different from the other can be statistically distinguished and decoded from the other emotional states by observing the corresponding property of tactile gesture sample data. The tactile gesture corresponding to angry emotion contains the mean value of intensity significantly higher than that of the other emotions. The mean value of temporal frequency corresponding to alarmed emotion is higher than that of the other emotions. However, spatial frequency and pattern correlation show less significant distinction in their mean values among the various emotions.

As shown in Fig. 1, the emotion group of excited, happy, angry and alarmed, which corresponds to high arousal according to Russell's dimensional model, is related with gestures with high intensity and high temporal frequency. The distributions of gesture samples in spatial frequency do not vary much among various emotions. However, gesture samples associated with happy emotion are placed low in spatial frequency as compared to those with excited, angry and alarmed. The emotion group of relaxed, sleep, tired and lonely is associated with patterned gestures such as drawing circles and lines. By observing pattern correlation values, this emotion group can be distinguished from the others. However, this procedure requires detailed pattern analysis for accurate decoding, which is the future work of this study.

CONCLUSION

In this research, the types of tactile hand gestures are categorized in terms of tactile signal properties and related to distinct emotions that the gestures originate from the findings. This investigation show opportunities and promises to use tactile hand gestures for the communication of emotions among people using online digital communication devices at a distance. From user experiments, we found that different emotions are statistically associated with different tactile hand gestures. However, the aspect of pattern correlation as one of tactile gesture properties needs to be further investigated to uncover more gesture information and to better define gesture-emotion relation. In future study, the relationship between touch hand gestures and emotions will be applied to emotional online communication devices, and a prototype design of weatable online tactile communication devices will be demonstrated.

REFERENCES

1. Dourish, P. Where the Action is, the Foundations of Embodied Interaction. MIT Press, Cambridge, MA, USA, 2001.
2. Moen, J. Aesthetic movement interaction: designing for the pleasure of motion. Doctoral Thesis, KTH, Numerical Analysis and Computer Science, Stockholm, Sweden, 2006.
3. Russell, A.: A circumflex model of affect. Journal of personality and social psychology, vol. 34, 1980.

ACKNOWLEDGMENTS

We thank all the participants to our studies for gathering tactile gesture data. We especially thank Randy Bernald who is a graduate project advisor.

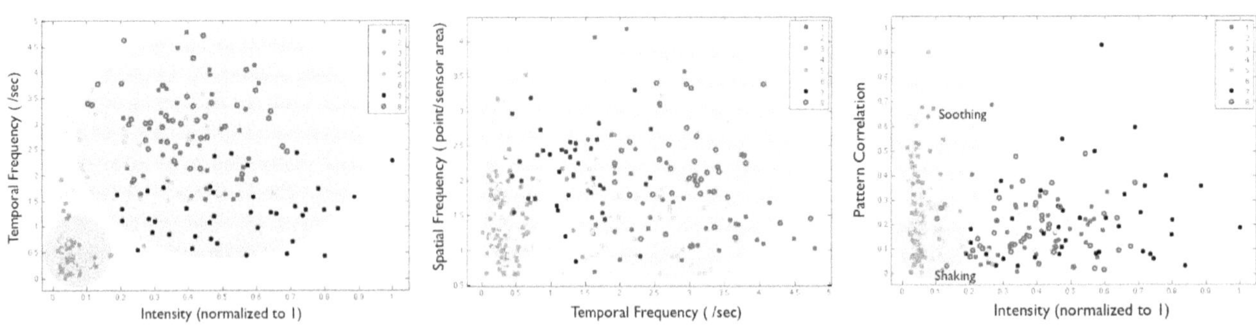

Fig. 1. Tactile gesture scatter plots: (1) excited (blue); (2) happy (green); (3) relaxed (red); (4) sleepy (light blue); (5) tired (magenta); (6) lonely (yellow); (7) angry (black); and (8) alarmed (blue/white).

Everyday Creativity in Novice E-Textile Designs: Remixing as Interpretive Flexibility

Yasmin B. Kafai
University of Pennsylvania
3700 Walnut Street
kafai@upenn.edu

Deborah A. Fields
University of Pennsylvania
3700 Walnut Street
stareyes@gmail.com

Kristin A. Searle
University of Pennsylvania
3700 Walnut Street
searle@dolphin.upenn.edu

ABSTRACT

We examine e-textile designs, a new domain combining crafts, circuitry, and programming with the LilyPad Arduino, to better understand how novice designers develop creative technical solutions. Our analyses draw from observation and interviews conducted with middle and high school students enrolled in e-textiles workshops. In the workshops, students created their own designs by re-interpreting e-textile creations from an online community or by re-purposing the conductive functionality of everyday objects. These remixes, popular in today's youth digital media culture, can also be seen as "interpretative flexibility" and promising indicators of the everyday creativity of novice designers.

Author Keywords

E-textiles, creativity, remixing, design

ACM Classification Keywords

K.3.0 [Computers and Education]: General

General Terms

Human Factors, Design

INTRODUCTION

Much of the research around creativity and technology has focused on understanding how software designers develop new solutions to overcome constraints. Smith [4] called this ability "computational flexibility," the capacity to invent software solutions when existing applications fail to solve new problems. While such flexibility can be expected of experienced designers, it is unclear how novice designers can engage in such creative designs. Yet though the creativity of novice designers may not look like those of experts, finding ways to recognize it may help us understand and promote the development of computational flexibility in design.

As a starting point for our investigations into the creativity of novice technology designers, we draw on Lewis' [2] understanding of creativity in the technology classroom and Roth's [3] suggestion of "interpretive flexibility" in his students' engineering designs. Lewis [2] argues that the technology classroom is an ideal site for creativity because it is not bound by traditional academic norms and provides a space for teaching problem solving, requiring creative thought processes. Similarly, e-textiles are a new domain that combines crafts, engineering, and programming with the LilyPad Arduino; students must combine knowledge from these multiple domains when problem solving. In the workshops, students created their own designs by re-interpreting e-textile creations from an online community or by re-purposing the conductive functionality of everyday objects. These remixes, popular in today's youth digital media culture, can also be seen as "interpretative flexibility" and promising indicators of the everyday creativity of novice designers.

Like the key aspects of the technology classroom as a site for creativity that Lewis discusses, e-textiles designers are put into an open-ended and ill-structured design situation where solutions are not pre-defined. The novice designers must match their desired designs with the affordances (and constraints) of the technology, combining old and new knowledge in creative ways. "Interpretive flexibility" [3], interpreting an object in different ways depending on local needs and the frames people bring to a situation is one way to understand young designers' emerging creativity in the new domain. The youth we studied were new to sewing, circuitry, and programming, all components of e-textiles using the LilyPad Arduino [1]. By analyzing the micro-changes made in their designs and expressed in their self-reflections, we study their remixing of materials and of images from an online archive and suggest these as a type of "interpretive flexibility."

CONTEXT

The case studies of novice e-textiles designers are drawn from a larger, ongoing study of creativity and computational design. As part of the study, we conducted a series of 6-8 week e-textiles workshops with middle and high school students from a range of racial, ethnic, and class backgrounds. With the 8 middle school students, we built simple circuits that required engagement with the crafting and circuitry domains. With the 27 high school students, we increased the level of complexity and included

C&C'11, November 3–6, 2011, Atlanta, Georgia, USA.
ACM 978-1-4503-0820-5/11/11.

the LilyPad Arduino, which required computer programming in addition to crafting and circuitry. Our data focus on participants' designs: careful documentation of design changes in their projects (daily/hourly pictures and observational notes) and interviews about their designs. We inductively coded the data with a focus on tensions and solutions as participants struggled to enact the aesthetic ideas they brought to the project and the affordances of the LilyPad technology they learned through the workshops. Finally, we compiled case studies based on particularly compelling examples that we found in the data set during the coding process. Here we share two of these case studies, one a 14-year-old high school girl and the other a 12-year-old middle school boy, engaged in design activities that illustrate the everyday creativity of novice e-textiles designers.

FINDINGS

In the following vignettes, we highlight the interpretive flexibility exhibited by students in e-textiles workshops as they moved through the process of conceptualizing, designing, and producing their own e-textiles projects. Our findings focus on how participants created their own designs by "re-interpreting" e-textile creations from an online community or by "repurposing" the functionality of everyday objects. For instance, Bailey's original idea came from browsing the LilyPond website, an online repository of many e-textiles projects. Intrigued by a simple circuit robot patch, she began to draft her own design based on this image. However, over time she changed the design in several ways in order to incorporate a LilyPad: making the robot rectangular instead of rounded, putting two LEDs as eyes instead of one in the heart, and using the LilyPad to make the lights blink. Further, through repeated iterations of designing and crafting, she discovered that the conductive thread only needed to be on the left side of the robot. However, she re-interpreted the conductive thread as an aesthetic element, going to great trouble to sew matching (non-conductive) lines on the right side (see Figure 1). Thus she remixed the original design that inspired her while still holding on to certain elements (a robot with a heart), and flexibly interpreting the conductive thread as both functional and aesthetic.

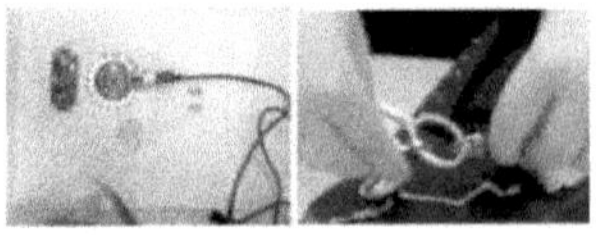

Figure 1: Bailey's robot design [left] and Aaron's shoe key [right]

In a different kind of remixing, Aaron repurposed everyday materials to build on his simple circuit design. In the workshop Aaron sewed a tri-color LED, a switch, and a coin cell battery on his a black canvas sneaker. Aaron's design is fairly simple, only sewing in one of the three potential colors of the LED, yet one aspect makes it a standout compared to many other designs: he used his own keys as a conductor to make the other two colors of the tri-color LED light up on his sneaker (see Figure 1). Most students worked solely within the confines of the e-textile construction kit, using the given switches, LEDs and conductive thread to make their designs. Aaron's repurposing of the key chain drew in his new understanding of what could act as conductive connector and allowed him to improvise with the color on his sneaker's LED. After his final project demonstration Aaron returned the key chain to his original place around his neck thus making it truly multi-functional.

DISCUSSION

These instances of youths' repurposing and reinterpreting designs and functionality can be seen as different types of remixes. Bailey's case suggests that remixing a prior design with new/additional materials can be a form of creative problem solving. Though there was imitation of the original robot with a heart, her design contained many different elements, including computation with the LilyPad that allowed the eyes to blink. Both Bailey and Aaron show interpretive flexibility in repurposing materials for non-traditional ends, the former using conductive thread both functionally and aesthetically, and the latter using a keychain as conductive material for improvisational lighting effects. While these remixes are not on the level of computational flexibility proposed by Smith [4], they do resemble Roth's "interpretative flexibility" [3]. This suggests one way to identify creativity in novice designers. Further, examining the hourly progress of the novice designers illuminated the ways their creative solutions emerged alongside their developing knowledge of the new domain of e-textiles. Indeed, we found that students' visual representations and physical manipulations of relevant objects made visible creative thinking that is often invisible in the final products. Finally, the cases suggest that the tension between aesthetics and function, perhaps most visible in youth new to specific technologies like e-textiles, may stimulate creativity. Studying how their original designs change as they learn a new domain, and how they 'solve' the dilemma of transforming their designs to be both aesthetically pleasing (to them) and functional with the technology may further illuminate novice creativity.

REFERENCES

1. Buechley, L. & Eisenberg, M. 2008. The LilyPad Arduino: Toward Wearable Engineering for Everyone. *IEEE Pervasive, 7*(2), 12-15.
2. Lewis, T. 2009. Creativity in technology education: Providing children with glimpses of their inventive potential. *International Journal of Technology and Design Education, 19,* 255-268.
3. Roth, W.-M. 1998. *Designing Communities*. Dordrecht: Kluwer Academic Publishing.
4. Smith, B. 2006. Design and Computational Flexibility. *Digital Creativity, 17*(2), 65–72.

Interpretation as Driver for Psychological Creativity

Nick Kelly
Design Lab
The University of Sydney
Sydney, NSW 2006 Australia
+61 9351 4107
nick.kelly@sydney.edu.au

John S. Gero
Krasnow Institute for Advanced Study
George Mason University
Fairfax, VA 22030 USA
+1 703 425 6503
john@johngero.com

ABSTRACT
This paper describes some acts of psychological creativity as phenomena arising from changes to a situation, brought about through interpretation. It presents a way of representing a situation as a schema of concepts made up from perceptual dimensions. It shows the utility of concepts as being changed by the situation within which they are used. An example of this is described, in which the information within a concept is unchanged yet its use becomes different through salience weighting. A computational implemented example is presented as a generate-and-interpret model that produces country growth indicators and then interprets them and repeats this process. The situation, and the space of possible designs, is changed through the act of interpretation. It is suggested that interpretation can be a driver for changing situations – something that looks like P-creativity to an outside observer.

Keywords
Situated cognition, interpretation, situated design, P-creativity

ACM Classification Keywords
J.4 Social and Behavoral Sciences: Psychology

General Terms
Design, Human Factors.

INTRODUCTION
When a designer has an idea that is both new and useful, an act of psychological creativity (P-creativity) has occurred [2]. This work suggests that an act of P-creativity can be described as a change of a designer's *situation* [4]. Consider the way that a designer looks at work they have just created and sees previously unobserved features [6]. For example, an architect suddenly decides that their recently sketched floor plan is 'not square enough'; an artist looks at their work and concludes that 'we could try distorting this more'; a musician suddenly decides that 'we could try syncopation here'. This kind of change to the design trajectory can be observed in designers [9]. This paper suggests one way of reproducing this class of phenomena, that constitutes an act of P-creativity, is through a change of the designer's situation brought about through interpretation.

C&C'11, November 3–6, 2011, Atlanta, Georgia, USA.
ACM 978-1-4503-0820-5/11/11.

Situated design [4,7] holds that design activity occurs within a situation, the current 'world view' of the designer, that can be considered as a network of concepts. As design activity progresses, this situation changes. This work frames the question: how does the situation of a designer change? It provides examples to support the claim that failed expectations during interpretation can be a driver for this change of situation, from which P-creativity can be observed.

In this work we describe a way of representing situations as well as how situations can become changed through interpretation. An example is provided in a model that uses a method of *generate-and-interpret.*

REPRESENTING SITUATIONS IN CONCEPTUAL SPACE
When we say that a designer 'knows about A' it can be considered the equivalent of saying that a designer 'holds a concept about A that has its basis in abstractions from the world' [1]. Concepts can be represented geometrically through the creation of conceptual spaces [3].

In this work, conceptual spaces are extended to represent situations. A situation brings a number of concepts together. Some concepts held by an agent are inside the current situation and some are not. Those concepts within the situation are not discrete units of knowledge, but rather are taken together as a 'situation' that alters all of the concepts – the whole in each of the parts. An example of how to achieve this computationally is presented, using salience weighting as an example.

Salience Weighting within Conceptual Space
Gärdenfors [3] describes that conceptual spaces can be distorted by dimensional scaling. Any operations carried out within this space, such as determining similarity through distance [5] are unchanged in process, but the result is different because they take place within an altered space.

One way to achieve this is formalized, in which the situation changes the use of each concept by determining the salient dimensions within the situation, and then scaling the conceptual space accordingly. This is done by extending the notion of salience weighting to introduce the effects of situation, Figure 1. Instead of changing concepts due to the situation, the space within which concepts are located is changed. Any future operations carried out within the space are now different.

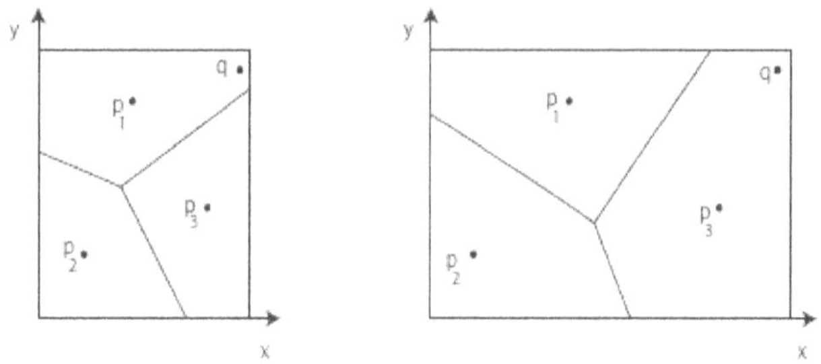

Figure 1 Voronoi tessellation of a space with three concepts, p_1, p_2 and p_3, before and after salience weighting, resulting in different classification of the external object q (after [3])

Changes to the Situation in Design Activity

The situation of a designer changes when it no longer works. The claim in this paper is that this can occur during interpretation, when the expectations held by a designer are unable to explain perceptions from the world. Examples are given of the way that this can lead to a change of the designer's situation.

IMPLEMENTING SITUATIONAL CHANGE

A model was implemented to demonstrate the way that a change of situation in this way can look like P-creativity to an external observer. It demonstrates situational salience weighting and the way that it alters the movement between different situations.

In one example, an agent is engaged in a cycle of generate-and-interpret, generating within a cycle of synthesis that has no fitness function – it continues this loop indefinitely. When interpretation occurs, there is an expectation to find the concepts that were held prior to generating. Sometimes these expectations will be met and at other times they will not. If the data from perception is distant from the expected concepts then it cannot be interpreted within the situation, leading to a change of situation.

The first implementation is in the domain of interpreting floor plans and is implemented using two linked self organizing maps. It shows the way that an agent moves around within its own knowledge, Figure 2. Whilst the situation is unchanged the agent is exploring within a limited space of possible designs. In interpretation the situation can change, leading to a new space of possible designs that may or may not overlap the previous space.

A second implementation demonstrates the way that the situation changes the use of a concept. The same concept, in two different situations, when considering the same data, results in two different interpretations due to salience weighting.

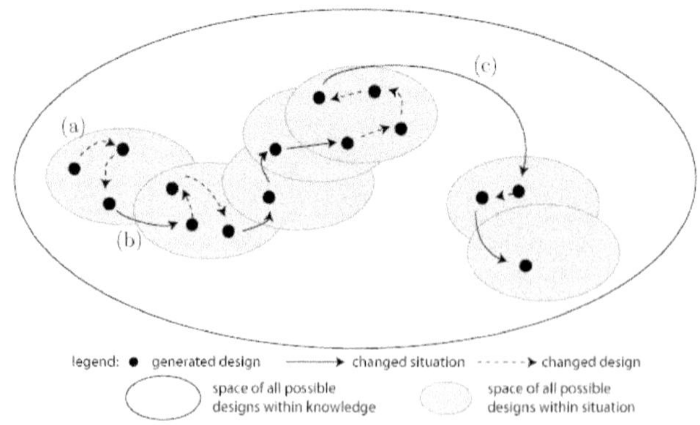

Figure 2 Generated designs and spaces of possible designs within changing situations in the model: (a) new generations within the same situation; (b) movement to an overlapping space of possible designs; and (c) movement to an entirely new space of possible designs

DISCUSSION

The claim made in this paper is that a change of situation appears to be like P-creativity to an external observer and that interpretation can trigger this change of situation. Two aspects of this have been demonstrated through computational implementation: (i) a generate-and-interpret model to demonstrate the way that situations can change; and (ii) the way that situations can change the use of concepts.

The work produces a link between the grounded experiences of an agent and the way in which it navigates its own knowledge during a task.

REFERENCES

1. Barsalou, L.W. Abstraction as dynamic interpretation in perceptual symbol systems. In L. Gershkoff-Stowe and D. Rakison (eds), *Building Object Categories. Carnegie Symposium Series*, Erlbaum, NJ (2005), 389-431
2. Boden, M.A. *The Creative Mind: Myths and Mechanisms.* Weidenfeld & Nicholson, London (1990)
3. Gärdenfors, P. *Conceptual Spaces: The Geometry of Thought.* MIT Press, Cambridge, MA (2000)
4. Gero, J.S. Situated design computing: Principles, in B.H.V. Topping (ed). *Civil Engineering Computations: Tools and Techniques.* Stirlingshire (2006), 25-35
5. Nosofsky, R.M. Attention, similarity, and the identification-categorization relationship. *Journal of Experimental Psychology: General* 15 (1986), 39-57.
6. Schön, D.A. *The Reflective Practitioner: How Professionals Think in Action*, Basic Books, NY, (1983)
7. Smith, G. and Gero, J.S. What does an agent mean by being "situated"? *Design Studies* 26 (2005), 535-5
8. Suwa, M., Gero, J.S. and Purcell, T. Unexpected discoveries and S-inventions of design requirements: Important vehicles for a design process. Design Studies 21(6) (2000), 539-567

Computing Indicators of Creativity

Kyu Han Koh
Dept of Computer Science
University of Colorado
Boulder, CO 80303
kohkh@colorado.edu

Vicki Bennett
Dept of Communication
University of Colorado
Boulder, CO 80303
Vicki.Bennett@colorado.edu

Alexander Repenning
Dept of Computer Science
University of Colorado
Boulder, CO 80303
ralex@cs.colorado.edu

ABSTRACT

Divergent thinking has been linked to creative processes leading to innovative artifacts. Measuring creative divergence can be difficult. Across the USA, the Scalable Game Design (SGD) Project includes thousands of student participants building their own games through learning computational thinking (CT). To evaluate these games, a technique, the Computational Thinking Pattern Analysis (CTPA) [1], was developed, refined and used successfully. Under three different learning conditions, divergence was computed through CTPA, and then analyzed and explored as an indication of creativity.

Author Keywords

Creativity Measurement, Game Design, Computational Thinking, Computational Thinking Pattern Analysis.

ACM Classification Keywords

K.3.m. Computers and education: Miscellaneous.

General Terms

Design, Measurement, Performance.

INTRODUCTION

Creativity and divergent thinking have been linked to ways of problem solving that increase the quality and quantity of viable solutions [2]. Programming, however, presents unique obstacles for creativity measurement. Analyzing programming manually can be time-consuming, and labor-intensive. The first obstacle to address is defining creativity. The creative process described in research investigations, includes the identifying or discovery of a problem and the selection of a solution with an identifiable outcome. However this outcome must be unique or divergent from most or all other possible solutions [3].

Divergent thinking tasks are currently the most recognized creative assessments [4,5]. Since computer programming lends itself to computational solutions, assessing a creative or divergent element in programming should be possible.

During the 2010/2011 school-year, we explored some early stages of mathematical measurement to calculate divergence in game programming with a sixth grade teacher participating in the Scalable Game Design Project. Among three of her classes, a highly divergent cluster pattern for the game programming element was shown.

METHODS

Computational Thinking Pattern Analysis

Computational Thinking Pattern Analysis (CTPA) [1] is a method to depict the semantic meaning, Computational Thinking Pattern [1] that is represented as an abstracted programming pattern of the submitted games/simulations to the Scalable Game Design Arcade, a cyberlearning infrastructure [3]. CTPA analyzes the implemented semantic meaning (CT patterns) of a submitted game/simulation with a similar technique as the Latent Semantic Analysis [6]. CTPA calculates high dimensional cosine similarity between a given game/simulation and nine canonical pre-defined computational thinking patterns. The value from this high dimensional cosine similarity calculation for each computational thinking pattern is displayed as a graphical representation (Figure 1).

Below equation represents a high dimensional cosine calculation for CTPA.

CTPA (u,v) (high dimensional cosine value between vectors)

$$= \frac{\sum_{i=1}^{i=n} u_i . v_i}{\sqrt{\sum_{i=1}^{n} u_i^2}\sqrt{\sum_{i=1}^{n} v_i^2}}$$

Equation 1 CTPA calculates the value of cosine ϕ between two n-dimensional vectors, u and v

Divergence Calculation

A divergence in programming among the student games would tend to show that each student approached the game programming from a unique perspective. Consequently, we surmised that creativity in programming could be shown as the divergence of a particular programming solution employed by one student, as opposed to another. Thus, we devised the divergence calculation to demonstrate student-programming creativity as a divergence calculation from the "norm" or SGD tutorial. Figure 1 depicts a student-submitted game in comparison to the official SGD tutorial game on a Computational Thinking Pattern Analysis graph [1]. The gap between the tutorial (brown) and the submitted artifact (green) illustrates the difference of that student's game from the "norm." The Divergence Score is calculated from the length (norm) of vector difference of the nine-element vector (nine computational thinking patterns).

$$\text{Divergence Score (u, v)} = \frac{\sqrt{\sum_{i=1}^{n}(u_i - v_i)^2}}{\sqrt{n}}$$

Equation 2 Divergence Score (u, v) where u and v represent nine-element vectors from a tutorial and a submitted game, and n stands the number of computational thinking patterns.

C&C'11, November 3–6, 2011, Atlanta, Georgia, USA.
ACM 978-1-4503-0820-5/11/11.

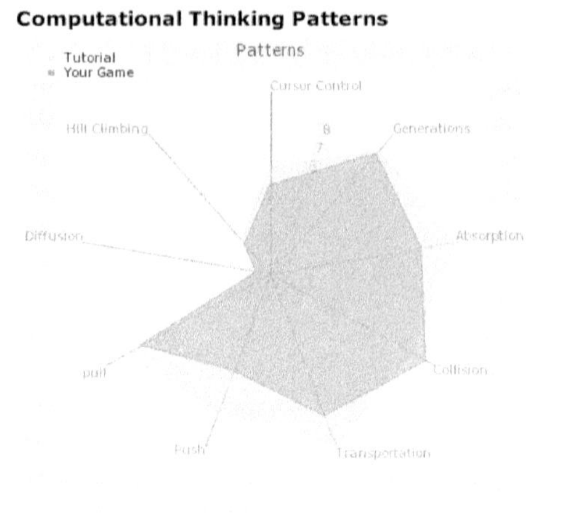

Figure 1 Computational Thinking Pattern Analysis Graph from a Tutorial and a Submitted Game

FINDINGS

Sheryle (pseudonym) was chosen for this analysis because she taught classes in three distinct conditions. Using the same teacher for all three conditions eliminates her as a variable in the calculations. The three class/learning conditions are as follows. The first learning condition is described as a standard type of technology/computer science class, taking place in a physical classroom. A standardized online tutorial provided by the SGD project is the basis for the class. The second class learning condition is similar to the first, except that the students are exposed to the teacher's own tutorial instead of the standardized version. In the third and last class/learning condition, the students are exposed to the teacher's own tutorial in an online environment, without her physical presence. The distribution graph for Sheryl's three different class conditions was drawn with the divergence scores from each class (Fig 2).

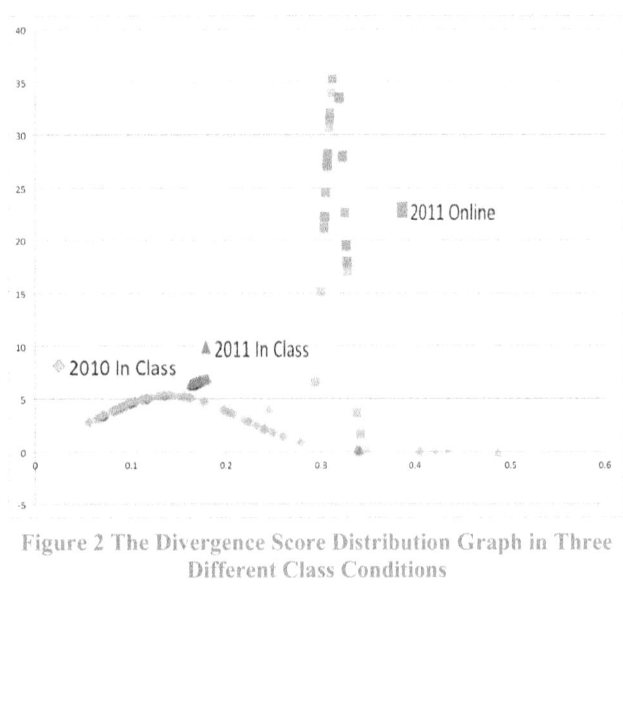

Figure 2 The Divergence Score Distribution Graph in Three Different Class Conditions

In this graph, x-axis means the divergence score, and y-axis means the number of students within set ranges. From this graph depiction, we speculate that there could be a significant difference between the in-class learning condition and the online one. Viewing all three learning conditions through the graph's perspective presents a new picture that highlights the revised tutorial and the "in-class" condition as significant factors among the three class conditions.

DISCUSSION AND CONCLUSION

Currently, the most common measurement of creativity is based on tests of divergence [4,5]. The larger the divergence from the standard, the more creative the solution is. Although the quality and quantity of the solutions to the task must be considered, divergence from the accepted "norm" is a significant indicator of creativity.

Looking at the Divergence Calculation graph (Fig. 2) there are three separate clusters. Even without the designating colors, the three class conditions stand apart. Although the implications and meanings of the different cluster spreads is a subject for future papers, the most significant feature of the Divergence Calculation graph is that each of the three separate class-learning conditions generated unique divergence patterns on the graph. The amount of creativity that each cluster pattern represents is not as important as the fact that it appears to demonstrate programming creativity, in general. So based on the idea that creativity can be shown through divergence in thinking and feeling [4,5], it stands to reason that creativity in programming can be shown through a similar divergence to a standard norm through calculating the divergence to that norm.

REFERENCES

1. Koh, K. H., Basawapatna, A., Bennett, V., Repenning, A. Towards the Automatic Recognition of Computational Thinking for Adaptive Visual Language Learning, IEEE International Symposium on Visual Languages and Human-Centric Computing 2010, Leganés-Madrid, Spain, September 21-25, 2010
2. Torrance, E.P. "Creative teaching makes a difference." In J.C. Gowan, J. Khatena, & E.P. Torrance (Eds.), Creativity: Its Educational Implications (2nd ed., pp. 99-108). Dubuque, IA: Kendall-Hunt, 1981.
3. Bennett, V., Koh, K. H., Repenning, A. CS Education Re-Kindles Creativity in Public Schools, ITiCSE '11: Annual Conference on Innovation and Technology in Computer Science Education, Darmstadt, Germany, June 27-29, 2011.
4. Runco, M.A. & Okuda, S.M. "Problem discovery, divergent thinking, and the creative process." Journal of Youth and Adolescence, 17:3, 211-220, 1988.
5. Williams, F.E. "Creativity assessment packet examiner's manual." Austin TX: PRO-ED, 1993.
6. Landauer, T. K., Foltz, P. W., Laham, D. Introduction to Latent Semantic Analysis. Discourse Processes, 25, 1998, 259-284

Dance in Augmented Reality: Calibration and Applications

Michael Korostelev
Temple University
Philadelphia, PA, USA
mike.k@temple.edu

Kathryn Knauth
Temple University
Philadelphia, PA, USA
kathryn.knauth@temple.edu

Dr. Li Bai
Temple University
Philadelphia, PA, USA
lbai@temple.edu

ABSTRACT
Dance expresses and translates human experience into meaningful body forms, transcending cultural barriers and language. Ideas and concepts can be portrayed through each dancer's movement on the stage. Mixing cutting edge technologies into contemporary fine arts creates opportunities for human imagination and advances development of futuristic technologies. Augmented Reality (AR) is this technology, and we envision the use of AR in avant-garde dance, interactive media, and story telling. Dance and Engineering in Augmented Reality (DEAR) is a collaborative effort between artists and engineers. Through this project, we will realize multiple creative works that take advantage of AR in an integral and non trivial manner. As part of this paper, we describe our application of the technology in dance and propose a simple projector camera calibration method for projection mapping installations. With an easier setup, we hope enable and inspire future AR pieces from talented artists, computer engineers and computer scientists.

Author Keywords
Augmented Reality, Human-Computer Interaction, Dance, Performing Arts

ACM Classification Keywords
J Computer Applications: J.5Arts & HumanitiesPerforming arts (e.g., dance, music).

General Terms
Design

INTRODUCTION
The goal of the Dance and Engineering in Augmented Reality (DEAR) initiative is to generate creative works that take advantage of Augmented Reality (AR). We have integrated AR with the art form of dance, enabling performers to incorporate technology into their works, allowing for augmentation of live scenes using visible projection of media onto dynamic surfaces in the real world. Our general process for augmenting a dance performance is as follows: We display a plain white panel marked off with infrared indicators which is tracked and augmented with video in real time. This gives us the ability to augment a live performance with computer generated special effects. Calibration is a very important procedure, as we must be able to project accurately for the AR implementation to be fully usable. The dancer and stage, the AR workspace, are tracked using a camera. The tracking allows us to have understating about the scenes geometry that we can then overlay with a projection that is fed back to the audience and performers through projected imagery. some

C&C'11, November 3–6, 2011, Atlanta, Georgia, USA.
ACM 978-1-4503-0820-5/11/11.

SYSTEM OVERVIEW
This AR system is made up of hardware and software subsystems. The software provides the means for the augmentation, processes data, and generates a model and a composite view of the AR workspace [4]. In our current system, the hardware consists of a white panel with infra-red LED makers at 5 locations on its surface, a simple webcam modified for infra-red vision, a high lumen projector and a computer with our software. During performance, a performer moves freely with the panel facing a projector some distance away. As the performer moves the panel, an IR camera tracks the position of the panel's corners, or fiducial points. These points' coordinates are then processed by our software within the timespan of one frame. Video is projected onto the panel so that it appears to lie upon it. As a result, when the performer moves the panel, the projected video moves along with it, making it appear as if he/she is carrying the object in the video.

Calibration
In order to accurately overlay objects in real space with projection once an object is detected, we need to figure out where this object is in relation to the projector. This is a problem, since the detection happens with a camera, and we only know where the objects are in the two dimensional camera space represented by a pixel coordinate system. A relationship must be derived that essentially converts the camera coordinate system into the projectors image plane.

To calibrate the projector and camera, at least four known image point pairs are needed, which are 2D coordinates of each image plane. By thinking of the projector as a camera, we can say that two cameras viewing the same scene see objects from a different perspective. To make a relationship between the two cameras views we have to consider perspective transformation. [3] Our task is to transform the camera view to the projector. This perspective transform is known as the homography [2], which is an invertible transformation from a plane in a projective space to another projective plane. Though invariant to scale, the homography maps straight lines to straight lines. A common approach to calibration involves examining an image with regular and known geometry. Using Zhang calibration, this known geometry is a chessboard pattern. When the dimensions of the squares are known, we can detect the corners of these squares in the camera image and create a mapping between the real points and the image points. OpenCV, an open-source computer vision library, provides us with easy functions to detect points of the calibration pattern as well as finding homographies. In a two camera system, calibration would actually be more difficult since pattern and feature detection would have to be implemented for both views. However, since the projector is a reverse camera, the information in its image plane is known without any sort of processing because we know what is being projected. To initiate calibration, a chessboard calibration pattern is projected onto a plane in space. A camera located close to the projectors lens then views this scene and attempts to detect the calibration pattern using a the chessboard detection function available in OpenCV [1]. Fitting media to the coordinates of detected objects (such as our projection plane) is made simple with the use of OpenGL. We draw vertices in the OpenGL environment using the projector points and fit a texture accordingly. In our software, this is defined as the WarpablePlane class that contains a warp method. Here the points of the quadrangle are transformed and normalized by the z coordinate. Textures are fit to the corners of the quadrangle. The corners vector contains the properly ordered projector points. The final result of the overlay appears accurately on the projection panel and follows with minor delay as the panel is moved through the projection space. This system is robust against occlusion and works in indoor lighting conditions, but suffers from interference from IR light.

Panel Detection

The plain white projection panel was described by 5 LED's. In order to improve frame-rate, especially with low cost cameras, the approach developed for DEAR does not implement any computational filtering for tracking. The tracking procedure uses only data in the current frame to recover the pose and orientation of the panel. This method is fast, practical and immune to problems from occlusion. To find the panel in the single frame, we assume that the position of each marker on the panel is known in the coordinate system of the panel and that the configuration of the LEDs is known to be four at each fiducial point with an orientation point off center. The detected blobs are classified by comparing the set to an ideal blob pattern. Each frame, we cycle through blob orders and compute a perspective transformation between the ideal and current pattern. Because of our five point configuration, it is known that the orientation point will always be enclosed between the other four. To determine which four points are on the outside, we use the convex hull algorithm. The last point is the orientation point. The problem with this is the order of the indexes is not necessarily correct with respect to orientation. It could be that the board is sideways or upside down and since the indices are just ordered clockwise, we need to find some way to recover and match the orientation. Different orders are chosen from these outside points. Since the outide points are fiducials, instead of permutation, we move through the indeces in a circular pattern. The orientation point should lie close to its image - plane analog, the combination with the smallest error between the orientation points will reveal the correct order of the points. Once identified, this combination will reveal the pose of the projection panel for warping media and projection overlay.

CONCLUSION

The DEAR Project initiative included equal input from engineers and dancers. Throughout the entire development process, our team worked closely with Dr. Luke Kahlich and fine arts students of the Temple University Boyer College of Music and Dance. This collaboration was certainly beneficial in that we maintained a realistic perspective of the needs and desires of dance professionals.In the past few years, artists have explored new technology and integrated it into their works. AR creates a rich medium for new immersive ways to present information, involve the audience and stimulate collaboration and creativity.

A critical requirement of the software package is re-usability. It should not be tailored to any specific performance, but provide a tool that can be integrated into different performances, and which adapts to the dancers' movements in real time. We want to harness creative motivation and use it to create a better artistic experience in the performing arts. Without formal education, people in fields of fine arts can become expert programmers and mathematicians.

As a result of this work, we have further pushed our exploration of this topic to include new technology presented by the the Microsoft Kinect RGBD sensor. Using this we are exploring better, full 3d calibration techniques as well as more efficient tracking that does not require infrared markers to describe the geometry of objects in the space.

REFERENCES

1. G. Bradski and A. Kaehler. *Learning OpenCV*. O'Reilly Media, Inc., 2008.
2. R. Hartley and A. Zisserman. *Multiple View Geometry in Computer Vision*. Cambridge University Press, 2nd ed. edition, 2004.
3. S.-Y. Park and G. G. Park. Active calibration of camera-projector systems based on planar homography. In *International Conference on Pattern Recognition.*, pages 320–323, 2010.
4. F. Zhou, H. Duh, and M. Billinghurst. Trends in augmented reality tracking, interaction and display: A review of ten years of ismar. In *7th IEEE and ACM International Symposium on Mixed and Augmented Reality*, 2008, pages 15–18. University of Canterbury. Human Interface Technology Laboratory., September 2008.

Collaborative Musical Improvisation in a Laptop Ensemble with LOLC

Sang Won Lee* **Jason Freeman*** **Andrew Colella*** **Shannon Yao**** **Akito Van Troyer†**
{sangwonlee, jason.freeman}@gatech.edu {ajcolella, shannonyao}@gmail.com
akito@media.mit.edu

*School of Music
Georgia Institute of Technology
840 McMillan Street
Atlanta, GA 30332 USA

**School of Literature, Communication, and Culture
Georgia Institute of Technology
686 Cherry St. Atlanta, GA 30332

†MIT Media Lab
75 Ames Street, E14-374D
Cambridge, Massachusetts
02142 USA

ABSTRACT
This paper discusses LOLC, a text-based collaborative music improvisation system for laptop ensemble developed by the authors. The paper evaluates LOLC in the context of a recent performance by professional classical musicians with minimal computer experience. Using qualitative data from interviews with the performers and quantitative data from server logs, the paper considers the degree to which LOLC facilitated collaborative improvisation among the musicians and the degree to which LOLC was accessible to non-programmers to learn and perform.

Authors Keywords
Live coding, laptop orchestra, improvisation, collaboration

ACM Classification Keywords
J.5. Arts and Humanities: Music

General Terms
Experimentation

INTRODUCTION
We designed and developed LOLC [6] to take advantage of the unique potential of text-based performance environments in larger-ensemble collaborative improvisation and to build upon the rich history of collaborative improvisation in jazz and avant-garde musical styles. In LOLC, musical patterns are coded symbolically and shared automatically, providing a foundation through which laptop musicians can effectively improvise and collaborate by borrowing and transforming the material created by others in the ensemble. In addition, we also wanted to make LOLC accessible to non-programmers, including skilled musicians without any experience in programming or computer music. LOLC is thus deliberately limited in complexity and scope: it is not a Turing-complete programming language and consists entirely of single-line expressions.

C&C'11, November 3–6, 2011, Atlanta, Georgia, USA.
ACM 978-1-4503-0820-5/11/11.

In this article, we briefly review the related work upon which LOLC builds and we then evaluate LOLC in the context of a recent performance by an ensemble of professional classical musicians who had no background in computer programming and little or no background in computer music. We consider the degree to which LOLC facilitated collaborative improvisation among the musicians and the degree to which LOLC was accessible to non-programmers to learn. For detailed information on the LOLC environment itself and our motivations for creating it, see [6].

RELATED WORK
The design and implementation of LOLC was influenced by existing models for collaborative text-based laptop performance and by approaches to collaborative improvisation in other types of ensembles.

Laptop-based musical ensembles can often collaborate more effectively when they share a common clock and code and/or music over the network [2,4], and some researchers have suggested environments that enable users to share actual code fragments among members of the ensemble [4,8]. The Hub's work *Borrowing and Stealing* [3] offers an intriguing model that served as a direct inspiration for LOLC. In addition to the ideas of live coding languages, LOLC was influenced by collaborative improvisation in other types of ensembles that have created structured strategies for ensemble improvisation in their works [1,7].

EVALUATION AND DISCUSSION
This section focuses on a single performance with LOLC in January 2011, in which musicians from a professional contemporary music ensemble performed with LOLC. These top-tier classical musicians have played with major symphony orchestras and also have considerable background with improvisation in experimental and/or jazz mediums. The musicians had no prior experience with LOLC, no (or negligible) background in computer programming, and little or no experience with using computer music software. The musicians started to learn LOLC through hour-long, one-on-one introductory sessions led by the authors, then practiced individually by following tutorial files and trying out LOLC on their personal

computers. The ensemble rehearsed together for a total of 12 hours in preparation for the public performance. During the rehearsal process, we provided technical assistance and guidance on the environment, but let the ensemble develop their own structure for the improvisation and decide how to build the piece collaboratively. Following the concert, we conducted an hour-long interview with each ensemble member to discuss his or her process of learning LOLC and experience of performing with it. In addition, we logged code and chat messages to disk and analyzed each log quantitatively.

Collaborative Improvisation

Since LOLC's primary goal is to facilitate collaborative improvisation within a laptop ensemble, our evaluation focused on how musicians borrow, re-use, and transform musical patterns. We found a healthy level of collaboration among all musicians. During the dress rehearsal, for instance, the musicians created a total of 61 musical patterns; 19 of those patterns (31%) were based on patterns borrowed from others. The musicians scheduled a total of 117 different variables for playback; 37 of these patterns (32%) were borrowed from another musician. Although these statistics do not necessarily correlate to the quality of collaboration, they indicate a critical degree of sharing that is prerequisite to effective collaboration in LOLC, and they demonstrate that musicians were responding to each other through the music they improvised.

Borrowing and transforming often became a chained process for the ensemble as musicians borrowed patterns that were themselves borrowed. One pattern from the dress rehearsal was based on 11 prior patterns (seven created from scratch) created by 5 different musicians in the ensemble over the course of nearly 15 minutes. To us, LOLC's ability to facilitate the integration of ideas from so many musicians over such a long time scale attests to its potential to facilitate collaborative improvisation in an ensemble, using its ability to preserve the history of creation and collaboration within the performance to enhance the ability of musicians to borrow, transform, combine, and recall musical material.

Accessibility

Despite the fact that the five musicians in the ensemble had no (or negligible) exposure to computer programming, all of these musicians were able to learn LOLC fairly quickly and mount a public performance with the environment. All of the musicians found the experience of learning and playing with LOLC to be straightforward, saying that it was "easier than I thought it would be" and that it was "pretty easy to use once you get the hang of it." They also found the combination of self-guided practice and group rehearsals to be an effective means to learn LOLC.

We also asked the musicians if they were musically satisfied with the performance. This quote from one of the musicians summarizes the attitudes of all of the musicians towards the experience: "I thought it was satisfying. Honestly, I had a great time working on this (...) and to me it was musically satisfying."

Apparently, for the musicians, LOLC was more than just accessible: they enjoyed the learning process and were proud of what they had accomplished.

FUTURE WORK

Based on our evaluation of a performance by professional musicians with no programming experience, we believe that LOLC has largely succeeded in facilitating collaborative improvisation within a laptop ensemble and in being accessible to use by non-programmers.

In the coming year, we are extending LOLC to the realm of real-time notation, in which musicians sight-read conventional or graphical notation live, in performance, as it is rendered on a digital display [5]. Performances with this extended system are already planned for 2012.

ACKNOWLEDGEMENTS

LOLC is supported by a grant from the National Science Foundation as part of a larger research project on musical improvisation in performance and education (NSF CreativeIT 0855758). We also thank all the musicians of Sonic Generator. Additional information is available at http://www.jasonfreeman.net/lolc/

REFERENCES

1. Allen, S. Teaching Large Ensemble Music Improvisation. *Radical Pedagogy* 4(1). Available at radicalpedagogy.icaap.org/content/issue4_1/01_Allen.html. 2002.
2. Brown, A., and A. Sorensen. Interacting with Generative Music through Live Coding. *Contemporary Music Review 28*,1(2009), 17–29.
3. Brown, C., and J. Bischoff. Indigenous to the Net: Early Network Music Bands in the San Francisco Bay Area. Available at crossfade.walkerart.org/ brownbischoff, 2002.
4. Collins, N., et al. Live Coding in Laptop Performance. *Organised Sound 8*,3(2003), 321–330.
5. Freeman, J. Extreme Sight-Reading, Mediated Expression, and Audience Participation: Real-time Music Notation in Live Performance. *Computer Music Journal 32*, 3 (2008), 25–41.
6. Freeman, J. and Troyer A.V. Collaborative Textual Improvisation in a Laptop Ensemble. Computer Music Journal 35, 2(2011), 8-21.
7. Lewis, G. *Virtual Concerto*. Unpublished musical score. 2004.
8. Wang, G., et al. CoAudicle: A Collaborative Audio Programming Space. In *Proceedings of the International Computer Music Conference*, 2003. 331– 334.

A Top-Down Design Methodology based on Causality and Chronology for Developing Assisted Story Generation Systems

Carlos León
Dpto. de Ingeniería del Software e I. Artificial
Universidad Complutense de Madrid
cleon@fdi.ucm.es

Pablo Gervás
Instituto de Tecnología del Conocimiento
Universidad Complutense de Madrid
pgervas@sip.ucm.es

ABSTRACT

Assisted story generation systems do not include automatic generation of content due to the fact that creating generation algorithms is a challenging task, usually carried out in research projects on Artificial Intelligence. This paper proposes a top-down design methodology in which the knowledge representation is based on causality and chronology. The proposed methodology partially eases the process by dividing the narrative generation system in two parts: a generic engine and a domain definition based only on a specific set of predicates. The theoretical model and an implemented case study with resulting stories are presented.

Author Keywords

Story generation, top-down design, assisted creativity, artificial intelligence, knowledge representation

ACM Classification Keywords

I.2.4 Knowledge Representation Formalisms and Methods: Representations (procedural and rule-based)

General Terms

Algorithms, Design

INTRODUCTION

There exist many methods for writing stories by hand, basically oriented to train storytellers. These methods basically give more or less generic rules to engage an audience or facilitate the understanding of the message being told. However, while these influence or improve the creativity of the generated narrative content, they fully rely on the effort of the storyteller and do not use computers.

In this paper we propose a design methodology for story generation systems. This methodology tries to offer a more general approach to story generation in such a way that the domain dependent knowledge and the generation engine are clearly isolated. The set of high-level relations that must be defined as the domain definition for the engine to work is kept to a minimum. In this way, the maintainability of the knowledge base in particular and the generation system in general is improved. The top-down approach makes it simpler to solve the growth of the knowledge base in the top levels which, by definition, are more intensely defined and thus less susceptible to changes at a large scale.

C&C'11, November 3–6, 2011, Atlanta, Georgia, USA.
ACM 978-1-4503-0820-5/11/11.

OTHER STORY GENERATION SYSTEMS

TALE-SPIN tackles story generation as a problem solving process [1]. This design proposes a basic core engine reasonably independent from the set of actions that can be performed. Grammar-based story generation systems also propose a top-down approach for the design of the generation systems [2,3]. They do not scale well because the dependency of the added knowledge with the rest of the knowledge base is not well managed. MINSTREL [4] domain-specific knowledge with TRAMS, which are base cases of narrative schemas that can be adapted to fit a new story. MEXICA [5] introduced tensional guidelines, which are typical progressions of some emotional variable in time. This has also inspired part of this work, as explained later. BRUTUS' engine consists on a large knowledge base that encodes a significant amount of common sense knowledge and narrative [6]. While this is powerful in principle, it suffers from the knowledge acquisition bottleneck and the inclusion of additional knowledge heavily restricts the improvement of the system. Another knowledge-intensive system is presented by León and Gervás in a story generation system based on evaluation and selection of stories [7].

DOMAIN INDEPENDENT PART OF THE STORY GENERATION ENGINE

One of the objectives of this research is to improve the ratio between the effort needed to improve the generation capabilities and the number of different stories that can be generated. In this research we have created a top-down design pattern for defining a domain definition without affecting the basic generation engine. This means that a new domain definition can be used to generate new types of stories without having to rewrite the engine. Additionally, the top-down definition makes it a bit easier to define the domain, as it will be explained. The basic engine relies on 5 relations that must be instanced for each implementation.

- *requirement* – this relation links a set of facts that must be true in a partial story with another one that requires them to be true.

- *cause* – this relation pairs a set of event descriptions with another one that *could* be caused by this set.
- *provoke* – this relation represents a stronger version of causality. When something is provoked, it means that it must happen in the story.
- *simultaneous* – this relation sets whether a fact can take place during the same interval as others or not.
- *duration* – this basic relation informs the basic engine about the basic duration of an event description.

These relations are defined in a state-independent way. This means that the domain-independent part of the engine expects a definition of these relations as generic rules that do not get instanced themselves, that is, the definition of the relations do not have access to the partial story. The core engine is responsible for finding a relation that helps to add a new event description to the partial story and for instantiating the variables.

Core Generation Engine

The proposed core engine performs story generation as a generic state space search problem. The story itself represents the state, and it is updated as the story is completed. According to this, the final objective is to generate a story that fulfils the user requirements, that is, to reach a state in which all user's constraints are satisfied. How these constraints are set is explained later. For the sake of understandability, it can be assumed that the user's constraints are a set of rules.

TOP-DOWN DEFINITION OF THE DOMAIN-DEPENDENT PART OF THE STORY GENERATION ENGINE

Since the relations are so high-level, definition of complex instantiations of the relations can be too complex. This is where the top-down approach shows its benefits. Instead of trying to describe a full computational representation of the content needed for creating a knowledge base for the generators, this research proposes a way to define the domain specific knowledge in a simpler, more straightforward way. This is possible due to the fact that a general scope knowledge base is not being created, but a knowledge base for narrative plot generation oriented towards assisted creativity. By restricting the range of application strong assumptions can be made, and this helps to reduce the amount of hand-input knowledge. The 5 relations defined in the previous section can be made more specific in many different ways. Instead of implementing the relations directly with rules, they can be implemented with more abstract definitions. These definitions help to manage the reduction of maintainability of a field-specific domain base. The relations can be further defined in terms of more specific relations.

DRIVING THE GENERATION THROUGH CURVES OF DESIRED VALUES AND RULES

Since the presented design is meant to ease the development of assisted creativity story generation systems, some means to let the user set what she wants the system to generate are proposed. Three different, complementary methods are considered in the model:

- A set of objectives for generation defined as logic rules. This set contains the characteristics that the final story must have.
- A set of constraints defined as logic rules. These constraints describe what the user does not want to be in the story.
- A set of curves that represent the sequential evolution of some set of user defined and domain dependent variables in time.

CONCLUSION

Automated story generation systems can reduce the amount of needed work in storytelling when used as an assisting tool, and this can help to spend the effort on the creative part. Since developing this kind of tools requires a complex handling of Artificial Intelligence techniques, this paper proposes a methodology to ease the creation of story generators. Several assumptions that can be made because of the constrained domain (narrative) help to restrict the constraints of the problem so that a simpler definition is possible. In this paper a detailed description of the model has been presented.

ACKNOWLEDGMENTS

Research funded by Spanish Ministry of Science and Innovation's TIN2009-14659-C03-01 and GR35/10-A (group 921332).

REFERENCES

1. Meehan, J. (1976). The Metanovel: Writing Stories by Computer. PhD thesis, Yale University.
2. Lang, R. R. (1999). A declarative model for simple narratives. In Proceedings of the AAAI Fall Symposium on Narrative Intelligence, pages 134–141. AAAI Press.
3. Rumelhart, D. E. (1975). Notes on a schema for stories. Representation and Understanding: Studies in Cognitive Science, pages 211–236.
4. Turner, S. (1992). MINSTREL: A Computer Model of Creativity and Storytelling. PhD thesis, University of California at Los Angeles, Los Angeles, CA, USA.
5. Pérez y Pérez, R. (1999). MEXICA: A Computer Model of Creativity in Writing. PhD thesis, U. of Sussex.
6. Bringsjord, S. and Ferrucci, D. (1999). Artificial Intelligence and Literary Creativity: Inside the mind of Brutus, a StoryTelling Machine. Lawrence Erlbaum Associates, Hillsdale, NJ.
7. León, C., Gervás, P. Towards a Black Box Approximation to Human Processing of Narratives based on Heuristics over Surface Form. AAAI 2010 Fall Symposium on Computational Models of Narrative. Arlington, Virginia, pp. 31-38.

LilyPond: An Online Community for Sharing E-Textile Projects

Emily Lovell and Leah Buechley
MIT Media Lab
Cambridge, MA 02139
emme, leah @media.mit.edu

ABSTRACT
LilyPond is a new online community that enables people to document, share and browse e-textile projects—projects that blend electronics, computation and textiles. It was designed to be a project repository and a community gathering place for students, educators, and hobbyists who are creating e-textiles. In this paper, we describe the developing website and its user community. We examine the demographics of this community, its patterns of site usage and its emerging tastes and preferences.

Author Keywords
E-textiles, electronic textiles, online communities, creativity, LilyPond, LilyPad, Arduino.

ACM Classification Keywords
K.3.0 [Computers and Education]: General. C.3

General Terms: Human Factors, Design

INTRODUCTION

Electronic textiles (e-textiles) are interactive artifacts created from a combination of soft, flexible materials like fabrics and threads and electronic components like lights, speakers, and sensors. New tools including the LilyPad Arduino [1], the iCatch [4], and the Sparkle kit (http://www.aniomagic.com) are enabling students, hobbyists, educators and other non-engineers to construct e-textiles. The LilyPond site is designed to be a place where these builders can document and share their projects, browse other projects for inspiration, and socialize.

The site is similar in spirit to other online communities that center around documenting and sharing creative work. In building the site we were particularly inspired by Ravelry (https://www.ravelry.com/)—a site where knitters share patterns and documentations of their knitting projects—Instructables (http://www.instructables.com/)—a site where a wide variety of crafters, engineers, and builders share how-to instructions—and Scratch (http://scratch.mit.edu/) [3]—a site where Scratch programmers (mostly children) share interactive media designs. Like each of these sites, LilyPond provides creators with a venue for showcasing their work and visitors a means to familiarize themselves with the medium and find inspiration.

E-textile projects are documented on other sites including Instructables, Flickr (http://www.flickr.com), and YouTube (http://www.youtube.com), but in these venues the projects are part of a mix of other content. LilyPond is intended to provide a place where e-textile crafters can encounter a critical mass of likeminded designers.

The LilyPond project is part of a larger research effort aimed at documenting and understanding the evolution of a creative community. We hope that developing a forum for a relatively young community will give us a unique opportunity to study how creative communities form, collectively establish evaluation criteria for their work, and reward exceptional contributions [2].

LILYPOND

Figure 1 shows a screen shot of the LilyPond homepage. Visitors to the site encounter three categories of user-contributed projects on the homepage: *Most Loved Projects*—the projects most often favorited by other users—*Most Recent Projects*—recent projects sorted in order of submission time—and *Workshop Projects*—projects created as part of organized workshops. Clicking on a project thumbnail takes a user to a page that displays more information about the project including: a media gallery of photos and videos, a description, a list of the components that went into the project, a copy of the source code that is controlling the project, and links to websites that have additional project documentation. A snapshot of a project page is also shown in Figure 1. After logging into the site, members can also comment on and love projects made by other users, as well as document and share their own projects.

LilyPond was launched in the Spring of 2010 and is now home to 158 projects and 81 users. So far, the site has been used primarily by members of our research team and affiliated students to document the outcome of e-textile workshops. We are receiving an increasing number of submissions from independent designers, educators, and hobbyists. Approximately 31% of site members are researchers or students directly involved in the project. Approximately 92% of projects on the site were created by students or researchers working on the project and 8% were created by independent developers.

Site usage

Members seem to be using the site in three primary ways: to document projects, find information and inspiration, and make community connections. Educators and researchers are using the site to document projects on behalf of students, and to share projects that they are testing in

C&C'11, November 3–6, 2011, Atlanta, Georgia, USA.
ACM 978-1-4503-0820-5/11/11.

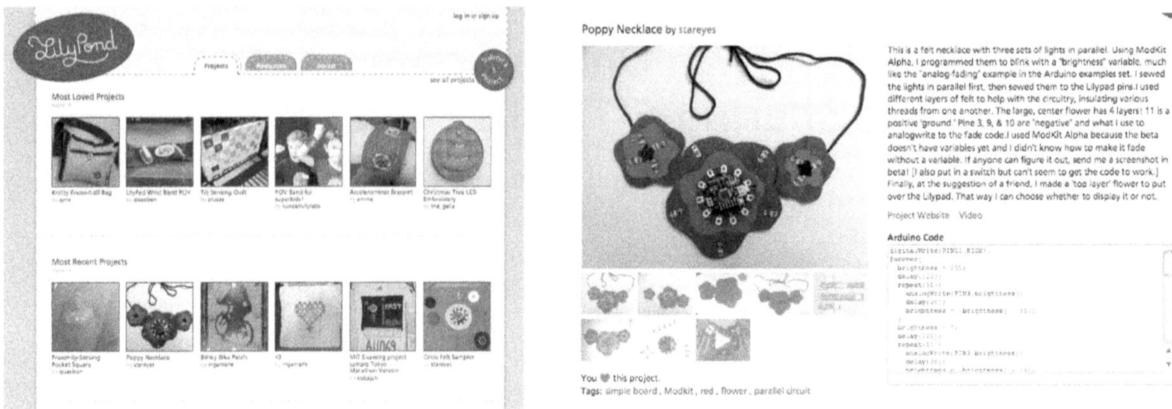

Figure 1: Screenshots of the LilyPond home page (left) and an individual project page (right).

advance of workshops. Independent hobbyists and designers are also posting projects to the site. In most cases these are projects that are also documented on the designers' personal web pages or other community sites like Instructables. These projects serve the important function of providing less experienced users with inspiration.

LilyPond generally allows people to browse projects for reference and inspiration. In workshops taught by the research team, students are encouraged to use the site in this fashion. Independent users seem to be employing the site in a similar manner. For example, Ravelry users *ingamarie* and *synemitchell* (independent LilyPond users *ingamarine* and *syne*) have linked to LilyPond from the Ravelry forums, citing it as a place to go for inspiration.

Finally, in addition to informational content, LilyPond provides users with access to a larger community of people who are creating e-textile projects—both other students and independent designers and hobbyists. Members can communicate with each other by loving projects and having conversations within project comment sections.

Community demographics and values

It is too early to draw clear conclusions about the character of the LilyPad community—particularly since a large percentage of users are associated with a research team that includes the site developers. However, what we do know about the users, their projects, and their viewing habits begins to paint an interesting picture. First, the majority of users (67%) are female (we have self reported gender data on 100% of our users), and a majority of LilyPond projects were constructed by girls or women. This kind of gender balance is unusual among technology focused communities.

It is also intriguing to examine the projects most loved by the community, which are not necessarily the most technically sophisticated. The community seems to value projects that are functional, beautiful, colorful, and well documented above those that are technically sophisticated but less aesthetically appealing. For example, a complex bike speedometer project was posted to the site around the same time as the most loved project of all time. The bike project received considerable attention from other blogs and is clearly an accomplished project, but is not in the top 10 of loved projects. Meanwhile, the project at the top of the most loved list is technically sophisticated but also decorative and beautifully documented.

In short, LilyPond seems to be supporting a female dominated community of people experimenting with electronics and computation that has different values than that of more traditional technical communities.

CONCLUSION

The LilyPond project is still in its early stages. As we move forward with the project we intend to expand the site in several ways and deepen our assessment of the activities and communities that it is supporting. In particular, we plan to investigate the evolution of the community and its evaluation standards, and we hope that this will eventually enable us to better understand how creative communities form and grow.

ACKNOWLEDGEMENTS

Thanks to Linda Delafuente for her assistance on this project. This material is based upon work supported by the National Science Foundation under Grant No. 0855773. Any opinions, findings, and conclusions or recommendations expressed in this material are those of the author(s) and do not necessarily reflect the views of the National Science Foundation.

REFERENCES

1. Buechley, L. et al., 2008. The LilyPad Arduino: using computational textiles to investigate engagement, aesthetics, and diversity in computer science education. In Proc. of CHI, pp. 423-432.
2. Csikszentmihalyi, M., 1987. Society, culture, and person: A systems view of creativity. In R. Sternberg (Ed.), The nature of creativity, pp. 325–338. NY, NY: Cambridge University Press.
3. Monroy-Hernández, A., 2009. Designing a website for creative learning. In Proc. WebSci.
4. Ngai, G. et al., 2010. i*CATch: a scalable plug-n-play wearable computing framework for novices and children. In Proc. of CHI, pp. 443-452.

mediPuppet: An Interactive Comforting Companion for Children While Visiting a Doctor

Szu-Chia Lu, Andy Wu, Ellen Yi-Luen Do
GVU Center
Georgia Institute of Technology
Atlanta, Georgia 30332
{ sj.today, andywu, ellendo }@gatech.edu

ABSTRACT
Young children often feel anxious when visiting the doctors. This paper presents mediPuppet, an interactive companion with an exploratory procedure map designed to help children feel more relaxed and comfortable during their medical procedure. The ultimate goal of this study is to transform an intimidating stressful situation into a joyful exploring game for children during hospital visits.

Author Keywords
Children, game, interactive puppet, pediatric patient, health.

ACM Classification Keywords
H.5.m. Information interfaces and presentation (e.g., HCI): Miscellaneous.

General Terms
Design.

INTRODUCTION

A regular medical exam can be an unpleasant event for young children and their parents. A hospital visit can quickly become a battle before, during or even after the exam. The reason why young children experience this anxiety is the fear of the unknown, which is often more frightening than the reality. A friendly comforting companion and a well-designed procedure informing system can help to put the child's mind at ease, and their parents' as well. A comforting object can provide further relief to help a child remain calm during the physical exams. An explanation before the procedure, including what to expect from the doctor or nurse, would be beneficial in helping a child to be mentally prepared for the upcoming exam. It also provides the parents information of how to assist in the next exam procedure for their child. Therefore, we built a prototype interactive comforting puppet to support emotional bonds and provide responsive interactions for children. We then conducted a user study to observe the interaction between young children and this interactive companion.

C&C'11, November 3–6, 2011, Atlanta, Georgia, USA.
ACM 978-1-4503-0820-5/11/11.

BACKGROUND

The Hays Medical Center in Kansas [1] gives "a Josh and Friends kit", which includes a plush puppy "Josh" and a book, called "I'll Be OK". The Emergency Department in Emerson Hospital in Massachusetts [2] distributed the Coping Kit with books and toys that varies by age group and color-coded by gender. However, these comforting kits cannot produce real-time responsive support for the children and the young patients might get bored easily.

The other therapeutic aspect called The Animal-Assisted Therapy (AAT) advocates the interaction between the young children and their pets can provide strong emotional bonds, promote the sense of security to the child pet owner. It can ease the anxiety of the young patients and quicken the medical procedure as well [3]. However, not all pediatric hospitals or parents can afford to have an animal companion for each child during their hospital visit.

PROTOTYPE DESIGN

The prototype of mediPuppet was made of foam boards with an Android phone embedded (Figure 1). The size and weight of this prototype is designed for young children to hold or walk around with them. The puppet has no small parts that could fall apart or cause choking hazard. An Android phone embedded provides a quick programmable platform to support interaction design so that a child can interact with the environment through the puppet.

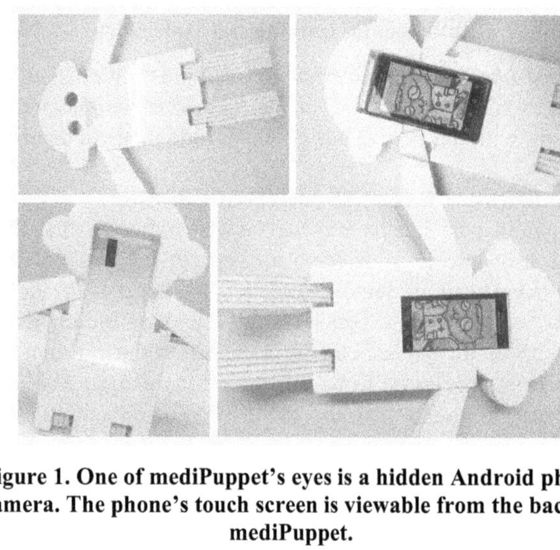

Figure 1. One of mediPuppet's eyes is a hidden Android phone camera. The phone's touch screen is viewable from the back of mediPuppet.

PILOT STUDY

We conducted a usability study to learn more about the interaction between the child and the puppet. Our young participants whose ages range from 3-5 years old who were paired interviewed with their parents. The experiments were in a pseudo hospital environment and took around 90 minutes in total for the three experiment sessions.

1) ***Pre-observation interview*** (30 minutes) Parents were asked to answer open-ended questions about the child's reaction and previous experience of visiting a doctor.

2) ***Field Observation*** (45 minutes) The child was given the puppet to play with, to name it, and to decorate it with one of the origami dresses (Figure 2). In the *examination phase*, the child explored the medical exam steps by scanning the QR code on the procedure game map (Figure 3) with mediPuppet's hidden camera. The whole session was recorded for data analysis.

Figure 2. Origami dresses used to decorate the mediPuppet

Figure 3. Procedure game map visualize the medical examination procedure and to support the interaction with mediPuppet for learning and exploration.

3) ***Post-observation interview*** (15 minutes). We asked the child to talk about his or her feeling and experiences from playing with the puppet during the pseudo medical exam.

PRELIMINARY RESULTS AND DISCUSSION

All parent participants we interviewed indicated that their child was able to understand and accept the concept why they have to see a doctor. However, unexpected or sudden exam actions from a doctor would still scare the child and bring about all the tears and screams. Both the children and the parents preferred to be informed beforehand. The field observation found that the children enjoyed naming and decorating the mediPuppet. Through engagement in the activity, they formed emotional bonds with the puppet. They called the puppet with names from their real life experience (e.g., naming it Baby because the mother is expecting). The children considered the puppet as a real person and posed the puppet into different poses to help it "see better" or "feel comfortable." All children in the post-test interview felt emotionally attached to the puppet.and expressed the desire to carry the puppet with them next time when visiting a doctor.

Figure 4. The QR code on the procedure game map can be scanned through the mediPuppet's hidden camera. Then, the information of next procedure pops up in the screen with images for the child and detail instructions for the parents.

CHALLENGES

The experiments were conducted in a mocked exam room of a child behavior study lab, not in a real hospital environment. In the continue user study could involve a trained professional in a real exam room. In addition, considering that young children may not verbally express their feelings or emotions clearly, the sessions were recorded to assist in analysis, taking into account together with the comments from the parents in the post-interviews.

SUMMARY

In this study, all children participants created a bonding relationship with mediPuppet, and engaged in the exam procedure through exploration and play. Emotion bonding and learning through exploration, help the young children (i.e., pediatric patients to be) overcome their anxiety during a hospital visit. Future version of mediPuppet could be a wearable version in the form of an attachable accessory, rather than limiting the features to be just one specific puppet. Preferably, children can bring their favorite toy to wear this device and accompany them during a doctor visit. Also, mediPuppet could include automatic recording of the hospital visit for procedure and data analysis or be incorporated into electronic health record

REFERENCES

1. Pediatric Patients at Hays Med Get a Companion. http://portal.haysmed.com/portal/page?_pageid=43,67257&_dad=portal&_schema=PORTAL.
2. Coping Kits Comfort Children in the Emergency Department. http://www.nursezone.com/nursing-news-events/more-features/Coping-Kits-Comfort-Children-in-the-Emergency-Department_20482.aspx.
3. Levinson, B.M. and Mallon, G.P. *Pet-Oriented Child Psychotherapy*. Charles C. Thomas Publisher, 1997.

Image Schemata in Animated Metaphors for Insight Problem Solving

Eric Luchian
School of Computing and Communications
Lancaster University
Lancaster, LA1 4WA UK
+44 (0) 1524 510 356
e.luchian@lancaster.ac.uk

Corina Sas
School of Computing and Communications
Lancaster University
Lancaster, LA1 4WA UK
+44 (0) 1524 510 318
corina@comp.lancs.ac.uk

ABSTRACT
While most of the work on metaphors has focused on conceptual ones, less attention has been paid to the visual metaphors for insight problems. This paper investigates the role of dynamism and realism in visual metaphors for cueing the insight problem solving process. To match the visual-kinesthetic feature of the eight-coin insight problem, the developed metaphors represented the insight cues, both kinetically and kinesthetically. An experimental study showed the superiority of metaphors as realistic and continuous animations over schematic and discrete animations.

Keywords
Visual insight problem, visual metaphors, animation, realism, image schemata.

ACM Classification Keywords
H5.2. Information interfaces and presentation (e.g., HCI): User Interfaces: Theory and methods.

General Terms
Human Factors

INTRODUCTION
By capturing the similarities between two domains, metaphors support the transfer of meaning from the source to the target. Different types of metaphors and predominantly conceptual ones have been investigated for their role in perception, learning, problem solving and creativity, whereas less work has focused on the role of nonverbal metaphors in insight problem solving. The existing work in insight problems offers conflicting findings on the effectiveness of different types of visual metaphors agreeing however that levels of dynamism and realism are important factors to be considered. Visual metaphors appear to be particularly successful when augmented with kinetic or kinesthetic information but no study has compared their effectiveness when such information is embedded in the metaphor's content. The paper reports the findings on the eight-coin insight problem using discrete and dynamic animations embedding image schemata to capture kinetic and kinesthetic information relevant for the insight.

C&C'11, November 3–6, 2011, Atlanta, Georgia, USA.
ACM 978-1-4503-0820-5/11/11.

METHODOLOGY
The experimental study explores three features of visual cues which may impact their success in supporting problem solving. Previous work on eight-coin problem suggests that the visual cues offering information about the initial and final state of the problem do not lead to higher success rate than those capturing only the final or solution state [10]. However, if well understood, the visual cues capturing more than the final state could be beneficial because they may allow better analogical transfer. To further explore this, we developed visual metaphors not as static images as in [10] but as *animations*, both continuous, i.e. computer-based simulations, and discrete, i.e. sequence of static pictures.

While the apprehension principle proposed by Tversky [11] argues that animations should be less realistic, the importance of *realistic* animations in learning has been emphasized by Höffler and Leutner's meta-analysis [2]. Michas and Berry [6] also argued that static pictures can in be more effective if they represent a set of key moments in the process or have a high level of realism. To further explore these outcomes, we considered two levels of realism: schematic for which we used only primary depth cues, and realistic which benefited from both primary and secondary cues, i.e., light, shadow, atmospheric perspective and gradients [9].

Previous findings have also shown the impact of animations on the acquisition of procedural-motor knowledge [2]. Interestingly, the expected superiority of animations in supporting problem solving has not been identified [5], and the link between the observational learning of motor skills and cognitive skills has not been investigated. Although the tied interdependence between *image schemata* and motor skills has been already advocated by Lakoff and Johnson [3], their role in insight problem solving has not been yet explored. A notable exception is Catrambrone et al. [1] who investigated the role of perceptual kinesthetic information in analogical reasoning. Our study is the first to investigate the role of animations in insight problem solving through visual representations of image schemata capturing both kinetic (i.e. force-based) and kinesthetic (gesture-based) information.

The reason for focusing on the eight-coin insight problem is twofold: the problem is delivered in a kinesthetic format, and each of the two insights involving object manipulation can be directly linked to available image schemata. To detail, the eight coins in the initial configuration are provided on the table in front of participants who are required to solve the problem by placing the coins in the right position. Solving the problem involves physical manipulations of the coins and the insights of grouping and stacking. We argue that these insights activate two specific image schemata: splitting schemata for the grouping insight, and verticality (up and down) schemata for the stacking insight. The sample consisted of 130 participants, 26 for each of the 4 experimental and control groups. The overall sample consisted of 55% males and 45% females and over 75 % were between 21 and 30 years of age. Participants were randomly assigned to conditions and after two minutes of working on the problem, they were stopped and advised to watch the first visual metaphor and then to resume the work for another two minutes. The procedure was repeated for the second metaphor and after a total of 6 minutes of solution attempts, the test ended and the result was marked as successful or unsuccessful.

FINDINGS

The most important outcome of this study is that each of the four conditions has led to success rates above 50%, with the highest value of 75% for the continuous realistic animation (Table 1). This is impressive given that visual insight problems are notoriously difficult to solve with a success rate for the control group seldom higher than 10%, i.e. 13% for radiation problem [8] or 9.4% for nine dots [4]. For the eight-coin problem, when stacking and grouping cues were verbally provided the success rate was 42.8% (Exp.1 in [7]), whereas the static visual cues enabled 50% success rate [10]. Exact binomial sign tests showed that the four types of metaphors enabled significantly higher success rate than the control group (7%) ($p < 0.01$), and that metaphors captured as continuous animations using secondary depth cues have led to significantly higher success rate (73%) than the metaphors depicted as discrete animations through primary depth cues (50%) ($p = 0.01$). The outcome is important given the limited engagement with the metaphors. For example, success rate over 80% was obtained in radiation problem [8] but participants had to recall each analogy through written descriptions, whereas in our study they were actively exposed for only 38 seconds to each of the two metaphors without being asked to recall them later.

The findings also emphasize the importance of image schemata and animations on motor knowledge for insight problem solving. An important aspect is the nature of the eight-coin problem both in terms of content, i.e., visual, spatial, three dimensional; and its form of delivery, i.e., visual-kinesthetic perception and object manipulation. It is this nature of the problem and the process of solving it which involves forces and gestures that makes image schemata a suitable candidate to represent the insight cues.

Condition	Force	Gestures	Total
Control group	NA	NA	2 (7)
Discrete animation primary 3D	5	8	13 (50)
Discrete animation secondary 3D	5	10	15 (57.7)
Continuous animation primary 3D	8	7	15 (57.7)
Continuous animation secondary 3D	8	11	19 (73)

Note: Numbers in parentheses are percentages, $n = 26$ in each condition

Table 1: Number of participants who solved the problem.

ACKNOWLEDGMENTS

This work is part of the DESIRE network and is supported by the Initial Training Network "Marie Curie Actions", funded by the FP7 People Programme (PITN-GA-2008-215446) entitled "DESIRE: Creative Design for Innovation in Science and Technology".

REFERENCES

1. Catrambone, R, Craig, D, and Nersessian, N. The role of perceptually represented structure in analogical problem solving. *Memory & Cognition*, 34, 5 (2006), 1126-1132.
2. Hoffler, T and Leutner, D. Instructional animation versus static pictures: A meta-analysis. *Learning and Instruction*, 17 (2007), 722-738.
3. Lakoff, G and Johnson, M. *Metaphors We Live By*. University of Chicago Press, Chicago, 1980.
4. Lung, C & Dominowski, R. Effects of strategy instructions and practice on nine-dot problem solving. *Journal of Experimental Psychology: Learning, Memory, and Cognition*, 111 (1985) 804–811.
5. Mayer, R and Moreno, R. Animation as an aid to multimedia learning. *Educational Psychology Review*, 14, 1 (2002), 87-99.
6. Michas, I and Berry, D. Learning a procedural task: effectiveness of multimedia presentations. *Applied Cognitive Psychology*, 14, 6 (2000), 555-575.
7. Ormerod, T, MacGregor, J, and Chronicle, E. Dynamics and constraints in insight problem solving. *Journal of Experimental Psychology: Learning, Memory, and Cognition* , 28, 4 (2002), 791-799.
8. Pedone, R, Hummel, J, and Holyoak, K. The use of diagrams in analogical problem solving. *Memory & Cognition*, 29, 2 (2001), 214-221.
9. Ramachandran, V. Perceiving Shape from Shading. *Scientific American*, 2 (Aug. 1988), 76-83.
10. Sas, C, Luchian, E, and Ball, L. Investigating Visual Analogies for Visual Insight Problems (2010), Proceedigns of *DESIRE Conference*, ACM. 90-100.
11. Tversky, B. Visualizing Thought. *Topics in Cognitive Science* (2010), 1-37.

Innovation is Built on the Obscure: Innovation-Enhancing Software for Uncovering the Obscure

Tony McCaffrey
University of Massachusetts
Amherst, MA 01003 USA
amccaffr@psych.umass.edu
+1 508 340 2655

Lee Spector
Hampshire College
Amherst, MA 01002 USA
lspector@hampshire.edu
+1 413 559 5352

ABSTRACT
Analysis of over 1,000 innovative inventions reveals that during the innovative process at least one rarely-noticed or new (i.e., obscure) feature is unearthed and built upon to create the solution (i.e., the *Obscure Features Hypothesis* for innovation: OFH) [6, 7]. Embedding the insights from this analysis into the structure of semantic networks creates *AhaNets*, which help optimize the search for the needed key obscure feature. Techniques to overcome cognitive aversions to noticing the obscure (i.e., *fixation effects*) further enhance innovation by improving the search process. Once implemented in software, *AhaNets* and counter-fixation techniques create an innovation-enhancing human-machine interaction.

ACM Classification Keywords
I.2.4 [Artificial Intelligence]: Knowledge Representation Formalisms and Methods—*Semantic networks*; I.2.6 [Artificial Intelligence]: Learning—*Concept learning*

General Terms
Experimentation

INTRODUCTION
Examining the solutions to all benchmark innovative problems used in psychology experiments (i.e., insight problems), 150 recent inventions, and 1,001 historic innovative engineering solutions [1] leads to several principles that when structurally placed in a semantic network increase the success rate for solving engineering problems requiring innovation. First, the solutions to all problems we analyzed involved at least one rarely-noticed or new (i.e., obscure) feature of the problem. Common sense stipulates that if the solution were based on commonly noticed features, the problem would have most likely been solved by now. Figure 1 places all common features of the concept in an inner basin while the obscure features reside outside the basin. The commonality of a feature is measured by the frequency that the feature is mentioned in a feature-listing task. Second, the key obscure feature needed for a solution was always just one or two links beyond the common features of the concepts of the problem—thus significantly reducing the search space. The height dimension of Figure 1 represents the probability of a feature being helpful in innovation with the features on the ridge having the highest probability of being helpful. Third, the key features for solving our collection of problems all fell into one of 32 categories of feature types for physical objects and materials (i.e., *Feature Type Taxonomy:* FTT) [6]. The FTT attempts to segment and span the possible feature space. The FTT also stipulates the reason that a link connects two concepts. For example, *candle* and *wick* are connected by the feature type *part*, while *candle* is connected to *motionless* by the feature type *motion*. Further analysis of our large sample of problems produces a probability distribution among the 32 feature types based on their degree of helpfulness in solving the problems. As more problems are solved, the probability distribution continually becomes more refined. The dotted lines of Figure 1 divide the feature space into sectors (only four of the 32 sectors are shown) and the ever-refining probability distribution makes the ridge of the different sectors have different heights. Together, the ridge and a probability distribution over the sectors of Figure 1 guide the search for the key obscure feature(s) to the most probable distance and direction from the initial concept.

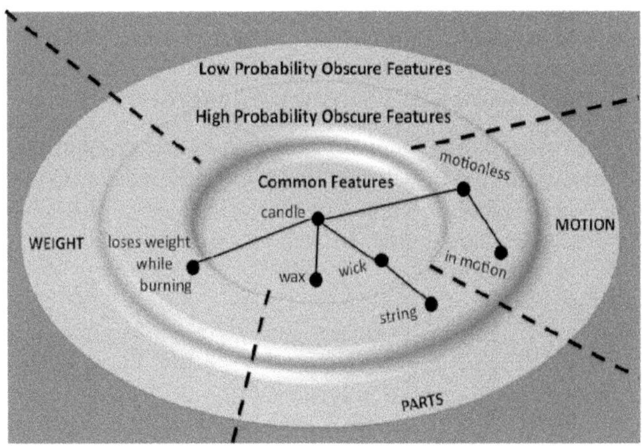

Figure 1. A simple *AhaNet* for a candle: The height shows the probability of a feature type being helpful for innovation.

FIXATION EFFECTS
Cognitive aversions to noticing the obscure are called *fixation effects* [3]. We present three *fixation effects* and effective countering techniques.

C&C'11, November 3–6, 2011, Atlanta, Georgia, USA.
ACM 978-1-4503-0820-5/11/11.

Functional Fixedness

Functional Fixedness is the tendency to fixate on the use of the object or one of its parts. The *Generic Parts Technique* (GPT) counters this habit by having subjects list the parts, shape, size, and material of each object in such a way that the descriptions do not imply a use (i.e., generic) [6]. For example, the prongs of a lamp cord's plug can be used as a screwdriver, but the word *prong* can hide this. Describing it as a *flat, rectangular metal piece one inch long and 3/8 inch wide* is more likely to trigger new uses.

Eight insight problems suffering from *functional fixedness* were solved 34% more often by a group using the GPT (83% solution rate) than a control group taught no technique (49% solution rate): $t(26) = 4.23$, $p < .001$. Subjects who used software that guided them through the GPT solved 100% of the problems.

Goal Blindness

Goal Blindness shields subjects from the many assumptions they make by their current phrasing of the goal. The *Goal Verb Technique* (GVT) focuses on the assumptions underlying the verb used in the goal description [7]. For example, an engineering firm presented us with the unsolved problem of adhering a coating to Teflon. Teflon is a no-stick surface and very aptly named. The verb *adhere* implies many features about a potential solution. Using the FTT, we articulated an extensive list of features for *adhere*. Three features from this list proved to be the crucial ones: *adhere* assumes a (1) chemical process between (2) two surfaces that are in (3) direct contact. Negating these three features opened up new options to explore including the critical combination: a sandwich of three surfaces in which the coating indirectly sticks to the Teflon due to its attraction to a magnetic surface behind the Teflon. Of course, the coating would need to possess the proper make-up in order to secure itself properly. The presenting engineering firm has affirmed the high probability that our novel approach or some variation of it will work.

An extensive list of verbs exists that covers almost all engineering goals [4]. By using the FTT on each verb in the list, we are creating a thorough database of assumptions that engineers can use during problem solving.

Design Fixation

Design Fixation is the tendency to fixate on the features of known solutions when trying to be innovative [5]. The *Feature Type Spectrum* presents a *spectral analysis* of sorts of an object's features—thus revealing the obscure features that should be focused upon to produce innovative designs.

For example, 96 subjects wrote down as many features and associations as they could in 4 minutes for each of a set of common objects. Categorizing their responses into the 32 types of the FTT and then averaging the number of responses in each category—as shown in Figure 2 for the object candle—reveals a clear pattern of underexplored and ignored feature types that can become the basis for innovation. The low bars and non-existent bars of Figure 2 point to the obscure feature types upon which to build new candle designs. Using this process, we have created many new candle designs that we are licensing to companies.

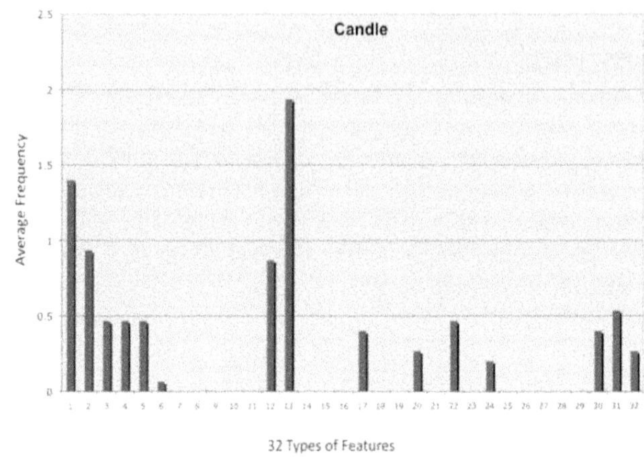

Figure 2. A Feature Spectrum Diagram for a candle.

REFERENCES

1. Challoner, J. (2009). *1,001 Inventions that changed the world.* Hauppauge, NY: Barron's Educational Series.
2. Duncker, K. (1935/1945). On problem-solving. *Psychological Monographs*, 58(5), Whole No. 270.
3. Hatchuel, A., Le Masson, P., Weil, B. (2011). Teaching innovative design reasoning: How concept-knowledge theory can help overcome fixation effects. *Artif Int Eng Des, Analysis, Manuf*, 25, 77-92.
4. Hirtz, J., Stone, R., McAdams, D., Szykman, S., & Wood, K. (2002). A functional basis for engineering design: Reconciling and evolving previous efforts. *Res Eng Design*, 13: 65-82.
5. Jansson, D., Smith, S. (1991). Design fixation. *Design Studies*, 12: 3-11.
6. McCaffrey, T. (2011). The obscure features hypothesis for innovation: One key to improving human innovation. Dissertation, University of Massachusetts Amherst.
7. McCaffrey, T. & Spector, L. (2011). How the Obscure Features Hypothesis leads to Innovation Assistant software. *Proc. of the Second International Conference on Computational Creativity*, 120-122.

Scaffolding Creativity with Open-Source Hardware

David A. Mellis
MIT Media Lab
75 Amherst St.
Cambridge, MA 02142
mellis@media.mit.edu

Leah Buechley
MIT Media Lab
75 Amherst St.
Cambridge, MA 02142
leah@media.mit.edu

ABSTRACT
In this paper we discuss the role of open-source hardware in supporting creativity. We use the case study of an open-source FM radio and explore the modes of creation that emerged from a workshop in which participants modified and produced the design: making, personalizing, designing, engineering, and experimenting. We contrast open-source hardware with other approaches to supporting creativity and explore some of its unique challenges and opportunities.

Author Keywords
Open-source hardware, creativity, digital fabrication.

ACM Classification Keywords
K.3.m [Computer and Education]: miscellaneous.

General Terms
Design, Documentation

INTRODUCTION
Open-source software supports a diversity of creative processes. Individuals are free to study a program's code to understand how it works, to create custom versions of the programs to suit their own needs, and to collaborate with others. Open-source hardware brings this same creative freedom to physical objects by making available their original design files for anyone to modify or manufacture. It is particularly relevant for objects made using digital fabrication processes (like laser cutting, 3d printing, or CNC milling) that allow for the creation of unique, one-off objects without significant setup time or tooling costs.

Other work [1, 2] has looked at the role of making and digital fabrication in creativity and education. Here, we focus on the role played by open-source hardware, using the example of an FM radio. We discuss the modes of creation that emerged from its making and modification. We then contrast them with those provided by other approaches. We list some challenges of open-source hardware and conclude with ideas about how they might be addressed.

FAB FM: AN OPEN-SOURCE FM RADIO
In order to explore the possibilities for creative expression provided by open-source hardware, we developed Fab FM, an open-source radio receiver housed with laser-cut wooden parts and fabric. We conducted a workshop in which participants customized and built their own versions of the Fab FM. We documented the project in a prior paper [3]; here, we specifically focus on the types of creative processes revealed through the workshop.

C&C'11, November 3–6, 2011, Atlanta, Georgia, USA.
ACM 978-1-4503-0820-5/11/11.

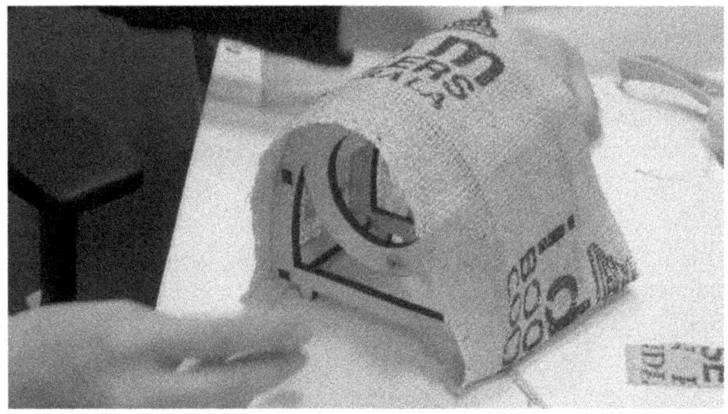

Figure 1. Making a Fab FM.

MODES OF CREATION
Open-source hardware supports many outlets for creativity: diverse processes and goals that can be applied towards its making and modification. These range from the simplest additions to the remixing of multiple designs.

Making
One direct – although not always easy – method of engagement with open-source hardware is the process of making the physical object from its digital design file. In making objects from design files, individuals gain a better appreciation of what they're are made of, how they're put together, and how they work. For example, by making a Fab FM, you find out which electronic components it requires and how they're connected together.

Personalizing
Because of the flexible fabrication processes we use with open-source hardware, it's possible to make many variations on a given design, even creating a unique appearance for each individual object. This creates opportunities for personalizing a design – simple modifications that may not effect the device's functionality or overall design but that create a personal connection between the object and its maker. With the Fab FM, one simple form of personalization is the selection of the fabric for the housing. Another is laser-etching decorations on the front or back faces.

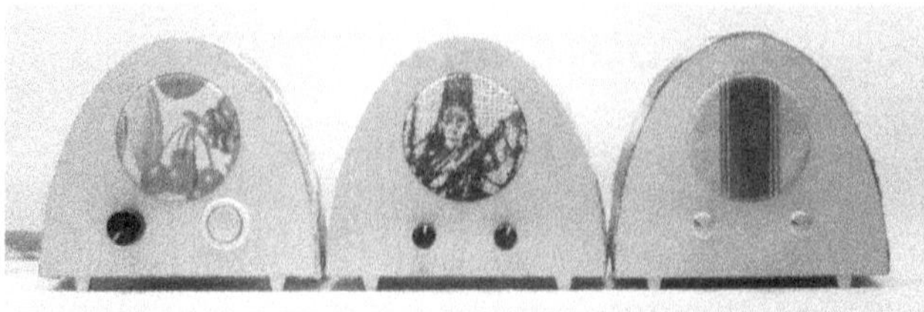

Figure 2. Personalized versions of the Fab FM.

Designing

Open-source hardware facilitates the exploration of the overall form and appearance of the object, including its shape and materials. This process is aided by the ability to use the original design as a template for the new form, maintaining those aspects required for the assembly or functioning of the object. For example, when modifying the design of the radio's wooden pieces, workshop participants could preserve the location and size of the openings for the electronic components while freely varying the overall outline. This freed them to focus on finding the right form while remaining confident that everything would fit together.

Engineering

Open-source hardware encourages technical exploration and learning by placing it within a context (the particular design) that motivates and inspires new abilities. For example, one workshop participant had never soldered through-hole electronic components before assembling the radio's circuit board. Another learned various programming and electronics skills in the course of creating capacitive touch sensing buttons for tuning the radio.

Experimenting

During the workshop, some participants used the radio as a platform for experimentation of various kinds. One modified it to switch back and forth between two stations, using what was originally the tuning knob to adjust the frequency of the switching. In this way, he experimented with the perception of this type of audio switching. Another participant used the plywood of the radio's frame as a speaker, using magnets attached to a flexure cutout in the frame with an electromagnet mounted behind it (driven by the audio signal).

COMPARISON WITH OTHER APPROACHES

Open-source hardware offers a very different set of qualities than other approaches to supporting creativity. Compared with construction kits, for example, it offers more flexibility in both design and function. Individuals aren't constrained to the system created by the maker of the toolkit. Instead, they work at the same level and with the same tools as the creator of the original design. Additionally, when you make something based on open-source hardware, it serves as a new master design or model, rather than a patch to or assemblage of other designs. This means that changes and improvements can be shared with and further modified by others, or integrated back into the original design, in ways that are difficult or impossible with construction kits.

Open-source hardware also allows an individual to easily retain portions of an existing design, allowing them to focus their creativity on those aspects of most importance to them. This contrasts with a more traditional craft or do-it-yourself (DIY) approach in which an individual creates the entire object for themselves. That requires the mastery of all the skills and techniques involved in the construction of the object, even those not of interest to the individual. Also, digital fabrication facilitates the scaling of open-source hardware design to larger volume production, as the original design files can be reproduced automatically, in contrast to craft approaches.

CHALLENGES

Open-source hardware faces a number of challenges as a creative process. The designs for an object might require a complex or expensive software tool to edit them. This can impose a significant barrier even for making small changes. (On the other hand, the desire to modify an open-source hardware design can be a useful motivation for learning these tools.) The separation of design and construction can also create difficulties: there may be a significant delay or cost involved in translating the digital file into a physical object; and, in the case of a problem, it may not be clear if the mistake is in the design or the construction.

CONCLUSION

Digital fabrication and open-source hardware provide an opportunity to take advantage of the aids to creativity offered by both software interfaces and physical making. In particular, bringing the notion of a modular construction kit into the digital (pre-fabrication) realm would allow for the combination of its higher-level abstractions and ease-of-use with the ability to customize or adjust details as desired. Moving back and forth between the digital and physical allows motivation or skill in one of the domains to scaffold their development in the other.

ACKNOWLEDGEMENTS

Thanks to Dana Gordon, Neil Gershenfeld, and the workshop participants.

REFERENCES

1. Do, E.Y.-L. and Gross, M.D. 2007. Environments for creativity: a lab for making things. Creativity & Cognition '07. 27-36.
2. Eisenberg, M. and Buechley, L. 2008. Pervasive Fabrication: Making Construction Ubiquitous in Education. Journal of Software, 3:4, 62-68.
3. Mellis, D., Gordon, D., and Buechley, L., 2010. Fab FM: the design, making, and modification of an open-source electronic product. TEI '10. 81-84.

The Impact of Design Media on Cognitive Load During Architectural Ideation Process

Ashraf Mohamed Ahmed
School of Architecture
Laval University
ashraf.mohamed-ahmed.1@ulaval.ca

Nathalie Bonnardel
Research Centre in Psychology of Cognition, Language and Emotion (EA3273)
Aix-Marseille University
& University Institute of France
Nathalie.Bonnardel@univ-provence.fr

Pierre Côté
School of Architecture
Laval University
pierre.cote@arc.ulaval.ca

ABSTRACT
Architectural design can be viewed as a process of solving ill-defined problems, requiring a constant dialogue between internal (or mental) representations and external representations based on the use of different media (sketches but also technologies) [4]. During the ideation phase or conceptual phase, this dialogue uses the resources of the working memory, which has to be discharged to process new information elements [1]. The objective of this research is to document whether different types of media traditionally used in architecture (physical models, freehand sketch or the use of a 3D software – in this case Sketch-Up) impose an additional cognitive load to the designer during the design process.

To address this topic, an experiment was conducted with 25 students in a school of architecture. Two kinds of measures of cognitive workload were performed: an objective measure using the paradigm of dual task and a subjective measurement based on a modified version of the questionnaire NASATLX.

The results showed no significant difference between media but the quantitative and qualitative measures allow us to point out tendantial differences between them.

Keywords
Architectural design process, cognitive load, design media

ACM Classification Keywords
H.5.2. Information interfaces and presentation: User Interfaces. Evaluation/methodology.

General Terms
Design, Experimentation, Measurement

INTRODUCTION
Design in general, and architectural design in this research, can be considered as a creative process since architects have to reach solutions that are both novel and adapted to the context of use [2] According to a cognitive approach, the design corresponds to a high-level cognitive process of solving "ill-defined" or "unstructured" "open" problems [2, 7]. Architectural design and, specifically, ideation or conceptual phase of design, treated as an iterative process (exploration, ideas generation and evaluation) of finding an "acceptable" solution from initial design assumptions [9] urges the need for representations. Both internal representations (depending on cognitive processes) and external representations (based on design media) are essential to any creative act.

ARCHITECTURAL DESIGN PROCESS: A DIALOG BETWEEN INTERNAL AND EXTERNAL REPRESENTATIONS

Internal Representations: The Importance of Cognitive Load for the Design Process
As recalled by Bonnardel and Piolat [3] the complexity of the design (ill-defined problems, imprecise and ambiguous mental representations, etc.) makes the designers' activity depending on Working Memory resources (WM). Current research in cognition argues that mental representations need to be externalised to free the WM. The conclusions of qualitative studies in the field of cognitive design studies, based largely on hand sketches studies [4, 5] highlight the importance of the cognitive load, defined as the amount of resources necessary to accomplish a given task. Researches on the WM have shown that the human attentional resources are limited. Consequently the externalization of ideas is necessary to reduce the cognitive load of MT.

External Representations: The Media as Design Aids
Hand sketches and ideation are two inseparable acts for most architects [6, 8]. The use of sketches has always been considered a medium of choice for the externalization of visual mental images: "Designing involves the interplay of sketching and imagery" [5]. However, little empirical research has investigated the ideation through 3D digital tools, such as SketchUp, as a design tool, dedicated to

C&C'11, November 3–6, 2011, Atlanta, Georgia, USA.
ACM 978-1-4503-0820-5/11/11.

ideation phase, which can allows objects manipulation and interactions in 3D and in real time. the objects that compose it, and navigate within it.

EXPERIMENT: THE INFLUENCE OF DESIGN MEDIA ON COGNITIVE LOAD

The objective of this research is to determine whether different types of media impose an additional cognitive load for participants during their design task.

Method

25 students in a school of architecture were asked to perform a full design task. Each participant completed three sessions using one of each of the three media: Physical Modeling (PM), Freehand Sketching (HD), and Sketch-Up (SU), the CAD software. For each medium, they performed randomly a twenty-two minute task to design either a bus station (BUS), a recycling station (RS) or a public restroom (WC).

To measure cognitive load, a dual task (performance based task) and a NASA questionnaire (subjective measure) were submitted to participants. The dual-task was conducted as follows. Throughout the 22-minute design task, the numbers from one to five were played randomly over headphones, at a rate of one every five seconds. The participant's task was to press on a foot pedal as quickly as possible whenever two ascending digits were repeated. The rate of correct responses and mean response time for correct responses are the two metrics used for data analysis.

Furthermore, the qualitative measure of mental load of the participants was achieved through a NASA TLX test, at the end of the main task. It takes into account six dimensions of load assessment: mental demand, physical demand, temporal demand, effort, performance and frustration.

Results and Analysis

Participants' Abilities with the Media

First, all participants considered themselves competent to use the media, with the highest score for the CAD medium (Responses Mean: PM = 3,85; HD = 3,39; and SU = 4,04; N = 25).

Dual Task Results

Two One-way Anovas were computed for correct responses and response time. The results for the correct responses show a tendancial difference between the three media ($p = .067$) (see Figure 1) although no significant difference is observed about the response time ($p = .17$).

NASA RTLX Results

One-way Anova was computed for the overall load TLX. The results show that there is a tendencial difference between the three media ($p = .067$). Five Anovas were also computed for the 5 dimensions of the TLX. The results show that there is no significant difference between the media for four of the five dimensions: mental demand ($p=.49$); temporal demand ($p=.35$); performance ($p=.78$); effort ($p=.72$). However, the frustration dimension presents a significant difference between the media ($p=.013$). Therefore, the use of Sketch-Up was considered as more frustrating than the two other media.

DISCUSSION AND CONCLUSIONS

The main issue about cognitive load measure is whether the externalization of cognitive activities is facilitated by one of the three design media. From the dual task results, although no significant difference was observed concerning the responses time, a tendency was obtained concerning the % of correct responses: the physical modeling seems to be the least demanding. One explanation could be that with physical modeling, unlike with the two other design media, the relatively slow pace of actions, which is intrinsic to the medium task (such as taking a craft knife, cutting cardboard, using glue and waiting until it sets, etc…) could give more time to react properly to the secondary task. In contrast, when using the CAD software (Sketch-Up), the participants have to focus on multiple areas, which require a distribution of attentional resources. This would be cognitively more demanding and it would increase the participants' workload. This may be also an explanation of the frustration feelings expressed by participants when they were using this tool.

REFERENCES

1. Bilda, Z., Gero, J.S. and Purcell, T. To sketch or not to sketch? That is the question. *Design Studies*, *27* (5). 587-613.
2. Bonnardel, N. *Créativité et conception : approches cognitives et ergonomiques*. Solal, Marseille, 2006.
3. Bonnardel, N., & Piolat, A. Design activities: how to analyze cognitive effort associated to cognitive treatments? *International Journal of Cognitive Technology*, *8* (1). 4-13.
4. Goel, V. Sketches of Thought. The MIT Press, Cambridge, 1995.
5. Goldschmidt, G. Visual displays for design: Imagery, analogy and databases of visual images. in A Koutamanis, H.T., I Vermeulen ed. *Visual Databases in Architecture,*, Avebury, Aldershot, 1995, 53-74.
6. Lawson, B. *How designers think : the design process demystified* Boston : Architectural Press, Oxford, 2006.
7. Lebahar, J.-C. *La conception en design industriel et en architecture : désir, pertinence, coopération et cognition*. Lavoisier, Paris, 2007.
8. Schon, D.A. *The Reflective Practitioner : how professional think in action* Temple Smith, London, 1987.
9. Simon, H.A. *Les sciences de l'artificiel*. Gallimard, Paris, 2004.

Mapping Seduction: Traditional Narrative Abstractions as Parameterized Story Systems

Janet H. Murray
Georgia Tech
Atlanta, GA 30338
jmurray@gatech.edu

ABSTRACT

Enduring story patterns provide a rich source of variation that can be exploited by the creators of multiform digital stories. Stories of seduction and courtship, for example, reveal variations based on the "moral physics" of the story world including characters serving similar plot functions, such as seducer or suitor, who contrast with one another in significant ways. Focusing on story structure at this level of abstraction can help authors to avoid arbitrary variation, by creating narratively consistent worlds that provide interaction choices that offer the possibility of dramatic agency

Author Keywords

Narrative Schema, Digital Narrative, Interactive Narrative

ACM Classification Keywords

J5 Arts and Humanities: Literature.

General Terms

Design

COHERENCE IN DIGITAL NARRATIVE

Digital affordances enhance the possibilities of storytelling by adding navigable space, encyclopedic capacity, participation, and procedurality to the representational strategies of legacy media forms. When participation and procedurality are well formed we get the characteristic pleasure of agency, and when all three are mapped to story elements we get dramatic agency [1]. Story patterns are encapsulation systems that work to increase dramatic compression: they eliminate the uninteresting actions and character attributes so that our attention can focus on the elements that are most salient to the story.

The procedural nature of interactive systems makes it possible to generate stories that include multiple instantiations of the same dramatic situations, and videogames make this possibility available through the affordances of saving and replaying challenging sequences. But the range of variations within videogames is rarely as expressive as that found in legacy story forms. World of Warcraft provides exciting first-hand play experiences but much of the game is monotonous, unlike the experience of reading Tolkien's novels which, though lengthy, have been crafted with dramatic compression and meaningful, consistent variation. To make an exciting game, we need only look for high action incidents and make them playable. To make a compelling narrative, we have to look for the underlying causal structures that motivate those actions.

Coherence in individual narrative choices comes from the interactor's orientation to the overall story schema. One way to identify the higher-level story patterns that make variation meaningful, is to examine the established legacy traditions, looking for the parameters along which characters and actions vary within and across representative stories. The goal of such an investigation is to identify characters, relationships, and event types that provide the strong narrative interest, and elements that are similar or parallel but different across versions of the story.

MAPPING SEDUCTION

For example let us consider the romantic triangle in which one woman has two possible male romantic partners. This pattern is the basis of two of the most lasting stories in Western culture, Helen of Troy, who chose the handsome Trojan Paris over her Greek husband Menelaus, precipitating the Trojan War, and Guinevere whose affair with Lancelot leads to the fall of her husband, King Arthur, and his Knights of the Round Table.

In both stories, the fulfillment of sexual passion leads to political turmoil. In the seminal account of the Helen-Paris-Menelaus story, Homer's *Iliad*, to the larger conflict between Hector as Paris's surrogate, and the Greek army, and especially Achilles. Paris is described as less manly than the warriors who face the consequences of his rash action. The patriarchal values of the time make the contest between the men more important than the happiness of the lovers.

C&C'11, November 3–6, 2011, Atlanta, Georgia, USA.
ACM 978-1-4503-0820-5/11/11.

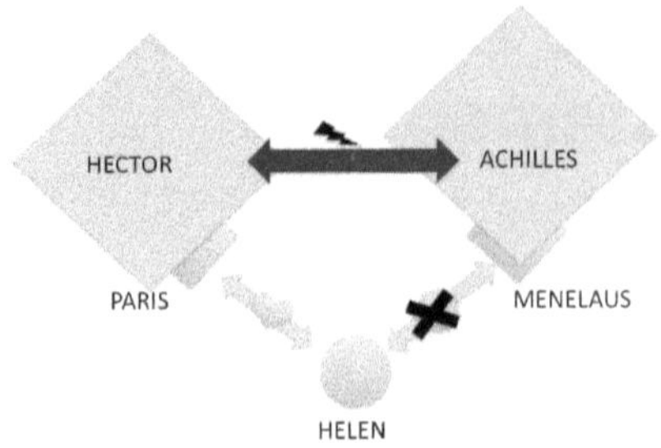

Figure 1 Helen of Troy story, showing Hector's role as a double for Paris, and Achilles as the avenger of the cuckolded Menelaus.

In the Arthurian legend, unlike Helen of Troy, emphasis falls on Lancelot's ties of duty to Arthur, and his attempts to resist temptation. The pattern of doubling that exists with Paris and Hector is repeated with Mordred serving as a double for Lancelot in his betrayal of Arthur and his designs on Guinevere. Characters like Paris and Mordred serve as "foils" to the heroes, an important function of character doubling and variation in mature narrative forms. The juxtaposition of the two characters is a cognitive shorthand, a way of encapsulating a range of possibilities within the same situation of forbidden sexual desire.

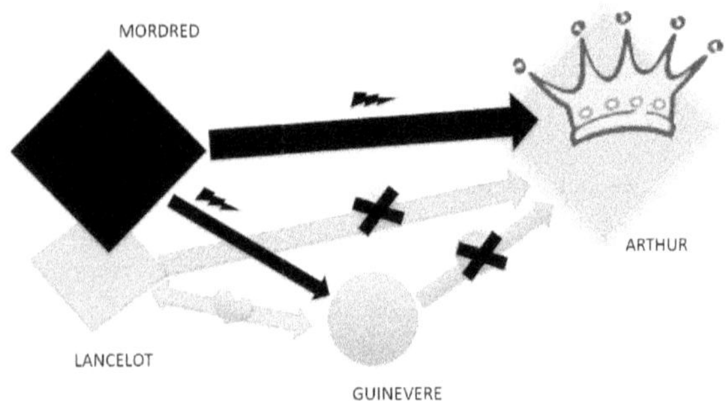

Figure 2 The King Arthur legend, in which Mordred doubles the roles of Lancelot, as a betrayer of the King.

Placing just these two legendary stories together we can create a spectrum of betrayal (Figure 3), a meta-schema that can be applied to multiple stories. We can identify points on the spectrum that characterize Lancelot's progress from a chaste knight, to an admirer of Guinevere, to actively seeking her attention, and eventually having dishonorable sex. We can locate Paris as not actively murderous like Mordred, but reckless in his actions which lead to violence which he is too weak to oppose. We can ask whether Hector belongs to such a spectrum or whether he is characterized by his indifference to sexual temptation.

A spectrum like this is also useful in locating other sexually transgressive characters from very different stories. For example Nicholas in the Miller's Tale, a raunchy Chaucerian story in which a cunning student tricks a landlord and has sex with his very willing wife, is certainly sinful and aggressive, but portrayed sympathetically because of the comic tone of the story which presents the adultery as a harmless prank. By contrast Mr. Wickham, a character in Jane Austen's *Pride and Prejudice* though is treated with much greater condemnation as a person who is careless of the consequences of his actions (like Paris) and driven by predatory ambition (like Mordred). His actions cause real harm, allowing the hero Mr. Darcy to rescue the victim and prove his character to the protagonist Elizabeth who had misjudged both men.

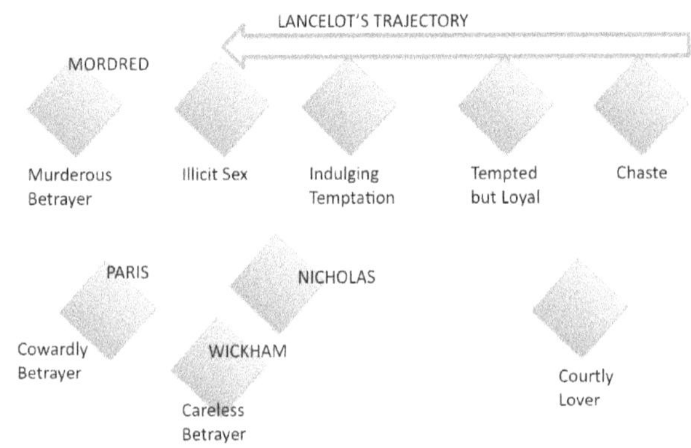

Figure 3 Spectrum of Betrayal.

Approaching digital narrative as an abstraction schema will give it the same cognitive coherence and dramatic intensity that we take for granted in more mature narrative forms. It will allow us to create stories of greater complexity in which variation is an expressive convention in itself, rather than just a novelty.

REFERENCES

1. Murray, J. H. *Hamlet on the Holodeck: The Future of Narrative in Cyberspace.* Simon and Schuster/Free Press, New York (1997).

Roles of Miniature Space in Hybrid Prototyping

Yasuto Nakanishi†‡, Koji Sekiguchi†
†Keio Univ., Faculty of Environment and Information Studies
‡JST Presto
naka, t07412ks@sfc.keio.ac.jp

Takuro Ohmori, Soha Kitahara, Daisuke Akatsuka
Keio Univ., Graduate School of Media and Governance
ohmori, soh335, dadaa@sfc.keio.ac.jp

ABSTRACT
We propose a hybrid prototyping approach that utilizes both virtual simulation and miniature simulation in designing spatial information systems such as public displays or sensors. In this paper, we describe a case study of the hybrid prototyping process and discuss roles of miniature space.

Author Keywords
Interactive System, Simulation, Prototyping, Design Process.

ACM Classification Keywords
D.2.10 Design: [Methodology]; H.4 Information Systems Applications: [Miscellaneous]

General Terms
Design, Experimentation.

INTRODUCTION
Recent years have witnessed an increase the use of various input and output devices in digital cameras, smart phones, mobile projectors, and large displays. Together with the real world around us, information systems are increasingly becoming a part of our everyday environment. When determining spatial positions for multiple devices that constitute such an environment, it may be difficult to perform practical tests in the case that the same number of devices must be used. In addition, the spatial arrangement of equipment and materials used for development of information systems may differ from that during operation. Some developers use low-fidelity techniques such as paper prototypes and mental walkthroughs, whereas others must wait for full-scale deployment. In other words, software developers are unable to accurately test the entire system in the early stages of system development.

To solve these problems, we have developed an integrated development environment for spatial interactive systems, called CityCompiler. A simulation in virtual space enables us to test a spatial layout and a combination of components. In addition, the system functionality allows for smooth switching between a virtual sensor and a real sensor, which enables hybrid prototyping by means of virtual simulation and miniature simulation. These features integrate the space design with the software design and allow the smooth deployment of spatial interactive information systems into the real world. In this paper, we detail one of the cases described briefly in [2], and discuss roles of miniature space in hybrid prototyping.

C&C'11, November 3–6, 2011, Atlanta, Georgia, USA.
ACM 978-1-4503-0820-5/11/11.

CASE STUDY OF HYBRID PROTOTYPING PROCESS
One of the authors developed a system in which a group of photos was captured using a smart phone and displayed on a map as a public display application. His hybrid prototyping process is as follows.

The prospective display location was first investigated. This entailed moving and installing the displays in the virtual space by using models of the interior and exterior spaces. During this investigation, the developer considered that the display should be visible not only to those inside the room but also to pedestrians on the street. Thus, it was decided that the most suitable position for the projection surface would be at a location where it could be seen from the street.

The developer assumed that a piece of white cloth would be used as the screen. He considered that if the application were to be projected on the actual cloth, it might introduce new problems that would not have been faced on the ideal display within the virtual space. Thereafter, possible problems were examined by reproducing a piece of cloth and a mini projector in the miniature space. A simplified model was built using Styrofoam; a piece of cloth was positioned

Figure 1. Verification of visibility in the model: A small camera was mounted on the doll (right).

Figure 2. Operation state of the installed application

on the room side of the window. The mapping application was projected onto the cloth using a mini projector. Our current system does not calculate the size of the Styrofoam and the cloth automatically, so we calculated the sizes of the parts on the basis of the 3D model and assembled them.

In the miniature space, we evaluated the systems operation by watching a movie that was sent from a wireless camera on the head of a doll. Accordingly, we matched the scale of the miniature space to the height of the doll. The visibility of the screen at the window, as viewed from the street, was investigated by moving the figure dolls 1). When a projection was made onto the screen with the maximum window size, there was an overlap between the projected application and the window frame and sash. This meant that there were hidden areas on the map. Some other problems also emerged; for example, while using the program prepared in advance, the displayed photo size became too small for viewing. To solve such problems, a feature was added to the program to enable modification of both photo size and the size of the overall application while the application was running.

When the projector was used at night, the inside of the room was bright and the outside was dark. However, the developer made an unexpected observation: the brightness levels both inside and outside the miniature space were the same. Therefore, the overall brightness in the room where the development was being conducted was lowered and white LEDs were lit inside the miniature model so that the miniature space matched the real space more closely. The model simulation was then performed again and the following problem was discovered: the visibility of the photo changed depending on the difference in brightness between the road and the room. It would be impossible to perfectly reproduce the difference in brightness in the actual scene, even if a precise model were used. Thus, in addition to the modification of the photo and application size, a new feature was added to the program so that the brightness of the application could be modified while the application was running. The miniature model simulation was then performed using the camera doll, which gave better results; this led the developer to conclude that the application could be installed in real space.

In the installation, it was possible to change the size and brightness over a wide range of values while prototyping in the miniature space. Because the actual appearance of the application is not perfectly identical to that viewed through the camera used in the miniature (Figure 2), the size and brightness were adjusted to what was considered ideal by the developer. These modifications were made while the application was running; amendments to the source code were not required.

DISCUSSION AND FUTURE WORK

In this case, we obtained the required parameters and the revised points of the program by carrying out the simulation in the miniature space. Flexibility in the adjustment of the three parameters (the size of photos and the size and brightness of the application) during operation was an advantage of this hybrid prototyping. In order to deploy devices that match the simulation, we have to implement virtual devices that have the same specifications as the real devices. However, it is difficult to fabricate devices that are the same as those used in the miniature space. In the case study, the problem regarding the differences between the virtual simulation and the miniature simulation paradoxically helped us to discover parameters and brought about spiral design cycles. The more imperfect the model, the more unexpected problems will surface. The developer gradually discovered such problems through a process of seeing the differences between a rough, imperfect model and the real space. Suwa examined the cognitive processes that enable an experienced architect to invent design requirements and found that design requirements were invented on the fly through cognitive interactions with sketches. Further, detection of unintended features has a significant bearing on the invention of design requirements [3]. Detection of unintended features is key to the invention of design requirements, which in turn is crucial to idea generation, and one role of the miniature simulation will be to bring such features to light. From this viewpoint, in order to bring about the flexibility and robustness of an application, our system should not help to automatically form an exact model with a 3D printer.

From the viewpoint of design model types, the relation between design sketch and computer graphics will be similar to that between miniature simulation and virtual simulation. Buur suggested new design models based on the model morphology for mechatronics design, which is a complex activity involving mechanics, electronics, and software [1]. In the future, our objective is to explore new design models that integrate virtual simulation and miniature simulation for a complex activity involving space, electronics, and software.

ACKNOWLEDGEMENTS

This research is supported by the JST PRESTO program.

REFERENCES

1. Buur, J. and Andreasen, M., M., Design models in mechatronic product development, Design Studies, 10(3), pp.155-162 (1989).
2. Nakanishi, Y, et.al. Hybrid prototyping by using virtual and miniature simulation for designing spatial interactive information systems, Proc. Pervasive2011.
3. Suwa, M., et.al. Unexpected discoveries and S-invention of design requirements: Important vehicles for a design process, Design Studies, 21(6), pp.539-567 (2000).

Beyond Eco-feedback - Using Art and Emotional Attachment to Express Energy Consumption

Valentina Nisi
Madeira-ITI, University of Madeira, Portugal
valentina@uma.pt

Diego Nicoletti
Independent Artist, Italy
diego.nicoletti@varedolab.com

Raffaella Nisi
Independent Artist, Italy
nisi.raffaella@gmail.com

Nuno Jardim Nunes
Madeira-ITI, University of Madeira, Portugal
njn@uma.pt

ABSTRACT
This paper describes several art based eco-feedback concepts conceived around the potential of emotional attachment between people and the natural environment. Starting from a sensor-infrastructure that looks at how families consume electricity in their homes, we investigate several artistic visualizations of the Madeiran local landscapes exploring the connection between families and elements of the endemic laurel forest. The approach described here leverages digital art as a means to go beyond traditional eco-feedback technology. By coupling people and the forest landscapes we intend to narrow the physical, temporal and psychological gaps between our everyday actions and nature. We explore how people can build a direct emotional connection between their daily energy consumption and the impact on the natural environment (such as climate change and related forest fires, mudslides, desertification and erosion).

Keywords
Art, case study, creative process, technology, visualization.

ACM Classification Keywords
H.5.m. Information interfaces and presentation (e.g., HCI): Miscellaneous.

General Terms
Experimentation, Design

1. INTRODUCTION
In this paper we discuss the challenges promoting a novel intersection between human-computer interaction (HCI) research, art and creativity. An artistic approach and mode of enquiry can often bootstrap and push existing technical developments, in our particular case in eco-feedback. In order to integrate an art-based approach with scientific led research we invested in an artist in residency program in connection with an HCI and technology driven research project [1] related to energy consumption in a domestic environment and sustainability.

Art is fundamentally a non-linear process resulting in an experience [2] that connects author and audience emotions (through aesthetic values) and critical points of view (concepts). These concepts are then used to express, criticize and represent the current and envisioned states of reality. The artist explores reality in an emotional way, through aesthetic and conceptual values and reaches its audience beyond what is rational - connecting directly with its core life meanings. This approach is hard to document, measure or replicate in a scientific setting but in accordance with Gromala and Bolter [3], the main task of Digital Art is to stimulate, inspire and move people connecting to their ethic as well as aesthetic human and social values. In a way we envision the artistic approach as a complementary way of motivating people from the inside (intrinsic motivation) rather than from the outside (extrinsic motivation).

C&C'11, November 3–6, 2011, Atlanta, Georgia, USA.
ACM 978-1-4503-0820-5/11/11.

2. RELATED WORK
Most people are concerned about the consequences of the unsustainable lifestyle but are also unaware of the impact of their daily activities and how can they change their behavior to reduce resources consumption. With the advent of new sensing technologies, eco-feedback has proven to be one of the most effective strategies in reducing electricity usage in the home [4]. The advancement and availability of sensing systems for environmentally related activities (e.g., human activity inference [5]) and interactive displays to feedback this data provides a rich space of prospects for new types of eco-feedback solutions [6].

3. TECHNICAL INFRASTRUCTURE
Under the context of the SINAIS project a pilot installation of about 30 families was deployed using a low-cost non-intrusive load monitoring (NILM) sensing system. The system reads voltage and current signals from the main power feed to detect and classify events at the appliance level. To reduce the cost of our NILM solution we are using a netbook as the data acquisition and processing components of the system.

During the evaluation of the system we found out that after 4 weeks the users stopped paying attention to the eco-feedback system. Even after changing the eco-feedback visualization with a new one the novelty effect only lasted for less than a week. We have witnessed similar results using other tangible eco-feedback prototypes [7]. This shows that current eco-feedback solutions based on simple qualitative and quantitative representations of consumption are not particularly effective in retaining people attention over time. To overcome this problem as well as the lack of connection between long term effects of sustainable or unsustainable actions, we are exploring different eco-feedback strategies.

4. DIGITAL ART ENHANCED ECO VISUALIZATION

Bolter and Gromala [3] claim that any digital artifact is meant to change something in the user's relationship to their physical and cultural environment; otherwise there would be no reason to produce an artifact at all. Based on this premise we refined several concepts during the Artist in Residency, which we report and describe here.

4.1 Coupling eco visualization feedback to families / home activities / appliances

The SINAIS infrastructure enables low-cost detection and classification of energy events. Using complex algorithms the system is capable of detecting power on/off events and classify those events at the appliance level (e.g. when was the microwave turned on and how much energy was consumed by it). These information enables various possibilities in terms of eco-feedback visualization mapping, in particular, feedback per family activity.

When faced with the rich data available, the artists proposed to map energy events and activities to the already complex, but yet very natural, elements of the existing local forest and trees. Differentiation of branches or trees in the virtual forest can be coupled with home activities (detecting in which room is the energy consumption activated). A different tree branch or a different tree in the forest can be mapped to different appliance. In the future, prior development of more accurate sensing technology and a more engaged choice of specific trees from the families, we envisage coupling each tree on the photographed landscape with a household and different branches to each of the household inhabitants.

4.2 Expressing Consumption

The real challenge in the domain of eco-visualization is how to express the energy consumption to the public. For a filmmaker, movement is what differentiates this art from other static forms of visualizations. The movement inside the image was proposed as a way to map variations in energy consumption by the users: i) consumption as movement in a landscape (e.g. clouds moving in the sky); ii) power events as elements the landscape (e.g. more or less animals moving next to the trees); iii) mapping consumption to weather changes (e.g. fog or rain).

4.3 Creating awareness

Without a specific message regarding the consumption, avoiding positive or negative feedback, the visualization will create and foster awareness towards preservation of nature in its endangered sites and landscapes. In order to reflect these different movements, behaviors and intentions of the users we have designed an installations that responds accordingly: first level of interaction - Coupling movement in front of the screen detected by a web camera to start the visualization or movie; second interaction – coupling moving clouds, glowing tree or flowers on the trees to the amount of energy consumed; third level of interaction – a detailed screen of the consumption data, per day, week and month, according to the level of details requested by the user.

6. CONCLUSION

With the growing impact of climate change and limited energetic resources, sustainability is becoming an important research theme. Several projects tackle the technical challenges of developing new renewable energy sources and eco efficient cities. Other projects look at ways to promote energy savings by motivating people to consume less through behavior change. All of these efforts are valid and important to promote a sustainable lifestyle.

Through this paper we explore digital art as a way to promote sustainability awareness. By drawing on previous experience [7] motivating sustainable behaviors through context awareness and social networks, we propose to take the challenge further and explore art as a way to inspire people to act sustainably. The approach described here combines the technical infrastructure developed in the project with innovative art explorations, in order to promote sustainable practices by drawing on intimate and emotionally connections between families and elements of the natural ecosystem - in this case trees in a forest.

REFERENCES

1. J.P. van Leeuwen, I. Oakley, N.J. Nunes, V. Nisi, and V. Kostakos, "Sensory Social Networks to Motivate Sustainable Behaviour," Presented at EuroIA 12 International Conference, 2009.
2. Dewey, J., Art as experience. Trade pbk. ed2005, New York: Perigee Books. viii, 371.
3. Bolter, J.D. and D. Gromala, Windows and mirrors: interaction design, digital art, and the myth of transparency. Leonardo2003, Cambridge, Mass.: MIT Press. xi, 182 p.
4. Gupta, S., Reynolds, M., The Design and Evaluation of an End-User-Deployable, Whole House, Contactless Power Consumption Sensor, CHI'2010, Atlanta, ACM
5. Froehlich, J., Findlater, L., Landay, J., The Design of Eco-Feedback Technology, CHI'2010, Atlanta, ACM.
6. Mankoff, J., Matthews, D., Fussell, S.R. & Johnson, M. (2007). Leveraging Social Networks to Motivate Individuals to Reduce their Ecological Footprints. In Proc. HICSS 2007.
7. Quintal, F., Nunes, N., Ocneanu, A., Berges, M., SINAIS: a low-cost eco-feedback energy-monitoring platform, in Proceedings of the Designing Interactive Systems Conference, 2010.

RE: Designing a Digital Sketchbook

Dr. Shaleph O'Neill
Duncan of Jordanstone Collage of Art and Design
University of Dundee
Dundee, Scotland
+44138286533
s.j.oneill@dundee.ac.uk

ABSTRACT

Why are digital tools not replacing traditional sketchbooks? Our research explores the fundamentals of sketchbook use by thinking about them as Creativity Support Tools that could be digitally replicated.

ACM Classification Keywords

H.5.2 [User Interfaces]: Prototyping, Screen Design, User Centered Design.

General Terms

Design, Human Factors, Theory

Author Keywords

Interfaces, iPad, Creativity, Sketchbooks, Csikszentmihalyi

RESEARCHING SKETCHBOOKS

The project was a research led teaching activity involving undergraduate students on the Digital Interaction Design Course at Duncan of Jordanstone College of Art and Design. The research phase involved a thorough examination of real sketchbook use, in terms of the role they play for creative practitioners as creative tools, repositories for information and communication devices. Three things were done during our research. 1. A survey of 10 popular digital sketching tools was performed in order to establish features that are already supported in digital form. 2. An analysis of 42 entries in Richard Brereton's book, "Sketchbooks: The Hidden Art of Designers, Illustrators & Creatives" [2] was conducted to establish some basic thematic codes that could be used to inform further investigations. 3. Our own semi-structured interviews were conducted with 15 sketchbook users based at the art college.

Methods

Answering Shneiderman's challenge to develop creativity support tools [3], we used Csikszentmihalyi's creative systems model and his adapted description of the creative process as a way to analyze the data [4]. In order to understand how sketchbooks find a place within this creative system, as a 'support tool', we mapped out our data in relation to both aspects of this model. This allowed us to group data in two complementary ways that helped to inform decisions about what elements of sketchbook use should be designed for. In doing so what emerged is a detailed picture of the role of sketchbooks in supporting creative practice across a creative system in terms of traditional and digital functionality.

C&C'11, November 3–6, 2011, Atlanta, Georgia, USA.
ACM 978-1-4503-0820-5/11/11.

A SURVEY OF SKETCHING APPS

Many existing apps provide a range of virtual pencils and brushes, all with varying levels of control and customizability. Some are simple to use, others require sophisticated interface components that must be carefully organized before a mark is even made. This can be a frustrating and sometimes off-putting experience for many creative practitioners as traditional sketchbooks are such a versatile medium. That said, there are many plus points that digital sketchbooks might have over traditional ones: Numerous sketches might be stored on one device rather than having to cart numerous sketchbooks around; Networking capabilities to share your ideas with your friends and perhaps even clients; Not forgetting the principles of digital multiples that can be distributed to wide audiences and the fundamentals of 'do', 'undo' and 'redo' that allow for multiple versions and streams of creative ideas to be explored in rapid succession.

ANALYSING THE LITERATURE

A number of sources could have been used for initial analysis purposes [5, 6, 7]. Brereton's book was chosen because it's format offered the clearest and most succinct material for analysis in the form of individual entries by a wide range of creative practitioners. A grounded textual analysis of these entries revealed 13 emergent codes, some of which were merged into 'supercodes' as we examined the data in more detail. For example, codes 10 and 12 ('need editing' & 'never edit'), though diametrically opposed to one another, were brought together under a new super-code called 'Editing'. Similarly, codes 11 and 13 ('Communication Tool' & 'Collaborative Tool') were brought together under 'Sharing', as one is often an extension of the other. 'Editing' and 'Sharing' are themselves very closely linked together with another code ('Freedom to Play'), which represents the way in which sketchbooks facilitate exploration and experimentation with ideas. Code 4 ('Private Journal') comes into play here too as privacy is essential for this sense of freedom. Privacy is the opposite of 'Sharing' and it would seem, though it is not always the case, that 'Editing' really comes into play when people think about sharing their sketchbooks with others.

SEMI STRUCTURED INTERVIEWS

Each team was asked to make a short film about sketchbooks using semi-structured interviews. The students then analyzed their film material (using post it notes) to pull out significant quotes, phrases, images and other observations that represented something significant about sketchbook use. This information was then filtered using the 'codes' developed from the analysis described above. This was an exhaustive process that helped to verify the kinds of requirements that a digital sketchbook should meet.

MAPPING TO THE MODEL

Csikszenmihalyi's system model, consists of three interrelated components: the domain, the person and the field, as well as phases of creativity: Preparation, Incubation, Illumination, Evaluation, Elaboration. In our analysis we systematically mapped our data in relation to both aspects of this model.

Engaging with the Domain

Sketchbooks allow creatives to engage with the domain as a form of preparation. This is all about getting to know what exists in the domain as a way of orienting yourself to a particular problem or issue. This involves collecting information and mapping it relationally to existing knowledge. In sketchbooks this tends to manifest itself in three ways: 1. Collecting reference materials for inspiration; e.g. collecting pictures, postcards and magazine cutouts etc. 2. Collecting physical materials; such as different papers, textures, colors or media. 3. Gathering observations, i.e. using drawing as an observational tool to gather visual data about a particular subject or situation. Sometimes it's about looking back at an archive of older sketchbooks as a source of inspiration, at others it's about making your own sketchbook from scratch in order to clear the decks.

The Creative Person

Incubation is about finding time and space to reflect on your ideas. Creatives often take breaks away from work to find this space. For many creatives, working in sketchbooks also provides this space, one that lets them freely play around with ideas in a private non-judgmental way. Several practitioners described sketchbooks in some way as an extension of their brains but more than that, they are cognitive tools that allow people to think and organize their thoughts in various different ways. Sometimes, consciously and at other times, subconsciously doodling. The latter activity is a kind of visual wandering that can seem unrelated to work but often leads to new ideas. Writing down or drawing elements from dreams is another common way of capturing some of this incubation process. Illumination is the output of incubation. It is about coming up with something new, something innovative. Many creatives talk about the 'Eureka' moment but this doesn't do justice to the work that has gone on during incubation. Sketchbooks keep track of incubation and support illumination by providing visual feedback about the development of an idea. Often illuminating ideas come to people after they have been working on sketchbooks or while they are taking a break somewhere else. Sketchbooks provide a handy 'always-on' mechanism to capture the important genesis of a new idea.

Facing the Field

Evaluation is a period of reflection on the quality of an idea. Is it good? Does it fit? Will it be accepted? Often this is done privately by the individual relating the new idea to older ideas or to existing knowledge in the domain. Sketchbooks facilitate the evaluation process in two ways: Ideas can be evaluated in relation to material gathered during the preparation stage and an evolutionary path can be traced from its origins to its realization. Sketchbooks can be shared with others and discussions can form around the ideas in them, allowing people to further explore their value and modify them accordingly. The elaboration of an idea is essentially it's end point, the turning of an idea into reality. Creative work in sketchbooks often has a painful birth during this 'transition' from one medium to another. Digital sketchbooks might be able to do this more easily than traditional sketchbooks due to the transferable nature of the digital medium.

REFERENCES

1. Kay, A. 1972. A Personal Computer for Children of All Ages. *Proceedings of the ACM National Conference*, Boston, 1972.
2. Brereton, R. 2009, *Sketchbooks: The Hidden Art of Designers, Illustrators & Creatives*, Laurence King, London.
3. Shneiderman, B. 2009. Creativity Support Tools: A Grand Challenge for HCI Researchers, In *Engineering the User Interface* , M. Redondo, et al (eds), Springer-Verlag, London, DOI: 10.1007/978-1-84800-136-7_1.
4. Csikszenmihalyi, M. 1996. *Creativity: Flow and the Psychology of Discovery and Invention*, Harper Collins, New York.
5. Gregory, D. 2008, *An Illustrated Life: Drawing Inspiration from the Private Sketchbooks of Artists, Illustrators and Designers*. How Books, Cincinnati, Ohio.
6. O'Donnell, T. 2009, Sketch Book: Conceptual Drawings from the World's most Influential Designers, Rockport Publishers, Beverly, Massachusetts.
7. Gunn, Wendy (ed.) 2009, Fieldnotes and Sketchbooks: Challenging the Boundaries Between Descriptions and Processes of Describing, Peter Lang International Academic Publishers, Frankfurt

Articulating Creativity in a New Domain: Expert Insights from the Field of E-Textiles

Kylie Peppler & Diane Glosson
Indiana University, Bloomington, IN, USA
kpeppler@indiana.edu; dglosson@indiana.edu

Yasmin Kafai, Deborah Fields & Kristin Searle
University of Pennsylvania, Philadelphia, USA
kafai@upenn.edu; stareyes@gmail.com; kristininutah@hotmail.com

ABSTRACT

Building on Csikszentmihalyi's conception of creativity as a system composed of the domain, the individual, and a field of experts who validate creative innovations, we examine a new domain of e-textiles to describe creativity. Further, we use our interviews with domain experts to outline some of the limitations of current assessment techniques to inform our understanding of creativity.

Author Keywords

Systems; Consensual Assessment Technique (CAT); Experts; E-Textiles.

ACM Classification Keywords

K.3.0 [Computers & Education]: General.

General Terms

Theory.

INTRODUCTION

While cognitive views of creativity have situated the source of creativity in the individual, more recent scholarship views creativity as the result of a systemic process. According to this view, creativity results from the interaction of a system composed of three elements: a culture that contains symbolic rules, a person who brings novelty into the symbolic domain, and a field of experts who recognize and validate the innovation. Csikszentmihalyi [3] further argues all three are necessary for a creative idea, product, or discovery to take place.

Of particular relevance to this poster is the role of the field in this scenario. In a systems view of creativity, the field includes all individuals who act as "gatekeepers to the domain". Social psychologists of creativity have further argued for new techniques that fit well with Csikszentmihalyi paradigm, including the Consensual Assessment Technique (CAT) pioneered by Amabile and colleagues [1]. This technique allows for the assessment of products' creativity by judges who are deemed to be "experts" in a particular domain. The panel is instructed to use their own subjective definition of creativity as they rate artifacts. Important to this technique, experts rate creativity relative to one another rather than against some ultimate norm. The CAT can inform what we know about the domain as well as what we understand about creativity more generally, especially since very few empirical studies have employed a systems view of creativity.

C&C'11, November 3-6, 2011, Atlanta, Georgia, USA.
ACM 978-1-4503-0820-5/11/11.

THE DOMAIN OF E-TEXTILES

The current study focused on an emergent domain of electronic textiles, or e-textiles, and employed a variation of the CAT analysis to stimulate a conversation among experts about creativity in this new domain. While e-textiles is a relatively new domain, the majority of its history was constrained to a small group of highly skilled artists capable of working with such materials. More recently, a construction kit called the LilyPad Arduino has enabled novices to embed electronic hardware into textiles [2]. The LilyPad Arduino toolkit is a set of sew-able electronic components, including a programmable microcontroller and an assortment of sensors that allows users to build their own soft wearable computers.

The recent launch of the first e-textile web community, LilyPond (http://lilypond.media.mit.edu), allows designers to share and display designs created using e-textiles. The community is currently being used by both a distributed group of Do-It-Yourself (DIY) e-textile designers as well as for youth participating in e-textile workshops across the United States to share the work created in these workshops. Because LilyPond is the only community of its kind within e-textiles, we limited our study to the discussion of just those projects displayed within the community (N=166).

ASSEMBLING A PROXY FOR THE FIELD

In order to better understand this emergent domain of e-textile designs, we assembled an external panel of pioneers in the e-textile domain. Each expert was chosen because of their contributions to the art and design of e-textiles, the creation of innovative materials for the industry, as well as their domain-specific teaching in higher education settings. This panel of experts met together to discuss work hosted in the LilyPond community and to better articulate what we know to constitute creativity within this domain.

The external panel independently rated a random selection of 25% of the artifacts contained in the LilyPond site, following procedures outlined in the CAT along three dimensions: (1) Overall Creativity; (2) Technique; and (3) Aesthetics. In addition, we asked them to define these categories, make suggestions for additional criteria, and comment on the individual projects. A quick analysis of inter-rater reliability revealed that there was relatively little consensus among our field of experts. This is in line with prior work that has established expert artists as problematic for establishing inter-rater reliability. To find the root of this, we had the experts share their thoughts on creativity within this particular domain as well as what constituted a creative contribution to the online community. Our analyses focused on experts' articulations of e-textile creativity.

FINDINGS

Moving Beyond the Obvious

Two tensions emerged in the discussions, including the constraints of the tools as well as the evident "workshop approaches" where a large number of the projects were designed. As one participant pointed out, workshops are "a great way to get somebody started. But seeing if someone goes beyond the suggested model then does something new and innovative" is the true measure of creativity. They also noted the constraints of the tools, remarking that "there is a set of obvious projects people can do." Among these more obvious solutions, they categorized the projects into discrete categories, including "my first LED" and "my first switch" projects. Beyond that, the panel saw projects that were "actually trying to make a piece of textile and conform it to the body." The connection between textiles, body, movement, and performance became an important part of the discussion as the inferred use or the history of the creation became an important consideration in their judgments. Lastly, the panel noted that there was "a huge leap" to the projects that became "much more considerate" and more "art projects as opposed to exercises." Taken together, these observations suggest several categories relevant in developmental trajectories in creativity.

Different Markers of Creativity

While the panel agreed upon these general categories, they didn't agree on how they ranked among one another or on the other qualities that made something creative. One member stated that creativity was marked by "subverting the first level assumptions that one might make…like putting the LED on the inside instead of the outside. Putting it really close to a sexual part of your body, which is delicate or forbidden." Other members of the panel argued that there is creativity in "use of form, design elements, color, form, and materiality". Others argued that it was important in their considerations that "things moved beyond the concept of the (simple) circuit and actually started to get into context." For example, thinking about not just a switch as a switch but as interaction, for instance a dance costume that placed sensors to detect movement. Lastly, another participant remarked, "I'm really into modularity and also iterations so those were two things that I thought". For each of the panel members, the core of their definitions of what defined a creative act differed and was deeply rooted in their own creative practice, which we assume is one reason that it was difficult to establish inter-rater reliability.

Evaluating Creativity in Diverse, Online Communities

While most prior studies have used the CAT to study parallel products and more recently non-parallel artifacts compiled from standardized tests, few studies have used these techniques to evaluate a more disparate online community, which is one alternative explanation for why we were unable to establish inter-rater reliability. However, online communities (as opposed to standardized tests) represent a more authentic domain for the study of creativity (rather than a controlled setting). While some of the panel members were frustrated by this, others remarked "it was interesting to actually question what I think creativity might be, by actually looking and accepting the fact that there are these different categories of projects." This sort of informed reaction closely parallels the role of experts in shaping the domain, and is more closely aligned with the original model outlined by Csikszentmihalyi [3]. Beyond the difficulties for evaluation, online communities also inject a few other layers of information important to the evaluation, including the quality and detail of the images (especially in considerations of craft and technique), the accompanying text (those that had nicely written statements or detailed the struggle with the materials were viewed more favorably), the positionality of the creator (non-traditional creators were viewed more favorably), as well as the choice of the textile itself (who made it and who chose the textile became a key consideration).

CONCLUSION

Few studies have tried to evaluate what it means to be creative in a new domain, particularly in the context of fast changing technology. For further studies, we suggest to focus on project-sharing online communities with shared affinity in a field like e-textiles as a more authentic domain for the study of creativity rather than a controlled setting that were favored in previous research.

ACKNOWLEDGMENTS

This material is based upon work supported by the National Science Foundation under Grant Nos. 0855868 and 0855886 and awarded to Yasmin Kafai and Kylie Peppler. Any opinions, findings, and conclusions or recommendations expressed in this material are those of the author(s) and do not necessarily reflect the views of the National Science Foundation.

REFERENCES

1. Amabile, T. M. 1982, 'Social Psychology of Creativity: A Consensual Assessment Technique', *Journal of Personality and Social Psychology* 43(5), 997–1013.
2. Buechley, L. & Eisenberg, M. (2008). The LilyPad arduino: Toward wearable engineering for everyone. Pervasive Computing, 7(2), 12-15.
3. Csikszentmihalyi, M. (1996), *Creativity: Flow and the psychology of discovery and invention*, HarperCollins, New York, NY.
4. Plucker, J. (2011). Personal communication.

Spielraum: Play, Chance and Creativity Across Disciplines

Diane Rosen
Morse Center for the Professional Education of Teachers, Teachers College, Columbia University
26 Sixth Avenue, Nyack, NY 10960 USA
rosenart@verizon.net

ABSTRACT
Creativity and technology share linguistic roots in "art, craft, making and method." But a more compelling substrate, increasingly evident in gaming culture, links the two. In the notion of *Spielraum*-- room-for-play— a common ground of emergent possibility may be discerned. This interactive space of memory, thought, affect and sensory perception allows the mind to wander creatively, i.e. purposefully and at the same time playfully. Integrating non-methods of play and chance (two variants of *spiel*) with goal-directed activity, this paper proposes, is an important way to foster creative problem solving across disciplines.

Keywords
Creativity, *Spielraum*, chance, play, problem solving

ACM Classification Keywords
J.O General; J.5 ARTS AND HUMANITIES; J.2 PHYSICAL SCIENCES AND ENGINEERING

General Terms: Human Factors, Performance, Theory

INTRODUCTION

"These are days when no one should rely unduly on his competence. Strength lies in improvisation. All the decisive blows are struck left-handed." Walter Benjamin [1]

These cautionary words from the 1920's are still valid today. With specialization increasingly required in every domain, many find themselves in virtual silos of expertise. As a result, competencies lose the robust flexibility to improvise, to seize and build creatively on the spontaneous and unexpected-- capacities governed by the brain's *right* hemisphere, which of course controls the *left* hand.

Throughout human history, agents of change have always, figuratively speaking, struck from the left. Defining creativity as "effective surprise"[2] that takes one beyond familiar ways of experiencing the world, Bruner says this of the synergy that drives it: "Reaching for knowledge with the right hand is science... Reaching for knowledge with the left hand is art. [But] the scientist and the poet do not live at antipodes, and I urge that the artificial separation of the two modes of knowing cripples the contemporary intellectual as an effective mythmaker for his times." Numerous studies support this view, touting flexible, creative thinking as *the* essential capacity for thriving in the 21st century.

Yet even amidst broad consensus about its pivotal role in personal, social and cultural growth, creativity is still often dismissed as irrelevant to core agendas, or simply impossible to assess. What seems to be needed is a new way of seeing creativity that synthesizes falsely polarized modes of knowing, and valorizes rather than avoids uncertainties of the inherently contingent creative process.

C&C'11, November 3–6, 2011, Atlanta, Georgia, USA.
ACM 978-1-4503-0820-5/11/11.

SPIELRAUM: AN UNSUSPECTED FIELD OF ACTION

Benjamin' seminal essay *Art in the Age of Its Technological Reproducibility* argues that cinema represented a vital new regime of perception which, by "its accentuation of hidden details in familiar objects, ...assures us of a vast and unsuspected field of action [*Spielraum*]" [quoted in 3]. Exploding the numbing sameness of the everyday, he said, film sets us off on uncertain journeys of adventure (play) among its far-flung debris. *Spielraum,* then, implies a dynamic action-space for unbounded imagination. Here, the dialectical relationship between creator as actor/ gambler/ player (*Spieler*) and creative process as improvisatory performance/ game (*Spiel*) is ignited.

In this porous sense-scape of possibility and probability, a version of the uncertainty principle holds sway. Teeming with multiple superposed states, all possibilities are open until the original intent or stimulus clicks with a set of conditions that may become the 'finished' state. In this stochastic formulation, interpenetrating subjectivity and objectivity, intent and randomness are essential to realization of the work. This suggests a fruitful approach for re-seeing creativity in terms of an aesthetic of play, chance and paradox, which by its energizing potential moves us beyond normative rules and paths.

WHERE REASON IS EXHAUSTED: ROOM-FOR-PLAY

Adventuring in the field of action that is *Spielraum*, a reciprocal relationship between control and randomness shapes the process of exploration and experimentation, producing unpredictable results that nonetheless feel entirely apt-- as if sprung form some region of collective unconscious. Stravinsky described it this way: "A composer improvises aimlessly the way an animal grubs about... suddenly stumbl[ing] against an unknown obstacle. It gives us a jolt, a shock, and this shock fecundates our creative power"[6]. While domain knowledge is necessary, it is not sufficient for either everyday or eminent creative work. What "shocks" us into contriving in the rift-spaces between familiar and strange, is a shift in perspective from logical to improvisatory, from predictable to open-ended.

Frequently this occurs automatically as "mind wandering," a de-coupling or shift of attention away from a primary task, toward internal information. Weaving memories, thoughts and emotions, the mind's default network is constantly at play with nascent patterns. Not surprisingly, studies suggest that mind wandering "may share important similarities with incubation processes related to creativity… by address[ing] more remote goals (e.g. discerning the solution to a heretofore unsolved problem)"[5]. Balancing in the tension of uncertainty— playing *with, from* and *in* its imminent possibilities— mind wandering entails the freedom to be nowhere and everywhere, to have a goal yet stray, to have no-way and therefore have access to all ways.

Within such complex systems as creative cognition, the unexpected and contradictory are driving mechanisms for synthesizing growth. Based on extensive research in the creative processes of prominent artists and scientists, Rothenberg theorized that the capacity to actively conceive of multiple antitheses simultaneously, what he termed *Janusian* process, is the foundation of all creative thinking [7]. Imagining in paradox to express a problem may be effective in initiating and facilitating creative tasks precisely *because* it transcends logic and throws us off balance.

To borrow a term from chaos theory, the creative-generative sequence is a kind of *far-from-equilibrium* system, losing stability when subjected to nonlinear (turbulent) conditions and then evolving into one of many available new states. Analogously, template-based processing instructions in the digital universe will say, "do X with the next copy of Y that comes around" without specifying which copy, or where [8]. The flexibility inherent in such dynamic systems, including the human neural workspace, is advantageous to development and adaptation to change. Outside our comfort zone, we become more responsive to new situations, more open to learning from contexts of ambiguity, more willing to explore new ideas. Drawing freely on information-rich spectra, open-ended questions and tasks increase the creative synergy between *what is* and *what could be.*

TOWARD VIABLE CREATIVE PRAXIS: PLAY-IN-ACTION

As the paradoxical nexus of creativity, *Spielraum* is where chance, play, purpose and context reciprocally engage. If uncertainty and ambiguity are allowed in the game, apparent anomalies or contradictions re-stimulate blunted perceptions so that things are seen anew and fresh meanings are forged. For Russian formalist Victor Shklovsky, the very purpose of art was defamiliarization *(ostranenie),* to make the familiar seem strange by subverting habitual perceptions of the everyday much as Benjamin had proposed regarding film.

My experience as a painter has taught me that a creative "product" comes to exist not as an end in itself, but as the trajectory through time of a particular search for answers to half-formed questions. Stirred by curiosity and the anticipation of discovery, I start from an interesting word or concept, then randomly select and arrange images. When a combination surprises me, aligning in some unforeseen way with the original stimulus, the composition is sketched out, paint is dripped and spattered to disrupt expectation and render the surface more evocative, and this knowing by not-knowing process of playful exploration proceeds.

For example, based on Mallarmé's free-verse poem "A Throw of the dice will never abolish chance," my painting *Throw of the Dice* improbably juxtaposes the flung dice of a game of chance (*spiel*) with an upside-down person in mid-fall. The poem's unorthodox form and content encapsulate what I sought to express graphically: thought, given its freedom of expression in playful ideation, converts moments of life into art, art into life, and chance into power.

Another painting, *Sound of One Hand,* also relies on the free interplay of ideas and images to tap sources of unmediated perception. It was inspired by a famous Zen *koan* or riddle, intended to teach the inadequacy of logical reasoning: the sound of a single hand "can by no means be heard with the ear. If… it is quite apart from seeing, hearing, perceiving and knowing… then in the place where reason is exhausted and words are ended," insight is attained [4]. Foreshadowing the neuroscience of mind wandering, this *koan* paints the unfettered mind as an essential mode of knowing.

CONLCUSION

Understanding creativity as a function of room-for-play is crucial, particularly in light of the dramatically enlarged *Spielraum* that is digital technology, "a virtual space [offering] hitherto unimaginable modes of playful innervation" [3]. What we call creativity, Arnheim writes, "is a kind of reasoning [that] can be either intellectual [abstract] or perceptual and, of course, is mostly a combination of both" [9]. Dualities and strictures of convention dissolve in the fluid state of play (*spielen)* and release the imagination, suggesting that the new creatives are those who will "wage an aesthetics of play"[3]. To do so requires a heuristic of radical ambivalence, indeterminacy and interaction, and the will to explore and shift between antithetical if not antinomic perspectives. In this view creativity is not only essential to problem solving across disciplines, it is a living perspective that enriches all things.

REFERENCES

1. Benjamin, W. *One-Way Street and Other Writings*, Jephcott, E.F.N. & Shorter, K. (trans.). Verso Books, Brooklyn, NY, 1997.
2. Bruner, J. *On Knowing: Essays for the Left Hand.* Harvard University Press, Cambridge MA, 1979.
3. Hansen, M.B. Room-for-Play: Benjamin's Gamble with Cinema. *Canadian Journal of Film Studies*. 13, 1 (2004) 2-27.
4. Seo, A. & Addiss, S., *The Sound of One Hand: Paintings and Calligraphy by Zen Master Hakuin*, Shambala, Boston, 2010.
5. Smallwood, J. and Schooler, J.W. The Restless Mind. *Psychological Bulletin*, 132, 6 (2006) 946-958.
6. Stravinsky, I. *Poetics Of Music In the Form of Six Lessons, Harvard University Press, Cambridge MA,* 2003, 55-56
7. Rothenberg, A. Creative Cognitive Processes in Kekule's Discovery of the Structure of the Benzene Molecule. *The American Journal of Psychology*. 108, 3 (1995) 419-438.
8. Dyson, G. "Richard Foreman vs. THE GÖDEL-TO-GOOGLE NET, *Edge/ The Third Culture (3.8.05),*
9. Arnheim, R. *Toward a psychology of art.* University of California Press, Berkeley CA, 1966, 287.

"I Reflect to Improve My Design" – Investigating the Role and Process of Reflection in Creative Design

Moushumi Sharmin, Brian P. Bailey
Department of Computer Science
University of Illinois at Urbana-Champaign
Urbana, IL, USA
sharmin2@illinois.edu, bpbailey@illinois.edu

ABSTRACT

Reflection is an integral part of the creative design process. However, reflection is often considered as an enigmatic, un-orderly, and irregular process, leading to a lack of support from existing design and creativity support tools. Through a contextual inquiry (N=12) of designers' reflection practice, we found that reflection is predominantly a systematic, intentional, and repeatedly practiced activity. We also found that artifacts play an imperative role in supporting reflective process. We offer guidelines for the design of better reflection support tools.

Keywords

Reflection, Creative design, Artifacts

ACM Classification Keywords

H.1.2. Models and principles: User/Machine systems.

General Terms

Design

INTRODUCTION

Reflection plays a critical role in creative design, helping designers' in problem formulation, idea generation, and self-evaluation. However, little is known about designers' reflection practice, making the process enigmatic; resulting in tools that offer little assistance for supporting reflection.

Schön described "reflection" as a set of activities that designers consciously or subconsciously engage in to get better understanding of the design problem (problem framing), to test the problem (hypothesizing), and finally, making sense of the situation by repeatedly framing and testing the hypothesis [4].

Researchers viewed reflection as not only a set of cognitive activities but also as a knowledge that we gain through our experience, which influences our assumptions and design choices [3, 5]. They emphasized the importance of reflecting on the design process to identify unconscious aspects of the design problem and to rethink dominant design choices. Design researchers also viewed reflection as a learning tool [1, 2] and suggested that designers utilizing representation of artifacts in the reflection process have a better understanding of their own design process [2].

C&C'11, November 3–6, 2011, Atlanta, Georgia, USA.
ACM 978-1-4503-0820-5/11/11.

Existing literature confirms the significance of reflection on design and creativity and acknowledges that artifacts are imperative for supporting reflection. However, they don't provide details of activities performed during reflection, types of artifacts associated with these reflective activities, and representations needed to support reflection. Our research aims to answer these questions.

In this paper, we present results from a contextual inquiry aiming to offer better understanding of designers' reflection practice. Our findings indicate that though sporadic, reflection is an intentionally practiced process and is aimed to recall design decisions, process, and context, to compare different projects, to get inspired, to remove creative block, to assess growth as a designer, and even to estimate effort invested for evaluating productivity and cost estimation.

METHODOLOGY

Our contextual inquiry utilized semi-structured interviews centered on understanding designers' reflective practices, utilization of artifacts, tools and techniques employed, and challenges faced during this process. Study participants came from Architectural (N=2), Industrial (N=4), and Graphic design (N=6) and are highly experienced professional designers (average experience> 7 years). Each of the interviews lasted around two hours, was audio-recorded, and transcribed for analysis. We collected screen grabs of the electronic design information archives and images detailing strategies utilized by our participants for supporting reflection and analyzed these to verify opinions expressed during the interviews and their actual practices.

STUDY RESULTS

We report key findings from our study of reflection practice, focusing on the process of reflection and why and how artifacts are utilized in this process.

Dimensions of Reflection

Reflective activities can be broadly categorized as: i) need-based reflection tied to an ongoing project, ii) intentional reflection for gaining an understanding about one's own design process, critiquing own work, evaluating past activities, reliving design experience, and getting inspired, and iii) unintentional and unplanned reflection resulting from any activity that spur design thinking. While need-based reflection is more frequent, designers consider it more as a process of reusing artifacts. Intentional reflection is sporadic in nature but is considered imperative for design success. All of our study participants mentioned engaging in less-frequent (ranging from once a week to three times a year) but repeated intentional reflection sessions throughout their design career. Artifacts are an integral part of these reflective activities. Here, we focus on intentional reflection and discuss the role artifacts play in this process.

Designers Sift through Artifacts to Relive Experience

Reflection is strongly tied to *memory* and *feelings* and a desire to *relive experience* rather than retrieving specific artifacts to satisfy an information need. Designers engage in reflection to get a glimpse of their own design at a point in time, often involving a combination of browsing and searching through the information archives. Artifacts work as a memory trigger in the reflection process, helping them to gain a holistic view of past activity. Designers try to utilize organization and descriptive filenames to access artifacts related to different types of design activities, but often abandon the process as it becomes increasingly complex with growing number of projects and artifacts.

Designers Want to Construct Stories about Design

Designers engage in reflection to get better sense of the overall design activity, often to reconstruct the design story for themselves or for communicating it to others. They explore stored artifacts to understand the process involved, rationale for choosing a particular direction, and project milestones in terms of ideas selected, prototypes generated and refined. However, it is extremely difficult to get a sense of the design flow, activity, and the underlying process by looking at the long list of files stored in existing information archives. Systems should thus provide a visual summary of activities (e.g., flow, alternatives, milestones) to support recall and construction of design story.

Designers Analyze and Compare Artifacts to Assess and Evaluate Changes in Their Design Process

Designers utilize stored artifacts as a proxy for analyzing and comparing their process employed in different projects, often to evaluate their growth as designers. Designers try to utilize information such as number and types of projects, artifacts collected and designed, and success and failure of the projects to gain better sense of their design activity. Gaining such insight is rather difficult if not impossible from information archives and requires investing a lot of manual effort and time. Designers access project folders and explore artifacts to get better sense of the materials, effort invested, and the processes utilized. This behavior suggests a need for tools that can generate a summary of intangible design activities (e.g., artifacts collected, ideas generated) to support analysis and comparison.

Designers Explore Related Artifacts to Understand the Design Context

Designers try to explore artifacts that share a common theme or are utilized to address a specific design issue. During reflection, designers often ask themselves, 'what was I thinking at that time' and believe that a set of artifacts utilized at that time would provide better access to the design context and would help to recall the thought process involved. At present, designers start with an artifact and continue exploring other artifacts that were accessed at that time – often combining search and browsing in one or multiple folders. This process continues until the designer finds artifacts that offer 'sufficient context' or abandons it after several unsuccessful tries. Systems should thus make temporal relationships among artifacts visible to offer cues of relatedness to assist recall of the design context.

Designers Estimate Effort Invested as a Function of Time Spent on Collecting, Creating and Refining Artifacts

Designers reflect on past projects to estimate how much effort will be required for a new and similar project. While design involves a lot of cognitive activities, lack of any external representation of such activities forces designers to consider time spent on collecting, creating, and refining artifacts in the different design phases of design as an approximate but useful estimation of their invested effort. However, it is almost impossible to estimate effort by looking at the file names or artifacts from the existing information archives. A better representation of time spent on artifacts and on different design activities is needed to supports designers' need for estimation of effort invested.

CONCLUSION

Reflection is an integral part of the creative design process, but design tools offer little support for reflective activities. Better technology can enhance designers' reflection experience; however, in-depth understanding of designers' reflection practice is critical before building such tools. We contribute deeper understanding of reflection practice, especially focusing on the process of reflection and the role of artifacts in this process. Our findings indicate that artifacts are an integral part of reflection and novel representation of artifacts and visual summary of design activities are imperative for supporting reflection.

REFERENCES

1. Adams, R. S., Turns, J. and Atman, C. J. 2003. Educating effective engineering designers: the role of reflective practice, *Design Studies*, 24(3): 275-294.
2. Ishii, N. and Miwa, K. Supporting reflective practice in creativity education, *Proc. C&C*, 2005.
3. Kinsella, E. A. 2007. Embodied Reflection and the Epistemology of Reflective Practice. *Journal of Philosophy of Education,* 41 (3):395–409.
4. Schön, D.A. *The Reflective Practitioner.* Basic Books, 84.
5. Sengers, P., Boehner, K., David, S., and Kaye, J. J. Reflective design, *Proc. Critical Computing*, 2005.

The Role of Iteration in the Design Processes of Middle School Students

Mark Sherman **Fred Martin**
Department of Computer Science
Michelle Scribner-MacLean
Graduate School of Education
University of Massachusetts Lowell
1 University Ave, Lowell, MA 01854 USA
+1 978 934 2705 msherman@cs.uml.edu
+1 978 934 1964 fredm@cs.uml.edu
+1 978 934 4672 michelle_scribnermaclean@uml.edu

ABSTRACT

This project studied the manner in which 7th and 8th grade students approach design problems, focusing on testing and iteration behaviors. Students were asked to solve design problems and create generalized processes for solving them. Observations of the students were analyzed using degree of design success with length and speed of iterations. The time spent exploring the problem before starting testing and iteration was the most significant factor to the success of the student's design. Future work exploring this property of design is needed to understand the causes of it.

Author Keywords

Engineering education, classroom design activities, design process

ACM Classification Keywords

K.3.2 [Computing Milieux]: Computers and Education

General Terms

Experimentation, Human Factors

INTRODUCTION

Research Focus

This study observed 7th and 8th grade students as they carried out short engineering design activities. The students were introduced to engineering activities spanning the disciplines of electrical engineering, mechanical engineering, math problem solving, and computer science. The students were asked to solve given problems, and also to create generalized processes for solving them. The focus of the data analysis was on the time students spent iterating through testing and improving their designs. Iteration has been shown to be an important component of the design process [1,2]. The time spent on the first iteration became of specific interest during the analysis.

Problem Statement

This study was an exploration, and as such was interested in multiple, closely related factors. The four questions of interest were:

Do 7th and 8th grade students exhibit patterns in testing and iteration? What are those patterns? What characteristics of a design activity elicit specific iteration patterns? What is the correlation between iteration in designing and success of the design?

METHODOLOGY

Approach

This research was conducted on a university campus with seven middle school students as research participants. The study consisted of five activities of 90 minutes, one per week. Each session provided one activity that represented a different discipline of engineering. The students worked in pairs, and were instructed and coached in thinking aloud [4]. From video recordings of the sessions, information about testing and iteration was extracted and methods of characterizing testing and iteration were developed.

Each activity was designed to meet certain criteria: it had to be process-oriented, have observable iteration behavior, and have defined metrics of success. The metrics of success for each activity was described in two levels. Completing the first level entailed the completion of a successful design that solved the problem. Achieving the second level was defined as a general process for arriving at a solution.

Working Definitions

A student was considered to be performing a "test" when a solution, or component of a solution, was applied to the problem in order to empirically ascertain how well that solution or component solved the problem. Iteration cycles were marked by the student performing a test, with the first iteration starting with the first test of the session. The time spent before the first test was considered to be "non-iterating time."

ANALYSIS

An approach to analyzing iteration patterns was developed using the total number of iteration cycles, average time for each iteration cycle, and non-iteration time before testing. These iteration data were compared with the degrees of student design success.

This analysis was applied to three of the five activities: Lights Optimization, Gear Reduction, and Elevator Control.

C&C'11, November 3–6, 2011, Atlanta, Georgia, USA.
ACM 978-1-4503-0820-5/11/11.

ACTIVITIES

Week 1: Rush Hour

"Rush Hour" is a sliding tile game where the player must manipulate cars on a 6x6 grid. The object of the game is to slide the cars so that a special car can escape through an opening in the game board.

Week 2: Light Optimization

The Light Optimization problem explored basic electrical principles and required students to balance between competing requirements. The design task was to connect eight small lights with alligator clip wires to a power supply in a way that minimized the amount of material used without sacrificing brightness.

Week 3: Gear Reduction

In this activity the students built a transmission from LEGO Technic gears and components between a fixed motor and load.

Week 4: Word Search

Students designed algorithms to solve word searches, where words were hidden in a two-dimensional grid of otherwise random letters.

Week 5: Elevator Control

Students designed and implemented an algorithm to govern the motion of a simulated elevator. The simulation acted as a microworld, allowing students to experiment within a dynamic but controlled environment [3]. The simulator used a drag-and-drop interaction method for code writing.

CONCLUSIONS

The most successful students were consistently slower to begin testing, possibly indicating that they spent more time in each activity trying to understand the problem before attempting a solution. The speed of iteration was also observed to relate to success, but not as strongly, where faster iterations were common among successful students.

FUTURE WORK

The future work to be conducted is best summarized by three potential research questions.

Why are some students spending more time exploring the problem than others? What are these students getting out of this expanded time that the others are not?

Can we make students become better designers by teaching or nurturing the problem incubation period?

ACKNOWLEDGMENTS

This material is based upon work supported by the National Science Foundation under Grants No. DRL-0624669 and No. DGE-0841392.

REFERENCES

1. C. Eckert, D. Wyatt, and P. J. Clarkson. The Elusive Act of Synthesis: Creativity in the Conceptual Design of Complex Engineering Products. *ACM C&C'09* (Berkeley, 2009).
2. Getzels, J. W., & Csikszentmihalyi, M. *The creative vision: A longitudinal study of problem finding in art.* Wiley, New York, 1976.
3. J. Levin and M. Waugh. Educational simulations, tools, games, and microworlds: Computer-based environments for learning. *International Journal of Educational Research,* 12(1):71–79, 1987.
4. Ericsson, K. A. & Simon, H. A. Verbal reports as data. *Psychological Review, 87,* 1980, 215-251.

Creative Feelings: The Effect of Mood on Creative Ideation and Evaluation

Paul T. Sowden and Leah Dawson
School of Psychology, University of Surrey, Guildford, Surrey, GU2 7XH, UK
p.sowden@surrey.ac.uk

ABSTRACT
Research has found mixed effects of mood on creative problem solving. Here we examined the effects of mood on two components of creative problem solving; ideation and evaluation. After induction of positive, negative or neutral mood participants completed ideation and evaluation tasks. Results showed that a positive mood facilitates ideation whereas a negative mood facilitated evaluation. Persons in a negative mood set their criterion for usefulness of ideas higher than did those in a positive mood. This would lead to continued search for optimal solutions and improve performance on creative problem solving tasks in which the quality, rather than quantity, of solutions is important.

Author Keywords
Creativity, affect, ideation, evaluation, usefulness

ACM Classification Keywords
Categories and subject descriptors: H.1.2 [Model and Principles]: User/Machine Systems --- human factors, human information processing

General Terms
Experimentation

INTRODUCTION
Creativeness is often defined in the literature in terms of novelty and appropriateness. That is, creative outcomes must be both original and useful [12]. In affect and creativity research, many researchers have found results supporting the "positive-mood-promotes-creativity" view [e.g. 9,11]. However, there are many other findings that cast doubt on this view [2,5]. Considering the type of task used in creativity experiments may help clarify some of the discrepancies found in the mood-creativity literature. One possibility, arising from cognitive tuning theory [6], is that a participant's mood signals to them the current situation. A positive mood indicates that the situation is safe and may encourage a relaxed and playful approach to situations, using simplifying heuristics, exploring novel possibilities, and elaborating on unusual, creative associations. In contrast, a negative mood informs the individual that the current situation is problematic and that negative outcomes are possible, which may encourage them to avoid such risky approaches, favouring instead a more exacting, detail oriented, processing style. This theory therefore predicts that the relaxed processing style of participants in a positive mood may favour performance on tasks requiring pure generation of ideas, such as divergent thinking tasks [cf. 3,7]. Conversely, the detail oriented processing associated with negative mood may lead to better performance when evaluating the usefulness of creative ideas is required. In agreement with this, positive moods worsen performance on insight problems, which require evaluation of whether a solution actually solves the problem, whereas negative moods enhance performance [10]. Here the effects of positive and negative mood on ideation and evaluation are explored. By explicitly testing the effect of mood on evaluation we extend previous work that has only been able to speculate post-hoc about an effect of negative mood on evaluation.

C&C'11, November 3-6, 2011, Atlanta, Georgia, USA.
ACM 978-1-4503-0820-5/11/11.

METHOD
Thirty six students from the University of Surrey aged 18 to 23 years (mean age 19.6) took part in the study. We adapted the GenEva task [8]. Participants were required to generate solutions to one of two problems: 1) what could be done to reduce aggressive behaviours of car drivers? or 2) if schools were abolished, what could you do to try to become educated? They also made ratings to evaluate another participant's answers to the other problem. Previously, the GenEva task has been used to evaluate originality of ideas but here we also evaluated usefulness as this is central to the definition of creativity. Participants were assigned to a positive, neutral or negative mood condition. Prior to completing the generation and evaluation tasks they watched one of three, 4-7 min, film clips to induce the relevant mood (positive condition – comedy with Mr Bean; negative mood - film clips relating to the genocides in Rwanda and Darfur; neutral mode – a film explaining how to watch TV through a computer monitor). After watching each film clip the participants completed the Self-Assessment Manikin [4], a pictorial method devised to assess the pleasure, arousal and dominance associated with a person's emotional reaction to an event. Analysis of participants' responses confirmed that the film clips led to the appropriate variations in mood across conditions ($F(2,33)=3.54, p=0.04$).

Scoring procedure
For the generative part of the task three variables were measured: fluency (the number of solutions generated),

flexibility (the number of different categories of ideas), and originality (1- the frequency of a given solution / the total sample size). For the evaluative part of the task, we assessed *accuracy* of both originality and usefulness evaluations. The difference between a participant's ratings of originality and the actual originality calculated above indicated their accuracy. The difference between their usefulness rating and those of a set of three judges (derived through the Consensual Assessment Technique [1]) indicated the accuracy of their usefulness evaluation.

RESULTS

In terms of idea generation, participants in the positive condition produced more solutions than those in the neutral and negative conditions ($F(2,33)=3.54$, $p=0.04$). They also produced solutions from more categories than participants in the neutral condition, who produced solutions from more categories than those in the negative condition ($F(2,33)=5.61$, $p=0.01$). However, there was no difference between conditions in originality ($F(2,33)=1.60$, $p=0.22$).

In terms of idea evaluation, there were no differences in accuracy of originality evaluation between conditions. However, participants in the negative condition were significantly more accurate in their evaluations of usefulness than participants in the positive condition who tended to overestimate usefulness ($t(33)=2.13$, $p=0.02$). In addition to these differences in accuracy of usefulness evaluation, participants in the positive condition gave higher ratings of usefulness per se than participants in the negative condition ($F(2,33)=3.62$, $p=0.04$). Note that this rating ignores the judges' assessments of usefulness and simply explores whether participants give different ratings of usefulness as a function of their mood state.

DISCUSSION

The current study has confirmed previous studies in which a positive mood improves performance on ideational tasks [e.g. 9,11] and, compared to a negative mood, worsens performance on tasks that require an evaluative component [e.g. 10]. Furthermore, the results extend previous research concerning the effect of negative mood on creative problem solving. Previous work has found that a negative mood is beneficial for success on insight problem tasks. The present findings suggest that a negative mood encourages evaluations of reduced usefulness. This is likely to encourage continued search for an optimal solution resulting in more useful solutions and more accurate evaluation of their usefulness. This may therefore improve performance on problem solving tasks in which the quality, rather than quantity, of solutions is important

From a practical viewpoint, these findings have implications for settings in which creativity and innovation are important. For example, changing mood state at different stages of the design process might enhance product design. Positive mood might support initial idea generation whilst switching to a negative mood state might enhance the evaluation of those ideas. Modern technologies provide many opportunities for inducing such mood switching and might be used to help realise the potential benefits of varying mood state on creativity.

REFERENCES

1. Amabile, T.M. Social psychology of creativity: A consensual assessment technique. *Journal of Personality and Social Psychology, 43*, (1982), 997-1013.
2. Bartolic, E.I., Basso, M.R., Schefft, B.K., Glauser, T., and Titanic-Schefft, M. Effects of experimentally-induced emotional states on frontal lobe cognitive task performance. *Neuropsychologia, 37*, (1999), 677-683.
3. Bass, M., De Dreu, C.K.W., and Nustad, B.A. A meta-analysis of 25 years of mood-creativity research: Hedonic tone, activation, or regulatory focus? *Psychological Bulletin, 134*, (2008), 779-806.
4. Bradley, M.M., and Lang, P.J. Measuring emotion: The self-assessment manikin and the semantic differential. *Journal of Behavioural Therapy and Experimental Psychiatry, 25*, (1994), 49-59.
5. Clapham, M.M. The effects of affect manipulation and information exposure on divergent thinking. *Creativity Research Journal, 13*, (2001), 335-350.
6. Clore, G.L., Schwarz, N., and Conway, M. Affective causes and consequences of social information processing. In R.S. Wyer & T.K. Srull (Eds.), *Handbook of Social Cognition* (Vol. 2, 2nd ed., pp323-417). LEA, Hillsdale, NJ, USA, 1994.
7. Davis, M.A. Understanding relationship between mood and creativity: A meta-analysis. *Organisational Behavior and Human Decisions Processes, 108*, (2009), 25-38.
8. Groborz, M., and Necka, E. Creativity & cognitive control: Explorations of generation and evaluation skills. *Creativity Research Journal, 15*, (2003), 183-197.
9. Isen, A.M., Johnson, M.M.S., Mertz, E., and Robinson, G.F. The influence of positive affect on the unusualness of word associations. *Journal of Personality and Social Psychology, 48*, (1985), 1413-1426.
10. Kaufmann, G., and Vosburg, S.K. "Paradoxical" mood effects on creative problem-solving. *Cognition and Emotion, 11*, (1997), 151-170.
11. Phillips, L.H., Bull, R., Adams, E., and Fraser, L. Positive mood and executive function: Evidence from stroop and fluency tasks. *Emotion, 2*, (2002), 12-22.
12. Sternberg, R.J., and Lubart, T.I. The concept of creativity: Prospects and paradigms. In R.J. Sternberg (Ed.), *Handbook of Creativity* (pp. 3-15). Cambridge University Press, Cambridge, MA, USA, 1999.

An Exploration of Creativity in School Children's Music Composition: Study, Software and Framework

Dr. Sylvia M. Truman
Faculty of Business and Management
Regent's College
London, NW1 4NS, UK
+44 (0)207 487 7614
trumans@regents.ac.uk

ABSTRACT

A question that has gained widespread interest is 'how can learning tasks be structured to encourage creative thinking in the classroom? This paper presents a generative framework which exists as a design support tool for planning creative learning experiences. A demonstration of the framework application is made through the design of SoundScape.

ACM Classification Keywords Creativity; Learning Theory; E-Learning, Music Composition, Education.

General Terms: Human Factors

INTRODUCTION

This paper reports upon a study which focused on facilitating collaborative creativity in a music composition task. Based upon theories of learning and creativity, a generative framework is presented. This framework exists as a design support tool to assist with the design of creative learning experiences within the classroom. In this instance it is applied to the domain of a collaborative music composition task and was used to inform the design of SoundScape. SoundScape was designed to explore the research hypotheses driving the study. The hypotheses focused upon explicitly supporting the preparation phase of the creative processes using music technology and using visual metaphors to specify music. The findings hold a number of implications for the design of meaningful and engaging learning experiences through considering aspects of the creative process.

THEORECTICAL BACKGROUND: THEORIES ON LEARNING

The framework take influence from constructivist learning theory.

C&C'11, November 3–6, 2011, Atlanta, Georgia, USA.
ACM 978-1-4503-0820-5/11/11.

The main assertions of this approach are; learning is contextual. Secondly, one needs knowledge to learn. It is not possible to assimilate new knowledge without having a previous knowledge structure. Thirdly, learning is a self-regulated process as every individual learns at a different rate depending on their prior knowledge and experience [1]. Finally, learning is viewed as an individual and social activity in which interactions with others and the external environment are conducive to learning [2][3].

THEORECTICAL BACKGROUND: THEORIES ON CREATIVITY

Although numerous models of the creative process have been proposed, certain points gain widespread agreement. Firstly, there is a need for preparation for the creative act. Preparation can have a number of aspects, this can involve accumulating existing facts and resources and preparing mentally for the creative process. Second, time is required for the incubation of ideas. Third, the verification of creative thoughts has both a personal and social element.

THEORECTICAL BACKGROUND: THEORIES ON CHILDREN'S MUSICAL COMPOSITION

Traditional music composition programs have been largely based upon staff notation, thus, in some instances excluding those with little to no music experience. Scholars have suggested that alternative forms of graphical notation have proven more effective in studies where the symbols used visually reflect the properties of musical sounds [4]. Symbol systems used in this way do not rely upon retrieval of previously learned meanings as visual elements are matched to auditory elements through readily identifiable representations.

A GENERATIVE FRAMEWORK FOR CREATIVITY

The framework assists the design of creative educational experiences for the classroom by providing scaffolding for supporting materials in terms of the six white component boxes of the framework (see figure 1). Wallas's four-stage model has been adapted as the fundamental basis for this generative framework, with the processes of preparation, generation and evaluation represented laterally across the

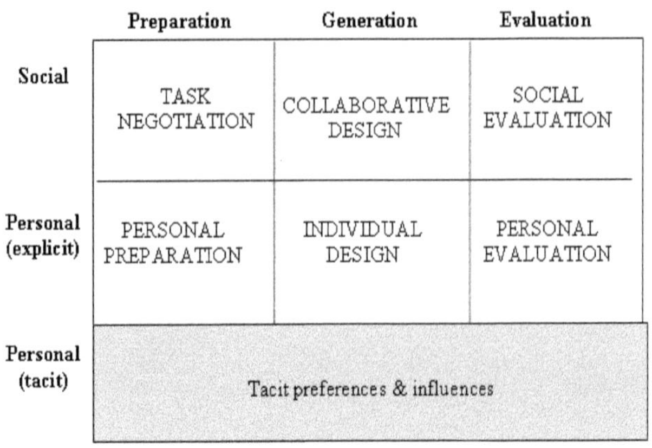

Figure 1 - A Generative Framework for Creative Learning

framework. The vertical dimensions reflect individual (denoted here as personal) and social components of creativity. The social level refers to others, peers and society and personal levels reflect explicit and tacit levels of thinking. Every creative act involves the preparation of ideas, whether in the form of tacit influences drawn from the environment, or conscious preparation for the task. The generation process of the framework encompasses social and personal design. The evaluation process concerns reviewing early creative ideas through to evaluating the final artefact.

RESEARCH QUESTIONS

Extending upon the motivation and the generative framework, two questions were raised. Firstly, what outcomes may arise when music composition software explicitly supports / does not support the preparation phase of the creative process? Secondly, what different outcomes may arise when real-world metaphors are used to specify music as opposed to using abstract representations? Lead to a greater depth of engagement for the student than those which do not.

DESIGNING SOUNDSCAPE

Four prototypes of SoundScape were developed to test the research hypotheses. Prototype one explicitly supported the preparation phase whilst using visual metaphors to specify music. With this prototype, students can select a 'theme' for their composition. Students select the theme they wish to use and prepare for the music composition task by specifying their 'composition' objects by associating real-world objects that one might expect to find within the theme to pre-recorded music samples. Students associate the metaphors to the pre-recorded music samples based on qualities they feel are shared between the two. Students then progress to the main composition environment within SoundScape where they drag and manipulate the composition objects to structure their musical work.

Prototype two does not explicitly support preparation. Students enter the program at the main composition screen and create a composition using pre-specified composition objects Prototype three uses abstract representation to specify music, preparation is explicitly supported within this prototype by allowing students to select eight music samples for use in their compositions. Students then progress to the main composition area of SoundScape Prototype four does not explicitly support preparation, students do not select composition objects to use, rather, they enter the task on the main composition. Here they use pre-define composition objects to create their composition using the abstract representation to specify music

STUDY AND FINDINGS

96 school children participated with this study, all eleven years of age. Twenty four participants were allocated to each condition, with twelve pairs of students in each. The study was conducted over a month and with one pair of students at a time to allow participants to work free from distraction. Results indicate that those working within preparation conditions spent significantly longer on the task than those in non-preparation conditions. Findings also indicate that those working with visual metaphors to specify music spent significantly longer on the task, used significantly more musical bars, moved significantly more objects and used significantly more of the eight composition objects than those using abstract representations to specify music.

CONCLUSIONS OF STUDY

Findings from the study indicated that preparation is a crucial element of the creative process and that support preparation in music composition can assist to encourage creative thinking in children's music composition. Outcomes also suggest that the use of visual imagery to specify music is also a useful too for learning, especially where the imagery used is consistent with real-world artifacts.

REFERENCES

[1] Bandura, A (1986) Social Foundations of Thought and Action: A Social Cognitive Theory. Englewood Cliffs; NJ Prentice Hall.

[2] Frank, C (2005) Teaching and learning theory: who needs it? College Quarterly. No. 2, Vol 8.

[3] Dewey, J (1916) Democracy and Education. New York. Macmillan.

[4] Walker, R (1992) Auditory-visual perception and musical behaviour. In Colwell, R. (Ed) Handbook of Research on Music Teaching and Learning. New York; Schirmer Books.

Beyond Fixing Bugs:

Case Studies of Creative Collaboration in Open Source Software Bug Fixing Processes

Jing Wang and John M. Carroll
College of Information Sciences and Technology
The Pennsylvania State University, University Park, PA 16802
{jzw143, jmcarroll}@psu.edu

ABSTRACT

Bug fixing is an important collaborative practice of open source software development. Creative collaborative bug fixing—collectively generating new and useful solutions to improve software quality—is important especially when bugs are difficult to fix. We find bug fixing practices are unavoidably creative by studying Mozilla and Python. We characterize their bug fixing process as four common subprocesses, problem identification, preparation, solution generation, and solution evaluation. We discuss the key challenges of creative collaboration during each subprocess, and recommend design implications to enhance creative collaborative bug fixing processes, including support for establishment of common ground, externalization of social networks, awareness of resolving progress, and articulation of design rationale.

Author Keywords

Bug fixing processes, creative collaboration, open source software development.

ACM Classification Keywords

H5.3. [**Group and Organization Interfaces**]: *Collaborative computing and Computer-supported cooperative work.*

General Terms

Human Factors

INTRODUCTION

Open source software (OSS) development is an important paradigm of collaborative knowledge work [3]. It involves globally dispersed experts, mostly voluntarily, collaborating over the Internet to produce software with source code freely available. OSS projects can hardly succeed without creative products and practices, as many other types of professional work. Creativity in OSS development is more commonly embedded in everyday problem solving activities, known as little c or everyday creativity, rather than revolutionary contributions [5].

C&C'11, November 3–6, 2011, Atlanta, Georgia, USA.
ACM 978-1-4503-0820-5/11/11.

Extensive bug fixing—detecting and repairing software defects or improving software deficiencies—is considered an advantage of OSS development [4]. Despite its importance, bug fixing has never been discussed as creative processes. In fact, creativity, generating novel and effective solutions or methods to defects or deficiencies, can be evoked from the collaboration of fixing bugs. Creative bug fixing is especially important when bugs are difficult to find, analyze, fix and/or verify. It may also lead to product innovation and organizational knowledge development. Therefore, we investigate how the creative collaborative OSS bug fixing is carried out, what challenges it, and what technical affordances may support it.

We conducted comparative case studies in two well-recognized and innovative OSS communities, Mozilla and Python. They differ at their product types, sizes, community scales and structure, and specific features of tools that support bug fixing activities. These differences enable contrasts that highlight consistencies [6].

DATA ANALYSIS AND RESULTS

The primary data source of the analysis presented in this paper is bug reports of Firefox and Python language from their respective bug tracking systems, which are the key places recording the important collaborative activities during OSS bug fixing. We retrieved bug reports created between two recent stable releases of Firefox and Python, including 7322 reports between the releases of Firefox 3.5 and 3.6 final and 1850 issues between the releases of Python 3.0 and 3.1 final. This sampling strategy was to accommodate the possible behavioral changes near releases [2].

Four subprocesses of the OSS bug fixing process emerged from our qualitative analysis, problem identification, preparation, solution generation, and solution evaluation, in accordance with previous literature on creativity [1]. Each bug can be fixed along different sequences or combinations of these subprocesses. Subprocesses are not perfectly clear-cut; some of them may be intertwined at times.

Problem identification involves different stakeholders judging and negotiating whether fixing the bug is consistent with community objectives and values. Specifically, a problem is found and described by an individual member experiencing a failure, discovering a product defect, or desiring a design enhancement. It is then elaborated, understood, verified and sometimes reframed through community effort.

Our data indicate that building common ground regarding a bug is a critical issue of the problem identification subprocess. Participants have heterogeneous knowledge of the problem—the reporter knows the local environment well, while other developers have the technical expertise to discover the cause of software dysfunction. However, collaborative identification cannot progress until all that unique information and knowledge is effectively shared, clarified and confirmed [5].

Preparation subprocess involves collecting and reactivating relevant information and resources for generating solutions. In OSS bug fixing practices, members actively search and gather information such as who has the best knowledge of the defective source code, what are the current technical constraints, and what methods may apply. Their interactions often appear in the form of asking for help or voluntarily introducing resources.

Creative collaboration requires appropriate domain knowledge and expertise [1]. Engaging appropriate experts is a simple and frequently used strategy of Mozilla's and Python's developers in preparation process for such purposes. Directly asking the author of the defected code works when someone in the discussion knows who the desired expert is. However, peripheral members, who rarely contribute to the community, often do not have such knowledge, whereas core developers have but can hardly participate in every bug discussion because of heavy workload. Therefore, externalizing the social networks connected based on members' shared work activities may enhance the effectiveness of the preparation subprocess.

During the solution generation subprocess, candidate responses to a problem are produced. In Mozilla and Python, collaboration on generating bug solutions usually appears as contributing design ideas or specifications for implementations, or sharing their implemented solutions. On the contrary, a group of developers working on different parts of the implementation rarely happens. This reduces the interdependencies between members, conducive to effective coordination and collaboration. Divergent thinking and convergent thinking may both be involved before a solution is implemented.

The ability of reflecting on the shared goals and progress, planning accordingly and taking actions is crucial to collaborative creativity [5]. During the solution generation subprocess in OSS bug fixing, keeping aware of resolution progress of a specific bug and all its interdependent bugs can facilitate discovering any demand of specific resources or help, adjusting developmental plans, and coordinating efforts across groups.

Solution evaluation process regards to the examination and validation of generated solutions, as well as the decision on integrating solution into current software products. In our context, we refer to the process when other community members critically review solution implementation to the defective software product rather than proposed ideas. At least one core developer has to participate in evaluation other than the solution author to accomplish the evaluation process. Mozilla supports explicit requests for specific reviewers, while Python highlights bugs pending for patch reviews.

Design rationale stimulates software developers to reflect on their design by explaining and elaborating their ideas to other members, helps others understand and review their design implementations, and may even facilitate developers explore or discover better design. It is not explicitly documented in OSS development. However, collaboration in bug fixing processes creates opportunities to articulate such implicit knowledge.

This study is our exploration of creative collaboration in OSS practices. We will include more data sources to refine and verify our current findings, for instance, mailing lists, commit logs, PEPs, and interviews with active members. Those sources will also provide the opportunities of triangulation. We will further speculate on designing tools that support collaborative software development and generating patterns of effective organizations.

ACKNOWLEDGMENTS

This work is supported by the US National Science Foundation (0943023). We thank our partners, the Mozilla and Python organizations for sharing their practices.

REFERENCES

1. Amabile, T.M. *Creativity in Context.* Westview Press, Boulder, CO, 1996.
2. Francalanci, C. and Merlo, F. Empirical Analysis of the Bug Fixing Process in Open Source Projects. *Open Source Development, Communities and Quality.* 187-196.
3. Moon, J.Y. and Sproull, L. Essence of Distributed Work: The Case of the Linux Kernel. *First Monday, 5* (11).
4. Raymond, E.S. *The Cathedral and the Bazaar: Musings on Linux and Open Source by an Accidental Revolutionary.* O'Reilly, 2001.
5. Sternberg, R. *Handbook of creativity.* Cambridge University Press, New York, 1999.
6. Yin, R. *Case study research: Design and methods.* Sage Publications, Inc, 2008.

Creative Storytelling Enhanced Through Social Media and Intelligent Recommendation

Yin-Li Wong
Faculty of Information Technology
Multimedia University
Cyberjaya, Malaysia
Mindy.ylwong@gmail.com

Chien-Sing Lee
Graduate Institute of Network
Learning Technology
National Central University, Taiwan
cslee@cl.ncu.edu.tw

ABSTRACT
Collaborative storytelling is an activity that would boost our creativity and imagination. However, collaborative storytelling systems are not popular and few efforts have been made to support its growth. This research presents *WriteYourJourney (WYJ),* a collaborative e-storytelling system integrated with social networking media and a recommender system. *WriteYourJourney* supports the idea of collaborative storytelling by adding in features that increase the interactivity between the users and the system. These features are story and link recommender, story tree visualization, diverse choices of story writing style and chat room. User testing results are positive with regards to usability, effectiveness, learnability and memorability. Users are keen to use the system in the future.

Keywords
Collaborative, Storytelling, Creative, Social networking media, Recommender, Implicit Rating, Story tree visualization.

ACM Classification Keywords
H.5.m. Information interfaces and presentation (e.g., HCI): Miscellaneous.

General Terms
Design, Experimentation and Human Factors.

INTRODUCTION
Bloom's Taxonomy [1] defines creative thinking as "creating something new and original". To create something new, one needs to be curious and think laterally [2]. Panqueve [3] agrees with [2] and adds that creative thinking is to look for new focus and explore all their possibilities. Some common techniques are brainstorming, elaboration, flexibility, imagery and associative thinking [1].

Storytelling, by its nature, is an activity that would push the storytellers to think creatively. Examples of collaborative storytelling systems are Protagonize.com [4] and Storybird.com [5].

C&C'11, November 3–6, 2011, Atlanta, Georgia, USA.
ACM 978-1-4503-0820-5/11/11.

In this paper, we address two problems related to meaningful interaction during collaborative storytelling. The first problem is the need to source for ideas, inspiration and references, be it real-life or not. There is a lot of information in the system and on the Internet. However, users often do not get the resources that they need.

Secondly, although we tell stories everyday, collaborative storytelling platforms are often not able to attract sufficient participation crucial to the generation, sharing, adaptation and creation of ideas

OBJECTIVE
WriteYourJourney (WYJ) addressed the above two problems by:

1. supporting online collaborative storytelling by incorporating social media to make collaborative storytelling more interesting.
2. providing a resource recommender that generates relevant and just-in-time recommendation in terms of image and stories.
3. adapting the Slope One algorithm to recommend stories based on implicit rating, which is based on the calculation between read frequency and time to create meaningful interaction.

WRITE YOUR JOURNEY's Story Recommender
Collaborative Filtering [6] is one of the approaches used to filter out information in order to recommend image resources or stories to the user. In WYJ, the Slope One Algorithm [7], a rating-based Collaborative Filtering item-to-item recommendation technique, is modified and implemented. The resulting recommendation is relevant to the user, thus, creating meaningful interaction between the user and the stories that he/she will be reading. Elaboration on the modified algorithm is provided in the subsection SLOPE ONE SCORE.

If a user clicks on a certain story, it will provide community-based recommendation. Else, it will provide user-based recommendation. Community-based recommendation refers to recommendation based on the community's interest pattern on the stories read by the whole community. User-based recommendation refers to recommendation based on the user's interest pattern over other users with similar interest patterns.

There are two types of rating, i.e. explicit and implicit. Explicit rating refers to ratings that would require users to determine it. For example, user rating on a rating bar of scale 1 to 5. Instead of Explicit Rating, as introduced in [8], WYJ will be adapting Implicit Rating, introduced by Oard and Kim (1998), in order to fit the nature of the data. In implicit rating, we take the frequency of a user reading the story as a rating. Thus, we will have a binary rating, where the story read is rated as 1, else, it would be rated as 0.

In order to make things work with Slope One, tracking of user's reading activity along with story read count tracking would be implemented in order to calculate the result. In this case, we will track using audit trail.

ADAPTED SLOPE ONE ALGORITHM

Slope One Score

First of all, we need to find the score for each user on every story that the user has read by using the following calculation:-

```
[[ (-e(-0.1*(number of times viewed on the same
   story)))+ 1]
+ [ e(-0.025*Average(Last Recorded View Dates –
   Current Date))]] / 2
```

The formula is adapted from the exponential formula [9]: Ae^{kx} ; It was calculated using addition("+") instead of multiplication("*") as we would cater for either cases of either higher read count of most recent read time to score high scores. Furthermore, since our database is not large, this is workable.

Slope One Result

Slope One Result tabulates the relationship score for every pair of stories. It will store the count of users who have read both stories and also tabulate the Slope One Score difference between 2 stories read by the same user.

User-Based Recommendation

The idea of user-based recommendation is to find similar user behavior or pattern between the user and the other users in the community and recommend relevant stories to them.

It is tabulated by the following formula. The top 7 stories with the highest score are recommended:-

```
Tabulate :
sum up ((cur_slopeOneScore *
Number of users that have read both
stories) - slopeOneResult)
/ Number of Users who have read both
stories
```

*cur_slopeOneScore = the current user's slopeOneScore.

Community-Based Recommendation

The system will calculate and tabulate the strength of the bond between 2 stories.

```
Calculate
(slopeOneResult /
Number of Users who
have read both stories)
```

Then, it will recommend the top 7 stories with the highest score.

CONCLUSION

The research shows that the implementation of social networking media tools, recommenders, story tree visualization tool and chat room have enhanced meaningful interaction. Consequently, this has enhanced users' experience during online collaborative e-storytelling.

REFERENCES

1. Bloom, B. Bloom's Taxanomy: Critical and Creative Thinking. 1956. Retrieved 3rd January 2011. From http://eduscapes.com/tap/topic69.htm
2. Panqueva, G. A. H. Play, Puzzles and Creativity: Learning engines for the knowledge society. Technical Document ACE-01-00, Version 2.0, March, 2000. Santa Fe de Bogotá.
3. DeBono, E. (1974). El pensamiento lateral. Manual de Creatividad. Barcelona: Ediciones Paidós.
4. Protagonize. Available at http://www.protagonize.com/
5. StoryBird – Collaborative Storytelling. Available at http://storybird.com
6. Goldberg, K., Roeder, T., Gupta, D. and Perkins, C. Eigentaste: a constant time collaborative filtering algorithm. *Information Retrieval 4* 2, 2001, 133–151.
7. Lemire, D. and MacLachlan, A. Slope One Predictors for Online Rating-Based Collaborative Filtering. *SIAM Data Mining Conference,* 2005, 21-23.

Creativity in Software Development in an Academic Research Lab

Andy Wu, Sam Mendenhall, Jayraj Jog, Ali Mazalek
Synaesthetic Media Lab
GVU Center, Georgia Institute of Technology
TSRB, 85 5th St. NW, Atlanta, GA 30318, USA
{ andywu, smendenhall3, jayraj.jog, mazalek }@gatech.edu

ABSTRACT
We review the creative activity in the software development process of the ROSS (Responsive Objects, Surfaces, and Spaces) API. The ROSS API is a tangible toolkit that allows designers and developers to easily build applications for many different tangible platforms while still accommodating the continued evolution of the underlying sensing technologies. We describe the ROSS API specification and discuss its use in application development.

Author Keywords
Software creativity, API, Toolkits, Tangible User Interface

ACM Classification Keywords
H.4.3 Communications Applications

General Terms
Design

INTRODUCTION
Most creativity research on software development focuses on the creativity of solutions during the development period. This paper focuses on three topics in the context of the a novel application programming interface called the Responsive Objects, Surfaces and Spaces (ROSS) API:

- The creative thinking that accompanied drafting the software specification of the API
- The creative methods supported by the ROSS communication architecture that developers can use to achieve software requirements during development
- The creativity involved in developing new applications using the ROSS API

RELATED WORK
There has been a variety of work on developing toolkits for physical sensors, tools to support co-located groupware, and other API frameworks within the areas of ubiquitous computing and tangible interfaces (see [1] for a summary). However there has been little work on toolkits that can integrate this range of interaction environments into a single application programming interface that would allow developers to create truly cross-platform applications. The ROSS API is a software package that extends our previous work in integrated toolkit development [1, 2].

ROSS: RE-THINKING SOFTWARE IN PHYSICAL SPACE
An application programming interface (API) is a software interface designed to enable communication between different software programs. While most software APIs target adjacent levels in the software architecture, ROSS is designed to communicate through several levels across multiple platforms that are very different but have common interactions. ROSS API is designed to establish communication between the hardware driver level to the software application level. To accomplish this, ROSS makes the interface between these levels abstract.

The nested structure of ROSS provides a common abstraction within which application developers can specify the particular configuration of their target platform. This is done using an XML configuration file that describes a given platform's nested structure of spaces, surfaces and objects, as well as its parameters such as ID, type and dimensions. When an application receives such a configuration file from a candidate platform, it can further analyze it and determine whether or not the platform satisfies its needs. This nested structure is best illustrated by an example as shown in Figure 1.

COMMUNICATION ARCHITECTURE
ROSS is designed to integrate different tangible interaction platforms. Developers can take advantage of the ease of the XML format to describe complex nested relationships of objects, spaces and surfaces. ROSS encapsulates all of a user's possible interactions with a device inside of a single representation, which can be fundamentally altered through the XML configuration file. Having the ability to quickly and easily swap out input methods adds an entirely different dimension of creative thinking to application development. Using the toolkit, designers gain a vocabulary for describing different sources of user input, and are free to

C&C'11, November 3–6, 2011, Atlanta, Georgia, USA.
ACM 978-1-4503-0820-5/11/11.

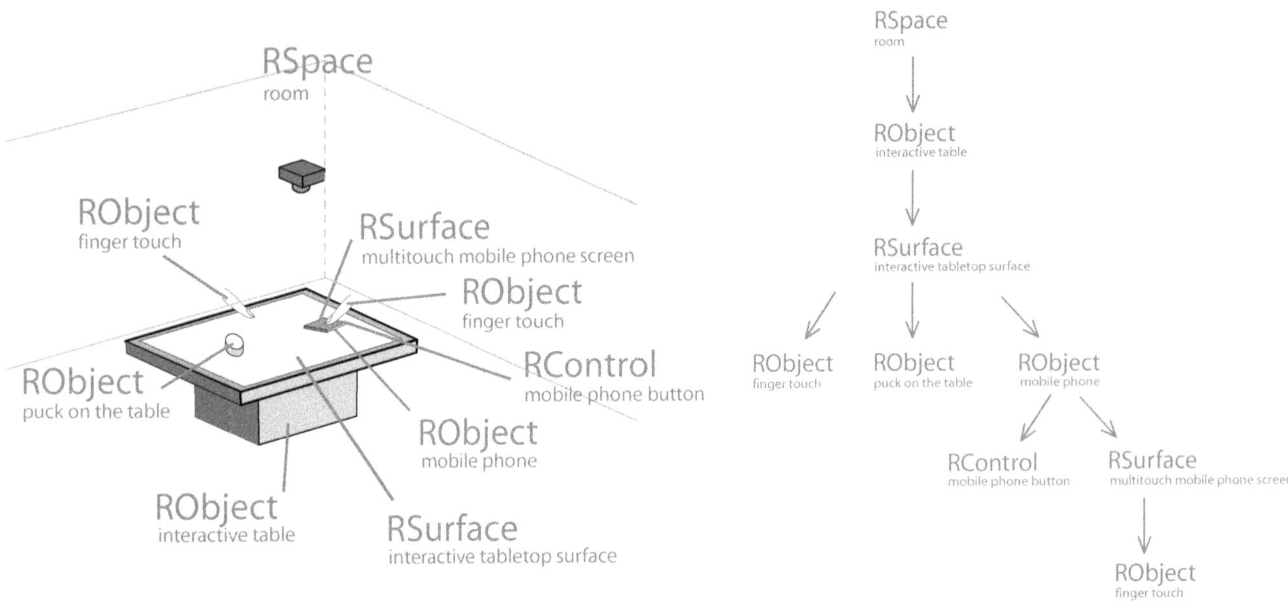

Figure 1. An example of ROSS's nested structure. In the left figure are the ROSS components in a room. There is an interactive tabletop with a puck and a mobile phone on its tabletop surface. Users interact with the tabletop and the objects on top of it. The right figure shows the hierarchical nested structure.

tinker and stretch the boundary between the physical and digital worlds.

APPLICATIONS AND LESSONS LEARNED

ROSS provides abstractions for tangible input devices. In addition, the library allows programmers to treat objects, surfaces and spaces with the same spatial relationships as they have in real life. A number of applications have been created at various stages of the ROSS API development process and demonstrate its flexibility. Examples include: the installation piece *Moons Over You* which tracks multiple people in a space and synchronizes their movements with the display of personalized moons overhead; the ROSS Paint application which allows multiple users to paint a shared drawing across various devices, such as mobile phones, laptops, and wall displays; and ROSS Ripple which demonstrates how the screen space of small devices such as mobile phones can nest into and interact with larger surfaces such as interactive tabletops.

The ROSS API makes programming for these varied platforms simple. It takes care of details such as networking, event handling and device management, allowing programmers to focus on making an engaging application. Some evidence of this is already available. For ROSS Paint and ROSS Ripples, the applications themselves perform very little of the common tasks of establishing connections, managing networking, events and subscriptions, and other necessary tasks. Instead the application code consists entirely of application logic.

Just as sketches and wireframes help GUI designers plan designs and physical models help architects visualize their buildings, we have found that tangibility promotes dialogue between developers and helps them think through design concepts. This is especially true for the ROSS API, since it is designed for integrating tangible user interfaces, many of which are graspable. Usually when we discuss an idea in the lab, we pick up the object and demonstrated it to other colleagues. This characteristic of the "tangible" user interface helps make project conversations more fluid.

SUMMARY AND FUTURE WORK

ROSS uses a fundamentally different design paradigm for specifying a networking API. Through its novel hierarchical nested structure, ROSS closely models the environments for which it is designed. These new concepts create a network of tangible user interfaces that promotes embodied interaction.

The unorthodox API architecture of ROSS opens another window for tangible user interface researchers to implement their applications in a different way. This novel method in API development has not yet been evaluated. Therefore, we cannot make claims about its efficiency. However, once a TUI developer follows the specification defined in ROSS, she can create applications that communicate with heterogeneous devices and benefit from being part of the entire ROSS tangible network.

REFERENCES

1. Mazalek, A. Tangible Toolkits: Integrating Application Development across Diverse Multi-User and Tangible Interaction Platforms. *Let's Get Physical Workshop, DCC'06*, (2006).
2. Reilly, D.F., Rouzati, H., Wu, A., Hwang, J.Y., Brudvik, J., and Edwards, W.K. TwinSpace: an infrastructure for cross-reality team spaces. *Proc. UIST '10*, ACM (2010), 119-128.

Perception, Insight, and Creativity in *Paradigm*, a Game of Pattern Exploration

William W. York
Indiana University
512 N. Fess Ave.
Bloomington, IN 47408
wwyork@indiana.edu

David C. Bender
Indiana University
512 N. Fess Ave.
Bloomington, IN 47408
dcbender@indiana.edu

ABSTRACT

We discuss Paradigm, a game of intuition and pattern exploration. We make a case for the game's relevance as a microdomain for studying creativity and related phenomena such as analogy-making, high-level perception, and aesthetic sensibility. Rather than focusing on creativity in the sense of "generating output" (e.g., writing stories or making up jokes), we emphasize its more exploratory and evaluative aspects, which we believe to be prerequisites for genuine "output creativity."

Author Keywords

Creativity, high-level perception, pattern recognition, analogy, induction, aesthetic judgment

ACM Classification Keywords

A.m. Miscellaneous

General Terms

Theory

INTRODUCTION AND BACKGROUND

Paradigm is a game of pattern exploration and discovery that also offers interesting avenues for the study of creativity. First, it serves as a challenging, yet tractable microdomain for computational modeling. Second, it lends itself to (empirical) psychological enquiry due to the gradually unfolding, interactive nature of the game. Here we aim to explain what is interesting about the domain and why it is well-suited for the study of creativity and related aspects of cognition. Finally, we outline some future directions for research involving Paradigm.

Creativity: Two Distinctions (and Continuities)

Rather than attempt to define creativity, we instead begin with a couple of useful distinctions, one between *input* and *output* creativity, and the other between *mundane* and *extraordinary* creativity.

According to [7], "Input creativity involves the analysis of incoming data, whereas output creativity involves the production of something new" (p. 212). Examples of input creativity include solving a puzzle or chess problem, interpreting a piece of music, or deciphering a joke; examples of output creativity include devising a puzzle or chess problem, writing a song, or making up a joke. Most AI projects dealing with creativity during the '80s and '90s [e.g., 5] emphasized output creativity, yet it would be hard to imagine a genuine model of creativity that did not account for the role of evaluation, sensibility, and aesthetic judgment, all of which are encompassed by the notion of input creativity. "To be a good writer, you have to be a good reader" [8], which is to say that input creativity is essential to true output creativity. The "central feedback loop of creativity" [8] depends on this iterative, back-and-forth relationship between input and output creativity.

Mundane and Extraordinary Creativity

Discussions of creativity tend to center on the extraordinary acts of genius one associates with the Picassos and Mozarts of the world. However, examples of creativity can be found in practically every aspect of life—for example, in the form of an offhand pun or joke, or a meal improvised out of spare assortment of ingredients from the refrigerator. Such examples are encompassed in the term *mundane creativity* [1]. Appreciating the creativity involved in seemingly mundane acts allows us to see it as something basic to cognition and pervasive in our daily lives, rather than as something rare and accessible to a select few.

Mundane and extraordinary creativity are best thought of as two endpoints along a continuum, rather than as sharply distinct phenomena. Our belief in this continuity between mundane and extraordinary creativity—and between input and output creativity—provides the rationale for our focus on Paradigm as a means of studying creativity.

Predecessors: Games and Models

Paradigm's predecessors include the card game Eleusis [7], the pen-and-paper game Patterns II [10], and the domain of Bongard problems [2], all of which were designed to highlight aspects of creativity, induction, and related cognitive phenomena. Relevant computational models include GENESIS [7], a model of (mostly) input creativity using a scaled-down version of Eleusis; Phaeaco [4], a model of pattern-recognition and high-level perception in the Bongard domain meanwhile; and Copycat [6], a model of analogy-making involving short letter-strings. In each case, a carefully circumscribed domain is used to study *domain-independent* aspects of cognition. The computer models operate *within* certain domains (or microdomains),

C&C'11, November 3–6, 2011, Atlanta, Georgia, USA.
ACM 978-1-4503-0820-5/11/11.

but they are ultimately not *about* those domains. Paradigm has been chosen with a similar approach in mind.

PARADIGM

Paradigm[1] is a digital extension of the pen-and-pencil game Patterns II. The game is played on a "board" consisting of a number of squares (or other shapes), which are blank to begin the game. The player begins by choosing any square and guessing its color from a set of possible choices—typically no more than a handful.[2] If the guess is correct, the player receives one point, and then can either continue the turn—risking any points gained from previous correct guesses during the turn—or pass. If the guess is incorrect, the correct color is revealed, the turn ends, and any points earned thus far on the turn are lost. A turn lasts for as many guesses the player is willing to make, as long as (s)he keeps guessing correctly. The final score for the entire game is the sum of all turn scores.

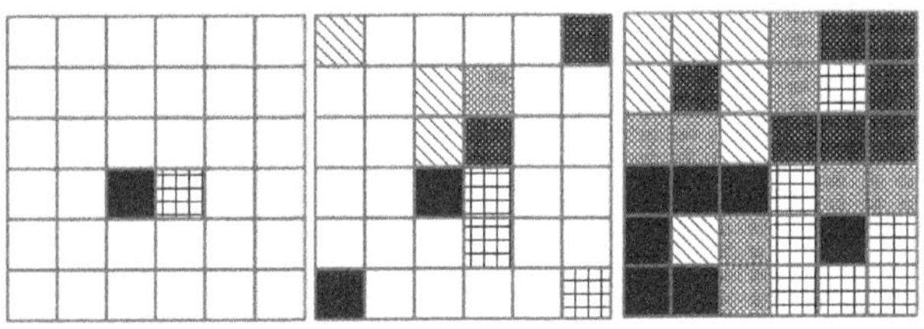

Figure 1. Three snapshots of a Paradigm game in progress.

Each guess yields one new piece of information: the color of the newly revealed square. This information may either trigger a shift in the player's perception of the overall pattern or simply reinforce an existing perception. Various competing pressures may be in play at any given point in the game, including the pressure to see horizontal, vertical, or diagonal lines of a given color; to perceive larger groups such as L-shapes or diamonds; to distinguish between background and foreground elements; etc. This gradually unfolding process leads to hypotheses about the colors of the unrevealed squares. (Making a guess is like testing a hypothesis.). Early in the game, guesses are tentative and often wrong; as more squares are revealed, they are less so. After each correct guess, the player must decide whether to stop—cashing in whatever points have been earned thus far on the turn—or to keep going and risk losing those points.

Observations on Paradigm

Let's consider some of the concepts that might become relevant as one works through a puzzle. First, there are concepts that are relevant in terms of the pattern itself, from the spatial (e.g., *center*, *corner*, *diagonal*) to the relational (e.g., *counterpart*, *pair*, *group*). Along with these pattern-level concepts, there are strategy-level concepts: *hypothesis*, *rule*, *guess*, *confident*, etc. Paradigm's scoring system rewards risk-taking, but only when it's well justified. Thus, players must have a sense for how well they understand the pattern and its underlying rules at each stage of the game. Finally, there are some more general aesthetic concepts that factor in: *interesting*, *tedious*, *surprising*, *elegant*, etc. Is the pattern visually appealing? Was the unfolding of the game interesting or boring? Players develop a feel for such aesthetic evaluations with experience, just as one does with any domain. This feel for the domain, which is a sophisticated form of input creativity, is a prerequisite to quality output creativity, which here means designing new patterns in the domain.

Having gained experience both playing patterns designed by others and creating new ones, we note a few basic characteristics of "good" patterns. Such patterns typically achieve a balance between complexity and order, ambiguity and clarity. The best patterns encourage oscillation between periods of uncertainty and periods of discovery, in which previously ambiguous aspects of the pattern suddenly "click." Finally, good patterns typically require players to revisit areas of the board that were previously "understood" and reinterpret them as new information comes to light.

CONCLUSION: FUTURE DIRECTIONS

Our research on Paradigm is taking place along three interrelated tracks. First, we are investigating the domain itself, identifying the various dimensions along which patterns can vary (e.g., emphasis on lines, paths, or shapes; symmetry; foreground–background distinctions; etc.). Second, we are designing more systematic empirical studies. Paradigm provides a built-in means by which to track players' decision-making, since it takes place one move at a time. In this sense, it allows for a finer grain of comparison between human-subject data and computer models. The third track is the development of a computer model of pattern exploration in Paradigm, building on the results of the first two tracks, along with ideas developed in models such as Copycat, GENESIS, and Phaeaco.

REFERENCES

1. Barsalou, L., & Prinz, J. Acquisition and productivity in perceptual symbol systems. In [3], 105–138.
2. Bongard, M. M. *Pattern Recognition*. Rochelle Park, N.J.: Hayden Book Co., Spartan Books, 1970.
3. Dartnall, T. (ed.). *Creativity, Cognition, and Knowledge*. Westport, Conn.: Greenwood, 2002.
4. Foundalis, H. *Phaeaco*. Ph.D. diss., Indiana Univ., Bloomington, 2006.
5. McCorduck, P. *Aaron's Code*. N.Y.: Freeman, 1991.
6. Mitchell, M. *Analogy-Making as Perception: A Computer Model*. Cambridge, Mass.: MIT Press, 1993.
7. Partridge, D., & Rowe, J. Creativity: A computational modeling approach. In [3], 211–238.
8. Rehling, J. Results in the Letter Spirit project. In [3], 273–281.
9. Romesburg, C. H. Simulating scientific inquiry with the card game Eleusis. *Sci. Ed.*, 63, 5 (Oct. 1979), 599–608.
10. Sackson, S. *Gamut of Games*. N.Y: Rand. House, 1969.

[1] http://www.koryheath.com/games/paradigm

[2] Here, we describe the one-player version of the game, although there is also a two player version.

Introducing Creativity Techniques and Software Apps to the Care of People with Dementia

Konstantinos Zachos, Neil Maiden, Kristine Karlsen and Sara Jones
Centre for Creativity in Professional Practice
City University London, UK
+44 20 7040 8994
kzachos@soi.city.ac.uk

Ian Turner, Malcolm Rose and Kevin Pudney
Registered Nursing Home Association
Birmingham B30 3JN, UK
+44 121 451 1088
ian.turner@rnha.co.uk

Julie MacManus
MediaTel Ltd
London W1B 5AJ, UK
+44 207 432 0874 telephone
juliemacmanus@gmail.com

ABSTRACT
This poster reports research to introduce creative problem solving techniques and software to the care for people with dementia in residential homes.

Author Keywords
Creativity; analogical reasoning; dementia care.

ACM Classification Keywords
J.3 [Life and Medical Systems] Health

General Terms
Human Factors

DEMENTIA CARE AND CREATIVITY

Dementia is a condition related to ageing. After the age of 65 the proportion of people with dementia doubles for every five years of age, so that almost one fifth of people over the age of 85 and a third of people over the age of 95 are estimated to be affected [2]. Two-thirds of all residents in care homes have a form of dementia [5], and caring for these residents can pose complex problems. Symptoms vary from person to person, requiring care to be individualized and care staff to think creatively to deliver the novel and effective treatments and support that individual residents need. The EU-funded FP7 *Mirror* Integrated Project is providing new capabilities to enhance care by offering care staff new forms of creativity training, techniques and software apps adapted to the care domain.

Research in *Mirror* aims to overcome two challenges in the care for people with dementia. The first is to implement creativity techniques that can support the care for dementia in residential homes effectively. These techniques need to be effective within the constraints that residential care homes impose, constraints such as the low status and limited training of the care staff [1]. The second is to develop new software apps that can support effective creative thinking with the techniques to be implemented in care homes. High turnover of staff means that sharing knowledge about good care practices that we perceive as a pre-condition to effective creative thinking is difficult. Therefore in *Mirror* we have developed mobile apps that enable care staff to undertake case-based reasoning with previous solutions to the same problem and creative thinking with analogical solutions to similar problems.

C&C'11, November 3–6, 2011, Atlanta, Georgia, USA.
ACM 978-1-4503-0820-5/11/11.

INTRODUCING CREATIVITY INTO DEMENTIA CARE

We observed and interviewed care staff in one care home to understand current care practices and introduce creativity techniques and software apps. Data collected revealed three distinct opportunities for creative problem solving:

1. Managing challenging behavior: creative problem solving can be used to analyze data about such behavior to discover its causes then compare with previous episodes of challenging behavior to propose possible resolutions to it.

2. Adapting to an evolving understanding of each resident: the process of understanding residents is not formulaic but requires care staff to react to individual situations, thereby establishing opportunities for creative problem solving.

3. Devising stimulation to residents with advanced stage dementia: creative thinking offers opportunities to discover new forms of stimulation through all five senses for these residents within one major constraint – limited staff time.

CREATIVITY TECHNIQUES FOR DEMENTIA CARE

Six care staff from the residential home experimented with different creativity techniques on a dementia case study, and the technique deemed most interesting and effective was *other worlds*, an exploratory creativity technique that encourages analogical reasoning in different domains. Its selection recognized the potential for case-based problem solving in the care for dementia [4]. The care staff generated ideas to solve problems analogical to ones encountered in dementia care in four domains - *social life*, *research*, *word of mouth* and *different cultures*, then transfer these ideas to the care for dementia. The staff then randomly picked a fifth analogical domain from *politics*, *tennis*, *flying* and *army* [6] and repeated the idea generation process. The success of *other worlds* can inform work redesign and new forms of training in the pilot care home

THE CARER SOFTWARE APP

A software app, called *Carer*, was developed to support creative thinking by care staff in situ based on the transfer and application of knowledge about previous similar episodes of challenging behavior. In particular it supports two forms of creative problem solving with previous strategies for managing challenging behavior. The first is case-based reasoning with descriptions of cases solved successfully in the same domain, i.e. challenging behavior in dementia care. *Carer* supports the care staff to adapt solutions developed initially for other people to residents in their own care, as reported in [4]. The second is analogical reasoning with descriptions of cases solved successfully in other domains such as policing and teaching. *Carer* supports care staff to reason analogically with then transfer and apply knowledge from the source domain to manage the current challenging behavior, as achieved with the *other worlds* technique. For example, a description of good policing practice to manage disorderly revelers can provide analogical insights with which to manage challenging behavior in dementia care. *Carer* distinguishes between these two forms of creative problem solving using two similarity measures specified in Gentner's [3] Structure Mapping Theory (SMT). These measures use attributional and relational predicates extracted from natural language descriptions of challenging behavior queries and descriptions of successful strategies.

Carer was implemented on an iPod Touch. Care staff enter natural language descriptions of the encountered behavior into the text box shown on the left hand side of Figure 1 using the device's keyboard, then refines it by selecting one of the observed behavior values such as *Resident is violent.* When the user presses the *Retrieve similar cases* button the app automatically generates a query that it fires at the central repository. A first version of the repository was seeded with 20 cases of published good care practice [Owen & Meyer 2009] and good care practices collected from experienced care staff at the pilot care home.

Carer's discovery service has two important capabilities from [9]. The first is *query expansion* – the addition of terms in the query that have the same or similar meaning to existing query terms, to make the query more complete. The second is *term disambiguation* – selecting the meaning, or sense of each term in the query to enable query expansion, thus making the query unambiguous. Therefore the description of an encountered challenging behaviour entered by care staff need not adhere to any lexicon or have same terms as the stored cases, making *Carer* more flexible. The right-hand side of Figure 1 shows how the three most similar retrieved case studies are displayed to the care staff, who receive an ordered list of case studies and view the details of each one by clicking on it.

FUTURE WORK

We are currently extending *Carer* with capabilities to retrieve good practices from domains analogical to dementia care by extending it with the AnTiQue discovery service [8]. To exploit these new capabilities we are populating the repository with managing challenging cases from other domains in *Mirror*, such as stroke care, as well as domains external to it such as policing and social care.

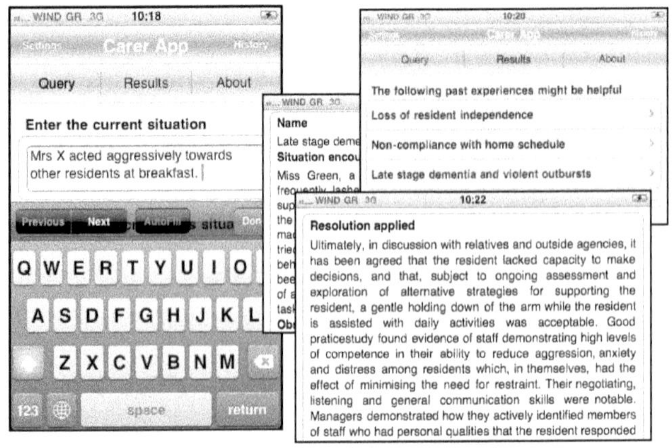

Figure 1. the *Carer* software app

ACKNOWLEDGMENTS

The research reported in this paper is supported by the EU-funded MIRROR integrated project 257617, 2010-14.

REFERENCES

1. All-Party Parliamentary Group on Dementia, 2009. Prepared to care: Challenging the dementia skills gap. June 2009, http://alzheimers.org.uk/site/scripts/download_info.php?fileID=735
2. Alzheimers Society, 2010. Statistics. http://www.alzheimers.org.uk/site/scripts/documents_info.php?documentID=341
3. Gentner D., 1983, 'Structure-Mapping: A Theoretical Framework for Analogy', Cognitive Science 5, 121-152.
4. Houts, P.S., Nezubd, A.M., Magut Nezubd, C, Bucherc, J.A., 1996. The prepared family caregiver: a problem-solving approach to family caregiver education. Patient Education and Counseling, vol.27, no.1, pp 63-73. Retrieved from Elsevier.
5. Knapp M., Prince M., 2007. Dementia UK; A report into the prevalence and cost of dementia prepared by the Personal Social Services Research Unit (PSSRU) at the London School of Economics and the Institute of Psychiatry at King's College London, for the Alzheimer's Society.
6. Michalko, M., 2006. ThinkerToys: A Handbook of Creative-Thinking Techniques, Second Edition. Ten Speed Press, New York. 132-136.
7. Owen T. & Meyer J., 2009, 'Minimizing the use of 'restraint' in care homes: Challenges, dilemmas and positive approaches', Adult Services Report 25, Social Care Institute of Excellence, http://www.scie.org.uk/publications/reports/report25.pdf
8. Zachos K. & Maiden N.A.M., 2008, 'Inventing Requirements from Software: An Empirical Investigation with Web Services', Proceedings 16th IEEE International Conference on Requirements Engineering, IEEE Computer Society Press, 145-154.
9. Zachos K., Maiden N.A.M., Zhu X. & Jones S., 2007, 'Discovering Web Services To Specify More Complete System Requirements', Proceedings CaiSE'2007, Springer-Verlag Lecture Notes on Computer Science LNCS 4495, 142-157.

Silent Barrage: Interactive Neurobiological Art

Riley Zeller-Townson
Georgia Inst. Tech.

Guy Ben-Ary
University of Western Australia

Phil Gamblen
University of Western Australia

Peter Gee
Telstra Corp

Stephen Bobic
Delta Airlines

Douglas Swehla
Georgia Inst. Tech.

Steve M. Potter
Georgia Inst. Tech.

ABSTRACT
Here we present Silent Barrage, a closed loop system in which a culture of rat brain cells is given a new body in the form of a small 'forest' of robotic poles located within an art space. This system allows us to study the relationship between brain and body in both scientific and artistic contexts.

Author Keywords
In vitro Learning, Biological Art, Neuroengineering

ACM Classification Keywords
J.5 [Arts and Humanities]: Arts, fine and performing

General Terms
Experimentation, Human Factors

INTRODUCTION
The concept of 'embodiment,' how intelligent agents use bodies, raises questions in both the arts and sciences. These questions range from philosophical investigations of what defines the boundary between mind and body, to the engineering task of designing artificial 'brains' to optimize the function of huge, highly complicated power systems [1]. We address these issues from the perspectives of Neuroengineering and Bioart.

Within the neurosciences, questions of how networks of neurons process information and learn have remained difficult to study. This is partially due to the difficulty of recording all the information necessary to characterize a network of neurons in a learning organism. One neuroengineering approach to further understanding of the learning process at this level has been to isolate networks of neurons and provide them an artificial body [2].

Within the arts, one main aim is to get the viewer to question their environment. By its very nature Silent Barrage allows the viewer to contemplate the existence of life from an ontological point of view. What does it mean to be alive and are accepted notions of 'living' and 'non-living' absolute or are there some levels that can fit in between? Silent Barrage raises these questions and many more. It is a semi-living entity that is unique in that it is both artistically and scientifically meaningful.

To address these questions, we provide a remote robotic 'body' to a culture of rat neural tissue. The body consists of 32 robotic poles located within a public art space. Each pole is 3 meters in height and spaced such that the audience can walk through the field of poles. Audience movements are captured through four overhead cameras, which form the sensory system of body. Data from these cameras is preprocessed on site in the exhibit, and then sent back to the neural culture through a MultiElectrode Array (MEA). Communication between the culture and electrophysiology (stimulating/recording) equipment in Altanta and the robotic (sensory/ motor) machinery in the exhibit is accomplished through a custom webserver. This embodiment shows a progression from previous work with similar technology [3], in that the audience interacts directly with the embodied culture by entering its 'field of view' and responding to its neural activity.

The primary form of activity of neural cultures that don't receive sensory input is a seizure-like barrage of electrophysiological activity [4]. These barrages are silent while inside the dish, but the robotic body allows the audience to experience the barrages as bursts of movement and sound, lending the piece its name.

METHODS
In order to produce this elaborate system, a variety of subsystems had to come together- the culture itself, the electrophysiology software and hardware used to communicate with the culture, the robotic body and sensory system, software to translate the neural data into movements of the robotic body and translate the movements of the audience into neural stimuli, and a webserver to allow two way communication between the robotic 'body' and living 'brain.'

Neural culture
Tissue from embryonic rat neocortex is dissociated to break down prior structure in the tissue, allowing the tissue to re-grow as a two dimensional monolayer of roughly 50,000 cells [5]. Neurons within this living network communicate with each other using short spikes in cell membrane voltage. This electrical activity can be recorded using electrodes spaced throughout the glass multielectrode array (MEA) that the neurons live on. This forms the 'read-out' or motor part of the electrical communication with the culture. By electrically stimulating these same electrodes, neural activity can be induced in select populations of neurons. This forms the 'write' part of the communication, i.e., sensory input from cameras to neurons.

C&C'11, November 3–6, 2011, Atlanta, Georgia, USA.
ACM 978-1-4503-0820-5/11/11.

Electrophysiology

Both neural activity and electrical stimulation occur on sub-millisecond time scales. To process neural data and stimulation tasks in real time, we created NeuroRighter, a free open source program available online. NeuroRighter uses National Instruments Data Acquisition hardware to record and stimulate the electrodes, and allows neural electrode data to be recorded, filtered, and displayed in real time through a graphical user interface. It also has the ability to stimulate the MEA electrodes using a custom multichannel stimulating circuit, and to control arbitrary additional hardware through a digital TTL signal. Lastly, the recording and stimulation capabilities can be used simultaneously through custom closed-loop 'plugin' programs. [6] This 'plugin' program has been changed for each exhibition of Silent Barrage, allowing for different scientific questions to be asked by changing the way sensory information (optical flow of the overhead cameras in the exhibit) is used to generate stimulation patterns and changing how motor commands (directions for when and how much the poles should move) are generated from network activity.

Exhibit

The webserver provides a constant connection to the exhibit, which has been be shown in USA (New York), Spain (Madrid), Brazil (São Paulo), Ireland (Dublin), and Beijing (China). On the exhibit side, a computer running MAX/MSP is used to connect to the webserver in Atlanta. The MAX module then normalizes the incoming data and relays this information to PICAXE® microcontrollers which serve as a central hub to communicate with and monitor each of the 32 poles.

Each pole, made from 80mm (3½ in.) PVC wastewater pipe, is wrapped in paper. Motors control a printhead, which moves up and down the pole, and the rotating pen for drawing on the paper. Each pole has its own microcontroller, allowing autonomous control of the head positioning as instructed by the master controller.

To attain the level of movement accuracy required, each pole controller has software which allows it to 'learn' the characteristics of its pole. Once 'learned', the response characteristics are stored in non-volatile memory and are constantly referred to as occurs in other living systems.

Over time during an exhibition, a series of lines are drawn on the paper covering the poles. The lines represent a simple graphic memory of past activity around each electrode in the neural network. Stimulus for the neurons around each electrode in the multielectrode array comes from audience activity in the area immediately around the robotic pole. The resulting drawings are "simple but beautiful data visualizations"[7], acting artistically as traces or documents the interaction between the viewers and the neurons. Audience members have reported that while walking through the poles "the feeling of physically travelling through an active brain is impossible to escape" [8] and that Silent Barrage "provides an immersive and somewhat overwhelming sensorial manifestation of questions that are at the core of our understanding of the stuff that make us think." [9]

ACKNOWLEDGMENTS

Funded by NSF grant "EFRI-COPN: Neuroscience and Neural Networks for Engineering the Future Intelligent Electric Power Grid", EFRI # 0836017, and by the Australian Council for the arts, The Department of culture and the arts, WA. The project is hosted by SymbioticA – The center for excellence in biological arts at the University of Western Australia.

AUTHOR CONTACT

Riley Zeller-Townson (phone +1 252 725 4344, email rtzt3@gatech.edu), Douglas Swehla (email swehla@gatech.edu), and Dr. Steve Potter (phone +1 404 385 0126, email steve.potter@bme.gatech.edu) are in the Laboratory for Neuroengineering, in the Biomedical Engineering department at the Georgia Institute of Technology, 313 Ferst Dr. NW, Atlanta, GA 30332. Stephen Bobic (email smbobic@gmail.com) is affiliated with Delta Airlines. Guy Ben-Ary (phone +61 8 6469 0019, email guy.benary@uwa.edu.au) is affiliated with the University of Western Australia. Peter Gee (phone +61 8 9271 2345, email pgee6@bigpond.com) is affiliated with Telstra Corporation, Australia. Phil Gamblen can be reached by phone at +61 408 151 664 and by email at pgamblen@hotmail.com).

REFERENCES

1. Johnson, C., Venayagamoorthy, G. K. Encoding Real Values into Polychronous Spiking Networks. *World Congress on Computational Intelligence 2010*, Barcelona, Spain, 1-7.
2. DeMarse, T. B., Wagenaar, D. A., Blau, A. W. and Potter, S. M. The Neurally Controlled Animat: Biological Brains Acting with Simulated Bodies. *Autonomous Robots 11*: 305-310. 2001.
3. Bakkum, D. J., Gamblen, P. M., Ben-Ary, G., Chao, Z. C., & Potter, S. M. MEART: The Semi-living Artist. *Frontiers in NeuroRobotics, 1,* 5,1-10. 2007.
4. Wagenaar, D. A., Pine, J. and Potter, S. M. An extremely rich repertoire of bursting patterns during the development of cortical cultures. *BMC Neuroscience 7:11*, 2006.
5. Potter, S.M., DeMarse, T. B. "A new approach to neural cell culture for long-term studies." *J. Neurosci. Methods 110*: 17-24. 2001.
6. Rolston, J. D., Gross, R. E., & Potter, S. M. A low-cost multielectrode system for data acquisition and real-time processing with rapid recovery from stimulation artifacts. *Frontiers in Neuroengineering, 2,* 12, 1-17. 2009.
7. Silent Barrage: Interaction and Cognition. http://thereisnowetware.wordpress.com/2011/05/10/silent-barrage-interaction-cognition/
8. Silent Barrage at the Science Gallery. http://www.boomingback.org/2011/02/silent-barrage-at-science-gallery.html
9. Australian Artists Acknowledged at Prix Ars Electronica. http://geekgirl.com.au/blog/tab/silent-barrage.html

Towards a Computational Model of Character Status in Interactive Storytelling

Jichen Zhu*
University of Central Florida
jichen.zhu@ucf.edu

Kenneth Ingraham
Interactor Simulation Systems, LLC
kenneth.ingraham@gmail.com

J. Michael Moshell
University of Central Florida
jm.moshell@cs.ucf.edu

Santiago Ontañón
IIIA-CSIC, Spain
santi@iiia.csic.es

ABSTRACT
In computer-based interactive narrative, a key challenge is the conflict between user agency and authorial control of the story quality. In this paper, we use the constructs of *character status* and *status shifts* from improvisational and interactive theatre to further engage users in the creative process of co-creating the story. Based on the cognitive semantics theory of force dynamics, we develop a computational model of status shifts.

ACM Classification Keywords
J.5 Arts and Humanities: Performing Arts; I.2.1 Artificial Intelligence: Applications and Expert Systems—*Games*

General Terms
Design

INTRODUCTION
Interactive narrative is a contemporary form of the age-old human creative activity of storytelling. One of its central challenges is what is known as the "narrative paradox" — the conflict between user agency and authorial control to structure the narrative. Generally speaking, the more freedom the user has to influence the story world, the harder it is to maintain the quality of the story, including narrative coherence, dramatic arc, etc. As Marie-Laure Ryan rightfully asks [4], will there ever be any user that, while playing the title character in a game version of Anna Karenina, decides to kill herself in order to make the story more interesting? To many, the answer is no. As a result, research efforts have been put into more sophisticated systems for interactive narrative, such as drama management.

However, algorithmic advancements alone are not the complete answer to Ryan's question. At the end, a truly interactive narrative piece relies on the user to make significant decisions for her character and hence to impact the story. If it takes professional storytellers years of experience to master their art, why should we expect an untrained user to create a great story without giving her the necessary clues and guidances? To us, the act of guiding and engaging the user without taking away their freedom of input and, ultimately, spurring their creativity in leading the story is as creative as constructing story content itself.

We can borrow useful insights from *interactive theatre* where human actors construct interactive stories with untrained audience participants. Similar to improvisation (improv) theatre, interactive theatre draws on improvisational tools and is spontaneous and unpredictable in nature. Some related study of improv for interactive narrative include [3] and [1]. However, unlike improv theatre performed by trained actors, an interactive theatre is designed specifically to be *experienced* by untrained audience participants (*spect-actors*), working together with the actors (*inter-actor*) to create stories in a loosely pre-defined format.

In this paper, we report our initial study of inter-actors' use of character status and status shifts to construct stories with untrained spect-actors. We identify the connection between status and force dynamics (FD) and propose a FD-based model of status and status shifts in the context of interactive narrative. We show how force dynamics provides a useful model to understand narrative strategies in interactive theatre and can potentially be used in computer-based interactive narrative.

A MODEL OF STATUS IN INTERACTIVE PERFORMANCE
In improv and interactive theatre, status is one of the core constructs that actors use to convey the social/professional standing of a character as well as her relation to other characters and the environment. Generally speaking, a high-status character dominates the situation whereas a low-status one submits. Seen as a top-down "motivation" to a character's actions, status determines the range of possible gestures (e.g. taking up a lot of space using one's body vs. sitting uncomfortably in order to leave space for others) and speech (e.g. "Get out of my way!" vs. "I'm not worth your time."). Johnstone [2] argues that a large proportion of drama comes from how characters attempt to raise or lower their social status

*Jichen Zhu is currently at Drexel University, Philadelphia, PA.

C&C'11, November 3–6, 2011, Atlanta, Georgia, USA.
ACM 978-1-4503-0820-5/11/11.

Status in performance	*Force Dynamics*
Main character	Agonist
Secondary character	Antagonist
Attempts to change status	Tendency to motion
Attempts to maintain status	Tendency to rest
Successful attempts	Stronger
Failed attempts	Weaker

Table 1. Comparison of Status and Force Dynamics

through different means. In interactive theatre, status also offers a means for the spect-actor to quickly engage in the process of co-creating the story with the inter-actors.

A useful framework to understand the working of status in narrative is the cognitive semantic theory of force dynamics [5] (FD). A basic FD pattern contains two entities, an *Agonist* (the focal entity) and an *Antagonist*, exerting force on each other. An Agonist has a *tendency* towards either motion (action) or rest (inaction), and it manifests its tendency if it is stronger than its Antagonist. To represent "The ball kept rolling because of the wind blowing on it," for example, the Agonist *ball*'s intrinsic tendency towards rest is overcome by the Antagonist *wind*'s greater force, and hence the result is the motion of the Agonist. Force dynamics can also be used to describe psychological and social interactions by conceiving such interactions as psychological "pressure." Time in force dynamics is represented by sequences of *phases*.

At the fundamental level, both force dynamics and status describe the power relationship between two or more entities and its changes throughout time. In a scene of two characters, we may select the one of primarily interest to us as Agonist and the other as Antagonist. The Agonist's attempt to change her status is defined as her tendency to motion, whereas her attempt to maintain her current status is defined as her tendency to rest. The character who manages to achieve her intended status is the stronger one in the force dynamics. The changing force dynamics relations across different phases therefore offer a cognitive model for status shifts. Table 1 lists the matching elements between status and force dynamics in our current model.

UNDERSTANDING INTERACTIVE THEATRE

Using the above FD-based model, we can analyze the dramatic structure of interactive theatre in terms of status shifts. Take the example of an interactive scene in which a spect-actor plays the role of a young musician. The first time the musician encounters the parent character, played by an inter-actor, the latter exhibits a controlling and dominating manner regarding various aspects of the musician's life. In a subsequent scene, other inter-actor characters set up external and internal influences over the musician, leading to her decision of leaving home and pursuing her dreams. In a final confrontation with the parent, the empowered musician overcomes the pressure of the parent and eventually departs.

This interaction can be divided into 2 phases, corresponding to different stages of the status shift. In Phase 1, the Agonist (spect-actor's musician character) has the tendency to move but is hindered by a stronger Antagonist (her parent). Phase 2 is composed of the following two scenes, in which the strengthened Agonist is able to overcome the Antagonist and initiate the motion. The change of FD relation (hence status shifts) is closely associated with the adrenaline rush and emotional satisfaction that spect-actors often report to experience in an interactive performance story. Having come up against the parent character in a visceral way and overcoming his/her control, the resulting status shift is essential to both the story development and the transformative feeling experienced by the spect-actor.

Our FD-based model not only identifies status shifts in the story, but also highlights the question of "why" and "how." From the perspective of the spect-actor, dramatic experiences, i.e. shifting FD relations, occur because of various external and internal pressures exerted on her character. The key question here, as in computer-based interactive narrative, is how to provide the right condition so that the spect-actor will (appear to) initiate the status shift herself. In the above scene, thanks to the clear personalities created in Phase 1, the tendency of the Agonist and her power relationship in relation to the Antagonist is implied. Phase 2 introduces the motivations, which leads to the Agonist's increased strength. The forward momentum of the narrative inexorably leads to the resolution, in which the intentions of the two characters clash and result in a shift in their FD relations. Our FD-based model calls attention to these creative endeavors and represents our initial attempt to model this process in computer-based interactive narrative.

CONCLUSION

In this paper, we discussed the importance and challenges of engaging the lay user in the creative process of interactive storytelling. We studied human interactive theatre regarding how human inter-actors guide, engage, and spur the creativity of untrained spect-actors on stage, especially in the use of character status. Using the cognitive semantic theory of force dynamics, we proposed a formal model for status and status shifts. As part of our future work, we plan to further explore this model in computer-based interactive narrative.

REFERENCES

1. D. Fuller and B. Magerko. Shared mental models in improvisational performance. In *Workshop on Intelligent Narrative Technologies*, 2010.

2. K. Johnstone. *Impro: Improvisation and the Theatre.* Theatre Arts Books, New York, 1979.

3. K. Perlin and A. Goldberg. Improv: A system for scripting interactive actors in virtual worlds. In *Proceedings of the 23rd annual conference on Computer graphics and interactive techniques (SIGGRAPH '96)*, pages 205–215, 1996.

4. M.-L. Ryan. Beyond myth and metaphor -the case of narrative in digital media. *Game Studies*, 1(1), 2001.

5. L. Talmy. Force dynamics in language and cognition. *Cognitive Science*, 12(1):49–100, 1988.

cartographs: the trans-sensory metaphor

Brian Evans
University of Alabama
Department of Art and
Art History
brian.evans@ua.edu

ABSTRACT

The visual music composition *cartographs*, a work in three short movements, is presented.[1] Each movement is an abstract animation—a visualization of a numeric process—that is then mapped into a single static image (a score)—that is then mapped into sound. Thus through the process of data mapping we hear and see a process unfold, each sense simultaneously experiencing a map (a metaphor) of what the other sense is experiencing.

Author Keywords

visual art, music, generative art, data map, metaphor, aesthetics

ACM Classification Keywords

J.5 Arts and Humanities: Fine arts, Music, Miscellaneous.

General Terms

Design, Experimentation

ART STATEMENT 1 (MAKING MAPS)

We are order-seeking creatures. Through our senses we receive signals from the world around us. Our senses convert these signals into electro-chemical data we then interpret, thus creating all of our experience. We try to make sense of these signals. What endures? What repeats? What changes? We look for structure. We recognize and compare patterns, trying to understand the sensory data. We build a basis from which we make choices. Living is the making of choices, based upon receiving signals and perceiving pattern within those signals.

Artists are order-making creatures. Sometimes we want to simply understand what order is. What establishes order? What defines pattern? Digital artists have number as their medium. Like homogeneous neural data, all digital representations of signals are in the same format. Digital data are binary numbers. As we create a digital experience it exists as numbers and we can map those numbers freely. If we use numbers to create aural experience we make a sonic map. A visual experience maps numbers into colors, making an image. It follows that we can create a sonic map of the numbers comprising a digital image and so hear the image. Of course the reverse is true. Monet's *Water Lilies* can be a symphony, Beethoven's *Ode to Joy* a wash of pigment on canvas. As a visual artist and music composer, crossing this sensory divide is of particular interest.

C&C'11, November 3–6, 2011, Atlanta, Georgia, USA.
ACM 978-1-4503-0820-5/11/11.

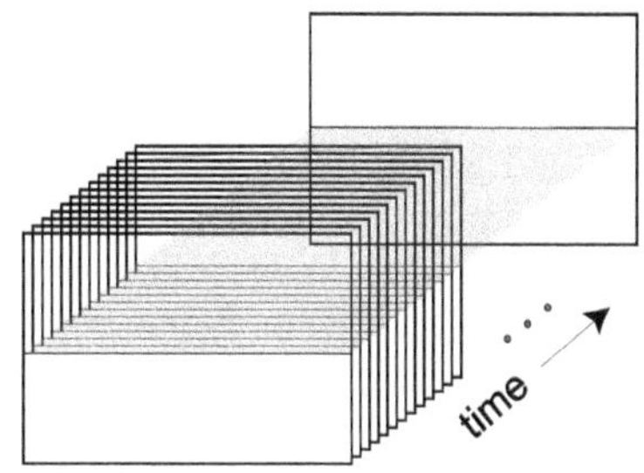

Figure 1. Time slice through a scanline of a series of frames.

SONIC MAPS (IMAGE TO SOUND)

In creating a sound score for an animation I start by making a time slice. A time slice is a static image built by extracting a single scan-line from each frame of the animation and stacking these lines sequentially. (Similar in result to the photographic slit-scan process.) Figure 1 shows a representation of an animation as a series of rectangular frames with time represented as depth. The time slice is constructed as a 2D cut through the time axis. Placing these scan lines on a single image, one after the other, gives a picture of the evolution of the animation on that line. The resulting image is a 2D graphic map of the 4D temporal object. See Figure 2 and Figure 3.

The image becomes a music score from which I then compose/perform a soundtrack. [2] Thus the static map (the score) is mapped again, this time into sound, carefully constructed with a duration that matches the animation. Sound is image, image is sound, data is mapped across the senses, a different kind of metaphor is constructed. (Time slices are created using tools creating with the Processing programming language. The sonic maps for *cartographs* were composed/created using U & I Software's Metasynth music synthesis software.)

ART STATEMENT 2 (MAKING METAPHORS)

Maps are metaphors. [3] Through metaphors we connect what we experience to what we remember. We create knowledge by connecting the new (the present) to what we know (the past) and so maybe predict what happens next (the future).

Our desire to predict fuels our desire to live, to survive. Desire is the foundation of narrative. Narrative reduces to desire, action and result—the structure of story. We exist in endless loops of desire—layer upon layer of stories of varying temporalities and shifting priorities—all synchronized to rhythms of breath and heart.

I make maps, in and out of time. I start with raw digital code—simple numeric models. As all is number in the computer I can map the numbers to the senses—turn numbers into tangible experience? The maps might loop in time (animation and audio) or freeze in a moment (a still image or print). There is synchrony in the sensory vertical and the temporal horizontal. Image and audio derive from the same numeric source. Each maps the other in the moment and through time. It's a visual music in a synaesthetic counterpoint.

Musical narrative developed over centuries, moving the listener through time with the Pythagorean struggle of harmonic conflict—dissonance seeking consonance. My little loops and images engage that struggle at various levels. Color shifts. Composition flows. Image and sound agree, complement, disagree and resolve.

Perhaps it's abstract expressionism, true to its digital materials, founded in musical traditions and Modernist formalism. But it's loosened a bit. It's jazz in color, shape, sound and computation. Relax. Hear the colors. Listen with your eyes.

ACKNOWLEDGMENTS

This work is done with the support of the National Science Foundation (award IIS 1002758) and the Leadership Board of the College of Arts and Sciences, University of Alabama.

REFERENCES

1. *cartographs* (2007) http://vimeo.com/25283010
2. Evans, B. Musical Connections and Heterophonic Maps. *Proceedings: Siggraph 2006*. ACM (2006).
3. Lakoff, G., Johnson, M. *Metaphors We Live By*. University of Chicago Press (2003).

Figure 2: *salia* graphic score (2nd movement), time slice through the center scanline

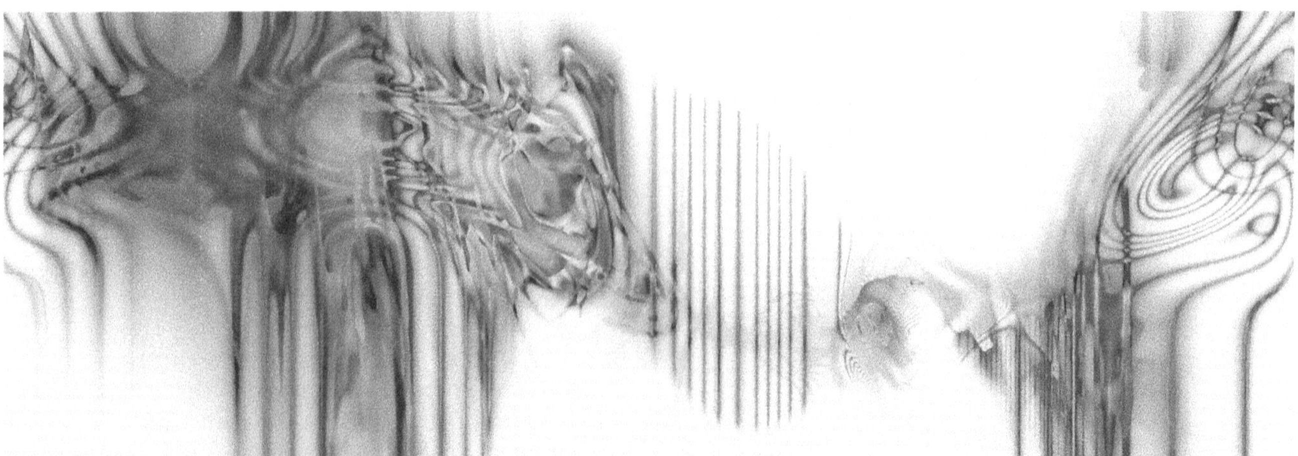

Figure 3: *pipilo* graphic score (3rd movement), time slice through the center scanline

The Zajal Programming Language

Ramsey Nasser
Parsons The New School for Design
ram@nas.sr

ABSTRACT
Computer programming opens up many exciting possibilities to the creative mind. These possibilities are limited by the mismatch between the organic, free-flowing nature of the creative process and the rigid, highly formal nature of machines. While the artist is concerned with presentation and content, the machine requires complicated setup, memory management, and precise programming before anything else can be considered. I have termed this mismatch *friction*; it is present in any software engineering project. Zajal's primary goal is to minimize friction, focusing on creative and audio/visual work. Zajal aims to take care of as much of the administrative code as possible while freeing the programmer to focus on what really matters – their idea.

Zajal is implemented as a language interpreter built on and compatible with the Ruby programming language while using the creative coding capabilities of openFrameworks. Although still very new, the responses in various user tests have been positive, with testers excited to use the language in future projects.

Author Keywords
User interface, Education, Creative Coding

ACM Classification Keywords
D.3.2 Language Classifications: Specialized application languages

General Terms
Design, Human Factors

INTRODUCTION
Creative coding tools developed over the past decade have allowed countless artists to explore the otherwise impenetrable world of computer programming for creative and aesthetic purposes. Processing made the graphical, computational, and web sharing capabilities of Java palatable to non-engineers. Arduino did the same for embedded microcontroller programming. openFrameworks brought high performance and iOS support to the creative coding community. These tools have fueled a generation of creative hackers that could not have existed otherwise.

Figure 1. "The Polygonal Flower" written in Zajal

Processing, openFrameworks, and the rest, however, are but *tools* in which to implement creativity. Code *itself* can be seen as human creativity, formalized and crystalized in the memory of a machine. The language in which we write code is the language in which we choose to represent our thoughts. A serious consideration for anyone interested in programming. Zajal strives make the transition from thought to code as seamless as possible. It is meant to be an extension of the programmer's natural creative impulses rather than a tool in which to awkwardly implement them in.

FRICTION DEFINED
One reason computer programming is difficult is because machines have no understanding of the work we ask them to do. To program a machine, one is forced to translate high-level creative ideas into the rudimentary instructions a processor can execute. The different natures of these two representations makes the translation tricky. Despite the myriad of tools and languages available to facilitate this processes, making the computer cooperate and implement one's vision remains difficult. I define *friction* as the need to worry about anything not directly related to the project at hand. The aforementioned translation difficulties are how friction manifests in software projects.

Examples of friction include manual memory management,

C&C'11, November 3–6, 2011, Atlanta, Georgia, USA.
ACM 978-1-4503-0820-5/11/11.

overly verbose syntax, languages that are not expressive, inconsistent idioms, and many others. Friction cannot be eliminated, but it can be minimized. This is the principal Zajal is built on.

CLEAN SYNTAX

To that end, the syntax of the language is designed to reduce non-essential elements as much as possible. Specifically, most administrative code required for the machine to behave correctly is generally managed by the interpreter. The primary interface of a language is its syntax. As a result, a user-interface design approach to the syntax was taken. Zajal makes heavy use of Ruby's syntax and idioms, which were designed in a similar fashion.

The syntax is structurally consistent across the whole language and an emphasis is made on optimizing common creative coding use cases. It also makes an effort to provide as many meaningful variations of all of its functions as possible. For example, the call `setup 200, 500` sets the sketch window's size to 200 × 500 pixels, while `setup 200` sets it to 200 × 200 pixels, reasonably assuming a square is intended.

LIVE CODING

To strengthen Zajal's role as an extension of the creative process, changes made to a sketch's code are seen in the sketch window as soon as the file is saved. This bypasses the normal code–compile–observe–repeat pattern and significantly changes a programmer's relationship with their code. Zajal analyzes exactly what changed in the code from save to save and updates the sketch accordingly.

This interaction makes for an intimate coding experience. The user becomes more of a sculptor who molds their code live, as opposed to an architect who carefully plans out every aspect of the project before breaking ground.

Live coding also has the added benefit of encouraging small changes, making the cause of an error introduced by new code easier to track down. It also has potential for live performative programming.

IT JUST WORKS

A major stumbling block and source of friction for beginners is the setup required by programming tools. Inspired by Processing and Arduino, Zajal sports a self-contained interpreter and an easy install process to get the programmer started as quickly as possible. It has no external dependancies and requires no additional setup.

BATTERIES INCLUDED

Like other creative coding languages, Zajal comes with features designed for audio/visual work. Vector graphics, images, videos, fonts, Arduino, and serial support are all standard in the language, using openFrameworks's implementation internally.

Beyond creative coding functionality, Zajal ships with and benefits from Ruby's standard library. Therefore, internet access, JSON and XML parsing, and other tasks that require setup in other languages work out of the box in Zajal. Combining these two feature sets results in clean sketches. As a proof of concept, a basic Twitter search client was written in under 30 lines of code.

Figure 2. "If Zajal Was Fairuz" video installation by Haitham Ennasr

These built-in features lower the barrier to entry for users, as complex applications can be written within minutes of downloading the language.

PACKAGE MANAGEMENT

No language can ship with every feature its users will need. Missing functionality is usually made available in the form of reusable code released by other programmers.

The problem with many existing languages, however, is that installing this third party code can be a hassle. To that end, Zajal is designed to use the popular Ruby Gems package management system to make this process streamlined. Ruby Gems is used by the Ruby community to share code, and is integrated into Zajal. This has the dual benefit of both allowing Zajal coders to exchange code, while exposing Zajal coders to the large repertoire of Ruby code already in Ruby Gems.

RUBY COMPATIBILITY

Advanced language constructs found in Ruby such as closures, lambdas, open classes, duck typing, and regular expression literals are available to Zajal programmers immediately. This both makes Zajal a great way to learn Ruby and invites Ruby hackers into the creative coding world.

THE MEANING OF ZAJAL

Zajal is the name of an ancient Andalusian form of poetry, traditional to my native Lebanon. At a Zajal performance, poets called *zajjaali* improvise complex and ingenious rhyming verse on the spot. My language is named after this art form, as it is meant to enable programmers to fluidly improvise their code as they go, the way the *zajjaali* create their poetry.

RESOURCES

Zajal can be found at `http://www.zajal.cc`. The code behind the projects pictured in this paper and more can be found at `http://sketch.zajal.cc/`.

RhythmSynthesis

Ryan Raffa
Parsons The New School for Design
2 W 13th Street, Room 1007
New York, NY 10011
ryan@ryanraffa.net

ABSTRACT
Originating as an investigation into the relationships between rhythm and technology, RhythmSynthesis applies color, shape, and sound to demonstrate how our understanding of visual music, computation, and tangible, audio-visual interactions can be applied as considerations in musical compositions. As an instrument, the final piece allows for experimentation, rewards for mastery, and is a vehicle for expression.

By asking questions about how visual music can be used to perceive rhythm, what ways visual rhythms can be used for composition, and what ways composition can be intertwined with performance and experimental notation, this project illustrates that sound is a reliable and effective way to provide users feedback for making visual composition decisions, judgments, and actions. From amateur to professional musicians, the instrument allows for unique, personal interactions and expressive choice.

ACM Classification Keywords
J.5 [Arts and Humanities]: Fine arts, Music, Performing arts

General Terms
Design, Experimentation, Performance

Keywords
Rhythm, Sound, Technology, Visual Music, Musical Performance, Composition, Design Research, TUIs, Computation

INTRODUCTION

New musical interfaces are necessary to further explore the complexities of rhythm. RhythmSynthesis proposes a new instrument for composition and performance to continue such exploration. Originating as an investigation into the relationships between rhythm and technology, RhythmSynthesis applies color, shape, and sound to demonstrate how our understanding of visual music, computation, and tangible, audio-visual interactions can be applied as considerations in musical expression.

There is a long history of investigation into rhythm (rhythm and sound, language, writing, etc) as well as the connections between the visual, sonic, and computational. The goals of this investigation are:

- reveal alternative models and interactions with rhythm composition using color, shape, and sound
- illustrate how physical objects can be encoded with sound
- design a new musical interface that allows for experimentation, rewards for mastery, and is a vehicle for expression.

C&C'11, November 3-6, 2011, Atlanta, Georgia, USA.
ACM 978-1-4503-0820-5/11/11.

Design Questions

This project began by asking what ways can visual music be used to understand rhythm. As the research progressed, additional questions surfaced such as how is rhythm embedded within our visually-dominated experiences, how is the visual encoded with sound, and what are ways visual rhythms can be used for composition.

The building and prototyping process was key to exploring these questions, and in doing so, the final question of what are ways in which composition can be intertwined with performance and experimental notation guided the completion of this project.

What is rhythm?

Concepts such as the Gestalt principles [1] and the multiplicity of speech cadence, the notion that we are perpetually in the process of attempting to perceive and create meaning out the rhythms that surround us, is paramount to this project.

Figure 1: Gallery visitors using the project

SIGNIFICANCE

In light of the constructivist view of learning [2], the mental models and templates that allow us to understand our experiences are based on what we hear, see, feel, and smell. We now have the opportunity to use technology, not as a singular lens, but as an addition to our current senses to perceive and apply meaning to rhythms.

Figure 2: Gallery visitors using the project

Much has been written about how we perceive and apply meaning to all that surrounds us. The French philosopher and music critic, Gabriel Marcel, wrote, "Meaning arises when an individual becomes aware, either affectively or intellectually, of the implications of a stimulus in a particular context."[3]

Similar to the process of viewing the color coding of a resistor (ex. a 4-band resistor with the color values red, red, brown has a resistance value of 220 Ω), the colors of an object are often used to understand the physical substance and characteristics of that object. This project proposes the use of technology to introduce, rehearse, and create dialogue around the associations of color and sound.

Similar to games and the playing of games, music is not something that resides outside of what it is to be human or social beings. Rather it is a direct comment on, a clear reflection of, and a contributor to our nature and our culture.

AUDIENCE

The objective is to provide an experience that allows the novice a low enough barrier of use so that they are able to participate and create, while at the same time providing the expert a balanced level of feedback so there is a reward for experimentation, mastery, and exploration. In addition, the process of using the instrument is a method for practicing and developing mental connections between the visual and sound.

There has been much work in the area of speech and learning (from Lev Vygotsky's *Thought and Language* to Noam Chomsky's *Syntactic Structures*), but research methods and practices need to be developed to map and document human's natural links between sound, perception, and understanding. There must be a set of standards put forth that can be debated and improved. "If they are to be useful, sounds must be generated intelligently, with an understanding of the natural relationship between the sounds and the information to be conveyed," Donald Norman writes [4].

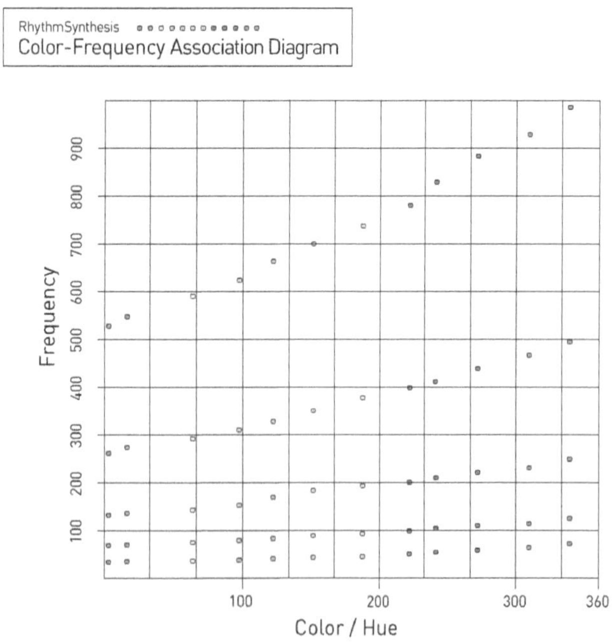

Figure 3: Color-Frequency Association Diagram

FINDINGS

Sound is a reliable and effective way to provide users feedback for making visual composition decisions, judgments, and actions. Early feedback from test sessions centered around providing users more visual feedback of the position of the rotating, play-head, but once the sounds became more distinct, represented a greater sonic range (specifically the mid-to-higher range), and had a pronounced attack, users relied less on a strictly visual association process and worked with combined senses to make expressive choices.

Both amateur and professional musicians, along with visual artists, engineers, programmers, and designers, found the experience enjoyable. Over sixty people (as individuals and groups) tested the instrument, and each testing session yielded an array of different strategies, approaches, and executions. From scientific approaches to more adventurous tactics, the testing sessions demonstrated unique and personal interactions.

There is more work needed to align the full spectrum of color to the full spectrum of sound (Figure 3). A fragment of the possible hue and frequency values have been associated and performed using the instrument. The spaces between the indicated values are an interesting space to play for future projects.

ACKNOWLEDGEMENTS

Thanks to my Thesis advisors Katherine Moriwaki and Scott Pobiner as well as my fellow MFA DT students, friends, and family who provided valuable insight, feedback, and assistance with this work. I am indebted to Matt Wright for the interview and feedback.

REFERENCES

1. "Gestalt principles of form perception by Mads Soegaard," http://interaction-design.org/.
2. Piaget, Jean. *The Psychology of Intelligence*. London: Routledge & Paul, 1950.
3. Marcel, Gabriel, Maddux, J. Stephen, and Robert E. Wood. *Music And Philosophy (Marquette Studies in Philosophy)*. Milwaukee, WI: Marquette University Press, 2005.
4. Norman, Donald A. *The Design of Everyday Things*. Cambridge, Mass.: MIT Press, 2002.

Conversing with a Computer – The Body Language of the Box

James Sheridan
Australian National University
Building 108 ANU
Canberra, ACT 0200 Australia
james.sheridan@anu.edu.au

ABSTRACT
This small performance looks at novel interactive ways for better understanding the attentive processes and there affects on things like perception. This is done via the user exploring an audio-visual environment that reacts to their attention in different ways. The users gaze and brainwaves (via EEG) are dynamically mapped to different visual and sonic objects based on the ways in which they pay attention. This allows them to setup and explore different feedback loops, which begin to resonate with each other allowing the users attentive patterns to be represented as a unique audio-visual structure.

Author Keywords
Attention, HCI, EEG

ACM Classification Keywords
H.5.2 User Interfaces (D.2.2, H.1.2, I.3.6)

General Terms
Design, Human Factors

INTRODUCTION

As society develops more and more ways to capture, organise and deliver data we are all feeling the pressures of information overload. These increasing demands upon our attention are driving the development of smarter interfaces and intelligent agents. Soon we will all be using these technologies to expand our mentalities and filter out information relevant to us.

Until the singularity occurs and we all turn into cyborgs we will need a way to interact with these new technologies. The constraints of our biological bodies means technologies are constantly adapting to take advantage of our natural communication mechanisms. Whilst an agent interface can easily be adapted its taken millennia for your cognitive functions to evolve. This not only leaves them predisposed to process information in certain ways but has resulted in complex emergent behaviour – attention[8].

C&C'11, November 3–6, 2011, Atlanta, Georgia, USA.
ACM 978-1-4503-0820-5/11/11.

This work explores the impact that different methods of tracking and modeling attention have on aesthetics and flow.

EMBODYING AN INTERFACE WITH ATTENTION

Attention is not only the gateway to our conscious selves it also plays a large part in communication. Gestures, body language and other paralinguistic cues (pitch, volume, intonation etc.) have all been shown to be important components of effective communication. They aid in the grounding process allowing people to reach a shared understanding more efficiently. But are computers currently capable of detecting and using these types of cues in a fluid conversation? Most would start thinking of research into virtual avatars, gestural interfaces and robotics, but even traditional GUI's can and do exhibit these characteristics.

When an application that we're not using is trying to tell us something, its icon flashes/bounces to let us know it's waiting for input, waiting to continue the conversation. When sound schemes are designed alert tones are often short and distinct – they have a certain tone and emphasis to them. Colour, form and position are also often used to set the tone of an alert or dialog box – are these not examples of paralinguistic cues?

Recent research into attentive interfaces has looked at not just *how* best to present information (e.g. screen vs. sound), but also *what* and *when*[7][1]. This is done to minimize distractions whilst improving information flow due to fewer context shifts. This requires the computer to be able to accurately know what we are paying attention to and why in close to real-time.

Measuring Attention

Being such a pervasive concept it's hard to accurately define attention let alone track it. It dictates how we view the world making its isolation close to impossible. The subjective father of American psychology, William James, suggested the effects of attention include five types of cognitive behaviour[5]. These are based around our ability to perceive, conceive, distinguish, remember, and shorten the reaction time of perceiving and conceiving.

Whilst we can easily use gaze tracking to know what someone's looking at, knowing what he or she perceived and why is much more difficult. For this reason past research into attentive interfaces has focused on track attention indirectly [7][4] or on very isolated tasks [9].

Giving a Computer Attention

Computational models of attention have been developed in a number of fields for a number of reasons. Cognitive neuroscientists use them to confirm our understanding of the brain. To validate the model they adjust its parameters and compare its performance to that of a human under similar circumstances.

AI researchers use them to improve the realism and performance of virtual avatars[6] or add functionality to robots. HCI researchers have created them to screen mobile phone and email communication based on things like perceived reward and/or relevance to current task[4].

Graphics researchers have used saliency maps based on how our visual cortex filters data to allocate rendering resources. Web and graphic designers also use them to evaluate the effectiveness of marketing material and information layout.

Just as the constraints of our brain caused attention to develop, the constraints of the computer dictate the attentive mechanisms it can use. It's not feasible to give every interface object the full range of behaviours related to attention. The Dynamic Neural Fields model by Rougier [2] has been chosen due to its modular nature.

The Conversational Environment

The audio-visual objects that users interact with in the interface allows for a number of different interactions to be explored:

- Active vs. Passive detection of attention – For example when someone is talking about a car you could either just assume they mean their own or ask them which car.
- Direct vs. Indirect sensing and display of attention – When you give someone an instruction they could either directly indicate they understood (e.g. a nod) or they could just do the action also indicating they were paying attention.
- Multiparty communication – You often want to observe or communicate with more than one entity at a time resulting in the need to split your attention. On the flip side you may need to use your attention to filter out irrelevant information – the cocktail party effect[3].

Figure 1: An early version of the system displaying brain activity in response to gaze activated musical objects.

REFERENCES

[1] Chen, D. and Vertegaal, R. 2004. Using mental load for managing interruptions in physiologically attentive user interfaces. *Conference on Human Factors in Computing Systems*. (2004), 1513–1516.

[2] Fix, J. and Rougier, N. 2010. A dynamic neural field approach to the covert and overt deployment of spatial attention. *Cognitive Computation*. (2010).

[3] Haykin, S. and Chen, Z. 2005. The cocktail party problem *Neural computation*. 17, 9 (Sep. 2005), 1875–1902.

[4] Horvitz, E. et al. 2003. Models of Attention in Computing and Communication: From Principles to Applications. (Sep. 2003).

[5] James, W. 1950. *The Principles of Psychology, Vol. 1*. Dover Publications.

[6] Kim, Y. et al. 2005. Modeling dynamic perceptual attention in complex virtual environments. *Intelligent Virtual Agents*. (2005), 266–277.

[7] Roda, C. and Thomas, J. 2006. Attention aware systems: Theories, applications, and research agenda. *Computers in Human Behavior*. 22, 4 (2006), 557–587.

[8] Rougier, N. and Vitay, J. 2006. Emergence of attention within a neural population. *Neural Networks*. 19, 5 (2006), 573–581.

[9] Santana, P. and Correia, L. 2010. A swarm cognition realization of attention, action selection, and spatial memory. *Adaptive Behavior*. 18, 5 (Nov. 2010), 428–447.

A Morphing Robotic Environment Shaped by and Shaping Kindergarteners, Reaching for the Stars

Anthony L. Threatt, Keith Evan Green
School of Architecture
Clemson, SC 29632
anthont, kegreen@clemson.edu

Jessica Merino, Ian D. Walker
Department of Electrical and Computer Engineering
Clemson, SC 29632
jmerino, iwalker@clemson.edu

Michelle V. Buckley, M. S. Ellison
School of Material Science and Engineering
Clemson, SC 29632
mvbuckl, ellisom@clemson.edu

ABSTRACT
Our world is digital, physical, social and technological. Informal learning environments that are likewise digital, physical, social and technological have the potential to afford children with creative, informal learning explorations. Following from Antle's concept of "embodied child-computer interaction" and Vygotsky's "cycle of creative imagination," we demonstrate an intelligent, robotic informal learning environment at room-scale targeted for K-3 visitors to a regional children's museum. Our reconfigurable environment is, in essence, co-adaptive, allowing the physical learning environment and young students to mutually change and develop through iterative interactions.

Author Keywords
Computer Support Tools; Children; Creativity; Intelligent Environments, Architecture, Design; Human Factors, HRI

ACM Classification Keywords
H.1.2 User/Machine Systems: I.2.9Robotics, K.3.1 Computer Uses in Education

General Terms
Design, Human Factors

INTRODUCTION
How can Intelligent Environments help cultivate in children creative exploration and life-long learning? Our response, a robotic informal learning environment at room scale, is informed by Alissa N. Antle's concept of "embodied child-computer interaction" [1]. According to Antle, "meaning is created through restructuring the spatial configuration of elements in the environment" [1].

While there is ample literature regarding creativity, learning environments, and the growing influence of technology on children, the literature on the important effects of the interactions of these domains has not yet emerged. Our research in child-computer interaction seeks to fill this gap by focusing on a reconfigurable, computationally-embedded physical environment fostering creative explorations and life-long learning in children K-3.

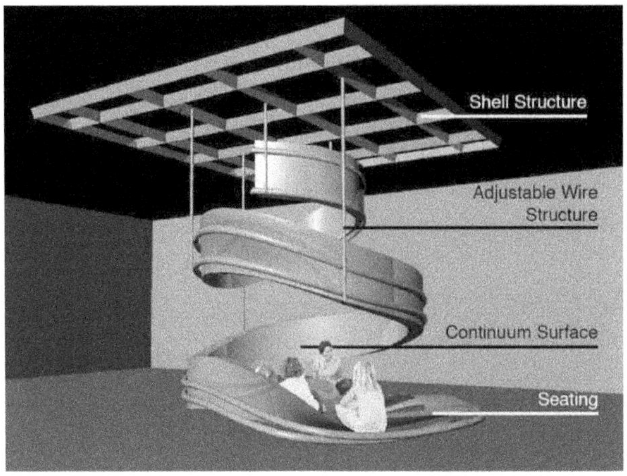

Figure 1. Our concept of a robotic learning environment

THE CYCLE OF SEASONS AND THE CYCLE OF CREATIVE IMAGINATION
Have you ever carefully observed the tendencies of children playing on a playground? What draws them? What goals do they exhibit? Our research team conducted observational sessions at a local playground focused on the behaviors children exhibit towards static and dynamic playground equipment. We noted, in verification of Antle, that children tend to shape their environment: when given the opportunity, children manipulate dynamic playground equipment to create an environment that satisfies their needs and wants, even if this means reaching outside the boundaries that playground designers envisioned. Children shape their surroundings to give form to their thoughts and ideas, and to make visible and tangible these thoughts and ideas for inspection by themselves and others. This energetic manipulation of the environment lends children a sense of ownership and control of their inner thoughts and their external surroundings, each

C&C'11, November 3–6, 2011, Atlanta, Georgia, USA.
ACM 978-1-4503-0820-5/11/11.

one made to reflect the other. These observations find theoretical validation in Antle as well as in the four-step "cycle of creative imagination" proposed by Vygotsky informing our research: exploration (a haptic, sensorial experience of the world), inspiration (an analysis of these impressions), production (a creative act informed by the analysis) and sharing (the presentation of an outcome) [5]. Vygotsky's cycle has informed related HCI work in non-robotic, informal learning environments [2].

Certain concepts are too abstract to be brought to reality by young children, given the character and equipping of their environmental surroundings [4]. Our research team comprised of faculty and students in Robotics, Architecture, Education and Human Factors Psychology are exploring, through working prototypes and virtual simulations, a digital-physical, robotic learning environment at room-scale (figure 1) supporting child-centered creative play, and advancing cognitive skills and understanding. This physical-digital learning environment features a continuum robotic surface embedded with an RGB display that morphs in shape and texture to facilitate a child's hands-on comprehension of such concepts. A video of our vision and our working prototypes is found at http://youtu.be/FXawb88FUhg.

Figure 2. Children and teacher using tangible interface; Interactive system display - in-concept.

One abstract concept identified as an important case in Education is "seasonal change" [3] which we test with our working prototype. Children, engaging our informal learning environment, physically manipulate spherical objects representing the Earth, sun, and moon by translating the two spheres representing Earth and moon about two rods representing their orbits (figure 2). In doing this, children explore the orientation of these celestial bodies to "create," for example, a summer day in Lima, Peru. Following changes made by the children to this tangible interface of spheres and rings of movement, the environment's morphing surface and RGB display exhibit sensations of colors, temperature, wind and even humidity - the atmosphere - of that summer day in Lima, or a harsh winter in northern Norway, or an early autumn storm on the coastline of Cuba. Setting the spherical objects to specific positions along the "orbital" rods morphs the environment's helical surface and alters the RGB display to create sensations of the seasonal conditions at points around our planet. This makes the abstract concept of seasonal change that much more tangible to young children.

Categorized as "continuum robots" for their infinite degrees of freedom, the "soft" pneumatic muscles employed here (figure 3) actuate the ribbon surface, helical in form to create activity towards the ceiling (engaging individuals at a distance) as well as closer to the floor (engaging children interacting more directly with the tangible interface). The shapes the morphing surface assumes depend on the length, diameter, number and configuration of the muscles and the material selected to comprise the helical surface. Our lab continues to test different configurations of muscles and materials to optimize movements that reflect, in three-dimensions, the character of seasonal change.

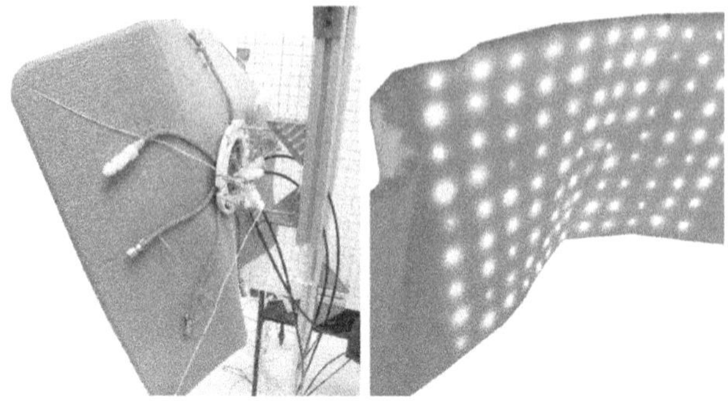

Figure 3. Our prototypes showing muscles and RGB display

CONCLUSION AND DEMONSTRATION

The reconfigurable nature of our informal learning environment makes it, in essence, co-adaptive, allowing environments and their inhabitants to change and develop through iterative interactions. "An environment... that supports multiple spatial configurations," as Antle offers [1], promises to advance a child's grasp of our universe through active, creative exploration.

Our demonstration includes a working prototype of one segment of the larger, helical morphing ribbon embedded with pneumatic muscles and the RGB display, as well as a video showing a virtual simulation and the full-scale physical working prototype.

REFERENCES

1. A. N. Antle. Embodied child computer interaction: Why embodiment matters. *interactions*, XVI.2:27–30, March / April 2009.
2. F. Decortis and L. Lentini. A socio-cultural perspective of creativity for the design of educational environments. *eLearning Papers 1 N 13*, April 2009 www.elearningpapers.eu.
3. T. Keating, M. Barnett, S. A. Barab, and K. E. Hay. The virtual solar system project: ... *Journal of Science Education and Technology*, 11(3):261–275, 2002.
4. P. Schwanenflugel. Why are abstract concepts hard to understand? In P. Schwanenflugel, editor, *The Psychology of Word Meanings*. LEA, Hillsdale, N.J., 1991.
5. L. S. Vygotsky. Imagination and creativity in the adoslescent. In R. W. Rieber, editor, *The Collected Works of L.S. Vygotsky*, volume 5: Child Psychology. Plenum, New York, 1998.

The Wheatstone Stereoscopic Random Line Pair Generator with Fitness Function for Non-objective Art

Gregory Patrick Garvey
Quinnipiac University
Hamden, CT 06518 USA
greg.garvey@quinnipiac.edu
203 582-8389

ABSTRACT
The Wheatstone Stereoscopic Random Line Pair Generator with Fitness Function for Non-objective Art is a proposal for an interactive installation. Viewers in the gallery wear stereoscopic glasses. The motion of each viewer will trigger the projection of randomly positioned stereoscopic pairs of lines projected on each wall of the gallery forming a dynamic, evolving, emergent, stochastic, "non-objective [1] composition."

Author Keywords
Interactive, art, installation, stereoscopic, random, generator, emergent, stochastic, non-objective.

ACM Classification Keywords
H.5.2. Interaction styles: J.5 Fine arts.

General Terms
Design, Experimentation, Human Factors, Theory.

INTRODUCTION

This proposal for an interactive installation is based on research undertaken during a residency at The Centre for Computational Neuroscience and Robotics (CCNR) and Department of Informatics at the University of Sussex, in Brighton, United Kingdom [2]. A brief outline of this research was included in a lecture entitled *Border Crossings: From The Real To The Half Real* [3]. This presentation was part of the Life and Mind Seminar Series sponsored by the Centre for Research in Cognitive Science (COGS), at the University of Sussex, Falmer/Brighton, UK

BACKGROUND

The motivation for this project stems from an interactive artwork called "Anita und Clarence in der Hölle: An Opera for Split Brains in Modular Parts." Supported by a residency in 1999 at the Banff Centre New Media Institute [4] in Alberta, Canada this work used documentary video of the 1991 United States Senate Judiciary Committee Hearings on the nomination of Clarence Thomas to the Supreme Court using a "split-brain" viewer interface [5].

C&C'11, November 3–6, 2011, Atlanta, Georgia, USA.
ACM 978-1-4503-0820-5/11/11.

The Split Brain Interface

Viewing this work required wearing a Virtual Research Systems' head mounted display to watch the 'she said, he said' drama where Anita Hill accused nominee Clarence Thomas of sexual harassment when she was Thomas' subordinate at the Equal Opportunity Employment Commission. The viewer watches Hill's testimony with the left eye while simultaneously watching Thomas' response with the right eye. Rather than seeing a stereoscopic pair of images the viewer sees two separate incongruous video streams. The image separation means that the left and right hemispheres of the viewer's brain simultaneously hear and see both sides of the story and induces 'artificial' cognitive dissonance.

The Split Brain Interface Revisited

This new project continues this research with a radical simplification by replacing media rich video with simple two-dimensional line drawings, which are perceived as stereoscopic pairs. These computer-generated drawings are based on a diagram presented by Charles Wheatstone [6] in his paper of 1838 used to demonstrate the principle of stereoscopy. This is referred to as the "Wheatstone seed."

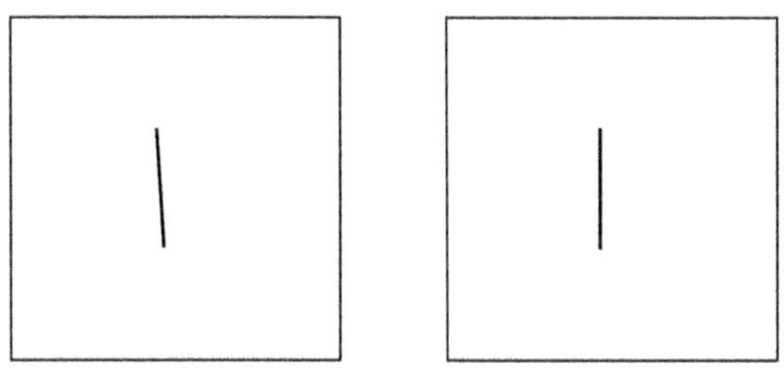

Figure 1. The Wheatstone Seed (1838)

The goal of *The Wheatstone Stereoscopic Random Line Pair Generator with Fitness Function for Non-objective Art* is the creation of dynamically generated wire-frame stereoscopic pairs that produce the illusion of three-dimensional depth. The "split-brain" interface uses a stereoscopic viewer to display a different image simultaneously and separately to each eye. Because these two source images have some features in common the brain attempts to fuse the two inputs into one coherent but virtual image. Perceived depth is seen only in the "mind's eye."

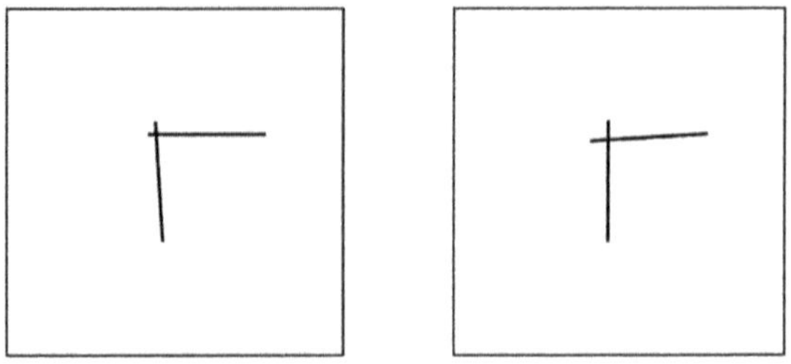

Figure 2. Random pair generation

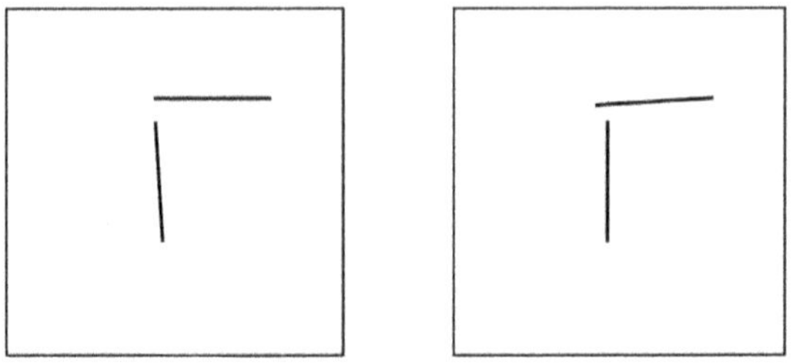

Figure 3. Discard overlap and determine best fit

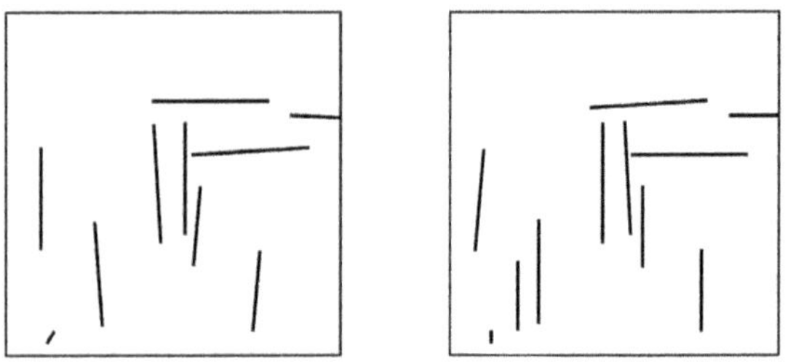

Figure 4. Generation 10 of random stereoscopic pairs

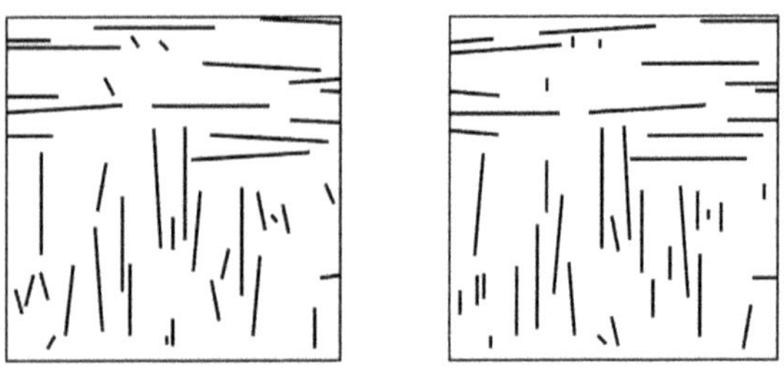

Figure 5. Generation 50

Operation

The motion of viewers wearing stereoscopic glasses will trigger the generation and projection of randomly positioned stereoscopic pairs of lines projected on each wall of the gallery. Line length will be mapped to frequency and Z-depth will be use to calculate amplitude of dynamically generated surround sound. Multiple viewers can each contribute to an emerging 'non-objective' composition through addition and erasure. If no one is present the 'drawings' fade and the system resets to the Wheatstone "seed" pair and the generation process begins anew.

The 2D Fitness Function

Overlapping lines will be discarded but the position of these lines will be used to generate a new pair that is constrained to a best fit without overlap. Surviving pairs are added to a database. The attributes (position, length) of 'parents' are inherited by next generation with random perturbations.

Emergence

There will be an emergent composition of stereoscopic effects. Any two pairs of two lines (with similar vertical or horizontal orientation) can contribute to the perception of 'virtual' stereo depth. Multiple viewers will "perturb" the system leading to additions, erasures and super-positions.

FUTURE DEVELOPMENTS

Visual illusions (e.g. Müller-Lyer or Zöllner illusions) may form the basis for fitness functions.

The 3D Fitness Function

True 3 dimensional stereoscopic pairs can be generated as wire frame and smooth shaded (Blinn) geometries. Discarding hidden lines and occluded polygons could be used as a fitness function based on point-of-view.

From Motion to Attention

Eye gaze tracking could be used, e.g. line pairs that are looked at for longer durations survive. Those ignored fade.

Invasive Interaction

When invasive, real-time fMRI (based on nano-bots impregnated into the brain) becomes available it will be possible to detect when a viewer experiences stereoscopic perception from the two separate line inputs. Lines pairs perceived stereoscopically will survive into the next generation. Line pairs, not seen stereoscopically perish.

ACKNOWLEDGMENTS

I am grateful for the support of Phil Husbands, Co-director of the Centre for Computational Neuroscience and Robotics, Professor of Artificial Intelligence, School of Informatics and also especially to Paul Brown, Visiting Professor at the Centre for Computational Neuroscience and Robotics, University of Sussex.

REFERENCES

1. Tate Collection. Glossary. Non-Objective Art. http://www.tate.org.uk/collections/glossary/
2. Centre for Computational Neuroscience and Robotics. http://www.informatics.sussex.ac.uk/research/groups/ccnr/
3. Life & Mind seminars. Archive for February 15, 2010. http://lifeandmind.wordpress.com/2010/02/15/
4. BNMI Archives Banff New Media Institute. http://www.banffcenter.com/bnmi/coproduction/archives/s.asp#thesplit
5. Garvey, G., The Split Brain Human Computer User Interface. *Leonardo Journal* 35, 3 (June 2002). (Select Conference Proceedings Creativity & Cognition, ACM-SIGCHI, Loughborough University, UK).
6. Wheatstone, C., Contributions to the Physiology of Vision. *Philosophical Transactions, Royal Society of London*, 128, (1838), 371-394.

Please Smile

Hye Yeon Nam
Digital Media,
Literature, Communication
and Culture
Georgia Institute of Technology
Atlanta, GA 30332 USA
hnam@gatech.edu

Changhyun Choi
Robotics & Intelligent Machines,
College of Computing,
Georgia Institute of Technology,
Atlanta, GA 30332 USA
cchoi@cc.gatech.edu

Sam Mendenhall
Human Computer Interaction,
College of Computing,
Georgia Institute of Technology,
Atlanta, GA 30332 USA
smendenhall3@gatech.edu

ABSTRACT
Nowadays, with reductions in manufacturing costs and a transition toward lifestyles of convenience, robots are becoming pervasive in our homes, museums, and hospitals. In addition to increased demands for robots in these domains, recently more artistic robots that interact with audiences on a personal instead of a practical level are now being exhibited in art exhibition. This paper explains how people interpret artistic robots as more than mere machines in the theory of intentionality and introduces the implementation of the artistic robot, *Please Smile*, which consists of five robotic skeleton arms that gesture in response to a viewer's facial expressions. The paper also explores how individuals can use experimental designs to create artistic robots that can express various ideas that traditional, practical robots can often not convey.

Keywords
Artistic robots, computer vision, skeleton arms, smile detection

ACM Classification Keywords
H.5.2 Information Interfaces and Presentation (e.g., HCI): User Interfaces; J.5 Arts and Humanities

General Terms
Design, Experimentation, Performance

INTRODUCTION
The production of robots has expanded to interdisciplinary fields that cover the design of mechanical and electrical components, sensor technology, computer systems, and artificial intelligence [5]. Denmark robotics scholars Luigi Pagliarini and Henrik Hautop Lund [7] suggested that groups from many walks of life such as philosophers, artists, scientists, engineers, and ordinary people are interested in and curious about robots because they have practical and sociable characteristics as well as various forms and designs.

Due to the complex interdisciplinary nature of the field, the definition of "robot" varies. Science journal describes robots as "microprocessor-controlled mechanical devices that perform functions or provide an intelligent interface between machines of processes. They can be intelligent enough to make on-the-spot manufacturing decisions. They can duplicate human manipulative skills with accuracy and precision" [6]. Another definition from the Robot Institute of America is "a robot as a reprogrammable, multifunctional manipulator designed to move materials, parts, tools, or specialized devices through variable programmed motions for the performance of a variety of tasks without human intervention" [4]. All of these definitions discuss the functionality and control of primarily industrial robots. However, by broadening the range of robotic categories, we can explore robots on a more personal level according to their features and relationships with people, which are often acknowledged when audiences appreciate them as art forms. This paper discusses how people interpret artistic robots as more than mere machines using the psychological theory of intentionality; it also introduces the implementation of the artistic robot, *Please Smile*, and explores how developers apply their ideas of experimental design form and function to create artistic robots that differ from traditional, practical robots.

THEORETICAL BACKGROUND
A philosopher and psychologist in the 19th century, Franz Brentano introduced the concept of "intentionality" used in philosophy and cognitive science to explain why people believe that machines can think without any human level intelligence. To explain mental phenomena, he used the phrase "intentional inexistence" [1]. German philosopher Edmund Husserl borrowed the term when he explained that consciousness is always intentional and links the mental and the physical world. Followed by Husserl, we detect the external physical world using our intentionality through our bodies.

The view is also supported by philosopher Daniel Dennett [3] in Intentional Stance. In his view, people applied three strategies to predict the behaviors of living organisms such as plants, animals, humans, and even artifacts. Whereas some are based on the laws of physics, or "the physical stance", others are determined by design, or "the design stance". Sometimes neither the physical nor the design stance is applicable, so another stance, "the intentional stance," can be adopted. The intentional stance treats plants, animals, humans, and artifacts as rational agents with beliefs and desires in order to further predict how they

C&C'11, November 3–6, 2011, Atlanta, Georgia, USA.
ACM 978-1-4503-0820-5/11/11.

are going to behave. In the same way, humans apply more meanings to a robot's perceived behaviors when the robot exhibits subtle predictable cues, so humans perceive robots as more intelligent agents.

IMPLEMENTATION

Please Smile combines artistic concepts and engineering technology to create a robot that interacts with humans. Compared to the traditional perspective of practical robots for manufacturing purposes, the new perspective of the artistic robot enables audiences to interact with robots on a more personal level and appreciate their aesthetic value as works of art.

Please Smile is an exhibit involving five robotic skeleton arms that change their gestures depending on a viewer's facial expressions. It consists of a microcontroller, a camera, a computer, five external power supplies, and five plastic skeleton arms, each with four motors (Figure 1). It incorporates elements from mechanical engineering and computer vision to create a more expressive robot. When people interact with the robotic arms, they encounter unexpected reactions.

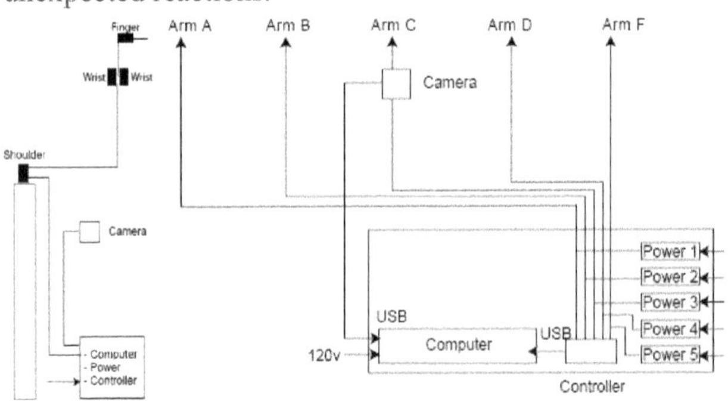

Figure 1. Structure of *Please Smile*

Audiences interact with "Please smile" in three different ways. When no human falls within the view of the camera, the five robotic skeleton arms choose the default position, which is bending their elbows and wrists near the wall behind them. When a human steps within the view of the camera, the arms point at the human and follow his/her movements (Figure 2, left). Then when someone smiles in front of it, the five arms wave their hands (Fig. 2, right). Through Please Smile, audiences foster positive behaviors such as smiling.

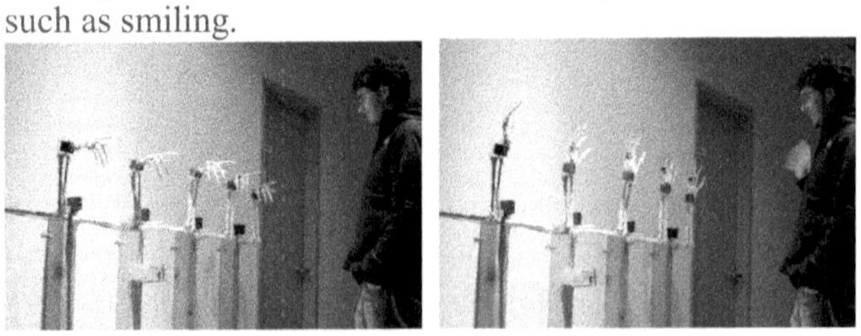

Figure 2. Interactions of *Please Smile*

From the sequence of images of the camera, the Smile Detector (SD) program (Figure 3) first detects frontal faces [9], and then the detected face regions are evaluated through our smile detection function. The function is trained in the SVM (support vector machine) algorithm in which HoG (histogram of gradient) [2] features are used as feature vectors. For training the SVM, we prepared training data from Genki-4K dataset [8], which contains 4,000 faces, smiling labels, and head poses. Since the faces are not preprocessed enough, we cropped the frontal face regions from the dataset using the head pose data. With HoG features defined as 6 X 6 cells and 8 X 8 blocks, our smile detection function showed 95.5963% accuracy.

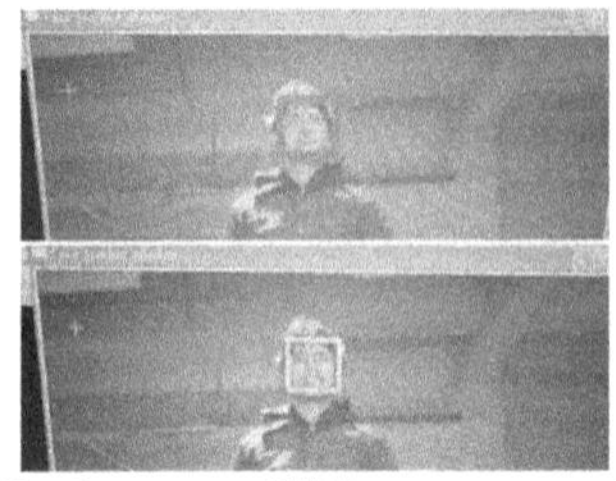

Figure 3. Smile detector (SM) program of *Please Smile*

CONCLUSION

Please Smile was exhibited at Buffalo Arts Studio, United States and FILE festival at Sao Paulo, Brazil in 2011. Hundreds of participants interacted with this artistic robot, and in their comments, they stated that it was sometimes "friendly" but also sometimes "scary." Because Please Smile's reactions to audiences' facial expressions imitate the movements of social creatures, it triggers people's imaginations and interpretations of intentionality, rendering the robot more life-like.

ACKNOWLEDGMENTS

This work is supported by the Next Generation Design Leaders Program, which is funded by the Korean Ministry of Knowledge and Economy (MKE) and administered by the Korea Institute of Design Promotion (KIDP).

REFERENCES

1. Brentano, F. *Psychology from an Empirical Standpoint*. Routledge, London and New York, 1995.
2. Dalal, N., Triggs, B. , Rhone-Alps, I. and Montbonnot , F. Histograms of oriented gradients for human detection, *IEEE Conference on Computer Vision and Pattern Recognition*, 1 (2005).
3. Dennett, D. C. *The Intentional Stance*. The MIT Press, 1989.
4. Dodd, J. Robots: The New "Steel Collar" Workers. *Personnel Journal*, 60 (September, 1981), 688-695.
5. Fu, K. S., Gonzalez, R. C., and Lee, C.S.G., *Robotics: Control, Sensing, Vision, and Intelligence*. Mcgraw-Hill Book Company, 1987.
6. Hudson, C. A. Computers in Manufacturing. *Science*, 215, 4534 (Feb 12, 1982), 815-825.
7. Pagliarini, L. and Lund, H. H. The development of robot art. *Artificial Life and Robotics*, 13, 2 (2009), 401-405.
8. The MPLab GENKI Database, GENKI-4K. Available at http://mplab.ucsd.edu/.
9. Viola, P. and Jones, M. Robust real-time object detection, *International Journal of Computer Vision*, 57, 2 (2002) 137–154.

Fitness Function: Turning the Loop Inside Out

David Norton, Derrall Heath and Dan Ventura
MIND Lab
Computer Science Department
Brigham Young University
dnorton@byu.edu, dheath@byu.edu, ventura@cs.byu.edu

Author Keywords
visual art, optimization, cultural expression

ACM Classification Keywords
J.5 [Arts and Humanities]: Fine arts; I.2.m [Artificial Intelligence]: Miscellaneous

General Terms
Measurement, Performance, Human Factors

ARTIST STATEMENT

The process of creating art is an optimization problem for which the objective function is probably unknown and possibly undefinable. That objective function is imposed on the artist by an environment which may be composed of any of a number of sources: peers, a jury, society, the self. This does not imply that the function is arbitrary nor that the optimization is impossible; however, it does suggest an interesting interpretation of the artist at work.

DESCRIPTION

Human-in-the-loop systems are a common hybrid approach to the solution of problems for which it is difficult to design an objective function. For example, evolutionary design often involves the automated production of design ideas that are then evaluated by a human before they may be propagated further downstream in the process [3]. Other recent examples include collaborative abstract artwork [2] and a system for jazz improvisation [1]. In all of these examples, the machine is relegated the mundane role of producing ideas while the human executes the role of judgment. We propose an art exhibit produced as a synergistic interaction between human and computer in which these roles are reversed—humans submit digital art to be juried by a computer system called DARCI. Feedback is immediate and those works accepted by DARCI are immediately printed and added to the dynamically growing exhibit.

DARCI (Digitial ARtist Communicating Intention) is a computer system designed to eventually produce original and meaningful images—to be an artist. This requires (among other things) the development of an appreciation of art, something that itself requires training and experience. DARCI experiences the world through images, and, much like humans, she receives training through interactions with people. Through this interactive process, DARCI forms associations between images and language. DARCI can currently only form associations between the low-level features of an image and adjectives. However, even given these limitations, with enough training, DARCI is capable of convincingly describing images with adjectives and can assign quantitative values to the image-adjective associations. These values act as the mechanism by which she can evaluate, and thus appreciate, her own artifacts as well as the works of others. (See `http://darci.cs.byu.edu` for more details.)

BIOGRAPHIES

David Norton is a PhD student in the Computer Science Department at Brigham Young University. His current research is in the field of computational creativity and his dissertation explores the significance of intention and evaluation in the creative process. His research interests include neural networks, evolutionary algorithms, and artificial intelligence.

Derrall Heath is an MS student in the Computer Science Department at Brigham Young University. His current research is in the fields of computational creativity and multi-label classification. His thesis deals with improving multi-label classification by avoiding implicit negativity with incomplete data.

Dan Ventura is an Associate Professor of Computer Science at Brigham Young University. His research interests include computational creativity, artificial intelligence, machine learning, neural networks and the application of intelligent systems to problems in medical domains.

REFERENCES

1. J. A. Biles. Genjam: Evolution of a jazz improviser. In *Creative Evolutionary Systems*, pages 165–187. Morgan Kaufmann Publishers Inc., San Francisco, CA, 2002.

2. `http://electricsheep.org`.

3. H. Takagi. Interactive evolutionary computation: Fusion of the capabilities of ec optimization and human evaluation. *Proceedings of the IEEE*, 89(9):1275–1296, August 2002.

C&C'11, November 3–6, 2011, Atlanta, Georgia, USA.
ACM 978-1-4503-0820-5/11/11.

Creating "Maybe Make Some Change"

Aaron A. Reed
UC Santa Cruz
1156 High Street, Santa Cruz, CA 95064
aareed@soe.ucsc.edu

ABSTRACT
"maybe make some change" is an interactive fiction incorporating video, audio, and animated text to explore a frozen battlefield moment from six violently conflicting perspectives. Inspired by a true story of Adam Winfield, a US soldier accused in 2010 of war crimes in Afghanistan, the piece was first exhibited in the spring of 2011 as part of the author's MFA exhibition in Digital Arts & New Media.

Author Keywords
interactive fiction, electronic literature, playable media, Afghanistan, Maywand District killings

ACM Classification Keywords
J.5. ARTS AND HUMANITIES: Literature.

General Terms
Design, Documentation

DESCRIPTION OF THE WORK
Exploring a frozen battlefield moment from a half dozen violently conflicting perspectives, "maybe make some change" merges text-based interactive fiction with video, sound, and images. Inspired by the currently unfolding trial of twelve US soldiers accused of war crimes in Afghanistan, the project asks what interactive stories can say about contemporary, real-world events, and what the role of documentarian becomes in a participatory space.

The core of the piece is a recurring moment of a soldier being unexpectedly confronted by an Afghani man who may or may not be holding a gun. This is described through text from varying perspectives, while in the background video clips from first-person shooters set during contemporary wars play on loop. The nouns of the text are highlighted, as well as a series of verb words the player slowly learns. The participant interacts by typing in verb/noun commands. The text is framed as from the point of view of a series of narrators from the soldier's past and future: an uncle warning him about the "savages" he'll face on his deployment; a lawyer cross-examining him about the incident; a threatening squad leader planning revenge; and three others. Each of the six narrators describes the scene very different, demands the player use his terminology to refer to the things and characters in the scene, and has his own expectation about what the appropriate action the player should take is: to shoot, to miss, to threaten. As the player cycles through this moment over and over again and learns the rules of each narrators vision of the scene, he or she learns more and more verbs that can be used to interact with the components of the vignette.

If the player performs contrarian actions (which are viewed as morally or practically wrong by the current narrator), a second layer of text behind the primary layer becomes increasingly visible. This second text describes not the story world, but the narrator telling this interpretation of the story world. With each contrarian action this text flares up and becomes more visible, eventually overshadowing the original text. Effectively this makes visible the distinction between the plot level and the discourse level of the narrative, the *fabula* and *sjužet* [2]. As with the nouns in the story-level text, the nouns in the discourse-level text are also highlighted. Eventually the player realizes they can use the verbs they've collected to interact with discourse-level nouns (the narrators). Each narrator is matched to one of the verbs: you can threaten your bullying staff sergeant, or miss your uncle. As the player uncovers these combinations, the verb and narrator annihilate each other: the verb disappears from the list and may no longer be used, and that narrator and his version of the story are removed from the cycling sequence. Once the player has eliminated every verb and narrator, a final concluding sequence plays which is based around a real-life transcript of a confessional Facebook chat between soldier Adam Winfield and his father from February 2010. Winfield was later accused of the murder of an Afghan civilian.

Drawn from research into the so-called "kill team" of soldiers accused of systematically murdering innocent civilians [1], "maybe make some change" hopes to draw attention to an underreported story in an underreported war, and asks participants to question their own sense of morality, duty, and complicity.

C&C'11, November 3–6, 2011, Atlanta, Georgia, USA.
ACM 978-1-4503-0820-5/11/11.

TECHNICAL CHALLENGES

The piece was written in Inform 7, a domain-specific language for creating textual interactive fiction. Since Inform 7 does not have strong support for multimedia or interaction with web-based components, a technical infrastructure had to be built up around the core story file. The Inform 7 code simulating the story world and narration was compiled to the Glulx format (a 32-bit virtual machine for interactive stories). A modified version of the extension Custom Library Messages by Ron Newcomb used to inflect verbs properly based on the temporal point of view of each narrator. Custom hacks allowed events within the Glulx VM to send text strings representing function calls to the browser's Javascript layer, which could then be executed with an eval() function. Within the browser, Andrew Plotkin's Quixe, a JavaScript Glulx interpreter, displayed the main text of the story and received keyboard input from the player, and a jQuery infrastructure was used to dynamically position elements, animate words, turn on and off video and audio streams, restart the story, and set up the introduction and conclusion. As the IF story file passed narrative state changes (such as a change in narrator) to Javascript, these could then affect the jQuery-driven display layer by, for instance, flashing verb words or changing the color and visibility of the various text layers. This framework should allow for eventual distribution of this project on the web, although the complex interconnections of systems and media files means this will take some effort to make cross-browser compatible. (Since the initial exhibition of this piece, several projects to make cross-browser frameworks for two way communication between web technologies and interactive fiction projects have begun [3].)

Authoring for "change" comprised of defining how the six narrators described the story world, and thinking up appropriate responses for every likely combination of action and narrator, as well as labeling which were complicit or contrarian from the perspective of each narrator. These responses are the way the player learns about the agenda of each narrator, which helps them understand the increasingly visible *sjužet* layer and also to determine which verbs to use to eliminate each narrator, so it was important for them to help characterize the narrators as efficiently as possible. As many responses as possible also had to work in one of the six verbs, to minimize the time spent by the player as they try to collect them all, which proved to be an interesting constraint: trying to repeatedly work the word "hug" into a bullying sergeant's jeers, for instance, took some effort. About 70% of responses ultimately incorporated one of the six verb words.

"maybe make some change" and its companion project, *what if im the bad guy*, are described more fully in my MFA thesis, *A Sequence of Possibilities* [4].

CONCLUSION

I had several opportunities to exhibit and refine "maybe make some change" before the MFA show, which pushed the piece towards being more transparent as to the underlying mechanisms and allowed modes of interaction. Many participants have been unwilling to engage with the piece by typing the first required command, shooting the Afghan (described by the first narrator using a racial slur). This is a reaction to the piece that I find completely acceptable, and has provoked a number of fascinating discussions as to why so many gamers are willing to engage in much more graphically realistic depictions of firing on foreign combatants (as in the first-person shooters playing in the background), but will not participate in the system presented here. I feel "maybe make some change" qualifies as a story system (although its narrative is not coherent to all participants), and uses the procedures of how the narrators relate to both the player character and the event they're retelling to tell a metastory about a soldier replaying an imagined or regretted incident over and over again in his mind. I am particularly proud of the way "change" demonstrates both how interactive fiction can be used as a platform for reflecting on current events, and a significant departure in both affordances and presentation from what most people think of as IF.

ACKNOWLEDGEMENTS

"maybe make some change" was supported in part by a Florence French Financial Aid Fund for Art grant. Thanks to Dannii, Phoenix Toews and my MFA thesis committee members D. Fox Harrell, Michael Mateas, and Noah Wardrip-Fruin for their input.

REFERENCES

1. H. Bernton. Stryker soldiers allegedly plotted to kill afghan civilians. Seattle Times `http://seattletimes.nwsource.com/html/localnews/2012712859_civiliandeaths25m.html`, August 24 2010.
2. S. Chatman. Towards a theory of narrative. *New Literary History*, 6(2):295–318, 1975.
3. J. Leinonen. Vorple, an interactive fiction user interface library. `http://vorple-if.com/`, 2010.
4. A. A. Reed. A sequence of possibilities: Constructive fictions, quantum authoring, and the search for an ideal story system. Master's thesis, University of California Santa Cruz, 2011.

Sympathy for Pacman

Matt Ruby
Parsons the New School for Design
19 Carroll Street, Apt 3F
mattaruby@gmail.com
603.767.5895

ABSTRACT
Our understanding of the digital world is influenced by the interfaces that we use to access it. Traditionally, interfaces are designed to be innocuous so that we do not question the role that they play in our experience. *Sympathy for Pacman*, addresses both the role and the potential for interfaces. This experimental interface which requires vigorous activity to control makes the user more aware of themselves and their actions. This work addresses interaction from the perspective of fine art, giving viewers a look at how digital elements and digital space can be translated into the physical world. By creating a piece that is not strictly practical, participants are given the opportunity to consider alternative connections and understanding of digital media while questioning their relationship to it.

Author Keywords
Art, Interaction, Interface, Video Games, Sculpture

ACM Classification Keywords
J.5. Arts and Humanities: Fine Arts.

General Terms
Experimentation, Human Factors

INTRODUCTION
Sympathy for Pacman (see Figure 1) is an artwork that explores the relationship between the physical and digital worlds. The work reinterprets control of the video game Pacman as an examination of the way we can interact with digital systems. The piece uses aspects of interaction design, interface design, fine art and popular culture to build the concept and experience.

Ease of use designed for most technology presents new tools that are constantly being embraced without evaluation. The user's role hasn't been questioned in regard to social implications. *Sympathy for Pacman* skews our understanding of usability in order to consider an alternative way of addressing human needs. The appearance of *Sympathy for Pacman* and the experience of interacting with it give new insight into often neglected aspects of interface design.

OVERVIEW
Sympathy for Pacman is presented with the video game Pacman, displayed on a television, mounted to a wooden stand which can turn 360 degrees. A large clear barrel of orange cheese puffs is mounted to the side of the television. A chrome tube dispenses the cheese puffs into a trough near the base of the television (see Figure 1 and Figure 2).

Figure 1. Sympathy for Pacman.

Interaction
Viewers are encouraged to interact with the work. Approaching the piece viewers can find a long handle that is conveniently attached to the trough where cheese puffs are dispensed and held. As a viewer approaches the piece cheese puffs are dispensed, enticing a viewer to engage. A single button is located on one of the four sides of the base which starts the game.

Once the game is started, as the user turns the television the onscreen Pacman character turns in relation to the direction the user is facing with the television. For instance, if

C&C'11, November 3–6, 2011, Atlanta, Georgia, USA.
ACM 978-1-4503-0820-5/11/11.

Pacman is moving up and the user turns the television 90 degrees to their right, Pacman will turn to the left.

The plane of the floor around the piece, mimics the onscreen plane of game play. The television turns on a horizontal plane, and the game is displayed on a vertical plane, this shift from horizontal to vertical is difficult to comprehend and exaggerates the gap between the physical and digital space. The viewer is forced to translate their three-dimensional experience into several different dimensions and react accordingly.

As a user stands in front of the piece, cheese puffs are being dispensed at a rapid pace, mimicking the dots being consumed by Pacman onscreen. The viewer is expected to eat the cheese puffs while playing, furthering their connection to the onscreen character.

Pacman

A video game was chosen to serve as the content for the system because of it's interactive nature. This allowed the work to serve as an interface for the existing video game. Pacman offered a prototypical and iconic video game, familiar and with a simple set of controls.

Early video games, such as Pacman, were some of the first digital media that was available by a mass audience. This is important because it was an introduction to digital media, and initiated the growing divide between user and content.

Television

The cathode ray tube television was chosen because it is typical of the kind of devices which this game was originally played on. The resolution of the television is able to display Pacman the way it was originally intended, and reminds the viewer of their familiarity to the game.

Stand

The stand is a mixture of arcade machine, and home furniture, making the stand familiar, warm, and inviting. The crafted wooden stand builds contrast with the technology and digital media.

Cheese puffs

The cheese puffs are a direct interpretation of onscreen elements found in the American landscape. They carry the significance of bringing onscreen elements into the physical world and hint at indulgent or idle behavior.

OPERATION

The piece is controlled by a hacked plug-and-play game system and an Arduino micro-controller. The game and cheese puffs are controlled by independent systems, that have no knowledge of one another.

Plug-and-play

The plug-and-play game system is a game controller that can be plugged directly into a television. Switches have

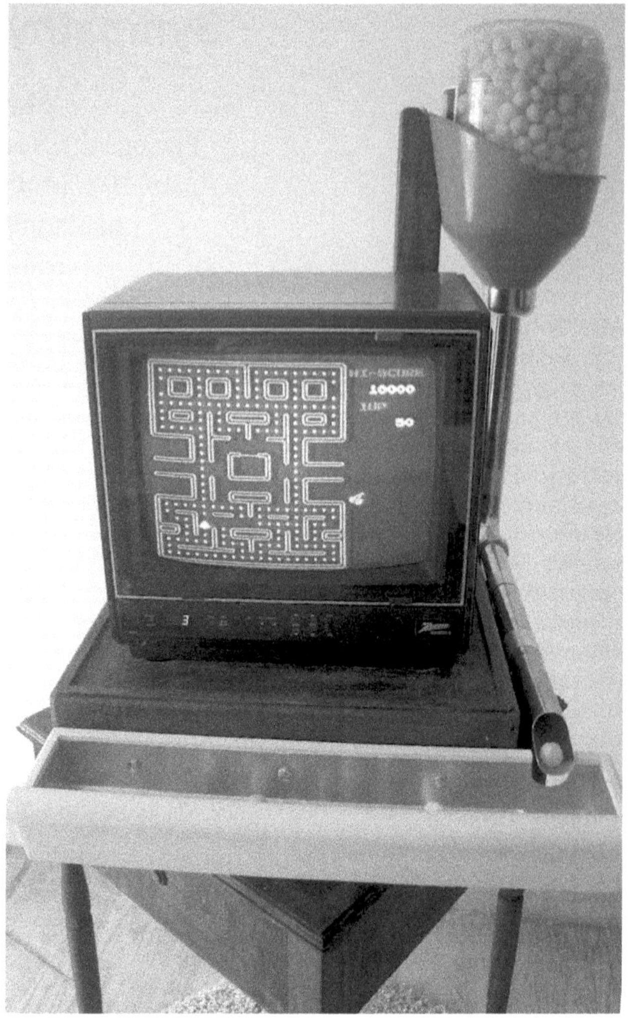

Figure 2. Sympathy for Pacman.

been wired directly to the game controllers circuit board, these switches make contact when a user turns the television 90 degrees in one of the four major directions. The game software is untouched and there is no micro-controller or logic in controlling the game.

Arduino

Dispensing cheese puffs is controlled by Arduino. A sensor alerts the system that a user is present turning a motor which controls the flow of cheese puffs. Cheese puffs are dispensed at a constant rate if a user is present.

ACKNOWLEDGMENTS

This project was conceived at Parsons the New School for Design in the Master of Fine Arts, Design and Technology program. Thank you to my instructors Katherine Moriwaki and Andrew Zornoza. Thank you to my wife, Joanie Turbek who helped work through these ideas and bring them to life.

Open House: Interaction as Critical Reflection

Jack Stenner, Ph.D.
School of Art + Art History
University of Florida
PO Box 115801
Gainesville, FL 32611 USA
stenner@ufl.edu

Patrick LeMieux
Art, Art History & Visual Studies
Duke University
PO Box 90764
Durham, NC 27708 USA
patrick.lemieux@duke.edu

ABSTRACT
This paper describes *Open House*, a networked art installation by Jack Stenner and Patrick LeMieux that allows visitors to telematically squat in a Florida home undergoing foreclosure after the U.S. housing collapse. Virtual markets transformed this otherwise livable property into a ghost house. Prior to the collapse, the movements of global capital seemed like a distant reality to most homeowners, but in the end it was imaginary systems of value, not bricks and mortar, that fell apart. Through computer interaction that integrates computational processes, mechanical relays, and human interactions, *Open House* implicates the tendency to separate virtual and physical activity, an enabling mechanism and proximate cause for the current U.S. economic crisis.

Author Keywords
Installation, body, affect, interaction, subjectivity, representation, immersion, aesthetics

ACM Classification Keywords
H.5.1. Multimedia Information Systems: Artificial, augmented, and virtual realities. H.5.m. Information interfaces and presentation, Miscellaneous. J.5 Arts and Humanities, Fine Arts.

General Terms
Design, Documentation, Experimentation

INTRODUCTION
The house at 1617 NW 12th Road in Gainesville, Florida was designed and built by M.H. Johnson in the late 1940s. The decorated World War II submarine officer and University of Florida architecture professor was able to realize his dream house despite post-wartime material shortages. After Johnson's death in 1968, this Mid-Century Modern, Florida-bungalow style home was maintained by his widow, Dr. Nedra Johnson, until 2006 when she sold it to Jack Stenner, a newly hired Assistant Professor of Digital Media Art at the University of Florida. As young Assistant Professors, Stenner and Johnson had markedly different experiences of the American Dream.

C&C'11, November 3–6, 2011, Atlanta, Georgia, USA.
ACM 978-1-4503-0820-5/11/11.

In the process of moving down the street, to a house with space enough to accommodate Stenner's art practice, the nearly $300,000 mortgage on 1617 NW 12th Road became worth only $150,000 overnight. Caught between two mortgages with no possibility of selling the house, Stenner had no choice but to default in 2009. Though the Bank of America motioned to foreclose, they could not produce the necessary paperwork. The deed had been so indiscriminately traded during the Housing Bubble that its paper trail had grown into an illegible labyrinth. As the foreclosure was delayed for months then years, 1617 NW 12th Road became an "open house."

CONCEPT
When the U.S. housing market collapsed in 2008, so did the dreams of many middle and lower-class Americans. Florida, California, Nevada, and Arizona were particularly hard hit, and not by a force of nature, but by the abstract and invisible hand of the market. Prior to the collapse, the movements of global capital seemed like a distant reality to most homeowners, but in the end it was imaginary systems of value and not bricks and mortar that fell apart. *Open House* is a networked art installation by Jack Stenner and Patrick LeMieux that allows visitors to telematically inhabit a "distressed" home in Gainesville, Florida. (see Figure 1).

Figure 1. Still of hybrid video stream and virtual environment, installation view.

The house at 1617 NW 12 Road is currently in financial limbo while undergoing the process of foreclosure due to the housing collapse. Virtual markets have transformed this otherwise livable property into a ghost house. *Open House* allows individuals to repopulate this disenfranchised space and assume the role of virtual squatters—opening the door, flicking the lights, rattling the shutters and remotely occupying the abandoned property. Live video feedback integrates real-time physical effects with one's virtual actions. Through *Open House*, virtual squatters can temporarily resist eviction by mirroring the market and becoming hybrid subjects occupying both virtual and physical space.

Figure 2. Initial application screen.

DESCRIPTION

Upon launching the *Open House* computer application downloaded from http://www.no-place.org/open_house, the viewer is presented with a networked interface to the house in Gainesville. The first screen is informational, providing a contextual overview and entryway into the project (see Figure 2). After clicking "enter" the software transitions to a black screen featuring dynamically loaded and recombinantly assembled texts from the no-place server. The user is instructed to "click to proceed," at which time the first image of the home appears.

This image is a composite of real-time streaming video from the physical site combined with a photorealistic, computer-generated (CG) model of the house and environs (see Figure 3). Through mouse interaction and particle effects, the viewer is lead to press and hold the mouse button, effectively "pushing" on the image of the Gainesville home.

Figure 3. House view showing composite imagery.

As the viewer "pushes," particle activity increases around the house and sound effects intensify. Feedback in the form of a text overlay is provided to assist the interaction and serves to prepare the viewer for the typical interaction utilized throughout the application. After holding the mouse for this short duration, the software transitions to another recombinant text screen followed by a new position at the front door of the home. Using the same interaction techniques as before, the viewer can "push" to open the front door (see Figure 4). Because this view is composed of live streaming video and CG imagery, the viewer witnesses the physical door in Gainesville opening before them.

Figure 4. Front door opening in Gainesville.

Another recombinant text composed from a constantly expanding database containing popular idioms, visitor testimonials, and selections from literary, theoretical, economic, and political texts relating to home, place, and virtuality is displayed before leading to a final view from inside the home. Once inside, the viewer can continue to interact by switching on a light and opening the blinds (see Figure 5). All of these interactions are simultaneously "real" and "virtual" and can be experienced by multiple participants logged in from remote, global locations. Of course, the viewer must leave the same way they entered, through the front door. This action leads to a final recombinant text, ultimately the most poetic of all, which randomly assembles fragments into a sort of haiku.

Figure 5. Interior view with viewer enabling light.

CONCLUSION

In 1981, Ronald Reagan's speechwriters popularized the idea that one could comprehend the U.S. national debt through the image of a billion thousand-dollar bills stacked 67 miles high. This idea was recalled during the U.S. bailout in 2008 where 67 miles turned into 67,000 miles, or the distance to the moon and back. The difficulty of these images is that they are designed to frame the totality of a virtual system in terms of a single human perspective. This desire for a monolithic and totalizing image of the virtual is constantly thwarted by systems like the global economy that can never be fully represented to the individual. In contrast to these images, *Open House* offers a complex series of computational processes, mechanical relays, and human interactions to create a more nuanced articulation of our implication in both physical and virtual reality.

LOLC for Laptop Music Ensemble

Jason Freeman, Sang Won Lee, Shannon Yao, Aaron Albin
School of Music
Georgia Institute of Technology
840 McMillan Street
Atlanta, Georgia 30332-0456
+1 404 385 7257
jason.freeman | sangwonlee | syao31 | aalbin3@gatech.edu

ABSTRACT
This statement describes LOLC, a text-based collaborative music improvisation environment for laptop ensemble developed at Georgia Tech and presented in performance by the authors at the Creativity and Cognition conference.

Author Keywords
music, improvisation, text, collaboration, laptop

ACM Classification Keywords
J.5. Computer Applications. Arts and Humanities. Music.

General Terms
Experimentation, Human Factors.

LOLC OVERVIEW

In LOLC [1], the musicians in a laptop ensemble use a textual performance interface, developed specifically for this piece, to create and share rhythmic motives based on a collection of recorded sounds. The environment encourages musicians to share their code with each other, developing an improvisational conversation over time as material is looped, borrowed, and transformed.

The LOLC software environment comprises server software that synchronizes pattern definitions across the ensemble and maintains time synchronization; client software that presents an integrated development environment (IDE) style interface for text-based performance and collaboration; and a visualization of performers' activities that is projected for the audience to watch.

LOLC's design is inspired both by live-coding systems and by traditional forms of ensemble improvisation, particularly in jazz and art music. Musicians type in simple one-line code statements to create rhythmic patterns based on sound files, to play and loop those patterns, and to transform and combine their own patterns and those of other ensemble members.

Our goal with LOLC was to create an environment that encouraged a conversational style of improvisational creativity within a large laptop ensemble, using the idea of borrowing and transformation as the core paradigm. Network functionality serves to make that collaboration easier, since this interaction paradigm can otherwise be difficult in a laptop ensemble, where each member would need to manually recreate the musical content or underlying algorithm in order to borrow from other musicians.

LOLC is also designed to be accessible to musicians with no experience in computer music or computer programming. The environment's easy learning curve and simple syntax guarantees that almost anyone can learn to perform competently with the environment after a few hours of practice, and we have successfully staged performances with musicians who have no technical background whatsoever.

In performances of LOLC, audiences are also able to relate to the performers via the projected visualization. The projection does not merely display code fragments, it also displays chat messages performers use to plan and comment upon the music as it unfolds. It also visualizes the collaborative relationships among the performers as they borrow and transform each other's material.

CREATING MUSIC WITH LOLC

Pre-recorded sound files serve as the base musical element in LOLC. Although any sound file can be used, short and percussive sounds tend to work best. Sounds are loaded as follows:

```
mySound : "sound.aif"
```

Another way to create a pattern is to specify the rhythmic repetition of an existing pattern through bracket syntax. For example, the following pattern definition plays mySound as two eighth notes at *fortissimo*, a quarter-note rest, one quarter note at *mezzo-forte* and four sixteenth notes at *pianissimo*:

```
myPattern : mySound[e.ff, e.ff,
   q.n, q, s.pp, s.pp, s.pp, s.pp]
```

Patterns can also be nested. In the following example, *myPattern* is played twice:

```
myNested : myPattern[w,h]
```


C&C'11, November 3–6, 2011, Atlanta, Georgia, USA.
ACM 978-1-4503-0820-5/11/11.

Each time the pattern is played, its note durations are stretched or compressed to match the target duration. In this example, the patterns remain unchanged for the whole note iteration and are halved for the half-note iteration.

The last but most important way to create a new pattern is to transform or combine existing patterns. Thirteen operations currently supported. These operations were chosen because of their importance in studies on improvisational interaction and musical pattern manipulations. The syntax for all transformations follows this example:

```
pattern1 : sound1[w,h,h]
pattern2 : sound2[q,q,q,q]
myConcat:cat(pattern1, pattern2)
myTrunc : trunc(pattern2, 2)
```

The operation cat places two patterns in succession, so myConcat combines patterns based on two different audio-file sources. The operation trunc removes the final n items from a pattern, so myTrunc removes the final two quarter notes from pattern2.

Patterns are not played immediately upon creation. Instead, musicians must use an LOLC scheduling expression to determine when and how they play. Typically, patterns are scheduled for playback at the next beat or measure:

```
play myPattern @nextBeat
play myPattern @nextMeasure
```

LOLC supports additional scheduling methods: preview will preview the pattern over headphones and loop will play it repeatedly:

```
loop myPattern @nextMeasure ~16
```

This example loops the pattern sixteen times. Additional mechanisms support shorthand notations, scheduling at specific points of time in the future, and prematurely killing playback. Scheduling commands are shared with other clients via the chat-inspired interface (Figure 1), but they are played solely on the local client machine.

Through LOLC's novel text-based, networked architecture for improvisatory music-making, we are exploring new mechanisms for musicians to collaborate with each other to create music in performance as well as new techniques for revealing their creative processes to audiences.

ACKNOWLEDGMENTS

LOLC is supported by a grant from the National Science Foundation as part of a larger research project on musical improvisation in performance and education (NSF CreativeIT #0855758). Additional documentation, software downloads, and videos are available at http://www.jasonfreeman.net/lolc/.

REFERENCES

1. Freeman, J. and Van Troyer, A. Collaborative Textual Improvisation in a Laptop Ensemble. *Computer Music Journal 35*, 2 (Summer 2011), 1-14.

Figure 1. Musicians use an Integrated Development Environment that is inspired by instant-messaging clients to create and share music and messages with LOLC.

A Reading of *Skeleton Seas of Mare Incognitum*: An Interactive Fiction Expedition in Curveship

D. Fox Harrell
Comparative Media Studies Program
Program in Writing and Humanistic Studies
Computer Science and AI Laboratory
Massachusetts Institute of Technology
77 Massachusetts Ave, 02139 USA
fox.harrell@mit.edu

Nick Montfort
Comparative Media Studies Program
Program in Writing and Humanistic Studies
Massachusetts Institute of Technology
77 Massachusetts Ave, 02139 USA
nickm@nickm.com

OVERVIEW

Skeletons of Mare Incognitum (The Unkown Sea) is an interactive fiction (IF) work developed by Fox Harrell. This work was written using Curveship [1, 2], a platform for implementing works of IF that offers a range of affordances for narrative variation such as flashbacks, temporal movement of the narrator, and changes in voice.

Author Keywords

Interactive Fiction, Narrative, Subjectivity, Artificial Intelligence

ACM Classification Keywords

J.5 [Arts and Humanities]:

General Terms

Design, Experimentation, Performance, Theory

SKELETONS OF MARE INCOGNITUM

In the IF work *Skeleton Seas of Mare Incognitum*, you awaken in a dark chamber – unaware that it is the belly of a sperm whale. Traveling is more figurative than literal – visiting and revisiting each location reveals more about the gastral nature of your predicament. Each location is the belly of a different denizen of one of the earth's oceans. After figuring out how to escape from a creature's stomach, you emerge to move from ocean to ocean, and must get back to your life. Ultimately, you confront that you have been swallowed by the sea, wondering if your predicament is reality or a fantasy of a lost soul adrift.

INTERACTVE FICTION

The basic IF components are a world model, simulating a fictional universe, and a parser, allowing limited natural-language-like input. During the 1980s, interactive fiction was highly successful as entertainment software and was written by some established authors (including Douglas Adams and Thomas Disch). Sales decreased in the 1990s, but a variety of free IF development systems, the ability to distribute interactive fiction using the Internet, and a community of players and authors have developed works in different lengths, languages, narrative voices, literary genres, and modes of collaboration.

C&C'11, November 3–6, 2011, Atlanta, Georgia, USA.
ACM 978-1-4503-0820-5/11/11.

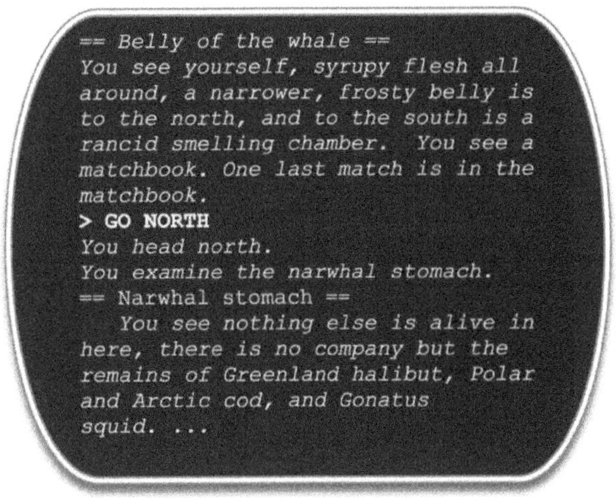

Figure 1: Sample Output

CONTRIBUTIONS

The narrative theory that Curveship is based upon is not specific to text. As an example of what Harrell calls *phantasmal media* and *subjective computing* practice, the innovations discussed here apply to graphical forms of computer gaming and AI-based interactive narrative and poetry. [3, 4] The work offers several innovations including:

- descriptions that change based upon the player character's current knowledge,
- descriptions that change upon repeated visits,
- tense determined algorithmically when narrated as a flashback,
- gender can be left ambiguous or adapted during play,
- person can be changed during runtime,
- figurative rather than literal content (a new poetic direction for IF), and
- narrative speed can affect the level of output detail

A priority in Curveship development has been a model of salience that can be specified for each actor. The need for such a model was highlighted while developing *Skeletons of Mare Incognitum*. It is currently difficult to change narrative speed to expand or contract descriptive text or text representing actions in a meaningful way, since this should be done by omitting the least salient information.

BRIEF BIOGRAPHIES

D. Fox Harrell, Ph.D., is Associate Professor of Digital Media at MIT, joint in the Program in Writing and Humanistic Studies, Comparative Media Studies Program, and in the Computer Science and Artificial Intelligence Laboratory (CSAIL). His research explores the relationship between imaginative cognition, digital media arts, and computation, developing new forms of interactive narrative, gaming, social computing, and other types of culturally engaged AI-based media. Harrell received the National Science Foundation (NSF) CAREER Award for his project "Computing for Advanced Identity Representation." He is currently completing a book, *Phantasmal Media: An Approach to Imagination, Computation, and Expression*, for the MIT Press.

Nick Montfort, Ph.D., is Associate Professor of Digital Media at the Massachusetts Institute of Technology and president of the Electronic Literature Organization, has collaborated on the blog *Grand Text Auto,* the sticker novel *Implementation,* and *2002: A Palindrome Story.* He writes poems, text generators, and interactive fiction. Montfort has co-edited *The Electronic Literature Collection Volume 1* (ELO, 2006) and *The New Media Reader* (MIT Press, 2003) and written *Twisty Little Passages: An Approach to Interactive Fiction* (MIT Press, 2003), *Racing the Beam: The Atari Video Computer System,* (with Ian Bogost, MIT Press, 2009) and *Riddle & Bind* (Spineless Books, 2010).

REFERENCES

1. Montfort, N., Curveship: An Interactive Ficiton System for Narrative Variation, in *New Narratives: Stories and Storytelling in the Digital Age*, R. Page and B. Thomas, Editors. University of Nebraska Press: Lincoln: NE, forthcoming 2011.
2. Montfort, N., *Generating Narrative Variation in Interactive Fiction, Ph.D. Dissertation*, Department of Computer and Information Science. University of Pennsylvnia: Philadelphia: PA, 2007.
3. Harrell, D.F., Toward a Theory of Phantasmal Media: An Imaginative Cognition- and Computation-Based Approach to Digital Media. *CTheory*, 2009.
4. Harrell, D.F., GRIOT's Tales of Haints and Seraphs: A Computational Narrative Generation System, in *Second Person: Role-Playing and Story in Games and Playable Media*, N. Wardrip-Fruin and P. Harrigan, Editors. MIT Press: Cambridge, MA, 2007.

Moori

Interactive Audience Participatory Audio-Visual Performance

Haeyoung Kim
MFA, Design and Technology
Parsons the New School for Design
Haeyoung.kim00@gmail.com
http://www.bubblyfish.com/thesis

ABSTRACT
Moori is a hybrid form of an audience-participatory dynamic narrative and an audio-visual performance system. By innovations in network-based personal mobile devices, users share their thoughts and stories to proposed questions by a performer. Through text inputs, buttons, and touch pads, user generated data is processed to create algorithmic audio and graphics. The dialogue between the performer and audience members results in a real-time audio-visual composition and a dramatic narrative. As authors, viewers transform the content in a collective narrative space.

Author Keywords
Audience participatory performance, dynamic narrative, story telling, algorithmic sound and graphics, live audio-visual performance, collaborative

ACM Classification Keywords
J.5. Arts and humanity: Arts, fine and performing, Music, Literature

General Terms
Algorithms, Performance, Design

INTRODUCTION
Live events promote a form of active participation to viewers. However, in many live audio-visual performances, audience participation is minimized. Moori proposes a form of participation in which an audience is invited to be a dynamic participant and to be more engaged in the performance and have an immersive experience.

Moori adapts available technology to effectuate the communication between the performer and participants.
It provides a framework for viewers to partake in the performance by employing dynamic interface and SMS on their personal mobile phones.

C&C'11, November 3–6, 2011, Atlanta, Georgia, USA.
ACM 978-1-4503-0820-5/11/11.

Figure 1. Questions from the performer displayed on the screen.

DESCRIPTION
Moori allows audience members to take part actively in narrative-building, which brings visuals and sound in a performance. Users tell stories in response to guided questions by the performer by interacting with multiple modes of messaging on mobile phones and portable smart devices. As audience members input data through their personal device, the user data is processed to generate audio and graphics while creating a larger narrative. This collaboration creates dialog between the performer and audience members and suggests new possibilities that can exist through the combination of algorithmic animation, audio and language.

The act consists of three chapters each beginning with the performer's monologue and background music followed by questions to audience members. The performer begins with the background music and narrative and establishes the tone before questions are proposed. Moori's visual content is solely created by audience participation. Most of the visual content is text art generated from questions and responses between the performer and participants. In addition to sending text messages, users are invited to accompany the performer with drawing and sound tools.

These tools are mapped to multi touch pads and buttons available on each user's device interface. The controllers allow participants to manipulate algorithmically generated images and sound. Moori's main visual system employs Openframeworks, while the audio system integrates Max/MSP and Ableton Live.

Both systems communicate with Mrmr, an OSC (Open Sound Control) control application available for mobile phones. Prior to the performance, audience members are asked to configure their devices. As users send text messages, they appear on the screen and words are spoken with text to speech software.

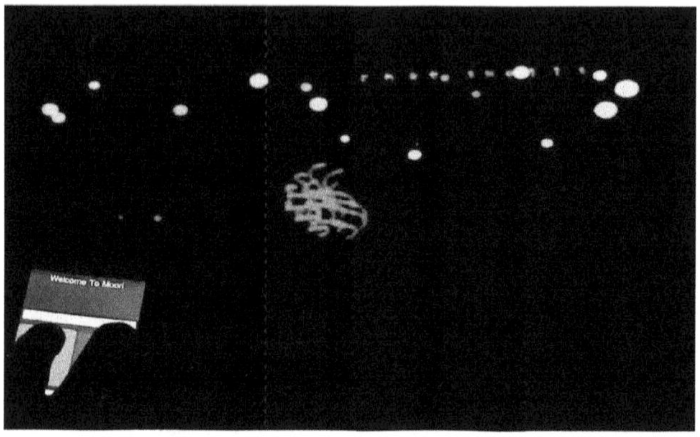

Figure 2. A user controls visual elements.

OSC messages are distributed to all users from the server where every participant receives the same interface on their devices. Subsequently, every participant uses this interface to control the performance and collaboration between the users is required.

ISSUES and APPROACH

To increase adaptability, Moori employs personal portable devices rather than custom-made hardware. To provide an OSC control application available for free to participants, the system integrates Mrmr, which is an open source OSC application for iOS products. To accommodate non-iOS device users, the SMS feature was added. However, the SMS feature only allows to text input. For other non-iOS smart phone users, NoBarrierOSC, a web browser based OSC application, is also integrated.

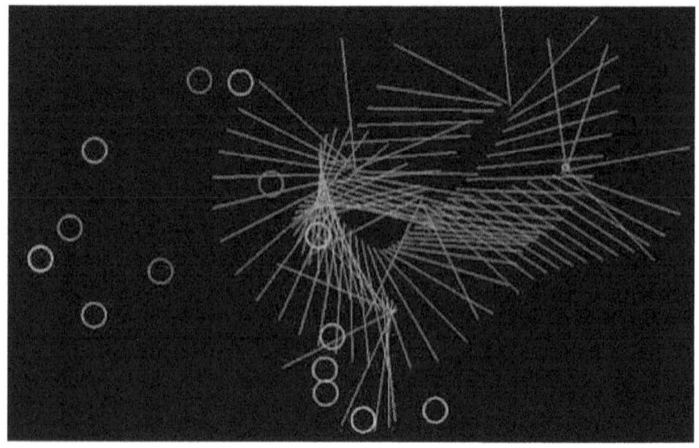

Figure 3. Graphical elements controlled by participants.

CONCLUSION

Moori distinguishes itself from other exemplary participatory performances by emphasizing collective narrative and incorporating closely interweaved sounds and images. In Moori, the performer initiates the formality of the performance and tells general story lines. This process helps participants to understand the narrative structure clearly. The primary goal of creating an engaging audio-visual concert experience is achieved by exchanging questions and responses. Providing controllers allow audience members to contribute. The text and computer voice provide users immediate feedback while interactive graphic/sonic control forces them to create audio-visual work collaboratively with other participants and the performer.

Regardless of the structure, the final result is left open to the participants. For larger audiences, the contributed content tends to be more divergent. Consequently, the narrative drifts from the theme that the performer framed originally. The openness of the result is part of the intended aesthetic, and the unpredictable consequences are conveyed as a form of participatory art. The artist remains merely as a mediator and the outcome is unique to each performance.

REFERENCES

1. Open Sound Control. http://www.opensoundcontrol.org/.
2. Mrmr http://www.mrmr.noisepages.com/.
3. NoBarrierOSC. https://www.masterbranch.com/nobarrierosc-project/815515

SoundPainter

Celine Latulipe,
David Wilson
Berto Gonzalez
Adam Harris
Erin Carroll
HCILab, UNC Charlotte
Charlotte, NC, USA
clatulip@uncc.edu

Sybil Huskey
Melissa Word
Robert Beasley
Department of Dance
UNC Charlotte
Charlotte, NC, USA
sdhuskey@uncc.edu

Nathan Nifong
Systems Science
Department
Portland State University
Portland, OR, USA
nifong@gpdx.edu

ABSTRACT
SoundPainter is an interactive dance performance that features a triad of dancers, musicians and projected visuals, where each of these three elements reacts to one another through improvisation, algorithmic representations of sound and vision-based technology.

Author Keywords
interactive performing arts, sound rendering, dance

ACM Classification Keywords
J.5 Computer Applications: Arts and Humanities—*Performing Arts*

General Terms
Human Factors.

Figure 1. SoundPainter with two dancers improvising, with visuals responding to their positions and the percussion sounds.

INTRODUCTION
Interactive performance pieces are exciting to many audiences because of the way they break through traditional boundaries, especially with respect to perceptual modalities. In dance, audiences expect to see dancers move and to hear some type of accompaniment. In interactive performance pieces, the addition of reactive elements on the stage that respond to performers, challenge traditional audience sensibilities. In the Dance.Draw project at the University of North Carolina at Charlotte, we have been working with dancers and choreographers to explore the space of real-time interactive digital elements in dance [3]. Through various technologies, our Dance.Draw system enables the dancers and audience members to act as inputs to our digital system.

PERFORMANCE
"SoundPainter" is a modern dance duet with an original choreographic structure accompanied by live percussions music. Choreographers Sybil Huskey and Melissa Word and percussionist Robert Beasley designed the parameters of both the choreography and the music to afford significant improvisation, allowing a conversation to take place between the dancers and the musician. The dancers' positions on stage are captured by an overhead camera in real-time and used as input to the Dance.Draw system which contains the SoundPainter visualization. The SoundPainter software listens to the incoming audio signal and draws an array of trailing color droplets to render various features of the sound. For example, volume is mapped to size, pitch to color and noisier sounds create scattered sets of droplets.

The SoundPainter visualization uses the camera-tracked positions of the dancers to decide where to draw the sound: if both dancers move upstage, the renderings of the sound will be projected at the bottom of the screen, behind the dancers. As the dancers move downstage, the renderings will move up the screen, as dancers move left and right, the renderings follow appropriately, see Figure 1. The semi-structured, improvisational nature of this dance is paired with a semi-structured improvisational musical composition, which allows for interaction between the triad of performers, musician and visuals. The dancers react to the musical accompaniment through movements within and through space, which in turn creates a visual pattern on screen that reflects both their kinetics and the features of the sound. The dancers can also react to and interact with the visuals that are created by their movements and the sound. The musician also reacts

C&C'11, November 3–6, 2011, Atlanta, Georgia, USA.
ACM 978-1-4503-0820-5/11/11.

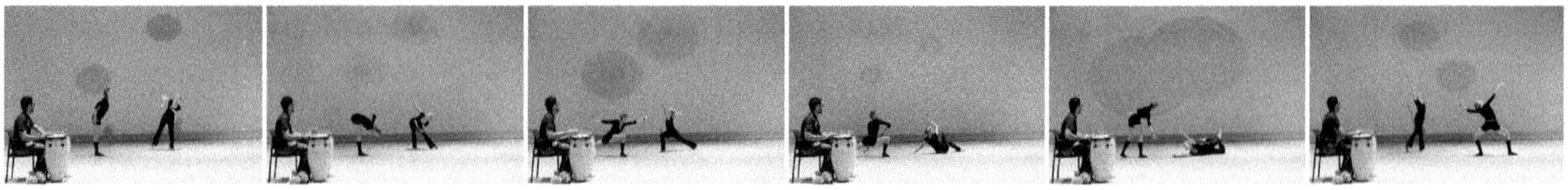

Figure 2. Rehearsal with percussionist.

both to the dancers' movements and to the visuals, creating an intricate, tri-directional interaction, see Figure 2.

AUDIENCE INTERACTION

One of the research goals of the Dance.Draw project is to investigate ways to involve the audience in dance performances, through the use of technology. This will happen in the SoundPainter production in two different ways. First, audience member noises are a natural part of performance settings, including the SoundPainter dance, and we purposefully anticipate rendering audience sounds. It is also possible that audience members who realize that the visualizations are responding to sound may explicitly make noises in order to see if they can influence the visualization.

The second way that audiences will be involved is in a direct, continuous, real-time, but nuanced manner using audience response technology. We have developed a system that allows the capture of galvanic skin response (GSR) data from multiple audience members simultaneously. GSR measures skin conductance, which is typically a measure of arousal, and is correlated to engagement with a performance, as shown by our previous work [2]. We will instrument audience members who wish to participate with GSR sensors. The average arousal (engagement) as they watch the performance will feed into the visualizations in real-time by affecting the color of the background. Initially, the background will be pale, but over time this background will vary, depending on the audience response, with higher engagement levels generating more saturated background hues.

PEOPLE

SoundPainter involves both performers and technologists:

Sybil Huskey Co-choreographer. Sybil is a Full Professor of Dance at UNC Charlotte and the Choreographic Lead on the Dance.Draw project.

Melissa Word Co-choreographer and Dancer. Melissa is a Dance graduate from UNC Charlotte. She has danced in and choreographed multiple Dance.Draw productions.

Jordan Stevens Dancer. Jordan is a Dance Major in her senior year at UNC Charlotte. She has danced in many Dance.Draw productions.

Robert Beasley Musician. Robert is a professional percussionist and a lecturer at UNC Charlotte. He regularly provides live accompaniment for modern and jazz dance.

Celine Latulipe Project Lead. Celine is an Assistant Professor of Human-Computer Interaction at UNC Charlotte and the Director of the Dance.Draw project.

David Wilson Technical Lead. David is an Associate Professor of Intelligent Systems at UNC Charlotte and is in charge of the software-hardware interfaces.

Berto Gonzalez Software Lead. Berto is a Doctoral Student at UNC Charlotte and does software development for the dance sensing and visualizations.

Nathan Nifong Visualization Coder. Nathan is a Masters Student at Portland State. He created the original SoundPainter application as an undergraduate at UNC Charlotte.

Erin Carroll Evaluation Lead. Erin is a Doctoral Student at UNC Charlotte and she facilitates audience evaluation.

Adam Harris Hardware Engineer. Adam is a Doctoral Student at UNC Charlotte and has developed the multi-person, real-time GSR monitoring system.

EVALUATION

We have put significant effort into the evaluation of longitudinal art-technology collaborations [1], and we continue to expand our repertoire of methods. The audience response system allows us to gage the unconscious reaction of audience members. Post-performance surveys and discussion will be used to evaluate the conscious audience response.

ACKNOWLEDGEMENTS

This work was supported by NSF CreativeIT (IIS-0855882).

REFERENCES

1. C. Latulipe, E. A. Carroll, and D. Lottridge. Evaluating longitudinal projects combining technology with temporal arts. In *Proceedings of the 2011 annual conference on Human factors in computing systems*, CHI '11, pages 1835–1844, New York, NY, USA, 2011. ACM.

2. C. Latulipe, E. A. Carroll, and D. Lottridge. Love, hate, arousal and engagement: exploring audience responses to performing arts. In *Proceedings of the 2011 annual conference on Human factors in computing systems*, CHI '11, pages 1845–1854, New York, NY, USA, 2011. ACM.

3. C. Latulipe, D. Wilson, S. Huskey, M. Word, A. Carroll, E. Carroll, B. Gonzalez, V. Singh, M. Wirth, and D. Lottridge. Exploring the design space in technology-augmented dance. In *CHI EA '10: Proceedings of the 28th of the international conference extended abstracts on Human factors in computing systems*, pages 2995–3000, New York, NY, USA, 2010. ACM.

Pictures at an Exhibition: A Physical/Digital Puppetry Performance Piece

Ali Mazalek[1], Michael Nitsche[1], Claudia Rébola[2], Andy Wu[1], Paul Clifton[1], Firaz Peer[1], Matthew Drake[1]
Digital Media[1] & Industrial Design[2]
Georgia Institute of Technology
Atlanta, GA USA
{ mazalek, michael.nitsche, crw, andywu, party, firazpeer, mdrake }@gatech.edu

ABSTRACT
Pictures at an Exhibition is a physical/digital puppetry piece that uses tangible interface puppets to modify a virtual scene projected at the back of the stage in real-time. Telling the story of a heist in an art gallery, the actions of the puppets are digitally reflected in abstract changes to an artwork in the scene. The piece merges traditional puppeteering practices with tangible interaction technologies and virtual environments to create a novel performance for the live stage.

Author Keywords
Performance, physical/digital puppetry, tangible interaction, virtual space.

ACM Classification Keywords
J.5 [Arts and Humanities]: *Performing arts*; H.5.2 [Information Interfaces and Presentation]: User Interfaces—*input devices and strategies, interaction styles*; H.5.1 [Information Interfaces and Presentation]: Multimedia Information Systems—*Artificial, augmented and virtual realities*.

General Terms: Design.

INTRODUCTION
Digital technologies are increasingly shaping novel performance practices [1,2]. Hybrid performance formats are found in traditional theatrical settings as well as in film and video games. For example, *It/I* was a theatre play in which a human character interacted with a computer-driven character on a computer-vision monitored stage [3]. For amusement parks, the Disney attraction *Turtle Talk with Crush* featured live puppeteers backstage controlling an animated performance that unfolds on a large projection screen in a theatre. Movie and TV productions use real-time digital puppetry interfaces (e.g. Waldos®) and motion capture technologies to animate virtual characters during the production process (e.g. for the TV series *Sid the Science Kid*). Finally, video games have adopted virtual puppeteering in titles such as the innovative *Little Big Planet* series and the Microsoft Kinect hardware performance.

C&C'11, November 3–6, 2011, Atlanta, Georgia, USA.
ACM 978-1-4503-0820-5/11/11.

Figure 1. *Pictures at an Exhibition* on stage during XPT 2011 at the Center for Puppetry Arts, Atlanta, GA.

Building on these ideas, our work explores the merger of traditional puppetry with tangible interfaces and virtual environments. In *Pictures at an Exhibition*, five physical puppets equipped with sensors communicate data about their movements to a virtual scene projected at the back of the stage, which changes in response (Fig. 1). The piece is inspired Rybczynski's *Tango,* which uses 36 overlaying loops to build a video performance. Our piece extends this concept into the computational realm. Instead of looping the recorded image, we capture animation data from the puppets during the live performance. This data directly affects the virtual background but can also be looped and layered much like the actions in *Tango*. The virtual space becomes a lasting reflection of the current and past story unfolding in the physical space. The mapping between puppet performance and virtual background is often abstracted but addresses key questions of digital performance that deal with the relationship of the body to the digital realm in hybrid performance pieces.

STORY AND PUPPETS
Pictures at an Exhibition tells the story of a heist in an art gallery, involving a security guard, a cat, a gangster, an old lady and a small boy. The piece is performed to a

specifically composed sound track that uses a different instrument for each character and helps to pace the performance.

All puppets are custom-designed variations on hand and rod style puppets with sensors at key points of articulation to capture expressive movements (Fig. 2). For example, accelerometers capture head movements on some puppets, while bend sensors and rotary potentiometers capture arm movements. The sensors are connected to an Arduino board and XBee, which transmit the data to a computer that controls the virtual space.

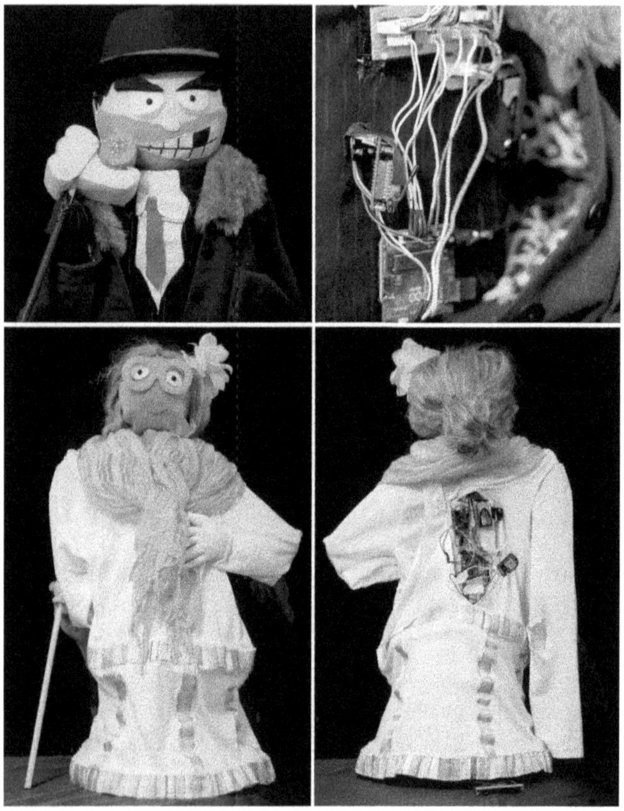

Figure 2. Front view of gangster puppet (top left) and electronics housed under his coat (top right). Front view of old lady puppet (bottom left) and electronics housed in her back (bottom right).

VIRTUAL ARTWORK

According to the setting of the piece (an art gallery), the virtual background consists of a 3D recreation of a famous art piece (Fig. 3). Four different artworks have been adapted for use in the piece: Warhol's *Silver Clouds*, van Gogh's *Starry Night over the Rhone*, Kandinsky's *On White II*, and French's *Summer*. They range from installation to impressionist to abstract art and cover a wide range of representational formats. The artworks were modeled in Maya as 3D scenes and run in the real-time Unity engine. Different mappings of the main characters were created to animate certain elements of each piece, including lights, colors, and movement.

The system reads and stores the animation data collected from the puppets. This can be re-played and looped to allow innovative layering of live and recorded animation. Some puppets can thus perform live on stage and affect the virtual backdrop, while looping animations of other puppets mix with these effects on the artwork.

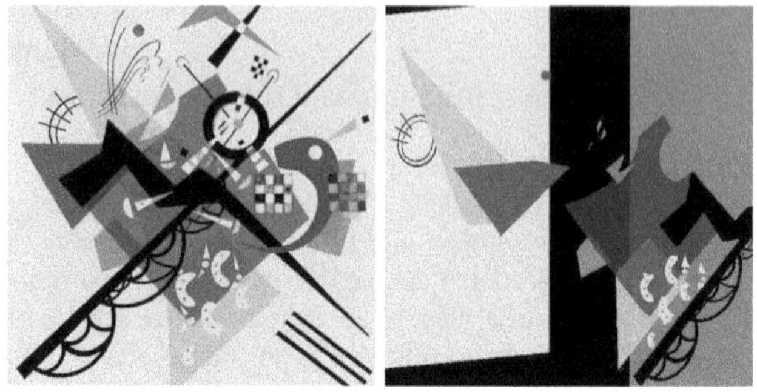

Figure 3. Virtual Kandinsky in the initial state (left) and animated (right).

PERFORMANCE

The tangible interface puppets are performed on a tabletop on stage by five puppeteers (one per puppet). A projection screen behind the table displays the virtual artwork that is altered by the actions of the puppets. To one side of the virtual artwork stands an easel with the physical painting prop that is the focus of the heist in the story. Off-stage, a computer receives data from the puppets and sends these to the 3D engine that drives the animation of the artwork.

The piece was a joint project from classes on experimental media, industrial design, and expressive virtual space and was developed for and performed at the 2011 Experimental Puppetry Theater (XPT) show at the Center for Puppetry Arts in Atlanta, GA.

ACKNOWLEDGEMENTS

We thank the students in our spring 2011 classes at Georgia Tech, our puppeteer collaborators Lee Bryan, Dolph Amick, Mauree Culberson and Lynn Talley, and the Center for Puppetry Arts for their support.

REFERENCES

1. Dixon, S. (2007). *Digital Performance. A History of New Media in Theater, Dance, Performance Art, and Installation.* Cambridge, MA / London: MIT Press.
2. Giannachi, G. (2004). *Virtual Theatres: An Introduction.* London, New York: Routledge.
3. Pinhanez, C., Bobick, A. (2002). "It / I: A Theater Play Featuring an Autonomous Computer Character." *Presence: Teleoperators and Virtual Environments*, 11(5): 536-548.

Being There, Doing It: The Challenge of Embodied Cognition for Design

Jelle van Dijk
Research Centre Technology and Innovation,
Utrecht University of Applied Sciences
P.O. Box 182, 3500AD Utrecht, Netherlands
jelle.vandijk@hu.nl
+31 6 23156597

Joep Frens
Department of Industrial Design
Eindhoven University of Technology
P.O. Box 513, 5600MB Eindhoven, Netherlands
j.w.frens@tue.nl
+312475966

ABSTRACT
This workshop investigates how to apply *embodied situated cognition* to the design for interaction. Participants combine embodied experiences, prototyping and theory. We aim for deep-level linkage of theory and practice by uncovering some of the more complex challenges that embodiment presents in the context of concrete design cases.

Authors' Keywords:
Embodied Cognition, Interaction, Cardboard Modeling.

ACM Classification Keywords:
H.1.2. Models and Principles: User/Machine Systems
H.5.2. User Interfaces: Theory and methods, Prototyping

General Terms:
Design, Human Factors, Theory

INTRODUCTION
In the past 20 years, the cognitive sciences have seen a dramatic shift from explaining cognition in terms of *knowledge*, internally represented and transformed by internal computations, towards understanding cognition as a local, situated and embodied achievement *in action.* 'Embodied and Situated Cognition' (ESC) explains how internal activity and external elements and activities all work in concert to create cognition, allowing for creative, improvisational ways of sense-making. [1,2,5,4,13]

ESC has become popular in cognitive science [3,15], but is not applied in a straightforward manner. Meanwhile, practitioners feel the need for 'embodied' and 'situated' designs [6, 7,11]. Don Norman's 'knowledge in the world' signaled a trend [12], and recent work discussed ESC more explicitly in relation to design [14, 17], culminating in Paul Dourish's seminal work 'Where the Action Is' [8]. Although Dourish's book has been influential, various underlying theories have not become accessible for most designers. Many writings are dense, and the theory's complexities are not easy to apply straightforwardly.

C&C '11, November 3-6 2011, Atlanta, GA, USA.
ACM 978-1-4503-0820-5/11/11.

For example, there is discussion on whether designed artifacts can actually have 'affordances' [9] or whether this term is to be reserved for natural settings. Or consider the idea that human beings develop local, *situated couplings* with artifacts. The question rises what defines the product: it's design, or it's use? [16]? It is not always clear how designers should deal with such issues in concrete projects.

We've seen many 'embodied interaction' concepts passing the scene, but at present a lively conceptual discussion in relation to theory seems to be lacking. Meanwhile, 'embodiment' has become a popular term, e.g. see [10]. This is understandable, with the many new technologies that allow for physical interaction, and the ever increasing role of digital computing in our daily lives. Yet we fear that, beyond catch-phrases, the theory and its consequences for design are often still not properly understood.

OBJECTIVES, APPROACH AND PARTICIPANTS
This workshop offers designers a deeper understanding of the way human beings, designed artifacts and the surrounding environment engage in situated and embodied couplings – and invites discussion of the role of artifacts within those couplings. As designer-researchers, we approach this discussion in a creative, 'designerly' way by combining embodied experiences, hands-on prototyping techniques and theoretical reflections [11]. Concrete design proposals will be designed, presented in the form of lo-fi prototypes and discussed within the theoretical context. The workshop aims to contribute to the further development and firm linkage of embodied theory and design practice.

Figure 1: Prototyping as a reflective design activity

We invite designers, researchers and artists, in particular those working with space, movement, tangible media, augmented reality, or related to participate.

WORKSHOP PROGRAM

The full-day program consists of the following activities:

1. Introduction to Embodied Situated Cognition
2. Experience-objects, activity & reflection
3. Introduction in cardboard modeling (figure 1).
4. Creating & presenting the concept in the form of a lo-fi prototype
5. Reflection, link to theory
6. Group learnings: defining the main challenges for applying ESC to design.

Theoretical introduction: We will discuss some differences between the various flavors headed under the umbrella of embodiment: embodiment in phenomenology, embodied cognition, situated cognition, distributed cognition, and activity theory. Attention is drawn to the difference between 'metaphor-based' embodied accounts, as applied in many 'Tangible Media' systems, where physical objects are designed to represent digital objects, and more 'radical embodied' accounts, where the goal is to design for interactions whose meaning exists 'in action', integrated deeply within people's actual embodied, situated practices.

Experience objects & reflection: We reflect on first-hand experiences of concrete objects and artifacts.

Design Case & Presentation: We apply learnings to a concrete design case of an interactive system supporting an everyday human activity. Teams evolve concepts through explorations in cardboard modeling and present their prototypes.

Reflection, link to theory: After each hands-on assignment we link back to theory and try to integrate our personal experiences with some of the theoretical concepts. Working with- and reflecting on the design assignment we aim to uncover on some of the more challenging (perhaps even problematic) aspects of how to apply ESC in design. Post-conference discussions may be found at www.jellevandijk.org/cc11embodied.

ABOUT THE ORGANIZERS

Jelle van Dijk is currently working on a Phd investigating the application of embodied cognition theory to the design of interactive media systems.

Joep Frens, did a Phd on *rich interaction,* is assistant professor in Industrial Design, and a skilled craftsman in designing and prototyping for embodied interactions.

REFERENCES

1. Anderson, M.L. Embodied cognition: a field-guide. Artificial Intelligence, 149 (1) (2003) 91-130.
2. Beer, R. D. The dynamics of brain-body-environment systems: A status report. In P. Calvo & A. Gomila (Eds.), Handbook of cognitive science: An embodied approach Amsterdam: Elsevier, (2008), 99–120.
3. Calvo P. & Toni G. (Eds). Handbook of cognitive science, an embodied approach. Amsterdam: Elsevier. (2008)
4. Clancey, W. J. Situated cognition: On human knowledge and computer representation. Cambridge, MA: Cambridge University Press. (1997)
5. Clark, A. Being there: Putting brain, body and world together again. Cambridge, MA: MIT Press. (1997)
6. Dijk, J.van, Lugt, R. van der & Overbeeke, C.J. Let's take this conversation outside: supporting embodied embedded memory. *Proc of DPPI09,* Compiegne, France. (2009)
7. Djajadiningrat, J.P., Wensveen, S.A.G., Frens, J.W. and Overbeeke, C.J. Tangible products: redressing the balance between appearance and action. Personal and Ubiquitous Computing, 8(5), (2004) 294-309. Dourish, P.. Where the Action Is: The Foundations of Embodied Interaction. Cambridge, MA: MIT Press. (2001)
8. Dourish, P. Where the Action Is: The Foundations of Embodied Interaction. Cambridge, MA: MIT Press. (2001)
9. Gibson, J.J. The Ecological Approach to Visual Perception, Houghton Mifflin, Boston (1979.)
10. Hornecker, E. (2011) The role of physicality in tangible and embodied interactions. *Interactions. 18*(2), 19-23.
11. Hummels, C.C.M., Overbeeke, C.J., Appleby, R.S., Frens, J.W. & Wensveen, S.A.G. (2008). The power of embodiment for design and vice versa. Form + Zweck, 22, 6-11.
12. Hutchins, E.. Cognition in the wild. Cambridge: MIT Press (1995)
13. Norman, D. A. (1988). The Design of everyday things. New York: Basic Books.
14. Robertson, T. Cooperative Work and Lived Cognition: A Taxonomy of Embodied Actions. In: Proc Fifth ECCSCW Dordrecht: Kluwer Academic Publishers (1997), 205-220.
15. Robbins, P. & Adydede, M. (Eds.) The cambridge handbook of situated cognition. New York: Cambridge University Press. (2009)
16. Steen, M. Human-centred design as a fragile process. *Design Issues*. Forthcoming.
17. Suchman, L. Plans and Situated Actions. Cambridge: University Press (1987)

Beyond the Binding: Exploring the Future Book

Natalie Freed
Jie Qi
MIT Media Lab
20 Ames St.
Cambridge, MA
{natfreed,jieqi}@mit.edu

Cristina Sylla
engageLab
University of Minho,
Guimarães
sylla@engagelab.org

Pedro Branco
Dept. of Information Systems/
engageLab
University of Minho,
Guimarães
pbranco@dsi.uminho.pt

ABSTRACT
We have reached a special moment in the story of the book: today's youngest generation will experience literature in a vastly different way than the generation preceding. What we call a book has always morphed over time, but digital capabilities and the ubiquity of mobile electronics are changing the landscape at an unprecedented pace. This workshop will be a forum for creative exploration and discussion of the future of the book, motivated by this particular historical moment and a desire to bring together researchers from diverse backgrounds who are working on book-related technologies. We will share and document visions, approaches, and techniques.

Author Keywords
Interactive Books, Augmented Reality, Augmented Books, Digital Manipulatives, Tangible Interfaces.

ACM Classification Keywords
H.5.m. Miscellaneous.

General Terms
Design, Human Factors.

INTRODUCTION
While the move to electronic book readers has been predicted for a long time, the past few years have truly demonstrated widespread adoption. These readers preserve the portable form factor and readability of bound printed pages while adding the ability to access any book at any time and features such as sharing and linking. The Internet now makes it possible to instantly obtain reference information that used to be accessible only through a collection of encyclopedia volumes and reference books. Much of children's fiction experience has moved online to interactive story-worlds and e-books. Finally, many people are reading stories and referencing information on general- purpose mobile devices such as phones and tablets.

Given this move to digital, interactive and interconnected media, we seek to examine how the traditional paper and page based book has evolved in the hands of designers and creators, and delve more deeply into where it could be taken in the future.

C&C'11, November 3–6, 2011, Atlanta, Georgia, USA.
ACM 978-1-4503-0820-5/11/11.

BACKGROUND
This workshop seeks to examine not only the book artifacts themselves, but also approaches, techniques, and the creative process around developing new book technologies. Designers and technologists have explored books from many angles and with a variety of purposes, only a small fraction of which can be touched on here.

One approach has been to preserve the aesthetic and emotional experience of reading a book while augmenting it with new technological capabilities. For example, the Listen Reader books take the physical form of traditional books, but allow readers to play narrative-related music and sounds by turning pages and tapping on printed pictures [1]. Here, actions normally done in the process of reading a traditional picture book are also read as electronic inputs for interactivity.

Researchers are also developing specific techniques for using traditional book form factors and materials in the context of modern technology; for instance, through embedding soft sensors and electronics on paper [3,5]. An example is Electronic Popables, a paper book that integrates traditional pop-up mechanisms with thin, flexible, paper-based electronics [7].

Some have taken a hybrid approach to blending dynamic digital information with physical books: the PhoneBook is an interface that integrates a phone screen into a traditional paper book, allowing users to interact with the story by tapping and swiping the display [6]. The MagicBook uses printed fiducials to incorporate augmented reality and virtual reality elements [2]. Finally, D-TOK is a storytelling book that reads physical cards at tokens for characters and actions which sent to a screen, so that a story unfolds as the cards are placed into the book [9]. In these, though the physical book form is present, actions associated with digital devices are introduced, thus transforming the experience of the book.

Many others shift away from the book form factor altogether but maintain the essence of page-based storytelling. These reading experiences are augmented with new ways to manipulate narratives, especially in ways that allow readers to create the story as it is read. For example Tink-R-Book is a touchscreen-based program that allows users to proceed in the narrative page by page while manipulating pieces of the story itself [4].

Finally, some designers take the reverse approach by analyzing the affordances of paper and books to leverage them in completely different contexts. For example, Rosner et al examine normal interactions with books to distill principles for designing technology [8].

CALLS FOR SUBMISSION

We are looking for creative explorations that preserve, reinvent, or repurpose the functions and affordances of the book. What forms will the spirit of "book" take many years from now? We encourage participants to think broadly about the question. A submission could serve a function that books have historically served but does not necessarily look like a book. It could look, feel, and function like a book but serve an entirely different purpose. It could explore creative approaches to expanding the definition of what a book could be. We encourage the submission of materials showcasing prototyped concepts and works-in-progress.

OBJECTIVES

The objectives of the workshop are as follows:

Bring together researchers from diverse disciplines to share ideas, techniques, and approaches.

Suggest directions for the research on book technology.

Produce a collection of book idea exemplars.

WORKSHOP STRUCTURE

The workshop will be divided into three sessions. First participants will present their book projects in a show-and-tell fashion. Next, to set a context for discussion, organizers will show a historical overview of the book and the more recent timeline of interactive books. Finally, participants will break into groups around proposed topics, which include hands-on technique learning, discussion groups for deeper exploration, or paper prototyping around specific areas of interest.

ABOUT THE ORGANIZERS

Natalie Freed is currently a researcher in the Personal Robots group at the MIT Media Lab. Her work centers on creating technology for children that leaves room for redefinition and user participation in the design process. Jie Qi is currently researching in the High-Low Tech group at the MIT Media Lab, where she blends electronics with traditional crafts with the goal of empowering traditional users of technology to become its creators. Cristina Sylla is currently a researcher at engageLab/ University of Minho where she works on the design of new learning materials that combine traditional pedagogical materials with embedded digital technology. Pedro Branco is Assistant Professor in the Department of Information Systems at the University of Minho, where he is currently director of the Masters Course in Technology and Digital Art.

ACKNOWLEDGEMENTS

This work is inspired by Fine Bookbinding Meets Electronics, held in collaboration with Daniela Rosner, Hannah Perner-Wilson and Leah Buechley [10]. It is also partially funded by "FEDER through the Operational Competitiveness Factors Programme - COMPETE and by National Funds through the FCT –Portuguese Foundation for the Science and the Technology within the Project: PTDC/CPE-CED/110417/2009, and the Doctoral Grant: SFRH / BD / 62531 / 2009.

REFERENCES

1. Back, M., Cohen, J., Gold, R., Harrison, S., Minneman, S. (2001), Listen Reader: An Electronically Augmented Paper- Based Book, in Proceedings of SIGCHI'01, ACM Press, 23-29.
2. Billinghurst, M., Kato, H., & Poupyrev, I. (1991), MagicBook: transitioning between reality and virtuality, in Proceedings of CHI '91, ACM Press.
3. Buechley, L., Hendrix, S., Eisenberg, M. (2009), Paints, paper, and programs: first steps toward the computational sketchbook, in Proceedings of TEI'09, ACM Press, 9–12.
4. Chang, A, & Breazeal, C. (2011). Tink-r-books. http://robotic.media.mit.edu/projects/robots/tinkrbooks/t inkrbooks.html
5. Coelho M., Hall, L., Berzowska, J. and Maes, P. (2007), Pulp- Based Computing: A Framework for Building Computers Out of Paper, in Proceedings of Ubicomp'07.
6. Mobile Art Lab. (2008), PhoneBook. http://mobileart.jp/phonebook_en.html
7. Qi, J., Buechley, L. (2010), Electronic popables: Exploring paper-based computing through an interactive pop-up book, in Proceedings of TEI'10, ACM Press 121-128.
8. Rosner, D. K., Oehlberg, L., Ryokai, K., (2008) Studying Paper Use to Inform the Design of Personal, Portable Technology." In Extended Abstracts of CHI'08. Work In Progress Submission.
9. Sylla, C., Branco, P., Coutinho, C., Coquet, E., Skaroupka, D. (2011), TOK - A Tangible Interface for Storytelling, in Proceedings of CHI '11, ACM Press, 1363-1368
10. Rosner, D., Perner-Wilson, H., Qi, J., & Buechley, L. (2011). Fine bookbinding meetselectronics. In *Proceedings of TEI '11*, ACM Press, 345-348.

Semi-Automated Creativity: Software as a Creative Collaborator

Jimmy Secretan
Korrelate
215 Celebration Place
Suite 150
Celebration, FL 34747
jimmy@korrelate.com

Author Keywords
Computer Supported Creativity; Artificial Creativity.

ACM Classification Keywords
I.2.0 ARTIFICIAL INTELLIGENCE: General.

General Terms
Design, Human Factors.

Extended Abstract

Creativity support tools are important to professionals and amateurs alike. Typically, these tools abstract away the mundane details of creative design to allow the user to focus on her creative process. However, emerging techniques in data mining, machine learning, and artificial intelligence all have the potential to enhance the efficiency, productivity, accessibility and usability of these tools. Leveraging these techniques, creativity support tools are poised to move from the role of an assistant carrying out chores for the user to a role as a creative collaborator.

The proliferation and importance of creativity support tools has never been so evident as it is now, with millions of Internet users generating creative works through image, sound and video editing software. At the same time, engineers leverage a different set of tools to design and engineer structures, electronics and cities (using a different, but no less valid mode of creativity). It is the aim of these tools, in the words of Ben Shneiderman, to have "more people, more creative, more of the time" [1].

At the same time, research into machine learning and artificial intelligence has accelerated in recent years, with industrial and academic organizations advancing both algorithms and applications in the field. Artificial Intelligence (AI) research has created systems capable of varying degrees of natural language understanding, game playing, planning, and problem solving. Machine learning (ML) and data mining techniques, including neural networks, genetic algorithms and support vector machines (SVM), have been leveraged to process audio and visual streams as well as large knowledge bases. All of these technologies have the potential to support the creative design of the user, not only in assuming mundane tasks that are seen to impede the creative process, but also to aid in the search for creative solutions.

In the past few years, several applications have emerged that have sought to elevate the role of software in the creative process. MySong [2] (now Songsmith) generates accompanying music to singers by mining databases of existing music. It substitutes the complexity of the song writing process with a few simple controls, which affect the parameters of the ML models responsible for generating the songs. In doing so, it empowers novices to participate and stokes the professionals' creativity in the song-writing process. Picbreeder [3] is a large scale, Internet-based experiment in Collaborative Interactive Evolution (CIE). It allows a user to evolve images by selecting ones that she likes, employing an evolutionary algorithm to produce the next generation. When the user is satisfied with her image after several generations, she can then publish it to the site, where other users can "branch" that image, thus copying it and continuing its evolution. This process begets a collaborative cycle of branching and publishing, resulting in a proliferation of interesting images. It too can serve as a tool to empower amateurs and inspire professionals. Both of these applications are indicative of a trend in using advanced machine learning technologies to augment the creative process, and they will hopefully encourage future development in this area.

Applications like these can force us to rethink our traditional models of how creativity works. The *Geneplore* model of creativity [4], for instance, bifurcates

C&C'11, November 3–6, 2011, Atlanta, Georgia, USA.
ACM 978-1-4503-0820-5/11/11.

creative thought into two frequently interleaving phases, *Generation* and *Exploration*. But how is the creative process changed when one of these phases is externalized to a piece of software, as in Picbreeder? Social models of innovation will also be impacted by the availability of these new tools. How will creative collaboration be affected when it can happen on an Internet-wide scale, or with one or more intelligent agents in the mix? Our already nascent models of the creative process will have to take these mechanisms into account to build a truly comprehensive understanding of creativity.

Creativity support tools will have numerous opportunities in the future to take advantage of AI, ML and data-driven techniques. Word processors may offer natural language processing and data mining techniques to help alleviate writer's block. CAD tools may employ evolutionary algorithms to suggest sound design alternatives that the designer may not have considered. And students may flesh out creative ideas using intelligent, interactive agents. Building these kinds of applications will require intensive, innovative and cross-disciplinary research. But considering the importance of creative endeavor in driving our society forward, the benefits will surely outweigh the costs.

References

1. Shneiderman, B., "Creativity Support Tools: Accelerating Discovery and Innovation," *Communications of the ACM*, Vol. 50, No. 12, December 2007.
2. Simon, I., Morris, D., Basu, S., "MySong: Automatic Accompaniment for Vocal Melodies," Proc. CHI 2008, Florence, Italy, April 5-10, 2008.
3. J. Secretan, N. Beato, D.B. D'Ambrosio, A. Rodriguez, A. Campbell, K.O. Stanley, "Picbreeder: Evolving Pictures Collaboratively Online," Proc. CHI, Florence, Italy, April 5-10, 2008, pp. 1759-1768.
4. Finke, R.; Ward, T. B. & Smith, S. M. (1992). *Creative cognition: Theory, research, and applications*. MIT Press.

The Intersection of Poetry and Design

Erin L. Beatty
Lancaster University
Lancaster LA1 4YF UK
e.beatty@lancaster.ac.uk

ABSTRACT

Despite parallels between the structure of poetry composition and design tasks, no research has explored these correspondences to better understand the skilled behaviour in these two domains. In Study 1 expert poets were interviewed about their creative practices and a thematic analysis was conducted comparing these practices to key findings concerning the nature of design expertise. In Study 2, poets wrote poems while completing a 'think aloud' protocol and in Study 3 award winning expert poets were interviewed in light of the findings of earlier studies. The results were examined in regards to: (1) the role of "sources of inspiration" [4] in contextualizing activity and informing the creation of novel solution ideas; (2) the involvement of "primary generators" [3] in scoping tasks to core objectives; and (3) the nature of self-questioning and the role that questions take in forming solutions.

Author Keywords

Creativity, inspiration, poetry composition, design theory, primary generator.

ACM Classification Keywords

H.1.m. Models and Principles: Miscellaneous.

General Terms

Design, Experimentation, Theory.

INTRODUCTION

People are capable of incredible feats of creativity, yet our understanding of the processes by which these creative acts occur remains limited (see [7] for a theories of creativity overview). Poetry's neglect as an area of research is surprising given its status as a key domain of creative expression from antiquity to the modern day. Most of our current knowledge about the nature of poetry writing derives from autobiographical accounts written by experts [2]. It is critical to validate and extend insights derived from these reports through in-depth empirical analyses of the imaginative processes of expert poets.

Existing empirical studies of poetry writing tend to adopt an educational perspective, focusing on how *novices* write poetry. For example, Groenendijk, Janssen, Rijlaarsdam, and Van den Bergh examined the writing processes of students to determine the impact of their writing processes on the final poems [5]. Their results indicated that production in the beginning of the session, and revision toward the end of the session, was associated with better quality poetry, whereas pausing and early revision had a negative effect. Most other poetry research centres on how students read and interpret poetry. The difficulty of poetry composition derives from its' ill-defined nature. Ill-defined problems are those where the goals are vague, where the optimal solution is unknown, and where the limitations of the problem space are not fully specified [9]. Poetry writing seems to exemplify this definition, with the poet typically starting from a point where they have uncertain goals, unclear constraints, and multiple actions that allow progression toward a final result. Poetry composition is most certainly an ill-defined problem in the same way that innovative design is typically conceived [1] [8] [9]. The overlap between poetry composition tasks and design tasks in term of their lack of definition is useful from a research perspective since it suggests that some common processes may underpin activity in both domains. The goal of the current research was to examine the design processes that occur in poetry composition looking for areas of overlap with design and areas unique to poetry.

C&C'11, November 3–6, 2011, Atlanta, Georgia, USA.
ACM 978-1-4503-0820-5/11/11.

Study 1

Five poets were interviewed on the topics of: inspiration, motivation, writing process, editing, and working with other writers and mentors. The results of this study focus on two orienting themes which have relevance in the context of expert poetry composition: (1) the possible role of "sources of inspiration" [4] in contextualizing poetic activity and in informing the creation of novel solution ideas; (2) the potential involvement of "primary generators" [3] in scoping the poetry-writing task in terms of core solution-oriented objectives. These themes derive from a wealth of design research conducted in the past few decades.

All the poets that we interviewed seemed to be heavily inspired by one common factor, which related to what was "familiar" to them and, thereby, in some sense what was "mundane" (e.g., daily experiences, family circumstances and personal conflicts). The commonality across the poets was striking, and shows that the familiar was also what they were passionate about as acknowledged by the poets when they explained successful poetry makes the audience "feel" something, and the best way to embody emotions within the poem is to feel something yourself about the writing.

In relation to the role of primary generators and solution focused processing in poetry composition, there seemed to be a wealth of evidence supporting the poets' tendencies to find an early way into the poem via a key objective or concept that paved the way toward subsequent solution exploration. Most of the poets commented on developing their poems from an initial idea or from a "first line" that had come to them. One poet spoke of the first line becoming redundant by the end of the writing process because the poem was now "saying" what had been originally inspired by the first line. This observation seems to validate the role of such primary generators in providing the poet with a platform to frame their subsequent exploration of a topic in a conjectural manner while providing a way to manage the complexity of the poetry writing task. Solution-focused behaviour and the conjectural aspect of poetry writing seems to reveal itself in the dominant role that revision plays in the process, with the poets describing revision as something that they needed to do as well as an aspect of the process that they enjoyed.

Study 2

Study 2 was a laboratory-based study of eight expert poets who wrote two poems while verbally reporting their thoughts using a 'think aloud' technique followed by an interview. The results of the study indicated that initial idea generation was quite associative and often related to items or instances that were close in proximity and/or time. Once an idea was selected another search was conducted around that idea and during this stage an initial line was produced. This first line was greatly influential to the progress of the poem. When writing was ongoing the poets seem to engage in self-questioning behaviour in response to writing blocks.

Initial exploration of the writing cues focused on rejecting available cues. This could reflect attempts to frame and restrict the problem space. Two poets commented on the quantity of cues and the lack of concrete specificity of some cues (i.e., love and a memory). Participants were strongly motivated to frame the task in such a way as to make it achievable given the time constraints. Participant 2 had a strong single anchor for their writing task and that was their idea of a child's drawing. This parameter was successful as they produced a full draft during their time.

Consistent with the concept of primary generators in design the present results seem to substantiate the findings of study 1 indicating that lines produced early on in the writing process tend to act in a highly generative manner, shaping how the poem is then developed. Moreover, such initial lines appear to remain in the poem relatively intact and unrevised. The poet seemed to make use of a single primary generator - a child's drawing of a house. A surprising finding was the use of sketching by one poet. The sketch appeared completely spontaneously and was closely connected to the insight into the writing problem. The direction of the entire exercise changed as a result of the idea that occurred while they were sketching for a 'lack of something else' to do. Sketching has a long history of investigation within the design literature [6]. We are interested to see if sketching allows for thought exploration that is not sufficiently formalized so as to be verbalized aloud. Though the hypothesis is supported here, only further study can determine if it holds beyond this case.

Study 3

Four national award-winning poets were interviewed about their creative process to investigate of the observed trends in the previous studies with high calibre poets.

In summary, these findings underline key parallels between design activity and poetry composition: first, the importance of problem framing and exploration; second, the use of primary generators; and third, the use of sketching. The presence of these three design-oriented processes in poetry composition suggests that they may be general aspects of creative endeavour for producing novel and valued outputs. These areas certainly warrant further research and I am currently building up the sample with the intention of being able to generalize conclusions when they are drawn from a larger number of individuals.

ACKNOWLEDGMENTS

Thank you to Dr Linden Ball, the Poets, the European Union Marie Curie Framework 7, and the National Science and Engineering Research Council of Canada.

REFERENCES

1. Ball, L.J., Evans, J.St.B.T., Dennis, I., and Ormerod, T.C. Problem-solving strategies and expertise in engineering design. *Thinking and Reasoning, 3* (1997), 247-270.
2. Curtis, T. (ed.). *How Poets Work*. Seren/Poetry Wales Press Ltd, Bridgend, Wales, 1996.
3. Darke, J. The primary generator and the design process. *Design Studies, 1* (1979), 36-44.
4. Eckert, C., and Stacey, M. Sources of inspiration: A language of design. *Design Studies, 21* (2000), 523-538.
5. Groenendijk, T., Janssen, T., Rijlaarsdam, G., and Van den Bergh, H. How do secondary school students write poetry? How creative writing processes relate to final products. *Educational Studies in Language and Literature, 8* (2008), 57-80.
6. Purcell, T. and Gero, J. 'Drawings and the design process: A review of protocol studies in design and other disciplines and related research in cognitive psychology', *Design Studies, 19* (1998), 389-30.
7. Runco, M. *Creativity - Theories and Themes: Research, Development, and Practice*. Academic Press, New York, 2007.
8. Simon, H.A. *The Sciences of The Artificial, Third Revised Edition*. MIT Press, Cambridge: MA, 1999 (Original work published in 1969).
9. Simon, H.A. The structure of ill structured problems. *Artificial Intelligence, 4* (1973), 181-201.

Investigating the Effects of Bimanual Multitouch Interaction on Creativity

Allen Bevans
School of Interactive Arts & Technology
Simon Fraser University Surrey
250 – 13450 102nd Avenue
Surrey, B.C. Canada V3T 0A3
allen_bevans@sfu.ca

ABSTRACT
Creativity is an important but difficult cognitive process to study. Recent findings from cognitive neuroscience suggest that inter-hemispheric interaction (the interaction of opposite brain hemispheres facilitated by the corpus callosum) is an important factor influencing creative output. We propose that bi-manual multitouch interaction may improve creative output because manipulating digital objects (an integral part of computer-supported creativity tasks) with two hands may facilitate inter-hemispheric interaction. This paper briefly describes the development of a computerized form of the Alternate Uses Task, a standardized creativity assessment tool, used in an exploratory study (n=65) investigating this theory.

Author Keywords
Input methods, multitouch, bimanual, comparative studies, divergent thinking, creativity.

ACM Classification Keywords
H5.2. User Interfaces: Input devices and strategies, J.4 Social and behavioral sciences.

General Terms
Design, Human factors.

INTRODUCTION
A significant body of work in psychological research has been devoted to developing a clearer understanding of the influences and outcomes of human creativity. While it is acknowledged that human creativity is expressed in a great variety of behaviors and contexts, specific creativity theories and measurable constructs have clarified the relationships between specific mental phenomena and creative output (see [5] for an overview). These theories and the instruments used to investigate them provide a rich foundation for exploring the effects of human-computer interaction on creative performance.

Recent findings linking changes in inter-hemispheric interaction (or IHI; the interaction of opposite brain hemispheres facilitated by the corpus callosum) to increased creative performance [15] suggest that interface designs and interaction methods which alter IHI could boost creative performance for users. In [15], bilateral eye movement (the movement of both eyes back and forth horizontally in sync) was used to alter IHI in study participants, which is thought to have led to the increase in creative performance in the context [15]'s study. Our research investigates whether the bimanual movements afforded by large multitouch displays could have a similar effect on users' creativity.

C&C'11, November 3–6, 2011, Atlanta, Georgia, USA.
ACM 978-1-4503-0820-5/11/11.

Bimanual and multitouch interfaces have been active areas of research within HCI since the early 1980's [1, 13], and have recently seen a resurgence of research interest, mostly attributable to technical innovation [9, among many others]. However, relatively little research investigating the effects of these interface technologies on user cognition (vs bio-mechanical performance) has been conducted [see 14 and 11 for notable exceptions]. Beyond specifically investigating the effects of bimanual multitouch interaction on creative performance, we hope to foster a discussion around further research into the cognitive aspects of using emerging interaction technology such as multitouch.

Our study design includes the development of a computerized form of the Alternate Uses Task, a standardized creativity assessment tool, used in a comparative study of three interface styles: unimanual mouse interaction, unimanual multitouch interaction, and bimanual multitouch interaction.

THEORETICAL BACKGROUND
In order to measure creative performance, [15] had participants complete the Alternate Uses Task (AUT) [3], which measures a person's ability to generate alternate uses for everyday objects. The specific creativity construct the AUT measures is a mental strategy called *divergent thinking* [7]. Divergent thinking consists of mental operations that produce multiple novel solutions to a problem. It is important to note that divergent thinking is not the same thing as creativity, but is a key mental strategy used in creative thought and behavior. Within HCI, divergent thinking has been examined within groupware contexts [8, 4] and in evaluating how information discovery may be supported by using image and text compositions as surrogates in representing information collections [12]. High performance on the Alternate Uses Task has been shown to correlate with creativity in the "real world" [16].

We use an experimental design closely modeled on [15] in order to assess the creative performance of participants using unimanual mouse-driven, unimanual multitouch, and bimanual multitouch interfaces with a computerized version of the AUT.

Our goal is not to determine if one interface style is "better" than another, or to establish our computerized version of the AUT as creativity-enhancing software – instead, we are primarily concerned with investigating the underlying psychological and physiological mechanisms that may boost creative thinking when augmented by bimanual multitouch interaction.

THE ALTERNATE USES TASK
The Alternate Uses Task is traditionally administered via paper and pencil. Participants are asked to generate novel uses for a set of 15 everyday objects (see [15] for the list) and given one minute per object to write down their alternate uses. In [15], participant

responses are scored along five dimensions: Appropriateness, Detail, Fluency, Originality, and Flexibility. Readers are encouraged to refer to [2] or [15] for a more detailed discussion of this scoring regimen.

RESEARCH INSTRUMENT

To facilitate the investigation of the effects of computer interfaces on divergent thinking using the Alternate Uses Task, we have created a computerized version of the AUT. The computerized AUT displays the name of an object from the AUT object list, as well as a 3d model of that object, which can be rotated and resized. Each interface style maps the rotate and resize functions uniquely to match the affordances of each interaction technique, as outlined in Table 1.

Table 1. Interaction specifics for the rotate and resize function of the AUT software.

AUT Function	Unimanual Mouse	Unimanual Multitouch	Bimanual Multitouch
Rotate	Click and drag mouse	Touch and drag on screen	Touch two fingers on screen and drag them in the same direction
Resize	Scroll up or down on mouse scroll wheel	Touch two fingers on screen and pinch together or apart	Touch two fingers on screen and move them closer or further apart

The Alternate Uses Task software differs from the traditional administration of the AUT in three significant ways: first, participants are shown a 3d representation of the object along with the name and normal use of the object. Second, participants are encouraged to manipulate the 3d representation of the object while they generate new uses for it. Third, participants are asked to speak aloud their new uses as they generate them, rather than writing them down (the traditional AUT method for recording responses).

The software handles audio recording through an external microphone, allowing us to record the participant's verbal responses while they interact with the software. Previous research [6] has found no difference in AUT performance due to verbal overshadowing (i.e. think-aloud responses are not measurably different than written responses). In order to ensure that participants do not passively view the object model and name while generating alternate uses, the session facilitators should continually prompt participants to interact with and explore the model as they generated alternate uses.

Experimental sessions using the computerized AUT (implemented in PyMT [10]) have been run with 65 participants, with 22 participants for both the mouse and bimanual multitouch conditions, and 21 participants for the unimanual multitouch condition. Analyzing responses to the computerized AUT involves transcribing the audio recordings of participants saying aloud their alternate uses for each of the 15 AUT objects. In our experiment, this translates to 975 minutes (or 16 hours and 15 minutes) of audio. These transcribed responses then are scored by multiple judges according the scoring criteria previously outlined here before they can be statistically analyzed for comparison between conditions. We are currently completing the scoring of the transcribed responses, which prevents a detailed statistical comparison of our experimental data from appearing here. Support for this research has also been provided by SSHRC.

REFERENCES

[1] Buxton, W., Myers, B. 1986. A study in two-handed input. SIGCHI Bulletin. 17, 4, 321-326.

[2] Chamorro-Premuzic, T., Reichenbacher, L. 2008. Effects of personality and threat of evaluation on divergent and convergent thinking. Journal of Research in Personality, 42, 4, 1095-1101.

[3] Christensen, P. A., Guilford, J. P., Merrifield, P. R., and Wilson, R. C. 1960. Alternate uses. Beverly Hills: Sheridan Psychological Services.

[4] Farooq, U., Carroll, J. M., and Ganoe, C. H. 2005. Supporting creativity in distributed scientific communities. In Proc. GROUP 2005, ACM Press (2005), 217-22.

[5] Fink, A., Benedek, M., Grabner, R.H., Staudt, B., Neubauer, A.C. 2007. Creativity meets neuroscience: Experimental tasks for the neuroscientific study of creative thinking. Neurocognitive Mechanisms of Creativity 42, 1, 68-76.

[6] Gilhooly, K.J., Fioratou, E., Anthony, S.H., Wynn V. 2007. Divergent thinking: strategies and executive involvement in generating novel uses for familiar objects. British Journal of Psychology 98, 4, 611-625.

[7] Guilford, J.P. 1967. The Nature of Human Intelligence, McGraw-Hill, New York.

[8] Hailpern, J., Hinterbichler, E., Leppert, C., Cook, D., and Bailey, B. P. 2007. TEAM STORM: demonstrating an interaction model for working with multiple ideas during creative group work. In Proc. C&C 2007, ACM Press (2007), 193-202.

[9] Han, J.Y., 2005. Low-cost multi-touch sensing through frustrated total internal reflection. In Proc UIST '05, ACM Press (2005), 115-118.

[10] Hansen, T., Hourcade, J. P., Virbel, M., Patali, S., and Serra, T. 2009. PyMT: a post-WIMP multi-touch user interface toolkit. In Proc. ITS 2009, ACM Press (2009), 17-24.

[11] Hinckley, K., Pausch, R., Proffitt, D., Kassell, N.F. 1998. Two-handed virtual manipulation. ACM TOCHI 5, 3, 260-302.

[12] Kerne, A., Koh, E., Smith, S., Choi, H., Graeber, R., Webb, A. 2007. Promoting emergence in information discovery by representing collections with composition. In Proc. C&C 2007, ACM Press (2007), 117–126.

[13] Lee, S.K., Buxton, W., and Smith, K.C. 1985. A multi-touch three dimensional touch-sensitive tablet. In Proc. CHI '85, ACM Press (1985), 21-25.

[14] Leganchuk, A., Zhai, S., Buxton, W.1998. Manual and cognitive benefits of two-handed input: an experimental study. ACM TOCHI 5, 4, 326-359.

[15] Shobe, E.R., Ross, N. M., and Fleck, J.I. 2009. Influence of handedness and bilateral eye movements on creativity. Brain and Cognition, 71, 3, 204-214.

[16] Torrance, E.P. 1988. Creativity as manifest in testing. In R.J. Sternberg (Ed.). The nature of creativity: contemporary psychological perspectives. Cambridge: Cambridge University Press.

Getting a Picture of Your Thoughts: Interactive Visualization for Creative Work

Marius Brade
Chair of Media Design, Technische Universität Dresden
01062 Dresden, Germany
marius.brade@tu-dresden.de
+49 351 463 37927

ABSTRACT
Creative work – especially in business – is often connected to highly complex data. While current software tools support manifold areas in working with complex data, they are very limited to support creative work. Little research has been done on what kinds of representations are supporting the externalization of mental efforts in the best way. Especially it is very challenging to give abstract mental concepts an appropriate representation. This doctoral research is creating and investigating novel approaches combining visualizations, interaction concepts and memory techniques to create design guidelines for interactive visualizations for creative work. First experiments have been conducted and the key principles are implemented partially in a prototype called BrainDump.

ACM Classification Keywords
H.5.2. Information interfaces and presentation: User Interfaces – Theory and methods

General Terms
Design, Experimentation, Theory

INTRODUCTION
Creative business work – such as decision making, problem solving, or planning – faces a continuous change between analysis and synthesis. This interdependent process has been coined *reflection-in-action* [p.21, 6]. Neither structure nor amount of data needed during this process is known in advance. A given task is incrementally structured and is subject to highly dynamic change. This results in conflicting goals: on the on hand as little effort as possible should be necessary for creating visualization patterns for creative work, while on the other hand the model should be as much expressive as possible.

The majority of current software tools imply that the goal of a task is clearly specified and the steps towards the solution are known in advance [4]. Thus the interaction is determined by the systems architecture and data constraints. This approach hinders the creative process in its early phase, what makes traditional materials such as whiteboards, pen and paper still most attractive for creative workers. Available software tools focus on displaying and modifying content. Thereby the structure of the mental state of a creative task exists only in the user's mind. However, internal mental representations perform poorly on reflecting upon them or making sense of complex and rich object relations or associations. Consequently, there is a need for well designed external representations that can support this process [5]. The aim of this doctoral research is to identify principles for the visualization of the structure of mental images and connections. As a result these findings shall lead to design guidelines for interactive mnemonic visualizations for creative work. These guidelines are identified through the development and evaluation of experimental setups and prototypes, which are based on initial requirements:

- Task based interaction: the interaction with the system should require as little cognitive effort as possible from the user. "People should learn the task, not the technology".
- Providing an overview: flexible visual shaping of the structure of the ideas, associations and mental concepts should be supported. Important information should be visually prominent.
- Modifying the overview: it should be possible to directly modify the overview (reflection-in-action) while it is being created.
- Flexible (re-)structuring of information: because of the constant dynamic changes, important information can be less important in a next step and vice versa. Thus focus and significance of information needs to be adapted in a dynamic way.
- History: the single steps of the creative process should be saved for later reuse and reflection.

INITIAL EXPERIMENT: THE EXPLORE TABLE
Experiments for inspiration on interface design were conducted using a self-made table setup called eXplore Table [2]. This setup uses a glass plate for the interaction with physical substances. Cameras were filming the experiments from the top and bottom of the glass. Participants had to use real physical substances such as rice, plasticine or eggs. Through their daily life, people have a natural way of interacting with those substances. For instance: plasticine is formed and rice is pushed. This is fundamentally different to the widely spread and dominant

C&C'11, November 3–6, 2011, Atlanta, Georgia, USA.
ACM 978-1-4503-0820-5/11/11.

paradigm of mouse and keyboard interaction. Touch-sensitive devices like touch-pads have no need for the cursor-hand-eye detour like desktop systems. Data can be shaped directly by hand. The participants were given the task to imagine that the physical substances on the table setup are like digital data. With these they should perform basic interactions like linking, separating, copy and paste, erasing and creating. Two main goals are pursued with these experiments:

- Visualization: Learning from nature and finding principles for optimal design of visualizations.
- Interaction: Identifying affordances for different substances to interact with them.

The filmed experiments and examples of the first digital prototypes can be seen in a video summary [2].

CASE STUDY: BRAINDUMP

Bringing the observed flexibility of changing fluid structures together with the idea of doing research in the internet, we created a first prototype named BrainDump [1]. The focused type of task is information gathering during web browsing sessions. While performing such a task, the structure and amount of required data is not known in advance. The system provides the possibility to create and manipulate visual images of mental connections in a dynamic way. This is done easily via one single step of interaction. Therefore the focus is on the user's creative work without being distracted by figuring out how to use the system. Further features are: keeping the links' entire information, i.e. source data, annotate content, and hierarchically group collected items. A first user test with 9 participants was designed and conducted, showing that participants understood the purpose of BrainDump completely. All of them would like to use the application more often in their daily work. Participants especially appreciated the easy way to visually change relations and associations between information [1]. An advanced follow-up version of the prototype for multi-touch interaction will be implemented on a tablet-pc.

FIRST CONCLUSION AND FUTURE WORK

In creative business work, problem analysis and solution synthesis are fundamentally interdependent. As they are alternating constantly, information structure is not predefined but changing in a highly dynamic way. It is essential for users to keep track of their mental efforts through visual externalization and to be flexible in changing the shape and structure of this visualization. The next challenge will be to identify implicit affordances for interaction of objects which can be transferred into rich interaction patterns. Since it might be hard for test participants to report on their own mental processes, it will be a further step to analyze methods for measuring results of such processes [3] using BrainDump or similar tools. Participants have already been filmed and asked questions using the first prototype of BrainDump.

Design guidelines for interactive visualization for creative work beyond mouse and keyboard will be derived using these results together with knowledge about affordances of objects for interacting as well as the conclusion of measuring the results of thought processes.

BIOGRAPHY

Marius Brade is a Ph.D. candidate in Media Design at the Chair of Media Design, Department of Computer Science at Technische Universität Dresden in Germany. His PhD program is a specific co-operation between industry and academia. The partner from industry for his research is the User Experience Research Practice at SAP Research. Before starting his doctoral study, Marius obtained a Diploma in Media Computer Science from the Technische Universität Dresden (2009). Next to his studies Marius attended several courses at the Academy of Fine Arts in Dresden. During his studies he developed a deep interest in how people think and memorize information.

ACKNOWLEDGMENTS

The author would like to thank his mentors and advisors Rainer Groh and Angelika Salmen for their valuable support. This doctoral research (contract no. 080951799) is funded by the European Social Fond and the Free State of Saxony as well as SAP Research.

REFERENCES

1. Brade, M., Heseler, J. and Groh, R. An Interface for Visual Information-Gathering During Web Browsing Sessions: BrainDump – A Versatile Visual Workspace for Memorizing and Organizing Information. Proceedings of the Fourth International Conference on Advances in Computer-Human Interactions (Le Gosier, France, 2011), 112-119.
2. Brade, M., Kammer, D., Keck, M. and Groh, R. Immersive Data Grasping Using the eXplore Table. Proceedings of the Fifth International Conference on Tangible, Embedded, and Embodied Interaction (Portugal, 2011), ACM Press, 419–420. Video: http://www.youtube.com/watch?v=ygAq8JHGtvM
3. Kerne, A., Smith, S.M., Koh, E., Choi, H. and Graeber, R."An Experimental Method for Measuring the Emergence of New Ideas in Information Discovery." Taylor & Francis. International Journal of Human-Computer Interaction. Issue 5, 2008, Volume 24, 460-477.
4. Nakakoji, K., Yamamoto, Y., Takada, S. and Reeves, B.N. Two dimensional spatial positioning as a means of reflection in design. Proceedings of ACM DIS '00. ACM, 2000, 154.
5. Russell, D., Stefik, M., Pirolli, P. and Card, S. The cost structure of sensemaking. Proceedings of ACM CHI '93. New York: ACM, 1993, 269-276.
6. Schön, D. A. The reflective practitioner: How professionals think in action. Basic Books, New York, 1983.

Convergence of Self-Report and Physiological Responses for Evaluating Creativity Support Tools

Erin A. Carroll
HCILab
University of North Carolina at Charlotte
Charlotte, NC, USA
e.carroll@uncc.edu

ABSTRACT

Creativity is a fuzzy, complex concept with a wide range of definitions and theories. Since there is no single agreed upon methodology for recognizing and evaluating creativity, this makes it particularly difficult to evaluate how well a creativity support tool (CST) supports the creativity of a user. My dissertation will be concerned with evaluating CSTs through the development of new quantitative metrics and methodologies. In this paper, I discuss research plans for my dissertation, which includes both existing work and new directions for my research.

Author Keywords

creativity support tools, creativity evaluation, physiological measures, self-report

ACM Classification Keywords

H.5.2 Information Interfaces and Presentation: User Interfaces—*Theory and methods*

General Terms

Human Factors

INTRODUCTION

The NSF Workshop on Creativity Support Tools (CSTs) addressed many critical issues surrounding CSTs, including evaluation [7]. The consensus was that: "A family of evaluation techniques [...] must be brought to bear in order to converge on the key issues involved in the study of Creativity Support Tools." The report also notes that CSTs should be evaluated using a mixed-methods approach, combining both quantitative and qualitative metrics.

There is much value to be found in taking a qualitative approach, as it often provides deep insight into the CST being studied, yet the analysis of this approach is often time consuming. Quantitative metrics offer equal value in evaluating CSTs, and these metrics are often easier to interpret through statistical methods. Many quantitative metrics for CSTs borrow heavily from metrics that are common to the evaluation of productivity software, such as time and error metrics and self-report surveys. Time and error measurements are rarely appropriate for evaluating CSTs. Based on our experiences with artists, choreographers, and dancers, we have observed that when something appears to be an 'error' in a creative task, it often turns into a serendipitous opportunity for the user. When users spend significant time on a creative task, it likely indicates immersion, rather than poor tool support. As for survey metrics, most are borrowed from other domains, or are metrics designed for assessing constructs like usability. While measurements from other domains may be useful to some degree, they are not beneficial for assessing the ability of a CST to support a user's creativity.

RESEARCH PLANS

Creativity Support Index

My first endeavor in evaluating CSTs was through the development of the Creativity Support Index (CSI), which is a survey metric specifically designed for evaluating CSTs. A preliminary version of the CSI was presented at Creativity & Cognition '09 [2], but a new version with supporting reliability measures is now being finalized. This new version is based on data collected from over 90 participants. The CSI, presented as 12 agreement statements, is made up of 6 factors that measure creativity support. These factors are: Results Worth Effort, Exploration, Collaboration, Immersion, Expressiveness, and Enjoyment. The survey also includes a paired comparison section, where each factor is compared against every other factor to determine which factors are most relevant. This generates weightings which are used in the final calculation of creativity support.

Physiology

It is a widely held position that emotion is represented by arousal and valance [3]. In work with my advisor, we measured people's autonomic nervous system arousal using galvanic skin response (GSR) to capture audience engagement, and this was presented to performing arts experts (Figure 1) [5]. We also gathered temporal self-report ratings of engagement using physical sliders, which resulted in correlations to support a relationship between physiological arousal and conscious engagement. Given our success in measuring audience responses, I intend to apply physiological measures to the evaluation of CSTs.

C&C'11, November 3–6, 2011, Atlanta, Georgia, USA.
ACM 978-1-4503-0820-5/11/11.

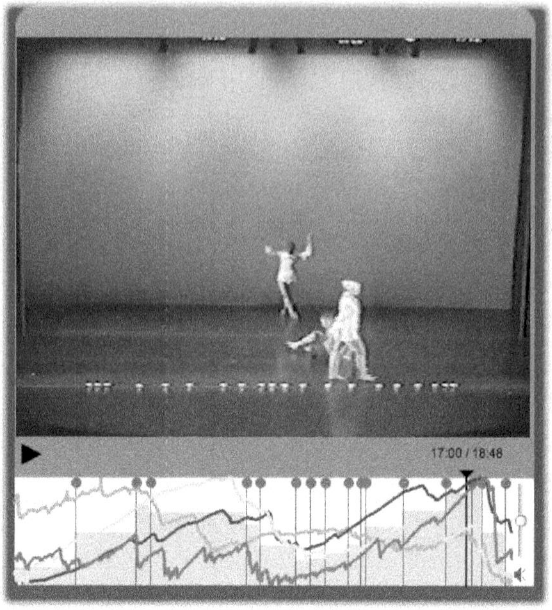

Figure 1. A custom tool built to allow performing arts experts to investigate audience members' physiological responses to performance.

A large body of research exists in neurophysiological creativity, where there are several accepted relationships between arousal and creativity, like 'creative' people having higher overall arousal than 'non-creative' people [6]. An explanation of this phenomenon is that creative people are able to defocus their attention, whereas non-creative people focus too much and spike their arousal. My future work will evaluate CSTs by looking at this relationship, while also looking at creativity and other extracted EEG features.

'In-the-Moment' Creativity

My most recent work includes the investigation of 'in-the-moment' creativity (ITMC), which is a temporal measure of the creative work process. The motivation behind capturing ITMC is that it enables investigation of the creative process during CST use – from creative inspiration to elaboration – and it also allows sources of creative interruption to be studied (e.g. frustration, mental overload, etc.). Accurately capturing ITMC, while challenging, has the potential to revolutionize creativity research.

In a recent study, we investigated ITMC by triangulating multiple sources of data [1]. We had participants watch screen recordings of sketches they drew using a digital tool and graphics tablet, and we built a tool that allowed them to retrospectively indicate moments in their sketching activity when they were being creative. While they sketched, we captured physiological responses using GSR and EEG. We also brought in external judges to watch the same screen recordings and rate each person's ITMC in order to see assess the validity of the self-reported ITMC ratings. Our preliminary analysis suggests that people and judges are reliably able to rate ITMC and that relationships exist between creativity and physiological responses.

RESEARCH CHALLENGES

There are several research challenges involved in the evaluation of CSTs. The most difficult challenges are related to validity issues and the scope of the work. The validity concern is whether we are measuring creativity or some other construct. Scope is also challenging because CSTs are found across a wide variety of domains, thus findings from a study in one domain may not apply to a different domain.

BIOGRAPHICAL SKETCH

Erin Carroll is a third year PhD student in the College of Computing and Informatics at the University of North Carolina at Charlotte. Before beginning her doctoral degree, she obtained a B.S. in Psychology and Cognitive Science (2008). Erin's research is concerned with evaluating creativity support tools using quantitative metrics and methodologies. To this end, she developed a survey metric called the Creativity Support Index for evaluating creativity software. Erin also had two related publications accepted at CHI 2011, which involve technology, performing arts, and physiological measurements [4, 5].

ACKNOWLEDGMENTS

This work was funded by an NSF CreativeIT grant (#IIS-0855882). I would also like to thank my advisor, Dr. Celine Latulipe, for all her support and encouragement.

REFERENCES

1. E. A. Carroll and C. Latulipe. Capturing 'in-the-moment' creativity through data triangulation. In *Proceedings of ACM Creativity & Cognition 2011*, 2011.
2. E. A. Carroll, C. Latulipe, R. Fung, and M. Terry. Creativity factor evaluation: Towards a standardized survey metric for creativity support. In *Proceedings of ACM Creativity & Cognition*, 2009.
3. P. J. Lang. The emotion probe: Studies of motivation and attention. *American Psychologist*, 50(5):372–385, 1995.
4. C. Latulipe, E. A. Carroll, and D. Lottridge. Evaluating longitudinial projects combining technology with temporal arts. In *Proceedings of ACM CHI 2011*, 2011.
5. C. Latulipe, E. A. Carroll, and D. Lottridge. Love, hate, arousal, and engagement: Exploring audience responses to performing arts. In *Proceedings of ACM CHI 2011*, 2011.
6. C. Martindale. *Handbook of Creativity*, chapter Biological Bases of Creativity. Cambridge University Press, 1999.
7. B. Shneiderman, G. Fischer, M. Czerwinski, M. Resnick, B. Myers, L. Candy, E. Edmonds, M. Eisenberg, E. Giaccardi, T. Hewett, et al. Creativity support tools: Report from a US National Science Foundation sponsored workshop. *International Journal of Human-Computer Interaction*, 20(2):61–77, 2006.

Gesture Modeling - Improving Spatial Recognition in Architectural Design Process

Chih-Pin Hsiao
College of Architecture
Georgia Institute of Technology
Atlanta, GA 30332 USA
chsiao9@gatech.edu

ABSTRACT
In this paper, we discuss the role of spatial cognition during the architectural design activity, and how it affects design creativity. Recognizing that current CAD applications' Windows-Icon-Menu-Pointer (WIMP) user interfaces do not fully support creative exploration in modeling geometries for design, we design a prototype system that incorporates a regular pc and a depth camera for gestural input. We present the implementation and use scenario of the system, and discuss why gestural input may advance creativity in the design process.

Author Keywords
Cognition, Computer Supported/ Mediated Creativity, Creative Process, Design, Embodied Interaction, Gesture Input

ACM Classification Keywords
H.5.2 [Information Interfaces and Presentation]: User Interfaces.

General Terms
Design, Human Factors

CREATIVITY IN DESIGN PROCESS
Spatial cognition in architectural design, involving the understanding of design forms, space functions and relationships between spaces, is one of the most challenging activities in the early architectural design process. It helps architects to discover problems associated with the contextual environment, which are ill-defined and difficult to be specified [1]. Usually, a skillful architect can infer proper mental representations from external representations, such as simple sketches or draft models to quickly discover design problems. The spatial cognition of an external representation could also stimulate new and unexpected design ideas and as a result, improve their designs. These new ideas usually came from an analogy-making process in which they may compare other cases in their minds to the external representations to improve their designs [2]. Thus, external representations can be at least partially inspired by their previous experiences. The experiences here could be in the form of any sensory inputs, such as visual, auditory, tactile, or even the motion in a space.

C&C'11, November 3–6, 2011, Atlanta, Georgia, USA.
ACM 978-1-4503-0820-5/11/11.

THE BODY IN OUR MINDS
Among the senses mentioned before, vision and motion are two senses most closely related to spatial cognitions. Many researchers have discussed the influences of visual/external representations during the design process. Because we have to experience the spaces, inspect drawings, and construct physical models through our eyes, there is no doubt that visual processing plays important role in spatial cognitions [3]. Another important factor of spatial cognition is the perception of motion in space. Johnson states, "*our understanding is our mode of being in the world*", and thus "*we are meaningfully situated in our world through our bodily interactions*" [4]. For building a physical model in the traditional design activities, architects rely on moving and modifying pieces of materials in different sizes and locations. All these interactions with physical objects or spaces require body awareness.

There have been many projects that employ the motions as the way of input when directly manipulating computer models, such as Gesture Modeling [5]. Some researchers also utilized hand motions to describe geometry for non-professionals [6]. Due to the ability of exchanging data and parameterizing model that a CAD system requires, we borrow some ways of creating geometries in the current modeling applications with the motion inputs in our proposed prototype.

SYSTEM DESCRIPTION
In our first implementation, we employ SketchUp as the host program with a plug-in for controlling geometries and navigating the cameras because SketchUp adopts many metaphors from our physical environments, such as push/pull, and drawing right on surface. The prototype supports users to use both hands to directly manipulate the geometries by representing the locations of users' two hands on a screen. When a hand "touches" an existing shape, the system will give visual feedbacks according to the gestures.

In the hand gesture part, each hand plays a different role. For example, the left hand serves as a 2-D reference plane in the 3-D space to let the right hand draw shapes on it. The drawing gesture for right hand is "Pointing" (frame C of Figure 1). This gesture allows users to draw any shape. After the camera detect the points of the right hand gesture, the host computer will recognize them as basic geometric shapes, such as rectangles, triangles, circles, and polygon shapes. These basic shapes could become the profile shapes for 3-D manipulations. In this version of the prototype, we implemented several fundamental 3-D modeling behaviors, such as extrude, scale, and Boolean operations.

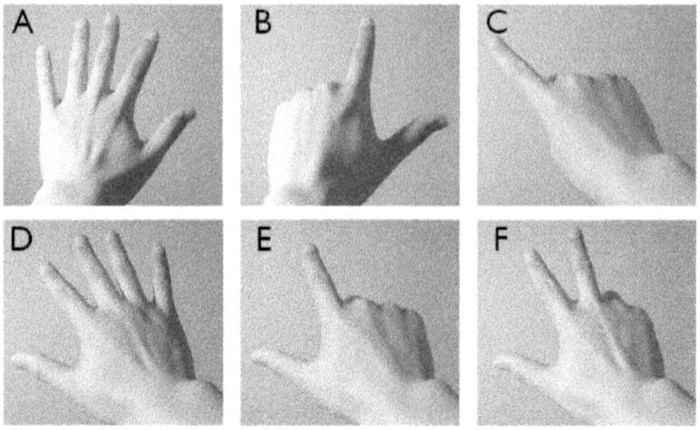

Figure 1. Basic Gestures in the Prototype System

Since the concepts of these modeling commands are actually based on our physical environment, we could let users perform some basic gestures, such as pulling for extruding in frame F of Figure 1, pinching for scaling by combining frame B and frame E of Figure 1, and grabbing for moving geometry by using right hand shown in frame D of Figure 1. Instead of only executing the commands by showing these gestures, the spatial information for these gestures is also detected by depth camera so that the system can know how far the user is pulling in scale, and toward which direction.

IMPLEMENTATION

In order to build the prototype, we employ a depth camera, Microsoft Kinect sensor for recognizing hand gestures and 3-D locations, and a host computer with a screen for computer vision analysis and visual feedback generations. There are two software components: (1) analyzing image stream from the device and (2) generating the geometry representations. In the first part, we adopt OpenNI as the middleware for natural interaction library, and OpenCV for analyzing each image frame. The former software library helps us to detect hand locations and managing image streams from the device. The depth camera can generate the regular RGB frames as well as depth raw data in 30 frames per second. The depth raw data not only gives the distance from the camera to objects in each pixel, but can also produce grey-scale images. These grey scale images are used for recognizing hands and fingers to produce the meaningful gestures in our prototype system. When the software in the first part recognizes the movements and gestures, the program in the second part will execute certain actions, such as generating a 3-D shape, or moving the scene or a shape.

In this program, we have two separated views for users to get the visualization feedback. One is a regular view for showing the perspective window, and the other one is to show a 2-D top view of the current scene.

We believe that these two views give designers the enough contextual information so that designers can imagine the spatial conditions in front of them.

In the navigation part, we simply restrict the view camera of the system on a fix height in order to reduce the complexity. For panning, users simply perform the gesture "Five" (Frame A of Figure 1) on a left hand and move their hand around. For rotating the view camera, users need to use their both hands to perform "Five" gestures and make a movement like a circle. The view will rotate in accordance with the center of the circle they perform. For zooming in and out, users have to perform "Gun" (Frame B and E of Figure 1) gesture on both hands. The scale of zoom is according to the distance between two hands.

DISCUSSION

This prototype system creates a new way of generating computer geometries for designers. Even though designers cannot create precise shapes in this system, they can use their hands freely to create shapes according to their imaginations and spatial perceptions. This prototype system adopts the movement of both hands to control the pushing/pulling, scaling, and panning/rotating view. These movements provide additional perceptions that the traditional modeling system couldn't provide. We are planning user studies to understand how these movements affect users' spatial cognition.

ACKNOWLEDGMENTS

I thank my advisor, Ellen Yi-Luen Do, and members of ACME Lab at Georgia Institute of Technology for giving me insightful feedback and suggestions.

REFERENCES

1. Eastman, C. M. Cognitive Processes And Ill-Defined Problems: A Case Study From Design, In *Proc. the International Joint Conference on Artificial Intelligence*, (Washington, DC, 1969), 671-690.
2. Boden, M. A. The Creative Mind: Myths and Mechanisms. Weidenfeld & Nicolson, London, 1990.
3. Logie, R. H. Visuo-Spatial Working Memory. Lawrence Erlbaum Associates, East Sussex, UK, 1995.
4. Johnson, M. The Body In The Mind. The University of Chicago Press, Chicago, 1987.
5. Gross, M. D. and Kemp, A. J. Gesture Modelling - Using Video to Capture Freehand Modeling Commands. In *Proc. CAAD Futures 2001*. (Eindhoven, The Netherlands). CUMINCAD, 33-46.
6. Holz, C. and Wilson, A. Data miming: inferring spatial object descriptions from human gesture. In *Proc. CHI 2011* (Vancouver, BC, Canada). ACM, 811-820.

Haptic Interaction Study and Application to Haptic Mobile Design for Online Communication

Hae Youn Joung
School of Industrial Design
Georgia Institute of Technology
247 4th St Atlanta, GA 30332, USA
joannejoung@gatech.edu

ABSTRACT

This study explores how individuals communicate emotions using tactile hand gestures and investigates the usability of applying tactile hand gestures for emotional online communication. Tactile hand gestures are used as the source of information to express emotions in distance communications. In this study, behavioral aspects of tactile hand gestures used for emotional interaction are observed through a sensory input device and analyzed using analysis of variance (ANOVA). In user experiments, subjects perform tactile hand gestures on the sensory input device to illustrate a list of 8 distinct emotions (i.e. excited, happy, relaxed, sleepy, tired, lonely, angry and alarmed). An analytical method is used to classify gestures in terms of signal parameters such as intensity, temporal frequency, spatial frequency and pattern correlation. I found that different emotions are statistically associated with different tactile hand gestures. From the research outcome data, I also introduce the design of online emotional communication devices that aim to mimic natural tactile hand gestures used in the face-to-face communication.

Author Keywords

Tactile hand gesture recognition, haptic interface, tactile communication device, and human computer interaction

ACM Classification Keywords

H.5.2 Information Interfaces and Presentation (e.g., HCI): User Interfaces

General Terms

Design, experimentation and human factors

INTRODUCTION

Touch, central to emotional communication, is the simplest and the most straightforward of all sensory systems [1]. The sense of touch is also capable of communicating and eliciting emotions [2]. Tactile gestures exhibit the natural capability and tendency of humans to move their hands to express and communicate emotions. In particular, in emotional communication, tactile hand gestures arouse human emotions through touch.

C&C'11, November 3–6, 2011, Atlanta, Georgia, USA.
ACM 978-1-4503-0820-5/11/11.

My research focuses on the study of tactile hand gestures for the use in affective online communication and on its application to wearable mobile design. I am interested in determining how emotions affect different parameters of tactile hand gestures and how I can code different emotions with tactile hand gestures in devices for online communication. The aim of this study is to better understand the relationship between hand gestures and emotions, especially those performed with fingers. Finally, I apply research results to designing a prototype tactile communication device that enables gesture-to-emotion conversion for the emotional interaction between people in distance through a new media and show how it can be used in online communication.

APPROACH

To analyze the emotion-gesture relationship, I obtain tactile hand gesture signals by asking 60 participants to express their emotions while holding and interacting with a wearable tactile user interface device as shown in Fig. 1. The device imitates the shape of a human arm so that the experimental subjects perform their hand gestures to express their emotions in the same way as they do on human arms, such as pinching, dragging, shaking and squeezing.

Figure 1. Developed wearable tactile interface device facilitating touch sensor arrays.

STUDY OF TACTILE HAND GESTURES

In this research, tactile hand gestures are used as the source of information to get to emotions. Behavioral aspects of tactile hand gestures being used for emotional interaction are observed through a sensory input device, wearable tactile interface device, and analyzed using a model-based analysis tool. In user experiments, the subjects perform tactile hand gestures on the sensory input device in the response of a list of distinct emotions based on Russell's dimensional model of emotions (i.e. excited, happy, relaxed, sleepy, tired, lonely, angry and alarmed) [3]. I obtain tactile hand gesture signals by asking participants to express their emotions while they are holding and interacting with the wearable tactile interface device. The participants were asked to perform tactile hand gestures on the interface device in response to the distinct emotions. The interface device records tactile hand gestures exerted on the device in terms of signal parameters such as strength, duration, temporal and spatial frequencies, and relative direction. Distinct tactile hand gestures are determined by a combination of these six signal properties. I analyze the recoded hand gestures and their corresponding emotions using a statistical analysis method called analysis of variance (ANOVA) to find the statistical relationship between the participants' emotions and their tactile hand gestures. The study results showing the relationship between the two are summarized in terms of a look-up table to be used in potential applications for online emotional communication device as shown in Table 1.

	Intensity		Temporal Freq.		Spatial Freq.		Pattern	
	μ	σ	μ	σ	μ	σ	μ	σ
Excited	0.41	0.11	2.7	0.90	1.8	0.81	0.19	0.13
Happy	0.17	0.16	2.3	0.69	1.4	0.72	0.21	0.12
Relaxed	0.052	0.024	0.50	0.40	1.7	0.58	0.26	0.19
Sleepy	0.049	0.030	0.31	0.20	1.4	0.44	0.29	0.18
Tired	0.054	0.044	0.31	0.17	1.3	0.62	0.24	0.19
Lonely	0.074	0.040	0.37	0.21	1.5	0.54	0.34	0.19
Angry	0.53	0.21	1.3	0.55	2.1	0.55	0.23	0.18
Alarmed	0.39	0.15	3.1	0.67	2.2	0.69	0.19	0.12

μ : Mean σ: Standard Deviation

Table 1. Mean and standard deviation of tactile gesture.

In the mapped table, I find that the emotional state of angry, alarmed, excited and happy, which correspond to high arousal and displeasure according to Russell's model of emotions [3], are related to tactile signals of high intensity and temporal frequency. The results also show that the emotional state of relaxed, sleepy, tired and lonely that contain to low arousal emotions correspond to tactile signals of low intensity and temporal frequency. Particular patterns such as linear and circular patterns are shown in low arousal states of emotions to express their emotions such as lonely, sleepy, tired and relaxed.

APPLICATION TO DESIGN

In this research, the types of tactile hand gestures are categorized in terms of tactile signal properties and related to distinct emotions that the gestures originate from. The findings from this investigation show opportunities and promises to use tactile hand gestures for the communication of emotions among people using online digital communication devices at a distance. From user experiments, I found that different emotions are statistically associated with different tactile hand gestures. The relationship between touch hand gestures and emotions is applied to emotional online communication devices and a prototype design of wearable online tactile emotion communication devices is demonstrated as shown in Fig 2. The prototype is suggested to wear on sender and receiver's wrest to communicate and share their emotions daily and seamlessly with those who are closely related in somebody such as husband/wife, girlfriend/boyfriend and mother/child. As the first prototype, a wearable tactile communication device called Tactile Bracelet is proposed. Five sensors, five motors and their LED indicators are connected with a digital controller (Arduino) as shown in Fig 2. Depending on how much pressure is applied to the pressure sensor by the sender, the vibration motor gives strong or gentle vibration to the receiver. All motors and sensors are connected with electronic threads.

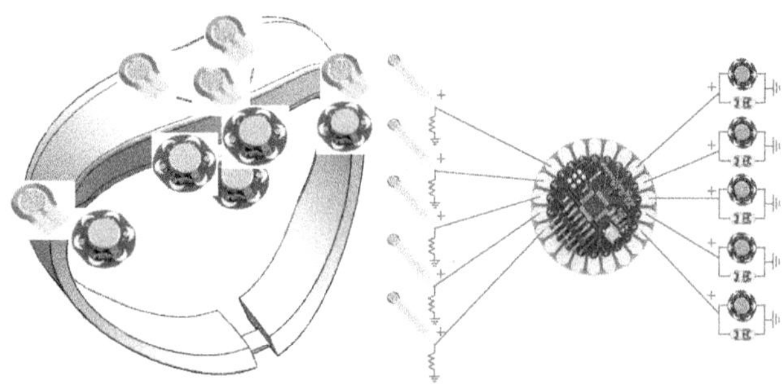

Figure 2. Tactile Bracelet: a wearable tactile communication device for sharing emotions using tactile hand gestures.

The sender and the receiver, who are closely related with each other such as husband-wife, boyfriend-girlfriend and mother-child, share emotions using the proposed tactile device at a distance. They wear Tactile Bracelets on their wrist and share emotions by applying their natural tactile hand gestures to the device as they use them in face-to-face communication. The sender device recognizes the user's gestures through pressure sensors that are placed on the surface of the device and transmits the emotion information embedded in the acquired gesture data to the receiver. The receiver device accepts the gesture information and generates the corresponding tactile gesture using motors vibration. For the prototype, I used vibration motors to generate tactile gestures. However, In the future, the gesture generation will be enhanced to implement more natural feeling of soothing, touching and squeezing.

REFERENCES

1. Geldard, A. Some neglected possibilities of communication. Science, vol. 131, (1960), 1583--1588.
2. Wolff, H. Observations on the early development of smiling. In: B.M. Foss (Ed.), Determinant of infant behavior II, London: Methuen & Co (1963), 113--138.
3. Russell, A. A circumflex model of affect. Journal of personality and social psychology Vol. 34 (1980).

Bridging the Design Time – Use Time Divide: Towards a Future of Designing in Use

Monica G. Maceli
Drexel University, College of Information Science and Technology
3141 Chestnut St, Philadelphia, PA 19104 USA
Monica.Maceli@drexel.edu

ABSTRACT

Meta-design theory emphasizes that future use can never be entirely anticipated at design time, as users shape their environments in response to emerging needs; systems should therefore be designed to adapt to future conditions in the hands of end users. In our increasingly complex technological environments, tomorrow's meta-designers must be able to anticipate the environment in which the end users will work in order to provide the flexibility for users to craft their tools. By exploring and projecting forward current trends in technology use, I have identified key principles for meta-designers and suggest that using them as design heuristics will aid meta-designers in crafting systems for future end-users. My doctoral research aims to validate and critique these meta-design principles.

Author Keywords

Design, meta-design, creativity, heuristics, context.

ACM Classification Keywords

H5.m. Information interfaces and presentation (e.g., HCI): Miscellaneous.

General Terms

Design

INTRODUCTION

At one time, design and use were closely entwined activities: *human crafters* designed tools through use and there was no distinctly separate design process. As technology advanced, industrialization introduced a divide between the goals of the setting of design (design time) and the setting of use (use time). Design time focused on experts creating a completed design artifact, while use time was oriented towards gradual user-driven evolution and change, responsive to environment and context. This tension between what could be accomplished at design time and what unpredictable situations the system would encounter during use has been an ongoing challenge to the evolving field of HCI.

When environments of use were constrained to the workplace, our early HCI methodologies could strive to match known work tasks with suitable interfaces; this *human factors* approach focused on the line between man and machine and the interfaces that afford interactions between the two. In the 1990s, when technology moved into the home and into more complex environments of use and practice, HCI methodologies began to take a broader view of interaction, supporting *human actors* who controlled the technologies used in their daily lives [2]. Our current HCI methodologies and theories are largely oriented towards this "human actors" relationship between technology, users, and use.

C&C'11, November 3–6, 2011, Atlanta, Georgia, USA.
ACM 978-1-4503-0820-5/11/11.

However, recently developed technologies have allowed for complex and shifting contexts of use [4] as well as empowered users to design their own technological environments. Novel means of information and technology production (e.g. open source software development, mash-ups, commons-based peer production [3]) have radically changed the technological landscape. Users are again behaving as *human crafters* – controlling, designing, and developing not only their relationships with technology, but the very form and function of this technology.

My dissertation research, which is currently in progress, seeks to understand *how we should design for a world that is increasingly full of human crafters*. Specifically, I seek to derive useful heuristics from key literatures and perspectives supporting systems that evolve in the hands of their users over their entire lifespan, exploring them first in a controlled laboratory setting and then on real-world design problems.

DESIGNING IN USE

Designing-in-use, by end-user "human crafters", is poorly supported by our current design methodologies which distance designers, both in time and space, from future scenarios of use and future users. The highly complex environments of use, consisting of rapidly evolving technologies and new means of information production, require a new focus for design activities. Earlier literature has focused on the requirement for design activities to continue throughout the life of the system [7], yet many of the issues raised remain unsolved. Technology has become malleable – often lightweight and able to be shaped, combined, and modified in use by real-world users. This behavior, however, is often poorly supported by our traditional design methods.

Fischer [5] suggests addressing these challenges by moving towards a future of *meta-design*, which emphasizes participatory co-design throughout the life of the system. Meta-design describes a future state of design consisting of open systems that evolve during use, with design activities redistributed across time and levels of interaction with the environment. The framework emphasizes that the design of socio-technical systems must support flexible and evolving systems, that are not (and cannot be) completely designed before use, and that evolve in the hands of their users.

Principles for Designing in Use

However, meta-design currently offers little practical guidance for designers creating tools for future end-users to craft their technological environments. The series of principles that follow, inspired by key literature in the area, intend to focus designer creativity on the core motivations and resulting modifications that may be desired by future end-user "crafters".

Principle #1: Connect with other people with similar needs and interests, both nearby and far away

John Thackara's [9] design frameworks emphasize the increasing importance of systems that allow people to connect and communicate both locally and across the boundaries of time and space.

Principle #2: Reach out and converse with other people in real-time, while they are using the system.

Prior research [e.g. 6] has explored the value of supporting spaces for reflective use-time conversations between designers and users, and users and users.

Principle #3: Combine it with other tools and systems they use regularly.

Theoretical frameworks such as distributed cognition [8] describe the intensely combinatory and situated nature of real-world use and problem solving.

Principle #4: Begin using it quickly, without a lot of help or instruction.

Christopher Alexander's unselfconscious culture of design [1] requires systems users can understand quickly and then contribute to confidently.

Principle #5: Tailor it to their personalized needs.

Henderson and Kyng's [4] early writings on designing in use identified tailorability as essential to systems supporting users acting as designers.

RESEARCH METHODS

The proposed principles for designing in use are currently being evaluated in a series of experiments testing the ability of the principles to serve as guidelines to focus and encourage design-time idea generation, in both a laboratory and real-world setting. The laboratory study will explore the main effects of the guidelines and end-user participation in a 2x2 between-subjects factorial design. In a real world setting, the guidelines will be used in an iterative design exercise with an existing websites' design team and several end-users. The end-users will be asked to keep diaries of desired changes while they are using the web-based system in the context of their daily lives. Preliminary results show that the guidelines are well-understood and often-referenced in design ideation exercises by both trained designers and end-users. A more in-depth analysis, to follow, will explore the quality of the ideas generated and critique the guidelines and their applicability to real world design activities.

CONCLUSION

The principles for designing in use are currently being validated and critiqued in a series of experiments. The experiments will explore how meta-design can help frame and inform the design of future meta-design systems, empowering users to shape their technology tools in use.

REFERENCES

1. Alexander, C. *Notes on the synthesis of form*. Harvard University Press, Cambridge, MA, USA, 1964.
2. Bannon, L. 1992. From human factors to human actors: the role of psychology and human-computer interaction studies in system design. In *Design at work*, Joan Greenbaum and Morten Kyng (Eds.). L. Erlbaum Associates Inc., Hillsdale, NJ, USA 25-44.
3. Benkler, Y. *The Wealth of Networks*. Yale University Press, New Haven, CT, USA, 2006.
4. Bødker, S. When second wave HCI meets third wave challenges. In *Proc. NordiCHI 2006*, ACM Press (2006), 1-8.
5. Fischer, G., and Giaccardi, E. 2006. Meta-Design: a framework for the future of end user development. In *End User Development*, Lieberman, H., Paternò, F., Wulf, V. (Eds.). Springer, Dordrecht, 427-458.
6. Fischer, G., Lemke, A. C., Mastaglio, T., and Mørch, A. I. 1990. Using critics to empower users. In *Proc. CHI 1990*, ACM Press (1990), 337-347.
7. Henderson, A. and Kyng, M. 1992. There's no place like home: continuing design in use. In *Design at work*, Joan Greenbaum and Morten Kyng (Eds.). L. Erlbaum Associates Inc., Hillsdale, NJ, USA 219-240.
8. Hutchins, E. *Cognition in the Wild*. MIT Press, Cambridge, MA, USA, 1995.
9. Thackara, J. *In the Bubble: Designing in a Complex World*. MIT Press, Cambridge, MA, USA, 2005.

Mind and Method: An Examination of Cognitive Activities in the Design Process

Amy Mattingly
Graduate Student
Colorado State University
Department of Design & Merchandising
Fort Collins, Colorado
amy.mattingly@colostate.edu

ABSTRACT

The creative process is a multifaceted and dynamic path of thinking required to execute a project in design-based disciplines (i.e., interior design, architecture). This research seeks to better understand the creative design process by investigating design student experiences during the course of a two week chair design project assignment. This study used an exploratory design to collect data from student demographic information, journal responses, and creative product results. The project deliverables were reviewed by external evaluators to identify level of creative output. High and low level output groups were identified and compared according to demographic data and journal responses. Grade point averages, transfer credits, and total credit hours were higher for the high creativity group in addition to evidence of higher levels of abstract thought and greater divergent thinking. Students in the high creativity group also demonstrated increased depth in thought and higher motivation throughout their creative process.

Author Keywords

Creativity, education, design process, creative output, creative process.

ACM Classification Keywords

A.0 Conference Proceedings

General Terms

Design, Performance, Verification.

INTRODUCTION

Entry level designers search for, and often require a competitive edge in seeking employment. Increased understanding of students' creative processes could enhance student preparation by more effectively teaching and preparing students in demonstrating creative thinking and production of creative output. A challenge is to concretely identify decision-making patterns distinguishing creative problem solutions from those simply solve the problem.

C&C'11, November 3–6, 2011, Atlanta, Georgia, USA.
ACM 978-1-4503-0820-5/11/11.

In this research, attention was focused on connections between process and product, and identifying differences and similarities in processes which result in creative products.

Purpose of the Study

The purpose of the study is twofold; to connect actions with outcomes to determine a best fit sequence for creative problem solving; and to test a proposed conceptual creative process model drawn from Amabile's (1996) Components of Creativity (motivation, creativity relevant skills, domain experience).

METHODOLOGY

The researcher examined contemporary and seminal design process models to understand the number of distinct stages conceptualized and the taxonomy between analysis and synthesis. From the review a new model was formulated which integrated the respective components of creativity within each proposed stage-*Analysis, Generation, Testing,* and *Reflection*. This study sought to examine the proposed model by uncovering subjective experiences, processes, and actions taken by a cohort of fourth year interior design students during a two-week design project consisting of a chair design and production of an accompanying design process board and scaled model. As a qualitative study employing an explorative case study framework (Creswell, 2009; Stake, 1995), data was collected from student records, reflective journal responses to pre-determined electronic prompts, and an external evaluation of the final outcome of the process.

Of 36 students enrolled in the course, 20 students both signed a letter of consent and completed each of the four journaling prompts within the required 24 hours provided for each intervention. Only participants who submitted within the 24 hour time frame for all four interventions were included. Timing of responses was important as participants who submitted their responses later had more time to reflect upon their entries or were possibly in later stages of the process; thereby skewing their data.

DATA ANALYSIS

Student academic records were used to obtain domain relevant skills including total and transfer hours taken, and external experiences attributed to design including credit hours for internships, and study abroad experiences.

Journal entries were examined using a deductive process to ascertain sequence of activities taken by students during the design assignment. The proposed model was tested using keywords derived from the responses to ascertain participants' task involvement and then associated with discrete stages in the model.

The construct of motivation used keywords from response prompts eliciting level of "interest in the task", and level of "excitement to continue" with the project. External evaluators-professors with sociology and fine arts backgrounds-were asked to assess product outcomes according to the seminal definition of creativity regarding relative degree of novelness and appropriateness for the project assignment. Each criteria was rated on a 5 point Likert scale resulting in 10 possible points per evaluator or 20 possible points total. Six individuals had scores of 15 or higher (the highest number of points awarded was 18) and five individuals had scores of 11 or lower (the lowest number of points awarded was 9). The group of participants with scores of 15 or higher was designated as the high creativity group and participants with scores of 11 or lower comprised the low creativity group. For evaluation these two groups were studied greater detail.

A statistical comparison of the groups illustrates several demographic differences between the two groups of students (see Table 1).

Cohort	Age	GPA	Transfer Credits	Total Credits
High Creative	**23.6**	3.83	46	152
Low Creative	**23**	3.29	21.2	127.4

Table 1, Group demographic comparison.

Participants deemed "*highly creative*" had higher grade point averages, and greater numbers of hours transferred into the school and total credit hours taken. This may suggest a relationship between creative output and success in assessments related to coursework requiring creative skills or creative thinking (i.e., interior design). Students with broad experiences (i.e., transfer credit hours) achieved relatively high creative output as did students with increased domain experiences (i.e., college-level credit hours). Following the demographic evaluation, the process of the participants in the high creative output group ($N = 6$) was compared to those in the low creativity group ($N = 5$). Evaluation was conducted by measuring frequency of task noted during each entry. Findings indicated both groups followed similar sequences of task in their respective processes.

From further comparison of prompt responses, characteristics of the student participants in the high creativity group included higher levels of:

Abstract thought

- ability to bring seemingly disparate ideas together
  - utilization of research multiple foci
- ability to relate the project abstractly to previous design problem solving experiences

Divergent thinking

- ability to utilize multiple research sources to develop a unified conceptual idea
- ability to utilize and synthesize multiple or diverse analysis techniques to solve the problem
- ability to formulate multiple design solutions

The students' processes also demonstrated:

Depth in thought utilizing domain experience

- ability to isolate and explore specific cognitive paths
- greater background knowledge (e.g. credit hours)

High work ethic exemplifying high levels of motivation

- ability to self examine and remove oneself from process to later revisit the design
- ability to deal productively and appropriately with frustrations

CONCLUSION

As an exploratory study this research began to examine the creative process and task conducted which result in higher levels of creative output. Findings from the study indicated similarities in process steps utilized by all students; however, differences arose when comparing the creative components of levels of motivation and domain experience. Students in the high creativity group described higher levels of motivation and had more transfer and total credit hours. These students also indicated a deeper level of task involvement by utilizing multiple analysis techniques.

ACKNOWLEDGMENTS

I would like to thank my advisor Dr. Katharine Leigh and my committee Dr. Ken Tremblay, Dr. James Banning, and Rob Work for their numerous contributions to this research.

REFERENCES

1.Amabile, T. M. (1996). *Creativity in Context.* Boulder, CO: Westview Press.

2.Creswell, J. (2009). *Research design: Qualitative, quantitative, and mixed method approaches.* Thousand Oaks, CA: Sage Publications.

3.Stake, R. E. (1995). *The art of case study research.* Thousand Oaks, CA

Tele-Improvisation: Cross-Cultural Creativity in Networked Improvisation

Roger Mills
University of Technology, Sydney
235 Jones St. Ultimo 2007 NSW
Roger.Mills@uts.edu.au

ABSTRACT
This paper summarizes the author's thesis investigating intercultural creativity and cognition in networked musical improvisation. The research is situated amongst scholarly studies of tele-musical interaction, highlighting the technological agenda that drives this enquiry and the need for a deeper examination of the experiential qualities of networked improvisatory practice. The advantages of distributed cognition as a theoretical perspective are considered in relation to evaluation of a preliminary pilot study. Incidences of creative interaction reveal the cognitive strategies that musicians employ to navigate the dispersed non-visual, improvisatory-networked experience.

Author Keywords
Telematic Music, Cyberformance, Networked Improvisation, Distributed Cognition

ACM Classification Keywords
Sound and Music Computing, Computer-supported cooperative work, Methodologies and techniques

General Terms
Performance, Theory, Human Factors

INTRODUCTION
The evolution of network technologies and high-speed broadband has led to the production of sophisticated multi-user audio visual interfaces, able to facilitate a range of remote synchronous collaborative expression. This has created unprecedented opportunities for musicians to improvise with collaborators from diverse cultures and disciplines. While network technologies eliminate distance in physical space, creative musical interaction occurs in a spatially dislocated and non-visual environment (i.e. without gestural cues and some of the modes of communication found in collocated musical interaction). For the remote improviser, this provides a liminal experience through which their performance is mediated, creating the imperative for a greater understanding of the nuances of dispersed musical interaction. Viewed through a perspective of distributed cognition, this paper examines the strategies that musicians of different cultures and musical traditions employ to collaborate in synchronous networked improvisation. Transferences of intercultural creativity are evaluated through methods of musicological analysis, participant observation and semi-structured interviews, highlighting the need for a framework for the description and analysis of creativity and cognition in networked inter-cultural improvisation.

C&C'11, November 3–6, 2011, Atlanta, Georgia, USA.
ACM 978-1-4503-0820-5/11/11.

Literature
Tele-communication technologies from the video-telephone of the late 1980s to present day A/V tele-conferencing are key to the development of computer-supported co-operative work (CSCW) [1]. However, much of the research has been technologically focused on facilitating "situation awareness" [2] in richer, visually perceptive and "smart" environments. Wang & Wang state that more experiential investigation encompassing the "context of mutual presence among multiple collaborators" [3] is needed, and this is also true of the networked improvisatory experience. A survey of research dating back to the local area network circuitry and tone generation at McGill University in the 1970s [4] to the current development of the high quality network software "JackTrip" [5] at Stanford University reveals a focus on technology driven enquiry, and a gap in an the understanding of dispersed creative intercultural interaction. This will be addressed by the thesis, motivated by the hypothesis that a greater understanding of networked improvisatory collaboration can enable musicians to develop new skills through intercultural creativity and pedagogical exchange.

Methodology
The aim of this research is to establish a framework for the description and analysis of networked intercultural improvisation. This involves developing a taxonomy of analytical classification and ontology, traversing the associated fields of, musicology, ethnomusicology, semiology and cognition. Drawing these strands together requires an interdisciplinary and grounded approach, combining methods for the analysis of cognition and perception of musical signs in dispersed cross-cultural interaction, ethnomusicology to codify transference, learning and cultural interpretation and reflective and musical methodologies that assess performers' approaches to intercultural networked improvisation. Distributed cognition theorists, Hollan et al (2000), argue that "cognition is embodied and that our perception of the world is a complex interaction of internal and external human

recourses e.g. mind–body and the artifacts of our immediate environment" [6]. Applied to the research of networked improvisation, it is not only culture, environment and history that inform the construction of social practice (improvisation) but also music technology and instruments (analogue or digital) that form part of our "distributed cognition" and become artifacts for analysis in the chain of investigation.

Pilot Study - Ethernet Orchestra

A preliminary pilot study focused on a networked performance by the Ethernet Orchestra [7], an intercultural group of skilled musicians who improvise remotely through networked audio interfaces. Spanning four time-zones, the performance was broadcast live on a Sydney community radio station in June 2010, and featured musicians at the University of Technology, Sydney (AU), Kunstmühle Gallery, Braunschweig (DE), and a home studio in Londrina (BR). The ensemble performed with a cross-cultural array of instruments including Turkish, oud & bendir, Mongolian horse fiddle and throat singing, guitar, trumpet and laptop electronics. Musicians also filmed their performances for evaluation and analysis purposes.

Data collection and Analysis

Original data was collected from field mixed audio and video recordings, post performance discussions and semi-structured interviews. Reviewing the recordings, the author compiled a descriptive narrative that drew detailed attention to instances of musical transferences between participants, highlighting interactivity in musical dialogues through a musicological analysis of melodic contour, range, timbre and meter. Comparisons were also made between what the musicians said in post performance conversations, and the musical events they identified in the recordings (i.e. a comparison of reflective thought and musical instance). A preliminary draft was forwarded to the musicians for comment and follow up responses were incorporated into the final description. A third tier of analysis was then applied, as individual performances were broken down event by event along the timeline. This then created new questions to which each musician qualified their responses until a "saturation of categories" was completed [8].

Preliminary Observations

Interview data and instances of melodic and rhythmic interaction illustrate that musicians begin a process of strategy building to mediate non-visual tele-musical improvisation. Approaches appear intuitive, responding to the situation at hand in a form of "knowing in practice", where musicians are able to reflect on their intuition in the process of improvising and "use this capacity to cope with the unique, uncertain, and conflicted situations of practice" [9]. Examples of this include extended note durations in the early construction of musical dialogues, attenuation of meter in rhythmic exchanges and timbral manipulation in signifying musical metaphor. In the midst of dispersed networked interaction, the author suggests that "intuitive knowing" emerges across cultures aided by embodied cognition. Just as the understanding of a "trembling" hand resonating vibrato on a guitar fret board or the timbre (tonal colour, warmth of sonority) of a musical sound, so gesture helps to codify qualities of sound in the minds of the musician. Cumming (2000) proposes that "bodily motion may account for the felt significance of sound" - and that what is 'heard in' the sounds, [...], has been heard according to a learned code of recognition" [10]. While Cumming is referring to collocated musical performance, this principal is even more salient in tele-musical improvisation.

Summary

Preliminary observations demonstrate emerging creative and cognitive strategies that cross-cultural musicians employ to engage in dispersed tele-musical improvisation. This research aims to map these strategies with musical examples of their implementation, developing a model for networked improvisatory cross-cultural learning and exchange. As network technology facilitates hitherto improbable meetings of diverse musical cultures and traditions, new methodologies that respond to this potential will provide the basis for innovative theories and practices in cross-cultural tele-musical improvisation.

References

1. Grudin, J. 2002, Computer-supported cooperative work: History and focus, Vol. 27 (5), 19, *IEEE Computer Society.*
2. Cowley, J. & Rhone-Alpes, I., 2006 *Social Perception, Magazine Queue*, Vol. 4 (5) July – August 2006, ACM New York.
3. Wand, W. and Wang, X. 2009, Improving Mutual Awareness and Distributed Cognition in Collaborative Design Communication *Proceedings of the 2009 13th International Conference on Computer Supported Cooperative Work.*
4. Bishoff, Gold, J.R., and Horton, J. 1978, Microcomputer Network Music. Computer Music Journal, Vol. 2 (3), 24-29.
5. Cáceres, J. and Chafe, C. 2009, JackTrip: Under The Hood of an Engine For Network Audio. Center for Computer Research in Music and Acoustics, Stanford University, 2009.
6. Hollan, J., Hutchins, E. and Kirsh, D. 2000, Distributed Cognition: Toward a New Foundation for Human-Computer Interaction Research. *ACM Transactions on Human-Computer Interaction,* Vol. 7, No. 2 (June 2000), 174-196.
7. Ethernet Orchestra, 2010. Viewed 1st April 2011. <http://ethernetorchestra.netpraxis.net>
8. Glaser, B.G. (1998). *Doing grounded theory: issues and discussions.* Mill Valley, Calif., Sociology Press.
9. Schön, D. (1983), *The Refelective Practitioner: how professionals think in practice*, Ashgate, 8-9.
10. Cumming, N. (2000). *The sonic self: musical subjectivity and signification.* Bloomington, Indiana University Press.

Shifting Between Modes of Thought: A Mechanism Underlying Creative Performance?

Andrew J. Pringle
a.pringle@surrey.ac.uk

School of Psychology, University of Surrey, Guildford, Surrey, GU2 7XH, UK

ABSTRACT
Creative-cognition has been viewed as involving both divergent and convergent modes of thought, with the former involved in generating new ideas and the latter in honing them into useful and appropriate outcomes [3]. It has been suggested that the ability to efficiently shift between modes may be an important feature underlying the capacity to be creative [4,6], and possibly, of particular importance in professions such as design [10]. However current measures of convergent and divergent thinking do not allow an examination of the dynamic deployment of these different modes on the same task. The present paper outlines a novel behavioral task examining dynamic shifts between modes of thinking, with pilot data tentatively suggesting more creative people are better able to shift between modes than less creative people. A better understanding of the link between shifting and creativity could inform the design of computer-based environments to facilitate shifting between modes [5].

Author Keywords
Creativity, divergent thinking, convergent thinking, cognitive control.

ACM Classification Keywords
J.4. Social and behavioral sciences: Psychology.

General Terms
Experimentation.

INTRODUCTION
It has been well established that creative-cognition involves both convergent and divergent thought [3]. Convergent problems are those with a single best solution while divergent problems involve the generation of multiple alternatives [3]. Different phases of the creative process may draw on different modes of thinking. For example, divergent idea generation on a previously performed task facilitated idea generation on an unrelated subsequent one [7], suggesting that the idea generation phase is supported by a divergent mindset. Conversely, the presentation of examples against which ideas could be honed and improved actually had a negative effect on idea generation [8], suggesting that convergent evaluative thinking operates more effectively outside the idea generation phase [6].

While it has been argued that both divergent and convergent modes cannot be present at the same time, it has been proposed that rapid movement between them is possible and doing so efficiently may be a facet of those with higher levels of creativity [4,6]. This could be of particular importance in professions such as design where idea generation is often followed by refinement and evaluation of ideas which may in turn necessitate further idea generation [10].

However, empirical evidence supporting this hypothesis is lacking. Evidence shows hormone induced improvements in convergent thinking at the expense of divergent thinking [9], suggesting a shift is possible. Evidence also suggests creative individuals are better able to move between a mindset that appears to mirror the divergent mode and one that appears to mirror the convergent one [11]. However an investigation of individual differences in the ability to shift modes of thought has yet to be examined on a task requiring rapid and repeated movement between modes.

The present paper outlines a novel word-based task designed to measure the ability to shift between modes and preliminary findings obtained from pilot work. Initial findings illuminate potential mechanisms underlying this ability and suggest how more creative individuals may differ from less creative ones in their ability to shift.

SHIFTING MODES ON A WORD-BASED TASK
The novel task designed to examine the shift between modes used compound remote associate (RAT) problems [1], each having only one correct answer hence drawing on convergent thought [3]. The present study adapted problems for presentation in two formats. In the first, convergent problem format (see first column, first row in figure 1 for an example) three target words were shown with the aim of identifying a solution word which can form a compound word or phrase with all three. For example, "ball" here links all three to form "basket-ball", "eight-ball" and "snow-ball". In the second, divergent problem format (first column, second row) single solution words, such as "ball", are used as seed words from which participants are asked to be as creative as possible in generating multiple compound words and phrases containing them. The current

C&C'11, November 3–6, 2011, Atlanta, Georgia, USA.
ACM 978-1-4503-0820-5/11/11.

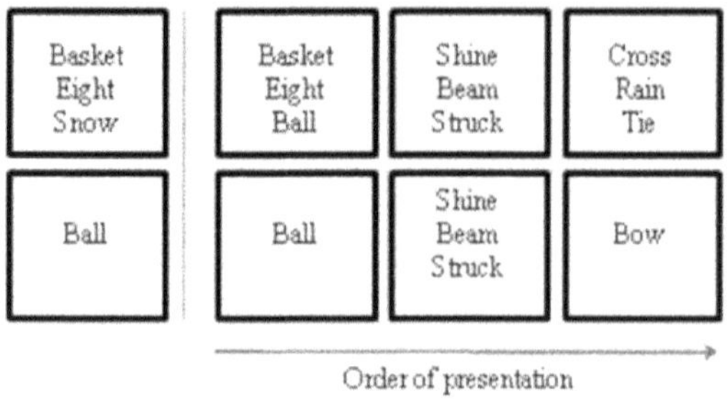

Figure 1. To the left of the dotted line are examples of problems in the convergent (above) and divergent (below) formats. Right of the dotted line is part of a pure block of convergent problems (above) and an alternating block containing both problem formats (below).

pilot compared performance on convergent problems within alternating blocks, where problems given in the convergent format were interspersed with those in the divergent one (as shown in the 2nd row, column 2-4 in figure 1), with performance on pure blocks, containing only problems in the convergent format[1] (as shown in the 1st row, columns 2-4).

Pilot data from 8 participants (*M*=27.38years, *SD*=4.34) showed solutions were generated significantly faster in pure (*Mdn*=10.49sec, *IQR*= 4.48sec) compared to alternating blocks (*Mdn*=13.17sec, *IQR*=4.82sec), z=1.96, *p*=.05, suggesting that alternating between problem types is a demanding process. Measures of creativity were obtained from a self-report measure of creative achievement, the creative achievement questionnaire (CAQ) [2]. Two groups, one of lower (*M*=4.67, *SD*= 4.05) and one of higher (*M*=26.5, *SD*= 11.61) creative achievement were formed (*N*=7[2]). The higher creative group solved more convergent problems in alternating blocks (*M*=48.86% correct, *SD*=17.61) than in pure blocks (*M*=38.90%, *SD*=15.95) while the lower creative group showed the opposite pattern with less problems solved in the alternating block (*M*=41.67%, *SD*=20.84) than in the pure block (*M*=45.84%, *SD*=14.84). While any interpretations based on such a small sample are extremely tentative, the data suggest that creative people don't suffer the decrement, observed at the sample level, when they perform sequences of problems requiring shifting between modes. They in fact perform better when having to shift modes than when they do not.

CONCLUSION

This paper outlines a novel task designed to provide a direct assessment of shifting between convergent and divergent modes of thinking and a means to test the hypothesis that creative people are better able to shift than less creative people. Findings from initial pilot work suggest that more creative people are better able to shift between modes. They also suggest a potentially interesting point concerning the mechanisms which may underlie this ability, with creative people going beyond merely resisting the possible detrimental effects of shifting, to the act of shifting itself actually improving their performance. Conclusions are extremely tentative at this stage due to the small sample size and because the effects of shifting on divergent problem performance have yet to be analyzed. Future work will examine if effects reported here extend to a full-scale study. A better understanding of the shifting-creativity link and its underlying mechanisms could inform the design of computer-based environments to support creativity by way of facilitating shifting [5].

ACKNOWLEDGMENTS

I would like to thank my supervisor, Paul Sowden, for his advice on the experimental work and a draft of this paper.

REFERENCES

1. Bowden, E. M., & Jung-Beeman, M. Normative data for 144 compound remote associate problems. *Behavior Research Methods, Instruments, & Computers 35*, 4 (2003), 634-639.
2. Carson, S. H., Peterson, J. B., & Higgins, D. M. Reliability, validity, and factor structure of the creative achievement questionnaire. *Creativity Research Journal 17*, 1 (2005), 37-50.
3. Cropley, A. In praise of convergent thinking. *Creativity Research Journal 18*, 3 (2006), 391-404.
4. Gabora, L. Revenge of the "neurds": Characterizing creative thought in terms of the structure and dynamics of memory. *Creativity Research Journal 22*,1 (2010), 1-13.
5. Hewett, T.T. Informing the design of computer-based environments to support creativity. *International Journal of Human-Computer Studies 63* (2005), 383-409.
6. Howard-Jones, P. A. A dual-state model of creative cognition for supporting strategies that foster creativity in the classroom. *International Journal of Technology and Design Education 12* (2002), 215-226.
7. Howard-Jones, P. A., & Murray, S. Ideational productivity, focus of attention, and context. *Creativity Research Journal 15*, 2 (2003), 153-166.
8. Jansson, D. G., & Smith, S. M. Design fixation. *Design Studies 12*, 1 (1991), 3-11.
9. Krug, R., Molle, M., Dodt, C., Fehm, H., & Born, J. Acute influences of estrogen and testosterone on divergent and convergent thinking in postmenopausal women. *Neuropsychopharmacology 28*, 8 (2003), 1538-1545.
10. Lawson, B. *How designers think: The design process demystified.* Architectural press, Oxford, UK, 2006.
11. Wild, C. Creativity and adaptive regression. *Journal of Personality and Social Psychology 2*, 2 (1965), 161-169.

[1] Analysis of performance on divergent problems in alternating vs. pure blocks is still to be conducted.

[2] One participant excluded due to incomplete CAQ.

Creativity Syntax: Codifying Physical Space's Impact on Creativity in the Workplace

Alison Williams
CITE, University of East London
London E16 2RD UK
alison@creativitysyntax.com

ABSTRACT
The impact of the physical environment on people's ability to be optimally creative at work is a research area which has only now, in the past decade, started to receive detailed attention. Although creativity in the workplace has been the subject of intensive research for over half a century researchers have stepped away from or minimized the effect that the physical environment may have on people's creativity and ability to innovate. Building on recent work done in the field, and on earlier theories of pattern language and shape grammar, this paper outlines work that moves towards a grammar of creative spaces identifying and codifying those elements of the physical environment which may optimize creativity in the workplace.

Author Keywords
Creativity, physical press, shape grammar, grammar of creative spaces, creative footprint.

ACM Classification Keywords
A.0 General Literature

General Terms
Design, Human Factors, Theory

INTRODUCTION
Exploring how physical space impacts people's creativity in the workplace has led me to hypothesize the need for, and endeavor to write, a grammar of creative spaces. In doing this I am seeking to identify and codify the three main elements of such a grammar: lexis, syntax and meaning [4], positioning the work as an explicit grammar rather than a pattern [1]. The content of each of these three elements is derived directly from the research data. Thus identified elements of physical space create the lexis; data categories of creative activities suggest the syntax governing the lexical elements' ordering; and the stimulus and support for small-c workplace creativity [18] identified by research respondents is the semantic and pragmatic meaning produced by that ordering.

BACKGROUND & RELATED WORK
Creativity research post-Guilford [8] has focused on the four Ps of creativity [16]: the creative *person,* the creative *product* or outcome, the creative *process*, and the *press* or environment within which creativity occurs [2], seen mainly, until recently, in terms of social rather than physical environment. My work draws on previous research in multiple areas, including McCoy's work demonstrating the link between physical space and creativity [14, 15], examinations by Lewis & Moultrie among others of creative spaces in organizations [11, 9], work on visual grammars by Stiny and others [19, 12], and work on patterns by Alexander et al in architecture [1] and Qian & Woodbury [17] in digital interpretation. I also draw on Gibson's theory of affordances [7] and linguistic grammar [4, 10].

In the field of creativity research, novelty and usefulness are, by consensus [13], seen as defining characteristics of creativity. Simonton [18] also posits different types or levels of creativity that can be graded on a continuous scale of creative activity: from big-C creativity which changes and contributes to both culture and history, to small-c creativity used by people in their daily and working life for improved problem-solving. In response to my research data, in which most subjects see their work creativity as novel and useful, and positioned on Simonton's continuum, I work from these definitions in my thesis.

METHODOLOGY
The grammar of creative spaces is emerging from research undertaken in a variety of office environments through a staged research process of interviews and case studies. I have used constructivist grounded theory [3] for both data collection and analysis. The final grammar version will be tested and refined in one or more work environments.

THEORY
As referenced earlier, the literature of linguistic grammar identifies three common elements: lexis, syntax and meaning (semantic and pragmatic). Chomsky's theory of a syntax-neutral grammar [4], i.e. one in which syntacticality is not dependent on meaning, enabled the creation of non-linguistic visual grammars such as shape and landscape grammars [19, 12]. Each of these visual grammars adheres to the same three-element structure. Thus Stiny's shape grammar has bounded shapes as its lexis, Euclidean transformations as its syntax, and good design as its meaning. I adopt the same structure in building a grammar of creative spaces, where the three-part structure has emerged from the data.

C&C'11, November 3–6, 2011, Atlanta, Georgia, USA.
ACM 978-1-4503-0820-5/11/11.

Physical Press

Having analyzed my data through the constant comparator method [3], I argue that *physical press* or environment is made up of three discrete and overlapping categories: *specificity* (where and what the place is), *properties* of the place, and its *affordances* (the possibilities for action that are afforded [7] to the space's users). In interviews and in case studies these three categories are consistently called forward, and are also present in the literature [15]. I further argue that these three categories form a key part of the basis for an explicit grammar of creative spaces.

Grammar of Creative Spaces

Categories of data pertaining to each of the three aspects of grammars – lexis, syntax and meaning – emerged from the data sets, becoming saturated [3] during analysis.

Lexis: Research subjects consistently identified aspects of physical press supporting their workplace creativity: *specificity, properties* and *affordances*. A wide range of elements appeared time and again in each of these three categories, populating the lexis of spaces necessary for people to be creative in the workplace. This quotation sits in the saturated categories of natural light and views: *"Here we get direct sunlight. [The office] just got a bright atmosphere about it [...] I see the water and it's nice."*

Syntax: Subjects consistently identified the same categories of activities supporting their creativity. *"Take notebooks, take a day [walking], think something, come back."* These are seen as those activities that led, by chance or deliberately, to an engagement between people, ideas and information; and those that led to a disengagement, allowing time for incubation [21]. These activities, I suggest, form the syntax or rule-base of the grammar which order the lexis of elements of physical space.

Meaning: *"It is important [...] to have meetings [in places] where [...] junior staff can feel very safe[...] You get some really good ideas."* I am currently working on this aspect of the grammar. *Meaning* in linguistics is categorized either as semantic: the association of words with their meaning [20] or pragmatic: the relationship of those words to an external context. Translating this to the context of a grammar of creative spaces, semantic meaning may be the association of a specific aspect of physical press with the degree to which it enables creativity in an individual. Pragmatic meaning in this context is, I would suggest, the way in which an individual or group identifies the precise lexicon they need in order to optimize their creativity.

DISCUSSION

My interim research findings indicate that everyone has their own unique creative process for generating and developing ideas. To do so, each person needs a physical environment that actively supports this uniqueness, their *creative footprint* [22]. These creative footprints are at one and the same time unique to the individual and composed of common elements. The grammar of creative spaces defines these elements and their structure, and simultaneously relates them to the context within which the individual is situated and needing to be creative.

CONCLUSION

The grammar is at a critical point of emergence, and I would welcome the opportunity to talk it through with my peers, including an anticipated technology development.

ACKNOWLEDGEMENTS

My thanks to the reviewers of this paper for their valuable contributions, and to Prof. Allan Brimicombe, Dr Helen Kennedy and Dr Deveril for their continuing inspiration.

REFERENCES

1. Alexander, C., Ishikawa, S.; Silverstein, with M.; Jacobson, M., Fiksdahl-King, I., & Angel, S. *A Pattern Language: Towns, Buildings, Construction.* New York: Oxford University Press, 1977.
2. Amabile, T. M. *Creativity in Context.* Oxford: Westview. 1996.
3. Charmaz, K. Grounded Theory: Objectivist and Constructivist Methods. In *Handbook of Qualitative Research*: Second Edition. Norman K. Denzin & Yvonna S. Lincoln (Eds.) pp 509-535. London: Sage, 2000.
4. Chomsky, N. *Syntactic Structures.* The Hague: Mouton 1957.
5. Csikszentmihalyi, M. *Creativity: Flow and the Psychology of Discovery and Invention.* New York: HarperCollins, 1996
6. Franck, K. A. Exorcising the Ghost of Physical Determinism. *Environment and Behavior, 16,* pp. 411-435. 1984.
7. Gibson, J. J. The Theory of Affordances. In Robert Shaw & John Bransford (Eds.) *Perceiving, Acting, and Knowing.* New Jersey: Lawrence Erlbaum Associates, 1977.
8. Guilford, J. P. Creativity. *American Psychologist, 5,* pp.444-454 (1950)
9. Haner U-E. Spaces for Creativity and Innovation in Two Established Organisations. *Creativity and Innovation Management, Vol 14* No. 3 pp. 288-298. 2005.
10. Langacker, R.W. *Cognitive Grammar: A basic introduction.* New York: Oxford University Press. 2008.
11. Lewis, M. & Moultrie, J. The Organisational Innovation Laboratory. *Creativity and Innovation Management, Vol. 14,* No.1 pp. 73-83. (2005).
12. Mayall, K. & Hall, G. B. Landscape grammar 1: spatial grammar theory and landscape planning. *Environment and Planning B: Planning and Design,* (2005) Vol. 32, pages 895-920.
13. Mayer, R. E. Fifty Years of Creativity Research. In *Handbook of Creativity.* R. J. Sternberg (Ed.). New York: Cambridge University Press. 1999.
14. McCoy, J. M. *The Creative Work Environment: The Relationship of the Physical Environment and Creative Teamwork a State Agency: A Case Study.* PhD thesis: University of Wisconsin-Milwaukee. 2000.
15. McCoy, J. M. Linking the Physical Work Environment to Creative Context. *Journal of Creative Behavior Vol. 39* No.3 Third Quarter (2005).
16. Mouchiroud, C. & Lubart, T. Past, Present, and Future Perspectives on Creativity in France and French-Speaking Switzerland. In *The International Handbook of Creativity.* J. C. Kaufman & R. J. Sternberg (Eds.) New York: Cambridge University Press. 2006.
17. Qian, Z. & Woodbury R. F. Between Reading & Authoring: Patterns of Digital Interpretation. *International Journal of Design Computing* 2004
18. Simonton, D. K. Creativity. In C. R. Snyder, Shane J. Lopez (Eds.) *Handbook of Positive Psychology.* US: Oxford University Press p 189-201. 2005.
19. Stiny, G. Introduction to shape and shape grammars. *Environment and Planning B,* Vol 7, pp. 343-351. 1980.
20. Vigliocco, G. Language processing: The anatomy of meaning and syntax. *Current Biology* 10: R78-R80 2000.
21. Wallas, G. *The Art of Thought.* New York: Harcourt, Brace, Jovanovich. 1926
22. Williams, A. The Creative Footprint: the impact of physical space on workplace creativity. In *Proc. Creativity & Cognition 09* 2009b

Crowd Creativity through Combination

Lixiu Yu
Stevens Institute of Technology
Castle Point on Hudson, Hoboken NJ 07030 USA
lisayu1103@gmail.com

ABSTRACT
The goal of this research is to perform large-scale experiments to see if the crowd, mediated by technology, produces creative designs by combining designs. To fulfill this goal, a sequential combination system is built. The system is a variant on a human based genetic algorithm, through which the crowd participates in an iterative process of design, evaluation, and combination. The study will provide a way of creatively solving problems in a number of different domains. It will also shed light on the mechanisms of social creativity: how individuals can build on each other's work and how technology can facilitate design by encouraging collaboration through shared designs.

Author Keywords
Crowdsourcing, creativity, design

ACM Classification Keywords
H5.3. Group and Organization Interfaces

ACM General Terms
Design

INTRODUCTION
How can a crowd be organized to generate creative ideas? Crowdsourcing makes it possible to assemble large numbers of workers in a short amount of time. It is a process that is part technology – an online marketplace with micropayments possible – and part organization – a coordination mechanism [10]. This process can be implemented with a wide range of possible structures, and many remain untried. In the proposed dissertation, I will look at a specific form of collaboration, in which members of the crowd combine the ideas of peers. This choice is motivated by the common claim made in management literature that innovation is at its heart the recombination of existing knowledge [3, 6]. Psychology researchers also claim that creativity results from a combination process [11, 12]. In a third literature, from the field of optimization, combination has been operationalized as crossover, a process in genetic algorithms [1, 4, 7]. In sum, these three different literatures suggest ways of addressing combination, but none in themselves are both specific enough to apply to design problems and flexible enough to tackle the types of ill-defined problems that characterize most product development.

C&C'11, November 3–6, 2011, Atlanta, Georgia, USA.
ACM 978-1-4503-0820-5/11/11.

Synthesizing ideas from the three fields, I propose such a process, calling it a sequential combination system: one crowd creates a first generation of designs, and then new crowds create successive generations by combining the designs made by previous crowds. I will describe the system in detail and report an experiment conducted with the system, one of several to be performed to complete my dissertation.

THE SEQUENTIAL COMBINATION SYSTEM
In order to clearly specify the sequential combination system, the way a genetic algorithm works will first be described. All variants of these algorithms start with a first generation population, and perform a fitness ranking. Then, members of the population are selected to become parents of the next generation. Most often, tournament selection is used: two parents are selected at random, and the fitter chosen. Another two parents are selected, and the fitter chosen. The two fit parents then produce offspring through a combination procedure. These offspring serve as a new population, which is then ranked, and the process repeats. Because combination can sometimes take the worst features of highly ranked parents, and thereby degrade the available genetic pool, a set of the strongest parents survive into the next generation without change, an attribute of the algorithm referred to as elitism [1].

The sequential combination system is based on the above description. It integrates together organizational processes, software tools, and a crowdsourcing market. The organizational process is based on the idea of a genetic algorithm [4, 7] implemented with human participants [9]: one crowd creates a first generation of designs, and then successive crowds create successive generations by combining the designs made by previous crowds. The fitness ranking in the system is based on the creativity scores of the designs, as evaluated by crowds. Tournament selection is used to pick the parents presented to the next generation crowds for combination. In each generation, 20 highest-rated designs are automatically promoted to the next generation in a process called elitism [1].

Specifically, the solicitation and management of participants are handled through Amazon Mechanical Turk. All participants receive nominal compensation for either generating or evaluating designs. When participants engage in idea generation, they are directed to a Google document page already opened as a drawing. This same page, in later generations, presents the designs to be combined. The drawing tool provides many menu choices including a freehand sketch option, a vector line, text, and pull-down shape palette. The system is run for three generations, as summarized in Figure 1.

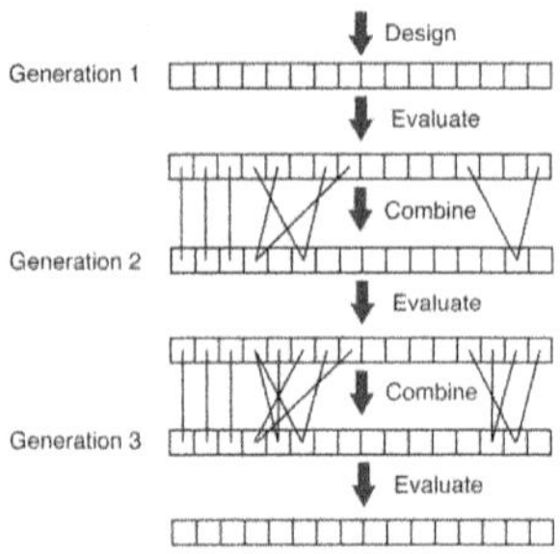

Figure 1. The generations of the experiment.

THE EXPERIMENT AND RESULTS

In the experiment, participants were asked to design chairs for children and present their designs through sketches. It was run through three generations with 1207 participants. The creativity of the designs from the last generation was compared to the creativity of the initial designs from the first generation. The consensus in the creativity literature is that only original ideas that are also practical should be called creative [2]. Operationally, this leads to a binary measure of creativity that includes only designs that exceed a certain threshold on both the scales of originality and practicality [2]. All designs were evaluated by the crowd on two scales: originality and practicality. The designs were then further classified as being creative or not based on the two scales. The results show that the number of creative designs in the last generation is significantly greater than that in the first generation, as shown in Figure 2.

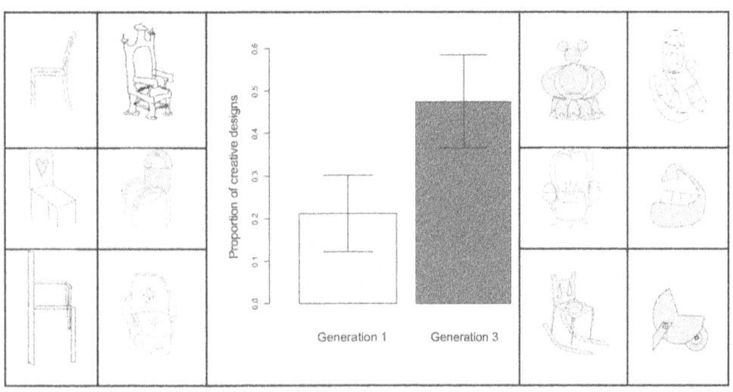

Figure 2. On the left and right are example chairs from the first and third generation. The bar chart shows the proportion of creative designs. The error bars indicate 95% confidence intervals.

FUTURE RESEARCH

Future research in the dissertation will focus on two directions. One direction considers a different evaluation mechanism, purchases in virtual worlds. The evaluation of designs in the reported experiments was based on the crowd's judgments. Another important test of a creative design, though, happens after it is implemented and becomes an innovation. That is, eventually the consumer or user evaluates the product for purchase and ongoing use. However, for many products, such as the chair example discussed here, production tests are probably infeasible. Some virtual environments have products and economies –so it would be possible to design and sell designs without the need for any physical manufacturing. Therefore, a future experiment will run sequential combination on a virtual worlds problem: three-dimensional products will be designed, combined and sold.

A second direction seeks to understand exactly how combination works. The current results show that the sequential combination system as a whole influences the creativity of the later combined designs. Several processes are involved in the system: combination, tournament selection, and elitism. To test whether combination leads to creativity—the hypothesis behind this work—future experiments will be run to control for the effects of tournament selection and elitism. And the ways features propagate in the different conditions will be examined to determine how exactly people combine ideas, and how such design ideas propagate.

ACKNOWLEDGMENTS

Funding for this research was provided by the National Science Foundation, awards IIS-0855995 and IIS-0968561.

REFERENCES

1. Deb, K. *Multi-objective optimization using evolutionary algorithms.* UK: Wiley, Chichester, 2001.
2. Finke, R. *Creative Imagery: Discoveries and Inventions in Visualization*, Lawrence Erlbaum, USA, 1990.
3. Fleming, L. Recombinant uncertainty in technological search, *Management Science*. 47, 1(2001), 117-132.
4. Goldberg, David E. *Genetic Algorithms in Search, Optimization and Machine Learning*, MA: Kluwer Academic Publishers, 1989.
5. Google Docs Drawing Application. http://docs0.google.com/demo/edit?id=scACRQalm3t83kVISWPhWfrqx#drawin
6. Henderson, R. M. & Clark, K. B. Architectural innovation: the reconfiguration of existing product technologies and the failure of established firms. *ASQ*, 35, 1(1990).
7. Holland. J. H. *Adaptation in Natural and Artificial Systems.* Ann Arbor: University of Michigan Press, 1975.
8. Kittur, A., Chi, E.H., & Suh, B. Crowdsourcing user studies with Mechanical Turk. In *Proc. CHI 2008, ACM(2008)*, 453-456.
9. Kosorukoff, A. Human based genetic algorithm. In *Proc. IEEE Conference on Systems, Man, and Cybernetics*, 2001.
10. Quinn, A. J., & Bederson, B. A Taxonomy of Distributed Human Computation. Technical Report HCIL-2009-23 [University of Maryland], 2009.
11. Simonton, D. K. Scientific creativity as constrained stochastic behavior: The integration of product, person, and process perspectives. *Psychological Bulletin*, 129, 2003, 475-494.
12. Thagard, P. *Conceptual revolutions.* New Jersey: Princeton University Press, 1992.

Author Index

www.ingramcontent.com/pod-product-compliance
Ingram Content Group UK Ltd.
Pitfield, Milton Keynes, MK11 3LW, UK
UKHW051414290926
15471UKWH00009B/1596

9 781450 313995